The OHIO ALMANAC™

AN ENCYCLOPEDIA OF INDISPENSABLE INFORMATION ABOUT THE BUCKEYE UNIVERSE

The OHIO ALMANAC™

AN ENCYCLOPEDIA OF INDISPENSABLE INFORMATION ABOUT THE BUCKEYE UNIVERSE

Edited by JOHN BASKIN & MICHAEL O'BRYANT

Drawings by JIM BORGMAN

Orange Frazer Press
Wilmington, Ohio

ISBN: 1-882203-29-1
ISSN: 0473-9760
Copyright 2004 by *Orange Frazer Press, Inc.*
All rights reserved

Ordering information: Additional copies of *The Ohio Almanac*™ may be ordered directly from:

> Customer Service Department
> *Orange Frazer Press, Inc.*
> Box 214
> 37$^1/_2$ West Main Street
> Wilmington, Ohio 45177

Telephone 1-800-852-9332
for price and shipping information

The Ohio Almanac™ is a registered trademark of Orange Frazer Press, Inc.

The information in this edition was compiled from the most current data available. Any errors, inaccuracies, or omissions are strictly unintentional.

For me the authentic, the resonant, the familiar extends only so far as Connecticut's old Western Reserve in Ohio, beyond which the country seems to dissolve in the glare of the western sun.
—*Out Here*, Andrew Ward

Ohio, the geography

44,828 square miles of land
(277.3 people per square mile)
3,499 square miles of Lake Erie
44,000 miles of rivers and streams
18,298.8 square miles of metropolitan areas
15,200,000 square miles of farm land
6,146,000 acres of forests

Length (extreme north to south)—205 miles
Width (extreme east to west)—230 miles
Geographic center—Centerburg, Knox County, approximate latitude 40 degrees, 18 minutes; approximate longitude, 82 degrees, 42 minutes

Ohio, the weather

Rainfall

Most—Chardon, average 45.22 inches per annum

Heaviest short term—Sandusky, 9.54 inches in eight hours, July 12, 1966

Snowfall

Most—Chardon, average 106 inches per season

Greatest single—Steubenville, 36 inches in three days, November, 1950

Temperatures

Highest—113°F, Centerville (Gallia County), July 21, 1934

Lowest—39°F, Milligan (Perry County), February 10, 1899

Warmest place—Ironton, average mean of 56°F

Coldest place—Dorset, average mean of 46.6°F

editors
John Baskin
Michael O'Bryant

managing editor
Leslie Frake

senior editor
Tammy McKay

department editors
Stephen Ostrander
Jane Ware

contributing editors
Thomas Bier, James B. Cash, Richard Coleman,
John Fleischman, Deborah A. Geier, Douglas
Graf, Jeffrey Hammond, C. Douglas Hurt,
George Knepper, Jay Paris, Thomas Suddes

design
John Baskin

illustration
Jim Borgman
Brooke Albrecht

photography
Ian Adams, Chris Smith, Andy Snow,
Eric Weinberg, Michael Wilson

special effects
Timothy Thrasher,
Thrasher Graphics, Vermont

proofreading
Cathy Edison, Leslie Frake,
Tammy McKay, Nikki Wilson

indexing
Amy Spicher, Shelby Wood

production supervisor
Tim Fauley

cover
©*Dan Patterson; the original 1903 Wright Flyer, photographed at the
National Air and Space Museum in Washington, D.C., for the Aviation
Century Project.*

Ohio, the people:
our nationality

German	2,866,565
Irish	1,447,735
English	1,016,67
United States of America	981,611
Italian	675,749
Polish	433,016
French (except Basque)	272,139
Dutch	200,850
Scottish	197,437
Hungarian	193,951
Scotch-Irish	165,741
Slovak	157,125
Welsh	132,041
Czech	86,892
Russian	73,863
Swedish	72,369
Swiss	70,302
Subsaharan African	65,250
Arab	54,650

Acknowledgements

The drawings were reprinted by special permission of King Features Syndicate, and **Jim Borgman**, the most gentlemanly of associates, whose characters, described as "dumpling-shaped Everyman and Everywoman," enliven Ohio's statistics with their special wit and supreme drollery.

Particular thanks to these writers, researchers, and comrades, who took time away from busy schedules to provide help, written and otherwise: **Denise Smith Amos**, columnist for the *Cincinnati Enquirer*; **Thomas Bier** of the Maxine Goodman Levin College of Urban Affairs at Cleveland State University; **James B. Cash**, author of *Unsung Heroes*; **Richard Coleman**, one of Ohio's best amateur historians; **Deborah A. Geier**, professor at Cleveland-Marshall College of Law; **Melissa Faye Greene**; formerly of Dayton and twice nominated for the National Book Award; **Jeffrey Hammond**, Distinguished Professor in the Liberal Arts at St. Mary's College of Maryland; **R. Douglas Hurt**, professor and director of the Graduate Program in Agricultural History and Rural Studies at Iowa State University; **Luke Knapke**, who translated Liwwät Böke's pioneer account of Ohio; **Dr. George Knepper**, author of *Ohio*, the definitive history; **Thomas Suddes**, the *Plain Dealer's* Statehouse reporter; **Will Underwood** and **Sandra Clark** at Kent State University Press.

Special thanks for invaluable assistance from *The Cleveland Plain Dealer* and particularly **Tom Coscarelli**, assistant managing editor.

Some of the almanac information was furnished by the generous permission of **Roy Wolford** and **Jean P. Kelly**—"Ohio Invents the Kitchen" by **Jean P. Kelly**; "The Governor's Cup"; "Why Oh, Why Oh, Christopher Columbus, Ohio?" by **John Fleischman**; "U.S, Supreme Court—The Ohioans" by **Dave Stephenson**; "Ohio Literary Favorites"; and "Ohio weather—the probabilities" by **Jay Paris**; as well as additional text by **John Fleischman**, **Sue Gorisek**, **Jay Paris**, and **Dave Stephenson**, drawings by **Brooke Albrecht**, and photography by **Jay Paris**.

And to the following: **Steven Kelley**, Ohio Department of Development; **Rosalie Beers**, Ohio Department of Agriculture; **Shelby Wood**; **Amy Spicher**; **Sally Shields**; **Joe Hammond**; **Dan Langen**; **Richard Gardner**; **Dr. Ann Dinkheller**; **Nikki Wilson**; **Jim and Jackie Colville**; **Dr. Kevin Bright**; **Mike Brannon**; **Pam Jones**; **Barb Yeary**; **Julie** and **Dave Lewis**; **Karen** and **Greg Mooney**; **Phyllis Hegner**; the staff at the Public Library of Cincinnati and Hamilton County, the staff at the State Library of Ohio; **Michelle Moore**; **Linda Hengst**, Director, Ohioana Library; **Christy Farnbauch & Jami Goldstein**, Ohio Arts Council; **Gary Gudmundson**, Ohio Department of Taxation; **Karen Ryan**, American Society of Civil Engineers; **John Paulson & Donna Smith**, Ohio Department of Health; **Asheely Clark**, Ohioana Library; **Sergeant Robin Schmutz**, Ohio State Highway Patrol; **Barbara Maslekoff**, editor, *Ohioana Quarterly*; **J. Curtis Mayhew**, Ohio Department of State.

And the original formatters of the almanac, **Annette Bickel and Michael Hauck** of Designer Set Studios of Wilmington, Ohio; as well as the compiler of the first edition, **Damaine Vonada**. Without them, the new edition would have been only marginally possible.

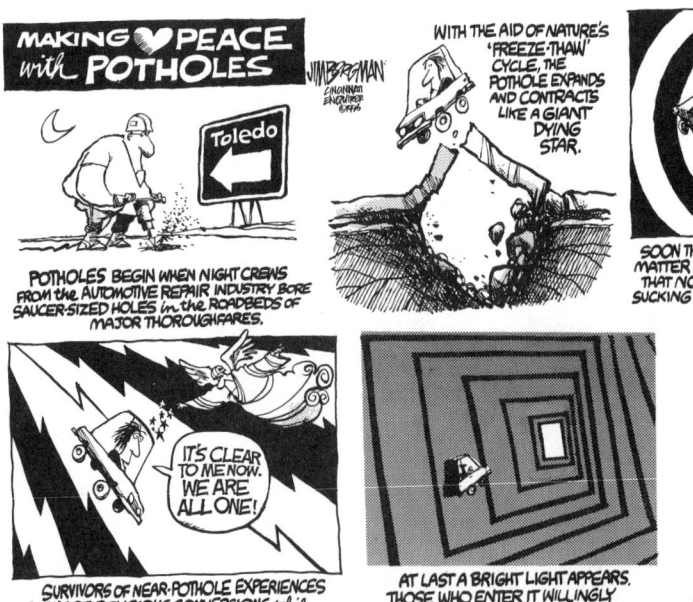

FOREWORD

Ohio has too many facts.

This peculiar state of affairs—unintentional pun—is something not entirely unexpected, for Ohioans are rather black-and-white folks, historically given to rolling up their shirtsleeves and getting down to work, whether it be clearing a pasture lot or inventing the rolled sheet steel process.

Most of the state's facts are in this book, which explains why it's so big. It's like *us*, actually (see page 86), a little overweight, factual, not too much abstraction, yet still with a little wry humor about ourselves. In other words, *Midwestern*.

This book attempts to cover every period of Ohio time, with special emphasis on the times in which we were most inventive. Making our facts work for us, one might say. There have been other times when Ohio has been at the mercy of its facts. You may judge for yourself which era we now inhabit. But whatever the era (and its attendant difficulty), rest assured that a considerable amount of whatever has occurred in America—"Greater Ohio," we call it—has either occurred here first, or was prompted by someone *from* here. For better or worse, we are a most American place, and many of America's definitions originated here.

This mammoth and somewhat oddly conceived almanac/encyclopedia is about our facts, and moreover, it is about our less apparent facts—the facts of who we are, where we came from, and how we've comported ourselves. The editors have tried to extrapolate the origins, methods, and ambition of Ohio from the raw data, and the book's various odd presentations demonstrate how many exemplary moments Ohioans have provided the rest of the country.

The final correction in our multi-year project was to repair Michael Gilb's name. It was something Freudian, no doubt, but the Findlay representative, at least in this book, is no longer Glib, which, one supposes, is a mixed blessing for a politician. It is not likely the final error in a multi-year project involving an estimated half-million Ohio facts—and over 6,000 hours—but it was the last one five different proofreaders found before shoving our bicentennial production out under the lights.

The sharp-eyed reader may notice discrepancies in facts from one place to another. From the last edition, for instance, Ohio seems to have gained 3,000 square miles of territory. Officials tell us the acreage of Ohio may or may not count a considerable portion of Lake Erie. Some statisticians count it; others prefer the dry land count. Different agencies correlate statistics differently, using differing criteria, and while we have tried to reconcile as many of these discrepancies as possible, the statistics outnumber us, and they do sneak in.

So here's to us, Buckeyes of all stripe (and fact), yet Buckeyes still.

—the editors

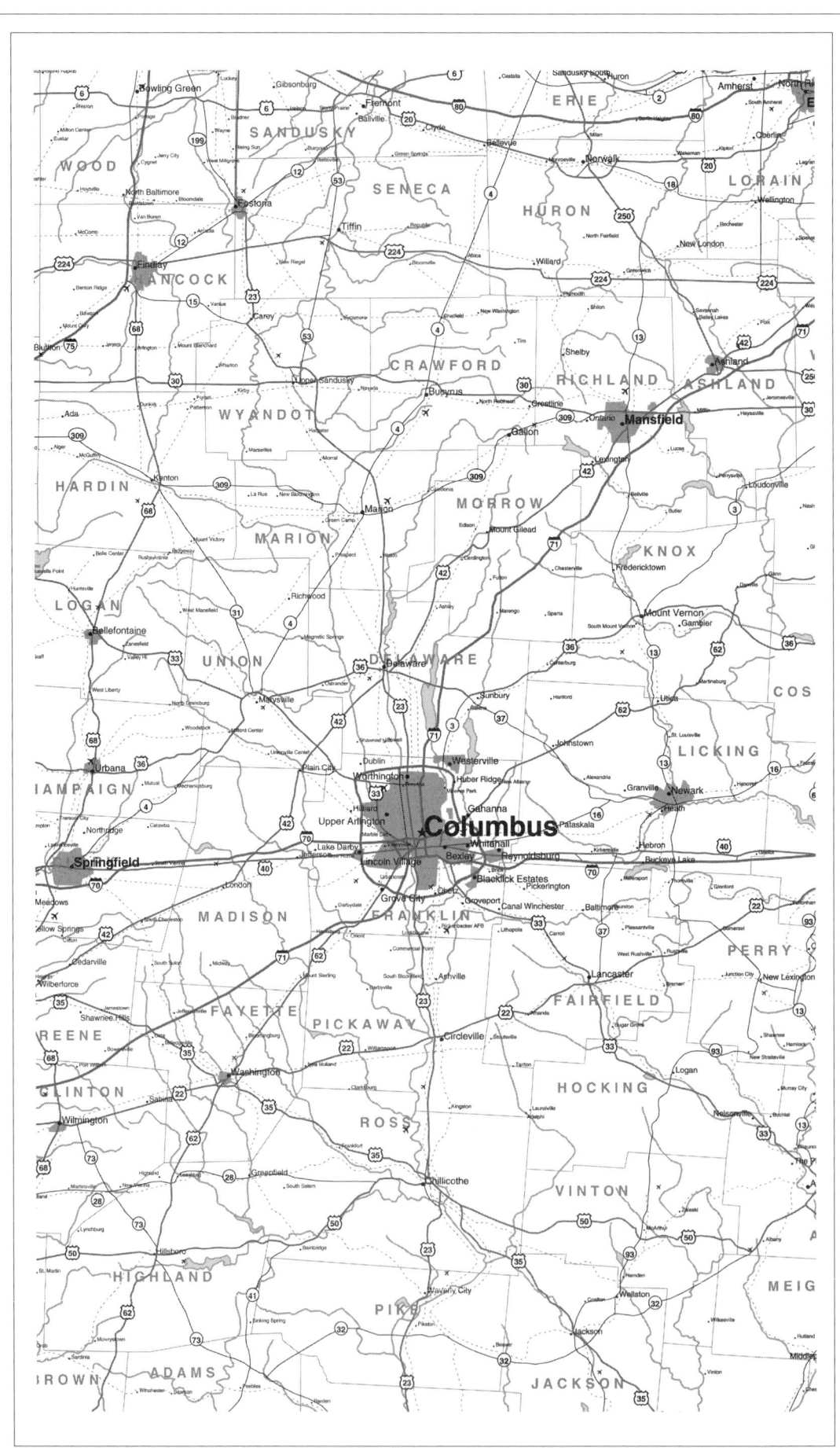

Table of Contents

The OHIO ALMANAC™

AN ENCYCLOPEDIA OF INDISPENSABLE INFORMATION ABOUT THE BUCKEYE UNIVERSE

A blizzard on the evening on November 29, 1802 delayed Thomas Worthington's departure from Chillicothe to Washington, D.C. A few hours earlier Worthington and other delegates approved Ohio's state constitution by a margin of 32 to 1, the lone dissenter being Ephraim Cutler, a rabid Federalist from Marietta who despised Worthington's Republican rabble. Before adjourning, the jubilant delegates deputized Worthington to whisk the document, a prerequisite for statehood, to Congress, but the eight-inch snowfall ("the deepest I ever saw in the month of November," Worthington wrote in his journal) forced the 29-year-old former Virginian to hunker down for a week in the territorial capital.

Worthington arrived in Chillicothe on July 4, 1796 from Berkeley County, Virginia (now West Virginia), with his brother-in-law Edward Tiffin, soon to be Ohio's first governor. Both men caught "Ohio fever," an affliction brought on by the prospect of easily finding power, prosperity, and adventure in a fresh wilderness. Forsaking slavery and small plantations in the Lower Shenandoah Valley, both men returned in 1797 to survey tracts and establish homesteads. By 1802, Worthington was a central figure in Ohio's body politick. Versatile, fit, quick-witted, ambitious, public-spirited, although controlling, he had enlarged a substantial inheritance with lucrative land speculations in Ohio.

The family, then consisting of wife Eleanor and two children (he would eventually sire ten) had recently moved into a substantial log cabin on a hilltop called Belle View overlooking the Scioto River. Folks addressed him as colonel, reflecting his social status as well as his rank in the militia. More important, Worthington, a

Republican, was well- connected in the nation's new capital, and a friend of President Thomas Jefferson, his political mentor. Ohio Republicans figured statehood would be a cinch because the philosopher-president wanted the state's three electoral votes in the 1804 presidential election. Worthington saddled up on December 7, and tracked northeast on Zane's Trace, still a crude bridle path after its blazing in 1796-97 by Ebenezer Zane. The long horseback ride to Washington, D.C. could take two to three weeks, depending on the weather and the fitness of stallion and rider. Colonel Samuel Huntington, a recent Republican convert from Cleveland and a future state supreme court justice and governor, and William Lytle, a land speculator possessing 39,000 acres in Clermont County, likely rode with Worthington as far as Zanesville, where on December 9 the trio lodged at an inn owned by John McIntire, the town's founder and Zane's brother-in-law.

Thereafter, Worthington mentioned no traveling companions in his diary, just his nightly

stopovers and the "weather, very cold." As he threaded alone across the gelid Ohio wilderness and Appalachian Mountains, he rehearsed his speech to Congress, considered what he would tell Jefferson, and reminisced about the events that lately unfolded in Chillicothe, the cradle of Ohio statehood.

Undoubtedly, he thought about Arthur St. Clair, still governor of the territory when Worthington left Chillicothe. Oligarchic and pretentious, St. Clair disgraced himself in 1791 by leading an army of 1,400 regulars and unruly frontiersmen into an Indian trap that resulted in 648 deaths and 271 wounded and abandoned soldiers, two-thirds of his entire command. The massacre still stands as the worst U.S. military defeat to Indian forces in history. St. Clair himself barely returned safely to Cincinnati. The tragedy touched many settlers on the frontier, including Worthington, who lost surrogate brother Joseph Darke, the son of his guardian, Colonel William Darke, also wounded in the fight. General Anthony Wayne avenged St. Clair's humiliation at the Battle of Fallen Timbers in 1794, then negotiated the Treaty of Greenville the following summer, without St. Clair's assistance, lest there be another disaster. St. Clair had neither aptitude nor willingness to march Ohio forward, militarily or politically.

Worthington and the Chillicothe clique of Tiffin, Michael Baldwin, and city founder Nathaniel Massie had been gnawing on St. Clair's power in the territorial legislature since 1800. That year, legislators chose the clique's candidate for the territory's non-voting representative to Congress, William Henry Harrison (Wayne's aide at Fallen Timbers), over Arthur St. Clair Jr., the governor's son. Harrison persuaded Congress to drastically cut the minimum size and down payment of land purchases to accelerate western settlement. Until then only 50,000 acres of Ohio's public land had been purchased under the Land Act of 1796, which required a $1,280 down payment for 640 acres, a hefty burden for cash-starved settlers.

Harrison also got himself named governor of the newly-formed Indiana Territory (including Michigan), thus acquiring more than half of St. Clair's former realm. Worthington, in charge of

the Chillicothe land office, made a fortune and many grateful friends. Meanwhile, St. Clair fumed and plotted a comeback.

In the lame duck days of his presidency, John Adams reappointed St. Clair to another three-year term as governor. Emboldened by the reappointment, St. Clair rallied Federalists and anti-Chillicothe representatives in the territorial legislature to vote 12-8 on December 21, 1801, for subdividing the Ohio Territory, with separate capitals at Cincinnati and Marietta. Drawing a border along the Scioto River was not a new idea. When Jefferson authored the congressional land ordinances in the mid-1780s, he envisioned a state called "Washington" east of the Scioto, and the states of "Metropotamia" and "Saratoga" blocked out of the rest of present-day Ohio and Indiana. St. Clair's coup, however, was meant to delay statehood by splitting the territory's population, fast approaching the requisite 60,000 people, and to vanquish the Chillicothe junto.

Ironically, Worthington saved St. Clair's hide on Christmas Eve 1801 by calming a pro-statehood mob, dubbed the "Bloodhounds," that intended to burn the governor's effigy (and perhaps the governor, too) outside his quarters in Chillicothe. Worthington threatened to shoot Baldwin, the Bloodhounds leader, until the mob dispersed. At a reception in Gregg House the next evening, William Rufus Putnam, a diehard St. Clair ally from Marietta, toasted the future of two states bordered by the Scioto River. Chillicotheans in an adjoining room overheard the salute. Hot words spewed, fists flew, blades flashed but cooler heads prevailed before blood spilled on the governor's floor.

Instead of seeking frontier-style justice with a noose, the Chillicotheans circulated statehood petitions and listed grievances against the governor, who had openly boasted that "a multitude of indigent and ignorant people [Ohioans] are but ill-qualified to form a constitution and government for themselves....They are too far removed from the seat of [national] government to be much impressed with the power of the U.S."

Privately, St. Clair muttered that his backwoods subjects, rootless debtors and simple-

minded schemers all, were toadies to "ambitious, designing and envious men." Worthington hand-delivered the petitions to Jefferson in January 1802, amidst preposterous rumors circulated by St. Clair that the statehooders planned to take possession of federal land.

His trip was personal and political, not sanctioned by the territorial assembly. That didn't matter to the Republican-dominated Congress, nor to Jefferson, who signed an Enabling Act on April 30, 1802, permitting Ohio to proceed toward statehood, and Congress restored the western border drawn by Harrison two years earlier.

Figuring that St. Clair, now desperate, prickly, and conspiratorial, would "hang himself" politically, the Chillicotheans let him address the statehood convention in early November 1802. They weren't disappointed. After challenging the competence and legality of the assembly, the 68-year-old patrician tried to bait delegates into sedition. "We have the means in our own hands to bring Congress to reason, if we should be forced to use them," he avowed. Worthington administered the coup de grace by mailing the intemperate speech to Jefferson, who fired the mutinous Federalist canker on November 22.

Worthington heard the good news about St. Clair when he arrived at Mr. Burch's boarding-house in Georgetown on December 19, amazing traveling time considering the "weather, very cold." The next day he sipped French wine beside a roaring fireplace and answered the questions of a very curious president. Indeed, Jefferson wanted to know everything because Ohio, in 1803, was the crucible for westward expansion.

WORTHINGTON'S BOOSTERISM ASIDE, Ohio was still a daunting, coarse wilderness in 1803, and would be for another decade. From a hawk's perspective, it resembled a horizonless sea of trees. Ohio was smack dab in the heart of one of the world's great hardwood forests, stretching from Canada's muskegs to Florida's tropics, eastward to the Appalachians and west to the Great Plains. An educated eye, however, could detect that the oaks holding sway in the hill country of southeastern Ohio seamlessly gave way to bulky beeches and maples in Cincinnati and the flatlands to the northwest. This deciduous, green ocean was interrupted by a prairie archipelago across central and western Ohio, gashes sliced by watercourses, and hundreds of scattered, mosquito-infested ponds and bogs born 12,000 years ago from chunks of melted glacial ice. A formidable and forbidding wetland, dubbed the Great Black Swamp, stretched across northwestern Ohio on both sides of the Maumee River. Mountain lions and black bears ravaged livestock, and sometimes settlers. (Wolves would attack Huntington, then an Ohio Supreme Court justice, at his Cleveland home in 1805; and kill 20 of Worthington's sheep in 1813.) Farmers even complained of hordes of meek squirrels menacing cornfields.

At McIntire's Inn in Zanesville, travelers heard amazing stories of the Muskingum River's largess: the man-sized muskellunge and catfish landed in 50-foot canoes carved from tulip trees; mussels as big as a dinner plate; sycamore hollows housing squatters and bandits; black walnut trees seven feet in diameter; and salt licks yielding crystals purer than the Atlantic's. Other stories rang truer. Come spring, warblers descended into the forests like drops of painted rain. Passenger pigeons, then the most abundant avian animal on the continent, darkened the skies during their migrations. Meriwether Lewis, one of Wayne's aides at the Treaty of Greenville, recorded such an event while navigating the Ohio River above Marietta, at the start of his famous adventure in 1803. Three years later, frontier ornithologist Alexander Wilson measured one flock to be a mile wide and 240 miles long. Traveling a mile a minute for two hours, Wilson estimated two billion birds winged overhead.

Such fond tales of flora and fauna served as metaphors of Ohio's boundless fecundity and fertility. However, to pioneers aiming to profit by raising grain and livestock, trees and critters were nuisances. They chopped down the forest, metaphorically and otherwise, to make their own horizon. Today, their labor seems both heroic and wanton, but at the time, in their minds, the contradiction did not exist. The land had to be conquered, cleared and cultivated—period. In doing so, they believed they were civilizing

The Harrison Land Act allowed sale of half-sections, 320 acres, to be paid for in installments over four years...These steps were the beginning of a policy of public land for the public, a policy that was liberalized in the Old Northwest and then enlarged in territories beyond the Mississippi. Under the 1796 law, less than 50,000 acres had been sold by 1800. In the first three years of the Harrison law, land sales surpassed a million acres.

—*Walter Havighurst,*
Ohio, A Bicentennial History

themselves and the nation. Two centuries ago, Ohioans were retouching the American Dream painted two centuries before them at Jamestown and Plymouth Rock.

In 1803, the earliest "gated" communities of Marietta, Cincinnati, and Steubenville had only recently spread beyond the timbered walls of frontier forts. Franklinton (Columbus), Zanesville, Cleveland, Dayton, Lancaster, Youngstown, Warren, and Ravenna, all staked out in 1796-97, remained clusters of log cabins. Toledo, Akron, Canton, Findlay, and Lima were not yet in anyone's imagination. Francois Andre Michaux, a botanist and frontier traveler, reported in 1802 that French inhabitants hoveling in 60 log cabins around Gallipolis, established in 1790, "breathe[d] out a miserable existence."

Deprivations and diseases, especially dysentery and malaria, killed more settlers than warfare with Indians. Restlessness was another frontier affliction. Even where Ohio had been settled there hadn't been much settling down. Twelve of 25 settlements built in Hamilton County in 1795 had been abandoned by 1803. One Ohio town counted 188 founding landowners in 1800, but a decade later only 82 of the original group remained. Some would-be pioneers, risking all, trudged across the wilderness, only to discover frontier life too burdensome and retreated home. Moses Cleaveland, for instance, returned to Connecticut after staking out his namesake in 1797.

Enterprising emigrants shed land like clothing when it wore out or no longer fit. They bought cheap land, cleared it, sold it for a profit, bought elsewhere, sold it again, hoping eventually to be rich. David Abbott was typical. He founded Willoughby in 1798, but moved to Milan ten years later. Indeed, if Ohio had the 60,000 people for statehood (nobody actually counted heads), then many of them were in motion.

Congress rubberstamped Ohio's statehood more on its prospects than its portfolio. Hard currency was scarce; few pioneers could rub two nickels together. Settlers paid off their debts, even land mortgages, with crops, livestock, or labor. Worthington accepted land from the federal government as payment for surveying tracts in the Virginia Military District in 1797. The U.S. government gave Ebenezer Zane land grants at Zanesville, Lancaster, and Chillicothe for blazing his famous path. Merchants, for example, would exchange cloth for corn, trade cornmeal for saddles, then sell the saddles to the army at inflated prices. Like most of its citizenry, Ohio entered the Union a pauper with just $10,950 in its budget.

Ohio's industrial output amounted to cornmeal, flour, and timber trickling from the cottage-sized gristmills and sawmills owned by affluent proprietors, Worthington included. Pioneers deep in the bush pulverized grain with hand-mills, which required two hours of labor to feed one adult per day. Marietta had a shipbuilder constructing flatboats of questionable quality, and the state's first iron furnace arose in 1804 near Youngstown. Blacksmiths, scarce in 1803, received land and other incentives to settle on the frontier. Manufacturing occured in the home on an as needed basis. Ohio's underground wealth—coal, oil, iron, natural gas, salt, limestone, clay—would be unrealized and untapped until the Industrial Revolution crossed the Alleghenies in the 1830s.

On the dawn of statehood, Ohio's transportation system consisted of the temperamental Ohio River and a few wilderness paths posing as roads, the main routes being Zane's Trace and the Lake Trail, an old Indian route between Cleveland and Buffalo. While these crude roads served emigrants with flexible timetables, they were inadequate for pack trains and wagons hauling perishable goods to distant markets. New routes and maintenance only happened on an as needed basis, with axes, oxen, and sweat.

It is no wonder then that internal improvements figured prominently in Worthington's conversations with Jefferson. Without roads, an isolated and independent-minded Ohio might develop close ties with England, Spain, or France, or go it alone. And then what? Roads promised to unify the nation, but who would pay for them, and how? The founders resolved the money problem in the

(*continued on page 6*)

www. *ohiohistory.org*

The Ohio Historical Society's site provides an online encyclopedia and other things adroitly historical, such as death certificates, a newspaper index, a site for kids to explore and get homework help, and a database where one may search and download—for a fee, of course—photo files.

4

Marietta, Ohio's first city: Conceived in greatness

The official line is that Marietta was the first organized settlement in the Northwest Territory. This takes some squinting at the facts to blot out the Americans at Fort Harmar, the British at Detroit, the French at Vincennes and the many Indian towns dotting the territory. If you narrow the claim to Marietta's being the first permanent white American settlement organized in the Northwest Territory, you come closer to the mark.

If they weren't leaping ashore into uncharted wilderness, Rufus Putnam and his followers did accomplish something historic. They brought ordinary life to the West. Marietta was the first test of the Ordinance of 1787 that set out the legal and civic structure of all the new territories to come. The Marietta pioneers brought lawsuits, taxes, politics and schools to the heartland. The Putnam party was well prepared to do things right.

Into their midst came Commodore Abraham Whipple, an ex-sailor joining the company of ex-soldiers, an unusual man in an unusual bunch. Whipple's naval adventures would make an implausible swashbuckling movie except they were real. He was a privateer and one of the first commanders in the U.S. Navy, driving the Royal Navy to distraction with his sheer nerve and appetite for danger. He emerged from the Revolution with great honors but poor prospects. At 55, he was considered an old man. When his son-in-law, a former Army officer, threw in with the Ohio Company's Marietta expedition, Commodore Whipple turned his back on the sea and went west to pass his declining years farming.

Marietta was far from peaceful. In 1791, the Indians rose up across the territory in one last desperate effort to throw back the tide of land-hungry Americans. Marietta became a fortified town. The main strength was Campus Martius, the powerful blockhouse fort that demonstrated why Rufus Putnam had been George Washington's most trusted military engineer. A smaller stockade stood on the Point, where the Muskingum flowed into the Ohio. Across the Muskingum was Fort Harmar. The garrison was shifted downriver to infant Cincinnati, leaving only invalid soldiers and the settlers themselves to hold it. The settlers farmed by day and withdrew into their strongholds at night.

Commodore Whipple, however, was more worried about his melons. Someone was raiding the splendid patch he had planted outside the walls in his son-in-law's garden. He suspected the boys of the settlement. Indian emergency be damned, no one steals with impunity from an old privateer. One moonlit night, the commodore took down his musket and slipped out of the fort. Towards midnight, three Indians glided over the garden fence and felt their way through the patch, seeking only the ripest of the commodore's melons. "Not expecting depredators of this kind, he looked quietly on, in silence," wrote Samuel Hildreth, Marietta's pioneer historian. "He could have easily killed one or more of them with his well-loaded musket but he felt no enmity toward them: but on the contrary, himself and countrymen were taking the land of their fathers and themselves from them. And as for the melons, they were not worth the life of a man, even of a savage…When they had selected such melons as suited them, they retired; and the commodore rested quietly the remainder of the night…He did not watch the melons again."

—John Fleischman

"No colony in America was ever settled under such favorable auspices as that which has just commenced at the Muskingum… If I was a young man, just preparing to begin the world, or if advanced in life and had a family to make a provision for, I know of no country where I should rather fix my habitation…"

—George Washington, 1788

5

Enabling Act of 1802, which put five percent of the revenues from public land sales into a road building fund. The cache, first used to build the Cumberland Road to Wheeling, would eventually seed the National Road in Ohio, starting in 1825.

While in Washington, Worthington heard about the crisis over New Orleans, the destination of most commodities produced in the Ohio River Valley, including the flour and timber from Worthington's mills. Access to New Orleans was vital to U.S. trade interests and to national unity. For years, Spain, Louisiana's titleholder, had granted Americans the right to unload goods at piers, then sell or trade them, and ship them out on larger vessels.

However, in 1801, France, now ruled by Napoleon, obtained ownership of the port city from Spain, run by Napoleon's brother. Recently, Spain, awaiting the arrival of the French, stopped the practice of offloading at docks, allegedly to curb smuggling. Americans could still transfer goods from keelboat to sailboat in the harbor, but Jefferson nervously wondered about Napoleon's plans for New Orleans. He bluntly told the French that blocking Mississippi River traffic or garrisoning a large army in New Orleans would be considered acts of war. While Worthington lobbied for statehood, Congress approved $9.3 million for the purchase of New Orleans.

In late July 1803, Ohioans heard the news of the Louisiana Purchase, which would double the country's size and keep Trans-Appalachian products flowing freely through New Orleans. In September, Jefferson's personal secretary, Meriwether Lewis, descended the Ohio River on the first leg of the Voyage of Discovery.

Low water slowed his progress above Wheeling, but thereafter the crew paddled 20-25 miles a day. Lewis camped at Clarington and Grandview on the Ohio side of the river before reaching Marietta on September 13. He spent the night there and visited with one of the settlement's founder, Colonel Griffin Greene, an "excelant republican" serving as postmaster.

Lewis reached Cincinnati on September 28 and for the next week accumulated supplies, rested the crew, sent a report back to Jefferson, and explored an archeological site in Kentucky along Big Bone Lick, where the remains of a mammoth had been discovered earlier in the year. The dutiful explorer mailed a 2,000-word description of the dig and some bone fragments to his sovereign.

On October 15, 1803, Lewis met the expedition's co-commander William Clark near Louisville. (Clark, one of Wayne's commanders at Fallen Timbers, had struck up a friendship with Lewis during the treaty talks at Greenville.) Four days later Senator Thomas Worthington would ratify the Louisiana Purchase and approve funding for the Voyage of Discovery.

BACK IN WASHINGTON, Worthington steered Jefferson's attention to hostile forces within Ohio. Native Americans still controlled the land ceded to them by the Treaty of Greenville, the region west of the Cuyahoga and Tuscarawas rivers and north of an invisible treaty line running from Fort Laurens (northeastern Tuscarawas County), to Fort Loramie (Shelby County) and to Fort Recovery in Mercer County, nearly a third of the state. Though peace generally had reigned after the treaty, Americans still saw the Shawnees, Delawares, Miamis, Ottawas, Wyandots, Mingos, and the others as a threat.

British agents openly operated in the treaty lands, providing Indians with guns, powder, musket balls, whisky, and encouragement. In the summer of 1799, a band of mounted Shawnees brandishing British rifles and wearing war paint had appeared at Fort Loramie. Alarmed settlers prepared for war, but the Shawnees withdrew to their side of the treaty line before a conflict ensued. Still, neither side let down their guard. Any Indian warrior, redcoat, or bluecoat soldier crossing the treaty line could provoke a panic.

Jefferson revealed his Indian policy to Worthington: Acquire their land by nibbling and negotiating, not by war. Employ cash, trinkets, bluster, and deception before the bayonet and cannon. Never mind the resultant resentment and hatred. Although Jefferson's frontier friends, including Worthington, did not share the president's altruistic view that the Indians would become yeoman farmers, the "bloodless" approach worked for awhile. The Indians ceded

land in the Western Reserve, from the Cuyahoga River to the western border of present Erie and Huron counties, for $18,000 on July 4, 1805, and a smaller parcel north of the Maumee River via treaty in 1807. However, there still were dangerous moments.

That year, after learning that a British ship, *Leopard*, had fired on the U.S. frigate, *Chesapeake*, Ohio's frontier settlers worried that Prophetstown, a multi-tribal village established south of the treaty line near Greenville, would become a staging area for a British and Indian invasion led by Shawnee war chief Tecumseh. Acting governor Thomas Kirker sent Worthington and Duncan MacArthur to Greenville to pow- wow with Tenskwatawa, the prophet at Prophetstown; Blue Jacket, the aged Shawnee war chief who masterminded St. Clair's defeat 22 years earlier; and Tecumseh.

RESORTING TO SABER-RATTLING, Worthington warned the Indian leaders not to take sides if war rekindled between the Americans and English. "But if they [the 5,000 American soldiers mustering for war] find you have let the British put the tomahawk into your hands to be used against them," said Worthington, "they will destroy you for your folly." Blue Jacket denounced the British for spreading war rumors and emphasized that "we have laid down the tomahawk never to take it up again."

Worthington brought the chiefs to Chillicothe on September 16, thereby comforting Kirker. In reality, though, relations with the Indians remained tenuous through the War of 1812. Ohio would not feel whole until the U.S. Senate approved the Treaty of Ghent in 1815, when Thomas Worthington, the father of Ohio statehood, would be governor.

Worthington's meetings with Jefferson and Congress had been cordial, productive, and encouraging. Writing to Massie on December 25, 1802 Worthington enthusiastically reported that "Our friends appear highly pleased with the proceedings in our quarter...He [Jefferson] informs me the most prompt measures have been pursued to do away the difficulties." Not prompt enough, however. As prescribed by the state constitutional convention, Ohio held elections for state offices in January, a month before Jefferson ratified a Senate bill enabling Ohio to apply for statehood.

For a month Ohio was the renegade state that St. Clair prophesied. (Oddly, Ohio never formally applied for statehood, nor did Congress formally grant statehood. That technicality was settled in 1953, during Ohio's sesquicentennial, when Congress approved statehood ex post facto). As expected, the Chillicotheans anchored Ohio's first state government. Tiffin was elected governor. Massie and Baldwin became speakers of the Senate and House, respectively, when the Ohio General Assembly convened on March 1, the official date of Ohio statehood. The legislature chose Worthington and John Smith of Cincinnati as U.S. senators, and Huntington as a supreme court judge.

Thomas Worthington lived long enough to ride a steamboat on the Ohio River, sire ten children, and break ground for the National Road, Ohio's canal network, and public school systems. After being governor, he served as U.S. Senator again, state legislator, Ohio canal commissioner, and trustee of Ohio University and the National Bank in Chillicothe. Every seventh grader in Ohio learns that the pastoral scene on the state seal mimics the dawn seen at Adena, Worthington's hilltop mansion in Chillicothe, now a state historic shrine.

This quintessential self-made man made and lost fortunes as a farmer, speculator, mill owner, distiller, meat packer, boat builder, stock investor, and military outfitter. He corresponded with eight of the first nine American presidents, including Washington, plus John Jacob Astor, Albert Gallatin, Thomas Paine, and Henry Clay. At Adena, he entertained myriad notables, such as President James Monroe, New York Governor DeWitt Clinton, and Tecumseh. Worthington's death on a business trip in New York City on June 20, 1827, marked the end of frontier Ohio.
—*Stephen Ostrander*

Isolated on the Western Frontier, Ohio emerged first as an agricultural power, then as an industrial one. For more than half a century, as America made itself into an international power, its native sons ran the White House. Its local ingenuity, meanwhile, transformed Ohio into a modern urban state. Today, Ohio seeks an identity for the new century.

Ohio is Mainstream America. Politically, economically, socially, it is at once North and South as well as East and West. At the same time the Buckeye state is both urban and rural, and like the Midwest in general it is industrial and agricultural—a place of rolling fields, small towns, and sprawling cities. Because Ohio has more metropolitan centers than any other midwestern state, it also has an urbane sophistication and a sordid ugliness that contrast sharply with the tranquility and beauty of the countryside. If a key exists to explain the cultural distinctiveness of Ohio, it is that Ohioans always have revered pragmatism, political traditionalism, Jeffersonian agrarianism, and the Puritan ethic. The resulting adherence to these philosophical ideals has created a people who exhibit the naiveté and the canniness that is characteristic of many midwesterners. The fruits of these guiding principles also have been the creation of a culture that has thrived on economic conservatism and political moderation.

That does not mean, however, that Ohioans have been unwilling to take risks. While supporting Henry Clay's American System, for example, the state embarked upon the ambitious if not reckless program of canal building that left it nearly hopelessly in debt. Ohio also has had its outspoken political reformers. Only Elijah P. Lovejoy in Missouri

and Illinois vied with Ohio's John Rankin, whose biting "Letters on Slavery," together with Benjamin Lundy's appeal for the universal emancipation of slaves, helped change the focus of American politics. Moreover, Ohio shared the messianic John Brown with Kansas and helped set the nation on the road to Civil War.

Still, Ohio has been ambivalent. During the antebellum period, most residents opposed slavery as well as abolitionism, at the same time supporting a host of black codes that were among the harshest in the Midwest. Ultimately, however, they feared disunion more than they opposed racial equality. In the 20th century, Ohioans welcomed the New Deal and the Great Society while preaching the merits of hard work and economy in government. They also have been peace-loving, but sometimes violent. The fire still burns in the Straitsville mine where labor and management fought bitterly over the right of workers to earn a living wage more than a century ago. Nor has substantive political change come without sharp division. Only in Ohio, for example, during the height of the student protests over the Vietnam War, did the National Guard fire on and kill students engaged in a lawful protest over a matter of principle. Yet for all these contradictions, the state has enjoyed political and economic stability.

Both of these features have contributed to material progress and social harmony and to the development of a typically midwestern state with its own special characteristics.

www. *ohiomemory.org*

The Ohio Memory Online Scrapbook is a collaboration among more than 300 Ohio libraries, museums, historical societies, and other archives which have assembled a large database of materials into, well, a *scrapbook*. Except that the viewer gets to use the images and other material to create his/her own. Great young adult site that helps alleviate the pain of history.

by R. Douglas Hurt

Immigrant dream meets Ohio real estate; inventive Buckeyes merge American agriculture and industry as more abundant life unfolds.

Early in the state's history, immigrants came to Ohio primarily in search of land. Their dream was little different from that of other frontiersmen in the Midwest. They did not stay for long, however, if they were burdened by "great, impossible dreams." Ohioans, of course, had inventive minds and skillful hands, as the work of the Wright brothers, Charles F. Kettering, and Thomas A. Edison clearly attests. But the vast majority of the men and women who created the state were not like those who painted "Pike's Peak or Bust" on their wagons, nor did they shout "California, here I come." Instead, they were the people who came to stay—farmers, shopkeepers, miners, and factory workers. They did not expect miracles but only the opportunity to work hard and to prosper.

The early pioneers of New England and southern heritage were not disappointed in the faith which they placed in the Puritan ethic. Their spirit, energy, and labor quickly created a leading agricultural state with a decidedly Jeffersonian philosophical foundation. Eventually, their work ethic led to the creation of an industrial economy that was slow to shed both the Jeffersonian tradition and the Puritan ethic. The resulting tug and pull between the agrarian past and the modern industrial state has shaped the main features of Ohio's development since the mid-19th century. Rapid economic change fostered by science, technology, and new business practices, however, created a state that exemplifies the best and the worst of American agricultural and industrial life.

In contrast to other midwestern states, however, Ohio did not develop a genuine provincialism. That is not to say that cultural distinctiveness did not emerge; indeed, it did. New Englanders commonly settled in the Western Reserve in northern Ohio. They built whitewashed Greek Revival homes around neat town squares and established a host of private academies to educate their children. In contrast, Virginians entered southern Ohio and brought the agrarian features of the rural South, while German immigrants developed bountiful farms and built solid stone churches in the northwest. Their cultural uniquenesses remains today, if only architecturally or linguistically. Even so, culture determined how the immigrants adapted, and it has left an indelible imprint on the development of Ohio. Still, a particular statewide provincialism did not emerge, primarily because Ohio is situated on a major line of immigration between the East and the West. Although tens of thousands of individuals passed through Ohio or stopped temporarily, each contributed to a cultural amalgamation which, if not a true melting pot, fostered social harmony while preserving local color.

The abundant life came slowly. No one ever spoke of Ohio as the land of milk and honey, only as a land of opportunity, if you worked for it. Prosperity came with a price, whether paid in the

fields, factories, or mines. From the beginning of statehood, they have been willing to pay it. Today, however, Ohioans are becoming increasingly uncertain about the hallowed values and truths of the past, particularly Jeffersonian agrarianism and the Puritan ethic. Economic events beyond the control of the family farmer have forced a decline in agriculture as a way of life. Moreover, a sagging industrial economy has made an increasing number of Ohioans question the value of the Puritan ethic. Hard work no longer is the absolute key to success; nor is the family farmer the epitome of independence and self-reliance or the guardian of democracy. If any cultural features of Ohioans remained intact as the state entered the 21st century, they were those of pragmatism and political traditionalism.

Early 19th century development oversees canals built in 1827; then railroads supplant canals at mid-century. Ohio becomes leading agricultural state in U.S.

 Until the completion of the Erie Canal in 1825, inadequate markets and insufficient transportation restricted Ohio's agricultural development. Farmers had little choice but to send their commodities to market over difficult roads and distant mountains or down the Ohio and Mississippi rivers to New Orleans for transshipment to the ports beyond. Either method involved time and expense. Moreover, once Ohio's farmers had money in their pockets, they had little access to the consumer goods that would enable them to improve their standard of living.

In 1827, after considerable political maneuvering, Ohioans responded to this economic isolation in a pragmatic fashion by building canals. Eventually, these canals linked Lake Erie with the Ohio River and created an interlocking network across the state, providing access to the markets that farmers desperately needed. When the digging stopped in 1847, state and private canals stretched across more than a thousand miles of Ohio. Even before they finished the canals, however, Ohioans turned to a new form of transportation—the railroad. By the end of the 1850's, the canals and railroads had opened Ohio to the outside world.

The canals and railroads also stimulated manufacturing. These new forms of transportation encouraged farmers to produce surplus crops for sale, and merchants were quick to buy, process, and ship agricultural commodities as well as to purchase the goods that farm families needed. Trading centers sprang up across the state. At the same time Ohioans were distrustful, even fearful, of industrialization, which many believed would corrupt society and, in turn, ruin the rural way of life. The first industries were, however, more necessary than threatening. By 1840 extractive industries, such as agriculture and mining, created the basis for an urban industrial network that extended from Cleveland in the north to Cincinnati in the south.

Akron was a shantyboat town made legitimate by the canal. There were 15 locks in 1 mile at Akron. Milan had Ohio's shortest canal—3 miles. But it made Milan into a major lake port. By the birth date of Milan's most famous citizen—Thomas Edison—Milan was second in the shipment of wheat only to the Russian port of Odessa.

While this occurred, Ohio, like others in the Midwest, stumbled through the Panics of 1819, 1837, and 1857. During each depression, the working class became more severely affected, in part because it grew in number. In 1837 the state's unemployment corresponded with the national average of between 6 and 8 percent. Ohioans felt the ramifications of major economic change on a national level, and whether this change would be for better or for worse, they were increasingly tied to a manufacturing economy.

Ohio, like other emerging industrial states in the Old Northwest, experienced divisions between skilled and unskilled workers as manufacturers relied more and more on outside capital, distant markets, and volume production. Impersonal and adversarial relationships among skilled and unskilled workers and between labor and management further stratified society and made the attainment of the American dream harder to achieve. Still, workers as well as farmers remained politically conservative. Radicalism was not part of their lives. In contrast to many states, for example, Ohio as late as 1835 had not yet embraced the movement for a ten-hour day.

Although manufacturing increased prior to the Civil War, Ohio became the leading agricultural state in the nation. By the mid-19th century, Ohio led the nation in the production of cereal grain, and was among the leading producers of wool, pork, and dairy products. Much of this production was the basis for the state's major manufacturing industries—flour, meat-packing, and distilling. The 1850s, however, were seminal, transitional years for Ohio as manufacturing superseded agriculture. The rapid increase in population, coupled with the development of regional markets, enabled Ohio to maintain a high ranking among the manufacturing states between 1850 and 1870. The value of manufactured goods quadrupled during this time, while the work force nearly tripled. In 1870 Ohio ranked first in the production of agricultural equipment and second in iron. Flour and gristmill products contributed the most value in dollars to the state's economy, followed by rolled and forged iron. The faith Ohioans placed in hard work and the Jeffersonian tradition remained firm.

Urban areas rise in late 19th century; ethnic minorities impact Ohio culture; age of big business arrives; agriculture declines; labor begins to organize.

By the last quarter of the 19th century, the growth of industry and the expansion of the railroad effectively fostered the concentration of population in cities over 5,000 inhabitants, 26 of which existed in Ohio by 1870. This growth gave Ohioans new concerns that were far removed from daily life on the farm—police and fire protection, sanitation, housing, lighting, water supply, street maintenance, and vice. Once in the city, an individual necessarily gave up a great deal of self-reliance and personal freedom. There, the communal needs of society superseded those of independent rural inhabitants.

After the Civil War, Ohio rapidly moved into the age of big business. By 1900 it epitomized all that was both good and bad about corporate, industrial America. As Ohio became more dependent on industry, agriculture continued to decline. Although approximately 75 percent of the work force held agricultural jobs in 1840, only 50 percent remained in farming by the Civil War. The industrialization and urbanization of labor continued to increase at a pace that far exceeded the national average. While the national work force engaged in nonagricultural pursuits did not reach 51 percent of the population until 1880, by that time 60 percent of Ohio's workers were employed in off-the-farm activities. Indeed, by 1880 the transformation of Ohio from an agricultural to an industrial state was complete. Even so, pragmatism, political

"If I were giving a young man advice as to how he might succeed in life, I would say to him, pick out a good father and mother, and begin life in Ohio."

—*Orville Wright*

traditionalism, Jeffersonian agrarianism, and the Puritan ethic remained basic features of Ohio's cultural distinctiveness.

Although agriculture declined as a way of life, most residents still believed that hard work and frugality eventually would provide a better living. That does not mean, however, that a great unity of purpose existed among the working class. Indeed, it often did not. The division of labor in the factory system, hostility to immigrants, and religious and ethnic differences, together with competition for jobs, inhibited the solidarity of the work force needed to build strong craft or industrial unions. In Cleveland, for example, squabbles among German, French, and Irish Catholics over the governing of their parishes carried over into the work place. The Poles in Toledo also were divided among themselves over religious issues. At the same time, white, native-born males frequently refused to work with immigrants, women, or blacks and openly discriminated against foreigners and Catholics. A high rate of geographic mobility among workers further hindered working-class cohesiveness and hampered the establishment of strong unions.

In addition, prosperity, coupled with periodic economic depressions, hindered the efforts of workers to unite. The independent proclivities of labor, together with Horatio Alger dreams of success, also prevented it from developing a working-class consciousness that soon would lead to unionization. The unity among workers that existed was ethnic, religious, and racial. It was not that of working men and women in general. Even so, by the last quarter of the nineteenth century, those barriers began to crumble as workers realized that they faced common problems that only cooperative action could solve. It was not by accident that Columbus hosted a convention of workers in 1886 that organized the American Federation of Labor.

Increased migration from farms to cities, coupled with the immigration of the foreign born, accelerated competition for jobs, kept wages low, promoted overcrowding, and changed the landscape in Ohio. Nativism and immigration, however, contributed to the development of isolated ethnic communities, such as German Village in Columbus and Over-the-Rhine in

Cincinnati. Although the foreign born never exceeded 14 percent of the population between 1860 and 1920, ethnic communities fostered segregation rather than assimilation. By the early twentieth century, Italians, Poles, Hungarians and other southern and eastern Europeans increasingly settled in the industrial cities of Cleveland, Toledo, Youngstown, Akron, Dayton, and Middletown. In 1920, Germany, Hungary, Poland, and Italy contributed the most foreign born to Ohio. This new ethnic mix had a major cultural effect on the composition of the cities. These immigrants and their descendents strengthened the Catholic parishes, established vibrant branches of the Eastern Orthodox Church, and built Jewish synagogues. The Greeks introduced their coffeehouses while the Slovaks transplanted their social halls to Ohio's urban scene.

As industrialization and immigration created a new urban landscape, Cincinnati self-consciously attempted to build an elite, sophisticated city far removed from the industrial grime that blighted most urban centers in the state. After the Civil War, for example, some people talked about moving the national capital from Washington to protect the federal government from another Southern insurrection. Although Chicago quickly bid for this relocation, Cincinnati sniffed that she would rather not be considered for the honor. The editor of the *Cincinnati Gazette* wrote: "Cincinnati offers all the beauties of site, climate and civilization, but Cincinnati does not need the capital. If the country desires to put it here . . . we shall acquiesce as a patriotic duty." This self-assurance and independence caused one reporter for a Louisville newspaper to refer to the Queen City as "our clever but rather vain sister up the river." If Cincinnati worried about its image, however, the other industrial-based cities did not. The city fathers of Toledo, Cleveland, and Youngstown, among others, welcomed industrialization, immigrant workers, and the political power that each helped create.

15 most Significant Ohio dates

by Dr. George W. Knepper

Ohio lacks almost nothing except an instantly recognizable symbol—perhaps because Ohio is not one thing but all things American, not distinctly north, south, east, or west, but some of each.

—*Ohio, The Spirit of America*, Diana Landau

Land ordinance of 1785

Congress established a rectilinear system of survey for the Northwest Territory. The grid of north-south lines intersecting east-west lines created ranges, townships, and sections, numbered in orderly sequence. Ohio's Seven Ranges is the first place this rational pattern was applied. It served as a model for all new states except Texas.

Northwest Ordinance of 1787

To encourage orderly and lawful settlement in the Northwest Territory, Congress enacted this ordinance establishing a "blueprint" for creating new states out of the wilderness. Articles of Compact preserved civil rights, freedom of religion, and freedom from slavery. Ohio was the first state formed under these terms, hence it became the model for all future states except Texas and California.

Founding of Marietta, 1788

Congress sold more than one and a half million acres at bargain prices to the Ohio Company of Associates, veterans of the American revolutionary armies from Massachusetts. It established Marietta at the mouth of the Muskingum River, the North-west Territory's first authorized settlement.

Treaty of Greenville, 1795

Mad Anthony Wayne's peace negotiations with the Ohio Indian tribes and their allies established a boundary line that opened two-thirds of eastern and southern Ohio to new settlers. Unlike earlier treaties that had coerced the Indians, the tribes vowed to honor this boundary–and they did. Thus began in this safe area the onslaught of immigration that tamed the wilderness into statehood in less than 20 years.

Ohio statehood, February 19, 1803

On this date President Thomas Jefferson signed a bill, passed by both houses of Congress, approving a constitution for the new State of Ohio. "The said state," it proclaimed, is "one of the United States of America," and all laws of the United States "shall have the same force and effect within the said State of Ohio, as elsewhere in the United States." Ohio, the nation's 17th state, was the first to be carved out of the national domain entirely under congressional direction.

Legislative session of February, 1825

After months of lobbying and politicking, the General Assembly authorized construction of the Ohio and Erie Canal and the Miami Canal (later the Miami and Erie). These vital internal improvements would soon bring Ohio much-needed access to eastern markets. Before voting in favor of the canal measures, representatives from Washington County demanded a new state tax in support of public schooling. A bargain was struck: canal votes in return for school tax votes.

Battle of Lake Erie, September 10, 1813

Commodore Oliver Hazzard Perry's tiny American fleet defeated a British fleet of similar

size in the waters off South Bass Island. Perry now controlled the British supply route to the West. The British, pursued by the American army, abandoned Fort Malden, from which they had supplied the western Indians.

During the retreat the British stood, but were soundly defeated by the Americans. Tecumseh, leader of Britain's Indian allies, was killed. After the War of 1812 ended, small remnants of the Ohio tribes were confined to small reservations located in the state's northwest quadrant.

8 Brough's victory, 1863

John D. Brough, the candidate of the prowar Union Party, defeated Clement L. Vallandigham, candidate of the peace Democrats, in Ohio's gubernatorial election. A victory by Vallandigham, the arch "Copperhead," would have been a crushing repudiation of Lincoln's war policies. A relieved President Lincoln wired Brough: "Ohio has saved the Union."

9 Birth of professional baseball, 1869

The Cincinnati Redstockings emerged as the first fully professional baseball team. Successful in the field of play as well as in the hearts of growing numbers of fans, they set the pattern for one of the world's greatest athletic enterprises.

10 The Standard Oil Company, 1870

Chartered by the State of Ohio, John D. Rockefeller's Standard Oil Company soon became the prototype of aggressive, monopolistic business enterprise. By organizing a "trust," Standard Oil showed the way to imitators trying to capture larger shares of America's great post-Civil War business growth, and Rockefeller's name became synonymous with enormous personal wealth.

11 Ohio Constitutional Convention, 1912

Ohio experienced the greatest concentration of social, political, and economic reform in its history during the first decades of the twentieth century. Progressive Republicans and Democrats controlled the 1912 constitutional convention which submitted 41 proposed amendments to the voters. They passed 33 of them, and the state legislature promptly acted to put most in force through statute law. The amendments addressed problems resulting in part from Ohio's evolution from an overwhelmingly rural state to a rapidly developing urban industrial state.

12 Ohio Conservancy Act, 1914

Disastrous floods in 1913 were especially severe in Dayton and the Miami Valley. Engineers proposed a plan to protect against future floods, but new state legislation was required. The Ohio Conservancy Act permitted formation of watershed districts. The first such district was the Miami Conservancy District in 1915. Its work became a model nationwide for flood control and regional rehabilitation projects including the mammoth Tennessee Valley Authority project.

13 State sales tax, 1935

In January, 1935, a new three-percent state sales tax went into effect. Its revenues were desperately needed to cope with unemployment and other social problems of the Great Depression. Though bitterly opposed by many, it endured. Today the rate is seven percent with counties permitted to add up to two percent in "piggyback" taxes for local purposes.

14 Ohio Civil Rights Commission, 1959

Established by legislative act in 1959, the commission was to prevent and eliminate the practice of discrimination in employment against persons because of their race, color, religion, national origin, or ancestry. Finding much discrimination within the state, the commission recommended new legislation putting teeth into antidiscrimination laws.

15 Man on the moon, 1969

When Neil Armstrong of Wapakoneta stepped onto the moon, it was indeed "one small step for a man; one giant leap for mankind." It was also the

culmination of accomplishment for generations of Ohio pioneers in the realm of flight. The Wright brothers, justly famed for pioneering powered flight, unleashed the imagination that led to an extraordinary list of aeronautical accomplishments by Ohioans.

Dr. George W. Knepper is a distinguished professor emeritus of history at the University of Akron, and the author of Ohio and its People

Political affairs remain stable throughout the 1800s; Republican Party replaces Whig and antislavery parties in 1855; two-party system returns by 1870; Ohioans remain Jeffersonian.

 While Ohio underwent a major transformation from an agricultural and rural to an industrial and urban state, it remained politically consistent and moderate. Ohioans always have been practical and traditional in politics. Although Democratic-Republicans dominated Ohio's early politics, between 1832 and World War I, the major political parties roughly shared the spoils of office and more commonly the vote. During this time, the size and composition of the two major political parties were remarkably stable. Between 1832 and 1855, for example, the Whig party won eight and the Democratic party nine of the 17 presidential and gubernatorial contests. Although Democrats were ardent supporters of Andrew Jackson, the Whigs represented two cultural entities. The New England tradition of John Quincy Adams characterized the first group, and settlers from the Northeast chose the Western Reserve for their homes. Southerners composed the second group. They settled in the Virginia Military District and southern portions of the state. These Whigs followed the banner of Henry Clay. Democratic strongholds centered in areas with a large German population, such as northwestern Ohio.

In 1855 the Republican party replaced the Whig and antislavery parties on the ballot. It did so, however, without upsetting the two-party system, because the Republicans essentially garnered the votes that formerly had been cast for their predecessors. Political continuity remained strong even during times of national crisis. In 1860, for example, when the Democratic party splintered, the Republicans garnered only 49.4 percent of the vote while the Democrats polled 46 percent. The Democratic tally was only three percentage points less than it usually totaled. Although Stephen A. Douglas, the nominee of the northern Democrats won 43 percent of Ohio's vote in 1860, the other Democratic candidates garnered 5.5 percent of the vote to give the collective party nearly a 49 percent share of the total vote. This tally was the best showing for the Democrats since the organization of the Republican party. Although the Republican party maintained large margins of victory during the war years, the Democratic party soon reasserted itself once the war ended. By 1870 a strong, vigorous, two-party system had returned to the Buckeye state.

Between 1870 and 1892, presidential elections remained closely contested. Even though the Republicans won all six presidential elections and seven of 11 gubernatorial contests, their average share of the vote was only 49.3 percent. During this time, the Democratic party averaged 47.4 percent of the vote. Clearly, both the Republican and Democratic parties survived the disunion of the Civil War with their constituencies intact. The Panic of 1893, however, began a decade-long decline for the Democratic party. Between 1893 and 1904, the party averaged only 43.6 percent of the popular vote in eight gubernatorial and presidential elections. That was the worst showing for the Democrats in 20 years. Still, with the exception of the aberrations caused by the Civil War and the most serious economic crisis yet experienced in the nation's history, the Republican and Democratic parties were evenly divided. After the Civil War, many Ohioans voted as they had shot, but nearly as many voters gave their traditional support to the Democratic party. The differences were less matters of substance or ideology than of emphasis and methodology. During the late 19th century, then, Ohio's voters responded to culture and traditional habits. No matter whether these customs were based on social

"Our position in the nation is peculiarly felicitous, as to soil, climate, and productions, and it will be our own fault if we are not the happiest people in the Union."

—Caleb Atwater, 1838

class, ethnicity, or occupation, tradition remained supreme.

In addition to being traditional in politics, Ohioans remained eminently Jeffersonian. Indeed, if Jefferson believed that the nation could profit from a revolution every 20 years, Ohioans provided for this possibility. In 1851 a new constitution enabled the voters to determine every twenty years whether the state should call a new constitutional convention. This Jeffersonian concept of democracy reveals that Ohioans still believed that government should remain close to the people. Moreover, it indicates that Ohioans maintained the assumption that the public was capable of determining whether systematic, constitutional revolution was necessary to safeguard personal freedom and democratic tradition. Still, this constitutional provision and ideological concept are inherently conservative. Ohioans were not afraid or reluctant to change the mechanics of their government in order to provide needed reform, but the change would come through a traditional process. While the results might be revolutionary, the process would be conservative. Ohioans cherished liberty and self-government, but they also favored law and discipline. They would maintain their liberty, but it would be an ordered freedom.

Thus a stable but growing economy and a conservative political system that provided for substantive reform tempered the public reaction to the changing conditions of the industrial age. Ohioans preferred the safe, known approach to social, political, and economic reform. Radical ideas, voiced through third-party politics, were anathema to most of them. Populism, for example, not only had no charm, it was dangerous. Jacob Coxey's call for major economic reform based on the federal government's issuance of non-interest-bearing bonds and support for a good-roads program was Ohio's weak answer to the slashing rhetoric of Jerry Simpson and Mary Elizabeth Lease and to the sharply honed, intellectual reasoning of John Davis in Kansas. In Ohio the Populists met scorn, ridicule, and neglect. With a diversified agricultural economy and few of the problems Populists experienced in the Great Plains, Ohio farmers marched to the drummers of their traditional political parties.

At the dawn of 20th century, Ohioans go to shops and factories; labor reform finally arrives. Reform candidates win in Toledo and Cleveland. Ohio's national political supremacy comes to end.

By the turn of the 20th century, Ohioans retained their cultural distinctiveness in relation to pragmatism, political traditionalism, Jeffersonian agrarianism, and the Puritan ethic. They were hard working, ambitious, and optimistic. Many believed that the agricultural life was the foundation of freedom and democracy. In contrast to other midwestern states with the exception of those in the Old Northwest, most Ohioans pursued the American dream in the factories and shops of the towns and cities. Corporate insensitivity to the needs of the worker, however, coupled with a blatant disregard for the consumer, stimulated a major reform movement in the early 20th century. With the leadership for reform coming from such individuals as Tom L. Johnson and Samuel M. ("Golden Rule") Jones, the Progressives swept away machine politics. They also improved social conditions through the political process by winning increased governmental regulation of corporate enterprise while gaining an expansion of public services. Although Democrats charged that Republicans could not serve as agents of reform, considering their past record, both political parties supported the Progressive movement.

Progressivism, however, increasingly restrained the individualism of the past and by so doing revealed the struggle Ohioans had adjusting to the industrial and urban world. This cultural realignment can be seen in relation to the constitutional convention of January 1912. This convention, the fourth for Ohioans, did not produce a new document, but the delegates drafted 41 prospective amendments for the voters. They responded in part by rejecting woman suffrage and by refusing to eliminate the word "white" from the qualifications for male voting rights—which placed the state constitution in violation of the Fifteenth Amendment to the Constitution of the United States.

Ohioans, however, adopted the provision of the initiative and referendum for state matters. Other amendments permitted workmen's compensation, minimum wages, maximum hours legislation and an eight-hour day on public works, the abolition of prison contract labor, and the conservation of natural resources. The voters also approved amendments requiring the merit principle in the state's civil service as well as a stricter governmental regulations of banking. Despite the setback for women and a perpetuation of the mentality of racism, these provisions enabled Ohioans to meet rapidly changing economic and social conditions in a practical fashion.

The Progressive movement did not radically upset the traditional response of the voters to the two major parties. The Democratic party, however, dominated the gubernatorial office by winning five of the six elections between 1905 and 1918. It also carried the state for Woodrow Wilson in 1912 and 1916. But in 1920, when James M. Cox and Warren G. Harding, both Ohioans, held the presidential nominations for the Democratic and Republican parties, respectively, a shift in voting behavior occurred. Although Harding won the presidential election by a vote of 58.5 percent to Cox's 38.6 percent, the large gap resulted from the abandonment of the Democratic party by many German voters because of its wartime policies.

Although party contests remained evenly divided on the state and national levels until the election of 1936, the age of Ohio's supremacy in national politics ended with the election of Harding to the presidency. Not since the Virginia dynasty dominated national government during the early years of the Republic had a state made such a mark on national political affairs. Between the Civil War and 1920, seven Ohioans were elected to the presidency, and many others came close to winning the nomination. During this same time, six Ohioans sat on the Supreme Court and two served as chief justice. The state also sent 19 men to hold cabinet positions. Moreover, several Ohioans, including John Sherman, George H. Pendleton, Marcus A. Hanna, and Joseph B. Foraker wielded substantial power in the Senate. Others in the House of Representatives also played instrumental roles in setting the course of national politics.

"The map and the history of America required the westward-flowing Ohio."

—*Walter Havighurst*

Ohio represents great American middle; continuity and tradition remain major feature of Ohio landscape. Depression brings New Deal to Ohio.

Ohioans dominated national politics for 70 years primarily because of the diversity of the people, the strength of the economy, and the balance between rural and urban populations. The individuals who played major roles in national affairs appealed to broad national constituencies because they learned their skills in Ohio, where political success required candidates to reconcile wide differences among the electorate. Ohioans were both northerners and southerners as well as easterners and westerners, depending on family background, economic interest, and the way an individual interpreted geographic location. Consequently,

Ohio politicians addressed constituencies at home that generally were the same as those across the nation. Because Ohio ranked third in population much of this time, it had great numerical strength in Congress, political conventions, and party caucuses. Moreover, in a leading industrial state the parties could find individuals who were willing to support candidates financially or could choose wealthy individuals who would run for office themselves.

Continuity and traditionalism remained major features of Ohio's political contest through the presidential election of 1932, when Franklin Delano Roosevelt carried 49.9 percent of the vote while Republican incumbent Herbert Hoover garnered 47 percent. In 1936, however, voters responded favorably to New Deal policies by giving Roosevelt 58 percent of the vote to Alfred M. Landon's 37.4. Democrats made the largest gains in industrial and urban areas where the working class appreciated the New Deal programs, particularly the National Labor Relations Act of 1935, which recognized the right of labor to organize and bargain collectively.

The New Deal substantially affected party alignment, but it also influenced economic structure and altered the views Ohioans held sacred concerning the relationship of government to the individual. When the stock market crashed in 1929, Ohioans faced an economic and social crisis of unprecedented magnitude. Like other Americans, they tried to solve it by political means. They recoiled from laissez-faire government policies and the capitalist economics that Hoover championed by giving Roosevelt a plurality and the Democratic party control of the state. The spirit of the New Deal soon permeated public affairs in Ohio. The legislature provided increased regulation of the banks, created a board of arbitration to establish minimum wages for women and children, provided old-age pensions, granted relief from foreclosure, and reduced property taxation. Ohioans also participated in a host of New Deal programs and, indeed, allowed the federal and state governments to regulate their lives in a remarkably un-Jeffersonian manner.

The New Deal also injected a mild dose of socialism into the lives of most Ohioans. In 1935, for example, Roosevelt created the Rural Electrifi-

cation Administration (REA) to provide long-term, low-interest loans to local cooperatives to help provide electricity to rural homes. Only 20 percent of the farms in Ohio had electric service. Consequently, farm folks could not use a wide variety of electrical appliances and implements that would make their farms more efficient and productive while easing the burdens of their daily lives. Ohio farmers greeted the REA with open arms. By May 1936, Ohio led the nation in the number of farmers and rural residents who contracted for electric service. At first some farmers believed that the REA was socialistic, and they hesitated to give their support to the agency even though they desperately wanted electricity. Once the lights turned on, however, their misgivings quickly disappeared. With REA service, the long trip to the outhouse in subzero temperatures came to an end, along with the Saturday night bath and cooking over a wood stove in the summertime. Electric pumps, hot-water heaters and stoves now became common features throughout rural Ohio.

By 1938, electricity comes to Ohio farms; New Deal affects voting habits; Ohioans send Republicans to White House, but Democrats to Statehouse.

If the REA represented socialism, no farmer cared. This attitude, however, reflected not so much a change in political, social, or economic ideology as it did the reaffirmation of the practicality of Ohioans. Because the utility companies failed to furnish adequate service at a reasonable price, rural Ohioans assumed the responsibility of organizing independent coopera-

tives and, with federal aid, provided electric service for themselves. In 1936, the president of the Lorain-Medina Rural Electric Co-Operative exhibited this practical and independent spirit when he remarked that farmers had "begged" Ohio Edison for electric service but that the utility company always refused to provide it because of the alleged high cost; with access to REA support, "We just told them to go to hell."

By 1938 REA lines were a common feature of the landscape. A year later the electric co-ops helped provide power to 43 percent of Ohio's farms while only 25 percent of the farms nationwide had electric service. The reception that Ohio farmers and other rural residents gave to the REA also reaffirmed their continued belief in the Jeffersonian concept of agrarian self-sufficiency, democracy, and cooperation.

The New Deal also affected voting habits in Ohio. Indeed, in 1934 the traditional voting patterns began to shift as the Democratic vote moved from the rural to the urban areas. This realignment occurred because of the New Deal's influence and because large numbers of the foreign born were employed in the steel and rubber industries. The industrial, ethnic vote has remained with the Democratic party ever since. Still, not all cities are inherently Democratic, nor are rural areas naturally Republican. Cincinnati, for example, remains a Republican stronghold while the Democrats are influential in northwestern Ohio. Traditional Republican areas such as southeastern Ohio retain strong Republican links while the central counties still lean toward the Democratic party. In short, the current voting patterns are historic—that is, traditional—and they involve settlement patterns.

During the 1970s, the Republican party dominated the governorship because James A. Rhodes had wide appeal to many Democrats. The elections since 1940 have been based on conservative principles, and, moreover, organized labor has remained fragmented among Ohio's many cities, and it has been more concerned with local issues than with statewide unity. As a result, urban, organized labor has not built a strong political organization with a liberal, issue-oriented base, much in contrast to Chicago, Detroit, and Milwaukee, places where the working class has

associated economics with politics and the ballot box. Nor has the ethnic vote responded favorably to issue-oriented campaigns. Both groups tend to support only bread-and-butter issues. Thus, Ohio remains a job-oriented rather than an issue-oriented state in contests between the major parties. As such, it is similar to Indiana and Illinois. In contrast, Michigan, Wisconsin, and Minnesota are issue-oriented states at election time. Consequently, job-oriented states like Ohio are more traditional and conservative in their political response to problems, and they spend far less for government services. Ohio, for example, customarily has been more interested in good roads than in public support for education, aid to dependent children, or old-age assistance.

Ohio politics remains sedate; rectitude favored over reform; agriculture becomes specialized and mechanized; only eight percent of Ohioans remain on farms by 1960.

 In many respects, then, Ohio remains the "great, Middle-class state." Job-oriented politics, together with a continued reverence for the virtues of hard work and political conservatism, govern daily affairs. Moreover, self-reliance and independence remain defined in terms of freedom from government. This Jeffersonian traditionalism in politics helps explain the caution which the state's politicians use when dealing with economic and social issues. Bold action or the advocacy of major alternatives might divide the electorate, hence the preference for meeting the traditional expectations of the people. Consequently, few differences exist among

candidates. The public tends to favor rectitude rather than reform from its representatives. The requirements of the postwar world, however, not only caused Ohioans to adjust or reaffirm their political loyalties, but it also led them to question, for the first time, the values of the Jeffersonian tradition. Ultimately, the postwar economy would destroy any lingering hope for the perpetuation of this traditional way of life in Ohio, the Midwest, or the nation. It also would seriously jeopardize Ohioans' faith in the Puritan ethic.

During the Second World War, for example, many farmers reared in the agricultural depression of the 1920s and 1930s experienced the first prosperity they had ever known. The postwar years also were a time of milk and honey for most Ohio farms. But while science and technology contributed to higher productivity, it also dramatically changed the emphasis and number of Ohio farms. Agriculturalists became increasingly specialized and mechanized, and specialization and technological change contributed to the continued decline of the farm population and to the number of farms. Moreover, while production remained high, prices were insufficient to enable many Ohio farmers to maintain full-time operations. More and more agriculturalists sought employment off the farm to make ends meet. By the mid-1950s about 37 percent of Ohio's agriculturalists worked away from their farms for a hundred or more days each year. Thus, by the late 1950s part-time farming no longer represented a period in which an individual worked in outside employment to build the capital to begin full-time farming. Now part-time agriculture was essential to preserve the family farm.

Despite the necessity to seek off-the-farm employment, many farmers remained on the land because they believed the values of rural living were superior to those of an urban environment. The family farm, like the church, the local school, and the Supreme Court, remained a symbol of freedom and democracy, and Ohio farmers strongly defended it. Throughout the 1950s, then, the Jeffersonian tradition remained strong. Nevertheless, the reality of its continued validity was open to question. Indeed, agriculture in Ohio, as elsewhere in the Midwest, could not escape the influence of science, technology, new manage-

ment practices, and government policy. By the 1950s farming had become more than a way of life. It was a business where only the most efficient survived. The days of the small-scale farmer were gone, and many of them went bankrupt or quit.

By 1960 only eight percent of Ohio's population were farmers. Three years later only six percent remained. More and more agricultural land was lost to cultivation each year, due in part to urban expansion. Despite the decline of agricultural population and good cropland, however, Ohio's farmers became more productive than ever. But increased productivity lowered prices and forced more farmers from the land. Thousands left the farms for the more economically secure life offered in the cities and towns, where the service industries expanded rapidly. By 1970 farmers represented only three percent of the state's population. Ohio farmers frequently felt helpless. No single farmer could change the economy by acting alone, and farmers were too independent, too conservative, and too diverse in their needs to act collectively.

Despite these problems, Ohio's farmers remained convinced that farming provided the good life. They continued to believe that the farm was the best place to raise their children and that it provided the foundation for democratic government. Despite sentimental attachments and nostalgic views of farm life, however, most agriculturalists regarded agriculture as a business. Nonetheless, by the late 1970s Ohio's farm income lagged far behind the national average. More farmers sought off-the-farm employment and nearly half of their income came from outside jobs. The Jeffersonian tradition remained, but it had less credibility than ever before. By the early 1980s Ohio had more part-time farmers than full-time farmers. Only the most productive and efficient farmers were able to marshal the resources needed to maintain operation in an economy where they did not control the prices that they received. As a result, more and more young men and women fled the farms. Their parents frequently encouraged them to go, and many parents left as well. No one can yet say with certainty what effects this upheaval will have on life in Ohio.

By last quarter of the 20th century, corn belt turns to rust belt; economy suffers through industrial decline and loss of high-paying jobs. White and black underclass grows.

 By the last quarter of the 20th century, Ohio was known more for being part of the "rust belt" than the corn belt. Like other industrial states, Ohio's economy suffered hard times as cheap, foreign competition, rampant inflation, and rapid technological change decimated manufacturing and heavy industry. As the cities withered economically, the American dream also faded for many Ohioans. Most, with advanced education or access to retraining programs, adjusted by entering such fields as computer science, and many shifted to the service industry. Between 1975 and 1980, however, more than 900,000 people fled the state in search of opportunities elsewhere.

Many of those who left Ohio were among the young and well-educated. Only Michigan lost more people in this category than Ohio between 1978 and 1984. By mid-1986 only Illinois had a higher unemployment rate than Ohio. Those who left the state did not relocate in the Midwest but rather sought employment and refuge in California, Texas, or Florida. The loss of population had serious political as well as economic consequences—the potential loss of two congressional seats and a corresponding reduction of political power and favor.

The social costs of the decline in Ohio's industrial base also are serious and incalculable. Unless a majority of the displaced industrial

workers can be retrained for jobs in the growing service and light-manufacturing industries, more and more families will fall beneath the poverty line. Moreover, with the loss of high-paying industrial jobs and the shift of workers to lesser-paying positions in the service industry, declining personal income will require an increase in taxation of some sort and the expansion of the state's bureaucracy to meet a host of social problems ranging from malnutrition to crime. Certainly, Ohio's future, both on the farms and in the cities, involves mastering new forms of science and technology. The brawn of the past no longer is sufficient to build new or to sustain old agricultural- and industrial-based economies.

The triple plagues of industrial decline, agricultural depression, and flight to the Sun Belt will not soon end, and the stigma of the "rust belt" will continue to mar the state's reputation as a pleasant place to live. Moreover, economic decline has widened the gap between the haves and have-nots. The increasing number of poor whites and poor blacks also is creating an underclass that is unified by economic plight rather than by race. Continued economic recession, high unemployment, and inadequate education may in time create a solidarity within the underclass that will have political, economic, and social ramifications for all Ohioans. Just what these ramifications may be are, of course, as broad and ill-defined as they are potentially dangerous.

Ohio is in the process of major cultural adjustment caused by economic factors beyond the control of the people. Farmers are no longer certain that they are working to gain a better living, and many doubt that agriculture ensures the best quality of life. Moreover, the laboring community no longer strives to gain new rights but rather works to preserve past gains. The strength Ohio drew from its natural resources also has waned. Coal, which once supported the state's heavy industry, now causes difficulties for others beyond Ohio's borders in the form of acid rain. For many, the American dream has escaped them. With a sluggish industrial and agricultural economy, people now speak of downward mobility on the social scale as a certainty. Children no longer expect to live more comfortably than their parents. The rapidly growing service

industry that replaced heavy industry, manufacturing, and mining as the chief employer pays far less than union-protected jobs. By 1980 the service industry employed approximately 67 percent of the work force. Consequently, the Jeffersonian tradition essentially is gone and the future of the Puritan ethic remains very much in question.

Ohioans, however, remain a practical people. And, despite the demise of the Jeffersonian tradition and the waning of the industrial state, they continue to be an optimistic people. Although Ohioans hold many of the same opinions held by other midwesterners, they are a moderate people in the heartland. If, as Woodrow Wilson proclaimed, the voice of the Midwest is the "voice of protest," then Ohioans stand alone. If the Midwest is generally against something rather than for it, or if it is the home of the native radicalism of the Right and the Left, then Ohioans are different. Although they have flirted with conservatism and liberalism, they are predominantly middle-of-the-roaders. Ohio is not, as one writer noted of the heartland, "a bizarre and uniquely American mixture of Rotarians and Wobblies."

In the waning years of the 20th century, however, Ohioans suffered an identity crisis.

Located on the eastern edge of the Midwest and on the western edge of the East, Ohioans were not sure where they belonged. Although they were certain that eastern effetism was not for them, they admired the cultural, economic, and political vibrancy of the eastern seaboard. The people of Ohio, like other midwesterners, also felt a sense of being under siege. They frequently were portrayed as naive, unsophisticated, bland hicks, particularly by easterners. At the same time Ohioans were certain that people with talent only *came* from the Great Plains, they did not *go* there. Still, Ohioans have a cultural affinity, forged over nearly 200 years of common experience, with the other people of the heartland.

Today, Ohio faces all the industrial, agricultural, and urban problems that plague the Midwest and the nation. Ohioans also enjoy the benefits of being part of the heartland—a moderate life-style, a pace that permits reflection, and a bountiful land. If the heartland is indeed the most American region of the United States, then Ohio is the key to the Midwest, economically, politically, and socially—that is, culturally. As such, the Buckeye state remains the epitome of midwestern distinctiveness.

—by R. Douglas Hurt, by permission of Indiana University Press

OHIO: HOME TO IMMIGRANTS

Ohio has become so synonymous with American normalcy that setting in the state a television show about aliens pretending to be human beings is an entirely predictable development. According to Terry Turner, one of the producers of *3rd Rock from the Sun*, "The aliens...looked at Earth and said, 'What's the best cross-section of America and people that we can find?'" Turner decided that Ohio was the obvious answer to that question during an initial visit in the 1970s. "It looked like what I thought America looked like. Los Angeles doesn't and New York doesn't...America, in my head, is Ohio."

Man on Moon

—Andrew Cayton, *Ohio, the History of a People*

Bobcats reminder: There's no U in Ohio

When Shakespeare wondered what was in a name and wrote that a rose by any other name would still smell as sweet, he never had to deal with the flower of the Hocking River Valley.

Ever since Ohio University put a full-court legal press on Ohio State over the Buckeyes' use of the word "Ohio" in merchandising, the four-letter, three-syllable word has been one of the preferred names for the university in Athens, Ohio. While Ohio State and Ohio University presidents worked out an amicable settlement, the dispute reflected Ohio University's wish to merge its identity with that of the state and simply be known as Ohio.

It's easy to see how Ohio University's hunter green shorts get in a twist when their fans see OSU football coach Jim Tressel, after a victory, leading the singing of "Carmen Ohio," the Ohio State alma mater, because the singers make semaphores of their arms in signaling O-HI-O.

An Ohio University spokesman left a message for me during the Mid-American Conference Tournament, complaining in part about the "Ohio U." and "OU" references in my stories. I was tempted to say, "Oh, you kid." Or maybe, "OU, kid."

To the average fan, the MAC school is not Michigan, Indiana, Wisconsin or Illinois, although it preceded the state universities of each of those places. In fact, it was the first institution of higher learning in the whole Northwest Territory, from which were carved those states, as well as Ohio.

Nor is it Texas, Florida, Colorado, Mississippi, or the other schools that Sports Illustrated's Frank Deford calls "University of Somewhere" schools. Deford's humorous essay drew a distinction between aristocratic "University of" schools and the bottom-dwelling A&M's, Techs, and State U.'s in their shadow.

The problem is that the state of Ohio broke the state-school mold with Ohio State and Ohio—the school, not the state. (See how confusing this is getting?) Ohio State, though established 66 years after Ohio University, considers itself the state's flagship school. In TV introductions before big games, its players go so far as to identify the place as THE Ohio State University. The capital letters are understood because of the vocal emphasis. Meanwhile, no one ever called the school in Athens the "University of Ohio."

The use of "Ohio," however, would create a lot of "Who's on first?" stuff, such as:

"Where do you go to school?"

"Ohio."

"Where in Ohio?"

"Ohio."

Let's cut this out before What's on second, I Don't Know's on third, and I Don't Care is at short.

The Athens School's graduates and fans use both "Ohio U." and "OU," presumably without official reprimand. On a national basis, however, "OU" would probably be considered Oklahoma, because of the Sooners' football success. Using "OU" below the Ohio River recalls former Boston Celtics' coach Red Auerbach's comment about the rival Bruins of the NHL: "A hundred miles outside of Boston, it means UCLA."

As for discarding the "OU" term, well, when the Bobcats were staging a late rally in the tournament quarterfinals to catch Miami of Ohio—oops, that's wrong too; according to the MAC Media Guide, it's Miami (Ohio)—their fans rose as one, chanting, in staccato bursts: "OU! OU! OU!"

Gee, you would have thought it would be "O! O! O!"

Uh-O! I think another reprimand is coming my way.

—Bill Livingston, by permission of The Plain Dealer

practical Ohio
moments

Ohioans remain a practical people. And, despite the demise of the Jeffersonian tradition and the waning of the industrial state, they continue to be an optimistic people. Although Ohioans hold many of the same opinions held by other midwesterners, they are a moderate people in the heartland.
—see R. Douglas Hurt, *Ohio Almanac*, page 22, first paragraph

Why here?
Why *Ohio*?

—dialogue,
The Faculty,
1998 horror
movie

Ohio was flat, like a headache.
> *Spoken in Darkness, Ann Imbrie*

The people...claimed they could hear the rustle of cornstalks in my voice, could see the roll of glacial plains in my walk, could detect in my manners and politics the domes of country courthouses and the steeples of country churches.
> *Ohio-born writer Scott Russell Sanders*

Ohio is the flat place between Hoboken and Malibu.
> *Ohio transplant John Fleischman*

When I moved to New York from Ohio in 1974 I thought of myself as a person from the continent.
> *Ian Frazier, New Yorker*

A real kid. A country Jake. A foozle from Ohio.
> *Tom De Haven, Funny Papers*

The Ohioans I've met have been very interesting, down-to-earth people. But if you ask me what Ohioans are like, I could only say that I know they're really into lawnmowers.
> *Robert Redford, after filming in Ohio*

He was surely from Ohio; no one immigrated here, ever, and I understood why. There was no body of water nearby, for one thing. Oceans and rivers, for us, were scenic features for nature shows and greeting cards. We had only vacant lots and alleys, and, on the outskirts of town, fields of soybeans that smelled when they were processed, for what, we could not imagine.

White Girls, Lynn Lauber

Somewhere, carved out of the cornfields of Nebraska
or Iowa or Ohio, are small towns where
no one is having sex.

Louise Kiernan, Chicago Tribune

Bring your family to the place where the Wright Brothers were born and would have stayed except they heard there was a high wind in North Carolina. So if you're looking for fun and do not particularly need wind, sand, or an ocean, then come to Ohio.

—slogan suggested for Ohio by Laura Pulfer

When I moved to New York from Ohio in 1974 I thought of myself as a person from the continent.

Ian Frazier, New Yorker

The Bertholdi statue must be modeled after some Ohio girl. The ears are three feet long.

New Orleans Daily City, commenting on the Statue of Liberty,
September 27, 1884

Oh, yes, we're in the north now. The barns are all bigger than the houses.

Eudora Welty's mother, upon crossing into Ohio, One Writer's
Beginnings by Eudora Welty

Born in Old Town

near Xenia,

his name meant

"Shooting Star,"

*and **Tecumseh** was*

indeed brilliant,

a courageous warrior

and intelligent

statesman who tried

to unite the Indians

against the white man's

frontier landgrab.

Widely respected and

admired, he was killed

during the War

of 1812 at the Battle

of Thames, where he

was a brigadier general

fighting in the

British army.

1670
French explorer LaSalle discovers the Ohio River.

1745
British fort erected on Sandusky Bay.

1748
Ohio Land Company formed, plans to colonize Ohio.

1750-51
Ohio Land Company sends **Christopher Gist** to explore Ohio.

1772
Missionaries **Zeisberger** and **Heckwelder** set up Schoenbrunn mission.

1774
Lord Dunmore's War forces Shawnees to surrender claim to lands south of the Ohio River.

1782
Ninety-six Delaware Indians, all of whom are Christians and peaceable,
slaughtered by a posse of frontiersmen at Gnadenhutten.

1783
Treaty of Paris ends the Revolutionary War—Ohio Valley ceded to emerging United States.

1784-86
Treaties remove Indians from southern Ohio.

1785
Land Ordinance of 1785—townships organized in Ohio; leads to orderly transfer of land and
sets pattern for land sales in the West.

1786
Ohio Company of Associates formed to purchase $1,000,000 worth of Ohio land.

1787
Northwest Ordinance establishes government for Ohio Territory;
General Arthur St. Clair appointed first governor.

1788
Forty-eight settlers establish Marietta, first permanent white settlement in Ohio.

1789
Fort Washington erected at present-day Cincinnati.

1790
Harmar's army of 1,420 regular soldiers and militia are defeated
by a much smaller Indian force commanded by Miami war chief **Little Turtle (Michikinikwa)**

1791
St. Clair's Defeat, 630 soldiers killed by Indian force under the command of **Little Turtle** and **Blue Jacket**
in worst single defeat ever suffered by an American army at the hands of Indians.

1794
General "Mad" Anthony Wayne defeats **Blue Jacket** at Battle of Fallen Timbers,
destroys much of the Indian power in Ohio. With threat of Indian attacks greatly reduced,
settlers pour into Ohio territory.

1795
Treaty of Greenville—Indians lose all but one quarter of Ohio.

1796
Town of Cleveland platted by **Moses Cleaveland.**

Zane's Trail, Ohio's first formal road, completed;
leads from Adams County to Jefferson City.

First book published in Ohio—*Maxwell's Code*, printed in Cincinnati.

1799
First Northwest Territory legislature meets in Cincinnati.

1800
Harrison Land Act makes possible sale of land
west of the Muskingum to individuals at $2 per acre;
Indiana Territory separates from Ohio, making land more affordable for average settler.

Connecticut gives up claim to land in northeast Ohio known as the Western Reserve .

1801
Cincinnati is site of first federal land sale in Ohio.

1803
Congress approves Ohio Constitution and admits Ohio as 17th state.

Edward Tiffin elected governor in first state elections.

1804
Ohio University founded; first college in Old Northwest Territory.

OHIO: APOGEE OF CIVILIZATION

Where would modern civilization reach its apogee? The Ohio Valley, of course. Progressing from savagery to civilization in less than a century, the region had an astonishing history. Christianity and representative government had made the place so special that many people chose to live in the Old Northwest even when there was more land south of the Ohio River. William Davis Gallagher, poet and editor who lived almost all of the 18th century in Cincinnati, proclaimed that "an experiment in Humanity, higher in its character and sublimer in its results" than any attempted elsewhere was happening in Ohio. Here there would be "the freest forms of social development and the highest order of human civilization." All signs pointed to "a Day...dawning upon this North-Western region" that would awaken all "to a just sense of their real dignity and importance in the social scale, by proclaiming to them that they are neither slaves nor nonentities, but true men and women." Here would Anglo-Saxons find their manifest destiny realized. Here would "Truth, Justice, Mercy, and Love" flourish.
—Andrew Cayton, *Ohio, the History of a People*

Setting of Ohio, Northwest Territory, 1788

1811
Battle of Tippecanoe—Harrison destroys Prophetstown, breaks **Tecumseh's** federation.

1812
War with the British.

Columbus named by Ohio legislature as site for state capitol.

1813
Fort Meigs, near Toledo, constructed by William Henry Harrison.

Oliver Hazzard Perry turns back British at Put-in-Bay; his success threatens to cut off British forces
in Western Ontario and leads to final British defeat in west at Battle of Thames.

1817
First abolitionist newspaper, *The Philanthropist,* published at Mt. Pleasant.

1825
Construction on Miami and Erie canals initiated; canal will open interior of state to commerce and boost
Toledo's fortunes when it is chosen over Sandusky as northern terminus.

National Road reaches St. Clairsville; road becomes nation's major east-west land route
aiding greatly Ohio's economic well-being.

1832
Cleveland and Portsmouth (on the Ohio River) linked with completion of Erie Canal; canal
opens part of Ohio's interior to commerce, aiding growth of Portsmouth and Cleveland (over Lorain)
as well as creating Akron.

1833
National Road reaches Columbus from Maryland.

Oberlin College founded; first coeducational college in U.S.,
and one of first to admit blacks.

1835
Ohio wins bloodless "Toledo War" with Michigan.

1836
Philanthropist press wrecked by Cincinnati mob.

1839
Construction begun on Statehouse in Columbus.

1842
Wyandottes, last Indian tribe in Ohio, sell lands and go west.

1851
New State Constitution approved by voters.

1857
Panic of 1857 initiated by failure of Ohio Life Insurance and Trust Company.

1858
Oberlin-Wellington Rescue—fugitive slave freed by mob in Wellington;
37 charged under Fugitive Slave Law; two serve short sentences.
Some historians cite event as beginning of Civil War.

1861-65
Civil War—346,326 Ohioans, three out of every five men in the state,
fight on Union side; 35,475 die.

1863
Confederate raiders led by **General John Morgan** captured in Meigs County;
raid has no military value and is little more than terrorist act.

1869
Cincinnati Red Stockings are first professional baseball team.

1870
Standard Oil Company organized by **John D. Rockefeller.**
Company grows into one of largest in the world, creating one of world's richest families.

1873
Ohio Agricultural and Mechanical College (later to become Ohio State University) opens.

1886
Electrolytic process of aluminum manufacture developed in Oberlin by **Charles Martin Hall.**

American Federation of Trades and Labor is founded in Columbus
with **Samuel Gomphers** as its president.

1892
Legislature resolution makes it illegal to terminate employees for membership in a labor union.
This legislation helps make Ohio one of nation's strongest union states.

1894
Populist Party leader and reformer **Jacob Coxey** leads protest march on Washington, D.C.;
it begins tradition of marching on Washington as a way of protesting the social order.

First rubber tire manufactured in Akron by B.F. Goodrich.

1900
Population: 4,157,545

1913
Spring floods kill 428, destroy $250 million in property.

1921
Bing Act passed—requires students to remain in school until graduation or age 18;
thus bars children under 16 from most employment.

1925
Dirigible **Shenandoah** crashes near Ava, Ohio, killing 14 people.

1929
Steel becomes Ohio's #1 industry.

1934
First—three percent—state sales tax imposed.

1937
Ohio River flooding leaves 750,000 homeless.

1938
Organization and construction of Muskingum Watershed Conservancy District completed.

Cincinnati-born

Robert Alphonso Taft

learned politics
at his presidential
papa's knee and served
in the U.S. Senate
from 1938 until he
died in 1953.
His conservatism and
isolationism—he
opposed the New Deal,
NATO, the UN, and
the Nuremberg
trials—earned him
the nickname
"Mr. Republican."
Taft didn't even
like Ike, losing the
1952 presidential
nomination to
Eisenhower after a
bitter struggle.

1953
Congress discovers it has neglected to officially recognize Ohio's statehood; passes formal resolution declaring official date of Ohio's entry into union as March 1, 1803.

1954
Frank Lausche's reelection makes him only five-term governor in Ohio history.

Ohio Constitutional Amendment extends governor's term to four years but no more than two consecutive terms at a time, effective 1959.

1955
Ohio Turnpike, 241 miles long, is completed giving northern Ohio quick access by highway to markets east and west.

1959
Lake Erie open to international trade with opening of St. Lawrence Seaway. Seaway makes Ohio lake ports seaports—able to ship by sea to every part of the world.

Official state motto—"With God all things are possible"—is adopted.

Nation's first truth-in-advertising law is adopted in Ohio.

1962
Marine Colonel ***John Glenn*** of New Concord becomes first American to orbit the Earth.

1963
Ohio's first black cabinet member, ***William O. Walker***, is appointed Director of Industrial Relations.

1967
Carl Stokes elected mayor of Cleveland, first black mayor in the U.S.

1969
Apollo 11 spaceflight—***Neil Armstrong*** becomes the first man to walk on the moon.

1970
Four killed, nine wounded by National Guardsmen during anti-Vietnam War protest at Kent State.

Ohio loan scandal causes Republicans to lose elections for governor, attorney general, treasurer, and auditor.

1971
In an attempt to lower the reliance on property taxes (middle class) and sales taxes (lower class), State income tax adopted. The bill only passed when coupled with property tax reduction.

1973
Voters approve Ohio State Lottery, a mixed blessing; although providing additional revenue to schools, the amount provided is much less than many voters expected.

1974
Xenia tornado kills 34, $100 million in damages.

15,000 acres of the Cuyahoga Valley become the first national park in Ohio.

1976
Ohio's last commuter train, Cleveland-to-Youngstown shuttle, is shut down. The idea of passenger trains serving Ohio would reemerge 30 years later.

1977
Cleveland Public Schools run out of money, teachers work for no salary.

A federal court rules that Ohio's method of funding schools through local
property taxes denies equal education to all.

1978
Blizzard causes $100 million in damages and clean-up costs.

James Rhodes becomes first four-time, four-year term governor.

Bankrupt Cleveland defaults on $14 million debt, first city to default since the Great Depression.

1979
Busing to eliminate segregation in Cleveland, Columbus, and Dayton Public Schools begins.

1980
In the U.S. Supreme Court Ohio wins the 14-year dispute with Kentucky over the Ohio River border.

1983
Marysville Honda plant dedicated—major step in Ohio's emergence as nation's
second-leading state in the automotive industry.

1988
An oil spill into Monongahela River from Ashland Oil Co. storage tank moves downriver
and into the Ohio, causing several Ohio towns to close down intake systems.

1989
Fernald nuclear plant shuts down; FBI investigates: cleanups estimated at $1 billion.

1990
Cincinnati's Contemporary Art Center indicted on obscenity charges for Mapplethorpe photography
exhibit; subsequently cleared on First Amendment grounds.

1991
Troubled Zimmer nuclear power plant in Moscow, Ohio,
becomes nation's first nuclear-to-coal conversion.

1993
Antioch College adopts written policy on sexual relations that requires both partners to give verbal
approval before moving to next level of sexual intimacy.

1995
The Bosnian peace agreement signed after negotiations at Wright-Patterson Air Force Base.

1997
The Ohio Supreme Court's *DeRolph I* decision rules 4-3 that state's method of school funding
discriminates against poor schools and is unconstitutional. In 2002, after two more decisions, Court
relinquishes jurisdiction, effectively ending legislation in state court system.
In 2003, case is appealed to United States Supreme Court.

2003
Ohio celebrates bicentennial, as well as
100th anniversary of Wright brothers' first flight.

Sophisticates detested **Jim Rhodes'** *practiced bumpkin's foolishness and both parties cursed his maverick ways— until they needed him—but even his enemies admired his roguish charm, the way he could make the most outrageous admissions with a smile and a wink. When reporters criticized him for doing the very things he'd once accused his enemies of doing, he'd say, "So what? That was then and this is now."*

—Sue Gorisek

The conventional group portraiture of the 19th century showed those stalwart Ohioans who held the Nation's highest office as somber, bearded fellows in frockcoats. They seem reticent, staring grimly at the camera as if the very act of posing were painful. They do not appear playful, or as hale-fellows-well-met, and to a man they suffered with image and public relations. And yet these Ohioans presided over the industrialization of America and its emergence as a world power. Why is the general impression of whiskers and small deeds? Why is their tenure in office largely unheralded? If you pronounce them a fuzzy lot, then read on. Try this primer on the personalities, the major events, and who did what (and to whom).

"All the presidents nobody ever heard of came from Ohio."

—Ann Imbrie,
Spoken in Darkness

They stare out of their official portraits—bearded, heavy bodied men with tall foreheads and dark, sensitive eyebrows. Dressed in black frock coats and posed before massive desks, they clasp a lapel in one hand, a rolled document in the other. If the light is right and the painter was good, they look immensely dignified. If not, they look stuffed. They are Ohio's gifts to the nation; presidents of the United States and native sons. They were born in rough Ohio frontier towns where the memory of a time when wolves and Indians haunted the edges of forest clearings was still fresh. They fought in the Civil War. They read the Bible, plowed, rode horseback and made speeches full of bombast and oratorical flourishes about large simple 19th century truths such as self-reliance, honesty, and patriotism. They didn't seem to notice that many of the lesser men around them believed only in self-interest. These Ohioans presided over government.

The beards disappear just before the close of the century. The cleanshaven Ohio presidents are plumper, paler men. They have urban habits and sophisticated tastes. They come from cities and up-to-date towns with electric lights and indoor plumbing. Their houses have wide front porches and flower gardens. They sit for their portraits, overfilling their chairs with their jackets open and gold watch fobs visible. They are the creators of the modern presidency—decisive, managed, and important. In con-

trast, their predecessors seemed to spend their time staring contemplatively out the window, formulating great axioms while the nation went unheeding about its own business. The 20th century presidents govern or at least, they are supposed to be governing. The lesser men are still around them.

In the 53 years between the Reconstruction Era and the Roaring Twenties, ten men inhabited the White House, and eight of them were from Ohio. No other state has had such a period of hegemony; no state but Virginia has put forward more presidents. In the 14 elections from 1868 to 1920 inclusive, the Republicans ran Ohioans 11 times. In 1920 Harry Daugherty supposedly talked Warren G. Harding of Marion into running on the grounds that an Ohio candidate was such a fixture of Republican conventions, the nation would think the state had seceded if one didn't come forward. That year, the Democrats finally read the handwriting on the wall and ran James Cox of Dayton. He lost.

The Republicans in 1952 considered Robert Taft, but it was Eisenhower, another Republican war

THE BUCKEYE BOYS CLUB—Rutherford Hayes (father and son), William Howard Taft, and Ulysses S. Grant, as they are pictured on a tranquil Ohio afternoon in this fanciful illustration for James Cash's book, *Unsung Heroes, Ohioans in the White House: A Modern Appraisal.*

hero, who won the day. John Glenn's campaign for the Democrats' presidential nomination also fizzled in 1984. Curiously, the nation that could rarely say no to an Ohioan president for so long has taken even longer to come close to choosing another Buckeye for the White House.

Perhaps the reason can be found in the historical record of Ohio presidents, because to be frank, their overall reputation leaves much to be desired. One is tempted to say that notoriety rather than fame is what sets them apart. Schoolchildren can rattle off with pride the great Virginia presidents, "Washington, Jefferson, Madison, Monroe . . . ," but when called upon to recite the Ohioans, they often get a fuzzy feeling behind the eyes. They either miss Hayes or count Cleveland (who was not a city but a Democrat from New Jersey). Read the roll—Grant, Hayes, Garfield, Harrison, McKinley, Taft and Harding—and the general impression is of whiskers and small deeds.

In 1948, Professor Arthur M. Schlesinger Sr., of Harvard University, invited fifty-five of his colleagues, historians, political scientists, and writers to rank the administrations of each of the American presidents. In 1962, he invited seventy-five experts to do the same. In both of these prestigious polls, the Ohioans fared very poorly. Two were excluded altogether because their terms were too short, several turned up in Lower and Middle Average; and two, Grant and Harding, were isolated from all the other presidents as the only failures in our history.

Although our high scorer, Rutherford Hayes, attained the third rung of Average in both polls, he, as well as Hayes, McKinley, and Taft—all decent men—seem to have been cut adrift in the national memory.

Ohio's presidents seemed dogged by bad luck and their records spotted with asterisks. If you count William Henry Harrison, (the original asterisk in the Ohio line because he was born in Virginia but lived his adult life on the Ohio frontier) as Ohio's eighth president, four of them died in office, including two who were assassinated.) Two were defeated in reelection. One left office under a cloud of scandal. One died in office a few months before the scandals broke.

The Ohioan claims to fame are often so dubious. Taft, for example, was the largest president— three hundred plus pounds—and the first to play golf. Garfield was the first left-hander in the White

House. Benjamin Harrison had two men named Foster in his cabinet. Hayes was the first president to assume office after having lost the popular vote.

On the other side of the coin Ohio presidents were often distinguished by the sheer peacefulness of their terms. Despite their impressive military credentials, only one—McKinley—took us to war.

Whatever the grievances of Indians, struggling trade unionists and disenfranchised blacks, the Ohioans presided over long periods of surface calm while the country went about its business of growing. New states came into the Union. New industries flourished. New inventions emerged. Immigrants rushed to climb into the American melting pot. The lofty quality projected by all those dignified Buckeyes on Pennsylvania Avenue was finally given a brand name by the last of the line, Harding, who promoted himself as the statesman committed to "a return to normalcy." How any one man could give ordinariness a bad name is a study in itself, but Harding did it so thoroughly that he left the nation Buckeye-shy for sixty years.

To play fair, William Henry Harrison shouldn't be counted as one of "our" presidents as he was born in Virginia in 1773, the last president born before the revolution. But Harrison's political career was an uncanny prototype of the Ohio presidential candidate formula perfected after the Civil War. Moreover, his grandson, Benjamin Harrison, was a fine specimen of the production model Buckeye president and owed much of his appeal to his grandfather's fame. William Henry Harrison was the first president whose image and career were tied to the Midwestern frontier. He was also a military hero—the victor over the Shawnee at Tippecanoe—who married well and settled at North Bend on a thousand-acre estate to live out his peaceful retirement in an elegant house overlooking the Ohio River. An educated, handsome man, he began the tradition of "log cabin" presidents because of a terrible tactical error on the part of his Democratic opponents. They sneered at his political simplicity (he had never voted in an election before his nomination by the Whigs in 1840), claiming Harrison would be content to live on a pension in a log cabin

with a ready supply of hard cider.

In the same way "I Like Ike" buttons and gourmet jelly beans have become modern political symbols, so too did miniature log cabins and cider barrels become the symbols of the "Tippecanoe-and-Tyler-Too" campaign. The "log cabin" campaign overlooked Harrison's patrician birth, his well-to-do lifestyle as well as his nebulous political convictions. It was the first triumph of modern advertising. Harrison won handily and set out for Washington, where he invited Daniel Webster to serve as secretary of state. Webster's first duty was to edit Harrison's inaugural speech. Webster was horrified when he saw the massive text that dwelt lengthily on the rise of the "proconsul" in ancient Rome. After a day of cutting, Webster returned, a shaken man, to his boarding house where his landlady asked solicitously what dreadful ordeal he had faced.

"You would think that something had happened," Webster told her, "if you knew what I have done. I have killed seventeen proconsuls, as dead as smelts, every one of them!"

Despite Webster's deletions, Harrison delivered the longest inaugural address in history. He did it bare-headed and coatless in the teeth of a blizzard. A month later, he was dead of pneumonia. But a pattern had been set. It fell to Ulysses S. Grant to perfect it.

 There was nothing bogus about Grant's log cabin Ohio origins. He was born in the crude settlement of Point Pleasant on the Ohio, grew up in nearby Georgetown, the horse-loving son of a tanner, and was packed off to West Point. He hated the place and when a bill to dissolve the military academy came before Congress, he prayed it would pass. Nonetheless Grant served with distinction in the Mexican War. Afterward, he slid into failure as a businessman. While the nation was tearing itself apart over the slavery issue, Grant was drinking heavily and serving as a clerk in his father's tannery in Galena, Illinois. He was known around town as an amiable man in a battered army overcoat. When the war broke out, the citizens of Galena remembered Grant's overcoat and his West Point background. They wanted him to be captain of the unit they were forming. Grant declined. Later, the governor of Illinois asked him to take over as colonel of the Seventh District regiment. He turned out to be the man of the hour.

In all the ineptitude and posturing that characterized the Union command in the early years of the war, Grant's star shone out like a beacon from the west. "I cannot spare the man—he fights," said Lincoln after Grant captured Fort Henry and Fort Donelson. When reports reached the White House that Grant was on the bottle again, Lincoln is supposed to have said, "Find out what he drinks, and send it to the rest of my generals."

Grant's abilities were decidedly mixed. As Woodrow Wilson wrote," Grant combined great gifts with great mediocrity." Historian Thomas A. Bailey divided them more precisely: "The great gifts related to war, the great mediocrity to government." As a general, Grant was a visionary. He saw the war in its national scale and victory at the end of a long bloody slog. Thus, he reached Appomatox Court House in the spring of 1865 to accept General Lee's surrender. Grant's terms were magnanimous and probably saved the country from a long, drawn out guerrilla war, preventing Lee's veterans from melting away to the mountains to revenge a humiliation. From that high point, Grant's career took him to the White House in 1869 and then straight downhill.

Grant's election had little to do with his political philosophy. (He didn't seem to have one.) It had to do with the war. The victors of the War to Save the Union were the North, in general, and the Republican Party, in particular. The GOP presented itself as the moral and political heir of Lincoln. For fifty years, they evoked the memory of the gallant Union dead who gave their full measure of devotion to crush the serpent of secession.

The War Between the States had moved indoors to the ballot box. With the South solidly Democratic (other than the increasingly disenfranchised black population) and New England "rockribbed" Republican, the growing Midwest became the "swing" region. With Ohio, the third-largest state in the Union between 1840 and 1889, an Ohio candidate came into the ring with a distinct "home field" advantage.

Grant was the first Republican presidential candidate to profit from the new political geography, but "waving the bloody shirt" was a potent charm for

"Papa says I may offer you twenty dollars for the colt, but if you won't take that, I am to offer twenty-two and a half, and if you won't take that, to give you twenty-five."

— *Ulysses Grant, age 8, buying a horse, Personal Memoirs of U.S. Grant, 1885*

the GOP until the end of the century.

Given his sizable mandate, Grant promptly squandered it. He filled his administration with disreputable cronies, relations, and speculators. He was an honest man in the center of a circus of graft and guile. Scandals came one after another—the Credit Mobilier, in which railroad officials bought favors from government officials; the Whiskey Ring, in which his personal secretary was implicated, the "Black Friday" Wall Street panic set off by secret information leaking from the White House to "friendly" investors. There were a few bright spots. He turned the government's policy from exterminating the Indians to putting them on reservations. Yet the endemic corruption of his administration sullied even that.

Grant was easily reelected in 1872, fumbled a nomination bid in 1880 and soon after went broke when his "friends" knocked the pins from under his banking firm. His final victory came in an unlikely arena—literature. To recoup his family's fortunes, he undertook to write his memoirs for Mark Twain's publishing house. Dying of a painful throat cancer, the old campaigner finished the last volume four days before his death in 1885. The Grant memoirs became a standard totem in every sound postwar Union household, set in place of honor next to the Bible. His clear, uncluttered prose set a new style for American writing, according to literary critic Edmund Wilson. It is only one of a hundred ironies of Grant's life that this Ohio president had such a salubrious influence on American letters while the last Ohioan president, Warren G. Harding, was to set new lows.

 Grant had given the Republicans a sure-fire recipe for the presidency—good looks, a good military record, and a blind eye to what was going on around him. The next of the Ohio line was Rutherford B. Hayes of Delaware. An alumnus of Kenyon College and Harvard Law School, Hayes was bearded, a war hero (he nearly died of wounds in Maryland) and a "hard money" Republican so much in favor with the wealthy backers of the party. He was the Gerald Ford of the nineteenth century. After the rampant chicanery of the Grant White House, Hayes was honest, forthright and the selector of a distinguished cabinet. "He had none of that tobacco-chewing, whiskey bonhomie which was very common among the mid-century- politicians," according to historian Rexford Tugwell. Unfortunately Hayes reached the White House because his behind-the-scenes supporters stole the election of 1876.

Hayes actually ran second in the popular vote by 250,000 votes behind Samuel Tilden of New York, who finished one electoral vote short of victory. Deadlock resulted. Republican operatives cut a deal with southern Democrats that allowed Hayes to take office in return for the withdrawal of federal troops from the South and a free hand in the crushing of black rights ensured by the Fourteenth and Fifteenth Amendments. "One of the ironies of history," wrote historian Bailey, "Is that this man of sterling honesty should have been the beneficiary of perhaps the most dishonest presidential election in our history."

If Hayes could never recover totally from the shadow over his election, he startled his Republican fellows in his inaugural with the novel notion that "He serves his party best who serves his country best." He then became one of the earliest civil-service reformers. His White House was a cheerful, domestic and teetotal home. The Hayeses moved in with their five children, the youngest being the first White House baby. The baby's mother, nicknamed "Lemonade Lucy," held evening hymn-singing meetings for members of the cabinet and staff. She also banned alcohol in all forms. Secretary of State William Evarts summed up a typical Hayes White House banquet: "It was a brilliant affair, the water flowed like wine."

Hayes, according to Bailey, "richly deserved reelection but he was an avowed one-termer . . . His great contribution was to restore faith in the integrity of the Washington regime and to prove, despite the Grant orgy, that a Republican could be honest, courageous, and a roadblock to designing thieves."

Hayes himself had no qualms about leaving. "Nobody ever left the presidency with less regret,"

MEN AT WORK—The fellows in background are William Henry Harrison, William McKinley, and Warren G. Harding. That's Benjamin Harrison and James Garfield in foreground. Between soldier-president W.H. Harrison in 1841 and Warren Harding, who died in office in 1923, Ohioans had been holding down the White House for a good portion of 82 years.

"One of the perplexing and confounding anomalies of existence was the fact that our neighbor, Mr. L——, was a Democrat. That fact perhaps explained to me why he walked so modestly, so unobtrusively, in the shade, so close to the picket fences of Reynolds Street, with his head bowed. I supposed that, being a Democrat, it was only natural for him to slink along.

—Brand Whitlock,
Forty Years Of It

he said, "less disappointment, fewer heartburnings, or any general content with the result of his term than I do."

After Grant, who was all outward propriety, and Hayes who was all inward integrity, the Republican chiefs came up with James Garfield, who was all sound and no fury. Garfield had it all—the last president actually born in a log cabin, he supported his widowed mother on their Cuyahoga County farm and drove mules on the Ohio Canal in his spare time. He was a ferocious self-educator. He made his own way through Williams College in Massachusetts and then came home to teach Greek and Latin at Hiram College, preach, and serve in the state senate. During the war, he climbed to the rank of major general in a little over two years and returned to Ohio the hero of Chickamauga. From that elevation he won nine terms in Congress.

Most of all, James Garfield was an orator. Rhetoric has a low reputation these days, but in the last century it was a public recreation as popular as television is today. Garfield was a genius. He was positively intoxicating to hear. "Garfield was remarkable because he said so little at such length and because it was done so purely with a view to its emotional effect," wrote Rexford Tugwell. "It poured out, apparently at extended length. He drew men's admiration and made himself glow with eloquence, not particularly to benefit anyone or any cause—although there was always an excuse, religious, moral or political—but just for the exercise. It was, in a very real sense, pure vocalization."

It was Garfield's eloquence that unintentionally landed him in the White House. At the deadlocked 1880 Republican Convention, Garfield rose to offer John Sherman of Ohio as a compromise candidate. The convention was spellbound by his speech and indifferent to its thrust. The delegates gave not a glance to poor Sherman, but rushed Garfield himself into nomination. In stunned immobility, Garfield watched his vote total climb toward the magic number until he was heard to mutter, "Get me out of here."

The party bosses and big money men saw in Garfield a handsome, pliable man, ideal for their

purposes. Warm hearted, and beloved by the public, Garfield was a weak chief executive, overwhelmed by the sharp men who gave him orders.

He was shot on July 2, 1881, by a frustrated office seeker and died on September 19. "The weaknesses of this amiable man," concluded Bailey, "were such that he had his feet firmly planted on the road to failure when Charles Guiteau's bullet ended his career."

James G. Blaine of Maine broke up the Ohio Republican candidate line in 1884 and Grover Cleveland broke up the Republican winning streak. In 1888 the Republicans decided to try a Buckeye again. Their candidate was a short thick man with a stodgy beard and an ancestral claim on the presidency. He was Benjamin Harrison, grandson of William Henry Harrison. Born at his grandfather's house in North Bend in 1833, he left Ohio at twenty-one for Indiana. He was a colonel in the Union army, a prosperous lawyer, a one-term U.S. senator and a stalwart Republican. His public speaking was everything a politician could hope for in those days, but his personal manner was chilly, formal and verged on the unfriendly.

"Don't think he means to insult you," an aide warned a group of supporters about to be led into his presence. "It's only his way."

In 1888, Blaine was the leading candidate for the Republican nomination but was too ill to accept. Recuperating in Scotland when he was told that the convention was stalemated without him, Blaine wired home, "Take Harrison." They took Harrison.

Harrison's successful campaign against Cleveland required some delicate stage management. At whistle stops, his staff noticed that the crowds cheered mightily at his speeches, but when the leading local lights were brought in for a handshake, they came away silent and melancholy. Thereafter, the moment Harrison's speech finished, the train's departure bell began ringing furiously. Startled well-wishers watched the candidate hastily depart but went to the polls that November none the wiser.

Harrison seemed aware of his isolation. "Now I walk alone with God," he said after his swearing-in. There were notable events during his administra-

FIRST THINGS FIRST

William Henry Harrison
—First (and only) Chief Executive who studied medicine
—president-elect who traveled by train to Washington, D.C.
—president photographed in office
—to die in office, April 4, 1841
—president who was the grandfather of a president, *Benjamin Harrison*

Ulysses Simpson Grant
—First to run against a woman, *Victoria Claflin Woodhull* from Ohio
—to receive a reigning king, *David Kalakaua* of Hawaii, on December 15, 1874

Rutherford B. Hayes
—First to take the oath of office in the White House; March 3, 1877
— who visited the West Coast while in office, San Francisco, September 8, 1880
—to use the desk in the Oval Office, a gift from *Queen Victoria* in 1880
—the first telephone was installed in the White House in 1878, when Hayes was President. His first call, fittingly, was to *Alexander Graham Bell*, and his first words were, "Please speak more slowly."

James Abram Garfield
—First to have his mother present at his inauguration
—left-handed—and ambidextrous—president

Benjamin Harrison
—First (and only) president who was the grandson of a president, Willam Henry Harrison
—first (and only) president to be preceded and followed in office by the same person, *Grover Cleveland*
—Chief Executive with a billion dollar budget appropriated by Congress
—to put up a Christmas tree in the White House, 1889

—to have electricity in the White House, 1891

William McKinley
—First presidential candidate to campaign via the telephone; in 1896 he called campaign managers from his Canton home

William Howard Taft
—First (and only) president to become Chief Justice of the U.S. Supreme Court

Warren Gamaliel Harding
—First newspaper editor elected president
—president chosen in an election where women voted nationwide
—chief executive whose election was announced on radio (November 2, 1920, at KDKA, Pittsburgh)
—to ride to his inauguration in an automobile
—president who could drive an automobile
—president who owned a radio (purchased in 1922 and placed in his study)
—post Civil War president to advocate Black civil rights while south of the Mason Dixon line (at the University of Alabama, 1921)

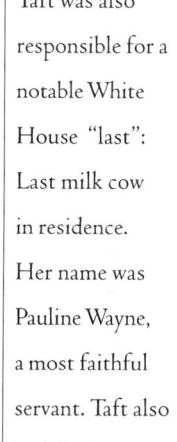

In addition to several firsts, Taft was also responsible for a notable White House "last": Last milk cow in residence. Her name was Pauline Wayne, a most faithful servant. Taft also had the last presidential mustache—a magnificent handlebar.

The swish of the big stick

tion—passage of the Sherman Antitrust Act, the McKinley Tariff and the admission of six new states, but none of this had much to do with the president nor did it seem to make much of an impression on him. He sat out his four years in his bleak White House, behaving in a dignified and gentlemanly manner that struck everyone as aristocratic, unfriendly, and very Republican. The country elected the next available Democrat—Grover Cleveland Part II—at the earliest opportunity.

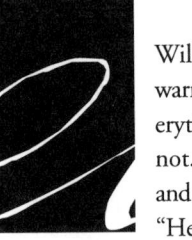

William McKinley was expansive, warmhearted, and cleanshaven, everything Benjamin Harrison was not. "He was handsome, portly, and sleek," wrote historian Tugwell. "He wore a frock coat and a spotless white vest and seemed never to lose the carefully stuffed look." He was the son of a Niles foundryman, a private under Rutherford Hayes in the Civil War and a prominent lawyer in Canton afterward. He clawed his way up in Congress to the chairmanship of the powerful Ways and Means Committee where he pushed through the stiff McKinley Tariff of 1890.

Defeated for reelection, he returned to Ohio to run for governor, with the blessings of industrialist Mark Hanna. Hanna threw his money and that of his friends Andrew Carnegie and John Rockefeller behind McKinley's presidential campaign, piling up something between $3-$16 million, a sum which is small today but was nearly obscene in 1896.

His "front porch" campaign of 1896 was a classic. (Harding copied it in 1920.) Each morning in Canton, McKinley rose, breakfasted, strode to his front porch, and waved affably to the crowds specially brought in by train to see him. Hanna shipped in entire labor union delegations, church congregations, fraternal organizations, and veterans' groups.

The Democratic candidate, William Jennings Bryan, meanwhile galloped across the country, shooting off sixty to 100,000 words of high oratory a day. The stately McKinley seemed more presidential somehow, simply gliding in and out his front door. He won the election by some 860,000 votes.

In 1896, McKinley promised no wars of expansion and no "jingo nonsense." In 1898, he endorsed Congress' declaration of war on Spain and ended up bagging the Philippines, Puerto Rico and Guam. What changed his mind was the explosion of the battleship Maine in Havana Harbor and a national hysteria whipped by the "yellow press," led by William Randolph Hearst. McKinley was always eager to retain his popularity—it was said he kept his ear so close to the ground, it was full of grasshoppers—and he rapidly saw the jingo light.

"Isolation is no longer possible or desirable," said the former isolationist as he notched up an even greater plurality against Bryan in 1900. His new global vision lead him to the Pan-American Exposition in Buffalo on September 6, 1901, where he was shot in a reception line.

He was always a kindly man even in death. "Don't let them hurt him," he begged as he lay bleeding and the crowd seized Leon Czolgosz. "My wife—be careful...," he whispered to an aide, "how you tell her—oh, be careful."

McKinley led America's emergence as a world power in an era of increasing prosperity and reconciliation between north and south. "He was the last of the old-fashioned caretakers," wrote Bailey, "and the first of the new-fashioned drivers."

McKinley's death brought Teddy Roosevelt to the fore, a catastrophe as far as the Republican bosses were concerned. They thought they had Teddy safely entombed in the vice-presidency. In his time, Roosevelt carefully considered his successor. He turned to Ohio and William Howard Taft.

Taft had never wanted to be president and never pretended that he did. He hadn't even wanted to be involved in politics, "but in Ohio," writes biographer Charles Willis Thompson, "one can hardly help it."

Taft graduated from Yale and returned to Cincinnati, where he finished law school and began moving up through the legal hierarchy in stately and regular fashion, from prosecuting attorney to city solicitor to superior court judge to federal judge. Historian William Allen White, puzzled by the phenomenon of the young man's facile success, visited Taft's brother to learn his secret and then wrote to Taft himself.

"I went to see your brother this evening in the

hope that he might tell me how you got the jobs at so young an age…I find…that you were given these appointments chiefly because you were an angel of light."

He was a big angel of light. He weighed 225 pounds at the age of twenty, and may have weighed one hundred pounds more than that as president. One of his biographers described him as, "a big blond man who had been molded between two six-foot parentheses, bulging gorgeously in the middle, his trousers wrinkled, his vest creased, his coat bumpy, his collar flaring at an angle of forty-five degrees above a decent dark tie."

His bulk became legendary. He was said to be so polite that he had once risen in a streetcar and given up his seat to three women. According to one story, some of his neighbors at Beverly Bay, Massachusetts, walked down to the shore to go swimming. Taft was in the water.

"Perhaps we'd better wait," said one. "The President is using the ocean."

When he was governor-general of the Philippines, he sent a cable to Secretary of War Elihu Root: "Took long horseback ride today, feeling fine." And

Root cabled back: "But how is the horse?"

Bent upon a judicial career, Taft was entangled in politics by having the peculiar fortune of impressing Teddy Roosevelt as the ablest man Roosevelt had ever met. One day in 1899, Taft had taken a train trip and conversed pleasantly with a fellow passenger. The passenger had been General Corbin of the United States Army who returned to Washington and reported to President McKinley that he had met the man who should govern the Philippines. Roosevelt sent Taft to Manila and made him governor-general of the islands. In 1904, impressed with his work, he made him secretary of war, and in 1907, still more impressed, he made him provisional governor of Cuba and, in 1909, unimaginably well impressed, he made him president.

On Inauguration Day, there was a fierce snowstorm. "I knew there would be a blizzard when I went out," said Roosevelt. "You're wrong; it's my storm," said Taft. "I always said it would be a cold day when I got to be president of the United States."

As president, Taft was a strong trustbuster and conservationist; he kept the United States out of participating in the Mexican revolution. Still, he left

CAMPAIGN TRAIL

•Democrat Ohio presidents—0

Whig Ohio presidents—1
William Henry Harrison

Republican Ohio presidents—7
Grant, Hayes, Garfield, Benjamin Harrison, McKinley, Taft, Harding

•Presidents elected without a popular-vote majority
John Quincy Adams, 1824
Ohioan *Rutherford B. Hayes,* 1876
Ohioan *Benjamin Harrison,* 1888.

•Republican Hayes got 4,036,298 votes in 1876. Democrat Samuel Tilden had more—4,300,590—but the 19 electoral votes of three southern states were in question. Congress appointed an electoral commission to settle the matter, and the members gave Hayes the disputed votes, by a slim 185 to 184 margin.

In 1888, Democrat Grover Cleveland won a majority in the popular vote (5,444,337) to Harrison's 5,439,853, but not in the Electoral College. Harrison carried 20 states with 233 electoral votes, while Cleveland's eighteen states tallied only 168.

"Nobody ever left the Presidency with less regret, less disappointment, fewer heartburnings, or any general content with the result of his term than I do."

—*Rutherford Hayes*

office in 1913 as the worst-defeated incumbent ever having placed a poor third after Woodrow Wilson and Roosevelt himself, who was back as a Bull Moose. By then, Taft had alienated the anti-Roosevelt forces for being Roosevelt's man and had disappointed the pro-Roosevelt forces for being so little like their hero. Roosevelt concluded that Taft meant well, but he meant well feebly.

Taft's resounding, unprecedented defeat for reelection in 1912 was a humiliation, but he mastered his disappointment and moved toward the only office he had ever wanted: Chief Justice of the Supreme Court. He was appointed by President Harding in 1921 and served until 1930.

After his election defeat in 1912, many people tried to cheer him up by telling him, "I voted for you." Taft told a friend: "Whenever anyone says that to me, I have an almost uncontrollable desire to say, 'Well, my friend, you are one of a select but small body of citizens whose judgment I heartily concur in and admire.'"

 The last Ohioan in the White House was Warren G. Harding and, by consensus, the worst. He was not an evil man, only a weak one. His own father told him, "If you were a girl, Warren, you'd be in the family way all the time. You can't say no." It was both prophecy and tragedy.

Harding was a self-made man, a newspaper publisher and the first president drawn from the country's business sector. He was a big fish in the small pond of Marion where he had risen from poverty and married the daughter of the town banker. He was an Elk and a Moose, played cornet in the town's marching band, and poker on Saturdays. His favorite activity was shooting the breeze, especially about politics. He called it "bloviating."

He was a master bloviator. His speeches struck critics as the worst abuse the English language had ever endured. H.L. Mencken, the literary power of the day, said it was a new language called "Gamalielese." Mencken declared, "Harding writes the worst English I have ever encountered. It reminds me of a string of wet sponges."

If Harding's failings had only been of the word, he might have fared better with history. His verbal muddle was only the shallowest mudhole in his administration. He had surrounded himself with a pack of unscrupulous men so heavily drawn from his home state they were called the "Ohio Gang." They made a mockery of enforcing the new Prohibition laws by selling permits for "medicinal" alcohol. They dumped the War Department's "surplus" materials and then turned around to replace the goods from grossly overpriced contracts. The crowning scandal was the Teapot Dome, in which government oil reserves were siphoned off with official connivance. Harding's secretary of the interior, Albert Fall, was the first and (until the Nixon Administration) the only cabinet member ever to be indicted and convicted of criminal activity. Harding grew dimly aware of the corruption around him in the final days of his life. On his last official trip in 1923, which included a trip to Vancouver, his ship had a slight collision with another ship, and he lay on his bed hiding his face in his hands and moaning, "I hope the boat sinks." He died in a San Francisco hotel room before the scandals broke in Washington.

Harding did perform a few decent acts while president: he freed from prison the outspoken Socialist presidential candidate Eugene V. Debs, who had been jailed for making antiwar speeches during World War I. He courageously spoke in support of voting rights for black citizens at a gathering in Birmingham. He appointed Taft chief justice. He helped organize an international disarmament conference. And he was influential in seeing the steel industry's twelve-hour day reduced to eight.

Yet the overall impression he left behind him of ineptitude, blundering, oversight, wrongly placed trust and illicit activities continues to impeach his memory 70 years later. "My God, this is a hell of a job!" he told historian William Allen White. "I have no trouble with my enemies. I can take care of my enemies all right. But my damn friends, my God . . . they're the ones that keep me walking the floor nights."

It is a warning that future presidents from whatever state in the union might keep in mind when they put their hand to the chief justice's Bible and begin to solemnly swear.

—*Melissa Faye Greene*

OHIO PRESIDENTS: A MODERN APPRAISAL

In general, academic historians have not ranked Ohio presidents very high, assessments with which Ohio author James B. Cash disagrees. He points out that six of the Ohio presidents were soldiers, and academics often do not understand or appreciate soldiers. His position is that by far the greatest national tragedy was the U. S. Civil War, one that reverberates still today with our problems of race and inequality. He thinks the worst presidents were those who served from 1841-1860 who allowed us to drift into that war, or even help bring it about: This list would include primarily: John Tyler, Franklin Pierce, and James Buchanan.

"The Civil War was caused by the failure to resolve the slavery issue which was exacerbated by the Dred Scott decision. People like Abraham Lincoln, Rutherford B. Hayes, James A. Garfield, and Benjamin Harrison joined the Republican party whose chief purpose was to prevent the spread of slavery.

"Five U. S. presidents from Ohio served in the front lines of the Civil War, to keep the country united and to free the slaves. They served with great courage and resourcefulness. Grant was the chief strategic general in victory; Hayes, recklessly courageous, was wounded five times; Garfield (at right) directed one of the earliest victories in the Big Sandy River valley of Kentucky, and as a staff officer rode between the lines to help prevent a total rout at Chickamauga; Benjamin Harrison was commended for his courage and resourcefulness as a part of Sherman's army in the campaign for Atlanta; McKinley joined as a private, served four years, advancing to brevet major, probably saw more front line action than any U. S. president.

"It is not well understood today that the Civil War was a close thing. There were crises in every year that threatened defeat. Only the resourcefulness of Lincoln and a few others prevented that. Were the Ohio presidents right to try to keep the country united, and abolish slavery? How could anybody today say they were not? Should we honor them for that? We honor Washington for his military victories before his presidency; Jefferson for his writing of the Declaration of Independence; Madison for his work on the Constitution; Eisenhower for his leadership in World War II.

"After the Civil War the Ohio presidents supported the 13th, 14th, and 15th Amendments to free the slaves and to try to assure them of equal rights. They also passed the first Civil Rights Act (still being used); they tried to reform the Federal Civil Service (politicized by the "near great" Andrew Jackson). The country was industrialized during their times, and great corporations got out of control. But they passed the Interstate Commerce Act for the regulation of railroads, and the Sherman Anti-Trust Act."—*James B. Cash, author of Unsung Heroes, The Ohio Presidents: A Modern Appraisal*

Evolution *of the* national clerk

by Michael O'Bryant

Conservative columnists—notably Paul Greenberg—have said that William McKinley's 1896 campaign from his front porch in Ohio was "the beginning of the modern, issueless campaign." McKinley, Greenberg has written, "mouthed respectable niceties, neither impressed nor frightened anyone, and was elected." An engaging thesis, accurate as far as it goes, but off by half a century, for the honor belonged to another Ohioan, William Henry Harrison, who ran the first Presidential campaign that was devoid of issues and high on image.

The Whig party, formed to oppose what they saw was the zealous democracy of Andrew Jackson, stood for a weak chief executive. Democracy, after all, was a messy business and too much of it frightened the horses, therefore Harrison was their man. Although he came from wealth and privilege, Harrison ran as the simple everyman. Patriotism, domestic affairs, and deference to Congress (as well as party leaders) rounded out the Whig view of the Presidency. When the party faded before the Civil War, Whigs formed the basis of the Republican Party, taking their philosophy with them. Republicans are Whigs without the Civil War.

The Whig approach, as absorbed into the Republican party of the late 1800s, found a wealth of willing candidates in Ohio., men who understood both their role and that of the chief executive. The Republicans wanted a win and Ulysses S. Grant could deliver it to them. At first, he was not sure *what* party he belonged to (witness Eisenhower and Colin Powell), but the Republicans saw him as an ideal candidate. He had the image; America has always had a love affair with military leaders. He was short on ideas: "Let there be peace." But he could win and restore the Presidency to where it was before events produced Johnson's disastrous challenges to Congressional power and the strong leadership of Lincoln. Grant's *laissez-faire* Presidency ushered in an era where, according

to Presidential historian Dr. Michael P. Riccards, the President's role is that of "National Clerk."

To fill that role, Ohio supplied a plethora of Republican presidents. When the country turned to Ohio for their leaders, they found men who made them comfortable. After a generation of sectional strife, these were men who had served the Union cause, but without the evangelical zeal of the radical Republicans. They were mainstream; they were safe. They could be trusted not to take extreme positions. They were for sound money and sound government. In short, they were from Ohio.

Whatever their political gifts, Hayes, Garfield, Benjamin Harrison, and McKinley each adhered to his party's view of the Presidency. Each respected Congress, except where it encroached on what they felt was the prerogative of the President (i.e. political patronage and foreign affairs). After Theodore Roosevelt—who was hidden in the vice-presidency where he would do no harm then became the powerful populist President unchecked by the conservative party regulars—the party returned to the same formula with William Howard Taft. Taft's Whig approach is seen in his conservative adherence to the law with its deep belief that the President could only do what was allowed by statute.

After a brief interruption by Roosevelt in the election of 1912, the Republican/Whig approach to the Presidency was restored with Harding. Harding had image and no ideas: an ideal front man. With a vague catchy slogan, "Return to normalcy," the *laissez-faire* Presidency reached its 20th century apogee. After history repeated itself with the scandal-ridden Harding administration, the Republicans corrected the problem by choosing men of more substance but who still filled the role of "National Clerk"—and Ohio presidents became the 20th century's Republican role models, a subset of almost interchangeable executives.

Aspects of the Ohio presidency can be seen in Eisenhower, Reagan, and both Bushes. Newt Gingrich suggested that even Presidential candidate Robert Dole was a lot like McKinley. By most ratings, the best of the group, McKinley—Ohio's top gun in the Presidential ratings—sits squarely in the middle. So it is surprising how much attention he has attracted. Democratic presidential candidate Bill Bradley characterized McKinley as having appealed to the masses by sitting "on his porch in Ohio carefully spinning sound bites that positioned him as a 'new Republican.'"

McKinley, in fact, preferred the clerk's role, but history thrust the modern world upon him, and being forced to deal with it, he became—of all his Ohio *confrères*—the *least* clerk-like. Dealing with the complexities of America as an emerging superpower, McKinley adequately acquitted himself. If only the new century's Republicans can do so well. ✍

illustration by Brooke Albrecht

"He is almost the ideal President. He looks like a somewhat decayed moving-picture actor, belongs to all the secret orders that plumbers and garbage-haulers belong to, and can scarcely talk intelligible English. Mr. Malaprop in the White House... I shall vote for him."

—H.L. Mencken on Warren Harding, letter to English novelist Hugh Walpole, 1921

HarrisonWilliam Henry

Term: *Ninth President of the U.S.*
Served: *March 4 - April 4, 1841*
Born: *February 9, 1773,*
Berkeley Plantation, Virginia
Married: *Wed Anna Symmes, daughter of a*
frontier Ohio land baron, 1795
Died: *April 4, 1841, in the White House*

President Harrison insisted on delivering his fatal hour-and-forty-five minute inaugural address without a hat or coat in a snowstorm, promptly caught cold, and died of pneumonia a month later. He thus set that most suspect of political laws: the inverse ratio between longwindedness and term of office. The president with the most to say also had the shortest term in which to say it.

Considering that he was the last president born a British subject, that his father signed the Declaration of Independence, and that the 1840 election putting him in the White House is considered the first modern presidential campaign because it focused on personalities rather than issues, Harrison might have become a pivot point in American history had not death aborted his month-old administration. At age 68, President Harrison was elderly by 19th century standards, and in fact, he held the record for being the oldest man elected President until Ronald Reagan occupied the Oval Office. Though Harrison served as a U.S. Congressman and Senator from Ohio between 1816 and 1828, the public knew him not for his Whig politics, but for his warrior past. In 1791, he quit school to join the Army, and in 1794, as an aid to General Anthony Wayne, he fought Indians in the Battle of Fallen Timbers, which resulted in the first white settlement rights in Ohio. President John Adams appointed him Governor of the Indiana Territory in 1800, and during his twelve years in that office, Harrison became one of the master land grabbers in American history. His tactics ranged from treaties to bribery and alcohol, but Harrison got the Indians to cede millions of acres to the U.S. government. When Tecumseh resisted by forming an Indian confederacy, Harrison burned his Shawnee village on the Tippecanoe River in 1811. The battle gave him both national renown as a war hero and the nickname "Old Tippecanoe," which was later adapted into a famed 1840 campaign slogan. During the War of 1812, he defeated the British and Indians in the decisive Battle of the Thames in which Tecumseh was killed. Harrison then resigned the army and returned to his own extensive land holdings at North Bend. He lived the life of a gentleman farmer and politician until 1840, when the Whig Party, unable to choose between Henry Clay and Daniel Webster, tapped him as a compromise presidential candidate to run against the incumbent, Martin Van Buren. Given Harrison's untimely death, the most significant result of his administration was that John Tyler became the first vice-president to succeed to the presidency.

> *All the measures of the Government are directed to the purpose of making the rich richer and the poor poorer.*

Himself on the presidency: "Some folks are silly enough as to have formed a plan to make a President of the United States out of this Clerk and Clodhopper."

Family Ties: Father of His Country: William Henry Harrison, the U.S. President with the most children born of one marriage—ten (six boys, four girls).
☞ Grandfather of His Country: William Henry Harrison, a record 48 grandchildren and 106 greatgrandchildren.
☞ Only man who was both the son and father of a U.S. President: John Scott Harrison of North Bend, Ohio; son of William Henry Harrison, father of Benjamin Harrison.
☞ Anna Symmes Harrison was the only woman who was the wife of one U.S. President and the grandmother of another, William Henry Harrison and Benjamin Harrison. ☞ She was the oldest woman to become First Lady at 65 years, 222 days.
☞ She is the only wife of an Ohio president who never lived in the White House; he died before she could arrive from North Bend. ☞ She became the first presidential widow awarded a pension, $25,000 from Congress in 1841.

The Martial Arts: Major General, Northwest Territory Indian wars and War of 1812

Alma Mater: Hampton-Sydney (three years); Medical School, University of Pennsylvania (no degree)

Term: *Eighteenth President of the U.S.*
Served: *March 4, 1869 - March 3, 1877*
Born: *April 27, 1822,*
Point Pleasant, Ohio
Married: *Julia Dent, daughter of a Missouri*
plantation owner, 1848
Died: *July 23, 1885,*
Mount McGregor, New York

When young Grant left his Georgetown, Ohio, home for the United States Military Academy in 1839, his appointment proved fateful both for himself and the nation. Few would have predicted that the lackluster lieutenant who graduated 21st in his class of 39 would one day command the Army of the United States in its most crucial hour, much less occupy the White House. Indeed, after West Point, Grant seemed doomed to failure. He served in the Mexican War under General Zachary Taylor, but when subsequent posts took him away from his wife, he started drinking and had to resign his commission in 1854. Grant then limped through a series of bad business ventures and probably would have struggled through life an obscure store clerk had not the rebellious shots fired at Fort Sumter pushed him into the national limelight as the North's most successful commander. When he captured Forts Henry and Donelson in 1862, it was not only the Union's first great victory, but also Grant's first real success in life. He demanded an "unconditional and immediate surrender" from the 15,000 Confederates at Fort Donelson, thus acquiring the nickname— "Unconditional Surrender Grant"—that captured the public's imagination. Grant steadily rose in rank as he scored victories at Shiloh, Vicksburg, and Chattanooga, and in 1864, Lincoln appointed him Commander-in-Chief. Grant forced Lee's

1865 surrender because he (1) doggedly pursued the enemy with every battlefield resource at his disposal; and (2) was a master strategist who formulated a comprehensive war plan that shattered the South militarily and economically. In 1868, Grant the War Hero was unanimously chosen on the first ballot to be the Republican Party's presidential candidate. He ran on a Radical Reconstruction platform and trounced Democrat Horatio Seymour in the Electoral College, a triumph repeated four years later when Grant won a second term by defeating Horace Greeley. President Grant mended diplomatic fences broken with Great Britain over the *Alabama* damage claims and kept the U.S. out of war during the Cuban rebellion, but left the setting of national policy to Congress. Given his indifferent leadership, the social ideals of Reconstruction began to collapse under the weighty commercial realities of the dawning Gilded Age. Because of his political naivete and soldierly sense of loyalty, Grant chose appointees badly, and scandal permeated and permanently stigmatized his administration: Gould's bond speculations, 1869; the Credit Mobilier railroad stock payoffs, 1872; the Whiskey Ring tax scam, 1875; and secretary of war Belknap's bribery at Indian trading posts, 1876. Grant left the White House and embarked on a world tour before settling in New York City in 1881. He backed his son in a corrupt brokerage house, went broke, and had to surrender his presentation swords and gold medal from Congress to repay a loan. Diagnosed with throat cancer almost surely caused by his 20 cigar-a-day habit, the dying Grant agreed to ensure his wife's financial security by writing his autobiography. Only days before his death, he finished *The Personal Memoirs of U.S. Grant,* a simply splendid military history.

At West Point, **Grant** *set a record for the horseback high jump and was elected president of the Dialectic Society but he also acquired a string of demerits for missing church, having an unkempt uniform, and being late. "A military life," he said later, "had no charms for me, and I had not the faintest idea of staying in the Army even if I should be graduated, which I did not expect."*

"Grant's imperturbability is amazing. I am in doubt whether to call it greatness or stupidity." —Garfield on Grant

Afflictions: The sight of blood made Grant so squeamish that he couldn't stand to look at the hides in his father's tannery. Meat cooked rare made him sick, and he refused to eat fowl. "I could never eat anything that went on two legs," he said. Ironically, Grant led the Union Army in the nation's bloodiest internal conflict: the Civil War cost more than 600,000 lives.

At Play: A friend of Grant's volunteered to introduce him to the game of golf. When they arrived at the course, a man was doggedly swinging at the ball, but couldn't quite manage to hit it. "That does look like very good exercise," said the President to his friend. "But what is the little white ball for?"

The Martial Arts: General, Civil War. Grant was the first person to command an army via telegraph and first four-star general in the U.S. Army.

Ill winds: Grant took his second oath of office on a bitter March 4, 1873. The inaugural parade bogged down under blizzard-like snow, guests at the inaugural ball danced with their coats on, and the champagne froze.

Alma Mater: U.S. Military Academy at West Point

Term: Nineteenth President of the U.S.
Served: March 4, 1877 - March 3, 1881
Born: Born October 4, 1822, Delaware, Ohio
Married: devout Methodist Lucy Webb of Chillicothe, Ohio, 1852
Died: Died January 17, 1893, Fremont, Ohio

"Presidents in the past have always been better than their adversaries predicted."

—*Rutherford Hayes*

Hayes's father, a storekeeper, died just weeks before his birth, and he was raised by his mother and uncle in Delaware. He was graduated from Harvard Law School in 1845, and four years later began a successful law practice in Cincinnati. There he met his wife, whose abolitionist beliefs influenced him to switch his politics from the Whig to the Republican Party. Participating in numerous Civil War battles, he was wounded several times and left the army as a much-decorated major general in 1865. Beginning in 1868 and again in 1876, he served as Governor of Ohio. Exercising the reform-minded leadership that later became the trademark of his presidency, he advocated establishment of the Ohio State University and improved conditions in schools, prisons, and asylums. His 1876 defeat of Tilden in the Electoral College was this nation's most hotly disputed presidential election. Recognizing the potential for violence in the streets, Hayes opted to take the oath of office privately two days before the public ceremony, and there was no inaugural ball or parade. While the politically disgruntled labeled him "Ruther*fraud,*" Hayes provided the nation with a sorely needed sure hand following the turbulent Grant years. With characteristic lack of fanfare, he returned the nation to the gold standard and began to abolish the blatant patronage of the spoils system with civil service reforms. In accordance with the Compromise of 1877, the deal that had appeased the Democrats into awarding him the Presidency, Hayes appointed a Southern Democrat to his Cabinet and ended Reconstruction by withdrawing all federal troops from the South. Though the Compromise virtually assured white supremacy, Hayes did appoint to the Supreme Court John Harlan, the "Great Dissenter" whose minority opinions provided a consistent voice supporting desegregation and civil rights for three decades. A fundamentally decent, though dull man, Hayes, as was always his intention, served one-term and retired at Spiegel Grove, his home in Fremont. He devoted himself to temperance, charity, and humanitarian works until heart failure claimed his life.

The melancholy thing in our public life is the insane desire to get higher.

Himself on the presidency: "I am not liked as a president by the politicians in office, or the press, or in Congress. But I am content to abide the judgement— the sober second thoughts—of the people."
Afflictions: maniaphobia (fear of going insane) as a youth
The Martial Arts: Brevet Major General, Civil War. In the Civil War, Hayes, a colonel, was commanding officer of McKinley, a brevet major.
Alma Mater: Kenyon College, Ohio. Post graduate: Harvard, Law

Point of Interest:
Lucy Webb Hayes, not Martha Washington, was the first First Lady. She acquired the title courtesy of Mary Clemmer Ames, a reporter who called her "the first lady of the land" in an account of President Hayes's inauguration. The working press liked the sound of it better than "Presidentess" and attached the name to not only Mrs. Hayes but also her White House successors.
Lucy Webb Hayes
☞ was the first First Lady with a college diploma, graduated with honors from Ohio Wesleyan Women's College, 1850
☞ banned liquor from the Executive Mansion
☞ started the White House Easter Egg roll

Term:	*Twentieth President of the U.S.*
Served:	*March 4 - September 19, 1881*
Born:	*November 19, 1831,*
	Orange, Ohio
Married:	*scholarly Lucretia Randolph of*
	Hiram, Ohio, 1858
Died:	*September 19, 1881,*
	Elberon, New Jersey

Garfield's father died when he was a baby, and he was raised by his mother, for whom he maintained a deep and lifelong devotion. Growing up poor on the family farm near Cleveland, Garfield worked his way through local preparatory schools and began to develop his gift for oratory. A champion debater at Williams College, he graduated with honors in 1856 and returned to Ohio to teach classical languages and study law. Admitted to the bar in 1860, Garfield served as a state senator before joining the Union Army, where he became General Rosecrans's Chief of Staff and the North's youngest general. From 1863 - 1880, Garfield was a U.S. Representative from Ohio. As a Radical Republican, he became an artful politician who served on the electoral commission that gave the presidency to Hayes. Garfield was elected a U.S. Senator in 1880, but before he took office, the Republicans nominated him for President. A dark horse candidate, Garfield ran against General Winfield Scott and won the popular vote by a nose. His attention in the early weeks of his administration was consumed by party members demanding patronage in return for their support during his campaign. Attempting to assert presidential prerogative in making appointments, Garfield locked horns with patronage boss Roscoe Conkling and succeeded in ending that New York Senator's powerful political clout. Ironically, the patronage issue proved Garfield's undoing when his presidency was only four months old. On July 2, 1881, he was shot in the Washington, D.C. train station by Charles Guiteau, an unstable political supporter whose request for a patronage position had been denied. After lingering for months, Garfield died and was buried in Cleveland. His assassination roused public interest in civil service reform, and Garfield's successor, Chester A. Arthur, inherited the unfinished business of ridding the nation of the spoils system.

"Assassination can no more be guarded against than death by lightning; and it is best not to worry about either." — *Garfield*

Himself on the presidency: "My God! What is there in this place that a man should ever want to get into it?"

Afflictions: Chronic depression in youth; indigestion; headaches and nightmares after elected president

Family Ties: First mother to attend her son's presidential inauguration and to live in the White House: Eliza Ballou Garfield
Garfield's first act as president: kissing his mother

At Play: Garfield's hobbies: hunting, fishing, billiards, and chess

Sizing Them Up: U.S. President with the biggest head: James Garfield, hat size 7 3/4
Big babies: Garfield and Harding both weighed 10 pounds at birth.

Martial Arts: Major General, Civil War

Ill winds: Garfield braved deep snow and high winds for his inauguration, but Washington boulevards were cleared in time for the inaugural parade.

Alma Mater: Williams College

Point of Interest:

☞ Garfield appointed Cincinnati author, General Lew Wallace, to diplomatic office, thinking of sending him to Paraguay. After reading Wallace's *Ben Hur*, however, Garfield decided to send him to Constantinople, hoping he might find proper inspiration to write another biblical epic.

☞ The beneficiary of a classical education, Garfield could write Greek with one hand at the same time that he wrote Latin with the other.

Garfield became President in a notably corrupt era. Whether he would have done better is unknowable. Less than four months after his inauguration he was shot by a disappointed office seeker. Interesting, though, are the topics that took the most space in his inaugural address: race and education. Faced with Southern arguments that freed slaves were incompetent to vote, thus creating bad local government, Garfield replied, "Bad local government is certainly a great evil—but to violate the freedom and sanctities of the suffrage is more than an evil. It is a crime."

Term:	Twenty-Third President of the U.S.
Served:	March 4, 1889 - March 3, 1893
Born:	Born August 20, 1833, North Bend, Ohio
Married:	witty, clever Caroline Scott of Oxford, Ohio, 1853 Married Mary Dimmick, his first wife's niece, 1896
Died:	March 13, 1901 Indianapolis, Indiana

"The manner by which women are treated is good criterion to judge the true state of society."

—Benjamin Harrison

Probably no American has ever possessed a finer political pedigree than Benjamin Harrison, whose great-grandfather signed the Declaration of Independence, whose grandfather was President, and whose father was a U.S. Congressman. Born into privilege on grandfather William Henry Harrison's estate, he grew up on an adjacent farm and attended a log schoolhouse. His family was thoroughly Presbyterian, and while attending Miami University, he met and courted his future wife, the daughter of a Presbyterian minister and professor. After his 1852 graduation, Harrison studied law in Cincinnati, then moved to Indianapolis, where his exceptional speaking ability helped build both his lucrative corporate law practice and his stature in the Republican Party. Harrison participated in Sherman's March to the Sea during the Civil War, afterward going home to Indiana, where his legal and political careers continued to prosper. A stiff and methodical man with a genius for detail, he served as a U.S. Senator from 1881 to 1887, and became known for his support of protective tariffs and veterans' pensions. The Republicans nominated him for President in 1888, and he won the office by vote of the Electoral College. Harrison's policies followed the party line as dictated by Republican leaders in Congress. In foreign affairs, he pushed the nation toward imperialism, convening the Pan American Conference, claiming Samoa for the U.S., and proposing annexation of Hawaii. Domestically, Harrison's middle-of-the-road civil service policy pleased neither the reformers nor the party faithful, and his political base was further eroded by his support of the McKinley Tariff Act, a stiff and unpopular levy on imports. Certainly the most colorful episode in his Presidency was the opening of the Oklahoma Territory on April 22, 1889, when gunshots signaled the start of "Harrison's Hoss Race," and one hundred thousand homesteaders bolted across the starting line to claim plots of land. A decidedly uncharismatic president, Harrison was defeated by Grover Cleveland in the 1892 election. Considered a legal expert, he returned to his Indiana practice, wrote for national magazines, lectured, and represented Venezuela in a territorial dispute with Great Britain in 1898. A widower, he remarried and fathered a daughter before his death from pneumonia.

"When I came into power, I found that the party managers had taken it all to themselves. I could not name my own Cabinet. They had sold out every place to pay for the election."
—Benjamin Harrison

Himself on the presidency: "Cheer up, everybody. This is no life and death affair. I am very happy here in Indianapolis . . . "
Afflictions: Physical exhaustion in 1867
Sizing Them Up: Last U.S. President to have a beard: Benjamin Harrison
At Play: A crony describes President Harrison up a creek: "When he's on a fishing trip, Ben takes his drink of whiskey in the morning, just like anyone else. He chews tobacco from a plug he carries in his hip pocket, spits on his worm for luck, and cusses when the fish gets away."
Ill winds: Benjamin Harrison took a page out of grandfather William Henry's book and rode an open carriage to the Capitol in a hard rain with strong winds. He survived, of course, although the fireworks scheduled for that evening did not.
The Martial Arts: Brevet Brigadier General, Civil War
Alma Mater: Miami University, Ohio

Point of Interest:
- Caroline Scott Harrison began the White House custom of using orchids at state receptions and put up the first Christmas tree. She also undertook the first White House renovation; armed with $35,000 from Congress, she attacked insects and rodents while fortifying the plumbing with sorely needed bathrooms.
- President and Mrs. Harrison were so leery of electricity that they refused to touch switches. They left the lights on all night and had the servants turn them off in the morning.

Term:	*Twenty-fifth President of the U.S.*
Served:	*March 4, 1897-September 14, 1901*
Born:	*January 29, 1843,*
	Niles, Ohio
Married:	*Ida Saxton, a belle*
	of Canton, Ohio, 1871
Died:	*September 14, 1901,*
	Buffalo, New York

Handsome and enormously well-liked, McKinley was raised in Niles and Poland, Ohio, the son of a successful iron founder. He dropped out of college and worked as a teacher and postal clerk before the Civil War, where he saw action at Antietam and served on the staff of Colonel Rutherford B. Hayes. Afterward, he studied law and opened a practice in Canton, Ohio, in 1867. He married the daughter of a prominent Canton banker. Tragically, the couple lost both of their young daughters, and McKinley helplessly watched his bright and pretty wife deteriorate into an epileptic invalid. His affection for her never waivered, however, and even in the White House, he devoted himself to her needs. McKinley's political career began in 1869, when he was elected the Stark County prosecuting attorney. From 1877 to 1883, and again from 1885 to 1891, he was a U.S. Representative in Congress. Highly influential, he favored the interests of business, minimal government interference in free enterprise, and strong protective tariffs. His 1890 sponsorship of the severe McKinley Tariff cost him his seat in Congress, but with the financial help of Cleveland business magnate and king maker Mark Hanna, McKinley won Ohio's gubernatorial elections in 1891 and 1893. When McKinley ran for president in 1896 and 1900, Hanna engineered and financed both of his victories over the populist Democrat Williams Jennings Bryan. His 1896 win was the first time since Grant that a President was elected by both the popular and Electoral College vote. The campaigns of McKinley and Bryan, which respectively pitted the interests of business against those of labor, also marked the first time that a presidential race mirrored the nation's emerging class struggle. As President, McKinley seized the moment during the 1898 Cuban insurrection and seized a global empire from the Spanish. In 1898, he annexed Hawaii, and in 1899, he instituted the Open Door policy toward China. His expansionism made the U.S. a world power, and the prosperity of a war time economy fulfilled his campaign promise of a "full dinner pail." McKinley was at the peak of his popularity when he was shot by anarchist Leon Czolgosz during a visit to Buffalo, New York. He died several days later. Though McKinley's second term was cut short, his was a presidency of remarkable transitions for the nation. With an administration spanning two centuries, his time in office represented the end of one chapter and the start of another in American history. Not only was he the last Civil War veteran to occupy the White House, but also the first postwar President with broad-based popularity enough to indicate the beginning of the end of North-South factionalism. The wounds of the Civil War were at last scarred over, and with McKinley pointing the way, the nation could divert its energy and resources to the challenge of becoming an international player.

"Hanna has advertised McKinley as if he were a patent medicine."

—*Theodore Roosevelt*

We cannot gamble with anything so sacred as money.

Himself on the presidency: "I have had enough of it, heaven knows! I have had all the honor there is in this place, and have had responsibilities enough to kill any man."

Afflictions: Physical exhaustion during college

The Martial Arts: Promoted from private to brevet major, Civil War

Ill winds: McKinley had a fine parade for his first inauguration. A good thing, because his second in 1901 was dampened by a deluge. Also rained-out: the evening's fireworks.

Alma Mater: Allegheny College (no degree)

Term:	Twenty-seventh President of the U.S.
Served:	March 4, 1909 - March 3, 1913
Born:	September 15, 1857
	Cincinnati, Ohio
Married:	ambitious Helen Herron of
	Cincinnati, 1886
Died:	Died March 8, 1930,
	Washington, D.C.

"I have one consolation," said the suddenly ex-President, after the returns were in. "No one candidate was ever elected ex-President by such a large majority."

—William Howard Taft

Outgoing and quite athletic despite his unusually large size, Taft played baseball during his youth in Cincinnati and his college years at Yale. After graduating as class salutatorian in 1878, he returned to his hometown, where it is said that he rejected an offer to catch for the Cincinnati Reds in order to study law at the University of Cincinnati. Since his father was a distinguished judge, Republican party leader, U.S. Attorney General, and ambassador, young Taft obviously intended to follow in his footsteps. He did, and then some. Taft was admitted to the bar in 1880, and with his sights set on becoming a justice of the United States Supreme Court, he married the daughter of a prominent judge and carved out a career in public service. Blessed with a genial personality and great administrative ability, Taft used family political connections and his friendship with President Theodore Roosevelt to obtain a series of appointments that took him from an assistant prosecutor of Hamilton County to Governor-General of the Philippines in only twenty years. Taft became Roosevelt's chief adviser, confidant, and troubleshooter, and in 1908, his service was rewarded when Roosevelt hand-picked him to be his successor in the White House. After accepting the Republican nomination from the steps of the Taft manse on Cincinnati's Pike Street, he rode Roosevelt's progressive coattails to an easy victory over William Jennings Bryan. His presidency, however, was anything but easy for Taft. A naturally prudent man with a jurist's studied detachment from the vagaries of the public opinion, Taft ran the government well and initiated Dollar Diplomacy abroad, but he failed to understand the power of the progressive movement. By aligning himself with conservative Republicans on tariff and conservation issues, he rapidly lost public approval. Ironically, his record on trust busting— especially the breakup of the American Tobacco and Standard Oil companies—was better than Roosevelt's, but his quiet, cautious administration paled in comparison to that of his flamboyant predecessor. Although he ran for a second term in 1912, Taft was unable to unite the liberal and conservative branches of the Republican Party. Roosevelt forsook their friendship and their party to run for President himself as a progressive Bull Moose, thus siphoning off enough of the Republican vote to insure Taft's defeat by Democrat Woodrow Wilson. Humiliated by carrying only the states of Utah and Vermont, Taft gladly left the White House to teach constitutional law at Yale. He reconciled with Roosevelt in 1918, and in 1921, President Harding granted him his fondest wish: appointment to the Supreme Court. Successfully clearing the court's overcrowded docket, he again proved himself an effective administrator and remained a respected justice until his death from heart disease at age 72.

"The nearer I get to the inauguration of my successor, the greater the relief I feel." –Taft

Himself on the presidency: "I have come to the conclusion that the major part of the President is to increase the gate receipts of expositions and fairs and bring tourists into the town."

Afflictions: Dengue fever in the Philippines, 1901; heart strain from overweight; depression during presidency

Family Ties: Helen "Nellie" Taft brought the cherry trees in Washington, D.C., on March 27, 1912, personally planting the first of 3000 cherry trees that she had persuaded the Japanese government to send to the United States. She is the only U.S. President's wife buried in Arlington National Cemetery, in 1943

The Martial Arts: Taft never served in the U.S. military

Alma Mater: Yale University; University of Cincinnati, Law

When Yale offered Taft its Chair of Law, he respectfully declined, saying that his considerable girth really required a "Sofa of Law."

Point of Interest:

Taft's prodigious pajamas — Neck, 19 inches; sleeve, 34 1/2 inches; chest, 53 inches; waist, 54 inches; hips, 58 inches

Taft's bulk
- inspired New York bakers to bake him a ninety-two-pound Christmas pie
- got him stuck in at least two bathtubs, once on a ship to Cuba and again in the White House

Term:	Twenty-ninth President of the U.S.
Served:	March 4, 1921 - August 2, 1923
Born:	November 2, 1865, Corsica, Ohio
Married:	divorcee Florence DeWolfe of Marion, Ohio, 1891
Died:	August 2, 1923, San Francisco, California

His father was a physician of quite modest means, and Harding lived in the village of Caledonia, Ohio, until the family moved to Marion when he was about 18. Upon graduating from college in 1882, Harding tried his hand at teaching and selling insurance, then in 1884, became co-owner of a newspaper, the Marion *Star*. Harding eventually acquired full ownership, built the circulation, and prospered into a well-known public speaker and whole-hearted Republican. Handsome and well-dressed, he attracted the attention of a strong-willed, older woman. They married, but it was an uneasy union. Harding called her "The Duchess," and he escaped her domination with extramarital affairs. In 1899, Harding met Harry Daugherty, a shrewd power broker who recognized the political potential of a self-made, small town editor with a statesman's visage. Daugherty boosted Harding into the state senate in 1899, into the office of Ohio lieutenant governor, 1903; and into the U.S. Senate, 1915. At their 1920 convention, the Republicans were deadlocked, and Daugherty lobbied hard for Senator Harding, a party regular who had voted for Prohibition and against the League of Nations. Allowing that Harding's good looks would be an asset when the nation's newly enfranchised women went to the polls, the party bosses made him their compromise candidate for President. His opponent was a fellow Ohioan and newspaper publisher, Democrat James Cox, who vociferously supported the League of Nations. With the nation in a war-weary isolationist mood, Harding swamped Cox and took office as the first President born after the Civil War. Harding promised "normalcy," but his administration was anything but normal. Unprepared for the task of leadership, Harding counted on Congress and his cabinet to set policy. The high point of his term was the 1921 Washington Disarmament Conference, but its success was largely the work of Secretary of State Charles Evans Hughes. Even his pardon of Eugene Debs has been credited to Mrs. Harding, who is said to have requested the Socialist's release as her Christmas present. Harding's administration unfortunately followed the same pattern as Grant's: patently bad appointments and duplicity on the part of intimates inevitably leading to wide-spread corruption. While he was on a transcontinental trip in 1923, the infamous Teapot Dome scandal was exposed. Worried and weakened by traveling, Harding died in a San Francisco hotel room and was spared from having to witness the ignominy of his administration.

"I don't know what to do or where to turn on this taxation matter. Somewhere there must be a book that tells all about it, where I can go to straighten it out in my mind. But I don't know where the book is, and maybe I couldn't read it if I found it."

—Warren Harding

I feel like a man who goes in on a pair of eights and comes out with aces full.

Himself on the presidency: "I am a man of limited talents from a small town. I don't seem to grasp that I am President."

Afflictions: Nervous breakdown, age 24, treated at Battle Creek sanitarium; frequent indigestion and heartburn

At Play: It was Harding's custom to play golf at least twice a week. On July 2, 1921, he formally ended World War I in his golf clothes. An aide called the President off a New Jersey golf course, and he signed the resolution ending hostilities between Germany and the U.S. "That's all," said Harding before heading back to his game.

Family Ties: Florence Kling DeWolfe Harding was the first wife of a president who worked with her husband, as circulation manager of the Marion *Star*. She edited her husband's inaugural address and was the first First Lady to accompany the outgoing President to the Capitol on Inauguration Day.

The Martial Arts: Harding never served in the U.S. military

Alma Mater: Ohio Central College

8 moments of Presidential homage
by James B. Cash

1 William Henry Harrison

Virginia aristocrat who advanced on his own merit through the army. Served in Indian wars and War of 1812; one of the five successful soldiers from that generally disastrous war to run for president. Another soldier from that war, Lewis Cass, of opposition party, called Harrison the bravest man he ever knew. In the Jefferson tradition, Harrison was interested in many things. He once wrote a scientific paper on the Indian mounds of southern Ohio/Indiana. He served 30 days as president. His loss may have been tragic for the country. He appointed an excellent cabinet, and as a Virginian and Ohioan he might have been a bridge between the slavery and slave free states.

2 Ulysses S. Grant

He was the great strategic general of the Civil War. (Lee may have been the greatest tactical general, and there is an important difference: Tactics win battles; strategies win wars.) For that Grant should stand next to Washington. After the war he reluctantly got involved in politics to serve the country. He tried to provide equal rights for ex-slaves. Many forces North and South worked against him and he was unsuccessful. He and Warren G. Harding are blamed for corrupt administrations. Corruption always comes out after a major war. The Truman and Wilson administrations were equally corrupt. The "near great" Wilson administration was also racist.

3 Rutherford B. Hayes

His father died before he was born; raised under difficult circumstances; became number 1 student at Kenyon College, and graduate of Harvard Law School. Became Cincinnati lawyer; helped defend runaway slaves. Joined Union Army because he believed country should not be split and slaves should be free. Was recklessly courageous leader of 23rd Ohio, one of outstanding regiments in Union Army. Was reform governor of Ohio; helped found The Ohio State University, and the Ohio Historical Society; campaigned for giving blacks the right to vote; elected over NY corporate lawyer Samuel Tilden in disputed election. There would have been no dispute if former Confederate states had given full right to vote to blacks like they said they would after reentering the Union. Served one term; man of integrity and intelligence. Apologized to American Indians for conduct of U. S. government; retired; he and his wife got involved in charitable and educational activities, (somewhat like Jimmy Carter).

4 James A. Garfield

Born in a log cabin; his father died when he was very young; family struggled; he became outstanding student, proficient in Greek and Latin; published a solution in a mathematical journal of a problem posed by Pythagoras; became ordained minister of Christian church at 18; involved in Civil War, becoming general then a leader on financial matters in Congress; his charismatic speech for John Sherman in the Republican convention led the convention to nominate him. He was shot after four months in office, lingered on, but ultimately died of sepsis. He would probably have been a good president: he appointed a good cabinet, and successfully tangled with the corrupt Republican NY state machine.

Benjamin Harrison 5

Benjamin was well-educated grandson of William Henry Harrison; attended Miami University, where he met his wife. They were both serious Presbyterians. He went to Indianapolis after graduation, where he became a successful workaholic lawyer. Joined Union Army in the Civil War, leading the 70th Indiana, another highly rated regiment; Harrison was fine speaker and writer; became Indiana senator; voted against Chinese Exclusion Act; supported land set-asides for national parks; and Civil War veterans' pensions; became dark horse president; generally acted with integrity and intelligence; supported Sherman Anti-Trust and Sherman Silver Purchase Acts. His fatal political mistake was supporting the "Christmas Tree" McKinley Tariff. He served one term, and then became a kind of national intellectual on government issues. He deserves a better evaluation, but he had no sense of humor, and was beloved only to his family. He has never had a worthy biographer.

William McKinley 6

William McKinley was a naturally kind and considerate individual beloved by all, even his political opponents. He joined the Union Army at age 18 and his pleasing ways, his industry, and his resourcefulness led him to advance to a brevet major. McKinley became a Congressman after the war. He was a natural, and had a career of success except for one loss, when the McKinley Tariff passed. He became a reform governor of Ohio and then president. He tried to avoid going to war, the implications of which he understood much better than his chief critic, Teddy Roosevelt. After a short intense war, he and William Howard Taft created a model for the Peace Corps in the Philippines. He was a gifted and practical politician. (Note: Teddy Roosevelt won The Congressional Medal of Honor posthumously for his well-choreographed advance up Kettle Hill. There are six Ohio presidents more deserving of that award, based upon combat service.)

William Howard Taft 7

Taft was an exemplar of American idealism tied to American ingenuity. After McKinley was assassinated, Taft became the key cabinet member for Teddy Roosevelt. He had many achievements as president: he started the National Parks System; the Postal Savings System; he established the Federal Children's Bureau, appointing the first woman bureau chief (before women had the right to vote); he also initiated more anti-trust cases in his four years than the Great Trust Buster did in his seven years. In 1921 President Harding appointed Taft as Chief Justice to the Supreme Court. Taft was not a great judge but he got a fractious court to work well together. He also got Congress to reorganize the Federal Court system and build the Supreme Court building, which gave a visible recognition to the court as a third coordinate branch of government.

Warren G. Harding 8

Harding was the amiable owner of a successful small city newspaper. He was not a great writer, but a good organizer and a thoughtful boss who shared profits with his employees. He successfully navigated Ohio's tricky political waters and became the Republican's dark horse candidate for president in 1920. After the Wilson years, he caught the right political winds by his advocacy of a return to normalcy. He was not a great president, but he had some accomplishments: He sponsored the Washington Naval Conference, the first strategic arms limitation talks; he established the Bureau of the Budget, to try to put some discipline in the federal budgetary process; he pardoned Eugene V. Debs, a labor leader harassed into prison by the Wilson administration; he intervened with big business for a standard 8-hour day; finally he made a pro-Civil Rights speech in Birmingham, Alabama in 1921. He died suddenly in 1923 when knowledge of scandals in his administration had just begun to develop. His scandals should be compared with those of Truman, a president now highly regarded.

James B. Cash is the Dayton author of Unsung Heroes, Ohioans in the White House: A Modern Appraisal, *in which he details the half-century between Reconstruction and the Roaring Twenties, evaluating the Ohio presidents from the vantage point of our own time.*

"Always have an icebox full of food and never let him travel without you."

—*Florence Harding, on how to keep a husband*

The Antietam National Battlefield in rural Maryland is a solemn place. The name looms large in history but the killing ground at Antietam is actually very small, a few acres here and there, a short hike between. In this narrow place, 23,000 men were killed or severely wounded in about 12 hours of a bright autumn day, the bloodiest single day in American history. The little farm lanes around Antietam are lined with monuments put up by the survivors, hailing this regiment and that battery. William McKinley was on the strangest marker of all—an obelisk, a good 18 feet tall, erected by the officers and men of the 23rd Ohio Volunteer Infantry, that declares, "Sgt. McKinley, Co. E. 23rd Ohio Vol. Infty, while in charge of the Commissary Department on the afternoon of the Day of the Battle of Antietam, Sept. 17, 1862, personally and without orders sent hot coffee and warm food to every man in the regiment on this spot & in doing so had to pass under fire."

Proportionally, no state put so much blood and effort into the Civil War; no state got so much back in power and prestige. That's the history. But why do we remember McKinley's coffee cup?

It is a monument to a cup of coffee delivered by a man who walked off this battlefield unharmed and lived another 39 years. It only makes sense if you can read the unwritten message; Ohio won the Civil War.

It is our state secret but the evidence of the Buckeye Ascendancy is before your eyes. Of all the victorious Northern states, Ohio proportionally put more into the war and proportionally got the most back.

New York and Pennslyvania sent more men in absolute numbers to the Union ranks but Ohio's 346,326 soldiers and sailors drawn from a population of only 2.3 million make it the largest percentage from any northern state. In the service of the Union, 34,591 Ohioans died, roughly a third in combat and two-thirds to disease and accidents.

From this investment in blood, Ohio drew massive economic growth and political clout. The war jolted Ohio manufacturing into the front ranks of world industry. It fired up Ohio transpor-tation, finances, and engineering. For 50 years after Appomatox Court House, money erupted from Ohio factories and mines, raining down as major industries, great family fortunes, large cities, and rich cultural endowments—museums, schools, and fantastical Victorian buildings. Only in recent decades has the post-Civil War ordering of Ohio begun to break up.

The Civil War also thrust a whole generation of Ohioans into leadership, both military and civilian. The list of winning Ohio generals from Grant, Sherman, Sheridan and on down is impressive enough but the state also had room for two of the North's biggest losers—George B. McClellan and Irwin McDowell. Salmon Chase of Cincinnati ran Lincoln's Treasury and Edwin Stanton of Steubenville the War Department. (In the hysteria following Lincoln's murder, Stanton ran the whole country for three days as America's only dictator until a fearful Vice President Andrew Johnson emerged from seclusion.) The war even launched the career

of New Rumley's George Armstrong Custer.

The crowning triumph of Ohio's victory was the *de facto* lease native Ohioans had on the White House in the second half of the 19th century. From Lincoln's assassination to McKinley's, Ohioans were in residence for 22 of those 36 years. The Ohio reign would have been even longer if two of the Buckeye presidents, James Garfield and the former Sgt. William McKinley, hadn't been murdered in office.

Ironically, McKinley's obelisk at Antietam celebrates the high water mark of the Buckeye Ascendancy. It was raised in the emotional aftermath following McKinley's death on September 14, 1901, six days after he was shot by Leon Czolgosz.

McKinley succumbed three days short of the 39th anniversary of his hazardous coffee run at Antietam. One of the men who drank McKinley's coffee under fire that day was another future White House tenant, Rutherford B. Hayes, thus making the 23rd OVI the only military unit in American history to muster two future presidents. (Hayes, it should be noted, reached the White House by accepting the Compromise of 1877. Southern Democrats threw the disputed election to Hayes in return for his agreement to withdraw federal troops from the South and end Reconstruction, leaving southern blacks, including thousands of Union Army veterans, to the tender mercies of Jim Crow laws and the Ku Klux Klan.)

After McKinley, the last president to serve in the Civil War, American demographics and politics moved on. Ohio was never so politically powerful again.

But that is the cold-blooded history. None of this explains why President McKinley, victor of the Spanish-American War, upholder of the Gold Standard and victim of an anarchist's bullet, seems as remote to us today as Vasco de Gama. Yet a full five generations later, Sgt. McKinley, deliverer of hot coffee under fire, steps alive into memory.

Other American events, wars, and myths have withered while the Civil War remains ever green. Cowboy stories are not so much fun now that we know what they really did to the Indians. No one digs authentic trenches to play Western Front as a hobby. Yet even as it recedes in time, the Civil War spreads like weeds in the popular imagination. It is watered by a never-ending river of Civil War books, television shows, and movies. It flows through the crowds at the national battlefield parks. It flourishes amongst tens of thousands of Civil War "reenactors" who turn out in authentically uncomfortable wool clothing to drill and skirmish away their weekends. Each generation renews the Civil War. And we refight it on our terms.

Ohio soldiers in the Civil War constituted three of every five Ohio males between the ages of 18 and 45.

57

Marching through *Ohio*
Civil War
A guide to historical sites

Beyond the books and the movies, the Civil War is still here to be touched and to touch us in Ohio. We are a state rich in relics—bullet-riddled tree trunks behind glass in local museums, statuary, cannonball garlands around courthouse flagpoles, and bewhiskered portraits of generals. Beyond that, we have the names, famed and almost forgotten.

Akron, Summit County—**John Brown,** who was a restless soul, was as much an Ohioan as anything else. He lived in Hudson, Richland, and from 1844-46, at 514 Diagonal Road in Akron. It was a period when he was recovering from his bankruptcy in the wool trade and brooding over America's moral bankruptcy in the slave trade. When he was hanged, flags flew at half-mast in Akron.

Athens, Athens County—**The Soldiers and Sailors Monument** with its four heroic bronze figures sits on the campus of Ohio University, commemorating the contributions of town, gown and county to the war effort.

Buffington Island Memorial, State Route 124 near the village of Portland, Meigs County—The site of Ohio's only significant battle is not completely in Ohio. The island, legally in West Virginia, was the center of a three-way fight on July 19, 1863, among **Confederate raider** John Hunt Morgan's troopers on the island, pursuing Federal cavalry on the Ohio side, and the gunboat, *U.S.S. Moose*, in the Ohio River. Losing half his men, Morgan escaped upriver. He was attacked by the *Moose* a few

hours later while trying to cross the Ohio River at Reedsville. Morgan and a further diminished force escaped yet again but he was still on the Ohio side of the river.

Cadiz, Harrison County—Birthplace of that "lucky slob" **Clark Gable** who played Rhett Butler, a highly important Civil War figure. Gable's presence in *GWTW* merely proves that you can't do anything important in Blue and Gray without Ohioans.

Canton, Stark County—Rising from private to brevet major, **William McKinley** served three long years of war, without sustaining serious injury. Taking up the law in Canton afterward, he served six terms in Congress before sustaining serious political injury over tariffs. Taken up by Ohio kingmaker Mark

Hanna, McKinley served as governor and then president before sustaining a fatal pistol wound. His tomb in Westlawn Cemetery is a sight to behold. **The McKinley Museum of History**, next door at 749 Hazlett Avenue NW, is a site to explore.

Cincinnati, Hamilton County, **Harriet Beecher Stowe House** at Gilbert and Foraker Avenue. "The little woman who made this big war," as Lincoln supposedly described the diminutive author of *Uncle Tom's Cabin* (at right), lived here while she was soaking up material on slavery.

Cincinnati, Hamilton County, **Burnet House**. When General Sherman came to talk war plans with General Grant in March 1864, they repaired to Parlor A of the swank Burnet House. Here they decided Sherman would take Atlanta and then march to the sea. The hotel was demolished in 1926 by the Central Trust Company. Rumors that "Gone With the Wind" refers to the Burnet House are entirely unfounded.

Cincinnati, Hamilton County, **Spring Grove Cemetery** has a magnificent larger-than-life bronze infantryman atop a stone column that was sculpted and cast in Munich, Germany. The soldiers stand guard over an extensive Civil War graves section encircling an usual decorative formation of cannon barrels. The cemetery has the graves of 35 Union Army generals.

Cincinnati, Hamilton County—When a Confederate army threatened the city in September 1861, a mob of "special police" rampaged through the black quarter seizing men for a black labor battalion. Colonel Dickson apologized, let the men go home to

"The first printing of 5,000 copies sold out in two days, a year later it had sold 305,000 copies and a pirated edition had come out in England...it would become the most popular American novel of the century, published in more than 40 languages, and read by millions...her hate mail was vast and violent—one small parcel from Dixie contained a black, human ear..."

● ●

prepare. The next morning, over 1,000 black men appeared for duty. Dickson presented them with a special American flag emblazoned, **"Black Brigade of Cincinnati."** The brigade served enthusiastically, building fortifications in the Kentucky hills and marching from job to job in military formation. When the Confederates withdrew, the Black Brigade tried to join the Army as a unit. They were refused.

Cleveland, Cuyahoga County, **The Soldiers and Sailors Monument** on Public Square is the state's most ambitious and energetic war memorial. It was designed by Levi T. Schofield who also did "These Are My Jewels" on the Statehouse lawn in Columbus.

One Mary Smith served in male disguise with the 41st Ohio Infantry, undiscovered until one day he/she was spotted "giving an unmistakeable twist to the dishcloth in wringing it out that no man could ever successfully counterfeit." Women masquerading as men in the war was not as uncommon as one might think: there were 135 documented instances in which the distaff testosterone count matched that of their male counterparts, and some historians believe there may have been as many as 400.

Cleveland, Cuyahoga County—**The Western Reserve Historical Society Museum and Library**, 10825 East Boulevard, has one of the finest collections of Civil War materials—diaries, letters, paintings, newspapers, etc.—in the country.

Columbus, Franklin County—The **Confederate Cemetery**, 2900 Sullivant Avenue, containing the graves of 2,259 Confederate prisoners, is all that's left of the sprawling military base that was once Camp Chase. Besides the Confederate prisoner-of-war camp, Camp Chase was also a military limbo for Union soldiers who'd been captured in battle but returned home on parole. The parolees couldn't legally fight until they were "exchanged" and they couldn't go home because the Army feared they would never come back. The graveyard at Camp Chase still exists because of William Knauss, a Union soldier from Columbus who was left for dead on the battlefield at Fredericksburg. A recovered Knauss became obsessed with honoring the graves of his onetime enemies. Through the 1880s, Knauss campaigned to protect Confederate cemeteries in the North, especially the graveyard at Camp Chase. His efforts made him a hero in the South and the object of various threats at home. When Knauss helped put up a new ceremonial cemetery gateway in 1902, an armed guard had to be posted for a time. The inscription on the arch still reads, "Americans." By the gate is a Confederate cannonball that was fired at William Tecumseh Sherman's headquarters during the siege of Vicksburg. It missed. Sherman's brother-in-law had it dug up for a souvenir and sent it home to Lancaster. Eventually the cannonball with its impeccable pedigree passed to Lt. Col. Herbert L. Snapp, U.S.A. Ret., who recently presented it to the cemetery.

Columbus, Franklin County,—Somewhere under Ameriflora, there is a monument to the site of **W. T. Sherman's 1880 "War is All Hell" speech** which he gave, in a suitably Shermanesque driving rainstorm to 5,000 uniformed veterans. "There is many a boy here today who looks on war as all glory," said the devastator of Georgia, "but boys, it is all hell. You can bear this warning to generations yet to come. I look upon war with horror, but if it has to come, I am here."

Columbus, Franklin County—If you are in any doubt as to who won the Civil War, go to the Ohio State Capitol grounds to admire Levi Schofield's bronze squadron of Ohio victors—Grant, Sherman, Sheridan, Hayes, Garfield, Chase and Stanton. It is a wedding cake of martial glory, topped by a statue of the legendary Roman matron who instead of gems had sons, declaring **"These Are My Jewels."** They don't make them like they used to anymore.

Dayton, Montgomery County—The Copperhead leader **Clement Vallandigham** was arrested at his home in the dead of the night of May 5, 1863, by soldiers who smashed in the door and dragged him away, leaving his wife and sister-in-law in hysterics. Vallandigham was carted off to Cincinnati, tried by a military court for uttering sedition and banished through the Confederate lines.

Fort Fizzle, Holmes County—Local farmers converged on a stone barn about a mile-and-a-half south of the present village of Glenmont and declared they would resist by force of arms any attempt to enforce the new draft act in Holmes County. The rebels were said to number 1,000 strong. On June 17, 1863, the federal provost for the area appealed for help. A motley force of infantry, militia and artillery was dispatched from Camp Chase. The rebels loosed off a few shots from behind a stone wall. The troops responded with a volley and a charge. The rebellion known as **Fort Fizzle** was soon over. It remained a sore subject in Holmes County well into this century.

Fremont, Sandusky County—**The Rutherford B. Hayes Presidential Center**, Spiegel Grove, is devoted to the study, not only of the Civil War general, U.S. president and devoted husband of Lucy Hayes, but to the study of

the so-called "Gilded Age" which was the big industrial and political pay-off for Ohio's victory in the Civil War. The Hayes term in the White House was the overstuffed and over-decorated peak of the American Victorian period. Lucy Hayes, an ardent temperance crusader, gave parties at which it was said, "The water flowed like wine."

Johnson's Island, Ottawa County—A half mile across Sandusky Bay from the city, Johnson's Island was leased in 1861 from Leonard B. Johnson, the eponymous owner, as the site of a **prisoner-of-war camp**. It became a camp for Confederate officers and political prisoners. Like all Union prison camps, it was hideously overcrowded. Two hundred died in captivity and never left the island. In 1864, the old sutler was fired and Leonard B. Johnson became the new sutler. He offered the hungry prisoners lithographic views of the island for $3. He refused to sell anything else to anyone who did not first buy a copy of his picture.

Lisbon, Columbiana County—A plaque just south of town on SR 518 marks where **John Hunt Morgan** and his remaining raiders finally gave up, 46 days after they crossed the Ohio and a week after the Battle of Buffington Island. Morgan surrendered with a promise of parole as a prisoner-of-war but was packed off, instead, to the Ohio Penitentiary as a common horse thief. Five months later, he busted out of the Pen, heading south to Dixie and his death in a Union counter-raid.

McConnelsville, Morgan County—Noted Civil War photography collector Larry Strayer says his favorite statue in the state is McConnelsville's bronze casting of a young infantryman in authentic gear. Strayer says that all too often, post-war statue makers took liberties with the equipment their subjects held. The **McConnelsville infantryman** is authentic down to his buttons.

Middle Bass Island, Erie County—A group of Confederate agents working from Canada seized the steamer "**Philo Parson**" in Sandusky

Bay on September 19, 1864, in an attempt to free the prisoners held on Johnson's Island. The "Parson" was nearly out of fuel so the Confederates turned her for Middle Bass Island. There they seized another boat, "The Island Queen," and put passengers and crew from both ashore. The Confederates now set out for Sandusky Bay again, scuttling the "Queen" in route. Then they spotted a federal warship riding at anchor near the prison camp. Nerves failed and the "Parson" turned for Canada where the agents ran her into shore and fled into the wilds of Ontario.

New California, Union County—**Jerome Township** sent 396 men to fight in the Civil War, the largest percentage from any township in the North. A memorial statue at the intersection of US 33 and 42 was hit by trucks so often, a concrete barricade was thrown up to protect it. Help came too late for the 80 Civil War cannonballs that once decorated the base of the memorial. According to James Cunningham, who lives in nearby Plain City and is active in the VFW, the cannonballs were all stolen. Once a year, the VFW gathers a firing party and color guard "to shoot over the old man, we say," says Cunningham.

Oberlin, Lorain County—**Oberlin College** was an abolitionist hotbed in the years leading up to the war. Three black students from Oberlin were with John Brown on his ill-fated Harper's Ferry raid. The body of one of them, John A. Copeland, is buried in Oberlin Cemetery. When word came of the firing on Fort Sumter, faculty and students surged to a mass meeting on Friday night at the First Church. By Monday morning, 130 students had volunteered for what became Company C of the 7th OVI. A week later, the number had been "trimmed to the regulation size of 100, chiefly by the refusal of parents' consent." Their captain was their Latin tutor, G. W. Shurtleff. Of the 150 Oberlin students who eventually served in Company C, 31 died and 15 were discharged with serious wounds. Shurtleff rose to Brigadier General and commanded the 5th U.S.C.T., a regiment of

Ohio blacks that earned four Congressional Medals of Honor. Shurtleff is immortalized in bronze just south of campus.

Pomeroy, Meigs County—While many Ohio towns bought mass-produced metal statues for their war memorials, Pomeroy commissioned **a rare stone statue of a sentinel** seated on a rock. Aficionados say his equipment is highly accurate.

Point Pleasant, Clermont County—The **birthplace of U.S. Grant** is a state memorial now, a log cabin in considerably better repair now than on April 27, 1822, when the future "Unconditional Surrender" Grant came into this world, the son of an overly-optimistic tanner and businessman.

Salem, Columbiana County—Home of the long-since deceased **A.H. Mullions Company**, caster of hundreds of "Tin Gods," Civil War memorials and other heroic statuary set up in honor across the land.

Sheffield Lake, Lorain County—The campground of the **103rd Ohio Volunteer Infantry**, the oldest regimental family association in Ohio, has a public museum open by appointment year round except during the third week of August when 300 and more descendents of the 103rd fall in for a week of fun and patriotism.

Urbana, Champaign County—Head bowed, hat in hand and sword at side, the Union officer stands at the center of Urbana. The bronze **Soldier's Monument** was the work of John Quincy Adams Ward, an Urbana native.

Yellow Springs, Greene County—Nearly all Ohio colleges sent students to the Civil War (Miami in Oxford sent contingents to both the Union and Confederate armies. In 1861, the Miami boys marched to the station together, shook hands, and went their separate ways.) **Antioch College** War Memorial is one of the few that honors students alone. The marble plaque in the lobby of Main Building lists 33 Antioch students "who gave their lives for their country." This was an extraordinary loss for a college that was nine years old in the 1860-1861 school year and had only 65 students.

Larger than life—the work floor of Salem's A.H. Mullions Company

Ohio did more to prompt the Civil War, fight it, win it—and figure out how to pay for it—than anyone. Ohioans pressed the antislavery cause by pen and sword. By pen, most notably by Cincinnati resident Harriet Beecher Stowe, whose *Uncle Tom's Cabin* was one of the nation's earliest publishing sensations. By sword, through the acts of one-time Ohio resident John Brown, a fanatic, though perhaps a useful one. For the first two years of the Civil War that followed, the Union cause suffered through the insufficiencies of its generals. When the North found the leadership it needed, it found it in the Buckeye state, where the three generals necessary to victory—Grant, Sherman and Sheridan—were born or raised. And it was in Ohio that the expertise was found to answer the question of the day—how to tax everyone and everything—for the survival of the Union. The war was between North and South, and it seemed painfully accurate that a state combining elements of both geographies would decide the conflict.

The Promptings

Harriet Beecher Stowe

Abolitionists preached mainly to the converted; often fervent, generally few. The circulation of the best-known abolitionist publication—William Lloyd Garrison's *The Liberator*—never topped 3,000. The gulf between the high-minded and the masses was bridged by a one-time Ohioan, Harriet Beecher Stowe, whose Cincinnati experiences were the foundation for her 1851 novel, *Uncle Tom's Cabin*, likely the most influential book ever written by an American. What she gave the public was not the high-minded argument of the abolitionists but a good low-church tale, rich in character, melodrama, and action. Her characters — slaveowners included— were sympathetically drawn. Her moral, however, was that one cannot in any way touch the slave system and remain a good Christian. In a highly religious age, this argument hit the public where it lived, and prayed. The book was a publishing sensation, selling 300,000 copies its first year, equal perhaps to six million today. The book's influence on shifting northern opinion against slavery was enormous. A story attested that when Mrs. Stowe met Lincoln, he greeted her by saying, "So this is the little woman who made this big war." If he didn't say it, he should have.

Oberlin

At least one historian termed Oberlin "the town that started the Civil War," a description earned for the town's sustained opposition to slavery. Oberlin was a center of the Underground Railroad; by one count, 3,000 escaped slaves passed through Oberlin in the decades before the Civil War. Much of the activism was the consequence of Oberlin College; three times, anti-abolitionists in the Ohio state legislature tried to have the college's charter revoked. The best known single event was the 1859 Oberlin-Wellington Rescue, when 37 townspeople rescued John Price, an escaped and recaptured slave, in

*In 1862, Ohio Medical School graduate **Richard Gatling** demonstrated the first rapid-fire weapon, subsequently known as the Gatling Gun. The prototype, manufactured in Cincinnati, had a crank-operated rotating barrel that could fire 350 .58 caliber rounds per minute—six per second. But formal adoption did not come until 1866. It saw sporadic use, however, in the trench warfare of the 1864-65 siege of Petersburg, Virginia. By report, Gatling considered his gun to be a small step for mankind. If, he reasoned, he could give one man the firepower of 100, then armies could be much smaller, and fewer would come in harm's way. The alternative—that armies would simply become that much more lethal—did not occur to him.*

Wellington, near Oberlin. All 37 were brought in to U.S. District Court in Cleveland for trial. Slavery opponents whipped up support for the accused, with marches and rallies. Eventually all defendants walked free: the federal government took the temper of the community and decided, on a technicality, not to press the prosecution. Not all got off so lightly. One Oberlin graduate went South to urge slaves to rebel and spent 17 years in prison. Quaker Thomas Garrett—who help hundreds of fugitives to safety—was fined almost everything he owned: "Judge, you haven't left me a dollar," he said, "but if anyone knows of a fugitive who wants a shelter or a friend, send them to Thomas Garrett."

From 1864 to 1884, the United States Army was commanded by someone born, or raised, in Ohio. By Ulysses Grant, from 1864 to 1869. By William Tecumseh Sherman, from 1869 to 1883. And finally, by Philip Sheridan, who, appointed as Sherman's successor, served the final year before his own death in 1884. Nineteen of those 20 years were peaceful.

Ripley

In the 1850s, John P. Parker ran a successful foundry in Ripley, securing three patents and employing 25 people. But Parker had a second career, equally successful. He was a slave-stealer. By Abolitionist account, Parker spirited between 900 to 1,000 escaping slaves to freedom. Commonly, he would cross into Kentucky, make contact with a rumored party of slaves, then get them across the Ohio to a safe house. This would have been extraordinarily hazardous work for a white man. For Parker, who was black, it was nearly suicidal. Once in Kentucky, he met up with the slave couple he was to lead north, only to learn that their owner was keeping the couple's infant child hostage. Parker sneaked into the slaveowners' bedroom and snatched the child from their bed. Parker was on terms with Ripley's white abolitionists, but did not collaborate. Said Parker, "I did not think it proper to ask white men how to conduct slaves from Kentucky." When war came, Parker boosted the recruitment of black soldiers. When peace returned, he ran his foundry, raised his family. A son graduated from Oberlin; a daughter from Mt. Holyoke. When Parker died in 1900, a local newspaper described him as "one of Ripley's energetic citizens."

"I am as content to die for God's eternal truth on the scaffold as in any other way."
—John Brown

John Brown

"I am worth inconceivably more to hang than for any other purpose." That statement, spoken by John Brown to his brother while Brown awaited execution for the raid on Harper's Ferry, was unhesitatingly correct. Like other figures of the age—notably Lincoln and Grant—Brown was for much of his life a notable failure. He failed as a land speculator, failed in business, failed in farming. He was not universally loved. From 1830 to 1849 he lived in Ohio, during which time 22 people filed lawsuits against him. It is not clear that Brown was sane; he had the monomania often associated with insanity. Brown had got hold of a very simple idea—that human slavery was wrong—and thought this wrong was the only truly important fact of the day. The response, to Brown, was to wash the guilty land with blood. This is what he did in Osawatomie, Kansas, in 1855, where with four of his sons, he hacked five pro-slavery men to death. To spark more blood, Brown in 1858 with 21 followers seized the

federal arsenal at Harpers Ferry, Virginia. The purported aim was to instigate a slave uprising. As insurrectionist strategy, the Harpers Ferry raid was hare-brained enough. Brown made no effort to alert the slaves he hoped would rebel; his party brought no rations, planned no escape route. Trapped, tried, and sentenced to be hung, Brown told the court, "I deny everything but what I have long admitted: a design on my part to free slaves." Wrote historian Stephen Oates, "His raid polarized the country as no other event had done, setting in motion a spiral of accusation and counter-accusation that bore the country irreversibly toward the Civil War..." Oates was correct; three years later, the Northerners who had condemned Brown's act were marching into battle singing "John Brown's Body."

The Victors

Ulysses S. Grant
Contrasted with the stoicism of Lee or the dour unreasonableness of Stonewall Jackson, Ulysses Simpson Grant is the great democratic figure of the Civil War. Grant attended his early schooling in Georgetown, Ohio. There, he later wrote, he was told that "'a noun is the name of a thing' so many times, that I came to believe it." It's an observation Tom Sawyer could have made, though Tom might have liked West Point more than Grant, who hated it. Grant represented the popular faith in the unrealized possibility. Whatever has happened in our lives up to this date, tomorrow may still present new possibilities that will allow us to realize our true selves. Ulysses S. Grant spent the better part of the 1850s failing: he failed as a soldier, failed as farmer, failed as a seller of wood, and failed as an insurance salesman. By decade's close, he was working for his father-in-law, in a leather store in Galena, Illinois. Then, civil war broke out. A rally was held in Galena. Grant went, and as a West Point graduate was asked to take charge. Whatever Grant's failures in previous life—whatever his subsequent failings as president—when thrust by circumstance into the military sphere, he entered a realm in which his touch was complete. For Grant, that first meeting in Galena was an epiphany.

William Tecumseh Sherman
The Civil War engendered a notion that war was a thing of romance. William Tecumseh Sherman would have none of it. Nothing romantic clung to him. Some argue he was the North's best general; more, that he was the first modern general. He is called this because he went Napoleon one better. Napoleon's dictum is that an army marches on its stomach; it is dependent on its supply of provisions. Sherman argued a step further, that that stomach was dependent on the civilian economy that created that supply. The Civil War, he believed, was not a contest between armies but between peoples; it would continue until the Southern people were exhausted. By marching across Georgia and northward through the Carolinas, Sherman did much to exhaust them. Curious, compared to the campaigning between Grant and Lee in Virginia, Sherman's advance was a relatively bloodless thing. He sought not to kill, but to rip out the underpinnings of war-making. There was no romance to it, and it was for the destruction of romance as well as for the destruction of things that the South has hated Sherman.

Johnny Clem: The boy, the man, the legend
The legend of Johnny Clem asserts that he ran away from Newark at the age of ten, attached himself to a Union regiment where he became a drummer boy, and rallied the troops at the 1862 Battle of Shiloh. The next year, during the Battle of Chickamauga the four foot, 40-pound lad managed to shoot a Confederate colonel off his horse. He became the youngest Army sergeant and, after the war, was commissioned a second lieutenant by his friend, General Ulysses Grant. Said one writer, "Though he lived to age 85, he was in the end remembered for what he had done at the age of 12." In the fall of 1989, the young Johnny Shiloh found himself facing a court martial, 127 years after the fact. A historian charged the boy wonder was a fake, and a local attorney arranged for a mock trial, the key players fitted in period costumes, including the young Clem. After charge and counter-charge, he was found not guilty. Wrote Jane Ware, "The legend now transcended any need for proof; it had become fact, at least in Newark."

Isolated at a California Army post in the early 1850s, Ulysses S. Grant turned to drink, eventually resigning his commission. Uncertain of himself early in the war, William Tecumseh Sherman more or less lost his nerve, returning home to recover. Shared near-failure was a tie between them.

Philip Sheridan

Philip Sheridan was born, by some accounts, in Albany, New York, although Whitelaw Reid, in Ohio during the War, claims Sheridan told him he had been born in Perry County, where in any case Sheridan grew up. A West Point graduate, he served with distinction in both the Civil War's western and eastern theatres. For his leadership in the Shenandoah, Sheridan was raised to the rank of major general. In a Union army noted for its caution, Sheridan was a driver. Once, mounted on Rienza, he encountered a Union soldier who had just been shot through the jugular. "You're not hurt," Sheridan shouted. "Get back in the line," a statement made with sufficient conviction that the soldier took two full steps before dropping dead.

Thomas Read and his epic

Philip Sheridan was a small man who rode a large horse, Rienza, with whom the federal cavalry commander co-starred in the Civil War's best-known epic poem—"Sheridan's Ride," by Thomas Buchanan Read. Born in Ohio, Read was a popular poet of the mildly epic school. In the fall of 1864, he was challenged by a speaker at a patriotic rally to come up with "something new and fresh that would arouse the audience." Three hours later, Read returned and presented a poem commemorating one of the war's great feats of battlefield leadership—Sheridan's 20-mile ride on Rienza from Winchester to Cedar Creek in Virginia's Shenandoah Valley to rally faltering Union troops to victory. The poem, when read aloud, gave the cadence of a galloping horse. It claimed an immediate popularity as an election ballad for the Republican's 1864 campaign. Read from the stage, one historian wrote, "it seldom failed to rouse crowds to roars of patriotic fervor." A sample:

Still sprang from these swift hoofs, thundering south
The dust like smoke from the cannon's mouth
Or the trail of a comet, sweeping faster and faster
Foreboding to traitors the doom of disaster.

Sherman's march to the sea in 1864 covered 300 miles—about the same distance for coalition forces moving from Kuwait to Baghdad in 2003. Sherman's men freed 40,000 slaves, targeting largely monuments to the Confederacy and plantations of wealthy slave-holders. In his entire march through Georgia, Sherman's men killed only about 600 Southerners.

—Victor Davis Hanson, professor of Military History, U.S. Naval Academy

"There is many a boy here today who looks on war as all glory, but boys, it is all hell. You can bear this warning to generations yet to come."
—*William Tecumseh Sherman*

The Money Men

Salmon P. Chase

Salmon Chase gained just about every office but the one wanted. He was governor of Ohio, senator from Ohio, secretary of the treasury and, later in life, chief justice of the U.S. Supreme Court. What he wanted to be was President. He looked the part—he was, one wrote, "a sculptor's ideal of a president." And he was energetic on his own behalf. In 1864, as a member of Lincoln's cabinet, he let his availability as a replacement to Lincoln be known: "I think a man of different qualities from those of the President will be needed in the next four years. I am not anxious to be that man, but..." Ambitions aside, Chase was quite able.

He secured passage of the National Banking Act, which created the national banking system that was the forerunner to the Federal Reserve System. And he introduced the first income tax. As of August 15, 1862, Americans with incomes of over $800 a year—a decent middle class figure at the time—were required to pay 3% of that income to the government. Given the government's wartime need for tax receipts, Chase also levied tribute on a few other things as well, among them liquor, tobacco, playing cards, carriages, yachts, jewelry, patent medicines, newspaper advertisements, on bank and corporation receipts and dividends, and added an inheritance tax and a tax on billiard tables.

Jay Cooke

In late 1861, treasury secretary Salmon P. Chase informed Lincoln that the government was nearly broke and he did not know where to turn for funds. Fortunately, Chase turned to Jay Cooke, the Sandusky-born banker who instructed Chase on the financial black arts. Cooke's first solution was to sell long-term bonds to the rich, many of whom he knew personally and was able to influence on behalf of purchase. Next, Cooke suggested that bonds be sold not just to the rich, but democratically to everyone else. To ease the public's way into high finance, Chase established bonds with denominations as low as $50, paid by monthly premiums. Jay Cooke and Company, granted standing as the government's sole agent in sales to the public, hired 2,500 agents nationwide to push the paper nationwide. That sale was boosted by patriotic advertising and gatherings that anticipated the bond rallies associated with the World Wars. Cooke's expertise came cheap: on bond sales of $1.2 billion, his company reportedly made only an actual profit of $700,000. The financial gods did not always favor Jay Cooke. Less than a decade later, the cash demands of the railway Cooke owned, the Northern Pacific, pushed his investment firm into bankruptcy, triggering the Panic of 1873.

Edwin Stanton

Abraham Lincoln appointed Edwin Stanton as secretary of war because the Steubenville-born attorney was bone honest. No incidental virtue. The Civil War prompted an unprecedented outpouring of federal funds; contracts to let, inspections to make, all highly susceptible to highly profitable bribery. Simon Cameron of Pennsylvania, Stanton's predecessor, had spent a considerable amount of federal money acquiring shoes with cardboard heels. Stanton was tight with a buck, a skilled manager and organizer.

"**An ironfisted martinet, Stanton saved the government $17 million in adjusted war contracts, streamlined army purchasing, reorganized the entire supply system, and assimilated a mass of technical data Lincoln found indispensible...**"

In 1863, he persuaded Lincoln to send idle eastern troops to the western theatre by train. Stanton called in the heads of various railroads, sent them to work hustling up trains and within 40 hours of Lincoln's decision had the first troops leaving Virginia. In 11 days, more than 20,000 men were moved over 1,100 miles, complete with their horses, artillery and equipment. Post-war, Stanton remained in the public eye. The one-time Democrat had turned Radical Republican, a formidable opponent of President Andrew Johnson. Johnson moved to oust Stanton, an act Congress branded a violation of the Tenure of Office Act. Johnson canned Stanton anyway, and the House impeached him.

15 Ohioans
you want on the next barstool
when the fight
breaks out.

Simon Kenton *the final frontier*

Simon Kenton, Zanesfield frontiersman, captured by the British *and* Indians, ran the gauntlet eight times, was tortured, thrice escaped burning at the stake, saved Daniel Boone's life, and died at 81—in bed. After everything else, death must have seemed fairly tame.

Tecumseh *civil warrior*

Tecumseh was our first macho-man. He *had* to be. He was contending with *us*. He fought us bravely in our first Civil War, our most feared enemy; he also seems to have been a superior man. For a time, he and his warriors virtually stopped river traffic on the Ohio. He got in William Henry Harrison's face. Tecumseh had the cheek, but Harrison had the brass. After he was killed at the Battle of the Thames, he became a legend. Harrison became famous for giving the longest inaugural address.

Mike Fink *to die as one lived*

Mike Fink, Ohio River keelboatman, was, at one time, a *real* man, even though *he* said he was half horse, half alligator, and could lick all comers, man or beast. The evidence seems to be that he probably could and may have. Even before the legend, Mike was the quintessential roughneck in a frontier world of roughnecks. When he died in a fight over a woman in 1823, he found himself just beginning to live.

Phil Sheridan *contender*

While **Phil Sheridan** was only five feet five, he was still tall in the Union saddle. Son of an Ohio mayor, he never shied from combat—he once threw a conductor off his own train—and someone once said he had seen more dead men than anyone alive. "Go in, sir, and get some of your men killed," he is said to have told one of his colonels. He did not say "The only good Indian is a dead Indian." But he *almost* did.

Grant *heavy hitter* 5

No American general ever lost so many men in so little time—7,000 in 30 minutes at the Battle of Cold Harbor—as **Ulysses S. Grant**. No American general ever had a greater aversion to the sight of blood. Blocked on his way to Richmond, Grant said to Lincoln, "I propose to fight it out along this line, if it takes all summer." It did. He did.

Sherman *float Like a butterfly* 6

Refusing to stand and fight, **William Tecumseh Sherman** whisked the props out from under the Confederate war machine. Some said he invented "total war," and was the spiritual father of the Vietnam War notion of "search and destroy." He used inglorious pillage and constant sidestepping, was macho without being murderous, and his enemies haven't forgiven him to this day.

Quantrill *bad boy, but our bad boy* 7

Although **William Clarke Quantrill** was from a Dover, Ohio, family, he fought with the Confederacy, a devoted family man who was called the "bloodiest man in American history." While leading a band of Confederate sympathizing guerrillas in Kansas and Missouri, the list of atrocities committed by him was topped by the 1863 raid he led on abolitionist Lawrence, Kansas, where his band murdered at least 185 men and boys, most of them unarmed, and burned most of the town's business district and at least a hundred houses. Some historians call the massacre the worst atrocity of the Civil War. For much of the 1900s, his shellacked skull remained in Ohio, the centerpiece for fraternity initiations. His gravesite in Dover did not have a tombstone until 1982 and even then a visiting priest had to be called in because the local priest refused to perform the burial ceremony.

Tom Custer *Custer's bluster* 8

Hays City, Kansas, was one of the roughest towns in the West during the late 1860s and part of its texture came from a transplanted Ohioan (New Rumley), **Tom Custer**, who was the first of only 18 Americans to receive the Congressional Medal of Honor *twice*. He also liked to ride his horse into saloons and make it jump up on the billiard tables. When the horse refused, he shot it. Tom's penchant for brawling was finally satisfied in 1871 at Little Big Horn, where he perished with his brothers.

Bully Hayes *aaaarrrrrgggg* 9

The most famous pirate of the Pacific was Bully Hayes, the son of a Cleveland saloonkeeper. A handsome man (though missing an ear), his vocation was terrorizing the ocean which he did for three decades after abandoning Cleveland in 1847, dodging a trial for horse-stealing. He earned an ocean-wide reputation for skullduggery, cheating, stealing, and hoodwinking, dying on a remote Pacific island after a crewman bashed his head in. A serendipitous ending to a misspent life.

Superman *steely man* 10

Macho is being able to leap a tall building in a single bound. Macho is facing off with Lex Luthor, mad scientist, as well as an Imp from the Fifth Dimension, not to mention your everyday sort of runaway train disasters. Superman, originally from Krypton by way of Cleveland, even returned from the grave. Being the kind of All-American fellow he was, he'd never be found on a barstool. Here was a man made for realllllllly *big* fights.

Ernest King *poster hellion* 11

Ernest J. King of Lorain was adversity's poster boy. He was rude, abrupt, overbearing, and humorless, which were generally considered his *best* qualities. Almost everyone disliked him, even the President, who made him Commander in Chief of the U.S. Fleet after the attack on Pearl Harbor. "When they get into trouble," King snarled, "they always send for the sons of bitches." The President wanted a tough guy to whip the Navy into shape, and in the person of King, he got one. King initiated the two-front war strategy and became one of America's great naval leaders. If he were your drinking campanion, you could safely wear a tu-tu into a biker's bar.

LeMay *flying leatherhead* 12

Curtis LeMay was a stumpy cigar-smoking bomber pilot from Columbus, Ohio, who at 37 became the youngest three-star general since U.S. Grant, another Ohioan. Called "Iron Ass" by his men, his ruthless B-29 raids with incendiaries wiped out over a hundred square miles of top Japanese cities, so much so that he thought the A-bomb would be only an afterthought. He was considered the architect of the Strategic Air Command, once called for a preemptive nuclear strike on the Soviet Union, and was reputed to be the model for the paranoid character of Jack D. Ripper in Stanley Kubrick's classic, *Dr. Strangelove.*

• • • • • • • • • • • • • • • •

"I don't know about you guys, but when I get in trouble, I try to act just as much like Paul Newman as I possibly can."
—*Terry Moore, Cincinnati drummer*

Shane *way out west on Western Avenue* 13

When Jack Schaefer wrote *Shane* in 1949, he hadn't been west of his rough-and-tumble industrial-frontier hometown of Cleveland. He learned about the west by reading old newspapers and diaries at Yale University, and invented the West's quintessential hero, Shane, a man with only half a name. Shane talked as straight as he shot, and even though we privately suspected the actor Alan Ladd wore platform shoes, Shane was still tall in the saddle. And he took on the greasiest villian in the entire Western genre—Jack Palance's black-hearted Wilson. So Shane *was* a bit taciturn. Still no better drinking companion when the crowd turned ugly.

Newman *cool stuff* 14

As *Cool Hand Luke,* Cleveland's **Paul Newman** maintained his poise on the chain gang despite brutal beatings, ate 50 eggs in one sitting, escaped and was captured and escaped again. His Herculean hard-headedness prompted his sardonic tormentor to utter the classic line: "What we have here is a failure to communicate." Each of us has suffered the failures of communication, but never with such panache.

Mr. Clean *big lug* 15

Mr. Clean was P&G's house enforcer, an exotic-looking brute with a shaved head, a muscle shirt, and an earring. If he could actually get rid of dirt and grime and grease in just a minute, imagine what he could do when the furniture starts flying.

ARISTOCRATIC ANTHONY WAYNE: HOW MAD WAS HE?

his omnipotence

Color overrides the man. *Mad* Anthony. While the name is omnipresent across Ohio even 200 years after the flesh-and-blood fact of him, who can recall whether Mad Anthony was, indeed, mad? And if not, what? In actuality, Wayne was a military aristocrat and despite his reputation for hot blood, he was careful and organized. He was also a romantic, a drinker, a bit of a dandy—he wanted a barber with each company—and he had an eye for the ladies.

In the war against Britain, his horse was shot from under him at the Battle of Germantown. He fought with Washington at Monmouth Courthouse, probably saving the Americans from being routed. Washington made him Commander of the American Army in 1792, and he immediately left for Fort Washington, near Cincinnati.

In 1791, the Indians had nearly wiped out Arthur St. Clair's undisciplined expedition, killing most of the officers and half the men, and Wayne came to build a chain of forts in western Ohio. He would not fight as St. Clair had; he patiently drilled his men in frontier fighting and late in 1793, led them up the western edge of Ohio and built a fort where St. Clair had been defeated. He called it Fort Recovery.

Here, he was combating—unknowingly at first—the machinations of one of his own commanders, Wilkinson, a backstabbing turncoat who plotted with the British in Canada to separate the Northwest Territory from the United States.

The Indians had rejected calls for peace, and the British governor of Lower Canada had told them the English would likely be at war with the Americans in the year, and then they could recover their lands. Wayne had some 2,000 men—about the number of the Indian confederacy, bolstered by the British. After building Fort Defiance, he tried unsuccessfully to make peace with the Indians. He referred to the coming encounter as an "interview."

Suffering from gout, wrapped in flannel under his uniform, he fought the Battle of Fallen Timbers on August 20, 1794.

The battlefield was in the path of a tornado, tangled with uprooted trees and Wayne's soldiers routed a thousand Indians who fell back until they reached Fort Miami, where the British betrayed their allies by closing the gates on them. He and his men—he lost only 33 of them at Fallen Timbers—remained near Fort Miami for a week, destroying crops and villages for miles around, and taunting the British, who stayed behind their gates.

The fate of the Indians—and Ohio—was set when on July 4, 1795, the Senate ratified the Jay Treaty, which meant the British were withdrawing from their forts and garrisons on the American side of the international boundary line. The Indians could no longer depend upon the British for any aid. On August 3, they reluctantly ceded to the United States a vast tract of land that encompassed much of Ohio and part of Indiana. The tribes were paid $20,000 plus annuities of $9,500, all in goods.

The Battle, and the subsequent treaty, ended the long years of Indian wars, and opened up the frontier to white settlement. It was one of the most significant American battles ever fought. Ask any realtor.—*John Baskin*

On the morning of August 20, Wayne woke in agony. His gout had returned in crippling force, so he told his men to wrap bandages around his arms and legs and to lift him onto his horse. Lt. William Henry Harrison said, "General, I'm afraid you'll get into the fight yourself and give the necessary field orders." Wayne replied, "And if I do, recollect that the standing order of the day is, 'Charge the damned rascals with the bayonets!'"

—Randy McNutt

Hemingway defined courage as grace under pressure. The Ohio variety of macho can be described as grace under posture. Sheer aggression or pigheaded willfulness is not enough. There must be additional elements, not only of style but of calculation behind the strutting. True macho also requires a dash of childish geewhiz to go with the blood, sweat and boorishness. In the Ohio tradition, its purest military expression was William Tecumseh Sherman. The worst embodiment of Ohio military macho was George Armstrong Custer who believed good publicity would cover any lack of tactical foresight. His uniforms seemingly designed for Grand Opera, Custer carried a cast-iron cook stove along on his campaigns, and succumbed to his own fatal self-definition of macho. He could not take seriously Indian nations that were home on the range without one.

Ohio Machismo. Think there's no such thing? Think again. We didn't invent it. But we almost did. Call it machio.

Buckeye machismo turns up where and when least expected. Flashes of it are in the careers of Howard Metzenbaum, who would take on anyone in the U.S. Senate, and James Rhodes, who would take on anyone for governor, and even Victoria Woodhull, the first woman to declare for the Presidency, who would take on *anyone.*

Macho can intoxicate grown men *and* women, leading to spectacularly foolish acts with dreadful consequences. For good or ill, Ohio *Machismo* is a force to be reckoned with, as any motorist who has ever tried to merge onto a stalled interstate will testify. We are prejudiced because we see it largely as a positive thing, the manifestation of a deeply Ohioan impulse toward contrarianism. Spit in the eye of the sensible thing. Root hard or die. In this rosy view, when Ohio macho goes awry or turns malicious, it is no longer the true spirit but a demented mutation. If you don't agree, you're probably in the grip of the macho molecules yourself. And if you want to make something of it, just step across this paragraph.

Men with balls

Hombre
Woody Hayes would take on anything: cameramen, players, writers, fans, yard markers—he'd even punch *himself.* He was the toughest coach in football. When frustration in the 1978 Gator Bowl aided Woody in punching Clemson's nose guard, he knocked himself out of football. Afterward, he offered no half-cocked rationales. Wrote one perceptive writer, "He thus spared himself the impossible task of explaining how it feels to be a man at war with something like time."

Arts and Crafts
Chris Spielman revealed the essence of the linebacker's art by tackling his grandmother when he was five years old. Said he: "She went to give me a hug, and I took her out. I knocked her down, but she bounced back up. You could tell she was a Spielman." What big hams you have, Granny.

Don Look Back
Don Zimmer of Cincinnati's West Side was "frighteningly beaned" in a Columbus, Ohio,

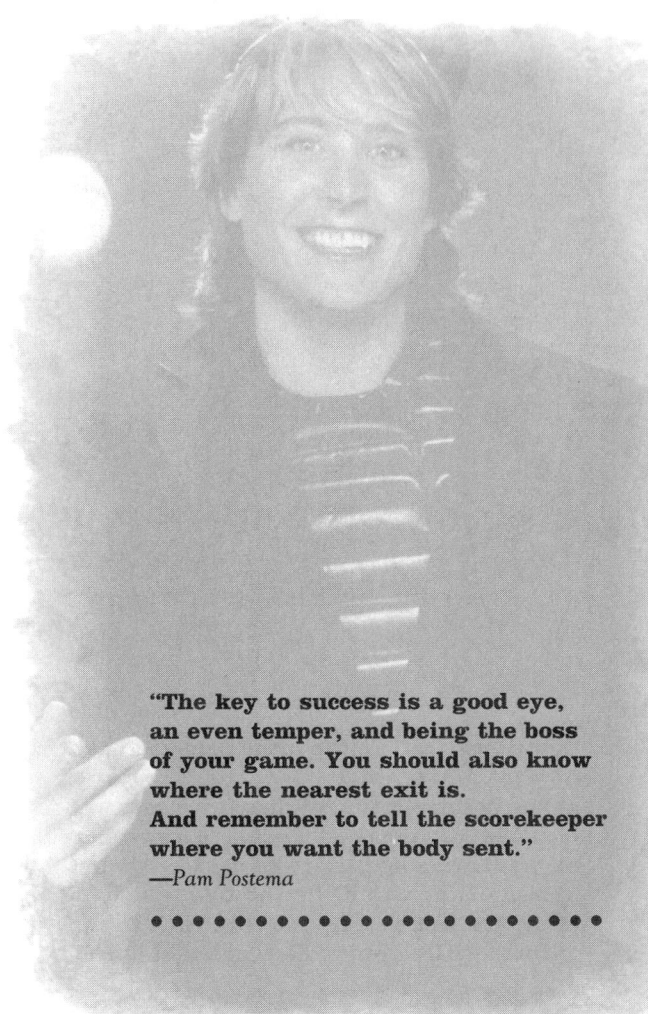

"The key to success is a good eye, an even temper, and being the boss of your game. You should also know where the nearest exit is. And remember to tell the scorekeeper where you want the body sent."
—Pam Postema

● ●

Women with balls

The Umpire Strikes Back
Pam Postema, tomboy daughter of a Willard vegetable farmer, umpired the first Triple A All-Star game but never got into The Show. One of her *confreres* said she was good enough "if only she had outdoor plumbing." At a Columbus Clippers game, when three OSU students heckled her about her chest size, she said to startled manager Dent, "How dare they say I have no ****?" She called Lenny Dykstra "a miserable little puke," and, all-in-all, gave as good as she got. Pam, bam, thank you, m'am.

Local Heat
Alta Weiss, of Ragersville, Ohio, was a cigar-smoking, spit-balling tomboy with a medical degree. The largest contradiction, however, was

1954 minor-league game. He stuttered for a year but returned to play and in 1956, his head still in the game, had his cheekbone broken with another pitch. That 1954 pitch brought about the mandatory batting helmet.

Trainman's Headache
"My idea of a good hit is when the victim wakes up on the sidelines with train whistles blowing in his head," said Jack Tatum, OSU's All-American safety. By the time he finished OSU he had, by his own admission, more knockouts than Muhammad Ali. At Oakland, they called him "The Assassin." Darryl Stingley would probably agree.

her ability to beat men at their own game— baseball. She had a man's windup, good speed and, in 1907 when she was 17 and playing against the semipro Vermilion Independents, she struck out 15 men. She also re-defined the taunt, "You throw like a girl," into a compliment.

Line of Most Resistance
At age 13, Amanda Cunningham became the first girl to play Massillon football. In 1992, she put on the pads as backup offensive and defensive lineman for her 7th grade team at Longfellow Middle School. We're talking Massillon football here, which for Amanda is roughly equivalent to Daniel suiting up for the lion's den wearing a pork chop belt.

Mythfits

In Your Face

The sport of gouging, imported from England, reached the height of its popularity in the Ohio River Valley during the early 1800s. Equipment requirement: one long and sharp thumbnail, used to gouge out an opponent's eyeball. Lots of testosterone all around; one-eyed Jacks were wild.

First Draft

General George Custer, New Rumley, Ohio, was an exhibitionistic loose cannon who ended up being canonized behind the bar of every saloon in America. That's where lithographs of The Battle—one of America's great macho moments—hung for half a century, courtesy of America's beer barons. It began an enduring advertising tradition of equating beer with guts (although not beer guts).

Custer was called 'the most famous goat in West Point history.' Meaning the man at the bottom of the graduating class, who traditionally received the loudest ovation at graduation because, 'it's not hard to get kicked out or to muddle through. But to slide along the knife's edge, to flirt with failure without failing out: this takes real spirit.'

• •

The New Rumley, Ohio, native who took up "the unholy profession of Indian fighter," George Armstrong Custer, was insured for $5,000 on the morning of 1876 when, as one writer put it, "his self-confidence exceeded his tactics." The policy was written by a New York Life agent who specialized in Army officers serving in remote forts, and became a business transaction that stands out as the ultimate metaphor for commercial folly.
The pay-out, in today's dollars, would be $83,395.

Mercenaries

Line of Fire

Outnumbered by Santa Anna at the Alamo, Colonel Travis drew a line in the dirt, asking Texas partisans willing to fight and die to step over it. Tapley Holland, an Ohioan—Scioto County—was the first to cross the line. If the phrase, "Step across this line" didn't begin there, it should have.

Cool Hand, Keen Eye

The Cincinnati Kid, in the novel by the same name, takes on dead-eyed Lancey Hodges in a stud game that begins on page 84 and doesn't end until page 140. It's one of sport's classic *mano-a-mano* faceoffs. Even those who know nothing about poker walk away in a wilt.

Man At Work

Mandingo, a *real* stud, has fathered more than 45,000 offspring. He's a history-making legend at Plain City's Select Sires, the world's largest producer of bull semen. Mandingo gives at the office three days a week and, according to the company newsletter, "continues to satisfy dairymen around the world." And, obviously, their charges. Unfortunately, his job is a little artificial; Mandingo has never, in the biblical sense, "known" a cow.

Underdog

Clarence Darrow, the attorney from Kinsman, made headlines taking on the odds. He took on the government for socialist Eugene Debs and the death penalty for thrill-killers Leopold and Loeb. In Tennessee's famed 1925 Scopes Trial, he even took on God. He lost that one and still managed to make a monkey out of William Jennings Bryan.

Leathernecks

Like a Fox

He liked a drink, he had an eye for the ladies; Mad Anthony Wayne wasn't mad at all. He was also one of the republic's most methodical soldiers. His moniker came from a dangerous but calculated counter-attack that saved Washington's army. In frontier Ohio, Wayne's regulars at Fallen Timbers broke the Indians—forever—with two well-aimed volleys and a bayonet charge.

Tribal Warfare

Brothers Dan and John McCook and their 17 sons charged out of Carrollton and Steubenville and into Civil War battles from Bull Run to Vicksburg. Dan was all of 63. They weren't called the Fighting McCooks for nothing.

Man O' War

With mostly unskilled labor, Oliver Perry (at right) built a fleet. With mostly landlubbers as crew, he sailed off to Lake Erie to engage the British. When his flagship sank, he rowed to another ship, and gave Captain Barclay the most thorough trouncing a British fleet had ever known. His dispatch: "We have met the enemy and they are ours." *That's* macho.

Steaming

In 1862, 16 Ohioans—Andrews' Raiders—stole a train in Georgia and, with Confederates in hot pursuit, tore up 90 miles of track and supply lines. That was The Great Locomotive Chase and the Ohioans were the first Congressional Medal of Honor winners.

Attitude

Grunge queen Kim Deal of Dayton, Ohio, once used a slab of bologna to tame her too-fluffy hair. "If anything, women should make better rock music than men," she said. "Pre-menstrual tension is perfect for making rock 'n' roll."

Tough guys

The Parting Shot

When Clark Gable, the Cadiz King, got in Vivian Leigh's face in *Gone With the Wind*, America's entire motion picture audience sat bolt upright. "Frankly, my dear, I don't give a damn," said Mr. Butler to Ms. Scarlett, politically succinct, if not correct. The men were envious and the women were, well, envious.

Real Men Don't

In an ill-fated attempt to combat his less-than-macho public image, William Henry Harrison insisted on braving a blizzard on inauguration day sans topcoat and hat. A month later he was dead from pneumonia. Tough guy, but dead guy.

Unchained

Terry Anderson of Lorain endured seven years—four on a six-inch chain attached to either a cot or the ankle of another man—as a Middle East hostage. He organized hunger strikes and needled his captors. When a guard held a gun to his chest, Anderson said "Go ahead. Shoot me." The guard didn't. Lebanon's loss, America's gain.

Tough As

Vernon Craig of Wooster is the kind of guy who can take things lying down and *still* be macho: he set world records for reclining on a bed of nails—25 hours and 25 minutes while holding 1,642 pounds on his chest.

A Name for Herself
Lucy Stones's father thought educating women a waste of money so she put herself through Oberlin College. A leading suffragette, she became the first known woman to refuse her husband's surname. Ms. Stone, with stones.

Gunsels

Macho Inc.
When Ohioan W.R. Burnett created *Little Caesar*, Rico Bandello became the premiere gangster of literature. The big little man, as Burnett wrote, loved but three things: "himself, his hair and his gun. He took excellent care of all three." When Rico finally expires in a burst of lead, he is incredulous. His last words: "Mother of God, is this the end of Rico?" Nope. The movie rights gave him eternal life.

**"One small step for a man.
One giant leap for mankind."**

• • • • • • • • • • • • • • • • •

Early to Rise
Allen Freidman, aspiring Cleveland punk, started his bomb-wary brother-in-law's Studebaker each morning for $2. "That was a lot of money for a 15-year-old kid," said young Friedman.

Dress Rehearsals
Dutch Zellers, a third-grade dropout, and his turn-of-the-century East Liverpool gang struck fear into the towns of the Ohio Valley. He once said it took two robberies a week just to keep his girlfriend, Amelia, dressed properly.

Right Stuff

Moonshine
Neil Armstrong of Wapakoneta, even before he took the Big Step, flew 78 combat missions in Korea and was a test pilot who talked about plummeting to Earth from 30,000 feet at Mach 2 "like he was walking down to the post office." They said his heart rate never accelerated when he landed on the moon. It did, of course. But having the Right Stuff means nobody could tell.

Skyrider
"I don't want any special treatment," said 2nd Lt. Sarah Deal of Pemberville when she became the first female pilot in the 266-year history of the Marine Corps. Spoken like a true Marine.

Hot Stuff
WWII flying ace Don Gentile beat fellow-Ohioan Eddie Rickenbacker's 26-kill-record with 30 of his own. As a boy in Piqua, "Captain Courageous" was famous for flying under the Main Street Bridge and buzzing St. Boniface's Church.

Heavyweights

Ringers
They staged a bayonet drill in the ring before the 1919 Jack Dempsey-Jess Willard championship fight in Toledo. The fight itself was at 3:30 on the afternoon of July the 4th. It was said to be 101 under an umbrella. Were Dempsey's hands

wrapped with plaster of paris and larceny? His right broke Willard's cheekbone in the first round, when Willard went down seven times. He broke Willard's ribs in the second round. He out-weighed Dempsey by 58 pounds and he never had a chance. Jimmy Breslin said the Roaring Twenties began in Toledo that day. The crowd was drinking the nation's first illegal hootch. Too bad Willard wasn't.

Streetfighters

No Man's Land

When he was U.S. Senator, Howard Metzenbaum was called everything from "Senator No" to a "pain in the ass" by his GOP sparring partners. Before he retired in 1994, he went out in a traditional blaze of glory: the old Clevelander, introduced a bill to expunge the name of J. Edgar Hoover from the FBI building in Washington.

First Lady

In 1872, Victoria Claflin Woodhull, Licking County's Distressing Damsel, the woman who never ducked a fight, advocated Free Love, legalized prostitution, and women's rights in becoming the first woman to run for President. By constitutional standards, she wasn't old enough, let alone the right sex. In your face, America.

Animal Rights

Akron singer Chrissie Hynde was punk before punk was popular. She once said you could pick her friends out of her high school yearbook because "every-body else is real kind of smiley, and my friends were a little bit...bewildered, 'cause they were too young

to look pissed off." She later made waves at an animal rights press conference when she suggested that someone ought to "go out and blow up a McDonalds."

Gloria In Excelsis

An early standard-bearer of the second feminist movement, Gloria Steinem of Toledo, popularized the term "Ms." as founding editor of *Ms.* maga-zine. She was at once man's worst enemy and his best friend. "Men should think twice before making widowhood women's only path to power," she said. *Ouch.*

Palookas

Earshot

Don King, on his way to fame as a boxing promoter, made a name for himself first as a Cleveland numbers operator. Called to testify in an extortion trial, King was hit in the back of the head with a shotgun blast that "blew holes in his ears big enough to see through." He was hurt but not enough to keep him from testifying.

Bantamweights

In 1991, Ohio Supreme Court justice Craig Wright grabbed Ohio Supreme Court justice Andrew Douglas, threw him into a desk, and jumped him until court workers sent them to neutral corners. Shining example of macho jurisimprudence.

The Ohio National Guard was born in Marietta, Ohio, July 25, 1788, when the first law passed in what was then the Northwest Territory provided for the establishment of the Militia. The Militia was ordered out in the spring of 1812 to garrison the American Post at Detroit, which was subsequently lost. In 1813, another force under General William Henry Harrison, commander-in-chief of the Northwest Army, defeated the British and Indians at the Battle of Fallen Timbers, ending forever the British encroachment in Ohio and the Northwest Territory.

In 1806, Ohio furnished 8,102 men for the War with Mexico, about one-eighth of the entire land forces. Ohio troops were engaged in the battles of Veracruz and Monterey. General Hammer, reporting to the Governor on the latter battle, wrote: "I am sure you would have been proud of them (the Ohio troops). They walked into the most galling and murderous cross-fire of the enemy with the coolness of regular soldiers, not a man or officer flinching."

Ohio's Constitution of 1851 provided that all white male citizens who are residents of Ohio between the ages of 18 and 45 were to be enrolled in the Militia.

Civil and Spanish-American Wars

In 1861, when President Lincoln asked Ohio for 13,000 troops, 30,000 responded. The first volunteers—among whom were James A. Garfield and Rutherford B. Hayes, later Presidents of the United States—came from such companies as the Cleveland Grays, the Columbus Vindettes, the Cincinnati Rover Guards, and the Dayton Light Guards. The Ohio forces served in the Virginia campaign, firing the first Union artillery after Fort Sumter and capturing the first Rebel cannon and Rebel stronghold. A total of 350,000 Ohio men served in the Civil War. At Virginia in 1861; at Shiloh and Kentucky in 1862; at Murfreesborough, Chancellorsville, Gettysburg, Chickamauga, Antietam, and Fredericksburg in 1864, Ohioans were there. The active Militia was given the new name of the

National Guard of Ohio on March 31, 1864.

In 1898, the state was asked to contribute soldiers for the Spanish-American War, and more than 15,000 men answered the first call. During that year, Ohio called up 102 companies of infantry, one troop of cavalry, eight light artillery batteries, and four Naval Militia divisions.

World War I

In 1916, most of Ohio's National Guard units were ordered to serve on the Mexican borders. They had scarcely returned from the fracas with Mexico, when the United States declared war on Germany. Ohio, then the fourth largest state, made the fourth largest contribution in men—an estimated 225,000—to the U.S. Armed Services in World War I. The two major contingents that Ohio furnished to the U.S. Army were composed of Ohio National Guardsmen: the 37th Buckeye Division and the 166th Infantry Regiment. The 37th Buckeye, which consisted of all the Ohio units except the 166th Infantry, served at Montfaucon, the Meuse-Argonne Drive, the Saint Mihiel sector, and Belgium. It was rated by the German General Staff as one of the five best American divisions. The 166th Infantry Regiment of the famous 42nd, or Rainbow, Division, performed admirably in the defense of Campayne and the Qurcq River and the Saint Mihiel, Meuse-Argonne, and Sedan offensives.

Between the World Wars, Ohio National Guard units were frequently called upon for relief duty in disasters, including the great tornado that

struck Lorain and Sandusky in 1924 and the Ohio River floods in 1936 and 1937.

World War II

By the summer of 1940, the federal government was calling troops into service for training to defend the nation. The Ohio National Guard—about 9,000 men—was federalized and sent to Camp Shelby, Mississippi. In 1941, the 37th Division received some 10,000 Ohio Selectees to bring it up to full division strength, and the 37th again achieved fame on New Georgia, Bougainville, and Luzon. Of the seventeen Medals of Honor awarded to National Guardsmen during World War II, seven went to members of the 37th Division. After World War II, all the Ohio units were reorganized, and a separate Air National Guard was formed.

Korea

With the outbreak of hostilities in Korea, the 37th Division in 1952 was ordered into federal service and sent to Camp Polk, Louisiana as a training unit that prepared more than 25,000 men for duty. After Korea, the Ohio National Guard was reorganized into five battle groups under the new pentomic Army concept, and the famous 166th Infantry Regiment again became part of the Ohio National Guard. Army National Guard antiaircraft artillery battalions were redesignated missile battalions, and selected personnel entered training with active Army missile units. In January, 1961, Ohio National Guard units took charge full-time of missile sites in the Cleveland area.

Berlin Buildup

In October, 1961, six major Ohio Air National Guard units and four Ohio Army National Guard units entered federal service in response to President John F. Kennedy's call for reserve strength to prevent, not fight, a war. Labeled "The Berlin Buildup," this was considered one of the most successful mobilizations in the recent history of the National Guard.

In 1963, consistent with the Army's program to update reserve component units in the event of an emergency, the Ohio National Guard was again reorganized to provide greater combat flexibility and recall readiness. With the escalation of the Vietnam conflict, emphasis was placed on the need for reserve forces available for immediate deployment to a combat area without the customary six weeks to six months delay.

Vietnam

In January, 1968, President Lyndon B. Johnson ordered the call-up of more than 14,000 reservists, including Ohio Air National Guard's 121st Tactical Fighter Group, which remained at Lockbourne Air Force Base near Columbus. The 121st's operational readiness and response capability provided successful sorties in support of the Southeast Asian Theater of Operations before being returned to state control in June, 1969. No units of the Ohio Army National Guard were activated for Vietnam.

From 1968 through 1970, the Ohio National Guard was reorganized with severe effect on the force structure in Ohio. The Ohio lost the 37th Buckeye Infantry Division, which had never suffered defeat at the hands of the enemy. Ohio's division base was moved to Indianapolis, and the Cincinnati-Dayton air defense network was phased-out.

Community Assistance

In the late afternoon of April 3, 1974, SFC Harry Osborne, of Detachment 1, 1st Battalion, 166th Infantry, was making a final check of the Xenia, Ohio armory when a roar was heard "like a hundred freight trains" just prior to the roof being blown off the building. The Xenia Tornado cut a path of death and devastation that killed thirty-five people. Assisting in the recovery operations, two of the Ohio Air National Guard members died in a fire.

In 1978, a crippling blizzard hit the entire state, stranding motorists, isolating homes, and curtailing public services. A total of 5,005 Ohio Army and Air National Guard members conducted rescue operations. Armories opened across the state, providing emergency food and shelter to the stranded and homeless. During the snow emergencies of 1978, a total of 32,319 State Active Duty man-days were used to rescue and support Ohioans, resulting in a military manpower expenditure of $1,238,125, or an average

of $1.60 per hour.

In June, 1990, more than 1,500 National Guard members responded to a flash-flood in Shadyside that claimed 26 lives. Initially called for search and rescue duties, the guard performed extensive recovery operations for more than three months, saving the State of Ohio and the citizens of Shadyside more than $3 million in cleanup costs.

Desert Storm and Beyond

When the military machine of the Iraqi dictator Saddam Hussein overran Kuwait in an unprovoked display of aggression, the Ohio National Guard again responded. A number of Ohio Air National Guard units were deployed almost immediately and performed yeoman service in providing the transportation of critical supplies and troops to the Persian Gulf theater. Additionally, fighter and air refueling components were key players in the air war, leading up to the ground assault. The Ohio Army National Guard also provided transportation, logistical and other combat support units to assist in Operation Desert Storm. Additionally, numerous individual Ohio Guardsmen with specialty skills volunteered and served in Operation Desert Storm. Despite long-standing questions as to the viability of the National Guard in a fast paced, rapid response combat environment, the Ohio Guard once again demonstrated that its citizen soldiers were equal partners with their active duty counterparts.

Although active hostilities ceased in February 1991, the continuing presence of Saddam Hussein required military presence in the Persian Gulf region. The Air National Guard units were routinely deployed to enforce the no-fly zones over Iraq as part of Operation Northern Watch. Other Ohio Guard units were periodically deployed to the Persian Gulf and Kuwait to engage in joint desert warfare training. Ohio Guardsmen also saw overseas service when deployed to the Balkans to provide peacekeeping support in war–torn Bosnia and Kosovo. Units of the Ohio Guard continued to take a leading role in providing humanitarian assistance in impoverished areas of Central America.

Engineering, transportation and medical detachments all acquired valuable experience by providing critical medical care as well as building roads, wells, bridges, schools and other needed infrastructure.

The Ohio Guard again met the call to duty in response to the attack upon the United States by Islamic terrorists on September 11, 2001. Aircraft from both the 178th and the 180th Fighter Wings were immediately scrambled to provide air cover and homeland security within minutes of being alerted. Numerous units from the Army Guard supplemented by security police units of the Air Guard were mobilized on short notice in the following days and executed security missions at various locations for extended periods of time. Other communications and engineering units deployed to the Persian Gulf area and Afghanistan in support of the war on terrorism.

Source: Office of the Adjutant General

Ohioans killed in Operations Desert Shield/ Desert Storm

Army Sgt. Tony R. Applegate, Portsmouth
Marine Cpl. Dennis W. Betz, Alliance
Air Force Capt. Thomas R. Caldwell, Columbus
Army Specl. Clarence A. Cash, Ashland
Army Sgt. Donald Danielson, Newark
Marine Capt. Kevin R. Dolvin, Mineral City
Navy Lt. Robert J. Dwyer, Worthington
Marine Capt. Jonathan R. Edwards, Terrace Park
Army Sgt. Mark J. Gologram, Alliance
Air Force Staff Sgt. Rande J. Hulec, Cleveland
Army Staff Sgt. Jonathan H. Kamm, Mason
Army Specl. Anthony W. Kidd, Lima
Marine Lance Cpl. James H. Lumpkins,
    New Richmond
Army Specl. Robert Noonan, Cincinnati
Army Specl. Brian K. Spackman, Niles
Marine Capt. David M. Spellacy, Columbus

Source: Department of Defense

Separated by 14 years of war and 58,190 American deaths, the names of Ohio's first and last casualties of the Vietnam War are almost side by side on the Vietnam Veterans Memorial. Airman Bruce R. Jones of Niles, killed in 1961, is on Line 4 of Panel 1 East, and Navy corpsman Ronald J. Manning of Toronto, killed in 1975, is on Line 131 of Panel 1 West. They are within a few feet of each other, surrounded by the names of 3,091 other Ohioans killed or missing in action.

Finest Moment

In the autumn of 1927, while prosperity reigned elsewhere in the state, the children of coal miners in southeast Ohio were starving. The mines had been shut down for six months, the work gone to non-union miners in West Virginia. Bitter and angry, the Ohioans rebelled. Mines were set afire and dynamited, coal company officials and guards shot at. The call came for Governor Donahey to dispatch Ohio National Guard troops to forcibly restore order. Instead, Donahey sent a team of Guard officers into Athens, Hocking, and Jefferson counties. Wearing no uniforms, brandishing no weapons, they managed a thin truce between management and labor, then reported to the governor the poverty and misery they found in the miners' shacks. Donahey asked the people of Ohio for money, food, and clothing, and as the donations came in, Adjutant General Frank Henderson organized supply stations in more than a hundred schools. The Guardsmen gave clothing to 18,000 children and every day fed 7,500 of them by issuing a benign bribe: anyone who came to school would be given meat, potatoes, vegetables, bread, and butter. "We are not asking whether they are miners' children, or what is their religion or color," said General Henderson about their mission of mercy. "All the governor cares about is that they are fed and clothed. This is not a miners' relief or even a miners' children's relief. It is a children's relief."

Blackest Moment

In the spring of 1970, the Ohio National Guard was again dispatched to a school but instead of rescuing the young, the troops ended up slaying them. On May 1, Kent State University students began to protest the U.S. invasion of Cambodia during the Vietnam War; as demonstrations escalated, windows were smashed in Kent's downtown and the campus ROTC building was burned. Governor James Rhodes, battling for Republican nomination to the U.S. Senate, denounced the protestors and sent in the Ohio National Guard. Ignoring a campus demonstration ban, some 500 students staged an anti-war rally on May 4. They hurled rocks and shouted obscenities at the armed Guardsmen. Twenty-eight Guardsmen formed a line at the top of a hill and fired into the crowd of students. The shots lasted only thirteen seconds, but four students—Allison Krause, Jeffrey Miller, Sandra Scheur, and William Schroeder—lay dead, another nine wounded. It was, as one writer noted, "an assault by the Establishment on the next generation; an assault unprecedented in American history." The Vietnam quagmire had spilled over, horribly, into the heartland, and the Kent State killings touched off a wave of protests on campuses across the country. Before the month was over, 448 colleges and universities were either shut down or on strike. A Presidential Commission determined that what had happened at Kent State was "unnecessary, unwarranted, and inexcusable," and Rhodes later called it "the most sorrowful day in the history of Ohio."

The first Congressional Medal of Honor recipients

1. **Pvt. Jacob Parrott**, Fairfield County
2. **Pvt. William Bensinger**, Wayne County
3. **Pvt. Robert Buffum**, Wood County
4. **Sgt. Elihu H. Mason**, Wood County
5. **Sgt. William Pittenger**, Jefferson County
6. **Cpl. William H. Reddick**, Adams County
7. **Pvt. Samuel Slavens**, Pike County
8. **Cpl. Daniel A. Dorsey**, Fairfield County
9. **Pvt. Wilson W. Brown**, Logan County
10. **Cpl. Martin J. Hawkins**, Scioto County
11. **Pvt. William J. Knight**, Defiance County
12. **Pvt. John R. Porter**, Hancock County
13. **Pvt. Samuel Robertson**, Muskingum County
14. **Sgt. Major Marion A. Ross**, Champaign County
15. **Pvt. John A. Wilson**, Wood County
16. **Pvt. Mark Wood**, Portage County
17. **John Wollam**, Butler County
18. **John M. Scott**, Stark County

Given for acts of "conspicuous gallantry and intrepidity" which are "above and beyond the call of duty," the Congressional Medal of Honor is the nation's supreme award for military bravery. The first Americans given the Medal were Ohioans, the volunteers for what one Southern newspaper called "the deepest scheme that ever emanated from the brains of the Yankees"—**the Great Locomotive Chase** of the Civil War.

In April, 1862, Ohio soldiers helped Union spy James Andrews steal a Georgia train out from under the noses of the conductor and crew, who were taking a coffee break in a hotel near Atlanta. As Andrews and his party headed north toward Chattanooga in the *General*, they lacerated critical Confederate supply lines by pulling up track and wreaking destruction. The chagrined conductor gave chase on foot and by hand car until he persuaded the engineer of a southbound freight to disconnect his locomotive and take after the Yankees going backwards. With the *Texas* bearing down on them, the Ohio volunteers couldn't refuel wood and water, so they ran out of luck when the *General* literally ran out of steam—about ninety miles after the chase began. Arrested and tried as spies, some of the Ohioans were hanged. Others escaped. The rest were imprisoned.

Soon after the Medal of Honor was created in 1863, Congress recognized the train wreckers' derring-do and bestowed the first ones on March 25, 1863, to **Parrott**, **Bensinger**, **Buffam**, **Mason**, **Pittinger**, and **Reddick**, who were followed within the year by the other Andrews Raiders.

Custers' Last Stand

Ohio also sired the first of only nineteen Americans who have received the Medal *twice*—**Capt. Thomas Ward Custer**, New Rumley native, Union soldier, and brother of the more famous George Armstrong Custer. The first time, he rode into Confederate fire and singlehandedly captured an enemy standard and fourteen rebels at Namozine Church, Virginia, in 1863. The second time, he had two horses shot out from under him while capturing two Confederate flags, which he ceremoniously presented to his commanding officer, who was none other than his brother, George. While earning his second Medal

The most recent recipient from Ohio was Airman First Class William Pitsenbarger, who in 1966 near Cam My in the Republic of Vietnam, assisted in the care and evacuation of wounded soldiers while placing himself at great risk. When escape helicopters were forced to leave the scene, Pitsenbarger stayed, providing medical treatment and taking up arms with infantrymen before being fatally wounded. His award, issued in December 2000, was presented posthumously to his family.

at Sailor Creek, Virginia, in 1865, the doughty Capt. Custer was shot through the head, the bullet penetrating his right cheek and exiting behind the ear. George ordered him off the battlefield twice, and twice he refused to obey. Finally, Tom had to be arrested and forcibly taken to a hospital where his cruel wound was treated. Tom cheated death long enough to serve under his brother eleven years later at the Battle of the Little Big Horn, which is known as Custer's Last Stand, but which is more accurately Custers' Last Stand, for three Custer brothers—George, Tom, and Boston—perished there at the hands of the Cheyenne and Sioux.

Ohio's Medal of Honor recipients: Vietnam

1. **LCpl. Joe C. Paul**, Dayton, 1965
2. **Sgt. Donald Russell Long**, Blackfork, 1966
3. **Sgt. Sammy L. Davis**, Dayton, 1967
4. **PFC. Douglas E. Dickey**, Greenville, 1967
5. **Capt. Michael J. Estocin**, Akron, 1967
6. **Sgt. Charles C. Fleek**, Cincinnati, 1967
7. **PFC. Melvin Earl Newlin**, Wellsville, 1967
8. **Sp4c. Frank A. Herda**, Cleveland, 1968
9. **Sp4c. Joseph LaPointe, Jr.**, Dayton, 1969
10. **Sp4c. Gordon Roberts**, Middletown, 1969
11. **PFC. David F. Winder**, Columbus, 1970
12. **Lt. Brian Miles Thacker**, Columbus, 1971

Of particular courage were **Pfc. Dickey**, **Sgt. Fleek**, **Sp4c. Herda**, and **Sgt. Long**, who saved others by throwing themselves on hand grenades.

Ohio's Heroes

Nearly 3,500 medals have been awarded since 1863, and including the first six, 319 recipients of the Medal of Honor have some connection to Ohio—more than any other state. Twenty-three Ohio recipients served in the Navy, one in the Air Force, 3 in the Army Air Corps, 17 in the Marine Corps, 275 in the Army.

—144 were born in the state and their medals are accredited to Ohio

—107 recipients were not native Ohioans, but their medals were accredited to Ohio

—68 men were born in Ohio, but their medals were accredited to other states .

More than half Ohio's recipients fought in the Civil War.

Award Winners by Conflict

Conflict	Recipients
Civil War	195
Campaigns against Native Americans	53
Spanish American War	4
World War I	4
World War II	32
Korean War	3
Vietnam War	13
Other conflicts and peacetime	15
Total	319

In the fall of 1996, seven African-American veterans of World War II —including 1st Lt. John Robert Fox of Cincinnati— received the Medal of Honor, after being ignored for over half a century. Lt. Fox was a forward observer with the all-black 366th Infantry, 92nd Division in Italy when he called an artillery strike on his own position after being overrun by the Germans.

We're a little older and a little smarter and making more money than 10 years ago, but here in the Heartland, probably few of us feel any richer. Household income jumped in the sizzling economy of the 1990s by about 38 percent, but so did inflation and expenses.

By 2000, Ohio households enjoyed no more buying power than a decade before, and neither did those in most of America, an analysis of figures using the latest U.S. Census Bureau shows.

Meanwhile, we went off to college in increasing numbers—but a step behind most everyone else. Last decade, 40 of the 50 states and the District of Columbia had a larger share of their residents attaining college degrees.

In fact, the Census Bureau survey found in Ohio a state in many ways average and struggling to remain so.

Yet it also found trends that may point toward better days ahead.

What once made Ohio a powerhouse—a manufacturing economy that produced the nation's steel, cars, tires and machine tools—has turned against us as plants close or move.

In a first-of-its-kind survey, the U.S. Census Bureau queried more than 32,000 households in Ohio, on everything from income to ethnicity to choice of heating fuels.

The so-called Census 2000 Supplemental Survey offers information traditionally supplied by the census "long form" that went to about one in every five households in the national head count.

Within that picture, Ohio emerges as a predictable middleager, a state more average than different and peculiar maybe only in its slowness to change.

We're a median 36 years old, compared with a median 35 for the nation, we have fewer college degrees than most of America, and we're more likely to work in a factory or foundry. We enjoy a good standard of living but buying power that is just holding its own.

The median household income in Ohio rose from $28,706 in 1989 to $39,480 in 2000.

That was about the same rate of growth experienced by the nation as a whole, census survey figures show. But the $10,774 increase in median income just roughly kept up with the rise in the cost of living.

Those who track our economy said they were not surprised by the lack of improvement.

"It's the change in the composition of the jobs, that's what's killed us," said George Zeller, a senior researcher for the Council for Economic Opportunities in Greater Cleveland.

Ohio's loss of thousands of manufacturing jobs hurt workers' income, Zeller said, because many of those displaced workers ended up in lower-paying industries.

Yet the census still found 20 percent of the Ohio work force involved in manufacturing, an industry area that now employs only 14 percent of workers nationally.

Manufacturing jobs have allowed people in Cleveland, Cincinnati and Columbus to enjoy a higher per capita standard of living than the national average, said Ned Hill, a professor of economic development at Cleveland State University. Hill says stagnant economies in Appalachia and in Ohio's midsize cities—like Lima and Youngstown—pulled down the state average.

Median household income is just one indicator of economic performance. Other factors, such as family income and the number of children and families living in poverty, appeared to show slight improvement in Ohio.

But the improvements are small enough that some of them could be a result of the survey's

www. *fermi.jhuapl.edu/ states/oh_0.html*

Color Landform Atlas of the United States: From shaded relief maps, to satellite maps, this link from the Color Landform Atlas of the United States has Ohio maps. Good links to Ohio sites as well.

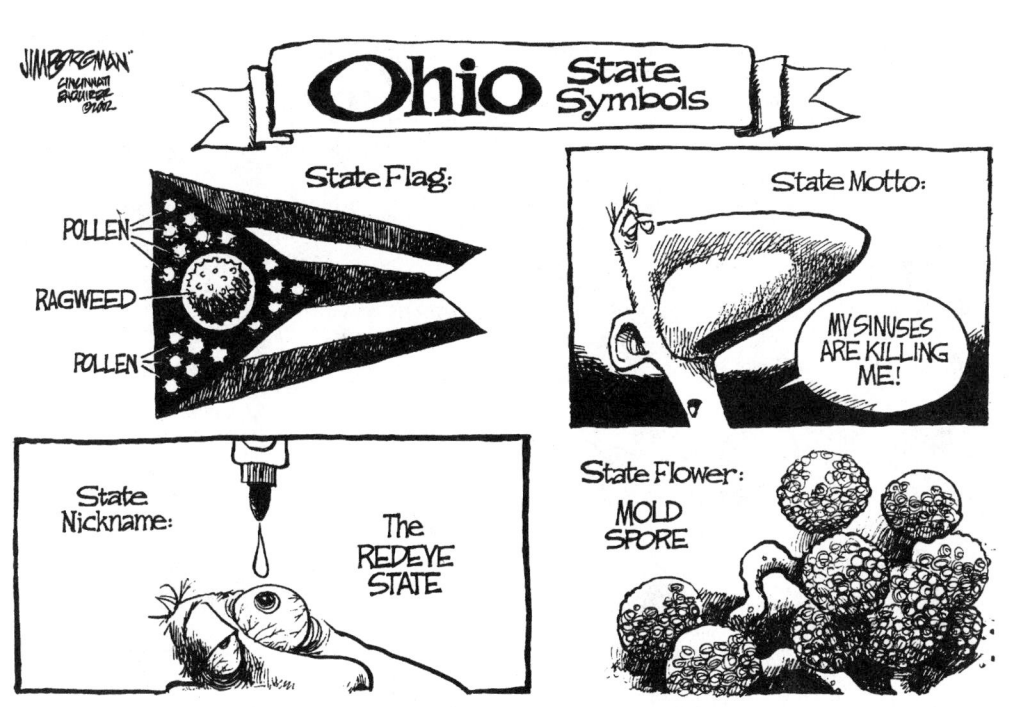

Ohio State Symbols

State Flag:
POLLEN
RAGWEED
POLLEN

State Motto:
MY SINUSES ARE KILLING ME!

State Nickname:
The REDEYE STATE

State Flower:
MOLD SPORE

JIM BORGMAN
CINCINNATI ENQUIRER
9/2002

sampling error.

The number of poor families dropped last decade from 10 percent to 8 percent of Ohio families, and the number of children living in poverty also fell slightly, from 18 percent to 16 percent of all Ohio children.

"We think that's indicative of the good economy," said Gretchen Holsinger Kunkel, director of research and administration at the Federation of Community Planning.

Erickson, Zeller and others said, however, that the economy has soured since the survey was done. If Americans were surveyed today, the economic information would be bleaker, with more people in poverty.

Meanwhile, Ohioans enjoy lower-than-average housing costs. Our homes in 2000 had a median value of $102,362, compared with $120,162 nationally. Ohio homeowners paid a median monthly mortgage of $1,101, compared with $1,307 nationally. Renters paid $511 a month, compared with the national median of $612.

But if Ohio is to join the affluent states and Ohioans are to avoid a drop in their standard of living, experts agree we must catch up academically.

In 2000, nearly 21 percent of Ohioans held at least a bachelor's degree, compared with 17 percent 10 years earlier. But the improvement was not enough to keep pace with America. In college-degree rankings, Ohio slipped from 40th to 41st.

Roderick G.W. Chu, chancellor of the Ohio Board of Regents, blames a lack of emphasis on higher education by parents and by state lawmakers.

"While we're getting better educated, and that's good news, we're not getting better educated as fast as the rest of the county," Chu said. "So we're falling behind."

He sees a glimmer of hope among the ranks of young adults. While older Ohioans are among the least likely people in America to hold a college degree, their children often follow the campus path. Ohioans ages 18 to 24 were slightly more likely than other Americans their age to hold a college degree, the survey shows.

Chu said that bodes well for the future.

"Education is the key to the new economy," he said. "I think our young folks are getting the message."

—by Robert L. Smith, Joan Mazzolini, and Dave Davis, of The Plain Dealer

The breadwinners	+plus	-minus
Average hourly wage for white males: $15		*In 1979, white males made $13.73 (adjusted for inflation); blacks now make $12, women $11.17*

The household		
Median income rose to nearly $44,000 in 2000, a 20% rise since the mid-1980s. This topped the median U.S. income by $1,700 and was higher than all surrounding states except Michigan.		*Parents are working 11 hours more each week than a generation ago. Single-parent families are working more than 18% longer than 20 years ago.*

The house		
69% of Ohioans own their own home which is three percent ahead of the national average.		*Median home value is $102,363; he national average is $120,162.*

Degrees		
21% of all Ohioans have at least a bachelor's degree.		*In number of bachelor's degrees, Ohio ranks 41st among all states; which means that Ohio needs an additional 408,575 of us completing college to bring the state to the national average.*

College costs		
The average student loan in Ohio is $3,597 a year.		*An Ohio family needs an average of 29% of its income to pay for an education at a four-year public campus (a private education takes about 54% of family income).*

The basics		
The average Ohioan eats 23 quarts of ice cream each year, 62.7 pounds of corn syrup, and drinks a barrel of beer.		*The average Ohio male weighs 187.2 pounds and his female Ohio counterpart, 151.3 pounds.*

Jobs		
20% of Ohioans still work in manufacturing, 6% ahead of the national average.		*Ohio lost 97,000 manufacturing jobs between 2000 and 2003.*

Life expectancy		
The life expectancy of Ohioans is 75.3 years, and more than 1,900 people in Ohio are 100 years old or older)— a 22% increase over the last decade.		*Ohioans are third in the nation to die of colon cancer, rank 5th-worst nationally in people who smoke, 14th in obesity, and even with new federal guidelines easing requirements, only 46% of us meet minimum activity standards.*

Moving on		
Between 1995 and 2000, 21,432 West Virginians moved to Ohio.		*In the same period, 25,801 Ohioans moved to West Virginia.*

Ferno-Washington Inc. in Wilmington added to its product line in 2002 a stretcher with a 650-pound weight capacity. Sales of the new model have almost doubled those of the older 500-pound capacity stretchers. Ambulance cots that can carry a patient weighing 600 pounds or more is becoming an industry standard.

—Associated Press

Homebodies	+plus	-minus
74.3% of those born in Ohio still live here (only four states have a higher percentage).		*86% of us were still living in the same residence as the year before.*

Wired		
57.6 of Ohio households have computers; 50.9% have internet access.		*We are 25th and 26th, respectively, among all states; only 7% of our households have high-speed connections.*

Alone		
83.6% of all Ohioans drive to work by themselves.		*We spend an average of 22 minutes getting to work; only two states have more drivers commuting alone.*

Wealth		
142,848 Ohio males make more than $100,000, and so do 23,521 Ohio women.		*The richest fifth of the Ohio population have incomes 9.7 times higher than the poorest fifth, which ranks us 40th nationally.*

Population		
Ohio's population increased 4.7% in the last decade, to 11,373,541.		*50,000 Buckeyes left the state between 2000 and 2001, and the state has now virtually stopped growing.*

Values		
Ohio ranks 12th among all states in lottery sales per capita.		*Ohio ranked 33rd for voter turnout in the 2000 election.*

Intangibles		
Ohio's public library system is rated as the nation's best.		*Ohio leads Midwest in number of white-supremacist groups—73.*

Pollution		
Between 1992 and 2000, toxic air emissions dropped 50%.		*More than 1,900 Ohioans die prematurely each year due to fine particulate air pollution, or soot, from power plants. Power plant pollution is also responsible for 37,000 asthma attacks and 1,600 hospital visits each year in Ohio.*

Air apparent		
63% of Ohio workers inhabit a smoke-free workplace (7th nationwide). The figure was 38% in 1993.		*More people smoke in Toledo—31.2% of the population—than in any other metropolitan area in America.*

Sources: Centers for Disease Control and Prevention, U.S. Census Bureau, U.S. Department of Agriculture, Bureau of Labor Statistics, National Center for Health Statistics, The Plain Dealer, Akron Beacon Journal, The New Yorker, Center for New Community, Small Business Survival Committee, Proctor & Gamble

The fine points

Ohio

has its semantic roots in the Iroquois word "O-he-yo," meaning "great river," but the first English appearance of the word in a book occurred in 1756 in *A Fourth Letter to the People of England on the Conduct of the M—rs in Alliances, Fleets, and Armies, since the First Differences on the Ohio, to the taking of Minorca by the French*, by John Shebbeare (printed for M. Collier, London).

The Capital

has a peripatetic history, having been variously located between 1788 and 1816 in Marietta, Cincinnati, Chillicothe, and Zanesville, according to the shifting political requirements of Territory and State, until it found a permanent home in Columbus.

Statehood

for all practical purposes was granted on March 1, 1803, when Ohio became the first state carved from the Northwest Territory; however, it was not officially admitted to the Union until August 7, 1953. Although Ohio has been sending Congressmen and Senators to Washington, D.C. since 1803, the U.S. Congress never actually voted on the formal resolution admitting Ohio to the Union. On what would have been the state's true sesquicentennial in 1953, this oversight was corrected when Representative George Bender introduced a bill for Ohio statehood. Meanwhile, Rep. Clarence Brown threatened that Ohio was going to apply for foreign aid if the bill didn't pass. But President Eisenhower swiftly signed the measure, noting that he wanted Ohioans to be able to celebrate their 150th birthday legally.

But even today, there are nay-sayers who claim that Ohio still is not a state because the Congress's *ex post facto* statehood resolution is unconstitutional. Samuel Pearce Holton, the president of a Georgia college, even filed a federal suit to prevent Ohioans from voting in the 1984 election. "The course of history of this country has been changed," he argued, "be it for better or for worse, by the unlawful votes of people of the

Territory of Ohio, masquerading as a state and sending delegates to Congress to vote, unlawfully, on issues of great importance."

The Ohio Flag

is the only burgee-shaped state flag in the United States. Architect John Eisemann chose the swallow-tailed shape because the triangular tips symbolize Ohio's hills and valleys. He designed the red and white stripes to represent roadways and waterways; the white circle with its red center, the initial "O" and the buckeye; the stars grouped around the circle, the original thirteen states of the Union; and the four extra stars, Ohio's status as the seventeenth state in the Union. The flag was created in 1901 only because one was needed to fly over the Ohio Building at the Pan-American Exposition in Buffalo. But what should have been a proud day for Ohio turned into a national tragedy on September 6, when the state's favorite son, President William McKinley, was shot at point-blank range as he stood in a receiving line. He died eight days later.

The Great Seal

is replete with symbolism. Designer William Creighton included a sheaf of wheat for Ohio the bountiful, a sheaf of seventeen arrows since Ohio is the 17th state; and the sun above the mountains because Ohio was the first state west of the Alleghenies. It is said that when Creighton was charged with designing the seal, he rode from Chillicothe to nearby Adena, where he consulted with the owner, Thomas Worthington, a future U.S. Senator and one of Ohio's founding fathers. Creighton and some other guests enjoyed an all-night game of cards, and when dawn broke, he stepped outside and was immediately taken with how the sun rising behind Mt. Logan cast a rosy glow upon the surrounding wheat fields. "Gentlemen," Creighton proclaimed, "there is our seal." The symbols, however, are standard-issue, maybe not intended as any physical reality, and Worthington never played cards. The founding story is most likely a founding myth.

Thomas Worthington was one of Ohio's first two senators and the man who fathered Ohio's statehood. Characterized by an opponent as a combination of "milk and honey and sour small beer," he was, nonetheless, one of America's first true Westerners and his anti-Federalist promptings helped give Ohio the most democratic constitution of the day.

The Lay of the Land

Northernmost place—near **Conneaut**, approximate latitude, 41 degrees, 58 minutes

Southernmost place—**South Point**, approximate latitude, 38 degrees, 24 minutes

Length (extreme north to south)—205 miles

Width (extreme east to west)—230 miles

Geographic center—**Centerburg**, Knox County, approximate latitude 40 degrees, 18 minutes; approximate longitude, 82 degrees, 42 minutes

Demographic Center—**Franklin Township**, Morrow County

Ohio owns 2,097,000 acres of **Lake Erie**

320 miles of shoreline

Largest county—**Ashtabula**, 711 square miles

Smallest county—**Lake**, 232 square miles

Counties with most crooked borders—**Washington** and **Noble**, approximately 30 corners each

Highest point—**Campbell Hill**, Logan County, 1,550 feet above sea level

Lowest point—**Ohio River**, near Cincinnati, 455 feet above sea level

Smallest incorporated town—**Miltonsburg** (Monroe), population 29

Largest city—**Columbus**, population 711,470

Counties with most bordering counties—**Stark**, 8
also Ashland, Ross, Licking, and Madison, 7

The Count
11,421,267   people,
(2002 estimate, based on 2000 census)

44,828 square miles of territory
277.3 people per square mile
40,948 square miles of land
Metropolitan areas take 18,298.8 square miles
339,185 acres owned by the Federal Government (1.29%)
3,876 square miles are water
3,499 square miles are in Lake Erie
376 square miles are inland water
State historic places take up 5,022 acres
44,000 miles worth of rivers and streams
Farms occupy 15,200,000 acres
Forests cover 6,146,000 acres
Foreigners own about 137,000 farm acres
60 percent of everybody else in U.S. is only a day's drive away

Only 35 percent of Americans 18 to 24 years old surveyed by the National Geographic Society in 2002 could correctly locate Ohio on a blank map. The survey also revealed that about one in ten could not locate their own country on a world map.

—National Geographic Society; Roper ASW

The Buckeye essentials

Mottos are a matter not to be taken lightly, or quickly, in the case of Ohio. After deciding on the Great Seal, it took the state another 62 years to come up with a motto, Imperium in Imperio, meaning an "Empire within an Empire." But that struck a lot of folks as entirely too pretentious, and the "too royal" motto was recalled after only a couple of years. Ohio was mottoless until 1959, when this deficiency was brought to the attention of the state's schoolchildren. When 9-year-old James Mastronardo of Cincinnati suggested a Biblical line, he accomplished what several generations of solons couldn't. Ohio, at last, had a motto.

State bird—the cardinal *(Cardinalis cardinalis)*, adopted 1933

State flower—the **red carnation**, William McKinley's lapel favorite, adopted 1904, as a posthumous tribute

State nickname—**The Buckeye State**

State slogan—**"Ohio, the Heart of It All,"** from a Columbus advertising agency, adopted 1984

State song—**Beautiful Ohio**, adopted 1969

State tree—the buckeye *(Aesculus glabra)*, adopted 1953

State animal—**white tail deer**, adopted 1987

State reptile—**black racer**, adopted 1995

State beverage—**tomato juice**, adopted with a nod toward Ohio's prodigious crop in 1965

State fossil—the trilobite *(Isotelus)*, adopted in 1985

State gem stone—**flint**, the crypto-crystalline type of quartz that was perennially favored by Indians for arrowheads, adopted 1965

State herb capital—**Gahanna**, designated 1972

State official location—**North Central Great Lakes Region**, according to U.S. Department of Commerce

State poetry day—**third Friday of October**, adopted 1938

State rock song—**Hang on Sloopy**, adopted 1985

State wildflower—white trillium *(Trillium grandiflorum)* adopted 1986

State motto—**"With God All Things Are Possible,"** from Matthew 19:26; adopted 1959

State insect—**ladybug**, adopted 1975.
According to the 1975 state law, the Ohio General Assembly chose the ladybug as the state insect because "the queenly ladybug is symbolic of the people of Ohio—she is proud and friendly, bringing delight to millions of children when she alights on their hand or arm to display her multi-colored wings, and she is extremely industrious and hardy, able to live under the most adverse conditions and yet retain her beauty and charm, while at the same time being of inestimable value to nature."

The Buckeye At A Glance

The Latin words in the Buckeye tree's scientific name mean oak and smooth, but the Indians called the species "hetuck," meaning buckeye because the seeds so strongly resembled the eye of a male deer. When Colonel Ebenezer Sproat arrived at Marietta in 1788 to be the new sheriff, the Indians were highly impressed and honored him with the name Hetuck, thus making Sproat the first recorded Buckeye. But not until a half century later did Ohioans in general acquire a national reputation as Buckeyes. During William Henry Harrison's 1840 presidential campaign, his opponent said that Harrison's Ohio roots suited him better for a log cabin than the White House. Harrison's people knew a good campaign gimmick when it got handed to them on a silver platter. His roots, of course, went deep into buckeye country, and soon log cabins made of buckeye wood were being towed from town to town while supporters sang a ditty that began, *Oh where, tell me, where/Was your buckeye cabin made?* Harrison's was the first staged political campaign. It not only got him elected, but also spread—and fixed—the image of Ohioan as Buckeye throughout the land.

Common Name: Ohio Buckeye.
Scientific Name: *Aesculus Glabra,* Willdenow.
Derivation of Name: the seed resembles the eye of a deer.
Plant Family: Hippocastanaceae (Horse Chestnut Family).
Official Designation: State Tree of Ohio; Symbol of The Ohio State University.

Characteristics:

Form: A small tree with a short trunk and narrowish crown, usually reaching a height of about 50 ft., but taller in old individuals.

Bark: Ashy gray and scaly at maturity.

Leaves: Compound, composed of five (or sometimes seven) elliptical leaflets attached to the leaf stalk at a single point.

Fall Color: Orange to yellow or yellowish brown.

Flowers: Small, pale yellow, in showy clusters at the ends of branches.

Blooming: Late April and early May.

Fruits: Brownish-green, one or two inches in diameter, covered with short spines, splitting open along two or three seams at maturity.

Seeds: Shiny dark brown, with a large tan spot on one side, about 3/4 of an inch in diameter, two or three per fruit.

Range: Western Pennsylvania south to central Alabama, and west to southeastern Iowa, Missouri, and eastern Arkansas, Oklahoma and Texas.

Data reprinted with the permission of The Ohio State University Herbarium

In 1930, a new Ohio State graduate, **Milton Caniff,** *who later drew the popular Steve Canyon comic strip, invented and began to promote a logo consisting of buckeye leaves and seeds. He continued doing this until September, 1950, when the University accepted the logo as its official symbol.*

A political party is a formal organization by which citizens attempt to affect government policies and actions. Parties nominate their candidates for office, establish positions on issues, and work to persuade the electorate to support their candidates and political agenda. In Ohio, a political party can be legally formed whenever a group of qualified voters either (1) nominates candidates for governor or presidential electors, and those candidates receive at least five percent of all the votes cast in the last preceding regular election for the offices they are seeking; or (2) files a petition of intent to nominate candidates in the next primary election and that petition has the signatures of registered voters equal in number to one percent of all the votes cast for the office of governor in the last preceding general election.

50states.com/ Ohio.htm

www.

Comprehensive web site with alphabetized information about all things Ohio, including deep list of public records, and both the Ohio constitution and the Ohio Revised Code. (Go to "public records," then to "Ohio constitution." The ORC is there.)

State law defines major, intermediate, and minor political parties according to how great a percentage of the total vote its gubernatorial candidate received in the last general election. Major parties have gubernatorial candidates who received at least twenty percent of the vote; intermediate parties have candidates who received between ten and 20 percent of the vote; and minor parties have candidates who either received between five and ten percent of the vote or filed a petition signed by one percent of the voters in the last gubernatorial election. The state has two major political parties: the Ohio Democratic Party and the Ohio Republican Party.

Major political parties in Ohio are legally required to have two controlling committees, a State Central Committee and a County Central Committee, whose members are elected during primary elections in even-numbered years. The State Central Committee oversees the business of the party within Ohio, including candidate endorsement and support, raising campaign funds, and organizing the state convention at which party policies and positions on issues are determined. State Central Committees consist of one man and one woman from each State Senate district in Ohio. Members of the County Central Committees act as liaisons between the party and the voters and are considered the foundation of a political party. They are responsible for conducting party business at the local level, including endorsing a slate of candidates, soliciting workers and financial support, and making recommendations for county board of elections members to the Secretary of State. One County Central Committee member is elected from each precinct in the county or from each city ward and each township in the county. An executive committee, chairman, and other officers are chosen by both controlling committees no later than 15 days after the election.

Anyone who is a United States citizen and at least 18 years old is eligible to vote in Ohio. Eligible persons must have both lived in the state and have been registered to vote in the precinct of their residency for at least 30 days prior to the election. Persons turning 18 on or before a November general election may vote for candidates but not issues in the May primary election.

Residency

For purposes of voter eligibility, a residence is considered to be the place to which a person returns whenever he has been absent. Such temporary absences as school attendance and military service do not constitute a change of residence. Students, however, may vote from their school address, if they consider it to be their place of residency.

Registration

Everyone, with the exception of members of the armed forces and their dependents who have left Ohio to accompany them, must register in order to vote. There are numerous places to register, including the office of the Ohio Secretary of State, any board of elections or board of elections branch office, state agencies that deal with the general public, the office of any motor vehicle deputy registrar, and any public high schools or vocational schools. Registration forms may also be requested in person, by mail, or by telephone; or they may be obtained from any office or individual designated to distribute registration forms.

Voters need not declare their political affiliations when they register, but registration forms are valid only if they are received by the county board of elections or the Secretary of State 30 days prior to the election.

Voters must re-register only if they have moved to another county or have not voted in any election for four successive years. Voters who change their names or change their place of residence within the same county must notify the board of elections or Secretary of State's office 30 days prior to an election. Voters who have moved within the same precinct need only complete a change of residence notice at their polling place on election day.

Voting Procedures and Ballots

Voters must cast their ballots at the polling places designated to serve the precincts where they reside. Voters who are unsure of the location of their polling places may obtain that information from their county board of elections. In order to cast a ballot, voters must sign their name and address on a poll list. Their signatures are compared to the signature on their registration cards for purposes of identification. Depending on the county, voters will use either voting machines or paper ballots. Instructions are given on how to mark the ballot. Should the ballot be spoiled or erroneously marked, voters may obtain a second ballot. Persons who are illiterate or mentally or physically disabled may receive voting assistance from poll workers or from anyone of their choosing, except their employer, an officer of their union, or a candidate whose name appears on the ballot.

The Ohio Constitution requires that an office-column ballot be used in general elections. On this type of ballot, the titles of each office are listed with the names of the candidates underneath of them. Since the candidates' names are not organized according to their political party affiliation, the office-column ballot precludes voters from voting a "straight ticket" for the candidates of a single party. In primary elections, however, each political party uses separate ballots bearing the party designation. Judges are elected on a separate nonpartisan ballot that carries no indication of political party affiliation.

"If you plan to run for office, get yourself neutered like a cat."

—Dick Feagler, Cleveland columnist

The questions and issues ballot, which contains no candidate names, is used to decide statewide concerns such as constitutional amendments and initiated laws and referenda.

Polls open at 6:30 a.m. and close at 7:30 p.m. Polls may be kept open for voters waiting in line, but no loitering is permitted near the voting area. Order is kept by elections officials, who post one copy of each precinct's unofficial vote count on the door of the polling place. The ballots cast are sealed and sent to the board of elections, where the official tally of the vote is made.

Absentee Voting

Voters may use an absentee ballot if they (1) will be absent from the county on election day; (2) are 62 years of age or older; (3) will be hospitalized on election day; (4) have a personal illness or physical disability; (5) cannot vote on election day because of religious beliefs; (6) will be in jail for a misdemeanor or are awaiting trial; or (7) will be serving as an election official.

Voters may obtain absentee ballots by visiting or writing to their county board of elections. Armed service absentee ballots are available to members of the United States armed forces serving outside the state, as well as spouses and dependents accompanying them. Unless a voting residence has been established elsewhere, the service member's voting residence is the place where he or she resided just prior to entering the service. Armed service absentee voters need not register.

Written requests for absentee ballots must be received by the board of elections by noon of the third day before an election. In order to be counted, completed absentee ballots must be returned to the board of elections by 7:30 p.m. on election day. Ballots mailed from out of the country will be counted if they are postmarked by election day and received by the board of elections up to ten days after election day.

Election Dates and Types of Elections

Special Elections are held in order to decide specific questions such as tax issues and bond levies. A special election may be held on the first Tuesday after the first Monday in the months of February, May, August, or November, or on any day authorized by a municipal charter for holding a primary election.

Primary elections are held so that (1) political parties can nominate party officials, delegates to national conventions for Presidential and Vice-Presidential candidates, and candidates to run in a General Election; (2) issues can be voted on; and (3) chartered municipalities can nominate municipal officials and municipal court judges. In primary elections, Ohioans vote for candidates according to their stated political party affiliation, except in the case of nonpartisan municipal elections and when voting on statewide issues. Primary elections are held on the first Tuesday after the first Monday in May in even-numbered years. In odd-numbered years, they occur on dates determined by each chartered municipality.

General Elections are held so that Ohio voters can select federal, state, county, and local officials. General elections are always held on the first Tuesday after the first Monday of November. State and local issues and amendments to the Constitution may be placed on the ballot in any year, but government officials are elected according to the schedule in the chart below.

In every even-numbered year:
All members of the U.S. Congress
All members of the Ohio House
　　　of Representatives
Half of the members of the Ohio Senate
One-third of the members of the State School
　　　Board
Two Justices of the Ohio Supreme Court
Court of Appeals Judges
Common Pleas Court Judges
County Judges

In some even-numbered years:
United States Senator
Chief Justice of the Ohio Supreme Court

In even-numbered years divisible by four:
United States President and Vice-President
Most county officers
Two County Commissioners (except for Summit
     County's County Executive and four
     County Council Members)
Prosecuting Attorney
Sheriff
Coroner
Treasurer
Recorder
Clerk of Courts
Engineer

In even-numbered years not divisible by four:
Governor and Lieutenant Governor
Secretary of State
Attorney General
Auditor of State
State Treasurer
County Auditor
One County Commissioner (except for Summit
     County's three County Council members)

In all odd-numbered years:
Municipal officers (such as city and village mayors
     and council members)
Township Trustees and Clerk
Local Boards of Education
Municipal Court Judges

Candidates

Candidates for office in Ohio must be qualified as voters in the state, specify their intention to seek an office, and pay a filing fee before election day. They may file as independent, nonpartisan, write-in, or party candidates. Independent and nonpartisan candidates must file nominating petitions; write-in candidates must file a declaration of intention to be a write-in candidate; and party candidates must file a declaration of candidacy and nominating petition. The deadlines for the required filings vary with the office being sought.

Nominating petitions must be signed only by qualified voters from the political subdivision in which the candidate is running for office. In the case of party candidates, the signatures must be those only of qualified voters who are also members of the same political party as the candidate. The number of signatures required varies with the office that is being sought. All signatures must be in ink, and all must be validated by the board of elections at which they were filed. Petitions remain open for public inspection, and protests against a person seeking candidacy must be filed and arbitrated at the board of elections.

Board of Elections

The Secretary of State of Ohio is the state's principal elections official, but the actual responsibility for planning and organizing elections lies with four people in each county who comprise the board of elections. The Secretary of State appoints two individuals nominated from each of Ohio's two major political parties, thus forming a bipartisan board of Republicans and Democrats whose competing political interests are intended to counteract each other. In fact, the boards of elections are quite probably Ohio's most universal and delicate balancing act. Not only are the members drawn from opposing parties, but the boards are also structured to enhance the equilibrium among them: the members choose both a chairman and director who are from different parties, and a deputy director whose party is different from the director's party. In case of a tie vote when the members are deciding an issue, the Secretary of State has the authority to vote and end the deadlock.

Five kinds of local government exist in Ohio. Three are political subdivisions of state government provided for by the Ohio constitution: counties, municipalities, and townships. State law also allows for two other local government units: school districts and special districts. School districts provide public education and are operated by an elected Board of Education in accordance with state regulations. Special districts are created by local officials or the vote of the electorate in order to fulfill specific needs and purposes. As independent government units with their own financing and budgets, special districts have various forms of appointed and elected governing bodies. County library districts, park districts, port authorities, and regional airport authorities are examples of Ohio's special districts.

First Ohio municipalities to adopt home rule charters

Cleveland, 1913

Dayton, 1913

Lakewood, 1913

Middletown, 1913

Springfield, 1913

Ashland, 1914

Ashtabula, 1914

Sandusky, 1914

Toledo, 1914

Cincinnati, 1917

Gallipolis, 1917

South Charleston, 1917

Xenia, 1917

Townships

Townships were the first kind of local government created in Ohio, but they originated with the Pilgrims, who brought the township form of government to the New World in 1620. Townships spread from New England to the Rocky Mountains, and today, Ohio is one of 22 states that still have this form of local government.

In Ohio, townships date back to the Land Ordinance of 1785, when Congress approved the survey and sale of the first public lands for the territory northwest of the Ohio River. At the point where the Ohio River crossed the Pennsylvania border, seven parallel parcels of land called the Seven Ranges were surveyed and divided according to townships six miles square in size that were subdivided into one-mile-square sections. Subsequent acts of Congress established other public land grants, which, except for the Virginia Military District lands, were all surveyed into townships five or six square miles in size. After Ohio became a state, townships were the obvious choice for the basic unit of Ohio government. In 1804, elected township officials consisted of three trustees, a clerk, two overseers of the poor, highway supervisors, constables, and justices of the peace.

Today, townships are subdivisions of county government in Ohio, and only those areas that have not been incorporated as municipalities (cities or villages) are under township jurisdiction. Ohio's 1,310 townships are governed by a three-member board of trustees and a clerk, who serves as the fiscal officer. All are elected to four-year terms. Elections for township officials occur biennially. Two of the trustees are elected simultaneously, and two years later, the clerk and third trustee are elected. The trustees take office on January 1 following the election, while the clerk takes office on April 1 following the election. The duties and responsibilities of the township officials are defined by the Ohio General Assembly and include providing such services as zoning regulation, police and fire protection, road and cemetery maintenance, and waste disposal.

Counties

Ohio's counties are a legacy from the Northwest Ordinance, which in 1787 allowed both to be established in the territorial wilderness of Ohio. In 1788, Washington was the first county organized in Ohio, and by 1802, Ohio had nine others. After Ohio achieved statehood in 1803, its Constitution provided that counties would be the primary subdivision of state government and gave the General Assembly the power to create new counties and determine their territory and political structure. Ohio now has 88 counties, the last of which—Noble—was organized in 1851.

Counties are not separate political entities but administrative agencies of state government with limited powers that serve on a local level certain specific purposes such as collecting taxes, administering justice, and overseeing elections. Since the Ohio Constitution guarantees that all general laws must have uniform operation throughout the state, the General Assembly cannot lawfully enact special purpose legislation that does not affect every county.

Ohio law provides for the organization of county government. State statutes specify a commission form of county government, unless the electorate in a county chooses to adopt a home rule charter or one of the alternate forms of government outlined by state law. Although home rule allows the electorate to control their own political affairs by creating an individual plan of local government structure and function, only the voters of Summit County have approved a home rule charter. Since 1981, Summit County has had an elected county executive and county council instead of the statutory county commission. No counties have adopted the alternate forms of government, which provide for either an elected or appointed county executive and grant the counties some leeway in the number and election of county commissioners.

The commission form of county government that is used by 87 of Ohio's 88 counties consists of a three-member board of commissioners who co-administer the county functions with eight other officers: auditor, treasurer, clerk of courts, coroner, engineer, prosecuting attorney, recorder, and sheriff. County commissioners and officers are elected at large in even-numbered years by the citizens of the same county to four-year terms. The commissioners serve overlapping terms, and the dates following the election when the other county officials take office vary. The salaries of county officials are determined by a state formula and differ according to county population.

County Commissioners

The Board of County Commissioners serves as the administrative and policy-making body of the county, but the members' authority is circumscribed by state law. The commissioners manage the county's employees, facilities, and finances. As administrators of the county funds, they decide an annual budget and any tax levies or bond issues. The commissioners are responsible for county lands, buildings, and other property, and they affirm all annexations and incorporations. The commissioners oversee and allocate moneys to other county departments such as building inspection, sanitary engineering, welfare, and animal control. Two of the commissioners are elected simultaneously, with one taking office on January 2 and the other on January 3 following the election. The third commissioner is elected two years later and takes office on January 1 following the election.

Auditor

As the county's chief accounting and fiscal officer, the auditor warrants all the money in the county treasury and monitors the accounts of the county treasurer. The auditor makes valuations of real property for tax purposes; keeps all records of location, ownership, and valuation for each county real estate parcel; and prepares and publishes the county financial report. The auditor is the county sealer of weights and measurements and oversees sales of dog licenses, vendor licenses, and licenses to cigarette and specialized goods dealers. The auditor takes office on the second Monday in March following the election. After 2002, Ohio county auditors' base salaries ranged from $45,573 to $80,164, plus an additional stipend for serving as an agent of the State Tax Commissioner.

Clerk of the Courts

An officer of the Court responsible to both the Common Pleas Court and Court of Appeals, the clerk of courts is responsible for keeping permanent accurate records of all civil, criminal, and domestic relations cases. The clerk of courts enters judgements, issues writs, collects court costs, serves summons, processes petitions, oversees

In 2001, Ohio county commissioners' salaries ranged from $31,860 to $78,874.

97

moneys granted to persons as a result of court cases, and issues and transfers automobile titles. The clerk of courts takes office on the first Monday in January following the election. In 2001, Ohio clerks of courts' base salaries ranged from $33,399 to $64,704, plus an additional stipend of 12.5 percent of their base salary, pursuant to the Ohio Revised Code.

County Coroner

The coroner must be a physician licensed to practice within Ohio for at least two years. The coroner investigates and determines the cause of death of unidentified persons and persons dying as the result of violence or a criminal act, by suicide, or in a suspicious manner. The coroner, who may conduct autopsies, must also keep records of the cause of death in all cases within the county and sign a medical certificate giving the reason for death. The coroner takes office on the first Monday in January following the election. In 2001, Ohio county coroners' salaries ranged from $18,842 to $64,451 with a private practice and $98,698 to $103,480 without.

County Engineer

The county engineer must be a registered professional engineer and surveyor licensed to practice in Ohio. The county engineer has responsibility for the construction, repair, and maintenance of county roads and highways, bridges, culverts, drains, ditches, and other public improvements with the exception of buildings. Part of the cost of operating the county engineer's office is obtained from motor vehicle license tax funds. The county engineer takes office on the first Monday in January following the election. In 2001, Ohio county engineers' salaries ranged from $48,300 to $71,182 for those with a private practice, and from $68,691 to $91,568 for those without a private practice.

Prosecuting Attorney

As the legal counsel to the county commissioners and other county and township officials, the county prosecuting attorney must be an attorney licensed to practice law in Ohio. The prosecuting attorney acts as the lawyer for the state in complaints and litigation involving felonies and criminal cases such as murder, rape, robbery, and fraud within the county. The prosecuting attorney takes office on the first

Monday of January following the election. In 2001, Ohio county prosecutors' salaries were $78,952 to $103,480 for those without a private practice and ranged from $46,245 to $73,700 for those with a private practice.

Recorder

The county recorder protects the real and personal property rights of Ohioans by acting as the custodian of all instruments and legal documents that are authorized by state law to be recorded. The public documentation that the recorder must maintain includes deeds, mortgages, powers of attorney, plat maps, leases, land contracts, mechanics liens, federal tax liens, and partnerships. The county recorder takes office on the first Monday in January following the election. In 2001, Ohio county recorders' salaries ranged from $32,543 to $63,479.

Sheriff

As the county's chief law enforcement officer, the sheriff is charged by state law with keeping the public peace. Although the sheriff is primarily responsible for providing police protection to unincorporated areas, his jurisdiction is county-wide. Aside from executing warrants, writs, and other legal processes, the sheriff is also the custodian of the county jail and county courthouse, subject to the respective control of the common pleas court and county commissioners. The sheriff takes office on the first Monday of January following the election. In 2001, Ohio county sheriffs' salaries ranged from $40,855 to $78,279.

Treasurer

Whereas the duty of the county auditor is to levy taxes, the primary duty of the county treasurer is to collect taxes and in turn disburse the money to meet expenditures. Charged with safeguarding the public's money, the treasurer's responsibilities include keeping accurate records of all incoming money, all money paid out, and the balance in the county treasury. These records are submitted for review to the county auditor. Money collected by the treasurer varies from real and personal property taxes to vendor and dog licensing revenue. The county treasurer takes office on the first Monday of September following the election. In 2001, Ohio county treasurers' salaries ranged from $33,399 to $64,704.

"THE CONSUMER CONFIDENCE INDEX ROSE TODAY ON NEWS THAT THE RETAIL OPTIMISM RATING WOULD REPORT AN UPTURN, SENDING THE WHOLESALE GIDDINESS METER SOARING."

Municipalities

Municipalities in the state also originated with the Northwest Ordinance of 1787, and by the time the Ohio Constitution was ratified in 1802, ten city governments had already been formed. The 1851 Constitution contained general laws regarding the government of villages and several classes of cities, but in 1912, Article XVIII of the Constitution limited all municipal corporations to two classifications: villages or cities. Municipal corporations with a population of less than 5,000 are defined as villages; those with a population greater than 5,000 are cities. Ohio now has 978 municipal corporations, of which 735 are villages and 243 are cities.

Incorporation of an area as a village occurs whenever a majority of the landowners petition and win the approval of the county commissioners. In order to become a village, the territory must have an area of at least two square miles, a minimum population of 600 persons per square mile, and an assessed property valuation of at least $2,000 per person. The territory in question cannot lie within three miles of another municipality, unless the municipality agrees or has refused to annex the territory. Any township having a minimum population of 25,000 can, with the approval of the electorate, incorporate as a city. Villages automatically become cities

whenever the population exceeds 5000. The Secretary of State verifies the number of residents in Ohio's municipal corporations after every federal decennial census and can proclaim a municipal corporation a city or a village. Villages that reach city status receive an official proclamation from the Secretary of State, which is sent to the mayor and read before the legislative authority of the municipality, where it becomes official within 30 days.

While counties are established by the state without popular consent, municipalities are created at the request of the people who live in them. Villages and cities epitomize self-government in Ohio, because the Constitution gives broad powers regarding matters of local concern to municipalities, except where their actions conflict with state laws. Ohio cities and villages provide such services to citizens as police and fire protection, municipal utilities, sanitation services, trash collection, traffic control, and public facilities such as hospitals, libraries, and jails. As a result, municipal governments more often than any other governments have the most immediate and personal influence on the lives of Ohio's citizens.

Ohio municipalities have three options for choosing the format of their government: (1) in accordance with the general plan prescribed by state law; (2) in accordance with alternative plans offered under state law; and (3) by creating a home rule plan. The general plan is the mayor-

council form of government; the alternative plans are the city-manager, commission, and federal forms of government, and the home rule option allows a municipality to construct its own form of government. Unlike counties, where the electorate must approve the adoption of home rule charters, the Constitution automatically grants the prerogative of home rule to every municipality.

The Mayor-Council Plan

The mayor-council plan is the most common form of government used by Ohio's municipalities. In this "split-executive" plan, the mayor is the CEO, but shares administrative functions with other municipal officials such as the auditor, treasurer, and law director. A council serves as the legislative authority. The mayor enforces municipal laws, and when a municipality lacks either a police or municipal court, the mayor presides over a "mayor's court." The mayor can approve or disapprove any city ordinance, but council can override the mayor's veto with a two-thirds vote. Village mayors do not have veto power. The council can determine its own operating rules and is not required to meet more than once a week.

In cities, the mayor is elected to a four-year term. According to a city's population, between seven and 17 council members are elected, three at-large and the rest from wards. Council members serve two-year terms, unless four-year terms have been voted upon.

In villages, all elected officials serve four-year terms. The Council has six members, and the mayor also serves as the council president. Other elected officials include the clerk, treasurer, a solicitor, and a three-member board of trustees in villages with utility services. The clerk serves as the chief fiscal officer and can assume other duties and responsibilities related to the village's operation. Council has the option of combining the clerk and treasurer offices.

The City Manager Plan

In this optional form of government, a council formulates municipal policies and the members hire a professional manager. The city manager's duties include executing municipal laws, supervising personnel, and submitting financial reports and budgets to council. Depending on the population of the municipality, the size of the council ranges from five to nine members, who are elected at-large to serve four-year terms. In addition to the city manager, council appoint-

ments include a clerk, a treasurer, an auditor, a director of law in cities, or a solicitor in villages. The council chairman executes judicial functions in cities and villages lacking a municipal court.

Commission Plan

This government option combines legislative and executive functions in a commission whose members are elected at large for four-year terms. The commission consists of three members in a municipal corporation with a population less than 10,000, and five members in all others. The commission plan is not in use in Ohio.

Federal Plan

This option includes an elected council and mayor. Elected to a four-year term in this "strong mayor" plan, the mayor serves as the chief executive, appoints department heads and other officials, and manages municipal finances. The council has legislative powers, and depending on a municipality's population, ranges in size from five to 15 members. In cities with less than 10,000 people, members are elected at-large to two-year terms; members in larger cities serve two or four-year terms depending on whether they are elected by wards or at-large. The federal plan is not in use in Ohio.

Home Rule Charter

The Ohio Constitution allows the electorate in municipalities considerable autonomy in determining their governments. Citizens in cities and villages can deviate from the plans prescribed by state law and write their own charters outlining the form and function of municipal government. Because home rule charters must accommodate the needs of varied electorates, they differ in particulars such as the number of council members and election methods.

In order to adopt a home rule charter, voters in a municipality must approve the creation of a charter commission, whose members have one year in which to prepare the proposed charter, a legal document describing the government structure. The charter goes into effect if a majority of the electorate votes to approve it. All municipal charters are filed with the Ohio Secretary of State.

Sources: Office of the Ohio Secretary of State, County Commissioners Association of Ohio, Ohio Municipal League, Ohio Township Association

Mayors in Ohio can perform weddings anywhere in their home county.

Home rule in Ohio

Ohio's progress is stymied by local fiefs that worked quite well when the state was all wilderness. But it's no longer wilderness. Although home rule might help us return to one. *An analysis by Thomas Bier.*

Our system of local government made perfect sense in 1803, when Ohio became the 17th state. After all, what other practical way was there to govern 40,000 square miles of wilderness? But today, the system has two serious defects:

(1) No jurisdiction has responsibility for an area larger than a county.
(2) "Home rule" isolates jurisdictions facing decline.

Local government in 1803 was the county. Ohio began with 17 of them. The founding fathers knew that more would be formed, but they did not know how many. They simply specified in the inaugural Constitution that a new county had to contain at least 400 square miles.

Eventually, Ohio would have 88 counties with an average size of 465 square miles.

Why 400 square miles?

Probably because of the pace of horse travel. The farthest that someone could live from the county seat and do a round trip in a day was 10 to 15 miles. That limited a county to roughly 20 miles by 20, or 400 square miles.

The principal of government "by the people" at the local level was reinforced by frontier conditions. Towns were small and far apart. By 1850, Cleveland was only 3 square miles with a population of 17,000. The largest settlement in the state was Cincinnati, with 115,000 residents on about 15 square miles.

It would have been quite a stretch back then to imagine a city extending over an entire county, 400 square miles; it would have been an oracular stretch to imagine a city (an urbanized area) of 2,000 square miles involving seven counties. But that is Greater Cleveland today. Ohio cities of 2002 do not match the governmental design of 1803.

The county was the original locus of home rule, but as hamlets grew into villages, and villages into cities, preference for rule that was even closer to home intensified. The phenomenal expansion of cities after the Civil War, and then the emergence of the first suburbs around 1900, forced the issue. The cities wanted county and state government out of their day-to-day affairs. They got their way in 1912, when the Constitution was amended to grant powers of local self-government to municipal corporations.

From then on, it was clear: cities were independent. Cleveland, Toledo, Dayton

Thomas Bier is on the staff of the Maxine Goodman Levin College of Urban Affairs at Cleveland State University

and all places from Aurora to Zanesville were free to govern themselves, in accordance with general state and federal laws.

It made good sense in 1912, and it still does—up to the point where cooperation is needed, or a city is faced with challenges for which its resources are inadequate. In those situations, home rule is a liability:

(1) Home rule means that there is no official governmental basis for cooperation or for assisting cities that face economic decline.

(2) Home rule means that cities have no responsibilities toward neighboring jurisdictions. None. When cooperation or assistance occurs, it is usually the result of political jockeying.

Home rule and county lines mean that nobody is officially responsible at the multicounty level for matters such as water and sewer systems, airports, parks, highways, public lands, ports, rivers, streams and air; and major singular assets such as convention centers, museums, athletic and recreational facilities. Nobody is responsible for considering what makes the most sense from a regional perspective.

Home rule means that every city is solely responsible for its fate. Cleveland, you've got problems. That's too bad, but they're yours—not the state's, not Cuyahoga County's, not Parma's, not Pepper Pike's, not Hudson's. Good luck.

Parma, you're losing tax base, that's too bad, but it's your tough luck.

Painesville, you have housing that is old and deteriorating. Sorry to hear that, but it's your headache, not ours. We wish you well.

Cities rise, reach their peak, and then become vulnerable to decline. Home rule is a blessing during the rise and at the peak, but after the glory days, it's not much of a friend.

A growing number of suburbs have begun to battle decline as age has weakened them. Their resources in that battle are severely limited. On their own, they're not likely to succeed. Letting them (and the original big cities) twist in the wind is a sure-fire way to a second-rate future for Ohio.

Over the last 40 years, the federal government has demonstrated far more responsibility for the condition of Ohio's cities than has our state government. Ridiculous. But that is what the mindset of home rule has done to us. It has provided an official way to ignore civic responsibility that is a fundamental principle of society. The well-being of each jurisdiction in a region is, first and foremost, the responsibility of those who live in that region. If that responsibility is not exercised, then the state's responsibility applies. And if the state fails to act, federal intervention is justified. For 40 years, the federal government has attempted to carry obligations that are regional in the first place.

Home rule is too deeply ingrained in who we are and how we are to be altered significantly, let alone to be replaced with regional government. Similarly, our county lines are fixed. But the need for cooperative endeavors within and across counties grows daily. It is unrealistic to expect county commissioners, mayors and township trustees to initiate more than cursory and sporadic cooperation.

Home rule obstructs them at nearly every turn. The situation calls for state intervention, or, more positively, state leadership.

But it is equally unrealistic to expect state legislators to address this matter, since they are locked in the same vise as local officials. The state administration—the governor—is singularly positioned to provide the way forward, by doing the following:

Request that the counties that comprise Ohio's metropolitan regions prepare jointly an assessment of the trend in economic condition of each city, village and township in their region and a regional plan for securing economic stability.

In order to confirm the seriousness of the request, the governor should direct that all state investments that affect economic development and land use be in accordance with the regional plans, noting that the state would be unable to make such investments in a region without an acceptable plan.

The advent of Ohio's 200th birthday would be a very appropriate time to make governmental adjustments that will propel the state into its third century.

TIMELINE: THE DEVELOPMENT OF THE OHIO BALLOT

1803

The new state of Ohio adopts the secret ballot, a legacy from the government of the Northwest Territory.

1845

First law requiring voters to register is passed.

1854

New law mandates ballots be printed and white paper of uniform size must be used to enhance the secrecy of each vote.

1886

Pugsley Law provides for nonpartisan boards of elections to handle voting in major cities.

1888

Law prohibiting loitering around the polls passed to curb voter intimidation.

1891

Ohio is one of the first states to adopt the Australian ballot, the prototype for ballots used today in the state. Named for the nation where it originated, this system insures secrecy and integrity of each vote by (1) having ballots printed at public expense at direction of public officials; (2) putting names of all candidates on each ballot or set of ballots; (3) identifying ballots with official markings to preclude counterfeiting; (4) providing private voting booths; (5) having voters fold ballots to conceal their choices; and (6) banning signatures or personal identification marks from ballots.

1898

Law allowing the use of voting machines passed.

1912

Constitutional amendment establishes primary elections in Ohio; electorate gains—party leaders lose—the ultimate say in candidate selection.

1917

Absentee ballots approved.

1949

Constitutional amendment bans party-column ballot, which fosters voting of "straight ticket" by listing candidates according to political affiliation. Ohio adopts the office-column, or Massachusetts ballot, which lists candidates by office sought.

1974

Constitutional amendment creates Ohio Ballot Board, charged with (1) determining ballot language for statewide issues such as constitutional amendments; and (2) writing and disseminating explanations as well as pro and con arguments concerning amendments put forth by General Assembly. ~

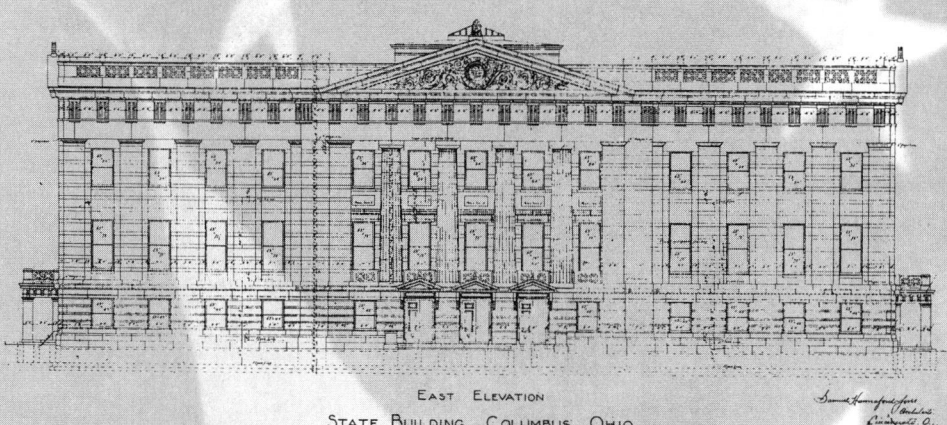

EAST ELEVATION
STATE BUILDING. COLUMBUS OHIO.

The original Annex elevation drawing shows the three original entrance doors into the lobby.

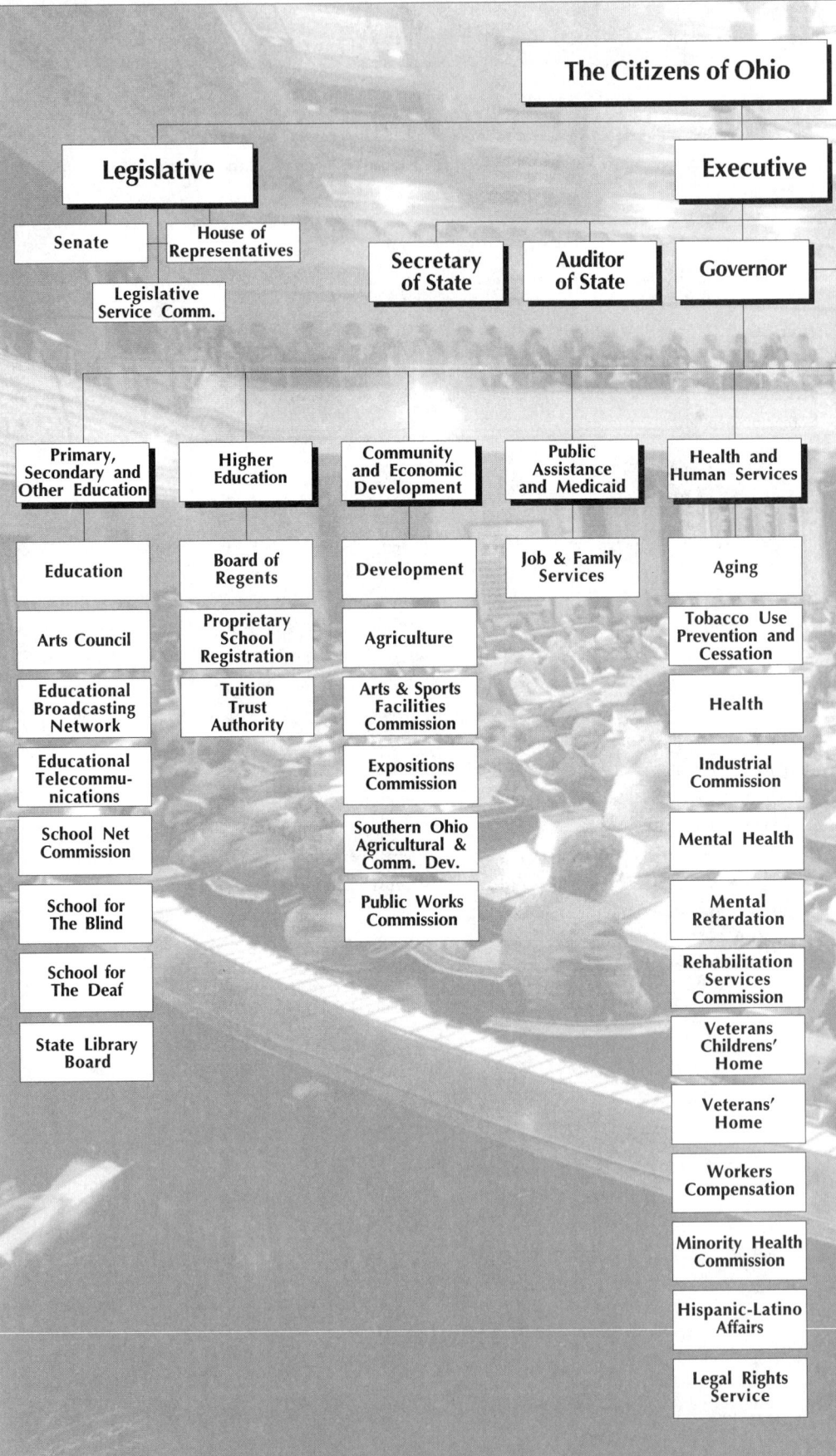

"All politics are based on the indifference of the majority."

—former Ohioan James Reston, *The New York Times*, June 12, 1968

The Citizens of Ohio

Legislative

Senate

House of Representatives

Legislative Service Comm.

Executive

Secretary of State

Auditor of State

Governor

Primary, Secondary and Other Education

Education

Arts Council

Educational Broadcasting Network

Educational Telecommunications

School Net Commission

School for The Blind

School for The Deaf

State Library Board

Higher Education

Board of Regents

Proprietary School Registration

Tuition Trust Authority

Community and Economic Development

Development

Agriculture

Arts & Sports Facilities Commission

Expositions Commission

Southern Ohio Agricultural & Comm. Dev.

Public Works Commission

Public Assistance and Medicaid

Job & Family Services

Health and Human Services

Aging

Tobacco Use Prevention and Cessation

Health

Industrial Commission

Mental Health

Mental Retardation

Rehabilitation Services Commission

Veterans Childrens' Home

Veterans' Home

Workers Compensation

Minority Health Commission

Hispanic-Latino Affairs

Legal Rights Service

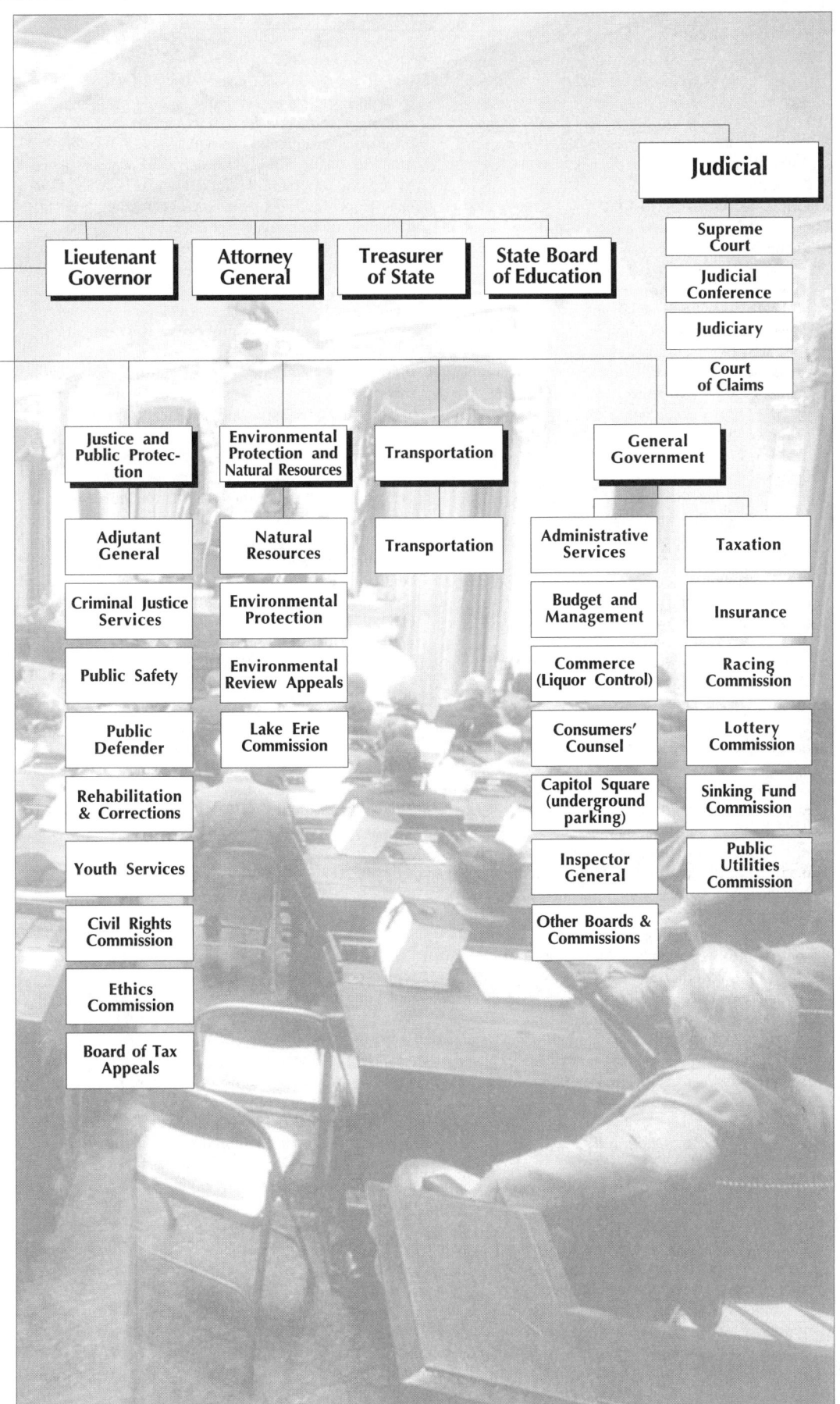

Judicial

Supreme Court

Judicial Conference

Judiciary

Court of Claims

Lieutenant Governor

Attorney General

Treasurer of State

State Board of Education

Justice and Public Protection

Environmental Protection and Natural Resources

Transportation

General Government

Adjutant General

Criminal Justice Services

Public Safety

Public Defender

Rehabilitation & Corrections

Youth Services

Civil Rights Commission

Ethics Commission

Board of Tax Appeals

Natural Resources

Environmental Protection

Environmental Review Appeals

Lake Erie Commission

Transportation

Administrative Services

Budget and Management

Commerce (Liquor Control)

Consumers' Counsel

Capitol Square (underground parking)

Inspector General

Other Boards & Commissions

Taxation

Insurance

Racing Commission

Lottery Commission

Sinking Fund Commission

Public Utilities Commission

Governor

Governor Bob Taft
30th Floor
77 South High Street
Columbus, Ohio 43215-6117

Phone 614-466-3555 or 614-644-HELP

I'm for a chicken

in every garage.

—John Fleischman,

election day, 1996

Among those offices provided by the Constitution of the State of Ohio within the executive branch of government is that of Governor. The governor is chosen by the electors of the state to serve for a period of four years and cannot hold office for a period longer than two successive terms of four years each. In the words of the Constitution, "The supreme executive power of this State shall be vested in the Governor."

The Constitution goes on to define certain of his duties and responsibilities:

1. To see that the laws are faithfully executed.

2. To require information in writing from the officers of the executive department upon any subject relating to the duties of their respective offices.

3. To communicate to the General Assembly by message at every session the condition of the state, and recommend such measures as he shall deem expedient.

4. To convene extraordinary sessions of the General Assembly by proclamation and determine the business to be conducted.

5. To adjourn the General Assembly in case of disagreement between the two houses, in respect to the time and adjournment.

6. To act as Commander-In-Chief of the military forces of the state.

7. To grant reprieves, commutations, and pardons.

The statutes of the State of Ohio have established more than 20 departments of government within the executive branch, the administrative heads of which are appointed by the governor with the advice and consent of the Senate. These department heads constitute the governor's cabinet. They are responsible to the governor and serve at his pleasure. The appointment powers of the governor are extensive and include the members of most of the boards and commissions provided by statute and some heads of divisions within departments as well. The governor may commission as many notaries public as he deems necessary.

Biography

Since being sworn in as Ohio's 67th Governor on January 11, 1999, Bob Taft has focused on rebuilding Ohio's schools, helping every child learn to read, attracting new jobs, positioning Ohio as a leader in technology, improving services for seniors, and restoring cities and rural communities.

Since his first day in office, Governor Taft's top priority has been to enable every child to succeed. Governor Taft is implementing his 12-year plan to provide $10 billion for new school buildings so every child has a good, safe place to learn. He is working to revise statewide academic standards and hold schools accountable for results, and his OhioReads program has recruited more than 45,000 volunteer tutors to ensure every child can read at grade level by the end of the fourth grade. He and his wife, First Lady Hope Taft, lead by example as reading tutors at a Columbus elementary school.

Governor Taft proposed The Clean Ohio Fund, which was approved by voters, to preserve green space, waterways and parklands, and revitalize urban centers through brownfield redevelopment.

The Governor has increased investments in research and technology to prepare Ohio to succeed in the New Economy. He is putting more state services online so Ohioans don't have to wait in line.

He also has expanded programs to help seniors remain in their own homes and has increased access to health care for thousands of children and families.

Governor Taft began his career in public service as a volunteer for the Peace Corps in East Africa. He has served Ohioans as a member of the Ohio House of Representatives, as a Hamilton County Commissioner and as Ohio's Secretary of State — the chief elections officer.

He graduated from Yale University with a bachelor of arts degree in government, received his master's degree in government from Princeton University and earned his law degree from the University of Cincinnati Law School.

Governor Taft's father and grandfather both served in the United States Senate, and his great-grandfather, William Howard Taft, served as the 27th President of the United States and Chief Justice of the U.S. Supreme Court.

The Governor and First Lady Hope Taft have one daughter, Anna.

Lieutenant Governor

Jennette B. Bradley
614-466-3636
www.com.state.oh.us/ltgov/index.htm

The Office of Lieutenant Governor was provided for by a Constitutional amendment in 1851. The lieutenant governor is elected every four years jointly with the governor. The lieutenant governor presides at cabinet meetings in the absence of the governor and assumes the governor's office in case of death, impeachment, resignation, removal, or any disability preventing the governor from executing his duties.

The lieutenant governor serves as the chairman of the State and Local Government Commission, which was created to review the federal, state and local government relationships. The governor may appoint the lieutenant governor as his representative on any board, agency, committee, or commission of which the governor is a member and has the authority to appoint a representative; or in an advisory capacity

to any non-elective board, agency, committee, or commission in the Executive Department; or give him any special assignment he considers in the interest of the state.

Biography

Jennette B. Bradley was elected in 2002 as Ohio's Lt. Governor with Governor Bob Taft, the first African-American woman to be elected as Lt. Governor in Ohio and in the nation's history. Ohio is the 7th largest state in the country.

Lt. Governor Bradley also serves as Director for the Commerce Department and as the Governor's liaison to county and local governments, to small businesses and as policy advisor for urban initiatives, community development and housing programs. As Director of Commerce, Bradley oversees the state's chief regulatory agency administering nine divisions which includes Financial Institutions, Industrial Compliance, Labor and Worker Safety, Liquor Control, Real Estate and Professional Licensing, Securities, State Fire Marshal and Unclaimed Funds and Administration.

Lt. Governor Jennette Bradley received her bachelor's degree in psychology from Wittenberg University in Ohio. Prior to being elected Lt. Governor, Bradley served 11 years as a City Council Member in Columbus, the nation's 15th largest city. In addition to serving on City Council, Lt. Governor Jennette Bradley was a Senior Vice President for a major Ohio bank. Lt. Governor Jennette Bradley is married to Michael C. Taylor and they reside in Columbus.

Secretary of State

J. Kenneth Blackwell
Ohio Secretary of State
180 E. Broad St. 16th Floor
Columbus, OH 43215

Client Service Center:
30 E. Broad St. Lower Level
Columbus, OH 43215

The Office of Secretary of State has been an elective office since the adoption of the Ohio Constitution of 1851. The secretary of state is often referred to as the chief elections officer in Ohio. His office appoints the four members of the bipartisan boards of elections in each of the 88 counties; the secretary casts the deciding vote when the members of a board of elections are equally divided on an action. In addition, all candidacy or nominating petitions for statewide office, all statewide initiative and referendum petitions and campaign finance reports are filed with the secretary. The secretary prescribes all election forms and encourages voter registration.

The secretary of state is responsible for filing the

articles of incorporation and granting corporate charters for all profit and non-profit corporations in Ohio; the secretary also files trade names, trademarks, service marks and marks of ownership. Foreign corporations doing business in Ohio must apply for a license from the secretary's office.

The secretary of state acts as the central filing officer for all secured transactions not involving farm equipment, fixtures, or consumer goods as collateral. He also carries out a number of minor duties: issues commissions to elected state and county officials and appellate, common pleas, probate, municipal, and county court judges; files rules and regulations of all state departments, boards, agencies, and commissions; issues licenses to ministers authorizing them to solemnize marriages within the state; and is the custodian of all laws and resolutions passed by the General Assembly.

Biography

J. Kenneth Blackwell has a distinguished record of achievement as an educator, diplomat and finance executive. As Ohio's 51st Secretary of State, he is the state's constitutional officer chiefly responsible for elections, the management of business records, and the protection of intellectual property and corporate identities.

Mr. Blackwell's public service includes terms as Mayor of Cincinnati, an undersecretary at the U.S. Department of Housing & Urban Development and U.S. Ambassador to the United Nations Human Rights Commission. In 1994, he became the first African American elected to a statewide executive office in Ohio when he was elected Treasurer of State. Mr. Blackwell is a Fellow of the National Academy of Public Administration. He is a member of the board of directors of the Campaign Finance Institute in Washington, D.C., a member of the Advisory Panel of the Federal Elections Commission, and a member of the Harvard Policy Group on Network-Enabled Services and Government. Mr. Blackwell is a member of the national advisory boards of the Princeton Review, Youth for Christ and the Jewish Institute for National Security Affairs.

In 2002, he received meritorious recognition from the Center for Digital Government, delivered the keynote address at *Governing Magazine's* National Conference on "Managing Technology", and was recognized by *Government Technology Magazine* as one of the top 25 public sector leaders in information technology. He is a past president of the National Electronic Commerce Coordinating Council. Over 20 years ago, he began his work in using technology to help government fulfill its mission and commitment to citizens as a member of the board of directors of Public Technology, Inc., located in Washington, D.C. He currently serves on the board of directors of the International City Management Association/Retirement Corporation and has served as president of the Ohio-Kentucky-Indiana Regional Council of Governments.

A certified government finance manager, Mr.

"The only thing worse than running for secretary of state would be being secretary of state."

—State Treasurer Ken Blackwell before running for Secretary of State, Cincinnati Enquirer, September 9, 1998

Blackwell was a 1999 recipient of the Government Finance Officers Association's Excellence in Government Award. He is on the board of directors of the National Taxpayers Union, the John M. Ashbrook Center for Public Affairs (Ashland University), and was formerly a domestic policy analyst at the Heritage Foundation in Washington, D.C. He has served on the U.S. Department of Labor's Advisory Council on Employee Welfare and Pension Benefit Plans. Mr. Blackwell was a delegate to the National Summit on Retirement Savings in both 1998 and 2002. During the 1990's he served on the National Commission on Economic Growth and Tax Reform, and in 1998, he co-edited a book with Jack Kemp, entitled, *IRS v. The People: Time for Real Tax Reform.*

Mr. Blackwell has also served on the boards of directors of Physicians for Human Rights, the International Republican Institute, the American Council of Young Political Leaders, and the Congressional Human Rights Foundation. He was a scholar-in-residence at the Urban Morgan Institute for Human Rights at the University of Cincinnati College of Law. As United States Representative to the U.N. Human Rights Commission, he led the U.S. delegation to all four of the preparatory meetings for the 1993 World Conference on Human Rights. He is a member of the Council on Foreign Relations, and the National Council of the United Nations Association of the USA. He presently serves on the Board of Governors of the International League for Human Rights and the National Council of the Lawyers Committee for Human Rights.

His international activities have taken him to 53 countries and strengthened his understanding of emerging international markets and the growth of democracy worldwide. Mr. Blackwell has held the nation's highest security clearance, and has twice received the U.S. Department of State's Superior Honor Award for his work in the field of human rights from the Administrations of Presidents George H.W. Bush and William Jefferson Clinton.

He holds Bachelor of Science and Master of Education degrees from Xavier University (OH) where he later served as a vice-president and member of its faculty. In 1992, he received Xavier's Distinguished Alumnus Award. He has been a Fellow at Harvard University's Institute of Politics, the Aspen Institute, the Salzburg Seminar in Austria and the School of Advanced International Studies at Johns Hopkins University (British-American Project). His continuing education has included executive programs at the Massachusetts Institute of Technology and Harvard.

Among his awards are honorary doctoral degrees from several institutions of higher education in Ohio, including Ashland University, Cincinnati Technical College, Urbana University, Wilberforce University, and Wilmington College, as well as from Franklin Pierce College in New Hampshire. He is a recipient of the Veritas Award from Albertus Magnus College in New Haven, Connecticut.

In 1998, Mr. Blackwell delivered the Beckett Lecture on Religious Liberty at Oxford University.

He has also lectured at Harvard, the University of Newcastle in England, the Moscow State Institute for International Relations in Russia, and the International Academy of Public Administration in Paris. Several of his speeches and lectures have been published in "Vital Speeches of the Day."

His commentaries have been carried in major newspapers across the United States, including The Wall Street Journal and The New York Times, as well as all major newspapers in Ohio. He has been a frequent guest on network and broadcast news and public affairs programs, including The O'Reilly Factor, Crossfire, Inside Politics, The Jim Lehrer Newshour, and Hardball with Chris Matthews.

Mr. Blackwell is a lifelong resident of Cincinnati. He and his wife of thirty-four years, Rosa, have three children, Kimberly, Rahshann, and Kristin. In 1994, the Blackwells were honored as one of The National Council of Negro Women's Families of the Year, and, in 1996, Mr. and Mrs. Blackwell together received the Martin Luther King, Jr. Dreamkeeper Award.

Auditor of State

Betty Montgomery
Office of Auditor of State
88 East Broad Street
Post Office Box 1140
Columbus, OH 43216-1140
Public Inquiries: 800-282-0370
Media Inquiries: 614-644-1111

The auditor of state is Ohio's chief accounting officer, responsible for auditing the financial records of political subdivisions of the state (cities and villages, schools and universities, counties and townships), as well as the many departments, agencies, and commissions of state government. The auditor also maintains an accurate cash accounting of expenditures and balances in each specific fund established by appropriation enactments of the General Assembly.

Additional duties include writing more than 11 million warrants (similar to checks) annually for such things as the state payroll, Aid to Families with Dependent Children recipients, and payments to the state's suppliers of goods and services. The auditor's office also makes monthly distributions of state revenues to Ohio cities, villages, counties, townships, school districts, libraries, and state supported institutions of higher education. Funds issued by the Auditor's office on a monthly basis constitute a major share of the financial needs of local governmental units—money to pay the costs of educating Ohio's youth; to construct, repair and maintain local roadways; and to pay civil servants responsible for maintaining the public health, welfare, and safety. The Auditor's office also maintains the inventory and deed records of state-owned real property.

The Office of Auditor of State traces its origins to the Northwest Territory, before Ohio was state. Its

responsibilities have continually increased from its inception in 1797, when the legislature of the Territory established the position of Auditor of Public Accounts, to assure the "legality and propriety" of territorial accounts. The Auditor was made an elective officer, serving a four-year term by vote of the people, under the current Constitution.

Biography

Betty Montgomery's entire career has focused on protecting Ohio's most vulnerable citizens. She has prosecuted criminals, helped victims, protected taxpayers, reshaped Ohio law, and continues to provide professional services to local government agencies as Ohio's first woman Auditor of State. Sworn in as Ohio's 30th State Auditor in January 2003, she has also served the public as a criminal prosecutor, state senator, and Ohio's first woman Attorney General. Auditor Montgomery is dedicated to meeting the commitments she has made to the people of Ohio — to serve as a watchdog of public funds by aggressively rooting out fraud and waste of public dollars and to provide taxpayers with the highest level of professionalism, service, and accountability.

Auditor of State Montgomery is a graduate of Bowling Green State University (1970) and the University of Toledo College of Law (1976). She began her career as a criminal clerk for the Lucas County Common Pleas Court. In 1977, she became assistant prosecuting attorney in Wood County. Later she became Perrysburg city prosecutor where she served until she was elected to serve as the Wood County prosecuting attorney. During her eight years as prosecutor she increased the felony conviction rate in her office by 250 percent.

The people of the 2nd Ohio Senate District (northwest Ohio) elected Montgomery to the Ohio Senate in 1988. She served as chair of the Criminal Justice Subcommittee, and the vice chair of both the Senate Judiciary Committee and the Ohio Criminal Sentencing Commission. In the Senate, her work included drafting Ohio's first living will law, its first brownfields legislation, and its Victim's Rights Law. Much of her work centered on crime and law enforcement, as well as efforts to help protect consumers, children, and the elderly. As Ohio Attorney General, Montgomery fulfilled commitments to provide increased state support for local law enforcement and to upgrade the state's crime labs, joining only four percent of the nation's law enforcement agencies by earning accreditation for both the Ohio Peace OfficerTraining Academy and the Ohio Bureau of Criminal Identification and Investigation. Among other top priorities, Montgomery emphasized the protection of Ohio's most vulnerable citizens — senior citizens, youth, and crime victims. Nationally, Montgomery has been recognized for excellence in service and advocacy, including:

Receiving the Best Brief Award for briefs filed with the U.S. Supreme Court an unprecedented six years in a row from the National Association of Attorneys General (NAAG). No other state ever received this award for more than two consecutive years.

· Receiving four national awards for the innovative Web Check background check program that eliminates potentially damaging delays on checks of individuals who work with vulnerable citizens.

· Receiving the annual Consumer Agency Achievement Award from the National Association of Consumer Agency Administrators. This award recognized Montgomery's Consumer Protection Section as the most outstanding in the nation.

Attorney General

Jim Petro
Ohio Attorney General
State Office Tower 30 E. Broad Street 17th Floor
Columbus, OH 43215-3428
614-466-4320

The attorney general is the state's chief legal adviser. He serves as legal counsel to the governor, the other elected officials, the Ohio General Assembly, and all state departments, agencies, boards, and commissions. He is responsible for providing legal representation to these clients and initiating litigation on their behalf. The attorney general also issues legal opinions on questions submitted to him by elected state officials, either house of the legislature, heads of state departments and agencies, and all county prosecutors. The attorney general may initiate legal proceedings in certain areas of state law, including enforcement of state environmental protection statutes, consumer fraud laws and rules, antitrust laws, Medicaid fraud statutes, and patient abuse.

Under Ohio law, the attorney general may provide legal advice only to the elected statewide officials, the General Assembly, the departments and agencies of state government, and the 88 county prosecutors. However, in its day-to-day activities the office provides a wealth of information to the citizens of Ohio, as well as specific suggestions to citizens in dealing with problems in such areas as consumer transactions, crime prevention, the crime victim's compensation program, insurance, and other areas of public interest.

Biography

In his first term as Ohio's chief lawyer, Attorney General Jim Petro continues to dedicate his career to professionalism and fairness. He serves as legal counsel to the state of Ohio, the governor, other statewide officials, the Ohio General Assembly, and all state departments, agencies, boards and commissions. In addition to those duties, Petro issues formal legal opinions on questions of law submitted by elected officials and prosecutors, and provides investigative support through the Ohio Bureau of Criminal Investigation.

"The sparse content of the candidate is directly proportional to the meager discernment of the voter."

—John Baskin, elections, 1997

Petro manages an office of attorneys and support professionals who handle approximately 35,000 active legal cases at a time, encompassing issues ranging from consumer fraud and criminal justice to environmental enforcement and constitutional challenges.

Before becoming Attorney General, he served for eight years as the Auditor of State, overseeing the financial health and legal compliance of nearly 5,000 units of Ohio government. During his tenure as Auditor of State, the office identified hundreds of millions in stolen, abused, or wasted tax dollars, and won wide praise for initiating new standards of government accountability.

Jim Petro has served Ohio in both the public and private sectors. His legal experience spans nearly 30 years as a practicing attorney, city law director and criminal prosecutor. He served eight years in the Ohio House of Representatives and four years as Cuyahoga County commissioner.

Jim resides in Columbus with his wife Nancy, president of a Columbus-based software company. Their daughter Cory is a graduate of Yale University and their son John graduated from Denison University. Both children are actively pursuing private sector careers.

Treasurer of State

Joseph T. Deters
Treasurer of State
9th Floor
30 East Broad Street
Columbus, Ohio 43266-0421

General Information	**614-466-2160**
FAX Machine	**614-644-7313**
	800-Line (TTY)
	800-228-1102
STAR Ohio 800 Line	**800-648-7827**
Electronic Funds Transfer	**877-338-6446**

The Constitution of Ohio provides that there shall be a state treasurer, elected by the people every four years. The treasurer's principal duty is to serve as the state's chief fiscal and investment officer, including the collection, protection, and investment of public funds. The treasurer receives and processes all payments to the state for taxes, fees, and licenses authorized by the Ohio General Assembly, with the exception of the State Income Tax, Horse Racing Wager Tax, Motor Transportation Tax, and Liquor Gallonage Tax, which are sent directly to the departments having the responsibility of processing and depositing them with the treasurer.

The treasurer maintains the various state accounts and processes payment of all state warrants for claims and expenses incurred in the operation of state government, and maintains custody of all funds of the Industrial Commission, the Bureau of Employment

Services, the Public Employees, State Teachers and School Employees Retirement Systems, the State Highway Patrol Pension Fund, the Police and Firemen's Pension and Disability Fund, and various other agency funds. The treasurer also safeguards securities purchased for the state for custodial accounts or deposited with the state by banks, trust companies, insurance companies, and other business organizations.

No taxes are levied by the state treasurer. The General Assembly is the sole taxing authority, and it enacts laws for payment of taxes, fees, licenses, and other revenues. Ohio's tax laws are administered and enforced by the Department of Taxation.

Biography

Joseph T. Deters was elected Ohio's 44th State Treasurer on November 3, 1998 and took office on January 11, 1999. He assumed duties as Treasurer with a commitment to put the safety of Ohio's financial assets above all other priorities.

As Treasurer, Joe Deters manages a staff of more than 160, safeguards some $170 billion in state funds, and serves as custodian for the accounts of Ohio's five public employee retirement systems and the state's workers' compensation account. He is also responsible for managing approximately $17 billion in state investments. In September 2000, he implemented a revised investment policy that placed unprecedented safeguards over Treasury operations and helped achieve an all-time record of $400 million in investment earnings in Fiscal Year 2001.

Deters is also committed to making the Ohio Treasurer of State's office a national model for increased efficiency through the use of the latest technology and modern banking practices. In October 1999, he launched BidOhio, the nation's first-ever competitive Internet auction for interim funds held by a state treasury. To date, BidOhio has generated more than $29 million in interest earnings, won four national awards for technological innovation, and served as the model for similar programs in several other states.

In order to share the Treasury's financial expertise with the people of Ohio, Treasurer Deters created "Women & Money"—a free financial planning workshop designed to help women take more control over their financial future. It served 1,600 participants in five cities during its inaugural year in 2000, and another 2,500 participants in six cities in 2001. In addition, *CommonSense*—the Treasury's free, monthly online financial newsletter—is now read every month by more than 30,000 Ohioans.

Joe Deters began his career in public service in 1982 as an Assistant Hamilton County Prosecutor. He was subsequently elected to the positions of Hamilton County Clerk of Courts in 1988 and Hamilton County Prosecutor in 1992. Treasurer Deters currently serves as a trustee for the University of Cincinnati. He is a graduate of the University of Cincinnati and the University of Cincinnati College of Law, which awarded him its Longworth Alumni Achievement Award for 1997. He and his wife, Missy, are the parents of three children.

A GOOD MAN'S WORTH

Annual salaries of Ohio's elected officials

Governor	$130,292	Secretary of State	$97,501
Lieutenant Governor	$68,295	Auditor of State	$97,501
Attorney General	$97,501	Treasurer of State	$97,501

Annual salaries of the Governor's staff members

Chief of Staff	$118,060.80
Chief Legal Counsel	$109,013.80
Director of Policy & Legislative Initiatives	$104,041.60
Communications Director	$100,006.40
Deputy Chief Counsel	$87,817.60
Press Secretary	$80,017.60
Special Assistant for Boards & Commisions	$74,006.40
Executive Assistant to the Governor	$59,592.00

Annual Salaries of the Governor's Cabinet Members

Adjutant General	$101,670.40
Department of Administrative Services	$117,072.20
Department of Aging	$98,685.20
Department of Agriculture	$103,688.00
Department of Alcohol and Drug Addiction Services	$98,862.40
Office of Budget and Management	$110,344.00
Department of Commerce (+Lt. Governor)	$120,016.00
Office of Criminal Justice Services	$81,910.40
Department of Development	$117,707.20
Environmental Protection Agency	$107,078.40
Department of Health	$144,081.60
Department of Job & Family Services	$125,008.00
Department of Health	$144,081.60
Department of Insurance	$120,016.00
Department of Mental Health	$144,081.60
Department of Mental Retardation and Developmental Disabilities	$117,707.20
Department of Natural Resources	$120,057.60
Department of Public Safety	$119,995.20
Ohio Lottery Commission	$101,982.40
Department of Rehabilitation and Correction	$120,057.60
Department of Taxation	$113,547.20
Department of Transportation	$116,459.20
Department of Workers' Compensation	$150,696.00
Department of Youth Services	$108,472.00

Adjutant General's Department
Major General John H. Smith
2825 West Dublin Granville Road
Columbus, Ohio 43235
614-336-7000
E-mail: pao@oh.ngb.army.mil
Website: www.ohionationalguard.com

Major General John H. Smith is responsible for the operation of the Adjutant General's Department and the military preparedness of the Ohio Militia. The organized militia consists of the Ohio Army National Guard, Ohio Air National Guard, Ohio Military Reserve and Ohio Naval Militia, totaling more than 18,000 personnel. He supervises four flag officer heads of these components and one deputy director in the day-to-day operation and management of the fiscal, personnel, equipment and real property resources of these military organizations and state agencies.

Department of Administrative Services
Director C. Scott Johnson
30 East Broad Street, 40th Floor
Columbus, Ohio 43215-3414
614-644-8151
614-466-6511 fax
E-mail: laurie.mitchell@das.state.oh.us
Website: state.oh.us/das

C. Scott Johnson became the director of the Ohio Department of Administrative Services (DAS) on June 4, 1999. DAS was established in 1973 from the former departments of Public Works and State Personnel as well as parts of the former department of Finance and Civil Service Commission. DAS centralizes many services that could be managed more efficiently and economically under one department. DAS offers services to state agencies, colleges and universities and local governments, as well as services for businesses and the general public.

Department of Aging
Director Joan Lawrence
50 West Broad Street, 9th Floor
Columbus, Ohio 43215-3363
614-466-5500
614-466-5741 fax
E-mail: odamail@age.state.oh.us
Website: www.goldenbuckeye.com

The Ohio Department of Aging serves and represents nearly 2 million Ohioans age 60 and older. The Department's role is to advocate for the needs of all older citizens. The emphasis is on improving the quality of life for older Ohioans, helping senior citizens live active, healthy and independent lives, and promoting positive attitudes toward aging and older people.

Department of Agriculture
Director Fred Dailey
8995 East Main Street
Reynoldsburg, Ohio 43058
614-728-6200
614-466-6124 fax
E-mail: agri@odant.agri.state.oh.us
Website: www.state.oh.us/agr

The mission of the Ohio Department of Agriculture is to provide regulatory protection to producers, agribusinesses and the consuming public; to promote Ohio agricultural products in domestic and international markets; and to educate the citizens of Ohio about our agricultural industry.

Department of Alcohol & Drug Addiction Services
Director Luceille Fleming
280 North High Street, 12th Floor
Columbus, Ohio 43215-2537
614-466-3445
614-752-8645 fax
E-mail: general@ada.state.oh.us
Website: www.odadas.state.oh.us

The mission of the Ohio Department of Alcohol and Drug Addiction Services is to promote, assist in developing and coordinate or conduct programs of education and research for the prevention of alcohol and drug addiction. The Department also has programs for the treatment, including intervention, of alcoholics and persons who abuse drugs. Programs established by the Department include abstinence-based prevention and treatment programs.

Office of Budget and Management
Director Tom Johnson
30 East Broad Street, 34th Floor
Columbus, Ohio 43215-2537
614-466-4034
614-466-3813 fax
E-mail: obm@obm.state.oh.us
Website: www.state.oh.us/obm

The primary mission of the Office of Budget and Management (OBM) is to provide fiscal accounting and budgeting services to state government. These services include the coordination, development, and monitoring of agency operating and capital budgets. OBM also reviews, processes and reports on financial transactions made by state agencies. OBM assists the Governor and other state agencies by providing policy and management support relative to the state's fiscal activities.

Department of Commerce:
Director and Lieutenant Governor
Jennette Bradley
77 South High Street, 23rd Floor
Columbus, Ohio 43215-0544
614-466-3636
E-mail: webadmin@com.state.oh.us
Website: www.com.state.oh.us/ODOC

In January 2003, Lt. Governor Bradley was appointed Director of the Ohio Department of Commerce by Governor Bob Taft and also serves as the Governor's liaison to county and local governments, to small businesses and as policy advisor for urban initiatives, community development and housing programs. As Director of Commerce, Bradley oversees the state's chief regulatory agency administering nine divisions which include Financial Institutions, Industrial Compliance, Labor and Worker Safety, Liquor Control, Real Estate and Professional Licensing, Securities, State Fire Marshal and Unclaimed Funds and Administration.

Office of Criminal Justice Services
Director Domingo Herraiz
400 East Town Street
Suite 300
Columbus, Ohio 43215
614-466-7782
614-466-0308 fax
Website: www.ocjs.state.oh.us

The Office of Criminal Justice Services comprises several sections: Administration, Fiscal Services, Grants Management, Information Systems, Policy and Research. The agency remains responsible for administering federal and state grant programs. However, it also coordinates comprehensive criminal and juvenile justice plans, addresses criminal and juvenile justice policy issues, recommends strategies and evaluates the impact of initiatives.

Department of Development
Director Bruce Johnson
77 South High Street
Box 1001
Columbus, Ohio 43215-6130
800-848-1300
E-mail: jbuchanan@odod.state.oh.us
Website: www.odod.state.oh.us

Made up of seven divisions, the Ohio Department of Development administers both short and long-term economic development programs to assist in the retention and expansion of job opportunities in Ohio.

Environmental Protection Agency
Director Christopher Jones
122 South Front Street
Columbus, Ohio 43215
614-644-3020
614-644-2329 fax
E-mail: info-request@www.epa.state.oh.us
Website: www.epa.state.oh.us

The Ohio Environmental Protection Agency (Ohio EPA) was created on October 23, 1972. It combined under a single agency the functions, which previously had been scattered throughout a number of state departments. Ohio EPA has authority to implement laws and regulations regarding air and water quality standards; solid, hazardous and infectious waste disposal standards; water quality planning, supervision of sewage treatment and public drinking water supplies; and cleanup of unregulated hazardous waste sites.

Department of Health
Director J. Nick Baird, M.D.
246 North High Street
Columbus, Ohio 43216-0118
614-466-3543
Website: www.odh.state.oh.us

The Ohio Department of Health strives to protect and improve the health of all Ohioans, through partnerships with 143 local health departments and the members of our medical and health communities. The Department works jointly with them to prevent disease, injury and premature death, support healthy lifestyles and assure the quality of health care services.

Department of Insurance
Director Ann Womer Benjamin
2100 Stella Court
Columbus, Ohio 43215
614-644-2658
800-686-4526
614-644-3743 fax
Website: www.ins.state.oh.us

The mission of the Ohio Department of Insurance is to protect the interests of the public through the consistent and fair application of Ohio's insurance laws and regulations, and to inform and educate the public on insurance issues.

Department of Job & Family Services
Director Tom Hayes
30 East Broad Street, 32 Floor
Columbus, Ohio 43215-3414
614-466-6282
614-466-2185 fax
Website: www.state.oh.us/odjfs

The Ohio Department of Job and Family Services was formed by the merger of the Department of Human Services and the Bureau of Employment Services. It develops and oversees programs that provide health care, employment and economic assistance, child support, and services to families and children. The programs and services offered are designed to help Ohioans be healthy and safe, while gaining and maintaining independence, and they are delivered at the local level in a manner that recognizes and preserves individual rights, responsibilities and dignity.

Lottery Commission
Director Dennis G. Kennedy
615 West Superior Avenue
Cleveland, Ohio 44102
216-787-3200
216-787-3313 fax
Website: www.ohiolottery.com

The Ohio Lottery Commission's mission is to adhere to all legal and ethical standards of the State of Ohio and to protect the integrity of the Ohio Lottery with its employees, sales retailers and, most importantly, its players. The Ohio Lottery strives to honor and maintain the annual commitment to the Lottery Profits for Education Fund and continues to offer to its players only games that are fair and equitable. The lottery also seeks to maximize the excess of revenues over expenses, judges all expenditures solely on the basis of their contribution to producing profits for the agency, and makes every effort to evaluate and improve operational efficiency. The Ohio Lottery's goal is to be always worthy of the public's trust and respect.

Department of Mental Health
Director Mike Hogan
30 East Broad Street, 8th Floor
Columbus, Ohio 43215-3430
E-mail: swank@mhmail.mh.state.oh.us
Website: www.mh.state.oh.us

The mission of the Ohio Department of Mental Health is to ensure that quality mental health care is available to all Ohioans — particularly individuals with severe mental illness — in their communities. Quality mental health services support consumer choice, build on natural supports, and embrace cultural diversity and clinical competence.

Department of Mental Retardation &
Developmental Disabilities
Director Kenneth W. Ritchey
1810 Sullivent Avenue
Columbus, Ohio 43223-1239
614-466-5214
614-466-3141 fax
Website: odmrdd.state.oh.us/

The Ohio Department of Mental Retardation & Developmental Disabilities' (MR/DD) role in the service delivery system is threefold. First, the Department distributes resources and funding to local county boards of MR/DD, which they administer at the local level to provide services to infants, children and adults with mental retardation and developmental disabilities. Second, it regulates county boards of MR/DD in order to ensure quality service to its consumers, best business practice, and maintains the confidence of Ohio´s taxpayers and citizens. Third, the Department provides technical assistance to county boards of MR/DD, in order for them to better serve individuals with MR/DD and their families.

Department of Natural Resources
Director Samuel Speck
Fountain Square
Columbus, Ohio 43224
614-265-6565
614-261-9601 fax
E-mail: dnrmail@dnr.state.oh.us
Website: www.dnr.state.oh.us

A department of incredible diversity, ODNR owns and manages more than 470,000 acres of land including 73 state parks, 20 state forests, 120 state nature preserves and 80 wildlife areas. The department also has jurisdiction over more than 120,000 acres of inland waters; 7,000 miles of streams; 481 miles of Ohio River; and 2.25 million acres of Lake Erie. In addition, ODNR licenses all hunting, fishing and watercraft in the state, and the Department is responsible for overseeing and permitting all mineral extraction, monitoring dam safety, managing water resources, coordinating the activity of Ohio's 88 county soil and water conservation districts, mapping the state's major geologic structures and mineral resources, and promoting recycling and litter prevention through grant programs in local communities.

Department of Public Safety
Director Kenneth Morckel
1970 West Broad Street
Columbus, Ohio 43223
614-466-2550
614-466-0433 fax
Website: www.state.oh.us/odps/default.htm

The Department of Public Safety includes the Bureau of Motor Vehicles, the State Highway Patrol, Emergency Medical Services and the Emergency Management Agency. Prior to being named Public Safety Director, Morckel served as the Superintendent of the Ohio State Highway Patrol from June 30, 2000, through January 10, 2003. While Patrol superintendent, he chaired the law enforcement sub-committee on the State of Ohio Security Task Force (SOSTF). Governor Taft formed the SOSTF after the September 11, 2001 attacks to develop a coordinated, comprehensive state strategy to address security issues.

Department of Rehabilitation and Correction
Director Reginald Wilkinson
1050 Freeway Drive North
Columbus, Ohio 43229
614-752-1159
614-752-1111 fax
E-mail: linda.diroll@odrc.state.oh.us
Website: www.drc.state.oh.us

The Ohio Department of Rehabilitation and Correction protects and supports Ohioans by ensuring that adult, felony offenders are effectively supervised in environments that are safe, humane and appropriately secure. In partnership with communities, the Department will promote citizen safety and victim reparation. Through rehabilitative and restorative programming, the Department seeks to instill in the offenders an improved sense of responsibility and the capacity to become law-abiding members of society.

Department of Taxation
Tax Commissioner Thomas M. Zaino
30 East Broad Street
Columbus, Ohio 43215
614-466-2166
614-644-6401 fax
Website: www.state.oh.us/tax

The Ohio Department of Taxation strives to provide quality service to Ohio taxpayers by helping them comply with their tax responsibilities and by fairly applying the tax law.

Department of Transportation
Director Gordon Proctor
1980 West Broad Street
Columbus, Ohio 43223
614-466-7170
614-644-8662 fax
Website: www.dot.state.oh.us

As director of the Ohio Department of Transportation (ODOT), Director Proctor oversees Ohio's $2.1 billion annual transportation program. The department is responsible for designing, building and maintaining Ohio's nearly 20,000 miles of state, U.S. and interstate highways. Ohio has the second largest inventory of bridges, the fourth largest interstate highway system and the tenth largest highway system in the nation. ODOT also helps coordinate and develop Ohio's public transportation and aviation programs. These include 56 public transit systems and nearly 200 public airports.

Bureau of Workers' Compensation
Administrator James Conrad
30 West Spring Street
Columbus, Ohio 43215-2256
800-644-6292
877-520-6446 fax
Website: www.ohiobwc.com

Since 1913 the Ohio Bureau of Workers' Compensation (BWC) has benefited employers and employees by providing medical and compensation benefits for work-related injuries, diseases and deaths. BWC has a central office in Columbus and 21 customer service offices located statewide. BWC directly provides insurance to about two-thirds of Ohio's workforce. The remaining workers receive coverage through a self-insurance program for large and financially stable employers who meet strict qualifications set by BWC. At $17.7 billion, Ohio's workers' compensation system has the largest exclusive state fund in the nation and is the second largest underwriter of workers' compensation insurance in the country.

Department of Youth Services
Director Geno Natalucci-Persichetti
51 North High Street
Columbus, Ohio 43215
614-466-4314
614-752-9859 fax
E-mail: goodmand@mail.dys.state.oh.us
Website: www.state.oh.us/dys/

The mission of the Ohio Department of Youth Services is to ensure public safety by providing and supporting a range of effective and cost effective services that hold youth accountable for their actions and gives them the skills and competencies they need to live crime free.

Republicans are the party that says government doesn't work, and then they get elected and prove it.

—P.J. O'Rourke

"If I were governor I would build a race track around the statehouse. What the people want is amusement."

—*failed gubernatorial candidate Col. John W. Bargar of Waverly, 1905*

Name	Party*	County of Residence	Name	Party*	County of Residence
Edward Tiffin 1803-1807	R	Ross	*Mordecai Bartley* 1844-1846	Whig	Richland
Thomas Kirker 1807-1808**	R	Adams	*William Bebb* 1846-1848	Whig	Butler
Samuel Huntington 1808-1810	R	Trumbull	*Seabury Ford* 1848-1850	Whig	Geauga
Return J. Meigs, Jr. 1810-1814	R	Washington	*Reuben Wood* 1850-1853	D	Cuyahoga
Othneil Looker 1814**	R	Hamilton	*William Medill* 1853-1856	D	Fairfield
Thomas Worthington 1814-1818	R	Ross	*Salmon P. Chase* 1856-1860	R	Hamilton
Ethan Allen Brown 1818-1822	R	Hamilton	*William Dennison, Jr.* 1860-1862	R	Franklin
Allen Trimble 1822**	Fed.	Highland	*David Tod* 1862-1864	R	Mahoning
Jeremiah Morrow 1822-1826	R	Warren	*John Brough* 1864-1865	R	Cuyahoga
Allen Trimble 1826-1830	R	Highland	*Charles Anderson* 1865-1866	R	Montgomery
Duncan MacArthur 1830-1832	NR	Ross	*Jacob Dolson Cox* 1866-1868	R	Hamilton
Robert Lucas 1832-1836	D	Pike	*Rutherford B. Hayes* 1868-1872	R	Hamilton
Joseph Vance 1836-1838	Whig	Champaign	*Edward F. Noyes* 1872-1874	R	Hamilton
Wilson Shannon 1838-1840	D	Belmont	*William Allen* 1874-1876	D	Ross
Thomas Corwin 1840-1842	Whig	Warren	*Rutherford B. Hayes* 1876-1877	R	Sandusky
Wilson Shannon 1842-1844	D	Belmont	*Thomas L. Young* 1877-1878	R	Hamilton
Thomas Bartley 1844**	D	Richland	*Richard M. Bishop* 1878-1880	D	Hamilton

** D denotes Democratic Party*
R denotes Republican Party
*** acting*

Name	Party*	County of Residence	Name	Party*	County of Residence
Charles Foster 1880-1884	R	Seneca	George White 1931-1935	D	Washington
George Hoadley 1884-1886	D	Hamilton	Martin L. Davey 1935-1939	D	Portage
Joseph Foraker 1886-1890	R	Hamilton	John W. Bricker 1939-1945	R	Franklin
James E. Campbell 1890-1892	D	Butler	Frank J. Lausche 1945-1947	D	Cuyahoga
William McKinley 1892-1896	R	Stark	Thomas J. Herbert 1947-1949	R	Cuyahoga
Asa S. Bushnell 1896-1900	R	Clark	Frank J. Lausche 1949-1957	D	Cuyahoga
George K. Nash 1900-1904	R	Medina	John W. Brown 1957**	R	Medina
Myron T. Herrick 1904-1906	R	Lorain	C. William O'Neill 1957-1959	R	Washington
John M. Pattison 1906—died	D	Clermont	Michael V. DiSalle 1959-1963	D	Lucas
Andrew L. Harris 1906-1909	R	Preble	James A. Rhodes 1963-1971	R	Franklin
Judson Harmon 1909-1913	D	Hamilton	John J. Gilligan 1971-1974	D	Hamilton
James M. Cox 1913-1915	D	Montgomery	James A. Rhodes 1974-1983	R	Franklin
Frank B. Willis 1915-1917	R	Delaware	Richard F. Celeste 1983-1991	D	Cuyahoga
James M. Cox 1917-1921	D	Montgomery	George Voinovich 1991-1998	R	Cuyahoga
Harry L. Davis 1921-1923	R	Cuyahoga	Nancy P. Hollister 1998-1999	R	Washington
Alvin V. Donahey 1923-1929	D	Tuscarawas	Bob Taft 1999-	R	Hamilton
Myers Y. Cooper 1929-1931	R	Hamilton			

The only two jobs where you start on the top are gravedigging and governor.

—*Cleveland Plain Dealer*

Bless them all, the long and the short and the tall governors, men whose names live on very quietly in Ohio history

The next time you're at a cocktail party or on a long airplane ride, try engaging your fellows in a discussion of "Ohio governors of the twentieth century." You might, however, want to block the exit first. Most Ohioans would be pressed to name, let alone discuss, even the last half dozen governors. It's not that our governors aren't colorful; it's just that gubernatorial coloring fades rapidly in the public mind. "Out of office, out of mind" could be the official slogan of Ohio's ex-chief executives. The trouble, says history professor George Knepper, author of the definitive *Ohio and Its People*, is that our governors reflect Ohio's basic political equation—stalemate. Ohio is a state of great diversity, Knepper says, where opposing factions cancel each other out, leading to a dull homeostasis. Urban interests block rural interests. Business checks labor. Big municipalities act like feuding city-states with little in common beyond license plates. In such a land, the high road to the governor's mansion has always been the middle of the road. Which is how Ohioans like their governors. As Knepper puts it in his book *Ohio Politics*, "Ohio entered the 20th century as a leader in nearly every important field of endeavor except, perhaps, political reform." Says Knepper, "Anyone with reform proclivities makes Ohioans nervous. That's not Ohio's style."

In this century, voters never spared the hook for a conservative governor who proved to be too conservative or for a reformer who waxed too reform-minded. Returned to their senses, voters tossed the bum out and steered the ship of state back into the center rut. The result is a long line of colorful Ohio governors who talked loudly and carried little sticks.

Still, with Buckeyes about to elect (or re-elect) yet another governor, a brush-up of the gubernatorial portrait gallery is in order. Here we throw light on men (and they were all men) whose names were once Ohio household words, and now they couldn't cash a check in a grocery store (assuming they were still alive) without photo I.D. *Sic transit gloria mundi.*

George K. Nash, 1900-04, Republican, Medina County

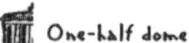 One-half dome

Forget the date. Nash was really the last of the 19th century, hand-picked and hand-packed governors selected by Ohio's legendary and ruthless political bosses.

At his best:
Property tax reform always a hit with Ohio voters. Supported a constitutional amendment giving the governor veto power.

At his worst:
Notorious for intervening in city governments to

spite his political opponents. Called out the Guard to stop a Cincinnati prize fight after Mayor Julius Fleischmann issued a license for the event. Seized control of the Toledo police force and appointed his own board.

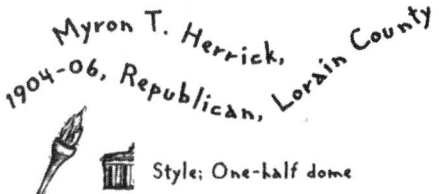

Myron T. Herrick, 1904-06, Republican, Lorain County

Style; One-half dome

A banker, he was allegedly born in a log cabin, an origin no true Republican would care to refute.

At his best: Reportedly a man of great charm and noticeable honesty.

At his worst: Tried the usual "business as usual" doctrine until social turmoil forced his hand. Pushed anti-saloon legislation that pleased neither the wets nor the drys. Vetoed a race track gambling bill that pleased neither the shearers nor the sheep. Lost bid for re-election.

John M. Pattison, 1906, Democrat, Clermont County

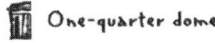 One-quarter dome

A lawyer in the insurance business, he proved a poor life risk.

At his best: Promised long-delayed action on temperance and urban home rule.

At his worst: Died in office after only five months, leaving promises unmet.

Andrew L. Harris, 1906-09, Republican, Preble County

Style; Two and a half domes

A lawyer and the last governor who served in the Civil War. His nickname was "The Farmer Statesman." They don't make nicknames like that anymore.

At his best: Startled everyone by bringing in real reforms. Passed pure food and drug legislation, established a bureau of vital statistics, and limited political contributions by big business.

At his worst: Ohio's version of Gerald Ford, he governed a full three years because of a constitutional change in the timing of elections without ever being elected.

Judson Harmon, 1909-13, Democrat, Hamilton County

Two and a half domes

A Cincinnati lawyer who saw himself above politics and political prudence.

At his best: Won election to second term by beating Warren G. Harding. Exposed corruption in state departments, centralized administration of state prisons and public utilities and passed Ohio's first employers' injury liability law, a forerunner of workers' compensation.

At his worst: Addressed Ohio's 1912 constitutional convention and lambasted reform proposals being pushed by his own party, not a wise move for a Democrat with presidential aspirations.

Politically correct

A woman turned up at the Statehouse with a 16-year-old daughter she claimed was fathered by Governor Herrick, who hired Pinkerton detectives to determine her "full history." Reasonable onlookers accepted innocence as the verdict after Governor Herrick pointed out that the woman was "decidedly homely."

James M. Cox, 1913-15, 1917-21, Democrat, Montgomery County

Style: Three domes

Dayton newspaper publisher Cox was the Democratic half of the All-Ohio Presidential Election of 1920. Republican Harding won.

At his best: Mapped out 56-point reform program in first address to legislature. Ninety days later, almost every point was successfully written into law.

At his worst: Became irrationally anti-German during World War I. Forbade German language instruction in primary schools and required teachers to take loyalty oaths. "People thought California was bad in the 1950s," Knepper observes, "but Ohio beat them to it."

Harry L. Davis, 1921-23, Republican, Cuyahoga County

One dome

A one-time Cleveland steel worker who became a true-blue Republican.

At his best: Effortlessly rode Warren G. Harding's presidential coattails into office. Nonetheless established state's first game reserve and first program to aid handicapped children.

At his worst: High-handed. Overly fond of executive actions and emergency legislation. Dismissed the legislature in 1921 to forestall an investigation of state contracts. Twisted the purpose of "emergency" legislation to get bill bringing all state departments under his direct control. Undercut opposition and bypassed voters.

Frank B. Willis, 1915-17, Republican, Delaware County

One-half dome

A college professor with a rich, booming voice.

At his best: Politically astute. Sensed that Ohio voters had once again lost their stomach for reform after Governor Cox, Part I. Reorganized and "retrenched" state government.

At his worst: Politically obtuse. Retrenched too far. Ohio's appetite for reform returned. Followed by Governor Cox, Part II.

A. Victor Donahey, 1923-29, Democrat, Tuscarawas County

Two domes

A one-time printer, he was alternately nicknamed "Honest Vic" and "Veto Vic."

At his best: A Democrat who won three successive terms while Ohio and nation went ardently Republican. More Republican than the Republicans on money matters, a route direct to the hearts

of Ohio voters. Progressive on social issues. Stopped a Ku Klux Klan bill requiring Bible reading in public schools. Pardoned 2,000 prohibition offenders because he believed the dry laws were unfair to the poor.

At his worst: Constantly at war with the Republican legislature. Vetoed 151 bills and $10 million in appropriations, including all legislation that raised taxes.

Myers Y. Cooper, 1929-31, Republican Hamilton County

🏛 One-half dome

A Licking County native but a well-heeled Cincinnati real estate developer.

At his best: Showed good timing. First (and last) race for public office was the governorship in 1928, a year Republicans swept every state office, save 11 House seats.

At his worst: Showed bad timing. Walked head-first into the Great Depression.

George White, 1931-35, Democrat, Washington County

 🏛 Style; One-half dome

An oil man who made his money around Marietta, White was a New York native and Ohio's only modern governor born outside the Great Buckeye State.

At his best: Proclaimed that government must live within its means even during a depression. Raised income for education and relief services by instituting first state sales tax.

At his worst: Early in administration, said that relief for the unemployed and destitute was a local problem. Cut state services and legislative salaries in worst of Depression.

Harry L. Davis, 1921-23, Republican Cuyahoga County

🏛 One dome

A somewhat-eccentric tree surgeon from Kent, Davey was once described as the "Joe Palooka of Governors."

At his best: Repealed the sales tax on take-out food.

At his worst: Had a reputation as a brawler. "His enemies hated his guts," explains George Knepper, "but even his friends despaired because he fought everybody." As commander-in-chief, he used the Ohio Guard to evict a troublesome penitentiary warden and to fund a limousine for himself, denied by the legislature, as a military necessity. Lurid headlines depicted him as the "grafting" tree surgeon, suspected of collusive bidding practices on state contracts, but never implicated personally.

The political event of 1920 was the notorious Baked-Potato Row between a court of appeals judge named Vickery and Ohio auditor Vic Donahey. The judge said food and lodging in Akron was $5 a day, including a 30-cent baked potato. Donahey turned down the expense account and said the potato was worth 10 cents. Donahey scored politically, was called "the watchdog of the Treasury," and went on to be elected governor, his career launched in part by a vegetable.

Style; Three domes

In 1944, Governor Bricker was nominated as vice president on the Presidential ticket with Thomas Dewey. He was called "a darling of the paleolithic right," and author John Gunther described him as "intellectually...like interstellar space —a vast vacuum occasionally crossed by homeless, wandering clichés." Still, Bricker was the last Ohioan chosen for national office by a major party.

John W. Bricker, 1939-45, Republican, Franklin County

Style; One dome

A farmer's boy from Mt. Sterling who became a Columbus lawyer and almost the GOP standard bearer in 1944.

At his best: After 1938 election, fired 2,000 state workers, immediately winning the hearts of Ohio voters. Always looked "presidential." Moved out of the governor's mansion with 92 suits; his successor moved in with one suit and two pairs of shoes.

At his worst: Took credit for state's economic recovery while riding wave of wartime prosperity.

The child of Slovenian immigrants, Lausche made good in Cleveland as a lawyer and crime fighter; he was nicknamed the "George Washington of Nationality Politics," "Fearless Frank" (for taking on organized crime), and the "Lincoln of Ohio" (for his rumpled look and rugged honesty).

At his best: His enormous personal popularity, independence of thought and fiscal conservatism cut across party lines. Served a record five terms until Republicans pushed constitutional amendment limiting governors to two consecutive, four-year terms (eventually shooting James Rhodes in the foot). Built Ohio Turnpike.

At his worst: Short-sighted penny-pinching hampered badly needed improvements in state services.

Thomas J. Herbert, 1947-49, Republican, Cuyahoga County

One-half dome

A Cleveland attorney and World War I flying ace.

At his best: Known mainly as an energetic campaigner with a hearty appetite for ice cream and corn-on-the-cob.

At his worst: Tried to "red-bait" Lausche by impugning his opponent's Slovenian roots and American loyalty. Not a good strategy. Ohioans elected Lausche again two years later.

John W. Brown, 11 days in 1957, Republican, Medina County

Style: One-quarter dome

Ohio's professional lieutenant governor, he stood by through four terms in all. In 1957, he saw his chance and took it.

At his best: Dazzled the state with its shortest and most bizarre administration ever. When Governor Lausche resigned on January 3, 1957 to get a seniority jump into the U.S. Senate, the newly elected governor William O'Neill could not legally be sworn in until January 14. Lieutenant Governor Brown seized the helm. Moved all his furniture into the Governor's mansion and portraits of Republican governors into Lausche's previously Democratically-decorated Statehouse office. Called a joint session of the General Assembly to deliver a State of the State address, insisted on a full governor's salary, and commuted the sentences of five convicted murders (denying the appeal, however, of Dr. Sam Sheppard).

At his worst: Brown's five bulging boxes of gubernatorial papers deposited at the Ohio Historical Society after his 11-day term include a letter to Vice President Richard Nixon asking for a federal job. He didn't get one.

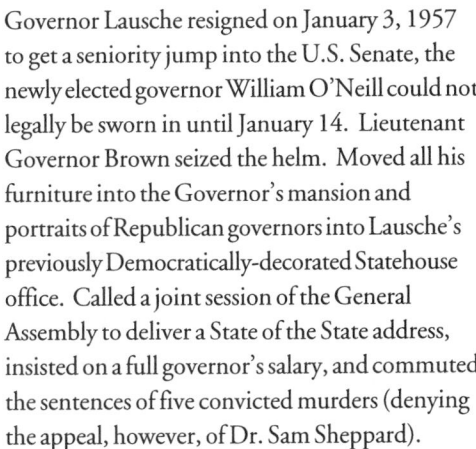

C. William O'Neill, 1957-59, Republican, Washington County

 One dome

At 5'4", the Marietta attorney ushered in era of short governors and ushered out the old short two-year governor's term. After O'Neill, it was four long years.

At his best: Probably the man who understood Ohio government best, having by the end of his career held top positions in all three branches. As governor, balanced budget and kept "no new taxes" pledge.

At his worst: A waffler who proposed a salary hike for state administrators, secured legislative approval and then rescinded it, all within four months. A maker of enemies whose support for "right-to-work" legislation effectively organized the up-until-then thoroughly disorganized union vote. Wrecked his own re-election. Fired-up unions may have cost John Bricker his U.S. Senate seat as well.

Michael V. DiSalle, 1959-63, Democrat, Lucas County

One and a half domes

The first Toledoan governor, the 5'5" DiSalle continued the non-partisan gubernatorial short line. His nickname, "Tax Hike Mike," signaled a short career as Ohio governor.

At his best: Faced up to the state's neglected social obligations that had been resolutely ignored by two bipartisan decades of penny-pinching governors. Instituted tax increases of nearly $500 million.

At his worst: Raised taxes, opposed capital punishment and shamed voters for their neglect of children and the aged—a politically lethal threesome in Ohio.

John Brown didn't know the meaning of the word "caretaker" when he approached his 11 days in office. He addressed the legislature on the need for school funds and soil conservation and warned them about urban sprawl before urban sprawl was an issue. He mediated a Portsmouth telephone strike and gave raises to state employees. All in all, he seemed to have done more in two weeks than many governors did in an entire term.

James A. Rhodes, 1963-71, 1975-83, Republican, Franklin County

Style; One and a half domes

A professional politician without college or law degree who always stressed his humble Jackson County beginnings, Rhodes raised the stature of the office to 6' even. His nicknames included "Dusty" (inevitable) and "Huckster" (unkind).

At his best: A shameless booster of all things Ohio. Talked poor but spent big on highways, colleges and airports.

At his worst: A knack for malapropisms ("No man is an Ireland"), a penchant for repeating himself (veteran reporters can still recite verbatim his "Gospel of Jobs") and a weakness for cheese and bologna sandwiches. Ran out of ideas and steam in later terms as state's heavy industrial base declined.

> "If a politician doesn't throw dead cats, he doesn't get elected."
>
> —John Gilligan

John J. Gilligan, 1971-75, Democrat, Hamilton County

Style; One dome

A 6'1" Cincinnati college professor descended from a family of undertakers.

At his best: A quick-witted, intellectual who pushed genuinely progressive social-welfare reforms.

At his worst: An arrogant intellectual who proved that you don't have to be stupid to put your foot in your mouth. Appeared at state fair just after instituting Ohio's first income tax.

Asked where he was heading at the fair, the not-so-bright governor said, "To the sheep shearing ...I shear taxpayers, not sheep." Ohioans didn't get the joke. Rhodes, Part II, laughed all the way to the Statehouse.

Richard F. Celeste, 1983-91, Democrat, Cuyahoga County

Style; One dome

At 6'4", the tallest of the century. Yale graduate and a Rhodes (both Cecil and James R.) Scholar who served as Peace Corps Director under President Carter.

At his best: High-minded platform attracted young starry-eyed liberal supporters nick-named "Celestials." Added a 40 percent increase to a 50 percent emergency income tax increase inherited from Governor Rhodes. Incredibly, three years later, was the first Democratic governor re-elected since Lausche. Ignored close ties to old crony Marvin Warner to push Home State prosecution.

At his worst: Celeste's close ties to Marvin Warner may have blinded state regulators to coming Home State Savings debacle. On state payroll, Celeste's Celestials fall to earth; Celeste's star sinks as both terms plagued by unqualified and dishonest appointees. Celeste's farewell address admits, "Good people can do bad things."

George V. Voinovich, 1991—98, Republican, Cuyahoga County

Style; One dome

Voinovich was the first of a new breed of Cleveland politicians, an ethnic Republican, but a return to the Ohio short form of governor at 5'9" (according to his driver's license, though aides claim 5'7" is closer to reality).

At his best: Impressed tax-weary Ohioans with 10-year "managerial" experience as

Cleveland's "Teflon" mayor and promised austerity in state spending as "Teflon" governor. Took advantage of good economic times to enhance his reputation as a sound manager by putting the state's fiscal house in order.

At his worst: Horse traded shamelessly with House Speaker Vern Riffe and Senate Majority Leader Stanley Aronoff just as he did with Cleveland Council President George Forbes, and pushed the tough problem—school finance—off on his successor when economic times made it harder to deal with.

Bob Taft, 1999—?, Republican, Unrated

Nancy P. Hollister, 1998—99, Republican, Washington County
Unrated

Womankind had to wait 200 years and outlast 60 men, but Ohio finally got a female governor, even if Nancy Putnam Hollister's term lasted only two weeks.

At her best: Provided an uneventful transition, moving into the Governor's mansion for security reasons but didn't rearrange the furniture and lived out of her overnight bag until the new governor—a male, of course—arrived. Hollister's brief tenure did prove, however, that a woman could occupy the office without the Scioto flowing backward.

At her worst: Gave away all the pens used to sign her lone piece of legislation (it preserved farmland), instead of saving the traditional one. Her husband (referred to by one newspaper as "the First Guy") called it "a rookie's error."

Although a member of Ohio's most illustrious political family, Taft is only the second member to win reelection to a major political office.

At his best: A good and honest man willing to embrace moderation.

At his worst: He was saddled with the worst economic conditions of two decades, an anemic opposition party, and few of the creative skills needed to move his hidebound party apparatus away from its more extreme positions. Party dominance appeared safe, but disagreement called into question its ability to govern effectively.

"Ask him what time it is, and he will tell you how to build a clock."

—*Howard Wilkinson, Cincinnati columnist, on George Voinovich, as governor*

The Ohio General Assembly is a bicameral legislature consisting of two houses, the Senate and the House of Representatives. The Ohio Constitution grants the General Assembly the power to make laws, but the people of Ohio also have the right to propose, change, or reject laws by petition initiatives and referendum votes. Ohio's Representatives and Senators deal primarily with two kinds of legislation: (1) bills, which are proposed to both enact new laws and amend or repeal existing laws; and (2) resolutions, which officially formulate the collective wishes and/or opinions of the General Assembly. A majority of the members of both houses must approve legislation before it becomes law, and bills must be submitted to the governor for his acceptance or rejection. The approval-of-two-thirds of the members is needed to pass emergency legislation, and three-fifths of their votes is required to countermand a gubernatorial veto. In addition to enacting laws, the duties of Senators and Representatives include proposing amendments to the Ohio Constitution, imposing or repealing taxes, appropriating money to operate the state government, and determining legislative districts.

The first regular session of the General Assembly begins on the first Monday in January of odd-numbered years. If that Monday is a legal holiday, the session convenes on the succeeding day. The second session commences on the same date of the following year. Although the length of each session varies according to the agenda of the General Assembly, the average session lasts about six months. Special sessions may also be convened by the Governor or the General Assembly's presiding officers, the Speaker of the House and the President of the Senate. According to the Ohio Constitution, all proceedings of the House and Senate are open to the public, unless two-thirds of the members vote to hold a secret session.

House of Representatives

Members of the House of Representatives are elected every two years from 99 legislative districts that have approximately equal numbers of constituents. Each member represents one legislative district. Representatives must be at least 18 years of age, qualified Ohio voters, and residents of their respective districts for at least one year prior to the election. The residency requirement is waived, however, if candidates have been absent while on the public business of Ohio or the United States. Representatives are elected in every even-numbered year, and their two-year terms begin on January 1 of each odd-numbered year. There is no limit on the number of terms a Representative may serve. If a vacancy occurs in the House, a replacement is selected by the Representatives who are members of the same political party as the person who last held the seat.

"LET'S GO PASS SOME STRINGENT LEGISLATION AIMED AT CURBING AMERICA'S MORAL DECLINE AND THEN EXEMPT OURSELVES."

The Speaker of the House is the leader and most powerful member of the House of Representatives. The Speaker is chosen after the November election by a caucus of the political party that won the majority of members in the House, and their selection is formally ratified by vote of the entire House on the first day of the session. The Speaker maintains order and decorum, determines procedures, presides over each day's session, controls the administration of the House, and, probably most important, names members and chairmen of all legislative committees. Committees are formed in the House to arbitrate various kinds of legislation, and the permanent committees deal with such matters as education, public utilities, and finance and appropriations. The Minority Leader heads the members who belong to the minority party in the House, and he can recommend his party members for committee appointments. Both Speaker of the House and Minority Leader are assisted by various political lieutenants, including Speaker Pro Tempore, Majority Floor Leader, Assistant Majority Floor Leader, Majority Whip, Assistant Majority Whip, Assistant Minority Leader, Minority Whip and Assistant Minority Whip. In the absence of the Speaker of the House, the Speaker Pro Tempore is charged with assuming his responsibilities.

The Senate

Members of the Ohio Senate are elected every two years from 33 legislative districts that have approximately equal numbers of constituents. Each member represents one legislative district. The rules concerning eligibility and vacancy are the same as those for the House of Representatives. Senators are elected in even-numbered years, and their four-year terms begin on January 1 of each odd-numbered year. Half of the Senators are elected every two years, and there is no limit on the number of terms a Senator may serve.

The President of the Senate is the leader and most powerful member of the Ohio Senate. The President is chosen after the November election by a caucus of the political party that won the majority of members in the Senate, and their selection is formally ratified by vote of the entire Senate on the first day of the session. Like the Speaker of the House, the President maintains order and decorum, determines procedures, presides over each day's session, controls the administration of the House, and makes the all-important appointments of committee members and chairmen. Senate committees are also formed to arbitrate legislation, and the standing, or permanent, committees deal with such matters as finance, commerce and labor, agriculture, and aging. The Minority Leader heads the members who be-

JIM BORGMAN CINCINNATI ENQUIRER ©1995

IN HIS LATER YEARS, DR. RORSCHACH DABBLED IN CONGRESSIONAL REDISTRICTING.

long to the minority party in the Senate, and he can recommend his party members for committee appointments. Both the President of the Senate and the Minority Leader are assisted by various political lieutenants, including the President Pro Tempore, the Assistant President Pro Tempore, the Majority Floor Leader, Majority Whip, Assistant Minority Leader, and Assistant Minority Whip. In the absence of the President of the Senate, the President Pro Tempore is charged with assuming his duties and responsibilities.

Legislative Districts

Representation in the Ohio General Assembly is based on population and determined according to a 1967 constitutional amendment. Article XI of the Ohio Constitution requires the Senate to have 33 members and the House to have 99 members, each of whom represents a single legislative district. Because each district must be substantially equal in size of population, House districts are determined by dividing the entire population of Ohio by 99, and Senate districts are determined by dividing the state population by 33.

The boundaries of the districts are organized by an Apportionment Board consisting of the governor, auditor of state, secretary of state, and one member of the General Assembly from each of the major political parties. The board must meet on a date designated by the governor between August 1 and October 1 of the year following every decennial U.S. census, and the apportionment of the districts must be published by October 5. Article XI requires that the Apportionment Board create districts that do not vary more than five percent from the respective population quotients for the House and Senate. The Senate districts consist of three contiguous House districts, and all the districts must also be compact, contiguous, and bounded by a single non-intersecting, continuous line.

Impeachment

According to Article II of the Ohio Constitution, the Governor, judges, and all state officers may be removed from office because of any misdemeanor. The House of Representatives has the sole power to impeach, or charge a public official with misconduct. If the majority of House members concur with the impeachment, the official must be tried in the Senate, where the vote of two-thirds of the members is required for a conviction.

Senate

125th General Assembly

STATEHOUSE
COLUMBUS, OHIO   43266-0604

SENATE CHAMBER   614-466-4884

LEGISLATIVE   INFORMATION
COLUMBUS   614-466-8842
TOLL FREE   800-282-0253
FAX   614-644-5466

Leadership: *President*
           Doug White
        President Pro Tempore
           Randall Gardner
        Assistant President Pro Tempore
           Jay Hottinger
        Majority Whip
           Jeff Jacobson
        Minority Leader
           Gregory L. DiDonato
        Assistant Minority Leader
           Mark L. Mallory
        Minority Whip
           C.J. Prentiss
        Assistant Minority Whip
           Teresa Fedor

District	Party	Senator

1st   **R**   **Lynn Wachtmann**
           Senate Building
           Room #40
           Columbus, Ohio 43215
           614-466-8150
           Website: www.senate.state.oh.us/
                senators/bios/sd_01.html
           Year Term Limited: 2006

2nd   **R**   **Randall Gardner**
           Senate Building
           Room #220
           Columbus, Ohio 43215
           614-466-8060
           Website: www.senate.state.oh.us/
                senators/bios/sd_02.html
           Year Term Limited: 2008

3rd   **R**   **David Goodman**
           Senate Building
           Room #125
           Columbus, Ohio 43215
           614-466-8064
           Website: www.senate.state.oh.us/
                senators/bios/sd_03.html
           Year Term Limited: 2010

4th   **R**   **Scott Nein**
           Senate Building
           Room #039
           Columbus, Ohio 43215
           614-466-8072
           Website: www.senate.state.oh.us/
                senators/bios/sd_04.html
           Year Term Limited: 2004

5th   **D**   **Tom Roberts**
           Senate Building
           Room #048
           Columbus, Ohio 43215
           614-466-6247
           Website: www.senate.state.oh.us/
                senators/bios/sd_05.html
           Year Term Limited: 2010

6th   **R**   **Jeff Jacobson**
           Senate Building
           Room #129
           Columbus, Ohio 43215
           614-466-4538
           Website: www.senate.state.oh.us/
                senators/bios/sd_06.html
           Year Term Limited: 2008

7th   **R**   **Robert Schuler**
           Senate Building
           Room #221
           Columbus, Ohio 43215
           614-466-9737
           Website: www.senate.state.oh.us/
                senators/bios/sd_07.html
           Year Term Limited: 2002

8th   **R**   **Louis Blessing**
           Senate Building
           Room #038
           Columbus, Ohio 43215
           614-466-8068
           Website: www.senate.state.oh.us/
                senators/bios/sd_08.html
           Year Term Limited: 2004

9th   **D**   **Mark Mallory**
           Senate Building
           Room #228
           Columbus, Ohio 43215
           614-466-5980
           Website: www.senate.state.oh.us/
                senators/bios/sd_09.html
           Year Term Limited: 2006

10th   **R**   **Steve Austria**
           Senate Building
           Room #041
           Columbus, Ohio 43215
           614-466-3780
           Website: www.senate.state.oh.us/
                senators/bios/sd_10.html
           Year Term Limited: 2008

"Watching the Senate work is like watching ham cure."

—*Ohioan Sam Stratman, press secretary to Henry Hyde, 1993*

11th	D	**Teresa Fedor** **Senate Building** **Room #226** **Columbus, Ohio 43215** **614-466-5204** Website: www.senate.state.oh.us/ senators/bios/sd_11.html Year Term Limited: 2012	18th	R	**Robert Gardner** **Senate Building** **Room #042** **Columbus, Ohio 43215** **614-644-7718** Website: www.senate.state.oh.us/ senators/bios/sd_18.html Year Term Limited: 2004
12th	R	**Jim Jordan** **Senate Building** **Room #** **Columbus, Ohio 43215** **614-466-7584** Website: www.senate.state.oh.us/ senators/bios/sd_12.html Year Term Limited: 2008	19th	R	**Bill Harris** **Senate Building** **Room #127** **Columbus, Ohio 43215** **614-466-8086** Website: www.senate.state.oh.us/ senators/bios/sd_19.html Year Term Limited: 2008
13th	R	**Jeffry Armbruster** **Senate Building** **Room #142** **Columbus, Ohio 43215** **614-644-7613** Website: www.senate.state.oh.us/ senators/bios/sd_13.html Year Term Limited: 2006	20th	R	**James Carnes** **Senate Building** **Room #222** **Columbus, Ohio 43215** **614-466-8076** Website: www.senate.state.oh.us/ senators/bios/sd_20.html Year Term Limited: 2004
14th	R	**Doug White** **Senate Building** **Room #201** **Columbus, Ohio 43215** **614-466-8082** Website: www.senate.state.oh.us/ senators/bios/sd_14.html Year Term Limited: 2004	21st	D	**C.J. Prentiss** **Senate Building** **Room #223** **Columbus, Ohio 43215** **614-466-4857** Website: www.senate.state.oh.us/ senators/bios/sd_21.html Year Term Limited: 2006
15th	D	**Ray Miller** **Senate Building** **Room #052** **Columbus, Ohio 43215** **614-466-5131** Website: www.senate.state.oh.us/ senators/bios/sd_15.html Year Term Limited: 2002	22nd	R	**Ron Amstutz** **Senate Building** **Room #140** **Columbus, Ohio 43215** **614-466-7505** Website: www.senate.state.oh.us/ senators/bios/sd_22.html Year Term Limited: 2008
16th	R	**Steve Stivers** **Senate Building** **Room #034** **Columbus, Ohio 43215** **614-466-5981** Website: www.senate.state.oh.us/ senators/bios/sd_16.html Year Term Limited: 2012	23rd	D	**Dan Brady** **Senate Building** **Room #056** **Columbus, Ohio 43215** **614-466-5123** Website: www.senate.state.oh.us/ senators/bios/sd_23.html Year Term Limited: 2006
17th	R	**John Carey** **Senate Building** **Room #134** **Columbus, Ohio 43215** **614-466-8156** Website: www.senate.state.oh.us/ senators/bios/sd_17.html Year Term Limited: 2012	24th	R	**Robert Spada** **Senate Building** **Room #143** **Columbus, Ohio 43215** **614-466-8056** Website: www.senate.state.oh.us/ senators/bios/sd_24.html Year Term Limited: 2008

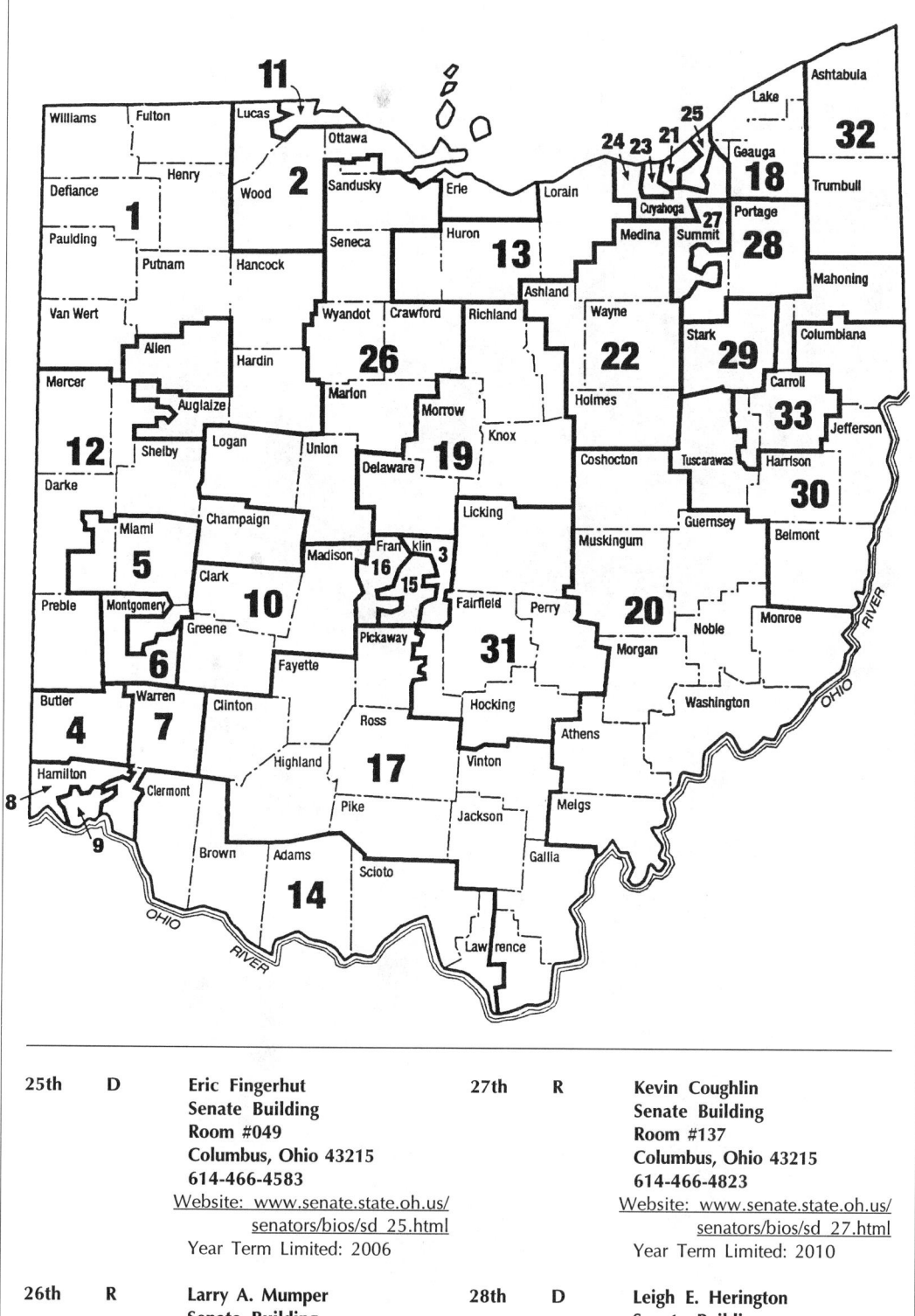

25th	**D**	Eric Fingerhut	**27th**	**R**	Kevin Coughlin
		Senate Building			Senate Building
		Room #049			Room #137
		Columbus, Ohio 43215			Columbus, Ohio 43215
		614-466-4583			614-466-4823
		Website: www.senate.state.oh.us/ senators/bios/sd_25.html			Website: www.senate.state.oh.us/ senators/bios/sd_27.html
		Year Term Limited: 2006			Year Term Limited: 2010
26th	**R**	Larry A. Mumper	**28th**	**D**	Leigh E. Herington
		Senate Building			Senate Building
		Room #035			Room #051
		Columbus, Ohio 43215			Columbus, Ohio 43215
		614-466-8049			614-466-7041
		Website: www.senate.state.oh.us/ senators/bios/sd_26.html			Website: www.senate.state.oh.us/ senators/bios/sd_28.html
		Year Term Limited: 2006			Year Term Limited: 2004

29th	R	**J. Kirk Schuring** **Senate Building** **Room #041** **Columbus, Ohio 43215** **614-466-0626** Website: www.senate.state.oh.us/ senators/bios/sd_29.html Year Term Limited: 2012	32nd	D	**Marc Dann** **Senate Building** **Room #057** **Columbus, Ohio 43215** **614-466-7182** Website: www.senate.state.oh.us/ senators/bios/sd_32.html Year Term Limited: 2012
30th	D	**Greg DiDonato** **Senate Building** **Room #303** **Columbus, Ohio 43215** **614-466-6508** Website: www.senate.state.oh.us/ senators/bios/sd_30.html Year Term Limited: 2004	33rd	D	**Robert Hagan** **Senate Building** **Room #050** **Columbus, Ohio 43215** **614-466-8285** Website: www.senate.state.oh.us/ senators/bios/sd_33.html Year Term Limited: 2006
31st	R	**Jay Hottinger** **Senate Building** **Room #138** **Columbus, Ohio 43215** **614-466-5838** Website: www.senate.state.oh.us/ senators/bios/sd_31.html Year Term Limited: 2006			*Source: The Ohio Senate*

oll.state.oh.us/ live.cfm

For those who feel distanced from their state legislatures, this site offers live, unedited, "gavel to gavel" broadcasts from the floor of the Ohio Senate and the House of Representatives, as well as texts from current and archived bills. If you're having trouble sleeping, this is your site.

125th General Assembly

OHIO HOUSE OF REPRESENTATIVES
Vern Riffe Center
77 SOUTH HIGH STREET
COLUMBUS, OHIO 43266-0603

HOUSE CHAMBER 614-466-4866

LEGISLATIVE INFORMATION
COLUMBUS 614-466-8842
TOLL FREE 800-282-0253
FAX 614-644-9494

Leadership: *Speaker*
Larry Householder
Speaker Pro Tempore
Gary W. Cates,
Majority Floor Leader
Patricia Clancy
Assistant Majority Floor Leader
Stephen Buehrer
Majority Whip
James Peter Trakas
Assistant Majority Whip
Jon M. Peterson
Minority Leader
Chris Redfern
Assistant Minority Leader
Joyce Beatty
Minority Whip
Dale Miller
Assistant Minority Whip
John Boccieri

District	Party	State Representative

1st **R** **Chuck Blasdel**
77 South High Street
11th Floor
Columbus, Ohio
43215-6111
Tel: 614-466-8022
Fax: 614-644-9494
Email Address:
district01@ohr.state.oh.us
Website: www.house.state.oh.us/jsps/
MemberDetails.jsp?DISTRICT=01
Term Limited: 2008

2nd **R** Jon M. Peterson
77 South High Street
14th Floor
Columbus, Ohio
43215-6111
Tel: 614-644-6711
Fax: 614-644-9494
Email Address:
district02@ohr.state.oh.us
Website: www.house.state.oh.us/jsps/
MemberDetails.jsp?DISTRICT=02
Term Limited: 2008

3rd **R** **Jim Carmichael**
77 South High Street
11th Floor
Columbus, Ohio
43215-6111
Tel: 614-466-1474
Fax: 614-644-9494
Email Address:
district03@ohr.state.oh.us
Website: www.house.state.oh.us/jsps/
MemberDetails.jsp?DISTRICT=03
Term Limited: 2008

4th **R** **John R. Willamowski**
77 South High Street
11th Floor
Columbus, Ohio
43215-6111
Tel: 614-466-9624
Fax: 614-644-9494
Email Address:
district04@ohr.state.oh.us
Website: www.house.state.oh.us/jsps/
MemberDetails.jsp?DISTRICT=04
Term Limited: 2006

5th **R** **Tim Schaffer**
77 South High Street
11th Floor
Columbus, Ohio
43215-6111
Tel: 614-466-8100
Fax: 614-644-9494
Email Address:
district05@ohr.state.oh.us
Website: www.house.state.oh.us/jsps/
MemberDetails.jsp?DISTRICT=05
Term Limited: 2008

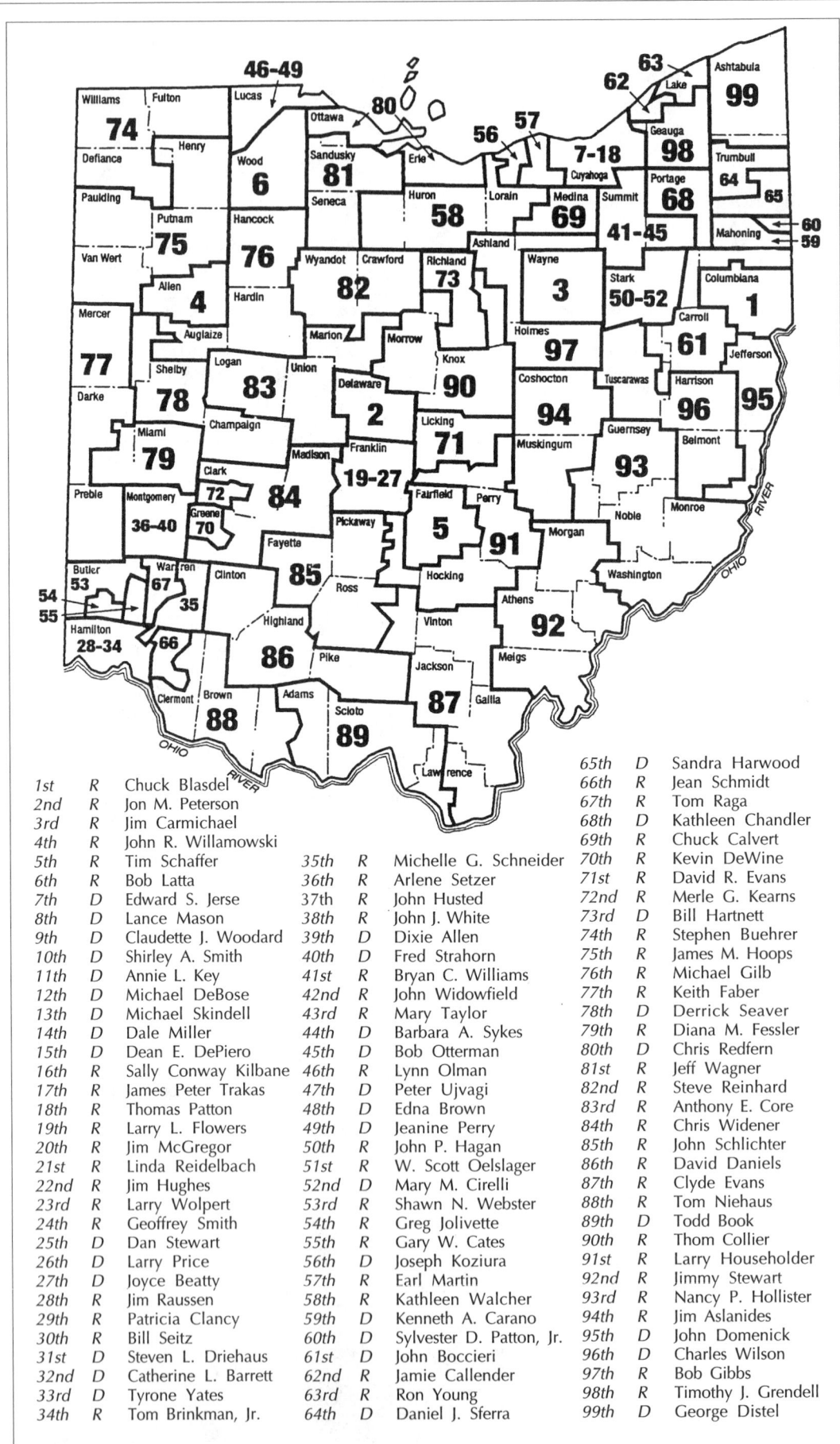

1st	R	Chuck Blasdel				65th	D	Sandra Harwood

1st	R	Chuck Blasdel			65th	D	Sandra Harwood
2nd	R	Jon M. Peterson			66th	R	Jean Schmidt
3rd	R	Jim Carmichael			67th	R	Tom Raga
4th	R	John R. Willamowski			68th	D	Kathleen Chandler
5th	R	Tim Schaffer	35th	R	Michelle G. Schneider	69th	R	Chuck Calvert
6th	R	Bob Latta	36th	R	Arlene Setzer	70th	R	Kevin DeWine
7th	D	Edward S. Jerse	37th	R	John Husted	71st	R	David R. Evans
8th	D	Lance Mason	38th	R	John J. White	72nd	R	Merle G. Kearns
9th	D	Claudette J. Woodard	39th	D	Dixie Allen	73rd	D	Bill Hartnett
10th	D	Shirley A. Smith	40th	D	Fred Strahorn	74th	R	Stephen Buehrer
11th	D	Annie L. Key	41st	R	Bryan C. Williams	75th	R	James M. Hoops
12th	D	Michael DeBose	42nd	R	John Widowfield	76th	R	Michael Gilb
13th	D	Michael Skindell	43rd	R	Mary Taylor	77th	R	Keith Faber
14th	D	Dale Miller	44th	D	Barbara A. Sykes	78th	D	Derrick Seaver
15th	D	Dean E. DePiero	45th	D	Bob Otterman	79th	R	Diana M. Fessler
16th	R	Sally Conway Kilbane	46th	R	Lynn Olman	80th	D	Chris Redfern
17th	R	James Peter Trakas	47th	D	Peter Ujvagi	81st	R	Jeff Wagner
18th	R	Thomas Patton	48th	D	Edna Brown	82nd	R	Steve Reinhard
19th	R	Larry L. Flowers	49th	D	Jeanine Perry	83rd	R	Anthony E. Core
20th	R	Jim McGregor	50th	R	John P. Hagan	84th	R	Chris Widener
21st	R	Linda Reidelbach	51st	R	W. Scott Oelslager	85th	R	John Schlichter
22nd	R	Jim Hughes	52nd	D	Mary M. Cirelli	86th	R	David Daniels
23rd	R	Larry Wolpert	53rd	R	Shawn N. Webster	87th	R	Clyde Evans
24th	R	Geoffrey Smith	54th	R	Greg Jolivette	88th	R	Tom Niehaus
25th	D	Dan Stewart	55th	R	Gary W. Cates	89th	D	Todd Book
26th	D	Larry Price	56th	D	Joseph Koziura	90th	R	Thom Collier
27th	D	Joyce Beatty	57th	R	Earl Martin	91st	R	Larry Householder
28th	R	Jim Raussen	58th	R	Kathleen Walcher	92nd	R	Jimmy Stewart
29th	R	Patricia Clancy	59th	D	Kenneth A. Carano	93rd	R	Nancy P. Hollister
30th	R	Bill Seitz	60th	D	Sylvester D. Patton, Jr.	94th	R	Jim Aslanides
31st	D	Steven L. Driehaus	61st	D	John Boccieri	95th	D	John Domenick
32nd	D	Catherine L. Barrett	62nd	R	Jamie Callender	96th	D	Charles Wilson
33rd	D	Tyrone Yates	63rd	R	Ron Young	97th	R	Bob Gibbs
34th	R	Tom Brinkman, Jr.	64th	D	Daniel J. Sferra	98th	R	Timothy J. Grendell
						99th	D	George Distel

6th	R	**Bob Latta** **77 South High Street** **13th Floor** **Columbus, Ohio** **43215-6111** **Tel: 614-466-8104** **Fax: 614-644-9494** Email Address: district06@ohr.state.oh.us Website: www.house.state.oh.us/jsps/ MemberDetails.jsp?DISTRICT=06 Term Limited: 2008	11th	D	**Annie L. Key** **77 South High Street** **10th Floor** **Columbus, Ohio** **43215-6111** **Tel: 614-466-1414** **Fax: 614-644-9494** Email Address: district11@ohr.state.oh.us Website: www.house.state.oh.us/jsps/ MemberDetails.jsp?DISTRICT=11 Term Limited: 2008
7th	D	**Edward S. Jerse** **77 South High Street** **10th Floor** **Columbus, Ohio** **43215-6111** **Tel: 614-466-8012** **Fax: 614-644-9494** Email Address: district07@ohr.state.oh.us Website: www.house.state.oh.us/jsps/ MemberDetails.jsp?DISTRICT=07 Term Limited: 2004	12th	D	**Michael DeBose** **77 South High Street** **10th Floor** **Columbus, Ohio** **43215-6111** **Tel: 614-466-1408** **Fax: 614-644-9494** Email Address: district12@ohr.state.oh.us Website: www.house.state.oh.us/jsps/ MemberDetails.jsp?DISTRICT=12 Term Limited: 2010
8th	D	**Lance Mason** **77 South High Street** **10th Floor** **Columbus, Ohio** **43215-6111** **Tel: 614-644-6721** **Fax: 614-644-9494** Email Address: district08@ohr.state.oh.us Website: www.house.state.oh.us/jsps/ MemberDetails.jsp?DISTRICT=08 Term Limited: 2012	13th	D	**Michael Skindell** **77 South High Street** **10th Floor** **Columbus, Ohio** **43215-6111** **Tel: 614-466-5921** **Fax: 614-644-9494** Email Address: district13@ohr.state.oh.us Website: www.house.state.oh.us/jsps/ MemberDetails.jsp?DISTRICT=13 Term Limited: 2012
9th	D	**Claudette J. Woodard** **77 South High Street** **10th Floor** **Columbus, Ohio** **43215-6111** **Tel: 614-644-5079** **Fax: 614-644-9494** Email Address: district09@ohr.state.oh.us Website: www.house.state.oh.us/jsps/ MemberDetails.jsp?DISTRICT=09 Term Limited: 2008	14th	D	**Dale Miller** **77 South High Street** **14th Floor** **Columbus, Ohio** **43215-6111** **Tel: 614-466-3350** **Fax: 614-644-9494** Email Address: district14@ohr.state.oh.us Website: www.house.state.oh.us/jsps/ MemberDetails.jsp?DISTRICT=14 Term Limited: 2006
10th	D	**Shirley A. Smith** **77 South High Street** **10th Floor** **Columbus, Ohio** **43215-6111** **Tel: 614-466-7954** **Fax: 614-644-9494** Email Address: district10@ohr.state.oh.us Website: www.house.state.oh.us/jsps/ MemberDetails.jsp?DISTRICT=10 Term Limited: 2006	15th	D	**Dean E. DePiero** **77 South High Street** **10th Floor** **Columbus, Ohio** **43215-6111** **Tel: 614-466-3485** **Fax: 614-644-9494** Email Address: district15@ohr.state.oh.us Website: www.house.state.oh.us/jsps/ MemberDetails.jsp?DISTRICT=15 Term Limited: 2006

| 16th | R | Sally Conway Kilbane | 21st | R | Linda Reidelbach |

16th   R

Sally Conway Kilbane
77 South High Street
13th Floor
Columbus, Ohio
43215-6111
Tel: 614-466-0961
Fax: 614-644-9494
Email Address:
district16@ohr.state.oh.us
Website: www.house.state.oh.us/jsps/
MemberDetails.jsp?DISTRICT=16
Term Limited: 2006

21st   R

Linda Reidelbach
77 South High Street
12th Floor
Columbus, Ohio
43215-6111
Fax: 614-644-9494
Fax: 614-644-6030
Email Address:
district21@ohr.state.oh.us
Website: www.house.state.oh.us/jsps/
MemberDetails.jsp?DISTRICT=21
Term Limited: 2008

17th   R

James Peter Trakas
77 South High Street
14th Floor
Columbus, Ohio
43215-6111
Tel: 614-644-6041
Fax: 614-644-9494
Email Address:
district17@ohr.state.oh.us
Website: www.house.state.oh.us/jsps/
MemberDetails.jsp?DISTRICT=17
Term Limited: 2006

22nd   R

Jim Hughes
77 South High Street
13th Floor
Columbus, Ohio
43215-6111
Tel: 614-466-2473
Fax: 614-644-9494
Email Address:
district22@ohr.state.oh.us
Website: www.house.state.oh.us/jsps/
MemberDetails.jsp?DISTRICT=22
Term Limited: 2008

18th   R

Thomas Patton
77 South High Street
11th Floor
Columbus, Ohio
43215-6111
Tel: 614-466-4895
Fax: 614-644-9494
Email Address:
district18@ohr.state.oh.us
Website: www.house.state.oh.us/jsps/
MemberDetails.jsp?DISTRICT=18
Term Limited: 2006

23rd   R

Larry Wolpert
77 South High Street
13th Floor
Columbus, Ohio
43215-6111
Tel: 614-466-9690
Fax: 614-644-9494
Email Address:
district23@ohr.state.oh.us
Website: www.house.state.oh.us/jsps/
MemberDetails.jsp?DISTRICT=23
Term Limited: 2008

19th   R

Larry L. Flowers
77 South High Street
13th Floor
Columbus, Ohio
43215-6111
Tel: 614-466-4847
Fax: 614-644-9494
Email Address:
district19@ohr.state.oh.us
Website: www.house.state.oh.us/jsps/
MemberDetails.jsp?DISTRICT=19
Term Limited: 2008

24th   R

Geoffrey Smith
77 South High Street
13th Floor
Columbus, Ohio
43215-6111
Tel: 614-644-6005
Fax: 614-644-9494
Email Address:
district24@ohr.state.oh.us
Website: www.house.state.oh.us/jsps/
MemberDetails.jsp?DISTRICT=24
Term Limited: 2008

20th   R

Jim McGregor
77 South High Street
11th Floor
Columbus, Ohio
43215-6111
Tel: 614-644-6002
Fax: 614-644-9494
Email Address:
district20@ohr.state.oh.us
Website: www.house.state.oh.us/jsps/
MemberDetails.jsp?DISTRICT=20
Term Limited: 2010

25th   D

Dan Stewart
77 South High Street
10th Floor
Columbus, Ohio
43215-6111
Tel: 614-466-1496
Fax: 614-644-9494
Email Address:
district25@ohr.state.oh.us
Website: www.house.state.oh.us/jsps/
MemberDetails.jsp?DISTRICT=25
Term Limited: 2012

26th	D	**Larry Price** **77 South High Street** **10th Floor** **Columbus, Ohio** **43215-6111** **Tel: 614-466-8010** **Fax: 614-644-9494** Email Address: district26@ohr.state.oh.us Website: www.house.state.oh.us/jsps/ MemberDetails.jsp?DISTRICT=26 Term Limited: 2012	31st	D	**Steven L. Driehaus** **77 South High Street** **10th Floor** **Columbus, Ohio** **43215-6111** **Tel: 614-466-5786** **Fax: 614-644-9494** Email Address: district31@ohr.state.oh.us Website: www.house.state.oh.us/jsps/ MemberDetails.jsp?DISTRICT=31 Term Limited: 2008
27th	D	**Joyce Beatty** **77 South High Street** **14th Floor** **Columbus, Ohio** **43215-6111** **Tel: 614-466-5343** **Fax: 614-644-9494** Email Address: district27@ohr.state.oh.us Website: www.house.state.oh.us/jsps/ MemberDetails.jsp?DISTRICT=27 Term Limited: 2008	32nd	D	**Catherine L. Barrett** **77 South High Street** **10th Floor** **Columbus, Ohio** **43215-6111** **Tel: 614-466-1645** **Fax: 614-644-9494** Email Address: district32@ohr.state.oh.us Website: www.house.state.oh.us/jsps/ MemberDetails.jsp?DISTRICT=32 Term Limited: 2006
28th	R	**Jim Raussen** **77 South High Street** **11th Floor** **Columbus, Ohio** **43215-6111** **Tel: 614-466-8120** **Fax: 614-644-9494** Email Address: district28@ohr.state.oh.us Website: www.house.state.oh.us/jsps/ MemberDetails.jsp?DISTRICT=28 Term Limited: 2012	33rd	D	**Tyrone Yates** **77 South High Street** **11th Floor** **Columbus, Ohio** **43215-6111** **Tel: 614-466-1308** **Fax: 614-644-9494** Email Address: district33@ohr.state.oh.us Website: www.house.state.oh.us/jsps/ MemberDetails.jsp?DISTRICT=33 Term Limited: 2012
29th	R	**Patricia Clancy** **77 South High Street** **14th Floor** **Columbus, Ohio** **43215-6111** **Tel: 614-466-9091** **Fax: 614-644-9494** Email Address: district29@ohr.state.oh.us Website: www.house.state.oh.us/jsps/ MemberDetails.jsp?DISTRICT=29 Term Limited: 2004	34th	R	**Tom Brinkman, Jr.** **77 South High Street** **11th Floor** **Columbus, Ohio** **43215-6111** **Tel: 614-644-6886** **Fax: 614-644-9494** Email Address: district34@ohr.state.oh.us Website: www.house.state.oh.us/jsps/ MemberDetails.jsp?DISTRICT=34 Term Limited: 2008
30th	R	**Bill Seitz** **77 South High Street** **11th Floor** **Columbus, Ohio** **43215-6111** **Tel: 614-466-8258** **Fax: 614-644-9494** Email Address: district30@ohr.state.oh.us Website: www.house.state.oh.us/jsps/ MemberDetails.jsp?DISTRICT=30 Term Limited: 2008	35th	R	**Michelle G. Schneider** **77 South High Street** **11th Floor** **Columbus, Ohio** **43215-6111** **Tel: 614-644-6023** **Fax: 614-644-9494** Email Address: district35@ohr.state.oh.us Website: www.house.state.oh.us/jsps/ MemberDetails.jsp?DISTRICT=35 Term Limited: 2008

36th	R	Arlene Setzer 77 South High Street 13th Floor Columbus, Ohio 43215-6111 Tel: 614-644-8051 Fax: 614-644-9494 Email Address: district36@ohr.state.oh.us Website: www.house.state.oh.us/jsps/ MemberDetails.jsp?DISTRICT=36 Term Limited: 2008	41st	R	Bryan C. Williams 77 South High Street 11th Floor Columbus, Ohio 43215-6111 Tel: 614-644-5085 Fax: 614-644-9494 Email Address: district41@ohr.state.oh.us Website: www.house.state.oh.us/jsps/ MemberDetails.jsp?DISTRICT=41 Term Limited: 2004
37th	R	John Husted 77 South High Street 13th Floor Columbus, Ohio 43215-6111 Tel: 614-644-6008 Fax: 614-644-9494 Email Address: district37@ohr.state.oh.us Website: www.house.state.oh.us/jsps/ MemberDetails.jsp?DISTRICT=37 Term Limited: 2008	42nd	R	John Widowfield 77 South High Street 13th Floor Columbus, Ohio 43215-6111 Tel: 614-466-1177 Fax: 614-644-9494 Email Address: district42@ohr.state.oh.us Website: www.house.state.oh.us/jsps/ MemberDetails.jsp?DISTRICT=42 Term Limited: 2010
38th	R	John J. White 77 South High Street 13th Floor Columbus, Ohio 43215-6111 Tel: 614-466-6504 Fax: 614-644-9494 Email Address: district38@ohr.state.oh.us Website: www.house.state.oh.us/jsps/ MemberDetails.jsp?DISTRICT=38 Term Limited: 2008	43rd	R	Mary Taylor 77 South High Street 11th Floor Columbus, Ohio 43215-6111 Tel: 614-466-1790 Fax: 614-644-9494 Email Address: district43@ohr.state.oh.us Website: www.house.state.oh.us/jsps/ MemberDetails.jsp?DISTRICT=43 Term Limited: 2012
39th	D	Dixie Allen 77 South High Street 10th Floor Columbus, Ohio 43215-6111 Tel: 614-466-1607 Fax: 614-644-9494 Email Address: district39@ohr.state.oh.us Website: www.house.state.oh.us/jsps/ MemberDetails.jsp?DISTRICT=39 Term Limited: 2006	44th	D	Barbara A. Sykes 77 South High Street 10th Floor Columbus, Ohio 43215-6111 Tel: 614-466-3100 Fax: 614-644-9494 Email Address: district44@ohr.state.oh.us Website: www.house.state.oh.us/jsps/ MemberDetails.jsp?DISTRICT=44 Term Limited: 2008
40th	D	Fred Strahorn 77 South High Street 10th Floor Columbus, Ohio 43215-6111 Tel: 614-466-2960 Fax: 614-644-9494 Email Address: district40@ohr.state.oh.us Website: www.house.state.oh.us/jsps/ MemberDetails.jsp?DISTRICT=40 Term Limited: 2008	45th	D	Bob Otterman 77 South High Street 10th Floor Columbus, Ohio 43215-6111 Tel: 614-644-6037 Fax: 614-644-9494 Email Address: district45@ohr.state.oh.us Website: www.house.state.oh.us/jsps/ MemberDetails.jsp?DISTRICT=45 Term Limited: 2008

46th	R	Lynn Olman 77 South High Street 13th Floor Columbus, Ohio 43215-6111 Tel: 614-466-1731 Fax: 614-644-9494 Email Address: district46@ohr.state.oh.us Website: www.house.state.oh.us/jsps/ MemberDetails.jsp?DISTRICT=46 Term Limited: 2004	51st	R	W. Scott Oelslager 77 South High Street 13th Floor Columbus, Ohio 43215-6111 Tel: 614-752-2438 Fax: 614-644-9494 Email Address: district51@ohr.state.oh.us Website: www.house.state.oh.us/jsps/ MemberDetails.jsp?DISTRICT=51 Term Limited: 2012
47th	D	Peter Ujvagi 77 South High Street 11th Floor Columbus, Ohio 43215-6111 Tel: 614-644-6017 Fax: 614-644-9494 Email Address: district47@ohr.state.oh.us Website: www.house.state.oh.us/jsps/ MemberDetails.jsp?DISTRICT=47 Term Limited: 2012	52nd	D	Mary M. Cirelli 77 South High Street 10th Floor Columbus, Ohio 43215-6111 Tel: 614-466-8030 Fax: 614-644-9494 Email Address: district52@ohr.state.oh.us Website: www.house.state.oh.us/jsps/ MemberDetails.jsp?DISTRICT=52 Term Limited: 2008
48th	D	Edna Brown 77 South High Street 10th Floor Columbus, Ohio 43215-6111 Tel: 614-466-1401 Fax: 614-644-9494 Email Address: district48@ohr.state.oh.us Website: www.house.state.oh.us/jsps/ MemberDetails.jsp?DISTRICT=48 Term Limited: 2010	53rd	R	Shawn N. Webster 77 South High Street 13th Floor Columbus, Ohio 43215-6111 Tel: 614-644-5094 Fax: 614-995-1863 Email Address: district53@ohr.state.oh.us Website: www.house.state.oh.us/jsps/ MemberDetails.jsp?DISTRICT=53 Term Limited: 2008
49th	D	Jeanine Perry 77 South High Street Floor Columbus, Ohio 43215-6111 Tel: 614-466-1418 Fax: 614-644-9494 Email Address: district49@ohr.state.oh.us Website: www.house.state.oh.us/jsps/ MemberDetails.jsp?DISTRICT=49 Term Limited: 2006	54th	R	Greg Jolivette 77 South High Street 13th Floor Columbus, Ohio 43215-6111 Tel: 614-644-6721 Fax: 614-644-9494 Email Address: district54@ohr.state.oh.us Website: www.house.state.oh.us/jsps/ MemberDetails.jsp?DISTRICT=54 Term Limited: 2006
50th	R	John P. Hagan 77 South High Street 11th Floor Columbus, Ohio 43215-6111 Tel: 614-466-9078 Fax: 614-644-9494 Email Address: district50@ohr.state.oh.us Website: www.house.state.oh.us/jsps/ MemberDetails.jsp?DISTRICT=50 Term Limited: 2008	55th	R	Gary W. Cates 77 South High Street 14th Floor Columbus, Ohio 43215-6111 Tel: 614-466-8550 Fax: 614-644-9494 Email Address: district55@ohr.state.oh.us Website: www.house.state.oh.us/jsps/ MemberDetails.jsp?DISTRICT=55 Term Limited: 2004

| 56th | D | Joseph Koziura
77 South High Street
10th Floor
Columbus, Ohio
43215-6111
Tel: 614-466-5141
Fax: 614-644-9494
Email Address:
district56@ohr.state.oh.us
Website: www.house.state.oh.us/jsps/
MemberDetails.jsp?DISTRICT=56
Term Limited: 2010 | 61st | D | John Boccieri
77 South High Street
14th Floor
Columbus, Ohio
43215-6111
Tel: 614-466-1464
Fax: 614-644-9494
Email Address:
district61@ohr.state.oh.us
Website: www.house.state.oh.us/jsps/
MemberDetails.jsp?DISTRICT=61
Term Limited: 2008 |
| 57th | R | Earl Martin
77 South High Street
12th Floor
Columbus, Ohio
43215-6111
Tel: 614-644-5076
Fax: 614-644-9494
Email Address:
district57@ohr.state.oh.us
Website: www.house.state.oh.us/jsps/
MemberDetails.jsp?DISTRICT=57
Term Limited: 2008 | 62nd | R | Jamie Callender
77 South High Street
13th Floor
Columbus, Ohio
43215-6111
Tel: 614-466-7251
Fax: 614-644-9494
Email Address:
district62@ohr.state.oh.us
Website: www.house.state.oh.us/jsps/
MemberDetails.jsp?DISTRICT=62
Term Limited: 2004 |
| 58th | R | Kathleen Walcher
77 South High Street
12th Floor
Columbus, Ohio
43215-6111
Tel: 614-466-9628
Fax: 614-644-9494
Email Address:
district58@ohr.state.oh.us
Website: www.house.state.oh.us/jsps/
MemberDetails.jsp?DISTRICT=58
Term Limited: 2010 | 63rd | R | Ron Young
77 South High Street
13th Floor
Columbus, Ohio
43215-6111
Tel: 614-644-6074
Fax: 614-644-9494
Email Address:
district63@ohr.state.oh.us
Website: www.house.state.oh.us/jsps/
MemberDetails.jsp?DISTRICT=63
Term Limited: 2004 |
| 59th | D | Kenneth A. Carano
77 South High Street
10th Floor
Columbus, Ohio
43215-6111
Tel: 614-466-6107
Fax: 614-644-9494
Email Address:
district59@ohr.state.oh.us
Website: www.house.state.oh.us/jsps/
MemberDetails.jsp?DISTRICT=59
Term Limited: 2008 | 64th | D | Daniel J. Sferra
77 South High Street
10th Floor
Columbus, Ohio
43215-6111
Tel: 614-466-5358
Fax: 614-644-9494
Email Address:
district64@ohr.state.oh.us
Website: www.house.state.oh.us/jsps/
MemberDetails.jsp?DISTRICT=64
Term Limited: 2008 |
| 60th | D | Sylvester D. Patton, Jr.
77 South High Street
10th Floor
Columbus, Ohio
43215-6111
Tel: 614-466-9435
Fax: 614-644-9494
Email Address:
district60@ohr.state.oh.us
Website: www.house.state.oh.us/jsps/
MemberDetails.jsp?DISTRICT=60
Term Limited: 2006 | 65th | D | Sandra Harwood
77 South High Street
11th Floor
Columbus, Ohio
43215-6111
Tel: 614-466-3488
Fax: 614-644-9494
Email Address:
district65@ohr.state.oh.us
Website: www.house.state.oh.us/jsps/
MemberDetails.jsp?DISTRICT=65
Term Limited: 2012 |

66th	R	**Jean Schmidt** **77 South High Street** **11th Floor** **Columbus, Ohio** **43215-6111** **Tel: 614-466-8134** **Fax: 614-644-9494** Email Address: district66@ohr.state.oh.us Website: www.house.state.oh.us/jsps/ MemberDetails.jsp?DISTRICT=66 Term Limited: 2008	71st	R	**David R. Evans** **77 South High Street** **13th Floor** **Columbus, Ohio** **43215-6111** **Tel: 614-466-1482** **Fax: 614-644-9494** Email Address: district71@ohr.state.oh.us Website: www.house.state.oh.us/jsps/ MemberDetails.jsp?DISTRICT=71 Term Limited: 2006
67th	R	**Tom Raga** **77 South High Street** **12th Floor** **Columbus, Ohio** **43215-6111** **Tel: 614-644-6027** **Fax: 614-644-9494** Email Address: district67@ohr.state.oh.us Website: www.house.state.oh.us/jsps/ MemberDetails.jsp?DISTRICT=67 Term Limited: 2008	72nd	R	**Merle G. Kearns** **77 South High Street** **11th Floor** **Columbus, Ohio** **43215-6111** **Tel: 614-466-2038** **Fax: 614-644-9494** Email Address: district72@ohr.state.oh.us Website: www.house.state.oh.us/jsps/ MemberDetails.jsp?DISTRICT=72 Term Limited: 2008
68th	D	**Kathleen Chandler** **77 South High Street** **10th Floor** **Columbus, Ohio** **43215-6111** **Tel: 614-466-2004** **Fax: 614-644-9494** Email Address: district68@ohr.state.oh.us Website: www.house.state.oh.us/jsps/ MemberDetails.jsp?DISTRICT=68 Term Limited: 2012	73rd	D	**Bill Hartnett** **77 South High Street** **10th Floor** **Columbus, Ohio** **43215-6111** **Tel: 614-466-5802** **Fax: 614-644-9494** Email Address: district73@ohr.state.oh.us Website: www.house.state.oh.us/jsps/ MemberDetails.jsp?DISTRICT=73 Term Limited: 2006
69th	R	**Chuck Calvert** **77 South High Street** **13th Floor** **Columbus, Ohio** **43215-6111** **Tel: 614-466-8140** **Fax: 614-644-9494** Email Address: district69@ohr.state.oh.us Website: www.house.state.oh.us/jsps/ MemberDetails.jsp?DISTRICT=69 Term Limited: 2006	74th	R	**Stephen Buehrer** **77 South High Street** **14th Floor** **Columbus, Ohio** **43215-6111** **Tel: 614-644-5091** **Fax: 614-644-9494** Email Address: district74@ohr.state.oh.us Website: www.house.state.oh.us/jsps/ MemberDetails.jsp?DISTRICT=74 Term Limited: 2012
70th	R	**Kevin DeWine** **77 South High Street** **12th Floor** **Columbus, Ohio** **43215-6111** **Tel: 614-644-6020** **Fax: 614-644-9494** Email Address: district70@ohr.state.oh.us Website: www.house.state.oh.us/jsps/ MemberDetails.jsp?DISTRICT=70 Term Limited: 2008	75th	R	**James M. Hoops** **77 South High Street** **13th Floor** **Columbus, Ohio** **43215-6111** **Tel: 614-466-3760** **Fax: 614-644-9494** Email Address: district75@ohr.state.oh.us Website: www.house.state.oh.us/jsps/ MemberDetails.jsp?DISTRICT=75 Term Limited: 2006

76th	R	Michael Gilb 77 South High Street 13th Floor Columbus, Ohio 43215-6111 Tel: 614-466-3819 Fax: 614-644-9494 Email Address: district76@ohr.state.oh.us Website: www.house.state.oh.us/jsps/ MemberDetails.jsp?DISTRICT=076 Term Limited: 2008	81st	R	Jeff Wagner 77 South High Street 12th Floor Columbus, Ohio 43215-6111 Tel: 614-466-1374 Fax: 614-644-9494 Email Address: district81@ohr.state.oh.us Website: www.house.state.oh.us/jsps/ MemberDetails.jsp?DISTRICT=81 Term Limited: 2012
77th	R	Keith Faber 77 South High Street 13th Floor Columbus, Ohio 43215-6111 Tel: 614-466-6344 Fax: 614-644-9494 Email Address: district77@ohr.state.oh.us Website: www.house.state.oh.us/jsps/ MemberDetails.jsp?DISTRICT=77 Term Limited: 2008	82nd	R	Steve Reinhard 77 South High Street 12th Floor Columbus, Ohio 43215-6111 Tel: 614-644-6265 Fax: 614-644-9494 Email Address: district82@ohr.state.oh.us Website: www.house.state.oh.us/jsps/ MemberDetails.jsp?DISTRICT=82 Term Limited: 2008
78th	D	Derrick Seaver 77 South High Street 10th Floor Columbus, Ohio 43215-6111 Tel: 614-466-1507 Fax: 614-644-9494 Email Address: district78@ohr.state.oh.us Website: www.house.state.oh.us/jsps/ MemberDetails.jsp?DISTRICT=78 Term Limited: 2008	83rd	R	Anthony E. Core 77 South High Street 11th Floor Columbus, Ohio 43215-6111 Tel: 614-466-8147 Fax: 614-644-9494 Email Address: district83@ohr.state.oh.us Website: www.house.state.oh.us/jsps/ MemberDetails.jsp?DISTRICT=83 Term Limited: 2008
79th	R	Diana M. Fessler 77 South High Street 13th Floor Columbus, Ohio 43215-6111 Tel: 614-466-8114 Fax: 614-644-9494 Email Address: district79@ohr.state.oh.us Website: www.house.state.oh.us/jsps/ MemberDetails.jsp?DISTRICT=79 Term Limited: 2008	84th	R	Chris Widener 77 South High Street 11th Floor Columbus, Ohio 43215-6111 Tel: 614-466-1460 Fax: 614-644-9494 Email Address: district84@ohr.state.oh.us Website: www.house.state.oh.us/jsps/ MemberDetails.jsp?DISTRICT=84 Term Limited: 2012
80th	D	Chris Redfern 77 South High Street 14th Floor Columbus, Ohio 43215-6111 Tel: 614-644-6011 Fax: 614-644-9494 Email Address: district80@ohr.state.oh.us Website: www.house.state.oh.us/jsps/ MemberDetails.jsp?DISTRICT=80 Term Limited: 2008	85th	R	John Schlichter 77 South High Street Columbus, Ohio 10th Floor 43215-6111 Tel: 614-644-7928 Fax: 614-644-9494 Email Address: district85@ohr.state.oh.us Website: www.house.state.oh.us/jsps/ MemberDetails.jsp?DISTRICT=85 Term Limited: 2012

86th	R	David Daniels	91st	R	Larry Householder

86th R David Daniels
77 South High Street
11th Floor
Columbus, Ohio
43215-6111
Tel: 614-466-3506
Fax: 614-644-9494
Email Address:
district86@ohr.state.oh.us
Website: www.house.state.oh.us/jsps/
MemberDetails.jsp?DISTRICT=86
Term Limited: 2012

91st R Larry Householder
77 South High Street
14th Floor
Columbus, Ohio
43215-6111
Tel: 614-466-2500
Fax: 614-644-9494
Email Address:
district91@ohr.state.oh.us
Website: www.house.state.oh.us/jsps/
MemberDetails.jsp?DISTRICT=91
Term Limited: 2004

87th R Clyde Evans
77 South High Street
11th Floor
Columbus, Ohio
43215-6111
Tel: 614-466-1366
Fax: 614-644-9494
Email Address:
district87@ohr.state.oh.us
Website: www.house.state.oh.us/jsps/
MemberDetails.jsp?DISTRICT=87
Term Limited: 2006

92nd R Jimmy Stewart
77 South High Street
11th Floor
Columbus, Ohio
43215-6111
Tel: 614-466-2158
Fax: 614-644-9494
Email Address:
district92@ohr.state.oh.us
Website: www.house.state.oh.us/jsps/
MemberDetails.jsp?DISTRICT=92
Term Limited: 2012

88th R Tom Niehaus
77 South High Street
11th Floor
Columbus, Ohio
43215-6111
Tel: 614-644-6034
Fax: 614-644-9494
Email Address:
district88@ohr.state.oh.us
Website: www.house.state.oh.us/jsps/
MemberDetails.jsp?DISTRICT=88
Term Limited: 2008

93rd R Nancy P. Hollister
77 South High Street
13th Floor
Columbus, Ohio
43215-6111
Tel: 614-644-8728
Fax: 614-644-9494
Email Address:
district93@ohr.state.oh.us
Website: www.house.state.oh.us/jsps/
MemberDetails.jsp?DISTRICT=93
Term Limited: 2008

89th D Todd Book
77 South High Street
10th Floor
Columbus, Ohio
43215-6111
Tel: 614-466-2124
Fax: 614-644-9494
Email Address:
district89@ohr.state.oh.us
Website: www.house.state.oh.us/jsps/
MemberDetails.jsp?DISTRICT=89
Term Limited: 2012

94th R Jim Aslanides
77 South High Street
12th Floor
Columbus, Ohio
43215-6111
Tel: 614-644-6014
Fax: 614-644-9494
Email Address:
district94@ohr.state.oh.us
Website: www.house.state.oh.us/jsps/
MemberDetails.jsp?DISTRICT=94
Term Limited: 2008

90th R Thom Collier
77 South High Street
11th Floor
Columbus, Ohio
43215-6111
Tel: 614-466-1431
Fax: 614-644-9494
Email Address:
district90@ohr.state.oh.us
Website: www.house.state.oh.us/jsps/
MemberDetails.jsp?DISTRICT=90
Term Limited: 2008

95th D John Domenick
77 South High Street
10th Floor
Columbus, Ohio
43215-6111
Tel: 614-466-3735
Fax: 614-644-9494
Email Address:
district95@ohr.state.oh.us
Website: www.house.state.oh.us/jsps/
MemberDetails.jsp?DISTRICT=95
Term Limited: 2012

| 96th | D | Charles Wilson
77 South High Street
10th Floor
Columbus, Ohio
43215-6111
Tel: 614-466-8035
Fax: 614-644-9494
Email Address:
district96@ohr.state.oh.us
Website: www.house.state.oh.us/jsps/
MemberDetails.jsp?DISTRICT=96
Term Limited: 2004 | 98th | R | Timothy J. Grendell
77 South High Street
13th Floor
Columbus, Ohio
43215-6111
Tel: 614-644-5088
Fax: 614-644-9494
Email Address:
district98@ohr.state.oh.us
Website: www.house.state.oh.us/jsps/
MemberDetails.jsp?DISTRICT=98
Term Limited: 2008 |
| 97th | R | Bob Gibbs
77 South High Street
11th Floor
Columbus, Ohio
43215-6111
Tel: 614-466-2994
Fax: 614-644-9494
Email Address:
district97@ohr.state.oh.us
Website: www.house.state.oh.us/jsps/
MemberDetails.jsp?DISTRICT=97
Term Limited: 2012 | 99th | D | L. George Distel
77 South High Street
10th Floor
Columbus, Ohio
43215-6111
Tel: 614-466-1405
Fax: 614-644-9494
Email Address:
district99@ohr.state.oh.us
Website: www.house.state.oh.us/jsps/
MemberDetails.jsp?DISTRICT=99
Term Limited: 2008 |

THE PECULIAR FITNESS OF GEORGE B. COX

the *Boss*

George Cox, the millionaire saloonkeeper, ran Cincinnati for nearly a quarter of a century. Corruption in the Queen City was so rife, Cincinnati was famous for it.

George B. Cox was the "Boss" in the grand old tradition of city political machines. From 1888 to 1910, observed the *Cincinnati Enquirer,* "no man had a chance to get on the Republican ticket without the approval of Cox;" his organization was "in its way, more complete, more exacting, and under more rigid discipline, than Tammany Hall." Actually, Cox had been to New York for some instruction at Tammany Hall, not that he particularly needed it. Though Cox was only elected to one public office (Cincinnati City Council, 1877), he held such an iron-clad grip on the city's politics that by 1905, 23 of the 24 ward captains he appointed were on a Cincinnati or Hamilton County payroll. The reform movement bloomed later in Ohio than in the rest of the nation, and the stories of Cox's corruption are legion. It was said that if someone had announced "Your saloon is on fire!" to the City Council, every member would have dashed out. But in all fairness, Cox did provide a sorely needed element of stability in a rapidly growing city where political factions, emerging suburbs, and new public utility, transportation, and communication systems were creating chaos. In 1911, Cox told a New York newspaper, "I had no ambition to become a boss when I entered politics... But because of my peculiar fitness, I became boss." And of his foiled enemies, Cox generously said, "Their failings were born in them, and they should not be blamed too much." ∾

In politics, how you see things often depends upon where you stand. To a reactionary, a conservative position may seem too liberal and a liberal stance might appear socialist. At the same time, far left-leaning individuals often see progressive ideas as too conservative. As for conservative ideas, well, they're viewed as reactionary. But no matter which side of the political fence you sit, you probably believe you exist among the mainstream—and that you're correct. To help you survey the political landscape, Ohio has two outstanding websites devoted to state policy, *Policy Matters Ohio* and *The Buckeye Institute*.

Both look at many of the same issues.

Both come to different conclusions.

Both think they're right.

If it's the conservative approach you like, *The Buckeye Institute* (www.buckeyeinstitute.org), which touts itself as "Ohio's only free market think tank," may be just the place to reinforce your beliefs and get the knowledge you need to debate your more progressive friends. *The Buckeye Institute* with its decidedly libertarian and pro-business approach to Ohio's economic situation draws from a team of over 50 Ohio college and university scholars. Predictably, they advocate low taxes, less regulation, and the other linchpins of conservative public policy. On their website can be found position papers on taxes, education, health care, and urban sprawl, all well-argued from the perspective of less government with a high reliance on private industry and the individual.

If you like opinions from the other side, try *Policy Matters Ohio* (www.policymattersohio.org). It has also amassed an impressive team of scholars from universities around the state. Their take on issues comes from a progressive perspective with a concern for the welfare of low- and middle-income workers. *Policy Matters Ohio* is more likely than its conservative counterpart to find economic solutions in the realm of government. Seeing itself as more "grass roots" than its conservative counterpart, it believes that it can "strengthen democracy by providing Ohio's citizens with the essential tools to participate in the public discussion on the economy."

The site is an excellent place to gather information to counter the arguments of your misinformed friends on the right. —*Michael O'Bryant*

BOB TAFT gets Governor JESSE VENTURA in his DREADED SLEEPER HOLD!

LET ME TELL YOU ABOUT MY COMMISSION TO STUDY EDUCATION FINANCE REFORM...

MUST.... REMAIN.... CONSCIOUS....

"Based on the campaign commercials you've seen, ask yourself this: If you washed your car, what would you rather have fly over it, a dove or a politician?"

—Dick Feagler, Cleveland Plain Dealer

state.oh.us/sos/ Voter/index.htm

From the office of the Ohio Secretary of State, this site offers information about registering to vote, how to vote, absentee voting for students, U.S Armed Forces members, and others; the site also provides answers to frequently asked questions about Election Dayand the polling place.

The vote for Ohio Elected Officials, 2000

Office	Candidate	Vote	Percent
Justice Ohio Supreme Court	Alice Robie Resnick	2,312,073	57.1%
	Terrence O'Donnell	1,740,516	42.9%
Justice Ohio Supreme Court	Deborah Cook	2,014,274	51.9%
	Tim Black	1,869,060	48.1%

The vote for Ohio Elected Officials, 2002

Office	Party*	Candidate	Vote	Percent
Governor	R	Bob Taft	1,865,007	57.8%
	D	Timothy Hagan	1,236,924	38.3%
		John Eastman	126,686	3.9%
		James Whitman	291	0.0%
Secretary of State	R	J. Kennith Blackwell	1,827,995	59.3%
	D	Bryan Flannery	1,256,428	40.7%
Attorney General	R	Jim Petro	2,007,411	64.1%
	D	Leigh Harrington	1,123,318	35.9%
Auditor of State	R	Betty Montgomery	2,010,022	64.3%
	D	Helen Smith	1,114,957	35.7%
Treasurer of State	R	Joseph Deters	1,666,844	53.3%
	D	Mary Boyle	1,459,113	46.7%
		Robert Martin	108	0.0%
Justice Ohio Supreme Court		Maureen O'Connor	1,709,673	57.3%
		Tim Black	1,276,497	42.7%
Justice Ohio Supreme Court		Evelyn Stratton	1,599,165	55.3%
		Janet Burnside	1,290,412	44.7%

Ohio Senators, 2000

Dist.	Party	Candidate	Vote
2	R	Randy Gardner	101,756 (100.0%)
4	R	Scott Nein	95,220 (66.6%)
	D	Arnold Engle	47,259 (33.4%)
6	R	Jeff Jacobson	80,340 (58.2%)
	D	Karl Keith	48,854 (35.4%)
	L	Tom Brown	8,960 (6.5%)
8	R	Louis Blessing, Jr.	80,340 (58.2%)
	D	Stuart Manning	40,656 (31.4%)
	L	Stephen Schulte	7,324 (5.6%)
10	R	Steve Austria	84,860 (63.8%)
	D	Roger Tackett	48,199 (36.2%)
12	R	Jim Jordan	99,803 (76.9%)
		Jack Kaffenberger	15,545 (12.0%)
	N	Debra Mitchell	14,373 (11.1%)
14	R	Doug White	105,321 (79.8%)
	L	Margaret Leech	26,813 (20.3%)
16	R	Priscilla Mead	104,454 (76.8%)
	L	William Kammerer	31,574 (23.2%)
18	R	Robert Gardner	73,529 (57.9%)
	D	Donna Mcnamee	49,385 (38.9%)
	L	Bart Hildebrant	4,091 (3.2%)
19	R	Bill Harris	102,539 (66.9%)
	D	Jack Campbell	50,758 (33.1%)
20	R	Jim Carnes	84,280 (64.4%)
	D	Randy Williams	46,644 (35.6%)
22	R	Ron Amstutz	91,542 (58.1%)
	D	Elizabeth Kelly	55,951 (35.5%)
		Randy Jotte	6,977 (4.4%)
	L	Cheryl Neufer	3,014 (1.9%)
24	R	Rob Spada	104,176 (64.8%)
	D	Ed Boyle	51,843 (32.2%)
	N	Richard Leirer	4,788 (3.0%)
26	R	Larry Mumper	83,509 (63.2%)
	D	Mary Fleure	48,823 (36.8%)
28	D	Leigh Herington	76,818 (62.3%)
	R	Judy Jones	41,771 (33.9%)
	L	Pearl Pullman	4,682 (3.8%)
30	D	Greg Didonato	101,320 (100.0%)
32	D	Timothy Ryan	67,853 (51.0%)
	R	Randy Law	47,402 (35.6%)
		Arthur Magee	14,328 (10.8%)
	L	Patricia Urquhart	3,485 (2.6%)

Ohio Senators, 2002

Dist.	Party	Candidate	Vote
1	R	Lynn Wachtmann	70,146 (67.9%)
	D	William Flanary	33,103 (32.1%)
3	R	David Goodman	56,989 (57.8%)
	D	Debra Payne	41,580 (42.2%)
5	D	Tom Roberts	45,412 (52.5%)
	R	Mike Osgood	41,159 (47.5%)
7	R	Robert Schuler	75,315 (71.4%)
	D	Tony Fisher	30,232 (28.6%)
9	D	Mark Mallory	53,356 (100%)
11	D	Teresa Fedor	56,760 (72.4%)
	R	Barbosa Phillip	21,605 (27.6%)
13	R	Jeffry Armbruster	47,857 (50.2%)
	D	Sue Morano	47,485 (49.8%)
15	D	Ray Miller	50,119 (73.0%)
	R	Lacey Lorena	18,497 (26.96)
17	R	John Carey Jr.	48,593 (53.9%)
	D	Michael Shoemaker	41,601 (46.1%)
19	R	Bill Harris	67,915 (67.9%)
	D	Jack Campbell	32,576 (32.4%)
21	D	C.J. Prentiss	50,922 (82.3%)
	R	Richard Norris	10,935 (17.9%)
23	D	Dan Brady	52,784 (67.0%)
	R	Ress Richard	25,998 (33.0%)
25	D	Eric Fingerhut	75,130 (84.6%)
	R	Jackie Huggins	13,665 (15.4%)
27	R	Kevin Coughlin	56,467 (53.9%)
	D	Tom Bevan	50,180 (47.1%)
29	R	Kirk Schuring	60,072(58.8%)
	D	Jan Schwartz	43,916 (42.2%)
31	R	Jay Hottinger	83,774 (100.0%)
33	D	Robert Hagan	71,469 (68.0%)
	R	Holly Hanni	33,571 (32.0%)

Registered Voters in Ohio

Year	Voters
1985	6,082,980
1986	5,996,430
1987	5,822,189
1988	6,275,638
1989	5,830,757
1990	5,912,746
1991	5,820,133
1992	6,536,936
1993	6,204,103
1994	6,231,724
1995	6,416,133
1996	6,879,687
1997	7,022,866
1998	7,096,423
1999	7,146,985
2000	7,531,555
2001	7,153,796
2002	7,104,549

Ohio Representatives, 2002

Dist.	Party	Candidate	Vote		Dist.	Party	Candidate	Vote
1	R	Chuck Blasdel	17,473 (56.8%)		22	R	Jim Huges	23,883 (65.3%)
	D	Frank Rivelle	13,299 (43.2%)			D	Ken Schweickart	11,592 (31.7%)
							Alan Amstutz	1,124 (3.1%)
2	R	Jon Peterson	27,347 (72.9%)					
	D	Andrew Mackey	10,143 (27.1%)		23	R	Larry Wolpert	24,370 (100.0%)
3	R	Jim Carmichael	19,936 (67.3%)		24	R	Geoffrey Smith	20,012 (60.2%)
	D	Tim Bradley	9,699 (32.7%)			D	Patrick Byrne	13,259 (39.8%)
4	R	John Willamowski	22,747 (76.5%)		25	D	Dan Stewart	12,338 (55.2%)
	D	Francis Matthew	6,978 (23.5%)			R	David Dobos	10,008 (44.8%)
5	R	Tim Schaffer	30,018 (100.0%)		26	D	Larry Price	20,043 (78.7%)
						R	Lionel Jones	5,421 (21.3%)
6	R	Robert Latta	25,493 (68.1%)					
	D	Scott McCarty	11,932 (31.9%)		27	D	Joyce Beatty	16,786 (82.4%)
						R	Stephan Reinhart	3,583 (17.6%)
7	D	Ed Jerse	21,039 (79.3%)					
	R	Steven Pressman	5,475 (20.7%)		28	R	Jim Raussen	20,381 (58.9%)
						D	Wayne Coates	14,242 (41.1%)
8	D	Lance Mason	26,788 (100.0%)					
					29	R	Patricia Clancy	24,474 (71.4%)
9	D	C. Woodward	21.673 (82.3%)			D	Danny Kenneweg	9,786 (28.6%)
	R	C. Wyssbrod	4,674 (17.7%)					
					30	R	Bill Seitz	28,907 (76.0%)
10	D	Shriley Smith	14,908 (100.0%)			D	Bob Klug	9,120 (24.0%)
11	D	Annie Kay	14,017 (78.0%)		31	D	Steve Driehaus	12,916 (65.2%)
	R	Tony Kaloger	3,943 (22.0%)			R	Sheryl Ross	7,425 (34.5%)
12	D	Michael DeBose	23,940 (86.5%)		32	D	Catherine Barrett	15,211 (70.5%)
	R	Dan Trif	3,738 (13.5%)			R	Randy O'Hara	6,363 (29.5%)
13	D	Michael Skindell	13,241 (63.9%)		33	D	Tyrone Yates	18,532(67.0%)
	R	Ryan Demro	7,495 (36.1%)			R	Sandra Hall	9,118 (33.0%)
14	D	Dale Miller	19,164 (70.8%)		34	R	Tom Brinkman Jr.	23,748 (63.1%)
	R	Michael Hoag	7,871 (29.1%)			D	Dave Schaff	13,896 (36.1%)
15	D	Dean DePiero	25,380 (100.0%)		35	R	M. Schneider	31,830 (100.0%)
16	R	Sally Kilbane	24,575 (59.1%)		36	R	Arlene Setzer	22,188 (60.2%)
	D	Kevin Kennedy	17,012 (40.1%)			D	Doug Orange	14,668 (39.8%)
17	R	James Trakas	27,511 (63.0%)		37	R	Jon Husted	22,468 (64.3%)
	D	Blair Melling	16,171 (37.0%)			D	G. Williamson	12,403 (37.6%)
18	R	Thomas Patton	19,875 (53.3%)		38	R	John White	22,974 (64.4%)
	D	Susan Adams	17,383 (46.7%)			D	Nick Gerren	13,678 (35.6%)
19	R	Larry Flowers	21,819 (65.2%)		39	R	Dixie Allen	16,994 (76.6%)
	D	Mary White	11,633 (34.8%)			D	Brian Whitaker	5,179 (23.4%)
20	R	Jim McGregor	19,940 (60.9%)		40	D	Fred Strahorn	19,725 (71.8%)
	D	Fran Dennis	12,788 (39.1%)			R	Martin Arbagi	7,744 (28.2%)
21	R	Linda Reidelbach	16,998 (54.9%)		41	R	Bryan Williams	22,219 (57.7%)
	D	Lori Tyack	13,964 (45.1%)			D	Kurt Landefeld	16,280 (43.3%)

42	R	John Widowfield	22,037 (55.6%)	63	R	Ronald Young	18,915 (61.7%)
	D	Libert Bozzelli	14,221 (35.9%)		D	Timothy Cassell	11,738 (38.3%)
		Harold Baer Jr.	3,375 (8.2%)				
				64	D	Daniel Sferra	17,898 (53.6%)
43	R	Mary Taylor	21.013 (53.6%)		R	Randy Law	15,492 (46.4%)
	D	Michael Grimm	18,180 (46.4%)				
				65	D	Sandra Harwood	21,882 (64.5%)
44	D	Barbara Sykes	19,655 (100.0%)		R	James Calko, Jr.	9,430 (27.8%)
						Werner Lange	2,632 (7.8%)
45	D	Robert Otterman	17,518 (70.3%)				
	R	Kathryn Culver	7,400 (29.7%)	66	R	Jean Schmidt	23,606 (100.0%)
46	R	Lynn Olman	26,628 (69.5%)	67	R	Tom Raga	26,574 (100.0%)
	D	Abbey Mortemore	11,680 (30.5%)				
				68	D	Kathleen Chandler	16,830 (55.6%)
47	D	Peter Ujvagi	17,991 (67.8%)		R	Terri Hauenstein	13,448 (44.2%)
	R	Roy Allen	8,558 (32.2%)				
				69	R	Charles Calvert	19,631 (60.2%)
48	D	Edna Brown	17,846 (69.5%)		D	Jack Schira	12,985 (39.2%)
	R	C. Voyles-Baden	4,827 (18.1%)				
		June Boyd	2,987 (11.2%)	70	R	Kevin DeWine	21,538 (71.7%)
					D	Lawrence Gordon	8,506 (28.3%)
49	D	Jeanine Perry	21,373 (70.4%)				
	R	Joseph Lipinski	8,991 (29.6%)	71	R	David Evans	27,441 (100.0%)
50	R	John Hagan	19,355 (57.1%)	72	R	Merle Kearns	15,293 (57.2%)
	D	Martin Olson	14,542 (42.9%)		D	Ron Rhine	11,463 (42.8%)
51	R	Scott Oelslager	19,936 (70.0%)	73	D	William Hartnett	19,411 (63.7%)
	D	Marylyn Scott	12,837 (30.0%)		R	Lisa Rathburn	11,083 (36.4%)
52	D	Mary Cirelli	14,052 (53.7%)	74	R	Stephen Buehrer	27,479 (100.0%)
	R	Scott Warner	7,574 (28.9%)				
		David Kidd	4,550 (17.4%)	75	R	James Hoops	30,653 (100.0%)
53	R	Shawn Webster	18,560 (64.5%)	76	R	Mike Glib	22,441 (68.9%)
	D	A. Mitchell	10,232 (35.5%)		D	Kenneth Ludwig	10,124 (31.1%)
54	R	Gregory Jolivette	20,700 (72.4%)	77	R	Keith Faber	28,353 (74.9%)
	D	Arnold Engel	7,881 (27.6%)		D	Benjamin Amstutz	9,483 (25.1%)
55	R	Gary Cates	23,756 (100.0%)	78	D	Derrick Seaver	20,434 (58.3%)
					R	John Adams	14,630 (41.7%)
56	D	Joseph Kozura	18,454 (71.0%)				
	R	Daniel Williamson	7,537 (29.0%)	79	R	Diana Fessler	23,793 (68.8%)
					D	Carol McKeever	10,805 (31.2%)
57	R	Jeffery Manning	19,904 (55.4%)				
	D	David Bruening	16,063 (44.4%)	80	D	Chris Redfern	20,635 (56.5%)
					R	J. Tom Lendrum	15,862 (43.5%)
58	R	Kathleen Walcher	18,365 (58.0%)				
	D	Kenneth Bailey	13,278 (42.0%)	81	R	Jeff Wagner	19,356 (54.1%)
					D	James Melle	16,443 (45.9%)
59	D	Kennith Carano	25,528 (58.4%)				
	R	Alberty Paul	18,211 (41.6%)	82	R	Steve Reinhard	19,705 (66.7%)
					D	Steven Chaffin	9,851 (33.3%)
60	D	Sylvester Patton	23,242 (80.1%)				
	R	William Sicfuse	5,759 (19.9%)	83	R	Anthony Core	21,956 (70.2%)
					D	Stacy Roberts	9,331 (29.8%)
61	D	John Boccieri	20,104 (62.8%)				
	R	Randy Pope	12,953 (39.2%)	84	R	Chris Widener	21,730 (62.2%)
					D	Natalie Tackett	12,974 (37.8%)
62	R	Jamie Callender	19,532 (62.8%)				
	D	John Hawkins	11,549 (37.2%)	85	R	John Schlichter	14,994 (58.1%)
					D	Joseph Sulzer	12,730 (45.9%)

Voter Turnout

in Ohio

1980 73.88%

1982 62.37%

1984 73.66%

1986 54.40%

1988 71.79%

1990 61.23%

1992 77.00%

1994 57.30%

86	R	David Daniels	17,779 (65.9%)
	D	Bill Horne	9,633 (35.1%)
87	R	Clyde Evans	17,996 (55.7%)
	D	Fred Deel	14,316 (44.3%)
88	R	Tom Niehaus	22,730 (100.0%)
89	D	Todd Book	19,337 (58.8%)
	R	Harold Sayre	13,556 (41.2%)
90	R	Thom Collier	21,491 (66.9%)
	D	Howard Hoffman	10,634 (33.1%)
91	R	Larry Householder	22,480 (66.7%)
	D	Brad Gothard	11,239 (33.3%)
92	R	Jimmy Stewart	19,423 (58.1%)
	D	James Pancake	14,015 (41.9%)

93	R	Nancy Hollister	20,188 (58.8%)
	D	William Moore	14,137 (41.2%)
94	R	Jim Aslanides	23,956 (100.0%)
95	D	John Domenick	21,354 (60.1%)
	R	Frank Sentich, Jr.	14,172 (39.8%)
96	D	Charlie Wilson	21,840 (62.0%)
	R	Greg Erb	13,397 (38.0%)
97	R	Bob Gibbs	18,182 (62.4%)
	D	Thomas Mason	10,939 (37.6%)
98	R	Timothy Grendell	26,363 (69.7%)
	D	Meg Cacciacarro	11,471 (30.3%)
99	D	L. George Distel	18,759 (65.8%)
	R	Robert Rennie	9,745 (34.2%)
		Donald Rogers	12 (0.04%)

OHIO FINALLY JOINS REST OF THE U.S.

One hundred thirty-five years later, Ohio is finally on board with the 14th Amendment to the U.S. Constitution, and it's about time.

In March of 2003, the Ohio House of representatives voted to endorse the amendment, which gives people born or naturalized in the United States full citizenship rights regardless of race. The amendment also ensures that the law treats people fairly, and it guarantees every American life, liberty and property under the law.

Ohio's resolution is a symbolic measure, but it almost didn't happen.

The 14th Amendment already is law. It was ratified by three-quarters of the states in 1868—three years after slavery was abolished. At first Ohio ratified the amendment, but a new state-house majority that opposed blacks' gaining rights rescinded Ohio's ratification the next year.

That's how it stood, until seven University of Cincinnati College of Law students discovered in 2002 that Ohio was the only state opposing the amendment.

The students convinced State Sen. Mark Mallory (D–Cincinnati) and Speaker Pro Tempore Gary Cates (R–West Chester) to sponsor a joint resolution.

At first things moved quickly. The Senate voted unanimously to ratify, and all the senators became co-sponsors. But in the House, several conservative lawmakers proposed adding provisos to the resolution, asterisks to ratification, to reflect their political and social views.

They said the 14th Amendment has had a checkered past that they didn't want to be on record as endorsing. It was instrumental, after all, in *Roe vs. Wade*, which ensured women's access to abortion. And it recently was used to prevent schools from forcing students to say "under God" in the Pledge of Allegiance.

Even for liberals, it hasn't always been kind. The 14th Amendment was used in *Plessy vs. Ferguson to* legalize Jim Crow, though in *Brown vs. Board of Education* the court struck down state-sponsored segregation. The U.S. Supreme Court used it to halt the hand count of Florida's ballots in the 2000 presidential election.

State Rep. Bill Seitz (R–Cincinnati) tried to cover many bases with language he proposed adding to Ohio's resolution.

"Resolved that the General Assembly rejects those judicial interpretations of the 14th Amendment that unreasonably restrict state governments from promoting the free exercise of religion, defending the sanctity of unborn life and ensuring the equitable distribution of educational dollars to aid students enrolled in schools sponsored by religious institutions."

Seitz explained that he was thinking of his constituency. "Nowhere is the Right to Life cause stronger than in Cincinnati," he said. He said he thought that the added language would silence opposition to the amendment. Instead it amplified it. The resolution's sponsors despaired that it might not pass.

After more debate and on-the-record posturing, the lawmakers, including Seitz, passed the 14th Amendment resolution—unadorned.

"Nobody has a problem with the 14th Amendment as written. Some of us just wanted to use it as a little educational experiment for our members," Seitz said.

The experiment didn't go over too well. Despite its mixed record, the 14th Amendment still deserves unqualified endorsement.

As Gabriel Chin, of UC's law school, put it: "I'm not saying America is perfect. But it's a freer and more just country because of the 14th Amendment."

—*Denise Smith Amos, permission of the Cincinnati Enquirer*

the 14th amendment

151

Convict labor, unused paper, a timely fire and a loser's painting all helped to produce Ohio's unusual "Hat Box Capitol." While 44 of the 48 continental United States have domed Capitols, and two others have modern skyscrapers, Ohio managed to produce a capitol design with the assistance of no less than 11 architects. What started out to be a building designed through a competition involving "the most eminent architects, and men of taste, which our country affords," turned out to be a structure designed by no one and everyone.

Ohio's first Capitol was a neat, clean and well-proportioned 30 x 30 foot stone building erected in the middle of the street in Chillicothe in 1800 to serve as a territorial seat of government. It was so well-regarded as fitting the needs of the new state legislature, that somehow an almost identical building was built in 1811 in Corydon, Indiana to serve the new Hoosier State. But while Ohio's Capitol was fine, the Capital city was not, for many of the citizens of the new state wanted Ohio's government to be in a more central location. The Capital was temporarily moved to Zanesville, where from 1810 to 1812, the legislators legislated in a new and larger Capitol that was dubbed "Old 1809." Though this brick Capitol was modeled after Independence Hall in Philadelphia, the legislators' first act in the building was to decide to locate Ohio's capital city within 40 miles of the state's geographic center, and while the solons searched for a site, they moved the Capital again, relocating back to Chillicothe in 1812.

The location of Ohio's present Capital is a logical one, being in the middle of the state at what was originally a small town named after Benjamin Franklin and that has since been renamed after Christopher Columbus, both good men and rather neutral politically. Columbus became the seat of Ohio's government in 1816. The first Capitol in the new Capital was a rather plain and small building for the legislature for a fast growing state. No one was very happy with it, and so there was great rejoicing in January 26, 1838, when the legislature voted to replace it

with its dream Capitol. They appointed a three-man commission (the first of seven to be involved) to conduct a competition among the "most eminent" etc., and thus began the long chain of circumstances that lead to the "Hat Box."

First prize in the competition and $500 was awarded to a good Cincinnati architect named Henry Walter. His was a nice clean design meeting all of the commission's requirements and specifications, and it included a dome supported by 26 forty-four foot high columns and a portico with eight massive columns on the west and east ends. Second prize and $300 went to architect Martin E. Thompson of New York City for a very similar design, except there were no columns supporting his 50 foot dome, and there were to be ten massive columns on the porticoes. Thompson's dome was lower but larger than Walter's, and both were judged better than the third place design of Thomas Cole, a painter from Catskill, New York. Cole's plan showed a much larger and higher dome supported by 24 columns without a portico.

From that point, having paid the prize and made the selection, one would think that things would have progressed into construction. There had been more than 60 designs submitted and the best designers had been consulted, but politicians are prone to "junket" and to justify their "junketing," they must make some changes. Two of the three commissioners thus went to Philadelphia and Boston and such places to consult some of the country's best and most qualified architects, including Alexander J. Davis

who had lost the competition. The plan that was finally submitted to the legislature and used for the construction was a "modification of the plans to which the premiums were awarded." The design, in fact, has been attributed to Davis more than anyone else, and it was a close modification of the third place design submitted not by an architect but the landscape painter Thomas Cole.

The huge new building was finally started on July 4, 1839, when the cornerstone was laid. The saving grace of the muddled design was the decision to use local limestone for the construction. Good limestone was available at nearby Marble Cliff, and it made a very distinguished appearance for a public building. There was also a decision to employ convict labor from the nearby penitentiary, which probably was part of the reason that it took 22 years to finish the building.

To complicate the situation even more, the commissioners hired the design winner, Henry Walter, to supervise the construction of a modification of the third place design. Mr. Walter then probably made a few more changes to favor his original design. To the untrained eye, the final building looked more like Walter's original plan than Cole's, but then the commissioners declared it, "Thomas Cole's plan as altered and executed," and "That adopted is Mr. Cole's

design, modified by projecting a portico on one of the sides instead of the recess."

Scandal, however, soon threatened to undermine the entire project. When the legislature moved to Columbus in the winter of 1839, Samuel Medary, editor of the *Ohio Statesman* and the *State Printer*, was accused of appropriating certain "unused paper" for his own purposes. In the end, Medary was found innocent, but the citizens of Columbus got into the act and presented a petition to the legislators that infuriated them almost to a man. The solons halted work on the new Capitol and began to look for a new Capital. By 1842, it looked very much like Newark, Ohio, would become Ohio's fourth official Capital and that the Capitol in Columbus would be converted to an insane asylum.

Cooler heads prevailed, and on March 6, 1843, the legislators decided to remain in Columbus. By then, however, the state was in a financial crunch caused in part by canal bond problems, and work did not resume on the Capitol until mid-1846. A new supervising architect, William Russell West, was retained, and the convicts went back to work. They might still be at it, except for a very timely fire.

In 1852, the old Statehouse burned to the ground. The legislature had no

THE NEW STATE CAPITOL BUILDING.

THE STATEHOUSE: AN ACCOUNTING

The renovation of the Statehouse—$40 million over budget—was pushed through by Richard Finian, the Senate president, after the Evendale fire chief came by for a visit and counted 69 fire violations walking from the garage to Finian's office.

—Cincinnati Enquirer, December 3, 2002

Style
Greek Revival with Doric columns

Location
Statehouse Square, ten square acres, 660 feet per side, bounded by Broad, Third, State, and High Streets in Columbus

Cost
$1,359,121.59; completed 1861

Cost of chairs in original House of Representatives: $8.50 each

Wage for mason laborers: $1.50 per day

Approximate cost of Statehouse restoration project, 1996: $121 million

Cost to taxpayer: 12 cents per month for 20 years

Outside dimensions
184 by 304 feet

Senate chamber dimensions
55 by 82 feet

House chamber dimensions
55 by 82 feet

Rotunda floor
4,982 marble blocks in white (from Italy), pink (from Portugal), black (from Vermont), and green (from Vermont)

Wiring
471 miles of wiring in statehouse

West portico flagpoles
Ohio state flags flown there show which chamber of the legislature is in session; an Ohio pennon on the north flagpole indicates the Senate; on the south flagpole, the House of Representatives

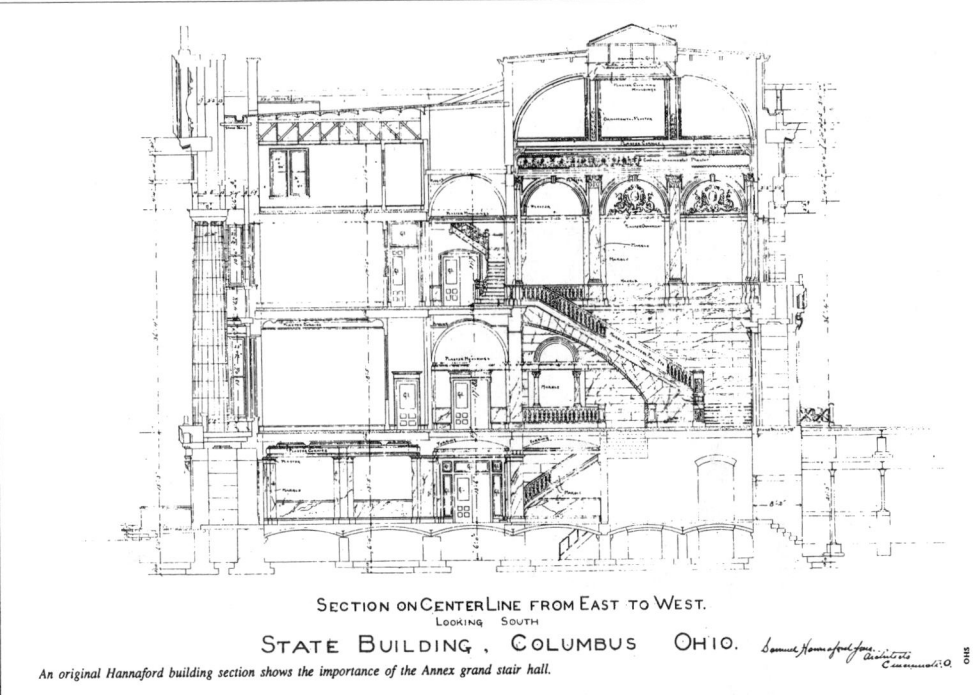

SECTION ON CENTER LINE FROM EAST TO WEST.
LOOKING SOUTH

STATE BUILDING , COLUMBUS OHIO.

An original Hannaford building section shows the importance of the Annex grand stair hall.

36 Ohio Statehouse Master Plan

place to meet, but found accommodations in other Columbus buildings that were at least as comfortable as the old Statehouse had been. By this time, there were new commissioners and of course a new governor (the third of five involved in the construction), and more changes were made to the Capitol. One of the smartest things they did in 1852 was build a small railroad from Marble Cliff to the construction site to transport marble blocks without the weather delays of muddy and corduroy roads.

With the new railroad and a new supervising architect, Isaiah Rogers, the work moved quickly and on January 6, 1859 (almost 20 years after the work began), the new building was dedicated and put into use, although not yet finished. The oldest member of the legislature was given the honor of the dedication. Al Kelley had first been elected to the legislature at age 24 in 1814, and he had served in Chillicothe as its youngest member. Kelley was still around in 1857, but ill and about to retire from public office.

Kelley was an honest man throughout his life and for that was not much loved, even by his own political party. He had mortgaged his own lovely Greek home on East Broad Street in 1837 to keep the State's canal bonds from going into default, and he had not only headed the canal construc-

tion but also had built a good many railroads across Ohio. If others expected Al Kelley to pay great verbal respect to the new Capitol and its architects, they were quite mistaken.

"The building in which we are now assembled," said Kelley, "combines that sublime massiveness, that dignity of room and feature, that beautiful symmetry of proportions which together constitute true architectural excellence in a high degree." Then, while the architects involved probably waited for their names to be raised in praise, he allowed, "True, it may have its imper- fections..."

Al Kelley expected and believed that the Capitol he was getting was a Doric structure with a dome, not a hat box. Although he and others applied pressure, the building that was completed in 1861 was a massive "Greek Revival" structure with a "Hat Box" roof. The Statehouse that had consumed $1.3 million dollars, 23 years, and eleven architects, and that Frank Lloyd Wright would later describe as "the most honest of state capitols, sincere and forthright," was, ironically, a hybrid that had neither been intended nor approved by the legislature.

— *by Richard Coleman*

Warning: DO NOT OPERATE HEAVY EQUIPMENT WHILE WATCHING THE POLITICAL CONVENTIONS!

The Democrats were for a lot more of something to be named at a later date. The Republicans were for less of whatever it was except the death penalty. The Democrats said, "We don't know what's wrong with America, but we can fix it." The Republicans said, "There's nothing wrong with America, and we can fix that."

—P.J. O'Rourke, Parliament of Whores

Year	Office	Political Party*	Candidate	Vote
1803	Governor	R	Edward Tiffin	4,564
1804	President	R	Thomas Jefferson	2,593
		Federalist	Charles C. Pinkney	364
1805	Governor	R	Edward Tiffin	4,783
1808	President	R	James Madison	3,645
		Federalist	Charles C. Pinckney	1,174
	Governor	R	Samuel Huntington	7,293
		R	Thomas Worthington	5,601
		R	Thomas Kirker	3,397
1810	Governor	RA	Return J. Meigs, Jr.	9,924
		R	Thomas Worthington	7,731
1812	President	R	James Madison	7,420
		Federalist	DeWitt Clinton	3,301
	Governor	R	Return J. Meigs, Jr.	11,859
		R	Thomas Scott	7,903
1814	Governor	R	Thomas Worthington	15,879
		R	Othniel Looker	6,171
1816	President	R	James Monroe	3,326
		Federalist	Rufus King	593
	Governor	R	Thomas Worthington	22,931
		R	James Dunlap	6,295
		R	Ethan A. Brown	1,607
1818	Governor	R	Ethan A. Brown	30,194
		R	James Dunlap	8,075
1820	President	R	James Monroe	7,164
		Independent	John Q. Adams	2,215
	Governor	R	Ethan A. Brown	34,836
		R	Jeremiah Morrow	9,426
		R	William H. Harrison	4,348
			Others	250
1822	Governor	R	Jeremiah Morrow	26,059
		Federalist	Allen Trimble	22,089
		R	William W. Irvin	11,060

Year	Office	Political Party*	Candidate	Vote
1824	President	R	Andrew Jackson	18,489
		R	John Q. Adams	12,280
		R	Henry Clay	19,255
	Governor	R	Jeremiah Morrow	39,526
		R	Allen Trimble	37,108
1826	Governor	R	Allen Trimble	39,526
		R	Alex Campbell	4,765
			Benjamin Tappan	4,192
			John Bigger	4,114
			Others	187
1828	President	D	Andrew Jackson	67,597
		NRepublican	John Q Adams	63,396
	Governor	R	Allen Trimble	53,971
		D	John W. Campbell	51,591
			Others	112
1830	Governor	NRepublican	Duncan McArthur	49,668
		D	Robert Lucas	49,186
			Others	226
1832	President	D	Andrew Jackson	81,246
		NRepublican	Henry Clay	76,539
		Anti-Mason	William Wirt	509
	Governor	D	Robert Lucas	71,251
		Whig	Darius Lyman	63,185
			Others	33
1834	Governor	D	Robert Lucas	70,738
		Whig	James Findlay	67,414
			Others	38
1836	President	D	Martin Van Buren	96,238
		Whig	William H. Harrison	104,958
			Others	1,137
	Governor	Whig	Joseph Vance	92,204
		D	Eli Bladwin	86,158
			Others	200
1838	Governor	D	Wilson Shannon	107,884
		Whig	Joseph Vance	102,146
			Others	7
1840	President	Whig	William H. Harrison	148,157
		D	Martin Van Buren	124,782
		Liberty	James G. Birney	903
	Governor	Whig	Thomas Corwin	145,442
		D	Wilson Shannon	129,312
			Others	8
1842	Governor	D	Wilson Shannon	119,774
		Whig	Thomas Corwin	117,902
		Abolitionist	Leister King	5,134
			Others	40
1844	President	D	James K. Polk	149,061
		Whig	Henry Clay	155,113
		Liberty	James G. Birney	8,050
	Governor	Whig	Mordecai Bartley	146,333
		D	David Tod	145,062
		Abolitionist	Leister King	8,008
			Others	11
1846	Governor	Whig	William Bebb	118,869
		D	David Tod	116,484
		Liberty	Samuel Lewis	10,797
			Others	46
1848	President	Whig	Zachary Taylor	138,359
		D	Lewis Cass	154,773
		Free Soil	Martin Van Buren	35,347
	Governor	Whig	Seabury Ford	148,756
		D	John B. Weller	148,445
			Others	742

Year	Office	Political Party*	Candidate	Vote
1850	Governor	D	Reuben Wood	133,093
		Whig	William Johnston	121,105
		Free Soil	Edward Smith	13,747
1851	Governor	D	Reuben Wood	145,654
		Whig	Samuel Vinton	119,548
		Free Soil	Samuel Lewis	16,918
1852	President	D	Franklin Pierce	168,933
		Whig	Winfield Scott	152,523
		Free Soil	John P. Hale	31,732
1853	Governor	D	William Medill	147,663
		Whig	Nelson Barrere	85,857
		Free Democrat	Samuel Lewis	50,346
1855	Governor	R	Salmon P. Chase	146,770
		D	William Medill	131,019
		Know-Nothing	Allen Trimble	24,276
1856	President	D	James Buchanan	170,874
		R	John C. Fremont	187,497
		Know-Nothing	Millard Fillmore	28,126
1857	Governor	R	Salmon P. Chase	160,568
		D	H.B. Payne	159,065
		American	P. Van Trump	10,272
1859	Governor	R	William Dennison	184,557
		D	Rufus P. Ranney	171,226
1860	President	R	Abraham Lincoln	231,809
		D	Stephen A. Douglas	187,421
		Constitutional Union	John Bell	12,193
		D	John C. Breckinridge	11,403
		Abolitionist	Gerritt Smith	136
1861	Governor	R	David Tod	206,997
		D	Hugh J. Jewett	151,794
			Others	109
1863	Governor	R	John Brough	288,374
		D	C.L. Vallandingham	187,492
1864	President	R	Abraham Lincoln	265,654
		D	George B. McClellan	205,599
1865	Governor	R	Jacob D. Cox	223,633
		D	George W. Morgan	193,797
			Others	360
1867	Governor	R	Rutherford B. Hayes	243,605
		D	A.G. Thurman	240,622
1868	President	R	Ulysses S. Grant	280,223
		D	Horatio Seymour	238,606
1869	Governor	R	Rutherford B. Hayes	236,082
		D	G.H. Pendleton	228,581
		Prohibition	Samuel Scott	629
1871	Governor	R	Edward F. Noyes	238,273
		D	George W. McCook	218,105
		Prohibiton	Gideon T. Stewart	4,084
1872	President	R	Ulysses S. Grant	281,852
		D and Liberal	Horace Greeley	244,321
		Prohibition	James Black	2,100
		D	Charles O'Connor	1,163
			Others	162
1873	Governor	D	William Allen	214,654
		R	Edward F. Noyes	213,837
		Prohibition	Gideon T. Stewart	10,278
			Isaac C. Collins	10,109
1875	Governor	R	Rutherford B. Hayes	297,817
		D	William Allen	292,273
		Prohibtion	Jay Odell	2,593
			Others	17

Year	Office	Political Party*	Candidate	Vote
1876	President	R	Rutherford B. Hayes	330,698
		D	Samuel J. Tilden	323,182
		Prohibition	G. Clay Smith	1,636
		Greenback	Peter Cooper	3,507
			Others	1,198
1877	Governor	D	Richard M. Bishop	271,625
		R	William H. West	249,105
		Greenback	Stephen Johnson	16,912
			Lewis H. Bond	12,489
		Prohibition	Henry A. Thompson	4,836
1879	Governor	R	Charles Foster	336,261
		D	Thomas Ewing	319,132
		Greenback	A. Sanders Piatt	9,072
		Prohibition	Gideon T. Stewart	4,145
			John Hood	547
1880	President	R	James A. Garfield	375,048
		D	Winfield S. Hancock	340,821
		Greenback	James B. Weaver	6,456
		Prohibition	Neal Dow	2,616
			Others	26
1881	Governor	R	Charles Foster	312,735
		D	John W. Bookwalter	288,426
		Prohibition	Abraham R. Ludlow	16,597
		Greenback	John Seitz	6,330
			Others	138
1883	Governor	D	George Hoadley	359,693
		R	Joseph B. Foraker	347,164
		Prohibition	F. Schumacher	8,362
		Greenback	Charles Jenkins	2,937
			Others	3,154
1884	President	R	James G. Blaine	400,082
		D	Grover Cleveland	368,280
		Prohibition	John P. St. John	11,069
		Greenback	Benjamin F. Butler	5,179
			Others	2,549
1885	Governor	R	Joseph B. Foraker	359,281
		D	George Hoadley	341,830
		Prohibition	Adna B. Leonard	28,081
		Greenback	John W. Northup	2,001
			Others	2,774
1887	Governor	R	Joseph B. Foraker	356,534
		D	Thomas E. Powell	333,205
		Union Labor	John Seitz	24,711
		Prohibition	Morris Sharp	29,700
			Others	2,820
1888	President	R	Benjamin Harrison	416,054
		D	Grover Cleveland	396,455
		Prohibition	Clinton B. Fiske	24,356
		Union Labor	Alson J. Streeter	3,496
			Others	1,580
1889	Governor	D	James E. Campbell	379,423
		R	Joseph B. Foraker	368,551
		Prohibition	John B. Helwig	26,504
		Union Labor	John H. Rhodes	1,048
			Others	195
1891	Governor	R	William McKinley, Jr.	386,739
		D	James E. Campbell	365,228
		People's	John J. Seitz	23,472
		Prohibition	John J. Ashenhurst	20,190
			Others	2

Year	Office	Political Party*	Candidate	Vote
1892	President	R	Benjamin Harrison	405,187
		D	Grover Cleveland	404,115
		Prohibition	John Bidwell	26,012
		People's	James B. Weaver	14,850
			Others	11,461
1893	Governor	R	William McKinley	433,342
		D	Lawrence T. Neal	352,347
		Prohibition	Gideon P. Macklin	22,406
		People's	Edward J. Bracken	15,563
1895	Governor	R	Asa S. Bushnell	427,141
		D	James E. Campbell	334,519
		People's	Jacob S. Coxey	52,675
		Prohibition	Seth H. Ellis	21,264
		Socialist Labor	William Watkins	1,867
			Others	3
1896	President	R	William McKinley	525,991
		D	William J. Bryan	474,882
		People's	William J. Bryan	2,615
		National Democrat	John M. Palmer	1,858
		Socialist Labor	Charles H. Matchett	1,165
		Prohibition	Joshua Levering	5,068
		National Party	Charles E. Bentley	2,716
1897	Governor	R	Asa S. Bushnell	429,915
		D	Horace L. Chapman	401,750
		Prohibition	John S. Holiday	7,555
		People's	Jacob Sechler Coxey	6,276
		Socialist Labor	William Watkins	4,246
		Liberty	John Richardson	3,105
		Negro Protection	Samuel J. Lewis	477
1899	Governor	R	George K. Nash	417,199
		D	John R. McLean	368,176
			Samuel M. Jones	106,721
		Union Reform	Seth H. Ellis	7,799
		Prohibition	George M. Hammell	5,825
		Socialist Labor	Robert Bandlow	2,439
1900	President	R	William McKinley	543,918
		D	William J. Bryan	474,882
		Prohibition	John G. Wooley	10,203
		Socialist Democrat	Eugene V. Debs	4,847
		Union Reform	Seth H. Ellis	4,284
		Socialist Labor	Joseph F. Malloney	1,688
		People's	Wharton Baker	251
1901	Governor	R	George K. Nash	436,092
		D	James Kilbourne	368,525
		Prohibition	E. Jay Pinney	9,878
		Socialist	Harry C. Thompson	7,359
		Socialist Labor	John H. T. Juergens	2,994
		Union Reform	John Richardson	2,718
1903	Governor	R	Myron T. Herrick	475,560
		D	Tom L. Johnson	361,748
		Prohibition	Nelson D. Creamer	13,505
		Socialist	Isaac Cowan	13,467
		Socialist Labor	John D. Goerke	2,071
1904	President	R	Theodore Roosevelt	600,095
		D	Alton B. Parker	344,674
		Socialist	Eugene V. Debs	36,260
		Prohibition	Silas C. Swallow	19,339
		Socialist Labor	Charles H. Corregan	2,633
		People's	Thomas E. Watson	1,392

Year	Office	Political Party*	Candidate	Vote
1905	Governor	D	John M. Pattison	473,264
		R	Myron T. Herrick	430,617
		Socialist	Isaac Cowan	17,795
		Prohibition	Aaron S. Watkins	13,061
		Socialist Labor	John E. Seitger	1,808
1908	President	R	William H. Taft	572,312
		D	William J. Bryan	502,721
		Socialist	Eugene V. Debs	33,795
		Prohibition	Eugene W. Chafin	11,402
		Socialist Labor	August Gilhouse	721
		Independence	Thomas Hissen	439
		People's	Thomas E. Watson	162
	Governor	D	Judson Harmon	552,569
		R	Andrew L. Harris	533,197
		Socialist	Robert Bandlow	28,573
		Prohibition	John B. Martin	7,665
		Socialist Labor	John Kircher	797
		Independence	Andrew F. Otte	397
1910	Governor	D	Judson Harmon	477,077
		R	Warren G. Harding	376,700
		Socialist	Tom Clifford	60,637
		Prohibition	Henry A. Thompson	7,129
		Socialist Labor	J. R. Malley	2,920
1912	President	D	Woodrow Wilson	424,834
		R	William H. Taft	278,168
		Progressive	Theodore Roosevelt	229,807
		Socialist	Eugene V. Debs	90,144
		Prohibition	Eugene W. Chaffin	11,511
		Socialist Labor	Arthur E. Reimer	2,630
	Governor	D	James M. Cox	439,323
		R	Robert B. Brown	272,500
		Progressive	Arthur L. Garford	217,903
		Socialist	C.E. Ruthenberg	87,709
		Prohibition	Daniel A. Poling	16,607
		Socialist Labor	John Kircher	2,689
1914	Governor	R	Frank B. Willis	523,074
		D	James M. Cox	493,804
		Progressive	James R. Garfield	60,904
		Socialist	Scott Wilkins	51,441
1916	President	D	Woodrow Wilson	604,161
		R	Charles E. Hughes	514,753
		Socialist	Allen L. Benson	38,092
		Prohibition	J. Frank Hanley	8,080
	Governor	D	James M. Cox	568,218
		R	Frank B. Willis	561,602
		Socialist	Tom Clifford	36,908
		Prohibition	John H. Dickason	7,347
1918	Governor	D	James M. Cox	486,403
		R	Frank B. Willis	474,459
1920	President	R	Warren G. Harding	1,182,022
		D	James M. Cox	780,037
		Socialist	Eugene V. Debs	57,147
		Single Tax	R. C. Macauley	2,153
	Governor	R	Harry L. Davis	1,039,835
		D	Vic Donahey	918,962
		Socialist	Frank B. Hamilton	42,889
		Single Tax	Earl H. Foote	1,497
1922	Governor	D	Vic Donahey	821,948
		R	Carmi A. Thompson	803,300
			Others	551

Year	Office	Political Party*	Candidate	Vote
1924	President	R	Calvin Coolidge	1,176,130
		D	John W. Davis	477,888
		Independent		
		Progressive	Robert M. LaFollette	357,948
		Socialist Labor	Frank T. Johns	3,025
		Commonwealth Land	W. J. Wallace	1,246
	Governor	D	Vic Donahey	1,064,981
		R	Harry L. Davis	888,139
		CommonwealthLand	Virgil D. Allen	11,776
		Socialist Labor	Franklin J. Catlin	8,468
1926	Governor	D	Vic Donahey	702,733
		R	Myers Y. Cooper	685,957
		Socialist	Joseph W. Sharts	5,985
		Socialist Labor	Anna K. Storck	1,597
1928	President	R	Herbert Hoover	1,627,546
		D	Alfred E. Smith	864,210
		Socialist	Norman Thomas	8,683
		Prohibition	William E. Varney	3,556
		Workers Communist	William Z. Foster	2,836
		Socialist Labor	Verne L. Reynolds	1,515
	Governor	R	Myers Y. Cooper	1,355,517
		D	Martin L. Davey	1,106,739
		Socialist	Joseph W. Shorts	7,149
		Workers Communist	William Patterson	2,184
		Socialist Labor	John D. Goerke	1,272
		Prohibition	Frank W. Stanton	1,085
1930	Governor	D	George White	1,033,168
		R	Myers Y. Cooper	923,538
1932	President	D	Franklin D. Roosevelt	1,301,695
		R	Herbert Hoover	1,227,319
		Socialist	Norman Thomas	64,094
		Prohibition	William D. Upshaw	7,421
		Communist	William Z. Foster	7,231
		Socialist Labor	Verne L. Reynolds	1,968
	Governor	D	George White	1,356,518
		R	David S. Ingalls	1,151,933
		Socialist	Joseph W. Sharts	32,288
		Prohibition	Aaron S. Watkins	19,575
		Communist	John Marshall	6,349
		Socialist Labor	William Woodhouse	1,784
1934	Governor	D	Martin L. Davey	1,118,257
		R	Clarence J. Brown	1,052,851
		Communist	I.O. Ford	15,854
			Others	64
1936	President	D	Franklin D. Roosevelt	1,747,140
		R	Alfred M. Landon	1,127,855
		Union	William Lemke	132,212
		Communist	Earl Browder	5,251
			Others	202
	Governor	D	Martin L. Davey	1,539,461
		R	John W. Bricker	1,412,773
		Communist	Andrew R. Onda	7,372
1938	Governor	R	John W. Bricker	1,265,548
		D	Charles Sawyer	1,147,323
1940	President	D	Franklin D. Roosevelt	1,733,139
		R	Wendell L. Wilkie	1,586,773
	Governor	R	John W. Bricker	1,824,863
		D	Martin L. Davey	1,460,396
1942	Governor	R	John W. Bricker	1,086,937
		D	John McSweeney	709,599

THE MIRACLE MAN OF CLEVELAND

He was called "Cleveland's Miracle Man," "Ohio's Lincoln," and "the most significant figure in post World War II Ohio." He was the first Catholic and the first son of immigrants to be elected an Ohio governor; the only man elected its governor five times; a political prodigy who served in all three branches of government; and one of the most successful and unconventional politicians the state has ever produced.

Frank J. Lausche learned politics, frugality, baseball, honesty, and ambition in the Slovenian section of Cleveland where he grew up at the turn of the century. A talented third baseman, he turned down a professional contract and went to law school instead. His work as a Democratic ward leader in the 1920s earned Lausche an appointment as a municipal judge, and he used his courtroom to clean out Cleveland's dirty politicians and mobsters.

With his impeccable reputation and knack for spinning tear-jerker stories about his widowed mother, "Fearless Frank" rode a tidal wave of popularity to become a Common Pleas Court judge in 1937; Cleveland mayor in 1941, Ohio governor in 1945, and U.S. Senator in 1957. His voter-appeal was so strong that Ohio's intimidated GOP, in a move that paralleled the national Republican Party's fear of the multi-term Franklin Roosevelt, devised the amendment to the state Constitution that limits the governor to two consecutive terms.

Ohio's electorate loved Lausche's plain talk, his plain looks, and his plain old-fashioned penny-pinching. He planted a victory garden outside the governor's mansion during World War II; he turned down political donations of more than a hundred dollars; he drove old cars and wore old suits; and he never smoked a cigar that cost more than a nickel. Lecturing President Kennedy on the national debt in 1962, Lausche declared, "Benjamin Franklin is said to have stated, 'Let us save the pennies, and the dollars will take care of themselves.' I suggest that we begin in this case to save millions of dollars, and the billions will take care of themselves."

Often described as a "conservative Democrat," Lausche was, in truth, an independent given to ignoring the party line and party stalwarts. He was always at odds with organized labor, and ultimately it was union money that undermined him in his humiliating defeat in the 1968 Democratic primary. In a self-doubting nation of flower children and flag-burners, the self-assured Lausche suddenly found himself out of date and out of work in politics. His swan song was short and utterly appropriate: "Have no sorrow for me. There is no distress in my heart and soul. ↩

Ohio's Lincoln

Teacher: "You have a holiday tomorrow. It is Columbus Day."

Schoolboy: "Who was Columbus?"

Teacher: "Columbus discovered America."

Schoolboy: "No Ma'am. America was discovered by Frank J. Lausche."

—Lausche campaigners' joke

The five most one-sided gubernatorial elections since 1942

1994, Voinovich (R) over Burch, 72 %;

1966, Rhodes (R) over Reams, 62.1%;

1986, Celeste (D) over Rhodes, 60.6%;

1942, Bricker (R) over McSweeney, 60.5%;

1982, Celeste (D) over Brown, 59.0%

Year	Office	Political Party*	Candidate	Vote
1944	President	R	Thomas E. Dewey	1,582,293
		D	Franklin D. Roosevelt	1,570,763
	Governor	D	Frank J. Lausche	1,603,809
		R	James Garfield Stewart	1,491,450
1946	Governor	R	Thomas J. Herbert	1,166,550
		D	Frank J. Lausche	1,125,997
		Social Labor	Arla A. Albaugh	11,203
1948	President	D	Harry S. Truman	1,452,791
		R	Thomas Dewey	1,445,684
	Governor	D	Frank J. Lausche	1,619,775
		R	Thomas J. Herbert	1,398,514
1950	Governor	D	Frank J. Lausche	1,522,249
		R	Don H. Ebright	1,370,570
1952	President	R	Dwight D. Eisenhower	2,100,391
		D	Adlai E. Stevenson	1,600,367
	Governor	D	Frank J. Lausche	2,015,110
		R	Charles P. Taft	1,590,058
1954	Governor	D	Frank J. Lausche	1,405,262
		R	James A. Rhodes	1,192,528
1956	President	R	Dwight D. Eisenhower	2,262,610
		D	Adlai Stevenson	1,439,655
	Governor	R	C. William O'Neill	1,984,988
		D	Michael V. DiSalle	1,557,103
1958	Governor	D	Michael V. DiSalle	1,869,260
		R	C. William O'Neill	1,414,874
1960	President	R	Richard M. Nixon	2,217,611
		D	John F. Kennedy	1,944,248
1962	Governor	R	James A. Rhodes	1,836,432
		D	Michael V. DiSalle	1,280,521
1964	President	D	Lyndon B. Johnson	2,498,331
		R	Barry Goldwater	1,470,865
1966	Governor	R	James A. Rhodes	1,795,277
		D	Frazier Reams, Jr.	1,092,054
1968	President	R	Richard M. Nixon	1,791,014
		D	Hubert Humphrey	1,700,586
		American Independent	George Wallace	467,495
			Others	603
1970	Governor	D	John J. Gilligan	1,725,560
		R	Roger Cloud	1,382,749
		American Independent	Edwin G. Lawton	61,300
		Socialist Labor	Joseph Pirincin	14,087
			Others	527
1972	President	R	Richard M. Nixon	2,441,827
		D	George McGovern	1,558,889
		American Independent	John C. Schmitz	80,067
		Socialist Labor	Louis Fisher	7,107
			Others	6,897
1974	Governor	R	James A. Rhodes	1,493,679
		D	John J. Gilligan	1,482,191
		Independent	Nancy Brown Lazar	95,625
1976	President	D	Jimmy Carter	2,011,621
		R	Gerald R. Ford	2,000,505
		Independent	Eugene McCarthy	58,258
		American Party	Lester G. Maddox	15,529
		Libertarian	Roger MacBride	8,961
		Communist Party	Gus Hall	7,817
		Socialist Workers	Peter Camejo	4,717
		U.S. Labor	Lyndon LaRouche, Jr.	4,335
1978	Governor	R	James A. Rhodes	1,402,167
		D	Richard F. Celeste	1,354,631
		Independent	Patricia H. Wright	35,164
		Independent	John O'Neill	29,418
		Independent	Allan Friedman	21,951

JAMES RHODES: THE LONG ROAD FROM COALTON

Ohio has probably never had a more enduring politician than the crafty, homespun *James Rhodes*. He was elected to his first office (a Republican central committeeman in Columbus) only two years after Franklin Roosevelt became President, and he won his last election (the 1986 Republican gubernatorial primary) when Ronald Reagan was in the White House. He grew up dirt poor in Coalton, but had the grit to make enough of the right friends and right promises to rise through the Republican ranks and serve four terms as governor in the 1960s, 1970s, and early 1980s.

He might even had held national office, but his designs on the U.S. Senate were nipped in the bud during Ohio's fateful spring of 1970. The May primary election was only a few days after Ohio National Guard troops that Rhodes sent to Kent State University killed four students protesting the U.S. invasion of Cambodia. Ohio's voters chose to nominate Robert Taft, Jr., instead of Rhodes, whose campaign was drowned by the tears of a nation sickened by the tragedy.

Rhodes political career seemed over, yet four years later he was running—again—for governor, delivering avuncular speeches in his familiar drawl throughout his

beloved state of "Ah-hi-ya" and selling the people—again—on the promise of jobs. Rhodes literally had a concrete vision of Ohio, for he left his multi-billion dollar stamp on the state in the form of new highways, state parks, airports (he wanted—and got—one in every county), untold vocational schools/technical/community colleges, two medical schools, and six new state universities (he wanted—and got—an institution of higher learning within 30 miles of every family).

Voters were true believers as long as Ohio had heavy industry and light taxes. Ironically, unemployment was the hallmark of his last gubernatorial years and his undoing as a politician. When Rhodes left the governor's office for the last time in 1983, the wake of a national recession had swamped Ohio with 13.2 percent unemployment and a $500 million debt. While Rhodes had continued his relentless pursuit of smokestacks, the American economy had been shifting to silicon. He had run too long on an idea that had lost its vitality.

In 1986, at age 77, he ran for governor for a fifth and final time. But Richard Celeste's easy victory proved that the Ohio electorate had finally lost all faith in Rhodes's ability to deliver jobs or progress.

staying power

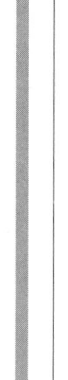

"I draw the pigeons."

—James Rhodes, commenting on his statue on the Statehouse lawn

Marginal victory

The closest election in Ohio history, in terms of the percentage captured of the overall votes cast, was the 1990 race between Democrat **Lee Fisher** and Republican **Paul Pfeifer** for the office of Ohio Attorney General. Fisher received 1,680,271 votes to Pfeifer's 1,678,891, a victory margin of only 1,234 votes, which was the equivalent of less than one vote per precinct.

Year	Office	Political Party*	Candidate	Vote
1980	President	R	Ronald Reagan	2,206,545
		D	Jimmy Carter	1,752,414
		Independent	John B. Anderson	254,472
		Libertarian	Ed Clark	49,033
		Communist Party	Gus Hall	4,729
			Richard H. Congress	4,029
		Workers World Party	Deirdre Griswold	3,790
1982	Governor	D	Richard F. Celeste	1,981,882
		R	Clarence J. Brown	1,303,962
		Libertarian	Phyllis Goetz	39,114
			Erwin J. Reupert	17,484
			Kurt O. Landefeld	14,279
1984	President	R	Ronald Reagan	2,678,560
		D	Walter F. Mondale	1,825,440
		New Alliance Party	Dennis Serrette	12,090
		Independent	Lyndon LaRouche, Jr.	10,693
		Libertarian	David Bergland	5,886
		Communist Party	Gus Hall	4,438
		Socialist Workers	Melvin T. Mason	4,344
		Workers League	Ed Winn	3,565
		Workers World	Gavrielle Holmes	2,565
1986	Governor	D	Richard F. Celeste	1,858,372
		R	James A. Rhodes	1,207,264
			Others	975
1988	President	R	George Bush	2,416,549
		D	Michael S. Dukakis	1,939,629
		New Alliance Party	Lenora B. Fulani	12,017
		Libertarian Party	Ron Paul	11,926
		National Economic	Lyndon LaRouche, Jr.	7,713
		Workers League	Ed Winn	5,401
			Others	350
1990	Governor	R	George Voinovich	1,938,103
		D	Anthony Celebreeze	1,539,416
1992	President	D	Bill Clinton	1,984,942
		R	George Bush	1,894,310
		Reform Party	H. Ross Perot	1,036,426
		Libertarian	Andre Marrou	7,252
		New Alliance Party	Lenora B. Fulani	6,411
		Populist Party	Bo Gritz	4,698
		Natural Law Party	Dr. John Hagelin	3,437
		Economic Recovery	Lyndon H. LaRouche, Jr.	2,446
			Others	42
1994	Governor	R	George Voinonich	2,401,572
		D	Robert L. Burch	835,849
		Independent	Billy R. Inmon	108,745
		Write-in	Keith W. Hatton	48
		Write-in	Michael Italie	24
1996	President	D	Bill Clinton	2,148,222
		R	Bob Dole	1,859,883
		Reform Party	Ross Perot	483,207
		Libertarian	Harry Browne	12,851
		Workers World Party	Monica Moorhead	10,813
		Natural Law Party	Dr. John Haglen	9,120
		Constitutional Party	Howard Phillips	7,361
		Green Party	Ralph Nader	2,962
		Write-in	Dan Burkhardt	11
		Write-in	Mark Snyder	4

1998	Governor	R	Bob Taft	1,678,721
		D	Lee Fisher	1,498,956
		Reform Party	John Mitchel	111,468
		Natural Law Party	Zanna Feitler	65,068
2000	President	R	George Bush	2,351,209
		D	Al Gore	2,186,190
		Green Party	Ralph Nader	117,857
		Reform Party	Pat Buchanan	26,724
		Libertarian	Harry Browne	13,475
		Natural Law Party	Dr. John Hagelin	6,169
		Constitutional Party	Howard Phillips	3,823

*D denotes Democratic Party

F denotes Federalist Party

R denotes Republican Party
Prior to the 1860s, R indicates the Republican Democratic Party, which was founded by Thomas Jefferson and from which the present Democratic Party claims descent. The present Republican Party was formed in 1854 by Democrats and Whigs dissatisfied with the Republican Democratic Party.

NR denotes National Republican party
Formed in the 1820s to oppose Andrew Jackson, the National Republican Party was replaced by the Whig Party, which was also formed to oppose Jackson. Henry Clay ran for President as both a National Republican (1832) and a Whig (1844).

Liberal denotes Liberal Republican Party
Formed by Republicans who opposed Grant, this party was led by Horace Greeley in his bid for President.

Article I of the United States Constitution provides for the legislative branch of the federal government, a Congress that consists of two chambers: the Senate and the House of Representatives. Members of the Senate are chosen by the vote of the entire electorate of the states. Since each state elects two Senators, the Senate has 100 members, and they serve six-year terms. One-third of the members of the Senate are elected every even-numbered year. The House of Representatives has 435 members who serve two-year terms. All the Representatives are elected every even-numbered year by voters in their respective congressional districts within the states. Each state has at least one Representative, but the total number of Representatives apportioned to each state is determined by its population and adjusted after each U.S. Census. Ohio has two Senators and eighteen Representatives in Congress. The 108th United States Congress commenced in January, 2003.

U.S. Senator

Michael DeWine

140 Russell Senate Building
Washington, DC 20510
202-224-2315
202-224-6519 fax

State Offices
312 Walnut St.
Suite 2030
Cincinnati, Ohio 45202
513-763-8260
513-763-8268 fax

600 East Superior Avenue
Room 2450
Cleveland, Ohio 44114
216-522-7272
216-522-2239 fax

37 West Broad Street
Suite 300
Columbus, Ohio 43215
614-469-5186
614-469-2982 fax

121 Putnam Street
Suite 102
Marietta, Ohio 45750
740-373-2317
740-373-8689 fax

420 Madison Avenue
Room 1225
Toledo, Ohio 43604
419-259-7536
419-259-7575 fax

100 West Main Street
2nd Floor
Xenia, Ohio 45385
937-376-3080
937-376-3387 fax

Casework Office:
Senators DeWine and Voinovich
37 West Broad Street, Suite 300
Columbus, Ohio 43215
614-469-6774
614-469-7419
800-205-OHIO   Casework Hotline

Senator Mike DeWine's reputation in the Senate is as a conservative who is willing to reach across the aisle and break with his party on issues that are important to him. Noted for studying the issues (he actually *reads* government reports) before reaching a conclusion, he is often guided by a pragmatic approach, asking staffers "Will it work?"

A father of eight, it is natural that much of the legislation he pushes involves children's issues. Drawing from this early political experience in the late '70s as prosecutor in Green County, children's issues have been high on his agenda. It has prompted him to partner with Democrats to successfully pass an antismoking bill aimed at reducing youth smoking. He also wrote a provision for a bill giving incentives to drug-makers for testing medications for children.

His biggest legislative success to date is a bill that he sponsored with Edward Kennedy and the late Paul Wellstone. The bill combined 50 federal job-training programs into block grants to states.

Born in Springfield, Ohio in 1947, this Miami University graduate received his law degree from Ohio Northern in 1972 and first won elective office in 1977 as Green County prosecuting attorney. After four years he was elected to the Ohio Senate and stepped up to national office when he began four terms in the U.S. House of Representatives in 1981.

He returned to state office in 1991 when George Voinovich tapped him to run on his ticket as lieutenant governor. While serving in that office from 1991 to 1995 his political career took a stumble when he challenged and lost a bid to replace Senator John Glenn in 1992.

In doing so, however, he fulfilled a saying in Ohio politics: You have to lose a statewide race before you can win one. He won one on his next try by defeating Joel Hyatt for the seat of retiring senator, Howard Metzenbaum. DeWine successfully defended his Senate seat in 2000 by defeating Ted Celeste, the brother of former governor Richard Celeste, and became the first Republican U.S. Senator in 48 years to be re-elected in Ohio.

Although DeWine's reputation as a moderate lies in the issues—such as children—that are close to him, in bread and butter conservative Republican issues such as taxes and social issues he is a reliable Republican vote. DeWine's conservative voting record is borne out by his AFL-CIO and Americans for Democratic Action ratings. Most years, the labor group gives DeWine a 0% rating while the ADA puts him at 10%. With the conservative ACU and the Chamber of Commerce of the United States, CCUS, DeWine usually ranges in the mid-80 percent range. His yearly votes measuring party unity range from 81% to 87%, and he supported President Clinton roughly half the time.

He and his wife, Fran, make their home in Cedarville.

U.S. Senator

George V. Voinovich

317 Hart Senate Office Building
Washington, DC 20510
202-224-3353

State Offices
36 East 7th Street
Room 2615
Cincinnati, Ohio 45202
513-684-3265
513-684-3269 fax

1240 East 9th Street
Room 2955
Cleveland, Ohio 44199
216-522-7095
216-522-7097 fax

37 West Broad Street
Room 310
Columbus, Ohio 43215
614-469-6697
614-469-7733 fax

420 Madison Avenue
Room 1210
Toledo, Ohio 43604
419-259-3895
419-259-3899 fax

Casework Office:
Senators DeWine and Voinovich
37 West Broad Street, Suite 300
Columbus, Ohio 43215
614-469-6774
614-469-7419 fax
800-205-OHIO

Anyone who was surprised at Senator George Voinovich's highly public opposition to President George Bush's 2003 tax cut had not followed his career. He ran for the Senate as a "deficit hawk" critical of Republican plans to cut taxes, and in 1999 was one of just two Republican Senators who originally voted against the party's plan.

In 2000 he opposed the end of both the estate and "marriage penalty" taxes. Again in 2001 he threatened not to support President Bush's tax cut, but the poor shape of the economy led him to reverse his position. A similar scenario was played out in 2003. This time Voinovich caved in to White House pressure and agreed to accounting tricks that masked the full impact of the tax cuts. He preferred to put off the tough decisions until a later date when the taxes are scheduled to return. Unlike earlier in his Senate career, when President Clinton could be counted on to stop Republican incentives, in a closely divided Senate his opposition to his party's tax policies will not go unchallenged.

Voinovich's reputation has developed largely from his successes in fiscal policy. He first gained national attention as mayor of Cleveland after turning around that city's finances. As governor, he earned a reputation for putting the state on sound financial footing—although he would leave the difficult problem of school funding to his successor. In 1994, Voinovich won a second term in a 20th century record landslide—72 percent of the vote—while running with Ohio's first female lieutenant governor. However, the Democratic challenger, little-known Dover senator Rob Burch, never raised enough money for television commercials. Voinovich avoided major scandals and ran on the sedate issues of improved management, progress in state services and, of course, frugal government. To Ohio's equally sedate voters, that seemed good enough.

After leading his party to its first sweep of the ticket since 1966, Voinovich found himself on the short list of vice-presidential nominees and began to get noticed nationally for opposing quick-fix solutions to government such as the balanced-budget amendment. Fiscal conservatives were less than enthralled, though, pointing out that Voinovich raised taxes his first term and

otherwise failed to hew the "Contract with America" line. Mid-1996, Voinovich said he hadn't thought much about the vice-presidency but planned to run for the U.S. Senate in 1998.

Voters seemed to like Voinovich's legendary frugality, evidenced in such things as $7 haircuts, shining his own shoes, brown-bagging lunch, and reusing office file folders. He learned early lessons on political survival in largely Democratic Cleveland with his ability to compromise. He also appeared to be a moderate from a blue-collar neighborhood who was also accepted by the city's corporate leaders. As governor of Ohio, he liked being compared to Frank Lausche, the *other* Slovenian govenor from Cleveland, a Democrat who sometimes appeared to be a Republican. Voinovich's carefully crafted image made him difficult to beat.

Much of his moderate reputation comes from his willingness to use tax increases to achieve balanced budgets. He attempted to increase sales taxes in Ohio, opposed the reduction of gasoline taxes, and is a supporter of finding ways to collect sales taxes on internet transactions.

On the national scene, he made headlines when he opposed the President's 2003 tax cut. He finally voted for it, however, and the Dems accused him of having budget cake and eating it, too, calling it a tax cut that benefited no one but the wealthy.

Despite his willingness to try and break with his party on red-meat Republican tax issues, Voinovich votes with the party nearly 85% of the time. His reputation as a moderate does not extend to social issues, and he can be counted on as being strongly pro-business on both environment and labor (the AFL-CIO rates him at about 20%; the liberal Americans for Democratic Action rates him at 15%). On the other hand, the Chamber of Commerce of the United States rates him at about 81% and the American Conservative Union in the mid-70s.

Since his days in the Ohio Statehouse, Voinovich has been a strong proponent of Federalism, and as a constant voice for the return of power to the states, he brings that philosophy with him to the Senate.

—*Sources: The Plain Dealer, Michael O'Bryant*

Ohio's Congressional delegation has lost some of its luster since the '90s. Where once we had two Senators of national prominence and members of the House who rode the coattails of a Speaker who revitalized the institutional dynamics of the institution, we now have the remnants of what was called the "Gingrich Revolution" and two Senators relatively new to the body. For we Midwesterners, living so far from the corridors of inside-the-beltway power, assessing the clout of our Senators or Congressmen (and women) is challenging work.

The web site www.yourcongress.com annually posts a power ranking that members (if rated highly) will gladly point out. But power is a difficult concept to quantify and while the ranking—based upon such things as leadership roles, committee assignments, and subjective polls—is admittedly flawed, it can still give insight to the Congressmen (and women) in power.

In the parlor game of Who's Up And Who's Not, it's probably unfair to compare the clout of Ohio's two current Senators to their immediate predecessors. Neither comes in with a national reputation even remotely equal to that of John Glenn, and neither has had the time to amass a Howard Metzenbaum's legislative record. Both sit well down in the Senate power rankings: Mike DeWine at 39 and George Voinovich probably frustrated at 92.

Mike DeWine has been quietly carving out a niche as a children's issues advocate. Willing to reach across the aisle to Democrats (sometimes breaking with his own party), he can mark several legislative accomplishments in that area. On major high visibility issues, he usually keeps his party bonafides. George Voinovich, meanwhile, has come to the Senate with a reputation as one of the GOP's effective governors in the '90s. Having served mostly as an executive, he has had some difficulty adjusting to the labyrinthine ways of the Senate, as well as being one-of-a-hundred equals.

While Voinovich has yet to live up to the reputation of Metzenbaum as Senate spending watchdog, he does have a reputation as a fiscal conservative. In his opposition to several of his party's early tax-cutting measures, his vote was not critical. During the 2003 tax-cutting season, however, he very visibly broke with the Bush administration to keep the tax cut at $350 billion. This time, in a closely-divided Senate, Voinovich had some leverage. After being thoroughly denounced by his own party members, the writers of the tax applied voodoo accounting (sun-setting many of the tax provisions in an effort to hide their full impact) and made the bill appear not to exceed Voinovich's ceiling. It passed with a tie-breaking "yea" by the Vice-President, and Voinovich claimed victory, thus preserving his reputation and avoiding party punishment.

Those on the other side of the aisle accused Voinovich of avoiding the immediate hard decisions, putting them off to other Congresses and playing into the hands of the party hard-core whose goal is starving the federal government of revenue. So, depending upon where one is standing politically, Voinovich is either the voice tempering his party's excess or an obstructionist hindering his party's progress.

Over the last 30 years, Ohio's clout in the U.S. House of Representatives has dropped. In 1970, Ohio sent 24 congressmen to Washington while today the number is 18. Still, the numbers

belay the fact that Ohio sends strong members to the House. Only Texas, with its 54 members, rivals Ohio when it comes to members exercising real power in the House.

Cincinnati-area Congressman Rob Portman has long been considered a rising star. First elected in 1993, he appropriated his earlier White House experience (he was a Bush appointee in the counsels office and later in legislative affairs) into a deep relationship with the current White House, and the election of the second George Bush has only enhanced Portman's influence. Portman advised Bush and his staff during the campaign, and he aided both Bush and Cheney in their debate preparation.

His stature in the White House can be measured by the rumor that the White House offered him the Chief of Staff position or the directorship of the Office of Budget and Management. Portman's strong ties down Pennsylvania Avenue are put to use as he chairs the Republican Leadership Committee, where he serves as the House's point man with the White House.

John Boehner roared into the House in 1990 as one of the "Gang of Seven," attacking members from both parties over check-bouncing, pay raises, and the House Post Office scandal. While his actions infuriated House veterans, Boehner became a top lieutenant to Majority Whip Newt Gingrich, managing Gingrich's campaign for Republican leader and becoming a major figure in the Contract with America.

For his efforts, the Gingrich-supported Boehner won the number four position in the Republican leadership, House Republican Conference chairman. His job was to enforce party discipline and spread the party message. But by 1997, Boehner was on the decline. The attempted ouster of Gingrich as Speaker—weakened by ethics investigations and political missteps—reflected negatively on Boehner.

Boehner denied supporting the coup, but he was criticized for not alerting the Speaker. After Republican losses in the 1998 elections, blame fell on Boehner, and he was replaced as House Republican Conference chairman. Once seen as Tom Delay's equal and rival for the attention of conservative Republicans, Boehner's stature in the House has declined while Delay has risen to position of Majority Leader.

Still, Boehner remains a formidable Congressman. He has continued to raise money for his fellow Republicans (over $1 million), gained the favor of Speaker Dennis Hastert, and become an effective legislator. Ironically, though, while he attacked the leadership of both parties for unethical behavior, he was criticized for handing out lobbyists' checks on the floor of the House chamber. He also proposed (in 1995) to abolish the Department of Education, yet drove into legislation Bush's 2001 No Child Left Behind program.

Cincinnatian Steve Chabot survived several tough reelection battles in one of the most Republican inner city districts in the nation. He did so by playing to his strong conservative record and despite voting against his district's interests in several high profile issues—money for the National Freedom Center and a study on mass transit.

He was most visible when he was selected as one of the Republican "managers" during the Clinton impeachment process. Since then, he has been unable to build upon that (or perhaps despite it) and remains a middle-of-the-pack Congressman.

Deborah Price is another Republican elected in the early '90s. She was interim president of her Republican class, helped write the Contract with America, and was elected to the Republican Conference secretary. She now heads the committee that sets the Republican agenda and also holds a seat on the important Rules Committee.

Four Republican members rank among the top 13 House power brokers: Hobson, Gillmor, Regula, and Ney. David Hobson was also aligned with Newt Gingrich in the '90s. He supported the Speaker during the 1997 coup and as a member of the ethics committee. He survived the fall of Gingrich, in part because of a long-standing friendship with present Speaker Dennis Hastert. In the current atmosphere of partisanship, Hobson has a reputation for pragmatic deal-making. Hobson's major source of power is as one of the House "Cardinals." They are the heads of the 13 Appropriations Committee subcommit-

tees, and all Federal spending must pass through one or the other of them.

Ohio is the only state with more than one Cardinal, Ralph Regula being the other. Regula, first elected in 1972, is credited with securing much of Ohio's power base. Said Congressman Steve LaTourette, a former prosecutor, "When I got here, I wanted to be on judiciary. He said, 'No, you're transportation.' Ralph made sure you were not going to find a major committee without an Ohioan on it."

Bob Ney, polling 11th most powerful in the House—highest among Ohioans—stayed clear of the ideological battles of his party. From the more Democratic part of the state, he often supports Democratic issues such as labor, trade restrictions, and the minimum wage. Coming as he does from a heavily Democratic district, Ney has shown streaks of bipartisanism that has served him well as chairman of the House Administration Committee. When named to that post, he was the first of his class to become a committee chairman, with it coming the nicknames "Governor" or "Mayor of the House."

Michael Oxley's advance in the House was slowed when he ended up losing a chairmanship fight to a Gingrich ally. Eventually, in 2001, he became chairman of the Financial Services committee, the second-largest committee in the Congress, placing him among Congress's top fifty power brokers.

When John Kasich retired, Ohio lost one of its most influential and highly visible members of Congress. Replacement Pat Tiberi, a former Kasich aide, has yet to establish himself as a major force in Congress.

Being in the minority party in Congress does not bring with it much power. Most survive by adhering to constituent services or finding a view-sharing Republican with whom to co-sponsor a bill. Most of Ohio's Democrats come from the northern "rust belt" where trade and labor issues reign supreme. Toledo's Mary Kaptur has made a career out of trade issues. She blocked the Clinton administration's attempt to bail out Mexico, opposed NAFTA, and urged the President to resign after the Lewinski scandal. Trade made her an ally of Ross Perot's United We Stand and her popularity crosses party lines. She sits on the Appropriations Committee with two of her Ohio Republican colleagues.

Northern Ohio Democrats—Dennis Kucinich, Stephanie Tubbs, Tim Ryan, Sherrod Brown, Tom Sawyer, Ted Strickland—suffer from a power vacuum created by being in the House minority. Most are too liberal to get much done in a Congress controlled by conservatives although some, like Kucinich, can be counted on to make a lot of noise. The leading Democratic dove—he opposed both Clinton's bombing of Kosovo and Bush's invasion of Iraq—he was especially vocal in his Presidential bid as the voice of opposition.

Ohio's delegation, from both parties, has shown a willingness to put aside partisan differences when it comes to benefiting the state. The delegation, according to Republican Steve LaTourette, has, "really worked well together and all like each other. Some delegations don't have that."

—Michael O'Bryant

United States Senate, 2000

Party	Candidate	Vote
D	Ted Celeste	1,597,122 (35.9%)
R	Mike DeWine	2,666,736 (60.0%)
	Michael Fitzsimmons	45 (0.0%)
	Patrick Flower	29 (0.0%)
L	John McAlister	117,466 (2.4%)

United States House, 2002

Dist.	Party	Candidate	Vote
1	R	Steve Chabot	110,760 (64.8%)
	D	Greg Harris	60,168 (35.2%)
2	R	Rob Portman	139,218 (74.1%)
	D	Charles Sanders	48,785 (25.9%)
		James Condit, Jr.	13 (0.01%)
3	R	Michael Turner	111,630 (58.8%)
	D	Rick Carne	78,307 (41.2%)
		Ronald Williamitis	14 (0.01%)
4	R	Michael Oxley	120,001 (67.5%)
	D	Jim Clark	57,726 (32.5%)
5	R	Paul Gilmor	126,286 (67.1%)
	D	Roger Anderson	51,872 (27.5%)
		John Green	10,096 (5.4%)
6	D	Ted Strickland	113,972 (59.5%)
	R	Mike Halleck	77,643 (40.5%)
7	R	Dave Hobson	113,252 (67.5%)
	D	Kara Anastasio	45,568 (27.2%)
8	R	John Boehner	119,847 (70.8%)
	D	Jeff Hardenbrook	49,444 (29.2%)
9	D	Marcy Kaptur	132,236 (74.0%)
	R	Ed Emery	46,480 (26.0%)
10	D	Dennis Kucinich	129,997 (74.1%)
	R	Jon Heben	41,778 (23.8%)
		Judy Locy	3,761 (2.14%)
11	D	Steph Tubbs Jones	129,997 (76.3%)
	R	Patrick Pappano	36,146 (23.7%)
12	R	Pat Tiberi1	16,982 (64.4%)
	D	Edward Brown	64,707 (35.6%)
13	D	Sherrod Brown	123,025 (69.0%)
	R	Ed Oliveros	55,357 (31.0%)
14	R	Steven LaTourette	134,413 (72.1%)
	D	Dale Blanchard	51,846 (27.8%)
		Sid Stone	113 (0.1%)
15	R	Deborah Pryce	108,193 (66.6%)
	D	Mark Brown	54,286 (33.4%)
16	R	Ralph Regula	129,734 (68.9%)
	D	Jim Rice	58,644 (31.1%)
17	D	Timothy Ryan	94,441 (51.1)
	R	Benjaman Womer	62,188 (33.7%)
		James Traficant, Jr.	28,045 (15.2%)
18	R	Bob Ney	125,546 (100.0%)

" LET'S GO PASS SOME STRINGENT LEGISLATION AIMED AT CURBING AMERICA'S MORAL DECLINE AND THEN EXEMPT OURSELVES. "

Tubbs Jones 11

Brown 13 **Kucinich** 10

La Tourette 14

Gillmor 5

Kaptur 9

Ryan 17

Oxley 4

Regula 16

Boehner 8

Pryce 12

Tiberi 18

Ney

Strickland 6

Hobson 7

Turner 3

Portman 2

Chabot 1

A good man's
worth

United States Senator
$125,100

United States
Representative
$125,100

*Salaries are subject
to annual cost
of living allowance
increases.

Ohio Members
U.S. House of Representatives

District 1
Steve Chabot (R)
129 Cannon House
Office Building
Washington, D.C.
20515
202-225-2216

District Office
3003 Crew Tower
441 Vine Street
Cincinnati, Ohio 45202
513-684-2723

Website: www.house.gov/chabot

Population 630,545
  Urban 597,890

Rural	32,655
Farm	830
White	69.1%
Black/African American	27.4%
American Indian/Alaska Native	0.2%
Asian	1.1%
Other Race (alone)	0.0%
Two or more Races	1.5%
Ohio born	470,653
Foreign Born	17,975
Income	
Per Capita Income	$20,427
White	$23,159
Black/African American	$14,170
American Indian/Alaska Native	$15,002
Asian	$21,199
Hispanic/Latino	$15,100
Median Household Income	$37,414
Median Family Income	$49,197
Income Below the Poverty Level	13.9%
Housing Units	276,443
Median Year Structure Built	1957
Median Real Estate Taxes	$1,388

Travel to Work
Drive Alone 225,070
Carpool 30,673
Public Transportation 16,589
Motorcycle 136
Bicycle 343
Walk 9,492
Work at Home 6,986
Education
High School Graduate 124,742
Associate Degree 25,495
Bachelor's Degree 57,495
Master's Degree 21,495
Professional School Degree 5,643
Doctorate Degree 3,954
Military Service
Vietnam Era Vets 16,802
Korean War Vets 9,154
World War II Vets 13,086

District 2

Rob Portman (R)
238 Cannon House Office Building
Washington, D.C. 20515
202-225-3164

District Offices
8044 Montgomery Road
Room 540
Cincinnati, Ohio 45236
513-791-0381
800-784-6366

175 East Main Street
Batavia, Ohio 45103
513-732-2948

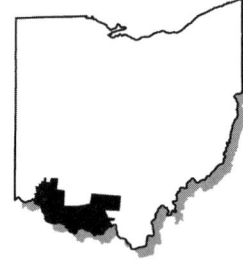

Website: www.house.gov/portman

Population 630,893
Urban 460,242
Rural 170,651
Farm 8,519
White 92.3%
Black/African American 4.3%
American Indian/Alaska Native 0.2%
Asian 1.1%
Other Race (alone) 0.6%
Two or more Races 1.5%
Ohio born 442,501
Foreign Born 16,517
Income
Per Capita Income $25,560
White $26,050
Black/African American $18,479
American Indian/Alaska Native $15,603
Asian $30,601
Hispanic/Latino $20,926
Median Household Income $46,813
Median Family Income $56,695
Income Below the Poverty Level 8.4%
Housing Units 263,542
Median Year Structure Built 1970
Median Real Estate Taxes $1,443

Travel to Work
Drive Alone 300,577
Carpool 28,531
Public Transportation 5,174
Motorcycle 140
Bicycle 375
Walk 4,847
Work at Home 10,288
Education
High School Graduate 125,895
Associate Degree 25,065
Bachelor's Degree 77,213
Master's Degree 29,969
Professional School Degree 9,796
Doctorate Degree 3,979
Military Service
Vietnam era Vets 18,584
Korean War Vets 8,927
World War II Vets 12,991

District 3

Michael Turner (R)
1740 Longworth House Office Building
Washington, D.C. 20515
202-225-6465
202-225-6754 *fax*

District Offices
120 West Third Street
Suite 305
Dayton, Ohio 45402
937-225-2843
937-225-2752 *fax*

15 East Main Street
Wilmington, Ohio 45177
937-383-8931
937-383-8910 *fax*

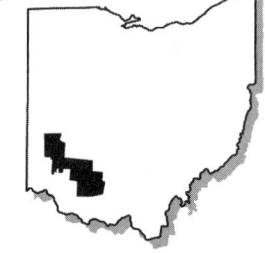

Website: www.house.gov/miketurner

Population 630,804
Urban 534,220
Rural 96,584
Farm 7,128
White 80.0%
Black/African American 17.0%
American Indian/Alaska Native 0.5%
Asian 0.1%
Other Race (alone) 0.3%
Two or more Races 1.3%
Ohio born 448,561
Foreign Born 13,474
Income
Per Capita Income $22,147
White $23,738
Black/African American $15,227
American Indian/Alaska Native $17,430
Asian $26,785
Hispanic/Latino $16,727
Median Household Income $41,591
Median Family Income $51,589
Income Below the Poverty Level 10.2%
Housing Units 273,270

Median Year Structure Built 1963
Median Real Estate Taxes $1,351
Travel to Work
Drive Alone 244,695
Carpool 25,569
Public Transportation 5,174
Motorcycle 156
Bicycle 361
Walk 6,779
Work at Home 7,726
Education
High School Graduate 132,405
Associate Degree 29,147
Bachelor's Degree 59,482
Master's Degree 24,810
Professional School Degree 6,918
Doctorate Degree 3,069
Military Service
Vietnam Era Vets 19,661
Korean War Vets 9,596
World War II Vets 14,486

District 4
Michael G. Oxley (R)
2308 Rayburn House Office Building
Washington, D.C. 20515
202-225-2676
800-472-4154
(from within Ohio)

District Offices
100 East Main Street
Findlay, Ohio 45840
419-423-3210
419-422-2838 *fax*

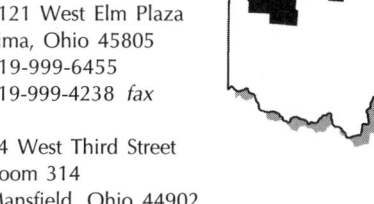

3121 West Elm Plaza
Lima, Ohio 45805
419-999-6455
419-999-4238 *fax*

24 West Third Street
Room 314
Mansfield, Ohio 44902
419-522-5757
419-525-2805 *fax*

Website: www.oxley.house.gov

Population 630,549
Urban 369,584
Rural 260,935
Farm 23,680
White 92.4%
Black/African American 5.0%
American Indian/Alaska Native 0.2%
Asian 0.5%
Other Race (alone) 0.5%
Two or more Races 1.3%
Ohio born 516,471
Foreign Born 8,120
Income
Per Capita Income $18,732
White $19,190

Black/African American $12,500
American Indian/Alaska Native $15,818
Asian $29,759
Hispanic/Latino $11,560
Median Household Income $40,100
Median Family Income $47,106
Income Below the Poverty Level 9.4%
Housing Units 258,216
Median Year Structure Built 1960
Median Real Estate Taxes $934
Travel to Work
Drive Alone 245,093
Carpool 28,264
Public Transportation 6,383
Motorcycle 152
Bicycle 712
Walk 6,779
Work at Home 8,531
Education
High School Graduate 184,757
Associate Degree 26,653
Bachelor's Degree 35,549
Master's Degree 12,646
Professional School Degree 4,294
Doctorate Degree 1,461
Military Service
Vietnam Era Vets 21,147
Korean War Vets 9,382
World War II Vets 13,506

District 5
Paul E. Gillmor (R)
1203 Longworth House Office Building
Washington, D.C. 20515
202-225-6405
Toll Free fax (only in Ohio)
800-278-8203

District Offices
613 West Third Street
Defiance, Ohio 43512
419-782-1996

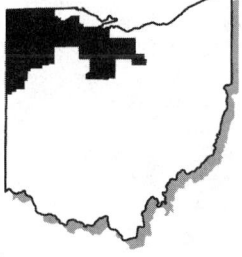

130 Shady Lane Drive
Norwalk, Ohio 44857
419-668-0206
(Tuesdays only)

96 South Washington
Street
Suite 400
Tiffin, Ohio 44883
419-448-9016

Website: www.house.gov/gillmor

Population 630,826
Urban 308,377
Rural 322,449
Farm 26,776
White 95.4%
Black/African American 5.0%
American Indian/Alaska Native 0.2%
Asian 0.5%

Ohio born 513,034
Foreign Born 8,858
Income
  Per Capita Income $19,031
    White $19,298
    Black/African American $14,199
    American Indian/Alaska Native $16,221
    Asian $19,872
    Hispanic/Latino $13,078
  Median Household Income $41,701
  Median Family Income $49,425
  Income Below the Poverty Level 7.6%
Housing Units 251,969
  Median Year Structure Built 1961
  Median Real Estate Taxes $948
Travel to Work
  Drive Alone 258,964
  Carpool 27,663
  Public Transportation 1,420
  Motorcycle 174
  Bicycle 753
  Walk 8,466
  Work at Home 8,204
Education
  High School Graduate 180,223
  Associate Degree 26,653
  Bachelor's Degree 38,012
  Master's Degree 13,677
  Professional School Degree 9,999
  Doctorate Degree 1,818
Military Service
  Vietnam Era Vets 18,202
  Korean War Vets 8,702
  World War II Vets 12,789

District 6
Ted Strickland (D)
336 Cannon House Office Building
Washington, D.C. 20515
202-225-5705
202-225-5907 *fax*
Toll Free (only from District 6):
888-706-1833

District Offices
374 Boardman-Poland
Road
Boardman, Ohio 44512
330-965-4220
330-965-4224 *fax*

254 Front Street
Marietta, Ohio 45750
740-376-0868
740-376-0886 *fax*

11692 Gallia Pike
Suite A
Wheelersburg, Ohio 45694
740-574-2676
740-633-2280 *fax*

Website: www.house.gov/strickland

Population 630,529
  Urban 315,278
  Rural 315,251
  Farm 10,614
White 95.6%
Black/African American 2.4%
American Indian/Alaska Native 0.3%
Asian 0.4%
Other Race (alone) 0.3%
Two or more Races 0.1%
Ohio born 435,689
Foreign Born 8,436
Income
  Per Capita Income $17,039
    White $17,256
    Black/African American $12,462
    American Indian/Alaska Native $10,603
    Asian $21,510
    Hispanic/Latino $15,334
  Median Household Income $32,888
  Median Family Income $40,511
  Income Below the Poverty Level 14.0%
Housing Units 270,497
  Median Year Structure Built 1963
  Median Real Estate Taxes $749
Travel to Work
  Drive Alone 219,515
  Carpool 23,184
  Public Transportation 1,267
  Motorcycle 170
  Bicycle 381
  Walk 9,307
  Work at Home 7,393
Education
  High School Graduate 182,991
  Associate Degree 24,251
  Bachelor's Degree 37,994
  Master's Degree 14,616
  Professional School Degree 9,999
  Doctorate Degree 1,818
Military Service
  Vietnam Era Vets 21,232
  Korean War Vets 10,521
  World War II Vets 17,099

District 7
Dave Hobson (R)
2346 Rayburn House Office Building
Washington, D.C. 20515
202-225-4324
202-225-1984 *fax*

District Offices
212 South Broad Street
Room 55
Lancaster, Ohio 43130
740-654-5149

5 West North Street
Suite 200
P.O. Box 269
Springfield, Ohio 45501
937-325-0474

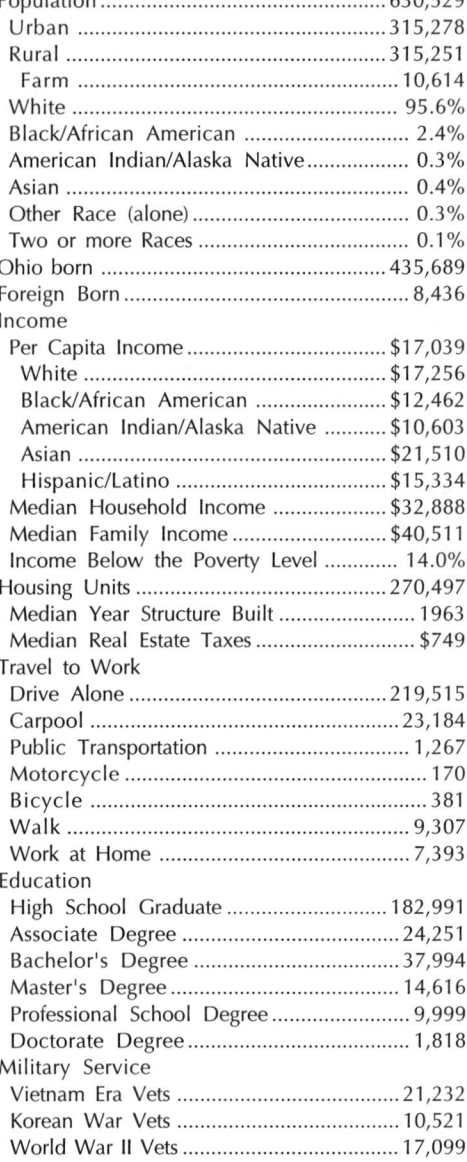

Website: www.house.gov/hobson

Population 630,805
  Urban 449,533
  Rural 181,272
    Farm 9,674
  White 89.3%
  Black/African American 7.3%
  American Indian/Alaska Native 0.3%
  Asian 0.4%
  Other Race (alone) 0.4%
  Two or more Races 1.6%
Ohio born 475,074
Foreign Born 12,394
Income
  Per Capita Income $20,194
    White $20,709
    Black/African American $15,823
    American Indian/Alaska Native $16,311
    Asian $22,898
    Hispanic/Latino $14,148
  Median Household Income $43,248
  Median Family Income $50,975
  Income Below the Poverty Level 8.8%
Housing Units 251,457
  Median Year Structure Built 1967
  Median Real Estate Taxes $1,196
Travel to Work
  Drive Alone 255,484
  Carpool 30,673
  Public Transportation 2,381
  Motorcycle 215
  Bicycle 379
  Walk 6,438
  Work at Home 7,505
Education
  High School Graduate 155,691
  Associate Degree 24,666
  Bachelor's Degree 48,048
  Master's Degree 20,546
  Professional School Degree 4,676
  Doctorate Degree 2,787
Military Service
  Vietnam Era Vets 24,073
  Korean War Vets 9,967
  World War II Vets 12,024

District 8
John Boehner (R)
1011 Longworth House Office Building
Washington, D.C. 20515
202-225-6205
202-225-0704 *fax*
Toll Free Number (within the 8th District only)
800-582-1001

District Offices
8200 Beckett Park Drive
Suite 202
Hamilton, Ohio 45011
513-870-0300
513-870-0151 *fax*

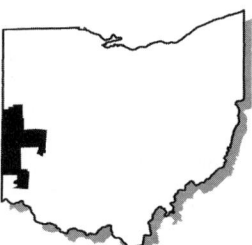

12 South Plum Street
Troy, Ohio 45373
937-339-1524
937-339-1878 *fax*

Website: www.johnboehner.house.gov

Population 630,805
  Urban 492,437
  Rural 138,358
    Farm 14,024
  White 92.3%
  Black/African American 4.4%
  American Indian/Alaska Native 0.2%
  Asian 1.2%
  Other Race (alone) 0.5%
  Two or more Races 1.3%
Ohio born 451,774
Foreign Born 13,760
Income
  Per Capita Income $20,725
    White $21,022
    Black/African American $16,844
    American Indian/Alaska Native $15,996
    Asian $24,925
    Hispanic/Latino $14,576
  Median Household Income $43,753
  Median Family Income $51,726
  Income Below the Poverty Level 8.8%
Housing Units 251,457
  Median Year Structure Built 1967
  Median Real Estate Taxes $1,177
Travel to Work
  Drive Alone 255,484
  Carpool 28,062
  Public Transportation 2,756
  Motorcycle 195
  Bicycle 502
  Walk 6,806
  Work at Home 7,796
Education
  High School Graduate 151,235
  Associate Degree 25,391
  Bachelor's Degree 49,353
  Master's Degree 18,819
  Professional School Degree 4,084
  Doctorate Degree 2,867
Military Service
  Vietnam Era Vets 19,986
  Korean War Vets 8,830
  World War II Vets 12,310

District 9
Marcy Kaptur (D)
2366 Rayburn House Office Building
Washington, D.C. 20515
202-225-4146
202-225-7711 *fax*

District Office
One Maritime Plaza
Sixth Floor
Toledo, Ohio 43604-1853
419-259-7500
800-964-4699
419-255-9623 *fax*

Website:
www.house.gov/kaptur

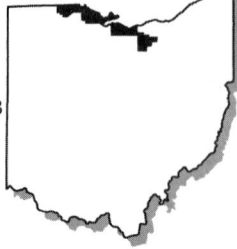

Population	630,795
Urban	542,576
Rural	88,135
Farm	3,607
White	81.4%
Black/African American	13.6%
American Indian/Alaska Native	0.3%
Asian	1.0%
Other Race (alone)	1.5%
Two or more Races	2.2%
Ohio born	486,830
Foreign Born	13,760
Income	
Per Capita Income	$20,885
White	$22,558
Black/African American	$13,307
American Indian/Alaska Native	$15,346
Asian	$24,579
Hispanic/Latino	$13,128
Median Household Income	$40,265
Median Family Income	$50,131
Income Below the Poverty Level	12.0%
Housing Units	253,359
Median Year Structure Built	1970
Median Real Estate Taxes	$1,271
Travel to Work	
Drive Alone	245,940
Carpool	25,317
Public Transportation	4,251
Motorcycle	341
Bicycle	736
Walk	6,639
Work at Home	6,274
Education	
High School Graduate	142,047
Associate Degree	28,445
Bachelor's Degree	52,548
Master's Degree	18,263
Professional School Degree	7,444
Doctorate Degree	2,766
Military Service	
Vietnam Vets	17,834
Korean War Vets	8,974
World War II Vets	15,370

District 10
Dennis Kucinich (D)
1730 Longworth House Office Building
Washington, D.C. 20515
202-225-5871
202-225-5745 *fax*

District Offices
14400 Detroit Avenue
Lakewood, Ohio 44107
216-228-8850
216-228-6465 *fax*

5983 West 54th Street
Parma, Ohio 44129
440-845-2707
440-845-2743 *fax*

Website: www.house.gov/kucinich

Population	631,003
Urban	627,377
Rural	3,626
Farm	2
White	89.4%
Black/African American	4.1%
American Indian/Alaska Native	0.2%
Asian	1.0%
Other Race (alone)	2.3%
Two or more Races	2.1%
Ohio born	469,669
Foreign Born	11,246
Income	
Per Capita Income	$22,455
White	$23,358
Black/African American	$14,134
American Indian/Alaska Native	$14,050
Asian	$25,061
Hispanic/Latino	$12,359
Median Household Income	$41,841
Median Family Income	$51,808
Below the Poverty Level	9.1%
Housing Units	277,699
Median Year Structure Built	1957
Medial Real Estate Taxes	$1,731
Travel to Work	
Drive Alone	244,332
Carpool	26,544
Public Transportation	13,500
Motorcycle	62
Bicycle	463
Walk	6,161
Work at Home	6,795
Education	
High School Graduate	139,733
Associate Degree	24,049
Bachelor's Degree	68,097
Master's Degree	22,036
Professional School Degree	8,587
Doctorate Degree	2,548
Military Service	
Vietnam Era Vets	13,643
Korean War Vets	13,495
World War II Vets	14,639

District 11

Stephanie Tubbs Jones (D)
1009 Longworth House Office Building
Washington, D.C. 20515
202-225-7032
202-225-1339 *fax*

District Office
2645 Warrenville
Center Road
Suite 204
Shaker Heights, Ohio 44122
216-522-4900
216-522-4908 *fax*

Website: www.house.gov/tubbsjones

Population	630,668
Urban	630,668
Rural	0
Farm	0
White	39.9%
Black/African American	55.7%
American Indian/Alaska Native	0.1%
Asian	1.6%
Other Race (alone)	1.0%
Two or more Races	1.6%
Ohio born	469,699
Foreign Born	33,696
Income	
Per Capita Income	$27,478
White	$27,478
Black/African American	$14,111
American Indian/Alaska Native	$19,921
Asian	$21,109
Hispanic/Latino	$13,152
Median Household Income	$31,998
Median Family Income	$40,406
Income Below the Poverty Level	19.5%
Housing Units	287,518
Median Value (owner occupied)	$89,900
Median Year Structure Built	1950
Median Real Estate Taxes	$1,454
Travel to Work	
Drive Alone	188,121
Carpool	26,129
Public Transportation	24,373
Motorcycle	100
Bicycle	629
Walk	8,885
Work at Home	6,521
Education	
High School Graduate	118,100
Associate Degree	19,977
Bachelor's Degree	54,983
Master's Degree	24,150
Professional School Degree	12,232
Doctorate Degree	4,800
Military Service	
Vietnam Era Vets	17,060
Korean War Vets	9,873
World War II Vets	17,659

District 12

Patrick J. Tiberi (R)
113 Cannon House Office Building
Washington, D.C. 20515
202-225-5355

District Office
2700 East
Dublin-Granville Road
Columbus, Ohio 43231
614-523-2555

Website:
www.house.gov/tiberi

Population	630,744
Urban	555,510
Rural	75,234
Farm	3,393
White	72.9%
Black/African American	21.7%
American Indian/Alaska Native	0.3%
Asian	2.1%
Other Race (alone)	0.7%
Two or more Races	2.3%
Ohio born	
Foreign Born	30,462
Income	
Per Capita Income	$28,106
White	$28,016
Black/African American	$16,050
American Indian/Alaska Native	$17,610
Asian	$30,178
Hispanic/Latino	$11,775
Median Household Income	$47,289
Median Family Income	$58,305
Below the Poverty Level	10.0%
Housing Units	268,159
Median Value (owner occupied)	$129,900
Median Year Structure Built	1974
Median Real Estate Taxes	$1,749
Travel to Work	
Drive Alone	260,504
Carpool	29,405
Public Transportation	7,564
Motorcycle	80
Bicycle	471
Walk	5,908
Work at Home	10,203
Education	
High School Graduate	112,349
Associate Degree	24,027
Bachelor's Degree	87,628
Master's Degree	27,549
Professional School Degree	8,959
Doctorate Degree	4,700
Military Service	
Vietnam Era Vets	19,062
Korean War Vets	7,380
World War II Vets	9,619

District 13

Sherrod Brown (D)
2332 Rayburn House Office Building
Washington, D.C. 20515
202-225-3401
202-225-2266 *fax*
E-mail: sherrod@mail.house.gov

District Offices
St. Joseph's Community Center
205 W. 20th Street, Suite M230
Lorain, OH 44052
440-245-5350
800-234-6413
440-365-5877
440-245-5355 *fax*

1655 West Market Street
Suite E
Akron, Ohio 44313
330-865-8450
330-865-8470 *fax*

Website: www.house.gov/sherrodbrown

Population	630,928
Urban	584,794
Rural	46,434
Farm	770
White	83.1%
Black/African American	12.2%
American Indian/Alaska Native	0.2%
Asian	1.2%
Other Race (alone)	1.4%
Two or more Races	1.9%
Ohio born	476,934
Foreign Born	23,021
Income	
Per Capita Income	$24,267
White	$24,267
Black/African American	$14,300
American Indian/Alaska Native	$15,473
Asian	$26,929
Hispanic/Latino	$10,299
Median Household Income	$44,524
Median Family Income	$53,761
Below the Poverty Level	9.4%
Housing Units	258,456
Median Value (owner occupied)	$116,400
Median Year Structure Built	1962
Median Real Estate Taxes	$1,428
Travel to Work	
Drive Alone	252,112
Carpool	25,686
Public Transportation	4,727
Motorcycle	149
Bicycle	304
Walk	4,081
Work at Home	7,826
Education	
High School Graduate	144,138
Associate Degree	25,308
Bachelor's Degree	62,116
Master's Degree	20,968
Professional School Degree	7,446
Doctorate Degree	2,941
Military Service	
Vietnam Era Vets	19,987
Korean War Vets	9,557
World War II Vets	14,941

District 14

Steven C. LaTourette (R)
2453 Rayburn House Office Building
Washington, D.C. 20515
202-225-5731

District Office
1 Victoria Place
Room 320
Painsville, Ohio 44077
440-352-3939
800-447-0529

Website: www.house.gov/latourette

Population	630,655
Urban	467,363
Rural	55,178
Farm	4,045
White	94.8%
Black/African American	2.4%
American Indian/Alaska Native	0.1%
Asian	1.2%
Other Race (alone)	0.5%
Two or more Races	1.0%
Ohio born	471,241
Foreign Born	23,523
Income	
Per Capita Income	$25,423
White	$25,706
Black/African American	$19,385
American Indian/Alaska Native	$17,640
Asian	$31,767
Hispanic/Latino	$14,814
Median Household Income	$51,304
Median Family Income	$60,292
Below the Poverty Level	5.7%
Housing Units	251,490
Median Value (owner occupied)	$139,100
Median Year Structure Built	1968
Median Real Estate Taxes	$1,668
Travel to Work	
Drive Alone	268,576
Carpool	25,092
Public Transportation	2,639
Motorcycle	62
Bicycle	267
Walk	4,250
Work at Home	10,093
Education	
High School Graduate	139,059
Associate Degree	21,325
Bachelor's Degree	74,451

Master's Degree	27,474
Professional School Degree	16,837
Doctorate Degree	3,624
Military Service	
Vietnam Era Vets	19,900
Korean War Vets	9,481
World War II Vets	14,628

District 15

Deborah Pryce (R)
221 Cannon House Office Building
Washington, D.C. 20515
202-225-2015
e-mail: pryce.oh15@mail.house.gov

District Office
500 South Front Street
Suite 1130
Columbus, Ohio 43215
614-469-5614

Website:
www.house.gov/pryce

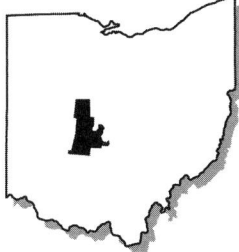

Population	630,710
Urban	464,056
Rural	166,664
Farm	10,681
White	86.2%
Black/African American	7.1%
American Indian/Alaska Native	0.3%
Asian	3.3%
Other Race (alone)	0.9%
Two or more Races	2.1%
Ohio born	444,975
Foreign Born	35,864
Income	
Per Capita Income	$23,902
White	$23,902
Black/African American	$14,322
American Indian/Alaska Native	$12,519
Asian	$19,413
Hispanic/Latino	$13,687
Median Household Income	$43,885
Median Family Income	$55,273
Below the Poverty Level	10.1%
Housing Units	272,972
Median Value (owner occupied)	$117,000
Median Year Structure Built	1968
Median Real Estate Taxes	$1,165
Travel to Work	
Drive Alone	266,033
Carpool	31,306
Public Transportation	8,947
Motorcycle	194
Bicycle	1,160
Walk	10,759
Work at Home	9,681
Education	
High School Graduate	169,208
Associate Degree	22,035
Bachelor's Degree	53,856

Master's Degree	17,187
Professional School Degree	6,456
Doctorate Degree	2,234
Military Service	
Vietnam Era Vets	16,845
Korean War Vets	7,034
World War II Vets	10,560

District 16

Ralph Regula (R)
2306 Rayburn House Office Building
Washington, D.C. 20515
202-225-3876
202-225-3059 *fax*

District Office
4150 Bleden Village Street,
NW
Suite 408
Canton, Ohio 44718-2553
330-489-4414
300-489-4448 *fax*
800-826-9015 *(Ohio only)*

124 West Washington Street
Suite A
Medina, Ohio 44256
330-722-3793
330-723-1319 *fax*

Website: www.house.gov/regula

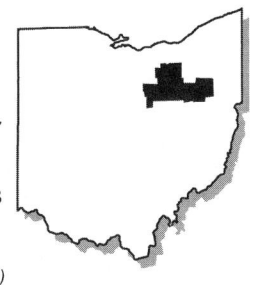

Population	630,710
Urban	464,046
Rural	166,664
Farm	10,681
White	92.9%
Black/African American	4.7%
American Indian/Alaska Native	0.2%
Asian	0.6%
Other Race (alone)	0.3%
Two or more Races	1.3%
Ohio born	504,074
Foreign Born	11,472
Income	
Per Capita Income	$21,041
White	$21,041
Black/African American	$12,860
American Indian/Alaska Native	$15,318
Asian	$26,199
Hispanic/Latino	$14,646
Median Household Income	$41,801
Median Family Income	$50,000
Below the Poverty Level	8.3%
Housing Units	254,335
Median Value (owner occupied)	$108,100
Median Year Structure Built	1963
Median Real Estate Taxes	$1,030
Travel to Work	
Drive Alone	255,572
Carpool	24,347
Public Transportation	2,446

Motorcycle 80
Bicycle 566
Walk 7,182
Work at Home 9,539
Education
High School Graduate 173,141
Associate Degree 20,141
Bachelor's Degree 44,879
Master's Degree 14,099
Professional School Degree 4,595
Doctorate Degree 2,124
Military Service
Vietnam Era Vets 18,744
Korean War Vets 8,900
World War II Vets 15,393

District 17

Tim Ryan (D)
222 Cannon House Office Building
Washington, D.C. 20515
202-225-5261
800-856-4152
202-225-3719 *fax*

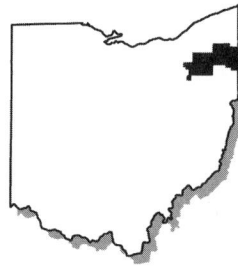

District Office
197 West Market Street
Warren, OH
44481-1024
330-373-0074
330-373-0098 *fax*

241 Federal Plaza West
Youngstown, Ohio 44503
330-740-0193
330-740-0182

Website: timryan.house.gov

Population 630,316
Urban 531,518
Rural 98,798
Farm 2,035
White 85.3%
Black/African American 11.5%
American Indian/Alaska Native 0.2%
Asian 0.7%
Other Race (alone) 0.6%
Two or more Races 1.6%
Ohio born 476,956
Foreign Born 14,404
Income
Per Capita Income $19,507
White $19,507
Black/African American $12,840
American Indian/Alaska Native $12,970
Asian $20,691
Hispanic/Latino $12,659
Median Household Income $36,705
Median Family Income $45,128
Below the Poverty Level 12.3%
Housing Units 268,881
Median Value (owner occupied) $84,500

Median Year Structure Built 1959
Median Real Estate Taxes $790
Travel to Work
Drive Alone 243,359
Carpool 24,686
Public Transportation 2,556
Motorcycle 136
Bicycle 319
Walk 5,963
Work at Home 5,204
Education
High School Graduate 185,714
Associate Degree 21,488
Bachelor's Degree 30,068
Master's Degree 10,959
Professional School Degree 39,79
Doctorate Degree 1,358
Military Service
Vietnam Era Vets 20,142
Korean War Vets 10,637
World War II Vets 16,286

District 18

Robert W. Ney (R)
2438 Rayburn House Office Building
Washington, D.C. 20515
202-225-6265
202-225-3394

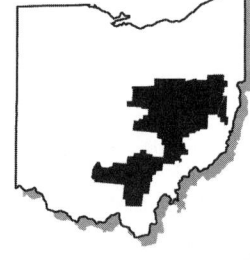

District Offices
800-866-4618

126 East Second
Suite D
Chillicothe, Ohio 45601
740.779.1634
740.779.1641 *fax*

200 Broadway
Jackson, Ohio 45640
740-288-1430
740-286-7630

Hilton Fairfield Building
152 Second Street, NE #200
New Philadelphia, Ohio
330-364-6380
330-364-7675 *fax*

146 A. West Main Street
St. Clairsville, Ohio 43950
740-699-2704
740-699-2769 *fax*

Masonic Temple Building
38 North, 4th Street
Room 502
Zanesville, Ohio 43701
740-452-7023

Website: www.house.gov/ney

Population 631,052	Median Year Structure Built 1964
Urban 273,399	Travel to Work
Rural 357,657	Drive Alone 220,705
Farm 19,760	Carpool 33,406
White 96.2%	Public Transportation 1,735
Black/African American 1.9%	Motorcycle 122
American Indian/Alaska Native 0.3%	Bicycle 824
Asian 0.3%	Walk 7,498
Other Race (alone) 0.2%	Work at Home 9,688
Two or more Races 1.2%	Education
Ohio born 530,851	High School Graduate 185,714
Foreign Born 5,262	Associate Degree 21,488
Income	Bachelor's Degree 30,068
Per Capita Income $16,725	Master's Degree 10,959
White $16,725	Professional School Degree 3,979
Black/African American $13,189	Doctorate Degree 1,358
American Indian/Alaska Native $11,662	Military Service
Asian $28,046	Vietnam Era Vets 20,698
Hispanic/Latino $15,310	Korean War Vets 9,985
Median Household Income $34,462	World War II Vets 14,214
Median Family Income $40,760	
Below the Poverty Level 12.6%	*Source: The United States House*
Housing Units 266,389	*of Representatives; U.S. Census Bureau*
Median Value (owner occupied) $81,700	

Voting Patterns, United States Senate and House of Representatives

		Party Unity		Presidential Support		ADA* Rating		ACU** Rating	
Senator		2000	1999	2000	1999	2000	1999	2000	1999
Mike DeWine (R)		86%	84%	52%	48%	10%	10%	80%	84%
George Voinovich (R)		78%	87%	59%	45%	10%	20%	64%	88%
Representative	District								
Chabot (R)	1	94%	89%	21%	22%	5%	10%	100%	96%
Portman (R)	2	91%	89%	31%	30%	0%	5%	87%	76%
Hall (D)	3	84%	76%	70%	71%	75%	80%	81%	12%
Oxley (R)	4	96%	89%	30%	28%	0%	5%	76%	80%
Gillmor (R)	5	91%	88%	32%	24%	10%	15%	76%	80%
Strickland (D)	6	85%	84%	67%	63%	90%	85%	12%	12%
Hobson (R)	7	90%	85%	33%	29%	0%	20%	72%	80%
Boehner (R)	8	95%	93%	30%	27%	5%	10%	87%	91%
Kaptur (D)	9	91%	87%	73%	68%	75%	85%	18%	4%
Kucinich (D)	10	89%	83%	76%	63%	80%	90%	16%	20%
Jones (D)	11	98%	96%	89%	87%	100%	90%	0%	0%
Tiberi (R)	12	n/a	n/a	n/a	n/a	n/a	n/a	n/a	n/a
Brown (D)	13	97%	95%	81%	80%	90%	100%	4%	0%
Sawyer (D)	14	95%	95%	93%	89%	90%	100%	4%	0%
Pryce (R)	15	90%	84%	35%	38%	15%	20%	80%	56%
Regula (R)	16	88%	83%	36%	32%	10%	25%	76%	64%
Traficant (D)	17	22%	43%	32%	44%	30%	60%	60%	52%
Ney (R)	18	88%	89%	29%	16%	20%	10%	83%	84%
LaTourette (R)	19	84%	77%	35%	31%	25%	35%	68%	64%

*Americans for Democratic Action (liberal)
**Americans for Conservative Union (conservative)
Source: Congressional Quarterly

ROB PORTMAN: RISING STAR IN THE OHIO CONSTELLATION

how Ohio works

Cincinnati Congressman Rob Portman leads no committee or subcommittee (he serves on only the Budget Committee and Ways and Means Committee), is into only his fourth full term in an institution that rewards longevity, and—by the political standards of the day—doesn't raise much money. He *does* chair the House Republican leadership but it's a post with no official House standing. He gets zero ratings from liberal and labor groups while pro-gun and business groups rate him nearly perfect. Yet even Tim Burke, chairman of the Hamilton County Democratic Party says, "He's a very bright, nice guy, easy to like and get along with." And Cincinnati Mayor Charlie Luken says, "If I was in his district, I'd vote for him." He is, simply put, the most powerful Ohio congressman—and one of the most powerful nationally.

So how did Portman get so far so quickly?

It wasn't really that far since Portman's power and influence comes not from the traditional ways of seniority or committee assignments. For Portman, it's been connections. He interned for Cincinnati Congressman Bill Gradison and after graduating from the University of Michigan Law School, he became a Washington lawyer, taking a job with the influential law firm of Patton, Boggs & Blow. After two years, he returned to Cincinnati to work for Graydon Head & Ritchey. In 1988, he spent a year campaigning for the first George Bush and was rewarded with a job as White House council. Later, he was a White House lobbyist. In those jobs, he worked closely with people from both ends of Pennsylvania Avenue, making connections that would serve him well in the future.

After Bill Gradison's seat opened in 1993, Portman won a difficult three-way primary, then won handily in the general election. He has not faced a serious challenge since. So solidly Republican is his district that in redistricting, fellow Republican Steve Chabot was given some of Portman's Republican-leaning precincts to make Chabot's seat safer.

During Portman's stint at the White House, he earned the respect and friendship of the president's son, the other George Bush. During the election campaign of 2000, Portman served as an informal consultant, so well-versed in policy that he played the Democratic role in both the presidential and vice presidential debate rehearsals. Today, a poster advertising the debate hangs in his office with a signature from Vice President Dick Chaney, "Bob—you were much tougher than my opponent."

With a voting record as conservative as the other two GOP congressmen—Chabot and John Boehner—Portman still does not stir the passions of those who disagree with him. Much of this is because Portman has managed to find issues with which to reach across the aisle to Democrats. Burke describes him as "less doctrinaire."

Speculation, a favorite Washington pastime, touts Portman as the next Ohioan to reach national prominence. He was reputed to have turned down the second President Bush for the position of Chief of Staff, believing he would be more effective in the House. The Senate seems to be closed to him since Ohio's two senators are settling in for the long run (Mike DeWine has indicated he will run again and George Voinovich, the lifetime politician, has nowhere else to go). Republican candidates for governor seem to be lining up like the planes at Port Columbus in the late afternoon and a lesser state office appears of no interest. When George Bush is out in 2008, it is probable that much of Portman's power base will be gone.

So what's next?

He's not saying, but many believe that Rob Portman will try for one of the top two spots.

—*Michael O'Bryant*

" I JUST REALIZED THAT I'M PAST THE AGE WHEN I GREET ELECTION RESULTS ENTHUSIASTICALLY. "

Senate, Key Votes 2000-1999

Senator	Increase Minimum Wage	Limit Federal Spending	Oppose Ending Kosovo Mission	Cut Taxes on Married Couples	Normal Chinese Trade Relations	Impeachment
DeWine (R)	Yes	Yes	Yes	Yes	Yes	Yes
Voinovich (R)	Yes	Yes	Yes	No	Yes	Yes

House Key Votes, 2000-1999

Representative	Increase Minimum Wage	Halt Kosovo Funding	Phase Out Estate & Gift Taxes	GOP Drug Plan	Impose Steel Import Quotas	Ban "Soft Money"
Chabot (R)	No	Yes	Yes	Yes	No	No
Portman (R)	No	Yes	Yes	Yes	No	No
Hall (D)	Yes	-	Yes	No	Yes	Yes
Oxley (R)	No	Yes	Yes	Yes	No	No
Gillmor (R)	No	Yes	-	Yes	Yes	Yes
Strickland (D)	Yes	No	No	No	Yes	Yes
Hobson (R)	No	Yes	Yes	Yes	Yes	No
Boehner (R)	No	Yes	-	Yes	No	No
Kaptur (D)	Yes	No	No	No	Yes	Yes
Kucinich (D)	Yes	Yes	No	No	Yes	Yes
Jones (D)	Yes	No	No	No	Yes	Yes
Brown (D)	Yes	Yes	No	No	Yes	Yes
Sawyer (D)	Yes	No	No	Yes	Yes	Yes
Pryce (R)	No	Yes	Yes	Yes	No	No
Regula (R)	No	Yes	Yes	Yes	Yes	Yes
Traficant (D)	Yes	Yes	Yes	No	Yes	No
Ney (R)	Yes	Yes	Yes	No	Yes	No
LaTourette (R)	No	Yes	Yes	No	Yes	Yes

U.S. Senate

Party	Mike DeWine U.S. Senator Republican	George Voinovich U.S. Senator Republican
2001-2002 Total Reciepts	$7,377,366	$8,288,943
2001-2002 Total Spent	$6,771,864	$7,518,639
Cash on Hand (11.25.2002)	$663,436	$2,067,098
Source of Funds		
Individual Contributions	$5,345,716 (72.5%)	$5,991,662 (72.3%)
Candidate Self-financing	$0	$0
Other	$527,245 (7.1%)	$670,653 (8.1%)
PAC Contributions	$1,504,405 (20.4%)	$1,626,628 (19.6%)
PAC Contribution Breakdown		
from Business	$1,405,588 (93.3%)	$1,528,145 (93.2%)
from Labor	$14,500 (1.0%)	$11,000 (0.7%)
from Ideological/Single Issue	$86,692 (5.8%)	$100,035 (6.1%)

U.S House of Representatives

	John Boehner	Sherrod Brown
District	8	13
Party	Republican	Democrat
2001-2002 Total Reciepts	$1,130,852	$1,149,860
2001-2002 Total Spent	$992,780	$578,703
Cash on Hand (11.25.2002	$123,780	$1,676,178
Source of Funds		
Individual Contributions	$535,768 (47.4%)	$508,343 (44.2%)
Candidate Self-financing	$2,200 (0.2%)	$0
Other	$204 (0.0%)	$134,242 (11.7%)
PAC Contributions	$592,680 (52.4%)	$507,275 (44.1%)
PAC Contribution Breakdown		
from Business	$574,385 (96.5%)	$335,651 (65.8%)
from Labor	$21,725 (3.7%)	$154,100 (30.2%)
from Ideological/Single Issue	-$950 (-0.2)	$20,075 (3.9%)

	Steve Chabot	Stephanie Tubbs Jones
District	1	11
Party	Republican	Democrat
2001-2002 Total Reciepts	$691,847	$401,633
2001-2002 Total Spent	$483,049	$409,722
Cash on Hand (11.25.2002)	$253,650	$19,174
Source of Funds		
Individual Contributions	$354,206 (51.2%)	$119,705 (29.8%)
Candidate Self-financing	$0	$0
Other	$7,973 (1.2%)	$7,614 (1.9%)
PAC Contributions	$329,668 (47.7%)	$274,314 (68.3%)
PAC Contribution Breakdown		
from Business	$281,324 (87.4%)	$141,987 (52.2%)
from Labor	$1,000 (0.3%)	$114,100 (41.9%)
from Ideological/Single Issue	$37,961 (11.9%)	$15,925 (5.9%)

www. *opensecrets.org/oh*

When someone says, "Show me the money," point them to this handy little site, which reveals who gives what to the politicians. And you thought they were *your* politicians. But then you probably knew that only five Ohio legislators raised a third or more of their campaign money from small grassroots contributors.

Campaign Phone Sex

	Paul E. Gilmore	Dave Hobson
District	5	7
Party	Republican	Republican
2001-2002 Total Reciepts	$448,404	$808,980
2001-2002 Total Spent	$650,588	$672,273
Cash on Hand (11.25.2002)	$259,474	$254,520
Source of Funds		
Individual Contributions	$65,026 (14.5%)	$433,580 (53.6%)
Candidate Self-financing	$0	$0
Other	$33,759 (7.5%)	$17,018 (2.1%)
PAC Contributions	$349,619 (78.0%)	$368,716 (44.3%)
PAC Contribution Breakdown		
from Business	$326,273 (95.2%)	$362,216 (98.2%)
from Labor	$12,000 (3.5%)	$500 (0.1%)
from Ideological/Single Issue	$4,500 (1.3%)	$6,000 (1.6%)

	Marcy Kaptur	Dennis J. Kucinich
District	9	10
Party	Democrat	Democrat
2001-2002 Total Reciepts	$415,373	$508,712
2001-2002 Total Spent	$329,092	$458,570
Cash on Hand (11.25.2002)	$774,357	$48,697
Source of Funds		
Individual Contributions	$118,793 (28.6%)	$263,960 (51.9%)
Candidate Self-financing	$0	$0
Other	$58,380 (14.1%)	$3,603 (0.7%)
PAC Contributions	$238,200 (57.3%)	$241,149 (47.4%)
PAC Contribution Breakdown		
from Business	$103,300 (41.1%)	$34,700 (13.8%)
from Labor	$141,500 (56.3%)	$210,250 (83.8%)
from Ideological/Single Issue	$6,575 (2.6%)	$5,986 (2.4%)

ZIP-a-dee-moolah

During the first six months of fund-raising for the President's re-election campaign, Cincinnati ZIP code 45243 was the nation's No. 2 contributor.

The 45243 ZIP is for tony northern suburbs, Madiera and Indian Hill, which is also the home of longtime Bush associate and former ambassador to Switzerland, Mercer Reynolds, principal Bush fund-raiser. Another Cincinnati ZIP, 45208, ranks 15th. It includes Hyde Park, Mount Lookout, and part of Walnut Hills.

—The Cincinnati Enquirer

189

	Michael G. Oxley	Rob Portman
District	4	2
Party	Republican	Republican
2001-2002 Total Reciepts	$1,253,240	$1,294,391
2001-2002 Total Spent	$1,121,999	$740,779
Cash on Hand (11.25.2002)	$460,676	$1,280,267
Source of Funds		
Individual Contributions	$359,669 (28.7%)	$1,239,299 (95.7%)
Candidate Self-financing	$0	$0
Other	$33,007 (2.6%)	$46,142 (3.6%)
PAC Contributions	$860,564 (68.7%)	$8,950 (0.7%)
PAC Contribution Breakdown		
from Business	$885,465 (98.7%)	$8,750 (140.0%)
from Labor	$4,000 (0.5%)	-$4,000 (-64.0%)
from Ideological/Single Issue	$7,000 (0.8%)	$1,500 (24.0%)

	Deborah Price	Ralph Regula
District	15	16
Party	Republican	Republican
2001-2002 Total Reciepts	$897,773	$282,642
2001-2002 Total Spent	$872,928	$245,748
Cash on Hand (11.25.2002)	$481,511	$121,501
Source of Funds		
Individual Contributions	$257,737 (28.7%)	$268,203 (94.9%)
Candidate Self-financing	$0	$0
Other	$56,514 ($6.3%)	$3,339 (3.9%)
PAC Contributions	$583,522 (65.0%)	$11,000 (1.2%)
PAC Contribution Breakdown		
from Business	$580,348 (95.5%)	-$500 (-2.1%)
from Labor	$13,000 (2.1%)	$2,000 (8.5%)
from Ideological/Single Issue	$14,200 (2.3%)	$22,000 (93.6%)

	Tim Ryan	Ted Strickland
District	17	6
Party	Democrat	Democrat
2001-2002 Total Reciepts	$536,285	$775,007
2001-2002 Total Spent	$502,575	$849,326
Cash on Hand (11.25.2002)	*$32,698*	*$159,018*
Source of Funds		
Individual Contributions	$157,310 (29.3%)	$196,658 (25.4%)
Candidate Self-financing	$2,000 (0.4%)	$0
Other	$9,400 (1.8%)	$44,724 (5.8%)
PAC Contributions	$367,575 (68.5%)	$533,625 (68.9%)
PAC Contribution Breakdown		
from Business	$54,250 (15.3%)	$239,609 (46.2%)
from Labor	$180,750 (51.1%)	$221,550 (42.7%)
from Ideological/Single Issue	$118,679 (33.6%)	$57,901 (11.2%)

	Partick J. Tiberi	Michael R. Turner
District	12	3
Party	Republican	Republican
2001-2002 Total Reciepts	$1,103,510	$1,042,699
2001-2002 Total Spent	$766,720	$1,026,328
Cash on Hand (11.25.2002)	$363,720	$16,369
Source of Funds		
Individual Contributions	$612,982 (55.5%)	$521,799(50.0%)
Candidate Self-financing	$0	$0
Other	$12,705 (1.2%)	$53,174 (5.1%)
PAC Contributions	$477,823 (43.3%)	$467,726 (44.9%)
PAC Contribution Breakdown		
from Business	$419,503 (93.5%)	$276,235 (69.3%)
from Labor	$2,000 (0.4%)	$6,000 (1.5%)
from Ideological/Single Issue	$26,972 (6.0%)	$116,227 (29.2%)

Source: Ohio Citizen Action

Top Campaign Spenders–U.S. Senate *(2000)*
(winners in bold)

	Party		Total Spending	Spending per Vote
DeWine, Mike	R		$5,619,163	$2.11
Celeste, Theodore	D		$475,007	$0.30

Top Campaign Spenders–U.S. House of Representatives
(winners in bold)

	Party	District	Total Spending	Spending per Vote
Tiberi, Pat	R	12	$1,609,422	$11.56
O'Shaughnessy, Maryellen	D	12	$1,151,414	$9.98
Boehner, John	R	8	$913,270	$5.09
Portman, Rob	R	2	$767,477	$3.76
Brown, Sherrod	D	13	$722,305	$4.25
Ney, Bob	R	18	$540,034	$3.55
Gillmor, Paul	R	5	$475,004	$2.80
Strickland, Ted	D	6	$433,979	$3.20
Oxley, Michael	R	4	$424,626	$2.71
Kucinich, Dennis	D	10	$411,107	$2.46
Guthrie, Marc	D	17	$189,162	$2.39
Walter, Randy	-	17	$350,172	$6.76
Pryce, Deborah	R	15	$346,603	$2.21
Sawyer, Thomas	D	14	$307,224	$2.06
Hobson, Dave	R	7	$295,096	$1.80
LaTourette, Steven	R	19	$273,768	$1.32
Kaptur, Marcy	D	9	$215,266	$1.28
Trafficant, James	D	17	$205,924	$1.71
Jones, Stephanie Tubbs	D	11	$201,347	$1.23
Cranley, John	D	1	$154,193	$1.57
Cabot, Steve	R	1	$136,797	$1.17
Hall, Tony	D	3	$125,193	$0.70
Alberty, Paul	R	17	$112,792	$2.06
Bryan, Dwight	R	9	$82,807	$1.67
Regula, Ralph	R	16	$82,765	$0.51
Wood, Rick	R	14	$33,416	$0.47
Parks, John	D	8	$27,371	$0.41
Jeric, Rick	R	13	$19,493	$0.21
Azinger, Mike	R	6	$5,877	$0.06
Dickman, Daniel	D	4	$5,315	$0.08
Smith, Bill	R	10	$4,369	$0.09
Sanders, Charles	D	2	$623	$0.01
Mitchel, John	I	7	$0	$0.00

Republicans outspent Democrats $6,121,616 to $4,161,423 in races for the United States House of Representatives.* Statewide, spending breaks down to $2.77 for each Republican vote and $2.38 for each Democratic vote. The two independent candidates spent a total of $962,302 or $5.32 per vote. Winners outspent losers at about 4 to 1 (no incumbent lost). The winners spent $2.77 per vote while losers spent $2.22 per vote. Only Randy Walter outspent his opponent and lost (James Trafficant).

* Six Democrats and one Republican candidate did not report their campaign spending.

Top Campaign Spenders–Ohio Senate (2000)
(winners in bold)

	Party	District	Total Spending	Spending per Vote
Jacobson, Jeff	R	6	$445,371	$5.54
Gardner, Randy	R	2	$407,484	$4.00
White, Doug	R	14	$301,049	$3.86
Jordan, Jim	R	12	$350,962	$3.52
Harris, Bill	R	19	$331,108	$3.23
Armstutz, Ron	R	22	$293,104	$3.20
Spada, Bob	R	24	$276,116	$2.65
Austria, Steve	R	10	$238,246	$2.81
Carnes, Jim	R	20	$221,175	$2.62
Herrington, Leigh	D	28	$215,273	$2.80
Mead, Priscella	D	32	$209,064	$2.00
Kelly, Elizabeth	D	22	$179,507	$3.21
Ryan, Timothy	D	16	$169,288	$2.49
Garder, Robert	R	18	$129,064	$1.76
Mumper, Larry	R	26	$132,566	$1.59
DiDonato, Greg	D	30	$115,321	$1.14
Nein, Scott	R	4	$106,893	$1.12
Boyle, Ed	D	24	$94,736	$1.83
Blessing, Jr.,Louis	R	8	$88,330	$1.08
Tackett, Roger	D	10	$87,990	$1.83
Keith, Karl	D	6	$52,130	$1.07
Magee, Arthur		32	$47,432	$3.31
Law, Randy	R	32	$36,606	$0.77
Fleure, Mary	D	26	$33,992	$0.70
McNamee, Donna	D	18	$27,939	$0.57
Engel, Arnold	D	4	$9,499	$0.20
Jones, Judy	R	28	$6,664	$0.16
Campbell, Jack	D	19	$2,155	$0.04
Williams, Randy	D	20	$1,750	$0.04
Kaffenberger, Sr., Jack		12	$632	$0.04
Schulte, Stephen	L	8	$287	$0.04
Kammerer, William	R	16	$0	$0.00
Leech, Margaret	L	14	$0	$0.00
Mitchell, Debra	N	12	$0	$0.00
Manning, Stuart	D	8	$0	$0.00
Brown, Tom	L	6	$0	$0.00

Republicans outspent Democrats over 3 to 1 ($3,364,738 to $1,073,824) in races for the Ohio Senate. On a per vote basis the Democrats spent $1.56 for each senate vote while the Republicans spent slightly less at $.49. Independent and nonaligned candidates spent $47,719, 42 cents per vote. There was a large discrepancy between winners and losers. Winners spent $4,030,414 while losers spent a little over a quarter of that amount—$581,319.

The cost per vote for winners was twice that of losers—$1.52 to $0.83.

Source: Ohio Secretary of State

Top Metro Areas in Political Contributions

Cincinnati (OH-KY-IN)	$8,961,134
Cleveland-Lorain-Elyria	$4,969,930
Columbus	$4,772,690
Akron	$2,894,269
Dayton-Springfield	$1,944,252
Canton-Massillon	$1,144,977
Youngstown-Warren	$803,235
Toledo	$664,392
Hamilton-Middleton	$435,018

Top 50 Campaign Spenders–Ohio House of Representatives (2000)

(*winners in bold*)

	Party	District	Total Spending	Spending per Vote
Householder, Larry	R	78	$1,032,450	$40.59
Trakas, James	R	15	$305,182	$9.16
Olman, Lynn	R	51	$225,215	$6.58
Boccieri, John	D	57	$211,018	$8.07
Ford, Jack	D	49	$197,179	$7.47
Cates, Gary	R	58	$189,968	$5.29
Husted, Jon	R	41	$188,554	$7.67
Smith, Geoffrey	R	28	$187,930	$6.93
Buehrer, Stephen	R	82	$187,693	$6.19
Carey, Jr., John	R	94	$173,103	$4.94
White, John	R	42	$172,924	$6.90
Mosher, Natalie	D	63	$168,955	$6.56
Raussen, Jim	R	32	$165,009	$7.84
Brinkman, Jr., Tom	R	37	$161,110	$4.57
Kearns, Merle	R	74	$160,306	$5.25
Peterson, Jon	R	80	$159,124	$3.78
Grendell, Timothy	R	68	$159,112	$5.85
Clancy, Patricia	R	35	$149,196	$5.05
Fedor, Teresa	D	52	$145,385	$5.50
Goodman, David	R	25	$141,587	$5.01
Hood, Ron	R	57	$139,417	$5.75
Hatch, Mark	D	27	$133,131	$6.00
Raga, Tom	R	2	$133,005	$2.74
Wilson, Charlie	D	99	$132,060	$3.78
Metzger, Kerry	R	97	$131,515	$3.99
Young, Ronald	R	69	$130,505	$5.45
Coughlin, Kevin	R	46	$128,077	$3.61
Hughes, Jim	R	27	$136,682	$5.28
Driehaus, Steve	D	33	$124,676	$6.47
Federico, Valerie	D	69	$123,484	$6.05
Distel, George	D	5	$122,245	$5.99
Webster, Shawn	R	60	$120,176	$4.21
Stapleton, Dennis	R	88	$119,518	$3.54
Hoops, James	R	83	$107,028	$2.63
Faber, Keith	R	84	$105,312	$3.28
Latta, Robert	R	4	$105,063	$3.26
Glib, Mike	R	86	$105,101	$3.54
Jolivette, Gregory	R	59	$104,032	$3.26
Eliason, Lisa	D	78	$102,997	$4.80
Seiz, Bill	R	34	$102,754	$3.26
Aslanides, Jim	R	95	$102,037	$3.73
Niehaus, Tom	R	72	$101,649	$3.78
Oakar, Mary Rose	D	13	$100,584	$5.11
Womer Benjamin, Ann	R	75	$100,362	$3.72
Condia, Tony	R	33	$92,652	$6.44
Rhine, Ron	D	73	$93,945	$4.51
Reidelbach, Linda	R	26	$88,393	$3.99
Lawson, Jones Pete	D	11	$88,490	$2.73
Mettler, James	R	52	$87,642	$4.40
Schneider, Michelle	R	36	$87,594	$2.49

Source: Ohio Secretary of State

Ohio's political parties

Political
Contributions
(2001-2002)

Total
Contributions
$31,660,797

Percent
to Republicans
78.1%
Percent
to Democrats
21.7%

Democratic Party
Dennis White, Chairman
271 East State Street
Columbus, Ohio 43215
614-221-6563
614-221-0721 fax
Website: www.ohiodems.org

Top 10 Contributors

Democratic	
National Committee	$1,220,882
Ohio House Democratic Caucus	$860,841
Democratic Senate Campaign Committee	$579,302
Cuyahoga County Democratic Party	$398,538
Everen Securities, Inc.	$345,000
AFSCME	$263,043
Ohio AFL-CIO	$226,690
Committee for a Democratic Majority	$194,197
Democratic Congressional Campaign Committee	$179,820
DLCC Hard Account	$150,000

Green Party
Paul Dumouchelle, secretary
1427 Northstar Road
Columbus, Ohio, 43212
Website: www.ohiogreens.org

Libertarian Party
Jeff Zweber, chairman
Suite 310
35 East Gay
Columbus, Ohio 43215
Website: www.lpo.org
e-mail: hg@lpo.org

Republican Party
Robert T. Bennett, Chairman
211 South Fifth Street
Columbus, Ohio 43215
614-228-2481
Website: www.ohiogop.org

Top 10 Contributors

Republican National Committee	$1,059,800
Ohio House Republican Campaign Committee	$965,000
Crown Equipment	$265,250
Republican National State Elections Committee	$250,000
Timken Company	$179,500
Montgomery Campaign Committee	$135,000
Republican Senate Campaign Committee	$133,000
Butler County Republican Party	$115,810
Ohio Republican Party	$79,250
Ohio Educational Association	$78,000

Natural Law Party
915 Washington Street
Genoa, Ohio 43430
419-855-1346
Website: www.ohiolp.org

Reform Party
2302 Buckley Road
Columbus, Ohio 43220
614-442-6641
Website: members.tripod.com/~reformohio
e-mail: chair@ohio.reformparty.org

Source: Ohio Citizen Action

Top Ten Campaign Contributors

American Financial Group	$2,044,058
United Transportation Union	$1,246,600
Cintas Corporation	$1,131,600
FirstEnergy Corporation	$911,951
Telantis Group	$596,155
Timken Company	$563,022
TRW, Inc.	$505,390
Limited, Inc.	$400,910
Pennsylvania Company	$400,000

Top Individual Contributors

	Total Contributions	D	R	National Rank
Linder, Carl & Edyth	$1,218,000	48%	52%	6
Farmer, Richard & Joyce	$721,000	0%	100%	15
Lerner, Alfred & Norma	$517,000	1%	99%	42
McConnell, John & Peggy	$372,500	0%	99%	83
Reynolds, Mercer & Gabrielle	$346,173	0%	99%	94
Belden, Marsh	$335,000	0%	0%	99

Ohioans Who Have Held National Office

Name	Term of Office	Residence or Place of Birth	Name	Term of Office	Residence or Place of Birth
President			**Secretary of the Interior**		
William H. Harrison	1841	North Bend			
Ulysses S. Grant	1869-1877	Point Pleasant	Thomas Ewing	1849-1850	Lancaster
Rutherford B. Hayes	1877-1881	Fremont	Jacob D. Cox	1869-1870	Warren
James A. Garfield	1881	Orange	Columbus Delano	1870-1875	Mt. Vernon
Benjamin Harrison	1889-1893	North Bend	John W. Noble	1889-1893	Lancaster
William McKinley	1897-1901	Canton	James R.Garfield	1907-1909	Cleveland
William Howard Taft	1909-1913	Cincinnati			
Warren G. Harding	1921-1923	Marion	**Secretary of War**		
			Lewis Cass	1831-1836	Marietta
			Edwin M. Stanton	1862-1867	Steubenville
Vice-President			William T. Sherman	1869	Lancaster
Thomas A. Hendricks	1885	East Fultonham	Alphonso Taft	1876	Cincinnati
Charles W. Fairbanks	1905-1909	Union County	Stephen B. Elkins	1891-93	NewLexington
Charles G. Dawes	1925-1929	Marietta	Russell Alger	1897-1899	MedinaCounty
			William H. Taft	1904-1908	Cincinnati
			Newton D. Baker	1916-1921	Cleveland
Speaker of the House					
Joseph W. Keifer	1881-1883	Springfield			
Nicholas Longworth	1925-1931	Cincinnati	**Attorney General**		
			Edwin M. Stanton	1860	Steubenville
			Henry Stanberry	1866-1868	Columbus
Chief Justice of the Supreme Court			Alphonso Taft	1876-1877	Cincinnati
Salmon P. Chase	1864-1873	Cincinnati	Judson Harmon	1895-1897	Cincinnati
Morrison R. Waite	1874-1888	Toledo	Harry W. Daugherty	1921-1924	Washington CH
William Howard Taft	1921-1930	Cincinnati	William B. Saxbe	1974	Mechanicsburg
Justice of the Supreme Court			**Postmaster General**		
John McLean	1829-1861	Lebanon	Return J. Meigs, Jr.	1814-1823	Marietta
Noah H. Swayne	1862-1881	Columbus	John McLean	1823-1829	Lebanon
William B. Woods	1880-1887	Newark	William Dennison	1864-1866	Columbus
Stanley Matthews	1881-1889	Cincinnati	Frank Hatton	1884-1885	Cambridge
William R. Day	1903-1922	Canton	Frank Hitchcock	1909-1913	Amherst
John H. Clarke	1916-1922	Youngstown	Walter F. Brown	1929-1933	Toledo
Harold H. Burton	1945-1958	Cleveland			
Potter Stewart	1958-1981	Cincinnati	**Secretary of Commerce**		
			Charles Sawyer	1948-1953	Cincinnati
Secretary of State					
Lewis Cass	1857-1861	Marietta	**Secretary of Defense**		
John Sherman	1897-1898	Mansfield	Charles E. Wilson	1953-1957	Minerva
William R. Day	1898	Canton	Neil McElroy	1957-1959	Cincinnati
John Hay	1898-1905	Cleveland			
			Secretary of Health, Education and Welfare		
Secretary of the Treasury			Arthur S. Flemming	1958-1961	Delaware
Thomas Ewing	1841	Lancaster	Anthony Celebrezze	1962-1965	Cleveland
Thomas Corwin	1850-1853	Lebanon			
Salmon P. Chase	1861-1864	Cincinnati			
John Sherman	1877-1881	Mansfield	**Secretary of Health and Human Services**		
Charles Foster	1891-1893	Fostoria	Donna Shalala	1993-2001	Cleveland
George M. Humphrey	1953-1957	Cleveland			
John W. Snow	2003-	Toledo	**Secretary of Housing and Urban Development**		
			James Thomas Lynn	1973	Cleveland

*William Allen is one of two Ohioans whose statue is in the U.S. Capitol. As U.S. senator from Ohio, he coined the slogan "Fifty-four / Forty or Fight!" in his support for U.S. expansion in the Oregon Territory. His likeness stands in Statuary Hall while the other statue, that of **James Garfield**, is located in the Rotunda.*

Name	Party	County of Residence	Term
Thomas Worthington	R	Ross	1803-1807
John Smith	R	Hamilton	1803-1808
Return J. Meigs	R	Washington	1808**
Edward Tiffin	R	Ross	1807-1809
Stanley Griswold	R	Cuyahoga	1809**
Alexander Campbell	R	Brown	1809-1813
Return J. Meigs	R	Washington	1809-1810
Thomas Worthington	R	Ross	1810-1814
Joseph Kerr	R	Ross	1814-1815
Jeremiah Morrow	R	Warren	1813-1819
Benjamin Ruggles	R	Belmont	1815-1821
William A. Trimble	R	Highland	1819-1821
Ethan Allen Brown	R	Hamilton	1822-1825
Benjamin Ruggles	R	Belmont	1821-1827
William H. Harrison	W	Hamilton	1825-1828
Jacob Burnet	F	Hamilton	1828-1831
Benjamin Ruggles	D	Belmont	1827-1833
Thomas Ewing	W	Fairfield	1831-1837
Thomas Morris	D	Clermont	1833-1839
William Allen	D	Ross	1837-1843
Benjamin Tappan	D	Jefferson	1839-1845
William Allen	D	Ross	1843-1849
Thomas Corwin	W	Warren	1845-1850
Thomas Ewing	W	Fairfield	1850-1851
Salmon P. Chase	R	Hamilton	1849-1855
Benjamin F. Wade	R	Ashtabula	1851-1857
George E. Pugh	D	Hamilton	1855-1861

Name	Party	County of Residence	Term
Benjamin F. Wade	R	Ashtabula	1857-1863
Salmon P. Chase	R	Hamilton	1861-resigned
John Sherman	R	Richland	1861-1867
Benjamin F. Wade	R	Ashtabula	1863-1869
John Sherman	R	Richland	1867-1873
Allen G. Thurman	D	Franklin	1869-1875
John Sherman	R	Richland	1873-1877
Stanley Matthews	R	Hamilton	1877-1879
Allen G. Thurman	D	Franklin	1875-1881
George H. Pendleton	D	Hamilton	1879-1885
James A. Garfield	R	Lake	1880
elected, declined seat to become President			
John Sherman	R	Richland	1881-1887
Henry B. Payne	D	Cuyahoga	1885-1891
John Sherman	R	Richland	1887-1893
Calvin S. Brice	D	Allen	1891-1897
John Sherman	R	Richland	1893-1897
Marcus A. Hanna	R	Cuyahoga	1897-1899
Joseph B. Foraker	R	Hamilton	1897-1903
Marcus A. Hanna	R	Cuyahoga	1899-1904
Charles Dick	R	Summit	1904-1905
Joseph B. Foraker	R	Hamilton	1903-1909
Marcus A. Hanna	R	Cuyahoga	1904-died
Charles Dick	R	Summit	1905-1911
Theodore E. Burton	R	Cuyahoga	1909-1915
Atlee Pomerene	D	Stark	1911-1917
Warren G. Harding	R	Marion	1915-1921

"I'M GOING TO GO VOTE AS AN EXPRESSION OF MY GRATITUDE TO THE CANDIDATES FOR SO DELIGHTFULLY ENHANCING MY TELEVISION-VIEWING EXPERIENCE, LO, THESE SEVERAL MONTHS."

"The first six months, I kept wondering how I got here. After that I started wondering how all of *them* did."

—Ohio Senator
William Saxbe

Frank B. Willis	R	*Delaware*	1921**		John W. Bricker	R	*Franklin*	1947-1953
Atlee Pomerene	D	*Stark*	1917-1923		Robert A. Taft	R	*Hamilton*	1951-1953
Frank B. Willis	R	*Delaware*	1921-1927		Thomas A. Burke	D	*Cuyahoga*	1953-1954
Simon D. Fess	R	*Greene*	1923-1929		George H. Bender	R	*Cuyahoga*	1954-1957
Frank B. Willis	R	*Delaware*	1927-1928		John W. Bricker	R	*Franklin*	1953-1959
Cyrus Locher	D	*Cuyahoga*	1928**		Frank J. Lausche	D	*Cuyahoga*	1957-1963
Theodore E. Burton	R	*Cuyahoga*	1928-1929		Stephen M. Young	D	*Cuyahoga*	1959-1965
Roscoe C. McCulloch	R	*Stark*	1929-1930		Frank J. Lausche	D	*Cuyahoga*	1963-1969
Robert J. Bulkey	D	*Cuyahoga*	1930-1933		Stephen M. Young	D	*Cuyahoga*	1965-1971
Simon D. Fess	R	*Greene*	1929-1935		William B. Saxbe	R	*Champaign*	1969-1975
Robert J. Bulkey	D	*Cuyahoga*	1933-1939		Robert Taft Jr.	R	*Hamilton*	1971-1976
Alvin V. Donahey	D	*Logan*	1935-1941		Howard Metzenbaum	D	*Cuyahoga*	1974**
Robert A. Taft	R	*Hamilton*	1939-1945		John Glenn	D	*Franklin*	1974-1999
Harold H. Burton	R	*Cuyahoga*	1941-1945		Howard Metzenbaum	D	*Cuyahoga*	1976-1995
James W. Huffman	D	*Franklin*	1945-1946		Michael DeWine	R	*Greene*	1995-
Kingsley A. Taft	R	*Cuyahoga*	1946-1947		George Voinovich	R	*Cuyahoga*	1999-
Robert A. Taft	R	*Hamilton*	1945-1951		**appointed upon resignation of elected Senator			

Why is it that most of our contemporary political men seem smaller? Does memory, that faulty instrument, play tricks on us, and we re-member our political organs as having more size than they really did? Does that explain why the great Midwestern moderate, John Glenn, appears positively saintly to us today? Leaving aside the larger philosophical questions—why *do* Mike and George seem half the size of Howard and John?—let us work on a gallery of folks whose legacy has been at least as large as life, folks who in our history have striven well and do not remain, as our contemporaries seem intent on remaining, smaller than life. Do you have suggestions for the larger-than-life vote? Please tell us. We'll make room.

"If you would succeed in life you must be solemn as an ass. All the great monuments on earth have been built to solemn asses."

—Thomas Corwin, Ohio congressman, to his colleague James A. Garfield (it was called 'Corwin's Law')

public **/ervant extraordinaire** *Thomas Corwin*

He was a public servant extraordinaire Prosecuting Attorney of Warren County (1818-28), State Legislator (1821-23; 1829-30), Governor of Ohio (1840-42), a five-term U.S. Congressman, Senator (1845-50), and Secretary of the Treasury (1850-1853). A loyal Whig who tirelessly supported William Henry Harrison's bid for the Presidency, Corwin was a man of wit and eloquence who in 1847 delivered an impassioned speech in the U.S. Senate denouncing the Mexican War as an act of conquest. "If I were a Mexican," Corwin told his fellow Senators, "I would ask you, 'Have you not room enough in your own country to bury your dead?'" His position was vindicated in 1861, when President Lincoln appointed him Minister to Mexico. Corwin, who died in 1865, once suggested that his tombstone should read, "Dearly beloved by his family; universally despised by Democrats; useful in life only to knaves and pretended friends."

the loyali/t *John Brough*

The 1863 Ohio gubernatorial contest was a distillation of the political conflict that per-vaded the North during the Civil War: loyal Unionist vs. hard-biting Copperheads who opposed the war; steadfast John Brough vs. powerful Clement Vallandigham. The eyes of

---

First Congressional investigation grills Ohio Territorial Governor Arthur St. Clair for disastrous outing against Indian armies; sets precedent of executive privilege and establishes 200-year pattern of conflict between the two branches.

1792

Ohio's first election is nationally significant because for first time in America those who were not landowners (except women) were able to vote.

1803

the nation focused on Ohio on election night, watching to see which way President Lincoln's delicate political balance might tip. When Brough notified Lincoln that he had won, the President telegraphed back: "Glory to God in the highest. Ohio has saved the nation." Brough was a big, beefy, workhorse of man, and probably the largest governor Ohio has ever had. People used to say, "If flesh is grass, then John Brough's a ton of hay." Unfortunately, the strain of leadership during the Civil War—he had delivered to Lincoln 35,000 Ohio volunteers in a hundred days—sapped even his considerable strength. In 1865, he had an accident, gangrene set in, and mighty John Brough was finally felled.

an honest man and more
Edwin M. Stanton

He was cold, and stern, and given to rudeness. It was said that he had once called Lincoln a "baboon." As Secretary of War during the Civil War, he was called "the most hated man in Washington." Yet, this lawyer who had dropped out of Kenyon College and begun a modest practice in Cadiz built a national reputation with his impeccable honestly, tenacity, and ruthless administrative ability. That, doubtless, is why Lincoln chose Stanton for such a critical cabinet post. It also explains, perhaps, how Stanton came to precipitate the first impeachment proceedings against a President. After Lincoln's assassination, President Andrew Johnson attempted to continue a benevolent Reconstruction policy, but his efforts were undermined by Radical Republicans—including Stanton—bent on punishing the South. When Johnson fired him, Stanton fought back, arguing that the Tenure of Office Act allowed only Congress to remove him, and thus giving the Radicals an excuse to impeach Johnson in 1868. With his former rival, Chief Justice Salmon P. Chase, presiding at the trial in the Senate, Johnson was acquitted—and the legislative-executive balance maintained—by a single vote. Stanton immediately submitted his resignation.

wordsmith John Hay

He was Lincoln's private secretary in the White House, and a decade after the assassination, he married a wealthy Ohio socialite and lived in Cleveland. A diplomat and writer, Hay penned poetry as well as newspaper editorials, and in 1890, co-authored the massive tome that was considered the definitive biography of the felled President: *Abraham Lincoln, a History.* President McKinley, mindful of Hay's campaign contributions as well as the custom of appointing men of letters as British ambassa-

Invention of the modern political campaign. With military hero as candidate and no clear issues, campaign is first to emphasize evasion and irrelevancy; floats, campaign hats, songs, and slogans come into use, help elect William Henry Harrison.

1840

Abraham Lincoln, on way to his inauguration, stops at Painesville railway station where he addresses young women from Lake Erie College. "Ladies," says tired President, "I see a great deal more beauty than you do."

1861

dors, chose him to represent the U.S. in London in 1897. A year later, Hay became Secretary of State and used his way with words to coin the phrase "splendid little war" to describe the Spanish-American donnybrook that began with the sinking of the Maine and ended with the U.S. a new world power presiding over an empire that spanned the Pacific from Hawaii to the Philippines. By 1900, Hays had another apt phrase—the Open Door—for his policy of gaining U.S. economic and military entrée into teetering, rebellion-ridden China.

northern light/*John Mercer Langston*

Along with Frederick Douglass, he was called the "Aurora Borealis" of the slaves, a fitting description indeed for one of the most visible black Americans of the pre and post Civil War eras. **John Mercer Langston** had been born in Louisa County, Virginia in 1829. His father was Ralph Quarles, a wealthy Virginia planter; his mother was Lucy Langston, a freed slave. Both died before he was five, and young John was sent to Ohio, where William Gooch, a friend of his father's in Chillicothe, oversaw his upbringing. Graduating from Oberlin College in 1853, he studied law, became one of the first blacks admitted to the Ohio Bar in 1854, and was elected clerk of Brownhelm Township in 1855. His ballot box victory marked the first time that a black had been elected to office in the United States, and Langston probably could not have chosen a better place to launch his political career—let alone make history—than Lorain County, where the town of Oberlin was a hotbed of abolitionism and a renowned terminus on the Underground Railroad. Langston coupled the cause of black civil rights with an extraordinary career in public service. He became a member of both the Oberlin town council and board of education; recruited black troops for the Union Army during the Civil War; urged Lincoln to issue a proclamation of emancipation; and helped start the National Equal Rights League. All the while, Langston crusaded to give his people the right to vote, proclaiming that enfranchisement was the instrument that would "stab the demon of slavery." After the Civil War, he was inspector general of the Freedmen's Bureau and became dean of newly-formed Howard University, where he started the law school. In 1877, he was named U.S. minister to Haiti and charge' d'affaires for Santo Domingo. Then in 1888, Langston ran for the U.S. House of Representatives, and secured what must have been his most gratifying achievement—election as the first black Congressman from his native state of Virginia.

noble works/*John W. Noble*

Although most folks think of Theodore Roosevelt as the first President bullish on America's national parks, TR actually built his conservation reputation on a foundation laid in Benjamin Harrison's administration. Harrison chose as his Secretary of the Interior a fellow Buckeye, **John Willock Noble**, who had been born in Lancaster in 1831 and educated in Cincinnati. Noble was at the zenith of a highly successful St. Louis law practice, when Harrison tapped him for his cabinet post. Noble's major achievement as Secretary of the Interior was initiating and promoting the Forest Reserve Act of 1891, which for the first time allowed the President to set aside land as national preserves. Thanks to Noble, the nation's national park system began when Harrison designated 13 million acres of timberland as national forests.

Robert Schenck of Franklin, Ohio, considered America's greatest poker player, is appointed minister to Great Britain, whereupon he acquires notoriety as having imported draw poker into British government circles.

1871

When disgruntled office-seeker Charles Giteau shot President Garfield, it became impetus for sweeping Civil Service reform. Said one historian: "The bullet that killed Garfield also killed the Federal spoils system."

1881

the *kingmaker*

After he got William McKinley nominated for President at the Republican Convention in 1896, **Mark Hanna** went home to Cleveland where a jubilant crowd waited at the train station to cheer his triumph. Hanna jokingly thumped his chest as he shouted to a friend, "Big Injun, Me big Injun." Indeed he was, the biggest Chief of them all, the Boss of Bosses, the savvy millionaire industrialist who bankrolled McKinley to the White House by putting the touch on his corporate friends, and probably the only man in the country powerful enough to tell Henry Cabot Lodge to go to hell and get away with it.

"The businessman in politics," said William Allen White, "was Hanna's American invention." Hanna, convinced that what was good for business was good for America, determined to proselytize that belief by putting "his boy" in the White House, and when he found McKinley, he found the perfect vehicle for his purposes.

McKinley, said White, had "a statesman's face, unwrinkled and unperturbed; a face without vision but without guile...He walked among men like a bronze statue... determinedly looking for his pedestal." Hanna provided that pedestal courtesy of a campaign fund conservatively estimated at $3,500,000, which bought speechwriters, speakers, and 300 tons of McKinley propaganda.

All Hanna wanted in return was an appointment to the most exclusive club in the world, the U.S. Senate.

McKinley, of course, obliged, though he did so at the expense of the incumbent, the faithful public servant John Sherman, who was thrown the sop of being a token Secretary of State. Hanna thoroughly enjoyed himself as Senator. He reportedly—and fittingly—got more mail than the President, and his offices were known as the "little White House." When the Constitution forced him to actually run for his Senate seat in 1897, Hanna's money greased his way again through probably the dirtiest campaign in Ohio history.

"Columbus, Ohio," wrote Hanna biographer Herbert Croly, "came to resemble a medieval city given over to an angry feud between armed partisans... Blows were exchanged in the hotels and on the streets. There were threats of assassinations."

Though political cartoons pictured Hanna covered in dollar signs and editorials decried bribery and corruption, Hanna was elected, and the scenario that he would succeed McKinley as President seemed written in stone.

However, McKinley was felled by an assassin's bullet, and the White House came to be occupied not by McKinley's mentor, but by his Constitutional successor, Theodore Roosevelt.

"Now, look," said Hanna, "that damned cowboy is President of the United States."

It was a blow from which Hanna never recovered. His health deteriorated, and on February 15, 1904—less than three years after McKinley's assassination—he died. ∼

hardboiled *Mary Grossman*

They called her "Hardboiled Mary," for as a jurist she was so strict that she made even grown felons grovel. Born in Cleveland in 1879, **Mary B. Grossman** was a suffragette who decided to become an attorney after working as a stenographer in a cousin's law firm. By 1918, she was not only one of the first women lawyers in Cleveland, but also one of the first women admitted to the American Bar Association. Five years later, Clevelanders elected her the nation's first woman municipal judge, and they continuously reelected her until she retired in 1959 at the age of 80. She was known as a "severe, rigidly honest" judge, and it is said that once when she took a day off, 39 bail jumpers seized the opportunity and turned themselves in, solely to avoid the righteous wrath of Judge Grossman.

legal access *Florence Allen*

Ms. Allen holds the distinction of being the first female judge to impose the death penalty, proving, among other things, that capital punishment had become by 1921—the date convicted Cleveland murderer Frank Motto was electrocuted—an equal opportunity employer.

She was trained as a pianist and had her musical ambitions not been thwarted, the nation almost surely would have been denied one of its foremost female jurists. **Florence Ellinwood Allen** was born in Salt Lake City on March 23, 1884, and before she turned six, she knew Greek and Latin. Her father had been a professor of languages at Western Reserve University in Cleveland, and in 1900, she enrolled there to study music. But when a nerve injury ended her hopes of performing, she turned her attention to political science and constitutional law and applied to Western Reserve's law school. Denied admission because she was a woman, Miss Allen went to New York University, then returned to Cleveland in 1914 with her law degree and a resolve to campaign for women's suffrage. When the 19th Amendment was passed in 1920, she was one of its first beneficiaries, receiving the votes of newly enfranchised women in her successful bid to become Judge of the Cuyahoga County Common Pleas Court.

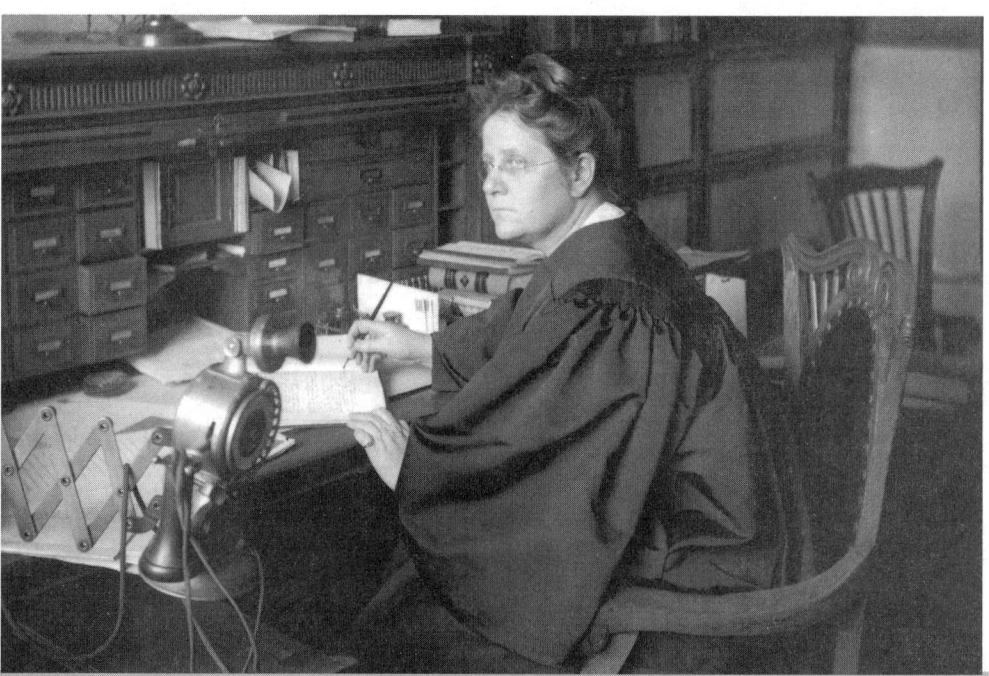

Ohioan John Sherman sponsors Sherman Anti-Trust Act. Deliberately vague, only 18 suits are instituted in its first 11 years, during which time monopolies flourish. A pro-business conservative, Sherman had little to do with the bill, except lend his name.

1890

Samuel L. Jones, one-time sucker-rod salesman, becomes mayor of Toledo and one of great reform mayors of American cities. He pushed 8-hour work day, end of political parties, required utilities to bury wires, and gave his salary to the destitute of Toledo.

1898

It was the first time in U.S. history that a woman had been elected a judge. It was not, however, the last judicial first for Miss Allen. She became the first woman to be a judge in a first degree murder trial and thus to sentence someone to death (1921); to be elected to a state Supreme Court (Ohio's, in 1922); to be appointed a judge in a U.S. Court of Appeals (the 6th Circuit Court of Appeals in Cincinnati, 1934); and to be Chief Judge of a federal court (the 6th Circuit Court of Appeals, 1958). In 1938, she handed down her most famous opinion: the landmark decision affirming the constitutionality of the Tennessee Valley Authority. Both Presidents Roosevelt and Eisenhower considered appointing her to the U.S. Supreme Court. When FDR choose William O. Douglas instead in 1939, a disgruntled Eleanor Roosevelt declared that when a woman finally was appointed to the nation's highest court, she should pause on the threshold of that august chamber and bow in tribute to the lady who had paved the way: Judge Florence Allen.

steely resolve *Charles Sawyer*

Although Cincinnati attorney **Charles Sawyer** prospered as a businessman, the self-described "conservative Democrat" also had a sterling parallel career in politics. In 1911, at age 24, he was the youngest person ever elected to Cincinnati City Council. In 1932, he was elected Lieutenant Governor; in 1938, Ohio's Democratic National Committeeman, in 1944, Ambassador to Belgium; and in 1952, President Truman's Secretary of Commerce. But Sawyer's name did not become a national household word until 1952, when Truman nationalized the steel mills. The Steelworkers of America had threatened to strike over wages, and because Truman feared a walkout while the U.S. was fighting the Korean War, he declared the situation a national emergency. Sawyer found himself in charge of 68 steel mills and 600,000 workers. When the mill owners cried foul and selected a Youngstown steel mill as a test case for taking the government to court, the legal fight went all the way to the Supreme Court as *Youngstown Sheet and Tube Company vs. Sawyer*. The Justices ruled that Truman's move was unconstitutional, promptly took the mills away from Sawyer, and placed the strongest ties on the hands of a President until the Watergate era in the 1970s.

industrial midas *George M. Humphrey*

George Humphrey was born in Michigan in 1890, but he was bred into a businessman in Ohio. Educated as a lawyer, Humphrey joined Cleveland's great mining and shipping firm, M.A. Hanna Co., as a general counsel when he was still in his twenties. Within two years, his reorganization saved the company from a lethal deficit, and he became a partner and its president. In the years before World War II, Humphrey was an industrial Midas who had a hand in the start of Republic Steel, National Steel, Consolidated Coal, and the Iron Ore Company of Canada. When Eisenhower recruited him as Secretary of Treasury in the 1950s, Humphrey applied his touch to the national economy. In the aftermath of World War II and the Korean War, the value of the dollar was dwindling, and he headed the administration's effort to cut federal spending and boost private enterprise. As St. George the Deficit Slayer, Humphrey achieved two fiscal feats that have been rarely equaled since: he halted inflation, and he bal-

President McKinley's government, without Departments of Commerce or Labor, Federal Trade Commission, or Federal Reserve System, spends half a billion dollars annually—less than the state of New York does 50 years later.

1900

Albert Beveridge, a Highland County farmer's son, sponsors Meat Inspection Act of 1906, written to remedy problems exposed by Upton Sinclair's muckrake, The Jungle.

1906

anced the federal budget. His putting the government back in the black—especially in light of today's uncertain economy—was all the more remarkable because Humphrey did it in three consecutive fiscal years: 1954, 1955, and 1956.

state fossil John Bricker

John Bricker, one of Ohio's most popular politicians, was Ohio's quintessential fossil, the ultimate defender of the Old Guard at a moment in history when the Great Depression had rendered nearly indefensible the status quo he loved so fervently. Bricker rose from Ohio origins so perfect he could have been cast rather than delivered: He was said to have been born in a log cabin—his descendants later disputed the claim—on a 50-acre farm south of Columbus where he grew up chopping wood and walking the prerequisite two miles down a dirt road to a one-room school house outside of Mount Sterling.

He put himself through Ohio State and law school with the same ethic, janitoring and teaching elementary school. He was elected to the governorship of Ohio three times between 1939 and 1945, each by increasing majorities, and served two terms in the U.S. Senate. In 1943, his conclusion as a three-time governor was marked by replacing a $20 million state debt with a $70 million surplus, although some of the mathematics was fueled by the wartime boom. He was honest and an able administrator; although organized labor called him "Breadline Bricker," complaining about him cutting out what he called "make-work" jobs.

When Ohio Senator Bob Taft and New York Governor Thomas Dewey removed themselves from presidential contention, Bricker went after the nomination. He clanked across the changing landscape, a man armored against any aspect of the modern world, and wishing to return the world into the 19th century. He was called "an honest Harding," and when he was accused of having no foreign policy, his stolid Midwestern isolationism replied, "Who has?"

His finest moment may, ironically, have occurred in defeat. Dewey re-entered the campaign and Bricker gamely stepped aside, his speech a hallmark of both innate selflessness and party loyalty. Bricker went

When Bricker went after the Presidential nomination, he was, writer Jean Kelly said, "an all-around ordinary guy with an American Legion pin in his lapel and a 33rd-degree Mason's ring on his well-manicured hand. 'A man in public office doesn't want to be pictured as being different in any way,' he said."

Federal Income Tax made possible by constitutional amendment proposed by President Taft, otherwise considered a good conservative: On $10,000, a married man paid $60.

1913

Warren Harding chosen as Republican Presidential candidate—for his looks, personality, and willingness to do party bidding, making him the first of the modern show-horse Presidential candidates.

1920

back to the Senate where he proposed his renowned "Bricker Amendment," a constitutional amendment that would restrict the President's treaty-making and foreign policy power. He lost a 1954 Senate roll call by one vote. Said his biographer Richard Davies, "Bricker had all the attributes necessary for political success—being from Ohio with strong political support. But once he went to the national level, he had no depth of background to draw on. He was just uninformed. He drew conclusions brutishly; they were almost doctrinaire. This rigidity...was born of his background and his personality." What Bricker himself called, "the Dutchman in me."

He was a man never at home very far away from home, which was Mt. Sterling, and 19th century America. He believed in certain mythologies because he had lived them, which was pointed out in his obituary in the *Cincinnati Enquirer.* "John Bricker," said the editorial, " had the good fortune to look precisely like what he was—a conservative Midwesterner who believed fervently in the American Dream, because he was one of its beneficiaries."

never a dull moment*Stephen M. Young*

Foes called him brash and acerbic; friends called him outspoken and independent; nobody ever called him dull. A liberal Democrat, millionaire lawyer, and friend of organized labor, **Stephen Young** served three terms as a U.S. Congressman and was Senator from 1958 to 1970. Both of his Senate victories were upsets, defeating conservative "right-to-work" John Bricker and Robert Taft, Jr. with the ultimate Republican last name. Crusty and not known for mincing words, Young helped derail John Glenn's run for the Democrat's Senate nomination by pointing out that all astronaut Glenn had ever proved was that he could go around the earth in the fetal position. Young considered his vote for the 1963 Limited Test Ban Treaty the most important of his career, but his colorful responses to Ohio constituents' letters made him legendary. To one critic he wrote, "Some idiot has sent me a telegram to which he has affixed your signature." And to the man who wanted the same free transportation for his horse

"Some idiot has sent me a telegram to which he has affixed your signature."

—*reply from Stephen Young to constituent*

Nicholas Longworth, of Cincinnati silk-stocking ancestry, is elected Speaker of the U.S. House, rebuilds the power of the Speaker through political skill rather than force, and creates modern template for his office.

1925

Presidential advisor Raymond Moley, son of a Berea, Ohio, clothier, distills basic content of New Deal program for President Roosevelt, including liberalization of Democratic Party.

1932

as had been accorded Pakistan's equine gift to Jacqueline Kennedy, Young replied:
"Dear Sir. Acknowledging the letter wherein you insult the wife of our President.
Am wondering why you need a horse when there is already one jackass at your address."

trailblazer *Carl B. Stokes*

The great-grandson of a slave, **Carl Stokes** was raised in a Cleveland public housing project by his mother, a cleaning woman, and grew up to become the mayor of his hometown—the first black mayor of a major American city, as well as one that was two-thirds white. It was an astounding political feat for its time—1967—and made him a pioneer in modern politics. For until his successful mayoral run, it was difficult for a black candidate to conceive of being elected to the top office in any major American city.

In 1962, he was the first black Democrat elected to the state legislature, and in 1965, had almost upset the Cleveland mayoral incumbent. No one knew quite what to expect but he allayed the fears of white voters with hard work and a moderate course in office. He was credited with opening jobs to blacks and women, establishing aggressive non-discrimination policies, and beginning clean-up measures for Lake Erie and the Cuyahoga River.

When Martin Luther King was assassinated in 1968, Stokes traversed the city asking for calm, and Cleveland was virtually the only major city to avoid racial turmoil. But the Glenville riot—ten people, including three policemen, were killed in a black militant shootout— also occurred on his watch, the guns purchased with arts and crafts money raised by the mayor's organization. He was re-elected in 1969 then left for New York City where he became the city's first black anchorman. He also won an Emmy. He returned to Cleveland in 1980, worked as a labor attorney, then served for a decade as a municipal judge.

In 1988, he walked away from a home improvement store with a $2.39 screwdriver he hadn't paid for but claimed absent-mindedness and made restitution. The next year, a jury found Stokes not guilty of stealing a bag of dog food from a Shaker Heights pet store. His detractors claimed he had lost his earlier charm and become an embarrassment to his profession by threatening lawsuits, once filing a libel action against a man who wrote a letter to the *Cleveland Plain Dealer* that was critical of Stokes. In 1994, however, President Clinton appointed Stokes ambassador to the Seychelles Islands in the Indian Ocean.

Whatever his slide from national prominence, there was a time, it was said, when nearly every black family in Cleveland had three portraits on their walls: John F. Kennedy, Martin Luther King Jr.— and Carl B. Stokes. At his death in 1996, columnist Dick Feagler recalled watching him campaign for Hubert Humphrey in California in

Representative Mike Kirwan devises grandiose pork scheme: a canal from Lake Erie to the Ohio River. "Yesterday we voted $3.5 billion to throw away on foreign aide," said one representative. "Let's build this ditch for Mike." It passes by one voice vote.

1947

Former Clevelander Maggie Kuhn, indignant at being forced into retirement because she had turned 65, launches Gray Panthers, America's Metamucil version of the Black Panthers; forces rewrite of retirement laws.

1970

206

1968. "He is so magnetic that when he enters a room," wrote Feagler, "its occupants move toward him, irresistibly, as if the floor has been tipped in his direction...He is criminally handsome and impeccably dressed and he moves like a dancer and the eyes of the white students shine with excitement and the eyes of the black students shine with hope. He is a man who, near the end of a harsh and cynical decade full of death, can kindle hope and enthusiasm in the eyes of young people by talking about the system...."

the last angry liberal *Howard Metzenbaum*

Before he retired in 1995 at age 78, **Howard Metzenbaum** was still known as the Tiger of the Senate, his only concessions the hearing aid and the slight stoop in his posture. But when he talked, he became pure energy, a fury of righteous indignation, one man against the 99, single-handedly defending against the sneak attacks of those other senators who, without his vigilance, would have pushed through their self-serving measures in the year-end rush to adjourn.

The Washington Post once figured Howard Metzenbaum had saved the United States Treasury a whopping $10 billion by blocking 26 separate year-end giveaways, an assessment that moved the headline writer to title the piece, "Thank God for Metzenbaum!"

He was called "a tiger" by Paul Simon of Illinois, and "a pain in the ass," by Senator Ted Stevens of Alaska. *The Wall Street Journal* described his legislative style this way: "In the U.S. Senate, where cooperation and comity are the grease that makes the wheels turn, Howard Metzenbaum is a bucket of sand." His tactics infuriated his colleagues but Ohio's voters were pleased. In 1988, he romped all over Cleveland mayor George Voinovich to win his third term in the Senate.

A certified millionaire and a genuine FDR–style liberal who toiled vigorously for civil rights and gun control, he could walk into any blue–collar union hall to a chorus of cheers. The same Ohio voters who voted for Reagan and Bush also voted for Metzenbaum, paradoxically giving this notoriously middle–of–the–road state a senator who was decidedly left of center. The voters admired his scrappiness and if they did not always know exactly what he was for, they knew what he was *against*: Big Oil, Giveaways for the Rich, Tax Breaks for Big Business, Insurance Industry Rip-offs, and Sweetheart Deals for Failed S&Ls.

If that sounded demagogic, it was; it was also the foundation of his broad appeal. Liberals supported

"Unafraid of incurring his colleagues's wrath, he ended up earning their respect with his guts and gall. He would not be stopped, and so he had to be dealt with."

—*Plain Dealer, on Howard Metzenbaum*

Lucille Perk, wife of Cleveland mayor Ralph Perk, refuses to accompany husband to White House dinner with President Nixon because it was her bowling night.

Bosnia peace talks held at Wright-Patterson Military Base. Said Serbian president Milosevic, "What, are you going to keep me locked up in Dayton, Ohio? I'm not a priest, you know."

1972

1990

him because they thought he was right on the Constitutional issues; working people, because he protected their jobs and promoted workplace safety; old people because he protected their pensions; minorities, because he always did the right thing, dating back to the 1950s when he first marched with Martin Luther King, Jr. Metzenbaum was the only Senator to get a near-perfect score from both the ADA *and* the readers of *Money Magazine.*

Once he made up his mind on an issue, Metzenbaum was rarely blown off course by the winds of fickle public opinion. He seldom pandered to voters, except in emergencies that occasionally arose during election years. But Senate campaigns came along only once every six years, and once safely re-elected, Metzenbaum was always quick to reclaim the liberal credentials that made him one of the last of his kind. Paul Simon went so far as to raise Metzenbaum to the level of one of the true "giants" of the Senate. "The real test of good government," said Simon, "is whether it helps people who really need help. People in this country who never heard of Howard Metzenbaum are better off today because he is in the Senate."—*Sue Gorisek*

above the fray/*John Glenn*

The folklore of our political process once romanticized that Americans of national political timber were born of sturdy pioneer loins and sprang forth from rude log cabins to their appointed date with destiny in the White House. This implied a highly egalitarian, quite democratic concept: any worthy American lad, no matter how humble his beginnings, could grow up to someday become president.

Of course, in the final quarter of the 20th century, worthy Americans are no longer routinely born in log cabins. Yet the land of the free and the home of the brave still values a certain humbleness in the origins of its elected leaders. In this country, after all, there is no royalty, and the Constitution forbids titles. The promises of the rhetoric about the land of opportunity ring a little truer when an everyday Joe or Josephine can be elected to Congress or the Presidency. We take a certain self-reassurance and pride when we send to Washington the poor boy from dusty Abilene, the rough-edged power broker from the banks of the Pedernales, the Georgia peanut farmer. Humble, small-town roots have supplanted the log cabin in the American political mystique. Modern political timber is rooted in the passions of working people and thrives in the simple, white-frame picket-fence houses of small towns not unlike New Concord, Ohio.

When **John Glenn** was growing up there, New Concord was so conservative a bastion of Presbyterianism that it was known as "Saint's Rest." The town was dry, and cigarettes were regarded as tools of the devil. Politically, New Concord leaned right and was overwhelmingly Republican. Glenn's father used to say that he could fit all the town's Democrats into his parlor, with room to spare.

New Concord provided the perfect backdrop for the unfolding series of Norman Rockwell-like scenes of which John Glenn's life seems to be made: freckle-faced young John swimming in Crooked Creek, and twelve-year-old John organizing the Ohio Rangers because New Concord had no Boy Scout troop. The Ohio Rangers liked to think they were tougher than Scouts and tried to do them one better. To earn their merit badges, the Ohio Rangers had to sleep outside in the rain, climb eighty-foot trees, and wade through knee-deep snow.

Bush-Gore Presidential recount recalls Florida recount of 1876 when Ohioan Rutherford Hayes used it to become 19th President. Losing Florida by about 90 votes, a recount gave him a 200-vote margin. Even with recounts in South Carolina and Louisiana, Hayes lost the popular vote. It was one of history's most fractious elections, coming just after the Civil War, and marred by deceit, deception, and deep rifts in the body politic. "His Fraudulency," Hayes was called.

2000

In high school, Glenn was an honor student, lettered in three sports, served on student council, was president of the junior class, marched in the band, sang in the glee club, and had the lead in the senior-class play. He gave his girlfriend, Annie Castor, a silver friendship ring and took her out on dates in an old jalopy dubbed "The Cruiser."

Every Memorial Day, Glenn's father, a World War I bugler, went to the local cemetery to play Taps. Young John, standing off in the distance, played the echo on his trumpet.

Glenn's father had moved to New Concord in the 1920s to start a plumbing business. John Herschel Glenn Sr. was a farmer's son with only a sixth-grade education. He figured that the farmers who plowed the rolling Muskingum County hills were ready to modernize with indoor facilities. While he traveled from farm to farm, his wife Clara stayed in town. She tended their plumbing store and their infant son, John Jr., whom she put down to nap in an old bathtub.

During the hard times of the Depression, Glenn Sr. and Homer Castor, the town dentist, had a discussion.

"Why is it that when a Depression comes, the first thing people give up is their bathtubs?" lamented old man Glenn.

"No," Doc Castor disagreed. "First they give up their teeth, then their bathtubs."

The Glenns and the Castors held on in New Concord to survive the Depression, and in 1943, the son of the town plumber married the daughter of the town dentist.

Years later, when the entire nation celebrated their son's successful return from earth orbit, when the President of the United States personally greeted their son, and when babies and highways and bridges were being named for their son, Clara and John Glenn, Sr. were flown to Cape Canaveral by President Kennedy for the arrival of their son, the new American hero. And, on the occasion of his trium-phant return from space, what poignant words did the proud parents have for their son?

"How're you doing?" asked old man Glenn, as simply as though John Jr. had just stepped off the bus from a trip to Zanesville. Clara Glenn made this down-to-earth observation about the space capsule: "I'd think your feet would go to sleep lying there so long."

In New York, some musicians presented the astronaut/hero with a trumpet. The Glenn family was staying at the Waldorf, and every now and then in the corridors, old man Glenn could be heard giving that trumpet a healthy blast. Back in New Concord, sightseers kept coming around to gawk at the Glenn home. The old man played a gentle trick on them, passing out miniature cardboard Bibles autographed by John Glenn, Senior, not Junior, of course.—*Damaine Vonada*

"I humiliated my family, gained sixteen pounds, and went millions of dollars into debt. Otherwise, it was an exhilarating experience."

—*John Glenn on his failed 1984 Presidential bid*

1850

Ohio's first Women's Rights Convention held in April in Salem, Ohio—the second women's right convention in America.

Ohio women seek to amend the state constitution, giving women the right to vote; it is soundly defeated.

Seventy-five years after women got the right to vote they account for 24.2% of Ohio's state legislators. The national average is 20.7%.

1851

Sojourner Truth, an illiterate ex-slave, gives her soon-to-be-famous "Ain't I a Woman?" speech at the second annual Ohio Women's Rights Convention in Akron. It sets tone for the rest of the century as women batter the solid door of male political dominion.

1869

The Toledo Women's Suffrage Association formed, making it the oldest local women's suffrage association in the nation.

The American Woman Suffrage Association is formed by **Lucy Stone**, a graduate of Oberlin—the only American college at the time to accept women—and Dr. Henry Blackwell, whom she marries while refusing to take his name. They issue a joint protest against inequalities of the marriage law, and feminists who follow her pioneering example are known as **Lucy Stoners**.

1872

Victoria Claflin Woodhull, suffragette pioneer and Free Love advocate from Homer, Ohio, becomes first woman to run for president, an ill-fated attempt against fellow Ohioan, Ulysses S. Grant.

1894

Ohio women win right to vote for and seek election to school boards. Fewer than two percent actually do. Usual explanation: "My husband votes for me."

1907

James Reynolds of Cuyahoga County introduces bill which allows women to vote in presidential elections. It passes and is signed by the governor but liquor interests—fearing that if women get to vote, they'll vote the country dry—successfully overturn the law through referendum in November of 1917. Their fears, of course, are not ungrounded.

1913

A Coshocton preacher says women should be content to remain on their pedestal rather than make "the fatal leap from the highest pinnacle to the seething cauldrons of political corruption."

1915

First woman political cartoonist—**Edwina Dunn**, *Columbus Saturday Monthly*, 1915

1916

East Cleveland writes suffrage into its city charter where it is approved by voters. It is refused by city board of elections but Ohio Supreme Court upholds it.

1917

Another suffrage vote fails at the state level; Ohio men are thus permitted to keep the seething cauldrons of political corruption all to themselves for three more years.

1919

U.S. Senate passes national suffrage bill, which moves to states for ratification. Ohio becomes fifth state to ratify. The amendment passes the Ohio House 76-6 and the Ohio Senate 27-3.

1920

Women vote in their first presidential election. Suffragist **Florence Allen** is elected judge in Cuyahoga County, the first woman judge in Ohio; two women are elected to the Ohio Senate; three to the Ohio House.

First woman delegate to a national political convention—Cleveland Democrat **Bernice Secrest Pyke**

1921

Ohio has first elected woman mayor—**Estelle Trippe**, Rochester, in Lorain County.

1922

Clevelander **Florence Allen** is elected to the Ohio Supreme Court.

1940

Frances P. Bolton, succeeding her late husband, wins special election to become Ohio's first female Congressperson; in 1953, she is the first congresswoman to serve as a United Nations delegate.

1961

Albina R. Cermak, a Cleveland customs collector and former precinct committeewoman, becomes first woman candidate for the mayor's office in a major American city. While she lost handily to popular incumbent Anthony J. Celebrezze, her trailblazing act set the stage for other women who wouldn't lose.

1970

Democrat **Gertrude Donahey** is elected state treasurer, thus becoming the first woman voted into a statewide executive office in Ohio.

1982

Democrat **Mary Ellen Withrow** wins treasurer's job, which remains the only statewide executive office held by a woman.

1992

In what is termed "The Year of the Woman," female candidates make historic gains statewide: 72 women now hold statewide elective office, including three governors, 11 lieutenant governors, 9 attorneys general, and 18 state treasurers. In Ohio, women make up more than one-fourth of the Ohio House of Representatives (26 of 99 members) and 18 percent of the Ohio Senate (6 of 33 members).

1993

Donna E. Shalala of Cleveland is confirmed as the U.S. Secretary of Health and Human Services.

1994

Mary Ellen Withrow becomes Treasurer of the United States, the first person to have held the post of treasurer at all three levels of government.

Marietta mayor **Nancy P. Hollister** becomes first woman in Ohio to occupy the office of lieutenant governor and **Jo Ann Davidson**, a suburban Columbus Republican who was the House minority leader during 1993-1994 session, becomes first woman in Ohio to be Speaker of the House. Ohio also has its first female attorney general, **Betty Montgomery**, two women on the Supreme Court, and 32 female legislators.

Jennette Bradley, a former Columbus bank executive, becomes first elected female African-American lieutenant governor in U.S.

2002

"If it has tires or testicles, you're going to have trouble with it."

—*attributed to Linda Furney, state senator from Toledo*

The judicial branch of government in Ohio is the system of courts established by Article IV of the Ohio Constitution in order to interpret the laws approved by the General Assembly and executed by the Governor. The Constitution places the judicial power of the state in the Supreme Court, Courts of Appeals, and Courts of Common Pleas. Only an amendment to the Constitution can change or nullify these constitutional courts.

Article IV also allows the state legislature to establish other courts, and the General Assembly has created Municipal Courts, County Courts, and the Court of Claims as adjuncts to the constitutional courts. Only the General Assembly can create or nullify such statutory courts.

The statutory courts and the Courts of Common Pleas are courts of original jurisdiction, that is, trial courts where cases are initiated. Article I of the Ohio Constitution assures the right of every accused person in the state to a speedy trial by an impartial jury. The Supreme Court and the Courts of Appeals, however, have appellate jurisdiction, which means that they primarily review the decisions arrived at in the trial courts. As the final court of judicial review in Ohio, the Supreme Court is the state's ultimate legal authority and "highest" court, followed by the Court of Appeals and the "lower" original jurisdiction courts.

Justices of the Supreme Court and judges of the Courts of Appeals, Courts of Common Pleas, Municipal Courts, and County Courts must be admitted to practice law in Ohio. All are elected to six-year terms on a non-partisan ballot in the general election. Except for the County Courts judges, they may seek nomination in party primaries or by filing petitions as independent candidates. County Courts judges are nominated only by filing a petition.

Justices of the Supreme Court

Supreme Court:
www.sconet.state.oh.us

Chief Justice Thomas J. Moyer
   Appointed: 1987
   Home: Sandusky
   Law Degree: The Ohio State University
   Background: Assistant Attorney General; Executive Assistant to Governor James A. Rhodes; Tenth District Court of Appeals, 1979-1986
   Biography: He was born in 1939 in Sandusky, Ohio, and received his undergraduate degree from The Ohio State University.
   On the bench: Justice Moyers believes that the intent of the framers of the Constitution can be reasonably interpreted. Still he cites Jefferson in stating that the general nature of the Constitution allows it to be applicable to changing circumstances. He believes that when the will of the legislation is clear that the law should be interpreted accordingly.

Justice Maureen O'Connor
   Appointed: 2002
   Home: Akron
   Law Degree: Cleveland-Marshall
   Background: She is the sixth woman to be elected to the Ohio Supreme Court. She served as an attorney in private practice, as a magistrate, and common pleas court judge. She was Summit County's prosecutor from 1995 to 1999, and in 1999 served as lieutenant governor.
   On the bench: Justice O'Connor ran on a platform of judicial restraint expressing the desire to shift the Court away from what she perceived as an activist role. She has come out for limits on

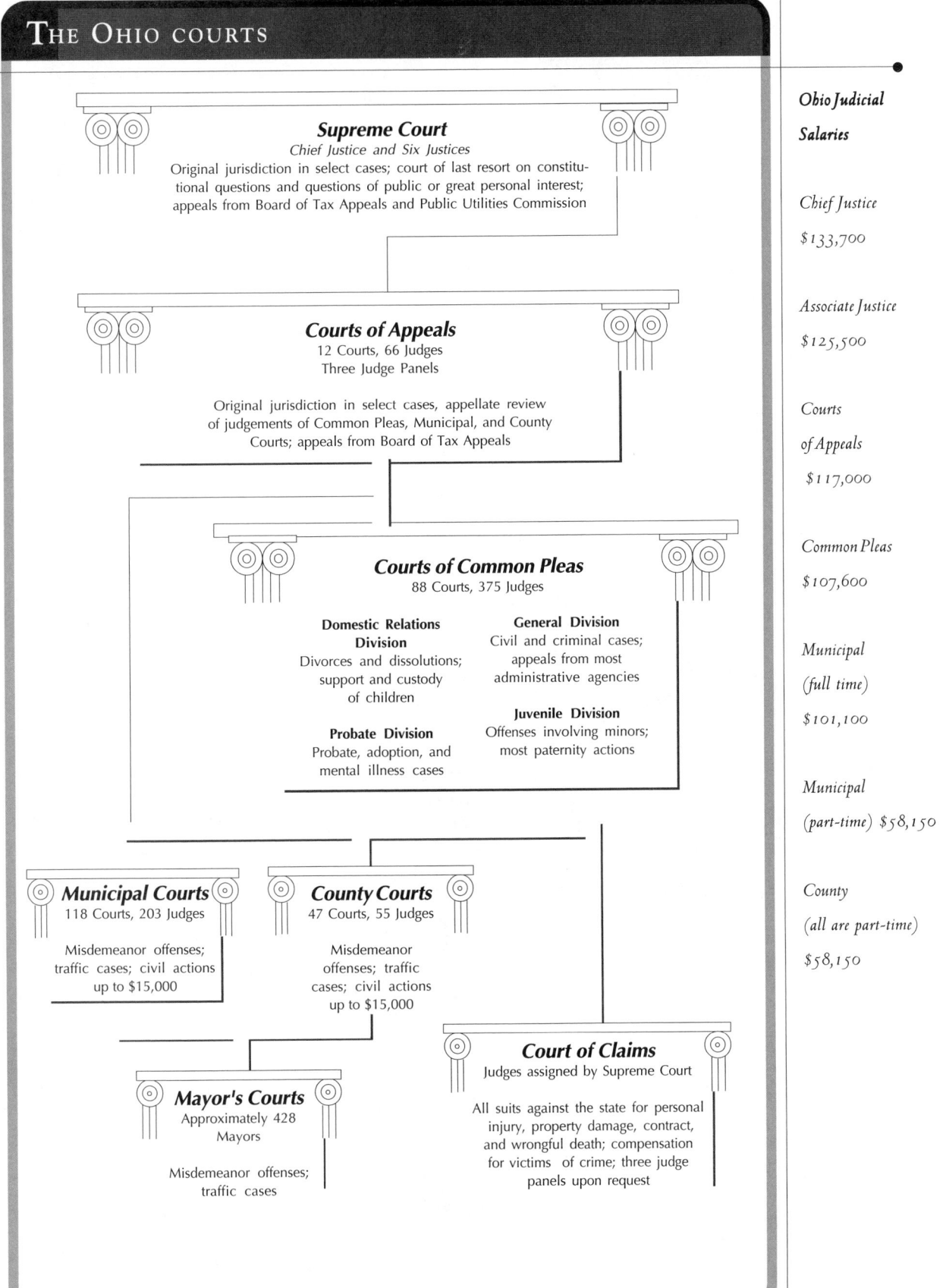

THE OHIO COURTS

Supreme Court
Chief Justice and Six Justices
Original jurisdiction in select cases; court of last resort on constitutional questions and questions of public or great personal interest; appeals from Board of Tax Appeals and Public Utilities Commission

Courts of Appeals
12 Courts, 66 Judges
Three Judge Panels

Original jurisdiction in select cases, appellate review of judgements of Common Pleas, Municipal, and County Courts; appeals from Board of Tax Appeals

Courts of Common Pleas
88 Courts, 375 Judges

Domestic Relations Division
Divorces and dissolutions; support and custody of children

Probate Division
Probate, adoption, and mental illness cases

General Division
Civil and criminal cases; appeals from most administrative agencies

Juvenile Division
Offenses involving minors; most paternity actions

Municipal Courts
118 Courts, 203 Judges

Misdemeanor offenses; traffic cases; civil actions up to $15,000

County Courts
47 Courts, 55 Judges

Misdemeanor offenses; traffic cases; civil actions up to $15,000

Mayor's Courts
Approximately 428 Mayors

Misdemeanor offenses; traffic cases

Court of Claims
Judges assigned by Supreme Court

All suits against the state for personal injury, property damage, contract, and wrongful death; compensation for victims of crime; three judge panels upon request

Ohio Judicial Salaries

Chief Justice
$133,700

Associate Justice
$125,500

Courts of Appeals
$117,000

Common Pleas
$107,600

Municipal (full time)
$101,100

Municipal (part-time) $58,150

County (all are part-time)
$58,150

civil lawsuits (tort reform) and restraint on worker's compensation decisions.

Justice Terrence O'Donnell
Appointed: 2002
Home: Cleveland
Law Degree: Cleveland State University, 1971
Background: Ohio Appeals Court Judge, 1995-2002; Common Pleas Court Judge, 1980-1995; Partner, Marshman, Snyder, Corrigan, 1974-1980; Clerk, Court of Appeals, 1972-1974; Clerk, Ohio Supreme Court, 1971-1972.
On the bench: O'Donnell has had the support of business groups in his previous race against Justice Alice Robie Resnick. O'Donnell is expected to support limiting jury awards (tort reform) and work against what he perceives as judicial activism.

Justice Paul Edward Pfeifer
Appointed: 1992
Home: Bucyrus
Law Degree: The Ohio State University
Background: In 1971-1972 he served in the Ohio House of Representatives, then moved on to the Ohio Senate for four terms. Before that, he served as Assistant Crawford County Prosecuting Attorney and was Assistant Ohio Attorney General from 1967-1970. He began serving on the Ohio Supreme Court in 1994.
On the bench: He believes that the language of the U.S. and Ohio State Constitutions rather than any attempt to determine "original intent" should determine the law. He is concerned with special interest groups attempts to sway the makeup of the Ohio Supreme Court. Pfeifer has shifted on the death penalty law that he helped write as a state legislator in the early '70s. While not openly opposing it he believes that the most cases deserve a closer review with reservations about how fairly it is applied.

Justice Alice Robie Resnick
Appointed: 1983
Home: Toledo
Law Degree: University of Detroit
Background: She practiced law while serving as Assistant Lucas County Prosecutor. Justice Resnick was elected Judge of the Toledo Municipal Court in 1975 and to the Sixth District Court of Appeals in 1982.

On the bench: Justice Resnick has been a target of special interest business groups that raised million of dollars to defeat her. These groups see her as opposing tort reform—she wrote an opinion striking down Ohio's tort reform law that attempted to limit personal injury lawsuit awards. Her decisions in Ohio's never ending school funding cases have also made her the target of groups who accuse her as one of the justices who attempt to legislate from the bench. In 2000 she won the election in one of the most expensive, bitter Supreme Court elections in history. Her opponent was Terrence O'Donnell, appointed to take the place of Deborah Cook.

Justice Francis E. Sweeney
Appointed: 1992
Home: Cleveland
Law Degree: Cleveland-Marshall, 1963
Background: Justice Sweeney began public service in 1963 by serving as the Assistant Prosecuting Attorney for Cuyahoga County. In 1970 he served as judge for the Court of Common Pleas in Cuyahoga County and in 1988 moved to the Court of Appeals, Eighth Appellate District Court.
Biography: After spending time in the army, he played professional football for the Ottawa Rough Riders.

Justice Evelyn Lundberg Stratton
Appointed: 1996
Home: Westerville
Law degree: The Ohio State University, 1976
Background: First woman judge in Franklin County Common Pleas Court in 1989, where her approach to sentencing in serious felony cases earned her the sobriquet, "The Velvet Hammer."
Biography: Born in Thailand of missionary parents, is considered an excellent Thai cook, and won the 1972 LeTourneau Stampede Girls Goat Tying Competition in Longview, Texas, while in college.
On the bench: Considered a leader in adoption reform, both nationally and in the Ohio legal system, authoring in 2000 the appellate rules and amendments to the Ohio Supreme Court's Rules of Practice that expedite appeals in adoption and termination of parental rights cases. Has taken pro-business stance in tort cases 67 percent of the time, according to the Ohio Chamber of Commerce.

MAPP AND BRANDENBURG: FUNDAMENTAL AMERICAN RIGHTS

ON MAY 23, 1957, SIX POLICEMEN banged on the door of Cleveland resident Dollree Mapp. The police suspected Mapp was harboring a bombing suspect, as well as gambling equipment. Mapp refused the police entry since they could not produce a search warrant, thus setting in motion a series of events that would forever change how law enforcement operates. After waiting three hours outside the home, the police forced their way in brandishing a piece of paper. Mapp seized the paper, which was blank, and was injured in the struggle. No evidence of a bomber or gambling equipment was found, only some obscene materials. Mapp was arrested and convicted of possessing obscene materials. The convictions, upheld by the Ohio Supreme Court, were appealed to the U.S. Supreme Court. There the Court ignored Mapp's primary defense—that Ohio's obscenity law violated her first amendment rights—and concentrated on the illegal search without a warrant. This argument centered on the exclusionary rule. The rule—that materials obtained illegally cannot be used as evidence against a defendant—had been a part of American law since 1914. Written by Supreme Court Justice William Day in his opinion for *Weeks v. the United States*, the exclusionary rule applied only to federal law enforcement officers. Justice Day, from Ravenna, Ohio, based his opinion on the Fourth Amendment. In *Mapp v. Ohio*, the U.S. Supreme Court overturned Dollree Mapp's conviction. For the first time, the Court extended the exclusionary rule to state law enforcement officers. Critics saw it as handcuffing law enforcement and allowing criminals to go free on "technicalities." Which would be true only if the Bill of Rights is considered a "technicality." Others believe that it forced the police to be more professional in their search techniques. The rule, despite having been weakened by subsequent exceptions, remains one of the fundamental rights of Americans.

ONE OF THE BASIC TENETS OF FREE SPEECH emerged from a literal field of fire and hatred in Hamilton County. In 1964, Clarence Brandenburg invited a Cincinnati television reporter to attend a Ku Klux Klan rally on a Hamilton County Farm. The reporter, accompanied by his cameraman, filmed 12 hooded figures around a burning cross. No one else was present. The men, one identified as Brandenburg, made speeches about sending Jews back to Israel and Blacks back to Africa. The speeches also advocated illegal actions against the government. The film was broadcast on the local station and later on national television. Brandenburg was arrested and convicted of violations under Ohio's Criminal Syndicalism Act by, "assembling to advocate crime, violence, or unlawful terrorism as a means of accomplishing political reform." He was fined $1,000 and sentenced to ten years in jail. The case was appealed to the U.S. Supreme Court, which used it to settle a 50-year struggle to develop a definition of illegal speech.

On June 9, 1969, the Court overturned Brandenburg's conviction in *Brandenburg v. Ohio*. In doing so the Court reversed a 1927 precedent that said that speech could be punished if it posed a "clear and present danger" with a "tendency" to encourage lawlessness or danger. The Brandenburg decision was less subjective. It said that speech was illegal only if "such advocacy is directed to inciting or producing imminent lawless action and is likely to incite or produce such action." The Ohio law violated free speech because it failed to distinguish between the advocacy of ideas and the advocacy of violence. In the opinion, Justice Douglas wrote that "The line between what is permissible and not subject to control and what may be made impermissible and subject to regulation is the line between ideas and overt acts." After Brandenburg, speech is distinguished from action and is protected unless it can be demonstrated to be dangerous.

—*by Michael O'Bryant*

The history of the Supreme Court of Ohio begins with the history of the state. When Ohio's first Constitution was adopted in 1802, the Supreme Court of Ohio was established as the highest court in the state. That Constitution, providing for a Court consisting of three Judges, required that a session of the Supreme Court be held each year in every county. Those early Judges spent major time riding horseback over the state, usually accompanied by members of the bar, who went along to present the cases to the Court. The Judges, in order to make room in their saddlebags for fresh linen, carried very few law books. They carried most of the law in their heads. Many of their early sessions were not held in the Statehouse—or even a courthouse—but were held in the homes of various individuals in the several counties.

From those early days until the amendment of the Constitution in 1912, the number of Judges on the Supreme Court varied from three to six. By the amendment in 1912, however, the membership of the Court was fixed at seven, comprised of a Chief Justice and six Judges. In 1968, the Constitution was further amended, and the Supreme Court is now composed of the Chief Justice and six Justices.

Today, the home of the Supreme Court of Ohio is the James A. Rhodes State Office Tower in Columbus. The building, completed in April, 1974, is the largest building in Central Ohio—41 stories high and containing 1.2 million square feet of office space. It is also one of the largest granite structures in the world. The Court occupies the lower floors of the building, with the Courtroom and offices of the Chief Justice and six Justices on the third floor.

The Courtroom has a long, elevated bench at which the Chief Justice and six Justices sit when the Court is in session. Behind them is the Seal of the Court made of stainless steel and Lucite. It was crafted by Ohio Sculptor David Black, as was the large Seal of the State of Ohio in the lobby of the building.

The Supreme Court usually hears oral arguments on Tuesday and Wednesday from 9 a.m. until noon. The four desks immediately in front of the bench are for the attorneys who will present oral arguments. Behind them are seats for the public. All sessions of the Court are open. Seats along both sides of the Court are for the law clerks of the Chief Justice and Justices.

At exactly 9 a.m., the Marshal of the Supreme Court asks the attorneys and spectators to rise and announces: "The Honorable Chief Justice and Justices of Supreme Court of Ohio."

Members of the Court, robed in black, file through a side door and take their places behind the granite bench. The Chief Justice is in the center with three Justices on either side. The most senior Justices sit nearest the center of the bench. The members of the Court remain standing as the Marshal opens Court:

"Hear Ye! Hear Ye! Hear Ye! The Honorable Supreme Court of Ohio is now in open session pursuant to adjournment."

The Chief Justice announces the first case and the name of the attorney who will make the first presentation. The attorney walks across the red carpet to the lectern in front of the bench and begins his argument. Normally arguments are limited to 15 minutes, but in some cases, the time is increased to 30 minutes. The Marshal keeps track of the time and turns on a white light on the

"IN AN OPINION HANDED DOWN TODAY BY THE UNITED STATES SUPREME COURT IN THE CASE OF HAROLD FLAGLER v. THE LAWN, THE COURT RULED 9-0 THAT EDITH FLAGLER HAD NO CONSTITUTIONAL RIGHT TO COMPEL HER BELEAGUERED HUSBAND TO MOW THE GRASS CONCURRENT WITH THE TELEVISION BROADCAST OF A MAJOR LEAGUE BASEBALL GAME."

lectern when the attorney has two minutes of time remaining. A red light indicates when the time has expired. Prior to the arguments, members of the court have read summaries of the case and briefs of the legal arguments of each side. The oral presentations of attorneys are often marked by sharp questioning from the bench.

The Court generally hears four or five cases in a day. When the final argument has been given in the last case on the day's docket, the Marshal asks those in the Court to rise and announces:

"Hear Ye! Hear Ye! Hear Ye! This open session of the Honorable Supreme Court of Ohio now stands adjourned."

The Justices file out and go to a conference room near the Courtroom to discuss the cases that have been heard. The only person with them in the conference room is the Court Reporter, who records the vote. The Chief Justice calls on each Justice to present views of the case. In cases where one of the Justices or the Chief Justice does not participate, a judge of one of the Courts of Appeals is chosen to sit on the Supreme Court. If the Chief Justice does not participate, the most senior Justice sits as Acting Chief Justice.

It takes at least four votes to decide a case. When the vote has been taken, small balls with the numbers representing the Justices in majority are put in a leather bottle with a thin neck. The

senior Justice shakes the bottle and pours out one ball. Another Justice looks at the ball and announces who has been selected to write the Opinion of the Court in the case. That ball is not put back in the bottle until each of the Justices has been assigned the writing of a case. The writing of the opinions is done by random selection and the work loads of the Chief Justice and Justices are nearly equal.

When the majority opinion is written, it is circulated to members of the Court for comment. Members in the majority may choose to write a concurring opinion. Those in dissent prepare a dissenting opinion. Opinions are announced Wednesday—except for some special releases— and become the governing law throughout the state. Several days after being issued, the opinions are printed in Ohio Official Reports Advance Sheets and the Ohio State Bar Association Report. They are eventually printed in the volumes of Ohio Official Reports and in North East Reports. These volumes are available in law libraries throughout the state, the nation and the world. The Ohio Constitution requires that all actions of the Supreme Court be published. There are no "unreported decisions."

Reprinted with permission from The Ohio Judicial System, a publication of The Supreme Court of Ohio

The eight Buckeye Presidents usually hog the limelight. Their considerable number and their ample physiques make the Ohio presidential impression hard to ignore. Yet, 13 other Ohioans have gone to Washington and left their mark on the body politic. They were Justices of the U. S. Supreme Court. In fact, during the 201 years the Court has existed, there has been at least one Ohioan sitting on the bench for 152 of those years. These Ohioans had critical roles in defining our rights and the legal limits of presidential actions, even in dissent.

One helped shape the decision that gave women the right to abortion. Another upheld the first federal wartime income tax, while another shot down the first peacetime income tax. One gave the government strong powers against corporate price-fixing, while others narrowed the government's ability to control child labor. Today, when the make-up of the Supreme Court is again a hot issue, who can recall the Buckeye Justices of yesteryear? How many know the famous definition of pornography—"I know it when I see it"—but not its author, Justice Potter Stewart? How many recall that Justice Morrison Waite died from an excess of charity? Who today remembers Justice John McLean, whose scorching dissent from the Dred Scott decision predicted the Civil War? If ignorance of the law is no defense, ignorance of the Justices should be not be an alibi either.

John McLean

(1785—1861)

Despite studying to be a lawyer, McLean almost left the profession in the early 1800s after buying a printing office and starting the Lebanon *Western Star*. He was appointed to the court by President Andrew Jackson in 1829 at age forty-four, one of the youngest ever, after another Ohioan, Charles Hammond, turned the job down. Some biographers claim that McLean really wanted the presidency more than anything, and, despite his judicial robes, he was a perennial

dark-horse candidate in 1836, 1848, 1852 and 1856. His vacillating personality and lack of warmth, however, worked against him.

Perhaps McLean's most important decision was his dissenting opinion in Dred Scott v. Standford, the pivotal pre-Civil War case that denied slaves the right to sue, saying they had no legal "standing" in court. McLean boldly countered, "All slavery has its origin in power, and is against right." McLean served 31 years, one of the longest terms to date.

Most negative quote about him:
"He cannot be accounted one of the leading Justices of the Supreme Court...his having one eye cocked toward the White House distracted him, thus preventing full application of his powers to the legal problems at hand."—Frank Gatell, history professor, University of California

Most positive quote about him:
"Able and efficient worker."—President John Quincy Adams

Noah Swayne

(1804—1884)

He had one of the most roundabout educations of any justice. He started first at a Quaker academy, then studied medicine but quit when his teacher died. He moved on to classical studies, but dropped those when his guardian couldn't support him. He finally settled on law.

Swayne became a Justice in 1862 at age 58, and served 18 years, resigning due to ill health at age 76. So far, Swayne is also the only Quaker to have served as a Supreme Court Justice. True to his beliefs, during the Civil War, Swayne intervened on behalf of a Confederate spy sentenced to death.

Swayne's summation of the Supreme Court's job would please certain conservative Justices today. "Our duty is to execute the law, not to make it," he wrote. His execution of that law did not please all his contemporaries. In a major decision, Springer v. United States, Swayne upheld the 1865 federal income tax. The case involved Illinoisan William Springer, who refused to pay his taxes, and the government, which refused to take no for an answer and instead took some of Springer's land. Swayne upheld the government's right to do so, saying "The prompt payment of taxes is always important to the public welfare. It may be vital to the existence of a government...if the laws...in question involved any wrong, it was for Congress...to see that the evil was corrected."

Most negative:

"Lincoln's first and worst appointment. Taking himself too seriously and overestimating his mediocre talents, Swayne flickered as one of the Court's lesser lights until a chill wind blew it out." — William Gillette, associate professor of history, Rutgers University

Most positive:

"Well-fitted to wear with dignity, and preserve without spot, the judicial ermine in the highest Court of the Nation." —National Intelligencer, 1862

Salmon Chase
(1808-1873)

Chase wasn't always a great problem solver. Once, his uncle, the imperious Episcopalian Bishop Philander Chase, asked young Salmon to prepare roast pig. Not wishing to pluck the bristles out one by one, young Chase merely shaved them off with his uncle's razor. At the meal, Chase's uncle and his guests got a mouthful of below-the-skin bristles, but Chase feigned innocence. The next day, Bishop Chase put two and two together when he tried to shave with his razor.

Chase served as a U. S. Senator, Governor of Ohio, and Secretary of the U. S. Treasury (where he issued the first "greenback" paper currency). Like Justice McLean from Ohio, he really wanted to be president, certain that he could do a better job than Lincoln. Nonetheless, he actively sought appointment to fill the seat of Chief Justice Roger Taney, who died in 1864. An early and fearless abolitionist, Chase always wanted to be Chief Justice so he could "overrule all the pro-slavery decisions."

He became a Justice in 1864 at age 56 and served eight years, until his death at age 65. During his term, he ironically had to decide the constitutionality of the act authorizing the first legal paper currency—which he had administered as Secretary of the Treasury. He actually voted against it.

Chase's most important act, however, may have been outside the Supreme Court altogether. Before the impeachment trial of President Andrew Johnson, Chase convinced Congressional leaders to follow strict courtroom procedures and standards in hearing the case. Johnson was acquitted (though only by one vote) in part due to Chase's moderating actions, thus ending the Constitutional crisis.

At top, Justice Swayne; Justice McLean at bottom

Most negative:
"Warped, perverted, shrivelled by the selfishness generated by ambition."—Fellow Justice Samuel Miller

Most positive:
"Chase is about one and a half times bigger than any man I ever knew."—Abraham Lincoln

Morrison Waite

(1816—1888)

The son of a judge, Waite was born in Connecticut, but moved to Maumee City, Ohio, after graduating from Yale. Noted for his support of charity, Waite nonetheless once defended a railroad on the grounds that the plaintiff, who had been orphaned by a train accident, wasn't entitled to damages because he was illegitimate. Waite was appointed to the court by fellow Ohioan Ulysses S. Grant in 1874 at age 57. Always a calm man, he received word of his Supreme Court nomination at the Ohio Constitutional Convention of 1873. Upon hearing the news, he simply put away the telegram and continued his work. An American journalist said of him, "a modest lawyer, from Ohio, little dreaming of the supreme honor that was soon to come to him."

Waite, who had never argued a case before the Supreme Court, was coolly greeted by fellow Court members at first, but on his second day he asserted himself. "I got on the box, gathered up the lines and drove, and I am going to drive and these gentlemen know it," he recalled.

One of his most important decisions was Munn v. Illinois, which decided the important issue for Midwesterners (and the entire nation) of whether states could regulate the charges of grain operators and thus of railroads. Waite eloquently wrote, "Their regulation is a thing of domestic concern, and, certainly, until Congress acts in reference to inter-state relations, the State may exercise all powers of government over them."

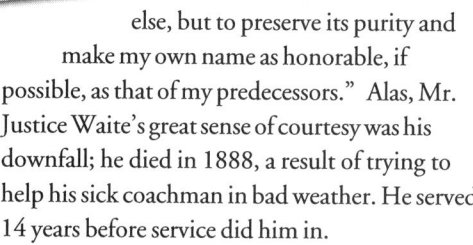

Some wanted Waite to run for president, but he would have none of it. "My duty was not to make it [his Supreme Court seat] a stepping-stone to something else, but to preserve its purity and make my own name as honorable, if possible, as that of my predecessors." Alas, Mr. Justice Waite's great sense of courtesy was his downfall; he died in 1888, a result of trying to help his sick coachman in bad weather. He served 14 years before service did him in.

Most negative:
"I can't make a great Chief Justice out of a small man."—Justice Samuel Miller

Most positive:
"This quiet, dutiful Justice, who drew up more than a thousand opinions...may have created a body of law with deeper ultimate effects than that of the more spectacular incumbents whose views and personalities have taken the fancy of reformers from time to time."—Louis Filler, Antioch College professor

William Woods
(1824—1887)

Often mistaken for a native "southerner" from Georgia, Woods actually was born in Newark, Ohio, and studied at Western Reserve College. It wasn't until after fighting in the Civil War that he settled in the South. There he was appointed to a federal circuit court post, standing up for the rights of newly emancipated blacks and, amazingly, earning the respect of white Southerners. President Rutherford B. Hayes (yet another Ohioan) made Woods a Justice in 1881 at age 56.

Some of Woods's decisions sound as timely as today's headlines. In the Supreme Court case, Presser v. State of Illinois, a man was convicted for parading without a license while armed. Woods upheld the conviction, writing, "The exercise of this power by the States is necessary to the public peace, safety and good order. To deny the power would be to deny the right...to suppress armed mobs bent on riot and rapine." Woods served only briefly, dying in office six years after his appointment.

Most negative:

"He reflected (the majority of the Court's) mundane compromises, but not their ideals or their more creative hopes."—Louis Filler, Antioch College professor

Most positive:

"We are proud of him because he is identified with us, and while serving as a judge in our midst has known nothing but the law, and been loyal to nothing but the law."—Chief Justice of Georgia

Stanley Matthews
(1824—1889)

As a student at Kenyon College, Cincinnatian Matthews became a longtime friend of future president Rutherford B. Hayes. When Matthews almost wasn't granted his degree because of his student antics, Hayes talked with the college's administrators on his behalf.

Needless to say, Matthews was a lifelong Hayes supporter. Matthews's defense of Hayes's disputed election in 1876 undoubtedly helped him win the 1881 Supreme Court nomination to fill a vacancy left when another Ohioan, Noah Swayne, resigned. Matthews's philosophy was an odd mixture of liberal and conservative, as evidenced by his pre-Civil War prosecution of a Cincinnati reporter who aided escaping slaves, and his support of the Cincinnati Board of Education's refusal to allow any sort of "religious instruction" in the schools.

Partly because of his help to Hayes in the bitterly disputed presidential election of 1876, Matthews has the dubious distinction of being one of only three Justices to, at first, be rejected by the U.S. Senate. When his first nomination stalemated, Matthews had to wait for Hayes to leave office and President Garfield of Ohio to reappoint him. He then squeaked through the Senate, 24-23.

In one of his most unusual decisions on the bench, Matthews upheld the right of American Indians to be tried by tribal, rather than territorial, courts; certainly a liberal stance only seven years after Custer's defeat at the Little Bighorn. Justice Matthews served only seven years before his death.

Most negative:

"Mr. Jay Gould [railroad magnate] has been appointed to the United States Supreme Court in place of Judge Swayne, resigned."—A sarcastic editorial in the *Detroit Free Press* about Matthews's alleged favoritism toward railroad companies.

Most positive:

"(Court members) recognized his great legal ability, but even more they appreciated the warmth of his affectionate nature. He was an industrious Judge, and his decisions exhibited wide research and thorough culture."—Justice Stephen Field

George Shiras, Jr.
(1832-1924)

Shiras started his education at Ohio University and attended Yale Law School. During his practice he developed a rather strange attitude for a lawyer: he "never raised a finger to collect his bills." Still, he earned $75,000 a year in the late 1880's, an astronomical sum.

Clockwise, Justices Waite, Matthews, and Woods

President Benjamin Harrison, a fellow Ohioan, appointed him in 1892 at age 60, partly because Shiras opposed a political group in Pennsylvania that had troubled Harrison. Despite strong opposition to Shiras, he was unanimously confirmed, partly because of newspaper support and because of his outstanding integrity. He served ten years before retiring.

While pictures make him appear a stern Victorian gentleman, Shiras had a quirky sense of humor. One day when he took his granddaughter shopping she was startled to see passersby chuckling at Shiras as he sat in what he called the "devil-wagon" (the automobile). She walked up to the car, only to see Shiras staring solemnly in the backseat—with her bonnet on his head.

Doubtless his major decision involved the first peacetime income tax enacted in 1894. The country was facing a fiscal crisis, but Shiras sided with the Justices who held the tax unconstitutional. When the 16th Amendment returned the income tax in 1913, one newspaper crowed, "He Made the Amendment Necessary." He was bitterly attacked by the press for changing his mind and thus deciding the issue, but the usually serene Shiras was truly shocked by the attacks for his role in the controversy, yet said nothing in his own defense. Years after his death a letter he prepared for the *Yale Law Journal* was discovered, explaining he hadn't changed his mind. In keeping with his laid back manner, he never sent the letter.

Most negative:
"Who the deuce is Shiras?"—Lancaster Intelligencer upon hearing of his nomination in 1892

Most positive:
*"It is a privilege to say that his integrity is unimpeached...In fact, he has a 'fine scorn' for mean things and mean men that warms my heart, though it may have prevented him from achieving a certain (dubious) success."—*Professor Matthew Riddle endorsing Shiras to President Harrison, 1892

William Day
(1849—1923)

As an attorney in Canton, Day became close friends with an up-and-coming Canton politician named William McKinley, and helped McKinley out of a huge debt shortly after he was elected governor. Later, President McKinley appointed the modest country lawyer first assistant secretary of state and then, in 1899, to the U.S. Court of Appeals for the Sixth Circuit, where coincidentally one of his fellow judges was another future Supreme Court member, William Howard Taft.

Taft was Theodore Roosevelt's first choice for the Supreme Court when Ohioan George Shiras Jr. resigned. Taft, however, felt he should fulfill

his duties as U. S. civil governor of the Philippines. With strong connections to both Taft and McKinley, Day was Roosevelt's next logical choice. In January, 1903, Roosevelt stood before a crowd in Canton and thanked "Mr. Justice Day" for his introduction. Day was 53 years old.

Day was a ferocious worker with a few eccentricities: During the World Series, he insisted that Supreme Court pages keep him constantly updated on the score. One of his most controversial decisions was in the case *Hammer v. Dagenhart*, which overturned the Keating-Owen Child Labor Act of 1916 that forbade the interstate shipment of items made by child labor. Day was outraged by the exploitation of children, but he drew a distinction between the federal government's right to regulate commerce and what he felt was its lack of powers to control manufacturing. He served 19 years on the bench, retiring at age 73. Although he always was a frail man, Day outlived the vigorous president who appointed him, Theodore Roosevelt, who died at age 60.

Most negative:

"*The head of the Department knows nothing; the First Assistant says nothing...*"—from Margaret Leech's book *In the Days of McKinley*

Most positive:

"*Throughout his life Day brought with him the values most celebrated in the American Dream—the Puritan value system, small-town respectability, the common touch, the ability to perform adequately any task set before him. This self-effacing man from Ohio fit the pattern perfectly...*"—James Watts Jr., assistant professor of history, City College of New York

Willis Van Devanter

(1859-1941)

Although born in Indiana, the great influence on Van Devanter was his legal education at the University of Cincinnati Law School, where he graduated second in a class of 65. He quickly learned how to make important "connections," and served as an assistant attorney general in President McKinley's administration.

President Taft appointed him to the Supreme Court in 1910 after he had served seven years as a Court of Appeals judge, despite his decidedly non-progressive decisions, such as one that overturned a decision in favor of a worker injured by a company's unsafe machinery procedures. He took the oath to become a Justice in 1911 at age 51, and was among the longest serving members: 26 years. He died at age 81, probably due to his workaholic attitudes.

One of his most crucial decisions was McGrain v. Daugherty, the case where the brother of Harry Daugherty, Harding's attorney general embroiled in the Teapot Dome Scandal, refused to appear at a Senate committee's investigation. The Court was faced with deciding if Congress could force witnesses to appear and if it could punish witnesses who balked. Van Devanter, often accused of "pen paralysis," wrote a simple, direct decision, saying "A legislative body cannot legislate wisely...in the absence of information respecting the conditions which the legislation is intended to affect...and where the legislative body does not itself possess the requisite information...some means of compulsion are essential." The important long term effects of Van Devanter's decision are obvious, as witnessed by such scandals as Watergate and Iran-Contra.

Most negative:

"*The judge that held that two railroads running parallel to each other for 2,000 miles were not competing lines, one of the railroads being that of the Union Pacific!*"—William Jennings Bryan

Most positive:

"*Van Devanter, master of formulas that decided cases without creating precedents.*"—Justice Louis Brandeis

John Clarke

(1857—1945)

Educated at Western Reserve College in Hudson, Clarke studied law under his father, a lawyer and judge. Clarke did well enough in practice to purchase half of the *Youngstown Vindicator*, which he turned into a major crusading newspa-

Clockwise, from left:
Justices Shiras, Day,
Van Devanter,
and Clark

223

per. He practiced what he preached, and became the first candidate for a major office in Ohio to release a full report of his campaign costs. In 1916, at age 59, he was appointed to fill a Supreme Court vacancy because President Woodrow Wilson believed Clarke was firmly antitrust.

A landmark antitrust decision of Clarke's was American Column and Lumber Company v. United States, a case involving a trade association that shared price, production and sales data. Clarke ruled the plan was an attempt to fix prices, pointing out that "This is not the conduct of competitors but is so clearly that of men united in an agreement...to restrict production and increase prices in interstate commerce."

On the bench, Clarke mixed sociology with law, sometimes ignoring precedents and even facts if they failed to fit his unconventional brand of progressivism. He became the only Supreme Court Justice to leave while in excellent health solely because of a desire to take part in "an idealistic crusade." When he resigned in 1922 after five years on the bench, people at first suspected he was planning a presidential campaign. They were wrong. Clarke wanted America to enter the League of Nations, and he fought hard to see it happen. Unfortunately, he died shortly before the conference that lead to the United Nations, never having seen his dream fulfilled.

Most negative:
"A nice fellow, I thought, who worked hard; but an obstinate and pedestrian mind."—Harold Laski, political scientist, University of London

Most positive:
"The public really has a grievance in Justice Clarke's resignation. He occupied a strategic place. He is a liberal among conservatives, and he was needed."
—*The New York Globe*

William Howard Taft
(1857—1930)

The Supreme Court was Taft's lifelong dream, a goal planted early by his father Alphonso, who also wanted to be a Justice and once said, "To be Chief Justice is more than to be President."

After Yale and Cincinnati Law School, young Taft began a meteoric rise through the Ohio legal system until he was spotted (indeed at 270 pounds, Taft was hard to miss) by Teddy Roosevelt. Taft became Roosevelt's all-purpose trouble shooter and Secretary of War. At a private White House meeting, TR is alleged to have tantalized Mr. and Mrs. Taft with the choice between the Supreme Court and the White House. Mrs. Taft opted for the White House.

After his election in 1908, Taft still wondered about the choice. "If I were now presiding in the Supreme Court," he wrote to a friend from the White House, "I should feel entirely at home, but... I feel just like a fish out of water." Taft and TR eventually fell out, and Taft was humiliated in 1912, finishing third behind the Democrat Woodrow Wilson and Teddy "Bull Moose" Roosevelt. When the Republicans finally retook the White House eight years later, Ohioan Warren G. Harding made good on Taft's lifelong ambition. Taft was sworn in as Chief Justice in 1921 at age 63, to date the only U.S. president to become a Supreme Court member. He served eight distinguished years on the bench before resigning due to ill health.

One of his most interesting dissents was in *Adkins v. Children's Hospital*, when the majority struck down the right of Congress to set minimum wages in the District of Columbia. In dissent, Taft said that "The evils of the sweating system and of long hours and low wages...are well known. But it is not the function of this court to hold congressional acts invalid simply because they are passed to carry out economic views which the Court believes to be unwise..."

To date, Taft holds the record for appointing or recommending more people—six—to the Supreme Court than any other president. As Chief Justice, he suggested or offered his endorsement on three other men to Harding. He is credited with dragging the federal judiciary into the 20th century by lobbying Congress to increase the number and staffs of federal judges. And he also pushed Congress into building a new Supreme Court Building. When the cornerstone was laid, Chief Justice Hughes praised

COPYRIGHT 1909 HARRIS & EWING WASHINGTON D.C.

Appointed Chief Justice of the U.S. Supreme Court in 1921, Taft achieved both his greatest desire and his best use. He Initiated judicial reform, reduced patronage, and eliminated the court's perpetual backlog. Some contend he was the first modern justice, as well as the architect of the modern judicial system.

Taft's "intelligent persistence." He had not lived to see it.

Most negative:
"I never saw anything that struck me as more than first-rate second rate."—Justice Oliver W. Holmes

Most positive:
"Bringing to the Chief Justiceship an almost majestic conception of its prerogatives, duties, and responsibilities, he seized the initiative and achieved substantial results. As judicial architect, Taft ranks second only to Oliver Ellsworth, who originally devised the judicial system."—Alpheus Mason, professor emeritus, Princeton University

Most positive:
"In doing so you have chosen an able nominee who is infinitely qualified in his own superb capacities and in his record and his experiences."—Senator Arthur Vandenberg to President Harry S. Truman

> "The dichotomy between personal liberties and property rights is a false one. Property does not have rights. People have rights."
>
> *—Potter Stewart, majority opinion in 4-3 ruling that upheld a district court's refusal to hear a case involving property rights, March 23, 1972.*

Harold Burton

(1888—1964)

A Cleveland attorney, Burton became director of law for the city in 1930. In the U.S. Senate, he was a middle-of-the-road Republican, willing to support the policies of a Democratic President if they were best for the country. President Harry S. Truman noticed this, and, in 1945 at age 57, Burton became the only Republican from Ohio appointed to the court by a Democratic President.

Burton's most important decision was in Henderson v. United States, a landmark civil rights case concerning segregated dining cars on interstate trains. Burton minced no words, "The right to be free from unreasonable discrimination belongs...to each...person. Where a dining car is available to passengers holding tickets entitling them to use it, each such passenger is equally entitled to its facilities." Justice Burton served 13 unflamboyant years, but in his quiet mediating way was a strong force for the civil rights of all Americans.

Most negative:
"Perhaps the worst selection in the last 100 years."
—*New Republic*

Potter Stewart

(1915—1985)

The last and most recent Mr. Justice from Ohio, Potter Stewart took the oath in 1958 at age 43, becoming the second youngest Justice since the Civil War. His 23 years of service, ending in 1981, made him the third longest serving Ohioan. Born in Michigan, Stewart was schooled in Cincinnati and later attended Yale Law School, where he joined the famous and powerful secret society, Skull and Bones. In an article about the secret society, noted journalist Ron Rosenbaum wrote, "You could ask Supreme Court Justice Potter Stewart if there came a time in the year 1937 when he dressed up in a skeleton suit and howled wildly at an initiate in a red-velvet room inside the tomb."

Judgeships ran in the Stewart family; Potter's father was an Ohio Supreme Court Justice. Stewart's chance at the nation's highest court came when fellow Ohioan Harold Burton retired. Although Stewart had no particular ties to President Eisenhower, Stewart had distinguished himself with well-written, carefully thought-out decisions at a circuit court.

When asked by reporters if he was liberal or conservative, Stewart replied, "I really can't say, except that I like to be thought of as a lawyer."

True to his word, he became the Court's "swing man" in close cases, confounding those who wanted to label him. In the still controversial abortion rights decision of Roe v. Wade, Stewart insisted that the majority opinion clearly state that a fetus is not a person, at least as far at the 14th Amendment is concerned.

His most famous legal dictum involved pornography. Legally, it was hard to define, Stewart wrote in a case involving a French film called *The Lovers*, but "I know it when I see it." In *The Brethren*, Bob Woodward and Scott Armstrong's book on the Supreme Court, the writers said of the famous definition, "It might not be the height of legal sophistication, but the remark expressed Stewart's Middle Western pragmatism." In their book, Woodward and Armstrong claim that when offered the position of Chief Justice by President Nixon, Stewart declined.

Most negative:
"Northern integrationist."—Comment from Southerners on his appointment

Most positive:
"At least in its early years, the Burger Court has seemed to represent the triumph of Potter Stewart. If not as opinion leader, as dominate vote, ...Stewart has been a central figure on the Court."—Richard Funston in Constitutional Counterrevolution
— *by Dave Stephenson*

Terry v. Ohio: The measure of 'reasonableness'

John W. Terry and Richard D. Chilton, walking back and forth along a Cleveland street on October 31, 1963, sometimes stopping to peer into a store window, were observed for ten minutes by police officer Martin McFadden. Suspecting they were armed and preparing to rob the store, McFadden stopped them.

McFadden identified himself and began questioning the two. After receiving only mumbled responses, McFadden frisked Terry, who had a .38 caliber revolver in his coat pocket. McFadden also found a revolver in Chilton's overcoat. Both Terry and Chilton were convicted of carrying concealed weapons, and the convictions were appealed. Since walking around the streets of Cleveland wasn't illegal, it was argued that there was no probable cause to "stop and frisk" the men. The procedure therefore violated the 4th Amendment right of unreasonable search without a warrant, meaning the evidence was obtained illegally.

The U.S. Supreme Court in *Terry v. Ohio* upheld Terry's conviction (Chilton died), rejecting the claim that "stop and frisk" needed probable cause. The Court stated that it only needed to be reasonable. While there was nothing unusual about two men standing on a streetcorner, it was more unusual for two men to pace an identical route, stare in the same store window 24 times, then hold a conference on the streetcorner. So, ruled the court, when the police observe suspicious activity, it is reasonable for the safety of the officers to stop and frisk the suspects.

If there is no illegal activity the suspects must be let go immediately. While the case has established the police right to "stop and frisk," the "reasonableness" of it remains subjective and open to further litigation. Some police use a very liberal definition of "reasonable," leading critics to contend that police abuse the ruling by stopping minorities for the suspicious behavior of "being black."
—*Michael O'Bryant*

Said the court, in wonderful understatement: "Street encounters between citizens and police officers are incredibly rich in diversity."

From left: Justices Burton and Stewart

President Bush has succeeded in balancing the 6th Circuit court's once-Democratic makeup— and, liberals fear, has a chance to take it to the right. The Court of Appeals is one step below the U.S. Supreme Court. "We will probably see a much more restricted and begrudging view of individual rights, women's reproductive rights and constitutional liberties," said Louis Bograd, counsel to the Alliance for Justice, an advocacy group that opposes Cook's nomination and also lobbied against Sutton. Bograd predicted that the addition of Deborah Cook and conservative lawyer Jeffrey Sutton, with other conservative nominees waiting in the wings, would bring "a very significant rightward turn" at the 6th Circuit. "You will probably see a court that is much more committed to protecting the authority of state government," he said.

Judges on the Cincinnati-based court work quietly in cities scattered over four states—Ohio, Michigan, Kentucky and Tennessee—and are largely invisible to the public.

But they have a big say in determining the rights, freedoms and culpability of their fellow citizens.

The judges, 16 in all, are nominated by the president, confirmed by the Senate and sworn in for a term that is lifelong if they choose. How they get there is a political process charged with emotion, litmus tests, and probing questions about political ideology.

Democrats, outnumbered 51-48 in the Senate, make no effort to stop every conservative nominee, since the president, by custom, is given some benefit of the doubt with his choices. As a result, no one tried to stop Cook, of Akron, and an ideological debate about Sutton ended with his confirmation.

As a lawyer with Jones Day in Columbus, Sutton represented a number of clients seeking to curb the power of the federal government. That won him the admiration of conservative activists and the scorn of disability groups that cited cases that Sutton won that restricted enforcement of

the federal anti-discrimination law for the disabled.

Cook is regarded as a conservative judge who often sides with business interests. With her confirmation, the appeals court reached political parity—six judges named by Democratic presidents and six by Republicans. But as of mid-2003, four seats remain to be filled.

Until now, the 6th Circuit court "has historically been a fairly moderate and closely divided court," said Bograd. But those four vacant seats are manned by semi-retired judges on temporary assignment, and Bush hopes to likewise fill those slots with his nominees.

Conservative analysts, such as Phyllis Schlafly and Dinesh D'Souza, have argued that Bush should seize the opportunity to halt a wave of judicial activism in rulings rendered by Democratic appointees to the bench who opened the Constitution to liberal interpretations.

David Goldberger, a civil rights lawyer who teaches law at the Ohio State University College of Law, already regards the 6th Circuit as conservative, if unpredictable, in its decision-making on controversial cases.

"Anyone that is arguing against the

government in a civil rights case has got an uphill battle in that court," he said. "That is not to say it is in the extreme. There are periodically decisions that go for civil rights plaintiffs."

Such was the case last May, when the 6th Circuit narrowly upheld the University of Michigan's affirmative action admissions plan. The 6th Circuit in 2000 ruled that Cleveland's school voucher program was unconstitutional, but the Supreme Court overturned that decision last year.

Goldberger believes Bush is trying to push the 6th Circuit and other appeals courts further to the right. He is representing prison inmates before the court in a case that could determine how far certain religious groups, including the Wiccans, can go in exercising their rights to practice religion while incarcerated.

Yet most cases don't involve big civil rights challenges or ideologically loaded questions. "In the overwhelming majority of cases, it does not matter which judges do the case—any competent jurist is going to decide most of the cases the same way," said Jonathan Entin, professor of constitutional law at the Case Western Reserve University School of Law.

Still, the political makeup of a court can make a difference, he said. In the conservative mid-Atlantic 4th Circuit in Richmond, Virginia, for instance, plaintiffs bringing a civil rights complaint or death penalty appeal face long odds, Entin said.

Typically, appeals on the 6th Circuit are considered by rotating three-judge panels assigned by a clerk of courts in Cincinnati. On rehearings or cases of significance, all 16 judges may decide the merits.

Democrats, believing the president is trying to pack the appeals court with right-wing ideologues, are likely to be even more grudging with Bush's nominees in 2004, an election year.

"I think it is important to keep them moving," said Ohio Republican Sen. Mike DeWine, a member of the Judiciary Committee. "It always gets tougher in an election year."

DeWine and Entin agree that prolonged, acrimonious debates on judicial nominees are unhealthy and leave understaffed courts gasping for help in trying to meet caseloads.

"Republicans played games with Clinton nominees; Democrats are playing games with Bush," Entin said. "We are getting to the point where every nominee is getting examined microscopically."

"It has deteriorated since I've been here," DeWine said. "It cannot be fixed unless it is done on a bipartisan basis. It is almost going to take a joint committee or commission."

—*Tom Diemer, by permission of The Plain Dealer*

NOTABLE COURT DECISIONS : *EUCLID V. AMBLER REALTY COMPANY*

When the Ambler Realty Company charged that the City of Euclid, Ohio, had decreased the value of its frontage along Euclid Avenue by intrusive city zoning, the case—*Village of Euclid v. Ambler Realty Company*—ended up before the U.S. Supreme Court. At issue was the question of public power vs. private use. And that is where Alfred Bettman came in. A Cincinnati city planner and Jewish social reformer, Bettman prepared an influential brief as *amicus curiae*, arguing that a zoning ordinance barring conversion of residential property to commercial and industrial use was not an exercise of the power of eminent domain, but an extension of the common law doctrine of public nuisance. His argument focused upon the question of public power being able to make regulations in the interest of health and safety, and persuaded the court to uphold the constitutionality of zoning. The 1926 decision read in part: "Until recent years, urban life was comparatively simple; but with the great increase and concentration of population, problems...constantly are developing, which require, and will continue to require, additional restrictions in respect of the use and occupation of private lands in urban communities...." *Village of Euclid v. Ambler Realty Company* thus led to widespread adoption of land-use regulation.

For those with deeper interest, Case Western Reserve Law Review held a symposium on the 75th anniversary of the famous case, exploring its historical context as well as addressing modern zoning law. Find it at: http://lawwww.cwru.edu/academic/lawReview/51-4/Leeintro%5B1%5D.lead.pdf

Slimmest gubernatorial victory—1848, Seabury Ford slid in past John Weller by 311 votes

Largest gubernatorial landslide—1994, George Voinovich defeated Robert Burch by 1,565,719 votes

Longest term as a State Representative—Vern Riffe, 1958-1995

First Ohio counties to approve women's suffrage—Ashtabula, Columbiana, Geauga, Lake, Lucas, Meigs, Portage, Summit, Trumbull; in the 1912 state referendum

First black elected to office in the United States—John Mercer Langston, Clerk of Brownhelm Township, Lorain County, 1855

First ballots cast by black Ohioans—April 4, 1870 (post ratification of the 15th Amendment to the U.S. Constitution, March 30, 1870)

First black U.S. Congressman from Ohio—Louis Stokes of Cleveland, elected November, 1968

First black judge in Ohio—Perry B. Jackson, Cleveland municipal court, appointed 1940; elected, 1945

First black judge of an Ohio appellate court—Charles W. White, Cuyahoga County, elected 1966

First black judge of an Ohio common pleas court—Perry B. Jackson, Cuyahoga County, 1964

First black elected to the Ohio House of Representatives—Hamilton County's George Washington Williams, 1879

First black elected to the Ohio Senate—Cleveland's John Patterson Green, 1892

First black mayor in Ohio—Robert C. Henry, Springfield, 1965

First black mayor of a major U.S. city—Carl Burton Stokes, the great-grandson of a slave, who in 1967 won Cleveland's mayoral race over Seth Taft, the great-grandson of President Taft

First black elected county commissioner in Ohio—James Ford, Greene County, 1964

First black woman elected mayor in Ohio—Ellen Craig, Urbancrest (Franklin County), 1971

First black woman elected to an Ohio city council—Canton's Esther Archer, 1947

First Ohio woman elected to U.S. Congress—Rep. Frances Payne Bolton, Cleveland, 1940

First mother and son simultaneously elected to U.S. Congress—Cleveland's Frances Payne Bolton and son Oliver Payne Bolton, 1952

First woman elected to public office—Catherine Hitchcock Tilden Avery, to the Cleveland Board of Education, 1896

First woman elected judge—Cleveland's Florence Allen, Common Pleas Court, Cuyahoga County, 1920

First woman in U.S. elected a State Supreme Court Judge—Florence Allen, 1922

First woman in U.S. elected municipal court judge—Mary B. Grossman, Cleveland, 1923

First women to serve in the Ohio House of Representatives—Nettie M. Clapp, LuLu T. Gleason, May Van Wye, and C.J. Ott, 1923

First women to serve in the Ohio Senate—Nettie B. Loughead and Maude C. Waitt, 1923

First woman President Pro Tem and Majority Leader in the Ohio Senate—Margaret A. Mahoney, 1949-50

First woman elected to State office—Gertrude W. Donahey, a Democrat from Tuscarawas County elected State Treasurer, 1970

First women elected county commissioners—Helen Baker, Athens County; Helen Jean Rofkar, Ottawa County; Harriet A. Fenner Stivers, Highland County; 1972

First women elected county treasurers—Mary Downs, Fulton County; Ova Ross, Crawford County; Ida Rothrock, Fayette County; 1922

First women elected county auditors—Ella Blizzard, Madison County; Pearl Pratt, Lawrence County, 1930

First women elected county recorders—Jennie Styer Bowman, Medina County; Eugenia Rosa, Muskingum County, 1922

First women elected county clerks of court—Mary Geiser, Fairfield County; Mrs. Brown Kettering, Delaware County; Amelia Waddell, Fayette County, 1922

First woman elected county coroner—Florence Lenahan, Delaware County, 1988

First woman elected sheriff—Katherine Crumbley, Belmont County, 1976

First governor to die in Office—John Brough, 1865

Only father to succeed his son as governor—Mordecai Bartley, who in 1844, followed Thomas Welles Bartley, the Speaker of the Ohio Senate, who became acting governor upon Wilson Shannon's resignation

Only father and son simultaneously elected to the Ohio House of Representatives—Democrats Robert E. Hagan (father) of Madison and Robert F. Hagan (son) of Youngstown, sworn in together in 1987

Oldest Ohio governor—William Allen, 1874-76, who took the oath of office at age 71

Youngest Ohio governor—Thomas Bartley, age 32, who served from April 15 to December 3, 1844

Youngest person elected to Ohio General Assembly—Twenty-one-year-old Representative Sherrod Brown, Mansfield, 1974

Youngest Ohio attorney general—Thirty-year-old William J. Brown, Youngstown, 1971

Most terms in the U.S. Senate—6, served by Lancaster native John Sherman, between 1861 and 1897

Most terms as governor—5, served by Cleveland's Frank Lausche; 1922-46; 1948-50; 1950-52; 1952-54; 1954-56

Most years as governor—12, served by Coalton native James Rhodes; 1962-70, 1974-1978

Most gubernatorial cabinet posts of any state in U.S.—Ohio's 25, 1991

A Comparison of Budgetary Revenues and Expenditures
For the Fiscal Years Ended June 30, 2002 and June 30,1999
(dollars in thousands)

Budgetary Revenues	Fiscal 2002	Fiscal 2001	Fiscal 2000	Fiscal 1999
Income Taxes	$7,982,461	$8,302,892	$8,302,892	$7,143,344
Sales Taxes	6,385,248	6,248,705	6,233,089	5,834,299
Corporate & Public Utility Taxes	1,640,433	1,726,263	1,697,970	1,817,641
Motor Vehicle Fuel Taxes	1,451,767	1,457,454	1,459,374	1,445,679
Other Taxes	895,414	930,338	913,086	917,505
Licenses, Permits, and Fees	1,521,736	1,219,605	1,156,379	1,137,577
Sales, Services, and Charges	94,597	83,891	86,981	81,731
Federal Government	11,734,436	10,433,688	9,321,234	8,697,800
Tobacco Settlement	368,588	315,812	412,270	–
Escheat Property	52,628	–	–	–
Investment Income	282,457	486,817	433,566	544,915
Other	635,812	514,544	481,856	481,748
Total Budgetary Revenues	$33,045,577	$31,719,989	$30,303,960	$28,112,239

Budgetary Expenditures

	Fiscal 2002	Fiscal 2001	Fiscal 2000	Fiscal 1999
Current Operating:				
Primary, Secondary and Other Education	$8,142,972	$7,194,833	$6,634,181	$4,497,568
Higher Education	2,449,614	506,511	439,137	377,868
Public Assistance & Medicaid	11,854,582	10,894,942	9,488,379	8,561,652
Health and Human Services	2,792,890	2,555,221	2,488,379	2,548,360
Justice and Public Protection	3,378,120	2,262,421	2,167,402	2,035,739
Environmental Protection and Natural Resources	355,576	340,574	354,180	330,069
Transportation	1,897,807	1,756,201	1,680,736	1,497,553
General Government	733,591	468,791	575,576	661,011
Community and Economic Development	748,185	541,166	452,516	398,905
Intergovernmental	3,563,306	3,361,184	3,257,632	2,898,094
Capital Outlay	465,843	411,817	629,753	1,256,271
Debit Service	1,193,604	1,137,537	1,053,995	1,024,125
Total Budgetary Expenditures	$36,576,090	$31,401,248	$29,347,340	$27,993,625

www. *state.oh.us/obm*

Ohio Office of Budget and Management site organizes and offers most of the data of the state's budget, from monthly financial reports to bond sales and long-range planning.

ALL THIS
DECIDING
MAKES A
CONGRESSMAN
HUNGRY...

PAY RAISE

BUDGET
PROPOSAL

BUDGET

PLAN 201

PROPOSAL

BUDGET PLAN

JIM BORGMAN
CINCINNATI
ENQUIRER
84787

The State Budget; by Departments and Agencies

	FY 1999 Agency Actual	FY 2000 Appropriations	FY 2001 Appropriations
Primary and Secondary Education			
Education, Department of	$6,225,005,944	$6,835,912,721	$7,238,462,894
Information, Learning & Technology Services, Office of	$130,558,800	$139,733,632	$56,590,285
School for the Blind, State	$6,955,139	$7,655,082	$7,839,254
School for the Deaf, State	$8,251,960	$9,132,562	$9,726,651
School Facilities Commission	$62,670,715	$58,009,726	$73,038,277
Colleges and Other Education			
Arts Council, Ohio	$15,674,757	$17,323,933	$17,151,665
Educational Telecommunications Network Commission	$9,826,186	$23,017,143	$11,370,188
Higher Education Facilities Commission	$2,744	$12,000	$12,000
Historical Society	$14,107,852	$19,482,139	$15,640,630
Library Board, State	$20,875,223	$25,656,179	$24,142,261
Ohioana Library Association	$223,130	$461,750	$316,461
Proprietary School Registration, Board of	$361,173	$486,524	$498,897
Regents, Board of	$2,306,812,990	$2,446,911,658	$2,603,176,133
Student Aid Commission	$2,017,906	$0	$0
Tuition Trust Authority	$3,241,637	$3,856,585	$4,126,546
Human Services			
African American Males, Commission on	$0	$885,622	$901,837
Aging, Department of	$253,811,533	$298,774,646	$321,265,693
Alcohol and Drug Addiction Services, Dept. of	$127,870,830	$145,166,860	$146,206,017
Employment Services, Bureau of	$274,225,586	$269,144,311	$0
Health, Department of	$398,938,880	$457,288,183	$461,700,835
Hispanic/Latino Affairs, Commission on	$189,137	$219,479	$224,747

	FY 1999 Agency Actual	FY 2000 Appropriations	FY 2001 Appropriations
Human Services, Department of	$8,726,201,561	$9,694,954,850	$0
Industrial Commission	$45,722,358	$52,450,358	$53,193,305
Job and Family Services, Department of	$0	$0	$10,442,347,266
Legal Rights Service	$3,148,582	$3,531,061	$3,524,887
Mental Health, Department of	$729,951,365	$795,941,368	$800,347,814
Mental Retard. and Develop. Disabilities, Dept. of	$709,204,634	$813,063,623	$820,462,334
Minority Health, Commission on	$1,815,968	$1,923,730	$1,966,714
Rehabilitation Services Commission	$219,033,348	$241,526,095	$243,078,809
Veterans' Children's Home	$0	$0	$0
Veterans' Home	$29,104,681	$31,879,090	$31,900,193
Veterans' Organizations	$1,257,397	$1,854,750	$1,433,876
Women's Policy and Research Commission	$245,164	$261,395	$261,836
Workers' Compensation, Bureau of	$272,852,090	$298,565,375	$294,812,105

General Government and Tax Relief

Accrued Leave Liability Funds	$141,084,234	$219,920,578	$237,776,728
Administrative Services, Department of	$1,860,909,257	$2,139,035,570	$2,237,462,966
Arts and Sports Facilities Commission	$28,265,577	$25,330,547	$33,562,698
Ballot Board	$321,680	$0	$0
Budget and Management, Office of	$15,455,910	$11,497,407	$11,427,960
Cancelled and Reissued Warrants	$1,695,720	$0	$0
Capital Items	$980,718,741	$0	$0
Capitol Square Review and Advisory Board	$6,987,037	$9,584,912	$8,336,413
Commerce, Department of	$375,560,553	$396,614,999	$403,455,751
Consumers' Counsel, Office of	$6,092,251	$8,131,725	$7,647,619
Controlling Board	$0	$34,922,000	$56,500,000
Deposit, Board of	$520,498	$818,400	$838,041
Elections Commission	$510,267	$573,950	$594,757
Employment Relations Board, State	$3,459,140	$3,698,984	$3,668,185
Insurance, Department of	$22,055,645	$24,421,886	$24,613,724
Liquor Control Commission	$603,440	$656,322	$671,416
Lottery Commission	$450,054,937	$483,498,815	$489,013,558
Personnel Board of Review	$911,949	$1,257,558	$1,115,978
Petrol. Undergnd Storage Tank Release Comp Bd	$697,786	$908,000	$927,924
Professional & Occupational Licensing Boards	$22,246,142	$25,685,776	$25,684,565
Public Utilities Commission of Ohio	$40,067,825	$45,807,616	$45,795,588
Racing Commission	$25,338,211	$24,004,820	$24,513,147
Revenue Distribution Funds	$3,768,493,247	$3,873,605,000	$4,010,877,800
Sinking Fund, Commissioners of	$154,251,115	$175,392,000	$201,756,000
State and Local Government Commission	$205,936	$258,143	$264,713
Tax Appeals, Board of	$2,225,575	$2,492,978	$2,441,955
Tax Relief Programs	$1,000,947,938	$1,075,200,000	$1,136,100,000
Taxation, Department of	$1,421,692,827	$1,159,635,698	$1,142,238,125

Public Safety and Corrections

Adjutant General	$35,145,430	$32,879,552	$33,065,930
Civil Rights Commission	$12,395,871	$12,866,901	$13,087,278
Criminal Justice Services, Office of	$38,251,715	$33,766,564	$35,796,899
Dispute Resolution and Conflict Mgt., Commission on	$544,409	$736,675	$754,355
Ethics Commission	$1,365,698	$1,651,135	$1,668,755
Inspector General	$500,206	$740,670	$736,253
Public Defender Commission	$51,772,328	$62,577,661	$66,815,521
Public Safety, Department of	$355,531,535	$405,151,775	$393,267,009
Rehabilitation and Correction, Department of	$1,329,387,457	$1,510,904,134	$1,578,220,366
Youth Services, Department of	$232,077,299	$248,940,853	$258,319,438

Environment, Development and Transportation

Agriculture, Department of	$33,774,011	$37,758,038	$37,641,420
Air Quality Development Authority	$352,793	$606,472	$621,079
Development, Department of	$346,868,112	$495,013,749	$475,877,965
Environmental Review Appeals Commission	$407,468	$463,373	$464,059
Environmental Protection Agency	$140,892,434	$159,743,513	$161,541,491
Expositions Commission	$13,495,024	$15,858,707 $	14,970,497
Lake Erie Commission	$1,295,159	$1,587,159	$1,625,251
Low-Level Radioactive Waste Facility Develop.			
Auth.	$10,210	$0	$0
Natural Resources, Department of	$237,901,888	$271,514,822	$271,143,437
Public Works Commission	$55,556,039	$63,325,810	$63,344,969
Transportation, Department of	$1,788,728,391	$2,248,055,179	$2,123,344,560

Executive, Legislative and Judicial Agencies

Agency Rule Review, Joint Committee on	$282,568	$381,126	$381,126
Attorney General	$115,548,483	$126,074,760	$129,985,883
Auditor of State	$62,586,443	$83,771,769	$87,237,475
Court of Claims	$23,652,993	$24,866,520	$25,797,779
Governor	$4,703,252	$5,215,903	$5,376,169
House of Representatives	$15,524,463	$19,311,456	$19,311,456
Joint Legislative Ethics Committee	$436,889	$611,500	$619,400
Judicial Conference of Ohio	$3,355,580	$1,200,000	$1,260,000
Judiciary/Supreme Court, The	$86,807,899	$98,006,843	$99,530,001
Legislative Service Commission	$14,704,681	$22,462,394	$21,649,140
Secretary of State	$10,545,847	$13,599,400	$13,829,402
Senate	$8,583,880	$11,722,769	$11,722,769
Treasurer of State	$256,336,752	$287,001,960	$307,634,577
Total All Funds	**$36,210,855,915**	**$38,736,405,256**	**$40,049,647,730**

Revenue from State Taxes

State-Collected Taxes*	2002	2001	2000
State Sales and Use	$6,343,538,289	$6,237,110,410	$6,213,961,851
Local Sales and Use	$1,348,123,199	$1,352,436,625	$1,321,129,345
Resort Area Excise	$665,407	$719,420	$718,624
State Individual Income	$8,157,146,924	$8,119,314,587	$8,084,576,329
Corporation Franchise	$774,367,410	$972,967,198	$1,029,883,951
Motor Vehicle Fuel	$1,383,330,324	$1,307,275,001	$1,404,945,725
Public Utility Excise	$299,950,367	$674,314,690	$675,339,746
Kilowatt-Hour Excise	$569,189,093	$38,026,261	$0
Cigarette Excise	$281,293,723	$282,481,419	$287,710,095
Local Cigarette Excise	$4,850,475	$5,037,137	$5,055,311
Intangible Personal	$18,498,916	$24,881,108	$22,333,722
Motor Fuel Use	$69,371,398	$75,311,561	$66,889,345
Alcoholic Beverage Excise	$56,446,131	$55,740,722	$55,993,783
Replacement Tire Fee	$6,304,162	$3,470,795	$3,339,367
Local Alcoholic Beverage	$6,196,901	$5,851,787	$6,284,465
Horse Racing	$17,411,384	$17,321,198	$16,582,056
Severance	$8,025,167	$7,967,438	$8,283,562
School District Income	$145,529,302	$153,238,001	$153,238,001
Total State-Collected Taxes	*$19,546,176,169*	*$19,333,465,359*	*$19,345,324,191*
Locally-Collected Taxes			
Tangible Personal Property	N/A	$1,802,487,778	$1,720,740,378
Public Utility Property	N/A	$715,307,242	$967,674,709
Estate	N/A	$375,411,087	$451,541,611
Total Locally-Collected Tax	*N/A*	*$2,893,206,107*	*$3,139,956,698*

* gross tax collected less refunds
Source: The Ohio Budgetary Financial Report

All State Tax Sources

Individual Income Tax	42.0%
Sale and Use Tax	32.7%
Motor Vehicle Fuel & Fuel Tax	7.5%
Corporate Fanchise Tax	4.0%
Public Utility and Kilowatt Hour Excise Taxes	4.4%
Cigarette/Alcoholic Beverages Taxes	1.9%
All other Taxes	7.5%

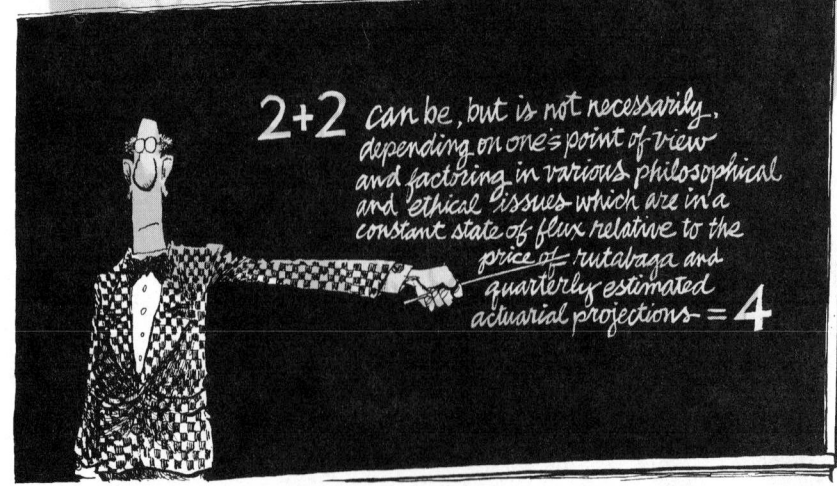

The NEW ACCOUNTING

ONCE AGAIN THIS YEAR, FRANK SMAGARINSKY CATCHES THE LATE FLIGHT TO THE WEST COAST IN ORDER TO GAIN THREE MORE HOURS TO FILE HIS TAXES.

Federal Taxes

Total Collections	$85,330,335
Corporation Income Tax	$46,787,736

Individual Income and Employment Taxes

Total	$75,061,668
Railroad Retirement Tax	$22,522
Unemployment Insurance Tax	$261,256
Estate Tax	$884,783
Gift Tax	$90,991
Excise Taxes	$2,505,157

Federal Income Tax Returns Filed

Total Tax Returns	9,265,655
Individual Income Tax	5,569,637
Individual Estimated Income Tax	1,462,285
Estate & Trust Income Tax	194,671
Estate & Trust Estimated Income Tax	32,315
Partnership	79,161
Corporation Income Tax	187,369
Estate Tax	4,675
Gift Tax	12,182
Employment Taxes	1,061,147
Tax-Exempt Organization	32,072
Employee Plan	39,396
Excise Taxes	29,204
Supplemental Documents	561,541

Total Returns Filed Electronically

Total E-filed Tax Returns	1,753,143
TeleFile Accepted	274,912
Online Accepted	286,106
Practitioner Accepted	1,192,125

Total Internal Revenue Refunds	8,342,818
Corporate Income Tax	91,847
Individual Income Tax	8,185,142
Employment Tax	62,133
Estate Tax	699
Gift Tax	146
Excise Taxes	2,851

"THE DEFENSE APPLIES PRESSURE.... HERE'S THE INBOUNDS PASS.... SNODGRASS HAS THE BALL! THEY'RE ALL OVER HIM!.... BUT WAIT! WHAT'S THIS? IT'S — YES! - ANOTHER BUSINESS DEDUCTION!..... SIX SECONDS, FIVE, FOUR.... HE TURNS! SHOOTS!... BRONNNK!".... IT'S GOOD!! HE'S COMPLETED FORM 9983B! HE GOES ON TO THE FINAL FORM!!" ".....THE CROWD GOES WILD!"

Ohio Individual Income Tax

Year	Number of Returns	Average Federal Adjusted Income*	Average Ohio Income Tax
2000	5,416,060	$49,435	$1,411
1999	5,366,304	$47,353	$1,395
1998	5,349,673	$45,550	$1,255
1997	5,226,526	$42,222	$1,222
1996	5,131,032	$39,385	$1,088
1995	5,080,488	$36,385	$1,092
1994	4,961,073	$34,861	$1,020
1993	4,887,049	$33,415	$983
1992	4,853,972	$32,568	$828
1991	4,842,551	$30,765	$858
1990	4,791,316	$30,825	$842
1989	4,704,060	$29,748	$812
1988	4,560,529	$29,194	$785
1987	4,410,441	$27,203	$722
1986	4,229,473	$25,436	$727
1985	4,106,441	$23,958	$643
1984	4,070,499	$22,882	$634
1983	3,935,354	$21,193	$554
1982	4,014,982	$20,449	$391
1981	4,051,687	$19,843	$293
1980	4,044,015	$18,473	$259
1979	4,064,255	$17,341	$232
1978	3,950,939	$16,082	$202
1977	3,861,468	$14,879	$178

*after deductions

www. state.oh.us/tax/ global_forms.html

Excellent resource for individuals, business owners, tax practitioners, and government officials. Tips, annual reports, forms (available to be printed through Adobe Acrobat), as well as free on-line state tax filing.

Income

Per Capita Income	$21,003
Median Earnings, Male	$37,692
Median Earning, Female	$26,400
Number of Households	4,446,621
Earning Less than $10,000	406,698 (9.1%)
$10,000-$14,000	285.372 (6.4%)
$15,000-$24,999	594,143 (13.4%)
$25,000 -$34,999	602,996 (13.6%)
$35,000-$49,999	771,129 (17.3%)
$50,000-$74,999	905,323 (20.4%)
$75,000-$99,999	444,599 (10.0%)
$100,000-$149,000	289,049 (6.5%)
$150,000-$199,999	71,062 (1.6%)
$200,000 or more	76,250 (1.7%)
Median Household Income	$40,956
Households with Earnings	3,538,957
Mean Earnings	$52,998
With Social Security Income (SSI)	1,175,559
Mean SSI	$11,376
With Supplemental SSI	186,579
Mean Supplemental SSI	$6,373
With Public Assistance Income	143,132
Mean Public Assistance Income	$2,550

With Retirement Income	841,456
Mean Retirement Income	$16,753
Number of Families	3,007,207
Earning Less than $10,000	156,828 (9.1%)
$10,000-$14,000	113,007 (6.4%)
$15,000-$24,999	309,926 (13.4%)
$25,000-$34,999	372,344 (13.6%)
$35,000-$49,999	549,998 (17.3%)
$50,000-$74,999	732,469 (20.4%)
$75,000-$99,999	386,861 (10.0%)
$100,000-$149,000	257,606 (6.5%)
$150,000-$199,999	62,842 (1.6%)
$200,000 or more	65,326 (1.7%)
Median Household Income	$50,037

Poverty

Families Living Poverty	235,026 (7.8%)
with Children under 18	185,813 (12.2%)
with Children under 5	94,763 (16.1%)
with Female Householder	137,052 (26.3%)
(no husband present)	
with Children under 18	124,213 (34.6%)
with Children under 5	64,025 (49.2%)
Individuals Living in Poverty	1,170,698 (10.6%)
18 Years or Older	762,013 (9.3%)
65 Years or Older	115,742 (8.1%)

The wealthiest Ohioans—incomes averaging $660,000 —pay 6.7% of their income in Ohio state and local taxes (after deductions). Middle-income Ohio taxpayers—earning between $27,000 and $41,000—pay 10.4% of their income. Ohioans earning less than $8,800 pay 10.9%.

—Ohio Department of Taxation; Institute on Taxation and Economic Policy

HOW WE EARN, SAVE, AND SPEND

The typical household:

Median pretax income★—$44,649
Average annual expenses—$38,045
Housing—$12,527
Transportation—$7,568
Food—$5,435
Utilities—$2,487
Apparel & services—$2,004
Insurance/pension—$4,308
Health care—$2,120
Entertainment—$1,958
Cash contributions—$1,344
Telecommunications—$2,073.60 ($517.20 cable; $391.60 internet access)
Daycare—$4,000-$10,000
Average family net worth—$395,000
Median credit card balance—$1,900
Average credit card percentage rate—13.37%
Average amount charged each month—$278
Average household charges during holiday season—$1,100

★'Median' means half of households are higher, and half are lower)
Source—Consumer Expenditure Survey; *www.billsaver.com*

Wages in Ohio: the good, the bad, the *ugly*

After a business downturn, Jerry and Julie Pickett, a Middletown, Ohio, couple, found themselves with a credit card debt that eventually reached $40,000. One card with an $8,000 balance—after late fees and interest, which jumped to 28 percent—reached $18,000. Between 1989 and 2001, credit card debt in America tripled, evidence indicating that people are using cards not for frivolous consumption but to cover gaps between earnings and essentials. Late fees are the fastest growing revenue source for the industry, and major cards are located in states that have no limit on rates they can charge.

—New York Times

Change in family income, after taxes, from late 1970s to late 1990s

Richest fifth
(Income now, and increase since 1970s)

$142,810
increase: $43,020

(The richest 5 percent now average $228,600, an increase of $83,470)

Middle fifth
$52,740
increase: $6,900

Poorest fifth
$14,680
decrease: $830

Since the late 1970s, the income gap between Ohio's richest families and its poorest has widened.

In Ohio, the richest fifth families have incomes 9.7 times higher than the poorest fifth (20 years ago the ratio was 6.4 times).

The increase in inequality was fifth greatest in the country.

The gap between the rich and the middle class also increased.

This increase was 15th greatest in the country.

While income disparities worsened almost everywhere, only five states—Ohio among them—saw the incomes of its poorest citizens actually go downward, when adjusted for inflation.

In 2001, the typical Ohio worker earned $12.81 an hour, which was 35 cents above the national average, but down from $13.73 (adjusted for inflation) in 1979.

Average hourly wage for white males: $15
Black males: $12
(For black men, wages have dropped 40 cents an hour since 1979)

Wages for working women increased to $11.17 an hour—10.3% more since 1979.

White women did better than black women.

240

Between 1997 and 1999, 71% of all Ohio men received health insurance from their private-sector jobs, down from 85.4% in 1981.

To afford a one-bedroom apartment in Ohio, one must earn $9.29 an hour (or 180% of the minimum wage).

While the income for Ohio families have risen, it did so because the families worked more hours, not because they earned more per hour.

Median income rose to nearly $44,000 in 2000, a 20% rise since the mid-1980s.

This topped the median U.S. income by $1,700 and was higher than all surrounding states except Michigan.

But married-couple families with children also worked almost one-fifth more per year from 1998 to 2000 than they did from 1979 to 1981.

This means parents are working 11 hours more each week than a generation ago.

Typically, parents worked 3,736 hours per year—the equivalent of one full-time job and a second person working more than four days a week. Single-parent families are working more than 18% longer than 20 years ago.

Analysts say Ohio's patterns are the result of its shrinking manufacturing base, and a subsequent growth in service jobs.

(By 2000, for instance, Ohio workers in unions dropped from 23 percent to 17 percent.)

Other problems: low minimum wages, and the lack of social safety nets such as child care and health insurance for low-wage workers.

The percentage of the working poor remains steady, 23.9% in 1979 and 23.5% in 2001.

More and more men take poverty-level jobs (less than $8.71 an hour), up more than 50% during the last 20 years.

The Economic Policy Institute, a national economic think tank, says that a median family budget—food, housing, utilities, non-recreational transportation, health care, child care, household items, and taxes—for a family of four in Ohio is approximately $33,490. This is more than twice the $16,895 poverty threshold for a family of four.

Sources: Economic Policy Institute Center on Budget and Policy Priorities, U.S. Census, Consumer Expenditure Survey of the Bureau of Labor Statistics; Coalition on Homelessness and Housing in Ohio

There are over 500 jurisdictions in Ohio with income taxes, what the tax commissioner calls "a compliance nightmare." Some argue that the tax laws should factor in Ohio's changing economy, which is shifting from manufacturing to services. "For better or worse," says one former commissioner, "you need a tax system that taxes economic activity."

241

Who carries the tax burden?

Cleveland-Marshall College of Law professor Deborah A. Geier says that those who write the biggest check may not be paying the most tax. Confused? Read her analysis on who pays what, and why.

As the tax filing deadline approached, we heard some politicians—and journalists—bemoan the heavy tax burden on the wealthy. For example, columnist Jerry Heaster asked, "How much tax do high income Americans need to pay before the class warriors will be satisfied?" He correctly reported that the top one percent of income earners in 1999 paid more than a third of "all federal personal income taxes."

But that's a little like saying that the wealthy drink the most alcohol in this country because they drink the largest percentage of 20-year-old port. What about beer?

The revenue collected under the regressive federal payroll taxes—Social Security and Medicare taxes—as well as state and local taxes, has exploded in the last 30 years. In 1963, for example, nearly twice as much revenue was collected in federal personal income taxes as in federal payroll taxes. Because of dramatic increases in the payroll taxes since then, however, by 1995 the federal government collected about the same amount of revenue in payroll taxes as it did in income taxes.

And these payroll taxes are extremely regressive, hitting the poor and middle classes the hardest. How does that happen?

Well, first, only wages are taxed, not investment returns, which are concentrated in the upper classes. About three-fourths of all capital gains income (realized on the sale of stocks, bonds and similar investment assets) comes from just 1.7 percent of taxpayers. These gains are not subject to the payroll taxes (and are subject to reduced taxation under the income taxes).

Moreover, only the first $84,900 of wages are taxed under the Social Security tax. Finally, the very first dollar earned is taxed; there is no personal exemption representing a bare-subsistence, tax-free amount, as under the income tax. These factors combine to make a very regressive tax that is borne predominantly by the wages of the poor and middle classes.

In other words, a waitress earning about $25,000 a year might pay only about $200 in federal income tax. But she would owe about $1,900 in the employee portion of the Social Security and Medicare taxes. Another example: Bill Gates pays the same amount of Social Security tax as a college professor earning $85,000 a year.

Provocative studies by economists Andrew Mitrusi and James Poterba show that nearly

two-thirds of families paid more in payroll taxes in 1999 than they paid in federal income tax, while only 44 percent of families did so in 1979. For families earning less than $50,000, more than three quarters paid more in payroll taxes than income taxes. Mean income taxes don't reach approximate parity with mean payroll taxes until one reaches $75,000 to $100,000 in income.

When you factor in payroll taxes, the percentage of federal tax paid by the top one percent plummets. A 2000 study by the Joint Committee on Taxation estimated that, under the law at that time, those earning more than $200,000 would pay 42.7 percent of the total federal personal income tax collected, while the top one percent would pay 33.6 percent.

If, however, all federal taxes are measured, including the regressive Social Security and Medicare taxes, the shares plummet to 27.5 percent for those earning more than $200,000 and 18.6 percent for the top one percent.

Because of the increased burden of payroll taxes on those earning less than $100,000, Mitrusi and Poterba have shown that the aggregate federal tax burden of the middle class in particular has increased between 1979 and 1999, while the tax burden of those earning more than $200,000 has decreased during that same time period. And these numbers will be far worse when the 2001 Bush tax cut for the super-wealthy is fully phased in.

The story doesn't end there, though. The Center on Budget and Policy Priorities recently released a study that shows that during the 1990s the states significantly decreased the percentage of revenue collected through progressive income taxes and significantly increased the percentage collected through regressive sales taxes. As a result, the wealthy pay a smaller percentage of state tax revenue than they did in the late 1980s and the poor and middle classes pay a larger percentage of that revenue than they did.

A regulated capitalist economy is the best economic system that man has thus far concocted, as it can lead to great societal wealth and well-being. But, by its very nature, it can also lead to great concentrations in wealth and income, which can lead to plutocracy and damage democratic values. The increased tax burden on the middle class and decreased tax burden on the wealthy over the last 20 years have occurred while both wealth and income concentration have reached levels not seen since 1929.

For example, the top one percent owns about 40 percent of private assets in this country, more than double the 19 percent it held as recently as 1976. Chief executives, on average, earn 475 times as much as the average factory worker today, up from 42 times in 1980. Between 1983 and 1999—the period that coincides with substantial increases in the payroll tax burdens on the labor income of the poor and middle classes—the richest one percent enjoyed 53 percent of the total gain in marketable wealth, while the bottom 80 percent enjoyed a mere nine percent.

Perhaps it is not unfair to ask those who disproportionately benefit the most from our regulated capitalist system to disproportionately pay the taxes that are necessary to support such a system. In other words, the right question to ask might not be how taxes should be distributed across income levels but rather how taxes affect the distribution of after-tax discretionary income.

The middle class has an increasingly hard time affording beer, while the top one percent's ever larger share of after-tax income allows it to stock up handsomely on that 20-year-old port.

It's not "class warfare" to point this out. It's basic fairness.

The tax bite (case studies)

	Family (2parents, one child)			Individual		
Average income	$16,600	$46,500	$162,000	$16,600	$46,500	$162,000
State Income Tax	$196	$3,132	$14,935	$229	$3,736	$15,764
Exemptions at						
$1,150 each	$3,450	$3,450	$3,450	$1,150	$1,150	$1,150
Ohio taxable income	$13,150	$43,050	$158,550	$15,450	$45,350	$160,850
Ohio tax	$319	$3,756	$15,784	$319	$3,756	$15,784
Exemption credit	$60	$60	$60	$20	$20	$20
Joint filing credit	$64	$563	$789	—	—	—
Local Income Tax (2%)	$285	$843	$2,407	$285	$843	$2,407
Property Tax	$548	$884	$2,916	$548	$884	$2,916
Projected annual property taxes paid	3.3%	1.9%	1.8%	3.3%	1.9%	1.8%
Sales and excise taxes	$996	$1,721	$2,592	$996	$1,721	$2,592
Projected annual sales/ excise paid	6.0%	3.7%	1.6%	6.0%	3.7%	1.6%
Total all taxes	$2,025	$6,579	$22,850	$2,129	$7,183	$23,679
Taxes as a percent of average income in group	12.2%	14.1%	14.1%	12.8%	15.4%	14.6%

Source: "Taxing Issues" (February, 2003), The Federation for Community Planning

Tax	Total, per capita	National rank
All state taxes	$1,733	34
All local taxes	$1,283	9
All taxes (state and local)	$3,016	20

How Ohio's major taxes rank nationally

Personal income (state and local)	$914	10
Corporate income (state only)	$67	39
Sales (state and local)	$883	37
Property (local only)	$829	25

State and Local Taxes as a Percentage of Personal Income

State taxes	6.2%	35th nationally
Local taxes	4.6%	5th nationally
All taxes, state and local	10.7%	17th nationally

Newly taxed services, as of August, 2003: Delivery charges; Laundry and dry-cleaning; Personal care (but not haircuts or perms); Satellite broadcasting (but not cable); Snow removal (if more than $5,000); Tattoos and piercing; Taxes and limousines; Towing.
—*Ohio Department of Taxation*

www. ohio.gov/phone/agency/

A time-saving list of links to most state agencies, from Aging, Ohio Department of, to Youth Services, Department of. Which may seem backward in chronology but there it is.

Accountancy Board
Website: www.state.oh.us/acc/
614-466-4135
614-466-2628

Adjutant General
Website: www.ohionationalguard.com/
614-336-6000

Administrative Services
Website: www.state.oh.us/das/
E-mail: laurie.mitchell@das.state.oh.us
614-466-6511
614-644-8151

African-American Males Commission
Website: www.state.oh.us/caam/index.htm
E-mail: greglewis@caam.state.oh.us
614-644-5143
614-387-0136

Aging
Website: www.goldenbuckeye.com/
E-mail: odamail@age.state.oh.us
614-466-5500
614-466-5741

Agriculture
Website: www.ohioagriculture.gov
E-mail: agri@odant.agri.state.oh.us
614-728-6200
614-466-4346

Air Quality Development Authority
Website: www.ohioairquality.org/
E-mail: mark.shanahan@aqda.state.oh.us
614-466-6825

Alcohol and Drug Addiction Services
E-mail: general@ada.state.oh.us
614-466-3445
614-752-8645

Ambulance Licensing Board
Website: www.state.oh.us/oalb/
E-mail: oalb@dps.state.oh.us
614-466-9451
614-728-6040

Apprenticeship Council
Website: www.state.oh.us/odjfs/apprenticeship/
E-mail: sicklesj@odjfs.state.oh.us
614-644-2469
614-644-2470

Architects Examining Board
Website: www.state.oh.us/arc/
E-mail: cmharch@aol.com
614-466-2316
614-644-9048

Arts and Sports Facilities Commission
Website: www.state.oh.us/afc/
E-mail: webmaster@oasfc.state.oh.us
614-752-2770
614-752-2775

Arts Council
Website: www.oac.state.oh.us/
E-mail: jamig@oac.state.oh.us
614-466-2613
614-466-4494

Athletic Commission
Website: www.state.oh.us/aco/
E-mail: oacpaul@riffe.ciec.state.oh.us
330-742-5120
330-742-2571

Attorney General
Website: www.ag.state.oh.us/
614-466-4320

Auditor
Website: www.auditor.state.oh.us/
614-466-4514
614-466-4490

Barber Board
Website: www.state.oh.us/brb/
614-466-5003
614-644-8112

Bicentennial Commission
Website: www.ohio200.org/
E-mail: obc@ohio200.org
614-752-0578
614-752-0584

Budget and Management
Website: www.state.oh.us/obm/
E-mail: obm@obm.state.oh.us
614-466-4034
614-466-3813

Building Authority
Website: www.state.oh.us/oba/
E-mail: fenlon@oba.state.oh.us
614-466-5959
614-644-6478

Bureau of Motor Vehicles (BMV)
Website: www.state.oh.us/odps/division/bmv/
bmv.html
E-mail: Webmaster@dps.state.oh.us
614-752-7500

Capitol Square Review & Advisory
Website: www.statehouse.state.oh.us/csrab/
E-mail: mdangaran@csrab.state.oh.us
614-752-9777
614-752-5209

Career Colleges and Schools Board
Website: www.state.oh.us/scr/
E-mail: bpsr@scr.state.oh.us
614-466-2752
614-466-2219

Chiropractic Examiners Board
Website: www.state.oh.us/chr/
E-mail: chirobd@mail.peps.state.oh.us
614-644-7032
614-752-2539

Civil Rights Commission
  Web site: www.state.oh.us/crc/
  E-mail: kautzmannm@ocrc.state.oh.us
  614-466-2785
  614-644-8776
Clean Air Resource Center
  E-mail: mark.shanahan@aqda.state.oh.us
  614-728-3540
College Advantage
  Web site: www.collegeadvantage.com/
  E-mail: info@otta.state.oh.us
  614-752-9400
  614-644-5009
Commerce
  Web site: www.com.state.oh.us/ODOC/
  614-466-3636
Community Service Council
  Web site: www.state.oh.us/ohiogcsc/
  E-mail: elizabeth.taggart@gcsc.state.oh.us
  614-728-2916
Consumers' Counsel
  Web site: www.pickocc.org
  webmaster@occ.state.oh.us
  614-466-8574
  614-466-9475
Correctional Institution Inspection
  Web site: www.ciic.state.oh.us/
  E-mail: webmaster@lis.state.oh.us
  614-466-1990
  614-466-2014
Cosmetology Board
  Web site: www.state.oh.us/cos/
  E-mail: ohiocosbd@cos.state.oh.us
  614-466-3834
  614-644-6880
Counselor and Social Worker Board
  Web site: www.state.oh.us/csw/
  E-mail: tracey.hosom@cswb.state.oh.us
  614-466-0912
  614-728-7790
Court of Claims
  614-466-7190
  614-644-8553
Criminal Justice Services
  Web site: www.ocjs.state.oh.us/
  E-mail: webmaster@ocjs.state.oh.us
  614-466-7782
  614-466-0308
Dental Board
  Web site: www.state.oh.us/den/
  E-mail: tabion@mail.peps.state.oh.us
  614-466-2580
  614-752-8995
Development
  Web site: www.odod.state.oh.us/
  E-mail: jbuchanan@odod.state.oh.us
  614-466-2480
  614-644-5167

Developmental Disabilities Council
  Web site: www.state.oh.us/ddc/
  E-mail: david.zwyer@dmr.state.oh.us
  614-644-5530
  614-466-0298
Dietetics Board
  Web site: www.state.oh.us/obd/
  E-mail: kay.mavko@exchange.state.oh.us
  614-466-3291
  614-728-0723
Dispute Resolution & Conflict Management
Commission
  Web site: www.state.oh.us/cdr/
  E-mail: website@cdr.state.oh.us
  614-752-9595
  614-752-9682
E-Commerce Center
  Web site: www.state.oh.us/das/dcs/odn/ecedi/
  index.htm
  E-mail: rick.dowell@das.state.oh.us
  614-995-4918
Education
  Web site: www.ode.state.oh.us/
  E-mail: contact.center@ode.state.oh.us
  614-995-1545
  614-752-3956
Educational Telecommunications
  Web site: www.oet.edu/
  E-mail: mirachi@oet.state.oh.us
  614-644-1714
  614-644-3112
Elections Commission
  Web site: www.state.oh.us/elc/
  E-mail: info@elc.state.oh.us
  614-466-3205
  614-728-9408
Embalmers & Funeral Directors Board
  Web site: www.state.oh.us/fun/
  E-mail: linda.clark@exchange.state.oh.us
  614-466-4252
  614-728-6825
Emergency Management Agency
  Web site: www.state.oh.us/odps/division/ema/
  E-mail: dkimmins@dps.state.oh.us
  614-799-3695
  614-799-3697
Emergency Medical Services
  Web site: www.state.oh.us/odps/division/ems/
  ems_local/default.htm
  E-mail: cldavies@dps.state.oh.us
  614-466-9447
  614-466-9461
Employment Relations Board
  Web site: www.serb.state.oh.us/
  E-mail: rkeith@serb.state.oh.us
  614-644-8573
  614-466-3074

www. auditor.state.oh.us

Found herein is
the complete Ohio
Revised Code,
as well as state &
local government
financial reports,
payroll records,
audits, manuals
of procedures,
and complete
documents of U.S.
and Ohio law.

Energy Efficiency
   Web site: www.odod.state.oh.us/cdd/oee/
   614-466-6797
   614-466-1864
Engineers & Surveyors Board
   Web site: www.ohiopeps.org/
   E-mail: mjacob@mail.peps.state.oh.us
   614-466-3650
   614-728-3059
Environmental Protection Agency
   Web site: www.epa.state.oh.us/
   E-mail: info-request@www.epa.state.oh.us
   614-644-3020
   614-644-2329
Environmental Review Appeals
   614-466-8950
Ethics Commission
   Web site: www.ethics.state.oh.us/
   ethicshome.html
   E-mail: ethics@ethics.state.oh.us
   614-466-7090
   614-466-8368
Exposition Commission
   Web site: www.ohioexpocenter.com/
   E-mail: c.minier@expo.state.oh.us
   614-644-4070
   614-644-4031

Family Support Collaborative
   Web site: www.state.oh.us/olrs/fsc/ASP/
   E-mail: fsc@olrs.state.oh.us
   614-466-7264
   614-644-1888
Financial Institution
   Web site: www.com.state.oh.us/ODOC/dfi/
   E-mail: webdfi@com.state.oh.us
   614-728-8400
Governor
   Web site: www.state.oh.us/gov/
   E-mail: governor.taft@das.state.oh.us
   614-466-3555
   614-752-4858
Governor's Council on People with Disabilities
   Web site: www.state.oh.us/gcpd/
   E-mail: lucille.walls@rsc.state.oh.us
   614-438-1391
   614-438-1274
Governor's Regional Econ Offices
   Web site: www.connectohio.com/
   bus_resources/gov_econ/
   E-mail: dlarzelere@odod.state.oh.us
   614-995-1895
   614-752-4858
Hazardous Waste Facility Board
   614-644-2742
   614-644-3439

Health
  Web site: www.odh.state.oh.us/
  E-mail: webmaster@gw.odh.state.oh.us
  614-466-3543
Hispanic/Latino Affairs Commission
  Web site: www.state.oh.us/spa/
  614-466-8333
  614-995-0896
Historical Society
  Web site: www.ohiohistory.org/
  614-297-2300
House of Representatives
  Web site: www.house.state.oh.us/
Industrial Commission
  Web site: www.ohioic.com/index.jsp
  E-mail: askic@ic.state.oh.us
  614-466-6136
  614-728-4795
Industrial Compliance
  Web site: www.ohioic.com/index.jsp
  E-mail: webdic@com.state.oh.us
  614-644-2223
  614-644-2618
Inspector General
  Web site: www.state.oh.us/watchdog/
  E-mail: oig_watchdog@oig.state.oh.us
  614-644-9110
  614-644-9504
Insurance
  Web site: www.ins.state.oh.us/
  E-mail: nancy.colley@ins.state.oh.us
  614-644-2658
  614-644-3743
Investigative Unit
  Web site: www.state.oh.us/odps/division/admin/
  liquor/liquor.htm
  E-mail: mkindle@dps.state.oh.us
  614-644-2415
  614-644-2463
Job & Family Services
  Web site: www.state.oh.us/odjfs/
  webmaster@odhs.state.oh.us
  614-466-6282
  614-466-2815
Joint Committee on Agency Rule Review
  Web site: www.jcarr.state.oh.us/
  614-466-4086
Labor & Worker Safety (OSHA)
  Web site: 198.234.41.198/w3/
  webwh.nsf?Opendatabase
  E-mail: webmaster@PERRP.com.state.oh.us
  614-644-2239
Labor & Worker Safety (Wage & Hour)
  Web site: 198.234.41.198/w3/
  webwh.nsf?Opendatabase
  E-mail: webmaster@wagehour.com.state.oh.us
  614-644-2239

Labor Market Information
  Web site: lmi.state.oh.us/
  E-mail: hayp@odjfs.state.oh.us
Lake Erie Commission
  Web site: www.epa.state.oh.us/oleo/index.html
  E-mail: oleo@www.epa.state.oh.us
  419-245-2514
  419-245-2519
Landscape Architects Board
  E-mail: cmharch@aol.com
  614-466-2316
  614-644-9048
Legal Rights Service
  Web site: www.state.oh.us/olrs/
  E-mail: webmaster@olrs.state.oh.us
  614-466-7264
  614-644-1888
Legislative Budget Office
  Web site: www.lbo.state.oh.us/fiscal/
  E-mail: webmaster@lbo.state.oh.us
  614-466-8734
Legislative Inspector General
  Web site: www.jlec-olig.state.oh.us/
  E-mail: info@jlec-olig.state.oh.us
  614-728-5100
  614-728-5074
Legislative Service Commission
  Web site: www.lsc.state.oh.us/
  614-466-3615
Liquor Control Commission
  Web site: www.state.oh.us/com/liquor/
  liquor.htm
  E-mail: Erika.Sowry@lcc.state.oh.us
  614-466-3132
  614-466-4564
Liquor Control Division
  Web site: www.state.oh.us/com/liquor/
  liquor.htm
  E-mail: agencyops@liquor.state.oh.us
  614-644-2360
  614-644-2480
Lottery
  Web site: www.ohiolottery.com/
  216-787-3200
  216-787-3313
Medical Board
  Web site: www5.state.oh.us/med/
  E-mail: med.recept@med.state.oh.us
  614-466-3934
  614-728-5946
Mental Health
  Web site: www.mh.state.oh.us/
  E-mail: swankd@mhmail.mh.state.oh.us
  614-644-8451
  614-752-6474

Mental Retardation & Developmental Disabilities
   Web site: odmrdd.state.oh.us/
   E-mail: robert.jennings@dmr.state.oh.us
   614-466-5214
   614-466-3141
Military Reserve, Ohio-OHMR
   Web site: www.state.oh.us/ohmr/
   614-336-6000
Minority Health Commission
   Web site: www.state.oh.us/mih/
   E-mail: minhealth@ocmh.state.oh.us
   614-466-4000
   614-752-9049
Motor Vehicle Collision Repair Board
   Web site: www.collisionboard.com/
   ez.php?Page=37
   E-mail: diane.hoenig@exchange.state.oh.us
   614-995-0714
   614-995-0717
Natural Resources
   Web site: www.dnr.state.oh.us/
   E-mail: dnrmail@dnr.state.oh.us
   614-265-6565
   614-261-9601
Nursing Board
   Web site: www5.state.oh.us/nur/
   E-mail: board@nur.state.oh.us
   614-466-3947
Occupational Therapy, Physical Therapy, &
Athletic Trainers
   Web site: www.state.oh.us/pyt/
   E-mail: diane.moore@otptat.state.oh.us
   614-466-3774
   614-644-8112
Office of Veterans' Affairs
   Web site: www.state.oh.us/gova/
   614-644-0892
Ohio Administrative Knowledge System (OAKS)
   Web site: www.state.oh.us/oaks/
   jennifer.leymaster@oaks.state.oh.us
   614-387-1865
Ohio County Profiles
   Web site: www.odod.state.oh.us/research/
   productListing.html#S0
   E-mail: osr@odod.state.oh.gov
   614-466-2115
Ohio Family and Children First
   Web site: www.ohiofcf.org/
   E-mail: info@ohiofcf.org
   614-752-4044
   614-728-9441
Ohio Judicial Conference
   Web site: www.state.oh.us/ojc/
   E-mail: clabornc@sconet.state.oh.us
   614-466-4150
   614-644-1296

Ohio Learning Network
   Web site: www.oln.org/
   E-mail: awoods@oln.org
   614-995-3240
Ohio Power Siting Board
   Web site: www.opsb.ohio.gov/
   E-mail: jeff.mcnaughton@puc.state.oh.us
   614-466-2871
Ohio State Fair
   Web site: www.ohiostatefair.com/
   E-mail: info@ohioexpocenter.com
Ohioana Library Association
   Web site: www.oplin.lib.oh.us/
index.cfm?id=773
   E-mail: ohioana@sloma.state.oh.us
   614-466-3831
   614-728-6974
Online Export Directory
   Web site: www.odod.state.oh.us/itd/
Optical Dispensers Board
   Web site: www.state.oh.us/odb/
   E-mail: ohioopticalboard@hotmail.com
   614-466-9709
   614-995-5392
Optometry Board
   Web site: www.state.oh.us/opt/
   E-mail: optometry.board@exchange.state.oh.us
   614-466-5115
   614-644-3937
Orthotics, Prosthetics and Pedorthics Board
   Web site: www.ohio.gov/bopp/
   E-mail: bopp@exchange.state.oh.us
   614-466-1157
   614-387-7347
Personnel Board of Review
   Web site: www.state.oh.us/pbr/
   E-mail: jeannette.gunn@spbr.state.oh.us
   614-466-7046
   614-466-6539
Petroleum Underground Storage Tank Release
Compensation
   614-752-8963
   614-752-8397
Pharmacy Board
   Web site: www.state.oh.us/pharmacy/
   E-mail: exec@bop.state.oh.us
   614-466-4143
   614-752-4836
Psychology Board
   Web site: www.state.oh.us/psy/
   E-mail: psy.license@exchange.state.oh.us
   614-466-8808
   614-728-7081
Public Defender
   Web site: www.state.oh.us/opd/index.htm
   E-mail: terri.wilson@opd.state.oh.us
   614-466-5394
   614-644-9972

Public Safety
Web site: www.state.oh.us/odps/odps.html
E-mail: webmaster@dps.state.oh.us
614-466-2550
614-466-0433

Public Utilities Commission
Web site: www.puc.state.oh.us/
E-mail: contactthepuco@puc.state.oh.us
614-466-3204
614-466-7366

Public Works Commission
Web site: www.pwc.state.oh.us/
E-mail: pwc_is@pwc.state.oh.us
614-466-0880
614-466-4664

Quality Services
Web site: www.state.oh.us/quality/
E-mail: stevew6296@aol.com
614-644-5154
614-644-6763

Racing Commission
Web site: www.state.oh.us/rac/
E-mail: mje@osrc.state.oh.us
614-466-2757

Rail Development Commission
Web site: www.dot.state.oh.us/ohiorail/
E-mail: susan.arduini@dot.state.oh.us
614-644-0306
614-728-4520

Real Estate
Web site: www.com.state.oh.us/ODOC/real/
E-mail: webreal@com.state.oh.us
614-466-4100
614-995-3310

Regents Board
Web site: www.regents.state.oh.us/
E-mail: regents@regents.state.oh.us
614-466-6000
614-466-5866

Rehabilitation & Correction
Web site: www.drc.state.oh.us/
E-mail: linda.diroll@odrc.state.oh.us
614-752-1159
614-752-1171

Rehabilitation Services Commission
Web site: www.state.oh.us/rsc/
E-mail: valerie.snavely@rsc.state.oh.us
614-438-1200
614-438-1257

Respiratory Care Board
Web site: www.state.oh.us/rsp/
E-mail: rcb.logsdon@rcb.state.oh.us
614-752-9218

Rural Development Partnership
614-466-5495
614-466-4346

Sanitarian Registration Board
Web site: www.state.oh.us/san/
E-mail: lynn.jones@exchange.state.oh.us
614-466-1772
614-644-8112

School Facilities Commission
E-mail: program.info@osfc.state.oh.us
614-466-6290
614-466-7749

School for the Deaf
Web site: www.ohioschoolforthedeaf.org/
E-mail: webmaster@osd.ode.state.oh.us
614-728-1422
614-728-4060

SchoolNet
Web site: www.osn.state.oh.us/
E-mail: glick@osn.state.oh.us
614-728-8324
614-728-1899

Secretary of State
Web site: www.state.oh.us/sos/
E-mail: guide@sos.state.oh.us
614-466-2655
614-466-3899

Securities
Web site: www.securities.state.oh.us/
E-mail: cary.dachtyl@com.state.oh.us
614-644-7381

Senate, Ohio
Web site: www.senate.state.oh.us/senators/
614-466-4900

Speech-Language Pathology & Audiology
Web site: www.state.oh.us/slp/
E-mail: deborahhoward@slpaud.state.us.oh
614-466-3145
614-995-2286

State & Federal Surplus
Web site: www.state.oh.us/das/gsd/surplus/ sfsur.html
E-mail: david.settlemire@das.state.oh.us
614-466-1584
614-752-0440

State Architect's Office
Web site: www.state.oh.us/das/gsd/index.htm
E-mail: StateArchOff@das.state.oh.us
614-466-4761
614-644-7982

State Controlling Board
Web site: www.state.oh.us/obm/information/ ControllingBoard/ControllingBoard.asp
E-mail: obm@obm.state.oh.us
614-466-5721
614-466-3813

State Fire Marshal
Web site: www.com.state.oh.us/ODOC/sfm/
E-mail: websfm@com.state.oh.us
614-752-8200
614-752-7213

State Highway Patrol
   Web site: www.state.oh.us/ohiostatepatrol/
   E-mail: wwwohp@dps.state.oh.us
State Library of Ohio
   Web site: winslo.state.oh.us/
   E-mail: refhelp@sloma.state.oh.us
   614-644-7061
   614-466-3584
Statehouse Museum Shop
   Web site: www.statehouseshop.com/index.htm?
   E-mail: museumshop@csrab.state.oh.us
Statehouse News Bureau
   Web site: statenews.org/
   614-221-1811
Supreme Court
   Web site: www.sconet.state.oh.us/
   E-mail: comments@sconet.state.oh.us
   614-466-3456
Tax Appeals Board
   Web site: www.state.oh.us/bta/
   614-466-6700
   614-644-5196
Taxation
   Web site: www.state.oh.us/tax/
   614-466-2166
   614-466-6401
Transportation
   Web site: www.dot.state.oh.us/
   E-mail: andy.eline@dot.state.oh.us
   614-466-7170
   614-644-8662
Travel & Tourism
   Web site: www.ohiotourism.com/default_f.asp
   askohiotourism@calltech.com
Treasurer
   Web site: www.treasurer.state.oh.us/
   E-mail: info@tos.state.oh.us
   614-466-2160
   614-644-7313
Tuition Trust Authority
   Web site: www.collegeadvantage.com/
   E-mail: info@otta.state.oh.us
   614-752-9400
   614-644-5009
Turnpike Commission
   Web site: www.ohioturnpike.org/
   E-mail: lhakos@ohioturnpike.org
   440-234-2081
Unclaimed Funds
   Web site: www.com.state.oh.us/ODOC/unfd/
   E-mail: unfd.claims@com.state.oh.us
   614-466-4433
   614-752-5078
Unemployment Compensation Review
   Web site: www.web.ucrc.state.oh.us/
   E-mail: webmaster@mail.ucrc.state.oh.us
   614-466-6768
   614-752-8862

Utility Radiological Safety Board
   Web site: www.state.oh.us/ursb/index.html
   E-mail: rhauenstein@dps.state.oh.us
Veterans Home
   Web site: www.state.oh.us/ovh/
   E-mail: jrallen@ovh.state.oh.us
   419-625-2454
   419-625-3207
Veterinary Medical Licensing Board
   Web site: www.state.oh.us/ovmlb/index.htm
   E-mail: info@vmlb.state.oh.us
   614-644-5281
   614-644-9038
Water and Sewer Rotary Commission
   614-466-4394
Water Development Authority
   Web site: www.owda.org/
   E-mail:
   614-466-5822
   614-644-9964
Workers' Compensation
   Web site: www.ohiobwc.com/
   614-644-6292
   877-520-6446
Youth Art Exhibition
   Web site: www.govart.org/
   614-272-1678
   614-272-1678
Youth Services
   Web site: www.state.oh.us/dys/
   E-mail: goodmand@mail.dys.state.oh.us
   614-466-4314
   614-752-9859

" WELL, WHADJA EXPECT THE ARMAND HAMMER COLLECTION TO BE ?!"

For years, arts and culture in Ohio have been a part of the very fabric that defines our local communities, serving to strengthen the infrastructure of the state. One of the major supports for this is the Ohio Arts Council, a state agency established in 1965, whose mission is building the state through the arts—economically, educationally and culturally—preserving the past, enhancing the present and enriching the future for all Ohioans. The council believes the people of Ohio should share the arts.

The OAC supports and encourages public, individual and organizational efforts via two primary methods. First, by funding council-operated programs providing support to artists and organizations for making arts activities available to a broad segment of Ohioans; and second, by providing services that support the growth of the arts

The budgets, staffs, boards, partnerships and planning of nonprofit arts organizations anchor Ohio's cultural landscape. How well they function in terms of budget, staff, board and audience affects the entire arts industry in Ohio.

The average nonprofit arts organization:

❏ Has revenues of $862,500 and expenses of $665,000

❏ Earns $246,800 in program revenues

❏ Earns $56,500 in investment income

❏ Secures $353,400 in contributed income

❏ Financial support from in-state foundations is ten times higher than support from out-of-state foundations.

❏ Most public support comes from local city funds exceeding both state and federal funding

❏ Average revenues per organization in Ohio are higher than in any nearby state except New York.

❏ Earned revenue accounts for the highest percentage of total income for nonprofit arts organizations.

❏ Many organizations rely heavily on part-time staff and volunteers. Paid part-time staff account for almost half (48%) of the hours worked at nonprofit arts organizations. Volunteer staff account for 23% of the hours worked.

❏ Two thirds (66%) engage in financial planning. The majority engage in program planning (62%) and marketing planning (58%). More than half (52.6%) plan very little in the area of technology.

❏ Nonprofit arts organizations tend to partner with a wide range of organizations, especially other nonprofit arts organizations and schools.

❏ The majority of nonprofit arts organizations give the arts and culture in Ohio a "B."

Small arts organizations

Small arts organizations face different issues and concerns than larger arts institutions. Of the typical small arts organization managers, few work full-time, and most do not receive adequate compensation for their efforts. They are diverse in their professional backgrounds, but share the common goal of connecting with their communities through the arts.

They know how to operate an arts organization regardless of budget size, staff or resources. Many have yet to establish nonprofit status and they turn to host organizations for fiscal purposes. Small arts organizations are rarely concerned with expanding their organizations. They tend to specialize, rather than diversify, programming. Some concentrate on a particular season of programs, while others focus on a specific concert, exhibition or festival. The life spans of these organizations vary from two to 90 years.

Small arts organizations creatively structure their boards with an equal number of artists and business people. This allows for the consideration of artistic risks, but also serves as a check for budgets and other sound business concerns. Board members, staff and volunteers often partner with schools, other arts and cultural institutions, universities, churches, civic clubs, businesses, senior groups and government, to supplement or subsidize limited resources. Many of these organizations would not be able to function without support in the form of building space, performance and exhibition spaces, fiscal agent services and administrative assistance.

Cultural organizations

Libraries, universities, festivals and other cultural oriented organizations are nonprofit organizations that may also provide arts programming.

Roughly one-third of Ohio's universities (32.3%) currently house, rent space, or act as a fiscal agent for arts organizations. The majority of universities (92%) have arts programs and exhibitions open to the public. The majority of libraries (93.9%) are wheelchair accessible. 89.7% have restrooms that are wheelchair accessible. 80.4% provide sign language, audio description or large print materials.

Ohio ranks second in the nation for attendance at festivals, according to a National Endowment for the Arts' survey. The majority of festivals (97%) are wheelchair accessible; about one-half of festivals (48.2%) publicize their accessibility. Libraries, universities, festivals and cultural organizations give the arts and culture in Ohio a "B."

Arts and cultural programs are offered at 59% of Ohio's libraries. Types of arts and cultural programming vary and include plays, theatre, music, readings, lectures and film. The majority of programs are for young audiences.

Ninety-two percent of university events are open to the public, and the majority of these events are concerts. More than half of colleges and universities offer lectures, exhibitions, concerts and plays to the public.

While the majority of Ohio's festivals offer arts and cultural programming, and there is much happening in the area of arts and culture at festivals, no particular type of event stands out.

Only about half (51%) of these organizations have cultural programs which are open to the public. Given the wide range of groups in this category—and the special audiences that they are likely to serve—this may not be a surprise.

For-profit arts organizations

The role of for-profit arts organizations in Ohio is complex and much is yet to be discovered about them.

There are three industries with unique connections to Ohio's arts and cultural environment: architectural firms, for-profit galleries, and music venues. Architecture is the art of the built environment. For-profit galleries mirror nonprofit galleries. They differ in their organizational structure and focus and much can be learned from comparing how they operate. Commercial music venues often serve as a primary point of exposure to the arts.

◼ *Architecture*

Many architects express a strong belief that architecture is an art. Architects believe that their art form is much more technical and functional than other art forms; and while other art forms are allowed to exist solely on their artistic merit, architecture must first and foremost serve a function. Architects believe that of all the arts, architecture has the strongest social function and utility. People live in buildings, drive over bridges and attend events in stadiums. The public's safety or welfare is rarely a factor in other types of art.

Architects see the public as a wise consumer of their product as well as a thwarting agent to their artistic creativity. They often view the public as being too conservative and intolerant of architectural innovation and complain that they have to sneak creativity into projects. Architects express frustration about the public's perceived desire for cheap and fast architecture. They believe that architecture has evolved into a field where projects are to be conceived and completed as quickly and cheaply as possible with little concern for lasting value or permanence. However, a minority of architects believe that they should serve the public and should not judge or try to enforce ideas of what constitutes good architecture.

Architects are involved in a variety of activities that enhance their communities. They visit public schools to inform children about their profession. Many enjoy designing schools because they enhance the education of youth and add to civic pride. They also take pride in designing public buildings because they have the potential to draw new people into their communities, enhancing the quality of life and the economy.

Most architects believe that technology has revolutionized architecture and will continue to do so in its artistic, creative and business functions. However, some architects believe that technology has a negative impact, inhibiting the creative process by automating drawing and designing. Architects see more design/build in their future and as a result work more with contractors. Unfortunately, they predict they will continue to design pre-fab buildings and share fees with construction managers. Architects see themselves as survivors, dedicated to an educational mission. They believe that if their profession is to survive they will have to continue to educate the public about architecture.

◼ *For-profit music venues*

Private music venues consider themselves substantially different from those that are supported with public dollars. They understand the need to package their product and underscore the benefits to corporate sponsors. As part of their business savvy they understand this. Proprietors of music venues stress the importance of their relationships with the broader community and in the civic roles they play, particularly in partnering with other organizations for benefits, fundraisers and public service. They are involved in a variety of community efforts including police safety programs, downtown housing programs, AIDS awareness efforts, hospital and other charity events. Some work with public entities, such as the Public Broadcasting System (PBS), provide a conduit for raising dollars.

Music venues have come to believe that the traditional arts community has misconceptions about their medium. They perceive this community as disdainful of the "rock focus" of most of these venues while unaware of the music venues' openness to collaboration and community inclusion. "If we can help, we're there," music venues say. But the traditional arts groups do not ask. Music venues struggle to capture people's time and have to focus on promotion, advertising and on being "in the right media." Operators of for-profit music venues recognize that there are significant barriers in the lives of potential audiences that prevent them from attending performances. They realize that people may not have the time and money to attend events and that parents of small children are constrained because they must find and pay for babysitters or find children-friendly events.

In Central Ohio, there is a sense that the audience is not as cosmopolitan as that in Cleveland or Cincinnati. In general, Central Ohio is considered to have a good music scene, but some formats don't work as well, such as country music concerts. The Central Ohio local music scene is vibrant and diverse, but it has been difficult to offer national talent in the past. In part, this is because Columbus is considered a secondary market. Music venues say this is because of the lack of arenas large enough to hold major national acts, and they hope this will change with the opening of two major venues in recent years. They also note the importance of community festivals as arenas for performers.

Music venues in Northeast Ohio praise their audiences. They feel they are in a good market and able to bring great performers to their venues. The Cleveland area is considered one of the best-kept secrets in the country for support of music. Northeast music venues see public, corporate and foundation support of the arts in this region as significant and comparable to other major cities such as Los Angeles, New York and Boston. However, as receptive as their audiences are, the venues believe that they constantly need to reinvent themselves. In Cincinnati, people identify strongly with their neighborhoods. While this is often a good thing, it means that it can be difficult to get people out of their neighborhoods or "comfort zones." On the other hand, it suggests loyalty to established venues. The managers of for-profit music venues express frustration with the performing artists. This is particularly true for Central Ohio music venues. They say their relationships with artists are hit and miss. While they consistently view the performers as artists and see art as encompassing a wide range of musical genres, they also feel that musicians need to understand that their art is a business as well as entertainment. For music venues, the future means meeting market demands. They must react to the ever-changing likes and dislikes in music and to varying audience demographics. They feel they must discover how to attract seniors to their venues, since this market will have more disposable income, will be technologically literate, and will seek convenience and speed in their transactions and attendance. Overall, music venues see themselves as a part of the music scene and are very passionate about what they do.

◼ *For-profit galleries*

While galleries face diverse issues, they share the goals of fostering relationships with artists, educating artists about what it means to be represented by a gallery, and selling art. Exceptions to this include gallery owners who deal in posthumous works and therefore, do not deal with the artist, but families or executors of estates; or a hair salon or restaurant whose priority is art exposure and not sales. Owners of for-profit galleries believe that Ohioans would rather purchase art from outside the state and that most Ohioans view purchasing art from the coasts as more prestigious.

Northeast and Central Ohio gallery owners feel the public perceives art galleries as elitist. Many go to great lengths to make people feel comfortable in their spaces and believe that their primary objective is to educate the client about owning a piece of original art or about art in general, rather than simply making a sale. The ultimate goal is to turn the public into collectors of art. "I'm not committed to just selling art, I'm committed to seeing that people live with art," said one gallery owner. "I think those are two very different things."

Knowing your market and finding your niche are important issues to for-profit gallery owners. Some galleries redesign storefronts to make their space more customer-friendly. In an attempt to lure younger, wealthier customers, organizations market original artwork as a status symbol. Other organizations disagree with that philosophy and view every person who enters their galleries as a potential customer. Gallery owners view location as a critical component to a successful gallery. Northeast and Central Ohio galleries are affected by the scarcity of parking. Southwest galleries feel that the lack of an artist district has impacted their business. Galleries outside metropolitan areas think their biggest obstacle is location and that a rural or suburban location makes it more difficult for them to be considered a legitimate gallery.

For-profit gallery owners believe that nonprofit art galleries can take more risks and present different types of work because they don't have to always be concerned with the market value of art. Others feel nonprofits do not have to promote personal interaction with people who enter their facilities because the sale of art is not their primary focus. However, some think that nonprofits educate the public more effectively

because they have other revenue streams. "Subsidy destroys the character in any type of organization," said one focus group member, in regards to public funding. For most for-profit gallery owners the belief is that government funding should be reserved for arts education.

Arts in the schools

School arts programs in Ohio are part of the arts and cultural environment and the role of the K-12 public and private schools is multifaceted. Research demonstrates that exposure to the arts will improve a child's creativity, self-esteem and overall capacity for learning. Further the role that the arts play in the life of a child directly correlates to the likelihood that the child will be involved in the arts as an adult.

Despite more than 4,000 public and private schools in Ohio the Ohio Arts Council finds that, in general, arts and cultural programming and opportunities in schools are inadequate. The money and staff allocated to the arts are not significant enough to affect a majority of students. With the exception of offering high school band programs, the existing structure to maintain and manage extracurricular arts activities for high school students is poor at best.

◼ One in ten Ohio schools has no funds budgeted for the arts
◼ Almost 90 percent of Ohio schools do not have a full-time theatre teacher
◼ Nearly half of Ohio schools do not offer theatre programs
◼ More than three out of four do not have dance programs
◼ Almost 64 percent do not have visual arts programs
◼ About one in four has one or two extracurricular music programs

High schools have more money budgeted for the arts than elementary and middle schools. Schools with large student populations have greater arts programming budgets than less populated schools.

Public schools appropriate more of the total arts budget for supplies, while private schools appropriate more of the arts budget for art teachers.

The most common field trips are outings to plays. Elementary school students are more likely to be given opportunities to visit museums of natural history, historical societies and zoos than higher-grade levels. High school students are more likely to be offered opportunities to visit art galleries and museums.

The majority of schools with 800 or more students (94%) provide at least one extracurricular music program, and 57% of these schools offer three or more music programs. Only 6% of schools with less than 300 students provide three or more extracurricular music programs.

Schools tend to partner with other organizations to provide arts opportunities for students. The most common partnerships (56%) are with parent-teacher organizations, particularly at the elementary level to assist with fundraising. Other partnerships include: hosting visiting artists; offering field trips to museums and galleries; working with local arts councils for student scholarships and grants; and organizing student exhibitions. 61% do not partner with nonprofit arts and cultural organizations.

The majority of schools (76%) market student arts performances to the public as well as to students and parents. The majority of schools (81%) market student exhibitions to the public as well as to students and parents.

Arts educators

Many arts educators do not see their profession or the arts in general as being valued within the schools. They often do not have assigned classrooms and their art rooms tend to be inadequate. Some are required to work between schools, with a large number of students. One arts educator works in two schools and teaches 1,000 students per week. Another works at four schools. Many arts educators feel they are not valued as professionals because of their perceived inability to increase proficiency test scores. They feel they are viewed as paraprofessionals, required to baby-sit students and to create bulletin boards or artistic additions to the school hallways. They sense a conservatism among parents and administrators regarding arts education programming, and feel that such conservatism prevents them from stretching students' imaginations and stifles creativity. One teacher received hate mail for putting on plays that some individuals thought to be too progressive.

Arts educators are strategic collaborators and often work with civic organizations, artists and private industries to bring students' artwork into the local community. Examples of community collaborations include student arts projects such as stained glass, photography and paintings for buildings, including historical societies, banks, malls and government centers. Many arts educators welcome technology, such as using the Internet for educational programming and e-mail service and listservs for networking with peers. They believe that technology has allowed them to present material in a more relaxed and didactic way, with greater emphasis on discovery and learning. However, some do not feel confident with the use of technology.

Overall, arts educators seem optimistic about the future of arts education. They see a need for the arts to be taken more seriously in education, but doubt that this will occur due to increased emphasis on proficiency tests scores and tighter education budgets. Despite some expressed hardships, arts educators are pleased with their profession and intend to remain in the field.

Many arts educators welcome technology, such as using the Internet for educational programming and e-mail service for networking with peers. They believe that technology has allowed them to present material in a more relaxed and didactic way, with greater emphasis on discovery and learning. However, some do not feel confident with the use of technology.

Arts administrators

Arts administrators function as managers, grant writers, fundraisers, marketing officers, publication designers, mentors, agents, promoters, facilitators, educators, counselors, social workers and sometimes janitors for their organizations. They support and manage devoted staff and volunteers to ensure that their organizations function effectively. Within their communities, they serve on boards, planning committees and as volunteers for a variety of organizations. They work with community agencies and form partnerships with schools, community centers, daycare centers, home-school groups, nursing homes, juvenile court systems, hospitals, churches and other social service agencies.

They believe there is a lost generation of arts supporters due to the lack of arts programming and opportunities in schools. They see public education as part of their primary focus, and feel they must continue to work with schools to nurture students' creativity. They defend innovative methods for getting people in the door, arguing that establishing a comfort level for the first experience will bring an audience back for more. "Whatever type of outreach you can imagine, get them into your buildings, get them into your spaces," said one arts administrator. "You can get them to come back once you bring down some of those walls."

Arts administrators recognize the importance of informal marketing as well as easy-to-understand, jargon-free information. Both urban and rural participants feel that word-of-mouth and one-on-one marketing are important for successful connections between community residents and arts organizations. In general, they believe people tend to be passive receivers of promotional information instead of active seekers. They value technology, specifically e-mail, and feel the Internet is a good tool for publicizing events and for staying informed about trends in the field. Regarding the future, they believe that one challenge will be to develop balanced boards that can generate dollars and support artistic products. Another challenge is to successfully articulate that experiencing art requires an investment of time and that this investment has a return—it is not only for the elite. They feel that people will commit the time and partake of the product if arts organizations commit to providing links to entertainment. "The educational element is easier to put forward," one administrator explained. "But you have to balance it with entertainment." Some arts administrators find it difficult to think about their organization in five years, but most are committed to being a part of their organization well into the future.

Artists

Arts professionals are the human capital of Ohio's arts and cultural environment. More than 52,000 Ohioans are working as artists or in arts-related jobs.

Artists in Ohio believe there is a social responsibility that comes with their profession. They feel there is a power that art can have on an individual and community, and that the arts promote self-expression and build self-esteem. Many artists also teach art because this philosophy leads them to work with children, at-risk individuals, individuals with disabilities and older adults. Many work with arts organizations, nursing homes, schools, hospitals, social services agencies and other community-based organizations. They believe in equal access to the arts for all people regardless of age, race, economic status or ability.

Artists often feel isolated from the communities in which they work. They tend to feel that people have misconceptions or hold negative stereotypes about them. They often struggle between community projects and personal work. One artist from Northwest Ohio dedicated time to creating public artwork with children, which left him little time for his own work. Many artists find it difficult to receive financial support for their work and often do not receive adequate compensation to cover the various costs associated with each discipline. Filmmakers spoke about the expense associated with making a film, and choreographers spoke about the cost of space to perform a piece once created. Some art forms lend themselves to collaborations; others do not. In general, artists feel they have become more entrepreneurial and business savvy in marketing themselves or their artwork. Many view the Internet as a great tool for communication and explore ways to use technology to market their work. However, some have not ventured into the world of e-commerce.

Artists from Southeast Ohio spoke about the number of craft and traditional artists in the area, the rural nature of the community, and how far away they were from a metropolitan area. They also spoke about Appalachia's economic and environmental difficulties. For example, a recent flood there caused serious damage that resulted in financial problems for schools, and therefore, the arts were not at the forefront of people's minds. Artists from Northeast Ohio spoke about using art to address larger community issues and that the arts should be accessible to all people. Many of these artists were involved with residency activities and worked with children. They also talked in-depth about how the arts bring neighborhoods and communities together and felt the arts played a large role in the revitalization of Cleveland.

Total Employment Figures and Salaries for Arts Professions in Ohio (based on a survey conducted by the Ohio Arts Council):

◗ There is a slight majority of females.

◗ The majority of the sample is White/Caucasian (87.3%); 11.6% are African American/Black; all other racial categories accounted for 1.1%.

◗ The average age is 45 years old evenly distributed across age groups: 18-29 (25.0%), 30-44 (26.7%), 45-59 (23.6%) and over 60 (24.8%).

◗ 58% are married; the others are single or never married (23.7%); divorced (9.9%) or widowed (6.5%).

◗ The majority does not have children living at home (63.0%). 37% have one child or more living at home most of the year.

◗ Approximately half (53.2%) of the sample have household incomes of $20,000 or less; 10.6% have household incomes of $20,001 to $30,000; 15.1% have household incomes of $30,001 to $50,000; 14.0% have incomes between $50,001 and $75,000; 7.2% have household incomes over $75,000.

◗ The majority of respondents work full time (56%); 20.4% had retired, 7.8% work part time and 8% describe themselves as "keeping house."

◗ The average amount of schooling is slightly more than 12 years; 19.3% are college graduates; and 17.2% never completed high school. The average number of years having lived in Ohio was 38 years.

Attendance

Ohioans attend various types of arts and non-arts events. The top ten types of events that are attended at least twice a year are: restaurant, shopping mall, library, movie, festival, historic site, sports event, art museum or gallery, amusement or theme park and health club or gym. The most common reasons for not attending events are financial, family obligations and time constraints. The following is a picture of the average Ohioan according to the Ohio Arts Council survey.

The Average Ohioan:
Thinks Ohio is a good place to live.
Gives the arts and culture in Ohio a "B."
Thinks that tax dollars should be used to support the arts in Ohio.
Spends some or a lot of time watching primetime television and engaging in recreational reading and outdoor activities.
Spends no time at all participating in organized sports; singing or playing a musical instrument; working on craft such as knitting, sewing, ceramics; and creative writing.
Has attended or visited in the last year:
A sit down restaurant (46 times)
A mall or shopping plaza (36 times)
A health club or gym (23 times)
A library (19 times)
A movie (8 times)
A historic site or park (7 times)
A professional or college sporting event (4 times)
A festival (3 times)
A gospel or religious music concert (3 times)
An art gallery or art museum (3 times)
A jazz or blues concert (once)
A classical music concert (once)
A science or history museum (once)
Has not attended or visited in the last year:
An ethnic dance or folk music performance
An R&B or hip-hop performance
A public literary or poetry reading
A ballet
A social spot such as a nightclub or bar

Museums

Cincinnati

Akron Art Museum
70 E. Market Street
Akron, Ohio 44308
330-376-9185
www.akronartmuseum.org

Launched with a founder¹s collection of American paintings from the turn of the 20th century, the Akron Art Museum has cut out a post-1850 niche for itself. Strengths include moderns, such as Frank Stella and Andy Warhol, and a noteworthy photo collection. These and traveling exhibits draw an annual attendance of 70,000. Housed in a handsome Renaissance building, originally a post office, the museum planned to start an adjacent and strikingly modern addition by the Danish firm Coop Himmelb(l)au in early 2004.

Butler Institute of American Art
524 Wick Avenue
Youngstown, Ohio 44502
330-743-1711
www.butlerart.com

www. *sculpturecenter.org*

Over 1,000 outdoor sculptures located throughout Ohio are inventoried on this site, including conservation efforts and histories, plus educational and promotional resources for sculptors, online newsletters and the current exhibition at The Sculpture Center in Cleveland.

Dubbed "America¹s Museum," the Butler Institute of American Art was the first structure in the United States built specifically to house a collection of American art; now it attracts 220,000 visitors a year. Over 40 temporary exhibitions of works by historic and contemporary American artists are on display each year, and since the mid-1930s the Butler has featured an annual juried National Midyear Show, bringing together paintings from artists across America. The exhibition program represents every aspect of American art. The Butler is housed in a Renaissance style monument of Georgian and Carrara marble, a building that is itself noteworthy architecturally.

Canton Museum of Art
1001 Market Avenue North
Canton, Ohio 44702
330-453-7666
www.cantonart.org

The Canton Museum of Art has a collection of American watercolors, other works on paper and contemporary ceramics, which, with temporary shows, attract an annual attendance of about 50,000. Previous exhibitions have included the works of American sculptor Bart Walter, paintings by the versatile August Biehle, Jr., and the vivid watercolors of American artists Joseph Raffael and Carolyn Brady. Traveling exhibition themes have included Ohio's Bicentennial, celebrating Stark County, and the Potters of Mata Ortiz in Mexico.

Cincinnati Art Museum
953 Eden Park Drive
Cincinnati, Ohio 45202
513-721-2787
www.cincinnatiartmuseum.org

In 1886, the Cincinnati Art Museum opened its original Richardsonian Romanesque building, which became the first permanent home of an art museum west of the Alleghenies. Today, after many additions to the building, the collection has grown to include some 100,000 works from 6,000 years of world art and attracts 275,000 visitors a year. In addition to the art of ancient Egypt, Greece and Rome, there are extensive galleries of Near and Far Eastern art, Native American, and African art. The painting collection includes works by European old masters as well as 20th-century works. The American collection holds works by major artists from the 1970s and 1980s. Areas of special strength include the only collection of ancient Nabataean art outside of Jordan, the renowned Herbert Greer French collection of old master prints, and a fine collection of European and American portrait miniatures. The Museum holds and displays many paintings from Cincinnati¹s "Golden Age" (1830-1900) as well as Cincinnati¹s own Rookwood pottery and over 40 pieces of Cincinnati carved furniture.

Cleveland Museum of Art
11150 East Boulevard
Cleveland, Ohio 44106
216-421-7340
888-262-0033
www.clevelandart.org

The Cleveland Museum of Art is "one of the nation¹s premier collections," says the *New York Times*. Every year 630,000 people come to sample some of its more than 40,000 works spanning 6,000 years and representing five continents. The museum is renowned for European and American paintings, medieval European art, and one of the world¹s finest collections of Asian and pre-Columbian art. It has

DAI

70 galleries and recital halls, all set in a 15-acre public park. Wrote one reviewer, "Even if art usually leaves you cold, it is hard not to be impressed by the rooms full of intricately wrought weapons and armor, bejeweled medieval artifacts, an Egyptian sarcophagus, and Central and South American stone carvings." Special exhibitions, films, lectures, and musical performances are extensive.

Columbus Museum of Art
480 East Broad Street
Columbus, Ohio 43215
614-221-6801
www.columbusmuseum.org

Ferdinand Howald was a Swiss-born engineer who lived in Columbus. With a fortune mostly from railroad stock, he retired at 50 in 1906 and began buying art. In the 1910s and early 1920s Howald was one of the few people acquiring the work of living American painters like John Marin and Marsden Hartley. Thus thanks to Howald, ever since the museum first opened its Broad Street building in 1931 with his collection, it's been an especially good place to see the work of early 20th-century Americans. The museum also has good examples of the work of European impressionists, post-impressionists and modernists; and it has the largest public collection of paintings by Columbus native George Bellows. Visitors average 160,000 a year.

Dairy Barn Cultural Arts Center
8000 Dairy Lane
Athens, Ohio 45701
740-592-4981
www.dairybarn.org

The official subtitle is the Southeastern Ohio Cultural Arts Center, but everyone still refers to it as "The Diary Barn," in reference to its origins as part of the regimen (patients milked cows as therapy) at the Athens Asylum, which sits on the hill above the barn. The residents had quite an operation here for nearly 50 years, regularly winning prizes for the dairy herd and the herd's products, but when the Asylum got out of the milking business, the barn was abandoned. A group of civic-minded types shoveled the place out, local artists, builders and designers donated their time, and the result is a true community arts center. A picturesque dairy barn, built in 1914 and now on the National Register of

Historic Places, it now has art exhibits and classes. Two shows, the Quilt National and Bead International are recognized internationally.

Dayton Art Institute
456 Belmonte Park North
Dayton, Ohio 45405
937-223-5277
www.daytonartinstitute.org

The Institute's modern incarnation began in the early days of the Great Depression, when Julia Shaw Patterson Carnell pledged nearly $2 million for a new museum if the community would endow its operational costs. She did, and it did. And in 1930, Dayton had a landmark building modeled after 16th century Italian Renaissance villas and set on a hilltop overlooking both Dayton's downtown and the river. Its collection of over 20,000 objects emphasizes Asian, 16th and 17th century European, and contemporary American art. The institute offers seasonal concerts for most musical tastes, as well as a variety of special exhibits. Yearly attendance is 300,000. The museum is rated "superb in quality" by the American Association of Museums, and its holdings are considered one of the best mid-size collections in the country.

Massillon Museum
121 Lincoln Way East
Massillon, Ohio 44646
330-833-4061

The Massillon Museum has a collection of photographs, Ohio quilts, Pueblo pottery and folk art, as well as one in local history and sports. It also has a miniature three-ring Immel Circus display. Visiting exhibits focus on contemporary art and photography.

CONTEMPORARY ARTS CENTER

Pyramid Hill Sculpture Park & Museum
222 High Street
Hamilton, Ohio 45011
513-868-8336
www.pyramidhill.org

Opened in 1997, Pyramid Hill is a 265-acre park with 48 modern sculptures by artists of international note. Located outside Hamilton on State Route 128, Pyramid Hill is one of only three parks of its scale in the U.S. Artists include George Sugarman and Alexander Lieberman, whose "Abracadabra" is generally regarded as the park's masterpiece. Although Pyramid Hill can be viewed entirely by car, the best way to view the sculptures is by walking the trails, which cover grassy hills sloping down to lakes, all of it surrounded by forests. The 1st Annual Pyramid Hill Art Fair was held on the second weekend of October, 2003.

Riffe Gallery
Vern Riffe Center for the Government and the Arts
77 South High Street
Columbus, Ohio 43215
614-644-9624
www.oac.state.oh.us/riffegallery

The Ohio Arts Council sponsors a little gallery offering an eclectic series of shows featuring Ohio artists and works from the state's museums and galleries.

Rosenthal Center for Contemporary Art
44 East Sixth Street
Cincinnati, Ohio 45202
513-345-8400
www.ContemporaryArtsCenter.org

The Lois and Richard Rosenthal Contemporary Arts Center is a museum without a collection, except for its spectacular new building, completed in 2003. The first U.S. work of Iraqi-born London-based architect Zaha Hadid, the Rosenthal Center is the first art museum in America to be designed by a woman. *The New York Times* called it "the most important American building to be completed since the end of the Cold War." The Center enlivens its Walnut Street corner with its black, concrete and glass facades; both inside and out, it relates well with its site. Windowless trapezoidal galleries have varying ceiling heights to accommodate art works, and the lower level features a black-box theater. Shows are all visiting works and installations.

Spaces
2220 Superior Viaduct
Cleveland, Ohio 44113
216-621-2314
www.spacesgallery.org

An artist-run alternative gallery exhibiting the works of emerging and experimenting artists in visual and performing arts.

Springfield Museum of Art
107 Cliff Park Road
Springfield, Ohio 45501
937-325-4673
www.spfld-museum-of-art.org

The Springfield Museum serves this small city with an impressive collection mostly of 19th and 20th century American paintings, prints, drawings and sculpture. With classes, gift shop, and 4500-volume art reference library, the holdings bring 40,000 people to the museum every year—this in a city of 65,000. Collections include works by two noteworthy Springfield natives: Berenice Abbott, a leading 20th century documentary photographer, and Thomas Worthington Whittredge, a prominent 19th century landscape painter.

Taft Museum of Art
316 Pike Street
Cincinnati, Ohio 45202
513-241-0343
www.taftmuseum.org

The Taft Museum, built originally in 1820 as a country house just east of downtown, ended up belonging to Charles and Anna Taft, who not only lived there but assembled an art collection that ultimately turned their home into one of America's great house museums. Besides the old masters, the fine furniture and ceramics, and the enamels, the house also has the impressive pre-Civil War murals of Robert Duncanson, who had been hired to decorate the walls of the house long before the Tafts occupied it. Duncanson, a Cincinnati artist, was one of the important landscape painters of the 19th century.

The Toledo Museum of Art
2445 Monroe Street at Scottwood
Toledo, Ohio 43620
419-255-8000
800-644-6862
www.toledomuseum.org

Ranked among America's top ten art museums, the Toledo Museum is particularly strong in European painting and the decorative arts. It draws about 250,000 people a year to its rich and varied collections, which include treasures from ancient Egypt, Greece, and Rome; paintings by old masters from Gainsborough to Turner; African and Asian art; and works by modern masters such as Matisse, Picasso, Hopper, and Nevelson. The collections contain a room from the Chateau de Chenailles in France (circa 1633), complete with its oil on canvas and wood panels, and what is called the largest collection of glass in any general art museum in the world. Founded in 1901 and holding its first exhibitions in rented rooms in a downtown building, the museum grew because of the Libbeys: Edward, patriarch of Libbey Glass, and his wife Florence, herself an heiress. They helped build the building, they acquired the art, and they left their enormous fortunes to run the museum and fund new purchases. The Libbeys believed art should be a part of people's education, so the museum did not charge admission, a practice it maintains more than a century later.

Zanesville Art Center
620 Military Road
Zanesville, Ohio 43701
740-452-0741
www.zanesvilleartcenter.org

Zanesville Art Center has a collection of 7,000 examples of American, Asian, and European art—including some old masters (Gainsborough, Rembrandt, Rubens) and an intact 400-year-old wood-paneled room from an English estate. It also has an extensive collection of Ohio art glass and art pottery, as well as Meissen, Tiffany and Wedgewood decorative arts. The center planned to move into its renovated and expanded building, a $3 million project, in fall 2003.

Allen Memorial Art Museum
Oberlin College
87 North Main Street
Oberlin, Ohio 44074
440-775-8665
www.oberlin.edu/allenart

The Allen Memorial Art Museum is one of the finest college or university collections in the nation. Its comprehensive collection holds over 11,000 works spanning the entire history of art, including 17th-century Dutch and Flemish painting, European art of the late 19th and early 20th centuries, contemporary American art, old master prints, and Japanese prints. The museum's lovely original building, with seven central arches in front, was designed by Cass Gilbert and its modern addition by Venturi & Rauch.

Cleveland State University Art Gallery
2307 Chester Avenue
Cleveland, Ohio 44114
216-687-2103
www.csuohio.edu/art/gallery

This is a small collection especially strong in African American prints and drawings from the early 20th century. Shows, curated in-house, include social themes and regional exhibitions.

Kennedy Museum of Art
Lin Hall, The Ridges
Ohio University
Athens, Ohio 45701
740-593-1304
www.ohiou.edu/museum

Among its holdings, Ohio University's Kennedy Museum has a unique and culturally significant collection of Southwest Native American textiles and jewelry and an internationally renowned contemporary print collection. The galleries are in Lin Hall, a renovated space in one of the monuments of Athens: the hilltop Administration Building of a one-time mental hospital complex.

McDonough Museum of Art
Youngstown State University
410 Wick Avenue
Youngstown, Ohio 44503
330-742-1400
www.fpa.ysu.edu/mcdonough/main.html

YSU¹s gallery is housed in a sleek modern
building, 1991, designed by Charles Gwathmey
of Gwathmey Siegel Associates, New York. It was
financed by benefactor John McDonough, a local
collector who sold a painting for $1 million to pay
for it. The museum shows the work of established
and emerging regional artists and examples from
other university and museum collections.

Miami University Art Museum
801 South Patterson Avenue
Oxford, Ohio 45056
513-529-2232
www.fna.muohio.edu/amu/

Much has been made of the stark contrast between
the modern, angular architecture of this award-
winning glass and limestone building and the
decidedly traditional structures that are a trademark of the Miami campus. But then, an exceptional collection deserves an exceptional building
and Miami can boast a range and variety of
holdings that is rare among collegiate collections.
As the university has been acquiring art since 1829,
the five galleries yield a rich display of paintings,
sculpture, prints, and decorative arts as ancient as
sixth century B.C. Greece and as modern as 20th
century America. A highlight of the museum is the
Charles M. Messer Leica Camera Collection, a
bonanza of some 1,200 items considered one of the
largest assemblages of Leicas in the world.
Representing one of the most important—to art as
well as science and journalism—cameras of
modern times, this prized collection is meticulously
maintained by the museum staff and displayed with
great pride and affection.

Wexner Center for the Arts
Ohio State University
1871 North High Street
Columbus, Ohio 43210
614-292-3535
www.wexarts.org

Conceived as a research laboratory for all the
arts, the Wexner Center set itself lofty goals when
it opened in 1989, and by and large it has realized
them. It has mounted shows of contemporary art
and artifacts that introduced many celebrated
artists and concepts to Columbus gallery goers.
The Wexner also encompasses art and cartoon
libraries, and film, music, dance and theater
performance programs. Director Sherri Geldin
has called the Wexner "one of the very few truly
multidisciplinary contemporary arts centers
anywhere." The building was the first large

structure designed by Peter Eisenman of New
York, a leading architectural theorist.

College of Wooster Art Museum
Ebert Art Center
1220 Beall Ave.
Wooster, Ohio 44691
330-263-2495
www.wooster.edu/artmuseum/

The Art Museum presents a series of rotating
exhibitions during the academic year, including
selections from the permanent collection of over
5,000 objects. Both nationally and regionally
recognized artists have exhibited at Wooster. The
most significant permanent holdings are in the
John Taylor Arms Print Collection, which includes
works from the 15th to the mid-20th century.
Other collections include African Art, ceramics,
and a large collection of Chinese bronzes and
snuff bottles.

Craft and glass museums

Fostoria Glass Heritage Gallery
109 North Main Street
Fostoria, Ohio 44830
419-435-5077
www.fostoriaglass.com

The Fostoria Glass Heritage Gallery is a colorful
glass museum featuring the glass made at the nine
factories producing glass in Fostoria, Ohio from
1887-1920.

National Heisey Glass Museum
169 West Church Street
Newark, Ohio 43055
740-345-2932
www.heiseymuseum.org

Produced in Newark from 1896-1957, Heisey
Glass is pretty enough that it's attracted collectors.
This museum has almost 5,000 pieces, showing
hundreds of patterns and all known colors.

Ohio Craft Museum
Ohio Designer Craftsmen
1665 West Fifth Avenue
Columbus, Ohio 43212
614-486-4402
www.ohiocraft.org

In addition to ongoing displays, the Ohio Designer
Craftsmen¹s Ohio Craft Museum presents six major
exhibitions a year, one on the year¹s best and the
other five devoted to a medium, like beads,
ceramics, or wood. Most items displayed are on
sale. This is the only museum in the Midwest
devoted to showing and collecting fine crafts.

Glass is one of those ubiquitous items: everywhere in our lives without us giving it much thought. In the hopeful dawning of a new consciousness, glass—as a container—may even be making a comeback. Therefore a notable haven for the cognoscenti of handmade glass is surprisingly close to most of us, in Newark, Ohio, the home of the Heisey Museum, the *national* museum, if you will, for this is the significant public American collection of what is arguably the finest handmade tableware America ever produced.

It's here because this area is the center of America's glassmaking industry, for it is here that both quality silica and cheap natural gas were found. The museum itself is an 1831 Greek Revival house filled with eight rooms of glass made by the Heisey Company during its tenure from 1896-1957, even to novice eyes an impressive collection.

With the company's closing, the handmade industry was virtually ended in this country. It was doomed by cheaper imports as well as a society that had quite unwisely decided to be "throwaway."

In its time, Ohio's Heisey was sold only by jewelry shops and the best department stores. It was such glass-with-class that it is likely the only folks of modest means who drank from its famous stemware were the people who made the glass and took the seconds home (not all of it legally). In Newark, for a time, people of ordinary means supped egalitarianly from fine crystal.

Today, many aficionados, who have both Heisey and Waterford in their cabinets, will choose Heisey as the better-made glass. Some Newark dealers contend the antique Heisey is a better bargain and, given some leeway for regional prejudices, they contend Waterford is overpriced. The Heisey cutters and engravers were, of course, noted for their perfection, particularly the master engraver of the 1930'a, Emil Krall, an Austrian who was considered one of the finest engravers in the world.

Heisey's extra process of fire-polishing—done in what glassmakers call "the glory hole"—was a notable process that lent the glass its brilliance. The Cambridge Glass Company was nearby and also made fine glass, but the Newark contingent contends Heisey is a bit superior. A gentle rivalry exists between the sister groups but every June, Newark is mecca to the nation's Heisey collectors and the entire place is viewed through a glass, lightly. It's the annual convention at which time there are auctions, flea markets—a notable one is held on the courthouse lawn—and swap meets.

The museum has most of the original Heisey molds—some 4,400 of them and a few are used to make small pieces for the museum shop. The old company is still standing, off East Main at Oakwood, although the great smokestacks are gone and there's not much to see. Where many people have seen Heisey glass, even though they might not have known, is in both the stage and film version of *The Glass Menagerie*; Laura's famous menagerie was a Heisey menagerie.

Warther Museum
331 Karl Avenue
Dover, Ohio 44622
330-343-7513
www.warthers.com

In 1913, when he was 28, Ernest Warther began making carvings to depict the history of the steam engine, which he considered history's greatest invention. He carved scale models with moving parts of ivory, walnut, and ebony; 64 are now on view, along with his wife's button collection.

Ethnic arts

African American Museum
1765 Crawford Road
Cleveland, Ohio 44106
216-791-1700
ourstory@aamcleveland.org

The African American Museum was founded for the preservation and dissemination of information regarding the contributions of individuals of African descent. Located in the historical Hough Community, the museum is a place of learning and a place to experience African and African American culture in the heart of Cleveland.

Croatian Heritage Museum and Library
34900 Lakeshore Boulevard
Eastlake, Ohio 44095
440-327-9498

The museum shows changing exhibits of Croatian and Croatian American fine and folk arts. It also offers lectures, a resource library, and programs to preserve ethnic traditions.

Karamu House
2355 East 89th Street
Cleveland, Ohio 44106
216-795-7070
www.karamu.com

Founded in 1915, Karamu House is the nation's oldest African-American cultural institution. Through theater and arts programs, it promotes understanding and interaction of diverse cultures and emphasizes development of new artists and new work.

King Arts Complex
867 Mount Vernon Avenue
Columbus, Ohio 43203
614-645-5464
www.thekingartscomplex.com

The King Arts Complex promotes increased awareness of African American artists' contributions, develops talents and preserves African

American culture. It has an art and sculpture collection and presents theater, dance, and other performances. The complex is housed in the restored Pythian Theatre, built in 1926 in an African-American neighborhood and designed by an African-American architect, Samuel Plato.

Temple Museum of Religious Art
1855 Ansel Road
University Circle at Silver Park
Cleveland, Ohio 44106
(mail: 26000 Shaker Boulevard
Beachwood, Ohio 44122)
216-831-3233
www.ttti.org/museum.asp

The Temple Museum is the fourth oldest museum of Judaica in the United States, and houses one of the most prominent and comprehensive collections of religious and Judaic art. The permanent exhibits include a collection of antique Jewish artifacts; fold art objects made and used by Jews in many countries; historic documents, manuscripts and bibles; and a collection of sculptures, paintings and lithographs by famous Jewish artists.

Ukrainian Museum-Archives
1202 Kenilworth Avenue
Cleveland, Ohio 44113
216-781-4329
www.umacleveland.org

Founded in 1952, the Ukrainian Museum-Archives is a large collection devoted to Ukrainian history and culture and the Ukrainian diaspora and community in Cleveland. Art, folk art, and artifacts are on display.

Summertime outdoor dramas

Blue Jacket
520 South Stringtown Road
Xenia, OH 45385
937-376-4318
www.bluejacketdrama.com

Presented in an amphitheater at Caesar Ford Park, *Blue Jacket* is one of the most popular outdoor dramas in the nation, a company of professionals that attracts some 40,000 patrons every summer. There really was a Blue Jacket, a young white man known as Marmaduke Van Swearingen until he was captured and adopted by the Shawnee Indians in the late 1700's. Since he became a war chief who led the Shawnee against his native people, the role of Blue Jacket synthesizes the cultural conflict between Indians as conservators of the earth and the settlers as exploiters. The production offers the audience plenty of frontier excitement and a cast of characters that includes live horses and the

legendary figures Daniel Boone and Simon Kenton. And because the Shawnee once thrived in the Xenia area, the play is also a wonderful dose of local—albeit romanticized—history, sweetened by a good story.

Tecumseh!
P.O. Box 73
Chillicothe, Ohio 45601-0073
740-775-0700
www.tecumsehdrama.com

Written by Allan Eckert, the historical drama about the great Shawnee leader Tecumseh and his conflicts with William Henry Harrison for control of the Northwest Territory is presented at the Sugarloaf Mountain Amphitheatre northeast of Chillicothe.

Trumpet In the Land
P.O. Box 450
New Philadelphia, Ohio 44663
330-339-1132
www.trumpetintheland.com

Written by Pulitzer Prize-winning playwright Paul Green, this is the story of frontier conflicts during the Revolutionary War, including the infamous Gnadenhutten massacre. It's been presented at Schoenbrunn Amphitheatre since 1970.

Bowling Green State University
New Music & Art Festival
MidAmerican Center for Contemporary Music
Bowling Green State University
Bowling Green, Ohio 43403
419-372-8171
www.bgsu.edu/colleges/music/MACCM

Festival celebrates current art and music with university and guest artists every October.

Cleveland International Film Festival
2510 Market Avenue
Cleveland, Ohio 44113
216-623-3456
www.clevelandfilm.org

In the biggest event of its kind between Chicago and New York, Cleveland International Film Festival presents 100 feature films and 100 shorts—new releases from around the world. The annual spring festival is held at Tower City Cinemas, usually includes a retrospective series on a genre or director.

Columbus Arts Festival
100 East Broad Street, Suite 2250
Columbus, Ohio 43215
www.gcac.org

Columbus's four-day June festival is held on the riverfront downtown and draws over 500,000 people. Attractions include 300 artist and craftsman exhibits, music on three stages, and 40 food vendors, including gourmet restaurants.

Lancaster Festival
127 West Wheeling Street
Lancaster, Ohio 43130
740-687-4808
www.lanfest.org

More than 70 performances of music, art, theater and dance are presented during this annual ten-day festival that sprawls all over town, from the university campus and the fairgrounds to St. Mary's Church and Public Square.

May Festival
1241 Elm Street
Cincinnati, Ohio 45210
513-381-3300
www.mayfestival.com

Cincinnati Music Hall was built in 1878 to accommodate the May Festival, founded in 1873 and now the oldest continuous choral festival in the Western Hemisphere. The chorus of 145 singers and Cincinnati Symphony join in five performances, four in Music Hall and one at the Cathedral Basilica of the Assumption in Covington, across the river in Kentucky.

Art festivals

Lancaster

Severance

Akron Symphony Orchestra
17 North Broadway
Akron, Ohio 44308
330-535-8131
www.akronsymphony.org

Taiwan-born music director Ya-Hui Wang has won prizes for her conducting in several international competitions. The orchestra is a professional one offering classical, pops and educational concerts. It also sponsors Symphony Chorus and Youth Symphony.

Ashland Symphony Orchestra
P.O. Box 13
Ashland, Ohio 44805
419-289-5115

Community orchestra performs five subscription and three pops concerts each year at Hugo Young Theatre and McDowell Auditorium.

Canton Symphony Orchestra
1001 Market Avenue North
Canton, OH 44702-1024
330-452-3434
www.cantonsymphony.org

Professional orchestra presents seven classical programs, holiday and spring pops and concerts for young people during its winter season. It also sponsors the Youth Symphony.

Central Ohio Symphony Orchestra
PO Box 619
Delaware, Ohio 43015
740-362-1799
www.delaware.org/comm/coso.htm

The Central Ohio Symphony Orchestra has 65 members from all walks of life, including music teachers, doctors, business people, students and others. They present a four-concert subscription series and other concerts in Gray Chapel at Ohio Wesleyan University. The conductor is Nicholas Perrini, professor of music at Capital University

and Columbus-born, a relatively rare feat for conductors.

Cincinnati Symphony Orchestra
1241 Elm Street
Cincinnati, Ohio 45202
513-381-3300
www.cincinnatisymphony.org

Founded in 1895, Cincinnati Symphony is the country¹s fifth oldest—old enough to have premiered works by Debussy, Ravel and Bartok. It¹s also one of the largest orchestras, with 99 instrumentalists; the music director is Estonian-born Paavo Jarvi. With the addition of two more instrumentalists, one playing a drum set and the other a banjo, the orchestra turns into the Cincinnati Pops, which has its own conductor and its own website (www.cincinnatipops.org). Both the Symphony and the Pops play at Riverbend Music Center in the summer. The Symphony also sponsors a Youth Orchestra.

Cleveland Chamber Symphony
CSU Department of Music
2121 Euclid Avenue
Cleveland, Ohio 44115
216-687-9243
www.csuohio.edu/ccs/

The 34-member professional ensemble-in-residence at Cleveland State University, the Cleveland Chamber Symphony performs only contemporary music, and that mostly American. In a season it does nine campus concerts, and of those, two are devoted to student composers.

Cleveland Orchestra
Severance Hall
11001 Euclid Avenue
Cleveland, Ohio 44106
216-231-7300
www.clevelandorch.com

Severance Hall itself is a Georgian landmark of Indiana limestone, its portico overlooking a major Cleveland intersection where streetcars once dropped off concert-goers. This Orchestra evolved into one of America¹s best under music directors like Artur Rodzinski, Lorin Maazel, and especially the feisty Hungarian maestro George Szell, who lifted it to international fame during his 24-year tenure ending in 1970. In 2002 Austrian conductor Franz Welser-Most took over the podium after guest appearances over nine seasons; he promises to carry on the Cleveland legend. The auditorium's distinctive acoustics have made the orchestra¹s signature sound. In 2000, the hall underwent an ambitious $36 million renovation and expansion that left the building completely refurbished, down to its Art Deco light fixtures and, of course, the famed acoustics. The orchestra also sponsors the Youth Orchestra and Orchestra

Chorus. In summer it performs at Blossom Music Center in Summit County.

Columbus Symphony Orchestra
55 East State Street
Columbus, Ohio 43215
614-228-8600
www.columbussymphony.com

A major orchestra with 54 full-time musicians, the Columbus Symphony Orchestra presents more than 130 performances a year, which adds up to yearly audiences of a quarter million people at live performances. The symphony does a 15-concert classical series, chamber programs, summertime Picnic with the Pops, and children¹s programs. It also sponsors a Youth Symphony and a Chorus.

Dayton Philharmonic Orchestra
109 North Main Street, Suite 200
Dayton, Ohio 45402
937-224-3521
www.daytonphilharmonic.com

The Dayton Philharmonic Orchestra has won awards for programming contemporary music. A professional regional orchestra, it presents classical, pops, chamber and family programs and a summertime Sunset Symphony Series at Fraze Pavilion in suburban Kettering. The orchestra performs in the Schuster Center for the Performing Arts and sponsors a Youth Orchestra and a 140-voice Chorus.

Firelands Symphony Orchestra
PO Box 2665
Sandusky, Ohio 44870
419-626-1950
www.state-theatre.com/orch/orch.html

Music director Jose Santos Perez takes pride in being at the helm of one of Ohio¹s fastest-growing regional orchestras: in 11 years, the budget rose from $2,000 to almost $300,000. Certainly, Firelands Symphony covers the region. Five winter concerts are held at Sandusky¹s State Theatre, with a second performance at either Elyria, Avon Lake or Lorain. A summer concert travels to Lorain, Huron, Put-in-Bay, Norwalk and Wellington.

Lima Symphony Orchestra
67 Town Square
PO Box 1661
Lima, Ohio 45802
419-222-5701
www.limasymphony.com

One of the ten largest orchestras in Ohio, the Lima Symphony presents a winter season of eight or nine classical programs and one pops concert. Founded in 1953, this professional orchestra serves a ten-county region.

Mansfield Symphony Orchestra
138 Park Avenue West,
PO Box 789
Mansfield, Ohio 44901
419-522-2726
www.rparts.org

Founded in 1930, the Mansfield Symphony Orchestra has up to 80 professional musicians and a regional stature, as its performances are broadcast. The orchestra does seven concerts in a winter season, four classical and three pops, with guest artists, and all in the Renaissance Theatre. It also sponsors a Symphony Chorus and Youth Orchestra.

Pro Musica Chamber Orchestra
243 North Fifth Street, Suite 202
Columbus, Ohio 43215
614-464-0066
www.promusicacolumbus.org

Pro Musica Chamber Orchestra has won many awards for adventuresome programming—such as Mahler's Symphony No. 4 performed by a small chamber orchestra. With a repertory spanning 300 years, ProMusica is directed by co-founder Timothy Russell. Performances are in the Southern Theatre.

Springfield Symphony Orchestra
PO Box 1374
300 South Fountain Avenue
Springfield, Ohio 45501
937-325-8100
www.springfieldsym.org

Counting ensemble presentations at schools, the Springfield Symphony performs 125 times a year. The 73-musician orchestra¹s main venue is the Kuss Auditorium at Clark State Performing Arts Center.

Suburban Symphony Orchestra
PO Box 22653
Beachwood, Ohio 44122
440-442-8914

The Suburban Symphony, a self-styled "avocational" orchestra, presents varied repertoire from Bach to Bartok, pops to young soloists. They do five free winter season concerts in Beachwood High School auditorium.

Toledo Symphony
1838 Parkwood Avenue, #310
Toledo, Ohio 43624
419-264-8000
www.toledosymphony.com

A major regional orchestra, the Toledo Symphony
does 500 performances a year with all or part of
the orchestra. Classical concerts are at the
Peristyle at the Toledo Museum of Art, which is
known for its fine acoustics. The orchestra also
does pops, family and chamber concerts, and has
a neighborhood concert series with performances
in Toledo-area spaces like churches.

Tuscarawas Philharmonic
PO Box 406
New Philadelphia, Ohio 44663
330-364-1843
www.tuscarawasphilharmonic.org

A semi-professional orchestra averaging 65
musicians a performance, the Tuscarawas
Philharmonic plays a six-concert series at Dover
High School Auditorium. Melanie Winn, general
manager and soprano soloist, says audiences total
almost 5000 people; and another several thousand
turn out for a summer concert in the park. The
orchestra also sponsors adult and children¹s
choruses.

Westerville Symphony Orchestra
PO Box 478
Westerville, Ohio 43086
614-890-5523
www.westervillesymphony.org

Community orchestra of 80 professional and semi-
professional musicians reaches audiences of 6,000
people a year with year-round concerts. The main
series is four classical performances at Cowan
Hall, Otterbein College.

Youngstown Symphony Orchestra
260 Federal Plaza West
Youngstown, Ohio 44503
330-744-0264
www.youngstownsymphony.com

A professional regional orchestra, Youngstown
Symphony presents masterworks and pops
concerts in beautiful Powers Auditorium. It has 34
contracted musicians and over 200 individuals
who perform as needed.

Yellow Springs Chamber Music Series
P.O. Box 448
Yellow Springs, Ohio 45387
937-767-1750

Yellow Springs is home to one of the nation's more
unusual chamber music concert series, primarily
because so many talented music-lovers have so
long resided there that the village virtually

constituted an audience waiting for an ensemble. In
1983, several music-lovers gathered in Ruth Bent's
kitchen and imagined their village having top-flight
chamber music concerts. The result of their
enthusiasm was Chamber Music in Yellow Springs,
Inc., a group of knowledgeable and discriminating
volunteers who invite the finest musicians from the
United States and abroad to give performances in
the Presbyterian Church. Over 200 people showed
up for the first concert, and today the series is so
popular with local patrons that the concerts are
often sold out in advance

Cincinnati Opera
1241 Elm Street
Cincinnati, Ohio 45202
513-241-2742
www.cincinnatiopera.com

Founded in 1920, Cincinnati Opera is the
second oldest company in the country. Its
Cincinnati Music Hall performances in June and
July offer the Cincinnati Symphony in the pit and
internationally renowned casts on stage. By and
large, the singing is the best to be found consistently in Ohio. Audiences know it; 30,000 people
come to Music Hall for eight performances of four
operas a season.

Cleveland Opera
1422 Euclid Avenue, Suite 1052
Cleveland, Ohio 44115
216-575-0903
www.clevelandopera.org

Cleveland Opera usually presents four productions
during its winter season, including operas (both
popular and rarely seen ones), operettas, and
classic musicals. The opera performs at Playhouse
Square's State Theatre, which it helped transform
into an opera house. General Director David

Bamberger has been with the company since 1976, when it was founded.

Dayton Opera
138 North Main Street
Dayton, Ohio 45402
937-228-7591
www.daytonopera.org

Dayton Opera celebrated its move to the Schuster Center with an *Aida* in March 2003; horses and 200 people crowded the stage. A regional opera, the company draws from the national pool of singers, while the chorus and smaller roles are filled with Daytonians, and the orchestra is the Dayton Philharmonic. They do one star gala and three productions a season, with a mix of standard, light, and unusual operas.

Lyric Opera Cleveland
PO Box 93046
Cleveland, Ohio 44101
216-685-5976
www.lyricoperacleveland.org

Lyric Opera Cleveland, a 1974 outgrowth of the Cleveland Institute of Music, has a reputation for innovative programming—"Our mission," says artistic director Jonathan Field, "is to perform new operas or standard operas in new ways." The company does three productions in its summer season, and two apprentice showcases. Performances are at Cleveland Play House¹s Drury Theatre.

The Ohio Light Opera
Freedlander Theatre
College of Wooster
Wooster, Ohio 44691
330-263-2345
www.wooster.edu/ohiolightopera

Founded anew by the College of Wooster in 1979 after an earlier beginning as the Kent State Light Opera Company, the Ohio Light Opera is now the darling of Wayne County tourism, for it brings audiences of over 20,000 every summer, all but 11 percent from out of county. Though the company has added a musical comedy to its summer program of seven works, it is essentially the country's only professional group devoted to operetta. Every summer it offers a nine-week season of 68 performances, with the same people appearing in up to seven different roles. The repertory includes not only all of Gilbert & Sullivan, but also American and other European works, all sung in English—through the years, the company has performed 80 different operettas. The ultimate goal, says manager-producer Laura Neill, is to reach at least some of the average American TV viewers who so far know nothing about the delights of light opera.

Opera Columbus
177 Naghten Street
Columbus, Ohio 43215
614-461-0022
www.operacols.org

Founded in 1981, Opera Columbus is a regional company with a history of extremes. Extreme highs have included the likes of sold-out performances of *Tristan and Isolde* in the 1980s—quite a coup for a fledgling company—and being named one of the country's fastest growing companies. The low came in 1991 when the board announced the opera's demise because of its debts, but enough money poured in to bring opera back from the brink. In 2001, the company merged with Columbus Light Opera, which offers a summer season of a light opera and a musical at the Southern Theatre.

Toledo Opera
425 Jefferson Avenue, Suite 415
Toledo, Ohio 43604
419-255-7464
www.toledo-opera.com

Toledo Opera, founded in 1959, offers three operas during its winter season and a festive Valentine¹s Day gala. In 2003 it was adding Christmas performances of *Amahl and the Night Visitors*. The opera hires professional singers for important roles, uses a volunteer chorus of local people, and members of the Toledo Symphony are in the pit. Except for the gala, which is in the Peristyle at the Toledo Museum of Art, performances are in the newly renovated Valentine Theatre—which is all but a new house because so little of the original theater remained.

The daughter of a Portsmouth steelworker, Kathleen Battle began her career in a church choir, going on to the University of Cincinnati and a 1977 debut in The Marriage of Figaro with the New York City Opera. Her pure soprano made her one of the most acclaimed singers of her time, with a repertoire ranging from opera, Baroque and sacred music, to jazz and spirituals.

Music venues

Blossom Music Center
1145 West Steels Corners Road
Cuyahoga Falls, Ohio 44223
330-945-9400
www.hob.com/venues/concerts/blossom/
www.cris.com/~jadato/blossom.htm

This is the architectural award-winning summer home of Cleveland Orchestra, which also hosts industry standard concerts in rock, pop, jazz, country and folk music. Located on 800 acres of rolling hills adjacent to the Cuyahoga Valley National Recreation Area, the heart of Blossom is the Blossom Pavilion, situated at the base of a natural bowl and acclaimed for both its distinctive architecture and its acoustical qualities. The pavilion seats 5,500 while another 13,500 people can be accommodated on the expansive hillside lawn seating area.

Cincinnati Chamber Music Society
PO Box 8403
Cincinnati, Ohio 44208
513-533-0451
www.cincychamber.org/index2.html

Presents chamber music concerts by nationally and internationally known ensembles at the Cincinnati Art Museum. October-April.

Columbus Chamber Music Society
PO Box 14445
Columbus, Ohio 43214
614-267-2267
www.columbuschambermusic.org

A volunteer organization which presents six world-class chamber music concerts each season on Capital University Campus. The CCMS celebrated its 50th season in 1997 and was begun in 1948 by James Cain, a 17-year-old West High School grad preparing to enter OSU, who recruited the Walden Quartet for its initial season.

Early Music in Columbus
2199 East Main Street
Columbus, Ohio 43209
614-861-4569
www.capital.edu/acad/cons/erly/earlymusic.html

Showcases soloists and ensembles of international repute performing music from the middle ages, renaissance and baroque periods on Capital University campus. September-May

Monday Musical Club
1000 Fifth Avenue, Suite 3
Youngstown, Ohio 44504
330-743-2717
www.mondaymusical.com/

Sponsors musical performances in historic Stambaugh Auditorium, including annual series of five pops concerts. September-May

Music & Performing Arts at Trinity Cathedral
2230 Euclid Avenue
Cleveland, Ohio 44115
216-579-9745
www.mandpa.org

Free noontime concerts of orchestra and chamber music, solo recitals and jazz.

Music in the Air
594 Franklin Avenue
Columbus, Ohio 43215
614-645-7995
www.musicintheair.org/

Free outdoor concerts in several locations. Presents festivals of Jazz, blues, zydeco, and world music along with dance, poetry, theatre and children's programs.

Oberlin Conservatory of Music
77 W. College Street
Oberlin, Ohio 44074-1588
440-775-8200
http://www.oberlin.edu/con/

Presents Artist Recital Series in acoustically renowned Finney Chapel and opera series in Hall Auditorium. September-May.

Sandusky Concert Association
107 Columbus Avenue
Sandusky, Ohio 44870
419-626-1950
877-378-2150
www.state-theatre.com/schedule2.htm

Presents classical music, dance and opera at State Theatre, which in its various incaarnations has been community gathering place for the Firelands region for nearly three-quarters of a century.

DAYTON'S SCHUSTER: GOING UPTOWN DOWNTOWN

The Benjamin and Marian Schuster Performing Arts Center, considered the linchpin in Dayton's downtown development, is Ohio's newest and most ambitious theatre construction—a $121.5 million, 2,300-seat auditorium in a Cesar Pelli-designed complex that covers most of a downtown block. While its theater is the new home of the Dayton Philharmonic, Dayton Opera, and Dayton Ballet, it is not only an arts forum but gathering place, restaurant, and luxury dwelling. Downtown advocates hope it will bring suburbanites back into the old city center.

When the Dayton Philharmonic Orchestra inaugurated its new home in March of 2003, the question was whether the sound in Mead Theatre would live up to its $121 million cost. Janelle Gelfand, the tough-minded Cincinnati critic, rendered the verdict immediately after the

Beethoven, Mendelssohn, and Stravinsky concert: "One of the most stunning acoustical spaces in Ohio" she said, "perhaps in the nation."

The stage can expand or contract to allow for opera or Broadway musical pit orchestra, symphony, or chamber orchestra, and on opening night, it extended 25 feet into the hall, giving the performance an intimacy even for a sold-out crowd of 2,155. A special feature is one of the most breathtaking views in Dayton—the blue domed ceiling, with concentric circles of fiber-optic lights depicting the constellations on the night of the first Wright Brothers flight 100 years ago. The orchestra played beneath an undulating acoustical canopy, surrounded by gently curved walls—similar to the treatment in Cleveland's newly renovated Severance Hall, designed by the same Norwalk, Conn., firm, Jaffe Holden Acoustics Inc.

The sound, Ms. Gelfand said, compared favorably with some of the best halls in the world.

Perhaps the most spectacular feature of the complex is the soaring Wintergarden, a seven-story, block-long, wrap-around glass lobby, its plaza containing 30-foot palms where patrons may have lunch or watch daytime performances on a public stage or have coffee before a concert. Adjacent is Performance Place, an 18-story office-and-luxury condominium tower, complete with upscale restaurant.

The Schuster is the center of Dayton's new entertainment district, one Main Street block that now contains five theatres, including the splendid old 19th century 1,141-seat Victoria Theatre and the 219-seat Loft Theatre.

Stephen Foster, working as an accountant near the Cincinnati docks and influenced by the city's cultural and racial tensions, writes "Oh! Susanna." It becomes *world's first bigtime popular hit song*, selling unheard-of 100,000 copies of sheet music and spurring Foster to turn his back on accounting. He becomes first fulltime professional pop music composer, dies alcoholic at 37, leaving behind a cautionary tale for aspiring songwriters (or, possibly, accountants) and a shabby leather purse holding 38 cents.

1847

Dr. Brewster Higley VI, having departed Meigs County, Ohio, for the Great Plains, writes "Home on the Range," later adopted by Roy Rogers, another Ohio cowpoke, as *"the national cowboy anthem."*

1872

Spurred by friend who bet him a barrel of apples, prolific Ohio inventor Thomas Edison sings "Mary Had a Little Lamb" into his new phonograph and makes *world's first record*.

1877

Cincinnatian Mamie Smith, a professional when she was 10, records "That Thing Called Love" and becomes *first African-American to record the blues*. Her "Crazy Blues" sold more than a million copies, began the jazz and blues revolution of the 1920s, and created a new marketing category called "race records."

1920

Frankie Yankovic records million-selling accordion songs "Just Because" and "Blue Skirt Waltz" by combining melodies from his native Slovenia with pop American beats. He remakes *Cleveland as polka capital of the world*.

1948

Alan Freed's Moondog Coronation Ball in Cleveland ends in riot after thousands of fans crash soldout show; becomes legendary as *the world's first rock concert*. Freed is credited with popularizing old blues euphemism for sex—"rock 'n' roll"—by applying it to "race music," as well as being the first major radio jockey to program black music for a white audience.

1952

James Brown (that dynamic showbusiness personality) records "Please Please Please" at King Records, a little Cincinnati recording independent that sat atop the early R&B charts and *inspires rock and roll's first generation of performers*. King becomes the first of the post-war record labels to seriously mix white and black music (as well as the performers), pioneered the country music house-band system known as "the Nashville sound," and recorded some of the best-known popular songs of the last half century.

1955

The Isley Brothers' song "Shout," becomes top hit and *rock classic*, its integration of gospel rhythm and pop lyrics causing instant sensation. Cincinnati's Isleys, who began their career singing in Lincoln Heights churches, have hit songs in each decade for rest of the century, an unprecedented feat.

1959

Cleveland's Henry Mancini, son of a flute-playing Cleveland steelworker, writes "Moon River," called one of most beautiful songs ever written for films. Composed for *Breakfast at Tiffany's*, the song and score wins Mancini the first two of his four Oscars as he becomes *most successful film composer of his time*. He made 85 albums, received 70 Grammy nominations (winning 20), 7 gold records, and his music was heard in nearly 250 movies.

1961

---

www. *acs.ohio-state. edu/download/ sloopy.html*

For the hardcore Scarlet & Gray, here's a download of *Hang on Sloopy*, by none other than TBDBITL. As added bonus, go to www.jacquedee63. com/sloopy.html for the lyrics and a brief on Ms. Sloop of Steubenville, who supposedly inspired TWDT (the whole damn thing).

1965 "Hang on Sloopy," by a Dayton group called The McCoys, reaches number one on charts, is adopted by the Ohio State marching band, and becomes twenty years later *the official rock song of the state of Ohio*. "It is to rock 'n' roll what Velveeta is to cheese," said one writer. Nonetheless, it is still sung during time-outs during OSU games.

1970s Cleveland punk quintet, the Dead Boys, release punk anthems such as "I Need Lunch" and "Son of Sam", roost at *forefront of Punk scene*, and perform behind chicken wire to deflect thrown bottles. Their classic: *Young, Loud and Snotty*. Said Dead Boys guitarist, Jimmy Zero: "We were ugly, we were mentally ill, we were [expletive]."

1971 Cincinnatian Bruce Iglauer records Hound Dog Taylor and the HouseRockers in Chicago, introducing tiny independent Alligator Records into an industry vacuum that had no exclusive blues labels. Alligator becomes *"the 800-pound gorilla of the blues recording industry."* Said Iglauer upon his company's 30th anniversary: "I'm proud that I'm the tallest of the midgets among the blues midgets."

1971 James Levine, a former child prodigy from Cincinnati who debuted with the Cincinnati Symphony at age 10, becomes conductor of the New York's Metropolitan Opera. He has made more than 150 recordings, won eight Grammys, and done nearly 2,000 performances of 75 different operas. In leading the Met to its unparalleled achievement, he *single-handedly increased the popularity of opera.*

1987 Marilyn Manson, a.k.a. Brian Warner, graduates from Canton's Glen-Oak High School after beginning musical career in the percussion section of the school band and does post-graduate work as *America's foremost advocate for teenage misfits* with songs such as "Fundamentally Loathesome."

1987 Director Paul Schrader *evokes Ohio rust belt* with *Light of Day*, a film about a dysfunctional Cleveland family, featuring Gena Rowlands as Christian mother trying to come to terms with her rock 'n roll spawn, Michael J. Fox and Joan Jett. Fox is near believable as the leader of Cleveland band, the Barbusters, but Joan Jett (in her film debut) carries the celluloid weight with her gritty leather-jacket music and attitude. Film features one of the best arguments for never being in a band: a tour, the highlights of which are Mansfield and Akron. "We know the magic words!" yells Jett at some point. "Rock and roll! Party! CLEVELAND!"

2002 "It Had to Be You", by Coalton native Isham Jones and Gus Kahn, is named *one of the most popular love songs of the 20th century* by the American Society of Composers, Authors, and Publishers (ASCAP).

2002 *Dr. Rock returns home, a half-century after the fact:* Alan Freed's ashes return to Cleveland in a brass urn, delivered in 2002 to the Rock and Roll Hall of Fame by the family.

OhioDance is the statewide service organization for dance and movement arts. Includes information about workshops, performances, rehearsal spaces, benefits of membership, and reliable links to organizations such as Ohio companies and schools of dance, Ohio college and university dance programs, and other arts links. Strong focus on traditional dancing such as ballet, but for the very adventurous, follow the link to Kai Kweol, the Caribbean Music and Dance website.

Short North Performing Arts Association
PO Box 8414
Columbus, Ohio 43201
614-228-6224
www.snpaa.org

Sponsors a chamber music series at Elevator Brewery and a Short North Folk Sampler series at Little Brothers. Winterseason.

Six String Concerts
PO Box 9330
Columbus, Ohio 43209
614-470-FOLK
www.sixstring.org

Promotes local, regional and national concerts in the Columbus area.

Xavier University Piano and Guitar Series
3800 Victory Parkway
Cincinnati, Ohio 45207-5144
513-745-3161

Presents the best established and young artists in an intimate theatre that seats 396. September-April.

Dance

Dayton Contemporary Dance

BalletMet
322 Mount Vernon Avenue
Columbus, Ohio 43215
614-229-4860
www.balletmet.org

With 27 dancers and annual audiences totaling 150,000, Columbus's BalletMet grew up in the 1990s to become one of the country's 15 largest professional companies. Performances include a range of dance from 19th century classics to world premieres. The company also has the support of its Dance Academy, which ranks among the nation's five largest professional dance training centers.

Canton Ballet
Cultural Center for the Arts
1001 North Market Avenue
Canton, Ohio 44702
330-455-7220
www.cantonballet.com

This pre-professional training company performs three programs a year with professional guest artists at Canton's Palace Theatre.

Cincinnati Ballet
1555 Central Parkway
Cincinnati, Ohio 45214
513-621-5219
www.cincinnatiballet.com

Cincinnati Ballet is a classically based professional company of 30 dancers. Every season they do six performances of classical and contemporary works, with major attractions like the Nutcracker at Cincinnati Music Hall and others at the Aronoff Center. The ballet also has a school, the Otto M. Budig Academy.

Dayton Ballet
140 North Main Street
Dayton, Ohio 45402
937-449-5060
888-228-3630
www.daytonballet.org

Founded in 1937, the Dayton Ballet is the nation's second-oldest professional company. Its 19 dancers present five programs a year, including three full-length story ballets and two of short works. The company commissions young American choreographers for one story ballet every other year, and for two short dances each season. There is also a school and a pre-professional company, Dayton Ballet II.

Dayton Contemporary Dance Company
126 North Main Street, Suite 240
Dayton, Ohio 45402
937-228-3232
www.dcdc.org

Dayton proves its mettle in dance with two full-fledged dance companies. Ohio's oldest modern and contemporary company, Dayton Contemporary Dance Company has 14 professional dancers performing modern classics by world renowned choreographers. It also owns the largest collection anywhere of classic dances by African American choreographers.

Ohio Ballet
354 East Market Street
Akron, Ohio 44325
330-972-7900
www.ohioballet.org

A professional dance company with 12 dancers, Ohio Ballet performs regularly at E.J. Thomas Hall in Akron and the Ohio Theatre in Cleveland, and presents free outdoor summer programs seen by 12,000 people in Northeast Ohio.

Toledo Ballet Association
5001 Monroe Street
Toledo, Ohio 43623
419-471-0049
www.toledoballet.net

Toledo Ballet is a school and preprofessional company performing three programs a year with visiting professional dancers.

Zivili
1753 Loudon Street
Granville, Ohio 43023
740-587-7715
877-906-8314
www.zivili.org

Zivili is the world's only professional company specializing in Southern Slavic dance, music and costume from the countries of the former Yugoslavia. Performances are in the summer.

Theatres

Actors' Theatre
1000 City Park Ave.
Columbus, Ohio 43206
614-444-6888
www.theactorstheatre.org

A free outdoor theatre in historic German Village. Presents Shakespearean productions in June and August and a classic American musical in July.

Amil Tellers of Dramatics
991 North Shore Drive
Lima, Ohio 45801
419-223-8866
800-944-1441
www.amiltellers.org/Theatre/

A volunteer theatre company, members present six productions at the Encore Theatre, with six special productions just for children.

Becky Thatcher Showboat
237 Front Street
Marietta, Ohio 45750
740-373-6033
www.marietta-ohio.com/beckythatcher/
Professional productions of showboat-era entertainment aboard the historic sternwheeler Becky Thatcher. Summer, Fall.

Cincinnati Playhouse in The Park
962 Mt. Adams Circle
PO Box 6537
Cincinnati, Ohio 45202
513-421-3888
www.cincyplay.com/

Professional resident theatre offers 11 productions yearly of established dramas, comedies and musicals as well as new works.

Cleveland Play House
8500 Euclid Avenue
Cleveland, Ohio 44106
216-795-7000
800-278-1CPH
http://www.clevelandplayhouse.com/

America's longest running regional theatre company presents original productions of plays and musicals, with emphasis on new American work.

Cleveland Public Theatre
6415 Detroit Avenue
Cleveland, Ohio 44102
216-631-2727
www.cptonline.org

Cleveland Public Theatre is an alternative performance company with a priority commitment to help develop original theatre artists from the area—particularly those whose work is experimental in form and/or challenging in content.
A venue for experimental & political performance, dance, music, poetry, and performance art as well as theatre. September-July

Cleveland Signstage Theatre
8500 Euclid Avenue
Cleveland, OH 44106-0819
216-229-2838
www.oac.state.oh.us/aie/artistsdirectory/
adtht_signstage.html

The only professional theatre in Ohio that employs both deaf and hearing actors and the only resident deaf theatre in the United States. Using American Sign Language, they adapt productions to reflect the deaf community's perspective.

Columbus Children's Theatre
512 North Park Street
Columbus, Ohio 43215
614-224-6672
www.colschildrenstheatre.org/

Theatre activities for youths of all ages, backgrounds and cultural heritages. June-May

Contemporary American Theatre Company
77 South High Street
Columbus, Ohio 43215
614-461-0010
www.catco.org

A professional resident theatre company which offers a diverse range of plays with an emphasis on new and contemporary American plays.

Dobama Theatre
1846 Coventry Road
Cleveland Heights, Ohio 44118
216-932-3396
www.dobama.org/

Challenges audiences with contemporary plays that entertain while they confront social and political issues. Encourages new playwrights. September-June.

Ensemble Theatre of Cincinnati
1127 Vine Street
Cincinnati, Ohio 45210
513-421-3555
www.cincyetc.com/

Cincinnati's only professional resident theatre develops and produces new works with emphasis on Cincinnati and Ohio artists. September-July

Senior Repertory of Ohio Theater Company
51 Jefferson Avenue
Columbus, Ohio 43215
614-228- 7458
www.glt-theatre.org/

Older actors create and perform theatre that illuminates issues of aging and speaks to audiences of all ages with vision, humor, and lasting impact. September-June

Mad River Theater Works
PO. Box 248
West Liberty, Ohio 43357
937-465-6751
www.madrivertheater.org/

The professional repertory company creates and presents plays that communicate regional ways of life and community concerns.

Mansfield Playhouse
95 East Third Street
Mansfield, Ohio 44902
419-522-2883
www.mansfieldplayhouse.com

Community and guest artists with professional director present six main stage, two second stage and a children's production each year. September-June

Paul W. Cassidy Theatre
6200 Pearl Road
Parma Heights, Ohio 44130
440-842-4600
www.cassidytheatre.freehosting.net/

A semi-professional community theatre offers mainstage and cafe-style productions, usually Broadway hits. September-June

Players Guild of Canton
1001 North Market Avenue
Canton, Ohio 44702
330-453-7619
www.cantonplayersguild.com/

One of the nation's largest non-professional theatres, in its 63rd season, performs new and classic works from the world's dramatic literature. September-June

Reality Theatre
775 N. High Street
Columbus, Ohio 43215
614-265-7337
www.realitytheatre.com/

This professional theatre company presents off-Broadway plays that deal with gay and lesbian issues.

Toledo Repertoire Theatre
1717 Adams St.
Toledo, Ohio 43624
419-243-9277
www.toledorep.org/home.htm

Presents mainstage performances at Tenth Street Theatre in downtown Toledo and Franciscan Life Center in Sylvania.

Youngstown Playhouse
600 Playhouse Lane
Youngstown, Ohio 44511
330-782-3402

Community theatre offers six main stage, four youth and several cabaret productions each year. September-June.

Community arts centers

Columbus Cultural Arts Center
139 West Main Street
Columbus, Ohio 43215
614-645-7047

Municipal facility gives adults, children and families opportunities to experience the arts through workshops, lectures, demonstrations, performances and exhibits.

Cultural Center for the Arts
1001 Market Avenue North
Canton, Ohio 44702
330-452-4096
www.cantonculturalcenter.org

Presents Funfest, Family Arts Festival, educational and outreach programs.

Mansfield Art Center
700 Marion Avenue
Mansfield, Ohio 44906
419-756-1700
www.mansfieldartcenter.com

Displays invitational exhibits; art school.

Pump House Center for the Arts
Enderlin Circle, PO Box 1613
Yoctangee Park
Chillicothe, Ohio 45601
740-775-3956
www.bright.net/~pumpart/

An art gallery and cultural center in a restored historic water pumping station featuring local artists.

Rosewood Art Centre
2655 Olson Drive
Kettering, Ohio 45420
937-296-0294
www.ci.kettering.oh.us/depts/prca/rosewood/events.shtml

Multi-disciplinary facility with performance theatre, contemporary art gallery and studios.

Wassenberg Art Center
643 South Washington Street
Van Wert, Ohio 45891
419-238-6837
www.vanwert.com/wassenberg

Displays works by local artists as well as traveling exhibits. Home of art, camera and wood carvers clubs.

Akron Recreation Bureau
1420 Triplett Boulevard
Akron, Ohio 44306
330-375-2804
www.ci.akron.oh.us/rec.html

Offers free music and dance performances for area residents. Sponsors arts and crafts programs, and a yearly Arts Expo in Hardesty Park.

Aronoff Center for the Arts
650 Walnut Street
Cincinnati, Ohio 45202-2517
513-721-3344
www.cincinnatiarts.org/venues/aronoff/

Cesar Pelli-designed, state-of-the-art facility for ballet, opera, theatre, contemporary dance, events and series. Three performance spaces, including Procter & Gamble Hall, which seats 2,719, and has a ceiling studded with 3,000 fiber optic lenses that create a starlight effect.

Ashtabula Arts Center
2928 West 13th Street
Ashtabula, Ohio 44004
440-964-3396
www.ashartscenter.org

Home of Straw Hat Theatre, GB Community Theatre, and a host of other drama, dance and music performances.

The Guggenheim in 1998 had major retrospective on Cincinnatian Jim Dine, attendee of Walnut Hills High and the Art Academy. His subject matter, it was said—hammers, axes, tools—were objects from his family's hardware store...

Beck Center for the Cultural Arts
17801 Detroit Avenue
Lakewood, Ohio 44107
216-521-2540
www.lkwdpl.org/beck/index.html

Visual and performing arts center offers community theatre, galleria, artists' collective, education departments, children's theatre and outreach programs.

Cain Park
40 Severance Circle
Cleveland Heights, Ohio 44118
216-371-3000
www.cainpark.com

This legendary summer theater program built in the middle of a residential neighborhood in the middle of the Depression has been consistently ranked among the top festivals in the country, and is said to be the only municipally owned and operated outdoor theatre of its kind in the United States. A kind of *uber*-park, it is at once an outdoor covered theater and art gallery, with a nationally-recognized arts festival, professional dance, childrens' programming, and concerts featuring both local and national performers. All this is surrounded by over 20 acres of bike-and-jogging paths, tennis courts, wading pool and picnic grounds, and skate park.

Cityfolk
126 North Main Street, Suite 220
Dayton, Ohio 45402
937-223-3655
www.cityfolk.org

Cityfolk, Ohio's only full-time, professional presenter of traditional and ethnic performing arts, began as a neighborhood event and grew itself into a national-class concert season and festival of musical diversity, featuring everything from jazz, Appalachian bluegrass, and Celtic music to African drumming and Greek dance. It features educational workshops, dance parties, cultural partnerships, and its top-quality performers and artists from throughout the U.S., allows it to draw increasingly from outside the Miami Valley.

JULY 5 & 6, 2003

Clark State Performing Arts Center
Springfield, Ohio 45501
937-328-3874
www.clark.cc.oh.us/pac

Hosts Clark State Community Performances as well as six area residential performing groups.

Cleveland Cinematheque
11141 East Boulevard
University Circle
Cleveland, Ohio 44106
216-421-7450
www.cia.eda/campuslife/cinematheque/default.asp

Located at the Cleveland Institute of Art, this commandeered classroom at the Cleveland Institute of Art presents as many as 200 films a year from all eras and countries, ranging from revival classics to the blatantly obscure. "What doesn't play here?" asked one reviewer. "The Cinematheque hosts short-subject collections, animation festivals, cutting-edge indies, underground efforts, and foreign titles that have to be shaken out of private collections or an embassy somewhere." Tradeoff for those spoiled by the amenities of new-age suburban theaters is the Cinematheque's striving for top-quality, widescreen purist prints.

Columbus Association for the Performing Arts
55 East State Street
Columbus, Ohio 43215
614-469-0939
www.capa.com/ohio/

Operates the Ohio, Southern, and Palace Theatres, manages Capitol Theater in the Riffe Center. Presents touring arts and entertainment including classical, folk, jazz, comedy, pop, children's concerts and classic films.

DanceCleveland
1148 Euclid Avenue, Suite 311
Cleveland, Ohio 44115
216-861-2213
www.dancecleveland.org

Founded in 1956, DanceCleveland presents contemporary dance programs in Northeast Ohio.

E. J. Thomas Performing Arts Center
198 Hill Street (at University Avenue)
Akron, Ohio 44325-0501
330-972-7595
http://destinationdowntownakron.com

Presents dance, music and theatre by international artists. Home for Akron Symphony and Ohio Ballet. September-May

Franciscan Center of Lourdes College
6832 Convent Boulevard
Sylvania, Ohio 43560
419-824-3975
www.franciscancenter.org

Presents a season of music and theatre, summer theatre arts camp. September-May

Freed Center for Performing Arts
Ohio Northern University
525 S. Main St.
Ada, Ohio 45810
419-772-2000
www.freedcenter.com/archive0102

Offers musical and dramas, lecture series and music series. September-July

Great Lakes Theater Festival
1501 Euclid Avenue
Cleveland, Ohio 44115
216-241-5490
www.greatlakestheater.org

Professional repertory company concentrates on Shakespeare, Shaw, Moliere, Chekov, Ibsen and the Greek dramatists, and modern classics. September-May.

Lakeside Association
236 Walnut Avenue
Lakeside, Ohio 43440
419-798-4461
www.lakesideohio.com

Traditional Chautaqua assembly with cultural programs in 3,000-seat auditorium. Operates for ten weeks each summer in historic enclave on Lake Erie. June-September.

Lorain Palace Civic Center
617 Broadway
Lorain, Ohio 44052
440-245-2323
800-889-4842
www.lorainpalace.org/

Civic center presents arts and theatre events, educational programs.

Miami University Performing Arts Series
102 Hall Auditorium
Oxford, Ohio 45056
513-529-6333
www.fna.muohio.edu/pas

Presents high quality musical, dance and ballet performances in subscription series at Millet Auditorium and Hall Auditorium. September-April.

Palace Cultural Arts Association
276 West Center Street
Marion, Ohio 43302
740-383-2101
www.marionpalace.org

Presents theatre, dance, music and film in restored historic movie theatre.

Playhouse Square Foundation
1501 Euclid Avenue
Cleveland, Ohio 44115
216-771-4444
www.playhousesquare.com

Five elegantly restored historic theatres present original musical productions and popular entertainment.

Renaissance Theatre
138 Park Avenue West
Mansfield, Ohio 44902
419-525-4884
www.rparts.org

Historic baroque movie palace serves as center for community cultural activities and touring shows.

Vern Riffe Center for the Arts
Shawnee State University
940 Second Street
Portsmouth, Ohio 45662
740-351-3600
www.vrcfa.org

$16 million theatre hosts music and plays.

**In 1965, tall, long-legged, fine-boned Cincinnatian Suzanne Farrell becomes star in Balanchine's <u>Don Quixote</u>...the role of Dulcinea, the Don's dream girl...Dulcinea, of course, is only what the Don wants her to be at any particular moment, and it gave Farrell the chance to appear as the Virgin Mary, a servant girl, and a gorgeous apparition...she was plucked out of a Cincinnati dance class by a former Balanchine ballerina, who was out in the hinterlands on a scouting tour, brought to New York as a scholarship pupil, and was dancing solo roles within a year...
<u>Holiday</u>, March, 1969**

Sorg Opera House
PO Box 84
Middletown, Ohio 45042
513-425-0180
www.sorgopera.com

Historic theatre built in 1891. Friends of Sorg
Opera house work with private owner to maintain
facility for live performances. September-May

Southern Ohio Museum and Cultural Center
P.O. Box 990
825 Gallia Street
Portsmouth, Ohio 45662
740-354-5629

Changing exhibits in fine arts and history.
Performing arts events, films and lectures.

Toledo Cultural Arts Center
and Valentine Theatre
Valentine Box Office, 400 North Superior St.,
Toledo, Ohio 43604
419-242-3490
www.valentinetheatre.com

The 900-seat Valentine Theatre is located within
the historic Renaissance Building in downtown
Toledo and serves as the home for Toledo's ballet,
opera and repertory theatre companies.

Victoria Theatre Association
138 N. Main Street
Dayton, Ohio 45402
(937) 228-7591
www.victoriatheatre.com

The Victoria Theatre Association, housed in what
was originally the 1866 Turner Opera House, is
Dayton's premier arts organization. In addition to
a Broadway Series, it offers a summer film series;
children's theatre; and Discovery, classroom
experiences for students and teachers.

Wayne Center for the Arts
237 South Walnut Street
Wooster, Ohio 44691
330-264-2787
www.wayneartscenter.org

Presents chamber music series, traditional arts
festival, dance programs, exhibits, classes and
workshops.

Wexner Center for the Visual Arts
North High Street (at 15th Avenue)
Columbus, Ohio 43210
614-292-3535
www.wexarts.org

Internationally acclaimed for unique architecture.
Features contemporary visual, performance and
media arts.

THE WEXNER: CUTTING EDGE INSIDE AND OUT

www. *wexarts.org*

The official Wexner
Center site is one of
the best arts sites
anywhere, as
befitting this
"spaceship that
crash-landed on the
prairies," as one
critic called the arts
center. Handsome,
fluid site takes one
through the building
of the building, with
panels-within-
panels, current
exhibitions, and an
online bookshop.

Built by Richard Trott of Columbus and Peter Eisenman, the famed architectural theorist
who had actually built only four avant garde houses (which might explain why the great
building began to leak), the Wexner Center for the Visual Arts (1989) quickly became an
architectural *cause célèbre*, certainly in the Ohio capital. Said Eisenman, "It's a great thing about
America that people in Columbus, Ohio, are building this crazy building." The architects
chose a narrow space between the small Weigel Hall and the large Mershon Auditorium,
spread out at the back where a parking lot was, as well as underground. Wrote critic Jane
Ware: "Fractured, abstracted brick towers herald the Wexner Center and recall the Armory on
this site until 1958. But the structure's most striking feature is the white steel scaffolding, an
oversized, multi-story jungle-gym-style scaffolding that forms a long exterior corridor
between the Wexner and Mershon. The path slopes, so the perception of the built lines and
their shadows hold surprises every time. This scaffolded corridor and its adjacent building
are aligned with the campus grid and true north, though that means they are a little askew
from nearby High Street, which diverges from true north by 12.25 degrees. Inside, it was
equally ambitious. Called "one of very few truly
multidisciplinary contemporary arts centers anywhere in
this country," it became OSU's multidisciplinary,
international laboratory for the advancement of
contemporary art, offering a wide range of cutting-
edge exhibitions, film and video screenings, music,
dance, and theater performances, as well as educational
public programs for all ages.

FROM SOUTHWEST

282

The phrase "starving artist" never had more literal meaning than during the Great Depression when the nation's economic malaise forced artists to stand in bread lines beside farmers and laborers. When Franklin Roosevelt's New Deal attempted a cure in the form of public projects, the government became a massive employment agency, putting people to work at not only building all manner of edifices but also decorating them. Post offices, the average citizen's most frequent point of contact with the federal government, were built throughout the land, including the 66 new ones in Ohio, embellished by specially commissioned murals and sculptures.

The federal programs fostered an unexpected kinship among craftsmen, for the artists celebrated the industry, enterprise, and pleasures of the common man with scenes from everyday life. "I don't give a damn about rich people. I don't even hold it against them," declared Columbus painter **Emerson Burkhart**, who did the murals at Ohio State University's School of Social Administration. Almost invariably, the themes of the artists were regional, their heroes working men and women, and their style strong, sinewy, and straightforward. It was indeed American art, and it served to lift the spirits of good people in bad times.

Since most of the new Ohio post offices were built in small towns, agrarian and bucolic settings were popular mural scenes. Thus, the Georgetown Post Office displayed *Tobacco Harvest* by Ohio native

Richard Zoellner; Herschel Levit did *Farm and Mill* in Louisville; **George Picken** created *Maple Sugar Camp* for Chardon; and **Robert Lepper's** *Noble County—Ohio* depicted a farm family in Caldwell. History, however, was the single most popular theme in Ohio's post offices, and a panoply of minor Buckeye epics were preserved in panoramas in places such as Amherst, Youngstown, and Orrville.

New Lexington's post office was graced by the exceptional talents of **Isabel Bishop**, whose works are in London's Victoria and Albert Museum and Paris's Muse Bibliotheque Nationale. But it is the village of New London that can claim the most distinctive post office mural in Ohio, if not the nation. **Lloyd R. Ney's** *New London Facets* was the only abstract art executed in a U.S. Post Office. His technicolor covered wagons, soldiers, and buildings formed a Cubist community mosaic, but because the federal government viewed abstract art with a jaundiced eye in 1940, Ney had to rally the town's support in order to obtain official approval for his work.

Happily, *New London Facets* still survives in the town post office, as do about sixty other of the state's murals and sculptures. They are a testament, of course, to grassroots Ohio, for they were inspired and born—and are now often sustained—by the will of the people. And yet, Ney's abstract still reminds us that this purposeful art was created for the most mundane of public buildings. In the forefront of his mural, he painted stamped letters and a humble box that bears the matter-of-fact message "Parcel Post. Fragile."

Modern mailmen will please take note—ZIP Codes had not yet been invented. ✍

art by mail

Inset is of Robert Lepper, professor of design at Carnegie-Mellon, working on the Caldwell, Ohio, mural in his Pittsburgh studio.

283

14 Cinematic moments in Ohio history

1 Hollywood, via Hicksville

When **Daeida Hartell Wilcox** landscapes the 120-acre Los Angeles fig grove she and her husband subdivided in 1887, a friend from Illinois insisted Daeida name it after the friend's summer home near Chicago: Hollywood. Daeida donates land for parks and city hall, builds the first sidewalks, and kickstarts Tinseltown—perfect counterpoise for a farmer's daughter from Hicksville, Ohio.

2 Sound (and fury)

Ohioan **Thomas Edison** premieres sound film in 1899, described as "a kind of peep show, " and shown in places without soundproofed walls. Because of the awful noise of the projectors, organs, phonographs, and music boxes are used to drown out the noise.

3 Brothers Warner

After **Harry Warner**—Youngstown, Ohio, circa 1900—talks his father into hocking his watch and delivery-wagon horse for a movie projector and print of *The Great Train Robbery*, he and his brothers launch themselves in rented storefronts across Northeast Ohio before moving west and starting their own studio.

4 Vamp

Theda Bara (real name Theodosia Goodman) was a nice Jewish kid from Cincinnati who in the late 'teens becomes Hollywood's first *femme fatale*, her vampire-like sexual persona creating both the term 'vamp,' as well as the movie archetype for seduction.

5 First star

Springfield's **Lillian Gish** begins her 75-year career as Baby Lillian in 1902 touring company production in Rising Sun, Ohio. Called "the first true actress," she was the superstar of the silent film era, collaborating with director D.W. Griffith to invent most of vocabulary of film.

6 Classic-maker

Dudley Nichols, an Irish idealist by way of Wapakoneta, Ohio, goes to Hollywood and hooks up with director John Ford, making 14 movies and one of filmdom's most creative partnerships. Nichols' screenplay for their 1935 film, *The Informer*, won an Oscar, but he turned it down in a battle of principle between the Screen Writers Guild—which Nichols helped found—and the Motion Picture Academy. He co-wrote the classic screwball comedy, *Bringing up Baby*, and in 1939 wrote *Stagecoach*, one of Hollywood's greatest westerns.

7 Mogul

Lewis Wasserman, Glenville High, class of 1930, begins entertainment career as usher in Keith's, the Cleveland movie palace at corner of 105th and Euclid. He goes on to become head of the Music Corporation of America (MCA) where he becomes Hollywood's original power-broker, for over 50 years the most powerful—and feared—man in Tinseltown. "To court Lew Wasserman successfully meant fame, influence, riches," said his biographer. "To cross Lew Wasserman meant the end of your career."

Ladies' man 8

After being rejected at Warner Brothers because Darryl F. Zanuck thought his ears were too big, **Clark Gable**, the son of a Cadiz, Ohio, oil driller, appears bare-chested in *It Happened One Night* (1934), causes panic in undershirt market, and becomes Hollywood's archetypal ladies' man.

He was so perfectly cast as Rhett Butler in *Gone With the Wind* that audiences thought the part had been written just for him, and his name became a household word: "Who do you think you are? Clark Gable?" His secret was his nonchalant American masculinity. "Hell, if I'd jumped on all the dames I'm supposed to have jumped on," he said, "I'd have had no time to go fishing."

Witch 9

Cleveland-born **Margaret Hamilton**, who debuted in 1923 at the Cleveland Playhouse, finds her greatest role as the Wicked Witch of the West in 1939 MGM classic, *The Wizard of Oz*. Her ominous performance as green-faced harridan, said the *New York Times*, "unnerved generations of children." As late as the 1970s, she was still receiving as many as 2,000 letters a year from fans of Hollywood's most famous sorceress.

Champ 10

Bob Hope, a one-time amateur boxer in Cleveland, creates the modern comedic monologue, moving fluidly from vaudeville to movies in an astounding career that covers most of the 20th century. One of the century's great entertainers, he was first multi-media star.

Native daughter, part I 11

Cleveland native **Dorothy Dandridge**, star of *Carmen Jones*, is first black woman nominated for a best actress Oscar. The 1955 trophy goes instead to quintessential white girl, Grace Kelly, for her role in *The Country Girl*. "If I were Betty Grable," Dandridge said, "I could capture the world."

Virgin 12

Doris Day, *née* Doris von Kappelhoff from Cincinnati, is nominated for Best Actress Oscar after her 1959 role as professional virgin in *Pillow Talk*, the first in a series of semi-sophisticated sex comedies in which she defends her virginity against assaults by a procession of Hollywood's leading men, making her four times the top box-office star in America.

Nobody's fool 13

Paul Newman, the son of upper-middle-class Jewish businessman from Shaker Heights, supplants that other Ohioan—Clark Gable—for a new generation's paradigm of male glamour. After a long and intelligent career in films, he finally wins Best Actor Oscar in 1987 for his role in *The Color of Money*. Afterward, he said, with characteristic *savoir faire*, "It's like chasing a beautiful woman for 80 years. Finally she relents, and you say, 'I'm terribly sorry. I'm tired'."

Native daughter, Part II 14

Halle Berry, Bedford High School class of 1984 and a former Miss Ohio, becomes in 2002 first African-American to win Best Actress Oscar, for her role in *Monster's Ball*. Beginning as a model, she wins Emmy for her 2000 HBO film, *Introducing Dorothy Dandridge*, the Clevelander playing, ironically, the Clevelander who *didn't* win the Best Actress Oscar.

Akron Civic Theatre

Akron

Atmospheric designer John Eberson used a Moorish theme for the Civic, his first challenge being the *real* atmosphere—the Ohio Canal running through downtown Akron. To solve that problem, he built the sumptuous Grand Lobby on large cement stilts. Eberson's design for the lobby resembles Charlton Heston's set for *El Cid*—darkly ornate and castle huge, while the auditorium looks like the middle of a Moorish garden. Above it all is a moonlit blue Mediterranean sky with 96 stars and a continuous group of moving white clouds. The "stars" are 10-watt bulbs with a flasher attached, and the "clouds" appear to move because they are cutouts passing through a beam of light. The Civic is one of the finest examples of the "atmospheric" theaters left in this country. *Now Showing: Bookings include concerts, Ballet, opera, proms, weddings, graduations and second-run movies; 2,672 seats. 182 S. Main St.; 330-535-3179, 330-253-2488. www.akroncivic.com*

Beachcliff Theatre

Rocky River

When the suburbia craze first surprised the cities in the 1930s, people who could scrape together a down payment moved out to the boonies, where they demanded fresh air, trees—and *movies*. Rocky River, west of Cleveland, the new Beachcliff subdivision obliged, with an art deco palace of brick and glass tile, plunked down in the midst of the tract houses. *The Plain Dealer* marveled at the size of the parking lot and the rain-or-shine marquee, lighted with the first weatherized neon in Greater Cleveland. The Beachcliff opened in 1937, with *Sing and Be Happy* with Tony Martin, and closed 39 years later with Mel Brooks' *Blazing Saddles*. But the theater was not empty long. Developers began a high-class adaptation, and the movie house reopened as Beachcliff Market Square, a specialty retail center. Suburbanites *still* love to shop. *Now Showing: Specialty shops. Beachcliff Market Square 19300 Detroit Rd.*

Canton Palace

Canton

Canton businessman Harry Ink made a fortune in sore-throat remedies and used his wealth to build one of the finest movie palaces of the 1920s. Architect John Eberson contrived this one to resemble a Spanish hillside garden on a summer night—complete with his trademark illusion of moving clouds and starry skies (96 stars lining up in perfect constellation). When Eberson couldn't find the craftsmen that suited him, he formed his own company—the Michael Angelo Studio—to do the tile and plaster work. Somewhere among the geegaws, there is a plaster giraffe, the trademark of Harry Ink's best selling product, Tonsiline, the elixir that paid for all this splendor. *Now Showing: Impeccably restored, the Palace is home to over 300 events each year. 605 Market Ave. North; 330-454-8172; http://thepalace.ezo.net/*

Bowling Green   **Cla-zel**

A banker from nearby Cygnet liked movies so much he built
lavish showcases in small towns in northwest Ohio. One, he
named the Cla-Zel, for Clark and Hazel Young, who operated
it. There were two other movies in Bowling Green, but none
could match the Cla-Zel for opulence: solid cherry doors
liberally carved, opening into a marble foyer and a high
Victorian lobby with cranberry carpeting, brass rails and ornate
plaster carvings. Above the stage, a plaster basket still overflows
with roses. The Cla-Zel put on the first talkies in 1929,
outshining the competition. The two other theaters have
long-since closed, but the Cla-Zel looks better than ever. The
newly renovate marquee flashes the name in script—red,
yellow and green—an enticing sight: people who want
elegance with their movies heed the invitation. *Now Showing:
First-run movies, numerous live shows and community events;
127 N. Main Street; www.cla-zel.com*

Marietta   **Colony Theatre**

The Colony's existence dates to 1911 when it was the old
Hippodrome vaudeville house, reopening in 1919 in a new
building as the *new* Hippodrome—with 1,200 seats, a cold-
water cooling system, a 50-foot fly loft, and room for the
chorus girls. It got sound in the initial year of the Great
Depression, officially became The Colony after a 1949
renovation, and in 1957 hosted the world premiere of *Battle
Hymn*, starring Rock Hudson as Marietta native Colonel Dean
Hess (a minister who flew 250 combat missions in Korea then
returned to build an orphanage). Hard cinematic times fell
after the mid-1970s, the theatre changed hands several times,
closing in 1985. The Hippodrome/Colony Historical Theatre
Association, a group of perseverant locals, secured in 2003
$300,000 from Senator Mike DeWine and the Save America's
Treasures program of the National Park Service, to be used
for restoration of the theatre. With the grant and contem-
plated tax credits, the group will have acquired approximately
$1 million dollars toward their campaign goal of $4.5 million.
*Now showing: Long run. The remaining funding necessary to renovate.
To help, contact the Hippodrome/Colony Historical Theatre Association, P.O. Box 1114 Marietta, OH 45750; info@colonytheatre.com*

Cincinnati   **Emery Theatre**

Philanthropist Mary Emery built her theater-style concert hall
in 1911 to house the Cincinnati Symphony Orchestra. After
the inaugural concert, the hall was pronounced acoustically
superb. Though the Symphony moved to Music Hall in 1936,
many people still feel the Emery is the best place in the city to
hear music. Bookings became scarce in the Fifties and the
Sixties, so in 1973 members of the local American Theatre
Organ Society asked the University of Cincinnati (beneficiary
of Mrs. Emery's estate) if they could install the "Mighty
Wurlitzer" organ in the Emery, since its home, the Albee
Theater, was doomed. In 1978, the Emery's weekend movies

Contributors:

Juliann Fleenor,

Lyn Goodwin, Sue

Gorisek, Marcy

Hawley, Pat

Jenkins, Linda

Queenan, and

Jane Ware

featured organ concerts before the show and at intermissions. It had a staff of 13 organists who took turns filling the cavernous theater and its cantilevered balconies with the power of nearly 2,000 pipes. The theatre is closed, but the contiguous old OMI-College of Applied Science Building has been renovated into 59 apartments, and in the future, the apartments will contribute $50,000 to the theater. *Now Showing: The few remaining apartments, and the forlorn hopes of 13 out-of-work organists. 1112 Walnut Street; www.emerycenter.com*

drawing by Frank Elmer

Holland Theatre   *Bellefontaine*

The 57-year-old Holland enjoyed four-and-a-half decades of architectural grandeur before its 1,400-seat viewing space was divided into five small screens. It was the only atmospheric theater in Ohio with a Dutch theme, and inspiration of mysterious origin. Today, some of the original architecture, like the windmills and royal lions, can be seen around screens 1, 2 and 3. In December, 1999, the Logan County Landmark Preservation, Inc., Save the Holland Theatre Project, received title with the intent to restore and renovate the theatre. *Now showing: Fundraising and tuckpointing. 127 E. Columbus Avenue; www.hollandtheatre.com*

Lorain Palace Civic Center   *Lorain*

When the State Theater was destroyed in Lorain's killer tornado, the balcony collapsed with crushing effect, trapping moviegoers under tons of debris. So, when the Warner Brothers built the Palace four years later, they made it "tornado-proof" and all on one floor, since people were nervous about balconies. It's still the largest one-floor theater of its type in the state. The size overwhelms: the two-story Venetian Gothic lobby, with a fireplace at each end; the nearly full-acre auditorium with its broad proscenium arch decorated by floral designs in a sunburst pattern; the three-quarter-ton crystal chandelier. On opening night, people heard the Vitaphone talkies for the first time in Lorain, and agreed with the sentiments on the program: it was indeed a "Temple of Amusement." *Now Showing: $1.50 movies on the largest screen in Lorain County; live stage shows; youth and community theatre. 800-889-2323; 440-245-2323; www.lorainpalace.org.*

Majestic Theatre   *Chillicothe*

A newspaper tells how Chillicothe's first "show" came about in the summer of 1806 when "a creaking vehicle, loaded with a large store box tied down with ropes" rolled into town. "The elongated, bewhiskered driver holding the reins of his bony horse" asked a tavern-keeper where he could display "the most terrible man-eating lion in captivity." Entertainment thus evolved through traveling shows, storerooms and taverns into the Masons' lodge hall in 1853. The fraternity paid a New York decorator $1,000 to paint a magnificent ceiling, then found themselves without funds to buy opera chairs. The place was

sold, remodeled and renamed the Majestic in 1915, featuring stock companies, vaudeville and, finally, motion pictures. In 1971, it was bought and restored by Harley Bennett. The richness and grandeur remain, with the lovely curved balcony and the highly ornate proscenium arch. *Now Showing: Community events, live performances, weddings. The Legacy Project of 2003—the theatre's 150th anniversary—continues theatre restoration. 45 E. Second St. 740-772-2041; www.majestic-arch.com*

Columbus

Ohio Theatre

In making Columbus' Ohio Theatre "a palace of the average man," Architect Thomas Lamb used damask and brocade wall panels, rose medallions, stars, gold leaf and flying horses on the chandelier. Furthermore, when it opened in 1928, the $865,000 structure had $1 million worth of trimmings—African animal skins on the walls, a grand player piano and live parrots. After 41 years of movies, vaudeville and OSU pep rallies, audiences waned, and an office tower was proposed for the site. Saving the theater turned out to be a matter of money ($1.8 million to buy it). The finished $2.76 million restoration draws hundreds of people every month just for tours and the Ohio has inspired theater restoration groups all over America. *Now Showing: The Columbus Symphony; Ballet Met; visiting performers, classic films. 29-39 E. State St.; 614-358-2222; www.capa.com/venues/ohio.html*

Columbus   **Palace Theatre**

Phil Sheridan is well suited to be manager of Columbus' Palace Theatre. He knows that the Palace opened in 1926 with the movie *Campus Flirt*, that in the late Twenties George Burns and Gracie Allen appeared in *Lambchops* and that in 1933 Ethel Barrymore scolded an audience for inattentiveness. Secondly, Sheridan has frequented the Palace since the Forties, when he found it a better option than North High School. Playing hooky, he heard the big bands and watched the famous striptease acts, including Gypsy Rose Lee. "She was a big disappointment," he says. "When she finished, she still had more on than many women on the street." After the theater languished in the late Seventies, owner Katherine LeVeque launched a $3 million renovation. *Now Showing: Opera/Columbus; touring Broadway shows; The Jazz Arts Group, The Broadway Series, and CAPA-sponsored shows. 34 W. Broad St.; 614-358-2222; www.capa.com/venues/palace.html*

Marion   **Palace Theatre**

After crowds thronged the Palace Theatre opening in August of 1928, a Star reporter wrote, "for 'lo these many years Marion has been reading about the wondrous opening nights of New York. But until last night, the city had no actual taste of the bliss of stepping on the other fellow's feet." An "atmospheric," the theater features an old Spanish skyline ornamented with classical nude statues; the dark-blue ceiling becomes a night sky with twinkling stars. The Palace owns a cloud machine, too, but Maintenance Superintendent Jim Obenour (a third-generation

employee) said it runs too fast. "It looks like a storm bearing down." Obenour grew up on stories about the live elephants in *Aida* years ago and the five tons of dirt delivered for Tobacco Road. Manager Jack Telfer said restoration of the 1,430 seat theater began in the mid-1970s and cost almost $1 million. *Now Showing: Local and visiting performing arts groups, theatre, plus movies occasionally. 276 W. Center St.; 740-383-2101; www.marionpalace.org*

Playhouse Square Center — *Cleveland*

Dedicated souls have pumped life into a sagging block that was once the heart of Cleveland's theatrical district. So much life, in fact, that the 1920s theaters—The Ohio, The State, The Palace, The Allen, and the Hanna—a six-acre, 7,000-seat complex became the largest theater restoration project in the country. The State's 320-foot lobby was the largest theater lobby in America, and The Palace, done in Imperial French style, was the home of Cleveland's first talking movie. No place was the size more evident than in The Palace service towers. Rising for seven stories on one side of the stage and for three on the other, the service tower provided both traditional dressing rooms and other services for the performers on the B.F. Keith vaudeville circuit— a beauty parlor and barber shop, a nursery complete with sandbox and billiard room with a putting green in the loft above the stage. The Playhouse Square revival, costing some $40 million (replacement value was estimated to be over $150 million) became the largest theatre renovation project in the world, resulting in the second-largest performing arts center, drawing a million people a year. *Now Showing: Everything from Broadway to resident theatre, opera, dance, movie classics, and professional magicians. 162 Euclid Ave.; 216-771-8403; www.playhousesquare.com*

Regent — *Springfield*

The marble walk is still in good shape, the original crystal chandelier still hangs in the lobby, and the plaster moldings look as good as new. But little else remains from owner Gus Sun's opening night in 1917. Gus, a famous booking agent, gave Bob Hope and Eddie Cantor some of their earliest dates, and old photos of the stars still hang in the dilapidated, upstairs offices, near an ancient vault full of old playbills and ads. There was an orchestra pit, balcony, box seats, a large mezzanine with a wood-burning fireplace and seating for 1,600. *Now Showing: No prospects. 117 S. Limestone.*

Renaissance Theatre — *Mansfield*

Stanley Warner outdid himself in Mansfield with the Ohio Theatre—a Grand Baroque palace with three lobbies and a lead-crystal main chandelier weighing a ton and a half. Its grandeur was put to the test when the movie version of Louis Bromfield's novel *The Rains Came* had its world premier in Mansfield, Bromfield's hometown. But it was downhill from there, and by the Seventies, the Ohio was home to X-rated movies until pickets made such a fuss the city shut it down. Industrialist

Warren Rupp bought the building launching a fund-raising effort ($3.5 million so far) to make it into the Renaissance Civic Center. By 1985, the Renaissance was flush enough to replace the Wurlitzer that had been lost and to add skywalks to connect the old theater to the new Holiday Inn. *Now Showing: Convention activities: big-name performers like Dionne Warwick and Ferrante and Teicher; classic movies; concerts. Home of the Mansfield Symphony Orchestra. 138 Park Ave. West.; 419-522-272; www.rparts.org*

Tiffin   The Ritz Theatre

Sixty years ago Tiffin added to its skyline the Italian Renaissance form of The Ritz, an idea conceived by theatrical promoters Ritzler and Kerwan. Inside, the wall tapestries, ornate furniture, houselights and blue carpeting are all gone. The owners had to sell the furniture to save the place during the Depression. The original houselights have been found in Upper Sandusky. But the gold plaster walls of the lobby, the 2,500-pound crystal chandelier, the marble steps and the toning chambers of the original organ remain. As does the original usher, Jack Roberts, who lives just down the street. He has his original usher's uniform, too. And it still fits. *Now Showing: Concerts and other live entertainment. Also: new Studio Theatre, with smaller venue and no fixed stage for audiences of under 100. 30 S. Washington St.; 419-448-8544; www.ritztheatre.org*

Cleveland   Shaker Square Cinemas

Architect John Eberson toned down his style considerably when he built the Colony at Shaker Square. It's surprisingly plain (classic Georgian brick with white trim), except for the sweeping ceiling and the elegant lounges. The Colony went dark in 1979, reopened by former employee Morrie Zryl, who once staged a chariot race around Shaker Square to publicize *Ben Hur*. In 2000, Cleveland Cinemas reopened it as the Shaker Square Cinemas. Renovation featured six new state-of-the art theaters with ergonomic Australian high-back chairs with moveable armrests and cupholders, digital sound, and a new concession stand complete with all of the "usual suspects"—food and specialty coffee. *Now Showing: First-run movies. 13116 Shaker Square; 216-658-1704; www.clevelandcinemas.com/shakersquare*

Middletown   Sorg Opera House

Paul J. Sorg arrived in Middletown in 1870 to establish the P.J. Sorg Tobacco Company, staying at the U.S. Hotel, where Jennie Gruver was a receptionist. He ended up buying the hotel and marrying the receptionist. Jennie was an avid theater buff, and Sorg was one to please. He hired architect Samuel Hannaford, designer of Cincinnati's Music Hall, and gave the people of Middletown the Sorg Opera House. Meanwhile, Jennie traipsed to New York to book top-quality performances. Opening night was September 12, 1891. The Richardsonian Romanesque structure held elaborate, frescoed walls and ceilings and was lit by 1,200 lights—probably because, by then Sorg owned the

utility company, too. The second balcony was not frequented by ladies. Men there were a bit rowdy, often inclined to pitching peanut shells over the railing to the first floor. But Nate Thomas "kept order with half a pool cue"; however, following a performance, the tobacco juice often had to be cleared from the floor with shovels. Silent movies came here in 1915, and for over 70 years the place remained a motion picture theater—the Colonial—for patrons—and for bats, who are still said to cast their shadows across the stage. Motion pictures ceased in 1986. Recently renovated and now on the National Register of Historic Places. *Now showing: Sorg Opera productions and other performing events. It is one of some 150 professional opera companies in the U.S. 65 S. Main St.; www.sorgopera.com*

The Southern Theatre   *Columbus*

The Southern Theatre, last of Columbus' downtown theaters actually showing movies, is closed and forgotten. The theater opened in 1896, before movies, but in time for James Whitcomb Riley, Victor Herbert, Lillian Russell and Sarah Bernhardt. Today the Columbus Association for the Performing Arts owns the Southern. In the dimness one can see the concentric arches that frame the stage, the orchestra denuded of seats, two neon signs (SOUTHERN and THEATRE) in the rubble on stage, a silent movie screen up in the fly loft. This theater has a second balcony, reached by a separate, uncarpeted stairway and once a haven for students and impecunious old ladies, who crowded together on wooden pew-like benches. *Now Showing: Shares performance billing with other Columbus CAPA theatres, The Ohio and The Palace, after $10 million renovation in 1998. S. High & E. Main Streets. 614-358-2222; www.capa.com/venues/southern.html*

State Theatre   *Sandusky*

William Seitz, a tailor, spent $965,000 to give Sandusky what he thought it needed—a movie palace. But he ran out of money before the theater was finished, and a family named Schine finished the job. So, it was the Schine name that shone from the marquee, and Seitz never saw his name in lights. The theater included an entertainment center, with billiard parlors and bowling alleys downstairs. The ambiance was vaguely Spanish, with turrets and arches outside and an abundance of red, gold, teal and amber tiles inside. The auditorium was fitted with "mood lights" that changed with the action, and a four-rank Page pipe organ that rattled the rafters at moments of high drama. *Now Showing: Theatre, concerts, and the Firelands Symphony Orchestra. 107 Columbus Ave.; 877-379-2150; 419-626-1950; www.state-theatre.com*

State Theatre   *Springfield*

The 9,126-sq.-ft. theater took a year to erect, furnish and equip, and cost over a quarter-of-a-million dollars. There were 1,200 leather upholstered seats and 1,300 yards of carpet, along with the finest Motiograph projection machines. And a piano sat in

the restroom for the public to play. The original Wurlitzer organ remains today, with pipes from 32' long to a unit 6" long and scarcely larger than a soda straw. It's used for the solos of Larry Blumenshine during intermission on Fridays, Saturdays and Sundays. *Now Showing: The theatre is now a bingo parlor. Come as you are. 19 S. Fountain.*

Oakley (Cincinnati)   **20th Century**

Opened in 1941, the 20th Century was the ultimate suburban movie house with all the latest innovations: "No tip auto hops" parked patrons' cars from the curb, theater seats flipped up by themselves for the first time, and there were "love seats" (aisle chairs made extra wide for large persons or two small ones). But what was really new about the 20th Century was its architecture. Restorers call this style "late deco automotive streamline." A huge serpentine wall of glazed blue terra cotta camouflages the theater above its marquee. Inside, there is hardly a right angle to be found. *Now Showing: Music, weddings, bar mitzvahs. 3021 Madison Road. 513-731-8000; www.the20thcenturytheatre.com/*

Cincinnati   **Union Terminal Theatre**

Inside the echoing concourse of Union Terminal was a small art deco theater located just inside the front doors. It was a haven for people with time to kill or in need of a nap. During World War II, servicemen would snooze in an aisle seat with a "Wake me at 6" sign hung under their chins. The only rail station in the country to have its own theater, it showed newsreels and travelogues—nothing long enough to make people miss their trains. Passers-through probably never took note of the classic deco details—torch lamps casting soft light on the walls, stylized chrome grills, the fluted, wine-colored marble of the screen's pedestal. Railroad policeman Cecil Scott checked the theater for runaways, pickpockets and "hanky-panky." When President Truman's private rail car was attached to a train that came through Cincinnati, he would have the Secret Service clear the theater so he could catch up on the news. *Now Showing: Now home of the Museum of Natural History and the Cincinnati Historical Society. The newsreel theater may reopen to show movies and for special presentations. 1301 Western Ave.; 513-278-7000; 800-733-2077; www.cincymuseum.org*

Toledo   **The Valentine**

In 1895, the Valentine opened its doors to reveal ecru walls and ceilings, rich green carpeting with golden fleur de lis, matching draperies, and Louis Quatorze divans. But the centerpiece was the theater's curtain. Apparently, the artist, Ludwig Bang, had a dispute with a prominent Toledoan—rumored to be a particular judge—and had painted the well-known face of his daughter on one of the struggling women in the foreground of the curtain, which featured The Rape of the Sabine Women. A legal battle ended by having the likeness painted out. The great stage was torn out to make room for more seats in 1942, and it became a movie house. The loss of the women and the proscenium arch

was barely noticed when the Navy Glee Club marched down the aisle singing "Remember Pearl Harbor." *Now Showing: Live performances: concerts, theatre, ballet, opera. 409 St. Clair St.; 419-242-2787; www.valentinetheatre.com*

Victoria Theatre — *Dayton*

Surviving is not new to the Victoria. Fires in 1869 and 1917, the Flood of 1913, a parking lot threat in 1975, and a financial crisis in the mid-1980s brought down the curtain only temporarily. There is, thus, a future, as well as a past, which includes two ghosts, residents from the 1800s. One is said to be an unnamed former actress; the other a girl who was beaten by an attacker in one of the opera boxes. "There are unknown incidents," says General Manager Jean Galan. "Things happen: footsteps on the stage, the rustling of taffeta, the smell of perfume." $10 million renovation began in 1988, resulting in new home for the Dayton arts community. *Now Showing: Events in conjunction with the new Schuster Center. 183 N. Main St.; 937-228-7591; www.victoriatheater.com*

Wapa Theatre — *Wapakoneta*

The Wapa was built in 1904 by Michael Brown, lumberyard owner, who named it the Brown Opera House, and its doors have been open ever since. The original piano is still on stage, an ancient upright with a wonderful sound. The only outside modification in the three-story building came in the 1940s when owner Emil George removed the columns and built a new marquee that featured an Indian head. The Georges had just returned from a vacation in Colorado where they had seen a theater with an Indian motif and, recalling their own chief, Wapakoneta, decided to add an Indian to their marquee. The theater had double balconies, although the top one had been closed, but all else remains much like it always has. The theater has been home to Spencer Tracy, the Barrymores, high school commencements, and Mrs. George, who lives there. *Now Showing: First-run movies, price $2. 700 seats, currently being painted and refurbished. 15 Willipie Street; 419-738-3718*

Youngstown Symphony Theatre — *Youngstown*

The Warner Brothers built their flashiest movie palace in Youngstown as a hometown memorial for their parents and their brother: a $1.5 million, 2,500-seat showplace that could make a poor steelworker feel rich as an emperor—just for the price of admission. They wanted the best, so they hired Rapp and Rapp, premier architects of the Renaissance/Rococo style. What they got was dazzling—a hall of mirrors that rivaled Versailles, with an art deco pastiche tossed in for good measure: Vaulted ceilings that shone with stars; carved classic figures; sweeping staircases; false balconies. Youngstown loved it, garish excesses and all. The Warner became one of the first movie palaces in America to be saved from urban blight and rehabilitated into a symphony hall. *Now Showing: live theater, performances, and the Youngstown Symphony. 266-268 Federal Plaza West; 330-744-0264; www.youngstownsymphony.com*

Mr. Murphy's monument on Main

The Murphy Theatre opened in Wilmington on a warm evening late in July of 1918, and although Charles W. Murphy's Chicago Cubs had won four pennants and two World Series between 1906 and 1914, the opening of his theater seemed to give him more pleasure. He owned the Cubs, of course, and at the time, it was said he was the best-known baseball man in the world. But when he built the Murphy, he owned his *hometown*.

There were 175 railroad carloads of material used in the construction, and Italian craftsmen came to Wilmington and worked for weeks on the interior. The best decorator from the Chicago interior design firm, the Mandel Brothers, came to Wilmington on the train, convinced he'd been put off at the wrong place. "Surely there can't be a theater in this town big enough to have the Mandel Brothers do the decorating?" he asked archly.

Each Saturday during the construction, folks from the countryside came to town to watch. Murphy had his name painted on the theater's rear wall, in letters so high they could be seen from the railroad. When the building was finished, at a cost of $250,000, Dan Foland, the druggist for whom Murphy worked as a boy, looked it over and said, "Charlie, that's a bad investment. It won't pay two percent."

"Dan," Murphy said, "that's not an investment. That's a *monument*."

It *was* a monument to Murphy, but it soon became the actual, as well as the symbolic, heart of the downtown. Everything went on there. John Phillip Sousa gave a concert there, and asked schoolgirl Pat Ballantine to button the clasps of his white gloves. The great Yiddish actress Bertha Kalish came to Wilmington and ate at the Carnahan Boarding House, greeted at the door by Mrs. Carnahan herself, in the midst of pie-making. Sarah Bernhardt's leading man, Lew Tellenger, came to town early and spent the afternoon fishing in Todd's Fork with Doc Hale. And a road company of the Passion Play came to town, using the Wilmington College students as extras. Big Jake Jacoby, a center on the basketball team, played a Centurian who was to carry Barabbas to his fate, picked up Jesus by mistake, and a scuffle broke out on the stage.

Theater folks said the Murphy could "hang any show in the country," meaning that it was large enough to accommodate scenery and sets. *The Music Box Revue of 1938*, for instance, polished its performance at the Murphy before opening on Broadway.

There were plays, vaudeville, lectures, minstrel shows and movies. The high school graduations were held there, and band concerts.

The high time of that kind of entertainment seems to be passed now, as are many of the theaters, victims to trends, economics and neglect. Men build for lesser reasons these days, especially in the small towns such as Wilmington, where the imagination runs by and large to the profit-loss statement.

The Murphy is, nonetheless, still the symbolic heart of the old downtown. For years, it was the flagship of the Chakeres chain of theaters, then it was purchased by a nonprofit community group and renovated into a multi-purpose arts center. Upon the proper occasion, its old-fashioned marquee still throws light over the center of town, and the absence of it would render Wilmington as lifeless in appearance as those other small, undistinguished towns across Ohio that grow dark and turn inward at nightfall.

—*John Baskin*

hometown boy makes good

Murphy had learned about the Cubs being for sale when he was an advance man for the New York Giants. He asked his old Cincinnati newspaper boss, Charlie Taft, for the money.

"What kind of security can you give me?" Taft asked.

"The club," Murphy said.

"I'll have to ask my wife," Taft said. "She has all the money."

When I was little, one of my favorite toys was an Ohio road map that my father picked up at a gas station. It was huge and when spread out on the living room floor, large enough to nap on—though I would never do that for fear of ripping it—and covered with an inexhaustible fund of words and colors and shapes. At first the map was simply a dazzling thing to look at, but once I understood what it was, it became magical. Here was an entire world cast into child-size, foldable form, gorgeous with red lines, yellow lines, hatched lines, double lines, bright hues clashing at the state borders, and the deep blue of mapped water. One starred city was our "capital," with other cities spreading out into irregular yellow shapes. There were hundreds of mysterious names and numbers and, here and there, tiny green pine trees and tents that meant, in one of my first experiences of legibility, "You can camp here."

I spent hours sprawled on my belly, tracing and retracing Ohio journeys with my finger. Once I learned that our house faced north (for a map-child, there was a profound rightness to that), I aligned the red, white, and blue Sohio ellipse at the top with our front door and imagined leisurely trips from this place to that and back again, always by a different route. These journeys usually started from our hometown, and always from a sense of well-anchored security that came from my opening ritual: Findlay, Ohio, is *here*. I am *right here*. When I was learning to read I practiced on the map names, eager to learn where I had been and where I would go next. Should I take the short, straight line up to Toledo, where the zoo was? Should I venture into the unknown, maybe south to wander a meandering black line leading to, say, Chillicothe? Or should I follow one of the many routes converging on the sprawling yellow of Cleveland? Cleveland had a cluster of names so tightly packed I could hardly distinguish them, and I instinctively moved my finger more slowly in order to take them all in.

If you spend time playing with an Ohio map, you will become a whiz kid of Buckeye geography without even trying. I knew what lay northwest of what, where the rivers ran, how to get from point A to point B without ever having to cross a bridge. These were not insignificant journeys; the map reinforced a child's sense of living in a manageable, self-contained world—in my case, a world of wall-to-wall Buckeyes. I thought we were lucky. We inhabited a state whose shape was particularly satisfying. No characterless rectangle like Colorado, no vast expanse like Texas, no pinched-in seeming afterthought like Connecticut or Rhode Island—Ohio seemed the perfect balance of nature and people, its boundaries a mix of lake and river and surveyors' lines. There was something for everybody, and as far as I was concerned, everybody lived within its confines.

I knew, of course, that people lived in places called Indiana, Michigan, Kentucky, Pennsylvania, and West Virginia, but those places dropped mysteriously off the edges of my map, its red and black lines extending into a child's terra incognita. I still get a muted thrill when I think of those first pointers to the unknown—

by Jeffrey Hammond

"To Erie," "To Detroit," "To Fort Wayne"—my versions, I suppose, of those ominous marginalia on medieval maps: *Here Be Monsters*. Not that I thought of Pennsylvanians or Michiganders as monsters, exactly, but I did assume that they were somehow different from us. Ohio's borders seemed to contain all that was knowable – and there was comfort in that. I didn't worry about these other places, because they were for later. I couldn't know it at the time, but this was a typical assumption for an Ohioan to make.

The Sohio map instilled a habit of feeling situated in a landscape larger than what I could perceive. Years later, when I rode my bike out to the reservoir, climbed the embankment, and looked north, I thought I could almost see the skyline of Toledo, forty-five miles away, so strong was my conviction that it was there. The world— or more accurately, Ohio—felt like a palpable, understandable thing. Just beyond those trees to the southeast lay Carey, and beyond Carey lay Upper Sandusky, and beyond Upper Sandusky lay Marion and Delaware and Columbus, the city with the star.

The map prompted considerable curiosity about my state, along with the natural assumption that this curiosity could be satisfied, that Ohio could be mastered. How could it not? After all, I lived there – or rather *here*, in this small town located on the thin black line of Route 68 between Bowling Green and Arlington. As it turned out, however, Ohio was not as easy to read as those pine trees and tents. Individual facts (entered the Union in 1803; home of the Great Serpent Mound and the Olentangy Caves; birth state of General Grant, Thomas Edison, the Wright Brothers) were straightforward enough, but not what those facts added up to. This became a problem, one that was especially disturbing to a child devoted to the legibility of things. The more I learned about other states, the harder it became to pin down the essence of mine. I remember feeling jealous of how *identifiable* other places seemed. Texas had beef and oil wells. Wyoming had cowboys. California had the movies. There was Iowa's corn, Wisconsin's cheese, West Virginia's coal mines, Michigan's car factories, New York's crime—and so on. But what did Ohio signify? What did *we*

stand for? The nickname "Buckeye State" offered little help; what did that brown, shiny nut say about *us*?

North Dakota, South Dakota and Kansas seemed to offer similar blanks, but I didn't live in those boringly squared-off places. I lived *here*: the meaning of Ohio was my problem.

As I got older my growing knowledge of Hoosiers and Golden Staters and Georgia Peaches, however slight, caused me to redouble my efforts to get a handle on us relative to them, and my search for the sum and essence of Ohio sent me back to the map. Maybe the town names would provide a clue. Like most children, I sensed the importance of names (just get a child's name wrong and watch the response: "I'm not John! I'm *Jonathan*!"). And if it's a big deal to have your own name or to name a pet, what if you had to name a town? This, I figured, was my key to Buckeye clarity. The people who had named our towns were pioneers, grownups who knew what they were doing. Surely they understood what Ohio meant.

My initial forays into Ohio's names boded well. My hometown, for instance, had been named for Colonel Findlay, a local hero of vague military significance. Heroes' names also graced Steubenville and Zanesville. Columbus honored an even earlier hero, though hardly a local one. It made sense, given my budding midwestern faith in progress and achievement, to name a place after a discoverer, a soldier, or a rich man who had coaxed a railroad or a canal to come *here* instead of there. These people had worked hard and played it smart and gotten ahead, all worthy activities. To name towns after such enterprising souls was a good deed, like respecting your elders.

This, then, was Ohio. Tennessee was the Volunteer State, and Florida was the Sunshine State, but I lived in the Respect-Your-Elders State. It was easy to picture a parade of distinguished elders named Tiffin, McComb, Worthington, and Kettering. In my mind these Buckeye luminaries all resembled President

Grover Cleveland, the inspiration, I wrongly presumed, for our biggest city. Mansfield gave me some trouble. Had a field once been owned by a man named Man? Had there once been a nearby town named Womansfield—the result, perhaps, a nasty frontier divorce, Debbie Reynolds and Eddie Fisher in buckskins?

I also discovered that you could name a town after what you found—or hoped to—once you got there. Defiance and Independence were stirring examples of this, but what the settlers found was usually more down to earth. There was no great mystery to Rocky River or Springfield and its etymological near-twin Bellefontaine, once I looked it up. I could guess what lay beneath the hills of Ironton. Upper Sandusky made sense too: it lay "above" Sandusky—that is, on higher ground than Sandusky, which was on Lake Erie and named, I assumed, for a distinguished elder called Mr. Sandusky. Middletown must have been halfway between two other places (absent, of course, a distinguished elder named Mr. Middle). Then there was Akron, which always had a harsh, un-Ohio sound to it. Once I learned that the name was Greek for "high place," the mystery vanished. Wasn't Akron the seat of Summit County?

So *this* was Ohio: the State of Respecting Your Elders in a New Place. But not all Ohio names started from scratch. People frequently named new towns after the ones they had left behind, though it seemed strange to anyone who had bothered to leave a place would want to use its name all over again. New Concord, New Boston, and New Philadelphia were obvious examples. I learned that there was a Dover in England, as well as an Arlington and a Kent. Once I saw in the dictionary that "Wooster" was how you pronounced the first two-thirds of Worcestershire—as in the steak sauce and the English county—another mystery was solved. Ohio also had a Cambridge, an Oxford, and a London, all of which must have been founded by Brits with big plans. East Liverpool made sense, too, until I remembered that it actually lay west of the Beatles' Liverpool. Maybe its founders had come to Ohio by way of China.

So far so good. Ohio was the State of Respecting Your Elders in a New Place but Without Forgetting Where You Came From. I soon realized, however, that Ohio's namers of things had embraced a far larger world than I had suspected. Toledo and Lima (pronounced *LY-muh*) were named for dreamy places where people wore colorful shawls, ate spicy food, and spoke Spanish. Milan (pronounced *MY-lun*) suggested elegant buildings and the Mafia. So did Parma, one of those squeezed-in names near Cleveland, and Ravenna, six inches southeast of Cleveland's sprawling yellow. Ohio also had a Lisbon, a Cadiz, and a Medina. And when I looked up Gallipolis, down on the Ohio River, I discovered that it meant "City of Frenchmen." This did nothing to further my progress toward Buckeye clarity. How did a city of Frenchmen, berets at a tilt and wineglasses on their gingham-covered tables, square with my hometown of slim farmers and beefy, narrow-tie Republicans? What American Dream was reflected in towns named after Spanish sword centers, Inca capitals, and Muslim holy cities? Arcadia, ten miles northeast of Findlay, looked nothing like that peaceful shepherd place described in our encyclopedia.

Clearly, the state of Respecting Your Elders in a New Place but Without Forgetting Where You Came From, or Didn't, was getting out of hand. Where was the "Ohioness" in all this? And what to make of all the Indian names, with their beautiful sounds and spooky reverberations? Although I had once believed that there had been a Chief Gallipolis, I soon learned that Ohio had plenty of legitimate Indian names to go around. Even *Ohio* was an Indian word, meaning "beautiful river." Ohio River, as our seventh-grade geography teacher pointed out, was a redundancy: the Beautiful River River. This was no help at all.

Echoes of the pristine, forested place that preceded this place—Ashtabula, Ottawa, Maumee, Miami, Wapakoneta, Coshocton, Cuyahoga Falls, Sandusky (there was no Mr. Sandusky, as it turned out), and Delaware—added to the incomprehensible mix of long-gone Buckeyes, a motley crew of Indians, easterners, Englishmen, Germans, Dutchmen, and Frenchmen forming a swirl of Ohio ghosts, a midwestern Babel whose capital city was named after an Italian who didn't get where he was

going and never really knew where he had been. I understood that the Indians had died off or headed out a long time ago. Their first stop westward must have been Indiana, where they managed to name another state before being shoved farther into the *real* West—the one that those clearly defined Californians showed us in the movies. Still, these names invoked tribal presences who spoke as loudly as the others, and not just in the Cleveland Indians' Chief Wahoo or in the warrior pictured on the label of the grape pop bottled in Wapakoneta, later famous as the birthplace of the first man on the moon.

Indian ghosts might be peering sullenly out from the trees, but there were ancient Greek and Roman ghosts, too. This new knowledge demanded adjustments. When I read the story of Cincinnatus, Chief Cincinnati joined Chief Gallipolis in the happy hunting ground of nonexistence. For a while I even thought that the real Ohio was Roman at heart. To be called from your plow to defend your people and then to return to your fields afterward sounded like a quintessentially "Ohio" thing to do, something that Grover Cleveland might have done. Never having been to Cincinnati, I imagined it as a gleaming cluster of temples and amphitheaters nestled on the banks of the Beautiful River River. The Romans, I learned, traced their ancestry back to the Trojans—and didn't Troy lie a little north of Cincinnati? Troy, Ohio, certainly had a ring to it, but was this the town that launched a thousand ships? When our family drove through on a visit to the great Smoky Mountains (a rare venture into terra incognita), I half expected to see spear marks on the storefronts. Instead, Troy looked a lot like Findlay.

Maybe, I thought, Ohio could be summed up more tersely than I had imagined: the State of Aiming High but Falling Short. Not far from Troy lay Urbana—"City Town". But despite its

founders' hopes, Urbana was hardly a city. There were lots of other remnants of lofty classical dreams: Attica, Delphos, Euclid, Utica, Bucyrus, Sparta, Macedonia, Minerva, Xenia, Antioch, Fostoria—Ohio's own "city of light, from the Greek—and more grandly, Athens, Rome and New Rome. I figured that Twinsburg must have been named for those wolf-suckled Roman boys, Romulus and Remus. But the towns I have seen gave off little of the glory that was Greece or the grandeur that was Rome. I was beginning to think that Ohio was less a place of new dreams than of old daydreams. I could still imagine Cincinnati looking like a set from *Spartacus*, because I hadn't been there. I had been to Fostoria, though, and seen its narrow streets and abandoned glass factories. Clearly, something had gone wrong in our City of Light.

Where was I now? I was a citizen of Ohio—the Aim High Like an Indian or a Roman Even

> When Ohioans leave home, we become Everybody: dependable, middle-of-the-road Americans bearing bread for other people's jam. It is an identity, however shapeless, that the nation cannot do without—and I am resolved to embrace it with honor and even a measure of relief. It's nice, at long last, to be somebody.

Though You Will Fall Short, and Respect Your Elders in a New Place and So Forth state. But forty miles southeast of the Greek high place where they made the tires lay the biblical high place of Salem. Ohio's rich supply of biblical names added yet another layer to the mix. Having learned something about the Bible from my grandmother, I guessed that those Salem settlers had aimed high with a vengeance. If you name your town after the Holy City, you probably aren't anticipating empty warehouses or juvenile delinquents. Ditto for the founders of

Zion. But how, exactly, did biblical holiness connect with my Ohio? Was there a balm in Mount Gilead? Was the Hebron east of Columbus a city of refuge, like its namesake? And what about Lebanon, Zoar, Goshen, Galatea, Damascus, Berea, Gilboa, Palestine, and East Palestine? Did the flinty-eyed ur-Buckeyes who settled these places hope to imitate the sanctity of those Bible lands? Did it make any difference that they would be substituting oats and winter wheat for date palms and olive groves?

I tentatively added Be Holy to Aim High Like an Indian or a Roman Even Though You Will Fall Short and So On and So Forth. After all, Ohio contained St. Marys (both a town and a lake, Marysville, Marietta, and Marion, the latter the home of Warren G. Harding, whose unpresidential behavior surely disgraced the Town of the Virgin. Curiously, I never ran across a Jesus, Ohio. I supposed that such a name would create too much pressure; if a town named Jesus ever had a corrupt mayor or lost its only supermarket, despair would surely be loosed upon the land. There was no God, Ohio, either—the closest was Lordstown, with its huge GM plant—but that was probably a good thing. If there ever were a God, Ohio, it would surely become the adopted hometown of every politician in the state. "Friends, I stand before you as a man of God." Warren G. Harding would have moved there just to save face, though it probably wouldn't have done any good.

Given all these biblical names, maybe Ohio was simply God's Country. That certainly sounded like a fine thing, and perhaps capable of encompassing all of the conflicting strands. But some Ohio towns seemed to reflect a flat-out opposition to God. Rome and Athens and Antioch might have been honorable classical places, but you couldn't be pagan and Christian at the same time, could you? Once I learned that these cities were also in the Bible and that Paul had tried to rescue them from false gods, I figured that a few old-time Buckeyes had intended to plant their crops and worship Mars. What about Gahanna, on the outskirts of Columbus? The fact that it sounded suspiciously like Gehenna, Jerusalem's valley of Hell, did not bode well. And

if Ohio was really the Devil's Country, what to make of all these Methodists and Baptists? Was there anything about my home state that wouldn't shimmer or break up, that wasn't canceled out by something else?

I began to suspect that no meaning was possible for a state that had been cobbled together from shards of this and that, a hopeless mix of conflicting dreams. Even individual dreams, on closer inspection, had a way of shrinking to insignificance. It was disturbing to learn that a number of proto-Buckeyes had established brassy, self-promoting towns. Moses Cleaveland—not President Cleveland—had founded our biggest city, in an act, I now thought, of monumental arrogance. A Connecticut lawyer, Cleaveland chose the site and immediately headed back east; a newspaper later dropped the "a" from his name to save space. The respectable President Cleveland, it turned out, wasn't even *from* Ohio. I darkly guessed that Colonel Findlay had probably pressured people to name my town after him. So much, I sadly concluded, for respecting your elders. So much for aiming high and being noble like an Indian or Roman and being honored for it. So much for the meaning of Ohio.

I couldn't know that I had bitten off more than any kid could chew. Ohio really *is* an enigma, and not without reason. It has always been a place in which the past and the future count for more than the present. If the present is diminished, people will consider the very ground on which they stand to be temporary. They will see themselves in a holding pattern, potentially just passing through. This is a natural legacy of Ohio's long-standing status as a way station. Once the original "West," Connecticut's Western Reserve to be exact, Ohio soon became the first Gateway to the West, a role that never ceased even as the frontier grew increasingly distant. Ohio was coming into its own just as those westward places were coming into *their* own, and the old thoroughfares—Zane's Trail, the

National Road, the tight nexus of railroads—soon became funnels to get you *through* Ohio to somewhere else. The Erie Canal, which linked the East with the Great Lakes and created the ports of Ashtabula, Cleveland, and Toledo, soon became like that. Lake Erie led to Lake Huron, which led to Lake Michigan, which led to that big-shouldered Hog Butcher for the World and rail lines leading still farther west, where the real action was. The old railroads—the Chesapeake & Ohio and the Baltimore & Ohio—quickly outgrew their Buckeye dreams, too. Within a few years of its founding, the C & O fossilized the O in its name by making Chicago its western terminus; the B & O did the same by extending to Chicago and St. Louis. Long before those Buckeye brothers Wilbur and Orville came along, Ohio was already becoming, in a phrase I've been hearing more and more lately, "flyover country."

Ohio's traditional role as the Not-Quite-West has always fostered among its citizens an acute awareness of impermanence. Even sixth and seventh-generation Buckeyes, whose ancestor shod horses and pumped gas for more adventuresome souls as they passed through, retain a feeling of just marking time, waiting for their own chance to move on. Born observers of a passing parade, most Ohioans grow up assuming, rightly or not, that they will someday join it. It's hard to resist such thoughts if you live in a place that remains nobody's destination. Even today the Ohio Turnpike serves as an extended bypass traversing a Lake Erie plain that exists merely as ground to be covered by the steady flow of East Coast-Chicago traffic. Travelers a little farther south on Interstate 70, which supplanted the old National Road and U.S. 40, pass through Columbus with Indianapolis beckoning as Oz and St. Louis as a greater Oz. Interstate 70 similarly connects Detroit with points south, good weather, and Florida beaches ahead—though not soon enough ahead. Ohio is a perennial midpoint between desired ends, an entire state as Middletown.

The University of Akron has an uplifting but oddly poignant slogan that could stand for the state as a whole: "You can get there from here." The slumping midwestern economy has aggravated the old Buckeye itch to get there from

here, or wish that one *had*. A charter member of the Rust Belt and a place of small farms unable to compete with modern agribusiness, Ohio has fallen hard during the past fifty years. Any middle-aged Ohioan will confess to nostalgia for better times. In 1950 Cleveland was the seventh-largest city in the country, with nearly a million kielbasa-eating souls. Cleveland has since shrunk to half a million and now ranks twenty-sixth, though its metropolitan area still ranks a respectable fourteenth. Houston, in 1950 an upstart at around half a million, is now pushing two million—the equivalent of two 1950 Clevelands. When I was growing up, Ohio's factories, buoyed by frenzied postwar production, were stamping out steel, auto parts, and heavy equipment in record quantities. All that money brought other, less tangible gifts. Ohio State was number one in basketball, and the Browns and Indians were champions in football and baseball. Jerry Lucas, Lou "The Toe" Groza, and Bob Feller were fabled warriors of the Buckeye Golden Age, but like all golden ages, ours didn't last.

Pushed by economic necessity, more and more of us have acted on the old impulse to join the caravan. Half the people you meet in Sun Belt cities seem to come from Ohio, though Michigan might run a close second. An astonishing number of Texans, Floridians, Arizonans, and Californians have Ohio roots, though they never describe themselves in such terms. Why proclaim yourself a former Buckeye, only to watch your face lose its features? When a Texan moves to Cleveland, he's a Texan in Cleveland. But when a Clevelander moves to Houston he's a Texan, then and forever. There's no mystery to this: If you have no identity, finding one will feel intoxicating. That's why you won't see anyone in the bars of Dallas, Phoenix, or Los Angeles hoisting a Coors to the ol' Buckeye State. You will hear no flushed, teary renditions of "Beautiful Ohio," even though its draggy waltz offers an ideal rhythm for drunks trying to sing. There will be no slurred toasts to Toledo or Dayton (the launching pads, respectively, of Gloria Steinem and Martin Sheen), no prayers for the deliverance of Steubenville (ditto for Dean Martin), Cadiz (Clark Gable), or Fredericktown

(*continued on page 305*)

The Midwest.
A dissonance of parts
and people, we are a
consonance of Towns.
Like a man grown fat
in everything but
heart, we overlabor;
our outlook never
really urban, never
rural either, we
enlarge and linger
at the same time.

—William Gass,
*In the Heart of the Heart
of the Country*

11 high cultural Buckeye moments

Buckeye

Ohio has forever suffered the slings and arrows of bi-coastal indifference. But after monumental research into the essence of Buckeyedom, we have but one cultural question: Who's your Daddy?

1836—Middle-class American world view. 1

When the first two editions of **William Holmes McGuffey's** *Eclectic Reader* were published, the Presbyterian minister and philosophy professor was paid $1,000 and promised a ham every Christmas if the books sold well. They sold so well they became the standard for reading in 37 states and can still be bought today. In them, McGuffey espoused a narrow but cheerful ethic that indelibly imprinted the Midwestern shirtsleeve values of hard work, thrift, sobriety—and conformity—into literally millions of American schoolchildren. "Nothing was left to the imagination," wrote historian Henry Steele Comager, "nothing to chance, and nothing, one is tempted to say, to conscience...it was a middle-class, conventional, and equalitarian morality.. if the *Readers* did not themselves provide the stuff of culture and morality, they were one of the chief instruments for weaving this stuff into the fabric of American life."

2 1869—Baseball.

They were not *from* Cincinnati but they were *of* Cincinnati, baseball's first team of paid mercenaries— and a payroll of $9,300. It proved to be one of sports' grand bargains, as the Cincinnati Red Stockings won what was probably 92 games, maybe as many as 130, and lasted a season and a half unbeaten, the prototype for all teams to come. They scored 2,395 runs to 575 that year; traveled by barge, stagecoach, and wooden railroad car; and the young women of the Queen City walked around town wearing red stockings. They revolutionized their sport "by nothing more than chutzpah

and happenstance," and from that 1869 season came the double-play, the switch-hitter, the terms 'ace', 'fan', 'the hot corner', and 'the seventh-inning stretch'. Where would the American idiom be without Cincinnati? Wrote Lonnie Wheeler, "If the game has a depot at which its makers had their tickets stamped, it is Cincinnati."

1889—the glory of Old Glory. 3

Depending upon your need for flagrant expression, 1889 was a flagship year. It was America's centennial celebration and Ohio president Benjamin Harrison wanted Old Glory to be glorified. He wanted flags in schools, waving from front porches, flying over the White House executive departments, and the White House itself whenever he was there. Before Harrison, the flag was given quiet due but it was not prominently displayed. After Harrison, it was the ultimate display of patriotism,

imprinted on salt and pepper shakers, ties, lapel pins, wallpaper, and teeshirts. There are now flag mousepads, flag beer steins, magnetic car flags, flag thongs, and somewhere, no doubt, a flag condom—*Stand up for America!* Patient and implacable, the flag serves with equanimity every purpose, the constant refuge of both patriot and scoundrel.

1913—faux America.

Formica began its omnipresent life in Cincinnati in 1913, the bugle (not real brass, of course) that played reveille for an emerging century of "faux" goods and events. Originally a substitute for mica (hence the name), which was a mineral used as an electrical insulator, this paper-based laminate had by midcentury cornered the market for kitchen countertops. In 1952, six million new homes were built; two million had Formica counters. It was the well-intentioned original that presaged an entire universe in which one thing masqueraded for another (whether it was vinyl siding or the personality of the nightly news anchor). Three-quarters of a century after its creation, Formica had become one of the world's ten most recognizable brand names.

1929—murder as entertainment.

When Springfield native **W.R. Burnett** absconded from his job as government statistician and wrote *Little Caesar*, his bestseller established the gangster as part of American culture's enduring iconography. The ensuing film made Edward G. Robinson a star and Burnett one of Hollywood's highest-paid screenwriters. It also launched a thousand tough guys in both book and movie, most of whom, existentially speaking, can trace their hard-boiled lineage back to Springfield, Ohio. Yet none of them ever surpassed Burnett's original tough guy, Rico himself, who gave the genre one of its great walk-away lines (speaking of himself in third person, no less): "Mother of God, is this the end of Rico?"

1933—the soap opera.

In the deeps of the Depression, Cincinnati's WLW debuted **Ma Perkins**, the saga of self-sufficient widow Perkins, manager of the Rushville Center lumberyard. Strictly speaking, *Ma* was not the first soap opera (that distinction belonged to one-time Dayton teacher Irna Phillips who wrote the short-lived *Painted Dreams* in 1930) but between Irna and P&G's Oxydol soap, Ohio cleaned up. "America's mother" washed her linen in front of America for 27 years—7,065 daily episodes. *Ma* was the country's classic washboard weeper and, suffice it to say, there wasn't a dry ear in the house.

1938—the modern comic book.

Created by two young Clevelanders, **Jerry Siegel and Joe Shuster**, Superman appeared on the cover of Action Comics #1 where he bashed a car against a large rock, on his way to loosing a spate of super-heroes on the American public, as well as becoming a kind of secular Messiah who would perpetually save mankind. The Big S arrived just in time for both the comic industry and World War II; since he was both Democratic savior and ultimate *mensch*, he was the perfect contrast for Hitler's idealized Aryan.

1951—the word 'ain't.'

When Clevelander **David Guralnik**, editor of the *Encyclopedic Edition of Webster's New World Dictionary*, added the word "ain't" to America's official vocabulary, it was considered a radical moment for the circumspect 1950s. Guralnik, who worked as an upholsterer to pay for his master's degree, refused to move to New York when Cleveland's World Publishing Company merged with Simon & Schuster; he thought the American language could be studied more effectively

In 1929, a Cleveland housewife originated one of America's greatest kitsch ideas: the bronzed baby shoe. The company Violet Shinbach started in Columbus in 1934, Bron-Shoe, is still bronzing shoes, which have been used as bookends and placed on a desk, mounted with an inkwell. Bron-Shoe also bronzes items such as jogging shoes, tennis rackets, and other paraphernalia.

in the Midwest. His work—including the temerity to say "ain't" in polite company—made him an internationally-known lexicographer. "English is the most hospitable of the languages," he said. "That's its glory."

1950s—the sectional sofa.

Russel Wright, born into a Lebanon, Ohio, Quaker family, became at mid-century the most famous designer in America. His name was a household word not only because he invented the sectional sofa but because he re-invented virtually the entire household itself. Wright was America's master of domestic Modernism, creating a new home-and-hearth lexicon as people struggled out of depression and war and into new ways of informal living. Wright introduced aluminum "stove-to-tableware" serving pieces and his *American Modern* dinnerware became the most popular dinnerware ever sold; 80 million pieces of it between 1939 and 1959, in spite of the fact that, as one critic pointed out, "it broke with alarming ease, the crevices and overhanging lips were remarkably difficult to wash, the neck of the water pitcher was too narrow to receive ice cubes, and the sugar bowl defied efforts to remove its contents." The odd thing: so much of Wright's designs adapted so perfectly to an emerging American taste that his ideas seemed like natural evolutions within various industries, and his own name was no longer connected to them. His ideas were so embedded within our lifestyles that they became almost *generic*. He was, it could be said, almost *too* successful. That in itself was the ultimate tribute to his inventive, original mind...."

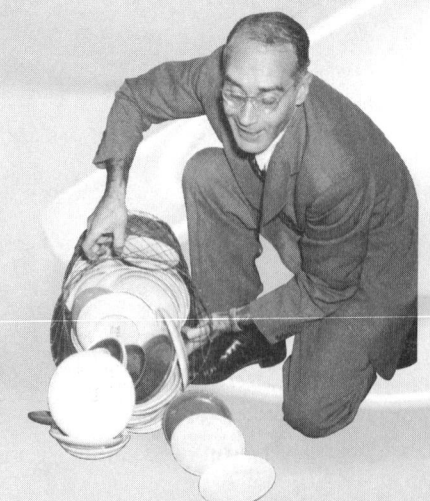

1967—the television talk show.

When *The Donahue Show* premiered in Dayton, Ohio, with its first guest, Madalyn Murray O'Hair—the atheist who got prayer kicked out of the public schools—television would never again be the same. It was a seminal moment in the democratization of the air waves, in which a procession of real-life folks sat in front of the camera and talked things over with the good Catholic boy from Cleveland. He was television's first "sensitive male," an unabashed liberal who spoke out on social issues important to women, and a radical addition to daytime television. Donahue's guests ran the gamut from Ralph Nader and Gloria

Steinem to Nazis, homosexual priests, and Ku Klux Klansmen. (Inherently serious, he *did* once ask 1,400-pound sisters, "What does it feel like to go shopping and find nothing that fits?") Said Erma Bombeck, his old Dayton neighbor, "He's every wife's replacement for the husband who doesn't talk to her." He led talk show ratings until deposed by *Oprah* in 1986, retiring in 1996 after nearly 7,000 episodes. In 1998, Oprah herself was tied by Jerry Springer, the former mayor of Cincinnati, whose tangled daytime offerings, a combination of sleaze, brawls, and low-rent angst, resembled Hieronymous Bosch at a trailer park. Donahue and Springer were a natural pair of Ohio cultural bookends: Phil started us talking, and Jerry left us speechless.

1974—the bar code.

At one minute after eight on the morning of June 26, a package of chewing gum with a bar code printed on it was scanned at the Marsh Supermarket in Troy, Ohio. The gum was the first product using the new computerized recognition system, and the retail industry was significantly altered forever. It meant that the time between ordering merchandise and receiving it was cut dramatically, inventory turnover was increased, while inventory itself—and the capital to maintain it—was reduced. The code appears on almost every retail item, and it's estimated some 4 billion codes are scanned every day.

(Luke Perry). I'm beginning to suspect that Barberton (City of Barbers?) is called "Magic City" because half its citizens have vanished into thin air—which is to say, into the suburbs of Houston and Atlanta. If *Ohio* has become a word that an increasing number of Americans use as a synonym for the past, it's important to remember that we Buckeyes were born to this long before the factories closed and the small farmers went bankrupt. When I was a child and assumed that those states off the edges of my map were for later, I had already absorbed every Ohioan's innate sense of the transient.

 When I moved to Washington, D.C., at the age of 27, I learned that my suspicions regarding Ohio's placelessness were true. In the past two decades I have heard people repeatedly confuse my state with Iowa or Idaho or Oklahoma.

As a college teacher I frequently hear colleagues—smart folks and holders of Ph.D.'s—conflate Ohio State and Ohio University into an apocryphal "University of Ohio," a thing to set Buckeye teeth on edge. For easterners, that old *New Yorker* cover in which the Hudson serves as a River Lethe to soft-focus oblivion was not far off the mark. Ask a New Yorker and a Philadelphian, if you can get them to stop badgering each other, and they'll agree that Buffalo and Pittsburgh are the ends of the line, twin gateways not to the West but to Palookaville. As for Ohio (East Coast people routinely infantilize the place by over pronouncing it: *Oh-HI-oh* rather than the native *Uh-Hi-yah*), "Fuhgettaboudit!" Cleveland is a blob somewhere between Here and Chicago. Columbus and Cincinnati, hovering in the uncharted ether between Here and St. Louis, are two more blobs in the vast blur of a continent that refuses to click into focus until L.A. smog and San Francisco fog render the world visible again.

Ohioans in exile are painfully aware of our nondescript origins. Whenever two of us meet on non-Buckeye soil, there is often a mutual cluck or a shrug, the subtle acknowledgment of people who once got minimally acquainted during a shared inconvenience like a delayed flight or a stuck elevator. Sometimes there is a hint of admiration for another soul who found a way out. About the old sod itself, though, we have little to say.

"I'm from Ohio, too."

"Oh? Whereabouts?"

"Zanesville."

"Ah."

We Buckeyes have always known that ours is one of those placeless places, the ones that aren't labeled on national weather maps because people don't go there unless they have to. Watch an Ohio flight boarding, and the first thing you'll notice is that nobody is cutting in line. Pasty-faced businessmen lugging sample cases wait patiently behind sunburnt Buckeye families whose vacations have just ended. Here and there, college-age Buckeye sons and daughters lug their backpacks through the gate with expressionless placidity. There are no reduced fares because as the airlines know, an Ohio flight is a captive market, like the post office on April 15. If your sales territory includes Cleveland and Cincinnati, you will be flying to Cleveland and Cincinnati. That week at Epcot was great, but if you live in Akron, you'll be returning to Akron. When grandma dies in Toledo, you'll be heading for a funeral in Toledo. This is the stuff of which Ohio journeys are made. Despite the recent hoopla surrounding the Rock 'n' Roll Hall of Fame and the Indians' Jacobs Field, when was the last time you saw an ad for a vacation package to Cleveland?

By the 1990s, tourism was bringing over eight billion dollars to the state—about the same as Michigan, with all its lakes and forests. But these numbers are inflated by the Buckeye law of just passing through. Most Ohio tourists are merely in transit, stocking up on Stuckey's pralines and Bob Evans sausage and Marathon gas on their way to—or back from—faster times and bigger things. In an attempt to sell more pralines, sausage, and gas, the state's tourism board recently adopted this slogan: "Ohio: The Heart of It All." That's pretty catchy, but doesn't a heart pump blood elsewhere? And if you're the

In 1967, Bowling Green State professor Ray Browne originated the phrase, "popular culture," and in 1972 developed the first— and only—academic department devoted to the study of what he called "the people's culture," which meant everything from bumper stickers to comic books. "If I had called it Everyday Culture or Democratic Culture," he said, "it would not have been so sharply criticized."

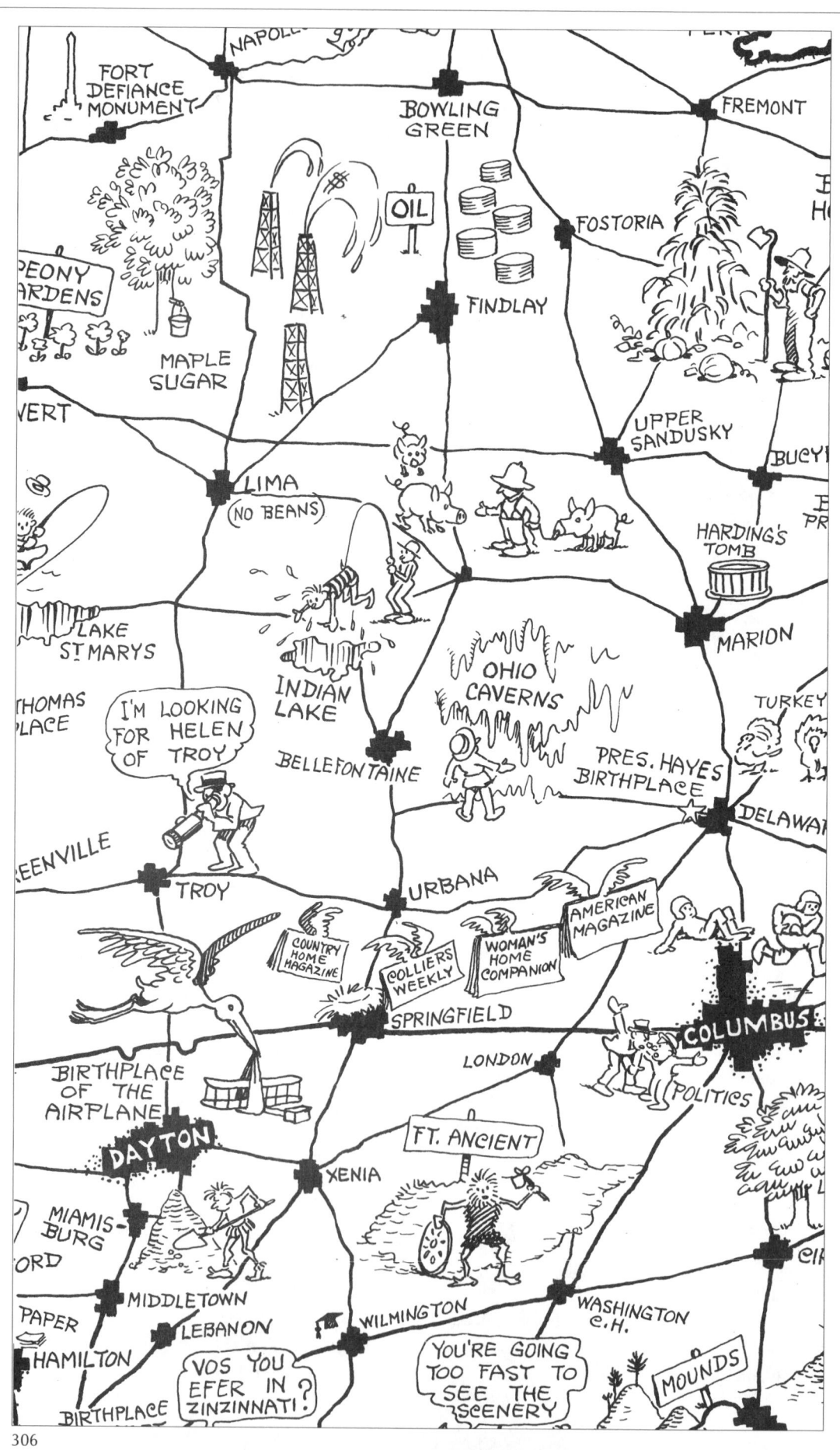

"Heart," then isn't the "All" somewhere else?

It would be easy for a Buckeye to feel bitter, to sulk invisibly in a tent that nobody sees. On those occasions when the burden of formlessness seems too heavy, I could almost say that I'm mad as heck (to use Buckeye-speak) and I'm not gonna take it anymore. Maybe all those Ohio jokes have taken their toll. The worst thing about them—the never-ending litany about Cleveland ("The Mistake on the Lake"), Woody Hayes, farmer savants, shoat-to-boar 4-H projects, the "Mother of Presidents," middle-class "normalcy" (Warren G. Harding's word")—is their fill-in-the-blanks quality. They have less to do with a specific place than with a general impression of incompetence and smallness. The fact that Ohio jokes actually say nothing *about* Ohio has renewed my old quest to redefine something that was never defined in the first place, to find the *quidditas* of Ohio and the core of my unsheddable identity as a Buckeye, through and through.

Lately I've been thinking that I had it right the first time, when I was lying on my belly and poring over that colorful, cryptic map and thinking of it as my whole world—or at least, my whole country. Maybe Ohio, in its stubborn indefinability, really *is* the whole country. This would offer a reasonable and honorable excuse for remaining imageless. A state could do worse than to play America in microcosm, to offer a hodgepodge so thoroughly and weirdly jumbled that its very "thereness" lies beyond recovery. Granted, we Ohioans seem bland. But can we truly *be* bland if we're the products not of nothing but of damned near everything, an entire spectrum blending into white light? And besides, who says that blandness cannot be redemptive?

I've wondered all my life whether a definable "Ohio" exists or does not exist, but I'm beginning to suspect that the question, so framed, poses a false dilemma. Why can't both options be true? If Ohio's being seems to edge

perilously close to nothingness, maybe its being resided *in* nothingness.

This revelation excites me. If Buckeyes are to achieve identities as crisp as those that descend upon Montanans, New Yorkers, and Californians as a birthright, we're going to have to embrace the distinguishing possibilities of indistinction, to accept shapelessness as our defining shape. The beauty part, especially for a middle-aged ex-Ohioan (and the "ex-" feels tellingly natural), is that this assertion of everything-through-nothing runs true to who we really are. Ohioans are nothing if not pragmatic ("Paint your feet blue? Why would you want to do that?"), and any solution that verifies what we already know will seem right as rain, as maddeningly down-to-earth as *we* are, our faces startlingly plain in reflections from Manhattan storefronts or the waters of San Francisco Bay.

Ohio's natureless nature makes us Buckeyes think of ourselves—when we think of ourselves at all—as unwritten pages, blank slates ready for anything and eternally poised to become something. We are, God bless us, an open people. If you grow up knowing that the City of Barbers is a suburb of the City of the High Mound of Tires, or that a drive eastward on Route 224 will take you, in fairly quick succession, through Tiffin, Attica, Willard, New Haven, Nova, Sullivan, Homerville, and Lodi, and juxtapositions that the world throws at you will not be unduly startling. You will find, in fact, that you have an innate taste for odd juxtapositions, that you are uniquely equipped to *see* them as juxtapositions in the first place. In practical terms, this means that you will possess a keen appreciation of the weird, even though—or more accurately, precisely because—the weird is utterly alien to you. Whenever people paint their feet blue, they are surely hoping that an Ohioan will be watching them with mild surprise. They are rarely disappointed.

This, I've come to believe, is an Ohioan's mission: to serve as a counterweight to whatever seems unusual, as a foil to whatever's happening once something actually starts happening. Wherever we go, we Buckeyes form a roving cultural ballast whose heraldic emblem might well be Beige Field with Nothing, *couchant*. An

The people claimed they could hear the rustle of cornstalks in my voice, could see the roll of glacial plains in my walk, could detect in my manners and politics the domes of county courthouses and the steeples of country churches.

—Ohioan Scott Russell Sanders

MAPPING THE INFINITE—Ohio of the 1930s was something of a simpler universe, as rendered by popular mid-century Buckeye cartographer, Claude Shafer, who included it in his 1939 *Cartoon Guide of Ohio.*

Ohioan is a walking zero at the intersection of America's *x* and *y* axes, a point from which everything else gains distinctiveness by veering away. Upholding this imagined, shifting center is what we were born to do.

This might seem a thankless job, but it is not without rewards. Among an Ohioan's blessings is the possibility, nowadays so rare, of being left blissfully alone. All those corny jokes about us— "Second prize, two weeks in Cincinnati!" —are too vague to cut very deep. Wouldn't it be worse to come from Tennessee and endure more pointed comments about moonshine, Elvis, and the Grand Old Opry? How often do uprooted Californians hear wisecracks about earthquakes, tofu, and Third Eye crystal fondlers? And what about the poor New Yorker who moves through life as everybody's Tough Guy, doomed to watch people constantly flinching in anticipation of the next rim-shot insult? This business of being known by total strangers, even through half-truths, strikes me as terrifying in its vulnerability—so public, in Dickinson's phrase, like a frog. I'd much rather be a Buckeye, gloriously swathed in anonymity.

Emerson once remarked that to be great is to be misunderstood. A Buckeye, who defiantly offers nothing to understand, surely embodies this greatness. Ohioans are pure mystery, human ciphers capable of sinking into whatever American place we enter. Take some well-known Clevelanders—Bob Hope, Arsenio Hall, Drew Carey, Teri Garr, Hal Holbrook, Tracy Chapman, David Birney, Tim Conway, Debra Winger, Jack Weston, Paul Newman, the Eagles' Joe Walsh—and ponder their collective affect, their steady projection of generic Americanness. Cleveland and Cincinnati together produced Phil Donahue, a kind of hyper-Ohioan, a Buckeye squared. Unassisted, Cincinnati gave us Roy Rogers, Steven Spielberg, and Doris Day (I wonder whether her forebears founded Dayton, until I remember that her real name was von Kappelhoff). Canton gave us Jack Paar; Columbus, James Thurber, Beverly D'Angelo, and Tom Poston; Toledo, Teresa Brewer and Jamie Farr. Lima, where I was born, produced Phyllis Diller. I'd like to claim Hugh Downs as

my spiritual kinsman because he grew up there, but he was born in Akron.

These are my people, their inscrutable but comfortable blankness shining through even in celebrity. Even Joe Walsh, long enshrouded in a mystique of rock 'n' roll hipness, looks like a hundred guys I used to see schlepping along Cleveland's Euclid Avenue. And speaking of hipness, what about Chrissie Hynde of the Pretenders and the robotic lads of Devo, Akronites all? What about Marilyn Manson, that skinny Canton boy who got tired of being Brian Warner, went Goth, and made a mint? These folks are exceptions that prove the Buckeye rule, If they ever checked out the Akron-Canton airport during their formative years (as they surely did when their sunburnt families returned from those Florida vacations), they learned precisely how *not* to look—how *not* to be—if you want to make it big. If you're seeking the Yin to which every self-respecting rebel must be a Yang, the Akron-Canton airport is not a bad place to start looking, And because Yin and Yang are locked in eternal embrace, Ohioans remain predictable even in dissent, the flip side of the standard-issue Buckeye. I get homesick whenever I see a picture of Chrissie Hynde. Not only was her Industrial Bad-Girl look already around when I was an Ohio teenage, but when I visit my parents for the holidays I see dozens of her younger sisters—pasty faces, low bangs, and owl eyes— scurrying through the malls buying presents for their little brothers.

The chief lesson that Marilyn Manson and I learned at the University of Ohio is that people who are nobody can be whoever they want. We Buckeyes have that freedom, and in full measure, because we are baggageless, devoid of particular expectation. Our job, after all, has always been to watch the other people passing through. A watched person might need a special outfit—a Stetson and boots, perhaps, or maybe one of those Gloucester fisherman's caps, or a floral print shirt that renders its wearer visible as a citizen of Miami (though probably born in Columbus). But if you're one of the watchers, it matters little whether you wear Armani or Sears off the rack. Occasionally, a Buckeye will don a contrived getup—a fright wig and a husband named

"Fang"? Gothic makeup? A British backup band?—and take the stage. However uncharacteristic this turning of the tables may be, a Buckeye will know exactly how to do it. All those years of watching are not lost on us.

 When I was a kid, the *Toledo Blade* ran Earl Wilson's syndicated column, with its chatty gossip about New York showbiz and nightlife. Its running title was "An Ohioan on Broadway," a phrase that brought a rush of pride whenever I saw it.

One of *us*—whoever *we* were—had somehow gotten himself to the center of it all and was now soaking up the energy and feeding it back to the home folks. Whenever the smart set gathered for after-theater drinks and repartee at Toots Shor's, Earl Wilson was our stand-in, a homegrown Edward R. Murrow reporting on the action from a far hipper front than Cleveland or Cincinnati. As I grew older, though, the notion of "An Ohioan on Broadway" began to stink of self-diminishment, of an intentional dumbing-down of who we were, whoever we were. Why should any of *us* play the star-struck yokel just to satisfy an easterner's notion of what an "Ohioan" is? How may New Yorkers were coming to Toledo to gaze at *us*?

Earl Wilson even looked the part: his picture revealed a nondescript man with a bovine face and a bland smile, like an Ohio insurance salesman. But now that I've turned fifty and look like an Ohio insurance salesman too, I've come to see Earl Wilson as a kind of pioneer, a model Buckeye. Could there possibly be light without shadow? Broadway wouldn't even exist unless somebody had a heartfelt acquaintance with slower, duller places. Places like Broadway need a steady supply of cultural and geographical centrists—solid, generic Ohioans—to crane our necks and take it all in. If life is to retain its spice, somebody has to be capable of viewing it from an undifferentiated, spiceless center. Somebody has to observe—to swell a scene or two—as a necessary foil for the observed.

It is this, finally, that makes Ohioans not only visible but indispensable. It is this that defines our niche in America's cultural geography. When a Texan leaves home, he becomes Somebody: a Texan in another place, encouraging or enduring all those faux drawls, cowboy jokes, and quips about the lucrative "erl bidness." When Ohioans leave home, we become Everybody: dependable, middle-of-the-road Americans bearing bread for other people's jam. It is an identity, however shapeless, that the nation cannot do without—and I am resolved to embrace it with honor and even a measure of relief. It's nice, at long last, to be somebody.

My Sohio map, of course, was telling me this all along. I should have heeded the clue embedded in those prominent words at the top: "Standard of Ohio." But I was young and green and had no way of knowing that the *real* Ohio lay in terra incognita, beyond the map's edges in those other places ("To Pittsburgh, "To Lexington," "To Indianapolis") where so many of us would live out our lives. With our special capacity for appreciating wherever we happen to end up, wherever we are *now*, we Ohioans make *your* place seem a little more interesting. Human antidotes to ennui, we expect little and are therefore pleased at most everything we find. If the first man to walk on the moon had not been Neil Armstrong of Wapakoneta, where my favorite grape pop was bottled, the first words uttered on lunar soil might well have been "Houston, there's nothing here." A farther-flung Earl Wilson, Neil Armstrong was only doing what comes naturally to every Buckeye. The instant his boot sank into the powdery surface and he found himself not bored, he had attained an Ohio state of mind. Ohioans, I now realize, become Ohioans only in diaspora. It is only after we have joined our fellow Buckeyes in the realm of elsewhere, a ghostly band of eager onlookers moving unobtrusively through an achingly palpable, non-Buckeye world, that we become our truest and noblest selves. After all, we got here from there.

—*Jeffrey Hammond*

Jeffrey Hammond is the George B. and William Reeves Distinguished Professor in the Liberal Arts at St. Mary's College of Maryland, and a transplanted Ohioan, which dislocation provoked his collection of essays, Ohio States, *published by The Kent State University Press, from which this one is taken.*

In the deeps of the great Depression, the Ohio-born Clarence Darrow, who had become one of America's most famous counselors, penned a notable article in which he delivered *instructions for successfully loading a jury*, to wit: "If a Presbyterian enters the jury box and carefully rolls up his umbrella, and calmly and critically sits down, let him go. He is cold as the grave..." Darrow's best advice was to choose a juror who could laugh. "A juror who laughs," he said, "hates to find anyone guilty." His good Midwestern drollery is still considered topflight courtroom advice.

1

Even Ohio folks do not generally regard him as such, but *one of the great Ohio wags* was OSU coach Woody Hayes. It *is* likelier that he became funnier after-the-fact, as in the remark made to a reporter who dared suggest the old coach had begun to mellow. "Don't you believe I'm mellow," said Hayes. "I'm a little older, a little meaner. I am *not* an innocuous old man." Hayes also said things such as, "Statistics always remind me of the fellow who drowned in the river whose average depth was only three feet." He once aroused his team, flying over to play Illinois, by telling them that Lincoln could have been a great defensive end. "He was tall and rangy, and strong," said Hayes, and turning to his tackle, John Hicks, continued by saying, "I think he could handle you, Hicks." Whereupon Hicks yelled back, "I can take Lincoln, Coach!"

2

When William Jennings Bryan was stumping the country before World War I on behalf of Woodrow Wilson's presidential candidacy, he found himself in Mowrystown, Ohio, addressing the crowd from the back of a manure spreader, which the locals had hastily pushed into the street for a makeshift dais. Said Bryan, "This is *the first time I have spoken from a Republican platform*."

3

Groucho Marx said that *the best bit of waggery he ever heard* about show business he heard in Ohio, in some little town whose name he had long since forgotten. It was delivered by a prospective customer as he stood outside the ticket office: "Before I buy the ticket," the man said, "I want to know one thing about this show: Is it sad or high-kickin'?"

4

The Wag of Baltimore, H.L. Mencken, had no ear for the prose style of President Warren G. Harding of Ohio. It pushed Mencken, in fact, to *an epiphany*: "It reminds me of a string of wet sponges," he wrote. "It reminds me of tattered washing on the line; it reminds me of stale bean soup, of college yells, of dogs barking idiotically through endless nights. It is so bad that a sort of grandeur creeps into it. It drags itself out of a dark abysm...of pish, and crawls insanely up the topmost pinnacle of posh. It is rumble and bumble. It is flap and doodle. It is balder and dash."

5

It is difficult to ever ascribe much humor to that immutable martial presence, William Tecumseh Sherman, but in one of his *reflections upon the nature of conflict*, we seem to discern, if not quiet waggery, then surely its distant cousin, irony: "Military history," said the old general, "is to die in battle and have your name spelled wrong in the newspapers."

6

Charley Weaver was once asked, on the Jack Paar Show, about juvenile delinquency in Mt. Idy, his hometown, and his answer nicely illustrated typical

7 ***Buckeye pragmatism toward problem-solving***: "We put on a ballet for the kiddies at Snyder's Swamp. The boys dress as kumquats and the girls are draped in creeping nussman. In the finale, they all circle the swamp and then dance into it. Bottom's all quicksand. Have to replace the whole cast every year—but we don't have any delinquency problems."

8 ***Leading Buckeye wag*** Jonathan Winters does Maudie Frickert, our timeless Miz Ohio: "I'll always remember the day that Lamargene went up to Wumler's Bluff above the stone quarry. He stood there—he musta been 6 feet 4 inches if he was a foot—and he had taped 147 pigeons to his arms. Suddenly he stepped off and he flew just fine for maybe 15 or 20 seconds. Then a kid come out of nowhere and throwed a handful of popcorn into the quarry and poor Lamargene's brains was bashed out."

9 ***Best example of 19th Century waggery***, by secretary of state William M. Evarts, and prompted by Ohioan Lemonade Lucy Hayes, after one of her teetotaling White House affairs: "It was a brilliant affair," Evarts said mournfully. "The water flowed like champagne."

10 ***Best waggish moment from Ohio vaudeville***, Fred Allen recalling his friend, Bert Yorke: "After one show, in Cleveland, when we had come off the stage, Bert followed me into the dressing room. He had a red nose on and a funny facial make-up, and was wearing a dirty streetcleaner's helmet, a yellow Inverness in the lapel of which he had a large sponge posing as a chrysanthemum, and on his hands he had red rubber gloves. He was wearing sailor pants with a watch fob that was the handle of a toilet chain; he had soiled spats over a big pair of shoes, and was carrying a cane, the ferrule of which reposed in a rubber plunger. Arrayed like a thrift shop come to life, and I quote, 'I ain't going to be no straight man for nobody!'"

11 It was in Ohio that ***one of show business' most immortal waggeries*** was first uttered, said Allen: "In Toledo, the Keith Theatre had been reduced to playing three shows daily. The orchestra leader, a little bald, acid-looking man, was so sick of looking at Bert and me that every time we walked on the stage he hung his head. To accommodate his drooping head he had to take his violin from under his chin and play it down around his navel. At one of the many shows we did I said to him, 'What would you charge to haunt a house?' This line has since been said by many comedians, but I said it first, on a really trying day in Toledo."

12 ***Best 20th Century wag***, as yet unsurpassed, is Alice Roosevelt Longworth, the wife of Cincinnatian Nicholas Longworth, i.e., "If you can't say something good about someone, sit right here by me."

13 Bob Hope grew up in Cleveland, an indifferent student, he said, writing so many test answers on his sleeve that "my shirt graduated before I did." When he headed west, he said, ***"The day I left Ohio is now an official holiday.*** This is the only state with two Thanksgivings." He made frequent homecomings, however, returning in the early 1930s to play the Palace Theatre where a group of neighborhood friends came to see him. They all sat together and when Hope appeared on stage, they pulled out newspapers and read through his act. In 1953, Cleveland gave him Bob Hope Day. "They gave me the keys to the city," he said. "The only thing they didn't tell me is that Cleveland locks from the inside."

When Bob Hope turned 100 in 2003, he was in the Guinness World Records as most honored entertainer on the planet: four stars on Hollywood Boulevard, two honorary Oscars, two knighthoods (the British Empire and the Vatican), and a Congressional Medal of Honor. He was the last great star whose work went from vaudeville to television, through radio, film, and stage.

The most waggish man in Ohio baseball in the 1970s was Cincinnati Reds manager Sparky Anderson. "One of these days they are going to have Spear Day at Riverfront Stadium, and the fan coming closest to my heart when I yank a pitcher will win a Buick." He also said, "So many players credit God with their swing after hitting a home run. I look at it this way: If God let you hit a home run last time up, then who struck you out the two times before that?" And:"My mother, I love her. But she don't pitch for me." **14**

Modern comics steel themselves for what they might find as they ply their wares on the club circuit. But few find themselves so adversarily misaligned with an audience as Cleveland comic Steve Harvey, who was working a Boston club and found himself the victim of group waggery: "I had been opening all week with a blues song that I said Ray Charles had given me. It went, *I got a big, fat, ugly woman/She's fat and ugly all the time/ And when I'm with that ugly woman/I thank the Lord he made me blind.* That was the punch line. It had been working well all week. This night, though, I got no response. I mean NO response. Nothing. So I reached down in the front row to shake a guy's hand and said, 'What's the matter, man, you blind?' And he said, "Yes, I am." I'm trying to recover so I say, 'What's the matter with the rest of y'all?' The first five rows were filled with the Cambridge School of the Blind and they all raised their white canes. It looked like a sequoia forest of canes, man. I apologized the best I could but I couldn't get anywhere with that crowd the rest of the night no matter what I did..."

Wagsmanship, 1st rule: Always try to see eye-to-eye with your audience. **15**

The largest fellow to ever occupy the White House was William Howard Taft, and it was quite an occupation. Once, he got stuck in the Executive bathtub. His Ampleness wore Executive jams with a 54-inch waist, and he was not able to tee up his own golf ball. One time, while he was vacationing in Beverly Bay, Massachusetts, one of the neighbors suggested to a friend that they go swimming. Noticing President Taft in the surf, the friend said, "Perhaps we'd better wait. The President seems to be using the ocean." **16**

Bob Hagan, the Lake County Democrat, was known during his tenure at the statehouse as *"the conscience of the legislature."* But before he entered politics he wrote for Danny Thomas, and he was also the political wag of the legislature. "He has a habit of putting his foot in his mouth," Hagan once said of Dan Quayle. "And that's not so easy considering where his head is." Hagan was also funny about his Catholic heritage. "My third-grade teacher was Sister Mary Ayatollah," he said. "They said she came over during the potato famine. Another rumor was that she started it." **17**

18   Jack Parr said ***the highest moment of waggery*** on his television show was delivered by Jay Silverheels, the Indian actor who portrayed Tonto on *The Lone Ranger*. Parr asked Silverheels how the actor had come about marrying an Italian girl. "As an Indian," replied Silverheels, "I'd been looking all my life for a way to get even with Columbus."

19   This is Kelly Monteith's ***favorite bit of Ohio waggery***:
A cheap, fleabag circus is playing a one-nighter in a small Ohio town. A local girl, adventurous and enamored of show business, ran off with the circus when it left. Being innocent and rather frightened, she confided in the ringmaster, 'I've never traveled with a circus before. Can you give me any advice?'
'Yes,' he replied *sotto voce*, 'don't undress in front of the bearded lady.'

20   ***Ohio's greatest modern domestic wag*** was Erma Bombeck. Born suburban—outside of Dayton—she escaped from its clutches by reversing field and pinning her environs with an unwavering waggish eye. "Garbage, if it's made right," she said, "takes a full week." She detailed the flat suburban detail, sparing no one: "If Mary had lived on our block, we would have said, 'Of course she has time to go to the dentist. She only has Jesus.'" And: "Those magazine dieting stories always have the testimonial of a woman who wore a dress that could slipcover New Jersey in one photo and 30 days later looked like a well-dressed thermometer." Her advice to the suburbs, and anybody anywhere else, since she's fairly positive no one today got too far away, was, "If you can't make it better, you can laugh at it."

1974

21   This is ***Myron Cohen's favorite bit of Ohio waggery***: The scene for this, he says, can be the lobby of any hotel in Columbus:
A very rich young man says to his girlfriend, 'If I had no money, would you still love me?'
'Yes,' she answers, 'but I would miss you.'

22   Michael DiSalle was also ***no stranger to a quick wag***. 1947
When the former governor was mayor of Toledo in the late 1940s, he was visited by the ex-king, Michael of Rumania, who walked the streets of Toledo with DiSalle and noted with humor that the commoners called the mayor "Mike." Said DiSalle, "If more people called *you* Mike, you might still be king."

23   The Democratic party chairman in Mahoning County, finding himself perpetually dealing with the propwash from his controversial congressman, Jim Traficant, made this ***waggish assessment*** to the congressman: "It's easy for your crocodile mouth to get your hummingbird ass in trouble."

24   Ms. Lula Riggs of Norwood, upon her 106th birthday, spoke to an inquiring newspaperman about her three husbands: ***"I like variety," she wagged.*** "I still have one of them, you know. The middle one. They had him cremated and I have him at home. I go over and shake him every now and then."

1992

Some LESSER-KNOWN NOBEL PRIZES AWARDED in OSLO LAST WEEK

PUBLIC SERVICE

MARY JANE STRUKE, FOR HER THEORY OF CAMPAIGN COMMERCIAL INTENSITY, WHICH STATES THAT ONLY DEADLY SERIOUS PEOPLE BUY TELEVISION TIME DURING LOCAL ELECTION SEASON.

COMEDY

MANNY BEAMER, FOR HIS RESEARCH in the FIELD OF MARGINAL HUMOR, WHICH LED TO the DISCOVERY OF the UNINTENTIONAL PUN.

LAUNDRY

GEORGE BRIGLEY, FOR TURNING MORE THAN 54,000 SOCKS RIGHT-SIDE-OUT in a CAREER SPANNING 8 CHILDREN.

NOBEL PEAS PRIZE

LOIS WANAMAKER, A CAFETERIA WORKER in PISGAH, OHIO, FOR HER RADICAL REINVENTION OF SUCCOTASH.

NOBEL

YOUR NAME HERE

JIM BORGMAN ©1997 CINCINNATI ENQUIRER

National Spelling Bee Winners (and their final word)

1964

William Kerek

Akron Beacon Journal

sycophant

1957

Sandra Owen

Canton Repository

schappe

1950

Diana Reynard

Cleveland Press

meticulosity

1949

Kim Calvin

Canton Repository

dulcimer

1948

Jean Chappelear

Akron Beacon Journal

psychiatry

The Pulitzer

Pulitzer Prizes, which were endowed by publisher Joseph Pulitzer and are awarded annually by Columbia University, recognize excellence in journalism, letters, and music. They have been won by the following Ohioans:

1918　History
　　　James F. Rhodes　　　Cleveland
　　　History of the Civil War, 1861-1865
1926　Biography or autobiography
　　　Harvey William Cushing　　Cleveland
　　　The Life of Sir William Osler, 2 vols.
1927　Literature
　　　Louis Bromfield　　　Mansfield
　　　Early Autumn
　　　Meritorious Public Service
　　　Canton *Daily News*
　　　Editorial writing
　　　Frederic L. Bullard　　Wauseon
　　　"We Submit" Boston *Herald*
1937　Journalism
　　　David Dietz
1937　Journalism
　　　Anne O'Hare McCormick　Columbus
1938　History
　　　Paul Herman Buck　　Columbus
　　　The Road to Reunion, 1865-1900
1944　Editorial Writing
　　　Henry Haskell　　　Huntington
　　　Kansas City *Star*
1945　Journalism
　　　James Reston　　　Xenia
　　　The New York Times

1946　Drama
　　　Russell Crouse　　　Findlay
　　　State of the Union
　　　History
　　　Arthur M. Schlesinger, Jr.　Columbus
　　　The Age of Jackson
1951　Fiction
　　　Conrad Richter　　　Cleveland
　　　The Town
1953　Editorial cartooning
　　　Edward D. Kuekes　　Cleveland
　　　"Aftermath" Cleveland *Plain Dealer*
1954　History
　　　Bruce Catton　　　Cleveland
　　　A Stillness at Appomattox
1957　Journalism
　　　James Reston　　　Xenia
　　　The New York Times
1958　Drama (adaptation)
　　　Ketti Fings　　　Columbus
　　　Look Homeward Angel
1961　Editorial cartooning
　　　Carey Cassius Orr
　　　"The Kindly Tiger" Chicago *Tribune*
　　　International reporting
　　　Lynn Heinzerling
　　　Drama
　　　Tad Mosel　　　Steubenville
　　　All the Way Home
1966　History
　　　Arthur M. Schlesinger, Jr.　Columbus
　　　A Thousand Days
1968　Correspondence
　　　Knight Newspapers

1970 Drama
    Charles Gordone   Cleveland
    No Place to Be Somebody
1971 Local Reporting
    Akron Beacon Journal
1972 Poetry
    James Wright   Martins Ferry
    Collected Poems
1975 Local Reporting
    Xenia Daily Gazette
1981 Editorial Cartooning
    Mike Peters   Dayton
1984 Poetry
    Mary Oliver   Cleveland
    American Primative
1985 Drama
    James Lapine   Mansfield
    Sunday in the Park with George
1987 General Reporting/News
    Akron Beacon Journal
    Poetry
    Rita Dove   Akron
    Thomas & Beulah
    Fiction
1988 Fiction
    Toni Morrison   Lorain
    Beloved
    Reporting
    Walt Bogdanich
    Wall Street Journal
1989 Commentary
    Clarence Page   Middletown
1991 Editorial cartooning
    Jim Borgman   Cincinnati
1993 Distinguished Criticism
    Michael Dirda   Lorain
1994 Public Service
    Akron Beacon Journal
1998 History
    Edward J. Larson   Mansfield
    Summer for the Gods
    Natonal Reporting
    Russell Carollo   Dayton
    Jeff Nesmith   Dayton
    Dayton Daily News
1999 Fiction
    Michael Cunningham   Cincinnati
    The Hours
    Journalism
    David Dietz
    New York Harold Tribune
2002 Poetry
    Richard Howard   Cleveland
    Talking Cures

National Book Award

The National Book Award is the nation's major book award. It is given by the National Book Foundation.

1964 Poetry
    John Crowe Ransom   Gambier
    Selected Poems
1982 First Novel
    Robb Forman Dew   Mt. Vernon
    Dale Loves Sophie to Death

National Book Critics Circle

Founded in 1974 the National Book Critics Circle has 700 members. It gives annual awards for the best book in fiction, general nonfiction, biography/autobiography, poetry and criticism.

1995 Poetry
    William Mathews   Cincinnati
    Poetry: Time and Memory
2002 Poetry
    Richard Howard   Cleveland
    Lifetime Achievement

Newbery Medal

The Newbery Medal is named for the 18th century British bookseller John Newbery. It is awarded annually by the Association for Library Service to Children, a division of the American Library Association, to the author of the most distinguished contribution to American literature for children.

1944 Lois Lenski   Springfield
    Strawberry Girl
1972 Alan Eckert   Dayton
    Incident at Hawk's Hill
1974 Virginia Hamilton   Yellow Springs
    M.C. Higgins the Great
1993 Cynthia Rylant   Kent
    Missing May
1995 Sharon Creech   Cleveland
    Walk Two Moons

1935

Clara Mohler

Akron Beacon Journal

intelligible

1933

Alma Roach, *Akron Beacon Journal*

torsion

1927

Dean Lucas

Akron Beacon Journal

luxuriance

—*Scripps Howard National Spelling Bee*

PEN/Faulkner Award

The award is named for William Faulkner who used his Nobel Prize funds to create an award for young writers, and affiliated with PEN (poets, playwrights, editors, essayists, and novelists). The award was founded by writers in 1980 to honor their peers and is the largest juried award for fiction in the United States.

| 1999 | Michael Cunningham | Cincinnati |
| | *The Hours* | |

Coretta Scott King Book Award

The award is presented by the Coretta Scott King Task Force of the American Library Association's Social Responsibilities Round Table. Recipients are authors and illustrators of African descent whose distinguished books promote an understanding and appreciation of the "American Dream."

1994	Angela Johnson	Kent
	Toning the Sweep	
2001	Jacqueline Woodson	Columbus
	Locomotion	

Hugo Award

The Hugo Awards are given to each year's outstanding science fiction works. They are voted on by the membership of the World Science Fiction Society.

1960	Short Fiction	
	Daniel Keyes	
	"Flowers for Algernon"	
1966	Novel	
	Roger Zelazny	Euclid
	...And Call Me Conrad	
	Short Fiction	
	Harlan Ellison	Cleveland
	"Repent Harlequin! Said the Ticktockman"	
1968	Novel	
	Roger Zelazny	Euclid
	Lord of Light	
	Short Story	
	Harlan Ellison	Cleveland
	"I Have No Mouth, and I Must Scream"	
	Dramatic Presentation	
	Harlan Ellison	Cleveland
	"City on the Edge of Forever" *Star Trek*	
	Special Award	
	Harlan Ellison	Cleveland
	Dangerous Visions	
1969	Short Story	
	Harlan Ellison	Cleveland
	"The Beast That Shouted Love at the Heart of the World"	

	Special Award	
	Neil Armstrong	Wapakoneta
	Moon Landing	
1972	Special Award	
	Harlan Ellison	Cleveland
	Again, Dangerous Visions	
1974	Novelette	
	Harlan Ellison	Cleveland
	"The Deathbird"	
1975	Novelette	
	Harlan Ellison	Cleveland
	"Adrift Just Off the Islets of Langerhans"	
1976	Novella	
	Roger Zelanzy	Euclid
	"Home is the Hangman"	
1977	Gandalf Award (Grand Master)	
	Andre Norton	Cleveland
1979	Campbell Award	
	Stephen R. Donaldson	Whooster
1982	Novelette	
	Roger Zelazny	Euclid
	"Unicorn Variation"	
1984	Novella	
	Roger Zelanzy	Euclid
	"Twenty-four Views of Mount Fuji, by Hokusau"	
	Novelette	
	Harlin Ellison	Columbus
	"Paladin of the Lost Hour"	
1987	Novelette	
	Roger Zelazny	Euclid
	"Permafrost"	
1989	Short Story	
	Mike Resnick	Cincinnati
	"Kirinyana"	
1990	Novella	
	Lois McMaster Bujold	Columbus
	"The Mountains of Mourning"	
1991	Novel	
	Lois McMaster Bujold	Columbus
	The Vor Game	
	Novelette	
	Mike Resnick	Cincinnati
	"The Manamouki"	
1992	Novel	
	Lois McMaster Bujold	Columbus
	Barrayar	
1995	Novel	
	Lois McMaster Bujold	Columbus
	Mirror Dance	
	Novella	
	Mike Resnick	Cincinnati
	"Seven Views of Olduvai Gorge"	
1998	Short Story	
	Mike Resnick	Cincinnati
	"The 43 Antarean Dynasties"	

Nebula Award

The Nebula Awards have been given since 1965 by the Science Fiction and Fantasy Writers of America for the year's best novel, novella, novelette, and short story.

1965 Novella
    Roger Zelazny   Euclid
    "The Saliva Tree"
    Novelette
    Roger Zelazny   Euclid
    "The Doors of His Face, the Lamps of His Mouth"
    Short Story
    Harlan Ellison   Cleveland
    "Repent, Harlequin! Said the Ticktockman"
1969 Novella
    Harlan Ellison   Cleveland
    "A Boy and His Dog"
1975 Novella
    Roger Zelazny   Euclid
    "Home is the Hangman"
1977 Short Story
    Harlan Ellison   Cleveland
    "Jeffy if Five"
1988 Novel
    Lois McMaster Bujold   Columbus
    Falling Free
1989 Novella
    Lois McMaster Bujold   Columbus
    "The Mountains of Mourning"
1994 Novella
    Mike Resnick   Cincinnati
    "Seven Views of Olduvai Gorge"
1999 Author Emeritus
    Daniel Keyes
2000 Bradbury Award
    Harlan Ellison   Cleveland

The Mystery Writiers of America

1948 First Novel
    Fredric Brown   Cincinnati
    The Fabulous Clipjoint
1969 Juvenile
    Virginia Hamilton   Yellow Springs
    The House of Dies Drear
1974 Short Story
    Harlan Ellison   Cleveland
    "The Whimper of Whipped Dogs"
1988 Short Story
    Harlan Ellison   Cleveland
    "Soft Monkey"
1980 Grand Master
    W.R. Burnett   Springfield

Bram Stoker Award

The Bram Stoker Award is given by the Horror Writer's Association. The awards (begun in 1987) are presented in twelve categories.

1987 Fiction Collection
    Harlan Ellison   Cleveland
    The Essential Ellison
1989 Nonfiction
    Harlan Ellison   Cleveland
    Harlan Ellison's Watching
1993 Novella
    Harlan Ellison   Cleveland
    "Mefisto in Onyx"
1995 Lifetime Achievement
    Harlan Ellison   Cleveland
1999 Other Media (audio)
    Harlan Ellison   Cleveland
    "I Have No Mouth, and I Must Scream"

HARLAN ELLISON: THE BEAST THAT SHOUTED

The Painesville, Ohio, writer **Harlan Ellison** did not define "speculative fiction," but he may have defined "prolific." His bibliography includes over 70 books, as well as 1,700 short stories, essays, articles, newspaper columns, two dozen teleplays, and a dozen motion pictures. He has won the Hugo award 8½ times, the Nebula award three times, the Bram Stoker award six times (including The Lifetime Achievement Award in 1996), and the Edgar Allan Poe award of the Mystery Writers of America twice. *The New York Times Book Review* said he had "the spellbinding quality of a great nonstop talker, with a cultural warehouse for a mind." And his friend, Michael Moorcock, said, "Harlan Ellison speaks about fifteen languages, all of them English. This gift is derived from a natural relish for words...It also enables him to work an audience. If he could produce his stories in front of about two thousand people at Circus Circus, Las Vegas, I think he would probably be in his element. The trouble with writing is that it is still a somewhat slow process, still essentially a solitary activity, and Harlan Ellison is still trying to beat those particular problems..." Known for a certain abrasive quality, he is remembered for saying, "The two most common elements in the universe are hydrogen and stupidity."

When Nobel laureate Robert Millikan attended Oberlin, he taught himself the elements of physics for nobody there knew enough to teach him. He was athletic and considered a career in physical education until one of his professors convinced him to attend Columbia University. Quote: "My idea of an educated person is one who can converse on one subject for more than two minutes."

Caldecott

The Caldecott Medal is given by the Association for Library Service to Children (a division of the American Library Association) to the artist of the most distinguished American picture book for children.

1942	Robert McCloskey	Hamilton
	Make Way for Ducklings	
1958	Robert McCloskey	Hamilton
	Time of Wonders	
1967	Evaline Ness	Union City
	Sam, Bangs, & Moonshine	
1993	Denise Fleming	Toledo
	In the Small, Small Pond	

Nobel Prizes

Nobel Prizes, endowed by the inventor of dynamite, Alfred B. Nobel, are annually given to individuals who have most benefited humanity in chemistry, physics, literature, medicine-physiology, and peace. Since 1901, the first year they were awarded, these Ohioans have won Nobel Prizes:

1923	*Physics*	
	Robert Millikan	B.A. Oberlin College
		M.A. Oberlin College
1925	*Peace*	
	Charles Gates Dawes	Marietta
		B.A. Marietta College
		L.L.B. Cincinnati Law School
		M.A. Marietta College
1927	*Physics*	
	Arthur Compton	Wooster
		B.S. College of Wooster
1974	*Chemistry*	
	Paul J. Flory	M.S. Ohio State University
		PhD. Ohio State University
1980	*Chemistry*	
	Paul Berg	PhD. Western Reserve U.
1981	*Medicine*	
	Roger Sperry	B.A. Oberlin College
		M.A. Oberlin College
1983	*Physics*	
	William A. Fowler	B. Eng. Ohio State University

1986	*Medicine*	
	Stanley Cohen	M.A. Oberlin Colege
1987	*Chemistry*	
	Charles Pedersen	B.S. U. of Dayton
1993	*Literature*	
	Tony Morrison	Lorain

Academy Awards

The Academy Awards, given annually by the Academy of Motion Picture Arts and Sciences, recognize outstanding achievement in the film industry. These Ohioans have won the golden "Oscar" statuette:

1928	Best Actor	
	Warner Baxter	Columbus
	In Old Arizona	
1934	Best Actor	
	Clark Gable	Cadiz
	It Happened One Night	
1935	Best Screenplay	
	Dudley Nichols	Wapakoneta
	The Informer	
1940	Best Screenplay	
	David Ogden Stewart	Columbus
	Philadelphia Story	
1949	Best Supporting Actor	
	Dean Jagger	Columbus Grove
	Twelve O'Clock High	
1961	Best Supporting Actor	
	George Chakiris	Cincinnati
	Wesr Side Story	
1971	Honorary	
	Lillian Gish	Lillian Gish
1972	Best Supporting Actor	
	Joel Grey	Cleveland
	Cabaret	
	Best Supporting Actress	
	Eileen Heckart	Columbus
	Butterflies are Free	
1986	Best Actor	
	Paul Newman	Cleveland
	The Color of Money	
1993	Directing	
	Steven Spielberg	Cincinnati
	Schindler's List	
2002	Best Actress	
	Halle Berry	Cleveland
	Monster's Ball	

Dudley Nichols: Top of His Game (and yet no hardware)

Dudley Nichols, a doctor's son from Wapakoneta, was one of the most highly regarded screenwriters of the mid-century. His early work with director John Ford grew into screenplays for some of Ford's best-known films, including *The Lost Patrol*, *Stagecoach*, and *The Informer*, for which he won an Oscar but at the ceremonies turned it down because of a dispute between industry guilds and the Academy over union matters. He was the first Oscar winner to refuse the award.

Miss Ohio Winners

Year	Miss Ohio	Hometown
1922-23	Mary Campbell	Columbus
1937	Jean Bernice Fadden	N/A
1938	Marilyn Meseke	Marion
1939	Jeanne Patricia Soboda	N/A
1940	Violet Berze	N/A
1941	Janice Sulzman	N/A
1945	Julia Ann Donahue	N/A
1947	Nancy Nesbitt	Cleveland
1948	Maxine Waack	Fairview
1949	Florence Bondi	Cleveland
1950	Irene Farren	Grand River
1951	Ruth Howell	Apple Creek
1952	Carol Koontz	Bolivar
1953	Martha Zimmerman	Salem
1954	Barbara Quinlin	Alliance
1955	Marguerite Garr	Cincinnati
1956	Roberta Palmer	Cleveland
1957	Linda Hattman	Mansfield
1958	Margaret Putnam	Ada
1959	Carole Weiler	Circleville
1960	Alice McClain	Marion
1961	Darlene DePasquale	Dayton
1962	Jacquelyn Mayer	Sandusky
1963	Peggy Emerson	Akron
	Bonne Gawronski	
1964	Diane Courtwright	Columbus
1965	Valerie Lavin	Canton
1966	Sharon Phillian	Delaware
1967	Pamela Sue Robinson	Beavercreek
1968	Leslyn Anita Hiple	Louisville
1969	Kathy Baumann	Independence
1970	Grace Elaine Bird	Alliance
1971	Laurie Lea Schaefer	Bexley
1972	Judy Jones	Oxford
1973	Karen Sue Sparka	Bowling Green
1974	Cheryl Ann Yourkvitch	Lorain
1975	Lorrie Janet Kapsta	Columbus
1976	Susan Kay Banks	Warren
1977	Janice Elaine Cooley	Portsmouth
1978	Susan Perkins	Columbus
	Joan Patricia Gilger	Ontario
	Sher Patrick	Centerville
1979	Tana Kay Carli	Alliance
1980	Kathleen Ann Vernon	Mansfield
1981	Juliana Marie Zilba	Toledo
1982	Debra Diane Gombert	Columbus
1983	Pamela Helean Rigas	Canfield
1984	Melissa Bradley	Mansfield
1985	Suellen Cochran	Heath
1986	Mary Elizabeth Zilba	Toledo
1987	Susan Kay Johnson	Ravenna
1988	Sarah Ann Evans	Van Wert
1989	Kristin Huffman	Canal Winchester
1990	Kristi Cooke	Marion
1991	Renee Autherson	Heuth
1992	Robin Meade	Mansfield
1993	Titilayo Acledokun	Cincinnati
1994	Lea Mack	Pickerington
1995	Ellen Pasturzak	Portsmouth
1996	Robyn Hancock	Grand Rapids
1997	Kelly Creager	Conneaut
1998	Cheya Watkins	Cincinnati
1999	Tiffany Baumann	Cleveland
2000	Stephanie Meisberger	Zanesville
2001	Natalie Witwer	Dublin

Warner Baxter, a "dashingly handsome actor with a resonant voice," portrayed in his academy award role the Cisco Kid, that happy-go-lucky South of the border Robin Hood. Baxter won the role by default, after intended star Raoul Walsh was injured in a car accident.

There

she goes

In 1929,
Ruth Burnam
of Cleveland was
named Miss America
in a Baltimore
pageant, after the
Atlantic City
pageant had failed
financially following
the 1927 pageant.
Burnam went on a
national tour after
the stock market
crashed and when no
one wanted to sponsor
the contest in 1930,
she kept the title and
continued the tour.
The Miss America
Organization,
however, regards
only its contestants as
true Miss Americas,
leaving Ms. Burnam
title-less.

—Cleveland Plain
Dealer

AMERICAN OBSESSION

| 2002 | Tiffany Hass | Cincinnati |
| 2003 | Janelle Couts | Akron |

N/A denotes not available
Source: Mansfield Jaycees

Miss Americas from Ohio

1922-23	Mary Campbell	Columbus
1938	Marilyn Meseke	Marion
1963	Jacquelyn Mayer	Sandusky
1972	Laurie Lea Schaefer	Bexley
1978	Susan Perkins	Columbus

Source: Mansfield Jaycees

Mrs. Ohio Winners

1979	Susan Kerr	Parma
1980	Deborah Kinsler	Marion
1981	Nora Zimmerman	Strongsville
1982	Victoria Boyer	Miamisburg
1983	Lula Mae Page	Bellefontaine
1984	Deborah McDaniel	Mansfield
1985	Cynthia Griswald	North Royalton
1986	Elisabeth Bell	Lucasville
1987	Cherlynn Kenke	Dayton
1988	Doreen Luke	Gahanna

1989	Tamara Epstein	Kettering
1990	Stacey Leigh Arthur	Sidney
1991	Rosemarie Mancuso	Cleveland
1992	Nancy Nelson	Marysville
1993	Dawn Baiko	Brecksville
1994	Kathy Shale	Springfield
1995	Nancy Huey	Harville
1996	Cynthia Pensiero	Cleveland
1997	Shawn Butz	Cincinnati
1998	Rose Marie Gibson	Cincinnati
1999	Marcy Fitzgerald	West Chester
2000	Teresa Rubio	Shaker Heights
2001	Darlene McKinney	Louisville
2002	Michelle Moore-Galvin	Upper Arlington
2003	Katherine Boyd-Golladay	RockyRiver

Mrs. America Winners

| 1996 | Cynthia Pensiero | Cleveland |

Source: Mrs. America pageant

National Aviation Hall of Fame Enshrinees

The National Aviation Hall of Fame is located at the United States Air Force Museum in Dayton, Ohio. Inductees listed below are either Ohioans, or those who had some significant career connection to Ohio.
www.nationalaviation.org

1962
Orville Wright
Wilbur Wright

On December 17 in 1903, they successfully made the first sustained controlled powered flight with Orville at the controls and flew 120 feet in 12 seconds. Four flights were made that day with Wilbur making the longest, flying 852 feet in 59 seconds. Orville and his brother continued their experiments and in 1908 Wilbur took their airplane to France, stunning the European aviation community. They soon received a contract with the U.S. Department of War for the first military airplane. They formed the Wright Company to manufacture their airplanes and opened a flying school.

1963
Frank Purdy Lahm

Frank Purdy Lahm was born in Mansfield, Ohio, and flew with Orville Wright in 1908, becoming the first American Army officer to fly in an airplane. The next year, after training for a mere 3 hours with Wilbur Wright, was pronounced a pilot for the U.S. Army. In 1920, he established the Air Corps Training Center at San Antonio, earning him the unofficial title, "Father of the West Point of the Air."

TOPICS OF THE TIMES.

Waiting for the Wrights. Reports of almost daily flights by the WRIGHT brothers are coming from North Carolina, and, accepting as true only those that claim the least in the way of present achievement, the indications are that the Ohio inventors have devised a real flying machine and have learned how to manage it over short distances.

They still must start from a stretch of railway track, but there are many birds, and some of the ablest among them, that cannot rise from the ground at all, and must have a water surface on which to acquire sufficient impetus to make their wings effective. The WRIGHTS, it is said, hope soon to overcome the present limitations of their machine in this respect, but that is a small matter and might well be left for later consideration.

No end of glory is theirs if they will only do in public what they are said to do when far from expert observation. We are all eager to acclaim them as the conquerors of the air, but their obstinate secrecy makes everybody suspicious and irritable.

1965
A. Roy Knabenshue

Toledo's A. Roy Knabenshue made outstanding contributions to aviation as an aeronaut making balloon flights; by being among the first to pilot a steerable balloon; as one of the pilots of the first successful American dirigible; as a builder and exhibitor of dirigibles of his own design; as manager of the Wright Brothers' Exhibition Team; and by building observation balloons during World War I.

Edward Vernon Rickenbacker

With 26 enemy kills in World War I, the Columbus, Ohio, native was America's first Ace of Aces. After the war he was co-founder of Florida Airways. In 1934 he set a transcontinental record of just over 13 hours in a DC-2, which he followed a year later by setting another trans-continental record in a DC-3 of just over 12 hours.

Charles Edward Taylor

Taylor is the "Unsung Hero of Aviation." As the first aviation mechanic in powered flight, he built the engine that powered the Wrights' first airplane. Taylor was the first aviation mechanic,

---

the airport manager at Huffman Prairie, and the man behind construction and maintenance of the early aircraft engines. In 1911, Calbraith Perry Rodgers decided to make a flight coast to coast in a Wright biplane. Taylor was the mechanic as the plane suffered 16 major crashes. After 49 days they arrived with only the vertical rudder and engine's drip pan left of the original plane, testifying to his skill as a mechanic.

1968
John Arthur Macready

Macready served as a test pilot at McCook Field in Dayton, Ohio, where he set an altitude record of 34,509 feet in 1921.

George Churchill Kenney

After World War I, Kenney attended engineering school at McCook Field, Ohio, and pioneered the mounting of machine guns on warplane wings to increase firepower. During a 1941 interview with a newspaper reporter, George Kenney recalled the two-year period from 1923 to 1925 when he held four jobs simultaneously, serving in Dayton as McCook field's chief of shops, chief of inspection, chief of production engineering and contracting officer. Kenney told the reporter, "One day I signed a letter as the chief of inspection, bawling out the chief of shops for some delay, and then went over to the shops office and found my own letter waiting for me." He returned to Dayton as chief of production at Wright Field in 1939.

1972
Curtis E. LeMay

Born in Columbus, Ohio, General LeMay was known for his gruff demeanor. During World War II, the then Colonel

---

Old Iron pants

Curtis LeMay, a Columbus native and Ohio State grad, became Chief of Staff of the Air Force. His finest hour was 1948, when he took charge of the Berlin Airlift. His worst was 1968, when he made a failed vice-presidential bid on George Wallace's American Independent ticket.

LeMay had organized and trained the 305th Bombardment Group and led them into combat in the European theater. He developed formation techniques that were later adapted to the B-29 Flying Fortresses over the Pacific. As the commanding General of the 3rd Bombardment Division in England, he led the famous Regensberg Raid deep into Germany and Africa. Following the war, as commander of the U.S. Air Force in Europe, he organized the Berlin Airlift, and in 1948 he assumed command of the new SAC (Strategic Air Command) where he laid plans for the ICBM (Intercontinental Ballistic Missile). From 1957 to 1961 he was the USAF vice chief of staff and was USAF chief of staff from 1961 to 1965.

1974
Leigh Wade
While assigned as a test pilot to the air service engineering division in 1919 at McCook Field, Ohio, he set an altitude record of 27,120 feet in 1921, and a three-man altitude record of 23,350 feet in 1922.

1976
John Herschel Glenn, Jr.
Glenn was selected as one of America's first seven astronauts in 1959, with the advent of the United States' space program. Glenn has flown two space missions and both times he was the oldest astronaut to do so: at the age of 40 in 1962, the first American to orbit the Earth Friendship 7, and in 1998 at the age of 77 he was a crewmember on the space shuttle Discovery 7. As a test pilot, on July 16, 1957, Glenn set a record for a transcontinental jet flight from Los Angeles to New York in 3 hours and 23 minutes. He also served in the Marine Corps during World War II and Korean conflict and flew 149 missions.

Albert Francis Hegenberger
While on assignment to McCook Field in Dayton, Hegenberger developed and tested flight instruments and taught the first course in navigation. After serving in Hawaii, he returned to Wright Field and planned a flight to Hawaii in the "Bird of Paradise," with Lt. Lester J. Maitland. After taking off from San Francisco on June 26, 1927, the Earth inductor compass and navigation radio failed. He used dead reckoning and celestial navigation to complete the first flight to Hawaii. His experience led him to develop a blind flight system at Wright Field. He made the first official solo blind flight on May 9, 1932.

1979
Neil Alden Armstrong
Armstrong became the first man to walk on the moon July 20, 1969. In the early '50s Armstrong, born in Wapakoneta, helped flight test America's new high speed aircraft, including the rocket-powered X-1, the first to break the sound barrier, and prototypes of the F-104 jet fighter and B-47 bomber, as well as the X-15 rocket plane.

Charles Franklin Kettering
Kettering was already famous by the time he became involved with aviation in 1912. During World War I, he designed the ignition systems for the "Liberty" aircraft engine and made the first synthetic aviation fuel. He helped form the Dayton-Wright Airplane Company that produced the DeHavilland, DH-4 warplane, and led its development of an unmanned guided missile. At the same time, the aircraft production board asked him to head the development of a pilotless "flying bomb" to carry explosives to a target 50 miles away. The flying bomb quickly acquired the name "Kettering Bug", and he devoted considerable time to its ingenious control. In 1923, his study of engine "knock" led to the development of tetraethyl lead in gasoline that increased aircraft engine horsepower and flight safety. He also pioneered developing high compression engines and improved fuels.

1983
David Sinton Ingalls
Born in Cleveland, Ingalls became the U.S. Navy's only ace during World War I. After the war, as a representative in the Ohio Legislature, he co-sponsored the Ohio Aviation Code, which became the model for other states. At the start of World War II, Admiral John Towers asked him to develop the Naval Air Station at Honolulu to handle the newly-established Naval Air Transport System. As a result, he reported for active duty on the staff of the commander of Naval Air Forces in the Pacific, and in mid-1943 became chief of staff for the Forward Area Air Center Command based on Guadalcanal, where he directed the transport of vital supplies to the Allies in the Pacific. Then after serving as plans officer for the Navy's South Pacific Air Force, he became Commander of the Pearl Harbor Naval Air Station, a major terminal.

1990
Hans P. von Ohain
Dr. von Ohain, who conceived the idea for jet propulsion in 1933, designed and built a liquid-fueled turbojet, which was flown successfully in August of 1939 near Rostock, Germany. He came to Dayton, Ohio, in 1947 and became a research scientist at Wright-Patterson Air Force Base. In September 1963, Dr. von Ohain was appointed Chief Scientist of the Aerospace Research Laboratories, while continuing his responsibilities as research leader in the field of energy conversion and propulsion. In this position, von Ohain was involved in virtually all Air Force in-house basic research conducted in the physical and engineering sciences. In 1975, he became Chief Scientist of the Aero Propulsion Laboratory of the Air Force Wright Aeronautical Laboratories. He assumed responsibility for maintaining the technical quality of the Air Force research and development in air-breathing propulsion, power and petrochemicals. His

accomplishments in these positions won national and international recognition. He retired from government work in 1979 and became senior research fellow at the University of Dayton Research Institute's Aerospace Mechanics division. During 32 years of government service, Dr. von Ohain published more than 30 technical papers and registered 19 U.S. patents. In 1990, the University of Dayton honored him by establishing in his name four graduate fellowships in aerothermodynamics.

1992
Lowell Thomas
Thomas, a tireless promoter of aviation, was born in Woodington, Ohio. As a broadcaster in Pittsburgh, Pennsylvania, he narrated the first aerial circumnavigation of the earth. Later he flew over Berlin in a P-51 Mustang, describing the final battle between the Germans and the Russians. He participated in the first flight across the Antarctic from Africa to Australia, from Cape Town to McCurdo Sound and on to New Zealand. With his son, he wrote a book in 1969 titled *Famous First Flights that Changed History*.

CLAYTON BRUKNER: CLASS OF 1997, HONORARY OHIOAN

Clayton Brukner grew up in Battle Creek, Michigan, but made himself into an Ohioan. Working briefly for Curtiss Aeroplane and Motor Corporation where he and his lifelong friend, Elwood "Sam" Junkin, helped build the Curtiss "Jenny", the two of them soon moved to Lorain, Ohio, and joined Buck Weaver at the Ohio Aviation School. It was there, in 1919, the three of them designed and built the first Waco—nicknamed the "Cootie."

In 1921, they built the Waco Model Four, capable of carrying three passengers, moved to Troy, Ohio, in 1923 and in the next year they had built the Waco 8, which carried eight people. The Model 9, built in 1925, became the first aircraft manufactured on an assembly line in the U.S. and the first Waco to use blueprints in construction. They also built the famous Waco Taperwing, which became the standard acrobatic plane of the commercial field. In this model, Waco's test pilot, Freddie Lund, performed the world's first outside loop by a civilian. In 1928, in order to keep the company from moving, the citizens of Troy gave the company 115 acres of land, and in 1929 it became the Waco Aircraft Company. It was the largest commercial builder of aircraft in the world.

All commercial aircraft production stopped in the early 1940s and went towards the war effort. Waco produced the UPF-7 trainer, and in the spring of 1941, the Army Air Forces asked Waco to design and develop several large troop and cargo–carrying gliders, which was the start of Waco's famous glider contributions to the United States' war efforts. More than 2,600 workers were employed by Waco during the "glider years" and nearly 1,100 military gliders were built by Waco. In all, almost 14,000 Waco–designed and contracted gliders were built.

After the war, Waco ceased commercial aircraft production and turned to the production of airplane parts. Later Brukner sold the company and turned his attention towards other inventions. He patented the "Lickity Log Splitter," still in demand, and devoted himself to the Brukner Nature Center. The center was built on the acreage he had bought over 30 years before. The Brukner Wing at Stouder Memorial Hospital was also a result of his generosity. "I made my money in Troy," Brukner once said, "and I am going to give all of it back." —*National Aviation Hall of Fame*

Flying housewife

Jerrie Mock, the "Flying Housewife," was the first female to solo a plane around the world—a 30-day, 1964 sojourn in a Cessna 180 that she dubbed "Spirit of Columbus." She landed to accolades and a place in history as the first American to receive the Louis Bleriot aviation medal.

1995

Dominic S. Gentile

At the beginning of World War II, Piqua-born Gentile was appointed a Royal Air Force Pilot Officer and began flying with various RAF squadrons out of Great Britain. In 1942, he joined No. 133, one of the legendary Eagle Squadrons in England. These fighter squadrons were manned by American pilots who wanted to fight the Germans before the United States even entered the war. When the United States entered the war, Gentile transferred into the United States Army and was assigned to the 336th Fighter Squadron, Fourth Fighter Group, of the Eighth Air Force in Europe. This unit destroyed over 1,000 German aircraft by the war's close. Several Eagles, including Gentile, became some of the war's most famous fighter aces. Gentile and his wingman destroyed more enemy planes then any other partnership of American fighter pilots, and Gentile broke the record set by World War One ace Captain Eddie Rickenbacker of 26 enemy aircraft downed in combat with a total of 30 enemy planes destroyed. After the war, Gentile came to Wright Field as a test pilot.

1996

Paul Tibbets Jr.

Paul Tibbets, Jr. was not a native Ohioan but came to Columbus in 1970 to join Executive Jet Aviation, an all-jet air taxi service company, where he eventually became Chairman of the Board. Earlier, he attended the University of Cincinnati in pursuit of a career in medicine but that was his parents' ambition rather than his own, which was to fly. At Fort Thomas, Kentucky, in 1937, he enlisted as a flying cadet in the Army Air Corps, got his pilot wings in Texas and was commissioned a 2nd Lieutenant. In 1942, he became the Squadron Commander of the 340th Bomb Squadron, 97th Bombardment Group, destined for England, flying 25 missions in B-17s, including the first American Flying Fortress raid against occupied Europe. In November of that year he was in Algeria leading the first bombardment missions in support of the North African invasion. He returned to the states in 1943 to test the combat capability of Boeing's new Super Fortress, the B-29, an airplane plagued with problems. He taught himself to fly the airplane and flew it about 400 hours in tests. In September 1944, Paul was briefed on the Manhattan Project, the code name for the development of the atom bomb. It was to be his responsibility to organize and train a unit to deliver these weapons in combat operations. He would also determine and supervise the modifications necessary to make the B-29 capable of delivering the weapons. Paul requisitioned 15 new B-29s and specified they be stripped of turrets and armor plating except for the tail gunner position; that fuel-injected engines and new technology reversible-pitch propellers be installed; and the bomb bay re-configured to suspend, from a single point, 10,000 pounds. Such an airplane would fly higher, faster, and above the effective range of anti-aircraft fire. At 02:30 A.M. August 6th, 1945, the Enola Gay—named after Tibbets' mother—lifted off North Field with Paul Tibbets and his crew enroute to Hiroshima. At exactly 09:15 plus 15 seconds the world's first atomic bomb exploded. The course of history and the nature of warfare was changed.

1997

Clayton Brukner

(see inset story, page 323)

1998

Harry Armstrong

Armstrong was assigned to the Air Corps Research and Development Division at Wright Field where he established a separate medical research laboratory in May of 1935. With co-worker Dr. Heim, he designed the first centrifuge in America to allow scientists to investigate the physiological effects of G-force on humans. The Physiological Research Unit, later renamed the Aeromedical Research Laboratory, with Dr. Armstrong as its director, designed new flight gear protecting aircrews from extreme temperatures and offering better oxygen supply at high altitudes. The pressurized aircraft so commonly accepted today are a direct result of Armstrong's work at Wright Field. Among the many items Dr. Armstrong developed at Wright Field were crash helmets, shoulder-type safety belts, and a horizontal altitude chamber. He also discovered that blood boils at 63,000 feet, an altitude limit now known as "Armstrong's Line."

James Lovell, Jr

Cleveland's Lovell was the first astronaut to make four space flights: pilot of Gemini 7; commander of Gemini 12; Command Module Pilot of Apollo 8; and commander of Apollo 13. His first, Gemini 7, was a record-breaking endurance flight in which Lovell and Borman orbited for over 330 hours. As the Apollo project developed, Lovell was chosen for Apollo 8, man's maiden voyage to the moon. Captain Lovell's next mission was in April of 1970, aboard Apollo 13, making him the first man to journey twice to the moon.

Sam Williams

Although Williams was born in Seattle, he grew up in Columbus, Ohio, where his love of tinkering with mechanical devices began. Without his invention of the small gas turbine engine, the cruise missile would not have been possible. His inventions have paved the way to development of a reliable yet low-cost fanjet engine for business aircraft.

Source: National Aviation Hall of Fame, Dayton

Neil Armstrong took his first airplane ride when he was six, and began flying lessons at 14. The lessons cost nine dollars an hour, which he paid for by working several jobs—at a drug store, a hardware store in Wapakoneta, and a bakery that hired him because he was small enough to fit into the mixing vats to clean them. As a boy, he dreamed that by holding his breath he could create a sensation akin to flying. It wasn't enough, of course. So at 16, he had his pilot's license and he didn't yet know how to drive a car.

He left Purdue for the Navy, flying combat missions over Korea when he was 21, 78 missions in all, surviving being shot down behind enemy lines, and he returned home with three Air Medals. "I didn't do much," he said later, with the Midwestern taciturnity that was always his trademark.

A co-worker recalled Armstrong describing a flight when he was a test pilot, and his X-15 was falling from 30,000 feet at Mach 2. "He told it like he was walking down to the post office," said the co-worker.

"Silence is a Neil Armstrong answer," his wife said. "The word *no* is an argument."

Once, at a press conference, he said, "I'm sorry. I'm afraid I did a great many ordinary things." Commenting on that press conference, writer Bob McKay said that was exactly the quality that got him to the moon. "It was," wrote McKay, "an ordinary guy, the uncommon common man, a thirty-eight-year-old citizen, who got there first, representing everyone."

And in 1969 when he became the first man to step onto the surface of the moon, this reserved and laconic Wapakoneta farm boy gave the best dramatic performance. First, with no display of uneasiness, he talking to Houston about finding "a parking place," flying the Eagle manually four miles past the designated landing spot because the surface was littered with boulders.

"That's one small step for a man," he said, "one giant leap for mankind." Some of the Houston people snickered because they knew there was "a good-sized hop" between the bottom rung of the ladder and the moon surface. (Someone else pointed out that the phrase was incomprehensible to the Japanese because their word for both 'man' and 'mankind' are the same.)

The phrase was Armstrong's own (tacit proof of the connection between a reserved man speaking only when he has something to say), and it became so famous that many subsequent articles referred to the quotation without actually using it, assuming, of course, that everyone knew what Neil Armstrong had said.

"The great achievement of the men on the moon," wrote fellow Ohioan James Reston, "is not that they made history, but that they expanded man's vision of what history might be."

Seeking solitude on his farm in Lebanon, Armstrong spoke again on the 20th anniversary of the historic flight. "There is a new frontier of substantial mystery, great promise, and unlimited size and variety," he said. Its exploration, he said, "is constrained by only our intellect, our courage and our resources."

His own presence—and Midwestern succinctness—had given us one of the singular images of the century. ✍
—*John Baskin*

Many people talked about how his heart rate did not accelerate when he landed the Eagle on the moon. In fact, his heart was thumping 156 times a minute. His heart was in his throat; he just didn't let on.

—*Bob McKay*

Ohio has been the home of thousands of writers, musicians, entertainers, and artists. The Ohioana Library Association serves as the caretaker and primary resource for that heritage. The Association is dedicated to encouraging and recognizing the creative accomplishments of Ohio's native sons and daughters; maintaining and preserving a permanent collection of books and music by Ohioans and about Ohio; and disseminating information about the work of Ohio writers, musicians, and artists.

The Association began in 1929, when Martha Kinney Cooper, the First Lady of Ohio, invited representatives of many groups from around the state to assist in gathering a collection of Ohio books for the Governor's Mansion. A few years later the collection outgrew the Mansion and was moved to the Ohio Departments Building at 65 South Front St., Columbus, where it is still located. A small rotating collection is still maintained in the Governor's Residence.

The Ohioana Library's current holdings include nearly 40,000 books; 4,000 pieces of sheet music; thousands of letters, photographs, journals, and news clippings; scrap books; and biographical files on more than 10,000 Ohio writers, artists, musicians, and other famous Ohioans. Special items include the works of William Dean Howells and Zane Grey, church and family histories, and personal memorabilia of noted Ohioans. The books cover nearly every topic: fiction, non-fiction, poetry, children's literature, county atlases, and local history. While new books are added to the collection daily, many that are rare and date back to the 1800s are unavailable to the public anywhere else. The collection does not circulate, but the Library is open to the public.

The Association recognizes and encourages the literary and creative accomplishments of Ohioans through nine different Ohioana Awards programs. The Awards are presented on Ohioana Day, a celebration held each autumn. Other events held around the state include the Hamilton County Authors and Composers Tea and the Central Ohio Authors Tea. The *Ohioana*

Quarterly, published since 1957, also disseminates information about the work of Ohio writers, musicians, and artists. The *Quarterly* features articles about Ohio events and people in the arts and humanities, book reviews, literary comment and criticism, and an annotated list of new books as they are received. The Association has also published the book, *Ohio Authors and Their Books*; the "Literary Map of Ohio," an illustrated guide to the birthplaces and residences of famous Ohio writers; and educational resources such as lists of Ohio Authors of Children's Books, Ohio Women Authors, Ohio Black Authors, Ohio Artists, Ohioana Award Winners 1942 to Present, and Famous People from Ohio.

The Ohioana Library is supported through memberships/subscriptions, contributions, and a subsidy from the State of Ohio. To obtain more information about The Ohioana Library, or to join the Association, call 614-466-3831.

The Ohioana Library
274 East First Avenue
Columbus, Ohio 43201
614-466-3831
Fax: 614-728-6974 fax
E-mail: ohioana@sloma.state.oh.us
Web Site: www.oplin.lib.oh.us/
index.cfm?id=773

Source: Linda R. Hengst, Director, Ohio Library Association

Ohioana Awards

Ohioana Career Award—awarded each year to a native Ohioan who has had an outstanding career in the arts and humanities.

Ohioana Citations—awarded for distinguished service in the arts and humanities in Ohio. Four Citations are given each year, including a special Music Citation.

Ohioana Pegasus Award—awarded for a unique and outstanding cultural contribution by a native Ohioan or long time resident of the state.

Ohioana Book Awards—awarded for fiction, non-fiction, children's literature, poetry, and books about Ohio or Ohioans. Six awards may be given each year.

Ohioana James P. Barry Award for Editorial Excellence—awarded to an Ohio-based serial that covers subjects of interest to the Ohioana Library, namely literature, history, culture or the general humanities.

Ohioana Poetry Award, Helen and Laura Krout Memorial—a monetary award to an individual whose body of work has made, and continues to make, a significant contribution to the poetry of Ohio; and through whose work as a writer, teacher, administrator, or in community service, interest in poetry has been developed.

Ohioana Award for Children's Literature, Alice Wood Memorial a monetary award to an author whose body of work has made, and continues to make, a significant contribution to literature for children or young adults.

Walter Rumsey Marvin Grant—a monetary award given to an unpublished writer under 30 years of age.

Florence Roberts Head Ohioana Book Award— award for literary excellence in fiction or nonfiction, with preference given to a woman author.

TONI MORRISON: MAJOR PROTECTOR OF AMERICAN REALISM

If William Dean Howells was nineteenth-century Ohio's literary emissary to the rest of the colonies, then his 20th-century counterpart was even more unlikely than a Brahmin from Martins Ferry: **Toni Morrison**, a feisty, black, ex-college beauty queen who grew up in the steel-town neighborhoods of Lorain.

The two of them were the oddest pair of cultural bookends produced anyplace, particularly Ohio, but there were more than passing similarities between them. Howells was widely read and acclaimed; so is Morrison. Howells was his party's standard-bearer, and in her own way, so is Morrison. He was the principal defender of American realism at its formative moment; she is one of the major protectors of American realism beset by the emerging theories of construct. Nearly a century apart, and several universes, Ohio gave each of them its compass points.

Morrison was one of four children, the daughter of a Great Lakes shipyard worker who signed his name to the sides of ships when he welded a perfect seam. Her grandfather, at age five, heard his folks say that "the Emancipation Proclamation was coming," and promptly crawled under the bed. It was, Morrison would say much later, the perfect and habitual response to the promises of white people. When she began the first grade, she had her father's pride, if not her grandfather's reactions—she was the only black but also the only child who could already read.

Her sense of language was a gift from the eloquent fabulists among her relatives, who told ghost stories each night; it is the same language that imbues all her novels, a unified language so filled with texture that it rises off the page in rebellion at such meager constraint.

Most of her books begin with the "village culture" of Midwestern places much like Lorain and travel to the larger geographies of men and women, both black and white, and to the cultural anomalies that constrict them both. The novels—her fifth, *Beloved*, has just reached the best-seller lists—are always *stories*, too, filled with sex and violence, wit, weather, mythology and nature, an ambitious amalgam of elements at once popular and literary.

In 1993, when she became the first African-American woman to win the Nobel Laureate in Literature, the academy said her work "characterized by visionary force and poetic import, gives life to an essential aspect of American reality."

Morrison said her education came from observing the outcasts and eccentrics of Lorain's underside. "Everything I write starts there," she said. "Whether I end up there is another question, but that's where I always start. Always."

Yr./Home Co.	Name	Award	Work
1942, Butler	Walter Havighurst	Book, nonfiction, honorable mention	*Long Ships Passing*
1942, Logan	Willard M. Kiplinger	Book, nonfiction, honorable mention	*Washington is Like That*
1942, Montgomery	James B. Reston	Book, nonfiction	*Prelude to Victory*
1943, Butler	Edgar Stillman Kelley	Career	Composer
1943, Erie	Marie E. Gilchrist	Book, juvenile, honorable mention	*The Great Lakes*
1943, Franklin	Eleanor Thomas	Book, juvenile, honorable mention	*Mr. Trotter & the Five Black Cats*
1943, Hamilton	Clarence A. Mills	Book, nonfiction	*Climate Makes the Man*
1943	Anna Bird Stewart	Book, juvenile	*Bibi: The Baker's Horse*
1943	Robert Emmett Taylor	Book, nonfiction, honorable mention	*No Royal Road*
1943, Hardin	Martin J. Freeman	Book, fiction	*Bitter Honey*
1943, Jackson	Ben Ames Williams	Book, fiction, honorable mention	*Time of Peace*
1943, Stark	William E. S. Flory	Book, nonfiction, honorable mention	*Prisoners of War*
1944, Butler	Philip Jordan	Book, Ohio scene	*Ohio Comes of Age*
1944, Clark	Lois Lenski	Book, juvenile	*Bayou Suzette*
1944, Greene	Fred Charters Kelly	Book, biography	*The Wright Brothers*
1944, Hamilton	Ann Steward	Book, fiction	*Take Nothing for Your Journey*
1944, Jefferson	Dard Hunter	Career	Publisher of fine books
1944, Licking	Gordon S. Seagrave	Book, war	*Burma Surgeon*
1944, Trumbull	Kenneth Patchen	Book, poetry	*Cloth of the Tempest*
1945, Butler	Dr. Joseph W. Clokey	Citation	Ohio composer
1945, Cuyahoga	Henrietta Buckmaster	Book, fiction	*Deep River*
	Michael DeCapite	Book, fiction, 3rd place	*No Bright Banner*
	Bob Hope	Book, humor	*I Never Left Home*
1945, Franklin	Robert S. Carr	Book, fiction, 2nd place	*Bells of St. Ivan's*
	Foster R. Dulles	Book, nonfiction	*The Road to Teheran*
	Florence R. Head	Career	Ohioana director
	James Thurber	Book, juvenile, 2nd place	*The Great Quillow*
1945, Greene	Algo D. Henderson	Book, nonfiction, 2nd place	*Vitalizing Liberal Education*
1945, Guernsey	Daphne McVicker	Book, humor	*The Queen Was in the Kitchen*
1945, Hamilton	Arthur Ernest Morgan	Career	Engineer/planner
1945, Henry	Joe E. Brown	Career	Actor
1945, Knox	Ralph Sockman	Book, nonfiction, 3rd place	*Date With Destiny*
1945, Licking	Eleanor Youmans	Book, juvenile, 3rd place	*Mount Delightful*
1945, Lorain/ Hamilton	Florence M. Fitch	Book, juvenile	*One God*

Mr. Havighurst and the Impertinent Detail

Ohio has escaped the stale loaf of regional literature, thanks to a literary club of yeasty old boys starting with Henry Howe—who canvassed the entire state on horseback—down through Harlan Hatcher to George Knepper, who is, thankfully, still writing. But one of the most estimable of this elite little fraternity was an old English prof whose resumé resembled something by one of those turn-of-the-century paper-stainers who couldn't write without first going to war or to sea. ***Walter Havighurst*** began his career by shipping out on the Great Lakes as a deckhand, then sailed the Pacific on a lumber schooner. Somewhere along the way, he also got a theology degree, and in 1927 discovered Miami University where his brother was teaching chemistry. Claiming no qualifications but "irregular employment, study, and reading," he spent 60-plus years in Oxford. In addition to teaching literature, Mr. Havighurst created it, absorbing all the history between the Ohio River and the Great Lakes and giving it a lively freshness. About the steamboat era on the Ohio, he once wrote, "Any man who owned a boat, a boiled shirt, and a blazing vocabulary could be a captain." His many books

included *Annie Oakley of the Wild West*, upon which the Broadway musical, *Annie Get Your Gun* was based. As the Midwest's literary historian, he wrote with wit, clarity, and elegance. So much for irregular employment and no qualifications. ✎

elite fraternity

Yr./Home Co.	Name	Award	Work
1946, Clark/ Hamilton	Philip R. Adams	Book, biography, honorable mention	Rodin
1946, Clark	William Burnett	Book, fiction, honorable mention	Tomorrow is Another Day
1946, Cuyahoga	Alice Monk Mears	Book, poetry	Brief Enterprise
	Ted Robinson	Book, poetry, honorable mention	Life, Love and the Weather
	Robert H. Schauffler	Book, biography, honorable mention	Florestan
1946, Franklin	Harriet Evatt	Book, juvenile, honorable mention	Mystery of Creaking Windmill
	Arthur Schlesinger, Jr.	Book, history	Age of Jackson, The
	James Thurber	Book, juvenile	The White Deer
	Carl F. Wittke	Book, biography	Against the Current
1946, Knox	John Crowe Ransom	Book, poetry, honorable mention	Selected Poems
1946, Lawrence	Harlan Hatcher	Book, history, honorable mention	Lake Erie
1946, Lucas	Ruth Southard	Book, fiction, honorable mention	No Sad Songs For Me
1946, Morgan	Fleming Crew	Book, juvenile, honorable mention	Splasher
	Alice Crew Gall	Book, juvenile, honorable mention	Splasher
1946, Muskingum/ Hamilton	Carl Hugo Grimm	Music Citation	Composer of the year
1946, Richland	Louis Bromfield	Career	Writer/conservationist
1946, Ross	Howard Riley Raper	Book, history	Man Against Pain
1946, Washington	Dorothy J. Roberts	Book, fiction	A Durable Fire
1947, Delaware	Edwin G. Conklin	Career	Dean of American biologists
1947, Belmont	Charles F. Harrold	Book, biography, honorable mention	Biography of John Henry Newman
1947, Butler	James M. Cox	Book, biography	Journey Thru My Years
	Walter Havighurst	Book, history	Land of Promise
1947, Cuyahoga	Charlotta Bebenroth	Book, juvenile, honorable mention	Meriwether Lewis, Boy Explorer
	Dr. Herbert Elwell	Music Citation	Composer of the year
	Frank C. Hibben	Book, history, honorable mention	The Lost Americans
	Jo Sinclair	Book, fiction	Wasteland
1947, Franklin	Harriet Evatt	Book, juvenile	The Snow Owl's Secret
1947, Hamilton	Janet Hart Diebold	Book, fiction	Mandrake Root
	Joshua Loth Liebman	Book, religion	Peace of Mind
	Arthur Ernest Morgan	Book, philosophy, honorable mention	Nowhere was Somewhere
1947, not Ohioan	Conrad M. Richter	Special citation, novels about Ohio	Novelist
1948, Belmont	William E. Livezey	Book, biography, honorable mention	Mahan on Sea Power
1948, Cuyahoga	Florence E. Allen	Career	Judge/suffragist
	Lillian Baldwin	Citation	Music appreciation
	Grace & George Crile	Book, biography	George Crile: An Autobiography
	Adella P. Hughes	Citation	Music appreciation
1948, Delaware	Alberta P. Hannum	Book, fiction, honorable mention	Roseanna McCoy
1948, Franklin	Jeanette Eaton	Book, juvenile, honorable mention	David Livingstone, Foe of Darkness
1948, Jackson	Romaine Alton Jones	Citation	County Chair of the Year
	Ben Ames Williams	Career	Novelist
1948, Medina	Carolyn Treffinger	Book, juvenile	Li Lun, Lad of Courage
1948, not Ohioan	Frederick Way, Jr.	Ohioana Fellowship	Story of Ohio River Life
1948, Stark	George Freitag	Book, fiction	The Lost Land
1949	Sr. Miriam Joseph	Book, nonfiction, honorable mention	Shakespeare's Use of the Arts
1949, Ashland	Charles F. Kettering	Career	Inventor/industrialist
1949, Athens	Ohio University	Citation	Ohio history for students
1949, Butler	Robert McCloskey	Book, juvenile	Blueberries for Sal
1949, Butler/ Cuyahoga	Howard Robinson	Book, history	The British Post Office
1949, Butler	William E. Smith	Ohioana Fellowship	Buckeye Titan
1949, Clark	Lois Lenski	Book, juvenile, honorable mention	Boom Town Boy
	John Ward Ostrom	Book, critical	The Letters of Edgar Allen Poe
1949, Clark/ Franklin	John H. Wilson	Book, biography, honorable mention	Court Wits of the Restoration
1949, Cuyahoga	May Hill Arbuthnot	Book, nonfiction, honorable mention	Children & Books
	Sally Carrighar	Book, nonfiction	One Day at Teton Marsh
	Grace Goulder Izant	Citation	Column on Ohio history
	Agatha Young	Book, fiction, honorable mention	Light in the Sky
1949, Franklin/ Cuyahoga	Virgil Scott	Book, fiction	The Hickory Stick
1949, Franklin	Ralph Fanning	Citation	Architectural history of Ohio
1949, Greene	Ridgely Torrence	Career	Biographer, dramatist, poet
	Ridgely Torrence	Book, Biography	The Story of John Hope
1949, Hamilton	Martha Kinney Cooper	Career	Founder of Ohioana
1949, Harrison	Mrs. H. B. McConnell	Citation	County Chair of the Year
1949, Huron	Norval Neil Luxon	Book, history, honorable mention	Niles' Weekly Register
1949, Lucas	Hilda Harpster	Book, nonfiction, honorable mention	The Insect World

She was considered a "belle" during her youth in Cincinnati, and she loved music, and when she married Myers Y. Cooper in 1897, her charitable works and enthusiasm for the Daughters of the American Revolution made her an altogether fitting wife for the highly successful businessman who built some of the Queen City's first and finest suburbs.

When Myers Cooper became Governor of Ohio in 1929, she might merely have become another member of the state's proud but rather anonymous legion of former First Ladies. But she spent an afternoon unpacking books in the Governor's Mansion, and there, she had the idea of grouping together and featuring all the works by Ohio authors.

For months, Mrs. Cooper devoted herself to personally gathering and shelving books by and about Ohioans, but when the task became too great, she called upon the Ohio Federation of Women's Clubs, whose members swelled the collection with all manner of information about Ohio writers, composers, and artists. Thus, Ohio became the first state in the nation to have a library dedicated to works by its native sons and daughters.

After only two years in Columbus, Mrs. Cooper returned to life as a Cincinnati society matron, but the Ohioana Library continued to be her pet project. She considered its founding to be her finest hour and lived long enough to see several other states—including California, Montana, and Kentucky—copy her idea.

But while some have tried variations, the Buckeye version is the only independent library of its kind in America.

The small—five—staff occupies space in an old manufacturing building at 274 East First Avenue where they share space with the State Library. The collection grows another 1,000 books every year, not to mention its biographical files on prominent Ohioans.

The bio files began years ago when an ardent library supporter, Mrs. Oliver Kuhn, began writing to and visiting Ohio authors, packing her children into her car and setting out across the state to beard Ohio's literary denizens in their Buckeye lairs.

When she died, her children donated her collection to the library. Through an assiduously maintained system of contacts across Ohio and beyond, most of the materials are donated to the Ohioana. Thus Ms. Cooper's unique Ohio Legacy today totals over 45,000 books and 10,000 musical compositions, as well as 20,000 bio files.

This undervalued resource—one of Ohio's most unique—while receiving a small stipend from the state, still relies hugely on patron generosity. Such as the visiting researcher, David Eastman, who donated the works of Cleveland children's author Hildegarde Frey—her ten-book "Campfire Girls" series—to the library. Or the patron who donated a first edition of Rita Dove's Pulitzer novel, *Thomas and Beulah*, which, at the time, cost $800.

Because of that generosity, the Ohioana has books found not even in the Library of Congress. But there's always a long list, in case there's some errant generosity out there looking for a home.

To find needed books and acknowledge generous donors, The Ohioana Library's new Book Builders Project posts books on its web page. The lists and accompanying bios are often informative and entertaining, a personal favorite being the encomium to Fredric Brown by his wife: "Fred hated to write. But he loved having written. He would do everything he could think of to delay sitting at his typewriter: he would dust his chair, tootle on his flute, read a little, tootle some more. After a time his conscience would begin to hurt, and he would actually sit at his typewriter..."

Yr./Home Co.	Name	Award	Work
1949, Richland	Ernest J. Wessen	Citation	Ohio bibliographies
1949, Ross	Burton Stevenson	Career	Novelist, librarian, anthologist
1950, Butler	Walter Havighurst	Book, juvenile	*Song of the Pines*
	Marion Havighurst	Book, juvenile	*Song of the Pines*
1950, Clark	T. A. Kantonen	Book, nonfiction, honorable mention	*Resurgence of the Gospel*
1950, Cuyahoga	Andre Norton	Book, juvenile, 2nd place	*Sword in Sheath*
	Louis B. Seltzer	Citation	Editor, *Cleveland Press*
	Hazel Wilson	Book, juvenile, 2nd place	*Island Summer*
1950, Delaware	Robert K. Marshall	Book, fiction	*Little Squire Jim*
1950, Franklin	Arthur C. Johnson	Citation	President of OHS
	Edward Nicholas	Book, history	*The Hours and the Ages*
	Andrew Rodgers, III	Book, biography	*Liberty Hyde Bailey*
1950, Greene/ Cuyahoga	James H. Hanford	Book, biography, honorable mention	*John Milton, Englishman*
1950, Greene	Mrs. Asa Messenger	Citation	County Chair of the Year
	Norman Vincent Peale	Career	Minister/writer
	Norman Vincent Peale	Book, philosophy	*A Guide to Confident Living*
	Arthur Schlesinger	Book, history, honorable mention	*Paths to the Present*
1950, Hamilton	Mary Margaret Deasy	Book, fiction, honorable mention	*Cannon Hill*
1950, Lawrence	Harlan Hatcher	Career	Historian, man of letters
1951, Portage	Earl N. Manchester	Citation	Librarian, bibliophile
1951, Clark	Marion Renick	Citation	Children's literature
	Mary Spining	Citation	County Chair of the Year
1951, Cuyahoga	Frank Siedel	Book, special	*The Ohio Story*
1951, Darke	Lowell Thomas	Career	Writer/broadcaster
1951, Franklin	Richard D. Altick	Book, literary history and critique	*The Scholar Adventurers*
1951, Harrison	Mary L. Jobe Akeley	Book, personal experience	*Congo Eden*
1951, Highland	Robert S. Harper	Special award	*Lincoln and the Press*
1951, Monroe	Edward Thomas	Citation	Teacher, friend of nature
1951, Morgan	Howard C. Christy	Career	Artist/illustrator
1951, Ottawa	Amy Kelly	Book, biography	*Eleanor of Aquitaine*
1951, Stark	Marie Kuhn	Citation	County Chair of the Year
1952, Allen	William Fridley	Book, fiction	*A Time to Go Home*
1952, Cuyahoga	Bruce Catton	Book, history	*Mr. Lincoln's Army*
	Ihna T. Frary	Citation	Teacher, author, artist
1952, Franklin	Wilbur H. Siebert	Citation	Scholar, college executive
1952, Hamilton	Mrs. James D. Murch	Citation	County Chair of the Year
	Anna Bird Stewart	Book, juvenile	*Enter David Garrick*
1952, Hancock	Russel Crouse	Career	Playwright
1952, Henry	Ernest G. Schwiebert	Book, biography	*Luther and his Times*
1952, Lorain	Stevan Dohanos	Career	Artist/illustrator
1952, Marion	Pansy Rauhauser	Citation	County Chair of the Year
	Norman Thomas	Book, autobiography	*A Socialist's Faith*
1952, Montgomery	Suzanne McConnaughey	Book, fiction	*Point Venus*
1953, Brown	Howard Swiggett	Book, biography	*The Extraordinary Mr.Morris*
1953, Cuyahoga	William D. Ellis	Book, fiction	*The Bounty Lands*
	Mrs. Elroy John Kulas	Citation	Kulas Foundation (music)
1953, Fayette	Grayson L. Kirk	Career	Education
1953, Franklin	James Thurber	Sesquicentennial Award	"Master of prose"
1953, Fulton	Charles Haubiel	Music citation	Composer
1953, Hamilton	Lynn J. Radcliffe	Book, philosophy	*Making Prayer Real*
1953, Knox	Gordon K. Chalmers	Book, nonfiction	*The Republic and the Person*
1953, Lucas	Mrs. Max Shepherst	Citation	County Chair of the Year
1953, Madison	Howard Barlow	Career	Conductor, music educator
1954, Athens	Ohio University	Citation	Education
1954, Cuyahoga	David B. Guralnik	Citation	Lexicographer, editor
1954, Hamilton	Ethel Glenn Hier	Citation	Music
1954, Huron	O.E. Jennings	Citation	Botany
1954, Knox	Ralph W. Sockman	Career	Preacher, interpreter
1954, Logan	Clarence E. Macartney	Book, history	*Grant and His Generals*
1954, Lucas	Milton A. Caniff	Career	Cartoonist
1954, Lucas/ Cuyahoga	Joseph H. Friend	Citation	Lexicography, editor
1954, Miami	Bertha C. Anderson	Book, juvenile	*Tinker's Tim and the Witches*
1954, Montgomery	Roger L. Shinn	Book, religion	*Christianity and the Problem...*
1954, Perry	Rollo W. Brown	Book, biography	*The Hills are Strong*
1954, Pickaway	Mrs. John Eshelman, III	Citation	County Chair of the Year
1955, not Ohioan	Harry Barnard	Special award	*Rutherford B. Hayes and his America*
1955, Cuyahoga	Jerome Lawrence	Merit award	*Inherit the Wind*

Yr./Home Co.	Name	Award	Work
	Arthur Loesser	Book, nonfiction	*Men, Women and Pianos*
	William E. Scheele	Book, juvenile	*Prehistoric Animals*
	Agatha Young	Book, fiction	*Clown of the Gods*
1955, Franklin	Clyde D. Moore	Citation	Newspaper humorist
	Robert Price	Special Award	*Johnny Appleseed: Man & Myth*
	Margaret C. Tyler	Citation	Education
1955, Logan	Willard M. Kiplinger	Career	Writer/columnist
1955, Lorain	Robert E. Lee	Merit award	*Inherit the Wind*
1955, Lucas/ Franklin	Randolph C. Downes	Citation	Ohio regional history
1955, Washington	Mrs. Raymond Guthrie	Citation	County Chair of the Year
	Sophia M. Russell	Citation	County Chair of the Year
1956, Athens	John F. Cady	Book, nonfiction	*Roots of French Imperialism*
1956, Cuyahoga	Jo Sinclair	Book, fiction	*The Changelings*
1956, Franklin	Mrs Fred Ellsperman	Citation	County Chair of the Year
	James Edward Pollard	Citation	Biography, William O. Thompson
1956, Hamilton	Nelson Glueck	Career	Archaeologist/rabbi
1956, Logan	James Flora	Book, juvenile	*Fabulous Fireworks Family*
1956, Washington	J. Dudley Chamberlain	Citation	Civic efforts
1957, not Ohioan	Marva Robins Belden	Book, Ohio subject	*So Fell the Angels*
	Thomas G. Belden	Book, Ohio subject	*So Fell the Angels*
	Anita Ruffing	Citation	Classroom Teachers of Ohio
1957, Champaign	Edna M. H. Clark	Citation	Ohio Art & Artists
1957, Cuyahoga	Bruce Catton	Book, nonfiction	*This Hallowed Ground*
	Herbert Gold	Book, fiction	*The Man Who Was Not With It*
1957, Fayette	Mrs. Frank Mayo	Citation	County Chair of the Year
1957, Franklin	Paul H. Buck	Career	Administrator
	Mary Hubbell Osborn	Citation	Music
1957, Lucas	Edward M. Eager	Book, juvenile	*Knight's Castle*
1957, Washington	Col. Dean E. Hess	Special Medal	*Battle Hymn* (book and film)
1958, Athens	Paul M. Kendall	Book, biography	*Warwick the Kingmaker*
1958, Butler	Adele DeLeeuw	Citation	Juvenile books, biographies
	Cateau DeLeeuw	Citation	Juvenile books, biographies
	Robert McCloskey	Book, juvenile	*Time of Wonder*
1958, Cuyahoga	David Dietz	Career	Science writer, editor
1958, Franklin	Ketti Frings	Career	Playwright, *Look Homeward, Angel*
	Arthur Schlesinger, Jr.	Book, nonfiction	*The Crisis of the Old Order*
1958, Hamilton	John Haussermann, Jr.	Citation	Music
1958, Seneca	Charles O. Locke	Book, fiction	*The Hell Bent Kid*
1958, Summit	Mary E. Earle	Citation	County Chair of the Year
	Mrs. Waldo L. Semon	Citation	County Chair of the Year
1958, Williams	Paul A. Siple	Citation	"Mr. Antarctica"
1959, Cuyahoga	Sally Carrighar	Book, nonfiction	*Moonlight at Midday*
1959, Fairfield	Mrs. Gerald Spitler	Citation	County Chair of the Year
1959, Franklin	Jeanette Eaton	Book, juvenile	*America's Own Mark Twain*
	James R. Hopkins	Citation	Art, art teaching
1959, Greene	Arthur M. Schlesinger	Book, nonfiction	*Prelude to Independence*
1959, Mahoning	Arne Oldberg	Career	Compsoer, teacher, administrator
1959, not Ohioan	Alfred B. Sears	Book, Ohio Scene	*Thomas Worthington*
1959, Ross	David K. Webb	Citation	Folklore
1959, Stark	Andrew W. Cordier	Career	Diplomat
1959, Washington	Anne Chamberlain	Book, fiction	*The Darkest Bough*
1960, not an Ohioan	Margaret Leech	Book, Ohio scene	*In the Days of McKinley*
1960, Belmont	James Wright	Book, poetry	*Saint Judas*
1960, Crawford	Carol Kendall	Book, juvenile	*The Gammage Cup*
1960, Cuyahoga	Bruce Catton	Citation	Spokesman/Authors of the year
1960, Franklin	Harry V. Jaffa	Book, nonfiction	*Crisis of the House Divided*
1960, Gallia	Mrs. W. A. Lewis	Citation	County Chair of the Year
1960, Hamilton	Nelson Glueck	Book, nonfiction	*Rivers in the Desert*
1960, Knox/ Franklin	Peter Taylor	Book, fiction	*Happy Families Are All Alike*
1960, Marion	James L. Morrill	Career	Educational statesman/spokesman
1960, Richland/ Franklin	Edith Myrtle Keller	Citation	Music education
1960, Washington	George J. Blazier	Citation	Library material/early Ohio history
1961, Allen/ Summit	Hugh Downs	Citation	TV personality/writer
1961, Butler	Roy Wilson Howard	Career	"Gatherer, editor of news"
1961, Carroll	Ralph Hodgson	Book, poetry	*The Skylark and Other Poems*
1961, Cuyahoga	Jack W. Schaefer	Book, juvenile	*Old Ramon*

Yr./Home Co.	Name	Award	Work
1961, Cuyahoga	Jo Sinclair	Book, fiction	*Anna Teller*
1961, Franklin	Tessa Sweazy Webb	Citation	Ohio poetry
1961, Greene	Louis Filler	Book, nonfiction	*The Crusade Against Slavery*
1961, Lucas	Grace Rhodes Dean	Citation	Ohio art
1961, Muskingum	Norris F. Schneider	Citation	County Chair of the Year
1961, Stark	Edward Thornton Heald	Citation	Local history
1962, Adams	Mrs. A.C. Palmer	Citation	County Chair of the Year
1962, Clark	Lawrence E. Laybourne	Citation	International journalist
1962, Cuyahoga	Bruce Catton	Book, nonfiction	*The Coming Fury*
	Raymond DeCapite	Book, fiction	*A Lost King*
	James J. Rorimer	Career	Art expert, art writer
	Marguerite Vance	Book, juvenile	Body of work
1962, Franklin	Suzanne de Borhegyi	Book, juvenile	*Ships, Shoals & Amphoras*
1962, Licking/ Franklin	Anne Grimes	Citation	Musician/balladeer
1962, Stark	Walter T. Brahm	Citation	In the cause of Ohio libraries
1963, Athens	Paul M. Kendall	Book, nonfiction	*The Yorkist Age*
1963, Cuyahoga	Hiram Haydn	Book, fiction	*The Hands of Esau*
1963, Erie	Mrs. Edward C. Lay	Citation	County Chair of the Year
1963, Franklin	Edward Rickenbacker	Career	Pilot/auto racer
	Walter Sutton	Book, Ohio scene	*The Western Book Trade*
1963, Hamilton	Cincinnati Symphony	Citation	Orchestra
	Caroline Williams	Citation	Artist/illustrator
	James H. Rodabaugh	Citation	Ohio history
1963, Lucas	Edward M. Eager	Book, juvenile	*Seven-day Magic*
1963, Richland	Ellen Bromfield Geld	Book, Florence Head Award	*Heritage: A Daughter's Memoirs*
1964, Champaign	Helen Krout	Citation	County Chair of the Year
1964, Cuyahoga	Louis B. Seltzer	Career	Editor
	Charles Allen Smart	Book, nonfiction	*Viva Juarez!*
	Western Reserve U.	Citation	School of Library Science
1964, Franklin	Ohio State University	Citation	School of Music
1964, Greene	Helen H. Santmyer	Book, Florence Head Award	*Ohio Town*
1964, Hamilton	Josephine W. Johnson	Book, fiction	*The Dark Traveler*
1964, Knox	John Crowe Ransom	Citation	Poet, critic, editor
1964, not Ohioan	H. Wayne Morgan	Book, Ohio scene	*William McKinley & his America*
1964, Ross	the Donald F. Hydes	Pegasus	Samuel Johnson collection
1964, Wayne	Lucy L. Notestein	Book, nonfiction	*Hill Towns of Italy*
1965, Athens	Jack Matthews	Book, fiction	*Bitter Knowledge*
1965, Butler	George Dell	Book, poetry	*Written on Quail & Hawthorne Pages*
1965, Carroll	Mrs. James Griffin	Citation	County Chair of the Year
1965, Cuyahoga	Sherman E. Lee	Book, nonfiction	*A History of Far Eastern Art*
	Randolph C. Randall	Book, biography	*James Hall: Spokesman*
		Book, Florence Head Award	*James Hall: Spokesman*
1965, Defiance	Francis Weisenburger	Citation	Historian/teacher
1965, Franklin	Evan J. Crane	Citation	Father of Chemicals Abstract
1965, Hamilton	Gustav Eckstein	Citation	Scientist/writer
1965, Madison	John W. Bricker	Career	Public servant
1966	Ohio Music Ed. Assn.	Citation	Music
1966, Allen	Leslie C. Peltier	Book, Ohio scene	*Starlight Nights*
1966, Clark	Lillian Gish	Career	Actress
1966, Cuyahoga	Florence E. Allen	Book, Florence Head Award	*To Do Justly*
1966, Franklin	Jim Baker	Citation	cartoonist, "Ben Hardy"
	Rutherford Platt	Pegasus	*The Great American Forest*
	Rutherford Platt	Book, nonfiction	*The Great American Forest*
1966, Hamilton	Karl H. Maslowski	Citation	Naturalist/author
1966, Licking	Quest Club, Pataskala	Ohioana $100 award	Craft exhibit on Ohio life
1966, Montgomery	Fletcher Knebel	Book, fiction	*The Night of Camp David*
1966, not Ohioan	Alpheus T. Mason	Book, biography	*William Howard Taft*
1966, Trumbull	Marie N. Martin	Citation	County Chair of the Year
1967, Butler	John B. Martin	Book, nonfiction	*Overtaken by Events*
1967, Franklin	Erwin C. Zepp	Citation	OHS Director
1967, Fulton	Charles Haubiel	Pegasus	Composer, pianist
1967, Greene	Louis Filler	Book, biography	*The Unknown Edwin Markham*
1967, Hamilton	E. Lucy Braun	Citation	Plant ecology, taxonomy
	Louis Kronenberger	Career	Author, critic, editor
1967, Lucas	Ms. Dale H. Fife	Book, juvenile	*Walk a Narrow Bridge*
1967, Montgomery	Katherine K. Brown	Citation	County Chair of the Year

Yr./Home Co.	Name	Award	Work
1967, not Ohioan	Conrad M. Richter	Florence Head Award	*Awakening Land, Country of Strangers*
1967, Washington	William Harrington	Book, fiction	*Yoshar the Soldier*
1967, Washington	Edith Stanley Reiter	Citation	Historian/author
1968, not an Ohioan	Richard O'Connor	Book, biography	*Ambrose Bierce*
1968, Athens	Jack Matthews	Book, Florence Head Award	*Hanger Stout, Awake!*
1968, Clark	Bentz Plagemann	Book, fiction	*Heart of Silence*
1968, Columbiana	William H. Vodrey	Citation	Lawyer, author, historian
1968, Cuyahoga	Burgess Meredith	Career	Actor
1968, Franklin	Capital U., Conservatory	Citation	Music
	Ed Mason	Citation	Lecturer, historian, author
	Amalie Nelson	Citation	Civic leader & educator
1968, Greene	Hollis Summers	Book, poetry	*Peddler and Other Domestic Matters*
1968, Hamilton	Dr. Howard L. Bevis	Memoriam	President of OSU & jurist
	Allan Eckert	Book, history	*The Frontiersmen*
1968, Montgomery	Elisabeth H. Friermood	Book, juvenile	*Focus the Bright Land*
1968, Tuscarawas	W. Desmond Cooper	Citation	County Chair of the Year
1969, Cuyahoga	James McConkey	Book, fiction	*Crossroads*
	Raymond Moley	Career	Journalist, educator
	Mrs. Darian Smith	Citation	County Chair of the Year
	Robert Ward	Citation	Music composition
1969, Darke	Merrill C. Gilfillan	Citation	Conservation & wildlife
1969, Franklin	Bill Arter	Citation	Cartoonist/writer
1969, Greene	Virginia Hamilton	Book, juvenile	*The House of Dies Drear*
1969, Hamilton	Nelson Glueck	Book, nonfiction	*The River Jordan*
	Ruth Lyons	Citation	Broadcaster
	Charles Sawyer	Book, autobiography	*Concerns of a Conservative*
	Carl Vitz	Career	Librarian
1969, Lucas	Dominick Labino	Citation	Creative art glass
1969, Montgomery	Jacob H. Dorn	Book, Florence Head Award	*Washington Gladden*
1970	Alfred B. Garrett	Citation	Vice-president for research, OSU
1970, Allen/ Franklin	Charles G. Rousculp	Book, nonfiction	*Chalk Dust on My Shoulder*
1970, Cuyahoga/ Summit/Hamilton	Robert L. Fish	Book, fiction	*The Xavier Affair*
1970, Cuyahoga	Jerome Lawrence	Pegasus	Playwright
1970, Darke	Jean Gould	Book, Florence Head Award	*Poet and her Book: ... Millay*
1970, Franklin	Novice G. Fawcett	Career	Teacher/administrator
	Fred Milligan	Citation	Civic leadership
1970, Hamilton	Mrs. C. C. Gaskill	Citation	County Chair of the Year
	Joseph Sagmaster	Citation	Editor, radio news analyst
1970, Lorain	Robert E. Lee	Pegasus	Playwright
1970, Lucas	Lawrence A. Frost	Book, Ohio scene	*The Thomas Edison Album*
	Jan Wahl	Book, juvenile	*The Norman Rockwell Storybook*
1970, not Ohioan	Robert M. Crunden	Book, biography	*A Hero in Spite of Himself*
1971, Clark	Marion Renick	Book, juvenile	*Ohio*
1971, Cuyahoga	Jesse Owens	Book, biography	*Black Think*
1971, Delaware	Alberta P. Hannum	Book, Florence Head Award	*Look Back With Love*
1971, Erie	Watt Marchman	Citation	Historian/Hayes Library
1971, Franklin	C. Burr Dawes	Citation	Horticulture & ecology
	Robert McKay	Book, juvenile	*Dave's Song*
	Robert C. McMaster	Citation	Engineer/research
1971, Hamilton	Edward Gould Mead	Citation	Music composition
	Janet Cutler Mead	Citation	Music composition
1971, Lucas	Foy D. Kohler	Career	Diplomat/educator
1971, Muskingum	William Manners	Book, biography	*T R & Will*
1971, not Ohioan	John Unterecker	Book, biography	*Voyager: Hart Crane*
1971, Trumbull	Mrs. Lucian J. Brown	Citation	County Chair of the Year
1972, Carroll	Clyde Singer	Pegasus	Art
1972, Clark	William Coyle	Citation	Editor: *Ohio Authors*
1972, Cuyahoga	Louis Lane	Citation	Music
	Kenneth S. Lynn	Book, Ohio letters	*William Dean Howells: An American Life*
	Mary O'Neill	Book, juvenile	*Winds*
1972, Franklin	Charles M. Cummings	Book, biography	*Yankee Quaker Confederate General*
	Stelias M. Stelson	Citation	"Good Will Ambassador"
1972, Greene	Louise Hutchison	Citation	County Chair of the Year
1972, Hamilton	Betty Zimmerman	Citation	Art & art education

Yr./Home Co.	Name	Award	Work
1972, Montgomery	Erma Bombeck	Book, humor	*Just Wait Till You Have Children of Your Own*
1972, not Ohioan	James M. Merrill	Book, Florence Head Award	*William Tecumseh Sherman*
	John M. Taylor	Book, Ohio scene	*Garfield of Ohio*
1972, Warren	Bergen Evans	Career	Etymologist
1973, Crawford	Boyd C. Shafer	Citation	Education & history
1973, Cuyahoga	Kenneth E. Davison	Book, history	*Presidency of Rutherford B. Hayes*
	Mary Oliver	Book, poetry	*The River Styx, Ohio*
	Dana Adams Schmidt	Citation	Pentagon correspondent
1973, Franklin	J. Allen Hynek	Book, nonfiction	*The UFO Experience*
	Francis Utley	Citation	Folklore
1973, Hamilton	John Alexander	Citation	Opera singer/teacher
	Hannah Green	Book, fiction	*The Dead of the House*
1973, Licking	Ada Clark	Citation	County Chair of the Year
1973, Lorain	Charles Holmes	Book, Florence Head Award	*The Clocks of Columbus*
1973, Muskingum	John Glenn	Career	Astronaut/senator
1973, not Ohioan	James T. Patterson	Book, biography	*Mr. Republican*
1974, Crawford/ Franklin	E. Richard Shoup	Citation	Music education
1974, Cuyahoga	Orville Prescott	Career	Author, literary critic
1974, Franklin	Battelle Institute	Citation	Science
	Weldon A. Kefauver	Citation	OSU Press, director
	Mahonri Sharp Young	Book, arts	*Paintings of George Bellows*
	Mahonri Sharp Young	Book, arts	*The Eight*
1974, Hamilton	Josephine W. Johnson	Book, Florence Head Award	*Seven Houses*
	Kenneth Koch	Book, poetry	*Rose, Where Did You Get That Red?*
1974, Licking/ Franklin	Ernest Cady	Citation	Journalism
1974, Lorain	Donald Smythe	Book, biography	*Guerrilla Warrior*
1974, not Ohioan	Donald F. Anderson	Book, Ohio scene	*William Howard Taft*
1974, Scioto	Ward M. Miller	Citation	County Chair of the Year
1975, Cuyahoga	George E. Condon	Book, Ohio scene	*Stars in the Water*
	Algis Ruksenas	Book, nonfiction	*Day of Shame*
1975, Fairfield	Michael Campbell	Book, technology	*Water-well Technology*
	John A. Ruthven	Career	Artist/ornithologist
1975, Franklin	Raymond Baby	Citation	Archaeologist
	Harold J. Grimm	Citation	History
	Jay R. Lehr	Book, technology	*Water-well Technology*
	Mrs. Marion Paoliello	Citation	Editor/State of Ohio
1975, Hamilton	Felix Labunski	Citation	Music composition
1975, Lorain	Patricia P. Leimbach	Book, Florence Head Award	*A Thread of Blue Denim*
	Toni Morrison	Book, fiction	*Sula*
1975, Summit	Mrs. Wm. J. McIntosh	Citation	County Chair of the Year
1976, Cuyahoga	the Russell Jelliffes	Pegasus	Karamu Theatre founders
	Ruby V. Redinger	Book, biography	*George Eliot*
1976, Fairfield	John Melvin	Citation	Conservation
1976, Fairfield	Ruth Melvin	Citation	Conservation
1976, Franklin	Ed Mason	Book, bicentennial	*Signers of the Constitution*
	Evan Whallon	Citation	Conductor
1976, Gallia	Joseph D. Pollitt	Citation	County Chair of the Year
1976, Hamilton	Nancy Lenz Harvey	Book, biography	*The Rose and the Thorn*
	Polk Laffoon, IV	Book, Ohio scene	*Tornado*
	Marjorie S. McKinney	Citation	Educational TV, administration
	Mary Jo Stephens	Book, juvenile	*Witch of the Cumberlands*
1976, Hancock/ Marion	William B. Thomas	Book, Florence Head Award	*The Country in the Boy*
1976, Licking	Minnie Hite Moody	Career	Journalist/writer
1976, Union	Gen. Robert Beightler	Career	Military
1976, Wood	Dr. Jane L. Forsyth	Citation	Geology
1977, Franklin	Robert Canzoneri	Book, autobiography	*A Highly Ramified Tree*
1977, Clinton	John Baskin	Book, Florence Head Award	*New Burlington*
1977, Franklin	Dr. Charles Doan	Career	Physician/teacher
	Bob Greene	Citation	Columnist/writer
	William E. Turner	Citation	Fine arts, history
	Terry Waldo	Book, social history	*This is Ragtime*
	Don E. Weaver	Citation	Journalist/editor
1977, Hamilton	Walter C. Langsam	Book, social history	*The World and Warren's Cartoons*

Yr./Home Co.	Name	Award	Work
	L.D. Warren	Book, social history	*The World and Warren's Cartoons*
1977, Muskingum	Walter F. Anderson	Citation	Music
1977, Stark	Brinton Turkle	Book, juvenile	*Deep in the Forest, Island Time*
1977, Summit	Thomas L. Vince	Citation	County Chair of the Year
1978, Athens	Thomas H. Smith	Book, history	*The Mapping of Ohio*
1978, Butler	Walter Havighurst	Pegasus	Writer, historian, teacher
1978, Columbiana	Jane Louise Curry	Book, juvenile	*Poor Tom's Ghost*
1978, Franklin	Roy H. Bowen	Citation	Theatre arts
1978, Franklin	Paul Colinvaux	Book, science	*Why Big Fierce Animals Are Rare*
	Eileen Heckart	Career	Actress
1978, Greene	Louise Hutchison	Citation	County Chair of the Year
1978, Mahoning/ Cuyahoga	Donald Erb	Citation	Music
1978, Montgomery	John Jakes	Book, fiction	Bicentennial series
1978, Sandusky	Elizabeth Boyer	Citation	Attorney/feminist
1978, Seneca	John I. Kolehmainen	Book, Florence Head Award	*From Lake Erie's Shores...*
1978, Summit	Mrs. Wm. J. McIntosh	Citation	County Chair of the Year
1978, Warren	Jared Lee	Citation	Illustrative arts
1979, Allen	John D. Unruh, Jr.	Book, history	*The Plains Across*
1979, Athens	Wayne Dodd	Editorial excellence	*The Ohio Review*
	Robert Winters	Citation	Theater arts
1979, Cuyahoga	George Crile, Jr.	Pegasus	Surgeon/writer
	Allan Peskin	Book, biography	*Garfield*
1979, Delaware/ Franklin	Janet Hickman	Book, Florence Head Award	*Zoar Blue*
1979, Franklin	Nicholas Guild	Book, fiction	*The Summer Soldier*
	James Westwater	Citation	Photographer
	John Weed	Citation	County Chair of the Year
1979, Hamilton	Gustav Eckstein	Career	Scientist/writer
1979, Lorain	Natalie Hinderas	Citation	Musician/teacher
1979, Perry	D.G. Sanders	Book, memoirs	*The Brasspounder*
1980, Ashland	Thomas Fensch	Book, biography	*The Story of a Friendship*
1980, Cuyahoga	Ruth Beebe Hill	Book, fiction	*Hanta Yo: American Saga*
	James T. Maher	Book, Florence Head Award	*Distant Music of Summer*
	Andre Norton	Book, juvenile	Body of work
1980, Franklin	Richard H. Hoppin	Citation	Music
	Ohio Science Academy	Book, science	*Ohio's Natural Heritage*
	David E. Black	Citation	Fine arts
1980, Hamilton	Mark Schneider	Music award	*Antimemoires*
	David J. McLain, Jr.	Citation	Dance
	Janis Gaskill	Citation	County Chair of the Year
1980, Hancock	Noverre Musson	Career award	Architect, planner, teacher
1980, Knox	Ronald Sharp, ed.	Editorial excellence	*The Kenyon Review*
	Frederick Turner, ed.	Editorial excellence	*The Kenyon Review*
1980, Stark	David Wagoner	Book, Sherwood Anderson Award	*The Hanging Garden*
1981, Ashland	Thomas Fensch	Book, biography	*Steinbeck and Covici*
1981, Cuyahoga	Ruth Beebe Hill	Book, fiction	*Hanta Yo*
	Frank J. Lausche	Career	Senator/governor
	George Loomis, Jr.	Book, Florence Head Award	*Billy Ireland*
	James T. Maher	Florence Head Award	*The Distant Music of Summer*
	Andre Norton	Book, juvenile	Body of work
1981, Franklin	David E. Black	Fine Arts citation	Sculptor
	Lucy S. Caswell	Book, Florence Head Award	*Billy Ireland*
	Charlotte Curtis	Pegasus	Journalist
	Lynn E. Elfner	Book, science	*Ohio's Natural Heritage*
	Richard H. Hoppin	Music citation	Musicologist/author
	Allan R. Millett	Book, history	*Semper Fidelis*
	David R. Wallace	Book, science	*Idle Weeds*
1981, Greene	Robert S. Fogarty, ed.	Editorial excellence	*Antioch Review*
	Suzanne P. Clauser	Citation	Creative writing
1981, Hamilton	David J. McClain, Jr.	Dance citation	Choreographer (ballet)
	Stephanie S. Tolan	Book, juvenile	*The Liberation of Tansy Warner*
1981, Ross	Robert Alan Gough	Fine Arts citation	Artist
1981, Summit	Mrs. Wm. J. McIntosh	Citation	County Chair of the Year
	Grace Reginald	Citation	Music
1981, Washington	Helen F. Rosenblum	Book, fiction	*Minerva's Turn*
1982, Ashland	Mrs. Rendell Rhoades	Citation	County Chair of the Year
1982, Cuyahoga	Elizabeth Adams	Marvin grant	Unpublished young writer
	Jerome Lawrence	Career	Playwright

Yr/Home Co.	Name	Award	Work
	Frances Beck		Composer/choral director
	Robert Fox	Citation	Writer/administrator
	Evan Whallon	Pegasus	Conductor
1982, Hamilton	Thomas Berger	Book, fiction	*Reinhart's Women*
	Robert Fabe	Citation	Artist
	Jacob Rader Marcus	Book, history	*The American Jewish Woman*
1982, Lorain	*Field Magazine*	Editorial excellence	
	Stuart Friebert	Editorial excellence	*Field Magazine*
	Robert E. Lee	Career	Playwright
	David Young	Editorial excellence	*Field Magazine*
1982, Miami	Carrie Young	Book, Florence Head Award	*Green Broke*
1982, not Ohioan	Milton Rugoff	Book, biography	*The Beechers*
1982, Stark	H.M. Hoover	Book, juvenile	*Another Heaven, Another Earth*
1982, Wood	Burton Beerman	Citation	Music
1983, Butler	Mrs. Wm. O. Cullen	Citation	County Chair of the Year
1983, Franklin	Jack Bickham	Book, Florence Head Award	*I Still Dream about Columbus*
	Gertrude Kuehefuhs	Music citation	Scholar/teacher
	Dorothy M. Littlehale	Citation	Painter
	Elijah Pierce	Pegasus	Folk artist
	Milton B. Trautman	Book	Body of work
	Sylvia H. Westerman	Career	TV-radio news executive
	James Westwater	Book	*Ohio*
1983, Greene	Helen H. Santmyer	Book, fiction	*"...And Ladies of the Club"*
1983, Hamilton	*Queen City Heritage*	Editorial excellence	
	Dottie L. Lewis	Editorial excellence	*Queen City Heritage*
1983, not Ohioan	Jerry Silverman	Citation	Fashion Museum, Kent State
1983, Tuscarawas	Shannon Rodgers	Citation	Fashion Museum, Kent State
1983, Vinton/ Ross/Pickaway	Tella Kitchen	Citation	Folk art
1983, Wood	Lawrence Friedman	Book	*Gregarious Saints*
1984, Athens	Robin Hemley	Marvin grant	Unpublished author
1984, Butler	John M. Dickinson	Editorial excellence	*The Old Northwest*
	Helen V. Worrall	Citation	Artist (enamel)
1984, Cuyahoga	Richard A. Hawley	Book	*The Headmaster's Papers*
	Dard Hunter, II	Citation	Publishing
1984, Delaware	F. Beverly Kelley	Book, Florence Head Award	*It Was Better Than Work*
1984, Franklin	Irma Cooper	Citation	Singer/teacher
	Ilsedore Edse	Citation	"Intercultural guide"
	Rosemary O. Joyce	Book, biography	*A Woman's Place*
1984, Greene	Virginia Hamilton	Book, juvenile	"Body of her work"
1984, Guernsey	Don E. Weaver	Career	Journalist/editor
1984, Hamilton	Mrs. Lowell P. Orr, Jr.	Citation	County Chair of the Year
1984, not Ohioan	R. David Edmunds	Book	*The Shawnee Prophet*
1985, Cuyahoga	David Citino	Krout Poetry	Outstanding Ohio poet
	Mildred Miller	Career	Mezzo-soprano
1985, Franklin	Michael J. Rosen	Book, poetry	*A Drink at the Mirage*
	Emmanuel Rudolph	Citation	Book collector/scientist
	Robert W. Wagner	Pegasus	Filmmaker
1985, Geauga	Hale Chatfield	Editorial excellence	*Hiram Poetry Review*
1985, Hamilton	Gloria Ackerman	Citation	Music
1985, Hancock	Emily Apt Geer	Book, Florence Head Award	*First Lady: Life of Lucy Hayes*
1985, Medina	Robert Skimin	Book, fiction	*Chikara*
1985, Putnam	John Nartker	Citation	Painter/print maker
1985, Summit	Allen G. Noble	Book, history	*Wood, Brick & Stone*
1985, Wayne	Thomas Clareson	Citation	Scholar/critic/teacher
1985, Wood	Michael Mott	Book, biography	*Seven Mountains of Thomas Merton*
1986, Butler	Ann Hinkle	Marvin grant	Unpublished young writer
1986, Cuyahoga	Glen Tetley	Career	Choreographer
	Alberta T. Turner	Krout Poetry	Poet/editor/teacher
1986, Franklin	Ellin Carter	Citation	Literature
	Donald A. Hutslar	Book, history	*Architecture of Migration*
	Freda Postle Koch	Book, biography	*Col. Coggeshall: The Man...*
1986, Hamilton	Don Dennis	Citation	Fine arts
1986, Montgomery	Ellen J.L. Porter	Citation	Music
1986, not Ohioan	Hugh Nissenson	Book, fiction	*The Tree of Life*
1986, Summit	Grace Goulder Izant	Book, Florence Head Award	*Hudson's Heritage*
1986, Summit	Frances B. Murphey	Citation	Journalism
1986, Washington	Nancy Pelletier	Book, fiction	*The Rearrangement*
1986, Wood	Robert Early	Editorial excellence	*Mid-American Review*
1987, Athens	Jack Matthews	Book, essays	*Booking in the Heartland*
1987, Butler	George Dell	Book, fiction	*The Earth Abideth*

Yr./Home Co.	Name	Award	Work
1987, Butler/ Cuyahoga	Phillip R. Shriver	Career	Educator/administrator
1987, Columbiana	Jane Louise Curry	Book, juvenile	*The Lotus Cup*
1987, Franklin	Charles A. Csuri	Art citation	Computer artist
	Christoper Duckworth	Editorial excellence	*Timeline*
	Ed Graczyk	Citation	Director/playwright
1987, Greene	Zenobia Powell Perry	Citation	Composer/teacher
	Hollis Summers	Krout Poetry	Outstanding poet
1987, Hamilton	Andrew R.L. Cayton	Book, history	*The Frontier Republic*
1987, Jackson	I. Max Hendershott	Citation	Fine arts
1987, Lucas	Virginia H. Eyster	Book, Florence Head Award	*Journey of the Heart*
1987, Montgomery	Josephine L. Schwarz	Pegasus	Dancer, choreographer, teacher
1988, Athens	Robert Newell	Citation	Composer/conductor
1988, Cuyahoga	Don Robertson	Book, fiction	*The Ideal, Genuine Man*
	David Young	Krout Poetry	Outstanding Ohio poet
1988, Fairfield	Frederick G. Ruffner	Career	Publisher
1988, Hamilton	John Alexander	Pegasus	Opera singer/teacher
	Nikki Giovanni	Book, essays	*Sacred Cows ... and Other Edibles*
	Don Heinrich Tolzmann	Book, history	*The Cincinnati Germans After...*
1988, Hancock	Doug Salveson	Fine Arts citation	Artist/teacher
1988, Huron	Larry Smith	Citation	Poetry
1988, Knox	Joseph Slate	Citation	Children's literature
1988, Lorain	David Edict	Marvin grant	Unpublished young poet
	Toni Morrison	Career	Novelist
1988, Mahoning	Frederick J. Blue	Book, biography	*Salmon P. Chase*
1988, Summit	Darshan Perusek	Editorial excellence	*Kaleidoscope*
1989, Athens	David Hostetler	Career	Sculptor
1989, Darke	Merrill Gilfillan	Book, nonfiction	*Magpie Rising*
1989, Franklin	Maurice Casey	Citation	Choral director/teacher
	J. Patrick Lewis	Book, juvenile	*The Tsar and Amazing Cow*
	George Myers, Jr.	Citation	Editor/critic/author
	Joy Reilly	Citation	Director/teacher
	Arthur I. Vorys	60th Anniversary citation	Attorney/volunteer
1989, Hamilton	Kay Boyle	Book, fiction	*Life Being the Best*
	Cincinnati Hist. Soc.	Ohio book	*Cincinnati Guide*
	Geoffrey J. Giglierano	Ohio book	*Cincinnati Guide*
	Deborah Overmyer	Ohio book	*Cincinnati Guide*
1989, Hardin	Charles M. Oliver	Editorial excellence	*The Hemingway Review*
1989, Lucas	Mildred Wirt Benson	Citation	Children's Literature
1989, not Ohioan	Gail R. Scott	Book, Florence Head Award	*Marsden Hartley*
1989, Sandusky	John Clarke	Krout Poetry	Outstanding Ohio poet
1989, Seneca	David Shevin	Book, poetry	*Discovery of Fire*
1990, Athens	Maya Lin	Pegasus	Architect/sculptor
1990, Cuyahoga	Dagmar Celeste	Special citation	Support of arts and literature
	George Klaus Roy	Citation	Composer/writer
	Helga Sandburg	Book, Florence Head Award	*... Where Love Begins*
1990, Franklin	Lee K. Abbott, Jr.	Book, fiction	*Dreams of Distant Lives*
	Robert Thomas	Citation	Journalism
	Bruce Peterjohn	Book, Ohio	*The Birds of Ohio*
	Christopher Ries	Citation	Glass sculptor
	David Rains Wallace	Book, nonfiction	*Bulow Hamock*
1990, Hamilton	Susan Tekulve	Marvin grant	Unpublished young poet
1990, Mahoning	Jim Villani	Editorial excellence	*Pig Iron*
1990, Portage	Cynthia Rylant	Book, juvenile	*But I'll Be Back Again*
1990, Summit	Rita Dove	Book, poetry	*Grace Notes*
	George W. Knepper	Career	Writer, teacher, historian
	Paige Palmer	Citation	Fitness and travel
1990, Wood	Howard McCord	Krout Poetry	Outstanding Ohio poet
1991, Athens	Wayne Dodd	Krout Poetry	Outstanding Ohio poet
1991, Cuyahoga	Bruce McCombs	Citation	Painter
	Louis T. Milic	Editorial excellence	*The Gamut*
	Eunice Podis	Citation	Pianist/teacher
	Gary E. Polster	Book, Ohio	*Inside Looking Out*
	Tricia Springstubb	Book, juvenile	*With a Name Like Lulu*
1991, Cuyahoga	Leonard M. Trawick	Editorial excellence	*The Gamut*
1991, Franklin	David Citino	Book, poetry	*House of Memory*
1991, Greene	Virginia Hamilton	Career	Author/teacher
1991, Hamilton	Rosemary Clooney	Pegasus	Singer/entertainer
	Suzanne Farrell	Book, Florence Head Award	*Holding on to the Air*
	Frederick Hauck	Citation	Inventor/philanthropist

Yr./Home Co.	Name	Award	Work
1991, Hancock	Barry Alexander	Citation	Theater
1991, Licking	Geoffrey C. Ward	Book, nonfiction	*A First-Class Temperament*
1991, Lucas	Mildred Taylor	Alice Wood Award	Body of work
1991, Montgomery	Nancy Zafris	Book, fiction	*The People I Know*
1992, Butler/Hamilton	Kay Sloan	Book, fiction	*Worry Beads*
1992, Cuyahoga	Jan Cigliano	Book, Florence Head award	*Showplace of America*
	Thylias Moss	Book, poetry	*Rainbow Remnants ...*
	Robert Wallace	Krout Poetry	Outstanding Ohio poet
1992, Franklin	Arthur Schlesinger, Jr.	Career	Historian/Author/Teacher
1992, Greene	Arnold Adoff	Citation	Children's Literature
1992, Greene	Virginia Hamilton	Alice Wood Award	Children's literature
1992, Hamilton	Roger Daniels	Citation	History
1992, Lorain	Ricky Clark	Book, Ohio	*Quilts in Community*
1992, Lucas	Samuel Paul Szor	Citation	Conductor/Musician/Teacher
1992, Montgomery	Melissa Fay Greene	Book, nonfiction	*Praying for Sheetrock*
1992, Portage	Cynthia, Rylant	Book, Juvenile	*Appalachia*
1992, Summit	George Knepper	Book, Ohio	*Quilts in Community*
1992, Wayne	Daniel Bourne	Editorial excellence	*Artful Dodge*
	Karen Kovacik	Editorial excellence	*Artful Dodge*
	Ellice Ronsheim	Book, Ohio	*Quilts in Community*
	Samrat Upadhyay	Marvin grant	Unpublished young writer
1993, Clinton	John Baskin	Editorial excellence	*Ohio Magazine*
1993, Cuyahoga	Eve Horowitz	Book, fiction	*Plain Jane*
1993, Cuyahoga	Mary Oliver	Book, poetry	*New & Selected Poems*
1993, Delaware	Robert Flanagan	Citation	Author, Teacher
1993, Franklin	Michael Feinstein	Citation	Singer/Pianist
1993, Franklin	John McFall	Citation	Dancer, Choreographer
1993, Geauga	Hale Chatfield	Krout Poetry	Outstanding Ohio poet
1993, Hamilton	Anita J. Ellis	Book, Florence Head Award	Rookwood pottery
1993, Hamilton	Suzanne Farrell	Career	Ballerina/Teacher
1993, Hamilton	John Fleischman	Editorial excellence	*Ohio Magazine*
1993, not Ohio	John Marszalek	Book, nonfiction	*Sherman: A Soldier's Passion*
1993, not Ohioian	Benjamin Townsend	Book, about Ohio	*Charles Burchfield's Journals*
1993, Pike	Dawna L. Buchannan	Book, Juvenile	*The Falcon's Wing*
1993, Portage	Alex Gildzen	Citation	Librarian, writer
1993, Portage	Cynthia Rylant	Alice Wood Award	Children's literature
1994, Athens	June Carver Roberts	Book, Florence Head award	*Season of Promise*
1994, Cuyahoga	Leonard Trawick	Krout Poetry	Outstanding Ohio poet
1994, Franklin	Mimi Brodsky Chenfeld	Citation	Education/Art
1994, Franklin	Thurber House	Citation	James Thurber
1994, Hamilton	Doris Day	Pegasus	Singer, actress
1994, Jackson	Benton Fletcher	Career	Sculptor/Artist
1994, Knox	Judith Sacks	Book, about Ohio	*Way Up North in Dixie*
	Howard Sacks	Book, about Ohio	*Way Up North in Dixie*
1994, Lorain	Abby Frucht	Book, fiction	*Are You Mine?*
	Margaret Young	Marvin grant	Unpublished young writer
1994, Lucas	Denise Fleming	Book, juvenile	*In the Small, Small Pond*
1994, Montgomery	Natalie Babbitt	Alice Wood Award	Children's literature
1994, Montgomery	Jeraldyne Blunden	Citation	Dance
1994, Montgomery	Clark Haines	Citation	Music
1994, Montgomery	Virginia K. Hess	Citation	Sculptor
1994, Portage	Scott R. Sanders	Book, nonfiction	*Staying Put*
1994, Summit	Rita Dove	Book, poetry	*Selected Poems*
1994, Wood	Pat Browne	Editorial excellence	*Journal of Popular Culture*
1995, Allen	Maidie Norman	Career	Actress, Teacher
1995, Clark	Imogene Bolls	Krout Poetry	Outstanding Ohio poet
1995, Cuyahoga	Richard Howard	Book, poetry	*Like Most Revelations*
1995, Fairfield	Nancy Crow	Citation	Quilter
1995, Franklin	Janet Hickman	Book, juvenile	*Jericho*
	Allan Wildman	Editorial excellence	*Russian Review*
1995, Hamilton	Cincinnati Symphony	Citation	100th anniversary
	George Laycock	Book, about Ohio	*John A. Ruthven*
	Roy Rogers	Pegasus	Actor
	Don H. Tolzmann	Citation	Humanities, education
1995, Knox	Bonnie Pryor	Alice Wood award	Children's Literature
1995, Montgomery	Richard P. Benedum	Citation	Organist, teacher
1995, Morrow	Merrill Gilfillan, Jr.	Book, fiction	*Sworn Before Cranes*
1995, Summit	Ian Frazier	Book, nonfiction	*Family*
1996, not Ohioan	Ari Hoogenboom	Book, about Ohio	*Rutherford B. Hayes: Warrior &President*

Yr./Home Co.	Name	Award	Work
1996, not Ohioan	Tim Page	Book, nonfiction	*The Diaries of Dawn Powell*
1996, Butler	Elizabeth Arthur	Alice Wood Award	*Antarctic Navigation*
	Edgar Marquess Branch	Pegasus	Educator, scholar, author
1996, Cuyahoga/Lake	Elizabeth Alder	Book, juvenile	*The King's Shadow*
1996, Franklin	John Matthias	Book, poetry	*Swimming at Midnight*
1996, Franklin	Jennifer Jackson	Marvin grant	Unpublished young poet
1996, Jackson	Lilly O. Goldstayn	Citation	Art
1996, Lucas	Deniese Fleming	Alice Wood Award	Children's literature
1996, Pickaway/Ross	Tony Ellis	Citation	Music
1996, Portage	John Hubbell	Editorial excellence	Civil War History
1996, Scioto/Franklin	Paul Bierley	Citation	Writer, editor, tubist
1996, Summit	Elton Glaser	Krout Poetry	Outstanding Ohio poet
1996, Wood/Medina	Tom Doyle	Career	Art
1997, Adams	Julie Salamon	Book, Florence Head Award	*The Net of Dreams*
1997, Cuyahoga	Herbert Gold	Career	Author
	Wayne Mack	Citation	Radio
1997, Franklin	Emily Foster	Book, about Ohio	*Ohio Frontier: Anthology*
	Charles A. Csuri	Pegasus	Artist, innovator, teacher
	Michael J. Rosen	Alice Wood Award	Children's literature
1997, Franklin	Han Xin	Citation	Art
1997, Greene	John Fleming	Citation	African American History
	Virginia Hamilton	Book, juvenile	*Her Stories: African American Folk Tales*
1997, Hamilton	Andrew Hudgins	Krout Poetry	Outstanding Ohio poet
	Erin McGraw	Book, fiction	*Lies of the Saints*
	David Quammen	Book, nonfiction	*The Song of the Dodo*
1997, Stark	David Wagoner	Book, poetry	*Walt Whitman Bathing*
1997, Wood	John G. Nachbar	Editorial excellence	*Journal of Popular Film and Television*
1997, Wood	Marilyn Shrude	Citation	Music
1998, Butler	Constance Pierce	Book, fiction	*Hope Mills*
1998, Clark	Steven Winteregg	Citation	Music
1998, Cuyahoga	Donald Erb	Career	Composer
1998, Cuyahoga	Salvatore Scibona	Marvin grant	Unpublished young writer
1998, Franklin	David Citino	Book, poetry	*Broken Symmetry*
1998, Franklin	Tracey Dils	Alice Wood Award	Children's literature
1998, Franklin	Wil Haygood	Book, nonfiction	*The Haygoods of Columbus*
1998, Franklin	Michael J. Rosen	Book, juvenile	*The Heart is Big Enough*
1998, Hamilton	Sister Jean Harrington	Citation	Education
1998, Hamilton	Walter E. Langsam	Book, about Ohio	*Great Houses...*
1998, Hamilton	Alice Weston	Book, about Ohio	*Great Houses...*
1998, Licking	David Baker	Krout Poetry	Outstanding Ohio poet
1998, Lucas	Gloria Steinem	Pegasus	Journalist and activist
1998, Montgomery	Ervin E. Beauregard	Citation	Education
1998, Montgomery	Herbert W. Martin	Citation	Theater
1998, Tuscarawas	Earl P. Olmstead	Book, about Ohio	*David Zeisberger*
1998, Wood	George Looney	Editorial excellence	*Mid-American Review*
1999, not Ohioan	Ron Chernow	Book, about Ohio	*Titan: Life of John D. Rockefeller*
1999, Cuyahoga	John Stark Bellamy	Ohio, Favorite Book	*They Died Crawling*
	Peter Morton Coan	Book, nonfiction	Ellis Island Interviews
	Victoria Crane	Marvin grant	Unpublished young writer
	Lynda Durrant	Book, juvenile	*The Beaded Moccasins*
	Jane Semple Wood	Editorial excellence	*Shaker Magazine*
1999, Franklin	Leland McClelland	Pegasus	Painter, cartoonist, teacher
	Geoffrey Nelson	Citation	Theatre
	Robert L. Stine	Career	Children's (Goosebump series)
	James Thurber	Ohio, Favorite Author	Nonfiction
1999, Greene	Virginia Hamilton	Ohio, Favorite Author	Juvenile
	Helen H. Santmyer	Ohio, Favorite Book	*"...And Ladies of the Club"*
1999, Hamilton	Nikki Giovanni	Ohio, Favorite Author	Poetry
1999, Jefferson	Larry Smith	Krout Poetry	Editor, *Bottom Dog Press*
1999, Licking	David Baker	Book, poetry	*The Truth About Small Towns*
1999, Lorain	Sharon Denslow	Ohio, Favorite Book	*Riding with Aunt Lucy*
	Toni Morrison	Book, fiction	*Paradise*
	Toni Morrison	Ohio, Favorite Book	*Beloved*
	Toni Morrison	Ohio, Favorite Author	Fiction
1999, Lucas	Christine Brennen	Book, Florence Head Award	*Edge of Glory*
1999, Medina	James Stuart	Citation	Ohio Light Opera founder
1999, Montgomery	Michale Major	Citation	Painter, sculptor
	Allan Eckert	Ohio, Favorite Author	about Ohio or and Ohioan

Yr./Home Co.	Name	Award	Work
	Allan Eckert	Ohio, Favorite Book	*The Frontiersmen*
1999, Portage	Angela Johnson	Alice Wood Award	Children's literature
1999, Sandusky	Grace Luebke	Citation	*Elmore, Ohio: A History Perserved*
2000, not Ohioan	Paul Mariani	Book, about Ohio	*The Broken Tower: Life of Crane*
2000, Clinton	Orange Frazer Press	Citation	Publishing
2000, Clinton	Marcy Hawley	Citation	Publishing
2000, Cuyahoga	A.Gomez-Jefferson	Citation	Theater
2000, Cuyahoga	Marilyn Greenwald	Book, Florence Head Award	*A Women of the Times*
2000, Fairfield	Elizabeth Spires	Book, juvenile	*The Mouse of Amherst*
2000, Franklin	Evelyn Freeman	Editorial excellence	*Journal of Children's Literature*
2000, Geauga	Anthony Doerr	Marvin grant	Unpublished young writer
2000, Hamilton	Alvin Greenberg	Krout Poety	Poet
2000, Hamilton	Will Hillenbrand	Citation	Illustrator
2000, Hamilton	Erich Kunzel, Jr.	Pegasus	Conductor
2000, Hamilton	Pat Mora	Alice Wood Award	Children's Literature
2000, Jefferson	Dard Hunter III	71st Anniversary Award	Papermaker, artisan
2000, Marion	Patricia Scharer	Editorial excellence	*Journal of Children's Literature*
2000, Montgomery	David Klingshirn	Citation	Music
2000, Montgomery	Terri Paul	Book, fiction	*Glass Hearts*
2000, Muskingum	John Glenn	Book, nonfiction	*John Glenn: a Memoir*
2000, Richland	Barbara Lehman	Editorial excellence	*Journal of Children's Literature*
2000, Seneca	Gene Logsdon	Career	Writer
2000, Summit	Rita Dove	Book, poetry	*On the Bus with Rosa Parks: Poems*
2001, not Ohioan	John Sugden	Book, about Ohio	*Blue Jacket*
2001, Athens	Erin Belieu	Book, poetry	*One Above and One Below*
2001, Athens	Mary L. Bowman	Citation	Genealogy
2001, Butler	Amy Sickles	Marvin grant	Unpublished young writer
2001, Cuyahoga	David Citino	Career	Educator, poet
	Lynda Durrant	Book, juvenile	*Betsy Zane*
	Philip Johnson	72nd Anniversary Award	Architect
2001, Franklin	Sunny Che	Book, Florence Head Award	*Forever Alien: Korean Memoir*
	Mardo Williams	Citation	Literary contributions, career
2001, Knox	P.F. Kluge	Citation	Literature
2001, Mahoning	William Greenway	Krout Poetry	Distinguished professor
2001, Montgomery	Willis H. (Bing) Davis	Pegasus	Artist, activist, educator
2001, Montgomery	Frank F. Mathias	Book, nonfiction	*The GI Generation: A Memoir*
2001, Richland	W.H. (Chip) Gross	Editorial excellence	*Wild Ohio and Wild Ohio for Kids*
2001, Summit	Tom Batiuk	Citation	Art
2001, Trumbull	Elizabeth George	Book, fiction	*In Pursuit of the Proper Sinner*
2002, not Ohioan	James Sallis	Book, about Ohio	*Chester Himes: A Life*
2002, Athens	Robert DeMott	Book, poetry	*Two Midwest Voices*
	Patricia Goedicke	Krout Poetry	Professor of English
2002, Cuyahoga	Dan Chaon	Book, fiction	*Among the Missing*
	Antwone Q. Fisher	Book, nonfiction	*Finding Fish*
	James Cross Giblin	Book, juvenile	*The Amazing Life of Franklin*
	Hal Holbrook	73rd Anniversary Award	Actor, director, educator
2002, Franklin	Ellis Avery	Marvin grant	Unpublished young writer
	Wayne Lawson	Career	Director, Ohio Arts Council
	Jerry Roscoe	Book, poetry	*Two Midwest Voices: Mirror Lake*
2002, Hamilton	Louise Borden	Alice Wood Award	Children's literature
2002, Lucas	Jon Hendricks	Citation	Music
2002, Montgomery	David Leach	Citation	Art
2002, Muskingum	Dave Longaberger	Book, Florence Head Award	*Longaberger: American Success*
2002, Portage	Thomas Schmidlin	Editorial excellence	*The Ohio Journal of Science*
2002, Stark	Audrey A.P. Lavin	Pegasus	Writer and educator
	Steven R. Smith	Citation	Education
2002, Wayne	Tami Longaberger	Book, Florence Head Award	*Longaberger: American Success*
	David Wiesenberg	Citation	Humanities
2003, Adams	Julie Salamon	Book, nonfiction	*Facing the Wind*
2003, Cuyahoga	Ian Adams	Book, about Ohio	*Ohio: A Bicentennial Portrait*
	Margaret Brouwer	Citation	Composer
	Anthony Doerr	Book, fiction	*The Shell Collector*
	Jen Hirt	Marvin grant	Unpublished young writer
	David Kaufman	Citation	Theatre critic
	Shelley Pearsall	Book, juvenile	*Trouble Don't Last*
	Melvin Unger	Editorial excellence	*Journal of Bach Institute*
2003, Fairfield	Elizabeth Spires	Book, poetry	*Now the Green Blade Rises*
2003, Franklin	Priscilla Hewetson	Citation	Historic interpretation

Yr./Home Co.	Name	Award	Work
	Stephen Ostrander	Book, about Ohio	*Ohio: A Bicentennial Portrait*
	Aminah B. Robinson	Career	Artist
	Ronald L. Stuckey	Book, Florence Head Award	*Lost Stories*
2003, Greene	Arnold Adoff	Alice Wood Award	Children's literature
2003, Hamilton	Charles Henry Parsons	Citation	Opera critic
2003, Montgomery	John Jakes	Pegasus	Author
2003, Portage	Maggie Anderson	Hrout poetry	Associate professor, KSU

THE BUCKEYE BOOK FAIR: OHIO'S OWN

In 1987, the Buckeye Book Fair in Wooster began bringing together dozens of Ohioans to meet the reading public. Now it's the state's premier event for writers who are from Ohio or who write about Ohio, bringing over 200 titles—and their authors—and thousands of bibliophiles to Wooster every November. It attracts nationally as well as regionally known novelists, journalists, historians, biographers, photographers, columnists, and cartoonists, much to the delight of the fair's growing legion of patrons, who spend the day stuffing bags, backpacks, and even baby buggies with books. Sponsored by Wooster's newspaper, *The Daily Record*, the book fair not only allows the public to meet authors and buy autographed books at a discount, but also raises thousands of dollars for Ohio literacy programs.

Novelists Allan Eckert of Bellefontaine, Les Roberts of Cleveland, and Scott Russell Sanders, formerly of Ravenna, have all come and expressed amazement at how many reading fans pack Fisher Auditorium on the campus of the Ohio Agricultural Research and Development Center for a chance to talk with an author. So, too, have sports figures Bob Feller, Jim Brown, and Sam Rutigliano; and cartoonists Tom Batiuk ("Funky Winkerbean" and "Crankshaft") of Medina, Art and Chip Sansom ("The Born Loser") of Lakewood, and Ryan Brown ("Teenage Mutant Ninja Turtles") of West Salem. Other native Ohioans who have participated include former Clevelander Lois Wyse, and Lorain native Terry Anderson.

Thousands of people browse through the nearly 250 book titles and 22 pallets of books, most from Cleveland, Toledo, Pittsburgh and even a few from the southern part of the state. For many, purchasing with the latest signed copies at the Buckeye Book Fair marks the start of the holiday shopping season.

The event is staffed with more than 50 volunteers and according to Stephen Badman, manager of the Buckeye Book Fair, proceeds from the event benefit literacy efforts in Ohio through the form of grants. More than $160,000 has been donated to Ohio libraries and literacy programs. ↩

www.buckeyebookfair.com

bookish occasion

343

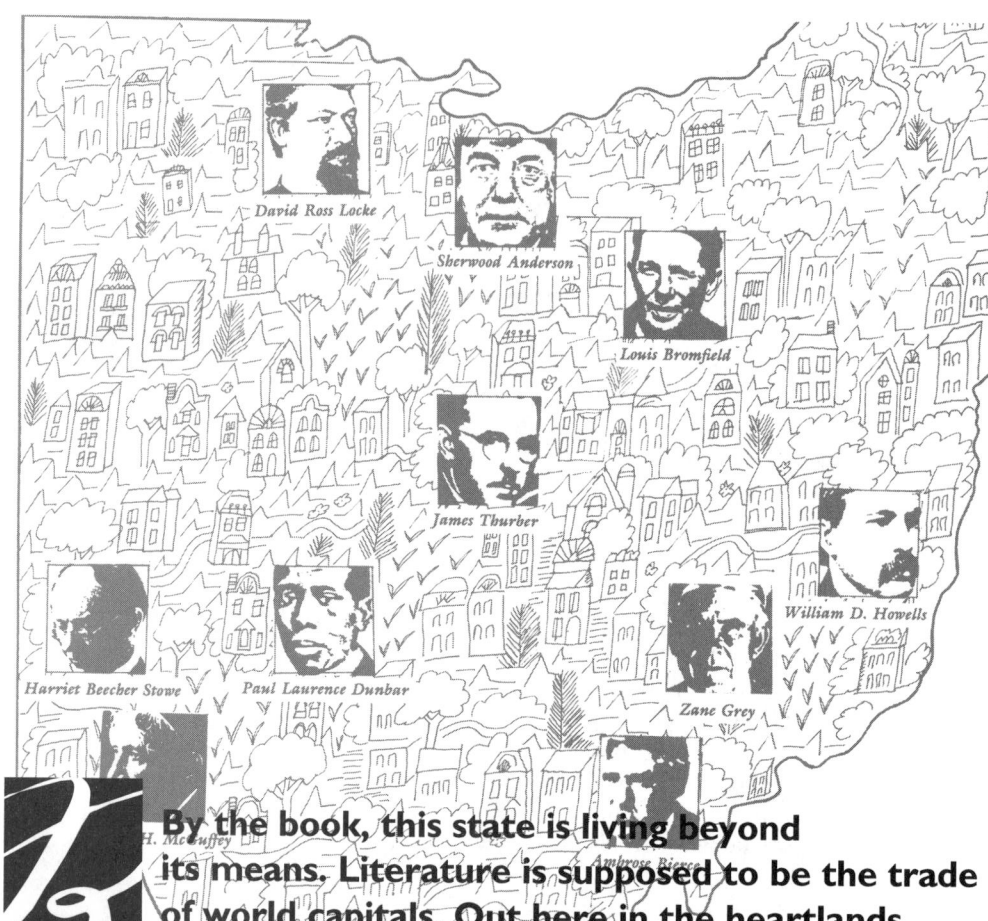

A readers"
digest of Ohio
writers, the
novel men and
women whose
pens and poesy
produced a
library's worth
of fiction, fables,
allegories, stories,
histories,
mysteries,
anecdotes and
accountings.

David Ross Locke

Sherwood Anderson

Louis Bromfield

James Thurber

William D. Howells

Harriet Beecher Stowe

Paul Laurence Dunbar

Zane Grey

H. McGuffey

Ambrose Bierce

By the book, this state is living beyond its means. Literature is supposed to be the trade of world capitals. Out here in the heartlands, our job is to export literary talent. We stake our young writers to their creative capital by giving them stifling childhoods, and then we ship them out to the literary stock markets. Fortunately, the balance of trade has not been entirely lopsided.

Ohio has done a surprisingly brisk business in the written word. True, many of our greatest penmen (and penwomen) have hotfooted out of the Great Buckeye as soon as their prose could carry them, but Ohio has a way of staying with a writer, an irritation surely provocative of great things, in the way sand provokes an oyster. Clasped to the bosom of Brahmin Boston like William Dean Howells or the talk of midtown Manhattan like James Thurber, the Ohio exile still hears unsung home melodies of flat vowels and flat fields.

If "never to return" is a standard line in many Ohio literary profiles, others find themselves drawn home. There are also outlanders who come

into the territory on other business and leave unaware of the metaphorical baggage they pick up in transit. Some came to Ohio against their will, such as William Sydney Porter (O. Henry), whose stay in Columbus was a three-year stretch in the State Pen. Some came *in utero* and left in diapers.

In Hollywood, that other lodestone of American literature (they can't read, but they can write checks), tourists are sold "Maps of the Stars" to guide them past the locked front gates and heavily watered lawns of filmdom. Here we provide *gratis* a map to some of our literary stars plus a few of our black holes. Most are dead. The rest don't need the company. Go by the book.

Sherwood Anderson—voice crying in the industrial wilderness

Born—Camden, 1876
Career—at 36, walked out of his position at an Elyria paint factory and into the annals of American literature with short stories that tried to "hear and render the voices of the common people," a people whose reality he saw cruelly violated by the Industrial Age; enormously successful as an American writer, his plain, but sensual, style inspired Hemingway and encouraged Faulkner.
Must read—*Winesburg, Ohio*, his classic anthology of small town portraits infuriated most of his hometown but charmed most of America.
To wit—"We Ohio men have taken as lovely a land as ever lay outdoors and...have, in our towns and cities, put the old stamp of ourselves on it for keeps." —*"Ohio, I'll Say We've Done Well."*

"As a matter of fact, Anderson is a man of practically no ideas. But he is one of the very best and finest writers in the English language today. God, can he write."
—*F. Scott Fitzgerald*

Ambrose Bierce—America's first significant writer of black humor

Born—Miegs County, 1842
Career—One of the most proficient literary craftsmen of the 19th century, his prose—acerbic and terse; decidedly modern in tone. Said one critic: "He is not afraid to call a spade a bloody shovel."
Must read—*"An Occurrence at Owl Creek Bridge"*
To wit—"Edible, adj. Good to eat, and wholesome to digest, as a worm to a toad, a toad to a snake, a snake to a pig, a pig to a man, and a man to a worm."
—*The Devil's Dictionary, 1911*

"For all our professed delight in and capacity for jocosity, we have so far produced but one genuine wit—Ambrose Bierce."
—*H. L. Mencken*

William Riley Burnett—wrote first realistic gangster novel

Born—Springfield, 1899
Career—skyrocketed to fame with first novel, *Little Caesar*, 1929.
Must read—*Little Caesar*, which at the start of the Depression sold 100,000 copies in six months.
To wit—in 1930, his book was made into a hit movie of the same name, starring Edward G. Robinson and starting the enormously popular "tough guy" movies of the 1930s.

Paul Laurence Dunbar—elevated black dialect into serious verse

Born—Dayton, 1872
Career—The son of ex-slaves, he was boosted into a national spotlight when William Dean Howells gave him a critical pat on the back; worked as elevator operator, a sad sign of his times, but influenced next generation of black poets.

Must read—*Majors and Minors*
To wit—his ambition was "to interpret my own people through song and story, and to prove to them that after all we are more human than African."

Hart Crane—"the greatest voice of his generation"

Born—Garrettsville, 1899
Career—a romantic caught in the jazz age, he was the heir to an Ohio candy fortune, although his turbulent personal life was anything but sweet.
Must read—*"The Bridge,"* the epic poem of 1931, which won a Guggenheim Fellowship for Crane, who invokes everyone from Rip Van Winkle to the Wright Brothers as a backdrop to his ultimate symbol of America, the Brooklyn Bridge.
To wit—"iridescently upborne through the bright drench and fabric of our veins."
—*"The Bridge"*

Ulysses S. Grant—in command of the language

Born—Point Pleasant, 1822
Career—the Union's Commander-in-Chief and former U.S. President was broke and dying of cancer when Mark Twain offered him $100,000 for his autobiography; hoping to secure his wife's future, Grant agreed.

Sherwood Anderson was an early victim of the literary cocktail party; he died of peritonitis and complications after swallowing a toothpick with an hors d'oeuvre.

Must read—*Personal Memoirs*, a masterpiece of unadorned style critically acclaimed both as a fine military history and as a watershed of simplicity in American prose.
To wit—"a man of sterling good-sense as well as of the firmest resolution."
—*Matthew Arnold*

Zane Grey—"Father of the Adult Western"
Born—Zanesville, 1872
Career—abandoned a career in dentistry for one in hyperbole, painting stark contrasts of good and evil, cowboy and tenderfoot, villains and heroes that in large part created the Wild West in the popular imagination; his own bountiful imagination produced some 90 books, enough so that even after his death, his publisher printed a new Grey title annually for two decades.

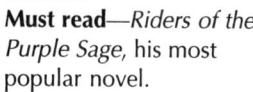

Must read—*Riders of the Purple Sage*, his most popular novel.
To wit—"I can never do anything reasonably. I always overdo everything."

Lafcadio Hearn—grandfather of the "new journalism"
Arrived—Cincinnati, 1870
Career—his detailed, descriptive copy about Cincinnati's back alleys made him a $25-a-week star reporter whose personal and professional fascination with the unconventional eventually landed him in Japan, where he established a world-wide reputation for his writings on Japan.
Must read—"Violent Cremation," *Cincinnati Enquirer*, November 9, 1874, his sensational account of a sensational murder appeared in newspapers nationwide.

To wit—"He prowled about the dark corners of the city, and from gruesome places he dug out charming idyllic stories."
—*Cincinnati Enquirer editor, John Cockerill*

"Literary success of any enduring kind is made by refusing to do what publishers want, by refusing to write what the public wants, by refusing to accept any popular standards, and by refusing to write anything in order."—Hearn

William Dean Howells—"Dean of American Letters"
Born—Martins Ferry, 1837
Career—editor, *Atlantic Monthly*, *Harper's*, *Cosmopolitan*; his prolific pen produced some 30 novels, 11 travel books, innumerable short stories, poems, essays, articles; crony of Henry James, Emerson, Twain, and Hawthorne; son of an itinerant, abolitionist father; child of the passing Ohio frontier; self-educated man who turned down professorships at Yale, Harvard, Johns Hopkins; patriarch of realism in fiction.
Must read—*The Rise of Silas Lapham*, a definitive portrait of the self-made man, 1885; Criticism and Fiction, in which Howells, the philosophical heir of the egalitarian values of "the West," presents his case for realism and its democratic roots.
To wit—"Real feeling is always vulgar."
—*Letters Home*

"Ah! poor Real Life, which I love, can I make others share the delight I find in thy foolish and insipid face?"
—*William Dean Howells,*
Their Wedding Journey

Toni Morrison—major protector of postmodern American realism
Born—Lorain, 1931
Career—richly lyric novels about the struggles of black women splendidly woven around the experiences of her kin and the family stories she heard in her Ohio hometown, "Where I always start."
Must read—*Beloved*, based on true story of Margaret Garner, a runaway slave who kills her child rather than "be taken back to slavery and be murdered by piecemeal."
To wit—". . . anybody white could take your whole self for anything that came to mind. Not just work, kill, or maim you, but dirty you. Dirty you so bad you couldn't like yourself anymore."
—*Beloved, 1987*

William Sydney Porter—created the "O. Henry ending"

Arrived—Ohio Penitentiary, Columbus, 1898

Career—he used a pen name so that his daughter wouldn't find out he was a prisoner in Ohio, but in that confinement, he began writing short stories with an ironic twist at the ending, an innovation in American letters that became his trademark.

Must read—"The Gift of the Magi," a Christmas classic: Della sells her lovely hair to buy Jim a watch fob; Jim sells his watch to buy her haircombs.

To wit—"And here I have lamely related to you the uneventful chronicle of two foolish children in a flat who most unwisely sacrificed for each other the greatest treasures of their house... Of all who give and receive gifts, they are the wisest. Everywhere they are the wisest. They are the magi."

It is said that the "Gift of the Magi" was inspired by Porter's wife, Athol. To escape prosecution for embezzlement charges in Texas, Porter fled to Central America, leaving his wife and young daughter behind. As Christmas, 1896, approached, Mrs. Porter was deathly ill, but she summoned the strength to fashion a lace handkerchief, which she sold for money to buy her absent husband presents. When Porter learned how ill she was, he went back to Texas, where he was arrested and convicted. Ironically, perhaps mercifully, his wife died before his trial, and Porter ended up in the Ohio Penitentiary on April 25, 1898, because federal prisons elsewhere were overcrowded.

Harriet Beecher Stowe—the nation's conscience

Arrived—in Cincinnati, 1832

Career—for years, she cast her Calvinist eye on Cincinnati, where the coming Civil War was already being fought on the streetcorners; thus inspired, she penned *Uncle Tom's Cabin*, the juggernaut that crystallized the nation's sentiments on slavery and made her an international celebrity.

To wit—"God wrote that book. I merely took his dictation."

"I hope Uncle Tom's Cabin will make enough so that I may have a silk dress."

James Thurber—an American original disguised as a humorist

Born—Columbus, 1894

Career—went from a *Columbus Dispatch* beat to the rarefied company of *The New Yorker* in a quantum leap of prose and drawings that brilliantly reflected his melancholy vision of love, marriage, and other absurdities of human relationships.

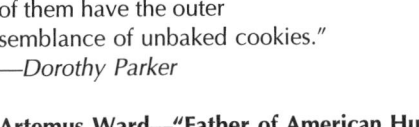

Must read—*My World— and Welcome to It,* and for his immortal clash of fantasy and reality, "The Secret Life of Walter Mitty.".

To wit—"These are strange people that Mr. Thurber has turned loose upon us ... All of them have the outer semblance of unbaked cookies."
—*Dorothy Parker*

Artemus Ward—"Father of American Humor"

Arrived—Cleveland, 1857, age 23

Career—writing tongue-in-cheek commentary sprinkled with "horse laugh spelling" for *The Plain Dealer* gave this former printer a fictitious identity, which he readily adopted as his own persona, setting first Cleveland to laughing and then the entire nation.

Must read—*Artemus Ward: His Book,* an anthology of his most popular sketches.

To Wit—"Be sure and vote at leese once in all elecshuns. Buckle on yer Armer and go to the Poles. See to it yer Naber is there ... This is a privilege we all possess, and it is I of the booties of this grate and free land."
—*"Fourth of July oration"*

James Wright—blue collar lyricist

Born - Martins Ferry, 1927

Career—world-renowned poet whose intense verses ring with gritty images forged in the mill town of his youth

Must read—*Collected Poems,* 1971

To wit—"The only tongue I can write in is my Ohioan."

Pen name

While in the Ohio Penitentiary, William Sydney Porter worked in the prison pharmacy where he read in a reference book the name of French pharmacist Etienne-Ossian Henry. This is said to be from whence O. Henry derived his nom de plume.

Source: American Literary Anecdotes, Robert Hendrickson

ZANE GREY: FATHER OF THE ADULT WESTERN

JUDKINS:
My name is Judkins.
I don't know you,
but I know... I've
heard what you
are... I heard you
killed some men in
the North.

LASSITER: Not
just in the North.

—from the
1996 film, *Riders
of the Purple Sage*

zanegreysws.org/
zgwsmenu.htm

www.

More than you ever
wanted to know
about Mr. Grey:
why you should
read him, and how
to get started;
explication of his
oeuvre, the value
of his first editions,
even his fishing
records. And
assorted links.

Born Pearl Zane Gray in Zanesville, he is said to have written his first story in a cave behind his house, not long afterward receiving an athletic scholarship to the University of Pennsylvania where he pursued baseball and dentistry, forsaking them both to write his first novel, *Betty Zane*, which was about his great-great aunt who saved Fort Henry during the Revolutionary War by carrying and apron full of powder through a hail of bullets. Which somewhat resembles a Zane Grey sentence, some of them being only slightly shorter than the Western migration.

When the novel was rejected, he published it himself, displaying an adventurous spirit that became his trademark. *Riders of the Purple Sage* was first rejected, too, because it was anti-Mormon, but ultimately it sold over four million copies, becoming the most famous popular western ever written.

In it, Grey set the pattern of the experienced westerner and the neophyte easterner. While the critics were seldom kind—Heywood Broun said that the substance of any two Zane Grey books could be written on the back of a postage stamp—there were those who said that Zane Grey shaped the American culture with his mythic creation of the West. It was a West of simple values, with a code that existed outside of the law, which was where the original West existed. And if it was a place that never existed, then it was still a fierce and enthralling notion. In the delineation of this West, *his* West, Zane Grey invented the Western novel.

There is one thing not in doubt: He brought escape and vicarious wish-fulfillment to millions by recreating the values of his boyhood in Zanesville. From 1915 to 1925, he was never off the best-seller list. He wrote some 90 books that sold an estimated 130 million copies, which—his son once pointed out—put him in the same league with The Bible and *McGuffey's Readers*, those other perennial best-sellers. Even though his popularity waned, more than a hundred films were based on his work, two with Grey playing himself.

One commentator observed that Grey's were "not necessarily the best books but the books that people liked the best."

348

Ohio best-sellers

Uncle Tom's Cabin, **Harriet Beecher Stowe**—first American novel to get best-seller status; after 1852 serialization in abolitionist *National Era,* sold 300,000 copies its first year, equal perhaps to six million today; later translated into 20 languages.

Martha Finley—This childrens' author from Chillicothe produced one of the 19th century's most popular caricatures, *Elsie Dinsmore,* a virtuous young girl who burst into "an agony of weeping" whenever a sinful thought entered her head. The series, though, produced a major readership, proving that, yes, virtue *was* its own reward—27 rather priggish books, 25 million readers.

Mildred Wirt Benson—in 1930, she penned *The Secret of the Old Clock,* the first of many books she ghost-wrote for the Nancy Drew series, which sold more than 80 million copies.

John Jakes—Daytonian whose series of Kent family chronicles outsold—more than 35 million copies—all other American Bicentennial fiction; in 1978, *The Bastard* became the first original paperback ever on *The New York Time's* best-seller list, and *The Warriors* had the largest first paperback printing, 3.5 million copies.

The Power of Positive Thinking, **Norman Vincent Peale**—the good doctor from Bowersville—wrote this early self-help book in 1952; it spent an unprecedented 98 weeks as Number One on *The New York Times* best seller list, which was 40 weeks more than the nearest runner-up: 15 million copies sold.

Accounting Principles—best-selling college textbook, published by South-Western Publishing, Cincinnati, 7 million copies sold since 1929.

Helen Hooven Santmyer—she began her ode to a thinly disguised Xenia, *"...And Ladies of the Club",* in the 1920s and finished the 1,344 page tome in 1982, whereupon her small town virtues—including, of course, tenacity, were rewarded with more than two million sales. At 87, she was the oldest woman to ever reach Number One on *The New York Times* best seller list.

General Grant's *Personal Memoirs*—100,000 sets of this two-volume hit were sold before publication, and more than 300,000 after, yielding royalties of some half-million dollars for Grant's survivors.

Sex and Racism, **Calvin C. Hernton**—the Oberlin College sociologist's book has sold more than 200,000 copies since 1966.

McGuffey's Eclectic Readers—Cincinnatian **William McGuffey** delivered his readers in 1836 and in the next hundred years they sold over 130 million copies, becoming the most famous pedagogical tool in America.

Emerson Bennett—Cincinnati's crackerjack of the dime novel produced hundreds of short stories, including *Prairie Flower* and *Leni-Leoti,* the 1849 works that each sold 100,000 copies.

Dictionary of Marks—Pottery and Porcelain, **Ralph and Terry Kovel**—the first book by the antique experts from Shaker Heights has had more than 35 printings since 1953 ("It has less plot than the telephone book, and it's a best-seller year after year," said Ralph).

The father of childrens' horror books, **R.L. Stine** of Bexley, Ohio, launched his **Goosebumps** series for young readers (ages 8-12) in the early 1990s and in three years more than 85 million were in print—plus another 30 million of his **Fear Street** series for teen readers. In 1995, his young fans were mailing him over 2,000 letters a week.

At the end of the century, more than 80 million people were using the college edition of the *New World Dictionary,* created by Clevelander **David Guralnik.** His dictionaries were the first to include colloquial usages and idioms, and when he began work as a lexicographer, he was famous for not even owning a dictionary.

What was it Louis Bromfield wrote? Was James Wright one of the Wright Brothers? How quickly we forget. And to see that you don't, here are 17 tough appraisals of folks who were once among the nation's very best.

James Thurber *the clocks of Columbus*

Columbus-born *James Thurber* began his writing career as a newspaperman for *The Columbus Dispatch*, eventually moving to *The New Yorker*, where he worked with Robert Benchley, E.B. White, Clarence Day and S. J. Perelman in what editor Harold Ross called "the bughouse."

Huge resigned dogs, determined and sometimes frightening women and globular men inhabited his drawings, and Dorothy Parker once said that his people have "the outer semblance of unbaked cookies." As he put it, his humor was about "beaten-down married people. The American woman is my theme, and how she dominates the male, how he tries to go away but always comes back for more."

For Thurber, "The clocks that strike in my dreams are the clocks of Columbus," and he wrote frequently about his Columbus family and neighbors. When Thurber was born in 1894, one of his neighbors, Margery Albright, a "woman's woman," was the midwife, telling the doctor, "He has too much hair on his head for a male child. Ain't it true that they don't grow up to be bright?" The doctor answered, "I believe that holds good only when the hair is thicker at the temples than this infant's. . . . By the way, I wouldn't discuss the matter with the mother." His material always bent back to his origins in Columbus, and he was, as one writer said, "the master of flat-footed fantasy, the fairy godmother in a union suit, and an everyday world that is quickly capable of becoming askew and magical."

Ambrose Bierce *black Bierce*

Ambrose Bierce was born in 1842 in a log cabin on Horse Cave Creek in Meigs County, the youngest of nine children, found himself engaged in a disappointing childhood and left it as soon as he could for the brighter prospects of the Civil War, where he was shot in the head.

It was a formative event, but we are uncertain if it gave Bierce his mordant wit; it is certainly likely it aided his sense of a world overseen by an unsympathetic God. At any rate, Bierce's adventurous spirit carried him westward, where he became one of the most proficient literary craftsmen of the 19th century. His careful prose was decidedly modern in tone, and he is best known for a short story, "An Occurrence at Owl Creek Bridge," and a stabbing collection of definitions, *The Devil's Dictionary* (1911). Its stinging precision led critic George Jean Nathan to call it one of the "powerful legends" of American literature. Another said Bierce was not afraid "to call a spade a bloody shovel."

His acerbic nature and his terse, contemporary style made him the first significant writer of black humor in America. When he was 71, he went to Mexico and was never seen again. Stories circulated about his suicide and/or his survival, but most think he died in the middle of the Mexican Civil War in 1913. Charles Fort, in a book called *Wild Talents*, noted that a man named Ambrose Small disappeared at nearly the same time and suggested that "some demonic force was collecting Ambroses." It is quite likely that Bierce himself, given his own startling and original expressions, would have admired and approved such a thesis.

William Dean Howells *a literary life*

Howells was born in 1837 in Martins Ferry and had little formal schooling as his family moved to Hamilton, Xenia, Dayton, Columbus and points elsewhere, this peripatetic childhood imbuing him forever with the rhythms of Ohio.

He was Ohio's first man of letters to earn a reputation of the first rank, and at the turn of the century he was one of America's three most important novelists. His rise occurred in Boston,

where he was editor of the *Atlantic Monthly* and lifelong friend to such disparate literary folk as Mark Twain and Henry James, and became the dean of American letters. His theory of fiction was "the truthful treatment of fiction," a somewhat radical notion for the ornamental Victorian Age, and his definitions and defense of realism in American fiction were major contributions.

He was the most prolific serious author of his day, his best novels being *The Rise of Silas Lapham* and *A Modern Instance* (1882), which was the first American novel to use divorce as a major theme. Both are still staples in graduate school classes in naturalistic fiction.

Although he lived abroad, and adopted the East as his home, he took with him the values he felt were of the "West," Ohio values, and he carried the traditional writerly ambivalence toward his native state. He could not wait to leave it, yet drew upon its formative richness all his life, and in his later years yearned for its tranquillity from the vantage point of his Boston apartment.

W.R. Burnett *a life of crime*

He was born in Springfield in 1899 and grew up mainly in Dayton and Columbus, those urban fleshpots that somehow managed to send him off on a life of crime. Out of such a formative background, Burnett soon produced *Little Caesar* (1929), which describes the life and death of Rico, who begins his gangster career in Toledo and ends there, gunned down on the streets.

"Rico was a simple man. He loved but three things: himself, his hair and his gun. He took excellent care of all of them." And, thusly, Rico

was the protagonist of what has been called the first realistic gangster novel.

While Burnett's imagination was best engaged by the netherworld of the big cities where men lived by jungle law, as in *High Sierra* and *Asphalt Jungle*, he also recalled the small towns of Ohio that offered, to him, escape from that world. In *Dark Command*, John Seton misses "the free and easy manners of Ohio, where a man could disagree with you without wanting to kill you."

Burnett stayed an expatriate, however, remaining under the law of the jungle and never returning to his more tranquil Midwestern origins.

Earl Derr Biggers *an unjust end*

Born in Warren, Biggers created Charlie Chan, Chinese detective, who in the end repaid him by killing his creator. His first Charlie Chan mystery, *The House Without a Key* (1925) featured the fat, chubby-cheeked Oriental with the dainty step of a woman, who was clearly not the major detective. By the time Biggers had finished his sixth Chan novel, Charlie had moved to his rightful position of chief detective.

Biggers struggled to make enough money to support his wife, children and parents, and after a nervous breakdown in 1919, he concentrated on short stories, selling four of them to film companies. The writing of mysteries was difficult for Biggers. His blood pressure soared while he struggled to complete *Keeper of the Keys*, the last Chan mystery (three of six Chan mysteries have the word "key" in the title). His blood pressure hit 240, and shortly after the completion of that last Chan novel, Biggers, age 48, died of a stroke, outlived by his healthier creation in film and books.

James Wright *an Ohio river of imagination*

Wright shook off the soot of Martins Ferry for world acclaim as a poet, but in some deeper actuality, he never left home, and the only language he ever really knew was Ohio. He even said it himself: "The one tongue I can write in is my Ohioan."

He was born in 1927, the son of working-

class parents who lived in half a dozen different places in Martins Ferry, and he grew up as a local roughneck, the least likely to win a Pulitzer, which he would do. When he went out into the world, his pragmatic steel town—and the Ohio River—dominated his imagination.

His poems, at once stark, clear and profound, are filled with Ohio imagery. It is this imagery that cancels the contradiction of such an event as the annual James Wright Poetry Festival, held each spring in Martins Ferry.

His poems are tough, fierce and intimate, exhibiting a wry, deeply pained empathy with the lives of ordinary people at extraordinary moments. "His true resilience," wrote one critic, "lay in his ability to turn blood into ink."

Paul Laurence Dunbar *black like him*

Born in Dayton the child of former slaves, Paul Laurence Dunbar wanted to be a lawyer but had no money to go to college. He was a friend of the Wright brothers, who printed his short-lived newspaper. Dunbar took a job running a Dayton elevator for $4 a week. He paid for the publishing of *Oak and Ivy* (1893) himself and then sold the books to passengers riding the elevator. His sales were thus both up and down.

His songs and stories in black dialect were an attempt to rescue the language of American blacks from the vaudeville jokes of whites by elevating it into an instrument for serious verse. His poetry was an influence on the next generation of black poets, including Langston Hughes. It was another Ohioan, William Dean Howells, who made Dunbar a national celebrity in 1896 with a laudatory review of *Majors and Minors*. Dunbar's health, however, failed in 1899,

and he died, aged 33, in 1906.

Today Dunbar's poetry is largely ignored by blacks and whites alike perhaps because it rings too vividly with the dialect of slavery days.

Harriet Beecher Stowe *cause célèbre*

Heaven only knows how Harriet Beecher came to write *Uncle Tom's Cabin: or Life Among the Lowly* but literary historians think it was her moving in 1832 to Cincinnati where her father, the redoubtable New England divine Lyman Beecher, took over the strife-torn Lane Seminary. The issue tearing cleric from cleric was abolition, and Cincinnati, at the frontier between slave and free soil, was in the thick of it. The papers were filled with runaway slave notices. Mobs chased an abolitionist editor from town and threw his press into the Ohio. Other mobs turned back slave hunters at gunpoint. The seminary nearly collapsed in the theological crossfire, and once when the mobs were on the street again, she came home to find her brother pouring hot lead into bullet molds. Why, she demanded? "To kill men," he replied.

By 1863, the killing of men was in full cry, and Harriet Beecher Stowe (she had married one of her father's disciples, Calvin Stowe, in 1836) was the most famous woman in America when she called on Lincoln at the White House. "So here's the little woman who started this great war," the Great Emancipator supposedly said, staring down at the 5-foot-tall Mrs. Stowe, whose anti-slavery novel was by then widely considered a *cause célèbre*.

Not many novelists can claim to have started a civil war, but Stowe's *Uncle Tom* hit America like a bomb, tipping Northern sentiment against slavery and convincing Southerners that against such vile propaganda the gun was the only recourse. By then the book itself had sold 300,000 copies in America and probably another million in England, ensuring British neutrality.

Jim Tully *the hard-boiled low life*

Irish-American Jim Tully's first novel was only one paragraph long, but that one paragraph was 100,000 words. Tully had been in prison, worked

in a circus, boxed professionally and wandered as a tramp. Pugnacious, indiscreet and a hard drinker, "a poet pelting you with manure" was how one acquaintance remembered him.

His fiction is hard, almost hard-boiled, abrupt, unsentimental, sometimes scandalous, and *Ladies in the Parlor* (1934) was attacked by censors.

Born in St. Marys in 1888, Jim Tully was put in an orphanage after his mother's death because his father, a "gorilla-built man" who dug ditches for 50 years, blamed the boy. His stories describe the family's hard, deprived life with its anger, pride, sadness, drink and fierce religion. He described his great-grandfather in *Shanty Irish* (1928) as "Five feet high, and nearly half that across the shoulders, his neck was a mass of muscle and according to my grandfather, 'Like steel ropes, be God.'"

Tully eventually worked his way to Hollywood and became a press agent. He described a skirmish with actor John Gilbert: "He was swinging away at me, and it looked to me as if he'd fan himself to death. So I just put him to sleep for his own protection." His vividness was a solid contribution to what one critic called "the development of the hard-boiled novel of low life."

Ulysses S. Grant *his best vocation*

Triumphant in war, nearly ruined in politics and finally bankrupted in business, U.S. Grant redeemed both his honor and his family with his pen. Writing his memoirs was an act of desperation, but by 1885 the former Ohioan, former General of the Armies and former president was desperate. Hung out to dry by unscrupulous business partners, Grant was broke and dying of throat cancer when Mark Twain approached him with a guarantee of $100,000 for an autobiography.

The old campaigner started dictating until the cancer took his voice. He had himself carried onto the porch of his rural New York home where, wrapped in blankets and fortified with painkillers, he slogged his way in pencil from his humble beginnings in the Ohio River hamlet of Point Pleasant, Ohio, straight through the Civil War from his first victory at Fort Donelson to accepting Lee's surrender at Appomattox Court House. He finished three days before his death.

The book was a colossal success, sold door to door by a grand army of Twain's subscription agents who pitched it as a monument that every patriotic Union household had to own and one that every reconciled Confederate household would be proud to display. But it was Grant's prose style that was the real victory. In clear, straightforward style, Grant set down the details of his campaigns in a distinctly American voice that literary critic Edmund Wilson later hailed as the salvation of American prose. Grant blasted away all the classical allusions, the floral diction and bombastic excess that had been the mark of the "educated" stylist in mid-century. Grant gave it to us straight.

Lafcadio Hearn *an eerie career*

Japan is the country that today claims Lafcadio Hearn as its own, but this half-Irish, half-Greek wanderer who became the first modern western interpreter of the Land of the Rising Sun began his eerie literary career in Cincinnati. Hearn had a wretched childhood. Virtually abandoned by his parents after they broke up, he was packed off to an English boarding school, where he was blinded in one eye in a gymnasium accident. After years of harrowing poverty in London, he turned up, stone broke, in Cincinnati in 1870. He lived for a time in an old boiler until a printer took pity on the young man, allowing him to sleep inside on the paper stacks. Hearn began to help out in the shop and then to scratch out little stories.

He soon caught on as a reporter with the *Cincinnati Enquirer* for his specialty was vivid and ghoulish accounts of macabre crimes. He also haunted Cincinnati's still-wild and roaring riverfront, writing about blacks, outcasts and petty

criminals in a way that titillated respectable Cincinnati but stopped short of outright offense. Then he committed an unforgivable sin—he took a mulatto woman as a common-law wife. The *Enquirer* promptly fired the best writer that newspaper would ever employ. Hearn was snapped up by the opposition, but soon after he left on assignment to New Orleans and never came back.

In all, Hearn was nine years in Cincinnati. The place was the making of him as a writer. He went on to national fame as a writer about the West Indies and then international fame as a writer about Japan, a culture he completely adopted as his own. He was especially fascinated by Japanese ghost stories. *Kwaidan*, a collection he called "stories and studies of strange things," is still extremely readable and haunting. Hearn died in Japan, aged 54, in 1904. Cincinnati's loss was the world's gain, and it was in Cincinnati that he became, as writer Tom Wolfe has indicated, the creator of what today is called the New Journalism.

12 Louis Bromfield *an agrarian heritage*

Born in Mansfield in 1896, Bromfield was still a young man when he won the Pulitzer Prize, and his life seemed charmed. He loved to do things with his hands, was a good conversationalist with an appetite for food, drink and people. Humphrey Bogart and Lauren Bacall were married in his Malabar Farm living room. He charmed his friends and an enormously wide reading public—

everyone, it seems, except OSU's large-farm adherents and the literary critics, the former because he didn't use enough chemicals in restoring his 400-acre farm, the latter because he persisted in the devilish notion that a writer's first duty was to entertain.

He won his Pulitzer for *Early Autumn* (1928), but his fame seems to rest more with his books on the natural reclamation of his worn-out Richland County farm, such as *Malabar Farm*. He was, wrote one critic, "an Ohioan determined to discover in his heritage a complete life."

13 O. Henry *an Ohio pen name*

His pen-name is a byword for a certain kind of story—a tale baited with an ironic hook lurking in the last paragraph to leave the unsuspecting reader goggle-eyed. An "O. Henry ending" is the way newspapers describe some bitter tale of charity exploding in the benefactor's face or of best intentions gone sickeningly awry. The story with a twist ending seems so simple that the structure has become an unforgivable cliché in the hands of anyone but the originator and master, William Sydney Porter, who comes into Ohio literary history through a twist nearly as awful as any in one of his stories.

The facts are simple. In 1898, Porter came to Columbus, bound for the Ohio penitentiary to serve out a five-year sentence, because prisons in Texas, where he was convicted (unfairly, say his later defenders) of embezzlement, were overcrowded. He served just over three years before he was released. Logically enough, he never set foot in Columbus again and took steps throughout his later successful literary life to obscure his past.

The confusion has provided O. Henry biographers with several lifetimes of unraveling. But one fact is clear: Porter's true literary career began in the penitentiary. His prison job as a pharmacy clerk gave him time and space to write. The troubles of his fellow inmates gave him material. His own fall from respectability gave him several lifetimes' worth of minimum irony requirements.

Josephine Johnson 14 *a piercing vision*

You won't find the Inland Island on any map, but it's a very real place. Physically, it's 37 acres of run-wild woodland out beyond eastern Cincinnati. Literally, it is a cycle of essays that Josephine Johnson wrote in the painful year of 1968. In that season of discontent, with her blend of sharp-eyed observations of the natural world played against the brutalities of the human world, it perfectly caught the nation's mood. Out of print for years, *Inland Island* was reissued by the Ohio State University Press as part of a rediscovery of Johnson that began in the late 1980s with the republication of her first novel, *Now in November*.

That book started her literary career with a bang in 1934 when it won the Pulitzer Prize. Since then, in a string of novels and short story collections and more recently in razor-keen essays, she brings an almost painfully clear vision to bear on ordinary things. She is by birth a Missourian, but by long residence an Ohioan, probably the best landscape word-painter we have of this "core-land state, Ohio, oceanless, mountainless, tempered by rivers," a homely beauty, but through Josephine Johnson's piercing eyes a beauty nonetheless.

Delia Salter Bacon 15 *an unjust end*

She scrapes into the Buckeye literary canon only by the merest accident of birth. Her father, a Congregational missionary, dragged the family from New England to the Western Reserve to join a short-lived Utopian Christian community at

WINESBURGERS: HOLD THE RELISH

As one journalist put it, "Not every town has the distinction of bearing the same name as a novel that changed the way literature was written, even if it was a case of mistaken identity." Winesburg, Ohio, it turned out, was not *Winesburg, Ohio*, after all. Its author, Sherwood Anderson, was from the little town of Clyde, Ohio, just east of Toledo, where the folks there didn't like what he'd done any better than the folks in Winesburg. But in innocent Winesburg, tourists stopped by the post office and asked about the whereabouts of Anderson's fictional characters. Needless to say, they got answers not literary in the least. At Winesburg's centennial in 1930, the locals chastised Anderson for his disservice and a local minister wrote Anderson and asked for an explanation. Anderson kindly wrote back, explaining he didn't know there was a *real* Winesburg. He asked the minister to convey his greetings to the real Winesburgers. "I trust they are all good, kind, God–fearing people," he said. "No doubt they are." His characters, meanwhile, were drawn from neither Winesburg nor Clyde, Anderson said, but from a Chicago rooming house. After a time, everyone in Ohio breathed easier.

Tallmadge in Summit County, where Delia was born in 1811. Utopia soon failed, and Delia Salter Bacon left her native state and its true literary history as a babe-in-arms. Nonetheless, her subsequent career was so startling that it would be churlish of Ohioans not to at least recall it, for Miss Bacon was the promoter of what writer Richard Altick calls "the biggest mare's-nest in the history of the English-speaking world;" namely that the works of William Shakespeare were not by Shakespeare at all, but by a secret literary confederacy led by Ms. Bacon's distant alleged ancestor, the Elizabethan philosopher Francis Bacon.

The idea, or at least the outlines of it, was not original with her. Literary detectives have tracked down 18th century references to the notion that Shakespeare, who was, according to all available documents a poorly educated provincial actor, might have had help. Yet it was Miss Bacon who fleshed out the conspiracy theory and then sprang it on a disputatious world. She put the notion first in 1852 to Ralph Waldo Emerson, who was appalled but mildly helpful. Miss Bacon was, by this time, a minor literary success and a major figure on the mid-century American lecture circuit. (A story by her had won first prize in an 1831 Philadelphia literary contest over entries by Edgar Allen Poe, a fact, says Altrick, "often recalled, either to illustrate the deplorable condition of taste at that time or to suggest that Miss Bacon was a better writer that she is usually given credit for being.")

Taking Emerson's ambiguous encouragement as a ringing endorsement, she convinced a New York lawyer to fund an expedition to England to track down the missing links. Whatever her powers as a writer, Miss Bacon had the extraordinary ability to drag great men into her service against their better judgment. Once in England, she dragged in the historian Thomas Carlyle, who on first hearing her Bacon theory supposedly "let out a shriek which, on her own authority, could be heard a mile away," according to Altrick. Still Carlyle was charmed by her sincerity if a little doubtful of her sanity and did his best to open important doors. One that opened to its owner's eventual regret was that of Nathaniel Hawthorne, who was then serving as American

consul in Liverpool. Miss Bacon promptly appointed him her unpaid literary agent and showered him with half-crazed letters of explanation and command. It was Hawthorne who finally pushed her 1857 *magnum opus* on the Shakespeare conspiracy into print, complete with a foreword in which he declared that he had not read it. "Nobody will blame him for this," Altrick says, "because it is one of the most unintelligible books ever printed."

By then, Miss Bacon had descended on Stratford-on-Avon, home of the great imposter Shakespeare, with a secret plan to break into his tomb by night and find hidden letters that would prove her theory. She went literally insane with indecision over the planned grave robbery and was shipped home in 1858, dying shortly thereafter. The Shakespeare-Wasn't-Shakespeare industry, however, was well launched and continues to this day.

Sherwood Anderson *Ohio's modernist*

Anderson was born in Camden in 1876, the son of a harness-maker when harness-makers were becoming obsolete. Then his father became a sign-painter at a time when, as Anderson put it, "the day of universal advertising had not yet come." The windbag in *Windy McPerson's Son* (1916), whose main occupation is spinning Civil War tales, is modeled on Anderson's father. His mother died of consumption at 42, and Anderson's two main themes—patricide and thwarted women—suggest what he thought of the both of them.

His *Winesburg, Ohio* (1919) was thought to have been modeled on Anderson's neighbors in Clyde, Ohio, although he swore they all were drawn from fellow-lodgers in a Chicago rooming house. His spare writing style influenced

Hemingway, among others, and he brought a strong, non-sentimental eye to his often-sentimentalized Ohio landscape, as in this observation from "The Egg": "Most philosophers must have been raised on chicken farms. One hopes for so much from a chicken and is so dreadfully disillusioned."

At 36, Anderson left his life as president of a mail-order paint company in Elyria, right in the midst of dictating a letter, commandeered by what turned out to have been, at least metaphorically, an appropriate Literary Transfiguration. Just before he took off, he supposedly said to his stenographer, "My feet are cold and wet. I have been walking too long on the bed of a river."

The painful moment signaled, in the least, that he should change his occupation, which he did, leaving us the immeasurable legacy of his graceful, unaffected prose.

Helen Santmyer *media darling at 88*

Helen Hooven Santmyer, for the last two years of her long and privileged life, was that rarity among Ohio creatures, a genuine East Coast media darling. She deserved it, too, if not for her writing then certainly for her example: a genuine, witty lady who marched to her own drummer and,

even in failing health, left an impeccable picture of independence and grace, before her death in 1986.

The book, of course, was her *magnum opus*, *"...And Ladies of the Club"*, a Tolstoyesque-sized, 1,344-page narrative that, said one critic, 'sent book vendors to the chiropractor and well-thumbed copies to serve as doorstops.' On at least one occasion, Miss Santmyer was amused to learn that her book served to bludgeon a misguided snake that had crawled into the farmhouse kitchen of one of her readers.

Ladies was Miss Santmyer's response to Sinclair Lewis' *Main Street*, that reckless piece of prose that besmirched the small-town life her beloved Xenia taught her to love. *Ladies*, begun in the 1920s, was also the most protracted case of labor that publishing had ever seen: She finished it in 1982.

Not long after, New York picked up her story of 64 years with the ladies of a small-town literary club; the book sold over two million copies, and Miss Santmyer was a celebrity. Which fooled her for not one moment. "Part of the interest," she said, "is because I'm an old lady."

There was another novelty, in addition to age actually having its rewards, and that was the notion of a writer working for years on something merely because she loved it. Miss Santmyer, said reviewer Trudy Krisher, was "the genuine article." She was "a person who knew who she was because she was *from* somewhere, a somewhere that Americans were in danger of losing...."

The somewhere was, of course, Xenia, which had lost Miss Santmyer, although she never lost it.

> "Her success seemed a plot for a silent film: First, an octogenarian spends a few decades of her life thinking about a book, then a decade or so writing it; and finally at the 11th hour, her health failing and her book's prospects slim, both are rescued by heroes in the form of virile publishers and adoring fans—a kind of Shirley Temple special for the <u>Modern Maturity</u> set."
> —Trudy Krisher

The best of Ohio architecture is places that work well, that are attractive by design: squares, riverfronts, cemeteries. The best of it is skilled builders who came early to Ohio from places like New England, England, and Switzerland, and gave frontier communities buildings of a sophistication that's startling today; or, it's towns, like Milan, built in prosperity and then saved by prosperity's passing. The best of it is the work of talented professional Ohio architects whose names are mostly forgotten, or sometimes even of gifted amateurs, also forgotten. And it's the work of many of America's great architects from places like New York and Chicago—or, for that matter, Spring Green, Wisconsin, which is where Frank Lloyd Wright lived when he designed a house for Oberlin's Welzheimer family in 1950. In the aggregate, the best of Ohio architecture is an amazing panorama.

Ohio has good architecture because, in the past, the state was relatively richer and more up-to-date culturally than it is today. Virtually every place in Ohio had money at some time, and some went into buildings. Early settlers came full of optimism for this new place: they laid out towns as if they would be important; they founded colleges; they built well. In the past people were more apt to build things that would last; they were more apt to see a building as an enhancement of their community. The result is an unusually strong architectural legacy.

Even so, preservation has lagged in Ohio. The private and institutional benefactors that, say, Indiana has, have not been evident here. In places where preservation has worked in Ohio, the benefits have been clearly evident. For example, one of the state's most enchanting areas today is Columbus's German Village. It's mostly small brick houses built for 19th-century workers; the houses look like those the immigrants had known in Germany. In the 1960s, German Village was threatened by decline and even demolition; it was rescued bit by bit by individuals, and now is a securely middle-class urban neighborhood.

In the 1990s, the General Assembly spent over $100 million on the two buildings in Capitol Square, including the Ohio Statehouse, which now sparkles. Counties have stopped tearing down their old courthouses, though in some cases, offices and courts have moved to other locations. But perhaps preservation lags here because too many Ohioans fail to recognize how many good older buildings Ohio has.

Granville

preservation
www.directory.com

This is the site for everyone in the U.S. (and Canada) interested in historic homes/ towns and how to help preserve them. Links to many different localized organizations, historic homes real estate listing service, tours, conferences, products, and services, including a listing of 20 historic house museums in Ohio.

by Jane Ware

"How much great stuff there is in Ohio. There's so much and it's so inspired. When Ohio towns were built, people were optimistic from the get-go—'This will be the new Rome!'

—Douglas Graf,
associate professor of
architecture
at Ohio State
University

Chateau LaRoche,
the Loveland castle
built by Harry
Andrews

Ohioans who designed fine buildings here are often little known today, in spite of the quality of their work. For example, one of the state's early builders was Lemuel Porter, who came from Connecticut to the Western Reserve at the age of 42. In 1825 he completed building Tallmadge's First Congregational Church, for which he also did the hand carving. The church is a beautiful building that's still one of the state's best. Lemuel Porter did even more for Ohio architecture when he sired Simeon Porter, who became an architect and practiced in Hudson and Cleveland.

Joseph Yost and Frank Packard were both Ohio natives, born in the mid–19th century. In Columbus during the 1890s, they formed a partnership, Yost & Packard, and built not only there but in towns all over the state, where even now their strong designs stand out in towns from Gallipolis to Piqua and beyond; their signature is on many of the state's best courthouses. A prime example is the wonderful Wood County Courthouse, 1896, in Bowling Green. Another example is the fascinating Toledo & Ohio Central Railroad Station, 1895, in Columbus, an exotic building with a tower and pagoda roof.

As a young child Samuel Hannaford came from England to Cincinnati with his parents; almost 40 years later he designed the Cincinnati Music Hall, 1878, red and black brick in High Victorian Gothic, 372 feet long and 14 stories high. It made his name which, after he and two of his sons formed Hannaford & Sons, endured in Cincinnati architecture until 1964. In 1893 Hannaford & Sons designed the Richardsonian Romanesque Cincinnati City Hall, and 40 years later, the Art Deco *Times-Star* Building.

Sometimes non–professionals came up with remarkable buildings. In Adams County's West Union, a woman named Tet

Woods ran a millinery and dry goods store. When she wanted a fancy premises, she designed it and had it built, with a high-ceilinged first-floor sales room fronted with windows, and an upstairs apartment with a balustraded balcony overlooking the street.

In suburban Cincinnati the dreamer who built Loveland Castle wasn't entirely an amateur because he was a structural engineer—he understood what would stay up. For over 50 years, until his death in 1981, Harry Andrews worked on his fantasy castle on the banks of the Little Miami River. The outside was built mostly of rocks from the river; the inside mostly from concrete blocks cast in quart-sized milk cartons.

Where the money came from gives another angle on buildings and their eras. Of course Ohio had coal; thus today the president of Ohio University lives in a fine Athens house built in 1899 by one mine owner; while all the town offices of Wellston, in Jackson County, are in the showy 1905 house of another. Oil, which built Bowling Green's courthouse, and gas, which built the houses of Findlay, seems to have been even more bounteous. (Many of Findlay's splendid 1880s gas-boom houses are on South Main and Sandusky Streets.)

Doctors and lawyers have done well for a

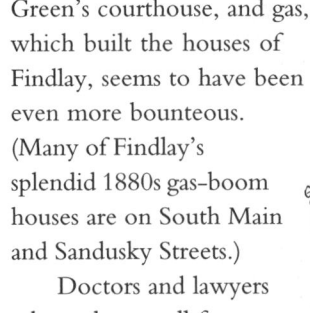

Wood County Courthouse

long time. In Kinsman in 1821 Dr. Peter Allen built himself a fine home and office with excellent carved woodwork; like Allen, his house's builder, Willis Smith, came from New England. The Greek Revival Glendower, 1835, in Lebanon was built by a lawyer; it's a house museum today. Agriculture enabled industrious Northwest Ohio farmers to build high-spired red-brick churches that stand out in the region's flat landscape, while in Springfield it was manufacturing machines to make farming easier that led to a wonderful array of buildings. Two examples are the next-door houses of farm machinery manufacturers John Foos, 1875, and Asa Bushnell, 1888. Bushnell's company was a precursor to International Harvester; his factories were down the hill behind his house.

And in Cleveland there was Samuel Mather. Mather was born rich, but he also founded his own business, shipping iron ore on the Great Lakes. Fortunately, Mather often hired architect Charles Schweinfurth. Because of Mather's money and Schweinfurth's design skills, Cleveland has Trinity Cathedral, 1907, and a few blocks away on Euclid Avenue, Mather's own house, 1910, now Cleveland State's alumni house. The story goes that Mather was so rich that once, when the president of Western Reserve asked him for $500,000, Mather agreed and asked his secretary to write the check. Said the secretary, "Which bank, Mr. Mather?"

For better or worse, how a town was laid out usually affects how it looks forever after. New England settlers would plan a central green or square with important buildings facing into it. An outstanding example is Cleveland's Public Square—no longer a green, but a grand public space dominated by the Terminal Tower complex and mostly enclosed by buildings. Northeast Ohio also has dozens of rural communities where buildings like a church, a town hall, and houses face into a central green; Mesopotamia and Gustavus Center are two examples in Trumbull County. On the other hand settlers from mid-Atlantic states like Virginia or Pennsylvania would lay out a green or square

and put the important building in it. A conspicuous example is in Columbus, founded by Virginians. There, in the middle of the ten-acre Capitol Square, the Statehouse is the heart of downtown.

The custom was also to center an important building at the end of a street. One example is the Meigs County Courthouse in Pomeroy on the Ohio River, where a one-block street lined with two and three-story commercial buildings leads to the splendid courthouse, which has columns and curving staircases on its white façade. Another example is Hughes High School in Cincinnati. Hughes is a large building with a central tower; its brown brick is frosted with dollops of cream-colored Rookwood terra cotta. Approached from the east on Calhoun, Hughes looms at the end of the street: an important destination.

And landscape architects have given Ohio splendid places. Akron's Stan Hywet Hall, 1915, is a prime example. Boston landscape architect Warren Manning picked the house's site, between spectacular vistas to the west and the north. At Cleveland's University Circle, the Museum of Art, 1916, faces across descending terraces and a man-made lagoon, to a formal stairway that rises up to the sidewalk at Euclid Avenue, a quarter mile away. It is a beautiful place, enhanced even more by other University Circle buildings, including Severance Hall, 1931, and Epworth-Euclid United Methodist Church, 1928. Still another example is Spring Grove Cemetery in Cincinnati. Adolph Strauch, a German who learned about gardens as a young man in Europe, ended up in Cincinnati, where in the 1860s he redesigned the cemetery to remove clutter and highlight handsome architectural monuments. Above all, he turned a swamp area into lakes that, amid trees and lawns, with handsome stone mausoleums, became a scene of beauty.

Ohio architecture provides an amazing panorama. What we really have to do now, is hang onto it.

Making lists of bests reflects the subjective choices of a moment, so here are two lists of the best buildings in Ohio cities, one preceding the other and including thumbnail descriptions, and the other afterward and without notations; but in fact all 63 sites are good candidates for a list of bests. Two lists for Ohio towns and rural areas follow; together, they include 69 sites, essentially all bests.

Stan Hywet Hall, 1915, and grounds
A grand Tudor Revival "cottage", Stan Hywet is a shoo-in for Ohio's best house museum; the marvelous setting, vistas, and gardens further exalt the place.

More Akron bests:
Akron Civic Theatre, 1929
First National Tower, 1931
Goodyear Airdock, 1929
Goodyear State Bank (National City Bank),
1918; and *Goodyear Hall*, 1919
John H. Hower House, 1871

Cincinnati Music Hall, 1878
Architect Samuel Hannaford's break-through project, the Cincinnati Music Hall is High Victorian Gothic, red brick, and huge, still used for symphony and opera. Flaws are remodeling outside (bricked-in windows, for example) and inside (as in some dreary corridors).

*Carew Tower and Hilton
Netherland Plaza Hotel, 1930*
An Art Deco tower and adjacent hotel, this is a landmark complex in downtown Cincinnati. Hotel lobby and adjacent Palm Court are great interiors.

*Cincinnati Union Terminal, now Cincinnati
Museum Center, 1933*
Many people call the Art Deco Union Terminal the best building in this city of wonderful architecture; it's spectacular inside and out, and now triumphs again as a museum complex.

Plum Street Temple, 1866
Gothic Revival and Moorish in design, the Plum Street Temple is wonderful inside and out. Here Rabbi Isaac Wise invented Reform Judaism—an American Judaism that would never be relegated to ghettos.

Rosenthal Center for Contemporary Art, 2003
The Center for Contemporary Art audaciously hired Iraqi-born, London-based architect Zaha Hadid to design their new building, and came up with a winner. Glass, concrete and aluminum building is striking but also meshes well with its site.

Spring Grove Cemetery, 1860s
In Spring Grove Cemetery in the 1860s, a German immigrant horticulturist named Adolph Strauch built a beautiful landscape and also revolutionized American cemetery design.

Mariemont, plat and 1920s sections
As a memorial to her late husband, Mary Emery built a town, hiring America's finest town planner and architects who would recreate English villages.

More Cincinnati bests:
Cincinnati City Hall, 1893
Clifton: Probasco House (1865)
 and Scarlet Oaks (1870)
Dixie Terminal, 1921
Glendale, 1851
Hatch House, 1851
*Over-the-Rhine Neighborhood, 19th century
 Schools, such as Hughes* (1910) *and
 Withrow* (1919) *High Schools*

Cleveland

(world's biggest bank lobby), Cleveland Trust, National City on Euclid at Ninth, Federal Reserve Bank, and Society for Savings, now Keybank, on Public Square.

Old Campus for Women, Case Western Reserve University, 1892-1912
This group of old college buildings includes Clark Hall, 1892, designed by Richard Morris Hunt; three by Cleveland architect Charles F. Schweinfurth; and the exquisite Mather Gym by Hubbell & Benes.

Peter B. Lewis Building, Case Western University, 2002
Frank O. Gehry gave the Weatherhead School of Management brick and glass walls under a roof of undulating ribbons of steel. The inside is even better, with details like curving drywall, beautiful wood, rounded classrooms, seven skylights.

University Circle and Cleveland Museum of Art, 1916
With its site, facing over terraces and the Wade Park lagoon, this Neoclassical museum becomes one of Ohio's finest architectural places. Severance Hall, 1931, The Temple, 1924, and Epworth-Euclid United Methodist Church, 1928, are also in the immediate vicinity.

To view one of Ohio's most spectacular new buildings, look for the $61.7 million Gehry-designed Lewis Building at http:// weatherhead.cwru.edu/ lewis/. Photographs, floors plans—the next best thing to being there. There's a live webcam and video at www.galinsky.com/ buildings/peterblewis/ index.htm

Cleveland Arcade, now Hyatt Regency Cleveland, 1890
Roofed in glass, its walls lined by four levels of balconies once fronting shops and now, hotel rooms, the Arcade began as an engineering marvel.

Terminal Tower, 1928
The crux of a mega-building complex, Terminal Tower is a monumental 52-story skyscraper that became a regional symbol.

Downtown Banks, 1890-1924
In a relatively small area, downtown Cleveland has a spectacular array of banks that can be seen inside (except for the closed Cleveland Trust) and out: Huntington National Bank

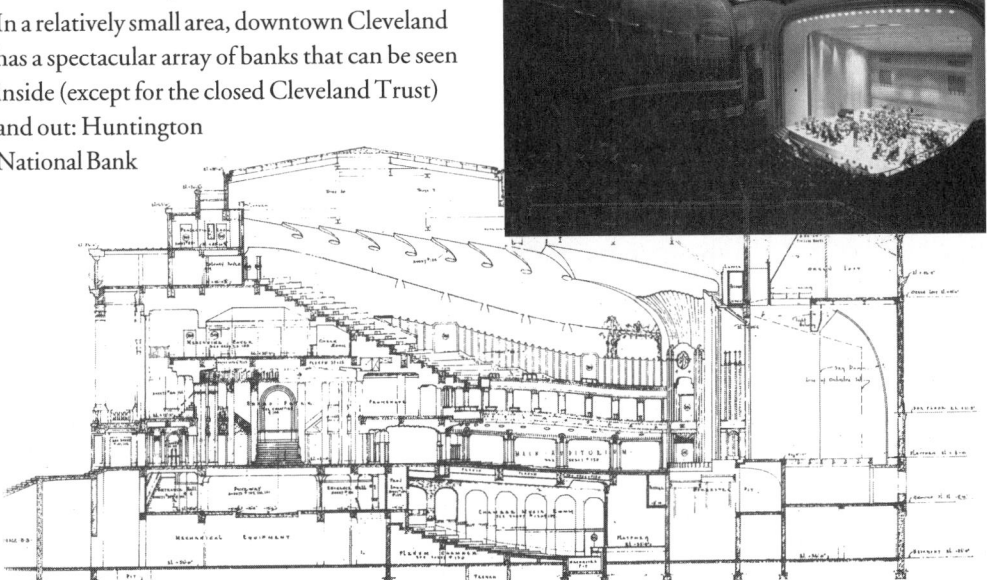

West Side Market, 1912
West Side Market is a working food market; the building, which has a vaulted ceiling and adjacent tower, is Ohio City's principal landmark.

Park Synagogue, 1950
Renowned architect Eric Mendelsohn's only Ohio building, Park Synagogue, in Cleveland Heights, has a marvelous round dome.

More Cleveland bests:
Carnegie West Branch Library, 1910
Old Cuyahoga County Courthouse, 1912
Federal Building, 1910
Rock and Roll Hall of Fame and Museum, 1995
Rockefeller Building, 1905, 1910
St. Ignatius High School, 1888, 1891
St. Theodosius Orthodox Cathedral, 1912
Tavern Club, 1905
Trinity Cathedral, 1901

Columbus

LeVeque Tower, 1927
For decades the 44-story LeVeque Tower, clad in terra-cotta tiles, was Columbus's only skyscraper; it's still the best.

Ohio Statehouse, 1861 and Senate Building, 1901
It took the State of Ohio over 20 years and eight architects to finish this monumental Greek Revival Statehouse. The adjacent Neoclassical Senate Building originally housed the Supreme Court.

Ohio Theatre, 1928
Sedate on the outside, the Ohio Theatre is unbridled lushness inside. In 1969 it was the first of hundreds of American theaters to be saved from demolition by a grass roots movement.

Southern Theatre, 1896
Tucked into the back of a downtown hotel, the Southern Theatre was shuttered for 20 years before the jewel-like auditorium was restored and reopened in 1998.

German Village, 1840-1920
German Village was a monumental rescue: a declining 233-acre neighborhood of mostly modest brick houses was turned into an enchanting urban village.

Wexner Center for the Arts, 1989
Architect Peter Eisenman gave Ohio State University a modern gallery and theater complex, with white scaffolding and brick towers outside, and a great hall inside.

More Columbus bests:
Ohio Departments Building,
        now Supreme Court, 1933
Ohio State University Oval,
        including Orton Hall, 1893
Sessions Village, 1927-1931
Toledo & Ohio Central Railroad Station, 1895
Wyandotte Building, 1898

Dayton

Old Montgomery County Courthouse, 1850
This Greek Revival courthouse is spectacular and
original both inside and out.

More Dayton bests:
Dayton Arcade, 1904
Dayton Art Institute, 1930
Forest Avenue Presbyterian Church, 1902

More Toledo bests:
National City Bank Building, 1930
Oliver House, 1859
Pythian Castle, 1890
Toledo-Lucas County Public Library, 1940

YOUNGSTOWN
Mill Creek Park, 1890s
Mill Creek twists through wooded ravines with
paths alongside, all as planned by young
associates of Frederick Law Olmsted.

More Youngstown bests:
Federal Plaza and Central Tower (1929)
Isaly Dairy, 1941
Wick Log House, 1886
Youngstown Historical Center of Industry
and Labor, 1989

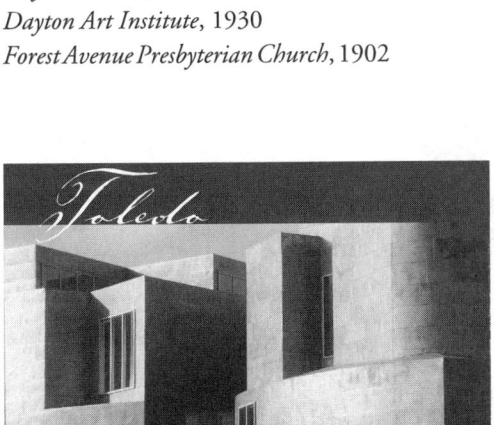

Toledo

Toledo Museum of Art, 1912, 1926, 1933
and University of Toledo Center for the Visual
Arts, 1992
This superb Neoclassical marble museum fronts
its lawn with 28 columns and, at its east end,
Frank O. Gehry's sculptural art school.

Old West End Houses, c. 1885-1910,
and Rosary Cathedral, 1940
Perhaps Rosary Cathedral's first miracle was
saving the adjacent Old West End neighborhood
of large and wonderful houses: a parade of the
work of Toledo's talented architects.

Central Ohio

Gambier: Kenyon College Campus, 1829-1910
The old south campus, with its lawn, Middle
Path, and Gothic Revival buildings, is one of
Ohio's most beautiful places.

Lancaster: Square 13
Square 13, a block in downtown Lancaster, has
an amazing array of fine houses dating from the
1830s.

terminal velocity

"It's a building often described as Cincinnati's best: the Art Deco train station that gave seven railroads one local terminal. Set on a flood plain, it was an engineering feat first, its site raised as much as 58 feet with 5.5 million cubic yards of fill. Then it was an artistic triumph."

—Jane Ware

Cincinnati's train station, Union Terminal, was the last of the great municipal train stations, built during the Depression for $41 million, and financed privately by the sale of stocks to the seven major railroads that had been using five different Cincinnati stations. When it opened in 1933, it was called the most beautiful railroad station in America.

The architects commissioned a German-American artist, Winold Reiss, to design the rotunda ceiling and create a series of massive murals depicting Cincinnati working life. His two 105-foot long panoramic murals in the rotunda—it contained 18,000 square feet—were among the largest artworks in the country.

The architecture was spectacular as well: a 120-foot high semicircle of limestone-and-glass front. Eight gigantic arched trusses, the largest of which weighed 380 tons, supported the half-dome, which was said to be the biggest such dome in the world, and tall enough to accommodate a ten-story building inside it. The soaring dome and its modern Art Deco architecture—one of the splendid American examples of the movement—caused local wags to say the station looked like a gigantic table radio made of concrete.

The structure contained wonderful details: contrasting paths in the terrazzo floors showed people where a gate was, or a ticket line, and it was here that baggage carousels were first used, later an airport commonplace.

It was astoundingly efficient—accommodating 17,000 people and 216 trains a day. During World War II, Cincinnati was a major north-south transfer point for troops and on some days as many as 20,000 passengers flooded through the station. Unfortunately, the figures were manipulated by the war. The truth was that train transportation had peaked before the first train pulled out of Union Terminal. The automobile had already rendered the magnificent station superfluous.

The last train left in 1972, and the station floundered through a series of well-meaning but futile exercises in usage, including a shopping mall—leased for $1 a year— that featured discount clothing sold in the great rotunda.

But in 1986, a serendipitous partnership put the Cincinnati Historical Society and the Museum of Natural History in the station, augmented by the passage of a county tax levy. The directors of the respective institutions had been sold in the Union Terminal basement: the station had been built on 5.5 million cubic yards of fill dirt, and underneath was 150,000 square feet of space with 24-foot ceilings—a vast arena large enough for two large museums.

A renovated Union Terminal would thus provide museum space 60 percent cheaper than new construction. In the bargain, one of America's great pieces of architecture would be saved. Said the history museum's director, DeVere Burt, "This Terminal is still devoted to transportation. In 1933, it was transportation from one geographic point to another. It has been rededicated to transportation to any point in time."

Oddly, the place has also become a real train station again. In 1992, Amtrak brought in its Washington-to-Chicago service to a remodeled rear platform. DeVere Burt had thus been proved doubly right. ↩

London: Madison County Courthouse, 1892
Madison County has a well kept courthouse with a grand hall, double staircase, and marvelous courtroom.

Marion: Harding Memorial, 1927
President Warren Harding's Memorial has two concentric white marble colonnades enclosing a green where his sarcophagus rests under an open sky, as he wished.

Newark: Licking County Courthouse, 1878
Licking County has one of Ohio's best courthouses, set well in a square, kept well, and favored with a wonderful courtroom that's a strong contender for Ohio's best.

Newark: Home Building Association Bank, now Tiffany's Ice Cream Parlour, 1915
Louis Sullivan's bank in Newark, gray stone like the courthouse across the street, has been improving gradually on the outside, while still serving ice cream in the altered interior.

More Central Ohio bests:
Circleville: Mount Oval, 1832
Delaware: Ohio Wesleyan's University (1893) and Elliott (1833) Halls
Granville: Avery Downer House, 1842 (*at right*)
Granville: Swasey Observatory, 1909
Mount Vernon: Central square; 19th-century houses, as on East High and East Gambier Streets
Newark: George Penney (1851) and Upham Wright (1851) Houses

Hudson: Western Reserve Academy Chapel, 1836, and Brick Row, 1830-1913
The handsome chapel, red brick with a white tower, anchors a row of fine old brick buildings.

Massillon: Five Oaks, Massillon Woman's Club, 1894
Cleveland architect Charles F. Schweinfurth gave a Massillon banker a luxurious house that the Woman's Club tends well today.

Mineral Ridge: Mahoning Valley Sanitary District, Purification and Pumping Works, 1932
Youngstown architect Charles F. Owsley designed a group of three spectacular Art Deco buildings facing into a green.

Niles: McKinley Birthplace Memorial, 1917
McKim, Mead & White designed a striking and unique memorial, with a central colonnaded courtyard and flanking library and auditorium buildings.

Hudson has true New England charm, and Hudsonites are uncompromised about preserving it, so passionate about the historic core of "the village" that when Hudson gained city status, they officially named it "The City of the Village of Hudson." Displayed on all the historic homes, you will see the distinctive double-H plaques of the Hudson Heritage Association, which works to preserve all the fine architecture (and keep newcomers such as McDonald's consistent with it). One story tells how a couple had to get approval simply to open the shutter on an attic window. And most residents wouldn't have it any other way.

St. Charles Seminary is the Catholic's Emerald City that rose out of an early black settlement's land of Oz. Augustus Wattles, a white Quaker, purchased the land around Carthagena in 1835 for newly freed slaves. Four hundred slaves made the settlement highly successful for 22 years until early Mercer county malcontents drove them out. The Seminary is either a righteous monument to the original black settlers or a powerful reminder of the hardiness of the Catholic pioneers who, when so many of them died in the cholera plague of 1849 and went to their graves by wheelbarrow, wagon, or stretcher, kept their faith in God and multiplied.

Oberlin: Tappan Square and Allen Memorial Art Museum with Venturi addition
Four Oberlin College buildings by architect Cass Gilbert face into Tappan Square. One is the Allen Memorial Art Museum, which has an addition by Robert Venturi. Another is Wallace Harrison's Hall Auditorium.

Kinsman: Dr. Peter Allen House, 1821
Mansfield: Oak Hill, 1847
Mantua: Hine House, 1895
North Bloomfield: Brownwood, 1819
Painesville: Dr. John Mathews House, 1829
Warren: Perkins House, now City Hall, 1871
West Andover: John Henderson House, 1850

Tallmadge: First Congregational Church, 1825
Designed and built by Lemuel Porter, who came from Connecticut, First Congregational Church is one of Ohio's best buildings.

Ohio Western Reserve, pre-1850
In some rural areas, Northeast Ohio's Western Reserve still has the stamp of New England. For example, see Kinsman, Gustavus Center, North Bloomfield, Hudson.

More Northeast Ohio bests:
Atwater: United Church of Christ, 1841
Barberton: O.C. Barber Farm Barns, 1909-1912

Carthagena: St. Charles Seminary, St. Aloysius and the Cross-Tipped Churches, 1878-1922
This Mercer County hamlet is the hub of Northwest Ohio's ensemble of cross-tipped Catholic churches, most in red brick. Altogether there are about 30 churches and other sites in a four-county area.

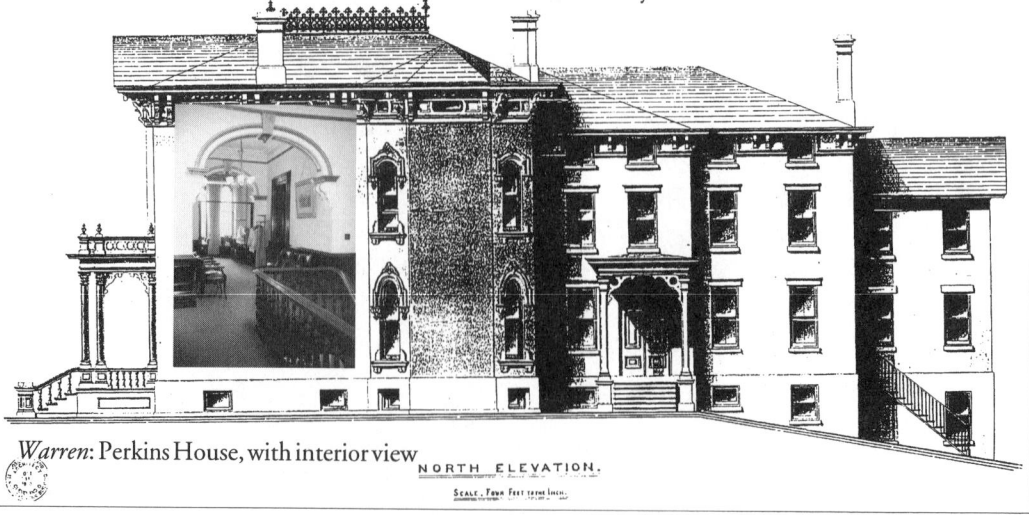

Warren: Perkins House, with interior view

NORTH ELEVATION.
SCALE, FOUR FEET TO THE INCH.

Bowling Green: Wood County Courthouse, 1896
An oil boom permitted Wood County this wonderful courthouse. Richardsonian Romanesque, adorned with fine stone carvings, it has the state's tallest courthouse tower, 185 feet.

Lima: Whemco Ohio Foundry Division, Roll Shop, 1939
Detroit architect Albert Kahn was known for sleek modern factories like this one.

Milan: Kelley Block, 1870
This Italianate commercial block, complete with its original iron columns dividing the large ground-floor shop windows, has a great site on Milan's square.

Napoleon: First Presbyterian Church, 1903, and others
This church is one of an ensemble of four Presbyterian churches in four towns and by three architects, all in similar Arts and Craft style, and all in a fabulous red Ohio sandstone. The others are Forest Avenue, Dayton, 1902; Barnesville, 1903; and Upper Sandusky, 1900.

New Hampshire: Manchester Barn, 1908
Eighty feet high and 100 feet in diameter, this spectacular round barn is Ohio's most celebrated.

Ottawa: Putnam County Courthouse, 1913
This farm county has an especially elegant stone Renaissance Courthouse.

More Northwest Ohio bests:
Findlay: Houses, South Main and Sandusky Streets
Glandorf: St. John the Baptist Church, 1878
Lima: Kewpee Restaurant, 1939
Marblehead: Lighthouse, 1821
Norwalk: Norwalk Female Seminary, 1848
Sandusky: Oran Follett House, 1837
Van Wert: Van Wert County Courthouse, 1876
Venedocia: Salem Presbyterian Church, 1898
Waterville: Columbian House, 1828, 1837

Southwest Ohio

Sidney: Peoples Federal Savings & Loan, 1917
Louis Sullivan's red-brick bank on Sidney's Courthouse Square is the best maintained of the eight small-town banks he designed.

Springfield: Warder Public Library, 1890
This former library is in a wonderful Richardsonian Romanesque.

Springfield: Westcott House, 1909
Frank Lloyd Wright's only Prairie style house in Ohio, the Westcott House is being restored prior to opening for the public.

Troy: Miami County Courthouse, 1888
Miami County has a showcase stone courthouse. In the mid 1990s the roof's nine superstructures, including the central dome, underwent the largest cast-iron restoration ever in the United States.

Other Southwest Ohio bests:
Greenville: Library, 1903, and Memorial Hall, 1910
Hamilton: Memorial Building, 1902
Hamilton: Lane Hooven House, 1863
Loveland: Loveland Castle, 1929-1981
Sidney: Monumental Building, 1876
Springfield: Bushnell Mausoleum, c. 1904
Springfield: Heritage Center of Clark County, 1890

The Piatt castles were not opened to public tours until about 1912. The story goes that curious people doing business at the estate repeatedly asked Abram Piatt's son, William, if they could go inside and see Mac-A-Cheek. Since that man's castle really was his home, William repeatedly turned them down. Eventually, the requests got so bothersome that William decided he could discourage his friends and neighbors by asking them for money when they wanted to see the castle. Much to his surprise, they paid willingly, and the castle tour business was born.

Springfield: John Foos (1875) and Asa Bushnell (1888) Houses
Urbana: 19th century Houses of Scioto Street
West Liberty: Piatt Castles, Mac-a-Cheek, 1871, and Mac-o-Chee, 1881
Xenia: Dodds Monuments, 1903

Athens: The Ridges, 1874-1920s
This is Ohio's only surviving 19th-century hospital complex, now being redeveloped by Ohio University. Thus today the central building houses the university art museum.

Chillicothe: Ross County Courthouse, 1858
Ross County has an elegant and exotic courthouse, complete with tower, one-story wings, and an excellent courtroom inside.

Chillicothe: Red-Brick Blocks of Paint Street, 1875-1896
Chillicothe has a distinctive group of large late 19th-century red-brick commercial blocks.

McConnelsville: Opera House, 1892
McConnelsville's Opera House, with its fine auditorium and its good site on the square, represents a charming, preservation-minded town.

New Lexington: Perry County Courthouse, 1886
This landmark courthouse, in brown sandstone with light-colored trim, is one of Ohio's best.

More Southeast Ohio bests:
Athens: Ohio University's Cutler, Wilson, and McGuffey Halls, 1818-1839
Athens: Galbreath Chapel, 1958
Chillicothe: Adena, 1807
Marietta: Plat, 1788, and 19th century houses on Fifth Street
Marietta: Colonel Joseph Barker House, 1811
Somerset: Old Perry County Courthouse, now Village Offices, 1828

COURT HOUSE, CHILLICOTHE, OHIO.

Places that matter

Ohio may be more unique than you would *ever* have thought.
Douglas Graf can tell you why.

Six-foot-three, Douglas Graf folds himself into his road-wise Civic and sets out to find the good stuff, architecturally speaking. He expects to find it in places others overlook—places, even, like Ohio.

He knows that Ohio has architectural masterpieces, and he names some. Union Terminal in Cincinnati. The Netherland Plaza Hotel ("spectacular"), also in Cincinnati. The Toledo Art Museum. Terminal Tower in Cleveland.

And he knows Ohio has wonderful places, like University Circle in Cleveland or Mill Creek Park in Youngstown or Spring Grove Cemetery ("second only to Boston in quality") and Eden Park in Cincinnati. And it has buildings and ensembles that are unique, like the Barberton barns, the many college campuses, Cincinnati's Dixie Terminal, the Western Reserve's New England villages.

Graf knows all this partly because of his profession—he's an associate professor of architecture at Ohio State—and partly because he travels. At every pause in the academic calendar, his Civic is out there; it's taken him all over Ohio and across the country. Beyond the United States, he's seen architecture all over Europe. He knows what's

been written. And he's observed that his students are among those who don't realize that Ohio has exceptional architecture, that Ohio was once on the cutting-edge. They discount this place, architecturally. And they are not alone.

Although Doug Graf grew up mostly in Washington, D.C., and studied at Princeton (architecture) and Harvard (a master's degree), he is an Ohio native. His passion for places began in Seven Mile, Ohio, between Middletown and Hamilton. Seven Mile was the right size for someone who was six. "It was just big enough to have some public space, a monument, and a flag pole," Graf says. It also had two stores, a bank, a barber shop, a consolidated school, a cement block plant, and a train he could watch passing through every day. After first grade his family moved away. Thirty years after he'd left Ohio, in 1984, he came back to teach at Ohio State.

He has some singular aptitudes. One is, that even on cloudy days, he always knows where north is, which means, he always has a good sense of where he is. So, when he walks into a house for the first time, he can comment on a window's having north light. He is voracious for new places, but then his sense of direction takes the kick out of it. "The deliciousness of a new place is lost so quickly," he says. "You get the layout and have to move on to the next one." Another of his aptitudes is, that when he looks at a good building, he finds a narrative. "There's a dialogue

Jane Ware is the indefatigable and well-traveled Columbus author of Building Ohio, companion handbooks to Ohio's urban and rural architecture. This essay is an excerpt from her handbooks.

With buildings
by Peter Eisenman
in Columbus and
Cincinnati, and
by Frank Gehry in
Toledo, Cincinnati,
and Cleveland, the
state of Ohio is
beginning to seem
as hospitable
to cutting-edge
architecture as the
Netherlands.

—*The New Yorker,*
June 2, 2003

between pieces," he says. "The design starts to discuss itself. It starts moving and changing. In good architecture, I should be able to make a long story happen."

The uniqueness of Ohio architecture, he says, is that Ohio is not just like everywhere else architecturally, for three factors have given it a unique stock of good buildings.

First, the state was located so that it was settled at the right time, when the nation was new, and moving west of the Alleghenies was not yet a commonplace. People came to Ohio with tremendous confidence in the future and in this new place. "Each town had the potential of being the new Athens," Graf said. Each town had to prepare for greatness with public space and public building (the green and the courthouse), with institutions (college, seminary, opera house), with quality structures. That sense of optimism diminished as settlement moved west; the farther west you go, the less interesting the towns are; and private colleges become rarer and rarer. "By the time you get to the West Coast," Graf said, "the optimism was completely dead. In San Francisco and Seattle there's almost no public space. They're just plats, with very little design."

Second, Ohio had industrialization that made it rich; at one time or another, every county had money. Agriculture and industry were strong and widely dispersed, an unusual pattern; in other places, wealth was more concentrated. As late as 1950, Ohio was the only state with so many as six cities with populations of more than a quarter million. Moreover, these large cities and many smaller ones stayed prosperous with industrial niches in, say, glass, cash registers, tires. Communities competed with one another.

Colleges were—and are—everywhere. "When you get to a small city in Indiana, you don't expect to find a college," says Graf. "But in Ohio, every town has a college, many of them fairly good. So you have money in a cultured venue that values the town. Then buildings will matter, will be thoughtful, will be a natural embellishment of the place."

Finally, Ohio has many examples of innovative hybridization, which depended on a general interest in what was going on in the rest of the world. The hybridization was reinterpreting styles or, say, combining elements of both New England and Virginia town layouts. The latter had central greens containing an important building, while New England towns had a central green with public buildings facing into it and a commercial street off to the side. Worthington, for example, has a side commercial street combined with greens reminiscent of Virginia.

Gambier has a wonderful, completely original layout—a hybridized concoction. This village, which is mostly the Kenyon College campus, has a mile-long Middle Path that links two pavilions, Kenyon Hall at one end and Bexley Hall at the other. The town is midway between, where two parallel two-way streets flank a green.

Or, says Graf, take the towns of Lancaster, Granville, Newark, and Mount Vernon, four central Ohio towns that are within an hour of each other. Three resemble other places. Thus Graf sees Lancaster as a Virginia town and Granville as a New England village. Newark has the broad streets and emphatic grid more typical west of Ohio—Newark could be Iowa. As for Mount Vernon, Graf calls it "a perfect Ohio town, which means it's actually quite unusual." Its central green is a neutral hub between commercial and governmental buildings. "These towns," says Graf, "are all very close but completely different. That wouldn't happen other places without incredible time differences."

Ohio's hybridization can be seen in building design too, Graf says, and he cites the Columbus architects J.W. Yost and Frank L. Packard, who practiced together in the 1890s. Yost's Orton Hall on the Ohio State campus is a very good Richardsonian Romanesque building, but, says Graf, "you'd never confuse it with H.H. Richardson's work. Yost didn't have the fine New England stone Richardson had, so he couldn't reproduce the style exactly. But he turned that into an opportunity. He transformed it into something wonderful."

When you add together optimism, money in cultured venues, and hybridization, Graf says, "You see that for a long time a lot of good architecture was being produced in Ohio." From the 1820s through the 1920s, Ohio was almost always part of what was happening nationally in architecture. Ohio buildings appeared in professional journals; good architects came here from other places; talented natives stayed.

But with the Depression all that came to a halt. The three major tower complexes that were being finished about 1930—Carew in Cincinnati, Terminal in Cleveland, LeVeque in Columbus—represented Ohio's last "big display of embellishment of the city for 50 years," Graf says. "Now, good things aren't being built here. We're getting deteriorating downtowns, unpleasant suburbs, and a disappearing rural landscape. It's funny when you think of it. There's been this cataclysmic decline from cutting edge to dreg and it's provoked no public scrutiny in the state. It's as though every organization and everybody here has been lobotomized."

Doug Graf is not about to coddle us.

The villages established in the 19th century are similar now: two dozen houses, a hardware store, maybe a small branch bank and a library, all huddled against an imposing Catholic church of Gothic or Romanesque design with a towering steeple, some of them over a hundred feet high and visible for miles across the fields. In some places, a half-dozen of them can be seen at once. There are dozens of them, strung magnificently across the western Ohio flatness, something like an ecclesiastical version of the modern landscape's utility tower, transmitting the ethereal.

With the Maria Stein Convent a stone's throw across the county line in Mercer County, this was the heart of Father Francis de Sales Brunner's empire. When the Cincinnati Diocese, the third one in America, had no priests to send to the new territory, Brunner made what amounted to a deal with the Bishop: *Give me complete authority, and I'll supply succor to the wilderness.*

"He built ten convents in ten years, on large holdings," says Mary Ann Olding, the native authority largely responsible for Brunner's handiwork being placed on the National Register of Historic Places. "He had no means of support but he would say, 'We are building a *convent*,' and the money would come in. He was the epitome of the reform movement of the mid-century and his Society of the Most Precious Blood built 42 parishes within a 22-mile radius of Maria Stein."

What Brunner actually did was colonize a large chunk of the western part of Ohio.

He was a proselytizing Catholic evangelical who spoke four languages and brought his mother's skull to Maria Stein on a silver chalice—today in the Maria Stein relic chapel. He was driven by his view of the decline of religious energy, and he would restore it. "If he were alive today," says Ms. Olding, "he would be a television evangelist."

Ms. Olding's nomination included 29 churches, 13 schools, 23 rectories, three convents, and a seminary. It is an extraordinary aggregation, the most concentrated settlement of German Catholics in America, 40 miles across, spilling into four Ohio counties and one in Indiana. Here, the old farmhouses, handsome and well-kept, mirror the architecture of the early convents and chapels.

By the time of Brunner's death in 1859, there were churches in all his parishes, but the ones there now are third-generation churches, marked by the architect's cross and gold ball. The architect and major builder was a remarkable Swiss-trained carpenter named Anton DeCurtins, who, along with his artisan offspring, built a third of the churches, as well as most of the pews, pipe organs, and frescoes.

The splendid 1920s St. Charles seminary building at Carthagena is no longer a

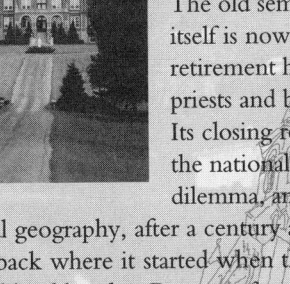

seminary; it closed in 1969. Several other of Ms. Olding's buildings have also been lost. The old seminary itself is now a retirement home for priests and brothers. Its closing reflects the national dilemma, and thus the local geography, after a century and a half, is back where it started when the formidable old zealot, Brunner, found a way to populate it.—*John Baskin*
(For a tour of the area, see:
www.grandlake.net/lctc)

Most of the parishes have the unmistakeable neatness that is characteristic of the Germans. Farm implements do not sit idly in the farmyards and weeds are cut. If things are not just so, there is a saying: "Infiltrated by the Yankees." The Yankees, Ms. Olding thinks, were the militia. They didn't have the farming skills of the arriving Germans, and they were afraid of the marshland. The Germans think the Yankees are a more relaxed people, not particular enough.

Ohio's built landscape

The American Society of Civil Engineers says these Ohio structures, machines, inventions, and events are outstanding historical engineering achievements. We could have told them *that*.

Civil Engineering

First Concrete Pavement
Bellefountaine, Ohio

The first engineering use of portland cement for street pavement was used in Bellefountaine in 1893. It was the precursor of thousands of miles of roads in the United States.

Cleveland Hopkins Airport
Cleveland, Ohio

Completed in 1925 it was the first major municipal airport to develop an integrated system of paved and floodlighted runways, and a terminal complex consisting of both operational buildings and hangers.

Goodyear Airdock
Akron, Ohio

When completed in 1929 (see above) this building was the largest in the world in terms of uninterrupted space — 55,000,000 cubic feet.

Ingalls Building
Cincinnati, Ohio

Built in 1902-1903 it was the first reinforced concrete skyscraper in the world. At 16 stories and 210 feet, it demonstrated for the first time the safety and economy of reinforced concrete for high rise construction.

John A. Roebling Bridge
Cincinnati, Ohio

Completed in 1866 by John A. Roebling this suspension bridge was the greatest structure of its kind in the world. With a span of 1,057 feet it became the proto-

type for his greatest achievement—the Brooklyn Bridge. *(See also page 586.)*

*Miami Conservancy District
Dayton, Ohio*

Following the 1913 flood Dayton developed the first regionally coordinated flood control system in the United States. Completed in 1922 it employs retention reservoirs for controlled release of flood waters. Five dams, levee and channel improvements, the removal of one village, and the relocation of roads, wire lines, water and gas lines.

National Road

The first use of federal funds to build a national highway. Surveyed by Jonathan Knight and Josiah Thompson it was built to the highest standards of road design and construction at the time.

Ohio Canal System

From 1825 to 1848, Ohio constructed a 1,015 mile canal system that included both locks and slack-water navigation. One of the greatest engineering feats of the early 19th century, it included the largest man-made lake (St. Mary's) in the world.

*Point of Beginnings
Liverpool, Ohio*

Following the Ordinance of 1785 Congress directed a team of surveyors to the Northwest Territory. Directed by Thomas Hutchins and working under difficult conditions with primitive instruments and techniques, they established the "seven ranges" of Ohio. It set the basis for similar processes to measure and disperse public lands in 30 other states.

Mechanical Engineering

The American Society of Mechanical Engineers (www.asme.org/history) recognizes existing artifacts of systems representing a significant mechanical engineering technology and are generally the first, oldest, last surviving examples, or they are

machines with some unusual distinction. Following are the designated landmarks in Ohio or developed in Ohio:

*ALCOA 500,000-ton
Hydraulic Forging Press
Cleveland, Ohio
United States Air Force Plant 47*

One of the world's largest fabrication tools it was built by the Aluminum Company of America for the government. Completed in 1955 it stands 87 feet high (36 of it below ground) and weighs 8,000 tons. A press of this size was built by the government to supply defense contractors with products for which there was no commercial market.

*Buckeye Steam Traction Ditcher
Findlay, Ohio
Hancock Historical Museum*

The earliest surviving example of the first successful traction ditching machine for laying agricultural drainage tiles.

*Cooper Steam Traction Engine Collection
Mount Vernon, Ohio
Knox County Historical Society*

The Engines built by Cooper & Co. of Mount Vernon are among the oldest surviving agricultural steam engines. They show the evolution from the portable, skid-mounted engine (ca. 1860), to the horse-drawn engine (1875), through the self-propelled, but horse-guided engine (1875), and finally to the self-propelled, self-steered traction engine (1883). Such engines powered the conversion to mechanized farming. Cooper built over 5,000 engines between 1853 and 1890, and other companies built thousands more based on the pioneering Cooper designs.

*First Hot Isostatic Processing Vessels
Columbus, Ohio
Battelle Memorial Institute*

An early fabrication vessel using gas pressure and temperature to produce advanced alloy and ceramic products.

Crawler Transporters
Kennedy Space Center

The two Crawler Transporters of the

The essential law of performance and diminishing returns—Murphy's Law—was named after a spit-and-polish young engineer at Dayton's Wright Field in the late 1940s. Traveling to Edwards Air Force Base for a rocket-sled test, Capt. Edward Murphy castigated a technician after a malfunction and said, "If there's a way to do it wrong, he will!" It became the axiom, "If it can happen, it will," then segued into its current expression: "Anything that can go wrong, will go wrong."

375

Kennedy Space Center's Launch Complex 39 were built by the Marion Power Shovel Company of Marion, Ohio. They are the largest ground vehicles ever built. Each six-million-pound transporter can carry a 12 million-pound Saturn V rocket and mobile launcher combination several miles to the launch pads.

So versatile are the transporters that, with small modifications, they are used to carry space shuttle vehicles.

Gravimetric Coal Feeder
Cleveland
Stock Equipment Company

The earliest known coal feeder, it represents innovations that influenced nearly all industries using coal-fired boiler.

Hulett Iron-Ore Unloaders
Cleveland, Ohio

The "Hulett," a highly efficient materials-handling machine unique to the Great Lakes, was invented by Clevelander George H. Hulett. The first, steam powered and with a 10-ton-capacity grab bucket, went into service at Conneaut, Ohio, in 1899. It could unload an ore boat at the rate of 275 tons an hour.

Like later Huletts, these were electrically powered. The various motions of the 17-ton bucket were controlled by an operator riding in a small cab in the vertical leg just above the bucket. Each machine could unload 1,000 tons an hour.

The Hulett's clear superiority over existing mechanical unloaders revolutionized ore handling and led to its rapid adoption throughout the lower-lake ore ports. Through 1960, more than 75 were built by Cleveland's Wellman-Seaver-Morgan company and its predecessor and successor firms. With the advent of self-unloading ore boats, most have been dismantled.

Icing Research Tunnel
Cleveland
NASA Research Center

Built during World War II it is designed to study and solve the icing problems that plagued aviation. The tunnel is essentially a refrigerated wind tunnel, the world's oldest and largest. Its test section is six feet high and nine feet wide and the airspeed can reach 300 miles per hour. It has spray nozzles to simulate natural icing conditions.

Jeep Model MB
Toledo, Ohio
Jeep House

Developed for the army by Toledo's Willys-Overland Company it brought together a series of engineering concepts that influence every four-wheel drive vehicle produced today.

Owens AR Bottle Machine
Toledo, Ohio

The world's first automated bottling machine that introduced cheap and plentiful supply of glass containers and ended child labor in those plants.

Pin-ticketing Machine
Miamisburg, Ohio
Monarch Marking Systems

This was the first successful machine for mechanizing the identification and price marking of retail merchandise. At a single stroke of the operating handle the machine formed a tag from a roll of stock, imprinted it with price and other information, formed a wire staple, and stapled the tag to the merchandise. This means for dispensing with handmade and written tags amounted to a minor revolution in the then rapidly expanding retail industry.

Steamboat William G. Mather
Cleveland, Ohio

The steamship *William G. Mather* represents the evolution of mechanical engineering innovation. Launched as a state-of-the-art ship for her time, the Mather later served as a prototype, incorporating the latest advancements in technology. The enhancements extended the Mather's economic life and included single oil-forced boiler, steam turbine propulsion, automatic power plant control, as well as, a dual propeller bow-thruster. As a result, the Great Lakes shipping remained efficient, productive, *(continued on page 379)*

THE OHIO CANALS: ONCE A GREAT NOTION

Blood, sweat and sky-high hopes went into the building of the Ohio canals. Their golden age lasted not quite 20 years, yet they hauled Ohio's isolated frontier economy out of the backwoods and into the national marketplace.

In the first quarter of the 19th century, Ohio was a nature preserve accessible to only the hardiest of tourists. The state was the Far West, a dark continent far from such Eastern refinements as navigable roads. Its entire population was considerably under a million lonely souls, and in 1825 the state's revenue was less than half the 2003 salary of the Cincinnati Red's reserve shortstop. Ohio, almost bankrupt, was thus an unlikely and threadbare suitor for the hand of America's commerce.

She was a promising stripling of a state, but without a transportation system, thus her products were largely relegated to the medium of barter. Wayne County was considered to have some of the richest land in America—and the poorest prospects. Wooster was the county's nearest point of trade, and historian Walter Havighurst wrote of one shoeless farmer arriving there with a groaning wagon full of wheat to find his only market a merchant who offered two bits a bushel for just enough to fill a mudhole in front of his store. In 1827, though, something changed all that forever. Overnight—July 5—wheat that had sold for 25 cents on July 4 jumped to 75 cents.

The dramatic agent of change was the opening of the Ohio canals, and behind that event stood an intractable Irishman with enough cast iron in his disposition to have

sunk an empty towboat. Alfred Kelley is the unsung hero of Ohio's canals, the man who presided over the finest—certainly the most difficult—moment in the history of Ohio's public-works projects. Kelley had resigned his prospering law practice and become canal commissioner for $3 a day. "Lonesome from a soaring intellect, dyspeptic from a gnawing canker of duty," wrote author William Ellis about him.

The canal system he and his Irish laborers built was in full operation for less than 20 years, but its benefits were incalculable; it brought Ohio out of the wilderness. In a decade and a half after the first canal opened, Ohio's population tripled. By 1850, it was America's third most populous state, and by 1860, led the nation in the value of its agricultural products.

One of the high ironies of the canals' brief but illuminating existence was that they carried many of the rails and ties—not to mention the coal—that built the railroad, which quickly replaced them. But in the early 1800s, a canal could be envisioned, while a railroad could not. The locomotives were slower than a canalboat, had little power, and could not climb a grade. Railroads were viewed with skepticism, right up until 1850.

In all of history did any other major transportation system so quickly replace another? And so, by 1860, Ohio also had more miles of railroad track than any other state. The thousand miles of canal, 32,000 acres of reservoir, and 294 lift locks fell into disuse. One of the nation's greatest physical feats—barely imaginable by today's standards—had virtually disappeared.

—*Richard Coleman*

The Ohio canals attracted at least one future president. He was a young mule skinner named James A. Garfield, who is said to have had his first fistfight at Lock 21, north of Akron. According to lore, his horses got their lines tangled with those of another boat, and the evolving brouhaha ended with Garfield being ignominiously launched into the canal. He dried off and headed for Washington, the only mule skinner to ever inhabit the White House.

THE BIRTH OF THE ELECTRONIC COMPUTER AGE

Considering the impact computers have had on the last half century, it is surprising that John Mauchley's name is not a household word. In 1971, a *New York Times* editorial said it was a gross injustice that the names of Mauchley and co-inventor Presper Eckert were unlikely to reach parity with "the Wright Brothers or Thomas A. Edison, let alone the Beatles." And since Mauchley's contribution was the world's first electronic computer, history has made the editorial an under-statement.

Born in Cincinnati, John Mauchley was a professor at Ursinus College in Pennsylvania when he conceived the idea of an electronic computer (using vacuum tubes) to solve meteorology equations. When he went to the University of Pennsylvania in the summer of 1941 to learn more about electronics, he found that its Moore School of Electrical Engineering had a contract with the government to provide ballistic tables for artillery guns. Mauchley realized that his idea for a computer could be applied to this problem, and he outlined his idea to the school.

Largely due to Mauchley's idea, the Moore School was awarded a contract to build the world's first electronic computer. It was called ENIAC (Electronic Numerical Integrator and Computer) and, with the help of Presper Eckert, a young engineer, completed the project in 1946.

The huge machine cost $400,000 and filled a room at the college. With its 18,000 vacuum tubes and 6,000 switches, it could do 5,000 additions per second—minuscule by today's standards but far exceeding anything on the drawing boards at the time.

Even before ENIAC was complete, Mauchley and Eckert began to work on a stored program computer. For that, they enlisted the aid of another Ohioan, Jon Van Neumann, who completed the work on the stored program.

John Watson, Sr., the president of IBM, who began as a salesman for Dayton's NCR Corporation, supposedly said in 1941, "I think there's a world market for about five computers." But Mauchley believed that computers could be adopted for many uses—by no means an accepted idea at the time—thus helping realize their vast potential.

In 1946, Mauchley and Eckert began designing UNIVAC for use in a wide variety of commercial applications. UNIVAC was the first commercially produced electronic digital computer, and their first contract was with the Census Bureau. UNIVAC gained public notice when it was used to predict the outcome of the 1952 presidential election.

Perhaps it was because of the patent fights that Mauchley hasn't received the credit he deserves. Or maybe it was just the nature of an invention that didn't produce a singular dramatic Kitty Hawk moment (even the Wright Brother's claim was disputed for years).

Whatever the reason for his relative obscurity, it was Mauchley that conceived the idea, foresaw its potential, and brought us into the computer age—changing irrevocably the world in which we live.

—*Michael O'Bryant*

and competitive with other modes of transportation. The savings realized helped local iron ore sources maintain an economical edge over foreign suppliers.

William Tod Rolling-Mill Machine
Youngstown, Ohio

Representative of steam-powered rolling-mill engine drives early in the transition to electric drive and typical of the largest work pieces produced by U.S. foundries and forges.

Wright Field Five-foot Wind Tunnel
Dayton, Ohio
Wright-Patterson Air Force Base

Wind tunnel testing of aircraft models is essential to determine aerodynamic parameters such as lift and drag. This early example of the modern wind tunnel was conceived and built by the Air Service Engineering Division when little aerodynamic theory or data existed as a basis for its design. Yet, when completed, this wooden tunnel was considered the most efficient in the world and precluded very smooth air flow. The final inspection team included Orville Wright. The model is mounted in a test section five feet in diameter. Air flow is provided by tow fans driven by electric motors totaling 1600 HP. The tunnel is still being used for teaching and research.

Wright Flyer III
Dayton, Ohio
Carillon Historical Park

The world's first practical airplane.

Xerography
Columbus
Battelle Memorial Institute

Chester Carlson developed a dry copying process for documents but had difficulty finding support to perfect and market it. After being turned down by several companies in 1944 he gained help from Columbus's Battelle Institute. Battelle was able to advance Carlson's process into a marketable product.

Electrical Engineering

ENIAC
Electron Numerical Integrator and Computer
Philadelphia, Pennsylvania
University of Pennsylvania

The world's first electronic digital computer was developed by the U.S. Army to compute World War II ballistic firing tables. Cincinnatian John W. Mauchley, who worked for the Moore School of Electrical Engineering between 1941 and 1946, conceived the computer's architecture. With the help of J. Presper Eckert, they built the machine that laid the foundations for the modern electronic computing industry.

United States Naval
Computer Machine Laboratory
Dayton, Ohio

In 1942, the U.S. Navy joined with the National Cash Resister Company to design and manufacture a series of code-breaking machines. This project was located at the U.S. Naval Computing Machine Laboratory. The machines built there, including the American "Bombes"— advanced code breaking machines—incorporated advanced electronics and significantly influenced the course of World War II.

Agricultural Engineering

The American Society of Agricultural Engineers recognizes important contributions and contributors to agricultural engineering.

Agricultural Aviation
Troy, Ohio

C.R. Neillie started agricultural aviation in 1921 when he used a military plane to dust catalpa trees near Troy, Ohio.

Ives Hall
The Ohio State University
Columbus, Ohio

In 1926 Ives Hall, Ohio State's original Agricultural Engineering building, became the first historic landmark recognized by the American Society of Agricultural Engineering. It was demolished in 2002. The building was dedicated to Frederick W. Ives (1884-1924) head of Ohio State's Department of Agricultural Engineering, 1920-24.

Slow Moving Vehicle Emblem
Ohio State University
Columbus, Ohio

In 1961-63 Kenneth A. Harkness of Ohio State's Department of Agricultural Engineering developed the slow-moving vehicle emblem that has now become standard.

Flights of fancy

Before they could make history flying the world's first powered aircraft, Wilbur and Orville Wright of Dayton first had to learn how to fly. They achieved a smaller—but no less significant—milestone when the first controllable glider sailed aloft over the dunes of Kitty Hawk in North Carolina. The brothers' 1902 glider was only their third unpowered aircraft, but it was backed by more sophisticated research than had been put into their first two gliders. While the 1900 and 1901 gliders had been based largely on existing theories of lift and drag—the flight principles that get planes off the ground—the 1902 glider was the result of the world's first wind tests, performed in the Wright brothers' bicycle shop. They made around 1,000 glides with the 1902 model, many of them lasting more than 600 feet. They sometimes tested the glider as a kite. Some of the glides were made in 36-mile-an-hour winds, unthinkable for other would-be aviators of the day. Here's a closer look at the science behind the 1902 glider. *Graphics and text by Stephen J. Beard, by permission of the Plain Dealer*

www. *wright-brothers.org*

Wonderfully complex site by the Wright Brothers Aeroplane Company in Dayton, a non-profit organization of aviators, historians, educators, and others who share an interest in the history of the invention of the airplane. Particularly focused on telling the story to young people, the site will capture anyone but the most jaded and earthbound. Everything amazingly Wright, from actual plans to build the brothers' full-sized 1902 glider (32-foot wingspan) to the history, music of the day, photographs, and assorted links.

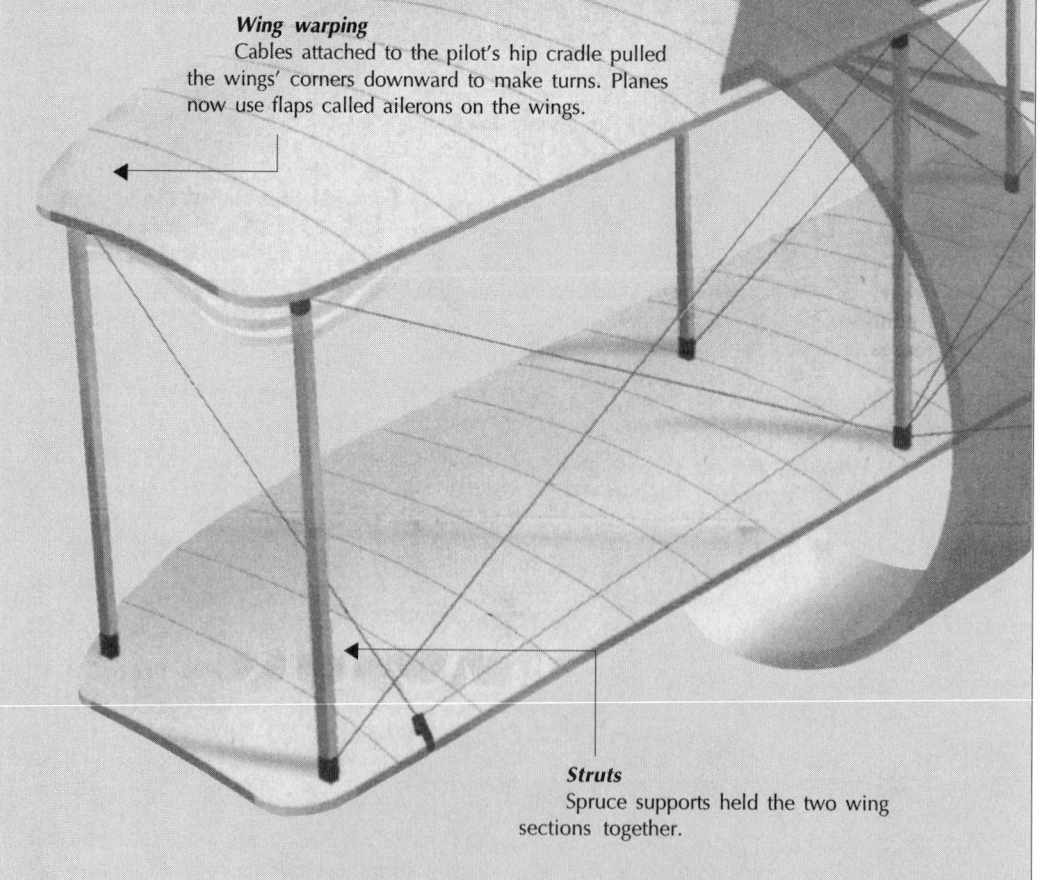

Tail
Added stability to the glider and gave the pilot more control in the turns.

Wing warping
Cables attached to the pilot's hip cradle pulled the wings' corners downward to make turns. Planes now use flaps called ailerons on the wings.

Struts
Spruce supports held the two wing sections together.

by Stephen J. Beard

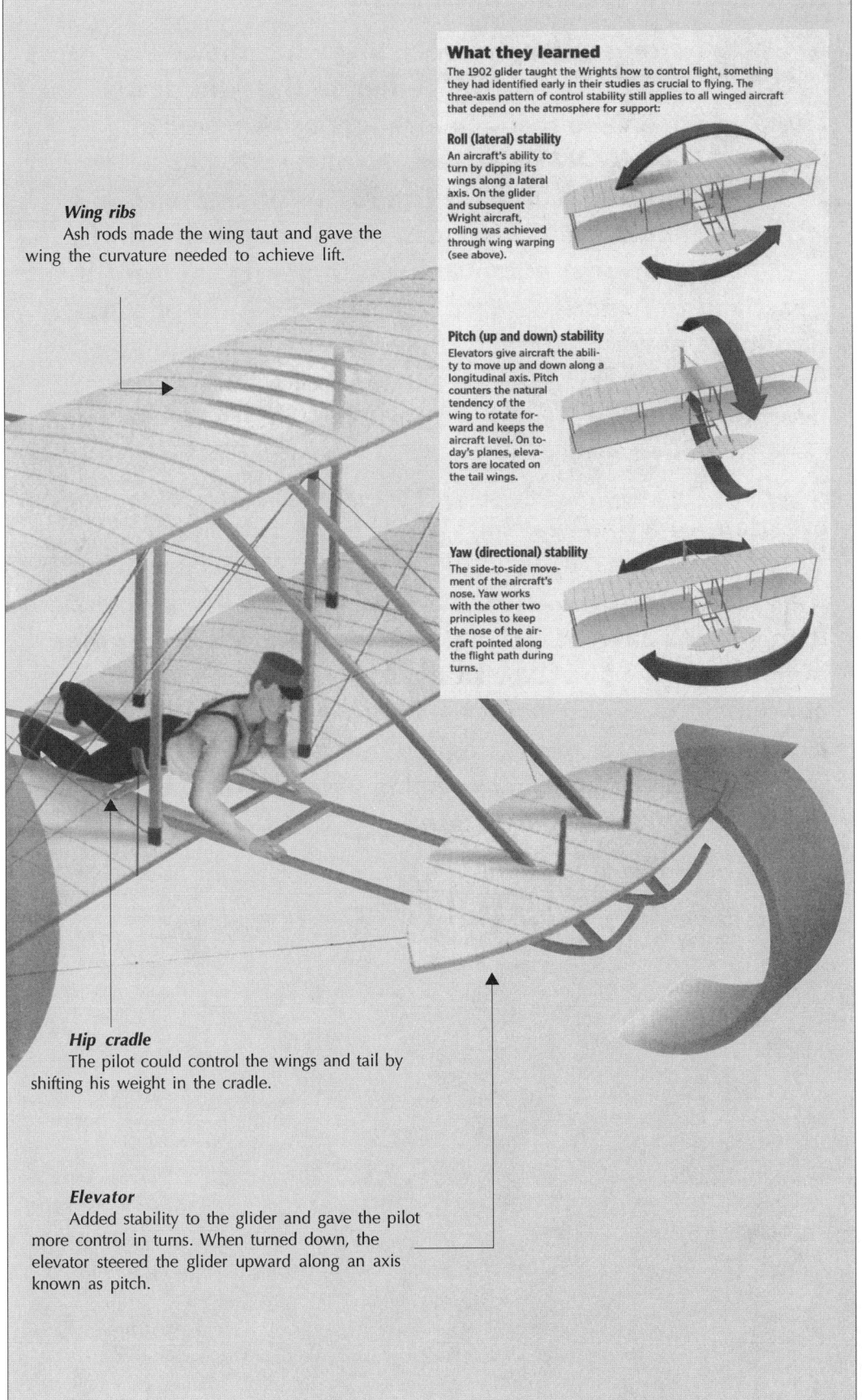

Wing ribs
Ash rods made the wing taut and gave the wing the curvature needed to achieve lift.

What they learned

The 1902 glider taught the Wrights how to control flight, something they had identified early in their studies as crucial to flying. The three-axis pattern of control stability still applies to all winged aircraft that depend on the atmosphere for support:

Roll (lateral) stability
An aircraft's ability to turn by dipping its wings along a lateral axis. On the glider and subsequent Wright aircraft, rolling was achieved through wing warping (see above).

Pitch (up and down) stability
Elevators give aircraft the ability to move up and down along a longitudinal axis. Pitch counters the natural tendency of the wing to rotate forward and keeps the aircraft level. On today's planes, elevators are located on the tail wings.

Yaw (directional) stability
The side-to-side movement of the aircraft's nose. Yaw works with the other two principles to keep the nose of the aircraft pointed along the flight path during turns.

Hip cradle
The pilot could control the wings and tail by shifting his weight in the cradle.

Elevator
Added stability to the glider and gave the pilot more control in turns. When turned down, the elevator steered the glider upward along an axis known as pitch.

What they learned

The 1902 glider taught the Wrights how to control flight, something they had identified early in their studies as crucial to flying. The three-axis pattern of control stability—roll (lateral) stability, pitch (up and down) stability, and yaw (directional) stability—still applies to all winged aircraft that depend upon the atmosphere for support.

Humility aside, it sometimes takes vision and imagination to spot Ohio's deft hand in great events. But if you know where to look, there it is.

Times and manners being what they were, not much had happened on the American beefcake scene before Johnny Weismuller, noted Olympian, was hired by the Piqua Hosiery Company in 1931 to pitch Piqua long johns. Piqua, of course, is the birthplace of the drop-seat union suit, another original from the heartland to America's *haute couture*. Soon to become filmdom's newest Tarzan, Weismuller traded Piqua for Hollywood and the drop seat for leopard skin, which prompted one more original: strange underwear for men.

Historians beware.

Like American beefcake, these Ohio origins are creations of a different ilk. They are not tidy firsts or simple inventions. Instead we find a timely occurrence that pushed history—not just Ohio history—in a direction it might not have otherwise traveled. And their common bond, a force, a power to shape and a momentum to continue, casts long shadows across America, shading from the limelight their fragile Ohio roots. If, as it's said, originality is the art of concealing your sources, Ohio, indeed, is a most original state.

The westward expansion   *1795*

Within a year of the signing of the Treaty of Greenville, a floodtide of immigration rolled across the territory; over a thousand boats went down the Ohio River. "Old America," wrote an Englishman, "seems to be breaking up and moving Westward." In this sense, Mad Anthony Wayne at Fallen Timbers, the battle that erased native title to the Northwest Territory, paved the way to a glorious westerly future, including the right of Sylvester Stallone to press his footprints into the wet cement of a Hollywood sidewalk.

Shakespeare in America   *1835*

Shakespeare in America didn't exist before the 1830s. The founders of New England never thought about him. It was William Holmes McGuffey, the son of Scotch-Irish parents who settled in the forests of Ohio, who actually brought Shakespeare to America. He created two school readers to be used as basic English textbooks, and Shakespeare was his favorite author to excerpt. Shakespeare's popularity then spread

to the strolling players who followed flatboats down the Allegheny. Actors were usually vagabonds and chronic debtors, but the frontier was a great place for one-night stands, sometimes not of their own making. In Florida, for example, in the late 1830s, a company was butchered by Indians who looted the costume trunk and galloped off dressed as Orlando, Macbeth and Othello. Thus, classical education via Shakespeare transformed illiterate frontier schoolchildren (with fears of Indians, gunfights and stabbings) into literate schoolchildren (with fears of ghosts, sleeping-walkings and suffocations).

The Civil War   *1851*

It was in Cincinnati that Harriet Beecher Stowe heard the story that later became the indelible image for slavery and the Underground Railroad: Eliza crossing the Ohio River ice. *Uncle Tom's Cabin* was quite likely the most morally persuasive American book of the century, and if it was apocryphal that President Lincoln once greeted Mrs. Stowe as being "the little woman who wrote the book that made this big war," it was also not much doubt that her book tipped Northern sentiment against slavery, and hastened the great Civil War.

America's sweet tooth   *1851*

An eccentric Methodist minister in Oxford, Ohio, showed the rest of the country how to solve its major beekeeping problem— how to harvest honey without killing the bees. Lorenzo Langstroth, after astutely observing the bee's own preferences for space, developed a rectangular hive with movable frames, inventing the modern beehive. It was a design so flawless it has yet to be changed.

The invention of total war   *1864*

In 1864, Lancaster's William Tecumseh Sherman extended the limits of acceptable wartime conduct. The irascible Sherman, a pro-slaver who was the Northern commander most sympathetic with the South, led his 60,000 men down a 50-mile-wide scorched path across the Georgia countryside, stripping farms of grain and livestock, spreading dread through the population and becoming the first American general on a massive scale to consciously demoralize a people in order to subdue its army, as well as the first to wreck an economy to achieve the same end. He thus became the spiritual forefather to the bomber aircraft of World War II. Ironically, Cump Sherman's march to the sea produced only about 1,400 Confederate casualties.

The re-election of President Lincoln

Phil Sheridan's famous 14-mile ride on his legendary horse, Rienzi, rallied the retreating Union troops at Cedar Creek, and the final control of the Shenandoah Valley was decided. But there were other repercussions from that day, one of the great battles in the annals of warfare. The feats of the 5'4", 115-pound Ohioan, called a "misshapen little terror of a man with an unholy aptitude for war," prompted the famous doggerel poem, *Sheridan's Ride*, which became the anthem of Lincoln's campaign, and Sheridan's success assured Lincoln the White House again. The battle also promoted a young cavalry officer, George Custer, to stardom and contributed to the future presidencies of another pair of Ohioans, officers Hayes and McKinley.

Modern Florida

1867

Handsome, roughish Henry Flagler and Cleveland refinery 1867 owner John Rockefeller created Standard Oil, quite an achievement in itself. Then Henry dealt himself out, looked southward to the gigantic alligator farm that Florida was at the time, and, unprecedented in the annals of American development, created out of his own wealth the East Coast Railway, which converted Florida from a wilderness into a 20th century superstate.

Solid-state electronics

circa 1879

When the most famous son of Milan, Ohio, died in 1931, he was called America's most useful citizen. Thomas Edison had begun with three months of formal schooling, and ended with 1,100 patents, an American record. His most famous one, the incandescent lamp, may have sprung from a boyhood image—the glimmer of whale oil lanterns on Lake Erie schooners. The light bulb, of course, was gloriously self-evident. But it had other, less apparent implications including the birth of solid-state electronics. The light bulb generated heat and light; its offspring, in the early 1900s, was the vacuum tube, which amplified sound. Both presaged a giant leap upward in the principles of modern computing design.

Realistic American fiction

circa 1880

While the old Brahmin from Martins Ferry, William Dean Howells, did not single-handedly forge the beginnings of Naturalism on American shores, he did forge its definition, calling his theories "the truthful treatment of fiction," a somewhat radical notion for the ornamental Victorian Age. His own novel, *A Modern Instance*, was the first American novel to use divorce as a major theme. The definition and defenses

of realism in American fiction were major contributions, and Howells became the dean of American letters, as well as Ohio's first literary man to earn a reputation of the first water.

The media event   *1881*

That high keening of the journalistic pack treeing its quarry, in one manner or another, has become a staple of contemporary life. Its origins are Ohioan and may be traced to a confluence of tragic events after the new president, Clevelander James Garfield, was shot by a deranged political aspirant. Garfield's death struggle coincided with a revolution in the communications industry—the evolving competencies of telegraphy and printing. Historian Allan Peskin calls this deathwatch "perhaps the best-known, most closely followed story of the century." Garfield's brave struggle became the first such event of modern times. Today, the struggle more often belongs to the besieged audience.

Modern salesmanship   *1885*

John H. Patterson, a Dayton toll-collector and coal merchant, bought the patent for the mechanical cash register and set about replacing the one cent pencil with his $125 machine. To overcome this lapse of economic logic, Patterson hired a sales force, teaching them how to dress, and how to make a difficult presentation. His innovation included direct-mail selling and exclusive territories for salesmen. He's also credited with developing the modern factory, along with most of the practices that distinguished modern American businesses, even though he sometimes told his men where to buy their neckties and was, in turn, called by one of them "a combination Julius Caesar and Alice in Wonderland."

The six-pack   *1886*

The U.S. Patent Office called the process of making aluminum commercially viable one of the 19 most important inventions in this country. It was made possible by Charles Martin Hall, the priggish son of a poor Ohio minister who discovered the process on a cookstove in an Oberlin woodshed in 1886. Hall, a piano-playing liberal-arts major, struggled through trial-and-error, fund raising and a mountain of litigation to begin Alcoa Aluminum. Thus, that indisputably modern social artifact, the six-pack, had its origin in an Ohio woodshed.

*In 1930, a new Ohio State graduate, **Milton Caniff**, who later drew the popular Steve Canyon comic strip, invented and began to promote a logo consisting of buckeye leaves and seeds. He continued doing this until September, 1950, when the University accepted the logo as its official symbol.*

The theory of relativity

Albert Michelson and Edward Morley, two Case Western Reserve professors with a basement experiment featuring rotating mirrors floating in a tub of mercury, failed in their search for an invisible ether they thought existed to conduct light. But what they did do was make astounding measurements accurate to one part in 100 million, and lay the foundation upon which Einstein would later build his theory of relativity and our modern theories of space, time and light. Michelson never gave up on ether, however. When Einstein made his last visit to Michelson in 1931, his daughter asked Einstein, "Please, just don't get him started on the subject of ether."

The mass-produced piano
1890

When Dwight Hamilton Baldwin took $2,000 and invested it in a downtown Cincinnati shop just before the Civil War, only the wealthy made their own piano music: the instruments were simply too costly. D.H., however, wanted a good instrument with a low price. When he couldn't find one, he decided to make his own, which he did, and in 1900 the Baldwin piano was exhibited at the International Exposition in Paris, where it received the Grand Prix, never before given to an American piano. If that was music to old D.H.'s ears, it was even more so to the rest of America, now better able to approach the piano as another piece of furniture, albeit one that occasionally needed both tuning *and* polishing.

The New Deal
1894

After the 1893 depression, a well-off Massillon quarry owner named Jacob Coxey, a currency reformer and better-roads advocate, devised a plan for federally supported public improvements. His ideas culminated in the famous Coxey's Army, which marched from Massillon to Washington to petition Congress. The Feds lent a deaf ear, but this was the first attempt at defining joblessness as a national problem that required government intervention. Coxey's march helped chip away at the prevailing notion that joblessness was the result of laziness, and its call for public works jobs anticipated a central element of the 1930s New Deal program.

Yellow journalism
1897

When the foreman for the printing presses at the *New York World* needed an illustration to test a new quick-drying yellow ink, Lancaster native Richard Outcault, the paper's cartoonist, drew a series about a gap-toothed, jug-eared munchkin who wore a nightgown. The pressman inked the gown yellow, and

the Yellow Kid's subsequent popularity fueled the Hearst-Pulitzer rivalry, with Outcault bouncing back and forth between the papers. The scenario gave birth to the pejorative description of journalistic competition we now know as "yellow journalism."

The assembly line   *circa 1900*

Henry Ford II always contended that it was Ohio's Porkopolis—Cincinnati—that gave the world the assembly line. He said his grandfather visited the Queen City at the turn of the century and saw the slaughterhouses with the pigs hung on belts, parts being removed as the carcass traveled along. He thought that if a pig could be disassembled in this manner, then perhaps other things—notably the auto—could be assembled in the same manner. The quintessential moment featuring the sow's ear.

The popularity of golf   *circa 1900*

John D. Rockefeller's 700-acre estate on Cleveland's east side had a nine-hole golf course where he obsessively played a sport most of America regarded—if they did at all—as a preposterous British eccentricity. Newspaper photographers followed Rockefeller everywhere, and for nearly 40 years, the image of Rockefeller on the greensward was a journalistic staple. Millions of Americans, rich and poor, were therefore led, wrote one historian, "into the same feverish chase." Ohio's revolutionary contribution to the game, however, was the invention of the modern golf ball itself, a ball with a rubber-wound core patented in 1899 by Clevelander Coburn Haskell. It replaced the universal gutta-percha ball of the day, giving golfers, in the best sense of the word, a better lie.

The American bungalow   *1902*

Two brothers from Cincinnati, Charles and Henry Greene, burst almost overnight out of obscurity and into the annals of architecture with their carefully articulated, wonderfully crafted, original houses that became known as the "California bungalow," houses that influenced the craft of home building across the country. Charles the artist and Henry the engineer complemented each other perfectly in their design, which integrated architecture, native materials, fixtures, fabric—even landscaping. With them, the Arts and Crafts movement achieved its highest moment.

The eradication of hookworm in America   1908

John D. Rockefeller's Cleveland oil legacy left him the wealthiest Baptist in America and turned his interests increasingly to philanthropy. One of his ventures, the prosaically named General Education Board, was a revolutionary force of Southern education, an offshoot of which was an attack on the hookworm parasite. The parasite, a warm–climate affliction, entered the body through the soles of bare feet and caused chronic weakness that the Northern press called "the germ of laziness." It was a formidable barrier to education. The old man donated $1 million for a ten-year war on the parasite, and his commission won it in five—over half a million people cured—one of the country's greatest cost-benefit ratios.

The modern college game   1913

During a seemingly uneventful summer on the shore at Cedar Point, two young collegians by the names of Gus Dorais and Knute Rockne learned how to toss—and catch—the over-inflated lump of leather that then passed for a football. The amusement park was paying them as lifeguards, but in reality, it was subsidizing a revolutionary development in college athletics. The pair took their new game east to play that Goliath of American sport, Army, and with a passing game no one had ever seen, pasted the troops, 35-13. That summer at Cedar Point established Notre Dame, and the forward pass. Said Rockne afterward, "We went out like crusaders. We were representing the whole aspiring Midwest."

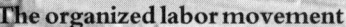

The organized labor movement   1934

It was called "The Battle of Toledo," and its aftermath made it one of the nation's most important military encounters. It began in the deeps of The Great Depression, with a third of all Toledoans on relief. When management of the Electric Auto-Lite Company refused to negotiate with workers, the workers set up picket lines, and the in the spring of 1934, the company brought in strikebreakers. Several thousand workers and their families blockaded the strikebreakers in the factory, deputies used tear gas and water hoses, and the National Guard came in. Two people died, another 200 were injured. At this, the strike was settled; the company recognized the union, rehired strikers and gave them a five percent wage increase. Some historians contend the strike was one of the three most important in the nation's labor history. They credit it with getting Congress to pass the 1935 Wagner Act, which gave workers the legal right to collective bargaining and prohibited employers from interfering with labor organizing, and that led to the development of the powerful United Auto Workers.

The integration of baseball   *1970*

It took a disparate set of circumstances to put blacks on
America's ball diamonds—the life of Branch Rickey and the
death of Judge Kenesaw Mountain Landis. Rickey, the son of a
fundamentalist Ohio farm couple who didn't allow him to play
baseball on Sunday, was the president of the Brooklyn Dodgers,
and the man who brought Jackie Robinson into the major
leagues. But that didn't occur until the passing of the
cantankerous old racist, Landis, another Ohioan, who for nearly
25 years was the most powerful figure in baseball. Rickey's
impulse was a combination of decency and business pragmatism:
Even white folks would one day pay to see blacks play baseball.

The ego of Donald Trump   *circa 1960*

According to Donald Trump's autobiography, he and his father,
while reading FHA foreclosures, came across Cincinnati's
Swifton Village, a troubled 1,200-unit apartment development.
They put in a minimal bid, and paid less than $6 million—
without putting down any of their own money—for a project
that two years before had cost twice as much. They repaired it,
established good management, then sold it for a $6 million profit.
Trump was still in college, and it was the seminal Trump deal.
What profiteth a man if he gain Swifton Village and lose any
sense of modesty? *Plenty.*

The popularization of Monday Night Football   *1970*

The skeptics said it would be an unmitigated disaster. The
networks thought the skeptics might be onto something. Never
one to turn away where angels fear to tread, Cleveland Browns'
President Art Modell agreed to host the first Monday Night
Football game—at his stadium, September 21, 1970. The Browns
beat Joe Namath's Jets in a heady one, 31-21, before ABC's
entranced home audience and an SRO local crowd of 85,000.
Another 10,000 were turned away, and Modell had soon caused
Monday night to be confused with Sunday afternoon, giving rise
to another legion of Astroturf widows.

Reaganomics   *circa 1980*

The doctrine that promised all things to all men was launched
in part by an eccentric Youngstown native. Arthur B. Laffer,
who sometimes appeared before press conferences with a parrot
on his shoulder, was said to have designed the "Laffer Curve"
on a napkin in a Washington, D.C., restaurant; it demonstrated,
Laffer said, that at a certain level more taxes mean a decline in
revenues, because taxable work is discouraged. The Reagan
administration then applied the Laffer Curve to the economy.
The country's longest span of economic growth followed, as did
the greatest deficit in history, which was more likely a promise
of *some* things to *some* men.

Bathsheba Rouse, an educated Massachusetts miss and a descendent from the famous Puritan union of Miles Standish and Priscilla Alden, came to Marietta, Ohio's first settlement, with other pilgrims in 1788. The following year the 19-year-old relocated to Belpre, ten miles downstream from Marietta, and agreed to teach school. The crude log schoolhouse had a sod floor, leaky roof, and planks nailed to wood stumps for benches. Sunlight beaming through an open window and slanting through gaps in the logs illuminated the classroom. Barnyard odors wafted through the same pores. Being summer, her barefooted pupils likely had their minds on outdoor fun.

ode.state.oh.us/

www.

Why go anywhere else than the Ohio Department of Education for educational news in Ohio? Excellent site for parents, educators, administrators, and board members. Something for everyone, including job opportunities, proficiency information, news updates, links to standards based education, certification, and more.

Nevertheless, she taught her pioneer prodigies manners, reading, arithmetic, and writing for three months, without the luxury of books and other materials. Miss Rouse, Ohio's first schoolteacher, endured her trial, and collected her salary of $1.67. She taught several more terms in Belpre before marrying Richard Greene and sinking roots in Marietta.

Like Bathsheba Rouse, Ohioans who had learned their ABCs back East found the newly-anointed state's school system non-existent in 1803, and its struggling and illiterate citizenry woefully suspicious and less than enthusiastic about public education. Although enlightened Yankee founders built schools in Cincinnati, Marietta, Zanesville, Warren, Steubenville, Hudson and other fledgling towns, learning on the frontier occurred in the log home after chores, often by candlelight, and only if a parent or older sibling proved capable, willing, and able to teach young ones.

Many pioneers only expected their children to write their name, read the Bible, and know enough math to keep merchants and millers honest. There wasn't much use for Latin, algebra, or poetry in the backwoods. Schooling wasn't a high priority in Ohio two centuries ago.

Although the Northwest Ordinance of 1787 had required land companies to set aside the revenues garnered from sales in Section 16 of each township for a public school, the document did not actually order the citizenry to construct and support schools. Consequently, many of those "school sections," totaling more than 700,000 acres, remained undisturbed, or they had been sold or leased by unscrupulous township officials to cronies or squatters at rates too low to fund a school. Back in "ought-three," Ohio had more trees than books, more yearning than learning.

There were exceptions. After staking out an 1,800-acre estate on a tributary of the Hocking River in 1799, Massachusetts-born Ephraim Cutler quickly became a prominent merchant, landowner, and farmer in Amesville. As a delegate to the state constitutional convention in 1802, Cutler wrote the antislavery and pro-education sections of the constitution, but then cast the only vote against statehood. Nevertheless, he brought a New Englander's intellectual refinement and curiosity to the frontier. It proved useful being the eldest son of the Rev. Dr. Manasseh Cutler, the Yale educated physician and minister who founded Marietta for the Ohio Company in 1787. At the time of statehood, Ephraim Cutler had all the wealth, military rank, and political office expected of the landed gentry. But his cupboard was bare of books.

To remedy that, Cutler and his learned neighbors, acting on the suggestion of not-so-learned pioneers George Ewing and Josiah True (the latter recently acquiring literacy in the local school), organized the Western Library Association

by Stephen Ostrander

in 1804. Lacking cash, the association figured it would sell animal pelts for books, including the "she bear" hide acquired by True and ten raccoon skins that represented the "accumulated wealth" of young Thomas Ewing, George Ewing's son and a future U.S. Senator and cabinet secretary of two presidents.

The association entrusted the furs to Samuel B. Brown and Cutler, both Boston-bound anyway on family business. (Brown was headed east to retrieve his family; Cutler to visit his father, who returned to the Bay State once Marietta was afloat.) In Boston, the duo sold their prizes to a fur company for $60 and purchased 51 books on history, biography, religion, travel—and one novel. The books, shipped for $13.50, arrived at the home of Sylvanus Ames, Amesville's founder, on December 4, 1804.

Association members elected Cutler librarian, a post he held until 1806 when he moved to a new home overlooking the Ohio River, six miles downstream from Marietta. Since horses and wagons towed the collection among subscribers, Ohio's first library, dubbed the Coonskin Library by Cutler, also can rightfully be called Ohio's first bookmobile. Thomas Ewing honored the library in his memoirs. "It seemed to me like an unbounded intellectual treasure...The library of the Vatican, and all other libraries of which I had

read were trifles, playthings, compared to it."

In 1818, forgiving or forgetting voters elected Cutler to the Ohio General Assembly, where he devoted much of three terms to establishing Ohio's educational system. In 1821, he crusaded for legislation requiring townships to establish local school districts, but his biggest victory came in 1825 when pro-canal legislators backed a property tax for schools in exchange for Cutler's support of canals. Cutler's savvy earned him the title of co-founder of Ohio's public education system, an honor he shared with Caleb Atwater of Circleville and Nathan Guilford of Cincinnati. The 1825 law also called for the election of school boards to administer the school districts established in 1821. (About this time, the Ohio legislature began trickling funds to a state library.) Four years later, state lawmakers established a three-month minimum school year.

The so-called Akron Law in 1847 allowed voters in cities and towns to pool resources and form larger school districts, the forerunner of the contemporary city school districts. Interweaving with other social and cultural movements before the Civil War, Ohio's education reforms ushered in a frenzy of school construction. This was the heyday of the one-room schoolhouse, the standard educational building for nearly a century, especially in the countryside.

These plain, sturdy and practical structures, similar in form and function to country churches, were inexpensive (an average of $340 in the 1850s) and easy to build. Typically, the clapboard or brick frame boxes featured tall windows, a bell tower, and twin privies. Austerity continued inside with a slate blackboard, double-pupil desks fastened to the floor, and bookshelves cramped with McGuffey's Eclectic Readers.

Usually there was an American flag tacked to a wall flanked by pictures of George Washington and, after the Civil War, Abraham Lincoln. Maybe a second-hand, out-of-tune piano occupied a corner. The state commissioner of common schools counted 12,602 school buildings in 1858, more than double the number just five years earlier. At the dawn of World War I, Ohio still had nearly 10,000 one-room schoolhouses.

To our elders, these vernacular stalwarts represent a simpler and more virtuous time. They fondly regaled their progeny with tales of frightful walks through rain and snow to answer the morning bell, of firing up the school's pot-bellied stove in January with staves of oak lugged from home, and of pranks pulled on classmates and the consequences they suffered for such boldness. Once ubiquitous, the one-room schoolhouse had virtually vanished by 1950, except in Ohio's rural Amish communities.

Privately-funded academies, seminaries, and institutes flourished in cities and county seats at this time too. These lofty two and three-story structures usually flashed some architectural ankle—Greek Revival and Federal being the favorites styles. Teachers trained back East taught lofty subjects, too, such as classical languages, geometry, rhetoric for boys; or music, sewing, and etiquette for girls. Many academies professed special missions, or boarded students for months, or dabbled in social reform. Twinsburg Institute, founded by the Rev. Samuel Bissell, a Yale graduate and Congregational minister, enrolled Native Americans. Hudson Academy featured the first astronomical observatory west of the Appalachians, while Stephen Strong's Manual Labor Seminary, housed in Chester Academy in Meigs County, focused on vocational training. The Marsh Foundation School in Van Wert

catered to orphaned and homeless children. Many graduates from the Steubenville Female Seminary became Presbyterian missionaries in the western U.S. and abroad. By the 1880s, however, tax supported high schools had supplanted most of the state's academies.

Ohio's early colleges also bloomed from the foresight of the Founding Fathers. To secure land grants from Congress in the 1787-88, the Ohio Company and John Cleves Symmes agreed to set aside the proceeds of sales in several townships for colleges. In December 1795, the Ohio Company dutifully earmarked a pair of scenic townships on the banks of the Hocking River for a university, wishfully naming the townships Alexander (as in Alexander the Great) and Athens, after the mecca of learning and culture in Ancient Greece. Athens, the village, was settled in 1797, but revenue for the college accumulated slowly.

The state issued a charter (an exclusive license to the Ohio Company to establish a college) for Ohio University in 1804, but classes did not start until 1808. That year students paid $2 a quarter, the cost of firewood and other expenses. The enterprising Tom Ewing of Amesville earned the school's first college diploma in 1815. Cutler Hall, a Federal-style brick eminence and Ohio's oldest college building, opened in 1816, when tuition amounted to $6 a session. Four years later, Ephraim Cutler, also one of the founders of the Underground Railroad, became a college trustee and kept the job until he died in 1853.

Miami University, chartered in 1809 in the Symmes Purchase at Oxford, began college instruction in 1823, thus fulfilling the educational obligation of its land grantors. Not surprisingly, the schools operated without a penny from the state for many years.

For the next half century, Ohio colleges would be founded and funded by diverse religious denominations, their mission being to dispatch an educated clergy and supporting cast into the westward frontier. Presbyterians erected Western Reserve, the self-proclaimed "Yale of the West" in 1826, Muskingum in 1837, and Wooster in 1866. Catholics started Xavier (1831) and Dayton (1850). Methodists began Ohio Wesleyan (1842), Baldwin (1845) and Mt. Union (1846). Wittenberg (1845) and Capital

SIGH!

PRINCIPAL

WATCH FOR TEENS EXHIBITING 'UNUSUAL BEHAVIOR' - EXPERTS

(1850) were founded by Lutherans.

Swedenborgians, whose most famous frontier disciple was John Chapman (a.k.a. Johnny Appleseed), built Urbana College in 1850. Congregationalists established Oberlin (1833), Marietta (1835) and Defiance (1850). Later, Baptists set up colleges at Rio Grande (1876) and Ashland (1878). Quakers built a campus at Wilmington in 1879, and the Church of God set up shop in Findlay (1882). Seed money for these colleges largely came from faithful followers in eastern states, the source of Ohio's school administrators and faculty for decades. Episcopalians, for example, started Kenyon in 1828 with money that Bishop Philander Chase, founder of Worthington Academy, raised in England.

Ohio briefly basked in the glow of college "experiments." Reform-minded Oberlin College raised eyebrows from the outset as the nation's first coeducational college and as the first campus to recruit African-American students. Its faculty and students harbored escaped bondsmen in defiance of federal law, the Fugitive Slave Act. An offshoot of the liberal Unitarian Church erected Antioch College in 1852, then stunned the nation by luring noted educator Horace Mann to Yellow Springs as its first president. Management

of America's first all-black college, Wilberforce, established in 1856, was transferred to the African Methodist Episcopal Church during the Civil War.

It took a hefty government gift to nudge Ohio toward a state-supported university. The Morrill Act, signed by President Abraham Lincoln on July 2, 1862, promised participating states 30,000 acres of federal land for each member of Congress, provided they use the land-sale revenues to establish and maintain a college "related to agriculture and mechanic arts" and other disciplines for the "practical education of the industrial classes."

The Ohio General Assembly finally accepted the offer of 630,000 acres in 1864. It then took nearly six years to charter the Ohio Agricultural and Mechanical College, and three more years to raise University Hall and commence classes. The Ohio State University, the land-grant institution's name after 1878, received state tax dollars for the first time in 1891, thus initiating the era of tax-supported universities. Ohio and Miami universities changed to state-run institutions in 1896, and Wilberforce in 1900. The "normal" schools for training teachers at Kent and Bowling Green became full-fledged state universities in 1935.

Aside from the Coonskin Library, the story of Ohio's public libraries was not a page turner until the richest tycoon in America, Andrew Carnegie, tossed millions of dollars over the Alleghenies. Carnegie had spent some of his youth in East Liverpool and worked briefly as a telegraph operator in Steubenville. In 1899, these were the first of 77 Ohio communities to benefit from his largesse for libraries. During the ensuing

quarter century, Carnegie's philanthropic foundation paid for more than a hundred libraries in Ohio. Villages as small as Bristolville and cities the size of Cleveland received grants. So his libraries would not stand idle and empty, Carnegie insisted that grant recipients pay for books, librarians, and maintenance with local dollars. Amazingly, 80 other Ohio towns built libraries before 1923 without the Great Scot's generosity (*see related story, page 453*).

The architecture of Ohio schools, symbolic of the value a community puts on knowledge and its aspiration for citizens, has changed as much as school curricula. Architectural fashions came and went and Ohio schools and libraries wore them all—Federalist, Greek revival, classical, neoclassical, Jacobean, Italianate, Gothic, octagonal, Romanesque, Renaissance, Victorian, Beaux-Arts, Georgian, Spanish mission, art deco, modern, post-modern, modular, cubism, deconstructionist, and their hybrids. Whether it's the weathered Federal face of Ohio University's Cutler Hall or the deconstructionist drape around the Aronoff Center for Design and Art at the University of Cincinnati, the architecture lifts all who enter them to a loftier plane, again and again.
—*Stephen Ostrander*

One of Ohio's grandest schools (although sadly neglected): Cincinnati's Hughes High, which "has so much terra cotta that it looks as though it were lusciously frosted—doors, windows, cornices all are in cream-colored terra cotta, as are gargoyles, griffins, hatchets and lo, books. The style is Collegiate Tudor, popular for schools in the early 20th century."
—Jane Ware

Educationplus&minus

The gap	+plus	-minus
Ohio high school dropouts—$8 an hour High school graduates—$11 an hour. College graduates—$18 an hour. People with a high school education or less lost 14% of their wages between 1979-2000.		Postgraduate degrees—$23.07 an hour. College graduates gained 14% in wages between 1979-2000.

The infrastructure

Ohio is second in the nation in the amount of money it borrows per capita to build university buildings.	Ohio's school building and technology needs are the third most expensive in the country—$25 billion. Only New York and California, with much larger enrollments, have larger needs.

The spending

Ohio is 33rd in the amount it spends per capita to provide academic programs at those universities. Ohio ranks 4th among all states in public university tuition costs—$5,058 (National average—$3,411)	An Ohio family needs an average of 30% of its income to pay for an education at a four-year public campus (a private education takes about 59% of family income). In the best-performing states, four years at a public institution takes about 18% of family income (32% at private institutions).

Degrees

Ohio average for those completing college—39%. U.S. average for those completing college—45%. Education deficit—408,575 (This is the number of additional Ohioans completing college required to bring Ohio to the national level).	Only 40% of Ohio's high school freshmen enroll in college within four years —14% less than the top states.

Salaries and systems

The Ohio college teacher's salary is $55,098, which is approximately the national average. Ohio professors average $79,889, slightly under the national average.	The average professor's pay at a public university in Michigan is $10,000 higher than in Ohio.

Jobs

Ohio is in the lower fourth nationally in the ability to retain and attract individuals with bachelor's and master's degrees.	Ohio ranks 33rd in the U.S. in progress toward an information age economy. Ohio's metro areas rated weak in workforce levels, which widens gap in economic growth, compared with regions with more educated workforces.

Scholarship

The average Ohio youth spends 900 hours in school each year.	The average Ohio youth spends 1,023 hours watching television each year.

Priorities

For the cost of incarcerating one person in an Ohio prison, the state could pay the annual tuition of four students at a public university.	From 1985-2000, the average increase in state spending on corrections was nearly double that of the increase to higher education.

Sources: National Education Association; Policy Matters Ohio; Akron Beacon Journal, The Cleveland Plain Dealer; the Ohio Board of Regents; National Center for Education Statistics; National Center for Public Policy and Higher Education; Case Western Reserve University's Center for Regional Economic Issues; Progressive Policy Institute; Southern Technology Council; TV-Turnoff Network.

Ohio has one of the largest and most comprehensive higher education systems in the country. It includes thirteen state universities, two free-standing medical schools, 13 community colleges, eight technical colleges, 24 university regional campuses, 64 independent non-profit liberal arts colleges and universities, and more than 70 specialized independent non-profit colleges (art and music academies, seminaries, nursing schools).

Within the state's public system of higher education are 2,218 buildings worth some $15.3 billion, and in the fall of 2001, these buildings were inhabited by upwards of half a million students—445,638, to be exact as we can be, with another 117,000 in Ohio's independent non-profit institutions.

This system was, at least in large part, the culmination of former governor James Rhodes' idea that a campus of higher education should be within 30 minutes of every Ohioan. There are now 1.14 educational institutions for every 100,000 Ohioans, a statistical measure (the national average is 1.2 per 100,000), and not an actual campus—although The Ohio State University seems to be close.

The average cost of tuition and fees is $5,734 at Ohio's four-year public schools , $3,150 for two-year colleges, and $16,304 for private schools. Seventy-one percent of private school students get financial aid, in the average amount of $14,675.

Over 100,000 students earn degrees in Ohio every year—65,000 from public institutions and over 26,000 from independent, non-profit institutions. More than one-half of those graduating receive baccalaureate degrees (which take an average of 4.3 years). Associate degrees (which take an average of 3.8 years) account for approximately 25 percent of the degrees awarded in any given year.

Class size in the public system averages 18 for labs and 27 for lectures.

Profiles of Ohio's Four Year Colleges and Universities

The University of Akron
381 Buchtel Common
Akron, Ohio 44325-2001
330-972-7077
800-655-4884
330-972-7022 Fax
E-mail: admissions@uakron.edu
Website: www.uakron.edu

This 131 year old university was a private institution called Buchtel College (after its number one benefactor, industrialist John R. Buchtel) and run by the Universalist Church of Ohio until 1967, when it became the University of Akron and began receiving full state support. The 160-acre campus is located within the City of Akron only 45 miles from Cleveland. The University of Akron offers 86 major programs of undergraduate study including anthropology, art education, electrical engineering, foods and nutrition, microbiology, and social science. Of special note is the internationally known polymer science program, which has received the Ohio Eminent Scholars Award.

Regional Campuses:
Community and Technical College
330-972-7077
800-655-4884

Wayne College
800-221-8308 ext. 8900

Allegheny Wesleyan College
2161 Woodsdale Road
Salem, Ohio 44460
330-337-6403
800-692-3153
330-337-6255 fax
E-mail: college@awe.edu
Website: www.awc.edu

A member of the American Association of Bible Colleges, Allegheny Wesleyan was founded in 1956. The college concentrates primarily on instruction in elementary education, religion, and theology.

Antioch College
795 Livermore
Yellow Springs, Ohio 45387
937-769-1000
800-543-9436
937-769-1111 Fax
E-mail: admissions@antioch-college.edu
Website: antioch-college.edu

This private, liberal arts college was established in 1852. The 100-acre campus is located within the village of Yellow Springs, 18 miles from Dayton. Students can choose from 54 programs of study in the liberal arts or design his or her own major.

Antioch offers an extensive cooperative education program, and students spend at least six quarters working off-campus in a job related to their major. Study or cooperative education abroad is also available.

Art Academy of Cincinnati
1125 Saint Gregory Street
Cincinnati, Ohio 45202
513-721-5205
800-323-5692
513-562-8778 fax
E-mail: admissions@artacademy.edu
Website: www.artacademy.edu

The Art Academy of Cincinnati has been in operation since 1882, offering programs of study in fine arts, painting, sculpture, printmaking, photography, communication design, graphic design, and illustration. This private, four-year institution also offers independent study and study abroad in addition to an accelerated honors program.

Ashland University
401 College Avenue
Ashland, Ohio 44805
419-289-5052
800-882-1548
419-289-5999 fax
419-289-5333 fax
Email: auadmsn@ashland.edu
Website: www.ashland.edu

Established by the Brethren Church in 1878, Ashland University is a private institution focusing on the liberal arts. The 98-acre campus is located in the town of Ashland, population 22,000. Among the 62 programs offered at Ashland are courses in art, art education, business, radio and television broadcasting, social science, and speech education. Study abroad in Spain, Singapore, Yugoslavia, England, and India is also possible. Special campus features include a Writing Center, the John M. Ashbrook Center for Public Affairs, and the Center for English Studies.

Baldwin-Wallace College
275 Eastland Road
Berea, Ohio 44017
440-826-2222
877-292-7759
440-826-3830 fax
E-mail: admission@bw.edu
Website: www.bw.edu

Baldwin-Wallace College was established by the United Methodist Church in 1845 and continues that affiliation today. The 53-acre campus of this liberal arts college is located in the city of Berea, 14 miles from Cleveland. Baldwin-Wallace has been professionally accredited in music and elementary and secondary education, and the college offers a total of 62 programs of study.

Ashland University, which uses a giant chocolate chunk cookie as its trademark, was named in 2002 by the National Association of College and University Food Services as having the best residence dining hall menu among all medium-sized U.S. colleges. Pasta is offered daily, eggs cooked to order, and the same meal is served only four times a semester.

More than half the student body is studying business. The college also offers dual majors, self-designed majors, cooperative education, and an honors program. There is an observatory, greenhouse, and electron microscope on campus.

Bluffton College
280 West College Avenue
Bluffton, Ohio 45817
419-358-3257
800-488-3257
419-358-3232 fax
E-mail: admissions@bluffton.edu
Website: www.bluffton.edu

Bluffton College was founded in 1899 and is affiliated with the Mennonite Affiliated Church. The 65-acre campus is located in the town of Bluffton, 60 miles from Toledo. Bluffton's 46 academic programs include study in accounting, education, nursing, social work, and peace and conflict studies. Pre-professional programs in medicine and law are offered, in addition to self-designed majors, independent study, internships, and study abroad in Mexico.

Bowling Green State University
110 McFall Center
Bowling Green, Ohio 43403
419-372-2478 (BGSU)
419-372-6955 Fax
E-mail: choosebgsu@bgnet.bgsu.edu
Website: www.bgsu.edu

Located 22 miles south of Toledo, BGSU is a state-affiliated university established in 1910. The 1,247-acre campus is within the city limits of Bowling Green. Students can choose from more than 103 majors including accounting, business administration, and elementary education. BGSU also offers an extensive course of study and facilities related to the pop culture major. Since 1984, the university has received three Ohio Eminent Scholars and five Program Excellence awards for chemistry, computer science, management, psychology, and visual communication technology. A planetarium is located on campus.

Regional Campus:
Firelands
419-433-5560 ext. 2-0607

Capital University
2199 East Main Street
Columbus, Ohio 43209-2394
614-236-6101
800-289-6289
614-236-6926 fax
E-mail: admissions@capital.edu
Website: www.capital.edu

Capital University was established in 1830 and retains an affiliation with the Evangelical Lutheran Church. The 48-acre campus is located in the City

of Columbus. The University offers 55 programs of study in areas like biology, computer science, criminal justice, music, nursing, and occupational therapy. Pre-professional programs in dentistry, theology, and law are also available as is study abroad in Italy, Mexico, Scotland, Africa, Jamaica, Japan, Tanzania, and a number of other countries. There is an art gallery located on campus.

Case Western Reserve University
Cleveland, Ohio 44106
216-368-4450
216-368-5111 fax
E-mail: admission@po.cwru.edo
Website: www.cwru.edu

Founded in 1826, Case Western is a private university occupying a 128-acre campus four miles from downtown Cleveland. Case Western Reserve offers a four-year degree in over 60 majors in addition to graduate or professional study. Conditional acceptance to one of the university's professional schools can be obtained in one's first year of undergraduate study if certain conditions are met. In addition, Case Western has developed a number of off-campus study and career experience opportunities including a Junior Year Abroad, Washington Semester, and a variety of cooperative education choices and professional practicums.

Cedarville University
251 North Main Street
Cedarville, Ohio 45314
937-766-7700
800-233-2784
937-766-7575 fax
E-mail: admissions@cedarville.edu
Website: www.cedarville.edu

Cedarville University is a private, liberal arts institution established in 1887 and affiliated with the General Association of Regular Baptist Churches. The 110-acre campus is located in the town of Cedarville, population 2,800, located 25 miles from Dayton. The University offers programs of study in over 40 areas including biology, English, international business, nursing, religion, and theology. An Honors program and opportunities for independent study, cooperative education, and study abroad are also available. Cedarville also specifies as a condition of admission that "students must present a testimony of their faith and exhibit a lifestyle consistent with college standards."

Central State University
P.O. Box 1004
Wilberforce, Ohio 45384-1004
937-376-6348
800-388-2781
937-376-6648 fax
E-mail: admissions@csu.ces.edu
Website: www.centralstate.edu

A public university established in 1887, Central State occupies a 550-acre rural campus located 18 miles from Dayton. Central State provides course options in more than 75 different programs of study including ancient history, communications, economics, journalism, physics, and social science. Independent study and cooperative education options are available. A performing arts center and language lab are located on campus.

University of Cincinnati
PO Box 210091
Cincinnati, Ohio 45221-0091
513-556-1100
513-556-1105 fax
E-mail: admissions@uc.edu
Website: www.admissions.uc.edu/

The University of Cincinnati was originally established in 1819 as a municipal university. It remained a state-affiliated municipal university until 1977, when it began receiving full state support. The 270-acre campus is located within the city of Cincinnati near the downtown area. Students may choose from more than 100 programs of study. An honors program, independent and foreign study, and cooperative education options are available. Since 1984, the University has received nine Program Excellence and ten Ohio Eminent Scholars Awards for its programs in architecture, chemistry, electrical engineering, interior design, nursing, pharmacy, physical therapy, and urban planning.

Regional Campuses:
Clermont College
513-732-5294
Raymond Walters College
513-745-5700

Cincinnati Bible College & Seminary
P.O. Box 04320
2700 Glenway Avenue
Cincinnati, Ohio 45204
513-244-8100
800-949-4CBC
513-244-8140 fax
Website: www.cincybible.edu

This member of the American Association of Bible Colleges was founded in 1924. The campus is located within the city of Cincinnati. The college offers a four-year degree in education, music, or religion. Independent study and cooperative education is also available. The college considers "Christian character . . . as the most important qualification for admission."

Cincinnati Christian College
3800 Reading Road
Cincinnati, Ohio 45229
513-281-2103

This four-year, private, religious institution has been in operation since 1921. It offers a bachelors program in religion and theology. Accordingly, candidates for admission should demonstrate "interest in Christian endeavors . . . and ability to comprehend subject matter," as well as possess "Christian virtues."

Cincinnati College of Mortuary Science
645 West North Bend Road
Cincinnati, Ohio 45224
513-761-2020
888-377-8433
513-745-1909 fax
E-mail: generalinfo@ccms.edu
Website: www.ccms.edu

The Cincinnati College of Mortuary Science is a member of the American Board of Funeral Services Education and offers a course of study leading to an

The average annual student loan in Ohio —$3,597

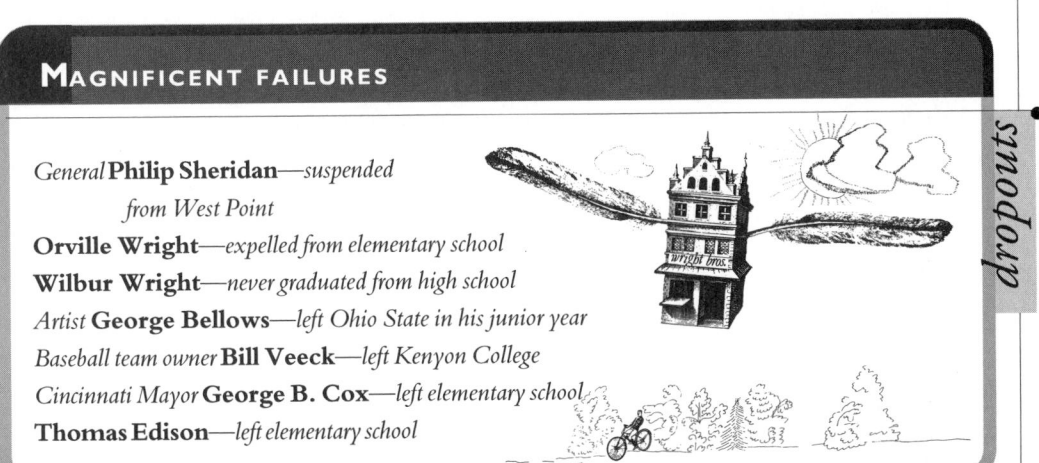

MAGNIFICENT FAILURES

dropouts

General **Philip Sheridan**—*suspended from West Point*
Orville Wright—*expelled from elementary school*
Wilbur Wright—*never graduated from high school*
Artist **George Bellows**—*left Ohio State in his junior year*
Baseball team owner **Bill Veeck**—*left Kenyon College*
Cincinnati Mayor **George B. Cox**—*left elementary school*
Thomas Edison—*left elementary school*

embalmer's or funeral director's license. Entrance requirements are based on the requirements of the state in which the applicant will be licensed.

Circleville Bible College
1476 Lancaster Pike
Circleville, Ohio 43113
740-474-8896
800-701-0222
E-mail: enroll@biblecollege.edu
Website: www.biblecollege.edu

A member of the American Association of Bible Colleges, Circleville Bible College was founded in 1948. The college concentrates primarily on instruction in elementary education, religion, and theology. Independent study and cooperative education options are available.

Cleveland Institute of Art
11150 East Boulevard
University Circle
Cleveland, Ohio 44106
216-421-7418
E-mail: credhead@gate.cia.edu
Website: www.cia.edu

This private college was founded in 1882 and is located in the University Circle area of Cleveland, six miles east of downtown. The institute offers a five-year program leading to the Bachelor of Fine Arts degree. Students can study all facets of visual art and design, including environmental design, industrial graphics, interior design, photography, and traditional art studies. An art teacher education program is also offered in cooperation with Case Western Reserve University.

Cleveland Institute of Music
11021 East Blvd.
Cleveland, Ohio 44106
216-795-5000
www.cim.edu

This private institute has been in operation since 1920 and is located within the city of Cleveland. The Cleveland Institute of Music offers a program leading to the Bachelor of Arts in Music. Study at the graduate level is also possible. Candidates for admission must audition and pass tests in aural skills and musical knowledge.

Cleveland State University
2121 Euclid Avenue, RTW 204
Cleveland, Ohio 44115-2114
216-687-2100
216-687-9210 fax
E-mail: admissions@csuohio.edu
Website: www.csuohio.edu

Cleveland State was established in 1965, and the 50-acre campus is located within the city of Cleveland. Cleveland State provides programs of study in more than 50 different areas, including

pre-professional programs in law and medicine. Independent study, a self-designed major option, and a year of study in Mexico, Spain, England, Germany, or Brazil are also available. Since 1986, Cleveland State has received three Program Excellence awards for its music program.

Columbus College of Art and Design
107 North Ninth Street
Columbus, Ohio 43215
614-224-9101
877-997-2223
614-232-8344 fax
E-mail: admissions@ccad.edu
Website: www.ccad.edu

The Columbus College of Art and Design was established in 1879 and is a member of the National Association of Schools of Art. The 14-acre campus is located within the city of Columbus. The college offers a number of programs related to the visual arts, including advertising, applied design, fashion design, graphic design, and photography. Independent study and cross-registration with OSU, Capital University, Otterbein College, Franklin University, and other colleges is also available.

David N. Myers College
112 Prospect Avenue
Cleveland, Ohio 44115
216-696-9000
877-DNMYERS
216-696-6430 fax
Website: www.dnmyers.edu

Founded as Dyke College in 1848, the campus is located within Cleveland. The college offers programs of study in 16 different areas, including banking and finance, business economics, industrial management, legal assisting, public administration, and social science. Honors, cooperative education and independent study programs are also available.

University of Dayton
300 College Park
Dayton, Ohio 45469-1300
937-229-4411
800-837-7433
937-229-4729 fax
E-mail: admission@udayton.edu
Website: admission.udayton.edu

The University of Dayton is a private, Roman Catholic institution founded in 1850. The 80-acre campus is located near downtown Dayton, 50 miles from Cincinnati. Among the more than 70 major options available are programs in biology, business, education, engineering, modern languages, philosophy, and social science. Independent study, internships, honors programs, and graduate and professional study are also available.

ANTIOCH COLLEGE: IDEAL OF DEMOCRATIC EDUCATION

Approaching Yellow Springs from the south on U.S. 68, the twin spires of Antioch Hall are visible in the distance, rising above the treetops like brick beacons to Horace Mann's ideal of democratic education. Because of those romantic spires, Antioch Hall—one of the first Victorian Gothic buildings in the United States—is an architectural cousin of the Smithsonian Institution. Along with adjacent North and South Halls, it was one of the original buildings erected when Mann took charge of the fledgling school in 1853.

Although coeducation was fundamental at Antioch, cohabitation was not; thus gentlemen students lived in South Hall and ladies in North. Today, as the college's revered version of Old Main, Antioch Hall is still the centerpiece that anchors the campus between Corry and Livermore Streets.

Antioch's campus is a green and lovely place, crisscrossed by student pathways and graced with enough ivy walls and erudition to satisfy the hoary academic stereotype. But it was not always so. Mann's campus was a barren field, which, unfortunately, also described the Antioch coffers. He struggled valiantly but, alas, in 1859, the woes of Antioch College killed the Father of American Education. An obelisk on a small mound behind Antioch Hall now marks his original burial site—the body was later removed to Rhode Island—and bears the moral exhortation that was the last sentence of his last address to his students: "Be afraid to die until you have won some victory for humanity."

Achieving victory for Antioch was thus left to Mann's successors in the college presidency. In the late 1860's, Thomas Hill put shovels in students' hands and had them plant saplings and woodbine; his legacy is the towering trees that shade the campus.

Eighty years later, Arthur Morgan again put students to work when he developed the first work-study program, and alternating semesters of academics and employment is now standard practice on American campuses. Morgan also started a strong student government at Antioch, a tradition most obvious at Maples Hall on Livermore Street where the College Fire Department is the only one in the nation manned entirely by students.

Glen Helen, the extraordinary natural asset unrivaled on any college campus, became part of Antioch during Morgan's presidency, and fittingly, both he and his wife were laid to rest in the peaceful Glen beneath an 80-ton memorial boulder near the start of the Inman Trail.

The remarkable Antiochiana Collection in the Olive Kettering Library attracts serious researchers with its volumes of original Morgan and Mann documents. But the archive, a combination museum and library, also serves as a fine stop for visitors to get a general perspective on the campus and, by association, Yellow Springs.

You'll find the letters of Massachusetts's famous Peabody Sisters (one married Horace Mann; the other Nathaniel Hawthorne); a bust of Morgan made by students working in a foundry; and a clock and dining room table belonging to Horace Mann (the educator is so revered in Japan that one Japanese visitor was nearly overcome by the honor of sitting at Mann's table). And in the college register of 1853, you'll find the name of Jane Andrews, who was not only Antioch's first student, but also one of the nation's first coeds.

"The modern attraction is not the water but the air—a freer social, intellectual, and political atmosphere. The geographic Yellow Springs is in Greene County, east of Dayton, south of Springfield, and north of Xenia. The cultural and political Yellow Springs is somewhere else—beyond ordinary, this side of Utopia, and just short of exasperation."

—John Fleischman

Kenyon is, in the words of one perspicacious writer, "an assertively high-toned, militantly liberal-arts, quintessentially eggheaded place, draped in social history and overgrown with ivy." It is also the oldest private institution of higher learning in the state of Ohio. Its first six graduates were in the Class of 1829 and graduation exercises were led by the founder, Philander Chase, a Dartmouth graduate and educational entrepreneur with strong financial ties in England. Hence, the British influence in architecture— High Episcopal, so to speak.

One professor has described it as living in "a sort of medieval Hamlet with modern plumbing, a kind of St. Disney-in-the-Fields." It has all of 1,550 students, became co-ed 20 years ago, and for the first time, in 1993, had more women than men graduating.

The campus has seen come and go poets, philosophers, prime ministers, presidents, and very good swimmers. It's the home of the famous literary journal, *The Kenyon Review*, and among its famous graduates are poets Robert Lowell and James Wright, novelists Peter Taylor and E.L. Doctorow, actor Paul Newman, President Rutherford B. Hayes, birth-control pill developer Carl Djerassi, the late Swedish Prime Minister Olof Palme, and cartoonists Jim Borgman and Bill Watterson (whose characters, Calvin and Hobbes, were drawn from Watterson's political science classes).

A bookish place, writer Doctorow once said, "Poetry was what we did at Kenyon, the way at Ohio State they played football." This may explain why the campus bookstore was once heralded by *Rolling Stone* magazine as the best campus bookstore in the country.

The school has a high a lofty academic reputation, a renowned faculty, and is also known for its small classes and high faculty-to-student ratio.

Visitors should take time to walk Middle Path, the gravelly institution built by students nearly a century-and-a-half-ago. Originally shorter and narrower, it runs north/south from Old Kenyon to Bexley Hall, the full course of the campus, and has carried the weight of many Kenyon traditions. In 1850, the Path was used as a football arena, with two sets of trees as goals. Later it was the fraternity brothers' forum to post-meeting singing, which became so popular that visitors would plan Tuesday evening trips to Gambier just for the occasion.

Before the Path was lighted it was the only way to get from one part of the campus to another without getting lost in the dark— students would merely follow the sound of their shoes on the crunching gravel.

There have been rumors that Middle Path is to be paved, all proven to be unfounded. Its tributaries, though, have been "poured," making alumni and students nervous that logic will outweigh tradition and the closest distance between two points will no longer be their lovely, gravelly, straight Middle Path.

The Defiance College
701 North Clinton Street
Defiance, Ohio 43512
800-520-4632
419-783-2468 fax
E-mail: admissions@defiance.edu
Website: www.defiance.edu

The Defiance College was established in 1850 and
is affiliated with the United Church of Christ. The
150-acre campus is located within the town of
Defiance, 55 miles from Toledo. Defiance offers
approximately 45 major programs of study
including pre-professional programs in dentistry,
law, medicine, engineering, and veterinary
science. Independent study, cooperative education,
and study abroad is also available. Special on-
campus features include the Eisenhower Archive
Room, an Art Gallery, and the UCC Media Center.

Denison University
Box H
Granville, Ohio 43023
740-587-6276
800-336-4766
740-587-6306 fax
E-mail: admissions@denison.edu
Website: www.denison.edu

Founded in 1831, Denison University is a private
institution whose 2,000-acre campus is located
within the small town of Granville, about seven
miles from Newark. In addition to an honors
program and opportunities for independent study
and study abroad, Denison offers more than 35
major programs of study; pre-professional programs
in engineering, forestry, law, and nursing; and
cooperative education.

The University of Findlay
1000 North Main Street
Findlay, Ohio 45840
419-434-4732
800-548-0932
419-434-4898 fax
E-mail: admissions@findlay.edu
Websites: www.findlay.edu

A private university affiliated with the General
Conference of the United Churches of God, the
University of Findlay was founded in 1882. The 25-
acre campus is located within the town of Findlay,
45 miles south of Toledo. The university offers 46
major programs of study, as well as opportunities
for cooperative education, independent study, and
study in Mexico, Spain, and the Holy Land. An
Equestrian Farm, Nuclear Medicine Technology
Institute, and the Mazza collection of children's
book art are located on campus.

Franciscan University of Steubenville
1235 University Boulevard
Steubenville, Ohio 43952
740-283-6226
800-783-6220
740-284-5456 fax
E-mail: admissions@franuniv.edu
Website: www.franuniv.edu

This private, Roman Catholic university was
established in 1946. The 100-acre campus is
located in the town of Steubenville, 40 miles from
Pittsburgh, PA. The university offers approximately
40 areas of study with opportunities for independent
study, as well as an honors program. Pre-professional program areas include medicine, dentistry,
optometry, pharmacy, and law. Certain students
may qualify to spend a semester abroad in England
or France.

Franklin University
201 South Grant Avenue
Columbus, Ohio 43215
614-797-4700
614-224-8027 fax
E-mail: info@franklin.edu
Website: www.franklin.edu

Franklin University has been in operation since
1902. The 12-acre campus is located within the
city of Columbus near downtown. Major programs
at Franklin University include business, communications, computer science, labor and industrial
relations, nursing, psychology, and public administration. Independent study and cooperative
education positions are also available, in addition
to cross registration with Mt. Carmel School of
Nursing, Otterbein College, Capital University, and
others.

Heidelberg College
310 East Market Street
Tiffin, Ohio 44883
419-448-2330
800-HEIDELBERG
419-448-2334 fax
E-mail: admission@heidelberg.edu
Website: www.heidelberg.edu

Heidelberg College, founded in 1850, is a private
institution located in the town of Tiffin, 50 miles
from Toledo. Heidelberg offers 43 programs of
study, including pre-professional programs in
medicine, engineering, and law. Independent
study, honors study, and study abroad in Germany
or Spain are also possible. A water quality
laboratory and sports medicine center are located
on campus.

Hiram College
Hiram, Ohio 44234
330-569-5169
800-362-5280
330-569-5944 Fax
E-mail: admission@hiram.edu
Website: www.hiram.edu

This private, Disciples of Christ-affiliated school was founded in 1850. The 245-acre campus is located in the small town of Hiram, 35 miles from Cleveland. The college offers approximately 35 academic programs including pre-professional programs in law, medicine, veterinary medicine, optometry, medical technology, and nursing. Opportunities for independent and foreign study in a variety of countries around the world and programs allowing the completion of a four-year degree in three years are available. Special campus features include two natural science field stations, an electron microscopy center, and computerized language laboratory.

John Carroll University
20700 North Park Boulevard
University Heights, Ohio 44118
216-397-4294
216-397-4981 fax
E-mail: admission@jcu.edu
Website: www.jcu.edu

John Carroll University, a private, Roman Catholic university, was established in 1886. The 60-acre campus is located ten miles from Cleveland. Students at John Carroll can choose from more than 40 programs of study at the undergraduate and graduate level. Pre-professional programs include law, dentistry, and medicine. An honors program, independent study opportunities, cooperative education, and foreign study are available as well. A seismology station and center for international studies are located on campus.

Kent State University
PO Box 5190
Kent, Ohio 44242-0001
330-672-2444
800-988-KENT
330-672-2499 fax
E-mail: admissions@kent.edu
Website: www.kent.edu

Kent State was established in 1910 as a public university. The 1,200-acre campus is located in the city of Kent, 12 miles from Akron. The university offers 93 different programs of study including pre-professional programs in law, medicine, osteopathy, engineering, and pharmacy. Since 1984, Kent State has won six Program Excellence awards for its programs in chemistry, electrical engineering technology, geology, graphic design and illustration, and speech pathology and audiology. The internationally known Liquid Crystal Institute has produced technologies used in cancer research and the development of electronic displays. Other specialized facilities, such as a planetarium and speech and hearing clinic, offer students unique research opportunities.

Regional Campuses:
Ashtabula Campus
440-964-3322
Geauga Campus
440-834-4187
East Liverpool Campus
330-385-3805
Salem Campus
330-332-0361
Stark Campus
330-499-9600 ext. 53252
Tuscarawas Campus
330-339-3391
Trumbull Campus
330-847-0571 ext. 58860

Kenyon College
Ransom Hall
Gambier, Ohio 43022
740-427-5776
800-848-2468
740-427-5770 fax
E-mail: admissions@kenyon.edu
Website: www.kenyon.edu

This private institution has been in operation since 1824. The 400-acre campus is located in the village of Gambier, 50 miles from Columbus. Students at Kenyon may choose from more than 40 programs of study in a variety of academic areas. An honors program, independent study options, and three semesters abroad in almost any European country, the Soviet Union, Japan, Columbia, or China are also available.

Kettering College of Medical Arts
3737 Southern Blvd.
Kettering, Ohio 45429
937-395-8628
937-395-8153 fax
E-mail: admissions@kcma.edu
Website: www.kcma.edu

Kettering College of Medical Arts (KCMA), located next to Kettering Memorial Hospital, is a co-educational college, chartered by the Seventh-day Adventist Church. KCMA offers associate and baccalaureate degrees in nursing and various allied health professions. Over 500 students receive exceptional clinical experience in the on-site hospital and other local health care facilities. Personalized instruction is the hallmark at KCMA.

Lake Erie College
391 West Washington Street
Painesville, Ohio 44077
440-639-7879
800-916-0904
440-352-3533 fax
Email: lecadmit@lec.edu
Website: www.lec.edu

This private, liberal arts college was founded
in 1856. The 57-acre campus is located in the town
of Painesville, 28 miles from Cleveland. Lake Erie
offers approximately 25 major courses of study
concentrating mostly on liberal arts areas. In
addition, opportunities for cooperative education,
independent study, and study in a foreign country
are available.

Lourdes College
6832 Convent Boulevard
Sylvania, Ohio 43560
419-885-5291
800-878-3210 ext. 1299
419-882-3987 fax
E-mail: lcadmits@lourdes.edu
Website: www.lourdes.edu

Established in 1958, Lourdes College is a private
institution located in the town of Sylvania, ten miles
from downtown Toledo. A liberal arts college,
Lourdes offers a selective but well-rounded
program of study, offering approximately 20
majors in addition to remedial and independent
study programs.

Malone College
515 25th Street
Canton, Ohio 44709
800-521-1146 ext. 8145
330-471-8149 fax
E-mail: admissions@malone.edu
Website: www.malone.edu

Malone College, established in 1892, is a private
institution operating under the auspices of the
Evangelical Friends Church Easter Region. The
78-acre campus is located in the city of Canton.
In addition to approximately 35 areas of study,
Malone College offers a medical technology
program and pre-professional programs in
engineering, medicine, and nursing. State certification for kindergarten, elementary, and secondary
education are also possible.

Marietta College
Marietta, Ohio 45750
800-331-7896
740-376-8888 fax
E-mail: admit@marietta.edu
Website: www.marietta.edu

This private liberal arts college was founded in
1835. The 70-acre campus is located just outside
the town of Marietta, 170 miles south of Cleveland.
More than 60 major programs of study are
available at Marietta College representing a
variety of academic interests. The college offers
an honors program and independent and foreign
study options as well. Special campus features
include a sports medicine clinic, mass media
building, and observatory.

MARIETTA-ON-THE-MUSKINGUM

This picture-perfect college was started in 1835 by the Congregationalist Church;
they snared the most desirable site in a town nearly 50 years old (no mean feat), and now
the campus sits, centered as if by the hand of God, on the banks of the Muskingum
River. The college has a marvelous and complicated history, but to the casual visitor, it is
most noteworthy, in the age of megaversity, that the campus is such a pleasurable place
to walk. It is built on a human scale, with a minimum of parking lots and a plethora of
footpaths and sidewalks; its corners are marked with inviting gates to the love of learning,
and the red brick, white-trimmed buildings are New England incarnate. Since it is such a
small college community (enrollment hovers around 1,300) visitors are often surprised
with greetings, offers of a tour, offers of lunch, offers to see the original territorial grants
and charters of the Ohio Company, which the College owns and displays at the drop of
a coonskin cap. And there is the crew—not the cleanup crew or the wrecking crew, but
the Thames River/Oxford Blues/Harvard/Yale/Princeton *crew*: healthy young men and
women in pencil-thin racing shells, sculling up the Muskingum. Aficionados of crew
know that the Marietta oarsmen are among the best in the nation; visitors know that
they are pristinely lovely to watch.

Mercy College of Northwest Ohio
2221 Madison Avenue
Toledo, Ohio 43624-1132
419-251-1802
888-806-3729
419-251-1462 fax
E-mail: admissions@mercycollege.edu
Website: www.mercycollege.edu

Mercy College offers degrees in nursing and allied health related programs. The school has immediate access to the Mercy Health System and balances professional and technical training with liberal arts studies.

Miami University
301 South Campus Avenue
Oxford, Ohio 45056-3434
513-529-2531
513-529-1550 fax
E-mail: Admission@muohio.edu
website: www.muohio.edu

This public university has been in operation since 1809. The 1,000-acre campus is located in the small town of Oxford, 30 miles from Cincinnati. Students may choose from more than 95 courses of study in a variety of academic areas. Miami also offers a three-year bachelors program, study abroad in Luxembourg, and cooperative programs in engineering with Columbia University and Case Western Reserve.

Regional Campus:
Hamilton Campus
513-785-3111
Middletown Campus
937-727-3216

Mount Carmel College of Nursing
127 South Davis Avenue
Columbus, Ohio 43222
614-234-5800
800-556-6942
614-234-2875 fax
E-mail: mmenefield@mchs.com
Website: www.mccn.edu

This private school of nursing was founded in 1903 but did not actually become a college until 1990. The campus is located in Columbus. The school offers a baccalaureate and certification in nursing. Some independent study is available.

College of Mount St. Joseph
5701 Delhi Road
Mount St. Joseph, Ohio 45233-1672
513-244-4531
800-654-9314
513-244-4629 fax
E-mail: Peggy_Minnich@mail.msj.edu
Website: www.msj.edu

This private liberal arts college is a Roman Catholic-affiliated institution founded in 1920. The 75-acre campus is located seven miles from downtown Cincinnati. A variety of liberal arts options are represented among the college's 31 major programs of study. Independent study and cooperative education are available, in addition to

GET YOUR FAITH LIFTED: OSU's COHESIVE ALUMNI

slightly scarlet

As of 2003, more than 123,000 of Ohio State's 340,900 living alumni were dues–paying members of the Ohio State Alumni Association, making it one of the largest organizations of its kind in the world. There are some 229 official Ohio State alumni clubs worldwide, and 1,200 alumni club meetings were held in 2002, meaning that somewhere in the world, on average, an Ohio State alumni club meeting was held every 7 hours and 18 minutes. The 84 alumni clubs in Ohio serve the 88 counties (some clubs do double duty such as Van Wert/Paulding), but Ohio State alumni activity also occurs in France, Germany, Israel, Turkey, South Africa, Taiwan, Hong Kong & the United Kingdom.

Source: Douglas A. Plummer, Assistant Director Biographic Records, The Ohio University

The Ohio State University is for that student looking for a veritable immersion into the "college experience," and whether that baptism is by plunge, dunk, or sprinkle, the Columbus conversion involves more than 170 undergraduate majors—from Aeronautical and Astronautical Engineering to Turfgrass Science and Portuguese—for its nearly 50,000 acolytes.

The college was founded in 1870 as part of President Lincoln's Land-Grant Act of 1862, originally devoted to agriculture and the mechanical arts but soon adopting a broader curriculum, and since expanded into an almost all-encompassing range of opportunities for B.A.'s, M.A.'s, and Doctorates alike.

Some of the most popular areas of interest are the arts and sciences, engineering, and business. The school ranked third among public universities in industry-sponsored research, and graduates have the opportunity for placement in such companies as Microsoft, Battelle, and General Motors. Due to pride and sense of community at the university, recent graduates can take full advantage of alumni ties.

Undergraduate students can easily feel lost in the school's academic labyrinth with teacher's assistants (TA's) instructing many classes, since the professors are often busy with research projects. Large classes are not as common as thought, however: 89% of first-year classes contain 50 or fewer students, and the undergraduate student-to-faculty ratio is 13-1. Scheduling has been simplified in recent years, and students can now register for classes over the phone in an average of seven minutes, although classes are often difficult to get into, even for priority students.

While OSU's history is one of prestige and intellect, its athletics are often the most visible part of the OSU iceberg, especially since the 110,000 seat-football stadium, commonly called the Horseshoe, is usually filled to capacity, and the Buckeyes have been recent national champions in sports as varied as synchronized swimming and football. The Schottenstein Center is home to not only the basketball team (which, with an average crowd of 16,057, finished in the top 10 nationally for the fifth straight year) but also big-name musical tours, concerts, and comedians.

Greek life is strong at the university, with 11% of students participating. Ranked 18th for partying by the Princeton Review's *Best 345 College Rankings* for partying, the school tries to play down that bit of down-time scholarship and bring the focus back to the overall OSU experience.

This cultural mega-center offers not only on-campus art shows, but also student exhibits and world-renowned artists, a variety of quality musical options such as the Glee Club, the Marching Band (commonly known as TBDBITL: The Best Damn Band In The Land), and several ensembles, such as Jazz and African. While OSU's galaxy of nearly 1,000 school-sponsored activities may intimidate some students, the college's size and diversity guarantees that there is, indeed, something for everyone.

—Leslie Frake

Columbus is rated eighth in the nation among healthiest cities for pets, largely because of the presence of Ohio State's College of Veterinary Medicine, which is itself rated sixth in the nation.

—U.S. News & World Report, Purina Pet Institute

LOSING OUR MINDS: GRADS WITH ADVANCED DEGREES LEAVE OHIO

A survey of 23 Ohio public and private institutions by *The Plain Dealer* in 2003 sought the validity to the following statements:

1. Most graduates of Ohio universities leave the state.

2. Departees are most likely to head south or west.

3. The better educated are more likely to stay.

4. Nurses and educators are more likely to stay than scientists.

(1.) false

The good news: More than 70% of those who graduated between 1991 and 2001 still call Ohio home.

The bad news: Those with master's degrees are roughly 30% more likely to leave than those with bachelor's degrees. Those with doctorates are more than twice as likely to go.

Perhaps worst of all, graduates with degrees in engineering, science and the arts—fields coveted by economic development officials for their putative link to innovation and the production of wealth—are among the most likely to depart, again with the most advanced degrees leading the way.

The study tracked alumni of Ohio schools only, and didn't compare Ohio departure rates with other states or account for the number of out-of-state graduates who were not residents to start with and perhaps more likely to leave. But for a state that ranks 39th in its share of adults over 25 with at least a bachelor's degree, evidence of substantial losses among those with coveted skills is a reminder of the daunting nature of Ohio's challenge.

(2.) false

Greater Chicago drew more departed Ohio graduates than any other metro area in the country, according to *The Plain*

Dealer analysis. The New York City area was No. 2, followed by Detroit; Washington D.C.; Pittsburgh; and San Francisco. In all, more than 42,000 Ohio graduates from the 11-year period studied moved to those six metro areas. At least 7,400 from the same graduate pool now live abroad.

In interviews, departees mostly say they were lured away by educational or job prospects that Ohio couldn't match. But they say the lifestyle and amenities of their new cities also make them want to stay. And therein lies a lesson for Cleveland and Ohio's other economically troubled cities.

Once considered an afterthought in the hunt for job growth and prosperity, regional amenities—like art, cultural diversity and recreational opportunities—are critical factors for the well-educated, highly mobile workers of the 21st century. And they appear to become even more pivotal over time.

(3.) false

65% of those with doctorates in engineering, the sciences, or the creative arts moved from Ohio, 51% of those with master's degrees in the same fields, and 31% of those with bachelor's degrees.

In other fields, 50% of those with doctorates moved, 28% with master's degrees, and 23% of those with bachelor's degrees.

(4.) true

Departure rates varied widely from discipline to discipline, with engineers more than twice as likely to leave as educators and nurses.

Percentage of graduates who moved:
Medicine—50%, 9,052
Music & fine arts —46%, 12,088
Engineering—39%, 32,673
Sciences—35%, 45,096

—*Sandra Livingston, by permission of The Plain Dealer*

The Ohio State University is spending $140 million to build what its peers enviously refer to as the Taj Mahal, a 657,000-square-foot complex featuring kayaks and canoes, indoor batting cages and ropes courses, massages, and a climbing wall big enough for 50 students to scale simultaneously.

—The New York Times

cross registration with the University of Cincinnati, Xavier University, Northern Kentucky University, and Thomas More College. One academic year at Lansdowne College in London is available for fine arts majors. A music therapy clinic and Institute for Marine Biology Research are located on campus.

Mount Union College
1972 Clark Avenue
Alliance, Ohio 44601
330-823-2590
800-334-6682
330-823-5097 fax
E-mail: admissn@muc.edu
Website: www.muc.edu

Mount Union is a Methodist-affiliated college established in 1846. The 72-acre campus is located 55 miles south of Cleveland. The college offers more than 30 major programs of study in addition to an honors program, independent study, and cooperative education. Pre-professional programs in dentistry, law, medicine, and the ministry are also available.

Mount Vernon Nazarene University
800 Martinsburg Road
Mt. Vernon, Ohio 43050
740-392-6868
866-462-6868
740-393-0511 fax
E-mail: admissions@mvnu.edu
Website: www.mvnu.edu

This private, liberal arts college is affiliated with the Nazarene Church and has been in operation since 1964. The 210-acre campus is located in the town of Mount Vernon, 50 miles from Columbus. Some 40 academic programs represent a variety of liberal arts subjects. Pre-professional programs in law, dentistry, engineering, medicine, agriculture, and nursing are also available.

Muskingum College
New Concord, Ohio 43762
740-826-8137
800-752-6082
740-826-8100 fax
E-mail: adminfo@muskingum.edu
Website: www.muskingum.edu

Muskingum, which has been in operation since 1837, is a private, liberal arts college affiliated with the United Presbyterian Church. The 215-acre campus is located in New Concord, 16 miles from Zanesville. The college offers 36 major areas of study, as well as pre-professional programs in medicine, engineering, veterinary science, law, dentistry, physical therapy, and Christian ministry. Independent study, self-designed majors, a three year bachelors program, and study abroad are also available.

Northeastern Ohio Universities
College of Medicine
4209 State Route 44, P.O. Box 95
Rootstown, Ohio 44272
800-686-2511
330-325-2511
E-mail: admission@neoucom.edu
Website: www.neoucom.edu

NEOUCOM is a public institution chartered in 1973 consisting of the Basic Medical Sciences Campus in Rootstown, three major state universities, and 17 community hospitals. The universities involved in the program are the University of Akron, Kent State University, and Youngstown State University, all located within 35 miles of Rootstown. Students may enter the program through a six-year BS/MD program or enter the MD program after completing a bachelor's degree in pre-medicine at any accredited university.

University of Northwestern Ohio
1441 North Cable Road
Lima, Ohio 45805-1498
419-998-3120
419-229-6926 fax
E-mail: klopp_d@nc.edu
Website: www.unoh.edu

The University of Northwestern Ohio is a co-educational, residential, private institution founded in 1920. It enrolls approximately 2,400 students in the Colleges of Business, Technologies, and Distance Learning.

Notre Dame College of Ohio
4545 College Road
South Euclid, Ohio 44121-4293
216-373-5355
877-632-6446
216-381-=3802 fax
E-mail: admissions@ndc.edu
Website: www.notredamecollege.edu

This private, all-female liberal arts college is affiliated with the Roman Catholic Church and has been in operation since 1922. The 54-acre campus is located twelve miles from downtown Cleveland. Notre Dame offers more than thirty-five programs of study reflecting the college's liberal arts background. The college also offers accelerated programs, internships, cooperative education opportunities, and study abroad.

Ohio ranks 6th among the 50 states in university patents issued from 1975-1998 and six Ohio universities are among the top 100 patenting universities: OSU (263), Akron (146), the University of Cincinnati (100) Case Western (93), the University of Toledo (64), and the University of Dayton (64).

—U.S. Patent and Trademark Office

Oberlin College
101 North Professor Street
Oberlin, Ohio 44074
440-775-8411
440-775-6905 fax
E-mail: college.admissions@oberlin.edu
Website: www.oberlin.edu

Oberlin is a private, liberal arts college established in 1833. The 440-acre campus is located in the town of Oberlin, 35 miles from Cleveland. Students may choose from more than 51 programs of study. An honors program, independent and foreign study are available, as are pre-professional programs in law, medicine, and business.

Ohio College of Podiatric Medicine
10515 Carnegie Avenue
Cleveland, Ohio 44106
216-231-3300
216-231-1005 fax
E-mail: klie@ocpm.edu
Website: www.ocpm.edu

The college offers a professional program leading to the degree of Doctorate of Pediatric Medicine (DPM). A balance of didactic and clinical instruction is provided. Clinical relations are conducted in the college's clinic and through externships, external clerkships and extension clinics.

Ohio Dominican University
1216 Sunbury Road
Columbus, Ohio 43219
614-251-4500
800-955-6446
614-251-0156 fax
E-mail: admissions@ohiodomician.edu
Website: www.ohiodominican.edu

This private, Roman Catholic-affiliated school was founded in 1811. The 43-acre campus is located in Columbus near the downtown area. The college offers approximately 35 academic programs, including pre-professional programs in law, medicine, veterinary medicine, medical technology, and pharmacy. Opportunities for independent and foreign study (in Spain) and for designing individualized majors are also available.

Ohio Northern University
525 South Main Street
Ada, Ohio 45810
888-408-4668
419-772-2313 fax
E-mail: admissions-ug@onu.edu
Website: www.onu.edu

Ohio Northern is a private university affiliated with the United Methodist Church and has been in operation since 1871. The 140-acre campus is located in the small town of Ada, 15 miles from Lima. Ohio Northern offers more than 45 different programs of study in a variety of areas. Independent study, cooperative education, and study abroad are also options for students.

The Ohio State University
Enarson Hall
154 West 12th Avenue
Columbus, Ohio 43210-1390
614-292-3980
614-292-4818 fax
Email: admissions@osu.edu
Website: www.osu.edu

Ohio State is a public university that was founded in 1870. The 15,057-acre campus (which includes 727 permanent buildings, two 18-hole golf courses, and a 1,376-acre airport) is located in the heart of Columbus. The Ohio State offers more than 150 major areas of study in addition to accelerated programs, honors programs, internships, a three-year bachelors program, and study abroad in almost any country. Special features include the Cancer Research Center, the Center for Polar Studies, the American Playwrights Theatre, the Barnaby Center for Environmental Studies, and radio and telescope monitoring for signs of life in outer space. Since 1984, OSU has won 17 Eminent Scholars Awards and eight Program Excellence Awards for its work in the areas of art and design technology, biological macromolecular structure, cosmology, experimental materials research, experimental physical chemistry, geodynamics, high temperature materials, and others.

Regional Campuses:
Agriclutural Technical Institute
800-647-8283
Lima Campus
419-995-8391 ext. 396
Mansfield Campus
419-755-4317
Marion Campus
740-389-6786
Newark Campus
740-366-9333

Ohio University
120 Chubb Hall
Athens, Ohio 45701-2979
740-593-4100
740-593-0560 fax
E-mail: admissions@ohiou.edu
Website: www.ohiou.edu

Ohio University is a public institution established in 1804. The 700-acre campus is located in the town of Athens, 68 miles from Columbus. OU features 107 major areas of study in addition to honors programs, opportunities for independent and foreign study (in more than 60 countries), and cooperative education. Students may also choose a self-designed major or other accelerated programs. Special features on campus include a nuclear

(continued on page 413)

Hotbed of intellect

Ten miles from Elyria, ten miles from original sin, and ten miles from normal American society, it is said. No other college in Ohio—say, *America*—has the traditions of Oberlin, which is still going strong.

Oberlin is the name of a town and a college in northeast Ohio, both founded in 1833 on the pure idealism of John Shipherd and Philo Stewart, two Christian evangelists hell-bent on changing the world through education. Inspired by John Frederick Oberlin, a French clergyman who devoted his life to educating impoverished people, they started Oberlin College to produce ministers and teachers for missionary work.

The town was initially a religious colony, a moral toehold on the untamed Ohio frontier that was—and still is—the social, economic, and philosophical consort of the College. The co-mingling of town and gown was perhaps best illustrated a century ago by Charles Martin Hall, a piano-playing chemist who was both a resident and alumnus. In the woodshed behind his house in Oberlin, he developed the first practical method for extracting pure aluminum from bauxite in 1886. His electrolytic process was the foundation for the Aluminum Company of America, and it made him a fortune, part of which still nicely feathers the nest of the College endowment.

Shipherd and Stewart had purposely picked a remote site about 30 miles southwest of Cleveland in order to avoid interference from sinful city people. More than a century and a half has passed since then, and Oberlin is now linked to the rest of the world by telephones, computers, and the pavement of State Route 58, but it is still very much a place apart. Physically and culturally, Oberlin remains off the beaten path—an island of ideals, art, and intellect tucked away in the flat countryside of Lorain County. Geoffrey Blodgett, the astute Professor of History at Oberlin College, once observed, "Oberlin often seems about ten miles from everywhere: ten miles from Elyria, ten miles from original sin, and ten miles from normal American society."

That distance from the mainstream has been the primary reason that this small college town—the current population is only 8,200—has historically wielded a large influence over national issues and social problems. In the mid-1830's, Oberlin was the first college in the United States to enroll women, and one of the first to enroll blacks. The three women in the Class of 1841 were the first in the nation to receive bachelor's degrees, and by 1900, nearly half of all black college graduates in the United States were Oberlin alumni. The unheard-of mixing of the races as well as the sexes made Oberlin notorious. The town was considered a "hotbed of abolitionists," and a primary stop on the Underground Railroad. By 1860, the black

population approached 20 percent, and Oberlin was probably the most integrated place in the nation.

Its "radical" reputation was sealed on September 13, 1858, when a group of townspeople and students raided nearby Wellington and blatantly defied the Fugitive Slave Act by forcibly taking a young black man away from some slave-catchers. The Oberlin-Wellington Rescue became a *cause clèbre* that synthesized the nation's moral and Constitutional dilemma over slavery, sparking passions and debates that would soon be settled on the battlefield. When the Civil War began, humorist Petroleum V. Nasby declared, "Oberlin commenst this war. Oberlin wuz the prime cause uv all the trubble." Even as recently as 1990, the respected historian Nat Brandt titled his book about the Rescue, *The Town That Started The Civil War*.

Today, the College has evolved into a private, liberal arts school with a tall reputation for academic excellence and innovation that disproportionately exceeds its small enrollment of 2,800 students. It not only boasts one of the best undergraduate libraries and campus art museums in the country, but since 1920 has also produced three Nobel Prize-winning scientists and more Ph.Ds than any other undergraduate, liberal arts college in the country. Oberlin is progressive and proud of it. The campus has no fraternities or sororities, but it does have student-operated dining and residential co-ops, an AIDS political action group, an animal rights organization, a pacifist society, and, of course, the infamous co-ed dormitories that were so controversial when they opened in 1970 they put the College on the cover of *Life Magazine*.

Oberlin students typically possess such a relentless spirit of inquiry and passion for pursuing ideas that the College has been dubbed "the Berkeley of Ohio." The town, on the other hand, is known as the "City of Music," thanks to the presence of the Conservatory of Music, a division of Oberlin College with an international reputation that vies with Julliard. The Conservatory has more Steinway pianos than any other place in the world except for the factory, and its outstanding performance facilities set the stage for so many orchestras, ensembles, operas, concerts, recitals, and theatrical productions that the Conservatory has needed a 24-hour hot line for schedule information. The Cleveland

Symphony comes to town every year to play in Finney Chapel, and residents often say that what they like best about living in Oberlin is being able to walk up the street and enjoy first-rate student and faculty performances, as well as world-class visiting artists and orchestras.

Their only complaint is that it is virtually impossible to find a free evening when something wonderful is not happening. The international array of artists who come to Oberlin and the geographic, ethnic, and religious diversity of the students—they come from virtually every state and more than 40 foreign countries—have produced one of the most cosmopolitan campuses and small towns in the nation. Long before the Berlin Wall crumbled or the Japanese were building cars in Ohio cornfields, the College was combining the fine arts and the liberal arts with a global vision that satisfied the abiding Oberlin impulse to better the world. When the College celebrated its sesquicentennial in 1983, the *New York Times* commented, "In its century and a half, while Harvard worried about the classics and Yale about God, Oberlin worried about the state of America and the world beyond."

That is a weighty responsibility for any place, but Oberlin continues to carry it well.

Notable Oberlin alumni

John Mercer Langston, Class of 1849, first black man elected to public office in the United States (Clerk of Brownhelm Township, Ohio, 1855); *Moses Fleetwood Walker*, Class of 1882, first black major league baseball player (from 1882-91 with the Toledo Mudhens). *John Langalibalele Dube*, Class of 1890, first president of the African National Congress. *Robert Millikan*, Class of 1891, winner of the 1923 Nobel Prize in physics for research on photoelectric effects. *Jack Schaefer*, '29, author of *Shane*. *Roger Sperry*, '35, winner of the 1981 Nobel Prize in medicine/physiology for his work on right brain/left brain functions. *Stanley Cohen*, '45, co-winner of the 1986 Nobel Prize in medicine/physiology for research on the relationship between proteins and cell growth. *Carl Rowan*, '47, syndicated Chicago Daily News columnist. *William Goldman*, '52, best-selling author and Academy Award-winning screenplay writer (*Butch Cassidy and the Sundance Kid*; *All the President's Men*). *James Burrows*, '62, television producer of *Taxi* and *Cheers*.

accelerator, telecommunication center, electron microscopes, and instrumentation center.

Since 1984 Ohio University has won three Ohio Eminent Scholar and eight Program Excellence Awards for its honors programs and other programs in journalism, telecommunications, visual communications, contemporary history, film, and molecular and cellular biology.

Regional Campuses:
Chillicothe Campus
740-774-7200
Eastern Campus
740-695-1720 ext. 208, 213, 215
Lancaster Campus
740-654-6711 ext. 238
Southern Campus
740-533-4612
740-533-4545
Zanesville Campus
740-453-0762 ext. 1439

Ohio Wesleyan University
69 Sandusky Street
Delaware, Ohio 43015
740-368-3020
800-922-8953
740-368-3314 fax
E-mail: owuadmit@owu.edu
Website: web.owu.edu

Ohio Wesleyan is a private, Methodist-affiliated college that has been in operation since 1842. The 200-acre campus is located in the town of Delaware, 20 miles from Columbus. In addition to approximately 60 areas of study available, Ohio

Wesleyan offers a pre-engineering cooperative program with California Institute of Technology and Georgia Institute of Technology; pre-professional programs in law, medicine, and veterinary science; and independent study and study abroad.

Otterbein College
One Otterbein College
Westerville, Ohio 43081
614-823-1500
800-488-8144
614-823-1200 fax
E-mail: uotterb@otterbein.edu
Website: www.otterbein.edu

Otterbein is a private, Methodist-affiliated college that has been in operation since 1847. The 70-acre campus is located in the town of Westerville, three miles from Columbus. The college offers more than 50 major programs of study as well as remedial training, an honors program, opportunities for independent study and study in a foreign country, and cross-registration. Individually designed majors are also available. An observatory, planetarium, and electronic music laboratory are located on campus.

Pontifical College Josephinum
7625 North High Street
Columbus, Ohio 43235-1498
614-885-5585
614-885-2307 fax
Website: www.pcj.edu

This private, Roman Catholic seminary is located within the city of Columbus. The Pontifical College

Lucy Webb Hayes of Chillicothe, Ohio, was the first Presidential wife to have a college degree, graduating—with honors—from Ohio Wesleyan Female College in 1850. A reporter referred to Mrs. Hayes as "the first lady of the land," and the sobriquet stuck not only to her, but to the wives of succeeding Presidents. Mrs. Hayes's road to the White House, by the way, supposedly began on the Ohio Wesleyan campus. Tradition says she met Rutherford B. Hayes while he was visiting the sulphur spring and that he subsequently proposed to her on the steps of Elliot Hall.

Josephinum offers programs of study in English, history, philosophy, psychology, and religion. Many of the students are studying for the Roman Catholic priesthood, but classes are open to students interested in the study of philosophy, scripture, and theology.

University of Rio Grande
Rio Grande, Ohio 45674
740-245-5353 ext. 7206
800-282-7201
740-245-7096 fax
E-mail: admissions@rio.edu
Website: www.rio.edu

This private university was established in 1876 and shares its 178-acre campus with Rio Grande Community College. It is located in the village of Rio Grande, about 15 miles from Gallipolis. Students may choose from approximately 40 major programs of study. The university also offers remedial study programs, independent study, and study abroad.

Shawnee State University
940 Second Street
Portsmouth, Ohio 45662
740-351-4778
800-959-2SSU
740-351-3111 fax
E-mail: to_ssu@shawnee.edu
Website: www.shawnee.edu

Shawnee State became a university in 1986. The campus is located in the town of Portsmouth. The university offers instruction toward a bachelors' degree in business, computer science, elementary education, English, humanities, physical science, plastics technology, science education, or social science. An honors program is also available.

Temple Baptist College
11965 Kenn Road
Cincinnati, Ohio 45240
513-851-3800
513-589-3052 fax
www.templebaptistcollege.net

This private institution was established in 1972. The college offers instruction toward a four-year degree in business, education, elementary education, liberal arts, religion, and theology.

Tiffin University
155 Miami Street
Tiffin, Ohio 44883
419-448-3423
419-443-5006 fax
E-mail: admiss@tiffin.edu
Website: www.tiffin.edu

Established in 1888, Tiffin University is a private four-year institution located in the town of Tiffin, 60 miles from Toledo. Students at Tiffin can receive a four-year degree in accounting, business management, computer science, criminal justice, hotel and restaurant management, information systems and processing, law enforcement, or office management. Independent study, remedial study, and graduate-level work is also possible.

The University of Toledo
Mail Stop 306
Office of Undergraduate Admission
1300 Rocket Hall
Toledo, Ohio 43606-3390
419-530-8700
800-586-5336
419-530-5713 fax
E-mail: enroll@utnet.utoledo.edu
Website: www.utoledo.edu

The University of Toledo is a public university founded in 1872 and located on a 420-acre campus a few miles from downtown Toledo. The university offers more than 90 major programs of study in addition to honors, independent study, and cooperative education programs. Pre-professional programs in dentistry, law, and medicine are available, as is work at the graduate level. Special campus features include an arboretum, the Kinesio therapy clinic, a planetarium, and two observatories. Since 1984, the University of Toledo has won seven Program Excellence Awards for programs involving chemistry, history, legal assisting technology, pharmacy, and respiratory care.

Regional Campus:
Community and Technical College
419-537-3157

The Union Institute
440 East McMillan Street
Cincinnati, Ohio 45206-1925
513-861-6400
800-486-3116
513-861-9968 TDD
800-486-9968 TDD
513-861-0779 fax
E-mail: lschrenger@tui.edu
Website: www.tui.edu

The Union Institute is a four-year, private institution, founded in 1964 and located in Cincinnati. The institute offers instruction in more than 40 different areas. Remedial study, independent study, and cross-registration are offered, and graduate-level work is also possible.

Urbana University
579 College Way
Urbana, Ohio 43078-2091
937-484-1356
937-484-1389 fax
E-mail: admiss@urbana.edu
Web site: www.urbana.edu

Urbana University is a private college founded in 1850 and affiliated with the Swedenborgian Church. The small town, 128-acre campus is located 45 miles from Dayton. Urbana offers instruction in more than 30 different major programs of study. Remedial study, independent study, and cross-registration with Dayton-Miami Valley consortium schools is also available.

Ursuline College
2550 Lander Road
Pepper Pike, Ohio 44124
440-449-4203
440-646-6138 fax
E-mail: admission@ursuline.edu
Website: www.ursuline.edu

Ursuline College is a private, women's liberal arts college established in 1871 and affiliated with the Roman Catholic Church. The 115-acre campus is located in the town of Pepper Pike, ten miles from Cleveland. Ursuline offers approximately 35 major programs of study including cooperative programs in podiatry and dietetics. Remedial instruction, independent study, and foreign study are also available. An art therapy center is located on campus.

Walsh University
2020 Easton Street, N.W.
North Canton, Ohio 44720
330-490-7172
800-362-9846
330-490-7165 fax
E-mail: admissions@walsh.edu
Website: www.walsh.edu

This private institution, founded in 1958, is affiliated with the Roman Catholic Church. The 58-acre campus is located in Canton. Walsh's 30 or more programs of study reflect a range of areas within the college's liberal arts curriculum. Remedial training, independent study, study abroad, and an honors program are also available. Walsh also has cooperative programs with the University of Michigan (forestry), Case Western Reserve (dentistry), and Stark Technical College.

Wilberforce University
P.O. Box 1001
Wilberforce, Ohio 45384-1001
937-376-7321
800-367-8568
937-376-4751 fax
E-mail: admissions@wilberforce.edu
Website: www.wilberforce.edu

Founded in 1856, Wilberforce is a private university affiliated with the African Methodist Episcopal Church. The 125-acre campus is located just outside the village of Wilberforce, about twenty miles from Dayton. Wilberforce offers a concentrated liberal arts curriculum to a predominantly minority student body. In addition to remedial study and honors programs and cooperative education opportunities, cross registration with the Air Force Institute of Technology, Antioch College, Central State University, Wright State University, the University of Dayton, and others is available.

Wilmington College
Pyle Center, Box 1325
Wilmington, Ohio 45177
800-341-9318 ext. 260
937-383-8542 fax
E-mail: admission@wilmington.edu
Website: www.wilmington.edu

This private, liberal arts college has been in operation since 1870 and is affiliated with the Religious Society of Friends. The 65-acre campus is located in the town of Wilmington, 35 miles from Dayton. Wilmington College offers more than 50 liberal arts-based programs. Remedial study, independent study, cooperative education programs, and study abroad are also available in addition to cross-registration with the member schools of the Southwest Ohio Council for Higher Education. An observatory, electron microscope, and greenhouse are located on campus.

Wittenberg University
PO Box 720
Springfield, Ohio 45501
937-327-6314
800-677-7558
937-327-6379 fax
E-mail: admission@wittenberg.edu
Website: www.wittenberg.edu

Established in 1845, Wittenberg is a private, liberal arts university affiliated with the Evangelical Lutheran Church. The 71-acre campus is located in the city of Springfield, 25 miles from Dayton. Wittenberg offers more than 75 programs reflecting a variety of academic areas. Study in a foreign country, independent study, an honors program, and cross-registration with the members of the Southwest Ohio Council for Higher Education are also available.

The College of Wooster
Wooster, Ohio 44691
800-877-9905
330-263-2621 fax
E-mail: admissions@wooster.edu
Website: www.wooster.edu/

The College of Wooster, which has been in operation since 1866, is a liberal arts institution affiliated with the Presbyterian Church. The 320-acre campus is located in the city of Wooster, 30 miles from Akron. Wooster offers approximately 30 programs of study. Independent study and a semester abroad in Spain, Africa, China, the Netherlands, Japan, Colombia, the Soviet Union, and several other countries are also possible.

Wright State University
3640 Colonel Glenn Highway
Dayton, Ohio 45435
937-775-5700
800-247-1770
937-775-5795 fax
E-mail: admissions@wright.edu
Website: www.wright.edu

Wright State is a public university founded in 1964. The 645-acre campus is located eight miles from downtown Dayton. Wright State offers more than 100 undergraduate programs in a wide range of academic areas and work at the graduate level is possible in most majors as well. Pre-professional programs in medicine, law, and dentistry are available as are self-designed majors, an honors program, internships, and cross-registration with the member schools of the Southwestern Ohio Council on Higher Education. The university operates its own radio and TV stations. Since 1984, Wright State has received three Program Excellence Awards for its financial services, motion picture, and theatre arts programs.

Regional Campus:
Lake Campus
419-586-0324

Xavier University
3800 Victory Parkway
Cincinnati, Ohio 45207
513-745-3301
877-982-3648
513-745-4319 fax
E-mail: xuadmit@xavier.edu
Website: www.xavier.edu

Xavier is a private, Roman Catholic institution that has been in operation since 1831. The 84-acre campus is located within the city of Cincinnati. Xavier offers more than 50 major programs of study in addition to work at the graduate level. Pre-professional programs in law, dentistry, medicine, pharmacy, and engineering are available, as well as internships, an honors program, study abroad, and cross-registration with a number of universities.

Youngstown State University
One University Plaza
Youngstown, Ohio 44555
330-941-2000
877-468-6978
330-742-3674 fax
Website: www.ysu.edu/

Youngstown State University is a public university founded in 1908. The 92-acre campus is located within the city of Youngstown. YSU's more than 80 major programs of study reflect a variety of academic areas. Graduate-level study in addition to cooperative education programs, an honors program, study abroad, and a three-year bachelors program are available. Special courses of study include a major in Black Studies and a self-designed major.

Ohio's Two-Year Colleges

Belmont Technical College
120 Fox-Shannon Place
St. Clairsville, Ohio 43950-9735
740-695-9500
800-423-1188
740-942-2222 (North Center)
740-666-3049 fax
Email: info@btc.edu
Website: www.btc.edu

Located approximately 15 miles west of Wheeling, West Virginia, on I-70, Belmont Technical College draws students from six Ohio and five West Virginia counties. Classes are also offered at North Center, Cadiz, Ohio.

Central Ohio Technical College
1179 University Drive
Newark, Ohio 43055
740-366-9222
800-963-9275 ext. 494
740-364-9531 fax
Email: jmerrin@cotc.edu
Website: www.cotc.edu

Located in Newark, Ohio, and shares the 177-acre Newark Campus with the Ohio State University at Newark. Classes offers associate degree programs in health, business, engineering and public service technologies.

Chatfield College
20918 State Route 251
St, Martin, Ohio 45118
513-875-3344
513-875-3912 fax
E-mail: chatfield@chatfield.edu
Website: www.chatfield.edu

(continued on page 418)

WOOSTER: MIDWEST IVY LEAGUE

Nationally known for its Independent Study program, this small (enrollment is about 1,800), private liberal arts college has graduated such a prodigious number of experts, executives, Ph.D.s, and all-around high achievers, that many regard it as a Midwest version of the Ivy League. The College's roots are 19th century Presbyterian and its endowment is very healthy, two circumstances that have resulted in a gracious 320-acre campus where impressive Collegiate Gothic buildings stand shoulder to shoulder with masses of trees high on a hill above the town of Wooster.

Trees have been a hallmark of the College ever since 1870, when it first opened its doors—to women, as well as men, by the way—on a 22-acre grove of oaks donated by Wooster banker Ephraim Quinby. The health and well-being of the 1,500 ashes, oaks, maples, sycamore, and elms currently on campus were recently assured by another donor, albeit anonymous, who started a most unusual endowment at the College—a fund for the conservation, maintenance, and replacement of its trees. The fund currently totals more than $300,000, which equates to a bank account of $204 for each tree on campus.

Abundant landscaping everywhere lightens the loftiness of the battlement-laden architecture, and the effect is an exceedingly attractive campus that, fittingly, encourages contemplation as well as perambulation along the network of brick pathways linking the mostly buff and cream-colored buildings.

Quinby Quadrangle, the square bounded by Wayne, Beall, University, and Bever streets was the original site of the College and is the location of two campus landmarks—Kauke Hall and The Rock.

Built in 1902 as a gift from the people of Wooster and Wayne County, castle-like Kauke is the home of the Delmar Archway, a pleasing passage through the heart of the hall that is lined with various plaques providing a veritable history of the College and its generously loyal alumni.

The enormous granite Rock, truly a sizable donation from the Class of 1874, is located just southeast of McGaw chapel. The Rock has long been a gathering spot for students, and in those innocent days when freshmen had to wear beanies, anyone caught hatless was required to climb The Rock and sing a song, presumably the *alma mater*.

Wooster's Nobel

A key discovery in the development of modern physics was made in the 1920s by Arthur Holly Compton, a 1913 graduate of the College of Wooster. His observation of wavelength changes in diffused X-rays—the Compton Effect—was fundamental to the development of the quantum theory of energy and resulted in his being awarded the Nobel Prize for physics in 1927. Born in Wooster on September 10, 1892, Compton throughout his life held sincere humanitarian principles that were undoubtedly rooted in his upbringing as the son of the first dean of the College of Wooster, whose motto is "Science and Religion from One Source." In addition to numerous technical studies, he also published several books that espoused his convictions, including *The Human Meaning of Science* and *Atomic Quest*, an account of the Manhattan Project.

One of the first things students learn is the local pronunciation of their new home. According to seasoned residents, the name should be said "Wuh-ster" and not "Woo-ster." If confused, just remember the phrase, "Welcome to Wooster where the cows say 'Muh.'"

—James Baumann, *Ohio Cum Laude, The Whole College Catalog*

417

Chatfield College is a two-year, private Catholic liberal arts college with a main campus in St. Martin, Ohio and a Cincinnati campus in North Fairmount. The Ursulines of Brown County, who settled in St. Martin in 1845, founded Chatfield in 1971. Chatfield is authorized to grant an Associate of Arts Degree in Liberal Arts with concentrations in business, human services, early childhood education, and liberal arts. A third year of study toward a bachelor's degree may also be completed at Chatfield.

Cincinnati State Technical and Community College
3520 Central Parkway,
Cincinnati, Ohio 45223
513-569-1544
513-569-1562 fax
E-mail: adm@cinstate.cc.oh.us
Website: www.cinstate.cc.oh.us

On September 1, 1994, Cincinnati Technical College became Cincinnati State Technical and Community College. It is the only autonomous, comprehensive state two-year college in Hamilton County. Cincinnati State offers over 40 associate degree and certificate programs in Arts & Sciences, business, health, humanities, and engineering technologies. The College offers a nationally acclaimed cooperative educational/clinical experiences program for associate degree students.

Clark State Community College
PO Box 570
Springfield, Ohio 45501
937-328-6028
937-328-6097 fax
Website: www.clarkstate.edu

A public, state-supported community college offering over 35 associate degrees and certificates in Arts and Sciences, business technologies, engineering technologies, health, human services and agriculture. In addition, Clark State students may transfer as a junior to four-year institutions. The newest programs at Clark State include stage production technology, corrections technology, and golf course maintenance.

Columbus State Community College
550 East Spring Street
Columbus, Ohio 43215-9965
614-287-2669
800-621-6407
614-287-6019 fax
Website: www.cscc.edu

Columbus State is a public, state-assisted community college, offering over 40 technical career programs, as well as transfer programs. Technical programs are offered in the areas of business, health, public service, and engineering technologies. Transfer programs allow students to complete

as much as the first two years of a bachelor's degree. Recently added Technical Communications and Environmental Technology.

Cuyahoga Community College
800-954-8742
Website: www.tri-c.cc.oh.us

Eastern Campus
4250 Richmond Road
Highland Hills Village, Ohio 44122
216-987-2024

Metropolitan Campus
2900 Community College Avenue
Cleveland, Ohio 44115
216-987-4200

Western Campus
11000 Pleasant Valley Road
Parma, Ohio 44130
216-987-5150

Edison Community College
1973 Edison Drive
Piqua, Ohio 45356
937-778-8600
800-922-3722
937-778-4692 fax
E-mail: info@edisonohio.edu
Website: www.edisonohio.edu

Located on 130 scenic acres in Piqua, near the intersection of I-75 and US 36. The College features interconnected buildings which are handicapped-ready. Students enjoy the friendly atmosphere and benefit from small classes and a faculty committed to teaching and learning. A strong university-transfer program (first two years of a four-year degree) is available.

Hocking College
3301 Hocking College
Nelsonville, Ohio 45764
740-753-3591
800-282-4163
740-753-1452 fax
E-mail: admissions@hocking.edu
Website: www.hocking.edu

Hocking College offers many programs unique in Ohio including: ceramic, compressor, forestry, juvenile corrections, materials, and telecommunications. Hocking's culinary arts and hotel/restaurant management programs use the Quality Inn-Hocking Valley as a training facility. Travel/Tourism students gain valuable experience working at the Uniglobe Hocking Hills Travel Agency.

James A. Rhodes State College
4240 Campus Drive
Lima, Ohio 45804
419-995-8000
419-995-8098
E-mail: enroll@RhodesState.edu
Website: www.RhodesState.edu

Located on a 545-acre setting near Interstate 75 the campus features a library, bookstore, career planning center, food services, placement services and a day care center. Day, evening and weekend classes are offered, as well as telecourses and internet courses. Its campus is shared with Ohio State University—Lima.

Jefferson Community College
400 Sunset Boulevard
Steubenville, Ohio 43952
740-264-5591
800-682-6553
740-266-2944 fax
Website: www.jcc.edu

Opened for students in 1968, the college offers technical training in over 25 programs leading to one-year certificated and/or associate degrees. College programs include careers in: allied health, business technologies, engineering technologies, public services, and Associate of Technical Study program.

Lakeland Community College
7700 Clocktower Drive
Kirtland, Ohio 44094
440-953-7100
800-589-8520
440-975-4330 fax
E-mail: tcooper@lakelandcc.edu
Website: www.lakeland.cc.oh.us

Offers modern, state-of-the-art facilities on a beautiful 400-acre campus. Lakeland offers university parallel programs and has written transfer agreements with major colleges and universities across the state. In addition, the college offers 42 career and technical programs designed for immediate job placement.

Lorain County Community Colleges
1005 North Abbe Road
Elyria, Ohio 44035
800-995-5222
440-366-4167 fax
Website: www.loraincc.edu

A comprehensive community college offering university transfer programs in Arts and Sciences and career programs in business, engineering technologies, allied health and nursing, and the public services. LCCC offers the following degrees: Associate of Arts, Associate of Science, Associate of Individualized Studies, and Associate of Technical

Studies. In addition, 15 short-term certificate of proficiency programs are available.

Marion Technical College
1467 Mount Vernon Avenue
Marion, Ohio 43302-5694
740-389-4636
740-389-6136 fax
E-mail: enroll@mtc.etu
Website: www.mtc.edu

Located 40 miles north of Columbus, Ohio, on a 180-acre campus that is shared with Ohio State University at Marion. The college offers programs in business, engineering, health, public service, and personalized technologies.

Muskingum Area Technical College
1555 Newark Road
Zanesville, Ohio 43701
740-558-1225
800-686-8324
740-454-0035 fax
Website: www.matc.tec.oh.us

The 179-acre campus is shared with Ohio University-Zanesville. In addition, the campus features a 125-acre land laboratory and new engineering technology center located in the city's industrial park. The college also features a branch campus in Cambridge, Ohio.

North Central State College
2441 Kenwood Circle
PO Box 698
Mansfield, Ohio 44901
419-755-4761
888-755-4899
419-755-4750 fax
Website: www.ncstate.tec.oh.us

This institution offers 31 technical programs in the business, engineering, health, and public service technologies. Placement rates for graduates have averaged 95 percent over the last ten years.

Northwest State Community College
22600 St. Rt. 34
Archbold, Ohio 43502-9542
419-267-5511
419-267-5604 Fax
Website: www.nscc.cc.oh.us

A progressive, two-year, state-supported institution serving five counties in northwest Ohio. Approximately 2,000 students are enrolled in associate degree and certificate programs in the business, engineering, health, and human services technologies, and in a rapidly growing general studies division.

Owens Community College
Oregon Road, PO Box 10,000
Toledo, Ohio 43699-1947
419-429-3500
800-466-9367 ext. 7777

300 Davis Street
Findlay, Ohio 45840-3600
419-423-6827
800-346-3529
E-mail: admissions@owens.edu
Website: www.owens.edu

Owens Community College offers more than 50 career oriented technical degrees, as well as the first two years of a bachelor's degree at half the cost of a university. Day, evening, and weekend classes are offered at the Toledo and Findlay campuses. Programs are in business, arts and sciences, health, public service, industrial and engineering technologies.

Rio Grande Community College
Rio Grande, Ohio 45674
740-245-7425
800-282-7201 ext.7425
E-mail: rlthomas@rio.edu
Website: www.rio.edu

The college, established in 1974, offers a wide range of services including career programs, arts degree, transfer programs, and continuing education.

Sinclair Community College
444 West Third Street
Dayton, Ohio 45402-1460
937-512-3000
800-315-300
937-512-2393 fax

Public, two-year community college serving Montgomery County and the Miami Valley region. It offers both career programs that are technical in nature as well as university parallel programs which are designed for the student to transfer to a four-year college or university as a junior.

Southern State Community College
200 Hobart Drive
Hillsboro, Ohio 45133
937-393-3431
800-628-7722
937-393-6682 fax
E-mail: info@sscc.edu
Website: www.sscc.edu

The college has campuses in Hillsboro, Sardinia, and Wilmington in addition to an extension center in Washington Court House. Over 1,600 students are enrolled in a variety of technical and general studies majors. Placement rates for graduates approach 100 percent in many technical fields.

Extensive adult and developmental programs allow students to start classes at a level appropriate for their skill.

Stark State College of Technology
6200 Frank Avenue, N.W.
Canton, Ohio 44720
330-966-5454
330-494-6170
800-797-8275
330-497-6313 Fax
Website: www.stark.cc.oh.us

Offers two-year programs leading to associate degrees in business, engineering technology, allied health and public service.

Terra Community College
2830 Napoleon Road
Fremont, Ohio 43420
419-334-8400 ext. 149
866-288-3772
419-334-9035 fax
E-mail: info@terra.edu
Website: www.terra.edu

Terra Community College offers convenient day, evening, and weekend course scheduling, as well as support offices for 34 technical majors, 24 certificate programs, and specialized training programs. The two-year, coeducational, state-supported technical college extends educational opportunities to everyone with a high school diploma or the equivalent. Terra offers several hard-to-find programs such as graphic communications, nuclear power technology, welding technology, sign-language/ interpreting, technical communication, total quality management and industrial electricity.

Washington State Community College
710 Colegate Drive
Marietta, Ohio 45750
740-374-8716
740-376-0257 fax
Website: www.wscc.edu

A public, state-supported community college. Washington State offers both baccalaureate transfer programs and technical education programs. The associate of arts and associate of science degrees are designed for students who wish to complete their freshman and sophomore years of a bachelor's degree locally, then transfer to a four-year college or university to complete the junior and senior years. The technical education programs prepare graduates with knowledge and skills that can be applied to jobs in important sectors of today's knowledge-based economy.

Sources: Handbook of Ohio Colleges and Universities, 2002-2003; The Counselor's Guide to Ohio Independent Colleges and Universities, 2002-2003; Associate Degree Preferred, A Guide to Ohio's Two-Year Colleges, 2002-2003

Costs, Enrollments, Standardized Test Scores
Four Year Colleges and Universities

College and University	Tuition & Fees	Room & Board	Enrollment	Middle 50% or Average SAT	Middle 50% or Average ACT
The University of Akron	$5,621	$4,550-$6,591	24,101	1012	20.4
Antioch College	$28,000*		682	N/A	N/A
Art Academy of Cincinnati	$6,500	N/A	210	997-1327	18-25
Ashland University	$17,270	$6,212	2,194	880-1150	19-24
Baldwin-Wallace College	$17,732	$6,022	3,974	1030-1250	21-26
Bluffton College	$16,430	$5,636	976	1060	23
Bowling Green State University	$7,408	$6,102	20,276	1012	21.6
Capital University	$18,980	$5,950	2,708	960-1180	20-26
Case Western Reserve University	$22,500	$6,750	3,381	1240-1440	27-31
Cedarville University	$8,004	$4,572	2,378	910-1150	22-27
Central State University	$4,044	$5,727	1,400	826	17
Chatfield College	$6,600	N/A	304	N/A	N/A
University of Cincinnati	$6.936	$4,933	33,085	920-1200	17-26
Cincinnati Bible College & Seminary	$5,088	$3,400	683	N/A	N/A
Cincinnati College of Mortuary Science	$15,345 (99hr)	N/A	N/A	N/A	N/A
Circleville Bible College	$8,320	$4,840	228	N/A	N/A
Cleveland Institute of Art	$10,987	$3,770	618	N/A	N/A
Cleveland Institute of Music	$20,625	$3,975	365	N/A	N/A
Cleveland State University	$6,072	$5,196	15,746	982	21
Columbus College of Art and Design	$17,160	$6,300	1,737	950-1166	18-23
University of Dayton	$17,450	$5,600	6,617	1050-1280	22-28
The Defiance College	$16,360	$5,020	906	870-1150	19-24

The average 18- to 24-year-old college student will spend $842.66 for back-to-school merchandise, ranging from computers and clothing to room furnishings.

—Back-to-College Consumer Intentions and Actions Survey

421

College and University	Tuition & Fees	Room & Board	Enrollment	Middle 50% or Average SAT	Middle 50% or Average ACT
Denison University	$23,680	$6,880	2,107	1110-1310	25-29
The University of Findlay	$18,114	$6,790	3,381	890-1160	19-25
Franciscan University of Steubenville	$14,020	$5,200	1,733	1020-1240	21-27
Franklin University	$6,420	N/A	4,650	N/A	N/A
Heidelberg College	$12,850	$6,034	1,173	1037-1197	23-27
Hiram College	$19,650	$6,820	1,190	1020-1260	20-27
John Carroll University	$18,832	$6,564	3,508	1050-1230	21-26
Kent State University	$6,882	$5,150	22,828	1007	21
Kenyon College	$27,900	$4,690	1,587	1180-1380	27-31
Lake Erie College	$16,370	$5,700	607	1005	21
Lourdes College	$13,700	N/A	1,288	870-1110	18-22
Malone College	$13,910	$5,830	1,900	990-1200	20-26
Marietta College	$19,762	$5,774	1,241	1086	23
Mercy College of Northwest Ohio	$6,104	$1,600	287	N/A	20-25
Miami University	$8,425	$7,600	16,219	1140-1290	24-28
Mount Carmel College of Nursing	$5,000	$870**	355	N/A	N/A
College of Mount St. Joseph	$14,950	$5,570	2,071	880-1090	18-25
Mount Union College	$16,240	$5,070	2,368	920-1148	20-25
Mount Vernon Nazarene College	$12,810	$4,527	2,106	1060-1200	19-23
Muskingum College	$13,500	$5,600	1,579	920-1200	19-25
David N. Myers University	$10,380	N/A	1,094	N/A	N/A
Notre Dame College of Ohio	$15,552	$5,906	735	N/A	20.6
University of Northwestern Ohio	$7,200	$2,400	2,130	N/A	N/A
Oberlin College	$27,880	$6,830	2,840	1304-1412	27-32

College and University	Tuition & Fees	Room & Board	Enrollment	Middle 50% or Average SAT	Middle 50% or Average ACT
Ohio College of Podiatric Medicine	$19,000	N/A	291	N/A	N/A
Ohio Dominican University	$16,200	$5,370	2,297	N/A	17-23
Ohio Northern University		$5,805	2,366	1030-1270	22-28
Arts and Sciences	$23,310				
Business Administration	$23,310				
Engineering	$24,900				
Pharmacy	$26,220				
The Ohio State University	$6,624	$6,291	48,477	1060-1290	23-26
Ohio University	$7,128	$6,777	19,195	1040-1210	22-26
Ohio Wesleyan University	$24,000	$7,010	1,886	1100-1320	23-29
Otterbein College	$18,993	$5,727	2,551	N/A	20-26
Pontifical College Josephinum	$9,640	$5,660	N/A	N/A	N/A
University of Rio Grande	$8,736	$5,362	1,932	N/A	N/A
Shawnee State University	$8,694	$5,754	3,464	N/A	17-21
Tiffin University	$12,850	$5,700	1,299	N/A	N/A
The University of Toledo	$6,415	$6,630	20,313	N/A	21.44
The Union Institute & University	$7,224	N/A	652	N/A	N/A
Urbana University	$12,554	$5,140	1,358	N/A	19
Ursuline College	$15,750	$5,030	1,019	850-1130	18-24
Walsh College	$13,450	$6,120	1,401	N/A	19-24
Wilmington College	$16,128	$6,240	1,876	870-1030	18-23
Wittenberg University	$23,604	$6,062	2,221	912-1322	19-29
The College of Wooster	$23,840	$6,320	1,823	1070-1290	23-28
Wright State University	$5,472	$5,400	15,810	930-1140	19-25
Xavier University	$17,780	$7,090	4,006	1060-1280	23-28u
Youngstown State University	$4,996	$5,320	12,250	N/A	20.4

The total bill:

Four-year cost

at a public university

in Ohio*

Tuition & fees

$78,349

Tuition, room

& board

$105,639

*assumes 10% annual

inflation for tuition;

3% for room & board

* full and part-time graduate and undergraduate students
Sources: The Association of Independent Colleges and Universities; the Ohio Private College Admission Directors; Council of Admission Officers of the State Assisted Universities in Ohio

Ohioans spend more of their state and local tax dollars on public elementary and secondary education than they do for any other government function. With only about 6 to 8 percent of Ohio's public school funding coming from federal sources with an equal amount coming from the Ohio Lottery, the remaining amount comes almost equally from state and local sources.

Another recent source of local income may come in the form of school district income taxes, but most of the income is from property taxes, on both real estate and tangible personal property. The tangible personal property tax is paid only by businesses on their furniture and fixtures, machines, equipment, supplies and inventory. The general property tax is levied upon land and buildings in the district, with the exception of property owned by governmental, charitable, and religious institutions or property abated by the local government.

Property taxes are set by the county auditor when he sets the market value of all the property, real and tangible, in a school district. Taxes are levied against the *assessed* value of the property, which is a percentage of market value, fixed at 35%. The local tax rate is computed in mills (one-tenth of a penny) so that a mill produces $1.00 in tax income for every $1,000 of taxable property.

In 1976—because the tax burden was being shifted from businesses to homeowners in times of high inflation—the state passed House Bill 920. It provided that the assessed value of property would not change more than once every three years and that the tax bill of the average homeowner would not increase due to inflation. An adjustment would be made after each reappraisal so that if an owner's property increased in value at the same percentage as the average increase in the district, his taxes would remain the same. Property taxes would go up if the property value increased *more* than the district average, and would go down if the property decreased more than the average. In addition there would be a 10% rollback (12.5% for owner-occupied homesteads) on property taxes.

There are three different kinds of property tax issues schools offer: operating levies; permanent improvement levies; and bond issues. Operating levies raise the funds that pay for the day-to-day costs of the school system. Permanent improvement levies can last up to five years and are used to raise money only for construction or repair. A bond issue can be used only to retire bonds issued for permanent construction. It cannot be used to pay for day-to-day operating expenses.

The state guarantees a certain amount of aid per pupil. If a school cannot reach this level by levying 20 mills on its taxable property, the state will make up the difference and will provide a lesser amount on the next 10 mills. There is also a "school district equalization factor" that gives schools in high cost areas additional money (up to 7.5%). Generally, it works like this: the higher the district's equalization factor, the more money it will receive per pupil from the state; the lower the amount of taxable property the more money a district will receive from the state.

The ABC's Of Public School Revenues

"Call me Ishmael. Some years ago - never mind how long precisely - having little or no money in my purse, and nothing particular to interest me on shore, I thought I would sail about a little and see the watery part of the world...."

ISHMAEL: "So we're going looking for a fish...?"
AHAB: "A whale, actually..."
(LAUGHTER)
AHAB: "... a white whale."
(UPROARIOUS LAUGHTER)
ISHMAEL: "A white whale, huh? You're sure you don't mean Roseanne...?"
(MORE LAUGHTER. APPLAUSE.)

Most of the financial support for Ohio school districts comes from local property taxes, generally paid twice a year. There are two forms of property taxes: general property taxes and tangible personal property taxes. General property taxes are levied on land and building values located within the school district. Tangible personal property taxes are paid by companies, based upon the value of the furniture, fixtures, machinery, equipment, supplies, and inventory used in their businesses. Governmental, charitable, and religious organizations are exempt from these taxes.

Property tax rates are based on mills, a mill being one tenth of a penny. A mill produces $1 for every $1,000 of taxable property value.

There are two types of mills levied for the benefit of school districts:

(1) *Inside mills* can be levied without a vote of the people, up to a maximum of 10 mills. These mills are normally shared between schools, municipalities, and other government agencies (schools usually receive between four to six of these inside mills).

(2) *Outside mills* are mills that are approved by a vote of the residents. *Effective mills* is a name given to outside mills that have been reduced when property values are reassessed due to inflation. This reduction prevents an automatic tax increase to the property owner due to inflationary property value increases. The effect is that less than 100% of the voted mills are applied to the re-appraised value of the property. The mills actually assessed are called *effective mills*. While district voters may have voted 40 mills for the schools, only 30 "effective" mills may be being collected. This reduction ceases when a

district reaches the 20 mill floor.

Once every six years, the county auditor is required to conduct a complete reappraisal of all property in the county. Once the market value has been determined, it is multiplied by the assessment rate (currently 35%) to calculate the assessed value for tax purposes. Thus, a house that has a market value of $100,000 would be assessed for tax purposes at $35,000. Both the owner and the school district can challenge the valuation to the Board of Revision and ask for an adjustment.

An example of a homeowner's property tax bill, assuming a countywide reappraisal increase of 10%, and an individual home increase of 15% is as follows:

	Year 1	Year 2 Reappraisal Year
Market Value	$100,000	$115,000
Assessed Value	$ 35,000	$ 40,250
Inside Mills	5.00	5.00
Outside Mills	25.00	22.73
Tax Bill:		
Inside Mills	$ 175.00	$ 201.25
Outside Mills	875.00	914.88
Total	$1,050.00	$1,116.13
Rollback (12.5%)	131.25	139.52
Net	$918.75	$976.61

Note that the reduction in outside mills is based on the countywide reappraisal of 10%, not on the individual property increase of 15%. The 15% increase in appraised value on the property resulted in an increase of only 6.3% for the property owner (because of the nature of the effective mills).

There are three types of property tax issues that a board of education may put before voters:

(1) *Operating levy.* The proceeds from an operating levy can be used for any legal expenditure by the board of education. These pay for the day-to-day expenses of running a school district and can also be used for building construction and facility improvements. Regular operating levies are requested in mills and can be either continuing (permanent) or temporary (for a period of up to five years).

Emergency operating levies are requested for a fixed amount of money annually and the millage is adjusted to collect only that amount. An emergency levy may be requested for a period of up to five years. It expires after the initial period of time unless the voters approve its renewal. Operating levies may also be requested in increments in which the amount of mills can change up to five different times in ten years. Another type of operating levy is a replacement levy. This levy is for the same purpose and the original millage of the levy it replaces. It normally raises more money than the expiring levy as it eliminates any reductions that have occurred due to reappraisal adjustments, which may have decreased the original mills to a lower effective rate.

(2) *Permanent improvement levy.*

Permanent improvement levies can only be used to construct, add to, or repair buildings and facilities (permanent improvements). Generally considered for items lasting five or more years, the funds cannot be used to pay operating costs. A permanent improvement levy can be requested for a continuing period of time or for a temporary period of up to five years.

(3) *Bond issue.*

Proceeds from a bond issue can only be used to retire bonds or notes issued by the board of education. The bonds can only be issued to pay the cost of permanent improvements and are the usual way most school districts pay for the cost of school construction and renovation.

Since 1989, in addition to property taxes, schools may collect income taxes on individuals who live in the district. The taxes may be used for any purpose for which property taxes are used. The taxes must be levied in increments of .25% and do not apply to corporations or non-residents working for businesses in the district. The income taxes may be combined with income taxes of local municipalities.

State Funding

In 1998, the state passed a "cost-based" model for school funding in which the state's contribution for funding education is determined. The state determines the amount of

OHIO'S SAT SCORES

Academic Record	Number of Students	Percent	Verbal	Math
A+ (97-100)	3,349	11%	622	638
A (93 - 96)	6,251	21%	580	592
B (80 - 89)	5,216	17%	553	563
C (70 - 79)	12,551	41%	502	503
D or F (below 70)	83	0%	422	418
HIgh School Rank				
Top Tenth	7,158	26%	607	623
Second Tenth	6,111	22%	551	562
Second Fifth	7,117	26%	515	521
Third Fifth	5,806	21%	474	473
Fourth Ffth	911	3%	440	437
Fift Fifth	172	1%	429	421
Senior Class Size				
750-1,000	329	1%	515	538
500-749	1,955	6%	527	539
250-499	13,221	41%	537	547
100-249	12,967	40%	528	531
Under `00	3,546	11%	554	553

Mean GPA, All Students: 3.38

Type of School				
Public	23,284	73%	530	539
Religous	7,831	24%	541	538
Independent	853	3%	603	614
Location				
Large City	5,316	17%	513	509
Medium Size City	3,486	11%	529	529
Town	4,988	16%	543	549
Suburb	16,465	51%	540	550
Rural	1,843	6%	537	541

by the numbers

From 1999 to 2002 about 62% of Ohio's students took the ACT test. The composite score each year was 21.4, about .4 above the national average.

" AND IF I EVER CATCH YOU DOWNLOADING DIRTY PICTURES FROM THE INTERNET AGAIN, YOUNG MAN, I'LL WASH YOUR MOUSE OUT WITH SOAP! "

basic education funding it believes is necessary for each student in Ohio. It then determines how much of this "foundation" is funded by the state and how much is funded locally. Through a complex process of comparing school districts of different financial levels and of different levels of achievement, the state determines a formula amount, which it considers to be a reasonable amount to educate every child in the state system. Because costs of services differ around the state, a "Cost of Doing Business" (CDB) index is applied to this funding. This per pupil funding amount is applied to the district's "Average Daily Membership" (ADM).

The state reduces the formula amount by the local share (called the charge off) that is determined by taking the total assessed property value within the district times 23 mills. That amount is subtracted from the state's basic aid calculation to arrive at the state's contribution. The effect is that the greater the value of the property in a district the less the state contributes to the foundation amount.

Districts may qualify for additional state funding called categorical aid. Categorical aid includes the following areas: Special Education, Gifted Education, Vocational Education, Disadvantaged Pupil Impact Aid, Transportation, Catastrophic Costs, Parity Aid.

In Ohio, local taxes are the source of about half of each school district's operating funds. The state accounts for about 44% while the federal government contributes about 6% (mainly through low income and special education programs). State law requires districts to spend at least 3% of their operating revenues for instructional materials and 3% for maintenance and capital improvements. Salaries and health insurance costs for the typical school district amounts to approximately 80 to 85 percent of total expenditures.

—Richard Gardner, Treasurer, Mason City Schools

State Board of Education

25 South Front Street
Columbus, Ohio 43215
614-466-4838
Website: www.ode.state.oh.us

The State Board of Education was created in 1956 to supervise public education in the State of Ohio, according to the acts of the General Assembly. One member from each of Ohio's congressional districts is elected to serve on the board through a non-partisan ballot. Terms are for six years. The board officially meets four times a year, once in January, April, July, and October, but special meetings may be called as necessary.

Board powers are outlined in the Ohio Revised Code and fall into three categories—leadership, regulatory, and administrative. Leadership powers give the board the ability to initiate special programs aimed at improving the quality of the educational system in general or some specific aspect (i.e., initiating special programs for gifted children). Regulatory powers allow the board to prescribe minimum standards for elementary and secondary schools (i.e., adopting standards for the education of handicapped children). Through the administrative powers, the board oversees the allocation and distribution of all state and federal funds for public education in Ohio.

Guaranteed Tuition Program and College Savings Bond Program

800-233-6734
Website: www.collegeadvantage.com

Since 1989, the Ohio Tuition Trust Authority, a state agency, has offered an affordable way to help Ohio families save for a college education through the Guaranteed Savings Fund. The Tuition Trust now offers additional market-based college savings options along with the original guaranteed option to form the CollegeAdvantage 529 Savings Plan.

CollegeAdvantage is offered and administered by the Ohio Tuition Trust Authority. The variable investment options of CollegeAdvantage are managed by Putnam Investment Management, LLC, and distributed by Putnam Retail Management.

Education
by the
numbers

School Districts

City School Districts 192
Exempted Village Districts 49
Local Districts.. 372
Joint Vocational Districts 49
Non-Public 14
Total *676*

Public Schools

Senior High Schools 807
Junior High Schools 121
Middle Schools 577
Elementary Schools 2,349
Adult Schools 6
Vocational Schools 12
Special Needs Schools... 47
Vocational Postsecondary 19
Technical Postsecondary 1
Total *3,939*

Nonpublic Schools

High Schools 167
Junior High Schools 4
Middle Schools 7
Elementary Schools 793
Special Needs Schools.. 5
Total 976

Enrollment

Total, Grades K-6 .... *946,231*
Total, Grades 7-8 .... *286,542*
Total, Grades 9-12 .... *544,264*

Ethnicity

African American 301,348 (16.5%)
Asian 21,426 (1.2%)
Hispanic 22,442 (1.8%)
American Indian 2,282 (0.1%)
Multi-racial 26,856 (1.5%)
White 1,445,281 (78.9%)

Pupil: Teacher Ratio (regular classroom) .... 14 : 6
Percentage Dropout Rate 5.2%
Percentage of Pupils in Average
Daily Attendance 94.3%
Graduation Rate.. 82.6%
Percentage of Students Enrolled in
College Prep Classes 60.6%

Staff

Average Teacher Salary $45,636
Average Teacher Experience (years) 14.6

Public School Operating Costs

Statewide Average per Student Served
Expenditure Per Pupil.................................... $7,589
  City $8,096
  Exempted Village $7,040
  Local $6,858

Source: State Board of Education of Ohio

One of every 20 children in Ohio— 5.2 percent of the children in the state— is growing up in a working-poor family, which means a family wherein at least one parent worked 50 or more weeks without making an income above the official poverty level. If you are this family of three, your maximum annual gross income is $1,000 monthly.

—Kids Count Data Book, the Annie E. Casey Foundation

NOSTALGIA MOVIES get REAL...

WARD, I'M WORRIED ABOUT THE BEAVER.

An Ohio glossary

School District—*a political subdivision and state agency created by the Ohio General Assembly to provide education via a public school system*

Board of Education— *a body of representatives elected in each school district to overlapping, four-year terms who are charged with (1) hiring a school superintendent, teachers, and staff; (2) providing equipment; (3) and overseeing school administration. This body may put tax levies and bond issues on the ballot in order to provide adequate funding to operate the schools.*

School District by County	Enrollment	Per Pupil Spending	Expenditures Instruction (%)	Admin. (%)	Average Teachers Salary	4-year Report Card*
Adams County						
Adams County/Ohio Valley Local	4,914	$7,681	55.6	10.7	$35,197	32
Allen County						
Allen East Local	1,082	$6,464	53.2	13.3	$37,112	74
Bath Local	1,977	$6,988	53.0	12.4	$42,966	75
Bluffton Ex Village	1,159	$6,591	55.4	10.8	$41,453	83
Delphos City	1,125	$6,837	55.5	12.1	$39,673	73
Elida Local	2,641	$6,505	57.4	12.6	$39,555	70
Lima City	5,514	$8,651	57.7	13.1	$37,654	27
Perry Local	820	$7,512	53.6	13.1	$38,709	59
Shawnee Local	2,469	$7,149	46.6	14.7	$40,483	84
Spencerville Local	1,036	$6,442	54.4	12.1	$37,845	78
Ashland County						
Ashland City	3,791	$7,361	60.8	11.3	$43,543	65
Hillsdale Local	1,156	$6,854	57.1	11.7	$42,393	71
Loudonville-Perrysville Ex Vil	1,341	$7,673	54.4	11.6	$40,997	72
Mapleton Local	1,042	$6,527	56.2	12.6	$38,980	64
Ashtabula County						
Ashtabula Area City	4,744	$7,707	61.5	10.5	$41,826	34
Buckeye Local	2,222	$7,590	58.9	11.4	$40,784	58
Conneaut Area City	2,469	$6,780	58.7	11.0	$44,141	49
Geneva Area City	3,123	$6,242	57.0	8.6	$46,306	54
Grand Valley Local	1,395	$6,219	54.9	12.1	$39,893	54
Jefferson Area Local	2,197	$6,375	55.2	15.1	$42,116	65
Pymatuning Valley Local	1,442	$7,000	55.5	14.6	$40,953	49

School District by County	Enrollment	Per Pupil Spending	Expenditures Instruction (%)	Admin. (%)	Average Teachers Salary	4-year Report Card*
Athens County						
Alexander Local	1,609	$6,762	56.0	12.2	$35,603	48
Athens City	2,892	$8,608	57.3	9.4	$39,413	73
Federal Hocking Local	1,409	$7,492	55.7	11.8	$34,921	35
Nelsonville-York City	1,320	$7,965	52.7	11.9	$37,804	51
Trimble Local	997	$8,249	59.3	10.2	$39,260	42
Augalize County						
Minster Local	917	$7,720	61.7	12.0	$45,283	94
New Bremen Local	951	$6,875	56.3	12.5	$44,049	98
New Knoxville Local	448	$7,134	52.1	16.7	$33,959	94
St Marys City	2,523	$6,867	57.8	9.7	$40,199	80
Wapakoneta City	3,188	$6,786	51.7	9.3	$41,263	73
Waynesfield-Goshen Local	588	$7,211	52.8	16.8	$36,243	67
Belmont County						
Barnesville Ex Village	1,349	$7,596	54.6	14.4	$38,065	53
Bellaire City	1,596	$8,336	53.9	11.3	$40,665	49
Bridgeport Ex Village	803	$7,150	60.0	11.0	$34,291	38
Martins Ferry City	1,481	$6,599	60.7	10.2	$36,725	70
Shadyside Local	904	$6,472	55.9	13.0	$38,403	71
St Clairsville-Richland City	1,727	$6,807	57.4	11.9	$40,575	73
Union Local	1,570	$7,020	58.3	9.0	$35,444	48
Brown County						
Eastern Local	1,429	$6,813	54.7	11.1	$40,037	59
Fayetteville-Perry Local	953	$6,105	49.8	14.5	$33,313	59
Georgetown Ex Village	1,173	$6,412	55.0	14.0	$37,867	65
Ripley-Union-Lewis-Huntington	1,388	$7,327	50.2	12.8	$33,847	52
Western Brown Local	3,152	$6,474	56.6	10.4	$38,505	46
Butler County						
Edgewood City	3,136	$6,805	55.7	10.6	$41,058	70
Fairfield City	8,346	$6,895	56.1	9.9	$43,791	73
Hamilton City	9,444	$7,589	57.2	8.7	$40,638	48
Lakota Local	14,380	$7,221	54.1	10.9	$43,397	92
Madison Local	1,514	$6,812	51.8	11.7	$34,408	70
Middletown City	7,296	$8,514	53.4	13.3	$41,984	37
Monroe	1,381	$5,643	72.3	7.1	$40,236	33
New Miami Local	867	$7,701	57.2	13.6	$41,030	32
Ross Local	2,456	$6,743	56.5	13.0	$42,765	85
Talawanda City	3,194	$7,121	54.4	9.5	$51,189	59
Carroll County						
Brown Local	931	$7,563	58.5	12.8	$38,261	54
Carrollton Ex Village	2,977	$5,836	54.2	10.4	$43,147	59
Champaign County						
Graham Local	2,133	$6,592	55.8	10.0	$42,270	68
Mechanicsburg Ex Village	806	$6,452	52.8	13.8	$35,020	61
Triad Local	1,045	$7,111	52.7	14.6	$37,550	56
Urbana City	2,306	$7,112	56.0	12.4	$41,960	50
West Liberty-Salem Local	1,127	$7,266	49.9	14.7	$40,982	76
Clark County						
Clark-Shawnee Local	2,441	$6,568	56.6	13.3	$46,880	77
Mad River-Green Local	1,985	$6,463	51.4	13.7	$37,953	71
Northeastern Local	3,395	$6,483	55.5	11.5	$41,939	66
Northwestern Local	1,867	$6,488	57.7	10.9	$39,790	76

City District— a school district whose territory usually, but not always, corresponds to the corporate limits of a city

Exempted Village District—a school district whose territory lies within the corporate limits of a village exempted from direction by the county district

Local District— a district whose territory is not within any corporate limits, but is generally within the boundaries of a county

County District— a school district that supervises and serves local school districts within a county.

431

School District by County	Enrollment	Per Pupil Spending	Expenditures Instruction (%)	Admin. (%)	Average Teachers Salary	4-year Report Card*
Southeastern Local	794	$6,944	55.0	14.8	$40,755	80
Springfield City	9,756	$8,643	53.6	12.0	$41,656	18
Tecumseh Local	3,586	$7,387	53.4	12.4	$43,098	52
Clermont County						
Batavia Local	1,713	$7,373	54.3	12.6	$43,569	64
Bethel-Tate Local	1,853	$5,688	57.8	15.3	$43,064	67
Clermont-Northeastern Local	1,928	$6,567	49.6	12.9	$41,106	56
Felicity-Franklin Local	1,204	$7,321	58.8	11.4	$40,525	52
Goshen Local	2,441	$7,191	49.5	19.5	$40,374	44
Milford Ex Village	5,604	$7,130	51.2	10.6	$44,637	88
New Richmond Ex Village	2,487	$9,255	52.3	11.8	$49,906	60
West Clermont Local	9,066	$6,171	60.8	9.4	$47,458	63
Williamsburg Local	1,054	$6,469	56.9	12.2	$41,210	48
Clinton County						
Blanchester Local	1,667	$6,258	51.6	12.5	$36,727	64
Clinton-Massie Local	1,582	$5,907	53.4	10.9	$36,901	74
East Clinton Local	1,481	$6,404	51.2	13.0	$35,492	51
Wilmington City	3,105	$5,895	62.8	10.0	$43,096	56
Columbiana County						
Beaver Local	2,408	$6,299	59.4	11.2	$37,012	58
Columbiana Ex Village	998	$7,097	57.7	14.2	$39,426	85
Crestview Local	1,101	$7,246	53.2	11.4	$37,774	72
East Liverpool City	3,133	$8,311	58.3	8.9	$40,458	30
East Palestine City	1,528	$6,398	54.0	9.6	$40,739	71
Leetonia Ex Village	895	$6,297	57.1	12.9	$37,707	66
Lisbon Ex Village	1,187	$6,047	57.8	12.2	$40,649	66
Salem City	2,475	$7,725	55.5	13.2	$41,346	70
Southern Local	841	$7,634	57.0	13.1	$32,128	57
United Local	1,436	$6,492	59.9	9.6	$41,426	71
Wellsville Local	1,022	$7,416	58.1	13.4	$37,897	60
Coshocton County						
Coshocton City	1,981	$6,872	56.8	12.2	$56,994	54
Ridgewood Local	1,460	$6,924	57.5	10.5	$36,150	65
River View Local	2,664	$7,201	51.2	12.1	$42,496	60
Crawford County						
Buckeye Central Local	521	$8,070	53.7	15.1	$36,081	70
Bucyrus City	1,768	$7,912	50.8	13.6	$36,432	57
Colonel Crawford Local	1,012	$7,420	55.3	13.8	$37,637	75
Crestline Ex Village	896	$9,135	50.7	13.8	$37,629	46
Galion City	2,207	$7,334	59.5	11.5	$39,789	48
Wynford Local	1,114	$7,076	55.1	11.4	$37,251	71
Cuyahoga County						
Bay Village City	2,229	$9,622	51.8	13.5	$49,269	101
Beachwood City	1,551	$17,590	49.6	14.4	$59,028	100
Bedford City	3,843	$10,358	48.8	11.4	$48,510	42
Berea City	7,727	$9,514	52.3	10.9	$44,790	74
Brecksville-Broadview Heights	4,075	$8,425	53.7	10.1	$51,702	103
Brooklyn City	1,328	$9,207	52.0	17.9	$44,211	52
Chagrin Falls Ex Village	1,862	$9,430	52.6	11.3	$49,513	102
Cleveland City	72,277	$10,352	53.9	10.5	$43,345	10
Cleveland Hts-Univ Hts City	6,891	$11,991	49.9	12.6	$53,674	44
Cuyahoga Heights Local	791	$16,340	44.3	14.1	$63,450	100
East Cleveland City	5,653	$10,400	57.0	14.6	$49,782	13

"OK, I'LL MOVE BALLET BACK AN HOUR, RESCHEDULE GYMNASTICS, and CANCEL PIANO...YOU SHIFT YOUR VIOLIN LESSON TO THURSDAY and SKIP SOCCER PRACTICE......THAT GIVES US FROM 3:15 TO 3:45 ON WEDNESDAY THE 16TH TO PLAY."

School District by County	Enrollment	Per Pupil Spending	Expenditures Instruction (%)	Admin. (%)	Average Teachers Salary	4-year Report Card*
Euclid City	6,051	$9,443	52.7	12.0	$47,366	36
Fairview Park City	1,857	$9,957	54.7	10.2	$50,713	80
Garfield Heights City	3,394	$8,116	51.1	12.9	$47,804	41
Independence Local	1,025	$11,619	52.5	12.0	$51,299	94
Lakewood City	7,121	$9,670	60.6	7.4	$49,265	72
Maple Heights City	3,799	$7,982	42.9	28.9	$40,946	30
Mayfield City	4,110	$10,387	52.2	10.3	$57,959	99
North Olmsted City	4,592	$9,076	58.4	11.3	$50,182	80
North Royalton City	4,221	$8,254	53.2	11.2	$51,069	96
Olmsted Falls City	3,015	$8,610	54.1	12.0	$47,955	102
Orange City	2,284	$13,556	52.8	11.2	$59,306	99
Parma City	12,698	$9,028	53.8	11.4	$49,150	68
Richmond Heights Local	1,034	$9,052	53.3	12.6	$49,641	71
Rocky River City	2,384	$9,236	55.1	12.2	$50,040	97
Shaker Heights City	5,497	$12,365	51.2	12.5	$59,095	74
Solon City	4,908	$9,909	57.1	9.8	$55,001	102
South Euclid-Lyndhurst City	4,212	$10,965	54.7	11.0	$48,065	73
Strongsville City	6,824	$8,815	59.1	12.0	$48,175	91
Warrensville Heights City	2,967	$10,761	55.2	14.7	$52,171	32
Westlake City	3,546	$10,125	56.2	10.0	$54,004	101
Darke County						
Ansonia Local	705	$7,995	50.7	12.3	$33,275	62
Arcanum Butler Local	1,181	$6,460	59.8	10.4	$40,396	76
Franklin-Monroe Local	711	$6,934	53.4	12.2	$42,069	89
Greenville City	3,374	$6,714	61.4	13.0	$40,108	67
Mississinawa Valley Local	721	$8,024	51.8	12.5	$34,272	59
Tri-Village Local	774	$7,756	53.6	11.4	$37,255	47
Versailles Ex Village	1,395	$6,277	57.2	12.4	$44,551	82

Attendance Rate for Ohio's Public Schools

K	94.2%
I	94.9%
2	95.5%
3	95.7%
4	95.7%
5	95.5%
6	94.8%
7	93.0%
8	92.4%
9	89.6%
I0	90.6%
I I	91.2%
I2	91.2%

School District by County	Enrollment	Per Pupil Spending	Expenditures Instruction (%)	Admin. (%)	Average Teachers Salary	4-year Report Card*
Defiance County						
Ayersville Local	885	$6,874	58.1	12.2	$44,725	89
Central Local	1,143	$7,495	53.9	14.5	$39,213	76
Defiance City	2,563	$7,165	58.3	11.4	$41,640	75
Hicksville Ex Village	953	$6,652	59.0	12.0	$37,960	80
Northeastern Local	1,141	$7,197	56.1	11.8	$38,629	83
Delaware County						
Big Walnut Local	2,570	$7,364	58.6	11.3	$42,227	70
Buckeye Valley Local	2,166	$7,398	53.4	12.3	$45,183	65
Delaware City	4,080	$8,363	55.4	9.7	$44,237	53
Olentangy Local	5,745	$7,902	53.1	11.1	$42,063	69
Erie County						
Berlin-Milan Local	1,755	$7,277	53.9	15.6	$39,137	85
Huron City	1,498	$8,934	46.7	11.0	$41,006	81
Margaretta Local	1,489	$7,161	52.2	11.9	$50,437	70
Perkins Local	2,123	$8,538	52.3	10.6	$47,258	90
Sandusky City	4,347	$8,712	59.0	10.7	$43,310	37
Vermilion Local	2,426	$8,083	49.7	9.6	$40,608	71
Fairfield County						
Amanda-Clearcreek Local	1,537	$6,541	57.6	10.6	$39,869	66
Berne Union Local	964	$6,703	50.6	12.9	$39,670	66
Bloom-Carroll Local	1,413	$7,152	53.0	15.2	$38,408	75
Fairfield Union Local	1,800	$6,797	55.1	11.8	$42,222	72
Lancaster City	5,832	$8,092	57.7	11.6	$46,050	55
Liberty Union-Thurston Local	1,301	$7,320	56.1	12.5	$44,445	84
Pickerington Local	7,372	$7,430	55.9	12.2	$48,455	102
Walnut Township Local	718	$6,435	54.0	14.8	$39,011	69
Fayette County						
Miami Trace Local	2,708	$7,522	47.3	15.2	$35,229	58
Washington Court House City	2,213	$6,648	55.8	11.5	$37,957	66
Franklin County						
Bexley City	2,246	$10,177	61.6	10.2	$58,486	100
Canal Winchester Local	2,078	$7,330	52.0	12.8	$38,031	77
Columbus City	63,630	$9,921	52.3	12.6	$48,103	19
Dublin City	11,100	$9,939	51.9	8.1	$48,880	91
Gahanna-Jefferson City	6,349	$8,129	62.3	12.0	$53,654	80
Grandview Heights City	1,232	$10,628	57.8	10.7	$50,270	99
Groveport Madison Local	5,762	$8,625	53.2	11.3	$50,433	44
Hamilton Local	2,639	$7,332	51.7	19.9	$36,521	39
Hilliard City	12,341	$8,366	57.5	10.6	$44,686	78
Plain Local	1,938	$9,106	46.8	16.4	$43,123	94
Reynoldsburg City	5,648	$7,321	56.5	12.8	$47,381	93
South-Western City	19,009	$7,533	52.8	12.4	$45,452	53
Upper Arlington City	5,399	$10,750	57.9	10.1	$54,540	99
Westerville City	12,994	$7,696	59.3	11.2	$53,104	80
Whitehall City	2,831	$7,723	57.7	13.2	$44,719	41
Worthington City	9,977	$9,953	57.0	11.9	$51,170	95
Fulton County						
Archbold-Area Local	1,431	$7,799	58.4	9.2	$42,821	91
Evergreen Local	1,269	$7,950	56.7	11.1	$40,418	67
Gorham Fayette Local	448	$8,738	51.3	20.3	$39,880	55
Pettisville Local	542	$7,358	53.0	12.1	$39,797	91

"OH, THAT'S MR. VINNY.... HE'S BEEN HERE IN FOURTH GRADE SINCE THE SCHOOL BOARD ENDED SOCIAL PROMOTION."

School District by County	Enrollment	Per Pupil Spending	Expenditures Instruction (%)	Admin. (%)	Average Teachers Salary	4-year Report Card*
Pike-Delta-York Local	1,574	$8,182	53.7	10.6	$42,466	65
Swanton Local	1,559	$7,408	57.2	12.1	$41,449	65
Wauseon Ex Village	1,980	$6,112	57.5	9.6	$41,395	79
Gallia County						
Gallia County Local	2,707	$7,202	57.1	9.3	$37,248	38
Gallipolis City	2,372	$7,136	59.3	10.8	$38,893	44
Greene County						
Berkshire Local	1,376	$8,039	50.5	11.6	$44,562	80
Cardinal Local	1,380	$8,860	53.2	11.1	$45,279	75
Chardon Local	2,947	$7,527	52.1	12.3	$45,780	98
Kenston Local	3,026	$8,351	53.6	10.5	$50,381	100
Ledgemont Local	608	$7,395	52.7	13.6	$40,993	63
Newbury Local	750	$8,913	52.6	14.0	$41,891	86
West Geauga Local	2,473	$8,307	50.4	12.5	$45,698	98
Greene County						
Beavercreek City	6,540	$7,526	56.9	9.4	$48,213	90
Cedar Cliff Local	622	$7,506	49.7	13.2	$44,584	87
Fairborn City	5,458	$7,341	58.3	10.4	$42,952	45
Greeneview Local	1,535	$6,532	52.4	14.7	$37,935	55
Sugarcreek Local	2,480	$7,430	49.8	10.3	$42,560	86
Xenia Community City	4,959	$7,852	51.6	14.1	$41,405	46
Yellow Springs Ex Village	630	$9,240	57.3	15.8	$42,847	85
Guernsey County						
Cambridge City	2,585	$7,351	60.5	12.6	$42,437	46
East Guernsey Local	1,167	$7,257	53.9	12.0	$37,881	57
Rolling Hills Local	2,078	$6,845	52.8	12.9	$40,684	45

The top ten

The counties ranked highest in how effectively they improve the quality of life for poor children, 1990-1993:

1. *Warren*
2. *Knox*
3. *Wyandot*
4. *Delaware*
5. *Coshocton*
6. *Ashland*
7. *Union*
8. *Medina*
9. *Defiance*
10. *Mercer*

The bottom ten:

79. *Sandusky*
80. *Logan*
81. *Stark*
82. *Jefferson*
83. *Summit*
84. *Franklin*
85. *Lucas*
86. *Clark*
87. *Pike*
88. *Cuyahoga*

—*Children's Defense Fund*

JIM BORGMAN
CINCINNATI ENQUIRER ©1997

Buddy's CARPET BARN ELEMENTARY SCHOOL

"DIDN'T YOU HEAR?.. WHEN THE SALES TAX HIKE AND LOCAL LEVIES GOT SHOT DOWN, THE SCHOOL BOARD DECIDED TO SELL NAMING RIGHTS."

For the third consecutive year, St. Xavier High in Cincinnati is Ohio's No. 1 school in the production of National Merit semifinalists. The Catholic all-boys school had 28 semifinalists in 2003. In 2002, the school had 32 and averages 24 semifinalists a year.

School District by County	Enrollment	Per Pupil Spending	Expenditures Instruction (%)	Admin. (%)	Average Teachers Salary	4-year Report Card*
Hamilton County						
Cincinnati City	40,167	$9,983	61.4	11.9	$49,474	24
Deer Park Community City	1,465	$8,221	53.1	13.1	$44,655	68
Finneytown Local	1,806	$8,331	57.8	12.7	$44,135	73
Forest Hills Local	7,363	$7,358	59.6	9.6	$48,644	100
Indian Hill Ex Village	2,185	$10,250	52.9	10.2	$50,222	102
Lockland City	640	$12,875	42.6	14.0	$43,467	51
Loveland City	3,777	$7,170	56.3	10.3	$44,182	93
Madeira City	1,429	$8,370	55.9	10.3	$47,654	103
Mariemont City	1,645	$9,557	54.2	11.1	$47,209	102
Mount Healthy City	3,778	$7,938	56.0	10.0	$44,232	38
North College Hill City	1,541	$6,521	55.8	12.2	$39,374	47
Northwest Local	9,976	$7,504	56.4	10.7	$45,309	64
Norwood City	2,907	$8,149	59.8	10.6	$45,779	51
Oak Hills Local	7,728	$6,652	59.8	10.3	$47,269	86
Princeton City	6,229	$11,051	49.9	11.9	$44,401	50
Reading Community City	1,165	$8,573	56.5	12.8	$44,594	67
Southwest Local	3,830	$6,891	55.9	11.8	$46,430	69
St. Bernard-Elmwood Place City	1,142	$9,053	52.5	13.5	$48,653	50
Sycamore Community City	5,754	$11,360	53.9	11.4	$55,701	101
Three Rivers Local	2,070	$7,916	56.1	14.8	$47,118	78
Winton Woods City	4,144	$8,644	55.2	13.0	$46,986	49
Wyoming City	1,896	$9,045	60.9	10.7	$47,806	103
Hancock County						
Arcadia Local	612	$7,241	52.3	13.3	$35,729	82
Arlington Local	652	$7,036	55.1	12.2	$38,390	84
Cory-Rawson Local	757	$7,622	53.1	14.9	$39,112	73
Findlay City	5,933	$8,143	58.8	9.3	$44,265	71
Liberty-Benton Local	1,258	$6,381	53.3	10.7	$35,362	73
McComb Local	829	$7,299	56.5	12.9	$33,236	57
Van Buren Local	863	$6,976	56.1	14.3	$38,134	84
Vanlue Local	313	$7,922	47.1	17.3	$27,760	60

School District by County	Enrollment	Per Pupil Spending	Expenditures Instruction (%)	Admin. (%)	Average Teachers Salary	4-year Report Card*
Hardin County						
Ada Ex Village	825	$7,069	55.5	13.1	$35,961	75
Hardin Northern Local	520	$6,877	50.8	19.3	$36,033	65
Kenton City	2,112	$7,374	61.0	11.7	$39,221	60
Ridgemont Local	584	$7,029	51.1	13.7	$32,016	64
Riverdale Local	1,030	$6,867	51.4	15.8	$34,342	57
Upper Scioto Valley Local	732	$7,434	53.7	17.5	$33,388	54
Harrison County						
Conotton Valley Union Local	530	$7,219	52.8	15.0	$28,153	59
Harrison Hills City	1,968	$6,816	58.2	12.7	$35,400	58
Henry County						
Holgate Local	514	$7,942	58.5	14.5	$38,379	84
Liberty Center Local	1,105	$6,411	55.8	12.9	$37,023	69
Napoleon Area City	2,225	$7,520	55.7	14.1	$38,651	84
Patrick Henry Local	1,128	$8,154	57.1	13.3	$38,445	85
Highland County						
Bright Local	855	$7,025	49.8	13.2	$33,081	41
Fairfield Local	732	$6,887	51.8	15.7	$36,159	57
Greenfield Ex Village	2,177	$7,105	58.3	10.1	$38,346	51
Hillsboro City	2,648	$6,727	54.0	12.8	$39,303	47
Lynchburg-Clay Local	1,248	$6,593	48.8	14.8	$35,368	49
Hocking County						
Logan-Hocking Local	4,096	$6,546	53.3	11.9	$37,298	50
Holmes County						
East Holmes Local	1,800	$7,182	58.5	12.1	$38,510	78
West Holmes Local	2,781	$6,433	54.6	13.1	$39,227	77
Huron County						
Bellevue City	2,240	$7,269	53.5	11.3	$40,397	61
Monroeville Local	665	$7,229	53.3	14.8	$35,630	66
New London Local	1,158	$7,503	59.7	10.5	$40,948	63
Norwalk City	2,598	$5,780	56.7	13.5	$41,182	59
South Central Local	879	$7,061	51.9	12.7	$35,645	65
Western Reserve Local	1,230	$7,699	56.8	10.3	$39,592	53
Willard City	2,173	$6,927	54.4	12.1	$40,388	60
Jackson County						
Jackson City	2,725	$6,284	57.5	12.1	$38,181	55
Oak Hill Union Local	1,235	$6,845	52.5	13.2	$35,886	43
Wellston City	1,727	$6,483	60.7	10.9	$36,753	28
Jefferson County						
Buckeye Local	2,480	$6,916	56.9	11.8	$35,634	60
Edison Local	2,589	$6,941	56.1	10.4	$37,100	66
Indian Creek Local	2,152	$7,207	54.3	12.7	$35,282	76
Steubenville City	2,439	$7,122	64.1	10.8	$41,406	56
Toronto City	958	$7,148	51.5	13.1	$32,318	57
Knox County						
Centerburg Local	1,023	$6,475	60.3	15.6	$40,209	83
Danville Local	638	$7,597	57.0	11.0	$30,713	67
East Knox Local	1,075	$6,165	54.6	12.3	$35,794	84
Fredericktown Local	1,152	$7,229	60.5	10.1	$41,072	67
Mount Vernon City	4,157	$6,533	58.7	12.2	$42,205	63

School District by County	Enrollment	Per Pupil Spending	Expenditures Instruction (%)	Admin. (%)	Average Teachers Salary	4-year Report Card*
Lake County						
Fairport Harbor Ex Village	543	$9,102	52.2	16.5	$43,683	59
Kirtland Local	984	$9,973	51.2	12.0	$41,453	84
Madison Local	3,409	$7,117	55.6	12.3	$49,997	68
Mentor Ex Village	9,881	$7,726	57.1	10.4	$51,612	80
Painesville City Local	2,611	$9,185	49.9	14.7	$48,862	43
Painesville Township Local	3,884	$8,062	49.8	11.6	$47,181	77
Perry Local	1,904	$15,160	44.2	11.2	$58,739	94
Wickliffe City	1,435	$10,158	52.8	12.5	$50,055	75
Willoughby-Eastlake City	8,684	$8,075	57.4	9.6	$51,417	77
Lawrence County						
Chesapeake Union Ex Village	1,334	$7,117	56.5	11.7	$38,993	62
Dawson-Bryant Local	1,330	$6,788	62.6	8.4	$35,815	57
Fairland Local	1,819	$6,138	61.2	11.6	$38,295	86
Ironton City	1,625	$7,593	54.9	13.1	$38,080	57
Rock Hill Local	1,948	$6,500	59.0	10.2	$34,264	46
South Point Local	1,903	$6,784	57.0	16.6	$41,309	63
Symmes Valley Local	910	$6,987	53.5	12.1	$37,287	62
Licking County						
Granville Ex Village	1,790	$7,956	57.0	11.4	$48,157	103
Heath City	1,527	$6,926	56.3	13.7	$40,764	77
Johnstown-Monroe Local	1,342	$6,513	55.3	12.1	$37,923	68
Lakewood Local	2,319	$6,683	55.3	12.4	$37,684	49
Licking Heights Local	1,346	$6,832	54.0	12.9	$36,515	56
Licking Valley Local	2,088	$7,234	49.4	15.9	$38,195	67
Newark City	6,708	$7,521	57.3	11.9	$42,047	43
North Fork Local	1,760	$6,492	53.0	13.5	$38,032	67
Northridge Local	1,320	$6,524	52.7	14.8	$36,370	73
Southwest Licking Local	3,132	$7,327	51.1	13.4	$44,634	68
Logan County						
Bellefontaine City	2,725	$6,920	58.1	12.1	$39,822	56
Benjamin Logan Local	1,931	$6,128	53.3	13.8	$40,149	67
Indian Lake Local	1,921	$6,907	54.4	11.4	$40,957	51
Riverside Local	743	$6,286	64.2	11.1	$39,627	61
Lorain County						
Amherst Ex Village	3,685	$6,781	56.3	11.0	$48,832	88
Avon Lake City	3,096	$8,299	54.8	12.5	$47,315	96
Avon Local	1,651	$7,094	51.6	11.7	$40,385	62
Clearview Local	1,441	$8,339	55.0	10.9	$41,673	46
Columbia Local	1,135	$7,318	51.0	13.3	$39,093	76
Elyria City	8,289	$8,103	56.1	11.4	$43,382	33
Firelands Local	2,018	$6,814	56.2	13.6	$41,028	65
Keystone Local	1,801	$6,192	55.9	13.1	$41,257	63
Lorain City	10,291	$8,555	62.8	9.8	$46,953	18
Midview Local	3,137	$6,479	52.6	15.6	$42,574	58
North Ridgeville City	3,262	$7,576	58.4	9.2	$47,087	65
Oberlin City	1,075	$9,986	52.7	12.9	$42,350	43
Sheffield-Sheffield Lake City	1,850	$8,413	56.0	11.6	$43,655	60
Wellington Ex Village	1,517	$7,053	56.3	13.7	$43,185	62
Lucas County						
Anthony Wayne Local	3,273	$7,412	56.4	11.7	$42,487	92
Maumee City	2,882	$8,784	60.3	11.4	$50,126	83

School District by County	Enrollment	Per Pupil Spending	Expenditures Instruction (%)	Admin. (%)	Average Teachers Salary	4-year Report Card*
Oregon City	3,615	$8,784	57.8	8.4	$46,707	71
Ottawa Hills Local	965	$10,020	63.6	11.2	$53,888	101
Springfield Local	3,365	$8,610	59.7	10.0	$48,155	68
Sylvania City	7,569	$9,249	51.2	9.8	$46,831	83
Toledo City	36,791	$8,726	55.1	11.2	$43,216	21
Washington Local	6,899	$8,813	55.8	10.6	$44,506	60
Madison County						
Jefferson Local	1,214	$6,707	54.6	14.6	$33,725	66
Jonathan Alder Local	1,679	$6,374	51.3	17.4	$38,595	69
London City	2,042	$6,852	54.5	13.8	$37,873	51
Madison-Plains Local	1,760	$6,612	52.1	14.5	$40,459	64
Mahoning County						
Austintown Local	4,888	$7,782	56.1	13.2	$44,903	71
Boardman Local	4,754	$7,668	56.2	8.8	$49,338	92
Campbell City	1,511	$7,474	60.2	12.3	$42,768	53
Canfield Local	2,920	$7,041	54.5	10.4	$46,455	90
Jackson-Milton Local	941	$8,140	56.1	13.3	$41,617	60
Lowellville Local	602	$6,536	52.2	17.7	$35,238	81
Poland Local	2,465	$6,962	56.5	11.6	$48,105	90
Sebring Local	741	$7,943	56.1	16.6	$37,568	70
South Range Local	1,269	$7,136	53.0	12.0	$40,518	101
Springfield Local	1,219	$7,088	53.3	17.2	$40,295	78
Struthers City	1,999	$7,295	62.8	11.9	$45,928	63
West Branch Local	2,306	$6,615	53.2	11.2	$41,231	70
Western Reserve Local	795	$6,737	47.7	15.3	$39,153	80
Youngstown City	10,589	$9,488	52.6	10.2	$41,611	17
Marion County						
Elgin Local	1,626	$6,259	56.3	12.2	$38,402	64
Marion City	5,569	$7,451	64.3	11.0	$42,662	38
Pleasant Local	1,398	$5,748	56.6	11.3	$38,337	70
Ridgedale Local	1,062	$7,700	50.3	13.5	$38,689	55
River Valley Local	1,648	$7,356	54.4	12.6	$40,861	65
Medina County						
Black River Local	1,483	$6,311	55.9	10.5	$38,695	68
Brunswick City	6,626	$7,633	58.3	10.6	$44,359	78
Buckeye Local	2,352	$8,199	52.6	15.0	$44,596	81
Cloverleaf Local	3,567	$7,088	55.0	8.8	$45,282	74
Highland Local	2,421	$6,971	53.5	12.0	$43,807	100
Medina City	6,363	$8,508	58.0	10.8	$50,289	86
Wadsworth City	4,231	$6,991	53.3	15.5	$47,985	90
Meigs County						
Eastern Local	788	$7,003	54.3	14.0	$29,101	53
Meigs Local	2,187	$7,669	57.8	14.1	$35,226	42
Southern Local	738	$7,766	54.8	12.5	$33,192	46
Mercer County						
Celina City	3,301	$7,472	58.9	10.3	$40,108	90
Coldwater Ex Village	1,592	$6,984	65.3	9.8	$41,091	96
Fort Recovery Local	943	$7,200	54.5	11.3	$36,085	102
Marion Local	959	$6,854	60.1	12.8	$45,002	98
Parkway Local	1,153	$7,566	56.6	12.2	$34,856	67
St. Henry Consolidated Local	1,131	$6,715	62.8	9.9	$42,134	97

School District by County	Enrollment	Per Pupil Spending	Expenditures Instruction (%)	Admin. (%)	Average Teachers Salary	4-year Report Card*
Miami County						
Bethel Local	864	$6,357	51.3	15.1	$36,192	75
Bradford Ex Village	589	$7,326	51.0	15.8	$34,705	41
Covington Ex Village	881	$7,351	52.5	13.8	$36,904	74
Miami East Local	1,321	$6,825	51.9	15.8	$38,313	73
Milton-Union Ex Village	1,834	$6,925	54.2	15.0	$39,548	79
Newton Local	589	$7,302	54.4	16.2	$35,423	83
Piqua City	3,710	$7,186	57.7	9.6	$45,077	46
Tipp City Ex Village	2,586	$6,502	59.2	12.3	$44,342	86
Troy City	4,475	$7,215	64.6	9.8	$48,299	68
Monroe County						
Switzerland of Ohio Local	2,814	$7,495	58.0	10.4	$35,466	55
Montgomery County						
Brookville Local	1,575	$6,910	51.7	13.1	$45,038	72
Centerville City	7,298	$8,088	59.4	9.2	$49,372	101
Dayton City	20,586	$9,854	47.6	14.1	$42,745	13
Huber Heights City	6,715	$7,256	60.6	9.2	$46,739	57
Jefferson Township Local	689	$10,992	43.3	18.9	$36,908	31
Kettering City	7,568	$8,247	53.3	12.8	$46,626	81
Mad River Local	3,836	$7,966	60.5	11.5	$43,584	42
Miamisburg City	4,833	$7,421	55.6	13.3	$43,337	87
New Lebanon Local	1,365	$7,745	54.2	15.2	$41,784	62
Northmont City	5,584	$7,100	57.3	12.0	$45,069	83
Northridge Local	2,005	$10,071	57.6	12.0	$46,643	37
Oakwood City	1,913	$8,487	59.7	15.1	$43,534	103
Trotwood-Madison City	3,634	$7,781	54.9	13.9	$38,203	28
Valley View Local	1,928	$7,621	55.8	13.2	$43,609	79
Vandalia-Butler City	3,355	$7,641	57.7	12.8	$43,105	69
West Carrollton City	3,783	$7,754	58.2	11.6	$42,815	50
Morgan County						
Morgan Local	2,382	$8,229	55.9	11.6	$37,479	42
Morrow County						
Cardington-Lincoln Local	1,190	$6,916	57.8	11.1	$36,628	52
Highland Local	1,688	$7,389	52.8	10.6	$39,366	53
Mount Gilead Ex Village	1,333	$7,525	56.3	10.2	$38,761	54
Northmor Local	1,243	$7,238	53.9	11.2	$37,585	60
Muskingum County						
East Muskingum Local	2,166	$6,652	57.4	12.4	$41,566	77
Franklin Local	2,397	$6,380	54.2	12.6	$39,872	41
Maysville Local	1,995	$6,440	52.3	15.5	$36,556	47
Tri-Valley Local	2,919	$5,924	56.4	16.9	$40,649	56
West Muskingum Local	1,735	$6,491	53.2	13.1	$37,853	70
Zanesville City	4,317	$8,579	60.3	11.8	$43,018	39
Nobel County						
Caldwell Ex Village	1,041	$6,626	56.3	12.6	$34,898	60
Noble Local	1,282	$6,682	52.4	13.5	$38,830	60
Ottawa County						
Benton Carroll Salem Local	2,066	$8,555	54.4	11.6	$53,450	86
Danbury Local	606	$10,682	54.0	11.0	$48,906	72
Genoa Area Local	1,674	$7,775	61.6	11.5	$42,479	70
Port Clinton City	1,914	$9,388	56.4	11.1	$49,217	59

REPORT CARDS FOR OHIO'S MAJOR SCHOOL DISTRICTS

Performance
Indicators*

Proficiency 4th Grade (75%)	State Average	Akron	Cleveland	Cincinnati	Columbus	Dayton	Toledo
Citizenship	67.4%	51.7%	44.2%	41.5%	43.2%	25.1%	34.7%
Mathematics	62.9%	46.7%	43.9%	34.4%	39.7%	23.9%	33.9%
Reading	67.7%	49.9%	40.1%	38.6%	45.1%	22.8%	41.2%
Writing	80.5%	73.3%	60.6%	67.4%	69.1%	53.3%	66.8%
Science	37.9%	44.0%	42.6%	37.1%	35.3%	21.2%	32.7%
Proficiency (75%) 6th Grade							
Citizenship	71.4%	46.7%	31.7%	47.6%	41.3%	31.7%	46.2%
Mathematics	61.7%	34.8%	23.6%	32.4%	41.0%	20.2%	38.4%
Reading	58.2%	35.6%	21.3%	33.1%	31.2%	19.2%	33.4%
Writing	87.2%	73.8%	66.1%	49.9%	76.1%	66.5%	77.8%
Science	60.5%	34.8%	21.4%	32.2%	28.0%	17.9%	31.4%
Proficiency (75%) 9th Grade							
Citizenship	83.9%	67.7%	53.3%	64.4%	66.5%	53.5%	65.3%
Mathematics	73.5%	50.7%	33.6%	45.1%	48.5%	31.5%	45.2%
Reading	91.6%	82.2%	73.4%	79.9%	81.2%	74.3%	82.0%
Writing	89.9%	80.8%	68.6%	78.7%	82.7%	72.3%	79.7%
Science	77.5%	57.7%	38.3%	52.1%	51.5%	39.9%	52.3%
Proficiency (85%) 9th Grade**							
Citizenship	92.6%	84.8%	70.6%	81.4%	82.0%	74.3%	87.1%
Mathematics	85.4%	69.2%	49.7%	64.2%	66.2%	52.2%	71.6%
Reading	96.5%	95.5%	85.4%	89.1%	91.4%	86.6%	94.1%
Writing	96.0%	94.2%	85.5%	85.0%	92.2%	85.6%	93.6%
Science	88.3%	79.0%	56.1%	70.5%	69.2%	60.8%	77.1%
Attendance (93%)							
Rate	94.3%	92.2%	93.8%	91.10%	91.5%	87.6%	90.9%
Graduation (90%)							
Rate	82.8%	73.5%	38.1%	82.8%	56.0%	62.6%	65.6%
Indicators Met	12	4	3	5	5	2	6
Improvement		1.8%	1.7%	7.7%	3.9%	1.4%	2.8%

*Performance indicators are the criteria that the state uses to determine a school's effectiveness. There are 22 indicators, 20 of them tests, the other two are graduation rate and attendance rate
**These results are for 10th grade students who took the test as 8th-, 9th-, and 10th graders.
Source: Department of Education

knowing the score

Number of Ohio schools meeting state standards:

Met 21 or 22 state standards:
109

Met 17 to 20 state standards:
191

Met 11 to 16 state standards:
257

Met 7 to 10 state standards:
33

"GOOD NEWS, DEAR! JENNIFER HAS BEEN ACCEPTED INTO THE ACCELERATED HONORS KINDERGARTEN PROGRAM ON THE STRENGTH OF HER PRE-SCHOOL PROFICIENCY TEST SCORES!"

Testing the tests

If you wonder why school testing is an ever-shifting field, a career history teacher puts the tests themselves to the test. His results? Fads, gimmicks, the rise of a new industry, politics—almost everything but education.

Ohio is changing its testing—again. Although we are asking more from students today than ever before, high-stakes testing is driven by the myth that student performance is down. But Ohio's students are doing more, and at an earlier age, than ever before.

Following the landmark 1983 report, "A Nation at Risk"—based on the country's poorest performing schools—Ohio jumped into the proficiency-testing fray, and many schools, sick or well, were given the cure. The "well" schools found themselves forced to scrap outstanding and innovative curriculums to meet new standards.

As the new high-stakes testing took hold, a cottage industry developed. Money was poured into test preparation, and as schools struggled to adapt to an ever-shifting landscape, they adopted the latest educational fad. Educational gurus flocked in, instructing teachers on the best (at that moment) methods. Materials were purchased to aid students (for most, their first exposure to a lifetime of self-help books). Successful schools

became Meccas where teachers from less fortunate schools made annual pilgrimages, and with evangelical zeal they sent their teachers out to spread the word.

The current wave of tests is just Ohio's latest, and this 20-year pursuit has been increasingly called into question. "There is not and never has been one best set of standards," says Ted Sizer, former dean of the Harvard Graduate School of Education. "Not one best array of disciplines, no one acceptable form of expression, no uniformly dependable single means of assessment. What endures in this inevitably confused and often high-charged situation is the struggle to ascertain the best of each, according to the intelligence and taste of the given time."

In the race to develop ever higher standards, some educators began to think that for many students the bar will never be cleared. These educators contend the bar is set, ultimately, by politicians: If too many students clear the bar, the bar should be higher.

If we are doing well, it must be too easy.

The new prescription includes diagnostic

www. ode.state.oh.us/ proficiency/ samples.asp

Little-known site for educators, parents, and students in need of extra help in passing Ohio's proficiency test. Links to free downloads of previous years' tests (in full) are published, along with answer keys and grading rubrics.

tests for every grade. Proficiency Testing occurs in the fourth, sixth, and ninth grades. The OGT is given to 10th graders and they will have at least ten other chances to pass or drop out. (High stakes testing increases the drop-out rate among those who fail to pass the test.)

If a student passes four out of five tests he has to be within only 10 points of passing on the fifth. Then—if he has passed all of the required classes in that subject; has a 97% attendance rate; a minimum GPA of 2.5 out of 4.0 in that subject; attended intervention programs (with a 97% attendance rate); and secured a letter of recommendation from each teacher in the subject area not yet passed—he may still earn a diploma.

The effect from all this?

Students are being forced to assimilate subject matter in a shorter amount of time. But weaker students find this difficult. The timing of the testing is to give them more chances before graduation to pass; the *effect* is that those who would benefit from a longer time period to assimilate the material are the ones pushed into taking the test prematurely. Then they must rely on less effective means of remediation to pass. What these students quite likely need are alternative approaches, more individual attention, and more time.

This testing mania also hides unintended consequences. One effect is that the curriculum has been narrowed. So much of our time and resources are diverted to the mandated, circumscribed process that we have watered down the educational experience for the majority of students whom the state deems competent.

Other "less important" disciplines are faced with dwindling resources. Passionate teachers outside the core curriculum are caught in a dilemma. Should they push for proficiency testing in their discipline—and with it the pressure and the loss of curricular control—or watch their subject regulated to second-class status in the educational hierarchy?

Art, foreign language and technology have chosen the former, opting for future inclusion into Ohio's inner circle of proficiency-tested subjects.

High-stakes testing is built on the false premise that schools can be tested into excellence. Mandating high standards does not, by itself, raise achievement. Even when the standards are adequate and appropriate, it is nearly impossible to measure—with an objective test or a short answer response—complex learning, problem solving, and conceptual understanding.

The current multiple choice/short answer tests being developed do not measure the skills a student needs to compete in today's economy. In the educational community, teachers are encouraged to break away from standardization, yet the state-mandated testing *requires* it.

Neither are one-size-fits-all standards appropriate for all schools in Ohio. Schools benefit from, or are at the mercy of their clientele. It is not as difficult for a wealthy suburban school to reach a passing level as it is for an inner city school. It is not inconceivable that inner city teachers and administration could be doing a superior job of educating students, yet fall far below the state's standards. Their hurdles may be too big.

One thing, however, is true: No matter its level of skill, the East Cleveland teaching staff would be perceived as immediately improved—and have better test results—if it began teaching Solon's student body. The Solon staff, meanwhile, its classrooms full of East Cleveland students, would see its results—and its image—drop.

No one denies that state testing is here to stay. While there is always a place for testing, our present method has dubious value and a punitive application. Social commentator Nicholas Lemann observed, "The first thing interesting about it (testing) is it's driven by real estate in suburban towns. When people try to buy houses in the town, they have a sheet listing of all the test scores in the town, and the test scores determine the value of the real estate. The realtors are the biggest business in these suburban towns, and for the typical family that lives there, their biggest asset is their house. So the kids are sort of foot soldiers in the local real estate wars because their third-grade reading scores will determine what their house is worth."

In his own children's district, after falling test scores, "There's an hour a day of test prep; they'd get protests; they'd be taught all of those tricks about eliminating two answers on the multiple choice; they would be sent home with drilling exercises that didn't have to do with learning to read; and sure enough our scores went up and our real estate values skyrocketed."

Schools need to be accountable; students need to be competent. It's the remedy that is questionable.

It's important to create tests that are meaningful. It's important to embrace alternative assessments, not just for our students but also for our schools.

It's important to find a way for districts to keep their creativity, as well as be accountable.

It's important for the government to help schools and not punish them.

In our undying passion for better schools—and a way to quantify them—we may be overlooking two important notions: (1) In the remarkable American educational experiment to educate everyone, we may be doing better than our present high-stakes testing tells us, and (2) even if we are not, it is highly doubtful that success in later life will ever be measured by 45 questions.

—*Michael O'Bryant*

Michael O'Bryant is an editor of the Ohio Almanac and a 31-year veteran of the classroom wars, teaching history and English.

443

School District by County	Enrollment	Per Pupil Spending	Expenditures Instruction (%)	Admin. (%)	Average Teachers Salary	4-year Report Card*
Paulding County						
Antwerp Local	770	$7,084	56.6	9.8	$37,562	77
Paulding Ex Village	1,805	$7,589	56.0	12.6	$37,322	71
Wayne Trace Local	1,092	$7,306	58.3	12.2	$45,653	77
Perry County						
Crooksville Ex Village	1,077	$6,837	54.5	11.2	$36,477	54
New Lexington City	1,888	$6,902	53.9	14.7	$39,442	38
Northern Local	2,398	$6,230	52.8	15.1	$34,585	72
Southern Local	1,082	$6,889	52.9	13.7	$33,002	33
Pickway County						
Circleville City	2,445	$7,403	58.1	12.0	$47,433	51
Logan Elm Local	2,293	$6,736	52.8	13.6	$39,521	62
Teays Valley Local	2,852	$6,523	59.3	11.6	$43,198	64
Westfall Local	1,688	$6,783	54.6	13.5	$41,080	52
Pike County						
Eastern Local	916	$7,430	53.1	13.3	$36,041	18
Scioto Valley Local	1,571	$7,189	54.4	11.9	$41,740	33
Waverly City	2,036	$6,471	54.9	11.1	$42,264	64
Western Local	912	$7,474	48.7	16.8	$36,842	40
Portage County						
Aurora City	2,356	$7,849	50.8	15.7	$50,545	101
Crestwood Local	2,743	$6,666	53.7	12.3	$42,736	74
Field Local	2,281	$6,971	57.3	12.9	$41,860	76
James A. Garfield Local	1,567	$6,310	50.8	13.1	$39,121	64
Kent City	3,663	$9,981	59.2	10.5	$50,156	72
Ravenna City	3,216	$8,032	57.5	12.8	$43,387	52
Rootstown Local	1,308	$6,686	58.0	10.3	$38,403	58
Southeast Local	2,337	$6,868	55.0	11.5	$42,402	61
Streetsboro City	1,869	$7,983	53.0	13.1	$42,728	62
Waterloo Local	1,421	$6,232	51.5	12.4	$36,693	58
Windham Ex Village	1,026	$8,766	53.9	10.7	$41,036	48
Preble County						
Eaton City	2,241	$6,748	56.1	13.8	$42,716	59
National Trail Local	1,190	$8,055	52.2	11.5	$38,879	49
Preble Shawnee Local	1,687	$6,937	54.1	11.0	$36,576	48
Tri-County North Local	1,189	$6,804	54.8	12.4	$36,208	64
Twin Valley Community Local	1,050	$7,022	53.2	14.3	$39,092	60
Putnam County						
Columbus Grove Local	817	$6,528	57.9	11.1	$37,209	92
Continental Local	752	$9,095	52.5	10.4	$38,667	74
Jennings Local	436	$6,669	54.1	16.9	$32,907	91
Kalida Local	741	$6,666	55.6	11.5	$37,284	95
Leipsic Local	668	$7,840	56.9	12.9	$37,538	74
Miller City-New Cleveland Local	466	$7,386	56.1	14.0	$36,128	97
Ottawa-Glandorf Local	1,640	$7,084	60.2	10.5	$39,475	89
Ottoville Local	643	$6,321	62.5	12.2	$32,864	93
Pandora-Gilboa Local	583	$7,603	51.3	16.3	$35,438	84
Richland County						
Clear Fork Valley Local	1,761	$6,318	50.6	11.0	$36,380	69
Crestview Local	1,230	$6,561	55.0	9.5	$34,988	71
Lexington Local	2,743	$6,554	54.0	11.5	$39,144	81
Lucas Local	597	$7,446	45.4	18.2	$32,650	75

School District by County	Enrollment	Per Pupil Spending	Expenditures Instruction (%)	Admin. (%)	Average Teachers Salary	4-year Report Card*
Madison Local	3,395	$8,375	59.1	9.4	$37,830	41
Mansfield City	6,033	$9,209	59.0	10.8	$41,653	28
Ontario Local	1,661	$7,068	50.3	11.5	$44,017	78
Plymouth-Shiloh Local	984	$7,743	54.6	14.3	$34,789	84
Shelby City	2,182	$7,575	54.9	10.9	$39,483	67
Ross County						
Adena Local	1,221	$6,717	53.1	13.4	$40,121	59
Chillicothe City	3,699	$7,200	54.2	11.6	$41,910	56
Huntington Local	1,350	$6,428	61.3	11.2	$39,830	32
Paint Valley Local	1,191	$7,010	58.7	11.5	$37,651	50
Scioto Valley Local	1,177	$6,250	49.8	15.2	$36,652	39
Union-Scioto Local	1,956	$6,000	59.8	13.4	$39,225	54
Zane Trace Local	1,471	$5,748	51.7	13.1	$37,003	51
Sandusky County						
Clyde-Green Springs Ex Village	2,240	$6,923	55.8	11.2	$42,082	73
Fremont City	4,566	$7,337	59.7	9.9	$44,349	56
Gibsonburg Ex Village	1,060	$6,564	58.4	13.4	$37,875	72
Lakota Local	1,283	$7,233	58.4	9.5	$30,221	59
Woodmore Local	1,203	$7,101	54.9	11.4	$42,366	75
Scioto County						
Bloom-Vernon Local	1,006	$7,433	48.8	12.6	$36,431	52
Clay Local	589	$6,427	54.9	14.3	$31,772	61
Green Local	700	$7,225	53.7	13.5	$33,938	51
Minford Local	1,626	$6,884	54.8	13.1	$39,631	60
New Boston Local	424	$8,381	51.9	19.3	$33,947	56
Northwest Local	1,773	$7,290	53.4	9.6	$38,856	45
Portsmouth City	2,631	$9,267	56.0	10.2	$39,662	34
Valley Local	1,235	$7,177	52.7	15.6	$40,417	59
Washington-Nile Local	1,691	$6,656	54.2	10.3	$35,477	47
Wheelersburg Local	1,463	$6,229	59.7	10.5	$38,795	72
Seneca County						
Bettsville Local	333	$7,009	48.7	16.1	$29,139	45
Fostoria City	2,349	$8,031	54.6	13.1	$41,113	39
Hopewell-Loudon Local	858	$6,401	53.4	11.7	$34,844	71
New Riegel Local	474	$6,453	59.5	11.6	$34,077	75
Old Fort Local	578	$7,046	50.1	12.7	$36,731	81
Seneca East Local	1,041	$6,940	56.3	10.1	$37,416	73
Tiffin City	3,193	$6,541	57.6	11.0	$40,680	69
Shelby County						
Anna Local	1,166	$7,011	51.4	12.3	$41,892	84
Botkins Local	599	$6,693	57.4	10.9	$37,006	82
Fairlawn Local	475	$7,253	52.2	13.7	$31,544	59
Fort Loramie Local	801	$7,143	53.1	10.9	$40,302	92
Hardin-Houston Local	899	$6,624	54.8	9.5	$36,962	63
Jackson Center Local	553	$6,736	54.7	13.7	$36,085	63
Russia Local	407	$6,840	56.3	12.6	$36,645	81
Sidney City	3,760	$6,552	55.6	11.6	$41,898	54
Stark County						
Alliance City	3,465	$8,062	62.6	9.7	$42,007	42
Canton City	11,929	$9,968	56.1	13.5	$47,005	27
Canton Local	2,451	$7,558	57.5	9.8	$41,602	65
Fairless Local	1,883	$6,514	54.8	11.8	$35,921	60
Jackson Local	5,283	$7,265	52.9	11.9	$43,933	97

School District by County	Enrollment	Per Pupil Spending	Expenditures Instruction (%)	Admin. (%)	Average Teachers Salary	4-year Report Card*
Lake Local	3,232	$6,260	55.0	12.6	$42,885	83
Louisville City	3,064	$6,191	61.4	10.0	$44,380	82
Marlington Local	2,634	$6,872	53.6	10.9	$40,429	66
Massillon City	4,572	$7,637	53.0	12.2	$41,207	40
Minerva Local	2,179	$6,771	58.6	11.2	$42,749	68
North Canton City	4,447	$7,239	55.7	10.5	$44,928	94
Northwest Local	2,401	$6,464	58.2	13.2	$43,793	73
Osnaburg Local	996	$6,820	53.0	12.8	$34,837	63
Perry Local	4,676	$6,667	58.4	10.0	$45,022	85
Plain Local	6,154	$6,559	57.6	9.4	$42,521	75
Sandy Valley Local	1,581	$6,502	56.4	11.1	$39,015	66
Tuslaw Local	1,422	$6,205	52.7	11.4	$36,920	82
Summit County						
Akron City	30,250	$8,986	57.9	11.1	$45,525	20
Barberton City	4,284	$8,264	57.7	9.4	$41,913	39
Copley-Fairlawn City	2,929	$8,462	56.6	10.4	$48,072	97
Coventry Local	2,277	$6,669	54.8	12.8	$40,269	65
Cuyahoga Falls City	5,222	$7,181	55.2	11.1	$41,011	60
Green Local	3,835	$7,205	55.2	9.6	$43,991	87
Hudson City	5,188	$8,873	55.6	10.8	$51,591	99
Manchester Local	1,395	$7,169	48.9	13.5	$42,389	77
Mogadore Local	835	$7,754	50.9	14.1	$41,190	72
Nordonia Hills City	3,595	$8,237	51.9	11.1	$45,262	75
Norton City	2,428	$7,350	55.9	10.8	$41,842	75
Revere Local	2,817	$7,868	55.5	11.6	$49,841	102
Springfield Local	2,935	$7,501	56.7	11.6	$40,425	49
Stow-Munroe Falls City	5,752	$7,521	61.2	8.8	$46,541	81
Tallmadge City	2,659	$7,218	58.7	12.6	$44,561	82
Twinsburg City	3,696	$8,173	59.1	11.4	$45,699	84
Woodridge Local	1,735	$8,594	54.6	12.3	$41,405	63
Trumbull County						
Bloomfield-Mespo Local	393	$8,166	56.2	13.6	$35,193	60
Bristol Local	895	$7,387	56.9	10.1	$38,162	60
Brookfield Local	1,520	$7,609	57.8	10.8	$42,170	67
Champion Local	1,773	$7,468	58.4	11.9	$43,885	87
Girard City	1,732	$7,295	57.2	11.4	$47,964	76
Howland Local	3,263	$7,450	56.4	12.0	$48,001	82
Hubbard Ex Village	2,325	$6,709	55.1	8.6	$40,807	66
Joseph Badger Local	1,161	$6,703	53.3	16.3	$39,436	65
LaBrae Local	1,485	$7,592	58.5	13.6	$43,894	73
Lakeview Local	2,237	$6,679	56.4	11.8	$44,219	89
Liberty Local	1,793	$7,736	56.1	12.6	$39,039	65
Lordstown Local	796	$10,056	58.6	10.8	$39,173	80
Maplewood Local	1,097	$6,874	56.3	10.7	$42,950	68
Mathews Local	981	$8,847	52.6	10.7	$42,943	70
McDonald Local	786	$6,663	65.5	12.5	$39,682	90
Newton Falls Ex Village	1,529	$6,934	54.4	15.4	$42,227	51
Niles City	2,850	$6,955	59.4	11.4	$40,732	55
Southington Local	649	$6,575	53.2	13.3	$41,113	65
Warren City	6,786	$9,121	55.4	10.3	$40,597	13
Weathersfield Local	1,072	$8,108	54.7	11.2	$40,228	73
Tuscarawas County						
Claymont City	2,283	$6,604	55.4	12.4	$38,098	44
Dover City	2,637	$7,007	56.2	10.5	$39,688	86
Garaway Local	1,176	$7,314	55.7	13.4	$36,557	92
Indian Valley Local	1,835	$6,525	55.1	12.0	$36,161	73

School District by County	Enrollment	Per Pupil Spending	Expenditures Instruction (%)	Admin. (%)	Average Teachers Salary	4-year Report Card*
New Philadelphia City	3,096	$6,461	57.4	12.8	$37,538	82
Newcomerstown Ex Village	1,319	$6,928	53.6	11.1	$35,452	75
Strasburg-Franklin Local	671	$6,172	57.0	14.0	$36,669	70
Tuscarawas Valley Local	1,600	$6,716	53.4	13.7	$36,981	80
Union County						
Fairbanks Local	900	$7,585	49.8	15.8	$41,114	73
Marysville Ex Village	4,169	$7,936	53.5	10.2	$44,418	74
North Union Local	1,372	$7,018	57.8	12.4	$37,845	56
Van Wert County						
Crestview Local	1,067	$6,246	57.9	11.1	$39,592	81
Lincolnview Local	833	$7,057	60.3	13.8	$36,185	79
Van Wert City	2,276	$6,845	61.5	11.7	$42,013	67
Vinton County Local	2,410	$6,793	51.7	11.6	$35,711	49
Warren County						
Carlisle Local	1,691	$7,823	55.6	10.6	$42,673	58
Franklin City	2,986	$7,177	57.7	11.8	$43,945	50
Kings Local	3,464	$7,924	52.9	11.1	$45,131	93
Lebanon City	4,336	$7,402	48.9	15.2	$41,816	78
Little Miami Local	2,606	$7,493	51.1	11.7	$39,985	77
Mason City	6,316	$7,487	53.7	10.5	$42,488	102
Springboro Community City	3,350	$6,231	55.5	10.5	$44,654	90
Wayne Local	1,290	$6,237	55.1	12.2	$38,842	75
Williams County						
Belpre City	1,288	$6,818	57.4	14.2	$38,646	63
Fort Frye Local	1,220	$6,855	50.3	15.3	$33,606	64
Frontier Local	994	$7,309	51.9	13.7	$29,923	52
Marietta City	3,297	$7,072	56.5	12.3	$38,631	63
Warren Local	2,490	$6,675	59.4	11.4	$40,099	71
Wolf Creek Local	656	$6,958	54.5	14.4	$35,432	63
Wayne County						
Chippewa Local	1,465	$7,314	49.7	11.7	$40,618	76
Dalton Local	1,003	$7,062	51.6	13.1	$39,290	86
Green Local	1,343	$7,162	58.0	12.6	$42,991	90
North Central Local	1,288	$6,277	56.9	11.3	$40,340	82
Northwestern Local	1,416	$7,388	58.0	10.4	$40,914	83
Orrville City	1,948	$7,208	56.9	12.5	$46,226	65
Rittman Ex Village	1,283	$7,316	55.6	11.0	$35,525	58
Southeast Local	1,663	$7,830	58.7	13.7	$41,407	75
Triway Local	2,101	$7,082	58.7	10.7	$43,122	75
Wooster City	4,157	$9,299	58.9	10.8	$49,428	71
Williams County						
Bryan City	2,206	$6,985	61.3	11.4	$43,131	72
Edgerton Local	713	$7,159	53.9	14.0	$35,730	76
Edon-Northwest Local	746	$6,172	54.1	14.2	$37,873	66
Millcreek-West Unity Local	773	$6,621	59.6	13.4	$39,905	69
Montpelier Ex Village	1,130	$6,802	58.8	12.5	$40,034	70
North Central Local	705	$7,509	56.6	12.6	$36,401	64
Stryker Local	554	$7,021	52.6	14.8	$38,094	74
Wood County						
Bowling Green City	3,240	$8,262	59.1	10.5	$47,969	75
Eastwood Local	1,863	$7,204	57.1	10.9	$42,796	82
Elmwood Local	1,244	$6,762	52.6	11.8	$36,620	69

School District by County	Enrollment	Per Pupil Spending	Expenditures Instruction (%)	Admin. (%)	Average Teachers Salary	4-year Report Card*
Lake Local	1,695	$6,460	50.0	12.8	$40,773	67
North Baltimore Local	778	$9,444	41.4	10.1	$32,561	63
Northwood Local	941	$8,003	53.2	12.7	$46,200	64
Otsego Local	1,602	$7,212	59.5	12.3	$43,790	73
Perrysburg Ex Village	4,060	$8,401	57.8	9.7	$49,709	95
Rossford Ex Village	1,929	$8,648	59.4	11.9	$48,413	65
Wyandot County						
Carey Ex Village	895	$6,668	53.8	13.1	$35,047	67
Mohawk Local	1,126	$6,790	53.6	13.0	$36,537	73
Upper Sandusky Ex Village	1,858	$6,983	48.8	14.0	$42,912	70

Ohio firsts

First school in Ohio—opened in Schoenbrunn, 1773, by Moravian missionary David Zeisberger for Indian children

First academy for higher (high school) education in Ohio—Muskingum Academy, Marietta, 1800

First school for higher education of women in Ohio—Mrs. Williams' School, Cincinnati, 1802

First industrial school in Ohio—founded 1821, at Upper Sandusky by James Finley, for educating Indians

First free public school system in Ohio—started in Cincinnati, 1825

Oldest college newspaper in U.S.—*The Miami Student*, started at Miami University, Oxford, 1826

First privately-supported high school west of the Alleghenies—Elyria, 1830

First coeducational college in U.S.—Oberlin, which first admitted women in 1837

First state school for the blind in U.S.—Ohio Institute for the Blind, Columbus, 1837

First kindergarten in U.S.—Columbus, 1838

Oldest Collegiate Bach Festival in U.S.—founded Baldwin-Wallace College, started 1845

First graded public schools in Ohio—started in Akron, 1847

First black American woman to earn a college degree—Lucy Sessions, Oberlin College, 1850

First institution of higher learning owned and operated by black Americans—Wilberforce University, founded 1856

First black American woman to earn a B.A.—Mary Jane Patterson, Oberlin College, 1862

First collegiate conservatory of music in U.S.—started at Oberlin College, 1865

First student transportation (busing) system in Ohio—Kingsville Township, Ashtabula County, 1890s

First junior high in U.S.—Indianola Junior High, Columbus, 1909

First cooperative education program in U.S.—Antioch College, 1921

First public Montessori school in U.S.—the Cincinnati Public Schools Sands Montessori, opened 1978

World's first College of Polymer Science Engineering—University of Akron, 1988

First woman president of any Ohio state college or university—Dr. Carol Cartwright, Kent State University, 1990

449

With apologies to the Bard, the good that men do isn't always buried with them, as shown by Ohio's libraries. These repositories are the dream come true of generations of public-spirited voters, and a couple of key leaders: Dennis G. Fedor; a Lakewood lawyer who died in 1994, and yes, oddly enough, that old skinflint the first Robert A. Taft, who presented himself to St. Peter in 1953. In the 2002 election season, bad news smashed Ohio harder than Lake Erie on its moody days. The economy stank. America was at war. But a national survey pierced the pall, reporting that Ohio still offered its residents the best libraries in the Union. Hennen's 2002 American Public Library Ratings, in the journal American Libraries, made its call largely, but not only, on the share of tax money Ohio's public libraries get to use.

And even beyond Ohio's No. 1 nationwide rank, Hennen's ratings of Ohio's individually top-notch libraries could write an AAA Trip-Tik for Greater Cleveland.

Thus, though it won't surprise patrons of Lakewood's library, where Fedor was a trustee, it ranks first in the United States in its population class (50,000 to 99,999). In the most populous class, the Parma-based Cuyahoga County library system ranks eighth in America.

Meanwhile, in the same class as Lakewood, Euclid's library ranked ninth in the nation, and the Cleveland Heights-University Heights system placed 10th. In other population classes, Twinsburg's library placed second in the country; the Westlake, Wickliffe and Medina County District libraries were third; Stow-Munroe Falls' ranked fifth; and Rocky River's was seventh. What's more, almost a dozen downstate Ohio libraries also made Hennen's list.

For that kind of quality, voters can thank a long line of shrewd library trustees and the constructive bipartisanship that once helped fashion public policy in Columbus.

Today's successes began in 1931, when Taft—Gov. Bob Taft's grandfather, who was then in the state Senate—won enactment of a new Ohio tax on investments, or "intangibles." Time was when Ohio Republicans weren't afraid to seek new taxes if they saw pressing needs.

Today, that would be unthinkably nervy to the wussies in Ohio's wheelhouse.

Also in 1931, Taft won passage of a bill that authorized creation of countywide library systems and, though the legislative details are complex, he let Ohio's public libraries benefit from his new intangibles tax. That poured the footers for today's libraries.

By the early 1980s, however, the intangibles tax was becoming tough to police (county auditors weren't about to search voters' bank boxes for stocks and bonds). And the way the tax money was allotted had the consequence (not intended by Taft) of making some well-off Ohio libraries even better off, while some poorer libraries stayed on short rations.

Accordingly, Gov. Richard F. Celeste—a Lakewood native—got the General Assembly to abolish the intangibles tax. He persuaded legislators to instead give libraries 6.3 percent of

OHIO'S GREAT PALACE OF BOOKS—At right is the grand atrium in the magnificent main Cincinnati library of 1874—five levels of cast-iron book alcoves taking up three stories with a skylight above. The library was built in an abandoned opera house and was considered one of the greatest American libraries. Minus the books, it fell to the wrecking ball in 1954. Photograph by Don J. Paevey, from *Free & Public, One Hundred and Fifty Years at the Public Library of Cincinnati & Hamilton County 1853-2003*.

JIM BORGMAN
CINCINNATI
ENQUIRER©1997

Net Search

FIND

MIDNIGHT IN THE GARDEN OF GOOD AND EVIL

Ohio's income tax. And he picked Fedor to chair a nonpartisan Public Library Financing and Support Committee to figure out how the income-tax money could help poorer libraries without dragging down better-off ones.

To make a long story short, Fedor's work proved to be such a great deal for all Ohio libraries that, in the 1990s, then-Gov. George V. Voinovich got legislators to prune libraries' 6.3 percent share of the income tax to 5.7 percent. That was a bad call. Nonetheless, because income tax collections grew, the libraries still did OK.

But in today's recession, linkage to income tax has a downside. The sputtering economy means libraries will get $458 million from Columbus this year; they got $496 million last year. True, librarians may ask voters for local property-tax millage, but three-quarters of Ohio's libraries depend entirely on state aid. So, as Thomas J. Hennen Jr. wrote in his survey, "a rising tide raises all ships, and a falling tide [can lower] them all."

To date, given bleak budget options, the General Assembly and Robert A. Taft's grandson haven't irrevocably imperiled Ohio's peerless libraries maybe because voters who love their library (and hundreds of thousands do) have been watching. But considering Ohio's seemingly unstoppable drive for mediocrity in every public service, they'd better not blink.

—by permission of *The Plain Dealer*

OHIO PUBLIC LIBRARY STATEWIDE SUMMARY

	2002	1994
Number of Tax-Supported Libraries	250	250
Total Volumes	48,074,614	39,839,294
Total Circulation	165,454,936	110,703,857
Total Tax Distribution to Libraries	$586,599,824	$314,758,294
Total Library Income	$645,382,899	$344,656,770
Total Expenditures for Salaries	$382,730,935	$170,338,818
Total Expenditures for Materials	$108,793,374	$56,676,679
Total Library Expenditures	*$612,284,965*	*$330,021,681*

Mary Ellen Armentrout's book, *Carnegie Libraries of Ohio, Our Cultural Heritage,* tells us that Andrew Carnegie revolutionized what she calls "the small and floundering public library system in this country." For in America B.C.—Before Carnegie—public libraries were usually subscription libraries to which patrons paid small fees for the privilege of borrowing books, and these meagre storehouses of books often moved across town, from one empty room to another.

In 1891, an Iowa senator went to Carnegie and asked him to build a public library in the senator's hometown of Fairfield, Iowa. Although Carnegie had no ties to Fairfield, he made an immediate counter proposal: Have the town buy the site and guarantee ten years of upkeep, and Carnegie would give Fairfield a $40,000 building.

This very quickly became the Carnegie mantra: Over the next 30 years, Carnegie gave $41 million toward the construction of 1,689 public library buildings in the U.S., and the Midwest was his largest recipient. Indiana was first—156 grants—but Ohio was not far behind with 111 libraries.

Ms. Armentrout's illustrated book documents what must be considered a rather monumental act of preservation; Ohio has lost but ten of its 111 libraries, and two of those were to fire. The author points out two dramatic success stories—the old Carnegie at Ohio University in Athens is now the Scripps School of Journalism and one in Oxford is Miami University's school of architecture. Sixty-one are still used for their original purpose,

while others have been preserved as offices for lawyers, county and city officials, and historical museums. There is one restaurant (Cleveland), one church (Toledo), a village hall (Madison), and a hair salon (Kenton).

Buried in Ms. Armentrout's accompanying text are several details that delineate the early library culture. Carey's first attempts at a library—B.C.—were begun by the Women's Christian Temperance Union and first located in a millinery shop. Lorain's first library was by subscription, formed in 1883, and located in a dentist's office. Mansfield's was in the opera house, and Middleport's was in a room over the hardware store.

The first library in Columbus—1797— consisted of a Bible and a small collection of other books. It had a book-to-mouth existence for most of the next century and in 1901, the librarian went to see Carnegie who was not inclined to help Columbus until the librarian addressed the magnate in Welsh, whereupon Carnegie replied in his native Scottish dialect and, in time, doled out $150,000. The Youngstown library had a disinfecting room in the basement where books were taken when used by diseased patrons, and the delivery desk wrapped books with paper and string on rainy days.

When the industrialist died in 1919, there were 3,500 public library buildings in the U.S., meaning that he built about half of them. (He also built another 830 libraries in other parts of the world.) He said a man had a right to make a huge fortune but an equal duty to give it away. And so he did.

Says an appreciative Ms. Armentrout, "As a public librarian in Ohio in the 1990s Andy Carnegie is God." ❧

Ohio gift horse

Founded in 1917 with a collection of 509 books, the State Library of Ohio was established to provide research and information services to state government and agencies. In 1895 the State Library opened its doors to the Ohio public. Since its establishment, the State Library has grown to a collection of more than two million books, journals, newspapers, and government documents. Through participation in various on-line bibliographic networks, the state library provides materials to other libraries across the state and the nation. In addition, the State Library acts as a liaison between state government and the libraries of Ohio.

Any Ohio resident may borrow materials directly from the State Library. Ohio residents must register in person and present at least one piece of identification which shows current address.

Materials circulate for three weeks and may be renewed for three weeks for as many times as needed providing no holds have been placed by other library customers.

The State Librarian
Michael S. Lucas

The State Library of Ohio
274 East First Avenue
Suite 100, Columbus, Ohio 43201
614-644-7061 or 800-686-6950

Monday-Thursday 8:00-5:00
Friday 9:00-5:00

Circulation
614-644-6950/ *fax* 614-644-7004
E-mail: circhelp@sloma.state.oh.us

Genealogy
614-644-6966/ *fax* 614-728-2789
E-mail: genhelp@sloma.state.oh.us

Government Information Services
614-644-7051/ *fax* 614-752-9178
E-mail: refhelp@sloma.state.oh.us

Reference
614-644-7054/ *fax* 614-644-7054
E-mail: refhelp@sloma.state.oh.us

Interlibrary Loan
614-644-6956/ *fax* 752-9178
E-mail: cirhelp@sloma.state.oh.us

Library Programs & Development
614-644-7061 or 800-686-1532
fax 614-728-2788

Talking Books
614-644-6895 or 800-686-1531
fax 614-995-2186

Branches

Southeastern Ohio Regional Library Center (SEO)
40780 State Route 821
Caldwell, Ohio 53724
877-552-4262
8:00-4:00

Southwest Regional Library Center (SWB)
4646 Park Road
Fayetteville, Ohio 45118
513-875-3757
8:00-5:00

Library Services

Data Collection

The State Library collects and compiles data from Ohio's libraries for use in federal and state programs. The information is published in the annual Directory of Ohio Libraries and is available on-line on the State Library's website.

Research Services

The Research Services staff can provide patrons with general reference services and state employees with in-depth information they need to perform their jobs efficiently and effectively. In addition to the general reference collection, the State Library has specialized research resources. It can:

• Access databases such as the American Business Directory, the Biography and Genealogy Master Index, the *Columbus Dispatch*, Computer Select, Ohio Revised Code, Books in Print, Facts on File, and the Harris Criss Cross Directory.

• Provide full-text articles from selected sources, including ABI Inform and Periodical Abstracts.

• Suggest avenues of research for patrons.

• Provide help with web access.

Talking Book Program

As part of a national network headed by the Library of Congress, the State Library coordinates library service for the blind and physically impaired Ohioans. Through contacts with regional libraries in Cincinnati and Cleveland, the State Library loans, free of charge, books and magazines in Braille and on cassette, as well as special playback equipment.

Specialized Collections

Genealogy—The State Library of Ohio's genealogy collection includes records for Ohio and New England, Middle Atlantic and Southern Border states. The Library is the Depository for the Ohio Daughters of the American Revolution and the Huguenot Society of Ohio.

Government Documents—The State Library of Ohio is the depository for federal and state government documents. In addition to printed information, the Government Information Services staff can help patrons explore many CD-ROM databases or search GPO Access and other Federal government websites.

History of Ohio Public Libraries and the Development of State Laws for Libraries

The first libraries in Ohio were those organized cooperatively and available to share-holders, subscribers, or members. These libraries were sometimes known as "social" libraries, "subscription" libraries, or "association" libraries. Individuals pooled their money in a common fund for the purchase of books. The General Assembly passed several separate acts of incorporation for libraries before 1817, and in that year it passed a general law providing for the incorporation of libraries.

It was also in 1817 that the General Assembly approved the establishment of the State Library by Governor Worthington.

By 1850, the year which American library historians have taken as the point at which the American free library movement got underway, some 187 "social" libraries had been established in Ohio.

The School Act of 1853 laid a base for tax support of school district public libraries in Ohio, and in 1869 the General Assembly enacted legislation authorizing municipalities to open and maintain free libraries and reading rooms. An 1898 act authorized county-wide library service, a result of a $50,000 gift to Van Wert County for establishment of the Brumback Library.

A public library could be established by a municipality, township, school district, or county

World's longest overdue library book

The Medical Reports of the Effects of Water, Cold and Warm, as a Remedy in Fever and Febrile Diseases, by James Curry; it was checked out of the University of Cincinnati Medical Library in 1823 and returned 145 years later by the borrower's grandson; the overdue fine of $2,646 was waived.

to provide free library service to the residents of the subdivision and support it by taxes collected on the duplicate of the subdivision. Association libraries opened their doors to the general public in return for a share of the public funds.

Before 1921, most public libraries were association or municipal but legislative action changed this. A 15-mill limitation enacted on real property taxes and subdivisions left many libraries without funding. In 1921, school districts were permitted to levy outside this limitation. Therefore, any library organized as part of a school district could levy a tax of one and a half mills. Many municipal and association libraries reorganized as school district libraries. All libraries were without support when a constitutional limitation of 10 mills was passed in 1934.

The desperate situation that resulted for libraries when they were thus cut off from property tax support made it necessary to find other means of library support. This was accomplished through legislation sponsored in the 1931 General Assembly by the late Robert A. Taft, then state Senator from Hamilton County, and in the 1933 session by Senator Frank E. Whittemore of Summit County. This legislation provided that any library board that would make the services of its library available to all residents of the county could receive funds from the intangibles tax through application to the county budget commission.

It then became possible for a community to establish a free public library without direct cost to itself because the intangibles tax was a county tax. The number of public libraries climbed from 197 in 1923 to 280 in 1947. In that year, the General Assembly took action, provided that after September 1, 1947, new public libraries would be established on a county-wide basis. The libraries already established by cities, townships, school districts, and associations were permitted to continue, but no taxing authority other than the county could establish new ones. In 1967, the Code was amended (Sec. 3375.121) to provide for the establishment of a municipal library under certain circumstances.

Funding for public libraries in Ohio changed again when the 115th General Assembly abolished the intangible personal property tax and created the Library and Local Government Support Fund. The fund consisted of 6.3 percent of the personal income tax collection, beginning January 1, 1986. A new funding plan was submitted January 1, 1985, the formula for distribution of these funds to counties developed by the Ohio Department of Taxation. Within each county, the plan for distribution remains the responsibility of the county budget commission.

Legal Organization of Public Libraries Today

Before 1931—when libraries were supported by real estate tax levies or by gifts and the income from endowments—libraries were organized as parts of political subdivisions (city, school district, township, county) and received their support directly from these subdivisions. Now all types of libraries receive their primary support from the County Library and Local Government Support Fund.

There are six types of public libraries under Ohio law: association, county district, county, municipal, school district, and township. The law provides for a seventh type, the regional district library (Sec. 3375.28), but no libraries are now organized under that law.

The board of an association library is appointed or elected in accordance with its state charter or the rules of the individual library association. The taxing authority for the association library is the county commissioners.

The county library board has six members appointed by the judge of the court of common pleas. The taxing authority is the county commissioners.

The county district library board has a membership of seven: three appointed by the common pleas judge or judges, and four by the county commissioners.

The municipal library has a board of six members appointed by the mayor. The taxing authority for the municipal library is the city council.

The school district public library has a board of seven members appointed by the local board of education. The taxing authority is the board of education.

The township library is governed by a board of three members appointed by the township trustees. The taxing authority is the township trustees.

Under certain conditions libraries may convert to a county district library status. The State Library has prepared these guidelines, which are available upon request to the State Librarian.

—*Source: Library Laws of Ohio, prepared by the State Library of Ohio*

The public rarely notices the Library's catalog except when entries are misleading or missing. Professional librarians regard the catalog as the soul of a library, and cataloging was once considered the highest skill in library science.

A great cataloger worked with the skill of a lapidary, reducing a massive book to its essence. A catalog entry highlighted the book's contents and its links to the broader themes of its field. It described its physical appearance and publishing history so precisely that the book in hand could not be mistaken for any other.

A catalog entry was a unique record and, at the same time, a standardized scientific source. In the 19th century, the Public Library of Cincinnati & Hamilton County did virtually all its own cataloging, generating an entry for every book in its collection. So did every other library. The duplication was enormous and wasteful.

In 1910, the Library began buying pre-printed cards with standardized catalog entries for new books from the Library of Congress. As data processing spread through libraries, they formed cataloging cooperatives like OCLC (once the Ohio Consortium for Library Cataloging but now legally the On-line Computer Library Center, Inc.) which now handles the vast bulk of new cataloging electronically.

But if new entries are mass-produced, every library's catalog is still slightly different. In a large, old, and active public library like Cincinnati's, the catalog is unique. The old card catalog especially, with its rows and rows of wooden filing cases, was a massive collective work, built up layer by layer, each generation of catalogers adding another level.

The proof was in the cards. Particularly on a subject the cataloger knew well or which was of intense local interest, an entry could run to three or more cards, all carefully typed or written and densely cross-referenced.

—John Fleischman, from his book, *Free & Public, One Hundred and Fifty Years at the Public Library of Cincinnati & Hamilton County 1853-2003*

County/Library	Registered Borrowers	Staff	Circulation Total	Per Borrower	Volumes	Per Borrower
ADAMS	12,868	22.1	294,349	22.9	103,164	8.0
West Union	12,868	22.1	294,349	22.9	103,164	8.0
ALLEN	95,879	95.2	1,187,386	12.4	470,349	4.9
Bluffton	6,572	7.8	85,490	13.0	32,651	5.0
Delphos	8,320	10.6	194,288	23.4	75,872	9.1
Lima	80,987	76.8	907,608	11.2	361,826	4.5
ASHLAND	38,759	39.6	677,584	17.5	175,290	4.5
Ashland	30,100	26.0	540,216	17.9	120,669	4.0
Loudonville	8,659	13.6	137,368	15.9	54,621	6.3
ASHTABULA	86,123	85.3	1,045,958	12.1	450,956	5.2
Andover	5,403	7.1	130,108	24.1	27,647	5.1
Ashtabula	36,868	31.1	289,375	7.8	140,909	3.8
Ashtabula Harbor	7,118	9.7	125,288	17.6	41,750	5.9
Conneaut	13,061	10.8	146,432	11.2	49,605	3.8
Jefferson	8,611	8.9	95,357	11.1	57,385	6.7
Kingsville	3,912	7.6	75,348	19.3	42,504	10.9
Orwell	7,600	5.8	97,317	12.8	60,500	8.0
Rock Creek	3,550	4.3	86,733	24.4	30,656	8.6
ATHENS	44,846	42.8	593,626	13.2	266,458	5.9
Nelsonville	44,846	42.8	593,626	13.2	266,458	5.9
AUGLAIZE	26,153	37.5	382,256	14.6	221,559	8.5
St. Marys	8,802	11.6	101,656	11.5	60,436	6.9
Wapakoneta	17,351	26.0	280,600	16.2	161,123	9.3
BELMONT	46,795	58.3	658,090	14.1	373,805	8.0
Barnesville	7,730	10.5	178,268	23.1	60,813	7.9
Bellaire	8,209	7.9	56,623	6.9	64,455	7.9
Martins Ferry	21,516	26.9	269,376	12.5	193,351	9.0
St. Clairsville	9,340	13.1	153,823	16.5	55,186	5.9
BROWN	24,743	36.2	392,686	15.9	148,661	6.0
Georgetown	18,109	22.5	224,726	12.4	96,988	5.4
Ripley	6,634	13.6	167,960	25.3	51,673	7.8
BUTLER	232,161	184.1	3,989,313	17.2	841,864	3.6
Hamilton	139,235	103.8	1,976,041	14.2	554,964	4.0
Middletown	92,926	80.3	2,013,272	21.7	286,900	3.1
CARROLL	14,056	19.3	275,747	19.6	78,414	5.6
Carrollton	14,056	19.3	275,747	19.6	78,414	5.6
CHAMPAIGN	35,242	34.6	415,822	11.8	175,032	5.0
Mechanicsburg	5,578	7.2	62,281	11.2	40,259	7.2
St. Paris	5,535	9.2	99,831	18.0	45,604	8.2
Urbana	24,129	18.2	253,710	10.5	89,169	3.7
CLARK	59,340	78.1	1,210,668	20.4	459,979	7.8
New Carlisle	8,190	7.3	155,105	18.9	60,374	7.4
Springfield	51,150	70.8	1,055,563	20.6	399,605	7.8
CLERMONT	120,207	120.8	1,416,416	11.8	424,650	3.5
Batavia	120,207	120.8	1,416,416	11.8	424,650	3.5

County/Library	Registered Borrowers	Staff	Circulation Total	Per Borrower	Volumes	Per Borrower
CLINTON	24,381	28.1	357,036	14.6	162,473	6.7
Blanchester	7,332	7.6	100,113	13.7	61,071	8.3
Sabina	4,328	4.4	64,215	14.8	33,173	7.7
Wilmington	12,721	16.0	192,708	15.1	68,229	5.4
COLUMBIANA	86,994	77.2	1,205,488	13.9	391,554	4.5
Columbiana	13,749	9.1	225,566	16.4	47,109	3.4
East Liverpool	23,403	21.9	201,848	8.6	92,397	3.9
East Palestine	8,623	4.2	132,004	15.3	42,300	4.9
Leetonia	2,714	4.8	80,401	29.6	27,016	10.0
Lisbon	15,471	11.4	132,117	8.5	82,020	5.3
Salem	16,548	19.5	379,087	22.9	65,729	4.0
Wellsville	6,486	6.3	54,465	8.4	34,983	5.4
COSHOCTON	19,691	25.6	529,429	26.9	119,912	6.1
Coshocton	19,691	25.6	529,429	26.9	119,912	6.1
CRAWFORD	45,206	30.8	481,230	10.6	220,393	4.9
Bucyrus	16,798	10.9	100,007	6.0	50,576	3.0
Crestline	11,281	9.4	135,029	12.0	71,180	6.3
Galion	17,127	10.6	246,194	14.4	98,637	5.8
CUYAHOGA	1,353,530	1703.1	27,204,716	20.1	7,580,739	5.6
Cleveland	558,799	600.3	5,346,487	9.6	3,036,081	5.4
Cleveland Hts.	52,512	111.1	1,908,017	36.3	340,403	6.5
Cuy. Co.-Parma	478,875	626.8	13,473,206	28.1	2,949,082	6.2
East Cleveland	17,801	44.2	436,292	24.5	191,264	10.7
Euclid	36,226	62.9	1,157,972	32.0	234,823	6.5
Lakewood	100,027	70.8	1,896,271	19.0	309,273	3.1
Rocky River	29,551	46.0	788,658	26.7	123,794	4.2
Shaker Heights	44,279	79.6	1,151,225	26.0	241,629	5.5
Westlake	35,460	61.4	1,046,588	29.5	154,390	4.4
DARKE	34,643	41.7	567,265	16.4	226,012	6.5
Arcanum	4,850	8.6	75,593	15.6	54,316	11.2
Greenville	20,266	17.9	273,603	13.5	87,055	4.3
New Madison	4,061	8.9	100,986	24.9	47,281	11.6
Versailles	5,466	6.3	117,083	21.4	37,360	6.8
DEFIANCE	22,175	25.5	260,451	11.7	119,028	5.4
Defiance	22,175	25.5	260,451	11.7	119,028	5.4
DELAWARE	68,218	48.5	844,747	12.4	286,302	4.2
Ashley	4,895	4.6	54,304	11.1	29,764	6.1
Delaware	45,390	30.4	520,463	11.5	157,637	3.5
Sunbury	17,933	13.5	269,980	15.1	98,901	5.5
ERIE	65,602	93.0	1,292,864	19.7	423,212	6.5
Huron	4,110	14.5	118,922	28.9	48,685	11.8
Milan	6,741	14.5	225,042	33.4	95,590	14.2
Sandusky	39,875	47.8	648,008	16.3	213,787	5.4
Vermilion	14,876	16.3	300,892	20.2	65,150	4.4
FAIRFIELD	111,270	81.6	1,530,995	13.8	353,468	3.2
Lancaster	77,080	63.1	1,164,268	15.1	250,325	3.2
Pickerington	34,190	18.4	366,727	10.7	103,143	3.0
FAYETTE	13,451	19.0	217,805	16.2	69,461	5.2
Washington CH	13,451	19.0	217,805	16.2	69,461	5.2

The Cleveland Public Library pioneered in 1890 the concept of open shelves for use by its patrons. The Cleveland system, one of the largest in the U.S., is also credited with originating the guide to current magazines, as well as the system of dividing a library into its various departments.

—The Plain Dealer

County/Library	Registered Borrowers	Staff	Circulation Total	Per Borrower	Volumes	Per Borrower
FRANKLIN	745,384	1127.5	22,965,957	30.8	4,225,867	5.7
Bexley	29,260	30.6	774,650	26.5	205,940	7.0
Columbus	440,614	751.0	15,323,568	34.8	2,419,952	5.5
Grandview Hts.	42,409	43.4	744,309	17.6	165,115	3.9
Grove City	45,724	77.0	1,278,571	28.0	290,371	6.4
Upper Arlington	57,891	80.6	1,563,527	27.0	400,040	6.9
Westerville	71,749	45.3	1,616,608	22.5	309,550	4.3
Worthington	57,737	99.6	1,664,724	28.8	434,899	7.5
FULTON	42,856	44.0	573,948	13.4	210,030	4.9
Archbold	7,199	7.8	159,731	22.2	31,200	4.3
Delta	7,943	9.5	97,916	12.3	52,631	6.6
Fayette	2,233	4.3	28,598	12.8	22,053	9.9
Metamora	3,261	5.1	63,225	19.4	35,781	11.0
Swanton	11,679	6.4	116,343	10.0	32,889	2.8
Wauseon	10,541	10.8	108,135	10.3	35,476	3.4
GALLIA	20,759	28.7	324,906	15.7	106,081	5.1
Gallipolis	20,759	28.7	324,906	15.7	106,081	5.1

THE EXACTING PRICE OF FRONTIER LITERACY

In the wilderness that was Athens County in the early 1800s, the only newspaper subscriber was one Josiah True, who, when his copy of the *American Gazette* arrived every three months, willingly shared it with his far-flung neighbors.

Given their lack of reading material, Mr. True proposed to the settlers in Amesville, Dover, and Sunday Creek that they start a library. Given their lack of cash, it was a most ambitious idea.

Undaunted, they set traplines all winter, and in the spring of 1804, dispatched Samuel Brown of Sunday Creek with a wagon load of bear, wolf, and raccoon skins.

He was to travel six hundred miles to Boston and barter the hard-won hides for books. Mr. Brown returned with fifty-one books valued at $73.50, his selections including an encyclopedia, *Butler's Analogy*, Lillo's *The London Merchant*, and the writings of Goldsmith.

The small, but treasured library was installed at Amesville, where the volumes were so meticulously kept that borrowers had to pay a fine if they put thumbprints on the pages.

The circulation reached 462 books by 1826, and the collection had grown to include the works of Locke, Shakespeare, and Scott.

When Lord Byron learned that his books were being lent by the frontier library, he wrote with delight, "These are the first tidings that have ever sounded like Fame to my ears—to be read on the banks of the Ohio!"

Many of the Coonskin Library books still survive, entrusted to the Ohio Historical Society in Columbus.

County/Library	Registered Borrowers	Staff	Circulation Total	Per Borrower	Volumes	Per Borrower
GEAUGA	70,149	118.6	2,100,974	30.0	522,326	7.4
Burton	7,610	15.1	203,290	26.7	73,659	9.7
Chardon	62,539	103.5	1,897,684	30.3	448,667	7.2
GREENE	46,890	109.5	2,256,630	48.1	506,405	10.8
Xenia	46,890	109.5	2,256,630	48.1	506,405	10.8
GUERNSEY	22,156	23.4	332,161	15.0	128,202	5.8
Cambridge	22,156	23.4	332,161	15.0	128,202	5.8
HAMILTON	404,655	747.8	14,403,659	35.6	4,977,386	12.3
Cincinnati	404,655	747.8	14,403,659	35.6	4,977,386	12.3
HANCOCK	45,645	54.2	1,181,090	25.9	302,323	6.6
Findlay	39,569	46.9	1,106,529	28.0	247,032	6.2
McComb	6,076	7.4	74,561	12.3	55,291	9.1
HARDIN	28,518	31.5	315,505	11.1	128,844	4.5
Ada	4,350	5.4	32,747	7.5	19,234	4.4
Alger	1,175	1.9	8,241	7.0	10,270	8.7
Dunkirk	1,019	1.5	12,603	12.4	7,039	6.9
Forest	1,974	3.1	42,682	21.6	14,486	7.3
Kenton	18,652	17.3	191,744	10.3	55,570	3.0
Mt. Victory	1,348	2.3	27,488	20.4	22,245	16.5
HARRISON	10,342	18.7	235,641	22.8	108,112	10.5
Bowerston	2,059	5.3	58,674	28.5	39,457	19.2
Cadiz	8,283	13.4	176,967	21.4	68,655	8.3
HENRY	24,767	28.9	284,757	11.5	235,958	9.5
Deshler	3,375	6.6	86,511	25.6	48,818	14.5
Holgate	2,832	2.3	13,519	4.8	32,344	11.4
Liberty Center	2,302	3.5	31,481	13.7	18,529	8.0
Napoleon	16,258	16.5	153,246	9.4	136,267	8.4
HIGHLAND	25,603	26.1	519,956	20.3	151,614	5.9
Hillsboro	25,603	26.1	519,956	20.3	151,614	5.9
HOCKING	25,528	13.4	404,694	15.9	147,767	5.8
Logan	25,528	13.4	404,694	15.9	147,767	5.8
HOLMES	17,312	25.3	621,071	35.9	147,131	8.5
Millersburg	17,312	25.3	621,071	35.9	147,131	8.5
HURON	52,032	70.0	915,533	17.6	291,937	5.6
Bellevue	10,579	14.7	246,378	23.3	66,820	6.3
Monroeville	924	4.3	42,993	46.5	20,830	22.5
New London	6,013	7.3	57,043	9.5	38,808	6.5
Norwalk	20,202	20.8	290,149	14.4	79,577	3.9
Willard	14,314	22.9	278,970	19.5	85,902	6.0
JACKSON	28,051	20.9	243,899	8.7	104,523	3.7
Jackson	11,940	11.1	122,110	10.2	45,115	3.8
Oak Hill	3,090	5.6	39,493	12.8	25,613	8.3
Wellston	13,021	4.1	82,296	6.3	33,795	2.6
JEFFERSON	39,994	53.1	736,297	18.4	188,552	4.7
Steubenville	39,994	53.1	736,297	18.4	188,552	4.7

Frequently replaced books at the Cleveland Public Library: *The Bible; The Koran;* Car manuals; *Best Loved Poems of the American People* by Hazel Felleman; *The Autobiography of Malcolm X.*

—*The Cleveland Public Library*

County/Library	Registered Borrowers	Staff	Circulation Total	Per Borrower	Volumes	Per Borrower
KNOX	30,657	54.7	829,344	27.1	207,539	6.8
Centerburg	5,537	4.4	81,705	14.8	28,282	5.1
Mt. Vernon	25,120	50.3	747,639	29.8	179,257	7.1
LAKE	184,241	232.4	3,956,662	21.5	944,748	5.1
Fairport Harbor	3,094	8.0	83,391	27.0	35,167	11.4
Kirtland	5,968	12.3	140,970	23.6	65,597	11.0
Madison	14,571	17.5	375,075	25.7	105,939	7.3
Mentor	59,927	55.3	971,567	16.2	209,739	3.5
Painesville	38,742	36.5	664,165	17.1	157,553	4.1
Perry	9,325	17.5	223,248	23.9	53,228	5.7
Wickliffe	11,384	20.1	468,890	41.2	100,148	8.8
Willoughby	41,230	65.2	1,029,356	25.0	217,377	5.3
LAWRENCE	46,892	48.8	590,547	12.6	167,566	3.6
Ironton	46,892	48.8	590,547	12.6	167,566	3.6
LICKING	127,465	117.3	1,663,961	13.1	566,492	4.4
Alexandria	5,899	6.8	96,353	16.3	52,087	8.8
Granville	14,702	11.3	162,529	11.1	62,110	4.2
Homer	2,683	3.4	41,713	15.5	32,407	12.1
Newark	92,558	82.5	1,153,243	12.5	346,087	3.7
Pataskala	11,623	13.3	210,123	18.1	73,801	6.3

Ten public libraries with most registered borrowers

bookworms

1. Cleveland Public Library—558,799

2. Cuyahoga County Public Library, Parma—478,875

3. Columbus Metropolitan Library—440,614

4. Public Library of Cincinnati and Hamilton County—404,614

5. Toledo-Lucas County Public Library—297,912

6. Dayton and Montgomery County Public Library—256,047

7. Akron-Summit County Public Library—224,494

8. Stark County District Library, Canton —210,292

9. Hamilton Public Library—139,235

10. Public Library of Youngstown and Mahoning County— 96,064

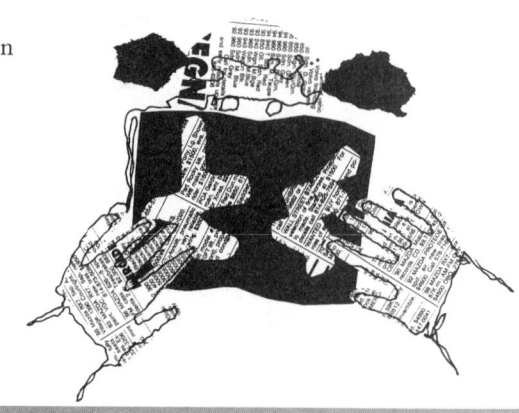

County/Library	Registered Borrowers	Staff	Circulation Total	Per Borrower	Volumes	Per Borrower
LOGAN	22,351	34.8	385,334	17.2	167,307	7.5
Belle Center	1,911	1.8	19,587	10.2	20,415	10.7
Bellefontaine	19,763	31.7	360,189	18.2	140,178	7.1
Zanesfield	677	1.3	5,558	8.2	6,714	9.9
LORAIN	211,105	250.8	3,699,549	17.5	1,240,938	5.9
Amherst	24,624	18.2	290,155	11.8	61,622	2.5
Avon Lake	19,958	34.4	600,935	30.1	90,338	4.5
Elyria	54,062	56.1	743,994	13.8	340,206	6.3
Grafton	13,718	15.9	180,402	13.2	63,783	4.6
Lorain	78,522	101.0	1,506,412	19.2	496,154	6.3
Oberlin	11,297	17.2	280,125	24.8	139,791	12.4
Wellington	8,924	7.9	97,526	10.9	49,044	5.5
LUCAS	297,912	342.0	6,603,030	22.2	2,469,168	8.3
Toledo	297,912	342.0	6,603,030	22.2	2,469,168	8.3
MADISON	27,386	35.4	395,473	14.4	182,548	6.7
London	9,617	13.5	127,262	13.2	42,409	4.4
Mt. Sterling	1,751	2.3	28,490	16.3	29,457	16.8
Plain City	7,999	10.0	160,080	20.0	58,043	7.3
West Jefferson	8,019	9.6	79,641	9.9	52,639	6.6
MAHONING	96,064	177.8	2,031,059	21.1	782,736	8.1
Youngstown	96,064	177.8	2,031,059	21.1	782,736	8.1
MARION	57,447	52.5	860,220	15.0	250,260	4.4
Marion	57,447	52.5	860,220	15.0	250,260	4.4
MEDINA	118,896	137.6	2,883,303	24.3	676,663	5.7
Medina	91,976	101.3	2,179,065	23.7	521,748	5.7
Wadsworth	26,920	36.3	704,238	26.2	154,915	5.8
MEIGS	7,017	20.3	207,436	12.2	113,421	6.7
Pomeroy	17,017	20.3	207,436	12.2	113,421	6.7
MERCER	25,046	34.9	550,539	22.0	206,062	8.2
Celina	14,726	21.2	282,142	19.2	112,439	7.6
Coldwater	6,004	7.1	144,414	24.1	53,108	8.8
Fort Recovery	2,574	3.3	63,943	24.8	20,677	8.0
Rockford	1,742	3.2	60,040	34.5	19,838	11.4
MIAMI	86,860	78.7	1,469,909	16.9	549,292	6.3
Bradford	2,499	3.7	67,627	27.1	33,789	13.5
Covington	2,035	5.0	144,831	71.2	52,857	26.0
Piqua	19,797	15.1	221,106	11.2	108,806	5.5
Tipp City	14,317	14.6	235,633	16.5	90,422	6.3
Troy	36,137	29.7	665,526	18.4	210,000	5.8
West Milton	12,075	10.6	135,186	11.2	53,418	4.4
MONROE	6,250	9.8	136,540	21.8	55,643	8.9
Woodsfield	6,250	9.8	136,540	21.8	55,643	8.9
MONTGOMERY	343,955	500.9	9,401,231	27.3	2,581,964	7.5
Centerville	55,466	97.7	1,968,103	35.5	349,628	6.3
Dayton	256,047	353.1	6,417,496	25.1	2,025,980	7.9
Germantown	9,185	14.1	230,600	25.1	80,203	8.7
Oakwood	23,257	36.0	485,032	33.8	126,153	5.4
MORGAN	7,820	11.3	132,254	16.9	60,890	7.8
McConnelsville	7,820	11.3	132,254	16.9	60,890	7.8

First library in Ohio: Farmer's Library, started in Belpre in 1796, with books—kept in a bushel basket —owned by the General Putnam family

First library incorporated under Ohio law —Dayton Library Society, 1805

First county-wide library in U.S. —Brumback Library, Van Wert, 1901

County/Library	Registered Borrowers	Staff	Circulation Total	Per Borrower	Volumes	Per Borrower
MORROW	20,656	21.0	226,403	11.0	113,735	5.5
Cardington	4,121	3.1	38,728	9.4	28,887	7.0
Chesterville	3,879	5.4	82,006	21.1	22,092	5.7
Mt. Gilead	8,759	7.5	69,851	8.0	30,395	3.5
Shauck	3,897	4.9	35,818	9.2	32,361	8.3
MUSKINGUM	66,642	54.0	856,733	12.9	306,684	4.6
Zanesville	66,642	54.0	856,733	12.9	306,684	4.6
NOBLE	5,726	11.2	107,957	18.9	43,653	7.6
Caldwell	5,726	11.2	107,957	18.9	43,653	7.6
OTTAWA	26,903	32.8	464,914	17.3	220,058	8.2
Elmore	6,027	9.4	101,613	16.9	98,634	16.4
Oak Harbor	6,020	5.2	96,871	16.1	33,327	5.5
Port Clinton	14,856	18.3	266,430	17.9	88,097	5.9
PAULDING	9,801	14.0	180,196	18.4	67,878	6.9
Paulding	9,801	14.0	180,196	18.4	67,879	6.9
PERRY	19,367	22.3	384,870	19.9	125,391	6.5
New Lexington	18,491	20.4	368,303	19.9	112,368	6.1
New Straitsville	876	1.9	16,567	18.9	13,023	14.9
PICKAWAY	24,721	34.2	317,577	12.8	131,948	5.3
Circleville	24,721	34.2	317,577	12.8	131,948	5.3

TEN PUBLIC LIBRARIES WITH HIGHEST AVERAGE CIRCULATION*

bookworms

1. Peninsula Library, Peninsula—87.7

2. J.R. Clarke Public Library, Covington—71.2

3. Greene County Public Library, Xenia—48.1

4. Monroeville Public Library, Monroeville—46.5

5. Wickliffe Public Library, Wickliffe—41.2

6. Newcomerstown Public Library, Newcomerstown—38.7

7. Mohawk Community Library, Sycamore—37.2

8. Bliss Memorial Public Library, Bloomville—36.6

9. Cleveland Heights–University Heights Public Library, Cleveland Heights—36.3

10. Public Library of Cincinnati and Hamilton County, Cincinnati—35.6

*average per card-holder

County/Library	Registered Borrowers	Staff	Circulation Total	Per Borrower	Volumes	Per Borrower
PIKE	15,815	19.6	260,171	16.5	89,005	5.6
Waverly	15,815	19.6	260,171	16.5	89,005	5.6
PORTAGE	83,336	103.1	1,474,916	17.7	524,413	6.3
Garretsville	36,997	64.6	950,710	25.7	247,722	6.7
Kent	33,634	18.7	336,999	10.0	179,537	5.3
Ravenna	12,705	19.8	187,207	14.7	97,154	7.6
PREBLE	24,972	30.7	341,725	13.7	200,974	8.0
Eaton	21,555	26.5	272,791	12.7	157,196	7.3
Gratis	555	1.1	8,787	15.8	15,486	27.9
Lewisburg	2,862	3.1	60,147	21.0	28,292	9.9
PUTNAM	17,761	32.0	274,408	15.5	131,037	7.4
Ottawa	17,761	32.0	274,408	15.5	131,037	7.4
RICHLAND	97,109	152.2	2,148,536	22.1	558,525	5.8
Mansfield	87,096	139.6	2,000,631	23.0	488,704	5.6
Shelby	10,013	12.6	147,905	14.8	69,821	7.0
ROSS	29,610	49.6	530,200	17.9	166,857	5.6
Chillicothe	29,610	49.6	530,200	17.9	166,857	5.6
SANDUSKY	33,276	40.6	528,521	15.9	192,480	5.8
Clyde	7,167	8.7	73,774	10.3	33,847	4.7
Fremont	26,109	31.9	454,747	17.4	158,633	6.1
SCIOTO	34,728	61.8	624,218	18.0	225,879	6.5
Portsmouth	34,728	61.8	624,218	18.0	225,879	6.5
SENECA	37,357	51.5	733,945	19.6	264,103	7.1
Attica	2,930	4.4	62,522	21.3	24,220	8.3
Bettsville	1,696	4.0	43,499	25.6	21,258	12.5
Bloomville	998	3.2	36,541	36.6	36,615	36.7
Fostoria	12,552	15.8	136,028	10.8	76,569	6.1
Tiffin	19,181	24.1	455,355	23.7	105,441	5.5
SHELBY	27,910	26.3	391,408	14.0	143,016	5.1
Sidney	27,910	26.3	391,408	14.0	143,016	5.1
STARK	347,371	369.1	5,812,468	16.7	1,327,577	3.8
Alliance	19,520	38.7	448,233	23.0	153,106	7.8
Canal Fulton	9,896	13.9	166,018	16.8	51,352	5.2
Canton	210,292	211.6	3,106,872	14.8	660,349	3.1
Louisville	17,428	13.4	247,002	14.2	122,740	7.0
Massillon	40,020	45.5	682,592	17.1	171,298	4.3
Minerva	9,887	13.2	212,730	21.5	72,672	7.4
North Canton	40,328	32.7	949,021	23.5	96,060	2.4
SUMMIT	402,512	524.4	8,223,469	20.4	1,955,423	4.9
Akron	224,494	355.5	5,119,005	22.8	1,275,451	5.7
Barberton	27,698	27.6	334,009	12.1	111,189	4.0
Cuyahoga Falls	63,181	32.7	624,470	9.9	193,544	3.1
Hudson	21,761	32.8	505,766	23.2	98,715	4.5
Peninsula	753	7.7	66,049	87.7	28,457	37.8
Stow	35,921	35.4	779,696	21.7	113,545	3.2
Twinsburg	28,704	32.7	794,474	27.7	134,522	4.7

County/Library	Registered Borrowers	Staff	Circulation Total	Per Borrower	Volumes	Per Borrower
TRUMBULL	165,987	182.2	2,467,209	14.9	743,689	4.5
Bristolville	6,761	10.8	194,777	28.8	50,038	7.4
Girard	23,092	14.4	274,740	11.9	74,840	3.2
Hubbard	14,385	18.0	178,238	12.4	64,755	4.5
Kinsman	8,723	12.5	228,164	26.2	71,499	8.2
Newton Falls	8,731	15.3	152,466	17.5	43,306	5.0
Niles	11,767	18.5	289,839	24.6	70,864	6.0
Warren	92,528	92.8	1,148,985	12.4	368,387	4.0
TUSCARAWAS	63,620	79.2	1,267,326	19.9	354,440	5.6
Dover	14,360	11.9	276,078	19.2	93,120	6.5
Gnadenhutten	2,060	5.1	33,306	16.2	23,860	11.6
New Philadelphia	34,319	45.8	632,782	18.4	152,684	4.4
Newcomerstown	3,622	6.8	140,078	38.7	41,775	11.5
Uhrichsville	9,259	9.5	185,082	20.0	43,001	4.6
UNION	18,336	25.6	403,098	22.0	158,621	8.7
Marysville	14,418	20.8	287,478	19.9	82,394	5.7
Richwood	3,918	4.8	115,620	29.5	76,227	19.5
VAN WERT	18,936	16.0	493,208	26.0	160,336	8.5
Van Wert	18,936	16.0	493,208	26.0	160,336	8.5
VINTON	11,352	8.8	98,228	8.7	47,981	4.2
McArthur	11,352	8.8	98,228	8.7	47,981	4.2
WARREN	91,042	78.9	1,519,197	16.7	537,439	5.9
Franklin	22,566	28.9	385,165	17.1	134,208	5.9
Lebanon	32,318	10.4	295,392	9.1	138,080	4.3
Mason	21,643	19.5	457,376	21.1	113,902	5.3
Morrow	6,085	6.8	199,826	32.8	86,393	14.2
Waynesville	8,430	13.3	181,438	21.5	64,856	7.7
WASHINGTON	35,379	52.9	N/A	—	208,416	5.9
Marietta	35,379	52.9	N/A	—	208,416	5.9
WAYNE	75,480	110.3	1,547,477	20.5	419,056	5.6
Orrville	13,482	19.4	386,321	28.7	67,054	5.0
Wooster	61,998	90.9	1,161,156	18.7	352,002	5.7
WILLIAMS	24,966	42.6	634,614	25.4	164,867	6.6
Bryan	20,958	37.3	567,548	27.1	120,183	5.7
Montpelier	4,008	5.3	67,066	16.7	44,684	11.1
WOOD	44,395	107.3	1,544,787	34.8	537,728	12.1
Bowling Green	—	28.4	449,920	—	153,843	—
North Baltimore	3,400	9.6	92,939	27.3	46,104	13.6
Pemberville	0	9.6	89,179	—	48,051	—
Perrysburg	28,686	25.7	538,982	18.8	101,156	3.5
Rossford	8,986	16.3	196,406	21.9	84,329	9.4
Wayne	—	6.5	93,885		51,337	
Weston	3,323	11.3	83,476	25.1	52,908	15.9
WYANDOT	16,716	21.8	352,161	21.1	104,375	6.2
Carey	7,009	8.9	149,014	21.3	45,654	6.5
Sycamore	2,962	4.9	110,061	37.2	31,225	10.5
Upper Sandusky	6,745	8.0	93,086	13.8	27,496	4.1
STATE TOTAL	*7,932,120*	*10085.2*	*165,454,936*	*20.9*	*48,074,614*	*6.1*

A guide to databases

Lost in dataspace? We've got news for you. The following list contains some of the best databases in Ohio, and how someone at the other end of the state may access them. Are *you* lucky.

Ohio has three of the nation's outstanding public information networks. Through Ohio's public, private, high school, and academic libraries the systems are linked to create an unparalleled research system. The Ohio Public Libraries Information System (OPLIN) serves primarily public libraries; INFOhio gives access to Ohio's schools, students, and parents; while OhioLink connects the state's academic libraries.

OPLIN

OPLIN, the most accessible of the three networks, is a comprehensive collection of databases and websites chosen by librarians, containing a wealth of information over a wide variety of subjects. The databases are, for the most part, beyond the reach of ordinary subscribers and range from encyclopedias to full-text collections of articles from scholarly journals.

Many of these databases can be accessed remotely by having a library card from a member library. Access may be through the member library's web site or directly from the OPLIN site. This access is limited to the databases subscribed to by your member library. However, any Ohio resident may become a member of any public library in the state, which requires only verification of residence. In most cases, this must be done in person, therefore, a Cleveland resident wishing a card from the Cincinnati library must visit the Cincinnati library in person, at least once (Toledo has an on-line registration form).

While every library's site is different, the databases—and their descriptions—are found in the "research" or "database" section of the site.

OPLIN publishes an on-line newsletter, *OPLIN Business Bytes: Ohio Public Libraries Serving Ohio Businesses*. The newsletter provides detailed information about business databases, websites, and other services that are provided by Ohio's libraries.

INFOhio

INFOhio is a free cooperative school library and information network service available to Ohio's parents, students, and teachers. Funded by the state, every student in every school in Ohio has access to the same core of up-to-date resource information with which to complete homework and research assignments.

These resources may be used during school and at home via the Internet. For home use, students must enter a username and password, which are provided by a school librarian, technology coordinator, or administrator.

Some of the databases and web sites available through INFOhio are:

American National Biography — Biographies of Americans no longer living

Britannica On-line: School Edition — Three encyclopedias

EBSCO Host — Full text articles from over 6,000 magazines and newspapers

MEDIANET — Book AV Material On-line

INFOhio Union Catalog — K-12 Curriculum Resources

OH! Teach — Web links for Educators

A.D.A.M. Health Illustrated Encyclopedia — In-depth information, color illustrations and animations on over 1,500 media topics.

American Memory — Primary source materials for U.S. history and culture from the Library of Congress

FirstGov — A search engine for more than 31 million U.S. Government Web pages

Librarians' Index to the Internet — Index to more than 10,000 Internet resources selected and evaluated by librarians.

MarcoPolo — Internet content for the classroom from a consortium of premier national education

organizations, state education agencies and the MarcoPolo Education Foundation

MEDLINE plus — Health information from the National Library of Medicine.

NetWellness — Health information from Ohio's major medical centers and much more.

OH! Kids — Activities, information and learning tools especially for tots, kids, and teens.

OH! Teach — Web links for teachers, library media specialists and other educators.

Ohio Landsat Satellite — Images. Satellite views of Ohio updated regularly; part of OhioLINK's Digital Media Center.

Ohio Memory Project — Ohio historical treasures in an on-line scrapbook of primary sources.

Ohio Resource Center — Links to resources that support best

practices in Math, Science and Reading.

OhioReads—Governor Taft's initiative to improve the reading skills of Ohio's K-4th grade students.

Sanborn Fire Insurance Maps— More than 40,000 maps (1847-1970) of Ohio towns and cities.

OhioLink

The nation's first statewide computer network of libraries and electronic information resources, OhioLINK is part of Ohio's ongoing tradition in pioneering library automation. In the 1960s, state funds supported the development of OCLC, then called the Ohio College Library Center, when The Ohio State University and others in Ohio began integrating campus library systems. OCLC has since grown into an international organization with a database of 30 million entries representing materials held in more than 10,000 libraries.

OhioLINK today is a consortium of the libraries of 84 Ohio colleges and universities, and the State Library of Ohio. Serving more than 600,000 students, OhioLINK's membership includes 17 public universities, 23 community/ technical colleges, and 43 private colleges, available to faculty, students, staff and other researchers via campus-based electronic library systems, the OhioLINK central site, and Internet resources.

OhioLINK's goal is to provide access to information and rapid delivery of library materials throughout the state. It offers six main electronic services: a central catalog,

research databases, an electronic journal center, a digital media center, a growing collection of e-books, and an electronic theses and dissertations center.

Central Catalog— OhioLINK offers access to more than 38 million library items statewide. The OhioLINK library catalog contains more than 8.4 million unique master records from its 84 institutions, encompassing a spectrum of library material including law, medical and special collections. The catalog systems throughout the state provide capacity for more than 4,500 simultaneous users. The central catalog is also available to outside users via the Internet. OhioLINK offers on-line borrowing through its statewide central catalog. Students and faculty have the ability to request items electronically while searching the catalog. OhioLINK also provides a delivery service among member institutions to speed the exchange of library items.

Research Databases— OhioLINK offers more than 100 electronic research databases, including a variety of full-text resources. These databases cover many academic areas at varying levels of detail. Many of the databases are citation indexes. Generally, the user can find out which OhioLINK members possess copies of the cited journal or link to the relevant full-text article. OhioLINK's electronic full-text resources include on-line dictionaries, literature, and journal articles. Access to the research databases is restricted to valid patrons at OhioLINK member institutions.

Electronic Journal Center (EJC)—OhioLINK launched the Electronic Journal Center, a

collection of full-text research journals, in 1998. The EJC contains over 4,700 scholarly journal titles from 34 publishers across a wide range of disciplines. More than 3.4 million articles are downloaded a year from the EJC, with a total of more than 8 million articles downloaded since its inception.

Digital Media Center (DMC)—The Digital Media Center is designed to archive and provide access to a variety of multi-media material. The DMC contains art and architecture images, satellite images of Ohio, historic Ohio city maps, social studies related materials, historic archival collections, foreign language videos, and physics demonstration videos. Several collections are accessible worldwide.

Ebooks—OhioLINK provides a diverse collection of e-books with more than 14,000 titles. A wide variety of titles purchased by OhioLINK, and public domain e-books are available in the net Library collection. The 24x7 collection contains technical and business reference books, journals, research reports and documentation from more than 80 of the world's top IT and business publishers. OhioLINK's growing Electronic Reference Book Collection contains more than 200 special-topic reference books, including encyclopedias, handbooks, biographical collections and guides.

Electronic Theses and Dissertations Center (ETD)—the ETD is a free on-line database of masters' theses and doctoral dissertations from graduate students in participating Ohio colleges and universities.

Following is a list of the databases with a short description and a list of the provider libraries. While the databases have been listed under topics, many go beyond their listing and cover multiple subjects.

Arts

Art Index Retrospective
A bibliographic database with citations to volumes 1-32 of the print edition of the *Art Index* (1929-1984) Articles from periodicals published throughout the world are cited.
The Public Library of Cincinnati and Hamilton County

Grove Dictionary of Art
Based on the 34-volume, 1936 *Grove Dictionary of Art.* Thousands of images in the Bridgeman Art Library, biographies, international coverage, prehistory to today. Selected web links.
*Columbus Metropolitan Library
Cuyahoga County Public Library
Dayton Metro Library
Public Library of Cincinnati and Hamilton County*

Grove Dictionary of Music On-line
Based on the 29-volume 2002 *New Grove Dictionary of Music and Musicians*, Second Edition and the *New Grove Dictionary of Opera*. Includes world, jazz, popular and 20th Century music coverage.
*Cuyahoga County Public Library
Dayton Metro Library*

Biography

American National Biography
A collection of 17,400 biographical sketches of American men & women throughout U.S. history whose lives have helped shape the nation.
Columbus Metropolitan Library

Biographies Index Plus
46,000 biographies and obituaries and more than 20,000 photographs from reference tools such as *Current Biography.*
Dayton Metro Library

Biography and Genealogy Master Index
Indexes current reference sources, such as Who's Who, as well as the most important retrospective works that cover individuals, both living and deceased, from every field of activity and from all areas of the world.
*Akron-Summit County Public Library
Cleveland Public Library
Cuyahoga County Public Library
Dayton Metro Library*

Biography Resource Center
A database of biographical information on more than one million people from throughout history, around the world, and across all disciplines and subject areas. Taken from 250 periodicals including the *Encyclopedia of World Biography*, The Complete *Marquis Who's Who*, and *Who's Who Among African Americans.*
*Cleveland Public Library
Columbus Metropolitan Library
Cuyahoga County Public Library
Public Library of Cincinnati and Hamilton County*

Business

Business and Company Resource Center
Detailed industry and company news and information with company profiles, histories, and financial; brand information; rankings; investment reports; and periodical articles.
*Akron-Summit County Public Library
Cuyahoga County Public Library
Public Library of Cincinnati and Hamilton County*

Business Dateline
Provides access to full-text articles from more than 530 newspapers, city business magazines, wire services in the United States and Canada. An essential business information tool for monitoring the latest trends in industry, health, environmental issues, and education.
Cleveland Public Library

Business Source Premier
Popular business magazines, trade and regional publications, scholarly journals, includes *Business Week, Forbes, Fortune, Harvard Business Review*, and *The Economist.*
*Cuyahoga County Public Library
Toledo Public Library
Dayton Metro Library*

Business Wire News
Full text newswires from all over the world.
Toledo Public Library

Careers

OCIS
The Ohio Career Information System, or OCIS is a career and job-finding tool for Ohioans
Columbus Metropolitan Library

Computers & the Internet

Computer Source
Periodicals covering computers, telecommunications, electronics, the Internet, and the latest innovations and trends in high technology.
*Cuyahoga County Public Library
Toledo Public Library*

Consumer Information

Consumers Index/First Search
Excerpts and abstracts for over 90,000 items.
Toledo Public Library

Dictionaries

Oxford English Dictionary
This is a searchable full text version of the OED, the undisputed authority on the history and development of the English language over the last millennium.
The Public Library
of Cincinnati and Hamilton
County

Directories

Acxiom InfoBase
Phone Directory
This database contains over 100 million business and residential listings from U.S. telephone directories, searchable by a number of fields including phone number.
Cleveland
Public Library
Cuyahoga County Public Library

Education

Ebesco High School
Designed for high school libraries it provides full text for over 500 popular interest and current events publications with information dating back as far as 1975 for magazines. Contains 550 full text pamphlets, 253 reference books, 100,000 biographies, 76,000 primary source documents, and 116,000 photos, maps and flags.
Dayton Metro Library

Live Homework Help
Provides homework help in a wide variety of subjects to students in the fourth through twelfth grades. Students work with tutors in the "On-line Classroom" on specific homework problems and questions during twenty-minute sessions. It can be accessed from 2:00 to 10:00 pm.
The Public Library
of Cincinnati and Hamilton
County

Education—Teachers

Education Index
A bibliographic database that indexes articles on the following subjects: Adult Education, Computers in Education, Continuing Education, Elementary Education, Government Funding, Higher Education, Instructional Media, Language Arts, Library Science, Literacy Standards, Multicultural/Ethnic Education, Parent-Teacher Relations, Student Counseling, Teacher Education, Teacher Evaluation, Teaching Methods, and Vocational Education.
Cleveland Public Library

Genealogy

Archives USA
Provides information for researchers from U.S. manuscript repositories.
Akron-Summit Public Library

HeritageQuest On-line
HeritageQuest On-line includes the complete text of more than 25,000 family and local history books, searchable by every word. It also includes the complete U.S. Census, 1790-1930.
Cleveland
Public Library
Columbus
Metropolitan Library

General Reference

EBSCOhost
MasterFILE 1000
Full text articles from nearly 1,800 general reference, business, consumer health, general science, and multicultural periodicals. It also offers indexing and abstracts for over 2,700 periodicals. Full text files go as far back as January of 1990, while indexing and abstracts files go as far back as January of 1984.
Akron-Summit County Public Library
Cleveland
Public Library
Dayton Metro Library
Public Library
of Cincinnati and Hamilton
County
Toledo Public Library

Encyclopedia Britannica
Includes all the text of the print set, plus thousands of additional articles, digital images, internet links tied directly to the articles,

SPENCER'S PEN: MIGHTIER THAN THE SWORD, AT LEAST FOR A TIME

Assaulted by the devices of modernity—typewriter and computer—penmanship has become a lost art. Today, few know its development in America came from a Geneva, Ohio, lad named Platt Rogers Spencer, who studied the common forms of nature along the Lake Erie shore and transplanted them into the graceful cursiveness of what would become known the world over as Spencerian Penmanship. Millions of students studied his methods, which, it is said, revolutionized the writing of common man, as well as spawned the development of business colleges in America. Spencer lives on in the hearts—and hands—of his advocates who have gathered for nearly 20 years at the week-long Spencerian Saga Penmanship Workshop held every fall at Geneva-on-the-Lake.
(For an online view of Spencer artifacts, try the Ashtabula Library archives at www.ashtabula.lib.oh.us/archives/tour/archtour1.shtm.)

statistics for over 190 nations, *Merriam Webster's 10th Collegiate Dictionary* and special multimedia databases.
Akron-Summit County Public Library
Cleveland Public Library
Columbus Metropolitan Library
Cuyahoga County Public Library
Dayton Metro Library
Public Library of Cincinnati and Hamilton County
Toledo Public Library

Electric Library (bigchalk eLibrary)
Full-text database of 800+ newspapers and magazines such as *USA Today*, *Consumers Digest*, and *Journal of the National Cancer Institute*. Over 18 reference books such as *Collier's* Encyclopedia CD-ROM and the *World Almanac and Book of Facts*, are included along with pictures, maps, television and radio transcripts, and classic books.
Cleveland Public Library
Columbus Metropolitan Library
Dayton Metro Library
Public Library of Cincinnati and Hamilton County
Toledo Public Library

Funk & Wagnalls New Encyclopedia
On-line version of resources for students: *Encyclopedia Americana*, *Grolier Multimedia Encyclopedia*, *The New Book of Knowledge*, *The New Book of Popular Science, Lands and Peoples, America the Beautiful*, and *Neuva Enciclopedia Cumbre en Linea* (Spanish-language encyclopedia).
Cuyahoga County Public Library
Dayton Metro Library
Toledo Public Library

SIRS Researcher
SIRS Researcher Contains thousands of full-text articles and graphics from more than 1,500 domestic and international newspapers, magazines, journals, and U.S. government publica-

tions. Additional content includes *Today's News, Maps of the World, World Almanac* Excerpts, *Spotlight of the Month, Issues in Government, Directory of Publications*, and *New & Updated Topics*.
Akron-Summit County Public Library
Columbus Metropolitan Library
Dayton Metro Library
Toledo Public Library

Government & Legal Research

FactSearch
A guide to statistical statements on current social, economic, political, environmental and health issues, derived from newspapers, periodicals, newsletter and documents such as the *Christian Science Monitor*, the *Congressional Record*, Congressional hearings. Daily Press Briefings of the White House, State Department and Department of Defense, and Australian, British, and Canadian Parliamentary Debates.
Cleveland Public Library

Health

NetWellness
Includes periodicals (indexing to over 150 titles with selective indexing and full text of health-related articles from over 2,500 general interest periodicals), pamphlets (full text coverage of over 500 medical education pamphlets) and reference books (full text coverage of *Mosby's Medical Dictionary, The People's Book of Medical Texts, Oryx Press Consumer Health Information Source Book*, USPDI Drug Information in Lay Language, and *Columbia University Complete Home Medical Guide*.
Akron-Summit County Public Library
Cleveland Public Library
Public Library of Cincinnati and Hamilton County
Toledo Public Library

History & Social Studies

Archives USA
For all researchers who use primary source materials, the Archives USA database provides information about primary source materials from nearly 4,800 U.S. manuscript repositories—records, complete with detailed indexes, of nearly 109,000 manuscript and other special collections.
Akron-Summit County Public Library
Cleveland Public Library

American National Biography
Full-text profiles of more than 18,000 people from all eras and walks of life who have influenced and shaped American History and culture.
Cleveland Public Library

Digital Sanborn Fire Insurance Maps
A century of maps for 400 Ohio communities. Originally intended to provide fire fighting information, now used at genealogical and historical research tools.
Akron-Summit County Public Library
Columbus Metropolitan Library
Cuyahoga County Public Library
Dayton Metro Library
Ohio Public Information Network
Toledo Public Library

Library Science

Library Literature
A bibliographic database that indexes articles and book reviews of key library and information science periodicals published in the United States and elsewhere. Subjects include: Automation, Cataloging, Censorship, Children's Literature, Circulation Procedures, Classification, Copyright Legislation, Government Aid, Internet software, Library Associations & conferences, Library Equipment & supplies, Personnel Administration, Preservation of Material, Public Relations, Publishing, Web sites.
Cleveland Public Library

Libraries

NetLibrary
Offers access to 2800 eBook titles in the OPLIN collection; eBooks are full-text electronic versions of published books that can be searched, borrowed, read, and returned over the internet.
Columbus Metropolitan Library Ohio Public Information Network Toledo Public Library

OCLC World Cat (World Catalog/First Search)
WorldCat is a database of library holding (books, manuscript, serials and other media) worldwide.
Columbus Metropolitan Library Toledo Public Library

Literature

Book Review Digest
A bibliographic database that cites and provides excerpts of reviews of current English-language fiction and nonfiction books for children and adults. An abstract of each book is also provided. Periodical coverage includes approximately 90 leading magazines from the United States, Canada, and Great Britain.
Cleveland Public Library

Contemporary Authors & Dictionary of Literary Biography
Provides access to biographical and critical information on authors from ancient times to the present. 120,000 U.S. and international authors as well as 10,000 critical essays on their lives, works and careers.
Columbus Metropolitan Library

Dictionary of Literary Biography
Provides access to biographical and critical information on authors from ancient times to the present.
Columbus Metropolitan Library

Discovering Collection— Shakespeare
A comprehensive electronic guide to the study of William Shakespeare's most-studied plays, life, and times. Each play covered in EXPLORING Shakespeare includes the complete text of the play. Also included with each play are descriptions of each character, a thematic index to all four plays, and a timeline of major world events. EXPLORING Shakespeare also focuses on Shakespeare's Life and Times, including a biography of the playwright, essays on the Globe theatre and the Elizabethan Theater and over 15 essays about contemporary society.
Cleveland Public Library

Newspapers & Magazines

Cincinnati Post
Full text access to all content from 1990 to the present.
Cleveland Public Library

Cleveland News Index
The on-line Cleveland News Index lists citation information for local news stories, feature articles, and reviews from the *Plain Dealer* (1983 - June 1999), *Cleveland Magazine* (1983-present), *Northern Ohio Live* (September, 1990-present), and *Ohio magazine* (October, 1990-present) Obituaries from the *Plain Dealer* and the *Cleveland Press* are included from 1976 to the present (does not provide full text access).
Cleveland Public Library

Dayton Metro Library Local Newspaper Index
Citations to newspaper articles of local significance from the *Dayton Daily News* (January, 1985-present);

Dayton Journal Herald, (January, 1985-87); *Dayton Magazine* (January, 1985-1995)
Dayton Metro Library

Ebsco News
Provides full text coverage for more than 240 newspapers. Includes cover to cover full text for *USA Today*, *The Christian Science Monitor* and *The Times* (London), as well as full text from more than 180 regional newspapers including: *Boston Globe*, *Detroit Free Press*, *Houston Chronicle*, *Miami Herald*, and the *San Jose Mercury News*. Full transcripts from *Face the Nation*, *CBS Evening News with Dan Rather*, *60 Minutes*, *O'Reilly Factor*, *Hannity & Colmes*, and National Public Radio are also included.
Dayton Metro Library

New York Times
Coverage of the U.S. newspaper of record. Offers superb coverage of national and international news, plus coverage of important speeches and documents, Supreme Court Decisions and presidential press conference transcripts. Full text coverage of the previous 90 days.
Cleveland Public Library

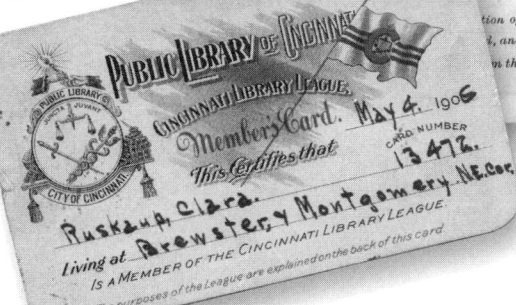

Rules for Visitors of the Library.

1. It is positively forbidden to spit on the floor or on the heaters.

2. Readers must not put their feet on the furniture.

3. Visitors are not permitted to talk in the reading-rooms, except in communicating with the Attendants.

4. Readers must return all books or per[iodic]als to the Attendant from whom procured.

...tion of the above rules will meet with in... ..., and persistence therein will be followed ...n the privileges of the Library.

"ARE YOU KIDDING?! DO YOU KNOW WHAT THEY SPRAY ON THOSE THINGS?!!"

Timeline

Acts of Faith

■ 1782—An Unholy War

Moravian missionary David Zeisberger founded Schoenbrunn and a handful of other villages to bring Christianity to the Delaware Indians who lived along the Tuscarawas River. Ironically, the pacifist Moravians soon found themselves in the middle of a war, for the American Revolution placed their settlements in a triple vice: the British to the west at Fort Detroit, the Americans to the east at Fort Pitt, and Indian tribes of sharply divided loyalties in between. The Moravians' earnest attempts to remain neutral incited hostility and suspicion on all sides and ultimately resulted in tragedy in March of this year. In one of the blackest incidents in American history, a ragtag volunteer militia from Pennsylvania methodically murdered the Delaware converts at the Gnadenhutten settlement, 62 adults and 34 children martyred for adopting non-violence in a violent time and place.

■ 1806—Religiously Recruiting

Preacher Peter Cartwright accepted the Methodist circuit along the Muskingum River. With their unexcelled ability to organize, the Methodists got a theological toehold in frontier America, and itinerant ministers such as Cartwright were the key to their reaching (in every sense of the word) isolated and independent-minded pioneers. The circuit-riding preachers worked cheap and hard. They typically traveled 475 miles per month; delivered sermons at noon on weekdays, twice on Saturday, and from morning to night on Sunday; and were paid $100 per year. By the mid-19th century, the Methodists had the largest church in the nation, thanks in no small part to Cartwright, who was generally regarded as the undisputed master at bringing folk into the fold.

■ 1814—The Power and the Glory . . . of the Press

The Reverend John Andrews began publication of Ohio's first religious newspaper, the *Weekly Recorder,* in Chillicothe. Its pages had a Presbyterian bent, and editorial prejudices leaned accordingly. *Pro*: missions and temperance. *Con*: slavery, circuses, and launching boats on Sunday.

1824—Shakers on the Scene

Among the many Utopian sects drawn to frontier Ohio, none would prove more prosperous or ingenious than the Millennium Church of United Believers in the Second Coming of Christ. Commonly called Shakers for the bodily frenzy of their worship, they had six communities in Ohio by 1824, but their notions of community property and equality of the sexes provoked hostility and even violence in citizens of more conventional persuasions. Their first and most successful settlement was Union Village in Warren County, where the plain and peaceable Shaker introduced animals—Merino sheep, Shorthorn cattle, and their own remarkable hybrid, the Poland China hog—that proved a boon to the agriculture of Ohio and the nation. But their communities disappeared within a century, doomed by the most unnatural of causes—their firm belief in celibacy.

"(The Shaker women) were all, without exception, of a pale and sickly hue. They were disfigured by the ugly costume, which consists of a white starched bonnet."
—Union Village visitor, 1840s

The Shakers of Union Village were so frequently attacked by mobs from nearby Lebanon that in 1820, Brothers Bedle and McNemar felt an Almighty justification to put a curse upon that offending place. Not so in Dayton, where folks found the Shakers' feverish rites and speaking in tongues more tolerable. There, they gave a blessing, and when word of that benediction spread, many farmers considered it a sign of certain prosperity and moved accordingly. As Dayton grew large and Lebanon stayed small, it was said that the Shakers had indeed determined their fates. The town of Kirtland likewise suffered the curse of Joseph Smith. When the Prophet made his hasty exit, he instructed the Mormons to "leave Kirtland to the owls and bats." It wasn't until 1979 that members of the Mormon church in Utah came to Ohio and officially wiped Smith's "scourge" from the town's brow.

1828—Deus ex Guernsey County

Out of nowhere, it seemed, a stranger appeared at a camp meeting held on the banks of Leatherwood Creek. "SALVATION!" he roared to locals, who were homespun enough to be impressed by his broadcloth suit and yellow beaver hat. They swallowed his claim of being God Almighty incarnate, and soon Joseph Dylks had followers in three counties. He warded off skeptics by threatening to destroy the universe, and the ploy might have worked indefinitely had Dylks not gotten too big for his britches, so to speak, by boasting that he could fashion clothing without seams. His miracle failed to materialize, and he departed the area with a mob at his heels. Ironically, Dylks eventually did become a deity of sorts, for William Dean Howells, the renowned writer born in a nearby corner of Ohio, immortalized him in a novel based on the incident, *The Leatherwood God*.

1831—The Beechers: Natural Preachers, Moral Teachers

Two munificent merchant princes from New Orleans, the Lane brothers, lent their name and their fortune to Cincinnati's new Presbyterian theological seminary, and the Reverend Lyman Beecher assumed the helm. A New Englander and founder of the American Bible Society, he opposed both alcohol and slavery, and the upstart Cincinnati school sprouted into a national abolitionist center. Dr. Beecher combated his indigestion by exercising on the parallel bars and shoveling sand in the cellar. He also played the fiddle and danced for the amusement of the Beecher children, who were prodigious in number as well as intellect. His progeny included Harriet Beecher Stowe, who later penned an American literary landmark, *Uncle Tom's Cabin*, and Henry Ward Beecher, an internationally celebrated preacher trained in Cincinnati. Unfortunately, Henry's brilliance in the pulpit was soundly tarnished by one of the most notorious scandals of the Victorian Era: an adultery lawsuit precipitated by Ohio's—and the nation's—foremost feminist, Victoria Claflin Woodhull.

Founding father

In the last half of the last century, Rabbi Isaac Mayer Wise launched the American Jewish Reform movement from his Cincinnati synagogue. This "American born in Bohemia" obtained a national forum and following with a singularly infectious idea: Judaism in the United States could and should be tailored to American tastes and traditions.

◗ 1831—Mr. Smith Goes to Ohio

In 1831, Joseph Smith came to Ohio from New York, where he attracted followers with his claim that the angel Mormon revealed a new religion to him. Though folks in Kirtland balked at his heavenly vision and speaking in tongues, the self-styled Prophet laid the foundation of his Church of Jesus Christ of Latter Day Saints, commonly known as Mormons. In that small Ohio town, Smith built a splendid temple on the premise of Divine direction, chose the first apostles and bishop, and increased the Mormon membership to 25,000.

"The fits usually came on during or after their prayer meeting, which was held nearly every evening. The young men and women were particularly subject to this delirium. They would exhibit all the apish actions imaginable, making the most ridiculous grimaces, creeping upon their hands and feet, rolling upon the frozen ground..."
—description of Mormon religious service, by Eber D. Howe, editor of the *Painesville Telegraph*, 1834

◗ 1832—Tar and Feathers

On the night of March 24, a mob seized Joseph Smith, leader of the highly suspect Mormon Church. They beat him, applied a humiliating coat of tar and feathers, and left him unconscious. Alas, this grim punishment was only the portent of things to come. When Smith started a bank, its failure during the 1837 recession was his Ohio undoing. His followers demonstrated a sudden concern for their worldly goods, and the simmering anger of his enemies boiled over. By fleeing to Missouri, Smith kept body and soul together, but only temporarily, for he met his death in 1844 at the hands of yet another mob. But Brigham Young, a follower from the Ohio days, picked up where Smith left off, leading the polygamous and unwelcome Mormon flock to permanency and prosperity in Utah.

"A new year dawned upon the church at Kirtland in all the bitterness of the spirit of mobocracy, which continued to rage hotter and hotter, until Elder Rigdon and myself were obliged to flee from its deadly influence, as did the apostles and prophets of old . . . we were obliged to secrete ourselves sometimes to elude the grasp of our pursuers, who continued their race more than two hundred miles from Kirtland, armed with pistols, etc., seeking our lives."— Joseph Smith, on his hegira

◗ 1837—The Great Debate

Alexander Campbell, who broke with the Calvinists to start the Disciples of Christ, arrived in Cincinnati for a debate with the Roman Catholic Bishop, John Baptist Purcell. The two men were at theological loggerheads, and their arguments consumed an entire week in January. The issue? Bibles in school. The outcome? Still debatable.

◗ 1844—The Final Countdown

Convinced by a New England man named Miller that the end of the world was imminent in 1843, thousands of people prepared to have their bodies taken directly into heaven. In Ohio, folks gave away their worldly goods, and hoping to be closer to their ultimate destination, sought out high places. Cincinnatians waited on Brighton Hill, while Millerites in Milan built a high platform. One man even cut off his coattails lest nonbelievers ride them into paradise. When the world failed to end as scheduled, Miller confessed a mistake in his math and announced October 22, 1844, as the new and improved Armageddon. Again, his Ohio followers impoverished themselves and took to the hills. Come October 23, they found themselves twice-fooled and considerably poorer in pocket if not in spirit.

◗ 1875—The Miracle Worker

Father Joseph Gloden so admired the statue of the Virgin Mary in his native Luxembourg that he had a copy made for the new Shrine of Our Lady of Consolation at Carey. Out of the blue, sunshine saved the statue's arrival procession from a driving rain. The

faithful called it a miracle, and visitors with troubled spirits and sick bodies soon credited the statue with remarkable cures. Pilgrims ever since have been going to Wyandot County, where they leave their offerings and, hopefully, their problems behind them.

▣ 1883—An Unorthodox Diet

The first years of Hebrew Union College were difficult ones. Founder Isaac Mayer Wise had only a few "noisy boys" to teach, but there were so many mice that he took to hiding his textbooks from them. But when the first American class of rabbis graduated, the largest number of Jews—Reform and Orthodox—ever assembled in this country gathered in Cincinnati for the occasion. A celebration banquet was planned, and the guests sat down at elegantly appointed tables. No sooner has the first course been served, than the Orthodox rabbis began to flee, leaving plates of shrimp—strictly verboten according to their dietary laws—untouched throughout the room.

▣ 1890—Beginning The Budget

Sugarcreek farmer John C. Miller started a newspaper to serve his Amish brethren. The Amish, whose origins go back to 17th century Switzerland, had a peripatetic history, staying one step ahead of their persecutors across Europe. But in northeast Ohio, the Amish put down solid roots and became eminently successful at agriculture. Though Mr. Miller intended to publish only local news, *The Budget* soon became an international newsletter for the widely scattered sect. The most human interest of stories— births, deaths, sickness, barn fires, and poison ivy cures—circulated from a tiny Ohio town to readers around the world, and today some 18,000 Amish from France to the Philippines read it.

The Old Order Amish are the most conservative segment of what is known as the Mennonite Church. They are direct descendants of the Anabaptists, a group that emerged from the Reformation in Switzerland in 1525. The Anabaptists felt that Zwingli, Luther, and other reformers compromised in their stand and did not go all the way in bringing the church back to a scriptural foundation. The Anabaptists differed especially with the popular reformers in that they rejected infant baptism and insisted that the church was to be a voluntary brotherhood of adult believers. They were the first to teach separation of church and state, an idea otherwise unheard of in those days. For three centuries after their origin, the Anabaptists were persecuted by both Protestant and Catholic authorities.

The name "Amish" is derived from the young Mennonite minister, Jacob Ammann, who led a division from the mainstream Mennonite church in 1693, primarily over the issues of the use of the ban (shunning former members) and plainer clothing styles. Doctrinally, the Mennonites and Amish remain close today except on interpretation of cultural issues. Driven by persecution from their homes in Europe, the Amish migrated to North America during a period of 150 years, beginning around 1720. Today,

A heavy rain doesn't seep into the ground but rolls off. Therefore when you preach to farmers, your sermon should be a drizzle instead of a downpour.

—basic tenant of the rural Ohio ministry

there are Amish congregations in at least 19 states and Canada, as well as Central and South America. The Amish population of Ohio is estimated at 35,000 out of a total U.S. and Canadian population of 90,000. This compares to Lancaster County, Pennsylvania, at 14,000.

The Amish feel strongly that the Scriptures teach a distinct separation between the church and the world. They believe that it is impossible for a church to maintain its beliefs and values if members associate freely with people who hold different values. Thus, they have not always accepted all the cultural changes introduced as progress.

They are still driving horse and buggies, not because they think the automobile is wicked in itself, but because they believe the trend of life the automobile brings with it is breaking down the family unit and the basic structure of society. They dress as they do because they do not care to be changing to styles designed to achieve more glamour and less modesty.

(Source: Mennonite Information Center, Berlin, Ohio. Reprinted with Permission)

❏ *1898—Paradise Lost*

The Society of Separatists disbanded, ending one of the nation's most successful experiments in communism. They had arrived in Tuscarawas County in 1818, when leader Joseph Bimeler rescued them from the wrath of their fellow Germans, who could not understand their pacifism or refusal to be baptized. With borrowed money, they bought land in Ohio and called their new home Zoar after the Biblical place of refuge. Life was so harsh that they resorted to communism and celibacy to survive. Instead of children, the industrious Zoarites conceived a grand garden, which literally and figuratively became a tree of life. With considerable help from the new Ohio Canal, their communal worth grew to a million dollars. Prosperity, of course, allowed them to resume reproduction, but apparently on a limited basis. When the Zoarites succumbed to the influences of free enterprise and divided up the community property, their

number after eight decades in Ohio has actually decreased—from 225 to 222.

❏ *1901—An Agnostic Sunday School*

Charles S. Sparks, a Cincinnati lawyer, started this contraction in terms with a class of ten. Weekly attendance eventually exceeded 100, boosted no doubt by such lively lessons as "What is Absolutely Known" and "Morals, Plants, and Lower Animals in Their Relation to Man and Themselves."

❏ *1913—The Land of Milk and Money*

The Columbus Campaign of William Ashley "Billy" Sunday shattered all revival records. More than 750,000 people turned out to witness the evangelist's histrionics against drink, dance, and the devil. Flamboyant and enormously popular, this master at pounding-the-pulpit enjoyed a national following. When he died in 1935, it was said that Sunday converted more than a million people and collected more than a million dollars, sums to which the good folk of Columbus added 18,000 and $21,000 respectively during his seven-week stay.

When Billy Sunday was preaching in Ohio, revival meetings were often labeled Butchers' Night, Bakers' Night, Mailmen's Night, etc. At that time, milkmen were widely suspected of upping their profits by watering down their products, and the theatrical preacher took advantage of the rumors to whip up the crowds. After mounting the pulpit, he shouted out, "What night is it?"

"Milkmen's Night," was the reply.

"Well, then," said Sunday, "we'd better open the hymnals to 'Shall We Gather at the River.'"

❏ *1930—A Christian for Christians*

In Toledo in 1930, the American Lutheran Church was formed by combining the synods of Buffalo, Iowa, and Ohio. A prime mover was Carl Christian Hein, a local pastor who became first president of the new church and served until his death in 1937.

www. *lib.muohio.edu/ mcguffey*

The site for the McGuffey Museum in Oxford is replete with photographs, bibliography, and the full text of McGuffey's first *Reader.* It begins, "John must not tear the book," which, 167 years later, is still good advice.

MCGUFFY: THAT GOOD OL' AMERICAN PIE

Among the fabled Three 'Rs of American education, Readin' became the indisputable province of William Holmes McGuffey, who teamed up with a Cincinnati publisher to produce the first of his *Eclectic Readers* in 1836. He was an obscure professor of moral philosophy at an equally-obscure college in Oxford, Ohio, when he launched his *Readers*, receiving $1,000 for the first two editions and the promise of a ham every Christmas if the books sold well.

Over his lifetime, McGuffey never wanted for Christmas ham. His celebrated series became the classic American textbooks, and during the ensuing century and a half they sold almost a yearly *average* of a million copies. They achieved a rare popularity second only to the Bible, and because of their pietistic lessons in manners, morality, and patriotism, the *Readers* have been credited with having more influence on the American mind than any book *except* the Bible.

The *Readers* were the primary elementary school textbooks in the United States for nearly a century, and the dour Scots-Irish teacher is credited with having more influence on the moral and social fabric of 19th century youth than any other single individual. His texts instructed his distant charges in history, biology, botany, astronomy, attitudes toward authority, and table manners; they were anthologies of rectitude and drew upon great authors from Shakespeare to Dickens.

His chapter titles— "Waste Not, Want Not;" "Look Before You Leap;" "Where There's a Will, There's a Way"—

became mantras for the shirtsleeve virtues of democratic capitalism and the rising American middle class.

The historian Henry Steele Comager called them materialistic and worldly, contending they taught a simplistic system of industry, sobriety, and conformity. Said Lesson XX, "Tom will not rob a bird's nest. He is too kind to do so." Or: "Brave boys do not cry when they fall on the ice." Comager's point was that in the emerging industrial America, there was little sympathy for spills on the ice of powerlessness and inequality, and *someone* was robbing the bird's nest.

The novelist Marilynne Robinson said, however, that the *Readers* acknowledged neither slavery nor the factory system, were contemptuous of war, and taught an ethic consistently opposed to both, all the while urging kindness and generosity.

The *Readers* helped form—for better or worse—the American character, providing a patchwork nation of immigrants with a common yardstick of conduct. They would educate at least five generations of Americans, making McGuffey's name a household word for decades. They were the oldest and best-selling textbooks in history, and it is estimated they have reached a *billion* students.

As late as 1985, there were 150,000 copies printed, and today a boxed set of seven *McGuffey Eclectic Readers* can be bought on *Amazon.com* for $41.96.

"Not bad for a collection of syrupy, preachy stories salvaged by marvelous illustrations," as the *Baltimore Sun* once said.

When you fall down, you must not cry, but get up, and run again. If you cry, the boys will call you a baby. Some boys use bad words when they are at play. The Bible says that you must not use bad words; and you must mind what the Bible says, for it is God's book. You must not play with boys that speak bad words or tell lies.

—McGuffey's Eclectic First Reader, page 17

Denominations

African Methodist Episcopal Church
Third Episcopal District
5300 East Main Street, Suite 101
Columbus, Ohio 43213-2580
614-575-2279

African Methodist Episcopal Zion Church
Mid-Atlantic One Area
2000 Cedar Circle Drive
Catonsville, Maryland 21228-3743
410-744-7330

American Baptist Churches of Ohio
Box 376
136 Galway Drive N
Granville, Ohio 43023
740-587-0807

Christian Church in Ohio
PO Box 299
38007 Butternut Ridge Road
Elyria, Ohio 44035
440-458-5112

Christian Methodist Episcopal Church
Second District
7030 Reading Road, Suite 211
Cincinnati, Ohio 54237-3842
513-772-8622

Christian Science Committee on Publication in Ohio
85 East Gay Street, Suite 400
Columbus, Ohio 43215-3118
614-222-8937

Church of the Brethren—Northern Ohio District
1107 East Main Street
Ashland, Ohio 44805-2806
419-281-8914

Church of the Brethren—Southern Ohio District
1001 Mill Ridge Circle
Englewood, Ohio 45322-8782
937-832-6399

Ohio Fellowship of Community Churches
2500 Nebraska Avenue
Toledo, Ohio 43607-3553
419-536-8440

OHIO AND THE SEEDS OF FAITH

God's acre

Other than a handful of mission districts in the western United States, Ohio is the only place where Congress ever set aside land to support religion. Even before the U.S. Constitution was ratified, Congress tried to prop up the weak finances of a fledgling nation by selling off land in Ohio. Surveyors carved out townships that contained 36 square miles, or sections, of 640 acres each. In land sales to the Ohio Company (1787) and John Cleves Symmes (1788), Congress stipulated that Section 29 of each township must "be given perpetually for purposes of religion." Thus, some 43,000 acres in Washington, Meigs, Gallia, Lawrence, Athens, Morgan, Hocking, Vinton, Hamilton, Butler, and Warren counties came to be known as "ministerial land." Income from the sale or rent of those lands was earmarked for churches until 1968, when Ohioans voted to spend the money on schools instead.

Ohio's formative years coincided with a time of religious transition in the nation. In the first half of the 19th century, the structured, intellectual doctrines of the New England Calvinists gave way to the more casual and emotional piety of personal conversion. The Protestant elect yielded to mass salvation as formal church services got competition from camp meetings. All in all, it was a change for the democratic, and why not? The folks who poured into Ohio had the First Amendment at their backs and openness in every sense at their feet. Evangelists arrived of every persuasion, and Ohio would often be their proving ground. They came painting Edens and sometimes Utopias, but always, always, carrying the seeds of faith. ⤶

Episcopal Diocese of Ohio
2230 Euclid Avenue
Cleveland, Ohio 44115-2405
216-771-4815

Episcopal Diocese of Southern Ohio
412 Sycamore Street
Cincinnati, Ohio 45202-4110
513-421-0311

**Evangelical Lutheran Church in America
—Northeastern Ohio**
1890 Bailey Road
Cuyahoga Falls, Ohio 44221-5259
330-929-9022

**Evangelical Lutheran Church in America
—Northwestern Ohio**
621 Bright Road
Findlay, Ohio 45840-6940
419-423-3664

**Evangelical Lutheran Church in America
—Southern Ohio**
300 South 2nd Street
Columbus, Ohio 43215-5001
614-464-3532

Greek Orthodox, Detroit Diocese
19405 Renfrew Road
Detroit, Michigan 48221-1835
313-864-5433

Greek Orthodox, Pittsburgh Diocese
5201 Ellsworth Avenue
Pittsburgh, Pennsylvania 15232-1421
412-621-5529

Moravian Church in America
P.O. Box 1245
Bethlehem, Pennsylvania 18016-1245
610-865-0302

Ohio Baptist General Convention
401 South Paul Laurence Dunbar Street
Dayton, Ohio 45407-3122
937-222-4373

**Jewish Communities, Government Affairs
Committee of Ohio Jewish Communities, Inc.**
50 West Broad Street, Suite 1915
Columbus, Ohio 43215
614-463-1835

**Presbyterian Church (U.S.A.)
—Synod of the Covenant**
1911 Indian Wood Circle
Maumee, Ohio 43537-4002
419-754-4350

Religious Society of Friends (Quaker)
PO Box 1194
251 Ludovic Street, Pyle Circle
Wilmington, Ohio 45177-4194
937-382-2491

**Roman Catholic Church in Ohio
—Archdiocese of Cincinnati**
100 East 8th Street
Cincinnati, Ohio 45202-2129
513-421-3131

**Roman Catholic Church in Ohio
—Diocese of Columbus**
198 East Broad Street
Columbus, Ohio 43215-3702
614-224-2251

**Roman Catholic Church in Ohio
—Diocese of Steubenville**
PO Box 969
422 Washington Street
Steubenville, Ohio 43952-5969
740-282-3631

**Roman Catholic Church in Ohio
—Diocese of Toledo**
Box 985
1933 Spielbusch Avenue
Toledo, Ohio 43697-0985
419-244-6711

**Roman Catholic Church in Ohio
—Diocese of Youngstown**
144 West Wood Street
Youngstown, Ohio 44503-1030
330-744-8451

United Church of Christ
6161 Busch Blvd. Suite 95
Columbus, Ohio 43229-2547
614-885-0722

United Methodist Church—East Ohio Conference
8800 Cleveland Avenue, Northwest
Box 2800
8800 Cleveland Avenue NW
North Canton, Ohio 44720-0800
330-499-3972

United Methodist Church—West Ohio Conference
32 Wesley Blvd.
Worthington, Ohio 43085
614-844-6200

*Source: Ohio Council of Churches
Government Affairs Committee of Ohio Jewish
Communities, Inc.*

Ohio has one church for each 1,000 people; 29th in the nation.

23 Facts of Ohio faith

First church west of the Allegheny Mountains—The Moravian Mission at Schoenbrunn, Tuscarawas County, 1772

First church bell in Ohio —sounded at Schoenbrunn, August 26, 1772

First Mormon Temple in U.S.—Kirtland, 1836

First Quaker Meeting House west of the Allegheny Mountains—Mt. Pleasant, 1814

First Disciples of Christ Convention —New Lisbon, 1827

First Roman Catholic Church in Ohio —St. Joseph's Priory, Somerset, 1818

First Episcopal Church in Ohio —St. Paul's, Chillicothe, 1817

First Heaven-on-wheels —St. Paul's Wayside Cathedral, a mobile trailer operated by the Diocese of Southern Ohio Protestant Episcopal Church, 1937

First traditional Islamic Mosque west of the nation's capital—Perrysburg, 1983

First Jewish house of worship west of the Allegheny Mountains—Congregation Bene Israel, Cincinnati, 1824

First U.S. Conference of Rabbis —Cleveland, 1855, Rabbi Isidor Kalisch presiding

First woman rabbi in the U.S. —Sally Jane Priesand, a Clevelander ordained at Hebrew Union College-Jewish Institute of Religion, June 3, 1972

First woman Presbyterian Elder —Sarah E. Dickson, selected at Presbyterian General Assembly Meeting, Cincinnati, 1930

First religious newspaper in U.S. —*The Weekly Recorder*, Chillicothe, 1814

First Conference of Methodists west of the Allegheny Mountains —Chillicothe, 1807

Only Byzantine Catholic Monastery in U.S.—Monastery of Our Savior, Steubenville

Only Papal Seminary in U.S. —Pontifical College Josephinum, Columbus, sanctioned by Pope Leo XIII, 1892

Only three cities in Ohio with Hindu Temples—Cleveland, Youngstown, Beavercreek

Oldest U.S. school for training rabbis —Hebrew Union College, begun in Cincinnati, 1875

Oldest Catholic newspaper in the U.S. —*The Catholic Telegraph*, published in Cincinnati since 1831

Last Shaker in Ohio—James Fennessy, died at Otterbein Home, formerly Union Village, 1928

Methodist Church's last circuit riding minister—Orval L. Hall, the Gallia County native who finally fell silent in Columbus, 1977

World's largest Amish community —some 35,000 Ohioans, who live mostly in Defiance, Geauga, Holmes, Stark, Tuscarawas, and Wayne counties

OHIOANS ON ASPECTS OF RELIGION

If chance sets you between a Methodist and a Baptist, you will move toward the Methodist to keep warm.
—*Clarence Darrow*

Everyone in the world is Christ and they are all crucified.
—*Sherwood Anderson*

God created man, but I could do better.
—*Erma Bombeck*

America has become so tense and nervous it has been years since I've seen anyone asleep in church—and that is a sad situation.
—*Norman Vincent Peale*

Thar's no foretellin' what a gent will do, once he's filled with grace.
—*Old Monte, in The Cowboy Humor of Alfred Henry Lewis*

God can't be a woman. If God were a woman, we wouldn't have tampons.
—*Karen Schneider, Cincinnati radio personality*

If Jesus were alive today, he would be at the Super Bowl.
—*Norman Vincent Peale*

I do benefits for all religions; I don't want to blow the hereafter on a technicality.
—*Bob Hope*

An altar boy is like a little Roman Catholic caddy.
—*Michael Flannery, Cincinnati magazine*

God can do anything he wants. But mostly he just eavesdrops.
—*Michael Heaton, Cleveland Plain Dealer*

I have noticed all my life that many people think they have religion when they are troubled with dyspepsia.
—*Robert Ingersoll*

Tale-bearing and distraction are discouraged.
—*New Burlington Friends, policy statement*

Catholic school kids were compelled to ask a lot of God, mostly through the Virgin Mother and enough saints to triple the population density of California, a place which is not of their natural habitat.

—*Joseph Ritz, Canton, Ohio,*
I Never Looked for my Mother

Churches and Church Membership in Ohio

Denomination	2000 Congregations	2000 Adherents	1990 Congregations	1990 Adherents
Total for Ohio	11,167	25,102,269	11,086	5,437,630
American Baptist Association	13	813		
Amish, other	34	2,479		
African Methodist Episcopal Zion Church	23	443	24	542
American Baptist Churches in the U.S.A.	323	117,757	337	127,219
Antiochian Orthodox Christian Archdiocese of North America	9	5,012		
Apostolic Christian Church (*American*)	9	2,899	8	2,043
Apostolic Christian Church (*Nazarene*)	13	1,729	13	1,490
Armenian Apostolic Church of America, Eastern Prelacy	1	105	1	350
Armenian Apostolic Church	2	665		
Assemblies of God	284	67,738	249	69,349
Associate Reformed Presbyterian Church	1	17		
Baha'i	21	2,004		
Baptist General Conference	15	4,001	17	3,504
Baptist Missionary Association of America	1	189	1	190
Beachy Amish Mennonite Churches	20	1,851	18	1,499
Brethren Church (*Ashland, Ohio*))	23	6,460	23	4,611
Brethren in Christ Church	15	906	14	978
Buddhism	34	N/A		
Bulgarian Orthodox Diocese of the USA	1	560		
Carpatho-Russian Orthodox Greek Catholic Diocese of the U.S.A.	5	1,035	5	546
Catholic Church	1,000	2,231,832	1,057	2,141,777
Cavalry Chapel Fellowship Churches	10	N/A		
Christian and Missionary Alliance	116	29,067	106	25,334
Christian Church (*Disciples of Christ*)	185	70,075	207	66,665
Christian Churches and Churches of Christ	477	142,571	480	135,830
Christian Reformed Church	6	1,044	8	1,418
Christian Church	62	3,413		
Church of God (*Anderson, Indiana*)	222	30,700	220	29,931
Church of God (*Cleveland, Tennessee*)	228	55,022	208	36,587
Church of God in Christ (*Mennonite*)	2	355	2	283
Church of God of Prophecy	51	1,824	63	2,844
Church of Jesus Christ of Latter-Day Saints	117	38,824	95	30,979
Church of the Brethren	103	18,836	109	20,765
Church of the Nazarene	410	87,767	419	90,659
Churches of Christ	428	47,472	432	47,949
Church of God, General Conference	33	4,318	35	4,349
Community of Christ	40	4,036		
Congregational Christian Churches (*not national*)	1	72	3	149
Conservative Baptist Association of America	12	2,357	12	N/R
Conservative Congregational Christian Conference	20	4,440	10	1,564
Conservative Mennonite Conference	26	4,287		
Enterprise Baptist Association	28	1,999	34	2,340
Episcopal Church	191	58,684	194	69,302
Evangelical Convent Church	10	1,904		
Evangelical Free Church of America	23	5,311	13	1,959
Evangelical Lutheran Church in America	640	301,749	658	320,02
Evangelical Mennonite Church, Inc.	6	1,726	4	1,640
Evangelical Presbyterian Church	4	1,202	4	764
Association of Free Lutheran Congregations	2	30		
Free Methodist Church of North American	43	4,630	45	3,921
Friends-USA	115	10,319	112	13,436
Greek Orthodox Archdiocese of North and South America	22	22,428	23	N/A
Hindu	19	N/A		

Denomination	2000 Congregations	2000 Adherents	1990 Congregations	1990 Adherents
Independent Charismatic Churches	28	22,781	27	22,755
Independent Free Will Baptist	1	25		
Independent, Non-charismatic Churches	55	73,680	92	93,332
International Churches of Christ	3	1,463		
International Church of the Foursquare Gospel	54	7,925	55	6,204
International Council of Community Churches	14	4,545		
International Pentecostal Church of Christ	21	2,232	24	1,451
International Pentecostal Holiness Church	19	2,201	11	1,3779
Jain	7	N/A		
Jewish (estimated)	114	142,255	138	124,832
Lutheran Church-Missouri Synod	189	79,976	186	83,336
Macedonian Orthodox	4	2,640		
Mennonite USA	83	16,673	135	22,580
Mennonite, other	36	4,190		
Universal Fellowship of Metropolitan Churches	4	322		
Midwest Congressional Christian Fellowship	11	719	10	674
Missionary Church	33	3,306	35	3,080
Moravian Church in America, Northern Province	7	2,067	7	2,409
Muslim (estimated)	36	41,281		
National Association of Congregational Christian Churches	19	6,170	20	6,858
National Association of Free Will Baptist, Inc.	167	12,687	150	14,222
Natural Primitive Baptist, USA	5	963		
North American Baptist Conference	7	2,521	7	2,180
"Old" Missionary Baptist Associations	3	186	2	168
Old Order Amish Church	324	24,613	238	35,200
Old Order Mennonite Church	10	1,342		
Orthodox Church in America: Albanian Diocese	1	200	1	N/A
Orthodox Church in America: Bulgarian Diocese	4	840		
Orthodox Church in America: Roman Diocese	7	1,911	7	N/A
Orthodox Church in America: Territorial Dioceses	21	4,957	27	N/A
Orthodox Presbyterian Churches	5	550		
Pentecostal Churches of God	40	4,461	38	3,166
Presbyterian Church (USA)	597	160,800	615	205,721
Presbyterian Church in America	16	2,982	12	1,580
Primitive Baptist Churches	35	N/A		
Primitive Baptist Eastern District	4	483		
Primitive Methodist Church, U.S.A.	3	183	3	293
Reformed Baptist Churches	5	N/A		
Reformed Church in America	7	2,280	8	2,110
Reformed Church in the U.S.A.	1	104	1	141
Reformed Mennonite	3	88		
Regular Baptist General Assembly	180	38,758		
Romanian Orthodox Abroad	1	700		
Russian Orthodox Abroad	5	N/A		
Russian Orthodox Moscow	1	N/A		
Salvation Army	77	21,547	63	6,455
Separate Baptist in Christ	1	99		
Serbian Orthodox USA	7	4,924		
Serbian Orthodox (New Gracanica)	5	N/A		
Seventh-Day Adventists	112	22,956	120	24,508
Sikh	9	N/A		
Southern Baptist Convention	514	187,227	511	3.5%
Southwide Baptist Fellowship	25	N/A		
Ukranian Orthodox Church of America	7	3,714	3	N/R
Unitarian Universalist Association	36	6,116	38	6,531
United Church of Christ	424	157,180	483	195,349
United Methodist Church	2,094	566,084	2,181	656,107
Vinyard	28	24,480		
Wayne Trail Missionary Baptists Association	11	2,385	11	2,467
Wesleyan Church	93	19,507	121	13,549
Wisconsin Evangelical Lutheran Synod	21	4,473	24	4,650

Source: Churches and Church Membership in the United States, 2000 Glenmary Research Center; this survey is done every ten years for the entire country

Seven score and eight years ago Ohio's iron furnaces, the state's first smokestack industry, employed hundreds of anonymous laborers, some of them poor immigrants who shared the American dream even though they couldn't speak the language. Today, the ruins of these and other early industries, such as gristmills and brick kilns, molder like statuary in a sonorous country cemetery. Consider, for example, the two 40-foot sandstone chimneys of Madison and Limestone furnaces just a mile apart in backwoods Jackson County. The narrow dirt road winding between them follows the Kanawha Trail, a route blazed by Indians then traced by pioneers. From 1854 to 1902, the life span of Madison Furnace, iron workers, charcoal makers, lumberjacks, mules, miners, and their minions wore down the path to bedrock. A swamp and youthful forest now spreads between the relics, now semi-protected in Cooper Hollow State Wildlife Area.

Study the stony shells of Bieber Mill, tottering on the bank of the Olentangy River, or ghostly Hambleton Mill beside Beaver Creek. Like the furnace stacks, they look sadly anachronistic, ancient without grandeur, primitive and awkward, and weirdly out-of-place in their surroundings. Nowadays, these silent sentinels recall Ohio's plunge into the Industrial Revolution. They outlasted manufacturers, millionaires, Congressmen and recessions. They honor the technological genius of their day and the unknown laborers whose bodies, after forging and preserving the Union, fell into weedy boneyards. All the enterprises, bruises, and sweat that have succeeded them are beholding to them.

Gristmills, the first industrial-sized machines on the frontier, represented the transition from wilderness to settlement, and from subsistence farming to market economy. Mills required streams, grain, and currency. Ohio had plenty of water and wheat, but little of the latter, so men with cash, credit or clout (not your run-of-the-mill miller) owned the first mills. Potts Mill, the state's first water-powered gristmill, opened in December 1790 at the confluence of Wolf Creek and Muskingum River, roughly 20 miles upstream from Marietta. A month later, Wyandot and Delaware warriors massacred pioneers at nearby Big Bottom, forcing frightened frontier settlers, including the occupants of Potts Mill, back to Marietta. Until that mill reopened in 1795, Marietta farmers took their grain to a floating mill anchored beside Blennerhasset Island in the Ohio River, a safe place with a steady current. The makeshift mill, funded by seven citizens, pulverized 25-50 bushels a day to the delight of settlers who previously had to grind corn by hand.

Mill-building accelerated when the Treaty of Greenville ended the Indian wars in 1795. Just about every Ohio watercourse featured a mill of some kind at one time. Before 1820 Thomas Worthington, the father of Ohio statehood and a wealthy Chillicothe landowner, had erected gristmills on Paint Creek, Hocking River, and Kinnickinnick Creek, sawmills on the Mad River and Paint Creek, and rope and cloth mills in Chillicothe, the latter being outlets for the wool and flax produced on his vast holdings. His brother Robert managed the Paint Creek flour

by Stephen Ostrander

mill; the rest he leased or employed operators. The number of water-powered mills peaked at 1,861 in 1840, the greatest concentration being 106 mills along the forks of the Mohican River. Only a handful of them stand today. Clifton Mill in Greene County still keeps its nose to the grindstone, as the nation's only full time, water-powered mill.

Ohio's iron-making industry fired up in Youngstown in 1804, but its growth stayed sluggish until high-grade ore was discovered in an area of Southern Ohio called the Hanging Rock Iron Region. In 1838, boosters with unrepentant optimism boasted that the furnaces in Jackson, Lawrence and Scioto counties alone could annually produce 400,000 tons of pig iron for 2,700 years. Nobody challenged the exaggeration because Ohio's belly swelled with the requisite raw materials—iron ore, limestone, and timber. It took 5,000 to 10,000 acres of forest and farm to feed one furnace and its workers each year. The typical furnace (making ten tons a day) consumed 25 tons of ore, a ton and a half of limestone, and an acre of virgin hardwood for charcoal. Nobody put much stock into the rowdy company shantytowns that throbbed around the furnaces because when local resources expired, companies relocated and left behind

abandoned smokestacks, buildings, and naked, chewed up ridges.

Twenty-two ovens baked iron in 1849, the most at any one time. During the Civil War, Ohio's forges worked at full blast to produce iron for cannons, railroads, ironclad ships, and armaments. Some historians rightfully argue that Buckeyes threw as much iron at the Confederates as lead. After the war, the furnaces resumed making iron for kitchen and farm tools, building supports, and locomotives, but one by one they closed. Timber became scarce and efficient coal-burning furnaces made high-cost charcoal forges obsolete. Most important, Michigan and Minnesota had richer ores. Jefferson Furnace, the last of Ohio's 46 furnaces, glowed for the final time in January 1917. By then Cleveland and Youngstown had emerged as major steel-making cities, thanks to railroads and ships that carted raw materials to the mills, then rolled finished products to markets. Even these seemingly impregnable industrial metropoli, which defined and dominated Northeastern Ohio for many decades, would show rust by the end of the 20th century.

Between the Civil War and First World War, Ohio flexed its burgeoning industrial muscle. It had all the tools for the new trades—excellent

transportation, abundant natural resources, cheap labor, and perfect location in the nation's heartland. Cities swelled with immigrants during the era. By 1900, Cleveland, population 326,000, had topped Cincinnati as Ohio's biggest city, and, with some 40 languages spoken in factories and streets, became its most culturally diverse. Small company towns in rural counties earned brief fame for specialities. Malvern Blue Granite Block, a polished paving brick produced in a Carroll County village, won a medal of excellence at the 1893 World Columbian Exposition in Chicago. Bricks and tiles, the material for cities and towns, put places like Zanesville, Logan, Haydenville, Roseville, Middleport, Nelsonville, and Sciotoville on the map, ceramically speaking. Just before World War I, quarries in Eastern Ohio, led by the Smallwood quarry near Empire, mined 90 percent of the nation's supply of pulpstone, the huge sandstone cylinders that paper mills needed to pulverize wood into pulp.

Ohio produced its crop of captains of industry, patriarchs of profit, and "rags to riches" royalty during the era. Arriving in Akron a poor German immigrant, Ferdinand Schumacher founded Quaker Oats and earned the title of Oatmeal King. Ohio Columbus Barber, who lent his named to Barberton, was dubbed the Match King after firing up Diamond Match Company. John Buchtel, a bankrupt farmer's son, made millions as head of the Buckeye Mower and Reaping Company in Akron, but the model company town he planned for Athens County, a place called Buchtel, never appealed to independent rural folks. None of these magnates reached the stratospheric status of John D. Rockefeller, the pious and penny-pinching Clevelander who founded Standard Oil of Ohio. A man reviled and revered, Rockefeller paradoxically set the national standard for corporate greed and individual philanthropy.

Ohio cornfields also sprouted wizards. Milan's Thomas Alva Edison, inventor of the light bulb and 1,093 other creations, and Dayton's Wilbur and Orville Wright, makers of the "flying machine," became storied heroes. Charles Kettering's self-starting ignition system for autos ended all that frustrating, arm-wrenching front-end cranking and literally put more women in the driver's seat. It was one of 200 patents credited to the lanky farmboy, who also concocted the first guided missile, diesel locomotive, and fast-drying auto paint. Curiosity, glory,

Welcome to the POST-BANKING REFORM WORLD...

"HONEY, DO WE WANT TO ROLL OUR IRA/LIFE INSURANCE/T-BILL/FREQUENT FLYER/COLLEGE FUND INTO A NO-LOAD MUTUAL FUND/CHRISTMAS CLUB/ORGAN DONATION/HBO PACKAGE/CHECKING ACCOUNT?"

and the almighty greenback, compelled other Ohio-born tinkerers to give the world the disposable diaper, space suit, durable elastic hoses, paper grocery bag, and the iron ore unloader. They pioneered the traffic light, refrigerated railroad car, radar detector, matchbook, windshield wiper, vacuum cleaner, formica, Freon refrigerant, aircraft de-icer, go-cart, tickertape machine, Play-Doh, blackboard chalk, Gatling gun, Teflon, PVC, talking doll (Mr. Edison, of course), gallon milk jug, household microwave oven, universal bar code, coffee maker, and railroad cowcatcher. Ohio techies gave the nation its first "gas hog" (eight-cylinder car engine), silk factory, made-in-America glass marbles, modern corporate trust (Rockefeller, of course), road striper, and electric street lights.

At some time during the last 200 years, Ohio has led the nation in the manufacture of ball-shaped lollipops, batteries, coffins, comic books, farm implements, footballs, golf clubs, dancing shoes, dirigibles, detergents, railroad cars, cereal, cash registers, tires (and related rubber products), household products, aircraft, fertilizer, playing cards, greeting cards, pottery, house paint, table salt, school buses, sewer pipes, reclining chairs, spark plugs, potato chips, machine tools, water coolers, and whistles.

Baskets too. Big baskets. A bit east of Newark, Ohio's strangest building—an eight-story basket with arching handles—sits beside State Route 16, like some Jurassic-sized berry picker just left it there and will pick it up later. A practical joke? Eyesore or icon? The stucco structure is headquarters of the Longaberger Company, the nation's leading basketmaker. It also is a memorial to Dave Longaberger, the fifth of a dozen kids raised at the edge of poverty in Dresden, an old canal and mill town north of Zanesville. Longaberger suffered from epilepsy, stuttered, and did not graduate from high school until age 21. After the army, he drove a truck, saved money, bought a restaurant in Dresden, then a grocery. In the late 1970s, he revived the town's lost basket business, upscaled the product, and sold millions of them. Baskets made the Longaberger Company a billion dollar business. Locals joke that Dave built that behemoth outside Newark before he died in 1999 so his money would be in one basket when he reaches down from Heaven and grabs it. —*Stephen Ostrander*

"I'VE HAD TO DO SOME DOWNSIZING OF MY OWN."

The gross state product is the final value of goods and services produced by labor and property located in the state. It is the state counterpart to the nations's gross domestic product. For reporting purposes, the economy is divided into ten major sectors: agriculture, manufacturing, mining, construction, transportation/utilities, wholesale trade, retail trade, finance/insurance/ real estate, services, and government. Ohio's Gross State Product (GSP) rose from $118.8 billion in 1979 to an estimated $390 in 2002. As a percentage of the U.S. total, Ohio's output was 3.7% and ranks seventh among the states in total GSP and third in manufacturing. If Ohio were a nation, its total economic output would rank 24rd in the world.

Share of GSP by Sector, 2002

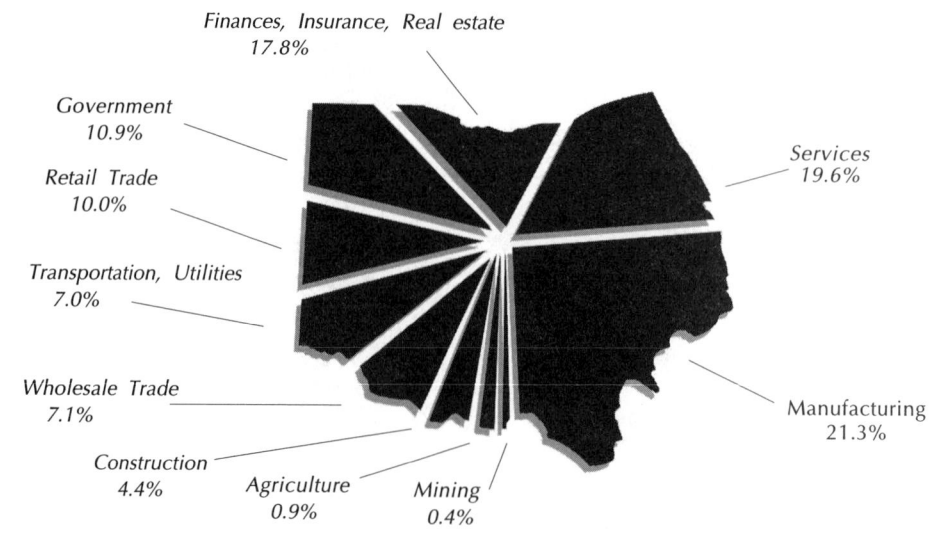

Finances, Insurance, Real estate
17.8%

Government
10.9%

Retail Trade
10.0%

Transportation, Utilities
7.0%

Wholesale Trade
7.1%

Construction
4.4%

Agriculture
0.9%

Mining
0.4%

Services
19.6%

Manufacturing
21.3%

Ohio Gross State Product, 2001 (in millions of dollars)

	Current Dollars	Chained Dollars*	Percent of U.S.	National Rank
Total Gross State Product	$373,708	$349,331	3.7%	7
Private Industries	$330,922	$312,623	3.7%	7
Agriculture, Forestry, Fishing	$3,506	$4,006	2.5%	11
Farms	$1,789	$2,538	2.2%	14
Agricultural Services, Forestry & Fishing	$1,717	$1,403	2.9%	8
Mining	$1,573	$1,472	1.1%	13
Metal Mining	L	$1	0.0%	N.A.
Coal Mining	$527	$700	5.0%	5
Oil & Gas Extraction	$564	$373	0.5%	14
Nonmetallic Minerals, except fuels	$481	$474	3.8%	7
Construction	$16,537	$12,813	3.4%	7
Manufacturing	$79,603	$83,767	5.6%	3
Durable Goods	$51,748	$58,975	6.4%	4
Lumber & Wood Products	$1,452	$1,444	3.7%	11
Furniture and Fixtures	$996	$890	4.0%	7
Stone, Clay, & Glass Products	$2,477	$2,285	6.7%	4
Primary Metals	$4,833	$5,730	10.7%	1
Fabricated Metal Products	$8,995	$8,241	8.9%	2
Industrial Machinery & Equipment	$8,833	$13,262	6.0%	4
Electronic Equipment	$4,563	$10,689	3.2%	10
Transportation Equipment	$16,893	$16,209	9.2%	2
Motor Vehicles & Equipment	$14,607	$14,223	13.1%	2
Other Transportation Equipment	$2,286	$1,986	3.2%	9
Instruments and Related Products	$1,524	$1,138	2.5%	13
Miscellaneous Manufacturing	$1,181	$1,114	3.9%	9
Nondurable Goods	$27,856	$24,992	4.6%	8
Food & Kindred Products	$6,396	$5,510	5.2%	4
Tobacco Products	$1	L	0.0%	23
Textile Mill Products	$268	$251	1.2%	13
Apparel & Other Textile Products	$510	$488	2.2%	12
Paper & Allied Products	$2,337	$2,078	4.2%	8
Printing & Publishing	$3,879	$3,129	3.9%	7
Chemicals & Allied Products	$8,405	$8,116	5.1%	7
Petroleum & Coal Products	$1,284	$778	3.2%	7
Rubber & Miscellaneous Plastics	$4,744	$4,778	8.4%	1
Leather & Leather Products	$33	$31	1.0%	22
Transportation, Communication & Utilities	$26,198	$24,273	3.2%	9
Transportation	$10,886	$9,420	3.6%	9
Railroad Transportation	$988	$959	3.8%	8
Local & Interurban Passenger Transit	$414	$373	2.2%	14
Trucking and Warehousing	$5,952	$4,694	4.7%	5
Water Transportation	$293	$248	1.9%	12
Transportation by Air	$2,202	$2,149	2.7%	13
Pipelines, except Natural Gas	$107	$100	1.7%	15
Transportation Services	$930	$882	2.8%	10
Communication	$6,826	$7,540	2.3%	12
Electric, Gas, & Sanitary Services	$8,487	$7,431	3.8%	7
Wholesale Trade	$26,507	$29,155	3.9%	8
Retail Trade	$37,261	$38,040	4.0%	6
Finance, Insurance, & Real Estate	$66,439	$57,571	3.2%	9
Depository Institutions	$17,817	$14,381	5.0%	5
Nondepository Institutions	$2,663	$2,757	3.0%	11
Security & Commodity Brokers	$2,197	$3,078	1.3%	13
Insurance Carriers	$7,178	$5,961	4.2%	9
Insurance Agents, Brokers & Service	$2,125	$1,708	3.2%	9
Real Estate	$33,251	$29,003	2.8%	9
Holding and Other Investment Services	$213	$609	2.7%	7

	Current Dollars	Chained Dollars*	Percent of U.S.	National Rank
Services	$73,297	$60,915	3.3%	9
Hotels & Other Lodging Places	$1,334	$990	1.5%	20
Personal Services	$2,694	$2,290	4.3%	6
Business Services	$15,176	$12,814	2.8%	13
Auto Repair, Services & Parking	$3,932	$3,455	4.0%	7
Miscellaneous Repair Services	$912	$600	3.4%	7
Motion Pictures	$303	$252	0.9%	13
Amusement and Recreation Services	$2,457	$1,940	3.1%	7
Health services	$25,538	$21,703	4.3%	7
Legal Services	$4,137	$3,415	2.8%	9
Educational Services	$2,590	$2,041	3.1%	8
Social Services	$2,714	$2,121	3.6%	8
Membership Organizations	$2,385	$1,761	3.8%	8
Other Services	$8,862	$7,381	2.8%	11
Private Households	$262	$223	2.2%	12
Government	$42,786	$36,696	3.5%	7
Federal	$8,078	$7,038	2.4%	12
Federal Civilian	$6,752	$5,879	2.9%	10
Federal Military	$1,326	$1,159	1.3%	22
State and Local	$34,708	$29,647	3.9%	6

L - less than $500,000
*chained dollars are adjusted for inflation; based on 1996 dollars

Top Sectors by Percentage of the American Economy

Manufacturing Primary Metals	12.8%
Motor Vehicles & Equipment	12.6%
Fabricated Metal Products	9.7%
Manufacturing Rubber & Miscellaneous Plastics	8.7%
Manufacturing Stone, Glass & Clay Products	7.5%

Top Sectors by Percentage Growth, 1999-2000 (current dollars)

Security & Commodity Brokers	234.4%
Nondepository Financial Institutions	166.1%
Motor Vehicles & Equipment	150.7%
Business Services	128.7%
Local and Interurban Passenger Transit	115.4%

Top Sectors by Real Change, 1999-2000 (percentage in chained dollars)

Security and Commodity Brokers	581.6%
Nondepository Financial Institutions	178.3%
Manufacturing Electrical Equipment	167.0%
Air Transportation	153.3%
Manufacturing Industrial Machinery & Equipment	124.3%
Coal Mining	120.5%

The economy	+plus	-minus

If Ohio's economy were ranked as a separate country, it would be the 23rd largest in the world.

In 2001, the typical Ohio workers earned $12.81 an hour, which was 35 cents above the national average; in 1979, however, the typical Ohio worker earned $13.73 an hour (adjusted for inflation).

The infrastructure

Ohio is ranked 12th nationally on *Inc.* magazine's 500 list of fastest-growing companies; we rank 6th on the *Forbes* 500 list with 41 of America's top companies.

Since 1969, Ohio has lost nearly one-third of its *Fortune* 500 companies—from 43 to 28 (in 1956, Ohio companies generated 7% of the total revenues of the *Fortune 500*).

Where the jobs were

Between 1969 and 1998, the *total* number of manufacturing jobs declined only slightly—from 1.4 million to 1.1 million. Manufacturing remained the largest of Ohio's 10 sectors

Many of the traditionally high-paying union jobs were in that decline, as 38% of Ohio's workforce was unionized in 1964—Ohio had the 8th most unionized workforce in 1960—and only 18% today. Between 2001-2003, Ohio lost 118,500 manufacturing jobs.

Where the jobs are

Only 12 states have more employment concentration in health care than Ohio does. (Cleveland ranks 14th among 300 metro areas, with 3 other Ohio areas in the top 50). Trends say Ohio's computer/data processing industry will grow over 100% by 2008, adding an expected 64,000 workers.

The state estimates that 73% of growth in Ohio's GSP will come in the service-providing sectors, and almost 100% of all job growth. These jobs pay between $6.72 and $9.54 an hour—food preparation, cashiers, retail sales, and waiters and waitresses.

And where else

The motor vehicle industry in Ohio produced $17 billion worth of goods in 1999, nearly a seventh of the U.S output. More than 170,000 people work in the industry, at an average annual wage of $46,208.

The industry's infrastructure is old; impending decisions could spur either reinvestment or plant closings.

Intimations about workforce

Ohio ranks 10th among all states in corporate research and development, No. 1 in plastics and rubber and No. 2 in primary steel. The state's private sector spent $6.5 billion on R&D in 1999; 2,255 companies were involved in some R&D activity. Ohio ranks 5th among all states in amount of federal R&D dollars received annually. The Battelle Institute says that Ohio's technology sector consists of over 28,000 businesses employing over 800,000 workers.

Ohio is in the lower fourth nationally in the ability to retain and attract individuals with bachelor's and master's degrees. Ohio's metro areas rated weak in workforce levels, widening the gap in economic growth, compared with regions with more educated workforces. Ohio ranks 33rd nationally in progress toward an information age economy.

Retail Trade in Ohio
(based on the U.S. Economic Census)

	Establishments	Sales	Employees
Retail Trade	**44,521**	**$102,938,830,000**	**630,098**
Motor Vehicle & Parts Dealers	5,053	$28,431,942,000	75,633
Automobile Dealers	2,151	$24,932,925,000	52,000
New Car Dealers	1,156	$23,295,280,000	47,940
Used Car Dealers	995	$1,637,645,000	4,060
Other Motor Vehicle Dealers	467	$930,013,000	3,545
Recreational Vehicle Dealers	111	$294,791,000	1,048
Motorcycle, Boat, & Other Motor Vehicle Dealers	356	$635,222,000	2,497
Motorcycle Dealers	150	$330,727,000	1,256
Boat Dealers	153	$235,103,000	978
All Other Motor Vehicle Dealers	53	$69,392,000	263
Automotive Parts & Accessories Stores	1,751	$1,742,811,000	14,311
Tire Dealers	684	$808,193,000	5,777
Furniture & Home Furnishings Stores	2,461	$2,975,212,000	21,398
Furniture Stores	1,188	$1,955,308,000	12,927
Home Furnishings Stores	1,273	$1,019,904,000	8,471
Floor Covering Stores	703	$641,036,000	3,947
Window Treatment Stores	49	$17,598,000	187
All Other Home Furnishings Stores	521	$361,270,000	4,337
Electronics & Appliance Stores	1,728	$2,898,383,000	15,429
Appliance, Television, & Other Electronics Stores	1,172	$1,927,792,000	11,180
Household Appliance Stores	387	$302,433,000	2,187
Radio, Television, & Other Electronics Stores	785	$1,625,359,000	8,993
Computer & Software Stores	434	$876,052,000	3,293
Camera & Photographic Supplies Stores	122	$94,539,000	956
Building Material & Garden Equipment & Supplies Stores	4,000	$9,427,187,000	50,717
Home Centers	151	$1,717,634,000	11,374
Paint & Wallpaper Stores	485	$379,278,000	2,239
Hardware Stores	685	$597,896,000	7,537
Lawn & Garden Equipment & Supplies Stores	855	$1,131,141,000	6,716
Outdoor Power Equipment Stores	252	$229,728,000	1,635
Nursery & Garden Stores	603	$901,413,000	5,081
Food & Beverage Stores	6,371	$15,806,582,000	125,217
Grocery Stores	4,266	$14,586,062,000	113,631
Supermarket & Other Grocery Stores	2,404	$13,501,350,000	102,279
Convenience Stores	1,862	$1,084,712,000	11,352
Specialty Food Stores	930	$428,126,000	5,671
Beer, Wine & Liquor Stores	1,175	$792,394,000	5,915
Health & Personal Care Stores	3,632	$5,645,857,000	43,774
Pharmacies & Drug Stores	1,846	$4,849,896,000	35,034
Cosmetics, Beauty Supplies, & Perfume Stores	62	$179,239,000	1,884
Optical Goods Stores	707	$259,524,000	2,961
Food (health) Supplement Stores	291	$123,831,000	1,468
All Other Health & Personal Care Stores	416	$233,367,000	2,427
Gasoline Stations	4,684	$8,318,200,000	38,213
Gasoline Stations with Convenience Stores	2,958	$5,491,073,000	24,981
Other Gasoline Stations	1,726	$2,827,127,000	13,232
Clothing & Clothing Accessories Stores	5,593	$4,322,174,000	46,151
Clothing Stores	3,180	$2,781,474,000	30,889
Men's Clothing Stores	459	$312,120,000	3,358
Women's Clothing Stores	1,314	$884,111,000	11,509

Children's & Infants' Clothing Stores	152	$165,534,000	1,538
Family Clothing Stores	633	$1,121,745,000	11,016
Clothing Accessories Stores	202	$50,615,000	770
Other Clothing Stores	420	$247,349,000	2,698
Shoe Stores	1,273	$779,336,000	7,852
Men's Shoe Stores	91	$40,277,000	341
Women's Shoe Stores	135	$55,583,000	832
Children's & Juveniles' Shoe Stores	43	$15,111,000	252
Family Shoe Stores	778	$428,395,000	3,944
Athletic Footwear Stores	226	$239,970,000	2,493
Jewelry Stores	1,089	$729,547,000	7,110
Luggage & Leather Goods Stores	51	$31,817,000	300
Sporting Goods, Hobby, Book & Music Stores	2,775	$2,216,042,000	21,757
Sporting Goods Stores	922	$641,480,000	6,453
General-line Sporting Goods Stores	296	$313,089,000	3,255
Specialty-line Sporting Goods Stores	626	$328,391,000	3,198
Hobby, Toy, & Game Stores	518	$590,033,000	4,836
Sewing, Needlework, & Piece Goods Stores	258	$139,046,000	1,756
Musical Instrument & Supplies Stores	195	$130,625,000	1,280
Book Stores & News Dealers	546	$714,858,000	7,432
Book Stores	459	$404,661,000	4,848
Book Stores, General	291	$255,464,000	2,821
Specialty Book Stores	118	$56,103,000	845
College Book Stores	50	$93,094,000	779
News Dealers & Newsstands	87	$29,801,000	403
Prerecorded Tape, Compact Disc, & Record Stores	336	$280,396,000	2,584
General Merchandise Stores	1,617	$15,028,178,000	129,491
Department Stores	505	$9,947,533,000	85,447
Conventional Department Stores	103	withheld	10 -24,900
Discount or Mass Merchandising Department Stores	322	$5,493,902,000	47,212
National Chain Department Stores	80	withheld	10 -24,900
Warehouse Clubs & Superstores	93	$4,120,676,000	29,294
Variety Stores	715	$677,805,000	7,220
Catalog Showrooms	31	withheld	2,500 -4,999
Miscellaneous General Merchandise Stores			
Miscellaneous Store Retailers	4,898	$2,642,242,000	31,706
Florists	1,085	$600,026,000	4,261
Stationery Stores	27	$13,963,000	181
Office Supply Stores	235	$586,063,000	4,080
Gift, Novelty, & Souvenir Stores	1,410	$531,343,000	9,072
Used Merchandise Stores	595	$176,417,000	3,596
Pet & Pet Supplies	359	$236,356,000	3,164
Art Dealers	164	$50,074,000	671
Manufactured (mobile) Home Dealers	137	$295,093,000	1,057
Other	886	$490,861,000	4,170
Nonstore Retailers	1,709	$5,244,831,000	30,612
Electronic Shopping & Mail-order Houses	383	$3,505,845,000	14,312
Vending Machine Operators	395	$570,239,000	7,749
Direct Selling Establishments	931	$1,169,747,000	8,251
Fuel Dealers	352	$718,858,000	3,228
Heating Oil Dealers	168	$319,445,000	1,121
Liquefied Petroleum Gas (bottled gas) Dealers	181	$396,898,000	2,100
Other Fuel Dealers	3	$2,515,000	7
Other Direct Selling Establishments	579	$450,889,000	5,023

*Source: U.S. Department of Commerce, Economic Census; these figures
are released every five years.*

Accommodation and Foodservices in Ohio
(based on the latest U.S. Economic Census)

	Establishments	Sales	Employees
Accommodation & Foodservices	**22,631**	**$12,410,978,000**	**401,206**
Accommodation	1,571	$1,665,805,000	35,400
Traveler Accommodation	1,159	$1,572,459,000	33,943
Hotels & Motels	1,099	$1,564,284,000	33,793
Hotels withe 25 Guestrooms or More	44	$1,236,097,000	26,666
Hotels with less than 25 Guestrooms	32	withheld	250 - 499
Motels	556	$254,578,000	5,783
Motor Hotels	65	$63,099,000	1,047
Organization Hotels	2	withheld	20 - 99
Bed & Breakfast Inns	49	$7,010,000	124
RV (recreational vehicle) Parks & Campgrounds	257	$56,507,000	776
Rooming & Boarding Houses	155	$36,839,000	681
Foodservices & Drinking Places	21,060	$10,745,173,000	365,806
Full-Service Restaurants	6,729	$4,522,501,000	168,038
Limited-Service Restaurants	9,689	$4,957,556,000	165,038
Cafeterias	7,932	$61,385,000	2,355
Snack & Nonalcoholic Beverage Bars	1,635	$380,304,000	13,082
Foodservice Contractors	633	$640,843,000	10,150
Caterers	327	$166,479,000	5,139
Mobile Foodservices	149	$64,539,000	742
Drinking Places (alcoholic beverages)	3,533	$624,273,000	16,487

Arts, Entertainment, and Recreation in Ohio
(based on the latest U.S. Economic Census)

	Establishments	Receipts	Employees
Arts, Entertainment, and Recreation			
Taxable	**2,902**	**$2,308,609,000**	**37,210**
Tax Exempt	**858**	**$907,677,000**	**19,582**
Performing Arts Companies			
Taxable	542	$823,504,000	7,891
Tax Exempt	200	$255,487,000	4,846
Opera Companies			
Taxable	1	withhed	1-19
Tax Exempt	50	$7,603,000	73
Theater Companies			
Taxable	19	$35,162,000	256
Tax Exempt	45	withheld	256
Dinner Theaters	5	withheld	250-499
Dance Companies			
Taxable	1	withheld	1-19
Tax Exempt	12	withheld	150 - 499
Musical Groups & Artists			
Taxable	53	$15,789,000	195
Tax Exempt	46	$83,040,000	1,800
Symphony Orchestras & Chamber Music Organizations			
Taxable	2	withheld	1 - 19
Tax Exempt	24	$78,172,000	1,662
Circuses	3	withehld	20 - 99
Other Music Groups & Artists			
Taxable	12	withheld	20 - 99

Tax Exempt	1	withheld	20 - 99
Spectator Sports	149	$519,421,000	4,583
Football Clubs	1	withheld	20 - 99
Baseball Clubs	4	withheld	500 - 999
Other Professional Clubs	8	$86,875,000	1,329
Auto Racetrack Operations	24	$20,700,000	255
Horse Racetrack Operations	11	$120,706,000	1,506
Other Spectator Sports	101	$47,520,000	451
Professional Athletes	23	$10,978,000	117
Racing (except racetrack operations)	78	$36,542,000	334
Promoters of Performing Arts, Sports & Similar Events			
Taxable	101	$115,562,000	1,372
Tax Exempt	91	$108,329,000	1,930
Agents/Managers for Artists, Athletes & other Public Figures	38	$111,885,000	469
Independent Artists, Writers, & Performers	160	$36,880,000	552
Museums, Historical Sites & Similar Institutions			
Taxable	20	$5,157,000	156
Tax Exempt	194	$284,263,000	4,488
Museums			
Taxable	10	withheld	20 - 99
Tax Exempt	133	$218,148,000	3,055
Historical Sites			
Taxable	1	withheld	20 - 99
Tax Exempt	39	$19,325,000	431
Zoos & Botanical Gardens			
Taxable	3	$182,000	2
Tax Exempt	10	$42,390,000	928
Nature Parks & Other Similar Institutions			
Taxable	6	$1,598,000	22
Tax Exempt	12	$4,400,000	74
Amusement, Gambling & Recreational Industries			
Taxable	2,340	$1,479,948,000	29,163
Tax Exempt	464	$367,927,000	10,248
Amusement Parks			
Waterparks	5	$7,653,000	73
Amusement Arcades	10	$329,520,000	1,989
Gambling Industries	18	$27,398,000	114
Golf Courses & Country Clubs			
Taxable	509	$409,017,000	6,786
Tax Exempt	134	$260,126,000	6,198
Skiing Facilities	8	$9,698,000	791
Marinas	140	$74,783,000	714
Ice Skating Rinks	8	$5,610,000	234
Roller Skating Rinks	96	$20,915,000	1,143
Bowling Centers	386	$175,649,000	5,898
Fitness & Recreational Sports Centers			
Taxable	694	$241,853,000	8,995
Tax Exempt	248	$84,934,000	3,595
Dance Studios & Halls	12	$4,449,000	45
Concession Operations of Amusement Devices & Rides	41	$21,151,000	339
Miniature Golf Courses	53	$12,925,000	269
Coin Operated Amusement Devices	108	$73,541,000	855

Source: U.S. Department of Commerce, Economic Census; these figures are released every five years.

Ohio has 66 breweries, mostly brewpubs or microbreweries, and two giants owned by two of the biggest beermakers in the world. Ohio thus produces twice as much beer as it drinks—16.8 million barrels of beer a year— a half a million barrels more than it drinks—making it a major exporter to other states.

—Associated Press

"WHEN WE BUILT IT WE THOUGHT IT WOULD SPUR ECONOMIC DEVELOPMENT IN THE AREA...."

The last 25 years have seen the largest economic restructuring of Ohio's economy since the Great Depression. In 1969, manufacturing accounted for 31.6 percent of the state's jobs but by 1998 that percentage had declined to 16.8. Even so, the total number of manufacturing jobs only dropped from 1,484,000 to 1,122,000 (this is because most of the new jobs in this period were created in the service industry; the point is that manufacturing jobs, in a relative sense, managed to hold). Based on gross state product, manufacturing is still the largest of Ohio's ten major sectors, led by transportation equipment, industrial machinery, and fabricated metals. The manufacture of machinery and that of motor vehicles also account for over half of Ohio's exports—53 percent.

While the state's reputation is not one of a high tech, "new economy" state, advancements in technology have allowed Ohio's manufacturing industry to increase productivity. Information and computer technologies are applied to the manufacturing process, often in the mature phase of the product cycle, creating what one Cleveland area manufacturer described as "putting new machines in old buildings."

Battelle Institute indentifies over 28,000 establishments with ties to technology in Ohio.

Harvard University's Cluster Mapping Project, which identifies concentrations of related industries, places Ohio at the top among the states as a Production Technology cluster. The state has many industries which are moderately intense users of technology (ones that use between two and five times the U.S. average of technologically-oriented workers). An exception is Ohio's chemicals industry, which is classified as

very intense technologically— employing at least five times the U.S. average of technologically oriented workers.

One key to Ohio's economic success lies with the partnerships among educational institutions, private research facilities, and the industrial sectors. Ohio State University, Case Western University, and the University of Cincinnati are each major research institutions that receive over $150 million annually in federal research grants. Wright-Patterson Air Force Base, NASA Glenn, and Battelle Institute also share a major part of the $8.1 billion annually Ohio receives for research and development.

While jobs in manufacturing have remained relatively flat, most of the state's job growth has occured in the service-producing sectors. These sectors account for 70 percent of the state's GSP and employ 75 percent of Ohio's workers. Analysts predict most of the state's future job growth will occur in this area.

Harvard University, in an attempt to assemble a picture of the location and perfor-mance of the nation's economy, has begun the "Cluster Mapping Project," which maps by state economic clusters in the United States as a way of measuring performance and competitive strength of regional economies, as well as giving an accurate picture of an industry's impact within a state's economy.

Clusters are geographically concentrated groups of interconnected companies, universities, and related institutions that arise out of linkages or externalities across industries. They are analyzed at various geographic levels including states, economic areas, and metropolitan areas.

An economic cluster may include producers, service providers, suppliers, universities, and trade associations.

The project looks at the geographic concen-tration of these groups. While there are several different types of clusters, state data is presented in narrow clusters that include only industries unique to that cluster. For example, telephones, telegraphs, radio and TV all fall exclusively into the communications cluster.

Going, going...

In 2002, there were 78,825 bankruptcy filings in Ohio; 96.4% were personal filings and 2,585 were business filings.

Number of filings

2000—54,184
2001—71,086

—American Bankruptcy Institute

Cluster	National Rank	1999 Location Quotient
Construction Materials	1	2.33
Metal Manufacturing	1	2.53
Production Technology	1	1.09
Automotive	2	3.02
Chemical Products	2	1.72
Lighting and Electrical Equipment	2	1.79
Motor Driven Products	2	1.77
Plastics	2	1.95
Building Fixtures, Equipment and Services	3	1.39
Heavy Machinery	4	1.30
Processed Food	5	1.09
Forest Products	6	0.89
Jewelry and Precious Metals	6	0.89
Power Generation	6	1.08
Publishing and Printing	6	1.03
Education and Knowledge Creation	7	0.83
Leather Products & Sporting Goods	7	0.80
Tobacco	7	0.65
Analytical Instruments	8	0.80
Distribution Services	8	0.78
Heavy Construction Services	8	0.75

Communications Equipment	9	0.69
Financial Services	9	0.99
Pharmaceuticals	9	0.84
Power Transition and Distribution	9	0.80
Medical Devices	10	0.71
Prefabricated Enclosures	10	0.82
Aerospace Vehicles and Defense	11	0.46
Furniture	11	0.65
Entertainment	12	0.51
Hospitality and Tourism	12	0.50
Transportation and Logistics	12	0.59
Business Services	13	0.72
Oil and Gas	13	0.39
Agricultural Products	15	0.41
Footwear	17	0.47
Information Technology	17	0.39
Textiles	18	0.15

The location quotient shows the percentage of Ohio jobs that are in a particular cluster relative to the national total. If the ratio is greater than one then Ohio has a greater share of employment than does the rest of the nation, showing a degree of specialization.

Aerospace and Defense Industry

Ohio's aerospace industry includes the manufacturing of aircraft, missiles, space vehicles, aerospace engines, propulsion units and aircraft or propulsion system rebuilding. It employs 17,642 Ohioans at 78 establishments. In 1999 the state ranked sixth nationally in the aerospace product and parts manufacturing industry and the subsector of aircraft engines and parts manufacturing ranked second in the U.S. Twelve of the top 50 companies with Air Force contracts have offices or headquarters in Ohio with the major employers in Ohio being Wright-Patterson Air Force Base, NASA Glenn, General Electric, Goodrich and Parker-Hannifin. Ohio companies received $2,471,715,000 in prime defense contracts in 1998 (eighth nationally) spread out among 38 Ohio counties. Hamilton County led the way with $762,342,000 followed by Greene ($570,452,000) and Montgomery Counties ($251,751,000). Wright-Patterson Air Force Base, located on the historic site of the Wright Brothers Flight Tests, is Ohio's largest single site employer in the aerospace industry employing 22,000 civilians and military workers. Its economic impact in 1999 was estimated to be over $2.7 billion. NASA Glenn is the premier facility for microgravity science, in-space transportation, aerospace communications and aeropropulsion and interdisciplinary research for bioscience. GE Aircraft Engines, headquartered in Cincinnati, produces 37 engine types for 91 aircraft systems. It is the world's leader in manufacturing jet engines. In Lima, Ohio the U.S. government owns the plant that General Dynamics uses to manufacture the Army MIA2 Abrams tank. The Harvard Cluster Mapping Project places Ohio 11th nationally in the Aerospace Vehicles and Defense Cluster.

"GOOD HEAVENS, WALTER... IT'S METASTASIZED!"

Food Processing

Its $6.8 billion food processing industry ranks Ohio fifth among the 50 states. Located between the grain belt of the Midwest and the markets of the East the state is well positioned as a leader in this sector. Frozen Specialty Food is a major success in Ohio. Pillsbury operates the world's largest pizza plant in Wellston helping Ohio lead the nation in that industry with 15.3 percent of the nation's production. Ohio ranks second in the Cookie & Cracker, Food Fats & Oil Refining, and Pet Food industries. It also ranks third in Fluid Milk and fourth in Snack Food. Major facilities in Ohio are the Campbell soup factory in Napoleon—the world's largest—and the Heinz plant in Freemont where more ketchup is made than anywhere else in the world. The Dannon yogurt plant, the world's largest, is located in Auglaise County. Wendy's Zanesville plant supplies a billion hamburger buns a year to restaurants in the Eastern half of the country. Major food processors headquartered in Ohio include Bob Evans Farms, Chiquita Brands International, Kroger, Lancaster Colony, Smuckers, Wendy's International and Worthington Foods. Harvard's study of economic clusters places Ohio 5th among the states in the Processed Food Cluster and 15th in the Agricultural Products Cluster.

Iron and Steel

Raw steel production in Ohio reached it peak in 1973 when the state's factories produced 26.5 million net tons. While this number has dropped—Ohio produces one-sixth of the raw steel made in the U.S.—it is the home to 292 iron and steel industry establishments. As judged by the dollar value-added at industry establishments, Ohio led the nation in:
- Iron and Steel Mill Products
- Electro-metallurgical Ferroalloy Products
- Pipe and Tube Manufacturing from Purchased Steel
- Rolled Steel Shapes
- Iron Foundry Output

It is estimated that 54,500 Ohioans are employed in the iron and steel industry. The largest employer in Ohio's iron and steel industry is AK Steel in Middletown with 7,300 employees. Republic Technologies International and LTV each employ over 5,000. In the Harvard Business School's Cluster Mapping Project, Ohio had the top-ranked Metal Manufacturing Cluster in which iron and steel is a large component.

Machinery Industry

As a producer of machinery, Ohio is the third highest producer in the U.S. with about $9.4 billion worth of goods—7 percent of the nation's total. It leads the nation in the sector of general purpose machinery (pumps, compressors, industrial trucks, power handtools, welding equipment, and scales). In the other six sectors, the state ranks second. Within those sectors, Ohio leads the nation in producing the following (percent of all U.S. production is in parenthesis):

- *Plastics & rubber industry machinery (34%)*
- *Welding & soldering equipment (29%)*
- *Machine tools, metal forming (25%)*
- *Machine tools, metal cutting (19%)*
- *Scales & balances (18%)*
- *Industrial trucks & tractors (15%)*
- *Measuring & dispensing pumps (13%)*
- *Industrial & commercial fans and blowers (12%)*
- *Fluid power pumps & motors (12%)*
- *Pumps & pumping equipment (11%)*
- *Power-driven handtools (9%)*

The industry is led in Ohio by Emerson Electric which employs 5,100 workers. Delphi Thermal (compressors for motor vehicles), Crown Equipment (industrial trucks), and Illinois Tool Works (food processing equipment) are also leading companies. Ohio companies account for one out of every three machines produced in the U.S.

Motor Vehicles

Of Ohio's Gross State Product, 3.8 percent comes from the motor vehicle industry in which Ohio ranks only behind Michigan nationally. Still, the GSP numbers do not reflect the entire scope of the state's auto industry. About 28% of the entirety of Ohio's manufacturing is related to motor vehicle production. In 1998, one-sixth of the nation's cars were assembled in Ohio (about 1,016,000) and one-seventh of its light trucks (840,000). In automobile stamping and vehicular lighting equipment, Ohio produces 20.3 percent and 18.2 percent respectively of the nation's total. Of the Ohio-produced vehicles, 37 percent are produced by Honda, 32 percent by General Motors, 16 percent, Ford, and 15 percent Daimler-Chrysler. Honda's Marysville plant assembled almost 456,000 cars—more than any other plant in North America. GM's Lordstown plant is the company's largest vehicle producer.

Petroleum and Chemical

Based on the transformation of crude petroleum and coal into usable products and forming products from organic and inorganic raw materials by a chemical process, Ohio produces 4.7 percent of the nation's total—the fifth highest of any state in the U.S. In the petroleum and coal products industry Ohio ranks third in total establishments with 176, sixth in employees with 5,697, and seventh in total receipts with $6.2 billion. Ohio has six refineries. In the chemical sector, Ohio ranks first in Paint, Coating and Adhesive manufacturing based on receipts ($3.3 billion) and employment

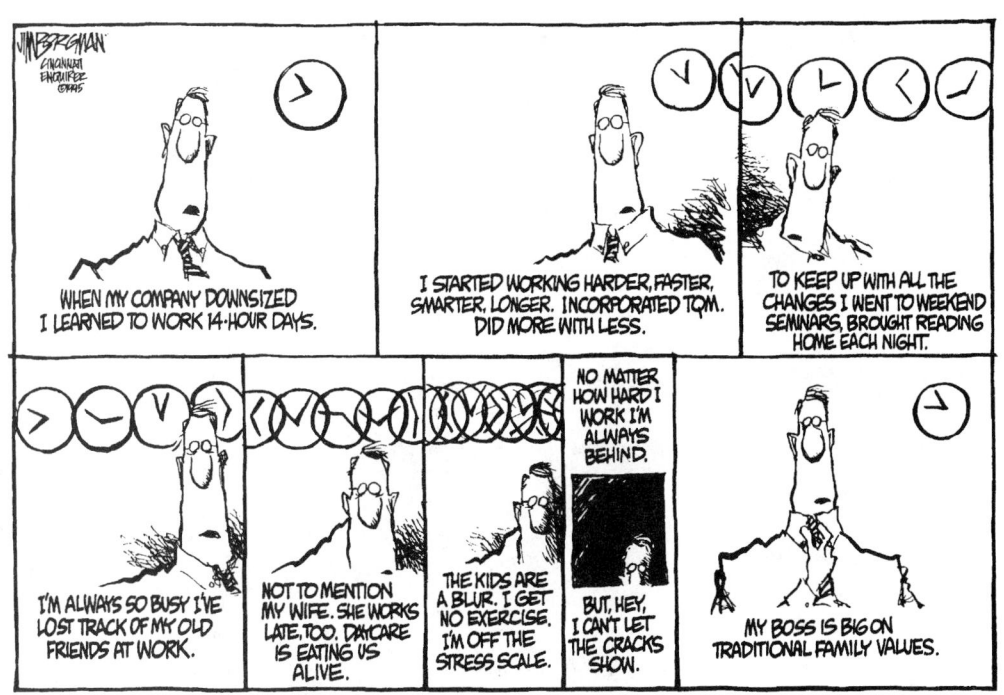

(9,037). It also ranked first in the Soap & Toilet industry with $6.1 billion in receipts. In Ohio, the sector is led by major companies such as Procter & Gamble, Sherwin-Williams, RPM, Inc., Lubrizol Corporation, Ferro, Borden, and Noveron. Harvard's Cluster Mapping Project ranks Ohio second in the Chemical Products Cluster and 13th in the Oil and Gas Cluster.

Plastics & Rubber Products

Ohio has historically had a strong rubber products industry. Today in Ohio this industry is twice as large as the second place state. Top ranked sectors in Ohio are:
- *Custom compounding—1st with 13% of U.S. production*
- *Tire retreading —1st with 7% of U.S. production*
- *Rubber & plastic hoses & belting—1st with 11% of U.S. production*
- *Rubber for mechanical use—1st with 24% of U.S. production*
- *All other rubber products —1st with 10% of U.S. production*
- *Plastics & rubber industrial machinery—1st 34% of U.S. production*
- *Synthetic rubber—2nd with 17% of U.S. production*
- *Unsupported plastic profile shapes—2nd with 8% of U.S. production*
- *Plastic bottles —2nd with 12 % of U.S. production*

In the industry, Goodyear Tire & Rubber and Cooper Tire & Rubber are the state's two largest employers. They are also the top two companies on the *Fortune* magazine list of rubber and plastics companies. From 1997 to 1999 Ohio ranked first in the nation in new capital expenditures in the rubber and plastics industry. Ohio's Plastics Cluster ranks second nationally in Harvard's Cluster Mapping Project.

Source: Ohio Department of Development; U.S. Census Bureau; Harvard University,
Ohio Manufacturers' Association

Procter & Gamble creates *moon and stars symbol* to identify products shipped across country; trademark is needed because many freight-handlers are illiterate and trademark distinguishes P&G products.

1851

Sherwin-Williams of Cleveland introduces *first specific purpose paint*, with a special paint for carriages. The company will soon patent a reclosable can and the first real money-back guarantee for its paint.

1874

1878 Carroll County's Theodore Vail is named general manager of the new Bell Telephone Company and over the next seven years creates a national network out of the chaos of many small, competing companies, thus bringing into being *the modern telephone industry.*

1878

When he founds the Edison Illuminating Company of New York, Thomas Edison of Milan, Ohio, has created *the modern electric power industry.*

1880

Edward S. Scripps buys the *Penny Post* and begins the *Cincinnati Post.* Describing his papers as "schoolrooms" for the working classes, he builds from his Cincinnati and Cleveland base *one of the nation's great media companies.*

1883

With his four Cincinnati stores, Barney Kroger places his first grocery ads, goes on to pioneer the technique of purchasing merchandise by the truckload and *underselling competitors with loss-leaders.* Kroger was also the first grocer to operate his own in-house bakery and to bring a meat department into a grocery.

1885

Procter & Gamble becomes *the first American business to offer a profit-sharing plan*; it is followed two years later by an employee stock purchase.

1887

Quaker Oats places *advertising sign on White Cliffs of Dover*. The sign, which can be seen three miles into the English Channel, generates a public outcry and is banned by the House of Commons.

1897

1907 James Murray Spangler, a janitor in a Canton department store and suffering from asthma, creates *a "suction sweeper"* out of a tin soap box, a sateen pillowcase, a broom handle, and a fan. He sells his patent to a boyhood friend, W.H. Hoover, a horse-collar manufacturer.

1907

Cleveland chocolate-maker Clarence Crane, looking for a product to boost warm weather sales, made a hard candy mint; to differentiate the *"Crane's Peppermint Life Savers"* from the conventional square-shaped mints of the day, he made his in the shape of the new round life preservers with a hole in the middle, which were just beginning to be seen on ships.

1912

Harry Burt, owner of a Youngstown confectionery shop, makes *the Good Humor Ice Cream Bar*, after his son suggests putting his frozen ice cream on a stick. Sold from a fleet of white trucks with bells and uniformed drivers, his ice cream bar becomes an American staple.

1920

1930	BFGoodrich of Akron develops one of the most important advancements in commercial aviation history; invents *de-icing mechanism* that enabled airplanes to take-off and land safely in winter weather.
1931	The Owens Illinois Glass Company begins eight years of experiments resulting in *the commercial manufacture of fiberglass*.
1933	Procter & Gamble introduces the *first synthetic detergent* for household use, Dreft; follows up next year with first synthetic shampoo.
1934	Fred Lazarus, Jr. arranges apparel according to size rather than color, price or brand; *changes face of retail clothing sales* in America. The system, adopted from the French, becomes an industry standard.
1935	Wooster Rubber Company comes up with the idea of *the rubber dustpan* and sets in motion the events, which will propel the company into the number one spot in plastic housewares
1937	Jack Green and Joseph Lewis found progressive Mutual Insurance in Cleveland. Company lured customers through innovations such as *installment payments of premiums and a drive-in claims service*, as the company was headquartered in a garage.
1944	The Battelle Memorial Institute invests $3,000 to develop *the first copying machine* and eleven years later sells the rights to the company that will become Xerox. The name was formed by an Ohio State University classics professor from two Greek words, *xeros* for dry and *graphein* for writing.
1960	Arnold Palmer enlists Cleveland attorney Mark McCormack to become his business agent, from which transaction came McCormack's International Management Group, which was one of the first to convince companies to *pay athletes to sponsor their products*. In 2003, IMG had 80 offices in 32 countries, $1 billion in revenue, a Who's Who client list of the world's most successful athletes, and once did promo for the Pope.
1979	Wendy's, the Columbus-based food chain named after Dave Thomas' 8-year-old daughter, reaches 1,000 restaurants faster than any of its competitors, and becomes *the first national chain to offer a salad bar*.
1995	Ohio becomes *leading state in nation for polymers*, surpassing California and extending its economic base beyonds steel and autos. Ohio was expected to ship nearly $9 billion of plastic products in 1996, nearly ten percent of the U.S. plastics product supply.

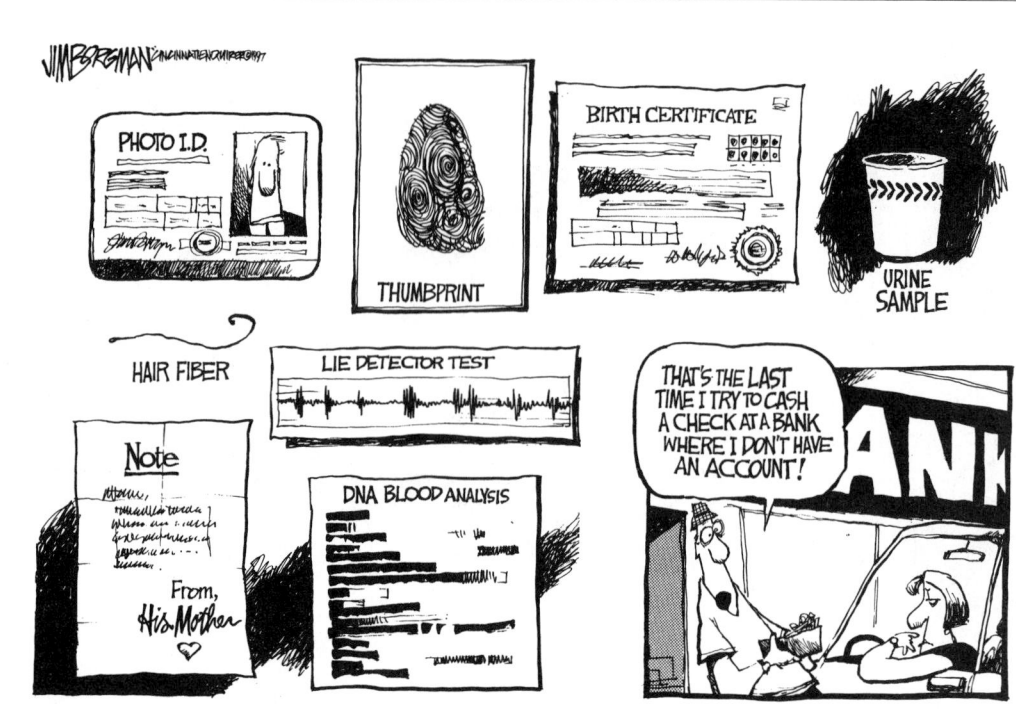

Estimated annual expenses on a million-dollar home

Mortgage:

$57,600

Property taxes:

$15,400

Insurance:

$3,000-$4,000

Association fee:

$780

Sportsplex fees (required):

$900

Golf course dues: (optional)

$6,000 (plus one-time $29,000 refundable deposit that may be financed with mortgage)

Cleaning:

$3,900

Landscaping:

$3,800

—Cincinnati magazine, June, 2003

Housing in Ohio

Average valuation of a home in Ohio: $103,700
Existing home sales, 2002: $207,800

Total housing units	4,783,051
Single detached units	67.4%
Multiple units	27.9%
Mobile homes	4.6%
Boat, RV, Van	0.1%
Median Number of Rooms	5.7

Housing Costs

Metro Area	Median Price	Affordable Homes**	Nat. Rank*
Akron	$109,000	79.9%	53
Canton-Massillon	$103,000	83.0%	28
Cincinnati	$125,000	83.6%	24
Cleveland	$123,000	79.9%	53
Columbus	$140,000	78.2%	63
Dayton-Springfield	$101,000	90.0%	6
Hamilton-Middletown	$133,000	83.9%	22
Mansfield	$90,000	83.5%	25
Toledo	$108,000	81.6%	35
Youngstown-Warren	$82,000	85.8%	15

* Rank is based on affordability
** Affordability is the percent of homes affordable to families based on median family income

Cost of Home Ownership (median cost)

With Mortgage	$963
Not Mortgaged	$289
Median Rent	$515

House Heating	
Utility gas:	68.8%
Bottled, tanks, or LP:	6.1%
Electricity:	18.3%
Fuel oil or kerosene:	4.7%

Lacking Complete Plumbing Facilities	0.4%
Lacking Complete Kitchen Facilities	0.5%
No Telephone Service	2.2%

Year Built	
1999-2000	1.8%
1995-1998	5.8%
1990-1994	5.7%
1980-1989	9.5%
1970-1979	5.8%
1960-1969	14.3%
1940-1959	24.6%
Before 1939	22.5%

Average Homeowners Insurance Premiums	
Akron	$362
Cincinnati	$412
Cleveland	$463
Columbus	$368
Dayton	$393
Toledo	$389
Youngstown	$419
Small town/Rural	$791

Source: National Association of Home Builders; U.S Census Bureau; Ohio Department of Insurance

Twenty years ago, the first Honda Accord left the assembly line in Marysville, Ohio, and the U.S. auto industry changed forever. Honda was the first Japanese automaker to build in America. Its move encouraged other Japanese automakers to follow, along the way destroying the myth that U.S. workers were inferior to their Japanese counterparts. Ultimately, Honda's move also affected almost every American autoworker.

The growth of Japanese auto plants in North America is one of the biggest auto industry stories since World War II, said Michael S. Flynn, director of the University of Michigan's Office for the Study of Automotive Transportation.

"Honda started it all," Flynn said.

Japanese automakers now have invested about $20 billion in auto plants in the United States and employ about 48,000 workers, according to the Japan Automobile Manufacturers Association.

Those 48,000 workers include about 13,000 Honda employees at plants in Marysville, East Liberty, and Anna in Ohio, building models including the Accord, the Civic, the new Element, and two Acura luxury models.

In 2001, Japanese auto plants in North America produced 3.4 million vehicles, or roughly 21 percent of the vehicles built in North America, according to Ward's AutoInfoBank, an automotive information service that is based in Detroit.

To some extent, the Japanese presence in the United States is a lesson in being careful about what you ask for. As Japanese vehicles became more popular, American auto executives counterattacked, saying that if the Japanese wanted to sell cars in America, they should build them in America.

The argument was that the playing field was not level because the Japanese automakers were building cars in Japan, where they had a currency and labor advantage, said David E. Cole, the director of the Center for Automotive Research. "The political pressure was enormous," Cole said.

Honda had been building motorcycles in Marysville since 1979. In 1980 it announced plans to build automobiles. When the plant opened roughly two years later, some doubted American workers could do as good a job as the seemingly invincible Japanese.

The idea was that the Americans "by heritage were sloppy and the Japanese were precise," the University of Michigan's Flynn said. As the first Accords left Marysville, some consumers insisted on having an Accord built in Japan, remembers Honda dealer Lee Seidman, president of the Motorcars Group.

Quality and productivity studies, however, quickly showed that the American workers were competitive with the best from Japan. Honda proved that with proper training and a thoughtful manufacturing system, American workers were capable of world-class manufacturing, Cole said.

Soon domestic automakers were trying to use some Japanese production methods in their plants. Those included giving workers more say in how they did their jobs and asking them for suggestions, not just hours.

But there would be a downside. As Japanese automakers increased their market share over the coming years, they would take sales and jobs from the Big Three. In 1982, the Big Three had 77.1 percent of the U.S. market; Asian automakers had 19.4 percent. At the end of 2001, the Asian automakers had 31.7 percent, and the Big Three had 64.2 percent, according to Ward's AutoInfoBank.

Honda's success led to the opening of assembly plants by Toyota, Nissan, Mazda, Subaru, Isuzu and Mitsubishi, some operated with domestic automakers.

Honda also grew. It increased its production and opened a second assembly plant in East Liberty and an engine plant in nearby Anna.

By the end of last year, Honda had about 16,000 workers in Ohio, including those at a transmission plant in Russells Point, the motorcycle plant in Marysville and engineers and researchers. That compares with about 17,000 hourly Ford workers throughout Ohio at the end of last year, according to a Ford spokesman.

Ford is expected to trim more jobs during the next few years. That makes it likely that Honda will soon have more workers in Ohio than Ford, something that was unthinkable in 1982.

It is also unlikely that in 1982 anybody imagined that last year most of the "Japanese" vehicles bought in the United States would be built by Americans.

In 1986, less than 12 percent of the Japanese vehicles sold in the U.S. were made in North America, but last year 64 percent came from North America, according to the Japan Automobile Manufacturers Association. About 78 percent of the Hondas sold in the United States last year were built in the United States or Canada, Honda said.

Meanwhile, Honda has continued to upgrade its East Liberty and Marysville plants, giving them updated flexibility so the automaker can switch among models to meet changing consumer demands.

But the Accord remains the heart of Marysville. By the end of last year the plant had cranked out 5.7 million Accords.

What happened to that first Accord?

It is on display at the Henry Ford Museum and Greenfield Village in Dearborn, Mich., the automaker's world headquarters.

—*by Christopher Jensen, The Plain Dealer Auto Editor*

Ohio's Job Growth by Industry
Ohio Employment Projections—Industry Totals

Industry Division	2000 Annual Employment	2010 Projected Employment	Change in Employment 2000 - 2010	Percent Change 2000 - 2010
Total Employment	5,997,900	6,659,900	662,000	11.0%
Goods-producing Industries	1,465,600	1,473,400	7,800	0.5%
Agriculture, Forestry and Fishing	125,800	129,800	4,000	3.2%
Mining	12,600	11,000	-1,600	-12.7%
Construction	246,100	286,900	40,800	16.6%
Manufacturing	1,081,100	1,045,700	-35,400	-3.3%
Durable Goods Manufacturing	726,200	693,000	-33,200	-4.6%
Nondurable Goods Manufacturing	354,900	352,700	2,200	-0.6%
Service-producing Industries	4,200,000	4,845,800	645,800	15.4%
Transportation, Communications & Utilities	247,500	280,000	32,500	13.1%
Trade	1,354,700	1,511,000	156,300	11.5%
Wholesale Trade	304,800	337,300	32,500	10.7%
Retail Trade	1,049,900	1,173,700	123,800	11.8%
Finance, Insurance & Real Estate	308,100	334,200	26,100	8.5%
Services	1,542,600	1,912,000	369,400	23.9%
Government (total)	747,100	808,600	61,500	8.2%
Private Households	14,400	10,700	-3,700	-25.7%
Nonfarm Self-Employed & Unpaid Family Workers	318,000	330,000	12,000	3.8%

Top 30 Industries—Job Growth, 2000-2010

Industry	Percent Change
Computer Data Processing Services	61.7%
Personnel Supply Services	50.0%
Home Health Care Services	48.2%
Other Health and Allied Services	45.4%

Public Warehousing and Storage	43.7%
Child Day Care Services	40.3%
Residential Care	39.1%
Veterinary Services	35.6%
Miscellaneous Equipment and Rental and Leasing	33.9%
Local and Suburban Transportation	33.8%
Offices of Other Health Practitioners	32.4%
Individual and Family Services	31.6%
Landscape and Horticultural Services	31.3%
Gaskets, Packing, Sealing, Hose & Belting	29.3%
Offices and Clinics of Medical Doctors	28.8%
Miscellaneous Shopping Goods Stores	28.0%
Offices of Osteopathic Physicians	27.8%
Air Transport, Scheduled	27.6%
Sanitary Services	27.5%
Producers, Orchestras, Entertainers	27.5%
Miscellaneous Amusement and Recreation Services	27.1%
Nonstore Retailers	27.1%
Retail Stores (not classified elsewhere)	27.0%
Auto and Home Supply Stores	26.6%
Lumber and Construction Materials	26.4%
Automobile Services (except repair)	26.1%
Accounting, Auditing and Bookkeeping	25.9%
Miscellaneous Business Services	25.8%
Museums, Botanical and Zoological Gardens	25.8%
Millwork, Plywood and Structural Members	25.6%

Top 30 Industries—New Jobs, 2000-2010

Industry	Projected New Jobs 2000-2010
Personnel Supply Services	82,000
Eating and Drinking Places	50,100
Computer and Data Processing Services	39,900
Local Government Education	36,000
Local Government (except Education & Hospitals)	23,200
Offices and Clinics of Medical Doctors	21,600
Nursing and Personal Care Facilities	19,400
Miscellaneous Business Services	15,000
Home Health Care Services	14,900
Miscellaneous Shopping Goods Stores	14,500
Residential Care	13,300
Miscellaneous Amusement and Recreation Services	12,700
Private Educational Services	10,400
Trucking and Courier Services (except air)	9,900
Private Hospitals	9,800
Child Day Care Services	9,800
Air Transportation, Scheduled	9,700
Other Health and Allied Services	8,900
Engineering and Architectural Services	8,600
Legal Services	8,400
Individual and Family Services	8,300
Management and Public Relations	8,200
Nonstore Retailers	7,800
Retail Stores (not classified elsewhere)	7,700
Miscellaneous Special Trade Contractors	7,300
Accounting, Auditing and Bookkeeping	7,100
Landscape and Horticultural Services	6,800
Other Miscellaneous Plastics Products	6,800
Religious Organizations	6,800
Offices of Other Health Practitioners	6,600

Source: Ohio Department of Job and Family Services; Bureau of Labor market Information

The percentage of low-wage jobs is growing, not shrinking. The growing sectors of the economy are the labor-intensive industries. By the end of the decade, the low end of the job market will account for more than 30% of the entire work force.

—Beth Shulman, The Betrayal of Work: How Low-Wage Jobs Fail 30 Million Americans

Employment Growth Relative to Educational and Training Levels

	Projected Employment Growth Rate 2000-2010	Annual Openings
First Professional/Doctoral Degree	17.1%	3,868
Master's Degree	19.3%	2,877
Work Experience plus Degree	13.0%	8,961
Bachelor's Degree	15.0%	22,453
Associate Degree	23.1%	9,065
Postsecondary Vocational Training	14.1%	8,936
Work Experience in Related Occupation	7.3%	11,092
Long-term On-the-job Training	6.1%	15,147
Moderate-term On-the-job Training	6.5%	32,378
Short-term On-the-job Training	12.1%	90,810

Occupations in Ohio—Most Annual Job Openings

Occupation	Annual Openings 2000—2010	Average Wage 2001
Food Preparation & Serving Workers (including fast food)	10,218	$6.72
Cashiers	8,434	$7.25
Retail Salespersons	8,281	$9.54
Waiters and Waitresses	5,539	$6.76
Laborers and Freight, Stock, and Material Movers (hand)	5,356	$10.92
Registered Nurses	3,806	$21.45
Office Clerks, General	3,206	$10.77
Stock Clerks and Order Fillers	3,073	$10.11
Customer Service Representatives	2,767	$13.31
Janitors & Cleaners (except maids & housekeeping cleaners)	2,708	$9.74
General and Operations Managers	2,700	$33.14
Packers and Packagers (hand)	2,429	$8.79
Truck Drivers, Heavy and Tractor-Trailer	2,368	$16.55
Nursing Aids, Orderlies, and Attendants	2,178	$9.27
Sales Representatives, Wholesale and Manufacturing	2,118	$23.43
Food Preparation Workers	2,094	$7.84
Elementary School Teachers (except special education)	1,830	$42,276*
First-line Supervisors/Managers of Retail Sales Workers	1,782	$14.48
Security Guards	1,775	$9.79
Computer Support Specialists	1,682	$19.96
Team Assemblers	1,640	$12.69
Receptionists and Information Clerks	1,595	$9.59
Secondary School Teachers (except special & vocational ed.)	1,577	$42,914*
Truck Drivers, Light or Delivery Services	1,529	$12.63
Landscaping and Groundskeeping Workers	1,486	$10.11
Bookkeeping, Accounting, and Auditing Clerks	1,446	$12.87
Licensed Practical and Licensed Vocational Nurses	1,442	$15.68
Secretaries (except legal, medical, and executive)	1,430	$11.73
Executive Secretaries and Administrative Assistants	1,413	$15.06
Teachers' Assistants	1,395	$20,920*

*average annual wage

Occupations in Ohio—Fastest Growing

	Growth Rate 2000 - 2010	Wage 2001
Computer Support Specialists	85.6%	$19.96
Computer Software Engineers, Applications	79.5%	$30.70
Computer Software Engineers, Systems Software	73.5%	$30.87
Network and Computer Systems Administrators	70.1%	$25.09
Network Systems & Data Communications Analysts	65.4%	$27.55
Desktop Publishers	62.8%	$13.88
Database Administrators	58.1%	$27.77
Personal and Home Care Aides	50.9%	$8.47
Social and Human Service Assistants	48.5%	$11.45
Medical Assistants	47.0%	$11.07
Audiologists	43.2%	$20.96
Physician Assistants	40.5%	$34.82
Occupational Therapist Aids	40.0%	$14.00
Mental Health & Substance Abuse Social Workers	38.8%	$14.65
Computer Systems Analysts	38.8%	$28.67
Home Health Aides	37.4%	$8.73
Computer Information Systems Managers	37.0%	$34.54
Pharmacy Technicians	36.9%	$9.70
Medical Records and Health Information Technicians	36.2%	$11.74
Substance Abuse & Behavioral Disorder Counselors	35.5%	$14.52
Special Education Teachers, Preschool & Kindergarten & Elem. School	35.3%	$42,156*
Education Administration, Preschool & Child Care Center/Program	35.3%	$15.76
Physical Therapist Assistants	35.1%	$18.48
Marriage and Family Therapists	34.6%	$19.97
Speech - Language Pathologists	35.5%	$24.44
Veterinary Assistants & Laboratory Animal Caretakers	33.5%	$8.37
Physical Therapist Aids	33.1%	$11.21
Veterinary Technologists and Technicians	32.7%	$11.26
Hazardous Materials Removal Workers	31.3%	$15.47
Ambulance Drivers & Attendants (except EMT)	30.2%	$8.92

*average annual wage

Employment Projections by Education and Training

Education & Training Level	2000 Annual Employment	2010 Projected Employment	2000-2010 Percent Change	Total Annual Openings
First Professional	68,660	79,940	16.4%	2,069
Doctoral Degree	41,670	49,210	18.1%	1,799
Master's Degree	68,960	82,290	19.3%	2,877
Work Experience plus Degree	284,010	320,790	13.0%	8,951
Bachelor's Degree	678,340	780,360	15.0%	22,453
Associate Degree	213,870	263,210	23.1%	9,065
Postsecondary Vocational Degree	255,810	291,900	14.1%	8,936
Work Experience in Related Occupation	444,440	476,780	7.3%	11,092
Long-term On-the-job Training	559,250	593,630	6.1%	15,147
Moderate-term On-the-job Training	1,269,430	1,351,600	6.5%	32,378
Short-term On-the-job Training	2,101,930	2,355,450	12.1%	90,810

Source: Ohio Department of Job and Family Services, Bureau of Labor Market Information

Minority and women-owned businesses in Ohio

All firms

781,284

women

205,044

black

26,970

Asian-Pacific Islander

11,398

Hispanic

6,448

Indian-Alaskan native

5,124

Asian Indian

3,697

Chinese

2,415

Mexican American

1,516

Korean

1,410

Filipino

1,242

Why it's a miracle you ever made a dime in the Stock Market

Ohio Unemployment

Year	Ohio Labor Force	Ohio Rate	Year	Ohio Labor Force	Ohio Rate
1960	3,920,200	5.3	1981	5,100,000	9.6
1961	3,883,500	7.4	1982	5,114,000	12.5
1962	3,852,100	5.7	1983	5,099,000	12.2
1963	3,855,300	5.1	1984	5,089,000	9.4
1964	3,900,000	4.3	1985	5,135,000	8.9
1965	4,009,900	3.6	1986	5,232,000	8.1
1966	4,139,900	3.0	1987	5,253,000	7.0
1967	4,075,000	3.8	1988	5,322,000	6.0
1968	4,155,000	3.4	1989	5,419,000	5.5
1969	4,252,000	3.4	1990	5,396,000	5.7
1970	4,391,000	5.4	1991	5,428,000	6.4
1971	4,419,000	6.5	1992	5,487,000	7.2
1972	4,513,000	5.5	1993	5,480,000	6.5
1973	4,623,000	4.3	1994	5,537,000	5.5
1974	4,710,000	4.8	1995	5,584,000	4.8
1975	4,723,000	9.1	1996	5,642,998	4.9
1976	4,751,000	7.8	1997	5,714,720	4.6
1977	4,833,000	6.5	1998	5,691,520	4.3
1978	4,959,000	5.4	1999	5,753,779	4.3
1979	5,059,000	5.9	2000	5,782,649	4.1
1980	5,089,000	8.4	2001	5,857,254	4.3

Source: Labor Market Information Division, Ohio Bureau of Employment Services

Ohio's Top Ranked Companies
(The Fortune 500 is based on revenues; The Forbes 500 is based on sales, profits, assets and market value)

Company		Fortune 500 Rank	Forbes 500* Rank
Kroger	Cincinnati	18	70
Cardinal Health	Dublin	19	54
Procter & Gamble	Cincinnati	31	21
Nationwide Insurance Enterprise	Columbus	111	301
American Electric Power	Columbus	120	187
Federated Department Stores	Cincinnati	122	160
Goodyear Tire & Rubber	Akron	139	320
FirstEnergy	Akron	159	103
Cinergy	Cincinnati	160	190
Dana	Toledo	182	375
Progressive	Mayfield Village	197	143
Limited Brands	Columbus	202	219
Eaton	Cleveland	258	274
National City Corp.	Cleveland	215	57
Fifth Third Bancorp	Cincinnati	278	67
Parker Hannifin	Cleveland	283	391
KeyCorp	Cleveland	285	102
Owens-Illinois	Toledo	298	420
NCR	Dayton	304	541
Sherwin-Williams	Cleveland	321	338
OM Group	Cleveland	331	571
Owens Corning	Toledo	338	501
OfficeMax	Shaker Heights	346	582
AK Steel Holdings	Middletown	376	593
Big Lots	Columbus	413	660
American Financial Group	Cincinnati	424	412
Cooper Tire & Rubber	Findley	459	722
Roadway Express	Akron	476	766
Charter One Financial	Cleveland		198
Huntington Bancshares	Columbus		265
Cincinnati Financial	Fairfield		305
Cintas	Cincinnati		417
Provident Financial Group	Cincinnati		479
FirstMerit	Akron		508
Sky Financial Group	Bowling Green		538
Wendy's International	Dublin		567
Abercrombie & Fitch	New Albany		601
Convergys	Cincinnati		758
HCR Manor Care	Toledo		775
Forest City Enterprises	Cleveland		794

*This list includes companies that didn't make the Forbes 500 list but ranked in the top 500 companies in the nation in one or more rating categories.

Procter & Gamble's chief executive, A.G. Lafley, received in 2003 a package worth over $19.5 million. That included salary and bonus of $4.6 million (a 27% increase), as well as stock ($7.2 million), stock options (estimated value of $6.9 million), stock dividends and other compensation. P&G's stock, since Lafley became CEO in 2000, has risen from the mid-$50s to nearly $90 a share.

—company documents filed with the SEC; The Cincinnati Enquirer

Forbes 500 Private Companies

		Rank
Travel Centers of America	Cleveland	98
Borden Chemical	Columbus	174
IMG	Cleveland	189
Nesco	Mayfield Heights	203
Battelle Memorial Institute	Columbus	206
Noveon	Cleveland	231
Primus	Dayton	255
Swagelok	Solon	257

INC 500 Companies

		Rank
Astute	Columbus	166
New Media Communications	Richfield	171
USA Instruments	Aurora	204
Dancor	Columbus	233
Montpelier Plastics	Montpelier	247
Diversitech	Cincinnati	294
Meritage Technologies	Columbus	303
Progressive Medical	Westerville	329
Fiber Network Solutions	Columbus	332
Learning Voyage	Cincinnati	397
L.E.M. Products	Miamitown	402
Process Plus	Cincinnati	422
Outta the Box Dispensers	Dayton	441
Kingston	Columbus	454
WRG Services	Willoughby	467
Cambridge Home Health Care	Akron	480

Business Week Top Performing Companies, 2002
(based on 8 factors including sales, profits and growth)

		Rank
Progressive Corp.	Mayfield Village	5
Cardinal Health Inc.	Dublin	11
Procter & Gamble	Cincinnati	29
Fifth Third Bancorp	Cincinnati	63
Manor Care	Toledo	79
FirstEnergy	Akron	94
Sherwin-Williams	Cleveland	110
National City	Cleveland	156
Wendy's International	Dublin	158
Kroger	Cincinnati	161
Charter One Financial	Cleveland	164
Cintas	Cincinnati	170
Cincinnati Financial	Cincinnati	179
Cinergy	Cincinnati	192
KeyCorp	Cleveland	254
Cooper Tire and Rubber	Findley	264
Big Lots	Columbus	273
Eaton	Cleveland	300
Parker Hannifin	Cleveland	303
Limited Brands	Columbus	308
Federated Department Stores	Cincinnati	326
Convergys	Cincinnati	350
Worthington Industries	Columbus	357
American Greetings	Cleveland	381
American Electric Power	Columbus	404
NCR	Dayton	413
Dana	Toledo	442
Goodyear Tire & Rubber	Akron	445

Ohio's Top Employers

Company	Estimated FTE Employees in Ohio	Headquarters Location	Sector
Wal-Mart Stores	37,000	Bentonville, AR	General Merchandise
Kroger Company	29,000	Cincinnati, Ohio	Food stores
Cleveland Clinic Health System	23,720	Cleveland, Ohio	Health
Wright-Patterson Air Force Base	22,000	Dayton, Ohio	Air Force Base
General Motors Corporation	21,350	Detroit, MI	Motor vehicles
Delphi Automotive	20,300	Troy, MI	Motor vehicles
General Electric Company	20,300	Fairfield, CT	Aerospace/Electrical Eqpt.
Ford Motor Company	17,800	Dearborn, MI	Motor vehicles
University Hospitals Health System	17,070	Cleveland, Ohio	Health
Ohio State University	17,000	Columbus, Ohio	Education
University of Cincinnati	15,400	Cincinnati, Ohio	Education
Ohio Health	15,000	Columbus, Ohio	Health
Procter & Gamble Company	15,000	Cincinnati, Ohio	Soaps and cosmetics
Meijer, Inc.	14,970	Grand Rapids, MI	Food stores
Honda Motor Company, LTD.	14,000	Tokyo, Japan	Motor vehicles
United Parcel Service of America, Inc.	13,500	Atlanta, Georgia	Package & Freight
Bob Evans Farms, Inc.	13,300	Columbus, Ohio	Restaurants
Health Alliance of Greater Cincinnati	13,140	Cincinnati, Ohio	Health
Banc One Corporation	13,000	Columbus, Ohio	Commercial bank
Nationwide Insurance Company	12,400	Columbus, Ohio	Insurance
National City Corporation	12,050	Cleveland, Ohio	Commercial bank
ProMedica Health System	12,000	Toledo, Ohio	Health
DaimlerChrysler Corporation	11,000	Highland Park, MI	Motor vehicles
KeyCorp	10,700	Cleveland, Ohio	Commercial rank
SBC	10,500	Addison, Texis	Utility communications
First Energy Corporation	9,500	Akron, Ohio	Electric utility
Whirlpool Corporation	9,400	Greenville, Ohio	Consumer Products
Bowling Green State University	8,900	Bowling Green, Ohio	Education
Airborne Express	8,100	Seattle, Washington	Air Delivery & Freight
Sears, Roebuck and Company	8,000	Chicago, Illinois	General merchandiser
Kohl's Corporation	8,000	Menomonee Falls WI	Retail Department Store
Fifth Third Bancorp	7,800	Cincinnati, Ohio	Commercial Bank
Kmart Corporation	7,500	Troy, MI	General Merchandiser
Schottenstein/Value City Stores Corporation	7,500	Columbus, Ohio	Department Stores
Longaberger Company	7,300	Dresden, Ohio	Home Furnishings
Limited	7,200	Columbus, Ohio	Specialist Retailer
Tri-Health	7,050	Cincinnati, Ohio	Health
Children's Hospital Medical Center	7,030	Cincinnati, Ohio	Health
J.C. Penney	7,000	Plano, TX	Retail Department Stores
Giant Eagle Incorporated	6,840	Pittsburgh, PA	Grocery Retailing
Progressive Insurance	6,800	Mayfield Village, Ohio	Insurance
Mercy Health Partners	6,780	Cincinnati, Ohio	Health Products & Services
American Electric Power	6,700	Columbus, Ohio	Utility Electric
Timken Company	6,600	Canton, Ohio	Industrial Equipment
Emerson Electric	6,600	Columbus, Ohio	Electrical Products
Federated Department Stores	6,200	Cincinnati, Ohio	Retail Department Stores
AK Steel Corporation	6,000	Middletown, Ohio	Manufacture Metals
Mill's Pride/Masco	5,850	Taylor, MI	Cabinets & Doors
Big Bear Stores Company	5,410	Syracuse, NY	Grocery
University of Toledo	5,200	Toledo, Ohio	Education
Case Western Reserve University	5,100	Cleveland, Ohio	Education
Ohio University	5,000	Athens, Ohio	Education
Miami Valley Hospital	5,000	Dayton, Ohio	Health
Newell Rubbermaid	5,000	Freeport, IL	Home Products
Wendy's International	4,900	Dublin, Ohio	Restaurants
Mount Carmel-East, West, & St. Ann's	4,877	Columbus, Ohio	Health

In the years 1995-1998, Procter & Gamble acquired 1,093 patents, more than twice the number by the second most-productive American firm (which was General Electric with 451).

—CHI Research

The Evolution of Retail — JIM BORGMAN Cincinnati Enquirer 1999

KIOSK — SHOP — DEPARTMENT STORE — DISCOUNT CHAIN

ERNWOOD TOWNE CENTRE — MALL

ernie.com — INTERNET

Company	Estimated FTE Employees in Ohio	Headquarters Location	Sector
Paramount's Kings Island	4,700	Cincinnati, Ohio	Theme Park
Parker-Hannifin Corporation	4,500	Cleveland, Ohio	Industrial Equipment
Berkshire Hathaway	4,500	Omaha, NE	Service/Finance
Miami University	4,270	Oxford, Ohio	Education
Goodyear Tire & Rubber	4,100	Akron, Ohio	Rubber & Plastic Products
Cinergy Corp	4,100	Cincinnati, Ohio	Energy
Alcoa	4,100	Cleveland, Ohio	Aluminum Forgings
Tops Friendly Market	4,000	Ashtabula, Ohio	Grocery Retailing
Sauder Woodworking	4,000	Archbold, Ohio	Home Furnishings
Siemans	4,000	Munich, Germany	Industrial Equipment
Cedar Point	4,000	Sandusky, Ohio	Theme Park
NASA Glenn	3,900	Cleveland, Ohio	Aerospace/Defense Products
Owens Corning	3,900	Toledo, Ohio	Home Products
Ohio State University Hospitals	3,770	Columbus, Ohio	Health
Eaton Corporation	3,700	Cleveland, Ohio	Industrial Clutches & Brakes
Cooper Tire & Rubber	3,600	Findley, Ohio	Manufacture Tires
Sherwin-Williams Company	3,400	Cleveland, Ohio	Chemicals
Worthington Industries	3,400	Columbus, Ohio	Metal/Plastics
Broadwing Inc.	3,400	Cincinnati, Ohio	Information Communications
Continental Airlines	3,360	Cleveland, Ohio	Transport
Wheeling-Pittsburgh Steel	3,200	Wheeling, WV	Manufacture Metals
American Financial Group, Inc.	3,000	Cincinnati, Ohio	Insurance
Navistar International Corporation	3,000	Chicago, IL	Motor Vehicles
United Dairy Farmers	3,000	Norwood, Ohio	Retail Dairy Products
Mead/Westvaco	3,000	Stamford, CN	Paper Products
U.S. Bank Corp	3,000	Minneapolis, MN	Banking, Finance
LexisNexis/Reed Elsevier	3,000	London, England	Information Date Retrieval

Source: Ohio Department of Development, Office of Strategic Research

Ohio's top 100

The Cleveland Plain Dealer *annually ranks the state's publicly held companies. To be included companies have to be based in Ohio with their common stock traded on a major exchange. To get the final rankings the* Plain Dealer *purchased customized information from Standard & Poor's which collected its data from company filings with the Securities and Exchange Commission. The seven criteria used to determine the final rankings were: 2002 revenues, two-year compound growth in revenues, two-year compound growth in net income, two-year return on average common equity, three-year total return, one-year percent change in profit margin, 2002 market value. The following is the list of the state's top performing companies.*

	Company	Sector	Headquarters
1.	Progressive	insurance	Cleveland
2.	Cardinal Health	distributes health care products	Dublin
3.	Thor Industries	recreational vehicles	Jackson Center
4.	J.M. Smucker	fruit spreads	Orrville
5.	Fifth Third Bancorp	banks	Cincinnati
6.	Charter One Financial	banks	Cleveland
7.	Procter & Gamble	consumer products	Cincinnati
8.	Sherwin-Williams	paint, paint stores	Cleveland
9.	Manor Care	long-term care facilities	Toledo
10.	Dominion Homes	home builder	Dublin
11.	Cinergy	electricity	Cincinnati
12.	RPM International	specialty coatings	Medina
13.	FirstEnergy	electricity	Akron
14.	M/I Schottenstein Homes	home builder	Columbus
15.	National City	banks	Cleveland
16.	Diebold	automated teller machines	North Canton
17.	Wendy's International	fast food	Dublin
18.	Scotts	lawn and garden fertilizers and products	Marysville
19.	Kroger	supermarkets	Cincinnati
20.	Cintas	corporate work uniforms	Cincinnati
21.	Lancaster Colony	auto products & salad dressings	Columbus
22.	Lanvision Systems	hospital soft ware systems	Cincinnati
23.	Too	clothing stores	Columbus
24.	Invacare	health care equipment	Elyria
25.	Cincinnati Financial	insurance	Fairfield
26.	Bob Evans Farms	restaurants	Columbus
27.	Max & Erma's Restaurants	restaurants	Columbus
28.	Reynolds & Reynolds	information management system	Dayton
29.	Steris	makes sterilization equipment for hospitals	Mentor
30.	Unizan Financial	banks	Canton
31.	Abercrombie & Fitch	retail	New Albany
32.	Lubrizol	additive chemicals	Wickliffe
33.	E.W. Scripps	media	Cincinnati
34.	Frisch's Restaurants	restaurants	Cincinnati
35.	Andersons	grain	Maumee
36.	Keycorp	banks	Cleveland
37.	Peoples Bancorp	banks	Marietta
38.	Eaton	transmissions	Cleveland
39.	Oak Hill Financial	banks	Jackson
40.	Multi-Color	printed labels	Cincinnati
41.	State Auto Financial	insurance	Columbus
42.	First Place Financial	banks	Warren
43.	Sky Financial Group	banks	Bowling Green
44.	A. Schulman	plastics compounds and resins	Akron
45.	Cooper Tire & Rubber	rubber and plastic products	Findlay
46.	Huntington Banc Shares	banks	Columbus
47.	Forest City Enterprises	commercial real estate	Cleveland

The American Whistle Company of Columbus is said to be the sole American manufacturer of metal whistles. It employs 11 and makes about a million traditional and custom whistles a year, including NFL commemorative gold-plated whistles for each year's Super Bowl officiating crew.

—Associated Press

	Company	Sector	Headquarters
48.	Second Bancorp	bank	Warren
49.	Royal Appliance	cleaning appliances	Glenwillow
50.	Limited Brands	retail stores	Columbus
51.	RTI International Metals	titanium products	Niles
52.	Park National	banks	Newark
53.	Roadway	trucking	Akron
54.	FirstMerit	banks	Akron
55.	American Electric Power	electric	Columbus
56.	Federated Department Stores	department stores	Cincinnati
57.	Ferro	industrial coatings	Cleveland
58.	Interlott Techs	lottery ticket machines	Mason
59.	United Community Financial	banking	Youngstown
60.	Provident Financial Group	banks	Cincinnati
61.	Convergys	billing and customer services	Cincinnati
62.	North Coast Energy	produces oil and natural gas	Twinsburg
63.	Lincoln Electric	welding and cutting equipment	Cleveland
64.	Midland	Insurance	Amelia
65.	Parker Hannifin	motion control products	Cleveland
66.	Nationwide Financial Services	Insurance	Columbus
67.	Jo-Ann Stores	fabric and craft stores	Hudson
68.	PVF Capital	banks	Solon
69.	Camco Financial	banks	Cambridge
70.	Myers Industries	plastic and rubber products	Akron
71.	LNB Bancorp	banks	Lorain
72.	First Citizens Banc	banks	Sandusky
73.	Big Lots	retail	Columbus
74.	Winton Financial	savings and loan	Cincinnati
75.	NCR	cash registers & automated teller machines	Dayton
76.	DPL	electricity and natural gas	Dayton
77.	Wayne Savings Banc Shares	banks	Wooster
78.	Greif	containers and container board	Delaware
79.	ASB Financial	banks	Portsmouth
80.	Home Loan Financial	banks	Coshocton
81.	Owens-Illinois	glass bottles & plastic containers	Toledo
82.	Libbey	glass tableware	Toledo
83.	Worthington Industries	processes steel and makes steel products	Columbus
84.	Gorman-Rupp	pumps and related equipment	Mansfield
85.	First Financial Bancorp	banks	Hamilton
86.	Timken	roller bearings and steel	Canton
87.	Stoneridge	electronic components	Warren
88.	Wayne Bancorp	banks	Wooster
89.	United Bancshares	banks	Columbus Grove
90.	Ohio Valley Banc Corp	banks	Gallipolis
91.	Great American Financial	insurance	Cincinnati
92.	REX	consumer electronics, retail	Dayton
93.	United Bancorp	banks	Martins Ferry
94.	LSI Industries	lighting fixtures	Cincinnati
95.	Robbins & Myers	fluids management systems	Dayton
96.	American Financial Group	insurance	Cincinnati
97.	Western Ohio Financial	banks	Springfield
98.	Nordson	industrial machinery	Westlake
99.	Applied Industrial Tech.	distributor	Cleveland
100.	Nacco Industries	forklift trucks, coal, small electric appliances	Mayfield Heights

Source: The Cleveland Plain Dealer, 2003

Coal Mining

History of Coal Mining in Ohio

Coal mining in Ohio began around 1800 and during its first 150 years, was an unregulated industry. Until the time of World War I, coal mining in Ohio was conducted almost exclusively underground and largely by manual labor. These underground mining operations gained access to coal seams by vertical mine shafts of up to 200 feet deep, by horizontal mine entries (drift entries) cut into hillsides at the coal elevation, or by sloping tunnels angling downward from the ground surface. Early underground mines were small, discontinuous, and poorly mapped. To maximize coal production, roof support was usually minimal. Further, coal pillars were often removed upon abandonment of the mines, making them highly prone to later subsidence.

With the advent of large, efficient excavating equipment, new drilling techniques, and newly developed explosives in the mining industry around World War II, large earthmoving operations became possible. Surface mining operations thus became an economic alternative to underground mining. Surface mining involves excavation of all of the rock and soil (overburden) above the desired coal seam, exposing the coal seam at the surface. The excavated rock and soil, known as "mine spoil," is placed in piles away from the excavation site. The exposed coal is removed in a way that includes as little non-coal rock as possible.

A very efficient recovery system of underground coal mining, known as longwall mining, was recently introduced into Ohio due to the development of automated mining equipment. The technique involves total removal of large blocks of coal which allows the overburden to collapse or subside in a controlled and predictable manner. This technique has significantly increased productivity and reduced costs so that underground mining can remain competitive with surface mining. It has the added benefit of allowing mitigation of subsidence impacts to occur while the mining company is still operating in the vicinity, rather than years after mining is complete.

Coal mining in Ohio today is a multi-billion dollar industry. Statewide production in 2000 totaled 22.4 million tons, with almost 47 percent from coal recovered through surface mining.

Coal in Ohio

The United States contains the largest recoverable coal reserves of any single country. It has been estimated that U.S. coal reserves will last over 500 years at current rates of onsumption.

Ohio is located in the northern portion of the Appalachian Coal Basin, which is one of the largest coal fields in the United States. It is estimated that Ohio has 11.8 billion tons of economically recoverable coal reserves.

Coal was produced by 41 companies at 111 mines in 21 Ohio counties in 2001. Production totaled 25.7 million tons, an increase of 14.7 percent from 2000. (Note: All tonnages are in short tons.) In 2001, 13.2 million tons were produced from 10 underground mines, and 12.5 million tons were produced from 102 surface mines.

Belmont County is the all-time coal production leader in Ohio. Once again it led the state in 2001, as in most years, producing more than 7.6 million tons of coal. Following Belmont County, the next four largest producing counties are, in order of decreasing production: Meigs, Harrison, Vinton, and Jackson. Together these four counties produced 71.3 percent of the total 2001 coal production.

Ohio ranks third nationally in the consumption of coal, following Texas and Indiana. More than 87 percent of the electricity generated in Ohio is coal-derived. Ohio used 43,856 million tons in 2000. Most of Ohio's coal is used for the generation of electricity, while some is used for making steel.

Down under

The record for longevity among Ohio miners belongs to Isaac Six of Nelsonville, who began working in Ohio mines in 1861 at age 13 and worked in the mines for 80 years.

—Ohio Department of Natural Resources

Minerals

A history of industrial minerals

The term "industrial minerals" refers to geological deposits that can be mined for commercial and industrial uses, as opposed to minerals used as gems or fuel (oil, gas, and coal). Ohio has a long history of industrial mineral production, but the exact date when minerals were first produced is unknown. It is known that Native Americans exploited raw materials long before the arrival of the first European settlers. They carried on extensive quarrying in the Flint Ridge area in Licking and Muskingum Counties; pottery fragments found at many archeological sites evidence the use of alluvial and glacial clays. The first mining of clay and shale by European settlers appears to have been for use in the brick industry in the late 1700's and early 1800's.

Gypsum was discovered along the shores of Lake Erie in the early 1800's and was first used as a soil conditioner. Gypsum is currently mined in only one location in Ohio, Ottawa County, and is used primarily in the manufacture of wallboard.

The first use of limestone and dolomite also occurred in the late 1700's and early 1800's. It is known that lime for whitewashing and plastering was being sold as early as 1817, and by the mid-1800's limestone was the most valuable building material among the State's natural resources. Its primary use was for building foundations, chimneys, and fireplaces.

Ohio became one of the major producers of sandstone in the nation in the early 1800's. Sandstone was used for building stone, foundations, and architectural purposes.

Sand and gravel were the last of the State's mineral resources to be developed extensively for commercial use. This did not occur until after the turn of the century. Since the primary use of sand and gravel is for construction, its production is tied closely to the economy and the expansion of our cities and highways.

Limestone and Dolomite

Limestone and dolomite were sold or produced by 65 companies at 121 operations in 49 Ohio counties in 2001. Production totaled 81.9 million tons, a .4 percent decrease from the previous year.

The total value of limestone and dolomite sold in Ohio during 2001 was $395.5 million. Average price per ton was $4.88. Ohio limestone and dolomite quarries directly employed 2,422 persons in 2001. Crushed stone for road construction/resurfacing was the primary use for Ohio limestone and dolomite in 2001. Ohio ranks 3rd nationally in the production of lime and 5th in the production of crushed stone.

Sand and Gravel

Sand and gravel were sold or produced by 218 companies at 302 operations in 64 Ohio counties plus Lake Erie in 2001. Sales totaled 56.8 million tons, a 2.0 percent increase from 2001. Sand accounted for 31.3 million tons sold, and gravel accounted for 25.4 million tons. Ohio ranks 4th nationally in the production of construction sand and gravel and 9th in the production of industrial sand and gravel.

The total value of sand and gravel sold in Ohio during 2001 was $263.8 million. Average price per ton was $4.64. Ohio sand and gravel operations directly employed 1,905 persons in 2001. Building, asphaltic concrete, Portland cement concrete, and road construction/resurfacing were the primary uses of Ohio sand and gravel in 2001.

Oil and Gas

With continued high prices in 2001, 677 (512 productive) oil and gas wells were drilled in Ohio. This was an increase of 20%. The depths range from 425 feet in Harrison County to 8,185 feet in Tuscarawas County with the most wells drilled in Muskingum County.

The market value of Ohio crude oil decreased 24.9% in 2001 to $43,795,452. At the same time the value of natural gas production increased 10.5% to $441,459,782.

Salt

of the earth

Because the state has more than 2,000,000 tons of rock salt and untold amounts of brine available, it is estimated that at current consumption levels, Ohio could supply the United States with salt for the next 150,000 years. In an average year, ODOT uses 1,550 trucks and approximately 365,000 tons of salt to clear snow on 43,000 lane-miles.

SECRETIVE FRED LENNON: ONE OF AMERICA'S GREAT BUSINESS STORIES

A one-time door-to-door encyclopedia salesman, Fred A. Lennon founded Crawford Fitting in 1947, bought out his partner less than a year later for $2,000, then ran the fledgling company out of his Cleveland apartment. That deal, said *Forbes*, "ranks with the purchase of Manhattan Island for a bag of beads as one of the great bargains of all time."

The innovative high-pressure fitting upon which the company was based was developed by Cullen Crawford, an engineer, who made at his kitchen table a fitting he called a Swagelok—to "swage" means to shape by applying pressure. But he and Lennon "butted heads," Lennon made his now-famous offer, and the rest is an incredible business history.

After finding unreliability in the local shops, he began the manufacture of his Swageloks in his own plants, and by the mid-1990s, he had 40 or so factories, all run with an almost overbearing attention to neatness and quality control. (Company officials were said to do a drive-by of the houses of prospective employee, to see if the lawn was mowed and the car washed.)

The Swagelok fittings, even though they cost about 25% more than the competition, were of undeniable quality in industries—space technology, nuclear power, oil pipelines—where precision and reliability was crucial. The Swagelok was called "the jewel of the fittings industry" and soon Crawford Fitting had become the sole supplier of fittings and valves to the Navy. By the mid-1990s, Lennon's company and its numerous related businesses made up an empire of 140 exclusive distributorships with reps in 39 foreign countries.

Lennon himself kept an almost obsessively low profile. His company motto was "Secrecy is success. Success is secrecy," and his public appearances were so infrequent that when he first made the *Forbes* list of wealthiest Americans in the early 1990s, the magazine had to settle for a 1957 photo. Said *Forbes*: "Fred Lennon inspires tenacious loyalty and bitter loathing after spending 48 years building one of the most impressive money machines in American industry." The magazine called him "one of the great untold business stories of the 20th century."

In the 1990s, *Mother Jones Magazine* reported that Fred Lennon was the largest single contributor to Republican political candidates (he also gave large amounts to the Catholic Church, educational institutions, and medical facilities). He was known for arm-twisting his distributors—and their spouses—into contributing to his right-leaning political causes—some of them being ardent Democrats.

He did not have a household staff, nor did he have air conditioning in his modest Hunting Valley home, which was marked only by an anonymous mailbox. At his death at age 92 in 1999, his estate was estimated, conservatively, at a billion dollars and Cleveland probate lawyer Steven Ott estimated that Hunting Valley could receive as much as $39 million in income taxes. ✐

—*Sources: Plain Dealer, Forbes, Mother Jones Magazine*

Clay and Shale

Clay from alluvial and glacial materials as well as from underclays associated with the coals of the Pennsylvanian System were first used in Ohio by Indians to make crude hand-fashioned pottery. With the advent of European settlers came the knowledge of brickmaking and the art of fashioning ware on the potter's wheel. The first use of common brick in Ohio was in the construction of Campus Martius at Marietta inn 1788-1791. Since then, the clays and shales of Ohio have supported a flourishing ceramics industry, which produces not only the familiar pottery, brick, and tile that are used in and around our homes, but also many less well known items that are vital to construction and to scientific and manufacturing concerns.

The bulk of the raw materials for these products comes from the clays and shales of the Pennsylvanian System in eastern Ohio. Devonian- and Mississippian-age shales and Pleistocene-age glacial clays in northern, western, and central Ohio also are important sources. Supplies of underclay, shale, and glacial clay are nearly inexhaustible, but the known reserves of flint clay are almost gone.

Clay is a fine-grained earthy material which becomes plastic when mixed with a limited amount of water, becomes firm when dried, and hardens when heated to a high temperature. The term fire clay indicates the ability to withstand high temperatures without warping. Flint clay is a hard nonplastic fire clay which breaks with a smooth conchoidal fracture like flint or fine-grained limestone. Chemical analyses show that clays and clay minerals are composed of silica, alumina, and water. X-ray analyses show that the clay minerals illite, kaolinite, and chlorite are the most common components of clays; vermiculite and montmorillonite are minor components. Common associated minerals are quartz, mica, feldspar, limonite, hematite, calcite, dolomite, and gypsum. Variable amounts of organic material may be present.

Shale is a fine-grained sedimentary rock with a distinct laminated or layered character and with essentially the same composition as clay. Most shales, however, do not develop plasticity unless they are ground very fine.

Clay or shale of some type can be found almost anywhere in Ohio. Nearly two-thirds of Ohio is mantled by clay-rich debris left behind by glaciers that advanced during the Pleistocene Epoch. In preglacial time Ohio was covered several times with lakes, swamps, and oceans in which muds were deposited. Over the years these muds were transformed into beds of clay and shale. These clays and shales now form much of the bedrock of Ohio and can be seen where they are not covered by soil or glacial deposits.

For many years Ohio led the nation in fire-clay production and in the total production of clay and shale. In 1978 Ohio production in these categories was 1.5 million and 3.5 million tons, respectively; production of glacial clay was 0.4 million tons. Total clay and shale production for 1978 was valued at $13.5 million. Tuscarawas, Paulding, Jefferson, Jackson, and Greene Counties were the leading clay-producing counties, accounting for 70 percent of the state's total production. Tuscarawas, Cuyahoga, Marion, and Medina Counties led in the production of shale, accounting for 64 percent of the state's total production. Most of Ohio's clay and shale is strip mined, but in a few places it is still being mined underground.

Economically, the most important fire clay is the Lower Kittanning or No. 5 clay, which is currently mined in about a dozen countries. In some places the Lower Kittanning clay is mined with the underlying and closely associated Lawrence clay. The Lower Kittanning clay is very versatile and is used in the manufacture of pottery, structural products, refractories, cement, and foundry bonding clay. The Clarion and the Brookville clays are probably the next most important clays in Ohio. They are mined in several counties and are used in the manufacture of stoneware, and as well-plugging clays. In some places shale and fire clay are blended together to obtain a low-firing plastic raw material; clay imparts plasticity, the shale a lower firing range.

Ceramic plants utilizing clays of glacial origin are scattered over the western two-thirds of Ohio and produce primarily drain tile and brick. The Silica and Chagrin shales of Devonian age have been used in recent times, the former in the manufacture of cement and the latter in the manufacture of light-weight aggregate and building brick. The Bedford and Cuyahoga shales of Mississippian age are used mainly in the production of face brick and tile.

www.dnr.state.oh.us/geosurvey/oh_geol/oh_geol.htm

This is—pardon us—for the hardcore geology folks out there (and you know who you are). But it's a splendid site, with back issues of *Ohio Geology*, as well as downloadable maps, publications, reports, and good fact sheets, such as the guide 'Where to see Ohio's Geology.' Added bonus: how to purchase an *Isotelus* belt buckle.

Flint

Ohio's official gemstone

Ohio flint is known to rock and mineral collectors throughout the country for its brilliant colors and its suitability for crafting into beautiful jewelry. It was appropriate, therefore, that in 1965 the Ohio General Assembly named flint Ohio's official gemstone.

Flint, a variety of quartz, is a hard, durable rock that is composed of silicon dioxide (SiO_2), or silica. Minor amounts of chemical impurities commonly impart a wide variety of colors to flint, in shades of red, pink, green, blue, yellow, gray, white, and black, which may be intricately intermingled. Its color, hardness, and ability to take a high polish make Ohio flint a coveted item among lapidarists, who produce unique jewelry items from this rock.

Flint (and its impure form, chert) is widely distributed in Ohio in rocks of Silurian (438 to 408 million years ago), Devonian (408 to 360 million years ago), and Pennsylvanian (320 to 286 million years ago) age. These rocks were deposited in shallow, tropical seas that covered the area that is now Ohio during the Paleozoic Era. Most flint deposits are associated with marine limestones, and it is thought that the silica necessary to form flint was derived from the siliceous spicules that formed the skeletal support for sponges that lived in the seas.

The most famous deposit of flint in Ohio is an area in eastern Licking and western Muskingum Counties known as Flint Ridge. The Vanport flint of Pennsylvanian age covers a ridgetop area of about 6 square miles. The flint deposit ranges in thickness from about 1 foot to 12 feet.

Flint Ridge flint is noted for its array of colors and suitability for jewelry making and for its long and widespread use by American Indians. Hundreds of pits dotting Flint Ridge are evidence of the extensive quarrying of flint by a succession of American Indian cultures. The earliest peoples to use this raw material for various tools, including knives, scrapers, and projectile points, were the Paleo-Indians, a culture that was contemporaneous with the last phases of the Pleistocene Ice Age and extinct animals such as mastodon and mammoth that roamed the area until about 10,000 years ago.

It is thought that American Indians from throughout the Midwest made periodic pilgrimages to Flint Ridge in order to obtain a supply of flint for tool making. The purity of this deposit permitted these skilled workers to fashion a wide variety of tools, weapons, and ceremonial pieces. Artifacts made from Flint Ridge Flint have been found as far east as the Atlantic coast, as far west as Kansas City, and as far south as Louisiana.

Ohio's first peoples also quarried flint from deposits other than Flint Ridge. Most notable are the Zaleski flint in Vinton and Jackson Counties and the Upper Mercer flint in Coshocton, Hocking, and Perry Counties. These units are of Pennsylvanian age. Other flint deposits of Silurian, Devonian, and Pennsylvanian age were also utilized in a minor way.

Flint was important to early European settlers in Ohio. These pioneers used impure, porous deposits of flint for buhrstones to sharpen tools and grind grain. In addition, flint was used in flintlock rifles and to start fires.

In 1933 the Ohio Historical Society established Flint Ridge State Memorial on a 525-acre portion of Flint Ridge. This area contains numerous pits dug by American Indians to obtain flint. In 1968 a museum was operated by the Ohio Historical Society, containing displays on the geology and use of flint. Trails through the memorial site pass by numerous ancient quarry pits. Flint Ridge State Memorial is located 4 miles north of Interstate 70 (exit 141 at Brownsville) on Licking County Road 668. The museum is open Wednesday through Sunday from Memorial Day through Labor Day and on weekends from Labor Day through October.

1. Ohio Division of Geological Survey, 2001 Report on Ohio Mineral Industries
2. U.S. Department of Energy, Energy Information Administration

Sources: National rankings: U.S. Department of Energy, Energy Information Administration. Ohio Division of Geological Survey, 2001 Report on Ohio Mineral Industries.

Ohio Exports, countries of destination

	1999	2000	2001	Share	Change 1999-00
World Total	$24,883,241,492	$26,322,241,431	$27,094,733,991	100.0%	2.8%
NAFTA Countries	$15,065,839,202	$16,050,344,526	$15,951,464,952	58.9%	-0.6%
Canada	$13,692,034,36	$14,091,727,132	$13,842,935,824	51.1%	-1.8%
Mexico	$1,373,804,833	$1,958,617,393	$2,108,529,128	7.8%	7.7%
Central America, West Indies	$145,251,637	$165,795,217	$210,398,318	0.8%	17.8%
South America	$594,778,793	$721,868,538	$754,592,535	2.8%	6.0%
Brazil	$251,838,052	$321,224,778	$370,901,071	1.4%	15.5%
Venezuela	$73,299,213	$85,643,058	$108,722,527	0.4%	26.9%
Argentina	$96,689,108	$146,453,022	$100,635,489	0.4%	-31.3%
Columbia	$49,588,520	$53,933,405	$63,166,586	0.2%	17.1%
Chile	$71,118,497	$65,093,265	$59,579,503	0.2%	-8.5%
Ecuador	$12,076,170	$11,366,287	$21,214,436	0.1%	86.6%
Peru	$22,774,357	$17,053,212	$17,950,277	0.1%	5.3%
Other South American	$29,481,046	$32,468,798	$12,422,646	0.0%	13.9%
Europe	$5,088,106,565	$5,024,111,019	$5,658,325,819	20.9%	12.7%
France	$1,393,298,115	$1,198,982,928	$1,448,486,062	5.3%	20.8%
United Kingdom	$1,031,877,405	$1,066,158,532	$1,284,253,668	4.7%	20.5%
Germany	$687,546,186	$702,525,493	$758,685,323	2.8%	8.0%
Netherlands	$352,433,215	$450,274,181	$474,919,816	1.8%	5.5%
Belgium	$311,827,091	$339,864,842	$389,705,542	1.4%	14.7%
Italy	$252,280,789	$227,476,277	$286,112,472	1.1%	25.8%
Ireland	$169,987,606	$176,274,181	$173,319,042	0.6%	-1.7%
Spain	$113,749,979	$149,793,787	$146,399,062	0.5%	-2.3%
Switzerland	$117,002,663	$149,896,402	$129,389,759	0.5%	-13.7%
Sweden	$126,881,100	$84,906,528	$97,073,101	0.4%	14.3%
Turkey	$102,479,459	$91,069,086	$70,298,412	0.3%	-22.8%
Other European	$348,742,957	$386,888,854	$399,683,560	1.5%	4.0%
Asia	$2,883,096,313	$3,167,700,590	$3,447,249,314	12.7%	3.6%
Japan	$1,329,959,024	$1,412,139,104	$1,389,018,062	5.1%	-1.6%
China	$244,756,283	$292,154,664	$449,613,992	1.7%	53.9%
Korean Republic	$391,484,855	$384,537,037	$409,166,211	1.5%	6.4%
Singapore	$212,799,625	$243,942,913	$257,927,861	1.0%	5.7%
Hong Kong	$189,537,107	$207,480,198	$216,292,595	0.8%	4.2%
Taiwan	$200,449,743	$223,447,811	$198,594,939	0.7%	-11.1%
Thailand	$103,091,321	$128,063,069	$153,010,491	0.6%	19.5
Malaysia	$126,380,949	$165,378,819	$123,756,157	0.5%	-25.2%
India	$65,737,316	$82,056,437	$105,595,547	0.4%	28.7%
Other Asia	$18,900,090	$28,500,538	$144,273,459	0.5%	-23.4%
Africa	$179,181,761	$169,168,801	$159,354,062	0.6%	-6.2%
South Africa	$93,321,695	$93,921,695	$78,196,142	0.3%	-16.7%
Egypt	$49,571,684	$32,901,832	$32,033,733	0.1%	-2.6%
Morocco	$4,457,626	$4,287,866	$10,976,856	0.0%	156.0%
Other Africa	$23,658,113	$24,948,019	$38,147,331	0.1%	-1.4%
Middle East	$383,932,973	$323,116,906	$390,479,613	1.4%	22.4%
Australia	$323,439,210	$354,892,749	$349,416,619	1.3%	-1.6%

Hands across the sea

Ohio is the nation's eighth largest exporting state sending goods to 194 countries and territories, five of which received at least $1 billion in Ohio exports. Ohio exports had a value of $27.1 billion, an increase over 2000 of 2.9 percent. Fifty-one percent of Ohio's exports go to Canada totaling $13.8 billion.

Six percent of the nation's total machinery exports originate in Ohio with about three-fifths of the state's exports concentrated in machinery, motor vehicles and electrical machinery.

Ohio ranks second in the nation in manufacturing jobs tied to exports. Because many of Ohio's products are first shipped to distribution facilities outside the state they may not be credited to Ohio's export total. For example, while Ohio is a leading exporter of jet engines its position would be higher if it were credited for engines made in Ohio but stored and shipped from warehouses in Kentucky.

Ohio leads the nation in exporting washing machines and paint and ranks either first or second in ATM machines, ceramic pigments, organic cleaners, steel tube and pipe fittings, rubber tubes, pipes and hoses, cleaning machinery, safety glass, air conditioning units, glues and adhesives, plastic making machinery, motorcycles, and auto engines.

—*Ohio Department of Development*

Ohio Exports, by Industry

Industry	1999	2000	2001	Change
Total	$24,883,241,492	$26,322,241,431	$27,094,733,991	2.9%
Machinery	$7,115,150,736	$7,603,105,736	$8,447,231,810	11.1%
Vehicles (not railway)	$5,805,299,063	$5,705,907,220	$5,893,438,812	3.3%
Electrical Machinery	$1,823,190,764	$1,961,368,238	$1,739,506,953	-11.3%
Plastic	$942,135,223	$1,023,406,978	$1,003,307,965	-2.0%
Optical/Medical Instrument	$796,368,130	$894,618,127	$921,208,431	3.0%
Iron/Steel Products	$729,011,237	$837,678,698	$806,046,457	-3.8%
Rubber	$716,481,801	$777,432,819	$771,504,497	-0.8%
Iron & Steel	$448,830,794	$571,924,751	$537,126,003	-6.1%
Paper/Paperboard	$406,599,595	$450,077,297	$452,744,997	0.6%
Misc. Chemical Products	$413,466,552	$409,732,322	$406,952,556	-0.7%
Glass & Glassware	$322,494,641	$389,751,246	$383,788,809	4.4%
Aircraft; Spacecraft	$348,976,786	$333,232,590	$380,164,321	15.2%
Tanning/Dye/Paint	$306,490,333	$405,705,261	$406,744,339	-6.3%
Inorganic Chemicals; Rare	$378,738,020	$327,940,989	$352,906,040	7.6%
Special Other	$242,999,084	$271,181,705	$392,872,456	13.4%
Misc. Articles of Base Metal	$268,609,406	$287,756,074	$307,496,892	5.9%
Organic Chemicals	$311,819,204	$267,265,518	$255,834,102	9.6%
Furniture & Bedding	$220,217,739	$270,946,431	$284,496,775	5.0%
Tool/Cutlery	$206,017,563	$248,226,192	$255,834,102	3.1%
Soap/Wax/Dental	$211,259,884	$241,819,213	$249,361,869	3.1%

Foreign investment

in Ohio

1. Japan

62,220 employees

268 locations

2. United Kingdom

40,651 employees

133 locations

3. Germany

36,803 employees

139 locations

4. France

16,740 employees

69 locations

5. Canada

13,676 employees

118 locations

6. Netherlands

10,413 employees

14 locations

7. Switzerland

9,544 employees

41 locations

8. Ireland

1,730 employees

11 locations

9. Finland

1,390 employees

10 locations

10. Sweden

1,218 employees

11 locations

"NOW THAT'S CRISP, RELIABLE, HASSLE-FREE TOAST, AND AT PEAK HOURS WITH NO LONG WAITS! WHO DID YOU SAY IS YOUR ELECTRICITY PROVIDER?"

Ohio Residential Energy Prices *(per million BTU's)*

	2000	1990	1980	1970
Total Energy	$12.73	$10.12	$6.33	$1.68
Primary Energy	$7.83	$5.49	$3.91	$0.98
Coal	$2.47	$2.80	$3.07	$1.05
Natural Gas	$7.39	$5.09	$3.49	$0.88
Petroleum (total)	$11.87	$9.18	$6.94	$1.54
Distillate Fuel	$9.24	$7.43	$6.63	$1.41
Kerosene	$9.22	$8.54	$8.07	$1.42
LPG*	$14.08	$12.05	$7.66	$2.14
Wood	$7.83	$5.49	$2.87	$0.57
Electricity	$25.23	$23.58	$16.29	$6.99

*Liquefied petroleum gases

Ohio Residential Utility Bills*

	Bill	Electric	Gas	Telephone
Dayton	$165.89	$71.54	$74.55	$19.80
Canton	$166.53	$53.14	$93.02	$20.37
Cincinnati	$183.76	$63.88	$96.79	$23.09
Cleveland	$194.44	$81.05	$93.02	$20.37
Columbus	$197.52	$64.77	$112.38	$20.37
Youngstown	$197.42	$84.03	$93.02	$20.37
Akron	$197.42	$84.03	$93.02	$20.37
Toledo	$217.13	$84.38	$112.38	$20.37
Marietta	$163.15	$49.76	$93.02	$20.37
Lima	$170.13	$53.14	$90.89	$26.10
Zanesville	$185.89	$53.14	$112.38	$20.37
Ashtabula	$191.81	$81.05	$93.02	$17.74
Chillicothe	$202.91	$64.77	$112.38	$25.76

*Based on 750 KHW, 10 MCF and Flat Rate Telephone Service; Source: Ohio Public Utilities Commission

pickocc.org/
handbook/

www.

The Ohio Consumers' Council electronic handbook, instructing the information-swamped Ohioan had to actually read and understand an electric or water bill, or—even *more* ambitious— how to read the meter itself. Everything from choosing a long-distance provider to utility assistance.

The Telephone in Ohio (and Elsewhere)

1860
1869—In Cleveland, Elisha Gray and Enos Barton start Western Electric.

1870
1876—Elisha Gray files at the U.S. Patent Office on St. Valentine's Day afternoon; unfortunately, another sweet talker, Alexander Graham Bell, already had his application in that morning.
1877—Ohio's first telephone line is a private enterprise, between wholesale and retail of Rhodes and Company, Cleveland coal dealers.
1878—Cincinnati gets Ohio's first exchange. Ohio Congressman James Garfield is among the first to have a phone in his home.
1879—Columbus's first switchboard—one operator, two lines, 17 phones—is installed at the corner of Long and High Streets. Cincinnati's first telephone book has 500 listings; operators must memorize them all.

Long Distance
1876—March 7, Alexander Graham Bell patents the telephone; three days later, he spills acid on his pants and places the first call—for help—to Thomas Watson.
1878—The nation's first central exchange opens in New Haven; the Bell company hires Theodore Vail as general manager.
1879—Western Union throws in the towel on its patent infringement litigation, and the Bell companies have a monopoly on the telephone until the original Bell patents expire.

1880
1880—Youngstown has 111 telephones.
1885—September 16 notice in the *Chillicothe Gazette*: "Dr. Hoyt may be called by telephone day or night-Number 98."

Long Distance
1880—James Garfield of Hiram elected president. U.S. has 48,000 telephones in service.
1881—The Bell company buys Western Electric, making it sole supplier of Bell phones and equipment.
1888—Supreme Court rules that Elisha Gray did not invent the telephone.

1890
1890—Canton has 200 Bell telephones.
1894—Central Union Telephone Company in Ross County issues formal invitation to

"IT'S SIMPLE. I JUST DIAL 10-10-9678833324589000 AND SAVE 10¢ A MINUTE BY COMPLETELY FORGETTING WHO I WAS GOING TO CALL."

opening of AT&T long distance lines "with the principal cities of the East and West."

1895—The nation's first independent telephone association begins in Newark, where Charles F. Kettering wires the exchange.

1896—William McKinley is the first man notified by telephone of his nomination for president. At home in Canton waiting for the phone to ring, "there were deep fires in his eyes and his intellectual pallor, always noticeable, now gave his features the stern grace of carved marble."

1898—Columbus gets its first common battery switchboard; Bell subscribers no longer need to turn a crank to summon the operator.

Long Distance

1891—A Kansas City undertaker who doesn't trust operators invents the dial telephone.

1895—The White House has only one telephone.

1900

1900—Canton has 1,200 Bell telephones.

1902—Telephone operators give Weather Bureau reports to farmers in Ross County, where the citizenry has joined the national debate on whether the telphone is making Americans "left-eared."

1903—Dayton gets Ohio's first dial telephone service.

1905—Cincinnati's first pay phone installed on the corner of Fifth and Walnut.

Long Distance

1900—Average daily phone calls made in U.S.: 7,600,000.

1903—Nationally, the Bell System counts 1,514 telephone exchanges and 1,278,000 subscribers; independent companies have 6,150 exchanges, 2 million subscribers.

1909—AT&T gobbles up independent companies and also grabs a controlling interest in former rival Western Union.

1910

1912—Harry Elliott, manager of Chillicothe's Home Telephone Company, climbs telephone pole to disconnect non-paying subscriber, dissatisfied customer begins chopping down pole with Elliott still on it.

1913—During the great flood, the Dayton Y.M.C.A. forever affirms the importance of the telephone. Workers trapped in Bell Telephone building try to get food by casting a cable across the street to the Y.M.C.A. Instead of sandwiches, Y employees send back basket full of phone messages.

1914—The Ohio State Telephone Company organized, nation's largest consolidation of independent companies.

Long Distance

1913—The Kingsbury Commitment: Under threat of antitrust legislation, AT&T opens long distance lines to independent companies. AT&T also forced to divest itself of controlling stake in Western Union.

1918—National security requires U.S. telephones to be nationalized. The Post Office takes over the telephone company, raises rates and goes $13 million into the red.

1919—National security requires Post Office give telephones back to private industry.

1920

1921—The Ohio State Telephone Company and Ohio Bell merge: start unified service at Dresden, Muskingum County.

1924—Ohio Bell installs telephone No. 500,000.

1925—Harry N. Case, Hudson Telephone Company, accepts jug of maple syrup in payment for a phone bill.

Long Distance

1920—U.S. has more than 13 million telephones; average daily calls: over 50 million.

1921—Congress passes Graham Act, which recognizes telephone as a "natural monopoly", subject to regulation but exempt from the Sherman Anti-Trust law.

1927—Commercial telephone service begins between New York and London.

1929—Stock market collapses.

1930

1937—Massive flooding in the Ohio Valley; Chillicothe operators handle 65,000 emergency calls in 18 hours.

1940

1942—Ohio Bell installs telephone No. 1,000,000.

1943—James Thurber publishes cartoon of woman asking, "Well, if I called the wrong number, why did you answer the phone?"

Long Distance

1940—U.S. has 22 million telephones; average daily calls: 96 million.

1950

1951—Ohio Bell offers world's first telephone answering service: $12.50 per month plus installation.

1954—About 85 percent of Ohio families have telephones, 2 million of which belong to Ohio Bell.

Western Reserve Telephone Company offers direct long distance dialing.

1960

1960—Ohio has more than 100 independent telephone companies.

1965—Chillicothe Telephone's Time and Temperature number gets 7,400 calls *daily.*

Long Distance

1960—U.S. has 75 million telephones; average daily calls: 273 million.

1963—"Hot line", actually a teletype, becomes operational between U.S. and Soviet Union.

1969—President Richard Nixon makes ultimate long distance call, talks to Ohioan Neil Armstrong on the moon.

1970

1971—Ohio Bell has over 4 million phones in service.

1980

1984—Ohio has 78,000 pay telephones. Average lifespan of Cincinnati pay-phone yellow pages: six weeks.

1985—Ohio has 44 local exchange companies, about 5 million access lines. Cost of a pay phone call in Wapakoneta: 5 cents.

1987—Average *daily* calls to Ohio Bell directory assistance: 150,000.

Long Distance

1980—U.S. has 180 million telephones; average daily calls: 717 million.

1983—AT&T is world's biggest business: $150 billion in assets, about 182 million telephones, $30 billion payroll, earns over $15 million per day.

1984—AT&T complies with anti-trust suit, divests itself of local operating companies.

BOSS KETTERING: INVENTING THE WHEEL

Ohio titan

After Boss Ket had perfected the high-speed diesel locomotive, he was asked to quantify its horsepower. "Strong enough," he said, "to pull 30 railroads out of the hands of receivers."

Before **Charles Kettering,** the automobile was merely an intriguing impracticality. Before him, there was no reliable way to start one. Working on evenings and weekends in the summer of 1909, he and his "barn gang," a club of what turned out to be America's first tech-heads, created a new ignition system—essentially what automobiles use today.

Within weeks, the old hand-crank was obsolete, Cadillac had ordered 8,000 of the new ignitions, and the automobile would soon be made available to virtually anyone. Depending upon one's viewpoint, Kettering was responsible either for one of America's most egalitarian monuments, or he had doomed civilization to choke in gridlock and a backwash of exhaust fumes.

Kettering was a lanky Ohio farmboy who, *Time Magazine* once said, resembled "both Ichabod Crane and Abraham Lincoln," and by 1915, the little company that grew out of his barn gang was making starters for a quarter of all the automobiles in the country. The Boss himself turned to other problems: he perfected the first quick-drying, weather-resistant paint finish for cars—painting a car could take a month— and one of his researchers, Thomas Midgley,

cured the problem of engine knock by inventing leaded, high-octane gasoline, which proved, in time, of course, to be a mixed blessing. Then, however, it lifted the ceiling on compression and engine performance.

Next, Kettering loosed Midgley on the problem of refrigerants and, soon, the world had freon—and air conditioning, which the inventors caused to become not the miracle it had seemed at the turn of the century, but a birthright.

Kettering held more than 200 patents. He developed the first lightweight, high-speed diesel locomotive, co-founded the Sloan-Kettering Institute, and was a major benefactor of Antioch College, where, nearby, he set up a research lab that for half a century probed the mysteries of photosynthesis, looking for an alternative fuel.

Before he died in 1958, he wrote, "A careful analysis will show that nine times out of ten a difficult problem is one we don't know how to solve. So we are blaming the problem instead of ignorance." Said author Mark Bernstein, "Beyond his inventions, the most useful thing Charles Kettering gave to the world was his unique way of sizing up a task."

—*John Baskin*

Inventive

Ohio

Number of patents

2001	3,995
2000	4,028
1995	2,986
1990	2,730
1985	2,522

Among all states since 1977, Ohio ranked seventh, with 71,979 patents issued

—*U.S. Patent and Trademark Office*

Matches were made possible by a mustachioed Akron-area entrepreneur with the absolutely splendid name of Ohio Columbus Barber. Mr. Barber, who a hundred years ago boldly founded and immodestly lent his name to the industrial town of Barberton, was called the Match King. Not only did his Diamond Match Company produce 250 million matches a day, but he also invented the modern matchbook.

Mr. Barber was the first to put the match striking surface on the outside of the cover, an improvement that made matches safer to use, gave him prime space to sell advertising, and brought the public's attention to what reportedly became the most frequently read phrase in the English language: "Close cover before striking."

But as impressive as matches might have been to the time, the greater magician was not Mr. Barber, but Thomas Edison, for it was Mr. Edison who put the magic and the power of electricity—the interior fire—at every man's fingertips. Mr. Edison was born in Milan, Ohio, in 1847, and as every schoolboy knows, he produced an array of inventions—the phonograph, the earliest motion picture cameras and projectors, the alkaline storage battery—that became hallmarks of our culture. His most well-known invention, of course, was the first practical incandescent electric light bulb, which by transforming night into day had such an impact on the world that the light bulb has become a symbol for an idea or inspiration. But even more important than the electric light itself, Edison developed a system to deliver electricity to that lamp. It was his system of efficient power distribution from central generators that truly ushered in the Age of Electricity and revolutionized life and work around the world.

Edison was an absolutely dogged inventor who adopted the motto, "Genius is one percent inspiration and ninety-nine percent perspiration."

(*continued on page 534*)

15 Ohio *classics*

"Ring up a sale"—this phrase entered the American lexicon after John H. Patterson put a bell on the cash register. According to Daniel Boorstin, "Americans had thus found a way to give a new publicity to the shopkeeper's smallest transaction. Shopping now was a semipublic, communal activity, announced by the ringing of bells."

1 Modern money *it isn't easy getting green*

The nation's currency was invented during the Civil War by Cincinnati lawyer Salmon P. Chase. As Lincoln's Secretary of the Treasury, he not only issued the first federal paper money good for legal tender, but also decided that the new bills would be green in color. And, Chase also literally coined the words "In God We Trust," when he placed the phrase on a 2-cent piece issued in 1864. One hundred and one years later, when silver coins got too expensive for the U.S. Treasury, the Battelle Memorial Institute in Columbus designed the nickel-copper "sandwich" now used for dimes, quarters, and, ironically, the latest silver dollars.

2 Rubber hose *elastic purposes*

In Akron in the 1870's, Dr. Benjamin Franklin Goodrich, a former surgeon, manufactured the first durable elastic hoses, which had the immediate effect of vastly improving firefighting, and which ultimately were adapted and adopted for use from backyards to operating rooms.

3 Phonograph *sound proposition*

In the 1870's, Edison thought he was merely inventing a device to record dictation and never anticipated that it would allow folks to enjoy sounds from Bach to rock in their living rooms.

4 Cash register *watching the drawer*

In 1878, Dayton saloon keeper James Ritty, inspired on a trip to Europe by a shipboard device that tallied propeller rotations, built a machine to automatically keep track of his daily receipts. He sold the patent rights to his "Incorruptible Cashier" to John Henry Patterson, a local sales and marketing genius who changed the name to "Cash Register," trained salesmen not to spit tobacco on the floor, and by systematically supplanting the pencil with millions of his machines, forever changed the way the nation did business.

5 Grocery bag *a sack in time*

Fremont native Charles Stilwell first designed and manufactured the free-standing, flat-bottomed brown paper in 1883. He called his invention the S.O.S., which stood for "Self-Opening Sack," although considering how indispensable the bags have become to grocers, those initials could arguably have meant "Save Our Supermarkets."

6 Aluminum extraction *woodshed moment*

In 1886, after months of experimentation in his woodshed in Oberlin, Charles Martin Hall developed an electrolytic process that solved the long-elusive problem of how to economically remove aluminum from bauxite; his discovery gave humanity all manner of 20th century sundries and yielded him a fortune in the form of the Aluminum Company of America.

7 Ore unloader *getting a move on*

The labor-intensive transfer of iron ore from ship to freight cars was mechanized by Conneaut's George Hulett in 1898, a transportation boon that expedited the growth of the nation's steel industry.

Airplane *the pitch and roll hall of fame*

Dayton's methodical bachelor brothers, Orville and Wilbur Wright, unlocked the secret of powered flight by controlling yaw, pitch, and roll, a 1903 achievement that would forever shrink time and distance.

Gasoline 'cracking' process

In 1913, Cleveland-born chemist William Burton was employed by Standard Oil, which ironically had a massive refinery but no oilfields. He dispatched the company's dilemma and started a revolution in the petroleum industry when he found a high-temperature-high-pressure method of making gasoline from fuel oil.

Automobile self-starter *fresh start*

In 1911, when the literally myopic Daytonian Charles Kettering started a car with an electric motor, he demonstrated a crystal clear inventive vision, turning the cumbersome hand crank into a dinosaur and making the automobile not only a useful but practical conveyance, especially for women, who at last could get comfortably—and therefore permanently—behind the wheel.

Continuous rolled steel *on a roll*

John Tytus started making strips of rolled sheet steel in Middletown during World War I, a process that raised the nation's standard of living by lowering prices on consumer goods from bicycles to Buicks.

Microencapsulation *smaller is better*

In 1953, Barrett Green of NCR Corp. developed in Dayton a process of controlled chemical release that yielded such modern amenities as time-released medication, digital thermometers, and carbonless copy paper.

Xeroxography *copy that*

In 1949, Battelle Memorial Institute agreed to help engineer Chester Carlson develop an electrostatic copying process that a score of other companies had turned down. Battelle joined forces with a fledgling New England company (now renowned as Xerox Corp.) and ten years later the first xerographic copy machine—the Xerox 914—went on the market, sending forth the first trickle in the tidal wave of copies that has since washed over the world.

Disposable diapers *cleaning up*

Though the bane of many an environmentalist, this invention from Cincinnati's Procter & Gamble has been a boon to mothers since 1962, alleviating parenthood's nastiest chore, increasing family mobility, and giving a fresh start to an estimated three-fourths of the nation's babies.

Liquid crystal display *small wonders*

James Fergason of Kent State University patented the nematic liquid twist cell (a.k.a. the LCD), and Daytonian John Janning cracked the conundrum of how to permanently align liquid crystal molecules in 1971, making possible such small wonders as digital watches and pocket calculators.

The Wright Flyer, the world's first airplane design capable of powered, sustained, and controlled flights, was brilliant in its time but roughly half a decade after it had first appeared, the brothers had nowhere to go unless they dramatically rethought their basic assumptions about design—but their vision did not extend beyond the Flyer's basic concept.
—Richard Hallion, Taking Flight, Oxford University Press

533

He once announced that at his New Jersey laboratory he could produce a new small invention every ten days and a "big trick" twice a year. Indeed, he has been called the "most useful American," simply because even now, nearly six decades after his death, he holds more patents than any other American: 1093.

One of those patents was a talking doll, which said "Mommy, Daddy," via a human voice recording. In 1880, it was the world's first talking doll. As inventions go, the doll was a minor one, but nonetheless it was symbolic of all inventions from Ohio, for in moments of inspiration, perspiration, enterprise, and surprise, our inventors have bestowed many things upon humanity. The following is a small sampling of the inventions Ohio has given the world.

Ohio On the Move

Traffic light—in 1923, Garrett Morgan of Cleveland greatly encouraged the nation's love affair with the automobile, expediting the traffic flow at intersections with both automatic "stop" and "go" signals and the yellow "caution" signal.

Refrigerated box car—Frederick McKinley Jones, an electrician and Cincinnati native, revolutionized the American diet in 1940, when he found a practical way to keep railroad cars and trucks cold for food transportation.

Ethyl gasoline—Engineer and Charles Kettering cohort Thomas Midgley developed the first anti-knock, high octane gasoline in the early 1920s.

Diesel locomotive—Kettering, after tinkering on his yacht engine, developed the two-cycle engine that delivered twice the power of previous Diesels in the early 1930s.

Cowcatcher—invented in 1851 in a workshop at the corner of Broad and Front streets, Columbus, by Lorenzo Davies, who later detested the name "cowcatcher," and always called it a "pilot."

Padded bicycle seat—Elyria banker Arthur Garford sold millions of the first soft—and therefore comfortable—bicycle seats in the 1880s; he quit his job, ran (poorly) for governor, and is now known in Lorain County as the man who "saved our butts."

Fuzzbuster—developed in the 1960s by Dale Smith of Tipp City, the truly speedy popularity of his invention made its very name a generic term for radar detectors.

Road striper—the machine that paints center and edge lines on roadways was developed at the Kelly-Cresswell Company in Xenia some 50 years ago.

Tubeless automobile tire—developed for Akron's BF Goodrich company in 1943 by Frank Herzegh, a bespectacled Cleveland native who thus softened the nation's blowouts.

Go-cart—Lee Richardson of Columbus is credited with building the first one, which he proudly displayed at the 1952 Ohio State Fair.

And: *the 8-cylinder automobile*, developed by Cleveland's Alexander Winton in 1903; *automatic windshield wipers*, patented by Fred and William Folberth of Cleveland; and *the hydraulic automobile shock absorber*—the Gabriel "Snubber"—patented by Cleveland's Claud Foster in 1914.

Around the House

Vacuum cleaner—invented by Canton janitor Murray Spangler in 1907, it was successfully manufactured by a relative, W.H. Hoover, whose name truly became a household word.

Disposable vacuum cleaner bag—this early 20th century convenience—a sign of our disposable times—was patented by Columbus native Robert Lay Hallock.

Synthetic detergent—the first heavy-duty non-soap detergent was Tide, made with a formula of phosphate compounds patented by Procter & Gamble in 1944.

534

Stepladder—it was patented in 1870 by John Balsley, an obscure employee of the Dayton water works, who some have speculated was seeking higher ground.

Formica—this plastic laminate adorns kitchens and baths across America, thanks to Cincinnati's Herbert Faber and Daniel O'Connor who in 1913 developed what they merely intended to be an electrical insulation substitute for mica.

Electric coffee grinder—the first one—Kitchen Aid model 10A—was introduced in 1937 by Hobart Manufacturing Co., Troy.

"Mr. Coffee" coffee maker—Vincent Marotta, Cleveland, invented this contemporary classic in 1972.

Air and Space

Wind tunnel—in 1901, Orville and Wilbur Wright built the first one that gave practical data, critical information that in two years resulted in the airplane.

Aircraft engine—without temperamental Charlie Taylor, the cigar-smoking Dayton machinist who built them a water-cooled, nine horsepower engine in 1903, the Wright Brothers—and perhaps humanity—might never have gotten off the ground.

Guided missile—the first one, a 300-pound, rail-launched airplane with detachable wings, was developed and tested in Dayton by Charles Kettering in 1918.

Aircraft de-icer—inflatable rubber "boots" that broke up ice were invented by W.C. Geer and first manufactured by BFGoodrich in 1932.

Helix antenna—now standard equipment on communication satellites, it was designed by electrical engineer John Kraus, Columbus, in 1946.

Space suit—Russell Colley, an engineer at BF Goodrich company in Akron, designed the first pressurized suits—based on the flexible anatomy of the tomato worm—worn by U.S. astronauts in the early 1960s.

Space helmet—Dayton sculptress Alice Chatham designed the helmets used by Capt. Chuck Yeager and the astronauts for the first supersonic and space flights.

"The English are not an inventive people; they don't eat enough pie."

—Edison

OHIOAN ELISHA GRAY—NUMBER TWO AND TRYING HARDER

The celebrity of Alexander Graham Bell and the prodigious companies he spawned tends to obscure the fact that the idea for the telephone was not exclusively his. In the 1870s, in fact, he and Belmont County native **Elisha Gray** were in a horse race to develop the apparatus, and their dash to the Patent Office ended in a photo finish with Bell arriving just hours before Gray to win what proved to be one of the nation's most valuable patents. Gray, the brilliant co-founder of Western Electric, charged that Bell and the patent office were in cahoots. The Supreme Court dismissed the case, and an embittered Gray spent his final days feeling cheated by the hands of the clock. ∾

call *waiting*

Busy Signal

535

Astronaut Maneuvering Unit—the combination life support and propulsion backpack that Gemini astronauts first used to move in space was developed at Wright-Patterson Air Force Base by Peter Van Schaik, who reportedly adapted the idea from a Buck Rogers comic strip.

What would we do without 'em?

Tickertape machine—the stock ticker, which was first used in the New York Stock Exchange in 1867, was invented by a Miami University valedictorian and gold broker, Samuel Spahr Laws, who had lived in both Troy and Cincinnati and who had the good sense to give the poor but promising Thomas Edison a job when he was only 22.

Day-Glo—the fluorescent colors that shine in daylight were invented by the Switzer Brothers—Robert and Joseph—of Cleveland.

Pre-mixed paint—developed by Sherwin-Williams Company in Cleveland, 1880.

Blackboard chalk—developed by the American Crayon Company of Sandusky in 1835.

At Work and War

Ratchet wrench—the double-action tool was invented by Robert Owen of Perry County, 1913.

Gun-boring lathe—Cincinnati machinist Richard LeBlond invented the first one in 1910, just in time to supply the demands of World War I.

Freon—the nonflammable gas that is now a universal refrigerant was invented in 1931 by Dayton's Thomas Midgley, who proved its safety by inhaling it.

Modern beehive—after Oxford's Lorenzo Langstroth discovered the phenomenon of beespace, the minister designed the first hive with a moveable frame in 1851; making it possible to reap honey without harming either the bees or their home.

Telephone switchboard—was perfected by Mt. Vernon native and multiple patent-holder Charles Ezra Scribner in the late 1800s.

Sakrete—ready-mix cement was developed in the 1930s by Arthur Avril of Cincinnati.

Patently number one

*According to U.S. Patent Office records, **Nathaniel Kirk** and **Sam C. Clark** of St. Clairsville became, on July 18, 1812, the first Ohioans ever to receive a patent, on a "machine for breaking, hairing, and fleshing every species of hides."*

bright ideas

BEING PRIVY TO INVENTIVE BUCKEYE MOMENTS

Rolling privy with removable vault, Patent No. 334,151 (January 12, 1886)
Inventor: Philip Anthony, Cleveland, Ohio

"In some rural districts, where, from the primitive habits of the people, there is but little call for a privy, except for an occasional visitor, and where a hole in the ground serves as a privy-vault...to meet the requirements for a generation or two, there would be but little call for my valuable improvement... [However] in the larger towns and cities...perhaps half of the expense and much of the annoyance [of cleaning privy vaults] may be saved." ～
—*U.S. Patent Office*

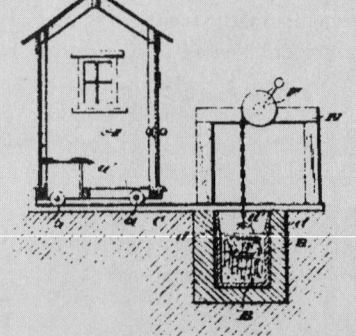

ACCIDENTAL OHIOANS

1. Floating soap—when workers employed by Cincinnati brothers-in-law William Procter and James Gamble mistakenly left a mixing machine on too long, so much air was beaten into their White Soap that it floated in water. After consulting the 45th Psalm—"out of ivory palaces, whereby they have made thee glad"—they rechristened the soap "Ivory."

2. Teflon—in 1938, Roy Plunkett, a New Carlisle native with a PhD in chemistry from Ohio State, was working for the DuPont Company when he found that some tetrafluoroethylene gas had inexplicably solidified into an exceptionally inert white solid. Discovering how to polymerize the gas in the laboratory, he named the new substance, Teflon, which *The Guinness Book of World Records* later pronounced the world's most slippery substance. Most folks associate Teflon with their no-stick cookware, but before it went on the frying pan, it was part of the fire: Teflon was

first used in World War II to make gaskets for the atomic bomb.

3. Plasticized polyvinyl chloride (PVC)—BF Goodrich researcher Waldo Semon was searching for a new adhesive in 1926, when he heated polyvinylchloride with another chemical and discovered that the PVC became malleable and chemically inert. Out of the material, he made an experimental golf ball, which to his great surprise bounced beautifully, and he immediately took off down the hall to show his colleagues. Thus Mr. Semon began the journey that would literally reshape—in hundreds of ways and means—the future in the image of PVC. ✎

Great Moments in Science:
LOUISE ZUCKER LOCATES THE JEANS ASSOCIATED WITH WEIGHT GAIN

not by the book

"I went out and sat on the dam near the old McCook Field and watched the Wright Brothers, came back home, and decided to make a glider. I got some two-by-fours, stole a bunch of mom's bloomers, and nailed it all together. I was trying to invent the lighter-than-air two-by-four, I suppose."

—Frank Irelan, Clinton County farmer

19 culinary Ohio moments

If it sliced, diced or otherwise eased the chore of scrambling up three squares a day, you can bet a Buckeye was behind it.

1 The grocery sack *in the bag*

These days, the bacon comes home in sturdy brown paper sacks, thanks to Fremont's Charles Stilwell who in 1883 patented the modern flat-bottom, self-opening grocery sack, known in the trade as the "SOS." Displacing the old hand-pasted, envelope-shaped bags, the SOS allowed grocers to pack more in without fear of the bottom falling out. Today the only distress signal on the horizon for the SOS is the question "Paper or plastic?"

2 The bar code *bar none*

Old-time grocers would add your total using a pencil stub on the side of a paper sack. Now a laser scans everything into the cash register (and the supermarket's computer inventory system) by reading the UPC "bar code." The bar code was the invention of what used to be called NCR of Dayton which previously popularized the cash register itself. NCR installed the first bar code scanner in a Troy supermarket in 1974. Today they are ubiquitous although the first President Bush hadn't seen one until a 1992 campaign "photo op" in a supermarket check-out line.

3 Aluminum foil *foiled no more*

The next time you crush a pop can for the recycling bin, you might recollect that aluminum was a rare and expensive metal until February 23, 1886 when Charles Martin Hall emerged from his makeshift laboratory in the woodshed behind his home in Oberlin. Hall had perfected a method for low-cost commercial aluminium smelting. The patent made a great deal of money for Hall (and for Oberlin College to which he gave a big block of Alcoa stock). In 1890, cheap aluminum gave Cleveland's Henry Avery the idea of replacing Mrs. Avery's cast-iron pots with aluminum pots. It wasn't long before Mrs. Avery was wrapping the leftovers in aluminium foil.

4 Teflon *letting it slide*

Not one to let a mistake slide, New Carlisle native and Ohio State graduate Roy Plunkett admitted that he'd botched a refrigeration gas experiment at DuPont in 1938. He tested the mysterious white powder left as residue, finding it slippery as ice but virtually impervious to heat. Teflon now coats over 500 million pots and pans, a few spacecraft, and the occasional Presidential metaphor.

Standardized yeast *getting a rise*

During an 1865 trip to the States as a wedding guest, Austrian Charles Fleischmann was appalled to be breaking bread leavened with rotting potato skins or stale beer. He went back to Vienna, returned with baking's manna and settled in Cincinnati. By 1868, the country had its first standardized yeast, in screaming yellow packets. A few years later, the yeasty Fleischmann discovered the martini: his Queen City-based distilling company was one of the first in the nation to bottle gin.

Crisco *frying times*

They say the name was inspired by the sound of food frying. Introduced in 1911, Procter & Gamble's 1911 all-vegetable Crisco became such a baking and frying staple that it was once sold in 50-pound tubs. Crisco which has an almost infinite shelf life if the familiar blue can is unopened gave us another first: the broadcast cooking show. "Crisco Kitchens" went on the airwaves in 1923 with an announcer reading aloud Crisco-based cookie and cake recipes.

Johnny Marzetti *lunchtime favorite*

From Teresa Marzetti's Italian restaurant at the corner of Broad and High in Columbus, pasta went out to generations of young Americans in the form of her ground beef and macaroni casserole that became a favorite of lunch ladies throughout the land; Johnny Marzetti is still a regular on school cafeteria trays. The T. Marzetti company is today the number-one maker of slaw dressing.

The gallon milk jug *got milk*

The once-familiar clinking sound of the milkman leaving bottles on the porch was replaced by a louder thud in the refrigerator after James J. Lawson introduced the gallon milk jug. As refrigerators became more common after the Depression, consumers abandoned home delivery to shop at Lawson's Akron dairy store. They found it more efficient and cheaper to buy larger quantities of fresh milk less often. In 1950, Lawson's gallon sold for 53 cents, compared to the 72 cents for the quart competitors.

The microwave *revolution in the kitchen*

In 1888, W. J. Tappan was selling cast-iron stoves door-to-door for the Ohio Valley Foundry Company in Mansfield. There had to be a lighter way, he decided. His Tappan Stove Company pioneered the domestic cooker, introducing the first all-porcelain range in decorator colors (1920s); the first window in a oven door (1930s); and a unique press-toe roll-out broiler (1940). In 1945, the company announced its engineering masterstroke, the "Jiffy Doodler," an all-in-one machine that could supposedly transform a live chicken into a five-course meal in only six minutes. While the Doodler never made it out of R&D, Tappan did revolutionize the way the world cooks with the first microwave oven for home use. Introduced in 1955, the "electronic range" was the size of a conventional oven and retailed for $1,200. The price—and the size—slowly went down, so that every evening Stouffer's Foods of Solon zaps its Lean Cuisine into several million microwaves.

Formica *where is the sin in synthetic?*

In 1913, two former-Westinghouse engineers Herbert A. Faber and Daniel J. O'Conor began experimenting in a downtown Cincinnati building with a synthetic insulating material intended to replace the mineral mica. The "faux" mica they created by coating paper with Bakelite became known as "Formica." Some 30 years later, Formica was the countertop of choice for suburbanites, available in such dreamy decorator colors as "Avocado Gossamer" and "genuine wood-grain Luxwood."

Rubber baron *cleaning up*

Knowing that every housewife dreamed of having her own maid, a penny balloon company in Wooster went into the housewares business in 1934, producing the world's first rubber dustpan. Mrs. America was swept off her feet. Rubbermaid followed up with time- and space-saving dish drainers, strainers, bathtub mats, drawer organizers, soap savers, trash cans and spatulas.

Refrigerator shelves 12

When radio pioneer, baseball team owner and inventor Powel Crosley Jr. of Cincinnati cast his powerful imagination on the kitchen of tomorrow, he created a well-organized home for salad dressing bottles. The Crosley "Shelvador" was the first refrigerator with shelves in the door. Crosley also marketed the "Icyball," a gas refrigerator but John M. Murphy of Oakwood did him one better by keeping ice off the Butterball with the invention of the first "frost-free" refrigerator.

The mixer 13

Cooks who were famed for their cake batter were often known for their forearms until KitchenAid of Troy marketed the world's first stand mixer in 1919. It weighed 65 pounds and was somehow sold door-to-door. To honor the mixer's 75th anniversary last year, KitchenAid paid $7,500 to Maud Humes of Pittsburgh for her original Model H. The honor of owning the second-oldest KitchenAid mixer went to Geraldine Mostinger of Middletown.

Hand-held vacuum cleaner 14

John Balch, a native of Coschocton, resurrected a Cleveland appliance manufacturer by creating a new niche in a market long dominated by Hoover of Akron. When Royal Appliance made dirt the devil, no kitchen was complete without a hand-held vacuum cleaner. The Dirt Devil is just the right size for sucking up spilt Cheerios or, as Balch himself pitches on television, pet hair.

The electric coffee grinder 15

For those not satisfied with coffee ground at the local A&P, KitchenAid of Troy introduced the first electric coffee grinder for in-home use in 1937. Model 10A sold for $112.75.

Mr. Coffee 16

Since 1975, he waits each morning for millions of bleary-eyed Americans to stumble into the kitchen for a steaming cup of eye-lid lifter. The automated "Mr. Coffee" first came for breakfast in Bedford Heights where it is still manufactured.

Oatmeal 17

Millions of children grew up with the exhortation "Eat your oatmeal," thanks to Ferdinand Schumacher, an Akron immigrant who hand-milled oats in his general store to create a breakfast food. In 1901, Schumacker's Quaker Oats went bigtime, eventually becoming world's foremost maker of processed cereal. Not only did the flaky cereal become a baking staple, its cylindrical cardboard container inspired countless elementary school craft projects.

The pick-up window 18

When your Teflon sauce pan burns the rice and the microwave is on the fritz, you can still turn to Ohioan Dave Thomas who perfected the drive-up "fast food" lane. Wendy's Old-Fashioned Hamburgers' second location in Columbus boasted the first successful pick-up window, installed in 1973; it featured a speaker system that allowed motorists to shout for their suppers and drive away with hot food and cold drinks wedged between their knees.

The safety bagel 19

In 2001, Cleveland Institute of Art student Bill Nottingham, after slicing his hand cutting a bagel, invented a machine that both cut and toasted the bagel. He won honorable mention in the national student design competition, but first place in the hearts—and hands—of bagel-lovers everywhere.

1995/Waldo Semon
Akron
PCV

1998/Henry Timken
Canton
Tapered Roller
Bearings

2002/Thomas
Midgley, Jr.
via Dayton
Ethyl Gasoline

2002/Sam Williams
via Columbus
Small fan-jet engine

The man with the biggest brain on scientific record was Edward Henry Knight, an early 20th-century Cincinnatian, who was an inventor, patent attorney, author, and watercolorist. His brain: 64 ounces, exactly 4 pounds. Your brain: about 32 ounces.

OHIO'S PATENT LIBRARIES

In strategic locations across the nation, the U.S. Patent and Trademark Office has established 68 Patent Depository Libraries, local outposts that receive all patents and publications issued by that office, to serve businesses, patent attorneys, and inventors. Ohio has four of these libraries, a number equaled only by California and Texas, an indication that what the Buckeye State lacks in sheer size, it makes up for in sheer ingenuity. The collections in some of Ohio's Patent Depository Libraries date back to the founding of the Patent Office in 1790, and contain about five million patents. These libraries are wonderfully equipped for conducting patent searches, a process that one of the Ohio patent librarians says is particularly useful "to keep people from reinventing the wheel."

Akron-Summit County Public Library
1040 East Tallmadge Avenue
Akron, Ohio 44310
330-643-9075

Cleveland Public Library (collection dates to 1790)
325 Superior Avenue
Cleveland, OH 44144
216-623-2870

Ohio State University (collection dates to 1870)
Science and Technology Library
175 West 18th Avenue
Columbus, OH 43210
614-292-3022

Paul Laurence Dunbar Library
Wright State University
3640 Colonel Glenn Highway
Dayton, Ohio 45435-0001
937-775-3521

Public Library of Cincinnati and Hamilton County (collection dates to 1790)
800 Vine Street
Cincinnati, OH 45202
513-369-6971

Toledo-Lucas County Public Library (collection dates to 1790, but 1910-1940 is incomplete)
325 Michigan Street
Toledo, OH 43624
419-259-5029

old money

Thomas Edison, the wizard of Milan, Ohio, more than a half century after his death, still holds more patents than any other American: 1,093. Said the New York Times, "His brain had the highest cash value in history."

Deep inside, each of us hankers for the mythical farm in the Ohio countryside. This whimsical place thrived in the 1880s, in the country of milk and honey, where the corn grew heavenward beyond a farmer's reach and cherry-red butchered beef hung in a barn. In this American Dreamland, contented and buxom cows grazed on bosomy hills and yielded creamy milk favored with clover. Add to this Rockwellian world a windmill, a commodious red barn, groomed and contoured croplands, and a whitewashed fence. The farmhouse facing the dirt road has a glider on the sprawling porch, flower boxes packed with petunias, a hound snoozing on the doormat, and shade from an elm and maple. Inside, bread dough rose on the kitchen table, a pie cooled on a window sill, and a cast-iron stove warmed a kitchen. Granny, her hair in a bun, hummed in the rocker with sewing and a new kitten on her lap. Yes, there was a cerulean sky above an amber wheat field, a cumulus cloud or two, and a teaspoon of Arctic ice in the air. Freeze that golden, timeless scene, and cherish it forever. It's the farm we measure all others against. It was a way of life born from a bale of way-back-when and a carton of make-believe.

Travel a century or more in either direction, however, and you'll find a different diorama. Farmers have been scratching the surface between Lake Erie and the Ohio River for at least 2,500 years. Ohio's first farmers, the Hopewell Culture natives cultivated goosefoot, little barley, erect knotweed, maygrass, sunflower, and squash. They boiled the seeds and mashed them into a gelatinous and edible porridge.

Adena Indians later raised pumpkins and gourds, then around 300 B.C. began planting maize (corn) by poking a hole in the ground with a Stone Age tool, depositing a few kernels, and tamping the hole with a calloused heel. They "cleared" the site by girdling trees (removing bark), trudging away fallen limbs, and burning. It amounted to farming in the forest, and in spite of the forest. Later, they grew beans and tobacco

on knowledge acquired via trade with southwestern cultures. Large-scale cultivation supported large permanent communities with ruling elites, settlements similar to the ancient "mound" cities preserved at Chillicothe and Newark. When the soil at these sites soured or other local resources became depleted (usually in five to ten years), then they moved elsewhere and repeated the practice. This prosperity went on for centuries.

Displaced elsewhere by white settlers and more powerful tribes, Wyandots, Shawnees, Delawares moved into Ohio early in the 18th century and jostled for position. Wise tribal leaders expanded the role of agriculture, essentially employing the techniques of their ancestors. They only needed to feed a village, not a market economy nor a burgeoning population in a faraway land. Incoming white settlers marveled at

by Stephen Ostrander

the thousands of acres ripened by the Indians. Consequently, invading white armies targeted corn as well as warriors. En route to their victory at the Battle of Fallen Timbers in the summer of 1794, General Anthony Wayne's soldiers ruined standing grain fields that stretched for miles along the Auglaize and Maumee rivers, including a 1,000-acre field near Defiance. The resulting famine, as much as the battle casualties and loss of British support, compelled the tribes to sign the Treaty of Greenville in 1795.

That peace treaty loosed a trans-Alleghenian stampede of agrarian settlers, most of them go-getter farmers seeking a patch of the Promised Land and a moment in the American Dream. They crossed the Appalachians lured by cheap land, frontier freedom, and tales of Ohio's fecundity. The first wave—call them the land clearers—girdled, grubbed, hoed, and sweated much like their Indian predecessors.

One healthy farmer could open two to three acres a year, but seven men needed 20 days for six acres and 16 months for 20 acres. Many land-clearers sold out at a profit, then cleared another parcel for gain, ad infinitum.

Ohio pastures drew mixed reviews. William Faux, traveling on the National Pike in 1819 near St. Clairsville, romantically observed that Ohio was "...a hilly country; all fine land in grain, corn, and pasture, with a beautiful clover face, white as with a shower of sleet; and an abundance of flourishing orchards full, above and below, of excellent fruit, although 16 years ago all was wild, and a complete forest...."

Three years earlier, however, Nathaniel Dike had reported the woes of retreating pioneers. "They were fatigued, impoverished, and sick almost to death of the Ohio [country]. They were very anxious to get home, to tell their friends the truth, and to dispell the delusions which led them to fancy the Western World...They said they would rather live on one meal a day in their native state than on three in Ohio."

Farming, then as now, strains body and spirit. Besides the constant, exhausting work, and the vagaries of weather, early settlers fell victim to malaria, isolation, and natural predators ranging from lethal mountain lions to grain-devouring turkeys, passenger pigeons, and squirrels. Some

arrived without a cent, but somehow endured. Preacher James Finley brought his young bride to his Highland County plot in 1801 possessing, literally, the clothes on their backs and hope in their hearts.

His father-in-law disapproved of the match so much that he denied his daughter her clothing when she departed with the frontier firebrand. Lacking horse, cow, bed, baggage, furniture, tools, and common sense, Finley failed spectacularly as a farmer. Instead, Preacher Finley provided for his frontier family by sowing the Word of God as Ohio's most celebrated circuit rider.

From the beginning, Buckeye farmers overproduced. Surplus grain, fruit and livestock were converted into products with a long shelf life, namely liquor and salted pork. Ohio "stills" produced more than a million gallons of spirits in 1810. Diversity also characterized early Ohio farms. Besides grain, farmers profited from flax, barley, vegetables, sheep, apples, cattle, potash, clay, and salt. Cattle and hog raising empires arose in the Miami and Scioto valleys, while northeastern Ohio got dubbed "Cheesedom" for its dairy delights.

As canals, roads, and railroads transported agricultural goods to markets, Ohio changed from primitive backwater to national breadbasket. On the eve of the Civil War, it ranked among the top four states in corn, wheat and oat production. Cincinnati, the West's premier farm entrepot, earned the double sobriquets of "Whiskey Capital of the Nation" and "Porkopolis," for its meat-packing industry.

By 1880, some 247,189 farms had nearly three-fourths of Ohio under cultivation. Ohio's cattle herd topped a million that year, and wheat and corn production had doubled since 1850. By now, Ohio also had become a major manufacturer of farm machinery. Indeed, agriculture revved Ohio's economy, and made it a national political power. That year, the nation elected another Ohioan to the presidency, James Garfield, who followed fellow Buckeyes Ulysses S. Grant and Rutherford B. Hayes. Four more Ohioan-born politicians—Benjamin Harrison, William McKinley, William H. Taft, and Warren G. Harding—would reach the nation's highest

office during the ensuing four decades. Today, at the threshold of a new millennium, feeding people (read agriculture and food processing) remains Ohio's chief enterprise, contributing more than $50 billion to the state's annual economy and employing one in six laborers. Paradoxically, Ohio ranks among the top ten breadbasket states even though it leads the nation in urbanized land area. Still fertile, Ohio is one of only four states with 50 percent or more of its land designated prime farmland. Indeed, farming is big business. Yet bottom lines fail to disclose farming's decline as a way of life.

Since 1900, Ohio has halved the acreage in cultivation. In the last half century alone it has lost about 30 percent of its farmland, at a clip of 77 acres a day. The number of farms has dwindled to 80,000, while the average size of a farm has increased to more than 200 acres. This puts more stress on the remaining tillers of soil, now only two percent of the population. They are expected to produce more food on less land, avoid environmental distress, and refrain from displays of consumer excess. Agribusiness has supplanted the family farm as the producing unit of commercial crops—except among the Amish and some contrarians who prove the old ways are still best. Others blame farming's decline on urban development and the attractiveness of lucrative enterprises requiring less capital and physical labor.

During the 20th century, two incurable romantics (or cranks) revolted against agriculture's mainstream. Ex-patriate Louis Bromfield harvested millions writing Pulitzer Prize-winning novels in France and Hollywood screenplays. However, on the eve of the Second World War, he returned to his roots in Richland County. With plow and pen, Bromfield quickly became the nation's leading advocate of diversified and scientific farming, and soil conservation. To prove his point, Bromfield turned a trio of used-up farms near Mansfield into a productive plantation that showcased his ideals, energy, and booming charm.

Pilgrims journeyed to Malabar Farm to see the prophet and his fecund fields. Although his prosaic, post-Victorian novels molder in libraries today, Bromfield's agricultural essays are studied like Scriptures, and stay fresh for every harvest. Now a state park, Malabar Farm keeps Bromfield's indomitable spirit and his farm alive.

Gene Logsdon picked up Bromfield's pen and plow in the 1990s, and became the groundhog hole that keeps twisting the agricultural establishment's ankle. Like Bromfield, Logsdon cured his agricultural angst by turning a 20-acre homestead in Wyandot County into a pocket paradise and then writing lovingly about it. Calling himself the Contrary Farmer, Logsdon rants against factory farms and the adherents of agribusiness who, he says, have imposed a kind of industrial totalitarianism on a passive peasantry. Instead, Logsdon hails the sustainable farming of the low-tech Amish, the intuitive wisdom and passion of Old School farmers, the grit and resourcefulness of organic practitioners, and the independent "aggies" who think outside of the prefab metal pole barns. At Logsdon's place the livestock still have names (not numbers), wild berries end up in Mason jars, Fido rides in the pickup truck, and the owner counts the blessings from his pond. —*Stephen Ostrander*

The Ohio Statehood Stamp features a hill-country farm scene by Ohio's pre-eminent nature photographer, Ian Adams of Cuyahoga Falls, (see www.ianadams photography.com) whose expert documentation of the state now entails a film archive of some 30,000 images. The farm on the stamp is the Knoch family farm, just north of Marietta (sold in 1997 to Marietta businessman John Lehman). It's Adams' smallest color print ever (1x1.5 inches), largest edition (50 million) and, says Adams, "at 37 cents, the most affordable."

Agriculture: the *regions*

The regional agricultural geography of western Ohio is more complex than that of eastern Ohio. The significant boundary is one which runs diagonally across the state, approximating quite closely the division between the two physiographic provinces of the Central Lowland and the Appalachian Plateaus.

On the basis of commodities produced, 12 distinct agricultural regions can be identified in Ohio:

1. **Cincinnati Urban Farming Region**. The unity of this agricultural region rests upon a mixture of three kinds of agriculture: dairying, truck gardening, and greenhouse and nursery operations. All of these activities exist because of the market which Cincinnati and nearby cities provide. The dairy farms tend to be located farthest from the urban centers. Alluvial soils and clay soils with high organic content tend to be associated with open-field vegetable raising; greenhouse and nursery operations dominate where there are more sandy soils.

2. **Southern Tobacco Region.** This is an extension of the Kentucky tobacco–growing area across the Ohio River. Tobacco accounts for almost a third of farm income; dairying ranks as the most important subsidiary of agricultural activity.

3. **Lake Erie Shore Vegetable and Fruit Region**. The emphasis here is on production of vegetables and fruits for which a soil and climatic advantage is present in this region. The state's most important concentration of greenhouse and nursery operations is found in this area. Throughout this region the emphasis is upon a variety of agricultural specialties. Celeryville, in Huron County, provides a good example of the importance that crop specialization assumes in this region.

4. **Northeast Dairy Region. Generally** there is a much greater emphasis in this region on livestock than on crop raising. Dairying accounts for most of all farm income, with beef cattle generally the second agricultural activity. Locally restricted areas produce vegetables on muck soils derived from glacial kettlehole deposits and small glacial lake beds. The emphasis on dairying has had some conse-

quences on the development of the rural landscape—the percentage of farms with silos and large barns for hay storage, the number of paved farm roads to move milk to market, the farm milkhouses and coolers, and the higher percentage of fenced pastures.

5. **Ohio Valley Dairy Region.** In many respects this area is similar to the Northeast Dairy Region. Dairying is the principal activity and cattle raising is second, although dairying does not produce quite as high a proportion of farm income as in the northeast. Two commodities, vegetables and tobacco, are widely produced from alluvial soils of the valleys of the Ohio River and its major tributaries.

6. **Southeast Beef Cattle Region.** Here in the heart of Appalachian Ohio, emphasis is on the production of livestock, especially beef cattle. Because of low soil quality and a generally sloping landscape, field crops are not grown. What little good land exists is in nearly every case devoted to corn, most of which is fed to livestock on the same farm. Other agricultural activities are dairying and the raising of hogs or poultry. Throughout the Appalachian area part-time subsistence farming is found on a greater scale than elsewhere. Some supplemental farm income is produced by sale of forest products.

7. **Northwest Mixed Farming Region.** Although the growing of corn and soybeans for sale predominates, a wide variety of agricultural activities is found in this area. Cattle raising is important, but so is dairying, vegetable production, and hog raising. The land is featureless and mechanization is greater than anywhere else in Ohio. Labor requirements are high for some specialty crops. Here in the northwestern corner of Ohio is found the most successful blend of favorable physical conditions and variety of agricultural responses.

8. **Corn Belt–Cash Grain Region.** Throughout western Ohio large fields of corn and soybeans constitute the basic unifying characteristic of the agricultural landscape; it is only in this region that production of grains (corn and soybeans, and to a lesser extent, wheat) makes up well over half of farm income.

9. **Corn Belt–Hog Region.** The dominant activity in this region of northwestern Ohio is the raising of corn and soybeans for cash sale, although fully a third to a half of the yield is consumed on the farm for animal feed. In all parts of the region the raising of hogs is the second most important type of agriculture, and beef cattle raising is generally a close third. This type of agriculture, which combines the raising of grains with the production of livestock, is commonly termed feeder-lot farming. It characterizes much of the eastern Midwest.

10. Corn Belt–Cattle Region. The main difference between this region of western Ohio and the Corn Belt–Hog Region is that cattle ranks as the second activity and hogs third. The dependence on corn for this region tends to be slightly less than in the hog-raising region and the significance of the second-ranking activity a bit higher. The feeder-belt landscape is a distinctive one, with stoutly fenced feeder lots crowded with livestock, grain cribs and storage bins, large barns (but not generally as large as in dairy regions), and long one-story machinery sheds.

11. Western Dairy Region. Dairying is normally the premier type of farming in this region, although the raising of corn and soybeans follows closely. The raising of hogs and cattle, although secondary, is characteristic of this region. The success of dairying is related in large part to the urban markets which lie nearby.

12. Southwest Hog Region. Here the raising of hogs is paramount. The raising of beef cattle is commonly the second-ranking activity. The fortunate situation of Cincinnati on the major water route of 19th century America and close to excellent agricultural frontier settlements made the city a major pork packing center well before the Civil War. The success of the packing plants and the over-coming of frontier conditions allowed farmers to concentrate on the most profitable item of their farming operation—hog raising. One of the most important products made in Cincinnati was lard. The demand was sufficient to encourage the development in the Miami River Valley of the first totally American hog variety, the Poland China breed.

*Source: excerpted with the permission of the Ohio Department of Natural Resources from **Ohio—An American Heartland**, by Allen G. Noble and Albert J. Korsok*

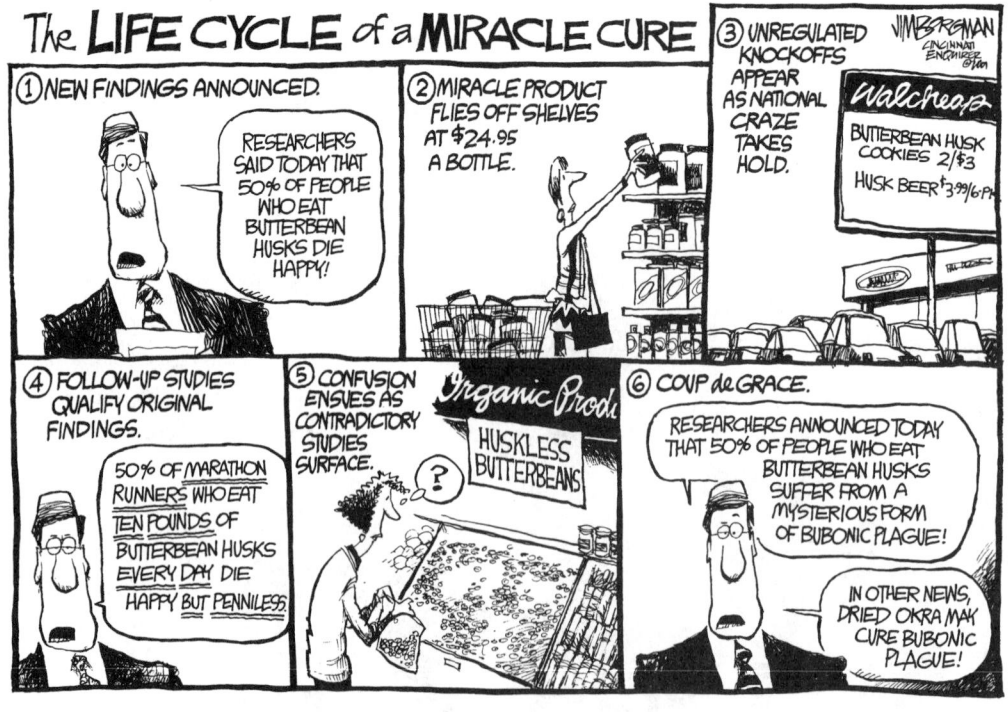

"NO, IT'S NOT GENETICALLY ALTERED EGGPLANT........ EGGPLANT JUST LOOKS THAT WAY."

Agriculture

Ohio 2001 Crop Summary

The 2001 planting season was ahead of schedule compared to the five year average; in addition, precipitation during the growing season was above average for the state. Farmers completed harvest of most crops a week or more ahead of the five-year average.

Planting progress for the 2001 Winter Wheat crop started off slightly above the five year average and was completed nine days behind the five year average. Even so the majority of the winter wheat was emerged by November 19, which was four days behind the five-year average. Producers harvested 900,000 acres, 210,000 acres less than the previous year. The yield, at 67 bushels per acre, was down 5 bushels from 2000 and production was down 25 percent from 2000.

The corn crop stayed ahead of the five year average throughout the growing season and ended up 25 days ahead of the 1996-2000 average. Corn harvested for silage finished around October 2, 11 days ahead of the average. Corn growers harvest was down 130,000 acres from the previous year and the yield decreased six percent while the total corn produced was down 47.6 million bushels from 2000.

Soybean planting also began a few days ahead of average and ended five days ahead; the harvest ended two days ahead of average. Acres harvested was up 140,000 from 2000 but yield was down two percent. Production still rose one percent to 187.8 million bushels.

Oat planting began three days behind but ended eight days ahead. The harvest was earlier than average but it was 5,000 acres less than the previous year. Yield was down four percent and total production down nine percent.

Alfalfa came in a few days early while other hay was a couple of days late. The yield from alfalfa fell four percent with the same acreage as the previous year. There was a slight drop in yield for other hay but the acreage harvested was up 14 percent increasing total hay acreage up nine percent. The all hay yield dropped 13 percent.

With fewer acres of burley tobacco in production in 2001 total production dropped 1.24 million pounds, despite a yield that increased by 200 pounds per acre .

Six hundred acres of sugar beets were in production, down from 800 the previous year. Coupled with a five percent drop in yield the total production fell 29 percent. Potatoes also saw a drop in acreage (down 100) and a decline in yield for a drop in total production of 13 percent.

The Ohio Department of Agriculture's crop forecast for the 2003 season put corn yields at 142 bushels per acre, near the state record of 147 in 2000. The estimate of 454.4 million bushels would be an 80% increase over that drought-diminished crop.

Cabbage, escarole/endive, onions, pumpkins, sweet corn and tomatoes led the way to an increase of 18 percent in the state's production of fresh market vegetables. The result: a 47 percent increase in total value to $134,700,000. At the same time the value of production for processing vegetables was down $5.6 million from the previous year to $26.2 million. An exception was processing tomatoes where despite a ten percent drop in yield, production rose four percent because of a 15 percent increase in acreage harvested. Another increase was in processing cucumber production which rose 28 percent following an increase in 200 acres harvested coupled with an increased yield.

Strawberry acreage remained stable but an increase of 2 cwt. per acre meant a five percent increase in production. Apples increased 4 million pounds; peach production increased while grape production decreased by 1,700 tons with a 22 percent drop in yield.

Livestock, Dairy and Poultry

In 2001 hog inventories fell to an all time low, dairy cows decreased by 5,000 head, sheep inventory dropped and cattle and calf numbers increased slightly. Honey production dropped ten percent.

Following an all time record low cattle and calf inventories rebounded slightly. For the second straight year cattle operations dropped by 1,000 leaving 27,000, a decline of four percent. The total value from cattle and calves rose due to a six percent increase from $800 per head to $850.

Ohio's milk cow population declined by 5,000 as milk production dropped three percent. This was offset by a 21 percent increase in milk prices.

Ohio's 1,420,000 hogs (half of what it was in 1970) were a decrease of five percent and hog operations declined the same percentage to 4,900. This decline was offset by higher prices as receipts increased six percent from the previous year.

Ohio's 3,600 sheep operations had 2,000 fewer sheep in 2001 and with 140,000 sheep is a long way from the 8,800,000 sheep that resided in the state in 1867. The value per head dropped $4.

Ohio's 38,000,000 laying hens supply 7,900,000,000 eggs, 9.2 percent of the nation's total. In addition Ohio has 4.8 million turkeys.

Ohio bee colonies produced over a million dollars for the state's beekeepers.

Profile

Commodity	Unit	Rank	Inventory 2001	Rank	Inventory, 2000
Field Crops					
Corn for Grain	Bu.	6	437,460,000	6	485,100,000
Corn for Silage	Ton	12	2,890,000	11	2,880,000
Oats	Bu.	9	6,205,000	7	6,840,000
Winter Wheat	Bu.	6	60,300,000	4	79,920,000
Soybeans	Bu.	6	187,780,000	5	186,480
All Hay (baled)	Ton	16	4,275,000	15	4,521,000
Sugarbeats	Ton	12	12,000	12	17,000
All Potatoes	Cwt.	26	984,000	25	1,134,000
Tobacco	Lb.	7	11,956,000	7	13,200,000
Fresh Vegetables					
Sweet Corn	Cwt.	5	1,309,000	5	1,302,000
Tomatoes	Cwt.	3	1,947,000	6	1,125,000
Storage Onions	Cwt.	10	169,000	10	168,000
Total Fresh Vegetables	**Cwt.**	**14**	**5,331,000**	**15**	**4,500,000**

Commodity	Unit	Rank	Inventory 2001	Rank	Inventory, 2000
Processing Vegetables					
Tomatoes	Ton	3	164,600	3	158,700
Cucumbers	Ton	6	29,400	6	22,900
Total Processing					
Vegetables	*Ton*	*8*	*231,100*	*8*	*205,400*
Fruit					
Apples	Lb.	11	120,000,000	10	95,000,000
All Grapes	Ton	8	6,000	9	7,700
Processed Grapes	Ton	8	5,900	9	7,600
Peaches	Lb.	17	11,200,000	18	10,400,000
Strawberries	Cwt.	9	46,000	10	44,000
Poultry and Poultry Products					
Chicken Layers	Head	2	38,009,000	2	35,832,000
Chicken Sold	Lb.	6	57,929,000	6	64,981,000
Broiler Production	Lb.	18	212,500,000	18	223,900,000
Turkey Production	Lb.	11	181,440,000	11	165,000,000
Egg Production	No.	2	7,900,000	1	8,163,000
Livestock and Livestock Products					
Hog and Pig Inventory 2001	Head	10	1,420,000	10	1,500,000
Hog and Pig Production	Lb.	9	770,745,000	9	774,738,000
Cattle and Calf Inventory	Head	27	1,250,000	28	1,240,00
Cattle and Calf Production	Lb.	29	427,488,000	27	459,350,000
Beef Cow Inventory	Head	29	3280,000	29	275,000
Milk Cow Inventory	Head	10	260,000	9	265,000
Sheep and Lamb Inventory	Head	14	140,000	13	142,000
Sheep and Lamb Production	Lb.	12	12,687,000	13	10,980,000
Wool	Lb.	13	1,200,000	13	960,000
Cattle Slaughtered	Head	19	133,400	19	137,000
Hogs Slaughtered	Head	14	1,166,500	14	1,206,000
Calves Slaughtered	Head	15	800	11	22,200
Sheep and Lambs Slaughterd	Head	13	16,300	14	11,300
Red Meat Production	Lbs.	24	297,000,000	24	315,300,000
Livestock Slaughter Plants	No.	2	163	3	160
Milk and Milk Products					
Milk Production	Lb.	11	4,319,000,000	11	4,461,000,000
Milk Equivalent Used for Manufactured					
Dairy Production	Lb.	9	2,556,000,000	5	2,430,000,000
All Cheese					
excluding cottage cheese	Lb.	10	146,184,000	8	139,073,000
Swiss Cheese	Lb.	1	90,223,000	1	80,656,000
Creamed Cottage Cheese	Lb.	4	19,447,000	4	17,735,000
Cottage Cheese Curd	Lb.	4	22,399,000	4	22,369,000
Ice Cream	Gal.	7	36,933,000	7	36,704,000
Milk Sherbert	Gal.	2	3,990,000	2	3,888,000
Manufactured Dairy Plants	No.	5	56	5	56
Miscellaneous					
Number of Farms	No.	8	78,000	8	80,000
Operations with Cattle	No.	12	41,000	11	28,000
Operations with Hogs	No.	4	4,900	3	5,200
Operations with Sheep	No.	3	3,600	3	3,600
Operations with Milk Cows	No.	5	5,200	5	5,500
Honey Production	Lb.	23	1,296,000	21	1,170,000
Maple Syrup	Gal.	4	96,000	9	34,000
Fertilizer Consumption	Ton	5	2,718,000	10	1,951,000

Source: Ohio Department of Agriculture

Corn yield went
from 54 bushes
per acre in 1954
to 147 in 2000
—an increase
of 170%.

Soybean yield went
from 22.5 bushels
per acre in 1964
and 1967
to 44 in 1997
and 1998
—an increase
of 96%.

Winter Wheat yield
went from 21
bushels per acre
in 1961 to 72
bushels per acre
in 2000
—an increase
of 242%.

Hay yield went
from 1.72 tons
per acre in 1956
to 3.23 in 2000
—an increase
of 88%.

Record Crops

Crop	Date series began	Record*	Harvest Acres	Year	Yield	Year	Total Production	Year	Unit
Corn for grain	1919	High	4,030,000	1985	143.0	1992	511,810,000	1985	Bu.
		Low	2,537,000	1961	27.5	1930	75,598,000	1924	Bu.
Corn for silage	1919	High	285,000	1981	20.0	1992	4,000,000	1982	Ton
		Low	106,000	1935	5.4	1930	823,000	1933	Ton
Soybeans for beans	1924	High	4,080,000	1979	44.0	1994	175,560,000	1994	Bu.
		Low	17,000	1925	11.5	1926	207,000	1926	Bu.
Wheat	1866	High	3,209,000	1899	62.0	1985	79,650,000	1990	Bu.
		Low	800,000	1987	6.0	1900	9,000,000	1866	Bu.
Oats	1866	High	2,374,000	1928	85.0	1985	92,400,000	1912	Bu.
		Low	150,000	1993	20.0	1890	9,000,000	1993	Bu.
Rye	1866	High	200,000	1913	43.0	1985	2,700,000	1913	Bu.
		Low	4,000	1985	10.0	1896	150,000	1993	Bu.
Alfalfa Hay	1919	High	1,052,000	1955	4.2	1994	2,800,000	1992	Ton
		Low	93,000	1920	1.3	1930	188,000	1919	Ton
Other Hay	1964	High	1,080,000	1968	2.6	1994	2,160,000	1989	Ton
		Low	700,000	1991	1.49	1965	1,328,000	1965	Ton
All Hay	1866	High	3,553,000	1908	3.43	1994	4,898,000	1916	Ton
		Low	1,260,000	1983	0.6	1895	1,755,000	1895	Ton
Apples	1934	High	N/A				7,886,000	1937	Bu.
		Low					780,000	1945	Bu.**
Peaches	1899	High	N/A				3,800,000	1901	Bu.
		Low					15,000	1982	Bu.**
Grapes***	1909	High	N/A				34,400	1935	Ton
		Low					4,900	1945	Ton
Potatoes-total	1866	High	225,000	1895	270	1985	12,269,000	1909	Cwt.
		Low	5,200	1992	27	1881	1,140,000	1991	Cwt.
Sugar Beets (no acres contracted in 1982)	1924	High	51,000	1938	21.7	1971	896,000	1971	Ton
		Low	9,500	1931	5.8	1937	72,000	1943	Ton
Burley Tobacco	1919	High	25,000	1919	2,680	1970	28,350,000	1982	Lb.
		Low	6,700	1971	715	1935	6,435,000	1935	Lb.
All tobacco	1866	High	106	1909	2,496	1970	94,575,000	1918	Lb.
		Low	7,350	1987	620	1875	12,044	1987	Lb.

*In case of ties, most recent year becomes record year
**42 lbs. (apples) or 48 lbs. (peaches)
***Utilized production

Source: Ohio Department of Agriculture

Historical Agricultural Statistics—acres harvested

Year	Farms	Corn	Soybeans	Wheat	Hay	Oats
2001	78,000	3,170,000	4,580,000	900,000	1,520,000	85,000
1990	84,000	3,450,000	3,480,000	1,350,000	1,400,000	230,000
1980	95,000	4,120,000	3,760,000	1,370,000	1,430,000	290,000
1970	118,000	3,249,000	2,550,000	925,000	1,440,000	528,000
1965	129,000	3,295,000	2,044,000	1,258,000	1,853,000	606,000

Historical Agricultural Statistics—livestock inventory

Year	Cattle	Milk Cows	Hogs	Sheep
2001	1,250,000	260,000	1,420,000	140,000,
1990	1,500,000	345,000	2,000,000	205,000
1980	1,825,000	375,000	2,150,000	265,000
1970	2,031,000	448,000	2,838,000	605,000
1965	2,204,000	630,000	2,191,000	662,000

Ohio's cattle population is 52% of what it was in 1956; its milk cow population 29%; hog population 53%; and sheep 13.5% of 1956 levels.

Agricultural Production

Maple Syrup	96,000 gal.
Milk	4,294,000,000 lb.
American Cheese	28,512,000 lb.
Cheddar Cheese	22,435,000 lb.
Swiss Cheese	90,223,000 lb.
Cottage Cheese Curd	22,399,000 lb.
Creamed Cottage Cheese	19,447,000 lb.
Lowfat Cottage Cheese	29,434,000 lb.
Ice Cream	36,933,000 gal.
Ice Cream Mix	17,654,000 lb.
Milk Sherbert, Hard	3,990,000 gal.
Water and Juice Ices	5,479,000 gal.
Wool Production	960,000 lb.
Mink Pelts Produced	58,500 (10 ranches)
Eggs Produced	7,900,000,000 lb.
Honey Produced	1,296,000 lb.
Chicken sales	57,929,000 lb.
Turkey Production	181,440,000 lb.
Sales from floriculture	$189,250,000
Sheep and Lamb Produciton	12,687,000 lb.
Hog Production	770,745,000 lb.

Average Prices of Commodities

Corn	$2.00 bu. (high $3.32, 1995)
Soybeans	$4.40 bu. (high $7.91, 1983)
Wheat	$2.50 bu. (high $4.08, 1979)
Oats	$1.50 bu. (high $2.61, 1987)
Hay	$91.50 ton (high $135, 1997)
Tobacco	$1.938 lb.
Milk	$15.20 cwt. (high $15.20, 1998 & 2001)
Fluid Grade	$15.40 cwt.
Mfg. Grade	$12.80 cwt
Milk Cows	$1,450 head
Hogs	$43.70 cwt. (high $53.90, 1982)
Sows	$35.50 cwt.
Barrows & Gilts	$44.70 cwt.
Cattle	$69.90 cwt. (high $73.10, 1987)
Cows	$39.80 cwt.
Steers & Heifers	$73.40 cwt.
Calves	$94.70 cwt.
Sheep	$32.80 cwt.
Lambs	$72.30 cwt.
Commercial Broilers	$0.39 lb.
Turkeys	$0.35 lb.
Eggs	$0.49 doz.
Tobacco	$1.938 lb.
Potatoes	$7.90 cwt.
Apples	$0.24 lb.
Peaches	$0.49 lb.
Grapes	$342.00 ton
Honey	$0.85 lb.

Bountiful Ohio: pertinent statistics

What is a farm?
"A farm is defined as an establishment that sold or normally would sell $1,000 or more of agricultural products during one year. This also includes government payments received."
—U.S. Department of Agriculture

Total Ohio Land in Farms
—14,800,000 acres (almost half of all land in Ohio is prime farmland—44%—one of only five such states in the U.S.) 394 acres of farmland disappear every day in Ohio.

Total cash receipts
—$5.3 billion

Total cash receipts per farm
—$73,214

Number of farms
—78,000

Average farm size
—190 acres

Employment
—41,899 (only mining had fewer, 13,217)

Average weekly earnings by an employee in agriculture
—$374.71 (lowest earning rate of any industrial sector)

Average per farm value, farmland and buildings
—$2,700 per acre

Average cash rent per acre for cropland
—$76

Net farm income per acre
—$71

Most farms
—Darke County,1,960

Largest Average Farms
—Fayette County, 442 acres

Most Land in Farms
—Darke County, 347,000
(Cuyahoga has the fewest farms, 170; and the least land in farms, 6,000 acres)

Ohio's Livestock Population
Hogs & Pigs	1,420,000
Cattle & Calves	1,250,000
Milk Cows	260,000
Sheep & Lambs	140,000

Oldest agricultural publication in Ohio
—The Ohio Farmer magazine, founded 1845

Ohio diversity
—Ohio grows more than 200 crops.
—Of the 78,000 farms in Ohio, more than 4,800 are actually managed and/or operated by women.

The ratio
The average farmer feeds 129 people.

Time being money
We work an average of 30 days to pay for a year's supply of food.

Ten Ohio Crops bringing in the most cash receipts

1. Corn for Grain	$19,209,312
2. Hay	$12,611,560
3. Soybeans	$12,439,597
4. Wheat	$5,553,815
5. Potatoes	$2,935,611
6. Grapes	$2,794,241
7. Tobacco - burley	$1,916,234
8. Apples	$1,514,301
9. Tomatoes	$1,116,982
10. Strawberries	$1,085,405

Ohio Farm Machinery, how many
Tractors	162,238
Trucks & Pickups	104,133
Balers	32,153
Combines	26,225
Mower Conditioners	25,612

—Sources: Ohio Department of Agriculture, Morgan Quitno Corporation, 2003

Agricultural Hall of Fame

(Ohio's highest tribute to individuals making outstanding contributions to the agriculture industry. Each year four prominent agriculturalists are honored and inducted into the Ohio Agricultural Hall of Fame)

1966 *Leo L. Rummell*—educator and farm writer
Glen H. Stringfield—plant breeder
Louis J. Taber—farm organization leader

1967 *Carl R. Arnold*—economist and finance expert
David W. Galehouse—seed producer, conservationist, and educator
Harry C. Ramsower—agriculture educator

1968 *L.P. Baily*—breeder of Jersey cattle
Oscar E. Bradfute—farmer, cooperative leader
John T. Brown—farmer and lawmaker
Howard M. Call—farmer and community builder
C.M. Ferguson—educator and administrator
A.B. Graham—founder of the 4-H Clubs
Perry L. Green—lawmaker and co-op leader
Henry P. Miller—writer and master farmer
Amos I. Root—evangelist of modern beekeeping
A.P. Sandles—booster of Ohio fairs
Charles E. Thorne—writer and soil scientist
Norton S. Townshend—educator and legislator
Allen Trimble—governor and livestock breeder
Joseph E. Wing—writer and alfalfa pioneer

1969 *Harold Anderson*—founder of grain business
Uri T. Cox—farmer and plant propagator
Leon M. Evans—farmer and banker
Lawrence A. Kauffman—teacher and sheep specialist
Forrest G. Ketner—co-op leader and marketing specialist
Edward H. Knight—farmer, inventor
Murray D. Lincoln—co-op founder and agriculture leader
Glen G. McIlroy—farmer and farm manager
Joseph Oppenheim—teacher and inventor
Virgil Overholt—teacher and drainage specialist
Charles Plumb—educator and administrator
Martin L. Ruetenik—vegetable specialist and innovator
Arthur L. Smith—vegetable grower and industry leader
Howard J. Ziegler—farmer and livestock breeder

1970 *Cosmas D. Blubaugh*—soil and water conservationist
Edmund Secrest—educator and forester
John A. Slipher—educator and soil conservationist
Samuel S. Studebaker—farmer and farm credit leader

1971 *Bryce. C. Browning*—conservationist and educator
Benjamin Basil Brumley—farmer and co-op leader
George L. Cooley—co-op leader and grape grower

Wheeler J. Welday—fruit grower and industry leader

1972 Charles A. Dambach—educator and conservationist
LeRoy Albert Demorest—inventor and beef cattle breeder
F. Edward Seitz—vegetable grower and industry leader
Charles Julius Willard—educator, agronomist

1973 Wilbur H. Bruner—educator and animal scientist
Max M. Scarff—farmer and seed producer
Lewis F. Warbington—co-op leader and humanitarian
Carlos Grant Williams—educator and administrator

1974 Lewis Charles Chadwick—educator and horticulturist
John M. Davis—dairy farmer and industry leader
Earl W. McMunn—agriculture editor and writer
Douglas Stanfield—educator and farm organization leader

1975 Wayne Brown—marketer and retailer
A.B. Evans—purebred livestock breeder, farmer
Walter R. Krill—educator and administrator
Thomas S. Sutton—educator and researcher

1976 A.Z. Baker—marketer and organization leader
Joel S. Coffey—educator and livestock industry leader
John H. Dunlap—farmer and conservationist
John D. Siebenthaler—nursery and landscape industry leader

1977 Walter L. Bluck—educator and farmer
Darwin R. Bryan—youth leader

John M. Grierson—farmer and farm credit leader
Warren G. Weiler—educator and administrator

1978 Max Drake—dairy and industry leader
Charles S. Latchaw—farm organization leader
Forest Don Loudenslager—farmer and hog producer
Lottie M. Randolph—agricultural leader and homemaker

1979 Joseph W. Fichter—teacher and lecturer
Elden R. Groves—farmer-communicator
C. Clayton Terrell—grain and livestock farmer
Dwight Wise, Sr.—grain, dairy, and beef cattle farmer

1980 Leonard M. Bettinger—pioneer in nursery industry
Martin Luther Howell—dairy industry leader
Thomas C. Kennard—innovative environmentalist
Kenneth N. Probasco—agri-business leader

1981 Beatrice J. Cleveland—4-H youth leader
Richard H. Kellogg—pioneer in artificial dairy breeding
Robert C. Miller—agri-newscaster and youth supporter
William H. Zipf—agri-business communicator

1982 Ralph E. Bender—educator and administrator
Harry A. Caton—farm organization leader
Willard W. Ellenwood—orchardist and livestock breeder
Everett G. Royer—farm manager and soybean leader

1983 Roy M. Kottman—educator, leader, and innovator

MARVELOUS MOLLY TURNS HEADS IN WELLINGTON

Marvelous Molly Baun was the making of many men in Wellington. She was a foreigner, an import from Holland, where she had caught the eye of some up-and-coming fellows from Wellington's Horr-Warner cheese factory. They brought her back home with them, and she not only became the most popular girl in town but also the most famous employee of the factory. Molly was a cow, and a most distinguished one at that. She was a Holstein-Friesian, one the first purebred cattle in Ohio, and thus quite superior to the local girls who gave at most 5,000 pounds of milk per year. Molly produced a record-setting 17,000 pounds, an accomplishment so astounding that she became the mother of cattle-breeding in Ohio.

JIMBORGMAN CINCINNATI ENQUIRER/1994

"BOVINE GROWTH HORMONE MILK....., GENETICALLY ALTERED BAKED POTATO WITH MARGARINE......
THE CRAZY FOOL WAS LIVING ON THE EDGE, CHIEF."

John Sawyer—environmentalist and industry leader

Henry H. Schriver—lecturer and co-op leader

John M. Stackhouse—government leader and farmer

1984 Robert P. Hester—farmer and cooperative leader

Ralph A. Howard—vocational educator

Suzanne Macino—government agricultural assistant

Harold L. Porter—government leader and plant specialist

1985 Robert O. Grieser—farmer and conservationist

Cecil H. Robinson—farmer and corn seed producer

Wilbur "Bill" Stuckey—educator and safety specialist

Charles E. Wyckoff—farmer and electric co-op leader

1986 Wallace Barr—educator and economist

Dale T. Friday—educator and exhibition leader

D.C. Kiplinger—educator, floricultural, and organizational specialist

Lawrence E. Kunkle—educator and meat specialist

1987 Samuel C. Cashman—journalist and organizational specialist

Floyd I. Lower—educator and potato specialist

Jacob McQueen—lecturer and soybean pioneer

Frank B. Sollars—organizational and financial specialist

1988 Earl F. Kantner—educator and youth leader

John H. Klippart—author, narrator, and organization leader

James M. Lewis—farmer and dairy breeder

Eugene C. Wittmeyer—educator, researcher, and horticulturist

1989 Louis Bromfield—author and conservationist

James E. Dougan—educator and vocational agriculture leader

Wilbur A. Gould—educator and food processing leader

Fred H. Johnson—beef cattle breeder and leader

1990 George G. Greenleaf—agriculture leader and consultant

Edward Huber—inventor and industrialist

Rueben R. Jones—dairy farmer, conservationist

Homer C. Price—educator, leader, and horticulturist

1991 Roy Battles—agricultural media and public relations leader

Shirley A. Brooks—educator and research leader

Ralph Grimshaw—author and sheep specialist

Oscar Share—agriculture leader and feeder calf marketer

1992 Eugene V. Endres—"Rose Man" of Ohio, promoter of the floriculture industry

George Gist, Jr.—former director of the Ohio Cooperative Extension Service

Dr. Berlin W. Kagy—leader in the development of the artificial insemination industry, bred the first cow by artificial insemination

William E. Krauss—agricultural research administrator

1993 Floyd Heft—soil and water conservationist

Earl Poling—promoter of the Ohio dairy farming industry

Dr. James Utzinger—founder and director of the Ohio Home Horticulture Center

Merlin D. Woodruff—auctioneer

1994 Bob Evans—businessman and environmentalist

Robert Gottesman—leader in the Ohio wine industry

William J. Richards—innovator in crop residue management and producing crops without plowing

Dean W. Simeral—legislative representative for the Ohio Farm Bureau Federation

1995 Clarence Durban—conservationist

Clifton Kerns Elliott—marketer for livestock producers, cooperative and independent markets and the packing industry

William D. Fulton—innovator in the fruit and vegetable industry

George W. Smidley—progressive farmer, businessman and inventor

1996 Carl S. Akey—livestock feed industry entrepreneur

Richard Dawson—pork industry leader

Freeman S. Hewlett—educator and horticulturist

J. Gordon Riel—cooperative leader

1997 Arnett J. Gordin—farmer and humanitarian

G. Edwin "Ed" Johnson—agricultural communicator

C. William Swank—leader and spokesman for agriculture

Vernon L. Tharp—DVM veterinarian and educator

1998 Richard H. L. Chichester III—animal geneticist

Edward Oxley Elliott—livestock marketer and restaurant entrepreneur

George R. Johnson—educator and animal scientist

Douglas J. Michael—potato grower

1999 Vernon R. Cahill—educator and meat specialist

Ralph Cobey—engineer and farm equipment dealer

Pat Leimbach—author and public speaker

James Patterson—fruit grower and organizational leader

2000 James F. Cavanaugh—dairy industry leader

Charles Ingraham—agricultural economist

Robert E. Jacobson—dairy marketing specialist and educator

Robert D. Scherer—agricultural advocate

2001 Richard Anderson—agribusiness, retail, processing and manufacturing

Gene Isler—pork breeder and educator

Mark List—agricultural public servant

John Mount—agricultural educator

OHIO WINE PRODUCERS HALL OF FAME

Nicholas Longworth—the "father of Ohio wine" he started Ohio's wine industry and in 1842 created America's first champagne called "Sparkling Catawba." Due largely to his efforts by 1860 one third of the wine produced in the United States came from Ohio.

Robert G. Gottesman—his purchase of Meier's Wine Cellars in Cincinnati as well as Sandusky's Firelands Winery and Mon Ami Wine Cellars in Port Clinton are credited with helping to bring about a renaissance in Ohio winemaking. In 1994 he was the first member of the Ohio wine making industry to be inducted into the Ohio Agricultural Hall of Fame.

James F. Gallander—an instructor at OSU's Ohio Agricultural Research and Development Center in Wooster, he has promoted the Ohio wine industry in both research, teaching and at wine industry conferences.

Dr. Garth Cahoon—assistant Chair of the Department of Horticulture at the Ohio Agricultural Research and Development Center in Wooster, he has been a strong supporter for the Ohio wine industry.

Ag Research

The Ohio Agricultural Research and Development Center (OARDC) is responsible for conducting basic and applied research in agriculture, home economics, natural resources, and related fields. It also has the responsibility of helping train Ohio State University graduate students in these fields.

It has its beginnings in 1862 when President Abraham Lincoln signed the Land Grant College Act proposed by Justin S. Morrill of Vermont. Each state would be given an amount of land that they could sell to provide funds for establishment of an Agricultural and Mechanical College. In 1868, Ohio accepted the provisions of the Morrill Act. The state received 630,000 acres of land script, which sold at an average of 54 cents per acre for a total of $340,894.70. In 1870, The Ohio Agricultural and Mechanical College was established on the "Neil Farm" north of Columbus, Ohio.

In 1878, the name was changed to The Ohio State University and the educational emphasis was toward a liberal arts education rather than agricultural and mechanical arts. This alienated the agricultural community within the state, and many boycotted the university. In 1882, an attempt was made to heal this rift with the establishment of an agricultural experiment station at the university.

The new experiment station (OAES) was incorporated with the university farm and the two agriculture professors, W. R. Lazenby and Norton S. Townshend, divided their time between classroom duties and directing research. The budget was a meager $3,000 per year. The work went slowly and was often in conflict with the OSU farm, which produced food for the college dorms. Moreover, the city of Columbus dug sewers through the plots, paved roads around two sides of the farm, and the river flooded the area each spring.

The only good farm foreman the station had found, Charles Thorne, quit to become editor of *Farm and Fireside Magazine* in Springfield, Ohio. From this position as editor, Thorne launched a vigorous campaign to separate the experiment station from the university and also to convince the university to offer more agricultural and mechanical courses rather than a liberal arts curriculum.

Since many land grant universities had moved to liberal arts institutions and away from the agricultural and mechanical arts, the U.S. Congress passed The Hatch Act of 1887, which provided funds for states to establish an agricultural experiment station under separate federal funding and to provide $15,000 annually for continued support. Dissatisfaction with the OAES's work had already caused a separate board of control to be named, and with the acceptance of the Hatch Act funds, the board in 1887 hired back Charles Thorne as the first full-time director. At Thorne's urging, the board received permission from the Ohio General Assembly to relocate the station by open bids from each county in the state. Warren, Clark, and Wayne counties submitted bids, and Wayne County's bid of $85,000 in monies and land was accepted as the high bid.

In 1892, the Ohio Agricultural Experiment Station moved to Wayne County. The station took possession of 470 acres of farmland just south of the town of Wooster. The bulk of the land was composed of the "Rice Farms" established by Barnhart and Simon Rice in 1822. Both of the original farm houses are still on campus and are historical landmarks.

Over the next three decades, Director Thorne supervised the growth of the station both physically and scientifically. The sandstone building complex on central campus was constructed, the Administration Building being dedicated in 1897. A large dairy barn was built and 26 miles of field tile were laid to prepare land for the Wooster test plots. These plots, hundreds of one-tenth acre fields, were to be used by Thorne and his staff to illustrate—for both the farmers of Ohio and the entire Midwest—how to bring old, farmed-out land back to maximum productivity. This work was to make Thorne famous throughout the country. The added work of the station staff in areas of pest control, animal nutrition and animal husbandry would make the station known worldwide.

In 1903, Director Thorne hired L.H. Goddard of Washington Court House, who set up the Department of Cooperative Experimentation at the research station. The following year the university hired A.B. Graham of Springfield, Ohio, to become the first director of Agricultural Extension. Graham and Goddard would map out the Ohio Cooperative Extension Service. Graham also brought with him his boys and girls clubs from Springfield, and these would evolve into the 4-H clubs of today.

Director Thorne retired in 1921 with a worldwide reputation as an agronomist and left behind a solid, well-operating agricultural experiment station with a similar reputation. That same year, Dr. C.G. Williams became the station's second director. Under his guidance, departments of agricultural engineering and home economics were established in 1926. Williams, also an agronomist, became an expert in breeding and the culture of wheat, oats and corn. Many new varieties, such as Trumbull, Gladstone, and Portage, were developed under his directorship. The station focused on the problems of mechanized farming and the disappearance of abundant farm labor.

Williams retired in 1937 and was succeeded by Edmund Secrest, a station forester. Director Secrest had been at the station since 1905 and developed most of the re-forestation programs in the state. He also developed the Wooster Arboretum (later named the Secrest Arboretum) into one of the best long-term plant repositories in the nation. Secrest was successful in obtaining funding and plans for building expansion of the station, which continued into the 1950s. During this period, the emergence of the high-tech laboratory brought investigations of many problems from the field inside to the laboratory bench. This has continued to the present day.

In 1948, Leo L. Rummell was named both dean of the College of Agriculture at The Ohio State University and director of the Ohio Agricultural Experiment Station at Wooster. Thus the directorship was transferred from Wooster back to the university at Columbus. Rummell had worked for Thorne as an editor in 1915-1917, and left the station's employ to become editor of the *Ohio Farmer* and a consultant in the emerging Ohio food industry. Rummell united the departments in the college of agriculture and the departments at the experiment station at the academic level, with the department chairman at Columbus and an associate chairman at Wooster. The funding for the college and the experiment station remained separate as both state and federal line items in their respective budgets. The OAES continued

LOSS OF STATE SOIL BLAMED ON SOD-BUSTERS

During the 1990s former state representative Jim Buchy occasionally got blamed for "dirty" politics. Four times the Greenville Republican introduced a bill in the Ohio General Assembly to designate the Miamian soil series as the official state soil. Four times his soil bill was plowed under in the House Agriculture and Natural Resource Committee.

Buchy claimed that the agriculturally-productive Miamian series was representative of Ohio, even though it is the fourth most common soil among the 475 different soil types in the state. Miamian soils spread over 750,000 acres, nearly all of it prime farmland in a 22–county region of Southwestern Ohio. It is named after the Native American nation that once thrived in the region.

Ohio's failure to dedicate a state soil distresses dirt devotees, who claim that such a designation would focus more attention on agriculture, land preservation, and soil conservation. Although pundits and detractors have jeered the "sod" proposal as frivolous, few of them mocked legislators when they adopted a state snake (*black racer*), state fossil (*trilobite*), state insect (*ladybug*), and state rock song (*"Hang on Sloopy"*). Fifteen states, including West Virginia and Michigan, have an official state soil.

to expand under the direction of Dr. Rummell until he retired in 1959.

Many professors, under Rummell, now divided their efforts between research, teaching and extension duties, with split appointments in each area. In 1948, with Rummell's appointment, Dr. William E. Krauss was appointed the first associate director of the experiment station, a post he would hold until 1969.

In 1960, Dr. Roy M. Kottman became the fifth full-time director of the OAES, replacing Rummell. Kottman would soon be named director of extension, thus becoming the first person to administer all three branches of the agricultural effort in the state—teaching, research, and extension. The OAES expanded rapidly with several new buildings, including Gerlaugh Hall (Animal, Dairy and Poultry sciences) in 1964, the 1,000-seat Fisher Auditorium in 1968, and Selby Hall (Plant Pathology, Electron Microscopy and Environmental Science) in 1972. Farming became a large agri-business during the Kottman era, and the station worked to solve problems and formulate advice to these areas.

In 1965, Kottman changed the name of the station from the Ohio Agricultural Experiment Station to the Ohio Agricultural Research and Development Center. In 1969, with the retirement of Dr. Krauss as associate director, Dr. James M. Beattie was appointed associate director. He was succeeded by Dr. Clive W. Donoho Jr. in 1973. Donoho would serve as associate director until 1982. In 1981, Governor James Rhodes signed legislation that merged the research center with Ohio State University. The merger took place officially in 1982, 100 years after the establishment of the station.

The center continued its primary mission of research targeted at better food and fiber production, environmental and water quality issues for both rural and urban populations, and continued emphasis on new, improved and safer products for use in the agricultural endeavors of both the state of Ohio and the world community.

The OARDC professional staff includes about 290 scientists, including 200 faculty members in Columbus on the main campus of The Ohio State University who devote part of their time to center research. About 400 projects are conducted by research workers in a number of scientific areas, including agricultural economics and rural sociology, agricultural engineering, agronomy (crops and soils), dairy science, entomology (insects), food animal health (diseases of livestock), nutrition, forestry, home economics, horticulture, natural resources, and plant diseases.

The Laboratory for Environmental Studies at Wooster coordinates environmental research and initiates additional studies on pollution and improvement of the environment. The U.S. Department of Agriculture has major research units at OARDC, including a Soft Wheat Quality Laboratory, Horticultural Insects Laboratory, and a prime engineering group probing into patterns of spray particle distribution on various crops.

In addition to the extensive research facilities on the Wooster campus, a number of attractions have proven popular with visitors. The 85-acre Secrest Arboretum, established in 1908, features collections of Taxus (yews), conifer trees (including the Dawn redwood planting), the Ollie Diller Holly Display, the John Ford Azalea Allee, the Rhododendron Display Garden, the collection of flowering crabapples, the shade tree evaluation plot, and the recently developed juniper and shrub evaluation plot. A formal rose garden, "The Garden of Legend and Romance" contains more than 1,500 plants representing 485 varieties of old roses.

Located near Secrest Arboretum on Williams Road, the rose garden was established in 1970 as a memorial to the late rosarian Michael H. Horvath. Thousands of people visit the center annually for field days, special events, or guided tours to learn about the current research efforts. The OARDC grounds are open to the public for self-guided tours during daylight hours seven days a week.

Source: The Ohio Agricultural Research and Development Center

Across the Fields—Site-Specific Research Laboratories of the Ohio Agricultural Research and Development Center

❏ Eastern Ohio Resource Development Center

EORDC was created to increase the agricultural income from the hills of eastern Ohio by making use of its vast natural resources. Unproductive land was to be revived for pasture and timber; gas, oil and coal energy; and a network of transportation systems to move the raw materials and finished products to market. In 1966 the Union Carbide Corporation and the Baker-Noon Coal Company donated an additional 1,325 acres of strip-mined land to the original 728-acre EORDC.

❏ Grape Research Branch

This 30-acre facility is used for horticultural research consisting of experiments on juice, wine, and table grape cultivars, rootstock-scion interactions, chemical growth regulators, nutrition, and general cultural practices. Entomologists evaluate methods of insect control, while plant pathologists study disease detection and control practices for grapes.

❏ Jackson Branch

Horticulturists have conducted cultivar trials and tests with apples, peaches, strawberry, and thornless blackberries on this area's 502 acres of rolling pastures and lowland along Little Salt Creek in southeastern Ohio near Jackson.

❏ Mahoning County Experiment Farm

This 275-acre research farm located at the edge of Canfield is the only remaining county farm that existed before 1950. The primary research here includes variety trials of wheat, oats, and forages plus hybrid corn performance trials. An interdisciplinary study of lactating dairy cows is being administered by dairy scientists. Long-term research includes Scotch pine, Douglas fir, and spruce plantings used as seed sources for Christmas tree plantings on selected sites and in different soil types.

❏ Muck Crops Branch

This branch is the smallest and oldest of the state-owned branches of the Ohio Agricultural Research and Development Center. Leafy vegetables and other crops such as radishes, carrots, onions, potatoes, and parsley make up most of what is grown on muck soils. Research in controlling disease and insect problems is conducted here.

❏ North Appalachian Experimental Watershed

OARDC scientists at this facility study the storage and movement of water, sediments, chemicals, and animal wastes within a watershed. Agronomists study soil and water conservation, tillage systems, and soil properties. Significant contributions to the body of knowledge regarding cattle feedlot run-off control and the non-point pollution potential of beef cow herds pastured at different stocking rates, varied levels of fertilizer application, and winter pasture management systems have been made here as well.

❏ Northwestern Branch

The majority of research at this 247-acre facility revolves around the agronomic crops of corn, soybeans, wheat, oats, sugarbeets, forages, and canola. OARDC agronomists evaluate varieties, herbicides, crop management and rotation, tillage methods, water quality, and soil fertility.

❏ Overlook Farm

Fruit production has remained the mainstay of research at Overlook Farm since its inception. Tree fruits, brambles, blueberries, and grapes are under continuous evaluation. Tree fruit research includes cultivar and rootstock evaluation, plant density, trickle irrigation methods, and raised bed plantings.

❏ Pomerene Forest Laboratory

These 227-acres of Coshocton County were donated to the OARDC by Warner and Walter Pomerene in 1971. Major research projects here focus mainly on forestry. Plant pathologists study production of plantation-grown Christmas trees, selection and breeding of forest tree species, and

the use of legumes as a nitrogen source in forest plantings.

◗ Southern Branch

This 275-acre farm in Brown County is the site of much agronomy, animal science, and horticulture research. Agronomists and horticulturists pursue the study of canola production, wheat and oats, apple rootstock, and the productivity of White Riesling grapes. Beef heifer nutrition and reproduction research focusing on feeder calves is conducted as well.

◗ Vegetable Crops Branch

Tomatoes are the primary crop at this branch, and the tomato breeding research program has resulted in a number of cultivars being released to Ohio's commercial tomato growers that increased yields and improved fruit quality.

◗ Western Branch

The Western Branch consists of 428 acres of highly-productive Miami, Celina, Crosby, and Kokomo soils that are widespread throughout the southern portion of west-central Ohio. The current agronomic research program features corn and soybeans. Experiments include variety evaluation, fertility studies, crop rotations, breeding programs, tillage, and weed control studies.

Source: The Ohio Agricultural Research and Development Center

---

4 - H

"I pledge my head to clearer thinking, my heart to greater loyalty, my hands to larger service and my health to better living for my club, my community, my country and my world."

This simple pledge is spoken by thousands of Ohio youngsters throughout the year. From Lake Erie to the Ohio River and across America, it vocalizes the purpose of 4-H to prepare young people to become productive adult citizens through hands-on learning experiences. Through 4-H, young people build self-esteem, cultivate decision-making and interpersonal skills and learn responsibility.

The 4-H movement was born in Ohio on January 15, 1902 in Clark County. There, Springfield Township school superintendent A.B. Graham organized 30 youths into what became known as the Boys' and Girls' Agricultural Club. Its goal, improve rural life with hands-on education. Topics included harvesting corn, planting a garden, testing soil samples, tying knots in rope and identifying natural wildlife such as weeds and insects. The successful program was aided by The Ohio State University's Agricultural Experiment Station and its College of Agriculture to help the club's research. Soon, agricultural clubs were being established throughout Ohio and by 1905 there were over 2,000 youths participating in 16 counties. Since that time the

---

SEEDING OHIO'S NURSERY INDUSTRY

Ohio's nursery industry was born in the 1850s on Fairport-Nursery Road, where Storrs & Harrison had 300,000 plants growing on 1,200 acres of Lake County's superior sandy loam. From this single root sprang dozens of "pocket nurseries," so called because they were started with the seedlings that Storrs & Harrison employees sneaked home in their pockets. Storrs & Harrison is gone, but the county is still a major wholesale supplier of nursery stock for the landscape trade, and there are dozens of family-owned fruit farms and farm markets. Depending on the season, you can pick your own berries, cherries, apples, and grapes. Watch for the roadside signs, or check the advertisements in local newspapers.

OHIO'S NATIONAL AGRICULTURAL STANDINGS

One
Swiss cheese

Two
Livestock slaughter plants; egg production; milk sherbert

Three
Fresh tomatoes; processed tomatoes; sheep farms

Four
Creamed cottage cheese; cottage cheese curd; maple syrup; hog farms

Five
Sweet corn; dairy farms

Six
Corn for grain; winter wheat; soybeans; processed cucumbers; chickens, sold

Seven
Tobacco; ice cream

Eight
Oats; total processed vegetables; grapes; number of farms

Nine
Strawberries; hog and pig production

Ten
Onions, storage; hog and pig inventory; milk cow inventory; all cheese (excluding cottage); fertilizer consumption

Eleven
Apples; turkeys; milk

Twelve
Corn for silage; sugar beets; sheep and lamb production; cattle farms

Thirteen
Sheep and lambs, slaughtered; wool

Fourteen
Sheep and lamb inventory; hogs, slaughtered

Fifteen
Calves slaughtered

Sources: Ohio Department of Agriculture, Ohio Agricultural Statistics Service; U.S. Department of Agriculture

4-H has spread nationwide to all fifty states. Today, Ohio's 4-H program is operated under the auspices of the Ohio Cooperative Extension Service at The Ohio State University.

The image of a 4-H club centered around cows and cooking is fast becoming passé. No longer confined to the farming community, it extends to suburbs and cities throughout America. More often than not, today's 4-H member is learning about computers, model rocketry, consumer skills, money management, health and nutrition. Educational experiences are as likely to take place in an inner city community center or middle school classroom as they are in a home or barn. And members are no longer just the rural offspring of the state's citizens. They may be more comfortable riding a city bus than sitting astride a horse.

OCES

The Ohio Cooperative Extension Service (OCES) is dedicated to enhancing agriculture, conserving natural resources, and improving quality of life for all Ohio citizens by linking the research and resources of The Ohio State University with the needs and concerns of Ohio's rural and urban citizens, communities, and organizations. A major component of Ohio State's College of Agriculture, OCES has both local and statewide educational programs with faculty and staff in county and district offices serving all of Ohio. The Extension disseminates research finding and technical information through timely teaching and counseling, group meetings, practical demonstrations, workshops, and short courses. It reaches all corners of Ohio with print and electronic media in the form of instructional bulletins and fact sheets, newsletters, radio and television programs, and computer information sources.

The OCES is a unique achievement in education—a partnership of Ohioans, their county governments, Ohio State University, and the federal government. County extension agents and district specialists provide a dynamic educational link with all these systems. OCES programs are in four major areas: agriculture, home economics, community and natural resource development, and 4-H and youth development.

Source: Ohio Cooperative Extension Service, OSU

ANOTHER OHIO FIRST: EAT MY DUST

In 1921, J.S. Houser, an entomologist at what is now the Ohio Agricultural Research and Development Center, recruited an aviator from Dayton's McCook Field to conduct the world's first crop dusting experiment. When Lt. J.A. Macready dropped lead arsenate from a modified Curtiss biplane onto a catalpa grove near Troy, sphinx moth caterpillars died by the millions. The *National Geographic* reported the successful "airplane dusting," and farmers had a new weapon for waging wars on insects: aerial application of pesticides.

Ohio: a transportation profile

The average Ohioian will drive about 500,000 miles in a 50-year period; this is equivalent to 80 round trips between New York and Los Angeles.

130,000 miles of highways

42,000 bridges

148 roadside rest areas

13 travel information centers

3,000 miles of bicycle paths.

1,000 airports and heliports

6,000 miles of railroad track

4,000 public transport vehicles

Total Public Road Length
—116,995

Rural area Interstate
—829

Urban Interstate
—3,794

Local roads, rural
—58,898

Local roads, urban
—23,368

Interstate highways
—1,572.07 total miles in Ohio
(includes the 241.20 miles of the Ohio
Turnpike)
State system
—17,970.13

County roads
—29,199.4

Township roads
—40,460.85

Municipal streets
—24,484.87

State park roads
—2,500

National park roads
—6.00

U.S. Forest Service roads
—25.20

Total roads
in Ohio
—116,218.81

Number of deer killed by vehicles
(and average insurance claim)
—27,000 ($2,000)

Linndale, a northeast village of 117 people and
1.5 miles of roadway, wrote over 5,000 traffic
citations in 2002; the village collected
$419,500 in fines and fees, which covered half
its government operations.

Ohio drivers who have work commutes
of 60 minutes or more—252,726

Ohioans who commute to work
by cab—4,815

The average Ohioan drives 9,847 miles a year,
uses 438 gallons of gasoline, gets 16.4 miles
per gallon, and spends 21.7 minutes getting
to work.

Sources: Ohio Department
of Transportation; Ohio Division of Wildlife;
Morgan Quitno Corporation; the Plain Dealer

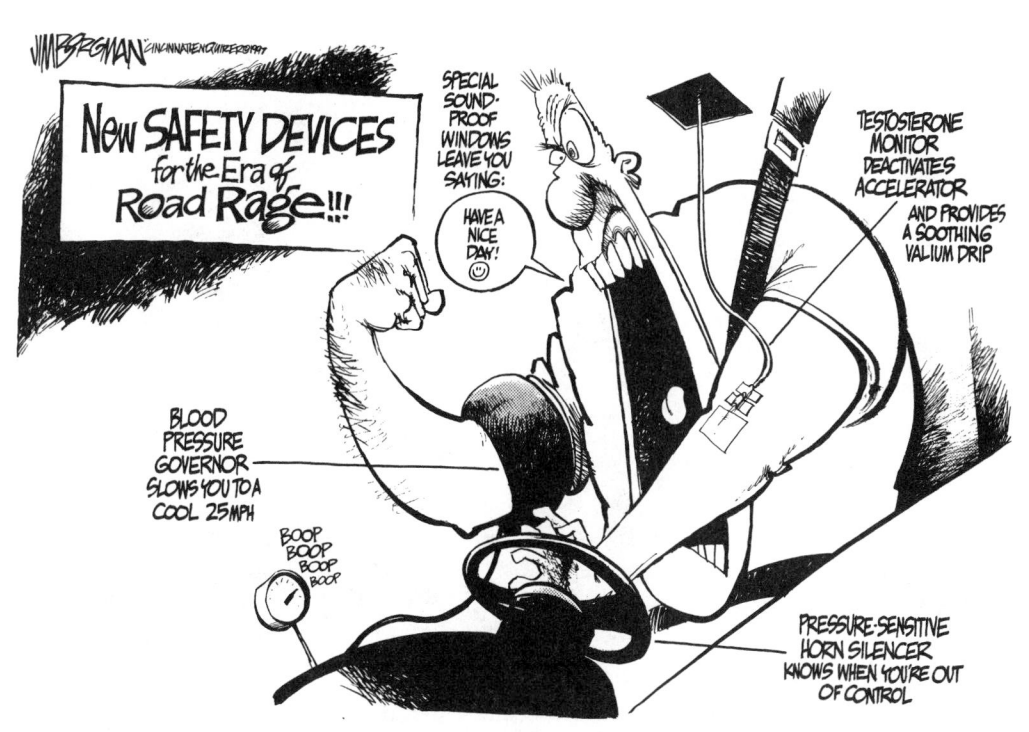

New SAFETY DEVICES for the Era of Road Rage!!!

SPECIAL SOUND-PROOF WINDOWS LEAVE YOU SAYING:

HAVE A NICE DAY!

TESTOSTERONE MONITOR DEACTIVATES ACCELERATOR AND PROVIDES A SOOTHING VALIUM DRIP

BLOOD PRESSURE GOVERNOR SLOWS YOU TO A COOL 25 MPH

BOOP BOOP BOOP BOOP

PRESSURE-SENSITIVE HORN SILENCER KNOWS WHEN YOU'RE OUT OF CONTROL

Ohio's geographic location puts 63% of the nation's manufacturing within 600 miles of the state's boarders. Since half of the Canadian market is within the same range, Ohio has easy access to a larger market than any other state.

Ohio is able to exploit this advantage because of its integrated transportation system: the 9th largest highway network of any state (and the fifth highest volume of traffic), the fifth largest interstate system, and the second largest number of bridges. The state has more railroad track per mile than any other state, and 700 miles of navigable waterways. Sixty percent of the nation's households lie within 600 miles of Ohio.

In 1882 the first Ohio Highway Commission determined that public highways would be better left to local governments, rather than the state. It wasn't until 1904 that the Ohio Legislature created the State Highway Department with a purpose defined as education. It was to study the physical makeup of the state's highways. By 1908 there were 10,649 cars and trucks registered in the state, and the department determined that the state should take the lead in planning the state's "main market roads." Two years later, the state took responsibility for 9,000 miles of roads (currently the state is directly responsible for 19,297 miles of roads). To help pay for the state system, a two-cent per gallon gasoline tax was enacted in 1925. In addition to the highways, the Ohio Department of Transportation is responsible for coordinating the state's entire transportation network.

HONEY? TALK LOUDER... YOU'RE BREAKING UP.

JIM BORGMAN CINCINNATI ENQUIRER © 2001

The genre of explicit driver-ed films began in 1950s Cleveland when photography hobbyist Richard Wayman began taking photographs of traffic fatalities. His graphic shock-cinema became such genre staples as Wheels of Tragedy *and* Mechanized Death, *used to scare the bejesus out of two generations of high school students. In 2002, the Ohio Department of Public Safety released an updated—and graphic—version of Wayman's 1959 original,* Signal 30, *this one filmed by the Highway Patrol, proving that inundation is the sincerest form of flattery.*

The responsibility of maintaining this system is divided among municipalities, counties, and townships, as well as the state and federal government, i.e., the Ohio Turnpike Commission, Ohio Department of Natural Resources, U.S. Forest Service, U.S. Department of Agriculture, and the National Park Service. Coordination of the entire system statewide is the responsibility of the Ohio Department of Transportation.

In 1991 the federal government called for the development of a National Highway System. Ohio contains 4,302 miles of the 163,000 mile system. A major part of this is the five interstate highways that bisect the state. Formed in 1944 as part of the Eisenhower National System of Interstate and Defense Highways, the funding for building the highways came from the Federal Aid Highway Act of 1956, paid for by Federal taxes on motor fuel and automotive products. While the first sections of interstate in Ohio were built in 1947 in Cincinnati and Cleveland, the majority of the construction program began in 1953 and was completed by 1968. In all, the state's original interstate system consisted of 549 separate projects designed to last 30 years.

Roads are classified based upon the type of service they provide. While this is not an exact science, streets and highways provide primarily different types of service. Therefore, they are part of an interconnected network and can be ranked accord-ingly. We do this intuitively. We know the difference between a "country road" and an "interstate." We know to use the "freeway" rather than the "local street" to get across town. We prefer to live on a "neighborhood street" rather than a "main thoroughfare." But classification can be difficult, confusing, and contradictory. "Expressways" may or may not charge a toll. "Freeways," "parkways," "interstates," "expressways," and even main highways may all mean the same thing, or something different.

Ohio's Functional Classification System for highways and roads is an attempt to group streets and highways based upon the service they provide. While it is not possible to do this exactly, it does provide guidelines for classifying and ranking the state's highway system. Arterials provide the most mobility through areas. Travel speeds and distances are the greatest on these types of highways. The highest classes of arterials—interstates and freeways—are limited access, so as to allow for the free flow of traffic. Access to places is the primary function of locals. Speeds, volumes of traffic, and distances on these are generally low, and through traffic discouraged. Between arterials and locals are the collectors. Collecting traffic from the locals and distributing it to the arterials is their primary function.

Source: ODOT

Ohio Highway System

Total Public Road Length	117,268

By Type

Rural	
Interstate	830
Other Principal Arterial	2,238
Minor Arterial	2,831
Major Collector	11,889
Minor Collector	6,742
Local	59,136
Urban	
Interstate	743
Other Freeways and Expressways	394
Other Principal Arterial	1,976
Minor Arterial	3,591
Collector	3,481
Local	23,417

By Owner

Rural	
State Highway	15,270
County	26,832
Town, Township, Municipal	38,120
Other	3,178
Federal	265
Total	83,665
Urban	
State Highway	4,024
County	2,338
Town, Township, Municipal	27,173
Other Jurisdictions	63
Federal Agency	5
Total	33,603

By Lane Miles

Rural	
Interstate	3,580
Other Principal Arterial	6,571
Minor Arterial	5,880
Major Collector	24,165
Minor Collector	13,485
Local	118,272
Total	171,953
Urban	
Interstate	4,010
Other Freeways/Expressways	1,664
Other Principal Arterial	6,512
Minor Arterial	9,956
Collector	8,513
Local	46,834
Total	77,489

Ohio's Daily Vehicle Miles Traveled

Year	Miles
1970	150,463
1971	167,263
1972	173,986
1973	178,511
1974	172,833
1975	175,710
1976	183,614
1977	192,005
1978	197,340
1979	N/A
1980	196,721
1981	196,512
1982	196,579
1983	200,589
1984	204,635
1985	206,984
1986	211,648
1987	216,843
1988	224,014
1989	231,288
1990	250,146
1991	254,799
1992	260,167
1993	263,472
1994	269,036
1995	276,132
1996	281,668
1997	289,594

Changes in Daily Vehicle Miles

1970-1997	86.75%
1980-1997	45.69%
1990-1997	14.57%

Average annual increase between 1970-1990
27.68%
Average annual increase between 1990-1997
1.96%

Annual Vehicle Miles Traveled in Ohio

Rural	41,884,000,000
Interstate	10,252,000,000
Other Principal Arterial	8,168,000,000
Minor Arterial	4,893,000,000
Major Collector	9,900,000,000
Minor Collector	2,125,000,000
Local	6,546,000,000
Urban	64,014,000,000
Interstate	19,767,000,000
Other Freeways & Expressways	4,804,000,000
Other Principal Arterial	11,895,000,000
Minor Arterial	11,537,000,000
Collector	4,384,000,000
Local	11,627,000,000
Total	105,898,000,000

Source: ODOT, most recent figures

A half-mile stretch of I-670 that crosses downtown Columbus was set for completion by the end of 2003 —the final half-mile of Ohio's more than 1,500 miles of interstate, first begun nearly 50 years ago. The national system of 42,800 miles is also nearly complete, awaiting final work on I-95 north of Philadelphia, as well as the "Big Dig" I-93 project underneath Boston.

—The Associated Press

10 Barnstorming moments
in Ohio history

1 Present at the disputed creation.

In 1890, John William Lambert spent $3,300 to purchase a stationary three-cylinder gasoline engine from one John Hicks in Cleveland. The local evidence is strong that he built a three-wheeled vehicle in an Ohio City farm implements store. It featured a radiator carrying seven gallons of water, a carburetor of Lambert's design, and a wooden axle. On May 20, 1891, he took an Ohio City druggist for a ride. If this ride occurred—and the evidence is good that it did—then it marks the birth of the nation's first automobile. Its top speed was five miles an hour, and Ohio City also carries the honor of holding the nation's first automotive accident, which occurred when Lambert drove over a stump root, lost control of his vehicle, and ran into a hitching post.

2 The road to good intentions is paved.

When George Bartholemew approached the Bellefontaine City Council and offered to pave the city's roads with the material he called concrete, it was hesitant. The roads were being chewed up by the steel-rimmed wheels of wagons, but concrete? But after George agreed to donate materials and labor, council let him pave, in 1892, an eight-foot section of Bellefontaine street. They also had him post a $5,000 bond that his product would last five years. It did, and it has.

3 Best man.

After James Packard, co-founder of the Packard Electric Company in Warren, Ohio, had his Winton towed several times for repairs, he gave Mr. Winton some suggestions for improvements. "Mr. Packard," said Winton, "if you are so smart, why don't you make a car yourself." He was, and he did. The first Packard, a one-cylinder, chain-driven runabout, hit the Ohio road in 1899 and soon became the industry bellwether for excellence. Its engineering was such that it used—without much fear of contradiction— the slogan "Ask the man who owns one."

4 Olds well that ends well.

Ransom E. Olds, the son of a Geneva, Ohio, blacksmith, built a runabout in 1901 that featured a curved-dash front. By 1904, his company produced 5,000 cars, which made it the leading auto manufacturer in the world. To stay up with demand, Olds improved efficiency by moving his vehicles along on wooden platforms mounted on casters, predicting some of Henry Ford's later techniques. The company's period of intense activity set the tenor for the coming automobile-building boom.

Fast and furious. 5

In 1903, barnstorming Barney Oldfield, of Wauseon, Ohio, became the first mortal to drive a mile a minute. He began his sensational career as a bicycle racer, and his first car—steered by handlebars—belonged to Henry Ford, who advised Barney to be prudent. "I'd rather be dead than broke," Oldfield is supposed to have replied, and his win helped establish the company's reputation. He raced anything with wheels, once driving a sub-minute mile on a farm tractor. By the considerable force of his personality he is credited with single-handedly advancing the growth of the fledgling auto industry, and for a century, his name became synonymous with speed.

Fishers of men. 6

In 1908, the offspring of a Sandusky, Ohio, blacksmith, were captivated with the bizarre notion that Americans would one day drive in bad weather, necessitating an enclosed automotive body, which their fledgling company would build. The auto industry thought otherwise: Americans were fresh air people and would not cloister themselves. By 1927, however, 85 percent of all cars had closed bodies, and the Fisher Brothers—there were six of them in the business—had almost single-handedly effected a major industrial transformation.

A self-starting man. 7

A near-sighted Loudonville farmboy and Ohio State dropout named Charles Kettering effected in 1912 perhaps the single most important automotive invention: the self-starter. It was installed on the 1912 Cadillac and replaced the hand crank, which because of its whimsical kickback instilled apprehension in a strong man's otherwise courageous breast. The crank required, said one critic, "the strength of Samson, the cunning of Ulysses and the speed of Mercury." Boss Kettering's new invention, however, required nothing but a key. It was also the key that opened the door to the mass production of the automobile.

Stop action. 8

In 1914, nation's first traffic light was installed at the corner of East 105th Street and Euclid Avenue in Cleveland. Light was not automatic; a policeman stationed on the corner flipped the lamp from stop to go.

Road warriors. 9

In 1940, the U.S. Army published specifications for a new General Purpose vehicle, or GP. With slight phonetic alteration, it got the Jeep, a vehicle so ubiquitous to military movement that it is claimed you may not legally fight a war without one. It was intended to be a go-anywhere reconnaissance vehicle, able to ford streams, and climb a 45-degree slope. Willys-Overland of Toledo won the contract and delivered 335,531 units. General Dwight Eisenhower declared the Jeep—along with the DC-3, the bazooka, and the atomic bomb—to be the greatest contributors to Allied victory. "The rolling embodiment of the GI," wrote no less an authority than *Rolling Stone*. And so the word 'Jeep' entered into the popular lexicon.

Engine Charlie's contract. 10

"Engine Charlie" Wilson of Minerva, Ohio, became president of GM in 1948 and worked out trail-blazing social contract in which big business conceded generous wages and benefits to unions in return for stability and control. Wilson introduced the cost of living adjustment and pay jumps as reward for increased productivity. As Eisenhower's secretary of defense, he was credited with the phrase, "What is good for General Motors is good for the country," a misquote that became one of the catch-phrases of the 1950s.

Fast company

In 1904, Harry Myers, Dayton, awarded Ohio's first traffic ticket after barreling down West Third Street at 12 miles an hour.

Ohio's Urban Highway System

	Highway Miles			Miles of Roadway per 1,000 Persons	Percent of Total Miles Serving as Freeways	Annual Average Daily Traffic on Freeways	Average Daily Traffic per Freeway Lane
	Interstate	Freeway	Total				
Akron	62	87	1,963	5.0	3.2	60,918	12,026
Canton	13	34	1,543	6.2	2.2	40,957	9,810
Cleveland	176	227	5,530	3.1	4.1	76,169	13,511
Cincinnati	147	176	4,887	4.2	3.6	89,495	16,194
Columbus	115	149	3,425	3.6	4.3	80,044	13,561
Dayton	70	92	3,102	5.2	3.0	62,502	12,308
Hamilton	0	3	431	3.7	0.8	21,987	5,497
Lima	11	11	408	5.8	2.6	35,901	8,495
Lorain-Elyria	33	53	1,027	4.4	5.2	37,724	8,975
Mansfield	0	15	439	5.5	3.3	21,006	5,521
Middletown	14	14	458	4.8	3.0	68,307	11,385
Springfield	2	6	399	4.7	1.6	29,384	7,950
Stubenville-Weirton	0	34	483	4.8	7.0	18,824	4,621
Toledo	67	71	2,120	4.2	3.3	56,794	12,615
Youngstown-Warren	26	46	1,822	4.8	2.5	35,258	8,403

(Urban Highway System: areas of over 50,000 persons in land areas delineated as urbanized by the Bureau of the Census; some may be in neighboring states)
Source: "Highway Statistics 1997" Federal Highway Administration, September 1998;
Ohio Department of Transportation Fact Book, 2001)

Travel Time *(national rank in parenthesis)*

	Cincinnati	Cleveland	Columbus
Percent of Peak Travel Spent in Congestion			
1982	17%	8%	10%
1990	40%	22%	30%
1994	48%	32%	42%
1999	61%	45%	52%
2001	62%	38%	52%
Percentage Point Change			
1982 to 2001	45	30	42
1994 to 2001	12	-2	3
Percent of Daily Travel During Congested Times			
1982	23%	23%	21%
1990	36%	30%	32%
1994	40%	36%	37%
2001	46%	44%	37%
Annual Delay (hours)			
per Person	20 (29)	17 (33)	7 (36)
Percent of Daily Travel in Congestion			
1982	8%	5%	4%
1990	20%	15%	11%
1994	24%	21%	16%
1999	31%	26%	22%
2001	31%	26%	19%
Percent Point Change—1982 to 2001	23 (6)	19 (21)	18 (25)
Percent Point Change—1994 to 2001	7 (12)	3 (51)	6 (20)
Hours Change in Annual Delay			
1982	2	1	2
1990	7	3	8
1994	14	10	17
2000	20	8	17
2001	20	7	17
Percent Point Change—1982 to 2001	18	3	15
Percent Point Change—1994 to 2001	6	-1	0
Cost of Congestion	$525,000,000	$275,000,000	$350,000,000
Delay	$465,000,000	$245,000,000	$315,000,000
Fuel	$60,000,000	$30,000,000	$30,000,000
per Person	$405 (26)	$145 (37)	$335 (31)
Annual Capacity to Increase Required to Prevent Congestion Growth			
Average Annual Vehicle Miles Traveled Increase	2.4%	0.3%	2.7%
Annual Lane Miles Needed			
Freeway	24	4	23
PAS	24	3	16
Annual Occupancy Increase Needed to Prevent Mobility Decline			
Growth in Daily Person Travel	2.4%	0.3%	2.7%
Additional Miles	598,000	83,000	566,000
Additional Trips	66,445	9,220	62,890
Occupancy Level Increase to Maintain 2001 level	1.28	1.25	1.28

I'll have what he's having

A 29-year-old woman was charged with driving on the Ohio Turnpike while breast-feeding her baby. The trial was held in 2003 in the Portage County Municipal Court.

—The Associated Press

Ohio has a mature highway system, much of it built in the 1950s and 1960s with a 30-year life cycle. It has aged prematurely. Suffering from too many vehicles with sections enduring up to six times the traffic volume it was designed to handle, it is in need of constant repair. As any Ohio commuter knows, he or she seems to drive in a perpetual cycle of orange alert as the ubiquitous barrels appear and disappear, only to reappear again.

Traffic congestion in Ohio is growing at a faster rate than the state's highway and transit systems. Over the past 30 years, traffic has grown about 2 percent annually. The result: traffic has doubled while capacity has remained nearly constant. Since 1976, traffic measured in vehicle miles has risen 69.6 percent—27 percent since 1990. Over the same periods, truck traffic has increased 78 percent—42 percent since 1990.

Obviously, most congestion occurs in the state's metropolitan areas. A Texas Transportation Institute study suggested that the average annual delay for Cincinnatians totaled 28 hours per person, with 17 hours for Columbus and 7 for Cleveland. The study estimated the cost of delay at $406 per person in Cincinnati, $340 in Columbus and $149 in Cleveland.

The TTI has also developed an index to track trends in urban traffic congestion. By using an index number to indicate the capacity of local roads to handle the traffic (1 meaning free-flowing traffic throughout the day), any higher number suggests periods of congested traffic. The increase in traffic in Ohio's three major urban areas since 1982 is shown next:

	1982	1987	1992	1999
Cincinnati	0.70	0.80	0.91	1.12
Cleveland	0.68	0.70	0.85	0.99
Columbus	0.63	0.76	0.90	1.05

Other statistics help paint a picture of Ohio congestion. One factor is to look at an area's roadway system in relation to the population it serves. Calculating miles of roads per person in Ohio's major urban areas tell us which metro areas have the most well-developed road systems:

Roads per Person for Ohio's Major Urban Areas

Canton	6.2
Dayton	5.1
Akron	5.0
Youngstown/Warren	4.8
Cincinnati	4.5
Toledo	4.3
Columbus	3.7
Cleveland	3.1

This figure indicates that the Canton area has the state's best developed highway system. Among the nation's major cities, Cincinnati is ranked 28th worst, Columbus 30th, and Cleveland 37th.

Another statistic is percentage of freeways in each urbanized area, and the percentage of total traffic those freeways share:

	Percentage of Traffic Served by Freeways	Percentage of Total Roads That Are Freeways
Columbus	48.2%	4.4%
Cincinnati	47.6%	3.2%
Cleveland	44.7%	3.2%
Akron	40.2%	3.2%
Dayton	35.3%	3.0%
Toledo	32.5%	3.3%
Canton	26.7%	2.1%
Youngstown-Warren	26.7%	2.1%

A third factor is daily miles traveled per freeway lane. This statistic indicates levels of congestion. The TTI believes that anything below 15,000 vehicles per day for each freeway lane indicates free-flowing traffic (at 60 mph). Traffic above that number reduces average speed down to 45 mph, meaning moderate congestion. A level above 17,500 vehicles daily is considered heavy congestion and traffic slows to 38 mph; at 20,000 (and 35 mph) congestion is severe and above 25,000 vehicles, traffic is reduced to an average speed of 32 mph under conditions of extreme congestion. Of the state's urban areas, only Cincinnati had reached the threshold of moderate congestion in the 1999 study.

Daily Vehicle Miles per Freeway Lane

Cincinnati	16,201
Columbus	14,185
Cleveland	13,723
Akron	12,417
Dayton	12,254
Toledo	11,931
Canton	10,051
Youngstown-Warren	8,101

The annual traffic growth rate, indicated by the TTI, was 3.1% for Cincinnati, 2.4% for Columbus, 2.1% for Cleveland. Given these numbers, Cincinnati reached heavy congestion in 2002. Its freeway system will suffer from severe congestion in 2007 and extreme congestion in 2014. Columbus is already at moderate congestion (2001); congestion will be heavy in 2008, severe in 2013, and extreme in 2023. Cleveland will reach moderate congestion by 2004; heavy in 2008, severe in 2013, and extreme in 2023. By way of comparison, the nation's most congested system is in the Los Angeles area and these Ohio cities will become like the LAs of today (at least in measurable traffic congestion): Cincinnati in 2010; Columbus in 2019; and Cleveland in 2022.

While the daily flow in Ohio's major urban areas has reached only low levels of congestion, there are times of the day when parts of the system become severely congested. The Ohio State Department of Transportation (ODOT) estimates that 27.6 percent of the time, the state's freeway system operates under congested conditions, 8.6 percent of the time under stop-and-go conditions.

Evaluated by cause, there are two kinds of congestion—recurring and nonrecurring. Recurring congestion consists of predictable backups at a location that is overcapacity, such

as an interchange. Non-recurring or incident delays are caused by events such as weather, accidents, or construction. It is estimated that 45% of all motorist delays in Ohio's cities are incident delays. Planning efforts, however, focus on locations that create recurring congestion.

A recent study by the American Highway Users Alliance identifying traffic bottlenecks rated Ohio as the third-worse state in the nation with 14. Major bottlenecks were found along I-480 in Cleveland, I-70 in Columbus, and I-75 in Cincinnati and Dayton.

Congestion, however, is not just in urban areas. With lower speeds and fewer passing opportunities, heavy truck traffic—up to 3,000 trucks per day on two-lane highways—can give a motorist the impression of congestion even when volumes of traffic do not exceed moderate levels. Ohio carries the nation's fifth-highest volume of trucks. Much of this is over rural two-lane roads such as U.S. 6, 20, 24, and 30, as well as SR 2.

We build out. We build more access. What was once an access point to a rural area or bedroom community now holds the office space of a mini-downtown. It has become a destination. But while parts of rural interstates have been converted to local use, making it easier to get from point A to point B, they also attract new development. Jobs leave the city core and relocate at freeway interchanges. These areas create an "Edge City" (or at least "Edge Village") where commercial development (with its mixture of retail, offices, and housing) resembles the urban core of several decades ago.

Using the theory that the majority of Ohio workers will not locate more than a 30-minute commute from work, the rise of "Edge Cities" allows many workers to move even farther out, taking the congestion with them. This cycle of "urban sprawl" puts a strain on the country roads and makes rural interstates flow like urban freeways, and the traffic problems often fall onto government agencies lacking the experience and resources to handle them.

For years, I-75 between Cincinnati and Dayton has been morphing into the state's longest urban freeway. At the same time, commuters in the older inner suburbs who once commuted almost exclusively to the downtown,

now find their jobs have moved to the newer suburban office parks. They are commuting away from the urban core, and the 4 p.m. rush hour now runs both ways.

Some would have us believe that Ohio exists in a kind of traffic "free market" system where road usage is governed by something akin to Adam Smith's "invisible hand" and road congestion is self-regulating. When it becomes bad enough, they believe, we'll find other ways to solve the problem, then point to "sprawl" as having improved congestion.

The conventional wisdom is that roads and highways are more efficient when the origins and destinations of travel are spread over larger geographical areas. As traffic congestion is spread out, the thinking goes, it will never reach critical levels because the population density in the newly-developed levels will never reach the mass of the old urban core. But this thinking has allowed us to avoid the hard and expensive problem of developing a real integrated transportation system.

Whether it is more lanes, car pooling, mass transit, or alternative work hours, there are plenty of ideas for solving Ohio's transportation problems. Other suggestions range from more sprawl to charging tolls for the use of "express lanes" during rush hours. Commuters would have a choice of staying in congestion, paying for a less congested lane, or changing their driving habits.

ODOT is aware that Ohio cannot build its way out of congestion. The cost and environmental impacts, such as neighborhood disruption, are too great. At present, 85% of the Department of Transportation budget is devoted to preservation of the highway network. ODOT knows that better control of incident management, traffic monitoring systems, and mass transit all have to be part of the program. How these are addressed will have a major effect on state funding and planning, as well as the habits of the traveling public. Meanwhile, Social Darwinists sit alone in their SUVs, waiting for the *other* driver to take the bus.

—*Michael O'Bryant, with the assistance of ODOT*

47.5% of Ohio drivers receiving or renewing licenses in 2002 made commitments to become organ/tissue donors.

Licensed Drivers

Total	*7,736,115*
by Sex	
Males	3,780,028
Percent Male	48.9
Female	3,956,087
Percent Female	51.1
16	58,971
17	90,466
18	114,800
19	128,874
19 and Under	393,111
20	133,029
21	125,380
22	127,360
23	126,041
24	129,424
20 - 24	641,234
25 - 29	627,665
30 - 34	720,311
35 - 39	782,460
40 - 44	852,629
45 - 49	802,429
50 - 54	737,797
55 - 59	531,921
60 - 64	434,512
65 - 69	363,553
70 - 74	335,357
75 - 79	269,934
80 - 84	161,122
85 and over	82,070
Licensed Drivers to Vehicles Regestered	0.74
Drivers per 1,000 Residents	681
Drivers per 1,000 Residents (driving age)	880

Six-point warning letters	201,514
Twelve-point suspension letters	31,456
Probationary suspension letters	10,968
Driver license suspensions	553,593

Motor Vehicle Registration (2000)

All Motor Vehicles	10,407,479
Private and Commercial	10,323,179
Public Owned	144,297
Automobiles	6,708,706
Private	6,662,157
Public Owned	47,549
Private and Commercial Autos per Capita	0.59
Buses	37,583
Private and Commercial	15,159
Commercial	12,290
School and Other	2,869
Publicly Owned	22,424
Federal	84
State, County, and Municipal	22,340
Trucks	3,720,187
Private and Commercial	3,645,853
Publicly Owned	74,324

Types

Truck Tractors	44,683
Farm Trucks	33,220
Pickups	1,588,069
Vans	995,034
Sport Utilities	837,443
Other Light	18,703
Trailer and Semitrailer Registration	731,913
Private and Commercial	722,271
Commercial Trailers	116,359
Light Farm Trailers, Car Trailers, etc.	495,827
House Trailers	110,085
Publicly Owned	9,642
by Federal Government	127
by State, County, and Municipal Government	9,515

Motorcycles

Private and Commercial	253,842
Publicly Owned	824

Special License Plates	638,521
Personalized	240,567
Reserved (Initial)	131,913
Wildlife	58,029
Lake Erie	49,941
Disability	23,549
Collegiate	19,093
CASA/Ad litem	16,119
Scenic Rivers	10,606
Hall of Fame	4,028
Bald Eagle	8,528

Motor Fuel Use (2000)

	Gallons
Gasoline	5,194,301,000
Highway Use	5,060,358,000
Private and Commercial	4,979,740,000
Public Use	80,618,000
Federal Civilian	5,538,000
State, County, and Municipal	75,080,000
Nonhighway Use	61,226,000
Private and Commercial	57,229,000
Agriculture	14,183,000
Aviation	8,958,000
Industrial and Commercial	8,402,000
Construction	7,422,000
Marine	35,125,000
Miscellaneous	18,264,000
State, County, and Municipal	3,997,000
Losses for Evaporation, Handling	72,717,000
Special Fuel	1,510,523
Total Fuel Use	*6,632,107,000*

Since 1992, the number of Ohioans 85 years old or older with valid driver's licenses has nearly doubled. There are also 127 Ohioans over 100 years old who have valid licenses.

—Ohio Department of Transportation

let me count the ways

Total Workers:
5,307,502

Car, Truck or Van—4,886,661
  Drove Alone—4,392,059
  Carpooled—494,602
    2-person—410,255
    7 or more—4,643

Public Transportation:110,274
  Bus or Trolley Bus—99,481
  Streetcar or Trolley Car—1,498
  Subway or Elevated—3,351
  Railroad—870
  Ferryboat—259
  Taxicab—4,815
Motorcycle—2,369
Bicycle—9,535
Walked—125,882

How Long?
Under 30 Minutes—3,703,651
60 or more Minutes—252,726

When?
12:00 a.m. to 4:59 a.m.—165,876

5:00 a.m. to 5:29 a.m.—138,561
5:30 a.m. to 5:59 a.m.—233,427
6:00 a.m. to 6:29 a.m.—418,394

6:30 a.m. to 6:59 a.m.—567,735
7:00 a.m. to 7:29 a.m.—729,122
7:30 a.m. to 7:59 a.m.—806,468
8:00 a.m. to 8:29 a.m.—518,682

8:30 a.m. to 8:59 a.m.—271,364
9:00 a.m. to 9:59 a.m.—262,742
10:00 a.m. to 10:59 a.m.—114,110
11:00 a.m. to 11:59 a.m.—57,549

12:00 p.m. to 3:59 p.m.—433,530
4:00 p.m. to 11:59 p.m.—443,689

An estimated
one million U.S.
workers commute
regularly to work
by bicycle.

—League
of American Bicyclists

Studying the BLACK BOX DATA RECORDER from CAR CRASHES...

WHAT?! MORE CONSTRUCTION?!
HAND ME MY COFFEE, BERNICE.
STOP FIGHTING, YOU TWO!!
GET IN YOUR OWN LANE, YOU *!@#$%!!
WAS THAT OUR EXIT?!!
DANG, THERE'S THE PHONE!!!
SONUVA-

JIM BORGMAN
CINCINNATI ENQUIRER©1997

Crashes

Crashes	2001	2000
Fatal	1,258	1,240
Injury	94,971	105,543
Property Damage	273,721	278,083
Unknown*	12,763	5,618
Total	387,075	386,122

Injuries		
Incapaciting	11,633	10,856
Non-incapacitating	55,221	60,945
Possible	71,933	94,987
Total Non-Fatal Injuries	138,847	166,788
Total Fatalities	1,379	1,361

Drivers		
Total Drivers in Crashes	620,903	644,284
Drinking Drivers in Crashes	16,698	20,802

Vehicles		
Passenger Cars	467,687	451,076
Sports Utility Vehicle	52,745	30,665
Trucks	126,425	127,897
Tractor Trailer Trucks	13,848	14,264
Motorcycles	4,040	3,534
Public Safety Vehicles	2,751	2,418
Public Transportation	1,709	1,654
Other Motor Vehicles	7,461	21,846
Bicycle (includes pedal cyclist)	2,603	2,613
Pedestrian (includes Skater)	3,561	2,069
Other Non-Motor Vehicles	522	289
Unknown	15,663	3,733
Total Vehicles in Crashes	699,015	662,058

Passengers		
Passengers in Crashes	237,517	238,626

Alcohol-Related Crashes		
fatal	342	320
injury	7,702	9,381
property damage	8,367	10,718
Total	16,794	20,582
Resulting deaths	375	350
Resulting injuries	11,131	14,293
Urban alcohol crashes	13,391	N/A
Urban alcohol fatalities	122	N/A
Urban alcohol injuries	10,093	N/A
Rural alcohol crashes	10,788	N/A
Rural alcohol fatalities	252	N/A
Rural alcohol injuries	8,690	N/A

*Investigation reveals no injury or property damage or damage less than $400
Source: Ohio Department of Highway Safety

Most Common Causes of Fatal Highway Crashes in Ohio

Excessive speed	234
Failure to yield	203
Failure to control vehicle	180
Driving left of center	119
Driving off the road	79
Running a STOP or YIELD sign	61
Driver Inattention	57
Other Driver Error	48
Following another vehicle too closely	39
Ran Red Light	29
Improper Passing	27
Improper Lane Change	12
Improper Turning	10
Stop / Park Illegally	2
Improper Backing	1

Type of Vehicle Involved in Fatal Crashes

Mid-Size Automobile	22.8%
Full-Size Automobile	19.3%
Compact Automobile	18.0%
Pickup Truck	12.5%
Semi-Trailer Truck	6.8%
Motorcycle	5.3%
Sub-Compact Automobile	4.0%
Panel Truck	3.4%
Straight Truck	2.5%

Ten Counties with Lowest Crash Rate

	Crash Rate*	Fatal Crashes
Monroe	18.91	1
Putnam	21.51	10
Columbiana	24.98	11
Champaign	25.33	2
Mercer	25.44	6
Medina	26.55	16
Geauga	26.87	10
Jefferson	26.94	12
Auglaize	27.18	10
Huron	27.27	9

Ten Counties with Highest Crash Rate

	Crash Rate*	Fatal Crashes
Vinton	47.40	2
Noble	46.81	4
Jackson	46.51	9
Muskingum	45.87	15
Hamilton	45.12	52
Gallia	44.61	5
Lucas	44.59	35
Ross	44.11	15
Defiance	43.06	14
Clinton	42.35	5

*Rate per 1000 people

Ten Cities with Lowest Crash Rate

	Rate	Fatal Crashes
Austintown	0.03	0
Blacklick Estates	0.11	0
Boardman	0.13	1
Mineral Ridge	0.26	0
Enon	0.38	0
East Clinton	0.61	0
Brimfield	0.62	0
Franklin Furnace	0.65	1
Neffs	0.88	0
New Washington	1.01	1

Ten Cities with Highest Crash Rate

	Rate	Fatal Crashes
Boston Heights	181.28	1
Cuyahoga Heights	170.28	1
Sheffield	136.32	0
Evendale	134.63	1
Brice	128.57	0
Bratenahl	109.95	1
Kirtland Hills	107.20	0
Lindale	102.56	0
New Rome	100.00	0
Springdale	96.66	0

Crashes by Month

	2001	Fatal 2001	2000	Fatal 2001
January	35,271	82	33,851	82
February	27,053	80	29,323	74
March	30,691	79	27,012	97
April	29,545	95	28,303	86
May	32,850	108	32,286	95
June	31,675	104	31,122	125
July	30,027	144	29,614	110
August	31,821	126	30,697	118
September	29,252	112	32,156	114
October	36,125	113	34,672	125
November	37,969	101	36,056	97
December	34,887	114	41,030	117

Crashes by Day of Week

	Crashes	Injury	Fatal
Sunday	38,659	9,967	178
Monday	55,523	13,361	143
Tuesday	55,493	13,215	152
Wednesday	56,689	13,912	160
Thursday	57,432	14,014	151
Friday	71,924	17,580	233
Saturday	51,355	12,922	241

Busiest interstate interchange in Ohio: Interstate 90 and Fairfield Avenue in Cuyahoga County has the most vehicular traffic in the state—an average of 146,640 vehicles passing through every 24 hours.

Source: Paul Staley, Public Information Officer, ODOT

Death Toll and Rates,* 1940-1998

Year	Annual Death Toll	Annual Travel	Death Rate	Year	Annual Death Toll	Annual Travel	Death Rate
1940	2,070	16,613,000,000	12.46	1970	2,575	55,978,000,000	4.60
1941	2,458	18,221,000,000	13.49	1971	2,381	61,151,000,000	3.90
1942	1,783	15,765,000,000	11.31	1972	2,451	63,497,000,000	3.86
1943	1,331	12,761,000,000	11.31	1973	2,385	65,164,000,000	3.66
1944	1,340	12,171,000,000	10.43	1974	1,900	63,123,000,000	3.01
1945	1,545	13,869,000,000	11.01	1975	1,930	64,149,000,000	2.82
1946	1,823	18,340,000,000	11.14	1976	1,809	67,014,000,000	2.88
1947	1,830	20,022,000,000	9.94	1977	1,873	69,888,000,000	2.68
1948	1,856	22,095,000,000	8.40	1978	2,048	72,113,000,000	2.84
1949	1,716	23,604,000,000	7.27	1979	2,281	73,109,000,000	3.12
1940-49	17,752	173,461,000,000	10.23	1970-79	21,633	655,086,000,000	3.30
1950	1,754	25,129,000,000	6.98	1980	2,033	71,837,000,000	2.93
1951	1,778	26,817,000,000	6.63	1981	1,780	71,774,000,000	2.48
1952	2,013	28,716,000,000	7.01	1982	1,618	70,655,000,000	2.29
1953	2,047	30,690,000,000	6.67	1983	1,585	73,380,000,000	2.16
1954	1,883	31,754,000,000	5.93	1984	1,645	75,114,000,000	2.19
1955	2,047	32,868,000,000	6.31	1985	1,644	75,413,000,000	2.18
1956	2,023	34,581,000,000	5.85	1986	1,673	77,097,000,000	2.17
1957	2,053	35,892,000,000	5.72	1987	1,772	79,107,000,000	2.24
1958	1,817	37,006,000,000	4.91	1988	1,748	81,765,000,000	2.14
1959	1,853	37,971,000,000	4.88	1989	1,772	84,054,000,000	2.11
1950-59	19,295	321,424,000,000	6.00	1980-89	17,270	760,196,000,000	2.27
1960	1,907	38,682,000,000	4.93	1990	1,637	88,197,000,000	1.86
1961	1,679	39,413,000,000	4.26	1991	1,635	93,002,000,000	1.76
1962	1,864	40,086,000,000	4.65	1992	1,440	94,961,000,000	1.52
1963	2,011	42,071,000,000	4.78	1993	1,479	97,522,000,000	1.52
1964	2,108	44,379,000,000	4.75	1994	1,368	97,522,000,000	1.40
1965	2,333	46,754,000,000	4.99	1995	1,357	99,679,000,000	1.36
1966	2,605	48,241,000,000	5.40	1996	1,395	102,809,000,000	1.36
1967	2,533	49,764,000,000	5.09	1997	1,439	104,839,000,000	1.37
1968	2,555	52,789,000,000	4.84	1998	1,423	106,029,000,000	1.34
1969	2,778	55,783,000,000	4.98	1990-98	13,173	884,560,000,000	1.49
1960-69	22,373	457,962,000,000	4.89				

* per 1,000,000 vehicle miles of travel

When stopped by the Ohio State Highway Patrol, drivers have a one-in-ten chance of not being cited.

Ohio State Highway Patrol

Number of Stations	61
Employees	2,548
Sworn officers	1,430 (56%)
per 100,000 residents	13
in Administration	13%
in Field Operations	87%
Nonsworn Employees	1,118
in Administration	18%
in Filed Operations	15%
in Technical Support	25%
other	43%
Nonsworn volunteer (part-time)	160
Officers assigned to respond to calls for service	1,251 (87%)
Calls received	205,327
Officers per call	164

Highway Death Toll

1940-9	1,775—6.36
1950-9	1,930—3.73
1960-9	2,237—3.04
1970-9	2,163—2.05
1980-9	1,727—1.41

The 50-year average death toll on Ohio's highways is 1,900 per year; a 2.58 rate.

Hot Wheels

	Total	Fatal
Motorist in Error		
None	3,861	8
Failure to Yield	49,086	144
Ran Red Light, or Stop Sign	14,785	76
Exceeded Speed Limit	400	22
Unsafe Speed	13,160	208
Improper Turn	9,69	8
Left of Center	5,1061	122
Followed Too Closely/ACDA	84,083	46
Improper Lane Change	21,083	114
Improper Backing	13,861	2
Improper Start	1,943	1
Stopped or Parked Illegally	419	1
Operating in Erratic Manner	5,284	70
Swerving to Avoid	3,155	5
Failure to Control	39,633	171
Vision Obstruction	688	0
Driver Inattention	2,385	27
Fatigue/Asleep	2,385	16
Operating Defective Equipment	3,644	6
Load Shifting/Falling/Spilling	1,939	1
Other Improper Action	3,256	13
Unknown (Motorist)	7,510	45
Subtotal	296,182	1,106
Non-Motorist Error		
None (non-motorist)	283	0
Improper Crossing	896	29
Darting	553	14
Lying and/or Illegally in Roadway	93	11
Failure to Yield Right of Way	303	7
Not Visible (Dark Clothing)	33	1
Inattentive	208	3
Failure to Obey Traffic Signs	192	4
Wrong Side of the Road	94	2
Other	239	0
Unknown	11,483	2
Subtotal	14,377	73
Animal in Error	34,224	6
No Error/Unknown	42,292	73
Total	387,075	1,258

Crashes by Weather Condition

	Total	Fatal
Clear	218,881	717
Cloudy	90,207	363
Rain	47,755	32
Sleet, Hail (Freezing Rain)	2,333	6
Snow	17,942	37
Fog, Smog, Smoke	3,189	32
Severe Crosswinds	358	2
Blowing Sand, Soil, Dirt, Snow	325	1
Other	386	2
Unknown	5,699	7

Crashes by Manner of Collision

	Total	Fatal
Not Collision Between Two Vehicles	117,180	650
Head On	10,139	182
Rear End	102,714	66
Rear to Rear	2,107	0
Backing	14,932	1
Sideswipe, same direction	26,907	15
Sideswipe, passing	7,706	21
Angle	97,750	312
Unknown	7,640	11

Crashes by Light Condition

	Total	Fatal
Daylight	250,595	646
Dawn	8,150	19
Dusk	10,640	32
Dark-Lighted Roadway	54,830	188
Dark-Roadway Not Lighted	54,123	364
Dark-Unknown Roadway Lighting	1,313	1
Glare	157	0
Other	252	0
Unknown	7,015	8

Number of Drinks

160 lb. Male	120 lb. Female	BAC*	
		.10	twelve times as likely to be involved in a fatal crash as nondrinking driver
4		.09	eight times as likely to be involved in a fatal crash
		.08	impaired speed control, braking, lane tracking judgement, attention
	4	.07	two and a half times as likely to be involved in a fatal crash
3		.06	twice as likely to be involved in a fatal crash
	3	.05	impaired traction, coordination, comprehension, divided attention,
		.04	impaired reaction time, and emergency response
2		.03	
	2	.02	
		.01	

* *Blood Alcohol Content*
One Drink—12 ounces of beer, 5 ounces of wine, or 1.5 ounces of 80-proof distilled spirits

"IT WASN'T MY FAULT, OFFISHA..., MY BUDDY HERE WAS DRIVING!"

Alcohol Related Crashes

Year	Crashes	Deaths	Injuries
1990	32,803	623	23,954
1991	27,095	594	27,172
1992	25,156	510	21,340
1993	23,642	435	19,531
1994	23,090	330	19,245
1995	23,456	400	19,270
1996	23,282	386	19,258
1997	24,360	390	19,310
1998	24,179	374	18,783
1999	23,156	394	17,800

Ohio Auto Repair Rates

	(Average Hourly Repair Rate)		
City	1997	2001	Increase
Akron	$30.25	$35.27	16.6%
Canton	$30.00	$35.27	17.6%
Cincinnati	$30.50	$35.78	17.3%
Cleveland	$30.25	$35.71	18.0%
Columbus	$30.25	$36.14	19.5%
Dayton	$30.00	$35.76	19.2%
Toledo	$29.75	$34.37	15.5%
Youngstown	$30.00	$35.00	16.7%
Ohio Average	$30.13	$35.41	17.5%

Ohio DUI Convictions

DUI Convictions Per Driver	Drivers Convicted of DUI
1	539,230
2	157,885
3	64,385
4	28,160
5	12,716
6	5,794
7	2,715
8	1,273
9	623
10	297
11	128
12	59
13	31
14	21
15	14
16	7
17	2
18	1

Auto Insurance Premiums

City	Average
Akron	$850
Athens	$734
Cincinnati	$816
Cleveland	$1,319
Columbus	$830
Dayton	$781
Shaker Heights	$941
Toledo	$880
Youngstown	$1,164
Small Town/Rural	$667

	Ohio Average	U.S. Average	Rank
1996	$617	$785	38
1997	$637	$803	29
1998	$648	$802	40
1999	$646	$783	41
2000	$646	$786	45

Between 1980 and 1999, 59% of the total number of drunk driving convictions were by repeat DUI offenders. Ohio's worst repeat DUI was a 43-year-old Daytonian, Curtis Sears, who in two decades was convicted 19 times. In 2001, he received a four-year sentence. In 1998, a Hillsboro judge sentenced repeat offender Dennis Cayse to live within walking distance of a liquor store or bar.

—The Cincinnati Enquirer

Columbus

I-270 & I71

163 crashes

I-270 & I-70

149 crashes

I-70 & I-71

132 crashes

Cincinnati

I-75 at Mile Marker 3

142 crashes

I-75 at Mile Marker 2

133 crashes

I-75 at Mile Marker 8

125 crashes

I-75 at Mile Marker 1

119 crashes

Lucas County

SR2, Mile Marker 10

138 crashes

Franklin County

I-270, Mile Marker 23

127 crashes

Dayton

I-75, Mile Marker 55

116 crashes

Fast company:
a cautionary compendium
on
speed

Tools of the trade
Radar—280,898 arrests
Laser—127,681
Aircraft—17,464

The leeway
MPH over limits   tickets given
1-9   14,410
10-15   179,536
16-25   154,258
25+   149,925

Average number of tickets given daily
—1,252

Tickets in 65 MPH zone
—161,766

Tickets in 60 MPH zone
—24,233

Tickets in 55 MPH zone
—225,747

Tickets issued
Men—312,394
Women—121,897

Warnings issued
413,195

Who gets most tickets, by age
20-year-olds, 19,027 tickets,
16.84 miles over the limit

Tickets by type of vehicle
Passenger car—315,002
Tractor & semi-trailer trucks—70,818
Vans—4,088

Motorcycles—1,142
Pick-up trucks—34,213
Buses—175

Day when most tickets written
Saturday—76,931
(More than half of all tickets are issued on weekends)

Best time to speed
4 a.m., on a Wednesday,
in the middle of the month

Months when fewest tickets given
January and December

Months when most tickets given
May

Time when most tickets are given
4 p.m.-6 p.m.

Time when fewest tickets are given
2 a.m.-6 a.m.

Most popular excuse:
"I have to go to the bathroom really badly."

Top ten speeding spots, statewide

Milepost	County	Tickets
I-71 & 152	Morrow	2,460
Trnpk & 141	Lorain	1,603
Trnpk & 198	Portage	1,477
I-75 & 64	Montgomery	1,407
Trnpk & 118	Erie	1,247
I-70 &131	Licking	1,206
I-70 & 4	Preble	1,158
I-70 & 170	Guernsey	1,157
Trnpk & 117	Erie	1,142
US30 & 6	Crawford	1.064

Turnpike
Profile

Official name
James W. Shocknessy Ohio Turnpike
Effective date of Ohio Turnpike Act
Sept. 1, 1949
Ohio Turnpike Commission organized
Sept. 8, 1949
Revenue bonds sold to construct turnpike
July 29, 1952
Easternmost 22-mile section of turnpike opened to traffic
December 1, 1954
Remaining 219 miles of turnpike opened to traffic
October 1, 1955

Length of Ohio Turnpike	241.26 miles
Number of lane miles	1,037 miles
Total land area of right of way	9,912.5 acres

Facilities

Interchanges	31
Toll	28
Non-Ttoll	1
Service plazas	16
Maintenance buildings	8
Administration building	1

Number of structures over or under turnpike:

Other highways or Interchanges ramps	399
Railroads	69
Rivers and streams	80
Total	548

Number of employees

Full-time	912
Part-time	313

Number of vehicles using the turnpike

Passenger cars	37,036,000
Commercial vehicles	8,864,000
Total	45,900,000

Percentage of vehicles

Passenger cars	80.7%
Commercial vehicles	19.3%

Number of miles traveled

Passenger cars	1,913,889,000
Commercial vehicles	803,853,000
Total	2,717,742,000

Percentage of miles

Passenger cars	70.4%
Commercial vehicles	29.6%

Toll revenue collected

Passenger cars	$74,710,000
Commercial vehicles	$99,616,000
Total	$174,326,000

Percentage of toll revenue

Passenger cars	42.9%
Commercial vehicles	57.1%

Average miles per turnpike trip

Passenger cars	51.7
Commercial vehicles	90.7

Toll revenue per trip

Passenger cars	$2.02
Commercial vehicles	$11.24

Toll revenue per turnpike mile

Passenger cars	$0.04
Commercial vehicles	$0.12

Activity by Interchange
(number of vehicles in thousands)

No.	Name	2001	1992
1	Westgate	7,118	5,768
13	Bryan-Montpelier	730	791
25	Archbold-Fayette	387	-
24	Wauseon	752	833
39	Delta-Lyons	456	-
52	Toledo Airport-Swanton	1,562	959
59	Maumee-Toledo	4,644	3,858
64	Perrysburg-Toledo	4,185	2,410
71	Stony Ridge-Toledo	6,121	5,148
81	Elmore-Woodville-Gibsonburg	621	-
91	Fremont-Port Clinton	1,728	1,945
110	Sandusky-Bellvue	1,370	-
118	Sandusky-Norwalk	1,815	2,316
135	Vermilion	933	-
142	Lorain County West	2,691	2,193
145	Lorain-Elyria	6,195	5,922
151	North Ridgeville-Cleveland	5,551	4,806
152	North Olmsted-Cleveland	1,888	1,372
161	Stongsville-Cleveland	5,971	4,887
173	Cleveland	5,013	4,144
180	Akron	3,986	3,105
187	Streetsboro	5,825	4,884
193	Ravenna	1,346	-
209	Warren	1,837	2,165
215	Lordstown West	488	-
216	Lordstown East	328	-
218	Niles-Youngstown	7,729	6,345
232	Youngstown	1,442	1,318
234	Youngstown-Poland	1,188	998
238	Eastgate	7,900	6,692

Accidents

	2001	1992
Accidents	2,092	1,755
Ratio per 100 million miles	77.0	78.5
Fatal accidents	13	8
Ratio per 100 million miles	0.5	0.9

Source: Ohio Turnpike Commission, 2001

The Ohio Turnpike was completed in 1955 and was expected to cut driving time across the state by five hours for truckers and three hours for other drivers.

ROEBLING'S MAGNIFICENT BRIDGE: MARVEL OF TWO CENTURIES

In the long and complicated building of one of America's great bridges—the Roebling Suspension Bridge—the patient genius of John Roebling barely outlasted nearly three decades of entrenched interests, political pugnacity, and cross-river rivalry. Looking back across time, the contention seems the harder part. Inventing twisted wire cable to replace the old hemp towropes Roebling had worked with on the building of the Ohio canals, then creating the technology for his new bridge—which did not exist at the time—well, all that seemed mere afterthought.

The hardboiled opposition of real-estate and steamboat interests thwarted Roebling in the mid-1840s, and even after he secured an Ohio charter in 1849, they managed to subvert the bridge's straight alignment, which would have created a magnificent thoroughfare through the heart of both Covington and Cincinnati and across the Ohio River.

Construction finally began in 1856, followed by a financial panic the next year, and Covington defaulted on its bridge bonds. It took a war to get construction started again. With Cincinnati under near-attack by 12,000 Confederates on the hills behind Covington, the Ohioans managed to cross on a pontoon bridge of lashed-together coal barges, and the bridge's necessity was demonstrated beyond any argument.

It was finished in 1866, a year after the war, and its 1,057-foot main span was the longest in the world. There were two enormous cables holding 303 horizontal iron suspenders, which, in turn, held up a roadway made of five inches of pine and three inches of oak. To brace it against crosswinds, wire stays radiated from the tops of the bridge's two towers. Roebling was the first to use these vertical suspenders and diagonal stays, and they became his trademark, next to be seen in his *magnum opus*, the Brooklyn Bridge.

The bridge was finished in December of 1866, and 120,000 people walked across it during the first Sunday of its operation. Pedestrians were charged three cents toll.

Two years later, Roebling returned to show off his creation to a conclave of New Yorkers who were considering his audacious proposal to span the treacherous East River in Brooklyn. The visitors needed little persuading; the Cincinnati bridge sold itself.

Roebling did not live to see his greatest creation. In the early building stages in New York, he crushed his foot in an accident. His resolve had kept him—and his projects—alive before, but it had no effect on tetanus. The Brooklyn Bridge was finished by Robeling's son, Washington.

So the Brooklyn Bridge became known as Roebling's Cincinnati descendant, but as the writer-historian, John Fleischman, pointed out, it had another, even grander one. Three years after Roebling first walked across his Cincinnati bridge, Joseph Strauss was born. The Cincinnatian grew up fascinated by Roebling's bridge, studied civil engineering at the University of Cincinnati, and went out to build bridges himself—over 400 of them. Strauss's *magnum opus* was the grandest of them all, for in 1937 he built the Golden Gate Bridge in San Francisco. Wrote Fleischman: "Strauss designed it, promoted it, and dragged it through 20 years of opposition, delay, and frustration that John Roebling would have recognized immediately as the price of genius."

In Cincinnati in 2001, a paint job was proposed for the suspension bridge; the estimate for the paint was $6 million—over three times the cost of building the bridge itself. When it first opened, it was a marvel of its century. Almost a century and a half later, it's still a marvel.

Ohio defines a bridge as any structure ten feet or more in length on, above, or below a highway.

Bridges
A History

From bridges built by the early settlers to the latest in engineering innovations, fine examples of bridge design and innovative use of materials can be found in Ohio. There are stone bridges on the old National Road; more than 135 covered wooden bridges of many different truss designs, including those still being built in Ashtabula County; examples of a variety of patent designs for wrought iron and steel trusses; and concrete beam and concrete arch structures.

The signing of the Greenville Treaty in 1795 ended the Indian wars in Ohio and resulted in an influx of settlers into the Ohio territory. Overland travel developed from well-used Indian trails, but the need for a road system for the burgeoning population soon became apparent. The first major road-building effort in the Ohio territory was the trail that Congress authorized Ebenezer Zane to build in 1796. Zane's Trace, as the road was known, was the first federally subsidized local construction. The road originally ran from Wheeling, in what is now West Virginia, to Zanesville, Ohio. It eventually passed through Lancaster, Kingston, Chillicothe, and extended as far as Maysville, Kentucky. In 1809, Congress set aside $12,000 for construction of the National Road, which reached Ohio in 1825 and was complete to Columbus by 1833. It reached the Indiana border in 1837. The National Road was the only east-west thoroughfare across Ohio connecting the eastern seaboard with the western frontier. Both covered wooden truss bridges and stone bridges, including the unique "S" bridges, carried travelers on the National Road across Ohio's many rivers.

In addition to the National Road, Ohio was served by a system of roads and bridges built by turnpike companies subsidized by the federal government. The first of these, the Boardman Turnpike Company, was incorporated in 1809. These companies built most of the roads and bridges in Ohio until 1843. Afterward, the Ohio General Assembly authorized county commissioners to provide free turnpikes constructed with funds raised by a tax on land within two miles of the road. These were known as the "Two Mile Turnpikes." Because timber was cheap and readily available, the covered wooden truss was the bridge of choice on these roads. These were built by the thousands from the early 1800s to 1920, the greatest number being built between the 1820s and 1880s.

During the late 18th and early 19th centuries, bridge designers and builders took the first tentative steps toward the construction of metal bridges. The first rational analysis of the stresses in the members of the truss spans came in a book published by Squire Whipple in 1847. The first long span truss of the Whipple type was built across the Ohio River at

Steubenville in 1864. The end posts and all other compression members of this bridge were cast of iron while all tension members were of wrought iron.

Modern bridge building can be said to have begun in 1855 with the development of the Bessemer process of steel making, followed a few years later by the open hearth, or Siemens-Martin, process. As steel replaced wrought iron, the most common type of short span bridge used the riveted built-up plate girder. In response to the growing demand for highway and railroad bridges, large numbers of bridge companies sprang up, many of them in Ohio, making the state a major builder of metal bridges. Many metal truss bridges still found in the state were built by these companies. Three Ohio bridge companies of this time are notable for their designs and technological contributions to bridge engineering and for the number of bridges they built: The King Iron Bridge Company, Cleveland; the Wrought Iron Bridge Company, Canton; and the Champion Bridge Company, Wilmington.

The years following the Civil War saw great activity on the part of Ohio bridge builders who were patenting new designs, such as the bowstring arch. These builders also experimented with designs of cast and wrought iron. The tragic collapse of a railroad bridge in Ashtabula County in 1876 marked the end of this era of large-scale experimentation of bridge design in Ohio.

The latter decades of the 19th century saw the development of the "Good Roads Movement" led by various cyclist groups that focused public attention on the need for better roads and bridges. In response to public demand, hundreds of short span pony truss bridges were built during this period over streams that formerly simply had been forded. In addition to wood and metal bridges, reinforced concrete bridges have been built in Ohio since the late 19th century, when the first reinforced concrete arch in America was built in Cincinnati in 1895.

The first decade of the 20th century was a time of standardization and consolidation in the bridge industry. Ohio's Department of Highways was created in 1904 and its Bureau of Bridges in 1911. This bureau was responsible for writing specifications for a wide range of standard bridge types to ensure uniformity of design and quality. Steel almost totally replaced iron during the early years of this century and pin connections were disappearing in favor of

riveted fastenings that were able to meet the demand of increased loads. The use of reinforced concrete for highway structures increased steadily. It was especially popular for short spans of about 20 feet because it was strong and durable. It was also replacing wood for the flooring in longer span steel structures.

A significant trend in the 1920s was the increased acceptance and use of reinforced concrete for bridge building. A concrete-filled arch could be used in much the same situation as a stone structure with analogous engineering effects. The solid concrete face allowed for decorative treatment such as recessed panels, elaborate railings, and decorative moldings. This decade saw the development and construction of the concrete arch bridge known as the "Rainbow Arch." Twelve of these visually appealing structures are still standing in Ohio.

Despite the economic effects of the Depression, the decade of the 1930s saw a great concern with the aesthetics of bridges. Engineers realized that the malleable characteristics of concrete allowed almost limitless possibilities for decorative treatment and some of the most ornamental bridges in the history of Ohio bridge building were conceived and constructed during this decade. On a more practical level, engineers began to design continuous beam bridges to eliminate deck joints.

During the 1930s, the Ohio Department of Highways became a leader in bridge design largely due to the creativity of its bridge engineers. Maintenance problems, a desire for aesthetics, and the need to use resources efficiently spurred the engineers to pour creativity and intellect into new bridge technology, design, and construction. Some of the most important innovations were the routine use of continuous construction and welded splices. These Departmental bridge engineers designed continuous bridges at about the same time that the instrumental theory of continuous construction was published by Hardy Cross. The concepts in his 1930 paper and their practical application revolutionized bridge design and construction. The desire to eliminate deck joints was the force behind the initial interest in continuous construction. Ohio began a new era in steel bridge construction when the first continuous girder was built in 1931, and only a year later the last non-continuous steel beam bridge was built. The detailed designs were created by the Departmental bridge engineers and the concept readily became

accepted. The first standard drawings were issued in 1939. In order to maintain continuity, the standard drawing incorporated the riveted splice concept, a design which improved the members' strength, stress, and rigidity.

The progress made by Ohio's innovative bridge builders during the 1930s came to a dramatic halt with the beginning of World War II. With the coming of the war the Department of Highways faced severe shortages of most materials; steel, rubber, copper, bituminous materials, and even timber were channeled into the war effort. In addition, the Department faced an acute shortage of personnel, including engineers, many of whom entered the service as engineering officers. Because of these wartime complications, many completed plans were scrapped and designs involving the use of a minimum of critical materials were used. Pavement and drainage structures were redesigned to allow for use of less materials. Wooden bridges were built on secondary highways and several bridges that were obsolete at their original locations were dismantled and used to replace weak or damaged bridges on less traveled highways.

As the war in Europe neared its end, Congress passed the Federal Aid Highway Act of 1944. With this far reaching legislation, Congress authorized $500 million for each of the first three post war years for road and bridge construction. Congress also authorized for the first time the use of federal aid highway funds in urban areas, provided authority for the construction of a secondary road system, and directed to design of a national system of interstate highways. In 1946, contracts in Ohio were awarded for more than $25 million worth of highway construction, as wartime engineering experience brought new uses of materials and new construction methods. Continuous beam construction and the use of high-strength steel changed the look of bridges as the 1940s gave way to the 1950s, and the era of the interstate highway systems dawned.

Source: excerpted with the permission of the Ohio Department of Transportation from the Second Ohio Historic Bridge Inventory, Evaluation, and Preservation Plan

BRIDGES: THE SHORT COURSE

Ohio has a total of 43,075 bridges statewide, second in number only to Texas. The total deck area for these structures is 141,369,943 square feet. The Ohio Department of Transportation (ODOT) is responsible for the ownership and maintenance of 14,956 bridges on the state highway system. The remainder of the state's bridges are owned and maintained by county and municipal governments. There are 25,981 county-owned bridges and 2,138 municipally owned bridges.

The ODOT bridges make up 35 percent of the bridges in the state but because these tend to be larger bridges, 72.6 percent of the total deck area is in the state system. Counties are responsible for 20.9 percent of the deck area and municipalities have 6.5 percent.

Ohio's interstate highways have 2,495 bridges. State law specifies that bridges on state system routes within cities are the responsibility of the cities, unless they are over water, in which case they are the responsibility of the county. Although not mandated to do so, ODOT funds these bridges, while local governments provide the routine maintenance. Ohio also maintains four structures spanning the Ohio River, and shares in the maintenance responsibilities for all the remaining structures on its borders with other states.

Ohio's longest bridge is 7,440 feet long and is owned by and located in Hamilton County. The longest state owned bridge is 6,580 and located in Cuyahoga County. The longest bridge span is 785 feet. The average age of a bridge in the state system is 35 years; for the county system it is 47 years, and the municipal system, 46 years.

number two

Some 7,072 of Ohio's bridges have been listed as deficient, ranking Ohio 5th among all states.

—Morgan Quitno Corporation, Ohio in Perspective, 2003

A System for the *traveler*

Early travelers in Ohio often had to stop and ask for directions. The farmers who were tired of repeated inquiries erected signs at intersections pointing toward the principal towns. The roads were named for the place to which they were headed, with the name changing as each destination was reached. For example, U.S. 68 was named Urbana Road going north and Limestone Road going south. In 1919, however, the state began stencilling digits on telephone poles to identify the roads by number. The first markers on U.S. highways were posted in 1925, and eventually roadways became known more by number than name.

Road numbering supposedly follows a simple system: all east-west highways have even numbers, and all north-south highways have odd numbers. The even numbers start in the south with Interstate 10 crossing from Jacksonville, Florida, to Los Angeles, California. The road numbers become higher towards the north, such as Interstate 90, which crosses Ohio. U.S. highway numbers, however, deviate within Ohio. High numbers, such as U.S. 90, are in the southern part of the state, and low numbers, like U.S. 20, are in northern Ohio. And, whereas the interstate numbering system has 5 low-numbered, north-south highways along the West Coast and 95 high-numbered, north-south highways along the East Coast, the U.S. system is reversed so that numbers are high on the West Coast and low on the East Coast. As a result, U.S. Highway 1 parallels Interstate 95 up the East Coast, and U.S.

www. *buckeyetraffic.org*

Your friend in the jungle of orange barrels, this site is the Department of Transportation's Road and Weather Information System, complete with web cams relaying instant traffic & roadway information, i.e., temperature, precipitation, wind, and visibility (from electronic sensors), as well as construction & detours.

JIM BORGMAN
CINCINNATI ENQUIRER ©2000
IF I EVER GET MY HANDS ON THE ★@#!%! WHO KEEPS DOING THIS TO ME...!
S.U.V. NATION

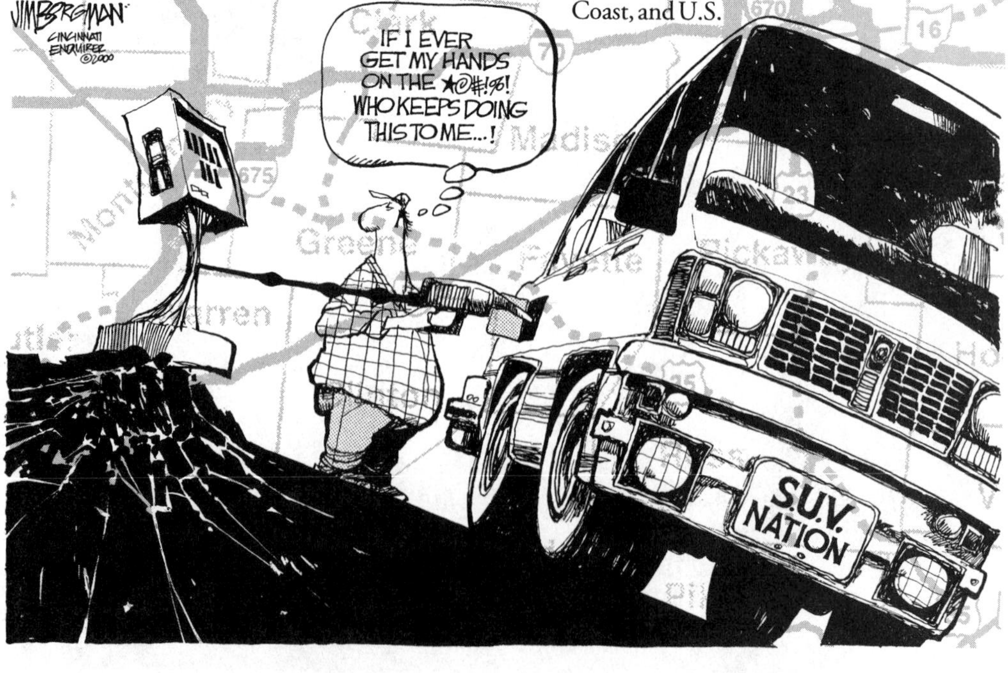

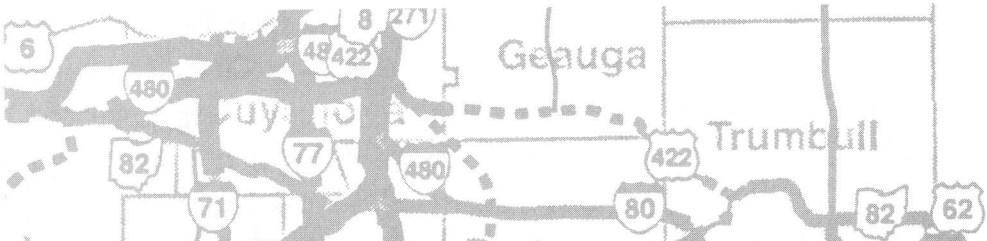

Highway 101 parallels Interstate 5 up the West Coast. Thus, the interstate numbers are the same as the U.S. highway numbers (odds north-south and evens east-west), but they start in different places.

In Ohio, we have the even-numbered Interstates 70, 76, and 80-90 (which run together) running east-west, and the odd-numbered Interstates 75 and 77 running north-south. Then there is the diagonal Interstate 71, which starts in Louisville and ends in Cleveland and runs more north-south than east-west and is, therefore, odd-numbered. Ohio's north-south U.S highways include 11 (from Liverpool to Ashtabula), 21 (from Marietta to Cleveland), 23 (from Portsmouth to Sylvania), 25 (from Cincinnati to Toledo), and part of U.S. 27 (from Cincinnati to Fort Wayne). Examples of east-west U.S. Highways are 52 (along the Ohio River), 50 (from Cincinnati to Belpre), 40 (from Wheeling to Richmond), 30 (from Liverpool to Van Wert), and 20 (from Conneaut to Columbia on the Indiana line).

But complications arise—again—with the diagonal highways. For example, U.S. 35 in Ohio enters the state near Gallipolis and leaves near Richmond. It is more east-west than north-south, but carries an odd number. U.S. 33 enters at Pomeroy and leaves at Willshire, having a little more north-south route but still carrying an odd number. Three other diagonal U.S. highways run in the opposite direction; that is, they run from the southwest to the northeast rather than from the southeast to northwest. While the southeast to northwest diagonals have odd numbers (33 and 35), the southwest to northeast diagonals carry even numbers: U.S. 22, 42, and 62. In truth, U.S. 42, which runs from Cincinnati to Cleveland, runs more north-south than east-west, but it is still considered a diagonal.

Another problem is the highways that have three- rather than two-digit numbers. A three-digit-numbered highway supposedly leads toward the highway numbered by its last two digits. For example, Interstates 270, 271, 275, and 280 respectively lead toward Interstates 70, 71, 75, and 80. But, U.S. 224 runs across Ohio to U.S. 24, which it finally reaches in Huntington, Indiana. U.S. 250 runs from Sandusky to Martin's Ferry to U.S. 50, which it meets in Grafton, West Virginia. The 4s or 6s, however, are even a little more complicated. Highways beginning with 4 are really alternate or substitute routes. Interstate 480 thus takes you away from 80 (the Ohio Turnpike) and kind of into Cleveland and then back out to Interstate 80, a detour that you really wouldn't want to take too often. Road numbers beginning with 6 are rare, but they are a part of the system. Interstate 675 runs around Dayton from Interstate 70 at Medway to Interstate 75 at West Carrollton. Therefore, if you are driving on a 6, you may get to the two-number road indicated in its three-number name, provided you are going in the right direction.

Another exception to the highway numbering system is U.S. 68. It runs north-south, yet has an even east-west number. Why? The road begins in central Kentucky and ends in Findlay, a route which is all north-south. The numbering problem arose because when 68 became a U.S. Highway, U.S. 23 and U.S. 25 were on either side of it, and there was no available odd number in between. The number 68 was not being used, so the U.S. highway got an even number, even though it runs north-south.

U.S. 68, in fact, is one of three U.S. highways that cross Xenia, the town that seems to be the epitome of Ohio's exceptions to the simple system. There, U.S. 35 and 42, as well as 68, break all the rules: the odd road is going east-west, while the two evens are running north-south.

—by Richard Coleman

The first metric distance markers on a state highway anywhere in the U.S. were put up by the Ohio Department of Transportation in 1973, on four spots along I-71, between Cincinnati and Columbus and between Columbus and Cleveland. The signs, for the first time, showed the distance in both miles and kilometers.

Attached to the front and back bumpers of every automobile registered in Ohio, there is a highly visible reminder that driving a motor vehicle in this state is not a right, but a privilege. The privilege is made manifest by the 6x12 inch, 0.017 inch-thick steel rectangles, which are officially called license plates, but are known in the driving vernacular as "tags." There are some 10.4 million sets in Ohio, symbols of the average citizen's most common contacts with the government in Columbus. In actuality, the tags represent the privilege of both driving, as well as paying taxes, for the tags are exactly that— a tax, the very sort of indirect users' levy that once incited our political forefathers to stage their famous Tea Party.

Yet there has been no Columbus Tea Party or Tag Party, with protesters dressed as Indians and chucking cartons of license plates into the Scioto, despite the fact that the Bureau of Motor Vehicles collects well over $600 million in vehicle registration fees each year. Actually, cars seem far more sacred to us than tea ever was to the Colonial tax protesters, and every year about 6.7 million automobiles require registration. There is the basic registration fee, of course, but nowadays there may be also be a premium for personalized "vanity" plates of $33.25 (for plain initials) to $58.25 (four to six letters with the sky, imagination, and public decency as the only limits).

It used to be that folks monogrammed only their bathrobes and their dinner napkins, but nowadays Ohio drivers can really indulge themselves, turning their cars into rolling billboards announcing their names, nicknames, messages, pet jokes, passions, or peeves. Some personalized plates proclaim the obvious: I AM OLD; or the esoteric: AN AV 8R (an aviator); the friendly: ICUIYQ (I see you, I like you); or the frosty: FOOE 2 U (phooey to you); the farm: EIEIO (eee-i-eee-i-oh); the field: GO OSU; the proud: DAD OF 4; and the professional: 2TH DOK (tooth doctor).

This combination—O2 BE ME—was found on a Corvette, and this one— 2BLND4U—on a convertible driven by—who else?—a striking blonde. A Ferrari sported personalized plates reading BIG BUX, and our own personal(ized) favorite: FIDL DD.

Of course, the BMV does not grant Ohio drivers complete—*ahem*—license concerning what they can display on their vanity tags. Applications for personalized plates are rejected when the characters are either already being used by someone else or appear on the BMV's list of verboten letter combinations and words. Ohio shares its risque license plate list with California and Texas, and along with some fairly blatant combinations, there are a few puzzlers such as HQR, KQX, MTW, and PAR, apparently because some folks have a talent for finding something offensive in unusual places.

In 1996, the bureau formed a six-person committee to review requests for personalized plates—and since in 2000 the BMV issued over 240,000 in 2001, that could mean the committee would be scrutinizing over 600 plates a day. Clerks in the regional bureaus were allowed to issue personalized plates, if the requests seemed innocuous enough, although with the growing ingenuity out there, it was hard to tell.

Folks were getting more creative, as witness the Californian who on his internet site (www.netscrap.com/netscrap_detail.cfm?scrap_id=700) retold the story of Oedipus by using 154 of California's more than one million

personalized license plates (sample: YEGODS WHYMEE? LIFSUX. IAMBAD. IMSOBAD).

An Ohio journalist, driving home to the suburbs from work in Cincinnati, fell in behind a motorist with such an odd combination of letters and numerals that he followed well past his exit, studying the plate ahead of him and trying to puzzle it out:

6UL DV8, it read.

Finally, it came to him: *sexual deviate*.

Exactly what the BMV tries to avoid.

In 2001, an Ohio skydiver's request for GETHIGH was denied, as was an earlier request for WINO, which was made by a member of Wine Investigation for Novices and Oenophiles.

In the last couple of years, the BMV has said you could not GONAKED. Neither could you be an IDIOT nor a WILD ONE. You could not ask anyone to TIE ME UP, you could not be a COP, a NUN, nor a US GUV.

You could not use PROZAC, have SEX, or be GAY. PEE was out, as was MAFIA1, GOT BEER, and H8MICH (Hate Michigan) was *verboten* because, said officials, it promoted violence (as opposed to the game itself, being the personification of violence).

But whatever they say, all Ohio plates have a common source: the Lebanon Correctional Institution, or more precisely the inmates there. In all, Ohio issued and renewed 769,065 special ones in 2002, in at least 56 categories, ranging from 21 different collegiate plates to veterans, professional firefighters, doctors, and members of the conservation group Ducks Unlimited. All this variety may seem excessive, but given the cacophony of vehicles and drivers that the BMV must harmonize, it is not prodigious. Aside from the standard passenger, personalized passenger, and initial reserve plates (specially requested tags with up to three letters and not more than six characters), the state also issues tags for buses, church buses, transit buses, television station owners, noncommercial trucks, historical motorcycles, trail bikes, mopeds, historic vehicles, snowmobile dealers, utility trailer dealers, watercraft trailer dealers, physicians, volunteer firemen, and such.

Cars, trucks, motorcycles, and mini bikes owned by the state or local governments get free license plates, along with certain Civil Air Patrol members, U.S. Senators, members of Congress, former prisoners of war, disabled veterans, (whose tags are red, white, and blue), and Congressional Medal of Honor winners. On the side of infamy, however, are some vehicle owners who have had their driving privileges suspended or revoked, usually for driving under the influence of alcohol. Only relatives may drive their cars, which must be licensed with the vehicular version of a "Scarlet Letter"—yellow "family" plates with bright red characters.

Voiture plates are reserved for exhibition vehicles owned by organizations chartered by Congress. Their name comes from World War I vintage French boxcars (*voitures*) that held forty men or eight horses. Today the Forty and Eight veterans' organization gets voiture license plates for its parade vehicles. Other special-issue Ohio tags include "Ace" plates, which display five bolts of lightening and are assigned to highway patrol officers who find five stolen cars; the "Blue Max," which has a cross and goes to the officer who tracks down the most stolen cars each year; and reserve plates bearing the numbers 1 through 999. In many states, license plate number 1 is reserved for the governor, but not so in Ohio, where number 1 is registered to a private citizen.

The State of Ohio began issuing standardized license plates 84 years ago with an initial run of about 10,000 tags. The first plate went to Thomas B. Paxton of Cincinnati for an H.H. Franklin Gasoline Car. Before 1908, municipalities marked the infant years of the automobile by issuing their own unique tags. Cincinnati in 1906 and 1907, for example, had beautiful brass licenses. Ohio's first official plates were also quite handsome, being made of steel coated with porcelain enamel until 1912, when the first all-metal tags were distributed.

The first time Ohio put a figure on its license plates was in 1938, when an ox pulling a covered wagon celebrated the 150th birthday of the Northwest Territory. It was the perfect iconic image for Ohio, a state that prided itself on pulling its own weight, and has yet to be adequately supplanted.

When Ohio expanded to seven-character vanity plates in 1996, the most popular request was for—you guessed it— BUCKEYE. The tags were reserved on a first-come, first-served basis, and Richard D. Callahan of suburban Columbus got it.

—The Plain Dealer

THE HIGHWAY PATROL: WHAT THEY HAVE THAT YOU DON'T

The Ohio State Highway Patrol was created in 1933 with 60 uniformed officers in six districts, communicating with "call stations," which were usually gas stations along the routes with attendants displaying a flag if there was a message. Speed traps were forbidden and Col. Lynn Black believed that speed itself did not constitute a hazard, only recklessness. There being no standard for drunkenness, suspect drivers were taken to a physician for examination.

—The Ohio State Highway Patrol

Engine:
8-cylinder, 4.6-liter or more, powerful enough to accelerate 0 to 60 in 10 seconds or less, and from 0 to 100 in 30 seconds or less. Top speed of 120 mph must be attained within a 3-mile distance.

Cooling system:
Must be able to operate without boiling over while the car is idling for 30 minutes in 120-degree heat with the air conditioner on.

Air bags:
Two front bags and two side bags.
Seats: Bucket seats, six-way power seat adjustor for driver's seat; cushion must have foam rubber pad, with minimum of 39 inches of head room and 42 inches of leg room.

Speedometers:
Must go to 140 mph.

Transmission:
Heavy-duty, suitable for police pursuit.

Tires:
P225/60R16 all-season radials speed-rated and certified for police use up to 149 mph.

Wheels:
Heavy-duty with safety rims to stay secure during pursuit driving.

Suspension:
Heavy-duty front and rear system with heavy-duty front and rear shock absorbers and stabilizer bars, giving best combination to prevent body roll and provide flat cornering, limit dive on harsh or severe braking and limit squat on fast acceleration to provide optimum handling.

Frame:
Must have additional welds and/or structural members to provide greater strength than a standard frame.

Axles:
Special, heavy-duty.

Brakes:
Anti-lock, power, four-wheel disc brakes.

Source: The Ohio State Highway Patrol; photograph is of patrol command officer with his 1934 Plymouth

Rails

Profile

Railroading has been essential in building the commerce and industry of America. From the Baltimore and Ohio Railroad's choice of the "Tom Thumb" steam engine over a team of horses in 1828, to the Civil War's "Great Locomotive Chase" of 1862, to the linking of our nation at Promontory Point, Utah in 1869, to the bustling rail booms that transported the country through both world wars, railroads have been part of the basic fabric of our culture. In the past, the railroad was "King," run by "rail barons" named Vanderbilt, Gould, and Hill. Few towns or businesses grew and prospered without the service of the "iron horse." In the 1950s and 1960s, the expansion and improvement of interstate highways, air travel, and inland waterways dethroned "King" railroad.

Railroading has now settled into its niche in American transportation, proving to be the most efficient ground transportation for bulk commodities and the least costly method of moving large quantities over a long distance. Based on these economics, rail not only is the preferred transportation mode for coal, grains, chemicals, plastic resins, and other such bulk materials, but also is highly competitive for long distance container and piggy-back traffic. The term "railroad" is becoming a misnomer, as railroading continues to shift with the times. Large railroads are now known as "transportation companies" that own trucking, barge, and shipping companies. Using a multi-modal approach, these companies are able to transport a customer's materials in the most efficient and cost effective manner possible.

The Staggers Act of 1980 largely deregulated railroads, allowing the industry to take its place in a relatively free-market transportation economy. This process of change is not always easy. Railroad management must take a hard economic look at lines with low-volume traffic to decide whether the return on investment is high enough to warrant the costs of continued maintenance and operation. Fortunately, rail service does not always cease if a major carrier withdraws from a line. In some cases, "short lines" or "regional" railroads can profit where major carriers cannot. Small railroads are generally able to have lower overhead costs.

Ohio is a leader in the development of small railroads. As Consolidated Rail Corporation (CONRAIL), CSX Transportation, Inc. (CSXT), Norfolk Southern Corporation (NS), and Grand Trunk Western Railroad (GTW) divest and consolidate their lines, new Ohio railroads such as the Ashtabula, Carson, and Jefferson; Ashland Railway; Ohio Southern; Ohi-Rail; Indiana and Ohio; Spencerville and Elgin; Temperance Yard; Youngstown and Austintown; and Ohio Central are providing needed rail freight transportation.

Class I railroads are those having adjusted annual operating revenues of $50 million or more for three consecutive years. Four Class I railroads operate in Ohio; CONRAIL, CSXT, GTW, and NS. In 1987, Ohio's Class I railroads made significant investments in Ohio's economy. Conrail invested over $328 million in taxes, employment, purchases and capital improvements; GTW invested $34,750,000 in taxes, employment, and capital investments; and NS invested $1,087,207,338 in taxes, employment, and capital investments. CSXT figures were not available. Class II railroads are those having adjusted annual operating revenues of $10-$50 million for three consecutive years. Two Class II railroads operate in Ohio: the Pittsburgh and Lake Erie Railroad Company and the Bessemer and Lake Erie Railroad Company.

Class III railroads are those having adjusted annual operating revenues of less than $10 million for three consecutive years. Twenty-three Class III railroads operate in Ohio.

Source: excerpted with the permission of the Ohio Department of Transportation from "Ohio Rail Map"

Aviation

Ohio's more than 800 airports (three international) range from large metropolitan facilities served by major airlines to small, private landing strips used solely by the owner. Ohio has four major air traffic hubs. A hub, which may have more than one airport in it, is not to be confused with an airline "hub and spoke" route system. A hub refers to a geographic area based on the number of passengers enplaned. Of the nation's 114 air traffic hubs, four serve Ohio. The largest, Cincinnati, is the only large hub in the state. Cleveland and Columbus are each medium hubs while Dayton is a small hub. The state is also a national leader in the air freight

In 2000, sales of the Ohio plate imprinted with the image of a cardinal, the state bird, funneled $820,000 to the Division of Wildlife for its wildlife diversity fund, which supported projects relating to endangered species.

Airport Activity in Ohio

| | Aircraft Departures | | | Revenue-tons | |
Service	Total	Scheduled	Passengers	Freight	Mail
Scheduled*	326,402	346,438	20,559,243	283,291.69	48,749.58
Nonscheduled	73,798		240,660	292,529.09	6,442.08
All Services	400,200	346,438	20,799,903	575,820.78	55,191.66

*Scheduled and nonscheduled refers to regular air service as opposed to private and charter flights

Ohio's Major Air Hubs

	Departures	Passengers	Freight (tons)	Mail
Cincinnati				
Greater Cincinnati	163,580	9,962,765	243,677.91	26,261.7
Lunken Field	22	170	10.65	
Total	163,602	9,962,935	243,688.56	26,261.7
Cleveland				
Burke Lakefront	10	290	0.9	
Cuyahoga County	2		.5	
Hopkins International	134,796	6,154,094	49,562.38	13,912.58
Total	134,808	6,154,384	49,562.97	13,912.58
Columbus				
Port Columbus International	45,104	3,104,695	2,257.95	8,506.68
Rickenbacker International	2,641	913	35,854.04	10.45
Total	47,745	3,105,364	38,111.99	8,517.13
Dayton				
James M. Cox/Dayton International	28,939	1,033,145	149,838.47	6,488.46
Montgomery County	7		.12	
Wright-Patterson AFB	1			
Total	28,947	1,033,145	149,838.59	6,488.46

Of the country's major airports Cincinnati's ranked first in 2001 with the fewest late departures (15.14%) after finishing third in 2000 (17.96). Its percentage of late arrivals ranked second in 2001 (16.98), dropping from the top spot in 2000 (20.23)

Top Airport Traffic Control Towers

Tower	National Rank	Total Operations	National Rank	Air Carrier Operations	Air Taxi	General Aviation	Military
Greater Cincinnati	22	401,367	26	189,762	196,072	14,155	1,378
Cleveland Hopkins	38	302,618	30	145,307	124,159	30,327	2,825

FAA Air Traffic Activity in Ohio

Airport Operations (Towers)	1,353,464
Aircraft Handled (Centers)	2,843,383

industry. Employing over 4,600 people, there are large air cargo operations in Wilmington (Airborne Express), Dayton (Emery), and Toledo (Burlington Express).

The Ohio Airport System

Public Use Airports in Ohio	165
Public Use Heliports	9
Public Use Seaplane Landing Areas	1
Private Use Airports & Heliports	741
State Registered Aircraft	5,753
Federal Registered Aircraft	9,661
FAA Registered Pilots	19,000

Economic Impact of the Ohio Airport System

Direct Economic Impact	$1,932,015,590
Indirect Economic Impact	$1,474,044,106
Induced Economic Impact	$3,993,639,454
Total Economic Impact	*$7,399,699,150*

Source: Ohio Department of Transportation, Office of Aviation: 614-793-5040
Website: www.dot.state.oh.us/aviation

Waterways

In the 18th century, the state legislature appropriated funds for the building of a canal system. This investment made Ohio a national leader, positioned only behind New York and Pennsylvania in the development of canal systems. During these early years, transportation via flatboats, keelboats, and Indian trails became inadequate for the needs of an expanding nation. Roads, canals, and railroads were built to meet these needs. When the National Road reached Wheeling in 1818, the Ohio River became, in effect, the road's western extension. It emerged as the avenue to new lands, new homesteads, and new opportunities.

Similarly, the Great Lakes played an important role in the making of America and in Ohio's development in the nation's heartland. The Great Lakes were a major theater of the War of 1812, and it was off Lake Erie's Put-in-Bay that Commodore Oliver Hazzard Perry won a turning-point victory against the British fleet in 1813. After peace was achieved in 1814, the Great Lakes formed a border between the U.S. and the British colony of Upper Canada. With the opening of New York State's Erie Canal in 1825, the region was unlocked to shipping activity and settlers. By the end of the 19th century, the southern lakes region was a magnet to industry, as the population and demand for manufactured goods and processed foodstuffs soared. For more than three-quarters of a century, the Great Lakes' ports, including Cleveland, emerged as steelmaking giants in the heart of the world's greatest concentrations of heavy manufacturing.

Today, Ohio's waterways are a critical link in the state's total transportation system and the state ranks as the fourth largest maritime state in terms of tonnage moved. Two-thirds of Ohio's boundaries—more than 700 miles—are navigable waterways, providing shippers with a low cost and safe mode of getting their goods to market. The state's ports account—directly and indirectly—for more than 21,000 jobs, adding $1 billion to Ohio's economy. Lake Erie, which is the 12th largest freshwater lake in the world, links Ohio to Midwest, Canadian, and world markets. As one of five inland seas which extend more than 800 miles from east to west, Lake Erie is on America's "Fourth Seacoast," providing access to European ports through the St. Lawrence Seaway. Distances from European ports to Seaway cities are actually shorter than distances to Atlantic ports. Ohio's nine deep-draft commercial ports, Toledo, Marblehead, Sandusky, Huron, Lorain, Cleveland, Fairport Harbor, Ashtabula, and Conneaut are dispersed along the state's 265-mile lake shoreline. Bulk cargoes such as coal, iron ore, and stone make up more than 90 percent of Ohio's Lake Erie port traffic.

Lake Ports

With billions of dollars in exports annually, Ohio is a major player in the global marketplace. Only 11 days from Rotterdam, the world's largest port, Ohio's leadership in international trade is due, in part, to an ideal location on the "Fourth Seacoast" shores of Lake Erie. Ohio's Lake Erie ports—Toledo, Marblehead, Sandusky, Huron, Lorain, Cleveland, Fairport Harbor, Ashtabula, and Conneaut—stretch along the state's 265-mile shoreline from Toledo in the west to Conneaut near the Pennsylvania border. Decades ago, many heavy industries, especially steel, located their mills on the rivers leading into Lake Erie because of the economy of waterborne transportation. Although changes in Ohio's industrial base have affected the ports, they have kept pace by diversifying their

Flyover country

The world's busiest air traffic control center is the Cleveland Air Route Traffic Control Center in Oberlin. Part of the Federal Aviation Administration (FAA), it has handled over 3 million air traffic operations every year since 1998 and on June 22, 2000 reached its peak when it handled 11,266. Located on the major east/west corridor it handles traffic between New York and Chicago in an airspace that covers parts of five states and Canada encompassing major airports in Cleveland, Detroit and Pittsburgh.

Ohio Waterborne Tonnage

State Totals	Total	Shipping Domestic	Shipping Foreign	Receiving Domestic	Receiving Foreign	Intrastate
	130,915,000	22,684,000	19,431,000	66,704,000	6,420,000	15,675,000

Major Ohio Ports

	National Rank	Total	Total Foreign	Imports	Exports	Domestic
Cleveland	44	14,390,802	2,475,365	2,262,104	214,261	11,914,437
Cincinnati	45	14,337,043	-	-	-	14,337,043
Lorain	46	14,180,191	274,562	274,562	-	13,905,629
Toledo	49	13,321,657	7,380,310	1,1915,302	5,465,008	5,941,347
Ashtabula	51	12,322,430	7,172,662	1,703,259	5,469,403	5,149,768
Conneaut	56	10,603,367	5,071,579	203,481	4,868,098	5,531,788
Marblehead	91	3,717,018	478,467	-	478,467	3,238,551
Sandusky	93	3,644,571	2,911,336	45,404	2,865,932	733,235
Fairport Harbor	112	2,538,850	-	-	-	2,538,850
Huron	143	1,275,242	86,456	15,157	70,299	1,188,786

Source: U. S. Army Corps of Engineers, 2000

Ohio River Locks

Lock Name*	River Mile	Date Open	Lift	Average Tow Size	Average Time in Locks
New Cumberland	54.4	1959	21 feet	11	61
Auxiliary Lock				3	36
Pike Island	84.2	1965	18 feet	11	56
Auxiliary Lock				2	36
Hannibal	126.4	1973	21 feet	12	52
Auxiliary Lock				3	38
Willow Island	161.7	1972	20 feet	12	57
Auxiliary Lock				6	54
Belleville	203.9	1969	22 feet	12	57
Auxiliary Lock				3	36
Racine	237.5	1969	22 feet	12	58
Auxiliary Lock				3	34
Robert C. Byrd	279.2	1993	23 feet	12	58
Auxiliary Lock				2	37
Greenup	341.0	1959	30 feet	12	51
Auxiliary Lock				6	49
Captain Anthony Meldahl	436.2	1962	30 feet	12	58
Auxiliary Lock				3	27

*There are two sets of locks at each location; the main locks are 1,200 feet long
and the auxiliary lock is 600 feet long
Source: U.S. Army Corps of Engineers

cargoes and seeking new business.

The Port of Toledo is the largest coal port on the Great Lakes, handling more than 12 million tons of coal in 1985. Other major cargoes handled in Toledo are agricultural products (including corn, soybeans, and wheat), iron, limestone, and petroleum products.

Cleveland and Conneaut are also major Great Lakes ports. In 1985, the Port of Cleveland, which is the first major, general cargo-port west of the Welland Canal, showed its fourth consecutive year of increases in overall shipping business. That same year, Conneaut was second largest Great Lakes port in the handling of coal, moving more than ten million tons over its docks.

Today, many millions of tons of commodities are shipped or received through Ohio's Lake Erie ports. Coal is the major commodity handled, along with metallic ores, sand and gravel, agricultural products, clay, concrete, glass and stone products, and pulp, paper, and allied products.

River Ports

The Ohio River forms the entire southern boundary of the state, extending 450 miles from East Liverpool to Cincinnati. The river is an integral part of a 25,000 mile system of inland and intercoastal waterways, and the channel is maintained by the nine locks and dams along Ohio's border. Commerce on the river is carried out by barge/towboat combinations which transport one-third of the nation's inland waterborne commerce and serves over 85 percent of the country's major cities. It gives Ohio shippers direct access to all major river communities and, via the Mississippi River, the Gulf of Mexico. The typical barge is 35 feet wide and 195 feet long and can carry 1,500 tons.

For more than 100 years, the Army Corps of Engineers has worked to improve navigation on the Ohio River. The first lock and dam project was completed on the river in 1885, and in 1929, the Ohio River was canalized to ensure a minimum channel depth. Today, it is maintained at a nine-foot minimum depth and a minimum width of 300 feet. Beginning in 1954, the U.S. Army Corps of Engineers began to modernize all the river's locks and dams. With the modernization of the Robert C. Byrd Lock and Dam near Gallipolis in 1993 the Ohio River is now fully capable of accommodating modern tows.

Today, more than two-thirds of the river's freight traffic is made up of bulk forms of energy: coal, crude oil, and petroleum products. Coal is the major commodity handled by terminals along the Ohio River.

Ohio has approximately 125 terminals along the river, while most are private designed for handling a single commodity there are 20 that will handle cargo for any customer wishing to ship by water. The most common products carried on the river are bulk forms of energy such as crude oil and petroleum products.

Land access on the Ohio River is achieved through Ohio's extensive highway and rail transportation systems. The need for these multimodal "connections" comes from the state's widely dispersed river traffic. In contrast to deepwater port traffic along Lake Erie, which is concentrated at eight major harbors, the Ohio River's terminals are dispersed along the river. All of Ohio's river terminals are privately owned and operated. Most are single purpose facilities designed to meet the needs of the owner. Twenty river facilities operate as public terminals, providing common carrier service to the public. East Liverpool and Wellsville in Columbiana county combine to make the largest river port complex in the state. Together they handle 15 million ton of cargo making it the 43rd largest port in the U.S. The Greater Cincinnati area is another active area. Several barge and towing companies operate out of the "Queen City," and the shipping time from Cincinnati to western Europe is just 18 days.

Source: excerpted with the permission of the Division of Water Transportation, Ohio Department of Transportation from "Water Transportation Map of Ohio"

In 2000, Ohio commercial fishermen landed 3,497,000 pounds of fish —down 11.1% from the previous year and about a tenth of what was caught in its banner year, 1936.

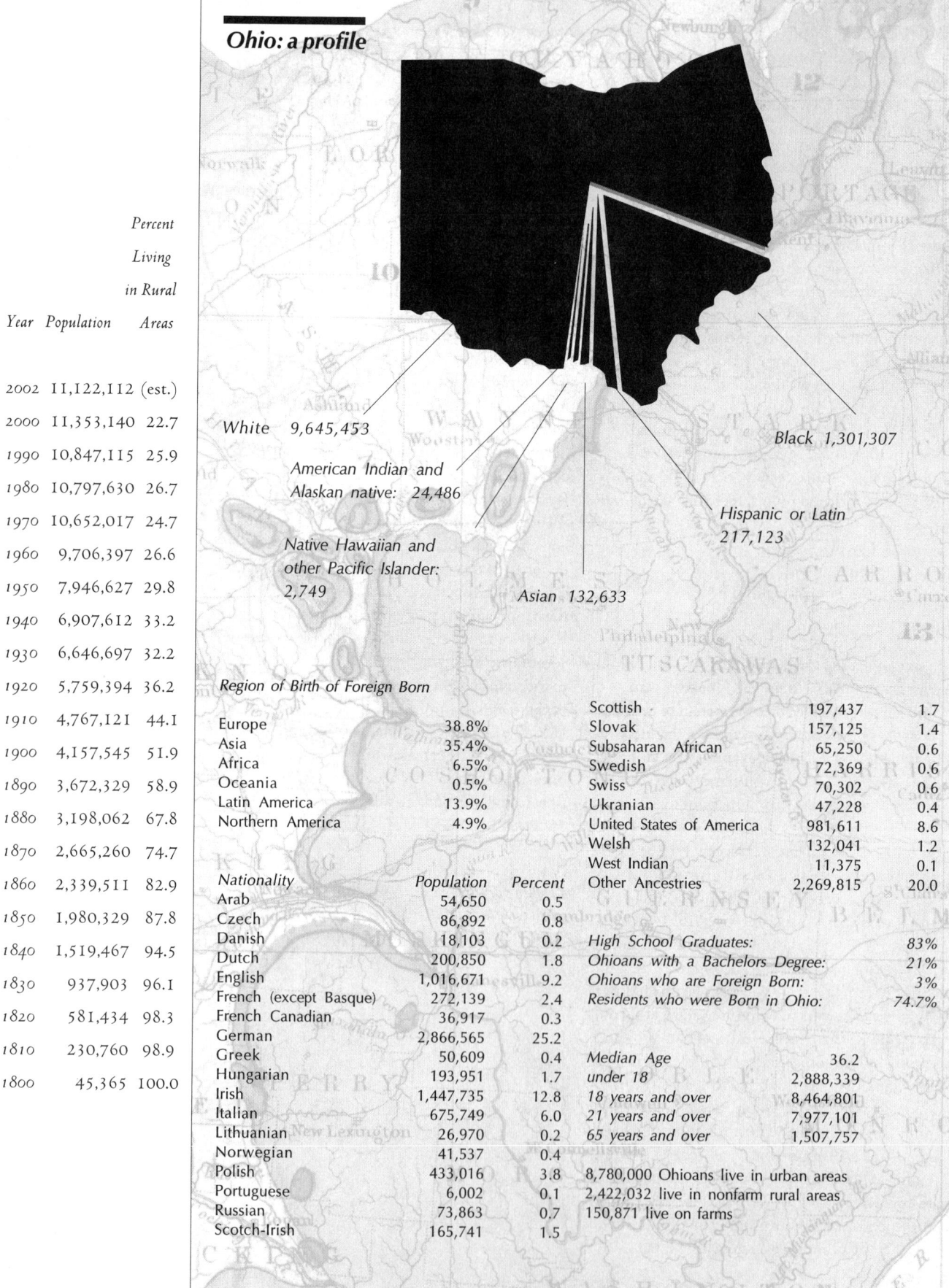

Ohio: a profile

Year	Population	Percent Living in Rural Areas
2002	11,122,112 (est.)	
2000	11,353,140	22.7
1990	10,847,115	25.9
1980	10,797,630	26.7
1970	10,652,017	24.7
1960	9,706,397	26.6
1950	7,946,627	29.8
1940	6,907,612	33.2
1930	6,646,697	32.2
1920	5,759,394	36.2
1910	4,767,121	44.1
1900	4,157,545	51.9
1890	3,672,329	58.9
1880	3,198,062	67.8
1870	2,665,260	74.7
1860	2,339,511	82.9
1850	1,980,329	87.8
1840	1,519,467	94.5
1830	937,903	96.1
1820	581,434	98.3
1810	230,760	98.9
1800	45,365	100.0

White 9,645,453

American Indian and Alaskan native: 24,486

Native Hawaiian and other Pacific Islander: 2,749

Asian 132,633

Black 1,301,307

Hispanic or Latin 217,123

Region of Birth of Foreign Born

Europe	38.8%
Asia	35.4%
Africa	6.5%
Oceania	0.5%
Latin America	13.9%
Northern America	4.9%

Nationality	Population	Percent
Arab	54,650	0.5
Czech	86,892	0.8
Danish	18,103	0.2
Dutch	200,850	1.8
English	1,016,671	9.2
French (except Basque)	272,139	2.4
French Canadian	36,917	0.3
German	2,866,565	25.2
Greek	50,609	0.4
Hungarian	193,951	1.7
Irish	1,447,735	12.8
Italian	675,749	6.0
Lithuanian	26,970	0.2
Norwegian	41,537	0.4
Polish	433,016	3.8
Portuguese	6,002	0.1
Russian	73,863	0.7
Scotch-Irish	165,741	1.5
Scottish	197,437	1.7
Slovak	157,125	1.4
Subsaharan African	65,250	0.6
Swedish	72,369	0.6
Swiss	70,302	0.6
Ukranian	47,228	0.4
United States of America	981,611	8.6
Welsh	132,041	1.2
West Indian	11,375	0.1
Other Ancestries	2,269,815	20.0

High School Graduates: 83%
Ohioans with a Bachelors Degree: 21%
Ohioans who are Foreign Born: 3%
Residents who were Born in Ohio: 74.7%

Median Age	36.2
under 18	2,888,339
18 years and over	8,464,801
21 years and over	7,977,101
65 years and over	1,507,757

8,780,000 Ohioans live in urban areas
2,422,032 live in nonfarm rural areas
150,871 live on farms

The average family in Ohio consists

Cities and Villages: location, population, ZIP code*

Name	County	Region	2000	1990	1980	Zip
Aberdeen	Brown	SW	1,603	1,329	1,566	45101
Ada	Hardin	NW	5,582	5,428	5,669	45810
Adamsville	Muskingum	SE	127	151	229	43802
Addyston	Hamilton	SW	1,010	1,198	1,195	45001
Adelphi	Ross	SW	371	398	472	43101
Adena	Jefferson	NE	815	842	1,062	43901
Akron	Summit	NE	217,074	223,019	237,177	44301-72
Albany	Athens	SE	808	795	905	45710
Alexandria	Licking	C	85	468	489	43001
Alger	Hardin	NW	888	864	992	45812
Alliance	Stark	NE	23,253	23,376	24,315	44601
Alvordton	Williams	NW	305	298	362	43501
Amanda	Fairfield	C	707	729	720	43102
Amberley	Hamilton	SW	3,425	3,108	3,442	45213
Amelia	Clermont	SW	2,752	1,837	1,108	45102
Amesville	Athens	SE	184	250	247	45711
Amherst	Lorain	NW	11,797	10,332	10,638	44001
Amsterdam	Jefferson	NE	568	669	783	43903
Andover	Ashtabula	NE	1,269	1,216	1,205	44003
Anna	Shelby	NW	1,319	1,164	1,038	45302
Ansonia	Darke	SW	1,145	1,279	1,267	45303
Antioch	Monroe	SE	89	68	113	43793
Antwerp	Paulding	NW	1,740	1,677	1,765	45813
Apple Creek	Wayne	NE	999	860	741	44606
Aquilla	Geauga	NE	372	360	355	44024
Arcanum	Darke	SW	2,076	1,953	2,002	45304
Arcadia	Hancock	NW	537	546	580	44804
Archbold	Fulton	NW	4,290	3,440	3,318	43502
Arlington	Hancock	NW	1,351	1,267	1,187	45814
Arlington Heights	Hamilton	SW	899	1,084	1,082	45215
Ashland	Ashland	NE	21,249	20,079	20,326	44805

*Only incorporated cities and villages are included in this section

Name	County	Region	2000	1990	1980	Zip
Ashley	Delaware	C	1,216	1,059	1,057	43003
Ashtabula	Ashtabula	NE	20,962	21,633	23,449	44004
Ashville	Pickaway	C	3,174	2,254	2,046	43103
Athalia	Lawrence	SE	328	346	367	45669
Athens	Athens	SE	21,342	21,265	19,743	45701
Attica	Seneca	NW	955	944	865	44807
Aurora	Portage	NE	13,556	9,192	8,177	44202
Avon	Lorain	NE	11,446	7,337	7,241	44011
Avon Lake	Lorain	NE	18,145	15,066	13,222	44012
Bailey Lakes	Ashland	NE	397	367	397	44805
Bainbridge	Ross	SW	1,012	968	1,042	45612
Bairdstown	Wood	NW	130	130	151	45872
Baltic	Tuscarawas	NE	743	659	563	43804
Baltimore	Fairfield	C	2,881	2,971	2,689	43105
Barberton	Summit	NE	27,899	27,623	29,751	44203
Barnesville	Belmont	SE	4,225	4,326	4,633	43713
Barnhill	Tuscarawas	NE	364	313	327	44663
Batavia	Clermont	SW	1,617	1,721	1,896	45103
Batesville	Noble	SE	100	95	129	44815
Bay View	Erie	NE	692	739	804	44870
Bay Village	Cuyahoga	NE	16,087	17,000	17,846	44140
Beach City	Stark	NE	1,137	1,051	1,083	44608
Beachwood	Cuyahoga	NE	12,186	10,677	9,983	44122
Beallsville	Monroe	SE	423	464	601	43716
Beaver	Pike	SE	464	336	330	45613
Beavercreek	Greene	SW	37,984	33,626	31,589	45430-32
						45440
Beaverdam	Allen	NW	356	467	492	45808
Bedford	Cuyahoga	NE	14,214	14,822	15,056	44146
Bedford Heights	Cuyahoga	NE	11,375	12,131	13,214	44128
Bellaire	Belmont	SE	4,892	6,028	8,241	43906
Bellbrook	Greene	SW	7,009	6,511	5,174	45305
Belle Center	Logan	C	807	796	930	43310
Belle Valley	Noble	SE	263	267	329	43717
Bellefontaine	Logan	C	13,069	12,126	11,888	43311
Bellevue	Huron	NW	8,193	8,157	8,187	44811
Bellville	Richland	NE	1,773	1,568	1,714	44813
Belmont	Belmont	SE	532	471	714	43718
Belmore	Putnam	NW	171	161	205	45815
Beloit	Mahoning	NE	1,024	1,037	1,093	44609
Belpre	Washington	SE	6,660	6,796	7,193	45714
Bentleyville	Cuyahoga	NE	947	674	381	44022
Benton Ridge	Hancock	NW	315	351	343	45816
Berea	Cuyahoga	NE	18,970	19,051	19,567	44017
Bergholz	Jefferson	NE	769	713	914	43908
Berkey	Lucas	NW	265	264	306	43504
Berlin Heights	Erie	NW	685	691	756	44814
Bethel	Clermont	SW	2,637	2,407	2,231	45106
Bethesda	Belmont	SE	1,413	1,161	1,429	43719
Bettsville	Seneca	NW	784	752	752	44815
Beverly	Washington	SE	1,282	1,444	1,471	45715
Bexley	Franklin	C	13,203	13,088	13,405	43209
Blakeslee	Williams	NW	130	128	136	43505
Blanchester	Clinton	SW	4,220	4,206	3,202	45107
Bloomdale	Wood	NW	724	632	744	44817
Bloomingburg	Fayette	SW	874	769	869	43106
Bloomingdale	Jefferson	NE	221	227	254	43910
Bloomville	Seneca	NW	1,045	949	1,019	44818
Blue Ash	Hamilton	SW	12,513	11,923	9,506	45242
Bluffton	Allen	NW	3,896	3,367	3,310	45817
Bolivar	Tuscarawas	NE	894	914	989	44612
Boston Heights	Summit	NE	1,186	733	781	44236

Name	County	Region	2000	1990	1980	Zip
Botkins	Shelby	NW	1,205	1,340	1,372	45306
Bowerston	Harrison	NE	414	343	487	44695
Bowersville	Greene	SW	290	225	329	45307
Bowling Green	Wood	NW	29,636	28,303	25,728	43402
Bradford	Miami	SW	1,859	2,005	2,166	45308
Bradner	Wood	NW	1,171	1,093	1,175	43406
Brady Lake	Portage	NE	513	490	470	44211
Bratenahl	Cuyahoga	NE	1,337	1,356	1,485	44108
Brecksville	Cuyahoga	NE	13,382	11,818	10,132	44141
Bremen	Fairfield	C	1,265	1,386	1,432	43107
Brewster	Stark	NE	2,324	2,307	2,321	44613
Brice	Franklin	C	70	109	93	43109
Bridgeport	Belmont	SE	2,186	2,318	2,642	43912
Broadview Heights	Cuyahoga	NE	15,967	12,219	10,920	44147
Brook Park	Cuyahoga	NE	21,218	22,865	26,195	44142
Brooklyn	Cuyahoga	NE	11,586	11,706	12,342	44144
Brooklyn Heights	Cuyahoga	NE	1,558	1,450	1,653	44131
Brookside	Belmont	SE	644	703	887	43912
Brookville	Montgomery	SW	5,289	4,608	4,322	45309
Broughton	Paulding	NW	166	151	171	45879
Brunswick	Medina	NE	33,388	28,218	27,689	44212
Bryan	Williams	NW	8,333	8,348	7,879	43506
Buchtel	Athens	SW	574	640	585	45716
Buckeye Lake	Licking	C	3,049	2,986	—	43008
Buckland	Auglaize	NW	255	239	271	45819
Bucyrus	Crawford	NW	13,224	13,496	13,433	44820
Burbank	Wayne	NE	279	289	365	44214
Burgoon	Sandusky	NW	199	224	244	43407
Burkettsville	Mercer	SW	254	268	295	45310
Burton	Geauga	NE	1,450	1,349	1,401	44021
Butler	Richland	NE	921	968	955	44822
Butlerville	Warren	SW	231	188	223	45162
Byesville	Guernsey	SE	2,574	2,435	2,572	43723
Cadiz	Harrison	NE	3,308	3,439	4,058	43907
Cairo	Allen	NW	499	473	596	45820

THE INCLINES AND DECLINES OF OHIO POPULATION

trendspotting

During the 1990s, Ohio's major urban centers and the areas adjacent to them experienced the most significant population growth in the state, particularly in the central and southwest regions. The fastest growing counties, with a few exceptions, were located next to the urban core of a metropolitan area. Thus, Delaware, Clermont, Brown, Warren, and Union counties, all located adjacent to Cincinnati or Columbus, grew rapidly, while Franklin County gained the largest number of people overal; 107,541 since 1990.

Nineteen of the state's counties saw a decline in population since 1990. Jefferson County lost the highest percentage—an eight percent drop in population—while Hamilton County's population lost the most people with 20,925 (2.4%) followed by Cuyahoga which declined of 18,162 (1.3%).

Source: United States Census Bureau

"MOMMY, WHERE DO DADDIES COME FROM?"

Ohio's Smallest Villages

(in square miles)

Jacksonburg (Butler)

0.2

Ithaca (Darke)

0.3

New Rome (Franklin)

0.3

New Bavaria (Henry)

0.6

West Rushville (Fairfield)

0.6

Nashville (Holmes)

0.7

Brice (Franklin)

0.8

Lakeline (Lake)

0.8

Lockington (Shelby)

0.8

Lower Salem (Washington)

0.8

Miltonsburg (Monroe)

0.8

Name	County	Region	2000	1990	1980	Zip
Caldwell	Noble	SE	1,956	1,786	1,935	43724
Caledonia	Marion	C	578	644	759	43314
Cambridge	Guernsey	NE	11,520	11,748	13,573	43725
Camden	Preble	SW	2,302	2,210	1,971	45311
Campbell	Mahoning	SW	9,460	10,038	11,619	44405
Canal Fulton	Stark	NE	5,061	4,157	3,481	44614
Canal Winchester	Franklin	C	4,478	2,617	2,749	43110
Canfield	Mahoning	C	7,374	5,409	5,535	44406
Canton	Stark	C	80,806	84,161	94,730	44701-35
Cardington	Morrow	C	1,849	1,770	1,665	43315
Carey	Wyandot	NW	3,901	3,684	3,674	43316
Carlisle	Warren	SW	5,121	4,872	4,276	45005
Carroll	Fairfield	C	488	558	641	43112
Carrollton	Carroll	SW	3,190	3,019	3,065	44615
Casstown	Miami	SW	322	246	331	45312
Castalia	Erie	NE	935	915	973	44824
Castine	Darke	SW	129	163	147	45304
Catawba	Clark	SW	312	268	317	43010
Cecil	Paulding	NW	216	249	267	45821
Cedarville	Greene	SW	3,828	3,210	2,799	45314
Celina	Mercer	SW	10,303	9,923	9,137	45822
Centerburg	Knox	C	1,432	1,323	1,275	43011
Centerville City	Montgomery	SW	23,024	21,082	18,886	45458-59 45475
Centerville Village	Gallia	C	134	128	148	45458
Chagrin Falls	Cuyahoga	NE	4,024	4,146	4,335	44022
Chardon	Geauga	NE	5,156	4,446	4,434	44024
Chatfield	Crawford	NW	218	206	228	44825
Chauncey	Athens	SW	1,067	980	1,050	45719
Cherry Fork	Adams	SW	127	178	210	45618
Chesapeake	Lawrence	SE	842	1,073	1,370	45619
Cheshire	Gallia	SE	221	250	297	45620
Chesterhill	Morgan	SE	305	309	395	43728
Chesterville	Morrow	C	193	286	242	43317
Cheviot	Hamilton	SW	9,015	9,616	9,888	45211

Name	County	Region	2000	1990	1980	Zip
Chickasaw	Mercer	SW	364	378	381	45826
Chillicothe	Ross	SE	21,796	21,923	23,420	45601
Chilo	Clermont	SW	97	130	173	45112
Chippewa-on-the-Lake	Medina	C	823	271	245	44215
Christiansburg	Champaign	SW	553	599	593	45389
Cincinnati	Hamilton	SW	331,285	364,114	385,457	45201-75
Circleville	Pickaway	C	13,485	11,666	11,700	43113
Clarington	Monroe	SE	444	406	558	43915
Clarksburg	Ross	SE	516	523	483	43115
Clarksville	Clinton	SW	497	485	525	45113
Clay Center	Ottawa	NE	294	289	327	43408
Clayton	Montgomery	SW	13,347	713	752	45315
Cleveland	Cuyahoga	NE	478,403	505,616	573,822	44101-49
						44178
						44181
						44185
						44188-99
Cleveland Heights	Cuyahoga	NE	49,958	54,052	56,438	44118
Cleves	Hamilton	SW	2,790	2,208	2,094	45002
Clifton	Greene	SW	179	165	182	45316
Clinton	Summit	SW	1,337	1,175	1,277	44216
Cloverdale	Putnam	NW	201	270	304	45827
Clyde	Sandusky	NW	6,064	5,776	5,489	43410
Coal Grove	Lawrence	SW	2,027	2,251	2,630	45638
Coalton	Jackson	SW	545	553	639	45621
Coldwater	Mercer	SW	4,482	4,335	4,220	45828
College Corner	Butler	SW	424	379	364	45003
Columbiana	Columbiana	NE	5,635	4,961	4,987	44408
Columbus	Franklin	C	711,470	632,910	564,871	43201-40
Columbus Grove	Putnam	NW	2,200	2,231	2,313	45830
Commercial Point	Pickaway	C	776	405	316	43116
Conesville	Coshocton	NE	364	420	451	43811
Congress	Wayne	NE	192	162	178	44287
Conneaut	Ashtabula	NE	12,485	13,241	13,835	44030

James Schul, a young postal worker at the U.S. Postal Remote Encoding Center in Dayton, can encode more than 1,000 pieces of mail an hour with a 99.65% accuracy rate, and he knows by memory the ZIP code for virtually any city in America.

—The Associated Press

GROWING PAINS, I

Ten largest counties in Ohio

Population	2000
Cuyahoga	1,393,978
Franklin	1,068,978
Hamilton	845,303
Montgomery	559,062
Summit	542,899
Lucas	455.054
Stark	378,098
Butler	332,807
Lorain	284,664
Mahoning	257,555

Ten fastest growing counties in Ohio

Percent population increase, 1990-2000	
Delaware	64.3
Warren	39.0
Union	28.0
Noble	24.0
Medina	23.5
Brown	20.9
Fairfield	18.7
Holmes	18.6
Clermont	18.6
Vinton	15.4

Name	County	Region	2000	1990	1980	Zip
Continental	Putnam	NW	1,188	1,214	1,179	45831
Convoy	Van Wert	NW	1,110	1,200	1,140	45832
Coolville	Athens	SE	528	663	649	45723
Corning	Perry	SE	593	703	789	43730
Cortland	Trumbull	NE	6,830	5,652	5,011	44410
Corwin	Warren	SW	256	225	276	45068
Coshocton	Coshocton	NE	11,682	12,193	13,405	43812
Covington	Miami	SW	2,559	2,603	2,610	45318
Craig Beach	Mahoning	NE	1,254	1,402	1,657	44429
Crestline	Crawford	NW	5,088	4,934	5,406	44827
Creston	Wayne	NE	2,161	1,848	1,828	44217
Cridersville	Auglaize	NE	1,817	1,885	1,843	45806
Crooksville	Perry	SE	2,483	2,601	2,766	43731
Crown City	Gallia	NE	411	445	513	45623
Cumberland	Guernsey	SE	402	318	461	43732
Custar	Wood	NW	208	209	254	43511
Cuyahoga Falls	Summit	NE	49,374	48,950	50,526	44221-24
Cuyahoga Heights	Cuyahoga	NE	599	682	739	44127
Cygnet	Wood	NW	564	560	646	43413
Dalton	Wayne	NE	1,605	1,377	1,357	44618
Danville	Knox	C	1,104	1,001	1,132	43014
Darbyville	Pickaway	C	293	272	282	43136
Dayton	Montgomery	SW	166,179	182,005	199,538	45401-90
De Graff	Logan	C	1,212	1,331	1,358	43318
Deer Park	Hamilton	SW	5,982	6,181	6,745	45236
Deersville	Harrison	NE	82	86	109	44693
Defiance	Defiance	NE	16,465	16,787	16,810	43512
Delaware	Delaware	C	25,243	19,966	18,780	43015
Dellroy	Carroll	NE	294	314	368	44620
Delphos	Allen	NW	6,944	7,093	7,314	45833
Delta	Fulton	NW	2,930	2,849	2,886	43515
Dennison	Tuscarawas	NE	2,992	3,282	3,398	44621
Deshler	Henry	NW	1,831	1,876	1,870	43516
Dexter City	Noble	SE	166	161	173	45727
Dillonvale	Jefferson	NE	781	857	912	43917
Donnelsville	Clark	SW	293	276	219	45319

Name	County	Region	2000	1990	1980	Zip
Dover	Tuscarawas	NE	12,210	11,329	11,526	44622
Doylestown	Wayne	NE	2,799	2,668	2,493	44230
Dresden	Muskingum	SE	1,423	1,581	1,646	43821
Dublin	Franklin	C	31,392	16,366	3,855	43016-7
Dunkirk	Hardin	NW	952	869	954	45836
Dupont	Putnam	NW	268	279	308	45837
East Canton	Stark	NE	1,629	1,742	1,721	44730
East Cleveland	Cuyahoga	NE	27,217	33,096	36,957	44112
East Liverpool	Columbiana	NE	13,089	13,654	16,687	43920
East Palestine	Columbiana	NE	4,917	5,168	5,306	44413
East Sparta	Stark	NE	806	771	868	44626
Eastlake	Lake	NE	20,255	21,161	22,104	44094
Eaton	Preble	SW	8,133	7,396	6,839	45320
Edgerton	Williams	NE	2,117	1,896	1,813	43517
Edison	Morrow	C	437	488	504	43320
Edon	Williams	NE	898	880	947	43518
Eldorado	Preble	SW	543	549	509	45321
Elgin	Van Wert	NE	50	71	96	45838
Elida	Allen	NW	1,917	1,486	1,349	45807
Elmore	Ottawa	NE	1,426	1,334	1,271	43416
Elmwood Place	Hamilton	SW	2,681	2,937	2,840	45216
Elyria	Lorain	NE	55,953	56,746	57,504	44035-39
Empire	Jefferson	NE	300	364	484	43926
Englewood	Montgomery	SW	12,235	11,402	11,329	45322
Enon	Clark	SW	2,638	2,605	2,597	45323
Euclid	Cuyahoga	NE	52,717	54,875	59,999	44117
						44123
						44132
Evendale	Hamilton	SW	3,090	3,165	1,195	45241
Fairborn	Greene	SW	32,052	31,300	29,702	45324
Fairfax	Hamilton	SW	1,938	1,955	2,222	45227
Fairfield	Butler	SW	42,097	39,709	30,777	45014
Fairlawn	Summit	NE	7,307	5,779	6,100	44313
						44333-4
Fairport Harbor	Lake	NE	3,180	2,978	3,357	44077

BRIGHT LIGHTS

Ten largest cities in Ohio (population, 2000)		*Ten fastest growing cities in Ohio* (increase, 1990-2000)		*Ten fastest growing cities in Ohio* (since 1950)	
Columbus	771,470	*Clayton*	1,772%	*Riverside*	6,264%
Cleveland	478,403	*Riverside*	1,500%	*Gahanna*	5,376%
Cincinnati	331,285	*Green*	542%	*Reynoldsburg*	4,329%
Toledo	313,619	*Hudson*	334%	*Hilliard*	3,872%
Akron	217,074	*Pataskala*	236%	*Clayton*	2,764%
Dayton	166,179	*Trotwood*	211%	*Centerville*	2,684%
Parma	85,655	*Hilliard*	105%	*Trotwood*	2,472%
Youngstown	82,026	*Mason*	92%	*Springboro*	2,299%
Canton	80,806	*Dublin*	92%	*Aurora*	2,274%
Lorain	68,652	*Springboro*	88%	*Pickerington*	2,161%

Name	County	Region	2000	1990	1980	Zip
Fairview	Guernsey	SE	81	79	125	43772
Fairview Park	Cuyahoga	NE	17,572	18,028	19,311	44126
Farmersville	Montgomery	SW	980	932	950	45325
Fayette	Fulton	NW	1,340	1,248	1,222	43521
Fayetteville	Brown	SW	372	393	478	45118
Felicity	Clermont	SW	922	856	929	45120
Findlay	Hancock	NW	38,967	35,703	35,594	45839-40
Fletcher	Miami	SW	510	545	498	45326
Florida	Henry	NW	246	304	294	43545
Flushing	Belmont	SE	900	1,042	1,266	43977
Forest	Hardin	NW	1,488	1,594	1,633	45843
Forest Park	Hamilton	SW	19,463	18,621	18,675	45405
Fort Jennings	Putnam	NW	432	436	538	45844
Fort Loramie	Shelby	NW	1,344	1,042	977	45845
Fort Recovery	Mercer	SW	1,273	1,313	1,370	45846
Fort Shawnee	Allen	NW	3,855	4,128	4,541	45806
Fostoria	Seneca	NW	13,931	14,971	15,743	44830
Frankfort	Ross	SE	1,011	1,065	1,008	45628
Franklin	Warren	SW	11,396	11,026	10,711	45005
Frazeysburg	Muskingum	SE	1,201	1,165	1,025	43822
Fredericksburg	Wayne	NE	487	502	511	44627
Fredericktown	Knox	C	2,428	2,443	2,299	43019
Freeport	Harrison	NE	398	475	525	43973
Fremont	Sandusky	NE	17,375	17,619	17,834	43420
Fulton	Morrow	C	264	325	378	43321
Fultonham	Muskingum	SE	151	178	281	43738
Gahanna	Franklin	C	32,636	23,898	18,001	43230
Galena	Delaware	C	305	361	358	43021
Galion	Crawford	NW	11,341	11,859	12,391	44833
Gallipolis	Gallia	NE	4,180	4,831	5,576	45631
Gambier	Knox	C	1,871	2,073	2,056	43022
Gann	Knox	C	143	179	173	43005
Garfield Heights	Cuyahoga	NE	30,734	31,739	33,380	44125
Garrettsville	Portage	NE	2,262	2,014	1,769	44231
Gates Mills	Cuyahoga	NE	2,493	2,508	2,236	44040
Geneva	Ashtabula	NE	6,595	6,597	6,655	44041
Geneva-on-the-Lake	Ashtabula	NE	1,545	1,626	1,634	44041
Genoa	Ottawa	NW	2,230	2,262	2,213	43430
Georgetown	Brown	SW	3,691	3,627	3,467	45121
Germantown	Montgomery	SW	4,884	4,916	5,015	45327
Gettysburg	Darke	SW	558	539	545	45328
Gibsonburg	Sandusky	NW	2,506	2,579	2,479	43431
Gilboa	Putnam	NW	170	208	220	45875
Girard	Trumbull	NE	10,902	11,304	12,517	44420
Glandorf	Putnam	NW	919	829	746	45848
Glendale	Hamilton	SW	2,188	2,445	2,368	45246
Glenford	Perry	SE	198	208	173	43739
Glenmont	Holmes	NE	283	233	270	44628
Glenwillow	Cuyahoga	NE	449	455	492	44139
Gloria Glens Park	Medina	NE	538	446	435	44215
Glouster	Athens	SE	1,972	2,001	2,211	45732
Gnadenhutten	Tuscarawas	NE	1,280	1,226	1,320	44629
Golf Manor	Hamilton	SW	3,999	4,154	4,317	45237
Gordon	Darke	SW	190	206	230	45329
Grafton	Lorain	NE	2,302	3,344	2,231	44044
Grand Rapids	Wood	NW	1,002	955	962	43522
Grand River	Lake	NE	345	297	412	44045
Grandview	Washington	SW	6,695	7,010	7,420	43212
Granville	Licking	C	3,167	4,244	3,851	43023
Gratiot	Licking	C	187	195	227	43740
Gratis	Preble	SW	934	998	809	45330
Graysville	Monroe	SE	113	89	112	45734

GROWING PAINS, II

Ten most densly populated cities in Ohio
(people per square mile)

Lakewood City (*Cuyahoga County*)	10,208.5
East Cleveland (*Cuyahoga County*)	8,761.8
Elmwood Place (*Hamilton County*)	8,106.5
Cheviot (*Hamilton County*)	7,753.5
University Heights (*Cuyahoga County*)	7,713.6
Deer Park (*Hamilton County*)	6,979.0
Norwood (*Hamilton County*)	6,956.5
Cleveland (*Cuyahoga County*)	6,166.5
Willowick (*Lake County*)	5,709.2
North College Hill (*Hamilton County*)	5,491.0

Ten most densely populated villages in Ohio
(people per square mile)

Golf Manor (*Hamilton County*)	6,896.3
Lincoln Heights (*Hamilton County*)	5,556.1
Gloria Glens Park (*Medina County*)	4,730.7
Newburgh Heights (*Cuyahoga County*)	4,101.3
Mariemont (*Hamilton County*)	3,991.7
Vallyview (*Franklin County*)	3,957.6
Shadyside (*Belmont County*)	3,844.6
Brookside (*Belmont County*)	3,714.7
Maineville (*Warren County*)	3,637.1
Timberlake (*Lake County*)	3,614.1

Ten most densely populated places in Ohio★
(people per square mile)

Lincoln Village (*Franklin County*)	5,074.8
Northbrook (*Hamilton County*)	5,713.1
Blacklick Estates (*Franklin County*)	4,775.3
Pleasant Run Farm (*Hamilton County*)	4,511.4
Huber Ridge (*Franklin County*)	4,492.5
Mount Healthy Heights (*Hamilton County*)	4,489.7
White Oak— East (*Hamilton County*)	4,393.1
Dillonvale (*Hamilton County*)	4,118.2
Cherry Grove (*Hamilton County*)	4,038.2
Bridgetown North (*Hamilton County*)	3,735.1

★Each of these are census designated places (CDP) by the Census Bureau

Least dense cities in Ohio

Pataskala	359.5
Kirtland	401.8
Monroe	459.9
Conneaut	473.4
Streetsboro	512.6
Avon	548.4
Norton	572.8
Aurora	583.8
Green	711.7
Clayton	723.7

Least dense villages in Ohio

Holiday City	36.9
Berkly	63.5
St. Martins	78.3
Kelly's Island	80.5
Hunting Valley	92.1
Harpster	104.3
Waite Hill	105.9
Kirkland Hills	106.9
Graysville	113.4
Summitville	116.0

"ON THE ADVICE OF MY ATTORNEY, I WILL NOT SUBMIT TO DNA TESTING."

Name	County	Region	2000	1990	1980	Zip
Green	Summit	NE	22,817	19,179	—	44720
Green Camp	Marion	C	342	393	475	43322
Green Springs	Sandusky	NW	1,247	1,446	1,568	44836
Greenfield	Highland	SW	4,906	5,172	5,034	45123
Greenhills	Hamilton	SW	4,103	4,393	4,927	45218
Greenville	Darke	SW	13,294	12,863	12,999	45331
Greenwich	Huron	NE	1,525	1,442	1,458	44837
Grove City	Franklin	C	27,075	19,661	16,793	43123
Groveport	Franklin	C	3,865	2,948	3,286	43125
Grover Hill	Paulding	NW	412	518	486	45849
Hamden	Vinton	SE	871	877	1,010	45634
Hamersville	Brown	SW	515	586	688	45130
Hamilton	Butler	SW	60,690	61,436	63,189	45011-13 45015-18
Hamler	Henry	NW	650	623	625	43524
Hanging Rock	Lawrence	SW	279	306	353	45638
Hanover	Licking	C	885	803	926	43055
Hanoverton	Columbiana	NE	387	434	490	44423
Harbor View	Lucas	NE	99	122	164	43434
Harpster	Wyandot	NE	203	233	239	43323
Harrisburg	Franklin	C	332	340	363	43126
Harrison	Hamilton	SW	7,487	7,520	5,855	45030
Harrisville	Harrison	NE	259	308	324	43974
Harrod	Allen	NW	491	537	506	45850
Hartford	Trumbull	NE	412	418	444	44424
Hartville	Stark	NE	2,174	2,031	1,772	44632
Harveysburg	Warren	SW	563	437	425	45032
Haskins	Wood	NW	638	549	568	43525
Haviland	Paulding	NW	180	210	219	45851
Hayesville	Ashland	NE	348	457	518	44838
Heath	Licking	C	8,527	7,231	6,969	43056
Hebron	Licking	C	2,034	2,076	2,035	43025
Helena	Sandusky	NW	236	267	307	43435
Hemlock	Perry	SE	142	203	197	43730
Hicksville	Defiance	NW	3,649	3,664	3,742	43526
Higginsport	Brown	SW	291	298	343	45131

Name	County	Region	2000	1990	1980	Zip
Highland	Highland	SW	283	275	284	45132
Highland Heights	Cuyahoga	NE	8,082	6,249	5,739	44143
Hilliard	Franklin	C	24,230	11,794	8,008	43026
Hills and Dales	Stark	NE	260	297	281	44708
Hillsboro	Highland	SW	6,368	6,235	6,356	45133
Hiram	Portage	NE	1,242	1,330	1,360	44234
Holgate	Henry	NW	1,194	1,290	1,315	43527
Holland	Lucas	NE	1,306	1,210	1,048	43528
Hollansburg	Darke	SW	214	300	339	45332
Holloway	Belmont	SE	345	354	459	43985
Holmesville	Holmes	NE	386	419	436	44633
Hopedale	Harrison	NE	984	685	857	43976
Hoytville	Wood	NW	296	301	315	43529
Hubbard	Trumbull	NE	8,284	8,248	9,245	44425
Huber Heights	Montgomery	SW	38,212	38,696	35,401	45424
Hudson	Summit	NE	22,439	5,159	4,615	44236
Hunting Valley	Cuyahoga	NE	735	799	786	44022
Huntsville	Logan	C	454	343	489	43324
Huron	Erie	NE	7,958	7,067	7,123	44839
Independence	Cuyahoga	NE	7,109	6,500	8,165	44131
Indian Hill	Hamilton	SW	5,907	5,383	5,521	45243
Irondale	Jefferson	NE	418	382	535	43932
Ironton	Lawrence	SW	11,211	12,751	14,290	45638
Ithaca	Darke	SW	102	119	130	45304
Jackson	Jackson	SW	6,184	6,167	6,675	45640
Jackson Center	Shelby	NW	1,369	1,398	1,310	45334
Jacksonburg	Butler	SW	67	50	58	45067
Jacksonville	Athens	SE	544	544	651	45740
Jamestown	Greene	SW	1,917	1,794	1,702	45335
Jefferson	Ashtabula	NE	3,572	3,331	2,952	44047
Jeffersonville	Fayette	SW	1,288	1,281	1,252	43128
Jenera	Hancock	NW	235	285	302	45841
Jeromesville	Ashland	NE	478	582	582	44840
Jerry City	Wood	NW	453	517	512	43437
Jerusalem	Monroe	SE	152	144	237	43747
Jewett	Harrison	NE	784	778	972	43986
Johnstown	Licking	C	3,440	3,242	3,158	43031
Junction City	Perry	SE	818	770	754	43748
Kalida	Putnam	NW	1,031	947	1,019	45853
Kelleys Island	Erie	NW	367	172	121	43438
Kent	Portage	NE	27,906	28,835	26,164	44240
Kenton	Hardin	NW	8,336	8,356	8,605	43326
Kettering	Montgomery	SW	57,502	60,569	61,186	45429
Kettlersville	Shelby	NW	175	194	199	45336
Killbuck	Holmes	NE	839	809	937	44637
Kimbolton	Guernsey	SE	190	134	255	43749
Kingston	Ross	SE	1,032	1,153	1,208	45644
Kipton	Lorain	NE	265	283	352	44049
Kirby	Wyandot	NW	132	155	158	43330
Kirkersville	Licking	C	520	563	626	43033
Kirtland	Lake	NE	6,670	5,881	5,969	44094
Kirtland Hills	Lake	NE	597	495	506	44060
La Rue	Marion	C	775	802	861	43332
Lafayette	Allen	NW	304	449	488	45854
Lagrange	Lorain	NE	1,815	1,199	1,258	44050
Lakeline	Lake	NE	165	210	258	44094
Lakemore	Summit	NE	2,561	2,684	2,744	44250
Lakeview	Logan	C	1,074	1,056	1,089	43331
Lakewood	Cuyahoga	NE	56,646	59,718	61,963	44107
Lancaster	Fairfield	C	35,335	34,507	34,953	43130
Latty	Paulding	NW	200	205	261	45855

Name	County	Region	2000	1990	1980	Zip
Laura	Miami	SW	487	483	501	45337
Laurelville	Hocking	SE	533	605	591	43135
Lawrenceville	Clark	SW	302	304	307	45502
Lebanon	Warren	SW	16,962	10,461	9,636	45036
Leesburg	Highland	SW	1,253	1,063	1,019	45135
Leesville	Carroll	NE	184	156	233	44639
Leetonia	Columbiana	NE	2,043	2,070	2,121	44431
Leipsic	Putnam	NW	2,236	2,203	2,171	45856
Lewisburg	Preble	SW	1,798	1,584	1,450	45338
Lewisville	Monroe	SE	233	261	285	43754
Lexington	Richland	NE	4,165	4,124	3,823	44904
Liberty Center	Henry	NW	1,109	1,084	1,111	43532
Lima	Allen	NW	40,081	45,553	47,381	45801-07
Limaville	Stark	NW	193	152	164	44640
Lincoln Heights	Hamilton	SW	4,113	4,805	5,259	45215
Lindsey	Sandusky	NW	504	529	571	43442
Linndale	Cuyahoga	NE	117	159	129	45135
Lisbon	Columbiana	NE	2,788	3,037	3,159	44432
Lithopolis	Fairfield	C	600	563	652	43136
Lockbourne	Franklin	C	280	237	373	43137
Lockington	Shelby	NW	208	214	203	45356
Lockland	Hamilton	SW	3,707	4,357	4,292	45215
Lodi	Medina	NE	3,061	3,042	2,942	44254
Logan	Hocking	SW	6.704	6,725	6,557	43138
London	Madison	C	8,771	7,807	6,958	43140
Lorain	Lorain	SW	68,652	71,245	75,416	44052-55
Lordstown	Trumbull	NE	3,633	3,404	3,280	44481
Lore City	Guernsey	NE	305	384	443	43755
Loudonville	Ashland	NE	2,906	2,915	2,945	44842
Louisville	Stark	NW	8,904	8,087	7,873	44641
Loveland	Clermont	SW	11,677	10,122	9,106	45140
Lowell	Washington	SE	628	617	729	45744
Lowellville	Mahoning	NE	1,281	1,349	1,558	44436
Lower Salem	Washington	SW	109	103	110	45745
Lucas	Richland	NE	620	730	753	44843
Luckey	Wood	NW	998	848	895	43443
Ludlow Falls	Miami	SW	210	300	248	45339
Lynchburg	Highland	SW	1,350	1,212	1,205	45142
Lyndhurst	Cuyahoga	NE	15,279	15,982	18,092	44124
Lyons	Fulton	NW	559	579	596	43533
Macedonia	Summit	NE	9,224	7,509	6,571	44056
Macksburg	Washington	SE	202	—	—	45746
Madeira	Hamilton	SW	8,923	9,141	9,341	45243
Madison	Lake	NE	2,921	2,477	2,291	44057
Magnetic Springs	Union	C	323	373	314	43036
Magnolia	Stark	NE	931	937	986	44643
Maineville	Warren	SW	885	359	307	45039
Malinta	Henry	NW	285	294	327	43535
Malta	Morgan	SE	696	802	956	43758
Malvern	Carroll	NE	1,218	1,112	1,032	44644
Manchester	Adams	SW	2,043	2,223	2,313	45144
Mansfield	Richland	NE	49,346	50,627	53,927	44901-07
Mantua	Portage	NE	1,046	1,178	1,041	44255
Maple Heights	Cuyahoga	NE	26,156	27,089	29,735	44137
Marble Cliff	Franklin	C	646	633	630	43212
Marblehead	Ottawa	NW	762	746	679	43440
Marengo	Morrow	C	297	393	329	43334
Mariemont	Hamilton	SW	3,408	3,118	3,295	45227
Marietta	Washington	SE	14,515	15,026	16,467	45750
Marion	Marion	C	35,318	34,075	37,040	43301-02
Marseilles	Wyandot	NW	124	130	164	43351
Marshallville	Wayne	NE	826	758	788	44645

Name	County	Region	2000	1990	1980	Zip
Martins Ferry	Belmont	SW	7,226	7,990	9,331	43935
Martinsburg	Knox	C	185	213	240	43037
Martinsville	Clinton	SW	440	476	539	45146
Marysville	Union	C	15,942	9,656	7,414	43040-41
Mason	Warren	SW	22,016	11,450	8,692	45040
Massillon	Stark	NE	31,325	30,964	30,557	44646-48
Matamoras	Washington	SE	957	1,002	1,172	45767
Maumee	Lucas	NW	15,237	15,561	15,747	43537
Mayfield	Cuyahoga	NE	3,435	3,462	3,577	44143
Mayfield Heights	Cuyahoga	NE	19,386	19,847	21,550	44124
McArthur	Vinton	SW	1,888	1,541	1,912	45651
McClure	Henry	NE	761	781	694	43534
McComb	Handcock	NW	1,676	1,544	1,608	45858
McConnelsville	Morgan	SE	1,676	1,804	2,018	43756
McDonald	Trumbull	NE	3,481	3,526	3,744	44437
McGuffey	Hardin	NW	522	550	646	45859
Mechanicsburg	Champaign	SW	1,744	1,803	1,792	43044
Medina	Medina	NE	25,139	19,231	15,268	44256
						44258-59
Melrose	Paulding	NW	322	307	315	45861
Mendon	Mercer	SW	697	717	749	45862
Mentor	Lake	NE	50,278	47,491	42,065	44060-61
Mentor-on-the-Lake	Lake	NE	8,127	8,271	7,919	44060
Metamora	Fulton	NW	563	543	556	43540
Meyers Lake	Stark	NE	565	493	222	44730
Miamisburg	Montgomery	SW	19,489	17,834	15,304	45342-43
Middle Point	Van Wert	NW	593	639	709	45863
Middleburg Heights	Cuyahoga	NE	15,542	14,702	16,218	44130
Middlefield	Geauga	NE	2,233	1,898	1,997	44062
Middleport	Meigs	SE	2,525	2,725	2,971	45760
Middletown	Butler	SW	51,605	46,022	43,719	45042-44
Midland	Clinton	SW	265	319	365	45148
Midvale	Tuscarawas	NE	547	575	654	44653
Midway	Madison	C	274	289	339	43151
Mifflin	Ashland	NE	144	162	203	44805
Milan	Erie	NW	1,445	1,464	1,569	44846
Milford	Clermont	SW	6,284	5,660	5,232	45150
Milford Center	Union	C	626	651	764	43045
Millbury	Wood	NW	1,161	1,081	955	43447
Milledgeville	Fayette	SW	122	120	162	43142
Miller City	Putnam	NW	136	173	168	45864
Millersburg	Holmes	NE	3,326	3,051	3,247	44654
Millersport	Fairfield	C	963	1,010	844	43046
Millville	Butler	SW	817	755	809	45013
Milton Center	Wood	NW	195	200	181	43541
Miltonsburg	Monroe	SE	29	56	109	
Mineral City	Tuscarawas	NE	841	756	884	44656
Minerva	Stark	NE	3,934	4,318	4,549	44657
Minerva Park	Stark	NE	1,288	1,463	1,618	43229
Mingo Junction	Jefferson	NE	3,631	4,297	4,834	43938
Minster	Auglaize	NW	2,794	2,650	2,557	45865
Mogadore	Summit	NE	3,893	4,008	4,190	44260
Monroe	Butler	SW	7,133	4,490	4,256	45050
Monroeville	Huron	NW	1,433	1,381	1,329	44847
Montezuma	Mercer	SW	191	199	200	45866
Montgomery	Hamilton	SW	10,163	9,733	10,088	45242
Montpelier	Williams	NW	4,320	4,299	4,431	43543
Moraine	Montgomery	SW	6,897	5,989	5,325	45439
Moreland Hills	Cuyahoga	NE	3,298	3,354	3,083	44022
Morral	Marion	C	388	373	454	43337
Morristown	Belmont	SE	299	296	463	43759
Morrow	Warren	SW	1,286	1,206	1,254	45152

The U.S. Census honored Miltonsburg, in Monroe County, as Ohio's smallest village—pop. 29. It is so small that when children sled down the village's hills, they slide to a stop in Malaga Township.

—The Plain Dealer

Name	County	Region	2000	1990	1980	Zip
Moscow	Clermont	SW	244	279	324	45153
Mount Blanchard	Hancock	NW	484	491	492	45867
Mount Cory	Hancock	NW	203	245	276	45868
Mount Eaton	Wayne	NE	246	249	289	44659
Mount Gilead	Morrow	C	3,290	2,846	2,911	43338
Mount Healthy	Hamilton	SW	7,149	7,580	7,562	45231
Mount Orab	Brown	SW	2,307	1,929	1,573	45154
Mount Pleasant	Jefferson	NE	535	498	616	43939
Mount Sterling	Madison	C	1,865	1,647	1,623	43143
Mount Vernon	Knox	C	14,375	14,550	14,380	43050
Mount Victory	Hardin	NW	600	551	667	43340
Mowrystown	Highland	SW	373	460	475	45155
Munroe Falls	Summit	NE	5,314	5,359	4,731	44262
Murray City	Hocking	SW	452	499	579	43144
Mutual	Champaign	SW	132	126	159	43044
Napoleon	Henry	NW	9,318	8,884	8,614	43545
Nashville	Holmes	NE	172	181	211	44661
Navarre	Stark	NE	1,440	1,635	1,343	44662
Nellie	Clermont	SW	134	130	150	43844
Nelsonville	Athens	SE	5,230	4,563	4,567	45764
Nevada	Wyandot	NW	814	849	945	44849
Neville	Clermont	SW	127	226	142	45156
New Albany	Franklin	C	3,711	1,621	409	43054
New Alexandria	Jefferson	NE	222	257	410	43938
New Athens	Harrison	SE	342	370	440	43981
New Bavaria	Henry	NW	78	92	135	43548
New Bloomington	Marion	C	548	282	303	43341
New Boston	Scioto	SE	2,340	2,717	3,188	45662
New Bremen	Auglaize	NW	2,909	2,558	2,393	45869
New Carlisle	Clark	SW	5,735	6,049	6,498	45344
New Concord	Muskingum	SE	2,651	2,086	1,860	43762
New Franklin	Stark	NE	2,191	—	—	44657
New Holland	Pickaway	C	785	841	783	43145
New Knoxville	Auglaize	NW	891	838	760	45871
New Lebanon	Montgomery	SW	4,231	4,323	4,501	45345
New Lexington	Perry	SE	4,689	5,117	5,179	43764
New London	Huron	NW	2,696	2,642	2,449	44851
New Madison	Darke	SW	817	928	1,008	45346
New Miami	Butler	SW	2,469	2,555	2,980	45011
New Middletown	Mahoning	NE	1,682	1,912	2,195	44442
New Paris	Preble	SW	1,623	1,801	1,709	45347
New Philadelphia	Tuscarawas	NE	17,056	15,698	16,883	44663
New Richmond	Clermont	SW	2,219	2,408	2,769	45157
New Riegel	Seneca	SE	226	298	329	44853
New Rome	Franklin	C	60	111	63	43228
New Straitsville	Perry	SE	774	865	937	43766
New Vienna	Clinton	SW	1,294	932	1,133	45159
New Washington	Crawford	NW	987	1,057	1,213	44854
New Waterford	Columbiana	NE	1,391	1,278	1,314	44445
New Weston	Darke	SW	135	148	184	45348
Newark	Licking	C	46,279	44,396	41,200	43055-58
Newburgh Heights	Cuyahoga	NE	2,389	2,310	2,678	44105
Newcomerstown	Tuscarawas	NE	4,008	4,012	3,986	43852
Newton Falls	Trumbull	NE	5,002	4,923	4,960	44444
Newtonsville	Clermont	SW	492	427	434	45158
Newtown	Hamilton	SW	2,420	1,589	1,817	45244
Ney	Defiance	NW	364	331	379	43549
Niles	Trumbull	NE	20,932	21,128	23,088	44446
North Baltimore	Wood	NW	3,361	3,139	3,127	45872
North Bend	Hamilton	SW	603	541	546	45052
North Canton	Stark	NE	16,369	14,904	14,228	44720
North College Hill	Hamilton	SW	10,082	11,002	10,990	452391

WELL, NOW WE KNOW THE KRAVITZES HAVE THE BOMB.

Name	County	Region	2000	1990	1980	Zip
North Fairfield	Huron	NE	573	504	525	44855
North Hampton	Clark	SW	370	417	421	45349
North Kingsville	Ashtabula	NE	2,658	2,672	2,939	44068
North Lewisburg	Champaign	SW	1,588	1,160	1,072	43060
North Olmsted	Cuyahoga	NE	34,113	34,204	36,486	44070
North Perry	Lake	NE	838	824	897	44081
North Randall	Cuyahoga	NE	906	977	1,054	44128
North Ridgeville	Lorain	NE	22,338	21,564	21,522	44039
North Robinson	Crawford	NW	211	216	302	44856
North Royalton	Cuyahoga	NE	28,648	23,197	17,671	44133
North Star	Darke	SW	209	246	254	45350
Northfield	Summit	NE	3,827	3,624	3,913	44067
Northwood	Wood	NW	5,471	5,506	5,495	43619
Norton	Summit	NE	11,523	11,477	12,242	44203
Norwalk	Huron	SW	16,238	14,731	14,358	44857
Norwich	Muskingum	SE	113	133	170	43767
Norwood	Hamilton	SW	21,675	23,674	26,342	45212
Oak Harbor	Ottawa	NW	2,841	2,637	2,678	43449
Oak Hill	Jackson	SE	1,685	1,831	1,713	45656
Oakwood City	Montgomery	SW	9,215	8,957	9,372	45409
						45419
Oakwood Village	Paulding	NW	607	709	886	45873
Oakwood Village	Cuyahoga	C	3,667	3,392	3,786	44146
Oberlin	Lorain	NE	8,195	8,191	8,660	44074
Obetz	Franklin	C	3,977	3,167	3,095	43207
Octa	Fayette	SW	83	78	74	43160
Ohio City	VanWert	NW	784	899	881	45874
Old Washington	Guernsey	SE	265	281	279	43768
Olmsted Falls	Cuyahoga	NE	7,962	6,741	5,868	44138
Ontario	Richland	NE	5,303	4,026	4,123	44862
Orange	Cuyahoga	NE	3,236	2,810	2,376	44022
Orangeville	Trumbull	NE	189	253	223	44453
Oregon	Lucas	NW	19,355	18,334	18,675	43605
Orient	Pickaway	C	269	273	283	43146

Name	County	Region	2000	1990	1980	Zip
Orrville	Wayne	NE	8,551	7,712	7,511	44667
Orwell	Ashtabula	NE	1,519	1,258	1,067	44076
Osgood	Darke	SW	255	255	306	45351
Ostrander	Delaware	C	405	431	397	43061
Ottawa	Putnam	NW	4,367	3,999	3,874	45875
Ottawa Hills	Lucas	NW	4,564	4,543	4,065	43606
Ottoville	Putnam	NW	873	842	833	45876
Otway	Scioto	SE	86	105	161	45657
Owensville	Clermont	SW	816	1,019	858	45160
Oxford	Butler	SW	21,943	18,937	17,655	45056
Painesville	Lake	NE	17,503	15,769	16,391	44077
Palestine	Darke	SW	170	197	213	45352
Pandora	Putnam	NW	1,188	1,009	977	45877
Parma	Cuyahoga	NE	85,655	87,876	92,548	44129
Parma Heights	Cuyahoga	NE	21,659	21,448	23,112	44130
Parral	Tuscarawas	NE	241	255	259	44622
Pataskala	Licking	C	10,249	3,046	2,284	43062
Patterson	Hardin	NW	138	145	153	45843
Paulding	Paulding	NW	3,595	2,605	2,754	45879
Payne	Paulding	NW	1,166	1,244	1,399	45880
Peebles	Adams	SW	1,739	1,782	1,790	45660
Pemberville	Wood	NW	1,365	1,279	1,321	43450
Peninsula	Summit	NE	602	562	604	44264
Pepper Pike	Cuyahoga	NE	6,040	6,185	6,177	44124
Perry	Lake	NE	1,195	1,012	961	44081
Perrysburg	Wood	NE	16,945	12,551	10,215	43551
Perrysville	Ashland	NE	816	691	836	44864
Phillipsburg	Montgomery	SW	628	644	705	45354
Philo	Muskingum	SE	769	810	799	43771
Pickerington	Fairfield	C	9,792	5,668	3,917	43147
Piketon	Pike	SE	1,907	1,717	1,726	45661
Pioneer	Williams	NW	1,460	1,287	1,133	43554
Piqua	Miami	SW	20,738	20,612	20,480	45356
Pitsburg	Darke	SW	392	425	460	45358
Plain City	Madison	C	2,832	2,278	2,102	43064
Plainfield	Coshocton	NE	158	178	221	43836
Pleasant City	Guernsey	SE	439	419	481	43772
Pleasant Hill	Miami	SW	1,134	1,066	1,051	45359
Pleasant Plain	Warren	SW	156	138	210	45162
Pleasantville	Fairfield	C	877	926	780	43148
Plymouth	Richland	NE	1,852	1,942	1,939	44865
Poland	Mahoning	NE	2,866	2,992	3,084	44514
Polk	Ashland	NE	357	355	351	44866
Pomeroy	Meigs	SE	1,966	2,259	2,728	45769
Port Clinton	Ottawa	NW	6,391	7,106	7,223	43452
Port Jefferson	Shelby	NW	321	381	482	45360
Port Washington	Tuscarawas	NE	552	513	622	43837
Port William	Clinton	SW	258	245	300	45164
Portage	Wood	NE	428	469	479	43451
Portsmouth	Scioto	SE	20,909	22,676	25,943	45662-3
Potsdam	Miami	SW	203	250	289	45361
Powell	Delaware	C	6,247	2,154	387	43065
Powhatan Point	Belmont	SE	1,744	1,807	2,181	43942
Proctorville	Lawrence	SE	620	765	975	45669
Prospect	Marion	C	1,191	1,148	1,159	43342
Put-in-Bay	Ottawa	NW	128	141	146	43456
Quaker City	Guernsey	NE	563	560	698	43773
Quincy	Logan	C	734	697	633	43343
Racine	Meigs	SE	746	729	908	45771
Rarden	Scioto	SW	176	184	199	45671
Ravenna	Portage	NE	11,771	12,069	11,987	44266
Rawson	Hancock	NW	465	482	477	45881

Name	County	Region	2000	1990	1980	Zip
Rayland	Jefferson	NE	434	490	566	43943
Reading	Hamilton	SW	11,292	12,038	12,879	45215
Reminderville	Summit	NE	2,347	2,163	1,960	44202
Rendville	Perry	SE	46	32	68	43730
Republic	Seneca	NW	614	611	656	44867
Reynoldsburg	Franklin	C	32,069	25,748	20,661	43068
Richfield	Summit	NE	3,286	3,207	3,437	44286
Richmond	Jefferson	NE	471	446	624	43944
Richmond Heights	Cuyahoga	NE	10,944	9,611	10,095	44143
Richwood	Union	C	2,156	2,186	2,181	43344
Ridgeway	Hardin	NW	354	378	388	43345
Rio Grande	Gallia	SE	919	995	864	45674
Ripley	Brown	SW	1,745	1,816	2,174	45167
Rising Sun	Wood	NW	620	659	698	43457
Rittman	Wayne	NE	6,314	6,147	6,063	44270
Riverlea	Franklin	C	499	503	528	43085
Riverside	Montgomery	SW	23,545	1,471	1,475	45424
Roaming Shores	Ashtabula	NE	1,239	775	581	44085
Rochester	Lorain	NE	190	206	207	44090
Rock Creek	Ashtabula	NE	584	553	652	44084
Rockford	Mercer	SW	1,126	1,119	1,245	45882
Rocky Ridge	Ottawa	NW	389	425	457	43458
Rocky River	Cuyahoga	NE	20,735	20,410	21,084	44116
Rogers	Columbiana	NE	266	247	298	44455
Rome	Ashtabula	NE	117	99	135	44085
Roseville	Muskingum	SE	1,936	1,847	1,915	43777
Rossburg	Darke	SW	224	250	260	45362
Rossford	Wood	NW	6,406	5,861	5,978	43460
Roswell	Tuscarawas	NE	276	257	264	44663
Rushsylvania	Logan	C	543	573	610	43347
Rushville	Fairfield	C	268	229	299	43150
Russells Point	Logan	C	1,619	1,507	1,156	43348
Russellville	Brown	SW	453	459	445	45168
Russia	Shelby	NE	551	442	438	45363
Rutland	Meigs	SE	401	469	635	45775
Sabina	Clinton	SW	2,780	2,662	2,799	45169
Salem	Columbiana	NE	12,197	12,233	12,869	44460
Salesville	Guernsey	NE	154	84	139	43778
Salineville	Columbiana	NE	1,397	1,474	1,629	43945
Sandusky	Erie	NW	27,844	29,764	31,360	44870-71
Sarahsville	Noble	SE	198	162	226	43779
Sardinia	Brown	SW	862	792	826	45171
Savannah	Ashland	NE	372	363	351	44874
Scio	Harrison	NE	799	856	1,003	43988
Scott	Van Wert	NW	322	339	340	45886
Seaman	Adams	SW	1,039	1,013	1,039	45679
Sebring	Mahoning	NE	4,912	4,848	5,078	44672
Senecaville	Guernsey	NE	453	434	458	43780
Seven Hills	Cuyahoga	NE	12,080	12,339	13,650	44131
Seven Mile	Butler	SW	678	804	841	45062
Seville	Medina	NE	2,160	1,810	1,568	44273
Shadyside	Belmont	SW	3,675	3,934	4,315	43947
Shaker Heights	Cuyahoga	NE	29,405	30,867	32,487	44120
Sharonville	Hamilton	SW	13,804	13,121	10,108	45241
Shawnee	Perry	SE	608	742	924	43782
Shawnee Hills	Delaware	C	419	423	430	43065
Sheffield	Lorain	NE	2,949	1,943	1,886	44054
Sheffield Lake	Lorain	NE	9,371	9,825	10,484	44054
Shelby	Richland	NE	9,821	9,610	9,645	44875
Sherrodsville	Carroll	NE	316	284	396	44675
Sherwood	Defiance	NW	801	828	915	43556
Shiloh	Richland	NE	721	778	857	44878

Name	County	Region	2000	1990	1980	Zip
Shreve	Wayne	NE	1,582	1,584	1,608	44676
Sidney	Shelby	NW	20,211	18,710	17,657	45365
Silver Lake	Summit	NE	3,019	2,756	2,915	44221
Silverton	Hamilton	SW	5,178	5,859	6,172	45236
Sinking Spring	Highland	SW	158	189	239	45172
Smithfield	Jefferson	NE	867	874	1,308	43948
Smithville	Wayne	NE	1,333	1,354	1,467	44677
Solon	Cuyahoga	NE	21,802	18,548	14,341	44139
Somerset	Perry	SE	1,549	1,390	1,432	43783
Somerville	Butler	SW	294	279	357	45064
South Amherst	Lorain	NE	1,863	1,765	1,848	44001
South Bloomfield	Pickaway	C	1,179	900	934	43103
South Charleston	Clark	SW	1,850	1,626	1,682	45368
South Euclid	Cuyahoga	NE	23,537	23,866	25,713	44121
South Lebanon	Warren	SW	2,538	2,696	2,700	45065
South Point	Lawrence	SW	3,742	3,823	3,918	45680
South Russell	Geauga	NE	4,022	3,402	2,784	44022
South Salem	Ross	SE	213	227	252	45681
South Solon	Madison	C	405	379	416	43153
South Vienna	Clark	SW	469	550	464	45369
South Webster	Scioto	SE	764	806	886	45682
South Zanesville	Muskingum	SE	1,936	1,969	1,739	43701
Sparta	Morrow	C	191	201	219	43350
Spencer	Medina	NE	747	726	764	44275
Spencerville	Allen	NW	2,235	2,288	2,184	45887
Spring Valley	Greene	SW	510	507	541	45370
Springboro	Warren	SW	12,380	6,574	4,962	45066
Springdale	Hamilton	SW	10,563	10,621	10,111	45246
Springfield	Clark	SW	65,358	70,487	72,563	45501-06
St. Bernard	Hamilton	SW	4,924	5,344	5,396	45216-7
St. Clairsville	Belmont	SE	5,057	5,162	5,452	43950
St. Henry	Mercer	SW	2,271	1,907	1,596	45883
St. Louisville	Licking	C	346	372	375	43071
St. Martin	Brown	SW	91	141	126	45118
St. Marys	Auglaize	NW	8,342	8,441	8,414	45885
St. Paris	Champaign	SW	1,998	1,842	1,742	43072
Stafford	Monroe	SE	86	89	98	43786
Steubenville	Jefferson	NE	19,015	22,125	26,400	43952
Stockport	Morgan	SE	540	462	558	43787
Stone Creek	Tuscarawas	NE	184	181	150	43840
Stoutsville	Fairfield	C	581	518	537	43154
Stow	Summit	NE	32,139	27,998	25,303	44224
Strasburg	Tuscarawas	NE	2,310	1,984	2,091	44680
Stratton	Jefferson	NE	277	278	356	43961
Streetsboro	Portage	NE	12,311	9,932	9,055	44241
Strongsville	Cuyahoga	NE	43,858	35,308	28,577	44136
Struthers	Mahoning	NE	11,756	12,284	13,624	44471
Stryker	Williams	NW	1,406	1,468	1,423	43557
Sugar Bush Knolls	Portage	NE	227	211	201	44240
Sugar Grove	Fairfield	C	448	465	407	43155
Sugarcreek	Tuscarawas	NE	2,174	2,062	1,966	44681
Summerfield	Noble	SE	296	295	299	43788
Summitville	Columbiana	NE	108	125	146	43962
Sunbury	Delaware	C	2,630	2,046	1,911	43074
Swanton	Fulton	NW	3,307	3,557	3,424	43558
Sycamore	Wyandot	NW	914	919	1,059	44882
Sylvania	Lucas	NW	18,670	17,489	15,527	43560
Syracuse	Meigs	SE	879	827	946	45779
Tallmadge	Summit	NE	16,390	14,870	15,269	44278
Tarlton	Pickaway	C	298	315	394	43156
Terrace Park	Hamilton	SW	2,273	2,133	2,044	45174
Thornville	Perry	SE	731	758	838	43076

Name	County	Region	2000	1990	1980	Zip
Thurston	Fairfield	C	555	539	527	43157
Tiffin	Seneca	NW	18,135	18,604	19,549	44883
Tiltonsville	Jefferson	NE	1,329	1,517	1,750	43963
Timberlake	Lake	NE	775	833	885	44094
Tipp City	Miami	SW	9,221	6,027	5,595	45371
Tiro	Crawford	NW	281	246	279	44887
Toledo	Lucas	NW	313,619	332,943	354,635	43617
						43620
						46601-15
Tontogany	Wood	NW	364	364	367	43565
Toronto	Jefferson	NE	5,676	6,127	6,934	43964
Tremont City	Clark	SW	349	493	374	45372
Trenton	Butler	SW	8,746	6,189	6,401	45067
Trimble	Athens	SE	466	441	579	45782
Trotwood	Montgomery	SW	27,420	8,816	7,802	45426
Troy	Miami	SW	21,999	19,478	19,086	45373
Tuscarawas	Tuscarawas	NE	934	826	917	44682
Twinsburg	Summit	NE	17,006	9,606	7,632	44087
Uhrichsville	Tuscarawas	NE	5,662	5,631	6,130	44683
Union	Montgomery	SW	5,574	5,501	5,219	45322
Union City	Darke	NE	1,767	1,984	1,716	45390
Unionville Center	Union	C	299	238	272	43077
Uniopolis	Auglaize	NW	256	261	259	45888
University Heights	Cuyahoga	NE	14,146	14,787	15,401	44118
Upper Arlington	Franklin	C	33,686	34,128	35,648	43221
Upper Sandusky	Wyandot	NW	6,533	5,906	5,967	43351
Urbana	Champaign	SW	11,613	11,353	10,762	43078
Urbancrest	Franklin	C	868	862	880	43123
Utica	Licking	C	2,130	1,997	2,238	43080
Valley Hi	Logan	C	244	217	60	43360
Valley View	Cuyahoga	NE	2,179	2,137	1,576	44125
Valleyview	Franklin	C	601	604	730	43204
Van Buren	Hancock	NW	313	337	342	45889
Van Wert	Van Wert	NE	10,690	10,922	11,035	45891
Vandalia	Montgomery	SW	14,603	13,872	13,161	45377
Vanlue	Hancock	NW	371	373	390	45890
Venedocia	VanWert	NE	160	158	161	45894
Vermilion	Erie	NE	10,927	11,127	11,012	44089
Verona	Preble	SW	430	472	571	45378
Versailles	Darke	SW	2,589	2,351	2,384	45380
Vinton	Gallia	NE	324	293	375	45686
Wadsworth	Medina	NE	18,437	15,718	15,166	44281-2
Waite Hill	Lake	NE	446	454	529	44094
Wakeman	Huron	NW	951	951	906	44889
Walbridge	Wood	NW	2,546	2,736	2,900	4346
Waldo	Marion	C	332	340	347	43356
Walton Hills	Cuyahoga	NE	2,400	2,371	2,199	44146
Wapakoneta	Auglaize	NW	9,474	9,214	8,402	45895
Warren	Trumbull	NE	46,832	50,793	56,629	44481-88
Warrensville Heights	Cuyahoga	NE	15,109	15,745	16,565	44122
Warsaw	Coshocton	NE	781	699	765	43844
Washington Court House	Fayette	SW	13,524	13,080	12,682	43160
Washingtonville	Columbiana	NE	789	894	865	44490
Waterville	Lucas	NW	4,828	4,517	3,884	43566
Wauseon	Fulton	NW	7,091	6,322	6,173	43567
Waverly	Pike	SE	4,433	4,477	4,603	45690
Wayne	Wood	NW	842	803	894	43466
Wayne Lakes	Darke	SW	684	671	—	45331
Waynesburg	Stark	NE	1,003	1,068	1,160	44688
Waynesfield	Auglaize	NW	803	831	826	45896
Waynesville	Warren	SW	2,558	1,949	1,796	45068
Wellington	Lorain	NE	4,511	4,140	4,146	44090

Name	County	Region	2000	1990	1980	Zip
Wellston	Jackson	SE	6,078	6,049	6,016	45692
Wellsville	Columbiana	NE	4,133	4,532	5,095	43968
West Alexandria	Preble	SW	1,395	1,460	1,313	45381
West Carrollton	Montgomery	SW	13,818	14,403	13,148	45449
West Elkton	Preble	SW	194	208	277	45070
West Farmington	Trumbull	NE	519	542	563	44491
West Lafayette	Coshocton	NE	2,313	2,129	2,225	43845
West Leipsic	Putnam	NW	271	244	298	45856
West Liberty	Logan	C	1,813	1,613	1,653	43357
West Manchester	Preble	SW	433	464	448	45382
West Mansfield	Logan	C	700	830	716	43358
West Millgrove	Wood	NW	78	171	205	43467
West Milton	Miami	SW	4,645	4,365	4,119	45383
West Rushville	Fairfield	C	132	134	159	43163
West Salem	Wayne	NE	1,501	1,534	1,357	44287
West Union	Adams	SW	2,903	3,096	2,791	45693
West Unity	Williams	NE	1,790	1,677	1,639	43570
Westerville	Franklin	C	35,318	30,269	23,414	43081
Westfield Center	Medina	NE	1,054	784	791	44251
Westlake	Cuyahoga	NE	31,719	27,018	19,483	44145
Weston	Wood	NW	1,659	1,716	1,708	43569
Wharton	Wyandot	NW	409	378	432	43359
Whitehall	Franklin	C	19,201	20,572	21,299	43213
Whitehouse	Lucas	NE	2,733	2,528	2,137	43571
Wickliffe	Lake	NE	13,484	14,558	16,790	44092
Wilkesville	Vinton	SW	151	151	189	45695
Willard	Huron	NW	6,806	6,210	5,674	44890
Williamsburg	Clermont	SW	2,358	2,322	1,952	45176
Williamsport	Pickaway	C	1,002	851	792	43164
Willoughby	Lake	NE	22,621	20,510	19,329	44094-95
Willoughby Hills	Lake	NE	8,595	8,427	8,612	44092 44094
Willowick	Lake	NE	14,361	15,269	17,834	44092 44094-5
Willshire	Van Wert	NE	463	541	564	45898
Wilmington	Clinton	SW	11,921	11,199	10,431	45177
Wilmot	Stark	NE	335	261	329	44689
Wilson	Monroe	SE	118	136	136	43716
Winchester	Adams	SW	1,025	978	1,080	45697
Windham	Portage	NE	2,806	2,943	3,721	44288
Wintersville	Jefferson	NE	4,067	4,102	4,724	43952
Woodlawn	Hamilton	SW	2,816	2,674	2,715	45215
Woodmere	Cuyahoga	NE	828	834	772	44122
Woodsfield	Monroe	SE	2,598	2,832	3,145	43793
Woodstock	Champaign	SW	317	296	292	43084
Woodville	Sandusky	NW	1,977	1,953	2,050	43469
Wooster	Wayne	NE	24,811	22,427	19,289	44691
Worthington	Franklin	C	14,125	14,869	15,016	43085
Wren	Van Wert	NE	199	190	282	45899
Wyoming	Hamilton	SW	8,261	8,128	8,282	45215
Xenia	Greene	SW	24,164	24,836	24,653	45385
Yankee Lake	Trumbull	NE	99	88	99	44403
Yellow Springs	Greene	SW	3,761	3,973	4,077	45387
Yorkshire	Darke	SW	110	126	146	45388
Yorkville	Belmont	SE	1,230	1,246	1,447	43971
Youngstown	Mahoning	NE	82,026	95,732	115,436	44501-15
Zaleski	Vinton	SE	375	294	347	45698
Zanesfield	Logan	C	220	183	269	43360
Zanesville	Muskingum	SE	25,586	26,778	28,655	43701-02
Zoar	Tuscarawas	NE	193	177	264	44697

Census Designated Place (CDP)

We live in cities and villages, counties and townships, and some of us in a Census Designated Place or CDP. We all know CDPs. Places that have a name, population and some businesses and are often mistaken for cities or villages. A CDP has no government structure and no definite boundaries and up until the last census had to have at least 1,000 residents. CDPs are the amoebas of the census with their boundaries changing from decade to decade depending on population patterns. Some disappear entirely—absorbed by a city while others become cities themselves. Local officials work with the census to determine if an area will be listed as a CDP. Many CDPs originated as housing developments or crossroads before they grew to a place with an identity. For many of us, it's not a city or village that we call home; it's a CDP.

Name	County	
Austintown	Mahoning	31,627
Bainbridge	Geauga	3,417
Ballville	Sandusky	3,255
Beckett Ridge	Butler	8,663
Beechwood Trails	Licking	2,258
Blacklick Estates	Franklin	9,518
Boardman	Mahoning	37,215
Bolindale	Trumbull	2,489
Bridgetown North	Hamilton	12,569
Brimfield	Portage	3,248
Brookfield Center	Trumbull	1,288
Burlington	Lawrence	2,794
Calcutta	Columbiana	3,491
Champion Heights	Trumbull	4,727
Cherry Grove	Hamilton	4,555
Chesterland	Geauga	2,646
Choctaw Lake	Madison	1,562
Churchill	Trumbull	2,601
Covedale	Hamilton	6,360
Crystal Lakes	Clark	1,411
Day Heights	Clermont	2,823
Dent	Hamilton	7,612
Devola	Washington	2,771
Dillonvale	Hamilton	3,716
Drexel	Montgomery	2,057
Dry Run	Hamilton	6,553
Easton Estates	Lorain	1,409
Edgewood	Ashtabula	4,762
Fairfield Beach	Fairfield	1,163
Fairview Lanes	Erie	1,015
Finneytown	Hamilton	13,492
Five Points	Warren	2,191
Forestville	Hamilton	10,978
Fort McKinley	Montgomery	3,989
Franklin Furnace	Scioto	1,537
Fruit Hill	Hamilton	3,945
Glenmoor	Columbiana	2,192
Grandview	Hamilton	1,391
Granville South	Licking	1,194
Green Meadows	Clark	2,318
Greentown	Stark	3,154
Groesbeck	Hamilton	7,202
Harbor Hills	Licking	1,303
Hilltop	Trumbull	534
Holiday Valley	Clark	1,712
Howland Center	Trumbull	6,481
Huber Ridge	Franklin	4,883
Hunter	Warren	1,737
Kenwood	Hamilton	7,423
La Croft	Columbiana	1,307
Lake Darby	Franklin	3,727
Landen	Warren	12,766
Leavittsburg	Trumbull	2,200
Lincoln Village	Franklin	9.482
Logan Elm Village	Pickaway	1,062
Loveland Park	Hamilton	445
Loveland Park	Warren	1,354
Lucasville	Scioto	1,588
Mack North	Hamilton	3,529
Mack South	Hamilton	5,837
Maple Ridge	Mahoning	910
Maplewood Park	Trumbull	321
Masury	Trumbull	2,618
Mineral Ridge	Mahoning	1,348
Mineral Ridge	Trumbull	2,552
Monfort Hghts East	Hamilton	3,880
Monfort Hghts South	Hamilton	4,466
Montrose-Ghent	Summit	5,261
Mount Carmel	Clermont	4,308
Mt. Healthy Hghts	Hamilton	3,450
Mount Repose	Clermont	4,102
Mulberry	Clermont	3,139
Neffs	Belmont	1,138
Northbrook	Hamilton	11,076
North Fork Village	Ross	1,726
Northgate	Hamilton	8,016
North Madison	Lake	8,451
Northridge	Clark	6,853
Northridge	Montgomery	8,487
North Zanesville	Muskingum	3,013
Olde West Chester	Butler	232
Park Layne	Clark	4,519
Perry Heights	Stark	8,900
Pigeon Creek	Summit	945
Pleasant Grove	Muskingum	2,016
Pleasant Run	Hamilton	5,267
Pleasant Run Farm	Hamilton	4,731

Portage Lakes	Summit	9,870	Wetherington	Butler	1,010
Rosemount	Scioto	2,043	Wheelersburg	Scioto	6,471
Ross	Butler	1,971	White Oak	Hamilton	13,277
Sandusky South	Erie	6,599	White Oak East	Hamilton	3,508
Sciotodale	Scioto	982	White Oak West	Hamilton	2,932
Shawnee Hills	Greene	2,355	Wilberforce	Greene	1,579
Sherwood	Hamilton	3,907	Withamsville	Clermont	3,145
Shiloh	Montgomery	11,272	Woodburne-Hyde Park	Montgomery	7,910
South Canal	Trumbull	1,346	Wright Patterson AFB	Montgomery	6,656
South Middletown	Butler	264			
Stony Prairie	Sandusky	836			
Summerside	Clermont	5,523			
The Plains	Athens	2,931			
Turpin Hills	Hamilton	4,960			
Uniontown	Stark	2,802			
Vienna Center	Trumbull	994			
West Hill	Trumbull	2,523			
West Portsmouth	Scioto	3,458			

Source: U.S. Census Bureau

THE RETURN OF BUCKEYE NATIONALISM

native stock

The state Division of Vital Statistics had never quite thought of it that way before, but the figures were there for the adding. Willing fingers and a calculator revealed the great truth. Between 1909 and 1988, 12,364,283 native sons and daughters of Ohio came into the world, entitled to all honors, privileges and advantages thereof. Not all of these happy few lingered here to enjoy their birthright; many of those native Buckeye lives were cut short by the Grim Reaper or the moving van. Still it is a stirring vision—12.3 million sprigs of sturdy Buckeye stock, joining hands across the generations, as it were, to hail what the attorney-poet John Milburn Harding called in 1903, "Ohio, name for what is good and grand, with pride we hail thee as our native land."

Who does not know that to be born under the metaphorical shade of the five-fingered buckeye leaf (or to have crawled under it at a tender age) is to be of the Elect? To pass one's infant years in these green (if largely flat) Ohio pastures is to swell to a maturity that dwarfs lesser breeds. From this heartland springs not merely Better Americans but representatives of a Higher Civilization.

Lest this scientific fact be dismissed as Ohio chauvinist moonshine, consult the dictums of the noted English philosopher and mathematician Alfred North Whitehead. In 1935, Whitehead propounded his theory of the emerging "Midwestern Man" to writer Lucien Price (he of Western Reserve nativity). "The only place I know where European man can still create another civilization on the grand scale," the great sage told Price, "is in the American Midwest, between the Appalachians and the Rockies, the Mississippi Basin." A wide territory surely, but Price took it as given that Ohio was the cradle of this new Midwestern civilization.

Whitehead declared that unlike the Atlantic and Pacific coasts, the Midwest was insulated from overseas influences that made the cultures of the American seaboards derivative. "A native culture must start from the ground up. In the Midwest you have those three preconditions to a flourishing civilization, a favorable climate, soil and food. Americans must not copy Europe. They must be themselves. American imitations of Europe will always lack interest and vitality, as all derivations do."

Whitehead's 1935 Buckeye contemporaries might have been a trifle startled to hear a cultured Englishman utter such evident good sense. His insight, however, was merely common knowledge to them. Ohio's pre-war native sons and daughters never doubted their role in God's plan for the United States. They were Buckeyes. They had grown up with the Fourth of July and School Speech Day rhetoric of their grandfathers ringing in their ears. Dressed in sailor suits and knee socks or buttoned into starched pinafores and scratchy woolen underwear, these children were the last generation to imbibe the principles of Midwestern regional nationalism from the clear (if gassy) fountainheads. The new Midwestern civilization wasn't coming, those long-dead picnic orators in their moist linen declared, it was already here in Ohio.

—by John Fleischman

Almost on crossing the Ohio line it seemed to me that people were more open and more outgoing. The waitress in a roadside stand said good morning before I had a chance to, discussed breakfast as though she liked the idea, spoke with enthusiasm about the weather, sometimes even offered some information about herself without my delving. Strangers talked freely to one another without caution...It seemed to me that the earth was generous and outgoing here in the heartland, and perhaps the people took a cue from it.

—John Steinbeck, Travels With Charley

Firsts

World's:

First teaching hospital—Dr. Daniel Drake's Commercial Hospital and Lunatic Asylum, Cincinnati, 1823

First city to be lighted electrically—Cleveland, where Charles Brush successfully demonstrated arc lights on the streets in 1879

First flash photo of lightning —taken by W.C. Gurley, Marietta, 1884

First horse track with night lighting —Fairfield County Fairground, 1889

First library with open shelves —Cleveland Public Library, 1890

First automobile advertisement—for a Cleveland-made Winton, in *Scientific American*, July 30, 1898

First skyscraper made of reinforced concrete —Ingalls Building, Cincinnati, 1903

First photo taken from an airplane—by Bill Mayfield, over Dayton, 1910

First person to fly over the Rocky Mountains —Columbus's Cromwell Dixon, 1911

First radio-controlled air traffic —Cleveland Municipal Airport, 1930

First gorilla bred and born in captivity—Colo, born of Millie Christina and Baron Macombo, at the Columbus Zoo, 1956

First American to orbit the earth—John Glenn, February 20, 1962, aboard Mercury 6. He did three orbits and went some 81,000 miles.

First person on the moon —Neil Armstrong, July 21, 1969

First free-net—Cleveland Free-Net, 1986, as a service of Case Western Reserve University

First joint U.S.-U.S.S.R. orchestra—American-Soviet Youth Orchestra, Oberlin College, 1988

First radio station playing only Elvis Presley music —WCVG-AM, Cincinnati, 1988

First facility dedicated solely to wildlife conservation and reproductive research—Carl H. Lindner Jr. Family Center, Cincinnati Zoo, 1991

First pregnant gorilla from in vitro fertilization —Cincinnati Zoo, 1995

Nation's:

First anti-slavery society—Benjamin Lundy's Union Humane Society, St. Clairsville, 1815

First air mail delivery—balloonist Richard Clayton's Cincinnati-to-Waverly trek, 1835

First silk factory—established on 25 acres of mulberry trees, Mt. Pleasant, 1841

First Christmas tree in U.S.—August Imward, a Bavaria immigrant, set it up in his Wooster home; it featured paper ornaments and a star designed by a local tinsmith. The first display of a Christmas tree in a church occured in 1851 in Cleveland's Zion Evangelical Lutheran Church, Dec. 24, 1851, after the Rev. Heinrich Schwan spent a year researching the tree's traditions in order to dispel heathen images from his parishioners.

First hospital with ambulance service —Commercial Hospital, Cincinnati, 1860s

First caramel color manufacturer—E. Berghausen Chemical Company, Cincinnati, 1860s

First mail carrier—Joseph W. Briggs, assistant to the Cleveland postmaster, made the first free home mail delivery; he became national superintendent of deliveries and began this system in 49 other cities.

First train robbery—A train near Anderson's Ferry, just outside of Cincinnati, was robbed on May 5, 1865

First woman dental school graduate—Lucy B. Hobbs, Ohio College of Dental Surgery, Cincinnati, 1866

First city to own its own railroad—The Cincinnati Southern Railroad was organized in 1869 by an act of the Ohio General Assembly, providing the first direct passenger service from the North to Chattanooga, a Southern rail hub.

First citizen knighted by the British—Cincinnati paint manufacturer and exhibition promoter Alfred T. Goshorn, by Queen Victoria, 1876

First government labor agency —Ohio Bureau of Labor Statistics, 1876

First modern corporate trust—created by Cleveland's John D. Rockefeller from Standard Oil of Ohio stocks, 1881

First made-in-the-U.S.A. glass marbles —manufactured by Akron's S.C. Dyke & Co., 1890

First gasoline-powered automobile —built by John William Lambert, Ohio City, 1891

First reinforced concrete bridge—Joseph Melan Arch Bridge, Eden Park, Cincinnati, 1894

First auto with left-hand steering —Baker Electric, made in Cleveland, 1898-1920

First assassin ever to be filmed—the deluded young anarchist, Leon Czolgosz, who killed President William McKinley, 1901, was caught on film by the Edison Company.

First comprehensive modern building code —adopted by Cleveland, 1904

First outdoor telephone booth—Cincinnati, 1905

First urban reforestation project —Cincinnati's Mt. Airy Forest, 1911

First community trust charity—the Cleveland Foundation, 1914

First black woman to record the blues—Cincinnatian Mamie Smith, in 1920: "That Thing Called Love"

First chapter, Disabled American Veterans —Cincinnati, 1920

First political photo opportunity—Warren Harding's "Front Porch Campaign," Marion, 1920

First electric traffic light—installed at Euclid Avenue and 105th Street, Cleveland, patent issued in 1923

First city-owned airport—Cleveland Municipal

First U.S. hotel with a drive-in parking garage —Starrett Netherland Plaza, Cincinnati, 1931

First police officer killed by Pretty Boy Floyd —Ralph Castner, Bowling Green, 1931

First department store with "no money down" credit —Lazarus Co., Columbus, 1934

First king-sized bottles of Coca-Cola—Columbus, 1955

First birth defects care center in a hospital —Children's Hospital, Columbus, 1958

First plastic credit cards —issued by six Cincinnati department stores, 1959

First Arby's restaurant—opened on Boardman-Canfield Road, Boardman, 1964

First 24-hour bank money machine—installed at what is now Bank One's Upper Arlington branch, 1970

First polka player awarded a Grammy—Cleveland's Frank "The Polka King" Yankovic, 1986

First college offering a bachelor's degree in hazardous waste management—University of Findlay, 1986

First state with a full-fledged trade office in Africa —Ohio, in Nigeria, 1987

First combination shopping/entertainment mall —Forest Fair Mall, Cincinnati, 1989

First all-fiber-optic campus network in nation —Case Western Reserve University, 1989

First felony indictment resulting from burning the U.S. flag—against Cheryl Lessin, Cuyahoga County Common Pleas Court, Cleveland, 1990

First university to open an Office for Social Responsibility in Washington, D.C. —Cincinnati's Union Institute, 1990

First firing of a Patriot anti-missile missile—by Patriot battery commander, Captain James Spangler, Enon, during Operation Desert Storm, 1991

First stamp in the U.S. to depict a comic book superhero—in honor of the 60th anniversary of Superman's creation in the Glenville neighborhood of Cleveland by two high school chums, Jerry Siegel and Joe Shuster, 1998

First city in America to ticket motorists who drive while talking on cellular phones —Brooklyn, Ohio, 1999

First mail center in U.S. to permanently install a biohazard detection center—Cleveland's Main Post Office, 2003

Geauga County's Jerry Rose harvested in October of 2003 a 1,370-pound pumpkin, beating the old Ohio record by 230 pounds. Rose's trophy measured almost 15 feet around and was nearly four feet tall. It was only 15 pounds shy of the world record.

A day of the life of Ohio

JIM BORGMAN
CINCINNATI ENQUIRER
8/2000

**In an average 24 hours
in the Buckeye state:**

One murder is committed.

47 robberies occur, and 265 burglaries.

49 Ohioans are assaulted.

12 rapes are committed.

115 vehicles are stolen;
two are recovered.

415 Ohioans die, including 3 infants;
411 of us are born.

Nearly 10 people die accidently,
including highway deaths, one
of which occurs every 6 hours and
24 minutes.

90 Ohioans die from heart-related
problems, slightly less than one person
every 4 minutes.

3,889,043 Ohioans drive alone to work.

The average worker takes 22 minutes, 54
seconds to drive to work, driving an
average of 36 miles, and using 2.6 gallons
of gas.

Traffic delays in Ohio's major cities
cost each of these drivers $1.62 and
6 minutes.

The average manufacturing worker
earns $169.19; the average construction
worker earns $138.98; and the average
retail worker earns $87.99.

74 new businesses are started and 2.5 new business facilities are built.

28 new fast food and food preparation jobs open.

Ohio exports $34,246.58 worth of washing machines.

$42,274,758 worth of goods is shipped to Canada.

5,432,876 lottery tickets are sold and $3,049,041 is awarded in lottery prizes, which means that each Ohioan spends 48 cents each day on lottery tickets and wins 27 cents.

Tourists spend $63,287.67.

46,849 Ohioans take an overnight trip to visit relatives.

17,260 Ohioans take overnight business trips.

249 Ohioans move to Florida; 130 of them move back.

25 immigrants move to Ohio.

78 Ohioans are arrested for DUI by the Ohio State Patrol, but 1,171 others are given traffic warnings

143 new houses are completed and 569 existing homes are sold.

The need arises for 3 more policemen, 10 nurses, and 9 new teachers.

11 jobs are created for PhDs, and 62 jobs are created for people with BA degrees.

There are 208 bankruptcies.

The average Ohioan pays $32 in homeowner costs, including 88 cents in homeowners insurance premiums.

Each automobile owner pays $1.77 in auto insurance.

Each Ohioan pays $4.42 in state taxes.

Each Ohioan spends 19 minutes each day working for food; he spends 3 hours and 20 minutes working to pay taxes.

Each renter pays $17.17.

Each Ohioan throws away 4.59 pounds of garbage.

Each Ohioan watches more than four hours of television.

49,871 gallons of alcohol are consumed.

240 Ohioans get married, and 130 other Ohioans get divorced.

About 68% of the immigrants arriving in Ohio late last decade had attended some college and 51% had graduated. Among the states receiving at least 50,000 immigrants from 1995 to 2000, Ohio immigrants ranked second in educational attainment. Unfortunately, a 'secondary migration' saw the state losing more immigrants than it gained in the late 1990s, causing some to call for a more aggressive public policy to retain them.

—Plain Dealer

AND THIS, JUST IN...

The average Ohioan drinks 2.3 gallons of alcohol a year, uses 438 gallons of gasoline, makes four trips a day, and generates one quarter ton of dirty laundry. 20% of Ohio households have three or more cars (8% have none). 3% of Ohio households have no telephone, the same percentage of Ohio households that use wood as a primary heat source. 4% of all Ohio residences are mobile homes, and 9% of Ohio homeowners have no mortages. 40% of Ohioans always—or often— watch television while eating dinner, and some 7% of all Ohioans experience some paruresis—otherwise known as stage fright—in public restrooms. As for Ohio itself, it has more tanning beds than any state in the union, edging out California by 245 beds.

—Sources: The New Yorker, Journal of the American Medical Association, TV-Turnoff Network, Morgan Quitno Corporation, International Paruresis Association, International Smart Tan Network

Nationalstandings

*How Ohio Stacks Up
with the Other Forty-Nine States*

First in
Eggs produced
Toxic waste sent out of state
Washing machine exports
Convenience store national headquarters
Toxic materials emitted into the air
Paint exports
Swiss cheese produced
SUVs per licensed drivers
Hazardous Materials Incidents

Second in
Number of savings institutions
Exports to Canada
Number of bridges
Automobile manufacturing
Number of roller coasters
Number of vans
Tire exports
Roller bearing exports
Number of motorcycles

Third in
Manufacturing workers hourly wages
Percent of residents who smoke
Number of visitors to state parks
Energy consumption
Number of pickup trucks
Spending for coal
Toxic waste received
Number of sheep farms
Exports to France
Light truck manufacturing
Number of books in libraries
Number of Commercial buses

Fourth in
Public high school graduation rate
Enrollment in the Head Start program
Number of trucks
Injuries from tornados
Lottery prizes per capita
Bigfoot sightings
Maple syrup produced
Number of libraries
Community revitalization—worst (*Sierra Club*)

Fifth in
Interstate highway mileage
Number of SUVs
Number of schools
Public libraries and branches
Number of National Board Certified Teachers
Federal money for the Head Start Program
Fortune 500 companies

Number of prisoners
The least amount of land owned
　　　　　　by the federal government
The number of deficient bridges
Police officers killed in the line of duty
Number of database administrators employed
Percent of people in poverty

Sixth in
Employees engaged in construction
Government workers
Number of colleges and universities
Size of the Reserve National Guard
Number of house trailers
Total military veterans
Prisoners under sentence of death
Total crimes
Lowest in spending (per capita) by the National
　　　　　　Endowment for the Arts
State income tax progressivity for single filers
Public libraries
Exports to Mexico
Response rate for Census 2000
Electricity expenditures
Toxic releases into the environment

Seventh in
State appropriated arts funding
Bankruptcy filings
Number of streets
Fatal truck accidents
Lowest violent crime rate
Ice cream production
Number in internet terminals per library

Eighth in
Full time law enforcement officers
Total exports
Number of farms
Open space protection (*rated by the Sierra Club*)
Percent of developed land

Ninth in
Number of private schools
Average student cost at public colleges/universities
Fewest gallons of gasoline used per capita
Adults on parole
Lowest percentage of government employees
Dumbest state (*rated by Morgan Quitno*)

Tenth in
Amount of land in metro areas
The size of the information technology workforce
Defense spending per capita, lowest

FOUNDERS: IT ALL STARTED HERE

The weather bureau

The U.S. Weather Bureau was an Ohio invention, after bewhiskered 30-year-old Cleveland Abbe proposed a weather telegraphy service out of Cincinnati's Mitchell Observatory and the Cincinnati Chamber had the temerity to fund him. His first weather bulletin was issued September 1, 1869, with reports for St. Louis; Chicago; Leavenworth, Kansas; and Cincinnati. Included was this forecast: "Cloudy and warm this evening. Tomorrow clear." It was a sterling forecast not yet improved upon.

4-H clubs

Albert Belmont Graham, an Ohio farmboy from the village of Conover, held the first organizational meeting of his agriculture experiment club in 1902. It arose from his wish to encourage youngsters into hands-on agricultural projects, and he told parents, "Please give your children your everyday problems arising from the selling of produce and purchasing groceries." His work linked all such clubs everywhere into what is now known as 4-H, which today is the largest youth organization in the world—300,000 members in Ohio, and six million in America.

Alcoholics Anonymous

Bill Wilson, a broker, and Dr. Bob Smith, both alcoholics, met in Akron for the purpose of each keeping the other away from the liquor cabinet. Dr. Bob took his last drink on June 10, 1935—the official founding date for AA. The early sessions were held in a room containing only Dr. Bob and a Bible, a stern solution designed to scare one to either salvation or more drink. Today, AA has two million members in 150 countries.

Boy Scouts of America

Daniel Beard, a noted Cincinnati illustrator with strong views on wildlife conservation and outdoor sportsmanship, turned his avocation into a famous manual, *The American Boy's Handy Book,* and a boys' movement that became in 1910 the Boy Scouts of America.

U.S. Civil Service

George Pendleton, a Cincinnati lawyer and legislator known in Congress as "Gentleman George," steered federal legislation for civil service reform resulting in the Pendelton Act of 1883, which created the modern civil service system. His stance so angered Democrat supporters of the old patronage system that they denied renomination to him the following year.

Women's Christian Temperance Union

A Hillsboro, Ohio, crusade in which women of the town prayed on the sawdust floors of saloons, became the birthplace of the WCTU. By the following summer, the women had organized themselves into what would become a potent political force and the world's oldest continuing non-sectarian woman's organization.

Reform Judaism

Isaac Mayer Wise, America's leading rabbi during the 19th century, introduced to America a Judaism that he considered responsive to modern American life. His Cincinnati synagogue incorporated sermons in the vernacular, a mixed choir, even confirmation. His definition of Judaism: "A religion, without mysteries or miracles, rational and self-evident, eminently human, universal, liberal, and progressive, in perfect harmony with modern science, criticism, and philosophy, and in full sympathy with universal liberty, equality, justice, and charity." Along the way, he founded—in 1875—Hebrew Union College, the first Jewish seminary in the U.S.

Christmas shopping season

Fred Lazarus Jr. of Columbus convinces President Franklin Roosevelt that changing the Thanksgiving holiday from the last Thursday of November to the fourth Thursday—and extending the Christmas shopping season—would be good for the nation's business. A 1941 Act of Congress perpetuated the arrangement.

The writer John McPhee once described Ohio topography as "looking like a bedspread on which someone has taken a nap." The rumpled blankets are a bit higher in the northeast and southeast, but the overall terrain speaks more of mattress than Matterhorn. We may not be the tops in topography, but Ohio has its high points. In this primer of perspective, overlooks, and the essential Buckeye long view, let's begin with giants upon the earth—the dozen tallest buildings in Ohio.

1. *Marriott Society Center*, Cleveland
   Height: 948 feet
   Stories: 63 stories
   Architect: Cesar Pelli & Associates,
       Kendal/Heaton & Associates
   Built: 1989-1991
   Costs: approx. $175-200 million

2. *Terminal Tower*, "Tower City," Cleveland
   Height: 709 ft., stands 786 ft. above
       Lake Erie
   Stories: 52, observation deck
       on 42nd floor
   Architect: Graham, Anderson, Probst,
   & White, Chicago
   Built: 1923-1928
   Cost: $11 million (1928)

3. *BP America Building*, Cleveland
   Height: 650 ft.
   Stories: 45
   Architects: Hellmuth, Obata &
       Kassabaum
   Built: 1985
   Cost: $200 million

4. *James A. Rhodes State Office Tower*, Columbus
   Height: 629 ft.
   Stories: 41, observation deck on 40th
       floor
   Built: 1970-1973
   Cost: $75.5 million

5. *Carew Tower*, Cincinnati
   Height: 574 ft.
   Stories: 49, observation deck on top
       floor

   Architect: Walter Ahlschlager, Chicago
   of Delano and Aldrich,
       New York
   Built: 1930
   Cost: $14 million

6. *LeVeque Tower*, Columbus
   Height: 555.5 ft.
   Stories: 46
   Architect: C. Howard Crane, Detroit
   Completed: 1927
   Cost: $7.5 million

7. *The Tower at Erieview*, Cleveland
   Height: 529 ft.
   Stories: 40
   Architects: Harrison & Abramovitz,
       New York
   Built: 1963-1964
   Cost: $24 million (1964)

8. *Huntington Center*, Columbus
   Height: 528 ft.
   Stories: 37
   Completed: 1984
   Architects: Skidmore, Owens, &
       Merrill, Chicago
   Cost: figures unreleased

9. *Vern Riffe Center for Government
   and the Arts*, Columbus
   Height: 503.5 ft.
   Stories: 32 floors, observation
       possible from Christopher's
       Restaurant on top floor
   Architects: Bohm-NBBJ. Columbus
   Built: 1985-1988
   Cost: $135 million

Tallest in town

Akron—First National Tower, 330 feet tall, 28 stories with a 160-foot TV antenna, built 1929-30 originally drawn for a Cleveland building, the design was used instead for the First National 41 miles away.

Cleveland—Marriott Society Center, 948 feet, 63 stories, built 1989-1991. The reigning state champ (and tallest building between New York and Chicago).

Columbus—James A. Rhodes Tower, 629 ft. tall, 41 stories, built 1970-1973. Has a heliport on top and Governor Rhodes in bronze at the base, one of the few statues on earth of a man carrying a briefcase.

Cincinnati—Carew Tower, 574 ft., 49 floors, built 1930. Built by the megabucks Emery family in the Depression to cheer up the town, the tower has bathrooms sheathed in two-inch-thick marble.

Dayton—Kettering Tower, 404 ft., 30 stories, named for the family of Charles F. Kettering, who invented the automotive self-starter.

Springfield—Credit Life Building, 175 ft., 11 stories, built in 1980. Designed by Skidmore, Owings, and Merrill. Still named for Credit Life, which is no longer a tenant.

Mansfield—Bank One Building, 152 ft., 12 stories, built 1928-29. A 20-foot observation tower on top was used by air raid wardens during World War II. The observation tower was torn down in 1992.

Toledo—One SeaGate Building (also known as the Owens-Illinois World Headquarters), 412 ft., 32 stories, built in 1981. This building is set apart (literally) on its own 6-acre fully landscaped lot complete with a 135-ton fountain.

Youngstown—Metropolitan Tower, 224 ft., 17 stories, built in 1929. Purchased by the Metropolitan Savings Bank in 1983, the old Central Tower underwent a face-lift—on the inside.

John Clubbe called the Carew Tower "America's finest Art Deco hotel"...He praised the decoration for its richness, sophistication, and unity—the interrelation of lighting, lettering, railings, carpets, wall and ceiling ornament. The lobby, upstairs from the sidewalk, is low-ceilinged; just off it is the two-story Palm Court, a room so good that it will take your breath away. Even on a weekday afternoon sightseers, one after another, come in gawking.

—Jane Ware,
Building Ohio

631

10. *One Nationwide Plaza*, Columbus
    Height: 482 ft.
    Stories: 40, "One Nation" restaurant
        on top floor
    Built: 1974-1978
    Architects: Harrison & Abramovitz,
        New York
    Cost: $78 million

11. *1 Riverside Plaza*, Columbus
    Height: 456 ft.
    Stories: 31
    Completed: 1983
    Cost: $77.5 million

12. *Franklin County Government Center*,
    Columbus
    Height: 453 ft.
    Stories: 27
    Architects: U.R.S. Consultants
    Completed: 1991
    Built: 1974-1978
    Architects: Harrison & Abramovitz,
        New York
    Cost: $78 million

From top to bottom

Absolute Tops

The highest man-made point in Ohio is the top of the WBNX-TV Channel 55 television tower in Parma. Although it is not the highest tower per se (that would be the WNWO tower in Toledo at 1,437 feet), the WBNX tower stands in Akron, which is already 1,052 feet above sea level. The top of the tower is thus 2,049 feet above sea level, which is as high as you can go in Ohio and still have one foot on the ground.

The Low Point

Standing at the water's edge of the Ohio River at the Ohio-Indiana border is as low as you can go in Ohio—455 feet above sea level.

The Pits

The Nelms Cadiz Portal Mine in Harrison County burrows 529 feet under Ohio, the deepest slope coal mine in the state.

Sky-High Rates

Under the Small Loan Act, 32 percent is the highest legal rate of interest.

Tall Timber

Yellow poplar, 164 ft. tall, listed in Ohio's Big Tree Registry from 1989. Located in Dysart Woods, near Centerville in Belmont County.

Twin Peaks

The tallest human couple was probably Captain Martin Van Buren Bates (7 ft. 9 in. and 470 pounds) and his wife Anna (7 ft. 11 in. and 413 pounds), who settled in Seville in 1873.

Not on Thin Ice

The last time Ohio was under the ice 20,000 years ago, the Wisconsinan glacier was probably fattest in the Erie basin, where it was a mile thick.

Falling Waters

Ohio's tallest waterfall is on a tributary of Crane Hollow in Hocking County, where, depending on the time of the year, the 122-foot falls is either a trickle or a roaring cataract.

Hypothetical Bear Goes Over Theoretical Mountain

If the bear in the song went over the tallest mountain in Ohio, he wouldn't see much. Ohio's highest natural point, Campbell Hill in Bellefontaine, is 1,549 feet above sea level. By the altimeter, that's higher than any building in Ohio, but unfortunately it doesn't look very impressive. Campbell Hill actually rises only about 50 feet above the surrounding landscape. It also illustrates just how flat Ohio is; in ranking the high points of each state, Ohio's highest point is 43rd out of the 50 states.

High Lifting

A 19th-century canalboat leaving Cleveland on the Ohio-Erie Canal would climb 395 feet over 35 miles, passing through 42 locks,
to reach Akron. It was done entirely with hydraulics and mules.

How Deep?

The deepest hole is not our share of the national debt but an oil well drilled 11,442 feet below the surface of Noble County in 1967. Ohio's deepest hole is roughly 12 times the height of our tallest building.

A Bridge So High

The twin bridges of the Jeremiah Morrow Bridge on Interstate 71 that span the Little Miami River valley Little Miami Bicycle Trail in Warren County are 2,230 feet in length and 239 feet above the valley floor.

Backboard Supremacy

The University of Cincinnati men's basketball team had 14 members on its '03-'04 roster; the tallest was Robert Whaley, listed at 6' 10". If all the team members stood head to toe, they would have measured 90' 4", as well as having an unblockable lay-up shot. Stacked up, the 14 members of the 2004 Cleveland Cavaliers were 93' 9" from the head of center Zydrunas Ilgauskas (at 7' 3" the tallest of four 7-footers), to the toes of guards J.R. Bremer, Kevin Ollie, and Dajaun Wagner (all 6' 2"). Thus, the Cavs had nearly three and a half feet on the Bearcats.

The Great TV Tower War

In 1962 WKRC-TV Channel 12 in Cincinnati billed itself as "Tall 12" on the merit of its 885 foot-tall tower. Now, with a new antenna on top, Tall 12 reaches 974 feet. Yet, several others tower over, including WOSU-TV in Columbus (1,124 feet), WBNX-TV in Akron (1,131 ft.), WRGT-TV (1,158 feet), and WPTD-TV in Dayton (1,170 feet), WKBN-TV in Youngstown (1,437 feet) and, the top, WNWO-TV in Toledo (1,437 feet).

Towers of Power

WLW-AM, which bills itself as "The Big One," had a pre-World War II signal of 500,000 watts, powerful enough to be picked up in Peru and strong enough to drown out another station in Montana. Today, the "Big One" has a mere 50,000 watts in the AM band, pretty run-of-the-mill in a state where every major city and most minor ones have 50,000 watt stations. WNCI (FM) in Columbus has the state's highest power, 175,000 watts.

The greatest of the Great Lakes freighters is the Paul R. Tregurtha, at 1,013 feet, six inches long. She was built in the American Ship Building yard in Toledo, launched in 1981, and if she were plucked from the water and stood upright, she would be decidedly taller than Ohio's tallest building.

Northeast Ohio counties have the lowest Ohio stroke-related death rates. Death rates in Ohio are 117 per 100,000, slightly below the national average. While Ohioans are overweight and smoke—two high risk factors—Ohio has good medical facilities so that stroke victims tend to receive quick care.

"YEAH, BUT I BET HIS PROSTATE IS IN GREAT SHAPE."

Some pertinent statistics

Physicians	30,880
percent female	25%
percent in primary care	34.2%
Community hospitals	166
percent in rural areas	52%
Non-government not-for-profit hospitals	139
Investor-owned hospitals	4
State and local government-owned hospitals	23
Average stay in community hospitals (days)	5.2
Occupancy rate in community hospitals	61.6%
Surgical operations - community hospitals	11,262
Population covered by private health insurance	76.9%
Population covered by employment based health insurance	69.9%
Population covered by government health insurance	25.6%
Population covered by military health insurance	1.6%
Population enrolled by HMOs	24.8%
Population not covered by health insurance	11.2%
Population lacking access to primary care	7.2%
Per capita Medicare benefit payments	$938
Per capita personal health care expenditures	$3,789
Per capita expenditures for hospital care	$1,492
Per capita expenditures for prescription drugs	$347
Per capita expenditures for dental services	$176
Per capita expenditures for vision and other durable products	$58
Per capita expenditures for nursing home care	$443
Medicaid expenditures per enrollee	$6,848
Average pay per health care establishment employee	$31,532
Diseases per 100,000	
Cancer	528.0
AIDS	6.7
E-Coli	1.6
Hepatitis A and B	3.9
Legionellosis	1.1
Lyme Disease	0.7

Malaria	0.2
Measles	0.01
Meningococcal infection	0.6
Rabies	0.3
Salmonellosis	12.7
Shigellosis	6.0
Tubereculosis	1.5
Whooping Cough	3.9
Chlamydia	331.7
Gonorrhea	186.4
Syphilis	0.7
Years lost by premature death	7,781
from cancer	1,847
from heart disease	1,425
from homicide	173
from suicide	310
from unintentional injuries	887
Average alcohol consumption per drinker (gallons)	4.58
per capita consumption (gallons)	2.3
per capita wine consumption	1.8
per capita distilled spirits consumption	1.3
Percent of adults who are binge drinkers	16.2%
Alcohol-induced deaths	548
Adults who do not drink	56.2%
Population who use illicit drugs	5.6%
Drug-induced deaths	534
Percent of adults who are overweight	37.7%
Percent of adults who are obese	22.4%
Percent who exercise vigorously	24.1%
Users of exercise equipment	1,814,000
Golf participants	1,572,000
Running or jogging participants	905,000
Swimming participants	2,416,000
Tennis participants	592,000
Percent of adults with no leisure time physical activity	26.2%

Source: Morgan Quitno Press, Lawrence, Kansas

Ohio is ranked as below average in end-of-life care; earned "B" grades for having 41% of its primary-care physicians certified in palliative care; earned "D" grades for poor pain management policies; confusing state policies on advanced-care directives; less than 30% of hospitals offering hospice and palliative care; and the low number of Ohioans—23%— who died at home.

—Last Acts, a coalition of health and aging groups

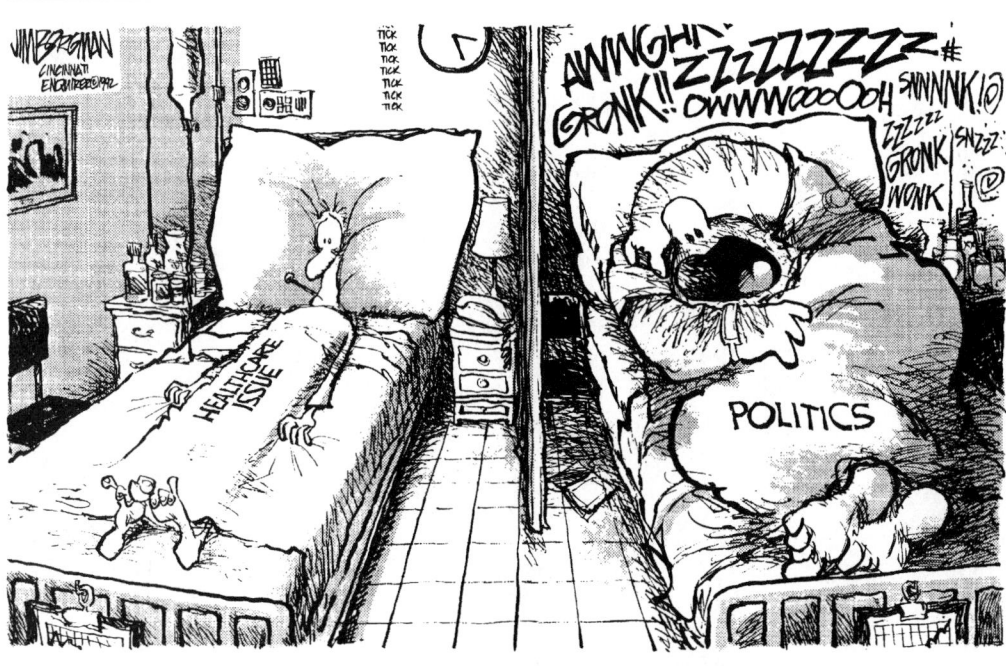

SEMI-PRIVATE ROOM

	Live births		Deaths		Marriages		Divorces	
	Number	Rate	Number	Rate	Number	Rate	Number	Rate
Ohio	**151,410**	**13.3**	**107,560**	**9.5**	**86,156**	**7.6**	**47,563**	**4.2**
Counties								
Adams	375	13.7	328	12.0	233	8.5	145	5.3
Allen	1,531	14.1	1,076	9.9	761	7.0	463	4.3
Ashland	708	13.5	474	9.0	396	7.5	234	4.5
Ashtabula	1,323	12.9	1,069	10.4	878	8.5	501	4.9
Athens	640	10.3	476	7.7	407	6.5	202	3.2
Auglaize	611	13.1	468	10.0	321	6.9	176	3.8
Belmont	667	9.5	902	12.8	472	6.7	274	3.9
Brown	541	12.8	386	9.1	308	7.3	166	3.9
Butler	4,808	14.4	2,665	8.0	2,453	7.4	1,378	4.1
Carroll	339	11.8	263	9.1	223	7.7	145	5.0
Champaign	494	12.7	370	9.5	285	7.3	175	4.5
Clark	1,880	13.0	1,702	11.8	910	6.3	737	5.1
Clermont	2,699	15.2	1,278	7.2	1,346	7.6	914	5.1
Clinton	589	14.5	366	9.0	317	7.8	208	5.1
Columbiana	1,308	11.7	1,152	10.3	796	7.1	405	3.6
Coshocton	482	13.1	351	9.6	276	7.5	165	4.5
Crawford	586	12.5	490	10.6	357	7.6	213	4.5
Cuyahoga	18,188	13.0	15,313	11.0	9,356	6.7	4,936	3.5
Darke	636	11.9	553	10.4	422	7.9	264	5.0
Defiance	472	11.9	324	8.2	339	8.6	200	5.1
Delaware	1,934	17.6	707	6.4	655	6.0	372	3.4
Erie	921	11.6	848	10.7	562	7.1	294	3.7
Fairfield	1,631	13.3	1,017	8.3	891	7.3	592	4.8
Fayette	372	13.1	313	11.0	277	9.7	229	8.1
Franklin	17,127	16.0	8,118	7.6	9,044	8.5	4,805	4.5
Fulton	574	13.6	359	8.5	341	8.1	188	4.5
Gallia	403	13.0	316	10.2	213	6.9	204	6.6
Geauga	1,092	12.0	687	7.6	549	6.0	249	2.7
Greene	1,723	11.7	1,069	7.2	1,003	6.8	576	3.9
Guernsey	536	13.1	404	9.9	333	8.2	197	4.8
Hamilton	11,788	13.9	8,273	9.8	5,686	6.7	2,900	3.4
Hancock	964	13.5	618	8.7	617	8.7	315	4.4
Hardin	357	11.2	292	9.1	211	6.6	137	4.3
Harrison	163	10.3	200	12.6	126	7.9	54	3.4
Henry	410	14.0	254	8.7	196	6.7	128	4.4
Highland	603	14.8	490	12.0	376	9.2	235	5.7
Hocking	377	13.3	308	10.9	209	7.4	134	4.7
Holmes	825	21.2	277	7.1	292	7.5	62	1.6
Huron	894	15.0	522	8.8	487	8.2	286	4.8
Jackson	413	12.7	355	10.9	260	8.0	156	4.8
Jefferson	725	9.8	1,017	13.8	539	7.3	295	4.0
Knox	702	12.9	518	9.5	399	7.3	30	0.6
Lake	2,656	11.7	2,131	9.4	1,576	6.9	812	3.6
Lawrence	740	11.9	730	11.7	260	4.2	415	6.7
Licking	1,964	13.5	1,308	9.0	1,082	7.4	691	4.7
Logan	602	13.1	440	9.6	396	8.6	238	5.2
Lorain	3,682	12.9	2,434	8.6	2,011	7.1	1,109	3.9
Lucas	6,459	14.2	4,487	9.9	7,206	15.8	1,987	4.4
Madison	503	12.5	366	9.1	273	6.8	185	4.6
Mahoning	2,953	11.5	3,091	12.0	1,589	6.2	777	3.0
Marion	829	12.5	629	9.5	579	8.7	419	6.3
Medina	2,103	13.9	1,078	7.1	1,008	6.7	563	3.7
Meigs	294	12.7	263	11.4	177	7.7	107	4.6
Mercer	516	12.6	348	8.5	277	6.8	125	3.1
Miami	1,279	12.9	871	8.1	761	7.7	453	4.6
Monroe	163	10.7	191	12.6	141	9.3	56	3.7
Montgomery	7,535	13.5	5,516	9.9	3,871	6.9	2,545	4.6
Morgan	172	11.5	170	11.4	100	6.7	77	5.2

Most likely ways an Ohioan will die on the job

1. Road accidents
   55
2. Falls
   52
3. Struck by object
   21
4. Murdered on job
   17
5. Electrocution
   13
6. Explosions and fires
   4

www. *odh.state.oh.us/*

This is the Ohio Department of Health site with everything from beach monitoring of waterborne diseases and fish reports, to disease outbreaks, food and product recalls, asbestos, and bioterrorism. Stunned by the malevolent possibility in the world-at-large, you might then be comforted by Ohio's health resources, as well as how to find death, birth, marriage and divorce records.

	Live births		Deaths		Marriages		Divorces	
	Number	Rate	Number	Rate	Number	Rate	Number	Rate
Morrow	445	14.1	268	8.5	304	9.6	138	4.4
Muskingum	1,029	12.2	854	10.1	698	8.3	464	5.5
Noble	112	8.0	110	7.2	77	5.5	50	3.6
Ottawa	404	9.9	454	11.1	319	7.8	186	4.5
Paulding	205	10.1	171	8.4	142	7.0	114	5.6
Perry	491	14.4	273	8.0	256	7.5	149	4.4
Pickaway	618	11.7	463	8.8	376	7.1	260	4.9
Pike	386	13.9	303	10.9	227	8.2	158	5.7
Portage	1,692	11.1	1,104	7.3	991	6.5	744	4.9
Preble	441	10.4	336	7.9	263	6.2	214	5.1
Putnam	447	12.9	282	8.1	252	7.3	103	3.0
Richland	1,630	12.7	1,250	9.7	1,049	8.1	598	4.6
Ross	875	11.9	706	9.6	616	8.4	393	5.4
Sandusky	883	14.3	586	9.5	501	8.1	279	4.5
Scioto	986	12.5	970	12.3	571	7.2	450	5.7
Seneca	699	11.9	534	9.1	382	6.5	260	4.4
Shelby	742	15.5	411	8.6	406	8.5	245	5.1
Stark	4,637	12.3	3,887	10.3	2,852	7.5	1,618	4.3
Summit	7,015	12.9	5,352	9.9	3,943	7.3	2,178	4.0
Trumbull	2,656	11.8	2,392	10.6	1,435	6.4	1,029	4.6
Tuscarawas	1,174	12.9	924	10.2	694	7.6	472	5.2
Union	619	15.1	277	6.8	286	7.0	207	5.1
Van Wert	322	10.9	271	9.1	262	8.8	114	3.8
Vinton	183	14.3	105	8.2	108	8.4	59	4.6
Warren	2,520	15.9	1,108	7.0	1,057	6.7	601	3.8
Washington	680	10.8	686	10.8	467	7.4	303	4.8
Wayne	1,567	14.0	925	8.3	829	7.4	491	4.4
Williams	435	11.1	358	9.1	374	9.5	227	5.8
Wood	1,369	11.3	950	8.4	794	6.6	462	3.8
Wyandot	287	12.5	229	10.0	196	8.6	99	4.3

*Per 1000 of population
Source: Ohio Department of Health

The day most likely that a baby will be born in Ohio —Friday

The day least likely that a baby will be born in Ohio —Sunday

Most Dangerous Occupations in Ohio

Occupation	Fatalities
Operators, Fabricators, & Laborers	87
Farming, Forestry, Fishing	32
Managerial & Professional	28
Precision Production, Craft, & Repair	27
Technical, Sales, & Administrative Support	21
Service Occupations	13

Most Dangerous Industries in Ohio

Industry	Fatalities
Transportation	42
Construction	34
Manufacturing	32
Agriculture	29
Retail Trade	26
Services	23
Government	13
Finance, Insurance, Real Estate	4

Leading Causes of Death in Ohio

Females

	Cause	Number of deaths	Rate 2000	Percent
1.	Diseases of Heart	16,827	225.0	29.9
2.	Malignant Neoplasms	11,963	174.6	21.3
3.	Cerebrovascular Diseases	4,307	57.2	7.7
4.	Chronic Lower Respiratory Disease	3,076	42.8	5.5
5.	Diabetes Mellitus	2,074	29.1	3.7
6.	Alzheimer's Disease	1,657	21.1	2.9
7.	Unintentional Injuries (Accidents)	1,431	21.9	2.5
8.	Influenza/Pneumonia	1,379	18.2	2.5
9.	Nephritis, Nephrotic Synd, etc.	1,017	13.9	1.8
10.	Septicemia	800	11.1	1.4
11.	Essential Hypertension	598	7.9	1.1
12.	Chronic Liver Disease	386	6.0	0.7
13.	Pneumonitis	361	4.7	0.6
14.	Atherosclerosis	354	4.5	0.
15.	In Situ Ca	312	4.3	0.6
16.	Aortic Aneurism	297	4.1	0.5
17.	Parkinson's Disease	291	3.8	0.
18.	Perinatal Conditions	253	4.8	0.4
19.	Congenital Malformations	218	3.8	0.4
20.	Intentional Self-Harm (Suicide)	214	3.6	0.4

56,239

Males

	Cause	Number of deaths	Rate 2000	Percent
1.	Diseases of Heart	15,438	345.4	30.1
2.	Malignant Neoplasms	12,778	266.5	24.9
3.	Chronic Lower Respiratory Disease	2,779	62.2	5.4
4.	Cerebrovascular Diseases	2,539	59.3	4.9
5.	Unintentional Injuries (Accidents)	2,353	45.7	4.6
6.	Diabetes Mellitus	1,672	35.6	3.3
7.	Influenza/Pneumonia	1,018	25.0	2.0
8.	Intentional Self-Harm (Suicide)	1,000	18.7	1.9
9.	Nephritis, Nephrotic Synd, etc.	884	20.4	1.7
10.	Alzheimer's Disease	711	18.2	1.4
11.	Septicemia	634	14.1	1.2
12.	Chronic Liver Disease	634	12.0	1.2
13.	Parkinson's Disease	388	9.5	0.8
14.	Assault (Homicide)	373	6.7	0.7
15.	Aortic Aneurism	362	7.9	0.7
16.	Perinatal Conditions	335	6.1	0.7
17.	Pneumonitis	330	8.3	0.6
18.	In Situ Ca	321	7.2	0.6
19.	Essential Hypertension	301	7.0	0.6
20.	Congenital Malformations	231	4.3	0.5

51,321

Rates are per 100,000, average annual rates, per 100,000

	Number	Rate*	Percent
Total Population	**102,573**	**945.6**	
1. Diseases of the Heart	35,451	326.8	34.6
2. Malignant Neoplasms	25,212	232.4	24.6
3. Cerebrovascular Diseases	6,802	62.7	6.6
4. Chronic Obstructive Pulmonary Diseases	4,865	44.9	4.7
5. Pneumonia and Influenza	3,386	31.2	3.3
6. Accidents	3,245	29.9	3.2
7. Diabetes Mellitus	3,182	29.3	3.1
8. Nephritis, Nephrotic Syndrome & Nephrosis	1,294	11.9	1.3
9. Suicide	1,234	11.4	1.2
10. Septiemia	904	8.3	0.9
11. Liver Disease and Cirrhosis	866	8.0	0.8
12. Atherosclerosis	860	7.9	0.8
13. HIV Infection	767	7.1	0.7
14. Homicide	720	6.6	0.7
15. Perinatal Conditions	717	6.6	0.7

Historical Vital Statistics

Year	Birth Rate	Death Rate	Infant Death Rate	Marriage Rate	Divorce Rate
1950	23.4	10.1	26.8	9.5	2.7
1960	23.6	9.6	24.0	7.0	2.4
1970	18.8	9.4	18.6	8.5	3.7
1980	15.6	9.1	12.8	9.2	5.4
1990	15.4	9.7	9.8	9.0	4.9
2000	14.0	9.5	7.5	7.6	4.2
2001	13.3	9.5	7.6	N/A	N/A

Fatalities

Total	207
Employee Status	
Wage & Salary Workers	157
Self Employed	50
Sex	
Men	180
Women	27
Age	
Under 20 years	5
20 - 24 years	11
25 - 34 years	40
35 - 44 years	43
45 - 54 years	47
55 - 64 years	38
65 years & over	23
Race	
White	167
Black or African American	22
Hispanic or Latino	5
Asian	3
Not Reported	9

Ohio ranks last among all states in percentage of adults who exercise regularly and the percentage who eat five or more servings of fruit and vegetables a day. Only 6.4% of Ohioans got regular and vigorous exercise, and 14% eat five or more servings of fruit and vegetables.
—American Cancer Society

Ohioans are some of the nation's heaviest users of perscription drugs, using on average over 11 perscriptions a year. Only two states use more.

Pro: Doctors may be doing a better job diagnosing and treating diseases, including anti-cholesterol drugs.

Con: Ohio's high death rate from diabetes, heart disease, and cancer suggest high drug use means health problems from sedentary lifestyle.

JIM BORGMAN
CINCINNATI
ENQUIRER@1988

"HEY, WHATTAYOU CRAZY?! YOU CAN SPREAD AIDS WITH THESE THINGS!"

The largest human baby on record was born in 1879 to Anna Bates and Captain Martin Van Buren Bates. Tragically, their 23-pound son lived only 11 hours.

In the mid-19th century, Henry Wadsworth Longfellow wrote a poem that immortalized the story of two lovers, Evangeline and Gabriel, who were separated during the French and Indian War and spent the rest of their lives searching for each other. It is said they both came looking in Ohio and passed through a Tuscarawas County village, where they missed each other by the hairbreadth that stretched into an eternity. Fortunately for the sake of the state's population, Ohio lovers have proven far better at getting together than poor Gabriel and Evangeline. Ohio now ranks among the top ten states annually in the number of marriages, and while all our love stories may not merit commitment to hexameter, many have indeed been the stuff of legend.

Winning Twosomes

Anna Swan and Martin van Buren Bates
He stood seven feet, nine inches and weighed 470 pounds. She was seven feet, eleven inches and weighed 413 pounds. They were the world's biggest couple and toured with the great showman P.T. Barnum, who had them presented to Queen Victoria. They made a huge impression, and the Queen gave Anna a diamond ring and Martin a pocketwatch. They retired in 1873 to the peace and quiet of a farm near Seville, where the doors in their house had a ten foot clearance. They also exerted a certain broadening influence on the local Baptists, who accommodated them by widening a pew.

Annie Oakley and Frank Butler

He was a previously divorced man of the world, professional marksman, traveling showman and ten years her senior. She was a Darke County girl with her hair still in braids, barely five feet tall and a hundred pounds and paying off the family farm by shooting game for Cincinnati hotels. Contrary to the Broadway musical, Annie did get her man with a gun, but more importantly, she kept him with her character. They met in 1875, at a Cincinnati shooting match, an impromptu battle of the sexes—demure damsel v. cool crack shot—in which Annie proved to be the sharper shooter. A year later, they were man and wife, and a few years after that the circus stars Butler and Oakley, "The Famous Far West Champion Rifle Shots." Annie had the star quality in the family, and Frank had the graciousness and good sense to take a back seat to her talent. They toured with Buffalo Bill's famous Wild West Show, Frank the manager and Annie the popular Superstar who performed for Queen Victoria and shot a cigarette from the lips of Kaiser Wilhelm. He taught her to read and write, and she gave him the foremost place in her thoughts and affection, and in their fifty years together, they were an unbeatable team.

Captains Mary and Gordon Greene

He was a tall steamboat captain. She was a short steamboat captain. From her birth on an island to her death in 1949 aboard the steamboat *Delta Queen*, Mary was surrounded by the Ohio River. She sealed her fate in 1890 by wedding a new steamboat captain. The bride wanted the groom to teach her the helm, and beginning with their shipboard honeymoon, the relationship turned into a threesome: Mary, Gordon and the River. Mary was a captain before she was a mother, and she plied the waters from Pittsburgh to New Orleans with the best of the steamer pilots and captains, though she was the only woman licensed as both. Mary and Gordon owned a steamboat line in Cincinnati, and after he died, her heart belonged only to the River. Mary ran the fleet, kept her license current, and lived her last years on the graceful decks of the *Delta Queen*, perhaps the only other lady in town who understood the pure pleasure of staying afloat.

Carol Heiss and Hayes Alan Jenkins

He was the U.S. and World Figure Skating Champion from 1953-1956 and an Olympic Gold Medalist in the sport in 1956. She was the U.S. and World Figure Skating Champion from 1957-1960 and an Olympic Gold Medalist in 1960. Hollywood couldn't have scripted it better—the handsome blade meets pretty ice princess, they pair up in 1960, and skate off to his hometown of Akron, where he practices corporate law instead of flying camels, and she still cuts a fine figure at the local rink.

Alice Roosevelt and Nicholas Longworth III

He was a short, balding Ohio Congressman, the scion of landed Cincinnati gentry and a Harvard man who enjoyed his liquor, his women and his Stradivarius. She was the young beautiful daughter of President Theodore Roosevelt, high spirited, outspoken, quite spoiled and never upstaged. Their nuptials were heralded as the wedding of the year in 1906, but then finding a suitable husband for irresistible Alice had been something of a national pastime. The wedding gifts included a snuffbox from a king, silver vases from an emperor and a mosaic from the Pope. The bride perhaps had encouraged this largess. "I'll accept anything but a red-hot stove," she declared. Alice acted as well as spoke her mind. She once took a pony up the White House elevator, and when the President asked her not to smoke under his roof, she climbed out a window and lit up on the roof of the White House. Such antics made her the darling of the newspapers, which dubbed her "Princess Alice." For her entire life she lived up to the title—launching a yacht for Kaiser Wilhelm, riding a tasseled litter chair into a Chinese Palace, trading dinner table *bons mots* with John Kennedy. Theirs was a marriage of the utmost convenience, and they spent only a token amount of time in the place Alice called Cincin-nasti. Nick became Speaker of the House, while Alice honed an unrivaled reputation as the acid-tongued grande dame of the Washington social scene. The Longworths did not quite live happily ever after, but as befits two good political animals, they were said to be "the best of comrades, always."

Mary Peabody and Horace Mann

He was a widower approaching 50, an educational and social reformer to the marrow who founded in Massachusetts the first U.S. teacher training school. She was intellectual, multi-lingual, given to attending lectures and reading literary journals; a New England schoolmarm, she set her cap for Horace from the table of their boarding-

The most-married woman in Ohio is Connie Post of Columbus, a former prison guard and truck driver. At 40, she has been married ten times. "I do believe in marriage," she said, "and I think the way I've lived my life proves it."

—Cleveland Plain Dealer

house. Horace was so busy becoming the "Father of American Education" that he put off siring a brood of his own. Mary patiently waited out their ten year courtship, and in 1843, he whisked her off on a socially conscious honeymoon touring prisons, asylums, and schools in Europe. Mary settled into blissful domesticity and rapidly produced three sons. The prospect of Horace at the helm of a new coeducational, non-sectarian college lured them to Ohio in 1853. However, his noble goals for Antioch College were woefully undermined by the difficulties of keeping the college financially afloat. The fight all gone out of him, Horace died in Yellow Springs in 1859. With children to support, Mary committed to the printed page her most valuable asset: the *Life and Works of Horace Mann*.

Harriet Beecher and Calvin Stowe

He was overweight and overwrought, a churchmouse-poor minister still grieving his first wife's death and though he was a gifted Biblical expert who spouted Hebrew and Greek, he was also a hypochondriac who openly discussed his frequent visits from assorted ghosts. She was his first wife's best friend, a diminutive, dutiful, and loving daughter, but also a broad-minded woman living under her father's narrow-minded roof. In 1836, Calvin Stowe married the boss's daughter, but even though Harriet was an offspring of *the* Reverend Beecher at Cincinnati's Lane Seminary, she considered his Calvinist sermons trying and much preferred to read. When enlisted to teach geography at her sister's new school, Harriet found every textbook lacking and solved the problem by handily penning one of her own. The articles Harriet sold to *Godey's Lady's Book* kept the wolf from their door, but with six children at her skirts, Harriet didn't take pen in hand seriously until the 1850s, when all of the sermons about slavery seemed lacking against the Fugitive Slave Law. Harriet solved the problem by using scenes and stories gleaned in Cincinnati to write a novel of her own, *Uncle Tom's Cabin*, which literally moved the nation. As for Calvin, he also built a mighty fortress in a single work—a report on education delivered to the Ohio legislature in 1837. Copies of his *Elementary Instruction in Europe* went to virtually every school district, and it became one of the pillars of free public education in the state.

Mary Ann Angel and Brigham Young

Mormonism brought him to Ohio on the heels of Joseph Smith, and his zeal would transform a New England carpenter into "The Lion of the Lord." She, a resident of Chardon Township, Geauga County, took up the Mormon faith and lived up to her maiden name, laboring at domestic chores while her husband helped build the great Temple of Kirtland. Since a previous Mrs. Young had died, Mary Ann was actually Brigham's second wife, albeit his first Mormon wife, when they married in Geauga County on March 31, 1834. Theirs was a peripatetic union, for Brigham was a top lieutenant in the Mormon hierarchy, and the Latter Day Saints were never welcome anywhere. A ruinous bank scheme got them run out of Ohio, and polygamy got their leader, Smith, killed in Missouri. Ah yes, polygamy, because of it, the mantle of Mormonism fell on Brigham, who led them all to the Great Salt Lake, a desert so hostile that no God fearing people had dared to live there. Because of it, Utah would be long-denied a place in the Union, and because of it, Mary Ann would not be the last—or only— Mrs. Young.

Loves Labors Lost

James Birdseye McPherson and Emily Hoffman

General Grant took James under his hawkish wing, General Sherman thought him a "bright, particular star," and by his mid-30s, James was a Major General in command of 30,000 men. An appointment to West Point had changed the life of this poor son of a widowed mother in Clyde, Ohio, and on the eve of the Civil War, James met the unlikely love of his life—a Baltimore lass from a well-off family. Though the Hoffmans had strong southern sympathies, Emily fully intended to marry her Union officer. They planned a wedding, but at the last minute, his leave was cancelled. General Sherman was starting his March to the Sea and needed him in Georgia. Just outside Atlanta, James was killed, and Emily grieved alone for the rest of her life.

Margaret and Harman Blennerhassett

They were Irish aristocrats, and they were also uncle and niece. The stigma of their union drove them from their native land, but the couple found another emerald isle on the Ohio River near Marietta, and there they built a grand estate and

First white couple wed in Ohio— Moravian missionary John Heckewelder to Sarah Ohneberg, daughter of a fellow missionary, in the Salem Church, Port Washington settlement, July 4, 1780.

lived, appropriately, like lords. Unfortunately, in 1805, the scoundrel Aaron Burr involved them in a revolutionary scheme, and an even blacker stigma— treason—ruined them. Their fortune was lost, their mansion destroyed, and their disgrace irreparable. Ironically, they both died, broke and broken, on islands—Harmon on Guernsey in 1831, and Margaret on Manhattan eleven years later. To the bitter end, she wanted money from Congress for the damage done to her Ohio dream home so many years before by the Virginia militia.

Deborah and Josiah Shackford

Josiah came to Ohio in 1802 to found the town of Portsmouth, which he named after his own hometown in New Hampshire. He was 68 and had enjoyed an adventurous life as a sea captain, once sailing alone to Surinam with only his dog for a companion. Josiah built a house on Front Street that looked and functioned like a ship. He had no door, but entered and exited by lowering a ladder through a hatch. His neighbors knew him

as an exemplary town builder who dedicated his time to civic improvements, paid his bills promptly, tried to invent a perpetual motion machine, and played archaeologist in the nearby Indian mounds. In fact, Josiah would have been a model citizen had he not been such a vehement woman hater. He avoided female company so religiously that he never let a woman set foot inside his "cabin" and even made the lady who did his cooking pass his meals in through a porthole. Only after he died at age 93 did folks learn the reason for the bitterness of the old salt. Stubborn Josiah had a stubborn wife back east, Deborah, who had refused to leave her mother and accompany him on his last great voyage west to Ohio.

Elizabeth and General George Custer

Custer did nothing without flourish, and so when the General bid farewell to his Libbie for what would be the last time, there were tears in his eyes as he poignantly reminded her that she was a soldier's wife. They had been married only twelve

---

Ohio Marriages

Marriages—81,224
Groom
  First marriage—64.0%
  Second marriage—26.7%
  Third marriage—7.2%
  Fourth (or more) marriage—2.1%
Bride
  First marriage—63.4%
  Second marriage—26.3%
  Third marriage—7.8%
  Fourth (or more) marriage—2.4%

Ohio Divorces

Divorces—45,909
Percent ending during the first year
  of marriage—3%
Percent of ending after over twenty years
  of marriage—14.4%
Month in which the most divorce decrees
  were finalized—October

Month in which the least divorce decrees
  were finalized—September
Percent of divorces involving minor children
  —50.3%
Percent of "no fault" divorces granted
  —42%

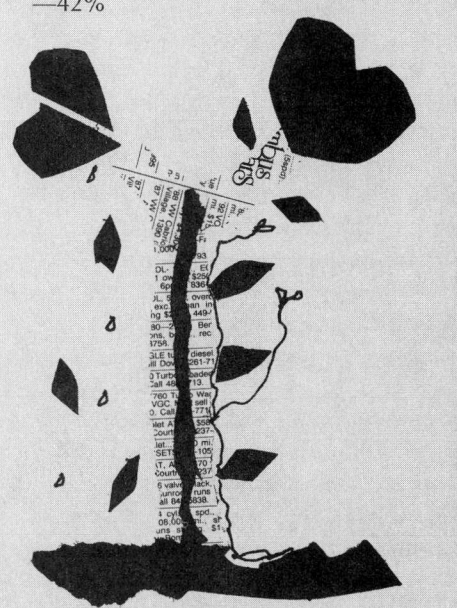

"Married:
In Berkshire Township
on Lord's Day, 12th
inst., by the Right
Reverend Bishop Chase,
Joseph Prince, Esquire,
to the amiable and
accomplished Miss Nobby
Shelton, daughter of Mr.
Selah Shelton.
Bachelors, go thou and
do likewise."

—Marriage
advertisement,
Delaware Gazette, 1820

years, but after his fatal June 25, 1876, battle, she would spend the remaining half-century of her life trying to vindicate his name and his decisions at Little Big Horn.

Uncommon Bonds

Humphrey Bogart and Lauren Bacall
On May 21, 1945, a Richland County telephone operator leaked the news that the two movie stars were going to be married in the manor house at Louis Bromfield's Malabar Farm. Bromfield wrote Hollywood screen plays and novels that were made into motion pictures. He loved to have house guests and collected autographed photos of his chums—Dorothy Lamour, Errol Flynn, Carole Lombard, Shirley Temple—that he displayed in a small, but star-studded gallery. Local folks should have been used to having celebrities come and go, but they weren't. By the time Bromfield's good friend Bogart had finished saying his vows beneath the mansion's magnificent double staircase, people were jamming the roads in all directions. Incidentally, Bromfield's business manager snagged Malabar's only double mattress, so "Bogie" and his "Baby" had to do as best they could with twin beds.

Mary Parson and The Prince de Lynar
Royalty came to Columbus in 1871 for their May 16 wedding. The bride, wearing white silk and orange blossoms, was on the arm of her father, real estate millionaire George McClelland Parson. The Prince, wearing a full dress uniform, arrived with a glittering delegation from the German embassy in Washington. Police had to keep the curiosity seekers in check, and as one reporter noted, Trinity Church was packed with enough fashion and beauty "to drive an impressible man raving distracted with delight." She had the money, he had the title, and immediately following the ceremony, they left for a life of privilege in Europe.

Elizabeth Walsh and Charles Colton
They were performers with P.T. Barnum's circus, and their names would surely have descended into obscurity had they not been the principals in the world's first airborne wedding. On October 19, 1874, a balloon was launched from Lincoln Park in Cincinnati. Inside the basket were Elizabeth, Charles, two witnesses, balloonist Washington Harrison Donaldson, and the requisite minister, Rev. Howard Jeffries. This marriage made in heaven had been arranged by Donaldson, a Barnum advance man who would be known to posterity as "the man on the flying trapeze."

Prisoners 9452 and 9453
When Nancy Jane Scott (alias Ann McFarland) and Thomas Miles were married in the chapel of the Ohio Penitentiary on February 1, 1875, theirs was the first prison wedding in Ohio, if not the United States. After both pleaded guilty to burglary in Licking County, they served two years. Warden Innis gave them permission to be married on their release date, and the prospect of a prison wedding in Columbus aroused such curiosity that tickets had to be issued. Eleven hundred prisoners witnessed the nuptials, but lest their credibility be suspect, also on hand were a host of state senators and representatives, city and county officials, and journalists from Ohio and the East Coast. The chaplain waived his fee, a hat was passed in the guard room, and the couple was last seen boarding a train for Newark with 30 fresh dollars in their pockets.

Souls of Devotion

John and Annie Glenn
In January, 1962, astronaut Glenn was sitting atop a rocket waiting for the countdown that would propel him into the history books. Outside the Glenn home, Lyndon Johnson was in a limousine waiting with a contingent of TV reporters for an invitation to come in. Annie balked; she not only had an exclusive contract with *Life* magazine but also a stutter severe enough to make her microphone-shy. As NASA officials wrung their hands, Glenn declared that Annie didn't have to open the door to anyone, not even the fuming Vice-President of the United States. Though Glenn would have to wait another month to become the first American in earth orbit, on that day, he was Annie's hero.

Ulysses and Julia Grant
When Julia wasn't around, he missed her so much that he took to drinking, and so the pampered Southern Belle became a willing army wife, following her "Ulys" from one bleak post to

Marital Status
in Ohio

Female

Married—52.1%

Never Married—23.5%

Separated/

Divorced—13.2%

Widowed—11.1%

Male

Married—57.0%

Never Married—29.2%

Separated/

Divorced—11.1%

Widowed—2.7%

—*Center for Family and Demographic Research & the U.S. Census Bureau*

another. Grant tried civilian life, but his finances constantly teetered on bankruptcy. Through all the hard and humiliating times, she believed he was destined for greatness, and then the Civil War proved her right. They were known to flirt publicly and hold hands in his headquarters. Julia insisted that he keep his beard neatly trimmed for the photographers, and Grant dissuaded her from corrective surgery, explaining that he was enormously fond of her crossed eyes exactly as they were.

Zane and Lina Grey

The Deep Blue Sea was as seductive as the Wild West to Zane Grey, who would go fishing at the drop of a paragraph. Lina kept him reeling out his lines, literary and otherwise. She acted as his grammarian, proofreader, editor, typist, and most importantly, ambassador with a world that demanded deadlines even if the marlin were biting. Her underpinning not only allowed him the frequent luxury of going fishing but also the freedom to become the legendary writer of the purple sage.

William and Ida McKinley

When they first met in Canton, Ida was a bright and beautiful young woman, but illness and deaths of their young daughters broke her health and her spirit. When they moved into the White House in 1897, her epileptic seizures were explained away as "fainting spells." But in McKinley's protective eyes, his faded and demanding wife was still the prettiest girl he had ever seen. Ida sat at his side during every state dinner, and if she suffered a seizure, he simply placed a napkin over her face until the episode passed. He was the center of her small universe, and friends considered him a saintly example of devotion. "President McKinley has made it pretty hard for the rest of us husbands here in Washington," said Mark Hanna. The brief memory of what was, the knowledge of what might have been—these were the McKinley bonds. And their mutual love and respect never faltered.

Their Families Disapproved

Anna Symmes and William Henry Harrison

Her prominent father thought nearby Cincinnati held better pickings than this poor soldier. After they eloped, he demanded to know how Harrison planned to support his daughter. The future President replied, "By my sword, sir, and my good right arm."

Julia Dent and Ulysses Grant

A *soldier*, sighed the Dents.
The Dents keep *slaves*, gasped the Grants.

Elizabeth Bacon and George Armstrong Custer

Libbie's father, the judge in Michigan, looked down his honorable nose at George's father, the blacksmith in Ohio.

Newborn boys in the Midwest are more than twice as likely to be circumcised as those born in other parts of the country— 81.4%.

HIGHS AND LOWS

Year since 1950 with the lowest marriage rate
—1957, 6.4 per 1000 of population

Year since 1950 with highest marriage rate
—1974, 9.6 per 1000 of population

Years since 1950 with lowest divorce rate
—1958, 1959, 1961, 1962, 1963; 2.3 per 1000 of population

Years since 1950 with the highest divorce rate
—1976, 1978, 1979; 5.6 per 1000 of population

Charlotte Rhodes and Marcus Alonzo Hanna

Hanna's oily Republican politics didn't mix with her vinegary dad, a diehard Democrat and Cleveland cousin of Stephen "The Little Giant" Douglas.

Florence Kling and Warren G. Harding

When Amos Kling, the richest man in Marion, heard that his daughter wanted to marry an upstart newspaper publisher, he went into an ugly rage, accused Harding of having negro blood, and didn't speak to either of them for seven years.

Katharine Wright and Henry Haskell

Katharine had truly devoted her life to getting her famous brothers off the ground. Finally, in her fifties, she consented to marry her old Oberlin classmate. Orville Wright went into such a snit at Katharine's "abandoning" him that he did not speak to his sister again until she lay on her deathbed in 1929.

Skirt chasers and heart breakers

Eagle Feather

This Delaware Chief should have been content with Mary Harris for a wife. A New Englander kidnapped in childhood, she was so respected by her Indian captors that they named their village White Woman's Town. Then Glowing Star, a younger woman, caught Eagle Feather's eye, and Mary derisively called the interloper Newcomer. When the two women eventually clashed, Eagle Feather got caught in the middle with a tomahawk in his brain. Glowing Star fled, but the Delawares caught and killed her. To this day, the place where she was captured in 1751, is called Newcomerstown.

Henry Ward Beecher

He trained for the pulpit at his father's Presbyterian seminary in Cincinnati, and though there only a few years, he got himself entangled with several women. Never mind that he was already engaged to a girl in New England. His ministry was smooth as silk, and Beecher, a glib and handsome figure of liberal righteousness, thoroughly enjoyed the fruits and financial rewards of success. Then Theodore Tilton, a member of his Brooklyn church sued the married minister for adultery with Mrs. Tilton. The nation was shocked, the trial juicy, and the jury hung. Tilton went into self-imposed exile in Europe, and Beecher, his ambitious stride interrupted but hardly broken, went back to the good graces of his forgiving flock. When Beecher died in 1887, 40,000 people came to pay their respects, and 90 percent of them were women.

Clark Gable

He limited himself to five wives, but a million women must have been in love with him. Gable could project more masculinity in sixty seconds on the silver screen than a barroom full of steelworkers on a Saturday night. The secret of his success was his utterly American brand of virility—raw, confident, energetic and a bit rough around the edges. And he never took himself too seriously. "I'm just a lucky slob from Ohio," said the King of the Box Office. In the 1934 film *It Happened One Night*, his bare chest annihilated undershirt sales across the nation. In *Gone With the Wind*, he gave a landmark performance as the dashing, realistic Rhett Butler, the archetype of a lady's man who was also his own man. Gable died in 1960, leaving behind his only child (a son born to him posthumously) and his legend, which, happily, has kept his image forever young.

Lottie Moon

She got herself betrothed to a dozen men, not all that surprising for a spirited ms. living in the small college town of Oxford, except that Lottie was engaged to them all at the same time. It must have been quite a juggling act, but Lottie was more than up to the challenge. She once left a young army officer, Ambrose Burnside, standing at the altar with his dander up and his dignity down, as she shouted "No siree Bob, I won't" to the minister's gentle query about taking a lawfully wedded husband. Little wonder that Oxford lawyer James Clark approached his and Lottie's 1849 wedding day with a precautionary pistol packed neatly in his pocket. He informed Lottie that if there were not a wedding that day, there would certainly be a funeral on the morrow, and given the circumstances, she displayed eminent good sense by going through with the ceremony. During the Civil War, Lottie put her energy and ingenuity to work for the Southern cause. Oxford was a veritable nest of Copperheads, and Lottie became an accomplished spy. With clever disguises and a deep bag of feminine tricks, she carried messages and documents from Canada to Virginia, and once slipped across

VICTORIA CLAFLIN WOODHULL: OHIO'S NOTORIOUS FEMINIST

She was born in Homer, in Licking County, Ohio, in 1838, of itinerant ne'er-do-well parents who made a paltry living telling fortunes and selling patent medicine. The family dabbled in spiritualism, and Victoria and her younger sister, Tennessee, were often enlisted for demonstrations. Married to a Dr. Canning Woodhull at 16, Victoria was uncommonly smart and pretty and blessed with a sixth sense when it came to advancing her own best interests. Those assets served her well after she was divorced in the 1860s. She and Tennessee moved to New York City, where they became fast friends with a kindred spiritualist, shipping magnate Cornelius Vanderbilt, who bankrolled them in a brokerage house, Woodhull, Claflin, and Company.

As stockbrokers, the women were a definite anomaly and caused something of a sensation, but with a little help from their friend Vanderbilt, they became phenomenally successful. In 1870, the sisters started *Woodhull and Claflin's Weekly*, a liberal magazine that promoted women's rights and published the first English translation of the *Communist Manifesto*.

Though well-schooled in the art of feminine wiles, Victoria, ironically, became a pioneer feminist and self-styled social reformer. As an unabashed advocate of Free Love, legalized prostitution, and identical moral and political standards for men and women, Victoria took her cause all the way to the U.S. Congress, where in 1871, she became the first woman to testify at a Congressional committee.

In 1872, the Equal Rights Party nominated her for President, and thus in her campaign against Ulysses S. Grant, Victoria achieved another feminine first as a woman out to win the White House. At the time, she was one of the most famous women in the U.S. Her party drafted the articulate abolitionist Frederick Douglass as her running mate, but the former slave wisely declined to participate.

She advocated an eight-hour work day, social welfare programs, profit sharing, and a graduated income tax. So she was not elected President of the United States (women, of course, were not yet allowed to vote) but she continued to make headlines—literally—in 1872, when her weekly alleged that the glib and handsome clergyman Henry Ward Beecher had had an affair with a parishioner's wife.

Beecher was not only the most famous preacher of his day, but also the brother of the icon of popular American literature, Harriet Beecher Stowe, who had, coincidentally, taken serious umbrage with Victoria's free thinking ways.

The article touched off one of the nation's most notorious scandals, which culminated in an adultery trial and a hung jury. In 1877, Victoria suddenly moved to England, apparently bought off by the Vanderbilt family.

She lived in great style, continued to write books and articles, and eventually married her banker. She died—sitting up—on her English estate in 1927. Said the *New York Times*: "She it was who blazed the trail for those more insurgent leaders who finally won victory."

—by Damaine Vonada

Victoria herself

There's a site for the Ohio suffragettes out there who want to see what Victoria was up to—whole issues of Woodhull & Claflin's Weekly— www.victoria-woodhull.com/ wcwarchive.htm. This, for instance: "Woman Items—The Nebraska men voted down infant education and woman suffrage, while they upheld free liquor. Do our readers take the idea?" And: "An Atlanta paper has the following statistics: 'Of the 69 young ladies who fainted away in Atlanta during the summer, 57 fell into the arms of gentlemen, 11 fell on the floor, and one into a water bucket.'"

Yankee lines under the unwitting protection of Secretary of War Edwin Stanton. When he learned how Lottie had played him for a fool, Stanton put a $10,000 bounty on her pretty head—dead or alive. Fate brought Lottie's jilted fiancé back to Ohio as General Burnside, commander of the Department of Ohio, which was headquartered in Cincinnati. Burnside was hell-bent on ridding Ohio of the Copperhead infestation, even if it meant putting offenders to death. When an invalid Englishwoman came to his office seeking a traveling pass, he recognized Lottie in disguise and placed her under benign house arrest in a Cincinnati hotel. She had plenty of company in the Burnet House, for also under arrest were her mother and younger sister Jennie. Jennie had followed quite nicely in Lottie's footsteps. It is said that she once shot every star out of a Union flag, not to mention her sending 15 Confederate boys happily off to the battlefield with her name on their lips and her solemn promise of marriage in their unsuspecting hearts. Though Burnside was a Union officer, he was also a gentleman, and a softhearted one at that. Word of Lottie's arrest never leaked to the newspapers. She never went to trial, and certainly never reaped Stanton's reward. When the war was over, Oxford no longer seemed big enough or perhaps friendly enough for the Copperhead Clarks. They went to New York, where James became a newspaperman and Lottie a foreign correspondent. In 1871, she left to report on the Franco-Prussian war, an assignment for which she already had considerable job training. As for General Burnside, he became best known for his distinctive whiskers. Folks simply reversed his name, and sideburns have been with us ever since.

Alice Pike Barney

Her father built Cincinnati's famous Pike Opera House, and Alice lived in a wonderland of celebrity. Understandably, she acquired a lifelong flair for the dramatic. Sir Henry Morton Stanley, who uttered the immortal "Dr. Livingston, I presume" at Lake Tanganyika was so smitten with her that he named his Congo boat "Lady Alice." But their romance sank abruptly when Alice decided that she was wild about Barney, specifically rich-as-Croesus Albert of Dayton's railroad car Barneys. Alice had considerable talents, and when Albert died, she got the fortune and freedom to live the life of an artiste. Her last liaison was with a much younger man, a relationship that she deliciously severed by cutting the word "Mr." out of her party invitations.

Warren G. Harding

His wife claimed, "I have only one real hobby—that's my husband." Unfortunately, Harding's many outside interests included at least two mistresses, one of whom allegedly bore him a child during their White House liaison.

Gloria Steinem

She grew up in a decrepit Toledo farmhouse where the furnace had been condemned by the health department and she became, during the last quarter of a century, America's most famous feminist. She was called "America's first smart blonde," and "the intellectual's pinup." She was witty and glamorous, encircled by powerful men, but as one writer put it, "she didn't have to wash their socks or clean up a nightly mountain of dinner dishes." She lived in a New York brownstone for nearly five years before she discovered the oven didn't work. Her suitors ranged from John Kenneth Galbraith to Mike Nichols, but she was just as renowned for her independence, as when she said, "Men should think twice before making widowhood women's only path to power." Or: "Some of us are becoming the men we wanted to marry." She also said, "In my own mind, I am still that fat brunette from Toledo, and I always will be." No one else saw her that way, however. In 1971, she helped found the National Women's Political Caucus, and in 1972 was the co-founder of *Ms. Magazine*, which was considered to be the voice of the women's movement. She and the magazine established the term "Ms." and her magazine became the only mass circulation feminist magazine in history. Writer, social activist, and lecturer for over a quarter of a century, she rose out of an unlikely Ohio background to become the most visible symbol of American feminism. "I have yet to hear a man ask for advice," she said, "on how to combine marriage and a career." Her wit and charm gave the feminist movement a credence that helped place the modern woman in a position where she could do both and sacrifice neither.

The story of Liwwät Böke, Mercer County pioneer, is an unusual Ohio ménage à trois involving two men and a woman spanning more than a century. Luke Knapke met Liwwät Böke in a garage in Columbus. He had been inveigled there by a distant relative, who arranged the meeting between Luke and the hundreds of pages of written record—old German script—that Liwwät Böke had left in the family.

Luke was a retired schoolteacher, welcoming the diversions of genealogy. What he found instead was a remarkable record of pioneer life in America, written in Plattdeutsch—a low German dialect Luke had grown up listening to, but a language that was largely spoken, by mostly older, rural people. There were over 1,100 pages in all, "an educated woman's impressions of the country."

Liwwät Böke came to Mercer County in the 1830s and left in her papers, written with a handmade quill pen, the best account of the forbidding landscape of Ohio anyone ever made: "Right up to our doorsill and to those of our neighbors reaches the huge, somber and vaulted forest," she wrote. "There are no openings to break up the overhang, nothing but endless miles upon miles of the shadowy wolf-haunted woodland...The sunlight cannot get through the arches of the murmuring leaves. Through the grayish shadow and down the pathways in the forest men walk, continually in a kind of midday gloom. In this thick forest we feel if our heads are hooded. All the countryside is monotonous in a tree-strewn land. Everything in it lies hidden...."

Liwwät was also among the very first liberated women, too, writing pamphlets such as, "What the Wives of Mercer County Wish Their Husbands Knew Better," and even instructing the Bishop that the parish priest was erroneous in dominating the "privileges and privacy in our married lifestyle." Wrote Liwwät, "He would forever like all people to live in the state of 'purity' and be considered like any harmless, innocent vegetation. Perhaps this human paradise here in the sexless forest can, generation after generation of people, make a new paradise of innocent and imperishable things come alive."

Shining through Luke's translation is the relationship of Liwwät with her beloved husband, Natz. When she despaired of the endless work, she sought solace in her journal and her drawings, many of them of Natz.

"In my own lifetime," she wrote, "Natz was always my beloved. He loved me, I him. As two we were in all things one, in work, viewpoint, suffering...Our relationship, experiences and sexuality delighted us both in the same way. That was to us another gift from God." Her frankness was astounding, her intelligence illuminated the darkness of the primitive forest around her.

Luke's translation—his own labor of love— left a remarkable pioneer document, an unknown diary tossed about in attics and garages for most of a century, but moreover, a diary written in a German dialect for which dictionaries do not exist.

Source: Liwwät Böke by Luke Knapke

pioneer liebestraum

"At a century and a half removed from us she is more authentic than most of us alive. We would like to know what she looked like but we know that she was beautiful to her husband, Natz. And the rest of us, we loved her spirit. We couldn't see what she looked like, but we could see that..."

—Luke Knapke

Harvey William Cushing is born in Cleveland, goes on to develop many of the basic surgical techniques for operating on the brain which establishes neurosurgery as a new and autonomous surgical discipline. Cushing becomes known as *the greatest neurosurgeon of the 20th century*.

1869

Cleveland's Dr. George Crile performs what may have been *the first successful total laryngectomy* in the U.S.

1892

Perrin Long, the son of a Bryan, Ohio, doctor, a pioneer in the study of infectious diseases and bacteriology demonstrates the effectiveness and safety of sulfa drugs, which bring about a *revolution in the management of bacterial infections*.

1936

Dr. Maurice Levine, an assistant professor of psychiatry in UC's College of Medicine, publishes the landmark *Psychotherapy in Medical Practice*, in which he contends that psychiatric knowledge is essential to all of medical practice; the book *helps legitimize psychiatry in America*, goes through some 18 printings and is translated into Swedish, Spanish, and Yugoslave, leaving Levine to assert that he had written a book that he, himself, could not read.

1941

Rollo May, of Ada, Ohio, graduates from Oberlin College in English, then finishes his doctoral thesis at Columbia which is published as *The Meaning of Anxiety*, helping May to become *one of the most important writers in the field of humanistic psychology in the 20th century*.

1950

Henry Rufus Biggs Smith of Cincinnati buys a home health care business and—noticing patients' difficulty drinking from straight straws— invents *the bendable accordion straw*.

1950s

William Howell Masters, Cleveland-born obstetrician and gynecologist, gives up study of prostitutes in 1956 as unsuitable for his studies of "normal" sexuality, hires sociology student Virginia Johnson to screen volunteers for what would become a pioneering effort that *made human sexuality a proper subject of scientific study.*

1956

In Cincinnati some 20,000 children receive, at no cost, a sugar cube soaked with the cherry-flavored vaccine—the first mass distribution of Dr. Albert Sabin's oral polio vaccine in the United States. At his death in 1993 it was called *medical science's greatest success story of the 20th century*: the vaccine was estimated to have prevented nearly 5 million cases of polio and 500,000 deaths.

1960

Dr. Rene Favaloro puts Cleveland Clinic on the medical map when he performs *the first documented coronary artery bypass graft;* it comes after his mentor, Dr. Mason Sones, discovers angiography after accidentally sending an opaque dye into the coronary arteries of a young patient which presented on the fluoroscope a splendidly outlined picture of the coronary circulation.

1967

The Heimlich maneuver is first described as a "subdiaphragmatic pressure," in an article by Cincinnati's Dr. Henry Heimlich; *an estimated 100,000 people have been saved* by Heimlich's application, including Ronald Reagan, Elizabeth Taylor, Cher, and broadcaster John Chancellor (who was saved by Tom Brokaw).

1974

In the cartoon:

THEY THINK WE'LL STOP SMOKING IF CIGARETTES COST ENOUGH.

LIKE WE WENT BAREFOOT WHEN SHOES GOT EXPENSIVE?

JIM BORGMAN
CINCINNATI ENQUIRER ©1998

Up in smoke

Can't break the nicotine habit to save your life?

For an incentive perhaps ever dearer, try putting it in economic terms.

To wit:

Figure an average smoker goes through a carton a week, at an investment of $30.

Assuming annual inflation of 2% and if the average smoker took that investment beginning at the age of 18 and invested it, realizing a return of 3%, he or she would have a nest egg of:

$22,901.32 at age 30
$44,998.14 at age 40
$71,934.05 at age 50
$131,943.87 at retirement, age 67

Want to reach retirement as a millionaire?

Investing a carton a week instead of smoking it, getting a 7.75 % return (Standard & Poor averages around 10%) the reformed smoker would have a nest egg of:

$36,498.23 at age 30
$108,244.88 at age 40
$266,435.22 at age 50
$1,060,212.91 at retirement, age 67

Taking more risk, although less a risk than smoking, and by gaining a 12% return, the smoker would realize:

$47,890.23 at age 30
$186,816.99 at age 40
$626,641.00 at age 50
$4,466,445.39 at retirement, age 67

—*Dr. Ann Dinkheller, math curriculum leader, Mason High School*

In Ohio, one woman in four smokes. Only two states have higher rates.

30% of all high school senior girls in Ohio smoked in 2000— only three percentage points behind the boys.

Ohioans smoke more than most of the rest of America—in 1999, 27.6% smoked, the third-highest rate in the U.S.

—Centers for Disease Control and Prevention

the dark side

I's wicked—I is.
I's mighty wicked,
anyhow. I can't help it.

Topsy, Uncle Tom's
Cabin, Harriet
Beecher Stowe

The Fugitive

It was one of the most famous murder trials in America. So famous that it was never really over. The **Sam Sheppard** case, as a matter of fact, is *still* playing in Cleveland. Socialite Marilyn Sheppard was bludgeoned to death in her Bay Village bedroom and her surgeon husband was convicted, spent a decade in prison, then—with the help of a brash attorney named F. Lee Bailey—retried and acquitted. The murder prompted a television series, *The Fugitive*, and a hit movie of the same name. Until he died in 1970, Dr. Sheppard maintained he was innocent. In 1996, using 42-year-old blood samples from the crime scene, a DNA expert checked the samples and found the blood on Dr. Sheppard's pants was neither his own nor that of his wife. In 2000, a jury refused to declare Dr. Sheppard innocent, voting in favor of the State of Ohio after a 10-week civil trial and insuring "the trial of the century" would live on. And on.

The Cleveland butcher

It was another Ohio murder without a satisfactory conclusion: Cleveland's "Torso Murderer," between 1935 and 1942, left a string of victims that even the untouchable **Eliot Ness**, Cleveland's director of public safety, was unable to solve. Most of the victims had been surgically dismembered.

The Dahmer serial murders

Jeffrey Dahmer's apartment was a crime scene to rival any special effects Hollywood could produce: It held seven skulls, four heads, and assorted body parts. Raised in a middle-class Akron community, Dahmer was a loner who confessed to committing 17 murders after luring the victims to his apartment where he drugged, strangled, and dismembered them.

Angel of death

Ohio's most prolific serial murderer, however, was a boyish nurses's aide in Cincinnati, **Donald Harvey**, who dispatched at least 37 people during the 1980s, most of them elderly or terminally ill.

Arsenic and old men

He was preceded in the Queen City by **Anna Marie Hahn**, convicted in 1937 of poisoning an elderly man by putting arsenic in his orange juice and forging her name into his will. "Do I look like the kind of woman who would do something like that?" she asked over and over. The answer was, apparently, yes. On Death Row, she said she had killed three others similarly, and in 1938 became the first woman to die in Ohio's electric chair.

The Kirtland cult

Jeffrey Lundgren thought he was the new Mormon prophet, sent to purify the old temple at Kirtland, Ohio. In this bizarre fervor in 1989, the charismatic cult leader sacrificed five of his followers—an entire family—and buried them in a single grave in an abandoned barn.

Easter massacre

On Easter Sunday of 1975, in a small frame house near Hamilton, **James Ruppert** killed his mother, brother, sister-in-law and their eight children while the church bells pealed outside. He fired something like 38 shots, placed his guns on a coffee table, and went to sleep. When he awoke, he called the police. Said the prosecutor, "He was this quiet little dude with glasses on and a coat and tie..."

JIMBORGMAN©1981CINCINNATIENQUIRER

"LET'S HOPE YOUR TIME HERE IN PRISON HAS TAUGHT YOU HOW TO ACT LIKE A HUMAN BEING, 430067-55831192!"

Crime Rates in Ohio*
2001

Crime	Total	Rate	Metropolitan Area Rate	City Rate**	Rural Rate
Violent Crime	40,023	351.9	36,939	1,978	1,106
Murder	452	4.0	409	21	22
Forcible Rape	4,466	39.3	3,929	325	212
Robbery	17,906	151.2	16,511	525	163
Aggravated Assault	17,906	157.4	16,090	1,107	709
Property Crime	435,115	3,825.7	327,621	38,701	22,401
Burglary	96,910	852.1	83,290	6,468	852.1
Larceny/Theft	295,976	2,602.3	251,374	30,781	2,602.3
Motor Vehicle Theft	42,229	371.3	39,349	1,452	371.3

Crime Rates in Ohio*
2000

Crime	Total	Rate	Metropolitan Area Rate	City Rate**	Rural Rate
Violent Crime	17,177	497.8	12,128	3,477	1,572
Murder	182	5.3	104	38	40
Forcible Rape	1,422	41.2	1,044	262	116
Robbery	2,615	75.8	2,253	312	50
Aggravated Assault	12,958	375.5	8,727	2,865	1,366
Property Crime	140,125	4,060.8	103,697	28,502	7,926
Burglary	31,661	917.5	21,464	7,038	3,159
Larceny/Theft	96,116	2,785.4	72,340	19,839	3,937
Motor Vehicle Theft	12,348	357.8	9,893	1,625	830

*Per 100,000 residents
**Cities outside metropolitan areas
Source: Uniform Crime Reports, FBI

Violent Crime

Of all violent crimes in Ohio:
40.4% are robbery
46.8% are aggravated assault

Of all robberies in Ohio:
46.0% use strong-arm
36.4% use a firearm
5.3% use a knife

Of all aggravated assaults in Ohio:
35.3% use fist or feet
17.7% use a knife
17.5% use a firearm

Crimes Committed in Major Ohio Cities*

City	Murder and Non-Negligent Manslaughter	Forcible Rape	Robbery	Aggravated Assault	Burglary	Larceny/ Theft	Motor theft	Arson
2002								
Columbus	41	304	1,688	1,064	7,450	17,508	3,347	107
Cleveland	42	298	1,556	1,153	3,895	6,198	2,655	216
Cincinnati	36	210	1,058	361	3,052	6,316	1,397	231
Toledo	14	93	643	777	2,812	6,412	1,536	247
Dayton	13	104	489	369	1,866	3,319	1,232	78
2001								
Parma	1	9	57	62	449	1,356	134	21
Youngstown	34	52	355	570	1,718	2,695	441	248
Lorain	1	22	105	151	626	1,536	149	19
Springfield	7	74	226	203	1,507	4,259	467	32
Hamilton	5	66	221	398	1,204	3,264	437	21
Kettering	1	32	31	27	409	1,629	170	21
Lakewood	0	7	51	57	243	1,019	108	5
Euclid	1	18	86	52	384	1,484	236	21
Middletown	2	18	61	56	518	2,444	166	12
Mentor	0	8	19	11	158	1,252	82	5
Cleveland Heights	0	1	10	1	120	621	85	0
Cuyahoga Falls	1	15	24	24	229	1,549	123	8
Mansfield	1	39	104	41	938	2,623	178	54
Warren	4	25	148	220	849	1,376	355	78
Newark	0	13	41	34	536	1,672	113	30
Strongsville	3	7	10	44	118	706	41	16
Union Township	1	2	26	11	226	1,280	27	13
Fairfield	0	16	22	120	239	1,535	131	8
Lima	6	72	108	235	847	2,107	147	40
Huber Heights	0	20	34	18	270	1,247	99	13
Beavercreek	0	6	14	9	191	1,150	72	12
Lancaster	0	21	30	18	253	945	82	17
Marion	2	5	25	29	469	1,514	63	28
Westerville	0	0	23	7	156	824	26	9
Upper Arlington	0	10	15	20	114	508	13	4
Gahanna	0	4	42	27	153	697	49	9
Stow	1	10	10	4	141	712	15	9
Fairborn	0	15	23	19	212	1,246	138	7
Westlake	0	6	9	11	66	346	19	5
Dublin	0	7	13	2	218	615	32	5
Delhi Township	0	4	13	0	66	507	18	2
Bowling Green	0	7	13	19	171	952	47	4
Shaker Heights	2	2	27	4	181	512	82	6
Perry Township (Stark County)	0	8	9	17	162	510	44	5
North Royalton	0	2	5	5	92	147	16	12
Kent	0	10	17	39	210	712	63	40
Barberton	0	16	29	49	259	1,093	97	14
Sandusky	1	13	42	136	373	1,663	53	11
Grove City	0	21	22	19	85	795	68	1
Zanesville	4	12	55	137	363	1,761	93	11
Sylvania Township	0	0	11	6	78	669	34	5
Delaware	0	17	7	16	163	709	45	9
Hilliard	0	5	15	9	124	553	24	12
Xenia	0	4	12	12	211	1,125	29	10
South Euclid	0	8	41	9	79	366	40	3
Alliance	0	8	38	110	255	953	30	25
Centerville	0	2	7	13	90	420	27	7
Hudson	0	2	0	4	54	235	6	10

Source: FBI Uniform Crime Reports
*Cities are listed by population, from Parma (85,655) to Hudson (22,439)

Making HANDGUNS safer still....

JIMBORGMAN
CINCINNATI ENQUIRER © 1997

CHILD-PROOF CAP
SQUEEZE TABS WHILE PRESSING DOWN AND TURN
CLOSE OPEN

In 1997, the entire prison population serving time in Ohio for drug offenses was 6,288; in 2000 alone, 6,302 drug offenders came into the system.

—Ohio Department of Rehabilitation and Correction

Arrests, 2001

	All Ages	Under 18
Total	*268,148*	*53,807*
Violent Crime	10,515	1,417
Murder and Non-negligent Manslaughter	167	10
Forcible Rape	647	154
Robbery	2,217	409
Aggravated Assault	7,484	923
Property Crime	31,282	9,366
Burglary	5,358	1,801
Larceny-Theft	23,819	6,554
Motor Vehicle Theft	821	1,738
Arson	367	190
Other Assaults	24,346	6,194
Forgery and Counterfeiting	2,041	89
Fraud	3,167	69
Embezzlement	283	89
Stolen Property; Buying, Receiving, Possessing	4,536	1,200
Vandalism	3,951	1,870
Weapons, Carrying, Possessing, etc.	3,078	596
Prostitution and Commercialized Vice	2,154	33
Sex Offenses (except Forcible Rape and Prostitution)	1,616	296
Drug Abuse Violations	20,464	2,948
Gambling	409	11
Offenses Against Family and Children	14,440	1,463
Driving Under the Influence	21,273	313
Liquor Laws	15,389	3,356
Drunkenness	9,142	216
Disorderly Conduct	14,457	3,213
Vagrancy	915	75
All Other Offenses (except traffic)	78,997	15,324
Suspicion	202	54
Curfew and Loitering Law Violations	3,053	3,053
Runaways	1,978	1,978

Murder in Ohio

	2000	1999	1998	1997	1996	1995	1990	1980
Sex of Victim								
Male	284	279	318	405	396	435	498	663
Female	132	118	124	118	142	165	165	208
Unknown	2	0	1	0	0	0	0	0
Age of Victim								
0-3	18	15	21	17	40	29	15	21
4 - 11	5	5	10	13	7	9	9	19
12 - 17	25	23	16	34	38	50	35	38
18 - 24	88	80	116	135	127	135	147	184
25 - 49	202	204	229	248	252	285	354	415
50 +	73	67	46	70	73	83	95	189
Unknown	7	3	5	6	1	9	8	5
Race of Victim								
White	206	157	174	215	198	225	246	426
Black	208	232	263	307	333	370	412	441
Native American	6	0	0	0	0	0	0	0
Asian	1	2	4	1	6	2	4	4
Unknown	3	6	2	0	1	3	1	0
Percent								
White	49.3%	39.6%	39.3%	41.1%	36.8%	37.5%	37.1%	48.9%
Black	49.8%	58.4%	59.4%	58.7%	61.9%	61.7%	62.1%	53.6%
Native American	0.0%	0.0%	0.0%	0.0%	0.0%	0.0%	0.0%.	0.0%
Asian	0.2%	0.5%	0.9%	0.2%	1.1%	0.3%	0.6%	0.5%
Unknown	0.7%	1.5%	0.5%	0.0%	0.2%	0.5%	0.2%	0.0%
Relationship to Victims								
Family	57	56	70	51	76	74	101	162
Acquaintance	162	148	167	192	177	224	272	306
Stranger	37	38	47	58	86	81	114	179
Unknown	162	155	159	222	199	221	176	224
Percent								
Family	13.6%	14.1%	15.8%	9.8%	14.1%	12.3%	15.2%	18.6%
Acquaintance	38.8%	37.3%	37.7%	36.7%	32.9%	37.3%	15.2%	35.1%
Stranger	8.6%	9.6%	10.6%	11.1%	16.0%	17.2%	17.2%	20.6%
Unknown	38.8%	39.0%	35.9%	42.5%	37.0%	36.8%	26.6%	25.7%
Weapon Used								
Firearm	213	226	261	326	351	383	404	580
Knife	57	45	54	58	45	74	120	123
Blunt Object	12	23	17	27	38	32	44	28
Personal	46	36	54	66	40	45	40	77
Other	90	67	57	56	64	66	55	63
Percent								
Firearm	51.0%	57.0%	58.9%	62.3%	65.2%	63.8%	60.9%	66.6%
Knife	13.6%	11.3%	12.2%	9.2%	8.4%	12.3%	18.1%	14.1%
Blunt Object	2.9%	5.8%	3.8%	5.2%	7.1%	5.3%	6.6%	3.2%

Ohio ranks 7th in the U.S. and No. 1 in the Midwest in exporting guns that end up in the hands of criminals in other states. Based on 2001 data, Ohio was the origin of 1,697 guns recovered in crimes committed in other states. Guns bought for $150 at Ohio gun shows bring $600 on the streets of Detroit where it's difficult to obtain a gun because of tougher laws.

—Americans for Gun Safety; Bureau of Alcohol, Tobacco, Firearms and Explosives

Law Enforcement

Number of Agencies	845
Total Law Enforcement Employees	36,863
Per 100,000 Residents	325
Sworn Personnel	25,082
Per 100,000 Residents	221
Officers Who Respond to Calls	15,689
Per 100,000 Residents	138
Local Agencies	712
Total	21,086
Per 100,000 Residents	186
Sworn Personnel	16,956
Per 100,000 Residents	149
Officers Who Respond to Calls	11,391
Per 100,000 Residents	100
Sheriffs' Offices	88
Total	10,199
Per 100,000 Residents	90
Sworn Personnel	5,366
Per 100,000 Residents	47
Officers Who Respond to Calls	2,146
Per 100,000 Residents	41
Special Jurisdiction	
Law Enforcement Agencies	44
Total	3,026
Per 100,000 Residents	27
Sworn Personnel	1,378
Per 100,000 Residents	12
Officers Responding to Calls,	
Per 100,000 Residents	138

Expenditures

Total Expenditure	$63,470,227
Total Justice System	$4,816,459
State	$1,396,010
Local	$3,120,449
Counties	$8,213,016
Muncipalities	$9,892,146
Police Protection	$2,036,446
State	$203,281
Local	$1,833,165
Counties	$394,827
Municipalities	$1,438,338
Judicial and Legal	$1,085,460
State	$181,224
Local	$904,236
Counties	$662,096
Municipalities	$242,140
Corrections	$1,694,553
State	$1,311,505
Local	$383,048
Counties	$359,351
Municipalities	$23,697
Per Capita	
Total Justice System	$424.25
Police Protection	$179.38
Judicial and Legal	$95.61
Corrections	$149.26

POLICE OFFICERS, PER CAPITA, MAJOR OHIO CITIES

Akron	469.9	Kettering	701.2
Canton	425.3	Lakewood	643.7
Cincinnati	323.2	Lima	450.3
Cleveland	245.8	Lorain	653.8
Cleveland Heights	458.3	Mansfield	508.7
Columbus	424.8	Mentor	661.6
Cuyahoga Falls	536.7	Middletown	554.9
Dayton	346.9	Parma	856.6
Elyra	601.6	Springfield	514.6
Euclid	527.2	Toledo	440.5
Fairfield	841.9	Youngstown	386.9
Hamilton	514.3		

Crime and punishment in Ohio

Murders, type of weapon

Total Murders	600
Total Firearms	437
Handguns	357
Rifles	7
Shotguns	33
Unknown	40
Knives or Cutting Instruments	54
Other Weapons	72
Hands, Feet, Fists, etc.	37

Police officers per square mile

Akron	7.3
Canton	8.7
Cleveland	22.7
Cincinnati	12.6
Toledo	8.8
Columbus	7.9
Springfield	8.2

Robbery, type of weapon

Total Robberies	19,169
Firearms	7,958
Knives or Cutting Instruments	1,103
Other Weapons	1,782
Strongarmed	8,326

Aggravated assault, type of weapon

Total Aggravated Assault	23,860
Firearms	5,976
Knives or Cutting Instruments	4,007
Other Weapons	7,266
Personal Weapons	6,611

Percent of crimes cleared by arrest

Type of Crime	Percent Cleared
Murder	74%
Forcible Rape	28%
Aggravated Assault	31%
Robbery	23%
Burglary	10%
Larceny-theft	14%
Motor Vehicle Theft	8%

Ten counties that send the most people to prison

	Total Prisoners	Percent of Ohio's Prison Population
Cuyahoga	5,104	25.3%
Hamilton	2,374	11.8%
Franklin	1,957	9.7%
Summit	1,235	6.1%
Montgomery	1,058	5.2%
Lucas	1,048	5.2%
Stark	517	2.6%
Lorain	508	2.5%
Butler	334	1.7%
Green	234	1.2%
Ten County Total	14,369	71.3%

Largest police departments

	Number Employees	per 10,000 Residents	Percent Responding to Calls	Nat. Rank
Cleveland	1,822	38	44%	21
Columbus	1,744	25	88%	24
Cincinnati	1,030	31	44%	44

Source: The Ohio Department of Rehabilitation and Correction

Crimes in Ohio
—475,138

**Average time
between crimes in Ohio**
—1 minute, 7 seconds

**Percentage of crimes
occuring in urban areas**
—95.1%

Murders in Ohio
—one every 19 hours, 22 minutes

A violent crime
—one every 26 minutes

A robbery
—one every 30 minutes

A forcible rape
—one every one hour, 57 minutes

A burglary
—one every five minutes

A stolen car
—one every 12 minutes

Top stolen vehicles in Ohio:
1. Oldsmobile Cutless/Supreme/Ciera
2. Oldsmobile Delta 88/Royale
3. Chevrolet Cavalier
4. Buick Century

Alcohol-related arrests in Ohio
—69,312 (22.9 percent of all arrests)

Sex offenders in Ohio
—5,423

**Arrests for prostitution
and commercialized vice**
—4,011

Physically abused children in Ohio
—14,960, or the equivalent population
of Mt. Vernon, Worthington, Marietta
or Greenville

Hate crimes in Ohio
—477

**Incendiary fires, including structures
and vehicles**
—4,317
(There were an additional 3,989
"suspicious fires", as well as 94 civilian injuries,
38 deaths, and over $55.6 million in losses
resulting from arson in 2000.)

Doing time in Ohio
Ohio locks up 45,000 people, more than
France and 10,000 less than Japan, which has
a population of 125 million.

The number of people incarcerated in
Ohio has quadrupled in the last 25 years, and
between 1985 and 2000, spending on corrections grew over $1 billion. Most of this expense
was because of mandatory sentencing for
nonviolent crime; only six states have a higher
rate of nonviolent, drug-related crime.

Overall, one of 11 Ohio males—one of
every 91 females and one of every four black
males—will spend time in a state or federal
prison.

The price of injustice—wrongful imprisonment—in Ohio is $25,000 per year, lost wages
(up to $30,000), costs and attorney's fees.

Number of Ohioans who use Marijuana
—485,000

Average daily population in local jails
—16,526

**State and local government spending
for Justice activities**
—$5.2 billion (or $459 per capita)

**What each of us pays
for police protection**
—$186.78

Longest sentence in Ohio history
—Lonnie Shelton, convicted in Cleveland
in 1989 of 49 rapes, 3,198 years

*Sources: ohioinsurancefactbook.org; Policy
Matters Ohio; Justice Policy Institute; Cleveland
Plain Dealer*

*If 2001
incarceration
rates remain the
same, about 6.6
percent of everyone
born that year can
expect to serve a
prison sentence.*

—Associated Press

Correctional Institutions of Ohio

Facility	County	Level of Security	Population	Cost per Prisoner	Year Built
Allen Correctional Institution	Allen	2	1,192	$60.20	1987
Belmont Correctional Institution	Belmont	1-2	2,110	$45.58	1995
Chillicothe Correctional Institute	Ross	2	2,414	$53.09	1966
Correctional Medical Center Columbus	Franklin	5	102	N/A	1993
Correctional Reception Center	Pickaway	3	2,133	$55.58	1987
Dayton Correctional Institution	Montgomery	2	471	$82.14	1987
Franklin Pre-Release Center (female)	Franklin	1-2	466	$61.94	1988
Grafton Correctional Institution	Lorain	1-2	1,368	$57.07	1988
Hocking Correctional Facility (older)	Hocking	1-2	408	$77.29	1983
Lebanon Correctional Institution	Warren	3	1,756	$65.70	1960
Lima Correctional Institution	Allen	1-2	954	$58.98	1982
London Correctional Institution	Madison	1-2	2,004	$50.93	1924
Lorain Correctional Institution	Lorain	3	2,094	$53.53	1990
Madison Correctional Institution	Madison	1-3	2,067	$53.33	1987
Mansfield Correctional Institution	Richland	3	2,308	$61.28	1991
Marion Correctional Institution	Marion	1-2	1,718	$56.39	1954
Montgomery Educational Pre-Release Center	Montgomery	1	321	$80.69	1994
Noble Correctional Institution	Noble	2	2,019	$48.97	1996
North Central Correctional Institution	Marion	1-2	2,034	$43.97	1994
Northeast Pre-Release Center	Cuyahoga	1-2	593	$42.97	1988
Oakwood Correctional Facility (female)	Allen	3	153	N/A	1994
Ohio Reformatory for Women	Union	1-4	1,851	$61.17	1916
Ohio State Penitentiary	Mahoning	5,4B &1	469	$149.59	2003
Pickaway Correctional Institution (female)	Pickaway	1	2,167	$63.09	1984
Richland Correctional Institution	Richland	1-2	2,245	$37.44	1988
Ross Correctional Institution	Ross	1-3	2,243	$54.05	1987
Southeastern Correctional Institution	Fairfield	1 & 3	1,377	$57.42	1980
Southern Ohio Correctional Facility	Scioto	4	1,350	$101.98	1972
Toledo Correctional Institution	Lucas	1 & 3	788	$86.35	2000
Trumbull Correctional Institution	Trumbull	1 & 3	1,413	$56.49	1992
Warren Correctional Institution	Warren	3	1,069	$71.09	1989
Private Prisons					
Lake Erie Correctional Facility		1	1,388	$62.58	2000
North Coast Correctional Treatment Facility		1	563	$39.96	2000

All figures are for Fiscal Year 2001; source: The Ohio Department of Rehabilitation and Correction

Levels of Security for Ohio Prisons

Level 1 (*Minimum*)—The perimeter is clearly designed by a single fence with no towers or external patrol. Detection devices are optional and the inmates are housed in single rooms, multiple rooms or dorms.

Level 2 (*Medium*)—The perimeter is walled or double-fenced with armed towers and mobile patrols. Detection devices are present and the inmates are housed in single cells or rooms or dormitories.

Level 3 (*Close*)—The perimeter is walled or double-fenced with armed towers and mobile patrols. Detection devices are present and the inmates are housed in single cells which are outside (a cell with a wall or window immediately adjacent to the outside of the building: i.e., if an inmate escapes from the cell, he has escaped from the building) or inside (a cell which is contained on four sides within a cellblock, i.e., if an inmate escapes from the cell he is still confined within the building).

Level 4 (*Maximum*)—The perimeter is walled or double fenced with armed towers, external patrols, and detection devices. The inmates are housed in single, inside cells.

Level 5 (*High Maximum*)—The same as level 4 with prisoners kept in cells 23 out of 24 hours.

It was all a big mistake between Vincent Wright's finger and his brain.

—*Dick Feagler, Plain Dealer columnist, commenting on a murder case in which the defendent explained that he didn't mean to shoot the victim*

DEADLY ENCOUNTER AT LUCASVILLE: OHIO'S WORST RIOT

It was the longest prison riot in modern U.S. penal history, and the third deadliest, right behind Attica and Sante Fe. Beginning on the afternoon of Easter Sunday in 1993, one guard and nine prisoners died in 11 days of siege at Lucasville's Southern Ohio Correctional Facility, a tense facility reserved for Ohio's most incorrigible inmates.

It began in midafternoon, after an edict from Warden Arthur Tate—called "King Arthur" by resentful inmates—that ordered the prison's Sunni Muslims to take tuberculosis tests. The Muslims said the injections violated their religious beliefs. There were other tensions, as well: overcrowding, prison gangs, and mentally ill inmates in the general population. In the system at large, the prisons were filled to nearly 180% of their intended capacity—more than 35,000, and guards were outnumbered 9-1, a ratio almost twice the national average.

Lucasville housed 1,819 prisoners, including 357 murderers and 279 rapists. Over 400 of them overwhelmed guards shortly after 3 p.m. and took control of Cell Block L. Some guards made it out, but others were stranded when central control slammed down the emergency gates.

Before the end of the day, officials recovered the bodies of five inmates—described by other inmates as "snitches"—who had been dumped in the recreation yard. Another inmate was killed on Monday, another found dead the following day, and on Thursday afternoon, the body of guard Robert Vallandingham was thrown into the rec yard.

On the following Sunday, even as townspeople circulated a petition asking officers to storm the prison, Cleveland lawyer Niki Schwartz, who had represented other inmates in federal suits, arrived to try and negotiate a settlement.

On April 19—the day Vallandingham is buried—prison officials aired taped messages over loudspeakers, telling inmates that 21 of their demands had been agreed upon, including a review of the commissary pricing system as well as FBI monitoring of their surrender. The surrender comes on April 21, at which time the bodies of two more inmates are found in their cells.

In the aftermath, millions of tax dollars went into a system called one of the nation's worst. The corrections budget nearly tripled, a dozen prisons were built, 900 new guards hired, and a range of inmate services were improved, from medical care to educational programming.

The costs—both direct and indirect—were estimated at $163.6 million, including a $41.8 million renovation of Lucasville complete with safety zones for guards, escape hatches, remote control locks, and a class action settlement of $2.7 million to the families of the nine inmates killed, and to non-rioting prisoners injured or with property damage. Five inmates were convicted of the murder of Robert Vallandingham and sent to Death Row.

The inmates no longer have free weights (they were used as weapons during the rioting), but there are relaxed phone privileges and nurses on each block—and 300 cameras inside the prison.

Said Reginald Wilkinson, Ohio Department of Rehabilitation and Correction director in early 2003, "Just about everything we do in some way or another has been touched by the riot. It changed the system and the way we think about the system." ꙮ

Sources: The Plain Dealer, Cincinnati Enquirer, The New York Times Magazine, Newsweek

"Living in extremely close proximity to a stranger frequently leads to stress, shortened tempers, impatience and what the committee has called a 'diminution of civility.'

— *Simon Dinitz, professor emeritus at The Ohio State University, the Governor's Select Committee on Corrections*

Doing Time in Ohio: The Numbers

Ohio statistics show that about 20 inmates a year are freed after their sentences are dropped or the courts determines a conviction was flawed. Forty-one former inmates have won settlements since 1975, the settlements being based upon a formula that takes into account the former inmate's skills, earning power, family status, and other factors. Awards of $25,000 per year are typical.

—Dan Horn, The Cincinnati Enquirer

Number of Jails	108
Rated Capacity	17,219
Percent Occupied	97%

Inmates per Employees

Total Staff	2.3
Correctional Officers	3.3

Prison Population

2002	45,349
2001	45,281
2000	45,833
Number in Private Facilities, 2002	1,936 (4.3%)
Number in Private Facilities, 2001	1,924 (4.2%)

Prison Admissions

2001	24,399
2000	23,780
1999	21,302

Prison Releases

2001	24,953
2000	24,793
1999	22,910

Largest Jail Jurisdictions, 2002

Franklin County
Average Daily Population	2,514
Percent Occupied	99%
National Rank	36

Cuyahoga County
Average Daily Population	2,150
Percent Occupied	123%
National Rank	44

Hamilton County
Average Daily Population	1,999
Percent Occupied	83%
National Rank	45

Female Prisoners

2001	2,829
2000	2,808
1995	2,793
1990	1,947
Change, 2001-2000	0.7%
Average Annual Change, 1995-2001	0.2%

Offenses of Persons Committed to Prison, 2000

Drug Offenses	6,302
Crimes Against Persons (excluding sex offenses)	4,752
Miscellaneous Property Offenses	3,343
Burglary Offenses	1,505
Offenses Against Justice/ Public Administration	1,265
Sex Offenses	1,239
Fraud Offenses	603
Motor Vehicle Offenses	160
Other Felony Offenses	1

Average Age of Prisoners Committed, 2000

Male	30.5
Female	33.3

Deaths Among Prisoners

Total Deaths	129

HIV Cases Among Ohio Prisoners

Male	363 (0.8%)
Female	28 (1.0%)

Inmates Receiving Mental Health Treatment

24-Hour Care	1,042 (2.2%)
Therapy/Counseling	7,165 (15.0%)
Psychotropic Medications	4,921 (10.3%)

Time Served

	Mean Maximum Sentence (months)	Mean Time Served (months)	Percent of Sentence Served
1999	165	64	39%
1996	226	71	32%
1993	237	61	26%

Prisoners Executed

	Total
1930-1934	43
1935-1939	39
1940-1944	15
1945-1949	36
1950-1954	20
1955-1959	12
1960-1963	7
1964-1998	0
1999-2003	8

Correctional Supervision

Probation
2002	195,403
2001	189,375

Parole
	17,885
2000	18,248
1995	7,432
1990	6,601
Percent Change, 1990-2000	176.4%
Supervision Rate (per 100,000 adults)	2,302

Parole Rate (per 100,000 adults)
2001	211
2000	216

Successfully Completing Parole Supervision

1999	43.6%
1995	50.0%
1990	52.4%

WHAT DOES A PRISON SENTENCE REALLY MEAN?

Q. When can 6 to 25 equal 4?
A. When it is a prison sentence in Ohio.

The minimum prison time imposed by a judge in open court is rarely the time served in Ohio. Decisions by prison officials and others can both shorten and lengthen the time. Although legitimate, these decisions are made in private. As a result, the public is often surprised when an offender is released from prison. One could say that prison time ticks, but it doesn't talk.

Let's follow a case. John Doe robs a store while armed with a gun. He is convicted of a first degree felony and sentenced to six to 25 years. The law lets prison officials reduce a sentence by 30% when an inmate follows rules ("good time"). Because of crowding pressures and the use of other tools to punish inmate misconduct, this reduction is virtually automatic.

Doe could also get another 3% "earned credits" reduction by attaining minimum security status or by participating in school, work, or substance abuse programs in prison. Together, good time and earned credits could make Doe eligible for release after serving two-thirds of his minimum sentence—about four years. In effect, each prison year may be only eight months long.

But it may be much longer. Good time and earned credits shorten an inmate's minimum sentence. As a higher-level felon, Doe received an indefinite term. Although he could be released early, as noted, he also could be kept until his 25-year maximum expires. Ultimately, the Parole Board decides how long Doe will spend in prison. If Doe's case is typical, he is likely to leave prison after four, five or six years of his six to 25 sentence. He will be supervised for a year or so once released. If caught violating conditions of release, Doe could be returned to prison.

In addition to his six to 25 year sentence, Doe could receive another three years for toting a gun. This is called "actual incarceration," not because Doe is actually incarcerated (his cellmate is actually incarcerated, too), but because Doe would actually serve the three years. The additional term could not be reduced by good time or earned credits. The Parole Board would continue to decide the time Doe would serve on the underlying six to 25 term.

Let's say Doe instead broke into a garage, unarmed. As a lower-level nonviolent felon, he could receive a definite sentence. The minimum and maximum would be the same. A flat 12-month term, reduced by good time and earned credits, would mean release after eight months, with no parole supervision.

Alternately, Doe could be sent to prison and released on shock probation by the judge after serving 30 to 90 days. Or he could be released on shock parole by the Parole Board after serving six months. Or he could receive a furlough from the board during the last months of his term. Or, in rare cases, he could have his term commuted to time served, or be pardoned, by the Governor.

Murderers, rapists, and offenders with guns are ineligible for probation. Almost everyone else is eligible. The judge could impose the 12-month prison term on Doe, then suspend it and place Doe in a community-based correctional facility or county jail for up to six months. Or the judge could suspend Doe's prison term and require him to participate in a nonresidential program with other restrictions on his liberty. In short, when it comes to prison sentences in Ohio, time certainly does not stand still. ✎

David Diroll, Executive Director
Ohio Criminal Sentencing Commission
The State of Crime and Criminal Justice
in Ohio

Cost of Prison
(based on average stay)

Prison
($54.39 x 7 months)
$11,421.90

Halfway House
($53.95 x 84 days)
$4,531.80

Community-based
Correctional Facilities
($79.00 x 125 days)
$9,875.00

Intensive Probation
($4.34 x 9-12 months)
$1,171,80—$1,562.40

Jail
($60.47 x 19.7 days)
$1,191.26

Day Reporting
($21.00 x 45 days)
$945.00

Electronic Monitoring
($5.43 x 60 days)
$325.80

The Ultimate Penalty

Death Row

Death Row is made up of 181 cells in Mansfield Correctional Institution. The cells are 91.58 square feet (10 feet, 10 inches by 7 feet with a 2 foot 3 inch shower). It includes a cot, desk, toilet, washbasin and 8-inch wide window. Inmates are allowed out of their cells up to three hours each day. They are fed through a slot in the door and may associate only with other Death Row inmates.

Last Hours

Executions still take place at the Southern Ohio Correctional Facility at Lucasville. The prisoner is taken from Death Row to the death house in Lucasville approximately 24 hours before execution. In the holding cell he may meet family, friends, and members of the clergy. He is given a last meal. At the proper time, the prisoner is taken to the execution chamber and placed on the lethal injection bed. He is strapped to the bed and intravenous injection tubes are hooked up. There is a telephone in the hallway between the death chamber and the executioner's room where a clemency call from the governor can arrive. The warden signals members of the execution team who begin the lethal injection. Twelve people may witness the execution: family, friends, members of the press and the clergy.

The History

The first recorded execution in Ohio was the 1812 hanging of John O'Mic, an American Indian convicted of murdering two trappers. Most of the village of Cleveland witnessed it. During much of the 19th century, hanging was the method of public choice, in the counties where the offense occurred. In 1885, the gallows at the Ohio Penitentiary consolidated county executions, and between that year and 1897, 28 people were hung.

In 1896, the General Assembly substituted electrocution for hanging, and the heavy wooden chair known as Old Thunderbolt was built; an engine and alternator cost $1,415. It was the final resting place for 315 inmates, including three women and several juveniles, between the years of 1897 and 1963. When the Ohio Penitentiary closed, the chair was moved in 1973 to the Southern Ohio Correctional Facility at Lucasville.

First

Willie Haas, 17, the "child murderer of Hamilton County," was convicted of killing the wife of a man who had befriended him. Haas was an orphan, executed in 1897, the year the state changed to electrocution. He was 16 at the time of the crime, to which he confessed, saying he choked and raped the woman, slit her throat and set her on fire. His execution was attended by a large crowd, said the *Columbus Dispatch*, many of them "pushing and shoving for a better view."

Last

Donald Reibolt, 29, was executed April 21, 1963, for the murder of a Columbus grocer.

In 1972, following the United States Supreme Court's

Willie Haas

declaration that the death penalty is unconstitutional, 65 Ohio inmates on death row had their sentences reduced to life in prison. The state's General Assembly revised the death penalty law in 1974 but this time a 1978 Ohio Supreme Court decision rejected the new law. The result, 120 condemned prisoners (including four women), had their sentences commuted to life in prison.

A new law setting the criteria for the imposition of the death penalty took effect in October, 1981. Leonard Jenkins of Cuyahoga County was the first to be sentenced to death under the law but his sentence along with three other men and four women was commuted to life imprisonment by Governor Richard Celeste during his last days in office.

Since 1993, prisoners under sentence of death are allowed to choose between electrocution or lethal injection. The prisoner had to decide the method a week before the scheduled execution. If the prisoner failed to choose the method would be electrocution.

On February 19, 1999, Wilford Berry became the first Ohio inmate since 1963 to be executed. After waving all appeals he selected lethal injection as his method of execution. Since November, 2001, condemned prisoners no longer have a choice as to the form of execution. All prisoners in Ohio are executed by lethal injection.

As of June, 2003, Ohio had executed 351 convicted murderers.

The electric chair has been donated to the Ohio Historical Society and a replica donated to the Mansfield Preservation Society.

Source: Ohio Public Defenders office, the Plain Dealer, the Columbus Dispatch

AND COULD I GET THAT TO GO?

Last meal, convicted murderer Alton Coleman, 2002:

well-done filet mignon, smothered with onions
fried chicken breasts
salad with French dressing
sweet potato pie with whipped cream
french fries
collard greens
onion rings
cornbread
broccoli with melted cheese
biscuits and gravy
cherry Coke
butter pecan ice cream

Last meal, convicted murderer Robert Buell, 2002:

one black olive

full man *walking*

Ohio's Death Penalty Criteria

In order for the death penalty to be imposed in Ohio the prosecution must prove aggravated murder which means that the defendant killed with prior calculation and design under at least one of the following circumstances:

(1) The assassination of the U.S. president or Ohio governor, and certain other top office holders and political candidates.

(2) Murder for hire.

(3) Murder for the purpose of escaping detection for another offense.

(4) A killing done by a jail or prison inmate.

(5) The defendant had a prior homicide conviction, or killed or tried to kill two or more people.

(6) The murder of a police officer.

(7) The murder committed during the commission of kidnapping, rape, aggravated arson, aggravated robbery or aggravated burglary.

(8) A murder committed to prevent testimony or retaliate for testimony in a criminal trial.

Hey. I'll get over it.

—Convicted crossbow killer Timothy Dunlap, after a jury recommended the death penalty, 1993

Defendants on Death Row

Males	206
Females	1
Total	*207*

Race of Defendants

African-American	104
Caucasian	95
Latino	2
Native American	2
Other	4

Race of Defendant/Victim

Caucasian/Caucasian	88
African-American/African-American	47
African-American/Caucasian	48
African-American/Other	5

Caucasian/African-American & Caucasian	3
Latino/Caucasian	2
African-American/ African-American & Caucasian	3
African-American/African-American & Caucasian & Other	1
Caucasian /African-American	3
Caucasian/Latino	1
Native American/Caucasian	1
Native American/Caucasian	1
Native American /Latino	1
Other/Caucasian	1
Other/Other	3

Source: Ohio Public Defender Commission

In June of 2001, Jay D. Scott, a career criminal and diagnosed schizophrenic, became the first Ohioan put to death against his will since 1963. Scott was convicted of gunning down a 75-year-old Cleveland deli owner in 1983. He died in the presence of his three brothers, from the effect of drugs costing $88.42. When a reporter asked afterward if the brothers wished to say anything, one of them replied, "I really think the Lakers are going to win tomorrow night."

Ohio Court Cases

Court	2001	2000	1999	1998	1997
Statewide	3,352,364	3,234,781	3,225,665	2,247,183	3,127,675
Supreme Court	2,284	2,355	2,327	2,728	2,730
Court of Appeals	10,480	10,394	10,762	11,713	12,488
Court of Claims	1,159	2,225	1,420	1,094	1,256
Courts of Common Pleas					
General Division	185,948	167,885	161,088	149,088	165,452
Domestic Relations Division	79,830	78,230	75,489	77,318	78,650
Probate Division	99,455	99,206	99,898	100,494	99,302
Juvenile Division	281,125	261,655	284,570	300,921	306,539
Municipal Courts	2,407,314	2,308,949	2,308,323	2,329,763	2,218,041
County Courts	284,769	383,882	281,788	274,064	243,217

The Ohio Department of Youth Services

The Department of Youth Services is the juvenile system of rehabilitation and correction for the State of Ohio. The Department of Youth Services confines juvenile felony offenders to help assure the public safety of the citizens of Ohio and maintains a system of institutions and aftercare (parole) programs that meet the physical, emotional, and educational needs of the youth during their commitment.

When a male or female between the ages of 12 and 18 is accused of breaking the law, the juvenile court judge has to decide if a crime has been committed. If the judge finds that a crime has been committed and, if the crime is a felony, the judge may commit the youth to the Department of Youth Services. The judge imposes a minimum stay, as prescribed by law. For minor felonies that stay is a minimum of six months. For serious crimes, a youth must stay a minimum of one year. In all commitments a youth may be held by the department until his/her 21st birthday.

Juvenile Crime

Property	31%
Violent	27%
Public Order	22%
Other Person	8%
Drug	8%
Status	4%

Juvenile Arrest Rate*

Violent Crime	218
Property Crime	1,488
Drug Abuse	422
Weapons	85

Juvenile Court Cases

Delinquency	
Petition	11,573
Rate	84.89
Nonpetition	329
Rate	2.27
Status	
Petition	25,632
Nonpetition	1,702
Dependency	
Petition	22,611

Juvenile Custody Rate

Number	*4,531*
Rate*	345
Male	564
White	340
Black	1,936
Hispanic	686
American Indian/Alaskan Native	466
Asian/Pacific Islander	166
Female	87
White	62
Black	238
Hispanic	99
American Indian/Alaskan Native	239
Asian/Pacific Islander	0

per 100,000

In Ohio, a "child" is defined as any person under 18 years of age—except that the juvenile court has jurisdiction over anyone under 18 who has been declared "an unruly child." That jurisdiction continues until age 21. Thus, an unruly child may be legally a child until he/she is 21.

—Ohio
Revised Code

Getting AND spending: a glossary of Buckeye boodle

1841—**Anna Harrison**, the widow of William Henry Harrison, becomes the first widowed presidential wife to receive a pension.

1862—**Salmon Chase**, the Ohioan who was Lincoln's Secretary of Treasury, issues first federal paper money, chooses green as its color because green couldn't be reproduced by cameras of the day, and put his face on the $10,000 bill, which is largest bill ever circulated. The following year he oversees National Bank Act, which moves country's monetary system under federal control.

Sandusky's **Jay Cooke**, one of the most powerful figures of the mid-century, invents modern investment banking by successfully marketing war bonds to the general public. Because of his wartime success, investments become a middle class pursuit and investment banking emerges as a specialized occupation following the war.

1870—**Victoria Claflin Woodhall** of Homer, Ohio, and her sister **Tennessee** become America's first women stockbrokers at a time when, "men stared at every woman on the pavement except the apple sellers."
They earned as much as $500,000 the first year before turning to suffragist politics where the risks were higher and the pay not nearly so lucrative.

1882—John D. Rockefeller and associates create **Standard Oil Trust**, the first such business trust in U.S. history. Move permits Rockefeller to legally thwart state laws restricting a corporation to activities in its home state. Trust controls 80 percent of refineries and 90 percent of oil pipelines in America. Company eventually evolves into Exxon.

1884—**John Henry Patterson** pays $6,500 for controlling interest in an obscure factory in a slum area of Dayton, Ohio, which manufactured an instrument for which there was no demand and no market. After trying unsuccessfully to back out of the deal, Patterson goes to work inventing an audience for the cash register, creating both modern salesmanship and his fortune.

1888—Under the Presidential administration of Ohioan **Benjamin Harrison**, the federal budget goes over $1 billion for the first time. When critics attack "the billion-dollar Congress", the Speaker of the House says, "This is a billion-dollar country."

1898-1914—**Oliver Hazard Payne**, son of a prominent Cleveland merchant and one of Rockefeller's major competitors, sails his yacht, *Aphrodite*, to Europe every summer for 16 years. When built, *Aphrodite* is largest, fastest, most luxuriously-appointed steam yacht in America.

1903—**Wright Brothers** launch aviation industry, and between that first flight and 1992 the country's airline companies make no money. "I'd like to think that if I'd been at Kitty Hawk in 1903 when Orville Wright took off," says Warren Buffett, "I would have been farsighted enough, and public-spirited enough—I owed this to future capitalists—to shoot him down."

1904—Wright Brothers offer U.S. government world monopoly on flight, including patents, for $10,000. Government says no.

1909—**William Howard Taft** receives what will be recognized as highest real pay of any President: his $100,000 would be worth $1,973,948 in 2003 dollars.

1928—Rockefeller Center construction begins in midtown Manhattan, supported by **John D. Rockefeller, Jr.**, the Clevelander who leases land on his personal liability as the Great Depression begins. He also pays for reconstruction of the Cloisters Museum, helps start the Palisades Park, donates land for the United Nations headquarters, and almost single-handedly creates Colonial Williamsburg. His philanthropic total is estimated at $537 million, only slightly less than his father's $540 million.

1933—"Don't ask for names, but one prominent woman in town helps unfortunates by collecting the cigarette butts her guests leave behind them. She then gives them to her husband with firm instructions to drop them on the sidewalk in front of his place of business for the penniless panhandlers to salvage."
—*Cleveland News,* 1933

1945—Treasury stops printing $10,000 bill; **Salmon Chase** drops from public view for first time in over a century.

1979—**Pete Rose**, after leaving Cincinnati and signing with Phillies: "I got so much money that if you stacked up all the cash, a show horse couldn't jump over it."

1985—Governor Celeste orders Ohio Deposit Guarantee Fund-insured banks closed after Cincinnati's **Home State Savings Bank** takes $275 million hit, hemorrhaging the insurer. Taxpayers bail out Home State with $129 million; Financier Marvin Warner does 28 months, retires to Florida.

1987-2000—**Ted Turner**, the CNN mogul from Cincinnati, buys 1.7 million acres in five Western states, including over a million acres in New Mexico—1.5 percent of the nation's fifth-largest state. He is said to be the largest private landowner in the United States. In 1997, Turner makes $1 billion pledge to the United Nations, the largest single pledge in philanthropic history. "I'm putting every rich person in the world on notice," he says.

1992—After **Bill Cruxton**, an 80-year-old customer at Dink's Colonial Restaurant in Chagrin Falls, has fatal heart attack, he leaves estate worth nearly $500,000 to his favorite waitress, **Cara Wood**.

1994—Ohioans are spending more than $1 million each week for rental space used by the state government, predominately in Franklin County.

There are 85,000 millionaires in Ohio; each has an average wealth of $2,661,811.76

1998—**Al Lerner** buys Browns expansion franchise for $530 million, most ever paid for a sports franchise at the time. Lerner, a one-time furniture salesman and ex-Marine, built MBNA Corp. into one of the largest credit-card empires in America, yet was defined by his generosity, giving millions to health and education, including a stunning $100 million gift to the Cleveland Clinic in what was called one of largest gifts in history of American philanthropy. Net worth at his death in 2002: at least $4.3 billion.

1999—Widow of *Superman* co-creator **Jerry Siegel** reclaims half of original copyright that Siegel and **Joe Shuster**, as Glenville teenagers, signed away in 1938 for $130. Estimated value of *Superman* over next decade: several billion dollars.

circa 2000—Guests to **John D. Rockefeller's** gravesite at Cleveland's Lake View Cemetery leave coins on his headstone.

2000—**Ki-Jana Carter**, the Columbus, Ohio, running back out of Penn State, was cut by the Bengals after five seasons, three of them ending with injuries in August or September. He signed for a rookie-record $7.125 million signing bonus (an overall seven-year, $19.2 million package), which nearly equaled the $7.2 million franchise cost in 1968. He played in 35 games, and gained only 747 career yards—$20,890.22 a yard.

Ohioan **Mary Ellen Withrow**, treasurer of the United States during the Clinton presidency, said at the Democratic Convention in Los Angeles that her autograph was the most valuable one on the block. "Mine," she said, "is the one on your money."

2001—Community Foundation Survey counts 68 such foundations in Ohio, making it the state with second-most number of such groups. Ohio foundation assets are above $3 billion.

Doctors at Wright-Patterson Air Force Base Medical Center in Dayton test local $1 bills for germs; they report nearly all have bacteria that can pose significant health risk to people with certain conditions. New meaning given to term *filthy lucre*.

2002—**Hunting Valley**, exclusive Cleveland enclave that has median income of $200,000, repeals its 0.75 percent income tax. "Under current conditions and projected conditions," says its finance director, "we do not need this cash." Which are words never before spoken in the English language.

After eights months of practice using 30,000 screws, **Jonathan Smith**, a 27-year-old carpenter from Delaware, Ohio, enters national hardware contest for fastest screwers in America, power-drills five screws into a pine board—1.2 seconds per screw—and wins $1 million. "You walk up and there is a big box of screws," said the winner, "touch each one to the drill bit, and screw it in. A hiccup would have cost me the contest."

2003—Basic services of full-time Ohio Mom, including "meals, cleanup and organization of the kitchen, procurement of equipment, supplies and food" are estimated by Columbus firm, the Professional Domestic Institute, at $24,000-$60,000 annually.

Akron prep basketball phenom LeBron James leaped from high school to the Cleveland Cavaliers (pocket change of $16-18 million over four years), then picked up his loooong green from a Nike shoe contract said to be worth upwards of $100 million—more than the *combined* shoe contracts of Michael Jordan, Shaquille O'Neal, Kobe Bryant, Allen Iverson, and Tracy McGrady. Feet, don't fail me now.

ROCKEFELLER: A BOOKKEEPER'S LEGACY

From humble Cleveland beginnings as an assistant book-keeper, **John D. Rockefeller** was in the 1920s and 1930s the richest man in the world. Establishing Standard Oil in 1870, Rockefeller became its largest stockholder. His business genius was to bring order to the boom-or-bust chaos that was oil's price cycle. He let others take the grave risks in finding oil while he sought to control the refining end. He was so dominant in the industry that Sohio, Exxon, Arco, Chevron, Mobil, Amoco, and Conaco were once just pieces of the company he built—Standard Oil.

A ruthless competitor, he was also a great philanthropist. He was notorious for unfair business practices but by 1892 his charitable donations were $1.35 million. His donations almost single-handedly eliminated hookworm in the U.S.—a formidable health problem in the early part of the century—as well as helping several hundred Jewish scientists escape the Nazis and come to America, which switched the center of scientific activity from Europe to America, and his funding pushed the development of penicillin into a wonder drug.

He was described as having the soul of a book-keeper, orderly and punctual, but he was also capable of eccentricity. He once demolished an entire college because it spoiled his view. Although Rockefeller never quite became a billionaire, he came close. His reported worth in 1892: $815,647,796.89, and it is estimated he gave half of it to charity. Historian Allan Nevins wrote that Rockefeller was likely "the most impressive single figure in the transformation of the American economy [between] 1865-1900," and his name even today is synonymous with great wealth.

Rockefeller was the richest American ever—worth $209.3 billion in present-day dollars, based on his 1913 worth. His wealth at the time was said to equal approximately one-fourth of all the money in circulation.

"I cheat my boys every time I get a chance. I want to make them sharp. I trade with the boys and skin them and just beat them every time I can."

—John D. Rockefeller's father, Big Bill

John D. Rockefeller and son, John Jr., to whom the old man transferred money in sums of $65 million or so, to which would be attached a note signed "Affectionately, Father." It is estimated that John Jr.'s philanthropic donations totaled $537 million, which nearly equaled those of his father.

Akron in Brief

Date Founded	1825
Area	62.1 square miles

Form of Government
Mayor-Council

Population	217,074
Per Square Mile	345.6

Percentage Increase

1990-2000	-2.7%
Median Age	34.2
Foreign Born	3.2%
Ranking among major U.S. cities	81
Segregation index*	61.0

Manufacturing

Establishments	370
Employees	12,822

Wholesale Trade

Establishments	334
Employees	4,956

Retail Trade

Establishments	908
Employees	11,912

Accommodation & Foodservice

Establishments	489
Employees	7,364

Education
High School

Graduates	80.0%

Bachelors Degree

or Higher	18.0%

Per Capita

Income	$17,596
City Taxes	$688

City Government

Expenditures	$1,223
Crimes	15,829
Violent	2,125
Property	13,704

Homes

Median Value	$76,500
Median Year Built	1950

Average Temperature

January	24.8
July	71.9
Elevation	1050 feet

Cincinnati in Brief

Date Founded	1788
Area	78.0 square miles

Form of Government
Mayor-Council

Population	331,285
Per Square Mile	4,427.2

Percentage Increase

1990-2000	-9.1%
Median Age	32.1
Foreign Born	3.8%
Ranking among major U.S. cities	54
Segregation index*	63.0

Manufacturing

Establishments	604
Employees	28,917

Wholesale Trade

Establishments	705
Trade	15,388

Retail Trade

Establishments	1,334
Employees	18,093

Accommodation & Foodservice

Establishments	829
Employees	16,006

Education
High School

Graduates	76.7%

Bachelors Degree

or Higher	26.6%

Per Capita

Income	$19,962
City Taxes	$841

City Government

Expenditures	$1,905
Crimes	21,469
Violent	2,475
Property	18,994

Homes

Median Value	$93,000
Median Year Built	1948

Average Temperature

January	29.8
July	76.4
Elevation	869 feet

Cleveland in Brief

Date Founded	1796
Area	77.6 square miles

Form of Government
Mayor-Council

Population	478,403
Per Square Mile	6,165.0

Percentage Increase

1990-2000	-5.4%
Median Age	30.6
Foreign Born	4.5%
Ranking among major U.S. cities	33
Segregation index*	78.3

Manufacturing

Establishments	1,270
Employees	44,400

Wholesale Trade

Establishments	921
Trade	16,936

Retail Trade

Establishments	1,607
Employees	15,454

Accommodation & Foodservice

Establishments	1,099
Employees	17,757

Education
High School

Graduates	69.0%

Bachelors Degree

or Higher	11.4%

Per Capita

Income	$14,921
City Taxes	$676

City Government

Expenditures	$1,285
Crimes	33,573
Violent	6,049
Property	27,524

Homes

Median Value	$72,100
Median Year Built	1940

Average Temperature

January	24.8
July	71.9
Elevation	777 feet

Columbus in Brief

Date Founded 1812
Area .... 210.3 square miles
Form of Government
Mayor-Council
Population 711,470
  Per Square Mile 3,383.1.0
  Percentage Increase
  1990-2000 .... 11.8%
  Median Age 30.6
  Foreign Born 6.7%
  Ranking among
  major U.S. cities 15
Segregation index* 61.0
Manufacturing
  Establishments 685
  Employees 32,243
Wholesale Trade
  Establishments 1,092
  Trade 24,483
Retail Trade
  Establishments 2,717
  Employees 51,028
Accommodation & Foodservice
  Establishments 1,508
  Employees 32,807
Education
  High School
  Graduates 83.8%
  Bachelors Degree
  or Higher 29.0%
Per Capita
  Income $20,450
  City Taxes $574
  City Government
  Expenditures $1,132
  Crimes 61,292
  Violent 5,755
  Property 55,537
Homes
  Median Value $101,400
  Median Year Built 1970
Average Daily Temperature
  January 26.4
  July 73.2
Elevation .... 833 feet

Dayton in Brief

Date Founded 1796
Area .... 55.8 square miles
Form of Government
Mayor-Council
Population 166,179
  Per Square Mile 2,978.1
  Percentage Increase
  1990-2000 .... -8.9%
  Median Age 32.4
  Foreign Born 2.0%
  Ranking among
  major U.S. cities 123
Segregation index* 78.3
Manufacturing
  Establishments 350
  Employees 20,112
Wholesale Trade
  Establishments 287
  Trade 5,256
Retail Trade
  Establishments 529
  Employees 6,801
Accommodation & Foodservice
  Establishments 327
  Employees 5,098
Education
  High School
  Graduates 75.1%
  Bachelors Degree
  or Higher 14.4%
Per Capita
  Income $15,547
  City Taxes $701
  City Government
  Expenditures $1,566
  Crimes 15,997
  Violent 1,789
  Property 14,208
Homes
  Median Value $67,300
  Median Year Built 1949
Average Temperature
  January 26.0
  July 74.2
Elevation .... 743 feet

Toledo in Brief

Date Founded 1837
Area .... 80.6 square miles
Form of Government
Mayor-Council
Population 313,619
  Per Square Mile 3,891.1
  Percentage Increase
  1990-2000 .... -5.8
  Median Age 33.2
  Foreign Born 3.0%
  Ranking among
  major U.S. cities 56
Segregation index* 67.0
Manufacturing
  Establishments 462
  Employees 25,466
Wholesale Trade
  Establishments 487
  Trade 7,731
Retail Trade
  Establishments 1,281
  Employees 18,732
Accommodation & Foodservice
  Establishments 737
  Employees 13,187
Education
  High School
  Graduates 79.7%
  Bachelors Degree
  or Higher 16.8%
Per Capita
  Income $17,388
  City Taxes $520
  City Government
  Expenditures $960
  Crimes 23,228
  Violent 2,158
  Property 21,070
Homes
  Median Value $73,300
  Median Year Built 1952
Average Temperature
  January 22.5
  July 72.1
Elevation .... 585 feet

From top, left:
Goodyear Airdock;
Mt. Adams;
Huntington Bank
lobby; Ohio Stadium;
Dayton Arcade; and
the National City
Bank Building

*The segregation dissimilarity index is based on 100 meaning complete segregation

AMERICA'S RUBBER CAPITAL MOVES ON

It was an unprecedented boom, for by 1905, Akron, Ohio, produced more automobile tires than any other place in the country and was fast becoming the world's Rubber Capital. A decade before, there was only one rubber factory in Akron, and it was not very large. That lonely plant, however, was brought to Akron by Dr. B.F. Goodrich, who relocated from New York in 1870, wisely leaving his competitors back east, even if only momentarily.

In 1910, the city consisted of 69,067 people but in another decade the burgeoning rubber industry had bounced it to 208,435. Akron couldn't build itself fast enough. In that decade, it grew 200 percent; for a time, it was said to be the fastest-growing city in America. Lines formed for a burlesque house that ran three shifts and some of the rubber workers wore silk shirts to the factories. "Boy, that smell of Akron!" wrote Vicki Baum, "it's a funny smell, warm and sweetish and burned, and sticks to you like green rubber..." Even Akron's aroma was large.

After the war, the zeppelin industry arrived in Akron and to manufacture the biggest rigid dirigibles in the world, the Goodyear Zeppelin Company built an airdock so big that sometimes moisture condensed inside it, causing rain. Covering over eight acres, it was the largest building in the world without internal supports. Frank Seiberling, who had converted an abandoned factory into the world's largest

tire company—Goodyear Tire and Rubber—escaped the prosperous smell of his own factory by heading west, out of the city, to build Stan Hywet, his English Tudor mansion that even today is probably the most splendid house in Ohio.

In World War II, Akron played a pivotal role in what some called one of the two most important breakthroughs of the war—synthetic rubber. (The other, said historian George Knepper, was atomic power.) Akron had the country's first plant to make these synthetics. But tire-making was leaving Akron soon after the war, headed to rural areas or overseas. The old tire plants weren't able to accommodate efficient, modern production lines.

Goodyear is still the biggest employer in Akron—nearly 6,000 people—but some recalled that before the war 15,000 workers struck Goodyear's Plant No. 2 and threw up a picket line 11 miles long. In 1993, Goodyear planted 85 acres of wildflowers—they were mostly blue and gold—on the previous site of two factories. Goodyear said it was the largest wildflower garden in America.

No single industry will likely dominate Akron the way rubber once did and most believe that's a good thing. Today, Akron is known for polymers, with over 35,000 people in the area employed in some 400 polymer-related companies. These statistics allow Akron to maintain its work-related superlatives: the place that gave the world polyvinyl chloride—the ingredient that makes up everything plastic, from toys to water pipes—is now one of the major polymer research and development centers in America.

Located in the heart of Northeast Ohio, Akron has been known for numerous things over the course of its history: Canal Town, Rubber Capital of the World, global center for research in polymers and liquid crystals, not to mention being the home of oatmeal, artificial fishing lures, the All-American Soap Box Derby, and the new National Inventors Hall of Fame. But one reputation that Akron has consistently retained through the years is that of "magnet to entrepreneurs with good ideas."

Ironically, the area was once considered the "end of the world" for America's first settlers. What is now one of Akron's finer neighborhoods was once the western boundary between the United States and the Indian nations of the Wyandot, Ottawa, Chippewa, and Delaware tribes. The 1785 treaty that set those boundaries stated that the Indians had all rights to land west of today's Portage Path Drive. Portage Path was the name of the route used by the Indians to "portage" their canoes between the Cuyahoga and Tuscarawas rivers. This may have been Akron's first "expressway," and it later gave way to major canal routes, wagon lines, and finally the intersection of two national highways.

When a Connecticut general named Simon Perkins surveyed the Akron area in 1807, he apparently liked what he saw, for he purchased a thousand acres of the land at a little over $4.00 per acre. In 1825, Perkins founded the village of Akron, derived from the Greek word "akro" meaning "high place." As Akron's first significant entrepreneur, Perkins encouraged development in his village, and one of his first interests was to link Lake Erie with the Ohio River, by way of a canal through Akron. Two years of digging, scraping and building 24 hours a day, seven days a week by more than 5,000 workers created the Ohio and Erie Canal that connected Akron with Cleveland and gave Akron a new image as a canal town.

The growing transportation system, from canoe to canal boat to railroad, brought men and women to Akron with new ideas and new dreams.

From General Perkins to abolitionist John Brown, from John F. Seiberling, who founded the Goodyear Tire and Rubber Company, to Benjamin Franklin Goodrich relocating his rubber factory to Akron, the city drew ambitious, creative people to the rolling hills and green valleys along the Cuyahoga and Tuscarawas rivers.

By 1895, Akron was where America bought its tires—for the enormously popular bicycle as well as for the first automobiles. It was also where America bought its breakfast cereal, for Ferdinand Schumacher's small enterprise eventually became the Quaker Oats Company. Akron was also one of the birthplaces of "lighter than air" travel. Dozens of huge airships, or "blimps," were constructed at the Goodyear Airdock, the largest building in the world without interior supports. Constructed in 1929, the Airdock is so large it can house the Eiffel Tower or ten football fields.

A strategic geographical location also enhances Greater Akron's successes. Excellent access from Akron to the entire Interstate Highway System is provided by Interstates 71, 76, 77, 80, 90, 271, 480 and the Ohio Turnpike. Known as "the trucking capital of the world," greater Akron is served by more than 150 trucking firms with terminals in all parts of the country. Two major airports, half of the nations population within a 500 mile radius and more than 150 of Fortune 500's top companies in the region allow Greater Akron to remain a vital heartland city.

Two major universities add to the Akron area's world-class reputation for research and

Hospital spending per capita

Dayton—$434

Columbus—$432

Toledo—$395

Cleveland—$380

Cincinnati—$290

Akron—$131

—Cincinnati Enquirer

675

creativity. The University of Akron, a state-supported institution, offers a wide array of studies from engineering and chemistry to music and speech education. The university is a center of significant research activity with a worldwide reputation in polymer research. The University of Akron works with many plastics and rubber-related corporations nationally on the development of new industrial and consumer materials. Kent State University, located just to the north of Akron, is home to the Liquid Crystal Institute, where massive research and development is taking place and targeting new uses for liquid crystals in the auto, electronics, glass, and medical industries.

Institutional research and development has attracted a number of high-tech firms to the Akron area, sparking an educational and economic renaissance that has made Akron's traditional "blue collar" image a bit whiter. But, small manufacturing and machining firms still make up a fairly significant section of the economy. In fact, the work in polymers has created a need for skilled machinists and molders among plastics manufacturing firms.

The Akron area is also attractive to business and individuals

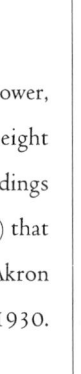

Central Tower, tallest of the eight Art Deco buildings (330 feet) that went up in Akron around 1930.

because of its high quality, but affordable standard of living. With a wide variety of new and existing neighborhoods, Akron has been listed as "one of the most affordable home buying markets in the country." Quality of life extends to the arts as well. Akron's E.J. Thomas Performing Arts Hall is home to the Ohio Ballet, the Akron Symphony Orchestra, and a host of Broadway shows and concerts. Just north of Akron in suburban Cuyahoga Falls is the Blossom Music Center, a huge open-air facility featuring a 16,000 seat amphitheater and a gentle hillside to stretch out a blanket for an evening of entertainment. Blossom is the summer home of the Cleveland Orchestra and the site of dozens of pop, rock, jazz, operatic, and country concerts. In addition, Akron attracts children from across the globe every August for the All-American Soap Box Derby at Derby Downs. The youngsters compete against each other in cars they have designed and built themselves.

The city of Akron is the new home of the National Inventors Hall of Fame. This unique facility features a museum with hands-on, educational displays and activities promoting the spirit of innovation and entrepreneurship in the United States. World-renowned architect and Akron native James Stewart Polcek designed this national center of excellence.

Source: William G. Jasso, Office of the Mayor

Distances from Akron to major markets:

Atlanta	658 miles
Boston	639
Chicago	348
Columbus	123
Detroit	178
Indianapolis	285
Nashville	500
New York	461
Philadelphia	393
Pittsburgh	101
St. Louis	519
Washington, D.C.	337
Toronto	318

OTHER SLOGANS FOR
Selling CINCINNATI !!!

NEW YORK.
NEW ORLEANS.
NEW CINCINNATI.*

*OFFICIAL NEW SLOGAN
(FOR REAL)

SINFUL FOOD.
SINCERE FOLKS.
SINCINNATI!

WHATEVER.

DELHI
Mili

Cincinnati
WE'RE IN HOG HEAVEN!

CINCINNATI:
OVER 75 DAYS OF
SUNSHINE
PER YEAR!

Cincinnati
JUST MINUTES AWAY FROM
NORTHERN KENTUCKY!

More people attended performing arts in Cincinnati in 2002 than Reds or Bengals games combined. While arts attendance is strongest among school children and adults aged 45-54, it is nearly as strong in the key demographic group of 25-34.

—Performing Arts Research Coalition

Longfellow dubbed Cincinnati the "Queen City of the West." Winston Churchill said it was "America's most beautiful inland city." Saturday Review called it one of America's "most livable cities." Cincinnati, which celebrated its Bicentennial in 1988, indeed has a proud heritage. The city began as a part of the Miami Purchase in 1788, when the town of Losantiville was founded by Mathias Denman, Robert Patterson, and Israel Ludlow. General Arthur St. Clair, commander of Ft. Washington, changed the name of Losantiville to Cincinnati in honor of the Society of Cincinnati, an organization of Revolutionary War officers founded by George Washington.

In 1802, Cincinnati was chartered as a village and in 1819, incorporated as a city. The city's greatest development came after the opening of the Miami and Erie Canal in the late 1820s. In the 1830s and 1840s, large numbers of Germans and Irish immigrated to Cincinnati, giving the city a rich European heritage. William Holmes McGuffey published his Eclectic Readers, which in 1836 Cincinnati became the educational touchstone of the nation. Cincinnati grew and developed into a major center for manufacturing, wholesaling, and retailing, as well as insurance, financial, and health services.

Its more successful manufacturing industries include transportation equipment, particularly aircraft engines and auto parts; food and kindred products; metal working and general industrial machinery; chemicals; fabricated metal products; and printing. Since no single company employs more than three percent of the population,

Cincinnati's diverse economy helps the city weather nationwide economic downturns better than many of its neighbors.

General Electric's Aircraft Engine Business Group is a major employer in the area. Cincinnati is also home to a number of well-known national and international companies, including Procter & Gamble, Kroger, Cincinnati Milacron, Federated Department Stores, Western-Southern Life Insurance, Scripps Howard, and American Financial Corp. Greater Cincinnati is, in fact, a growing center for international business.

Greater Cincinnati owes much of its business success to its location within 600 miles of much of the nation's population, purchasing power, and manufacturing establishments. Cincinnati International Airport, approximately 12 miles (15 minutes) from downtown Cincinnati, is one of five major U.S. hubs of Delta Air Lines, and 59 percent of the nation's population is within one hour of flight time from Greater Cincinnati. Three interstate highways (I-71, I-74 and I-75) pass through the city, and the port of Cincinnati is generally navigable the year round. More Ohio River barge traffic flows past Cincinnati each year than through the Panama Canal. Good rail facilities are also available.

Other assets in Cincinnati's "blue chip" portfolio include comparatively low energy rates, high worker productivity, a strong and relatively young labor force, and high quality of life. Cost-of-living runs very close to the national average, while Cincinnati housing costs have historically ranked below the national average. Among the region's colleges and universities, the University of Cincinnati is nationally known for its College of Medicine, School of Engineering, and Conservatory of Music. Other colleges in the area include Xavier University; Northern Kentucky University; Thomas More College; the College of Mount St. Joseph; Cincinnati Art Academy; The Union Institute; and Hebrew Union College, a graduate seminary for rabbinical studies. In addition, there are many specialized institutions for vocational and technical training, including Cincinnati State Technical & Community College.

Greater Cincinnati is a regional leader in health care. At the center of Cincinnati medical expertise is the University of Cincinnati Medical Center. Another widely known facility is the Children's Hospital Medical Center, one of the largest pediatric facilities in the U.S. and one of the top children's hospitals in the country. It was there that Dr. Albert Sabin developed the oral polio vaccine and Dr. Leon Goldman established the first laser laboratory.

Not surprisingly, this storied and diverse city is home to a wide array of cultural opportunities: the world-famous Cincinnati Symphony Orchestra, Cincinnati Opera, Cincinnati Ballet Company, Playhouse in the Park, and the annual May Festival, the oldest continuing choral music festival in the Western Hemisphere. Cincinnati is well-known for its festivals, including the famous Oktoberfest Zinzinnati, Summerfair, Riverfest, A Taste of Cincinnati, and Summer on the Square. Riverbend Music Center, on the Ohio River, is the summer home of the Cincinnati Symphony Orchestra and the site of many other concerts. Greater Cincinnati also has more than 100 museums and galleries. The newly constructed Contemporary Arts Center is gaining worldwide attention for its design. Others include the Art Museum in Eden Park, the Taft Museum, and Krohn Conservatory. The Aronoff Center for the Performing Arts is the home of a variety of cultural activities. The Museum Center at Union Terminal is located in the fabulous train station that was once the hub of transportation for the region. After extensive renovation, Union Terminal is the new home of the Museum of Natural History, the Children's Discovery Center, the Cincinnati Historical Society, and the Robert D. Lindner OMNIMAX Theatre.

Cincinnati's riverfront is undergoing a revalidation. The city's NFL team, the Cincinnati Bengals, recently moved into Paul Brown Stadium and the Cincinnati Reds opened Great American Ball Park in 2003. Between the two will be shopping, entertainment, parks and the National Freedom Center.

The city is also distinguished as the home of the Cincinnati Reds, the world's first professional baseball team. The Reds' record boasts seven National League West titles, nine National League pennants, and five World Series championships. The Cincinnati Bengals compete in the Central Division of the National Football League's

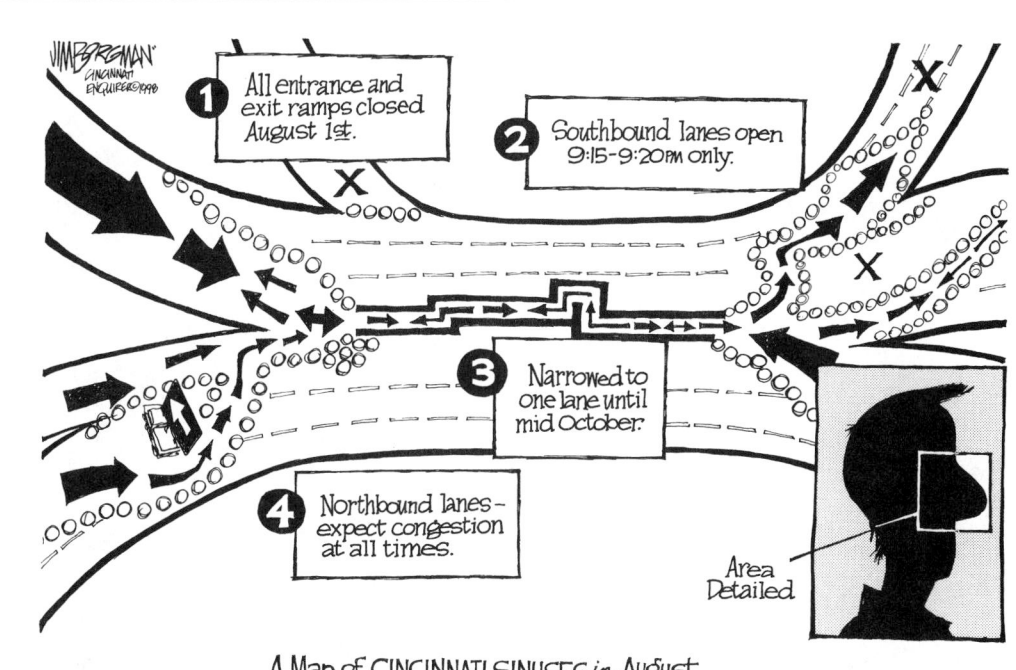

A Map of CINCINNATI SINUSES *in* August

American Football Conference and have twice represented the AFC in the Super Bowl. Horse racing is available at Turfway Park, River Downs, and Lebanon Raceway, while just over an hour's drive away are beautiful Keeneland and Churchill Downs in Kentucky.

Numerous city parks and recreation areas afford more than 7,000 acres of green space in Cincinnati, and the Cincinnati Zoo, one of the top ten zoos in the U.S., is famous for its great success in breeding many species of animals. A Greater Cincinnati attraction for millions is Paramount's Kings Island Amusement Park, set in 1,600 acres of woodlands, along with Timberwolf Amphitheater, numerous campgrounds, and The Golf Center at Kings Island, site of the Association of Tennis Professionals Tournament. Other area theme parks include Americana, Coney Island, The Beach, and Surf Cincinnati.

Greater Cincinnati is filled with unexpected dining treasures from the elegant Masionette to the hip Jeff Ruby's Steak House. The Masionette, the nation's longest running Mobil 5-star restaurant (38 consecutive years) is joined by many other fine dining establishments. At the lower end of the palate Cincinnati boasts of its famous chili parlors serving distinctive Cincinnati style chili (served over spaghetti and topped with beans, onions and cheese). Other Cincinnati favorites are Graeter's and Aglamesis Brothers ice cream parlors. Both family-owned, they've served Cincinnatians for generations.

Airtime from Cincinnati to:

Atlanta	65 minutes
Boston	105
Chicago	60
Cleveland	50
Denver	180
Houston	160
Los Angeles	296
Minneapolis	94
New York	90
Washington, D.C.	70

Source: Greater Cincinnati Chamber of Commerce

a tale of two Cities

Cincinnati

More car crashes per registered vehicle than any other city in Ohio—1 per every 14.2
(Or, 48 accidents a day, one every 30 minutes)

Cincinnati—Blue Ash, 10% of its 12,755 residents are foreign-born (national rank, number 14) Statewide: 3%

Cincinnati—safest of 49 major urban areas for pedestrians—0.7 pedestrian deaths per 100,000)

Percentage of Cincinnatians who smoke, ranked nationally—21.5%, 59th

Most segregated metropolitan areas in nation: Cincinnati, number 6

Most densely populated cities in Ohio: Cincinnati's Norwood, 4th, at 6,992 people per square mile (Cincinnati, 19th, at 4,247 people)

Highest per Capita Income in Ohio —Montgomery, $45,460

Number one blue–collar city in Ohio: 111,451 factory workers

Gen X young adults lost during last decade —5.8% (10th in nation)

Grandparents raising their grandchildren —5,073

Rank among nation's top 50 fall allergy cities —17

Cleveland

Cleveland car crashes—1 per every 15.6

Cleveland—Mayfield Heights has highest percentage of foreign-born residents in Ohio—18% of the city's 19,386 residents.

East Cleveland—largest percentage of Ohio residents who use public transportation, 18%

Percentage of Clevelanders who smoke —29.8%, 4th highest in country

Most segregated metropolitan areas in nation: Cleveland, number 3

Most densely populated cities in Ohio: Cleveland's Lakewood. 1st, at 10,299 per square mile (Cleveland, 6th at 6,165 people)

Lowest per Capita Income in Ohio —East Cleveland, $12,600

Number two blue–collar city in Ohio: 101,451 factory workers

Gen X young adults gained last decade —2.2% (19th in nation)

Grandparents raising their grandchildren —7,355

Rank among nation's top 50 fall allergy cities —33

www. *derfmagazine*.com

This e-zine is dedicated to the removal of self-importance in Cincinnati's self-portrait. It's a satirical site that reports on nonexistent occurences that seem to have actually happened—the Bengals scout with seeing-eye dog, the man from Norwood who set a new world record for standing in front of vending machines, and the man who avoided losing his place in line at the Cincinnati airport by removing his own appendix. For neither the inherently sober nor the Visitors Bureau.

Cincinnati

Percentage with high school degree—81.8%

Percentage with college degree—19%

High school dropout rate—11.2%

Language spoken other than English
—14,184

Of German ancestry—66,668

Walking to work—7,023

Median household income—$30,851

Literacy ranking, nationally—10th

Percentage of individuals in poverty—19.8%

Houses with nine rooms—8,406

People living alone—47%

Lacking plumbing facilities—0

Value of owner-occupied homes—$99,671

Bag of groceries—$100

Most generous cities:
Cincinnati—20th most generous region
in country, 7.2% of discretionary income
to charity

Average Homeowners Insurance Premiums
—$412

Most wired moms:
Cincinnati moms average 18 hours, 35 minutes
online each week, making Cincinnati 10th
most-wired city in the country.

Cleveland

Percentage with high school degree—72.4%

Percentage with college degree—5%

High school dropout rate—24.8%

Language spoken other than English
—47,252

Of German ancestry—44,788

Walking to work—7,620

Median household income—$26,543

Literacy ranking, nationally—20th

Percentage of individuals in poverty—25.9%

Houses with nine rooms—15,061

People living alone—38%

Lacking plumbing facilities—871

Value of owner-occupied homes—$75,134

Bag of groceries—$116.60

Most generous cities:
Cleveland community foundations—$1.5
billion in assets, gave away $62 million

Average Homeowners Insurance Premiums
—$463

Highest ratio of people to taverns and bars of
50 major cities (13th fattest city in America,
ranking from 47th to last among states in
percentage of adults who exercise regularly).

*Since 1996, the
seven-county
Northeast Ohio
region has lost nearly
$3.4 billion in
household incomes
to other places.
In seven years
through 2002,
Cuyahoga County
lost more than
52,000 people
and $1.5 billion
in income to its six
neighboring counties.
Planners say the
affluent elderly head
for Florida, while
educated professionals
go to Charlotte,
Atlanta, and Ohio's
white-collar
capital—Columbus.*

—The Plain Dealer

*Sources: Ohio Insurance Institute, AOL Digital City, Centers for Disease Control and Prevention,
Plain Dealer, Ohio Manufacturers' Directory, Surface Transportation Policy Project, Digital Marketing
Services Inc., Asthma and Allergy Foundation of America; Men's Fitness magazine, Chronicle
of Philantrophy, U.S. Census, University of Wisconsin-Whitewater*

In 1796, at the propitious place where the Cuyahoga River empties into Lake Erie, Moses Cleaveland started the city that bears his name (minus, of course, the first "a," which, it is said, was dropped some years later by a newspaperman short on masthead space). General Cleaveland and his 50-man crew surveyed the Western Reserve for the Connecticut Land Company and platted the settlement on the pattern of a New England town square, but they were soon driven away by insects and disease. In a few years, Lorenzo Carter and other Connecticut militiamen returned to the area and used land grants to settle both sides of the Cuyahoga River. Cleaveland never returned to see how his rough, but ideally located frontier town grew from a mosquito-and-malaria-infested swamp into an industrial and trade giant.

Growth was slow until the completion of the Ohio and Erie Canal made Cleveland a mercantile trade center. After the Civil War, the city's accessibility to iron ore and coal made it a perfect spot for the steel industry. Cleveland's first oil refinery, the Excelsior Works started by John D. Rockefeller in 1862, was the beginning of the famous Standard Oil Company of Ohio. By the time Rockefeller retired in 1895, the companies that he had organized as the Standard Oil trust controlled 90 percent of the U.S. petroleum industry.

By the turn of the century, Cleveland's population skyrocketed to nearly 400,000, and it became one of the nation's largest cities. The mixture of Catholics, Jews, Protestants, and people of more than 50 nationalities gave the city a diverse flavor that defied its New England roots. Given its advantageous location, Cleveland thrived on its waterways, railroads, and heavy industries, and its merchant princes and captains of industry displayed their wealth in lavish and extravagant mansions that lined Euclid Avenue. The bustling metropolis wielded political power at both the state and national levels. Shipping magnate Marcus Hanna bankrolled William McKinley's election as President of the United

States but the political burr under his Republican saddle was social reformer Tom Johnson. Elected Cleveland's mayor in 1901, Johnson campaigned for "home rule, three-cent (trolley) fares, and just taxation." With liberal, populist reforms such as municipally owned utilities and transportation, Johnson made Cleveland into what Lincoln Steffens called "the best governed city in the United States."

After World War II, Cleveland, like most industrial cities, began losing population. Its industrial economy eroded, and people left for the suburbs. Once-gracious neighborhoods fell into disrepair and the air and water surrounding the city became polluted with industrial waste. Cleveland experienced a series of economic setbacks that culminated in 1978, when the city defaulted on its municipal bonds and declared bankruptcy.

About that time, civic and business leaders encouraged former Cuyahoga County Commissioner George V. Voinovich to run for mayor. The Voinovich decade, 1979-89, is best known for the public-private partnership that paved the way for business and government leaders to rally around their ailing city. Voinovich brought with him to the mayor's office solid support from the

business community, which loaned 90 of its best executives to scrutinize city operations. They submitted 650 suggestions for improvements, 500 of which were used to save the city $200 million in a decade, and Cleveland won the All-American City award three times in a seven-year period.

One of the largest ports on the Great Lakes and the leading cargo port on Lake Erie, Cleveland is also a major Midwest transportation hub. The city is situated at the intersection of several interstate highways, including I-71, I-77, I-90, and I-80, the Ohio Turnpike. State Route 2/State Route 6 follows the Lake Erie shore line through Cleveland and is part of Ohio's Lake Erie Circle Tour. Known as "The Great Lakes City on America's North Coast", Cleveland is the commercial and cultural center of an area that extends 100 miles along the shores of Lake Erie and more than 40 miles inland.

Long known for its manufactured goods, Cleveland is not only capitalizing on its diversified industrial base, but also on its varied cultural offerings. Tourism is becoming a major industry, as renovation and restoration have fostered a variety of cultural, shopping, and educational opportunities. Cleveland is home to Case Western Reserve University, Cleveland State University, John Carroll University, and a host of other schools. University Circle, located four miles east of downtown, has one of the highest concentrations of cultural institutions in the nation. There visitors can explore the world-class Cleveland Museum of Art, Museum of Natural History, Crawford Auto-Aviation Museum, and the Western Reserve Historical Society. They can also experience the world-renowned Cleveland Orchestra and the Karamu Performing Arts Theatre, one of the pioneer African-American theatres.

Among Cleveland's top visitor attractions are the International Exposition Center, the largest exhibition facility in the world; and Playhouse Square Center, three restored, 1920s-era theaters that are home to the nationally acclaimed Cleveland Ballet, Cleveland Opera, and Great Lakes Theater Festival. Visitors also enjoy the Cleveland Center for Contemporary Art, Cleveland Playhouse (the nation's first resident professional theatre company), and Blossom Music Center, the summer home of the Cleveland Orchestra located 30 miles south of the city. Along with the only Sea World in the northern United States, Cleveland also claims Geauga Lake amusement park, the Rock and Roll Hall of Fame, NASA Lewis Visitor Center, the Cuyahoga Valley Line Steam Train, and Hale Farm and Village. There is Cleveland's famous "emerald necklace" of Metroparks, and several state parks offer recreation on Lake Erie. Manicured Lakeview Cemetery literally is the last resort for many of Cleveland's past elite, as well as President James Garfield, whose three-story monument is open to the public.

Three professional major league sports teams call Cleveland home. The Cleveland Browns of the NFL play in the state-of-the-art Cleveland Browns Stadium. The Cleveland Indians baseball team, which belongs to the American League, calls Jacob's Field home. The Cleveland Cavaliers are part of the National Basketball Association.

The Flats entertainment district, along the Cuyahoga River, features more than 30 clubs and restaurants, most of which become standing room only on hot summer nights. The glass-topped Arcade provides shops and restaurants in an old-fashioned, genteel setting while the ultra-modern Galleria offers shopping in an eye-popping atrium. The butchers, bakers, and greengrocers of the West Side Market are a Cleveland tradition, as is Shaker Square, the vintage shopping center located in Shaker Heights, a tony suburb started by the Van Sweringen Brothers who built Terminal Tower.
—*Source: Convention & Visitors Bureau*

Distances from Cleveland to major markets:

Atlanta	728 miles
Buffalo	191
Chicago	348
Cincinnati	244
Columbus	144
Detroit	172
Indianapolis	318
New York	471
Pittsburgh	129
Toledo	112
Washington, D.C.	360

"You know you're from a special place when your editor says, 'More Cleveland, less sex.'"

—*novelist Eve Horowitz, speech at the Ohioana Awards, 1993*

TERMINAL TOWER: AN OHIO MASTERPIECE

The Terminal Tower complex was the world's largest multi-building, multi-use project; it predated Rockefeller Center and incorporated more facilities. "As a megabuilding," says Ohio State's Douglas Graf, "it's unparalleled." He puts it on his short list of Ohio masterpieces. Terminal Tower succeeds above all because for ordinary people, it became an image for a region.

So avers Walter Leedy, architectural historian and Cleveland State University art professor. "How many buildings try to create an image for a city and fail?" says Leedy, who has a populist approach to architecture. "This building has the most meaning for Clevelanders. People talk about taking the train and eating at Harvey's. Every day thousands of people walked through that space. They would come in on a train, walk up the steep ramps, and then suddenly Public Square burst upon them."

Two brothers built the whole Terminal Tower complex, though their original intention was merely to develop suburban Shaker Heights. Oris P. and Mantis J. Van Sweringen's projects did have a way of ballooning. What became Terminal Tower was conceived initially as a downtown station for interurban trains to Shaker Heights. Then in 1916, to acquire the right-of-way for that interurban, the Van Sweringens bought the Nickel Plate Railroad; 13 years later they owned a $3 billion transcontinental rail system. And by then, the interurban rail terminal had grown to include a union terminal and the Terminal Tower complex itself.

The Van Sweringens gave Cleveland a skyline second only to those of New York and Chicago, writes historian John R. Stilgoe; they were credited with making Cleveland into a real city. The Depression brought it all to an end for the Van Sweringens. It bankrupted them, and both died in the mid-1930s. But Terminal Tower, their monument on Public Square, is still going on.

The tower itself is a 52-story skyscraper on 20-story piers anchored on bedrock, set on the diagonal at the southwest corner of Public Square. Sixty years later, long abandoned by railroads and serving only local transit, the railroad station was remodeled into Tower City shopping mall. In back the complex has three Art Deco

255:—TERMINAL TOWER BLDG. CLEVELAND, OHIO.

skyscrapers and a former post office; two new high rises flank the shopping mall. Critics have made much of Terminal Tower being out-of-style when it was built; echoing the New York Municipal Building. But Walter Leedy says the use of the dated Neoclassical style was deliberate. For the Terminal Tower to make money, it had to be monumental, Leedy says. And therefore it had to be Neoclassical.

—*Jane Ware, from Building Ohio, Vol. I*

As Ohio's capital city, Columbus is not only a thriving metropolis but also the only major city in the nation's Northeast quadrant to experience continuous growth during the last twenty years. Despite declining population in Ohio and throughout the Northeast, Columbus experienced a 12 percent population increase between 1980 and 1990, and the number of households jumped 16.2 percent in that same period. Columbus is now Ohio's largest city, and population projections anticipate commensurate growth through 2110.

Columbus experienced its first boom virtually as soon as it was platted in 1812. In 1813, a U.S. Post Office was established; in 1814, a public school was built on what is now the Statehouse Square; and the first Statehouse was built in 1817. By 1831, the first boat traveled the Columbus Canal, built by inmates of the state penitentiary, and three years later the "new" Ohio Penitentiary opened on Spring Street. With twenty factories producing buggies by the late 19th century, Columbus earned the nickname "Buggy City."

During the 1920s, Ohio Stadium opened, and City Hall construction commenced. What is now the LeVeque Tower, the signature building of Columbus's skyline, was erected at the corner of Broad and Front Streets. By the mid-20th century, the center city was pushing outward, increasing its geographic area from about 50 to nearly 150 square miles.

Today, Columbus is the state's largest city and the 15th largest in the nation. It is the fastest growing city in the northeast quadrant of the country and lies within 550 miles of half the nation's population. Columbus is located at the intersection to two of the nation's major highways, I-70 the nation's major east-west highway and I-71. Port Columbus Airport provides nonstop flights to 33 destinations.

Two of the most unique of the city's neighborhoods are German Village and the Short North. German Village dates back to 1867 and is a collection of 19th century homes, restaurants,

and shops. The recently revitalized Short North district boasts Victorian homes, numerous art galleries, and trendy restaurants. Two major shopping areas have been developed along the outskirts of the city: The Polaris Fashion Place and the Easton Town Center, which attract visitors from all over the state.

Columbus's population enjoys extensive recreational opportunities. Central Ohio boasts more useable park space per capita than any other community in the United States. The Columbus and Franklin County Metropolitan Park System operates eight developed and three undeveloped parks totaling some 11,200 acres. In addition to major collegiate sports at Ohio State University, the city has the Columbus Clippers baseball team of the International League; the Columbus Horizon of the Continental Basketball Association; the Columbus Chill of the East Coast Hockey League; the Little Brown Jug championship harness racing; and the Columbus Marathon, a major competition for runners. With the most extensive network of diamonds and leagues in the nation, Columbus is also considered to be the softball capital of the Midwest.

Unique annual events augment the Columbus calendar: the Ohio State Fair; Jack Nicklaus Memorial Golf Tournament at Muirfield; the Greater Columbus Arts Festival; Octoberfest; Red, White and Boom, and the spectacular Fourth of July city-wide celebration. Other attractions include the Center of Science and Industry, the historic German Village and Brewery Districts,

"Columbus is a town in which almost anything is likely to happen and in which almost everything has."

—*James Thurber*

and a zoo renowned for its successful breeding of endangered animals.

The Ballet Metropolitan, the Thurber House, Opera Columbus, the Columbus Symphony Orchestra, the Contemporary American Theater, and events held in the historic Ohio and Palace Theatres affirm Columbus's commitment to the arts. The Columbus Museum of Art is home to the Sirak Impressionist/Post-Impressionist collection, and The Wexner Center, designed by internationally-acclaimed architect Peter Eisenman, provides performance space for the avant-garde.

Columbus has a solid educational tradition being the home of the first junior high school, the first kindergarten, and the first school safety patrol. Central Ohio has more than 40 colleges, universities, and technical schools. The Ohio State University, the largest single campus in the country, enrolls more than 55,000 students, while urban education centers such as Franklin University, Columbus State College, DeVry Institute of Technology, Capital University, and the Columbus College of Art and Design offer diverse curricula. Other institutions in the Columbus area include Ohio Wesleyan University, Otterbein College, Denison University and the Pontifical College Josephinum.

With eleven hospital systems, the Wexner Institute for Pediatric Research, and the Arthur C. James Cancer Hospital/Research Institute at Ohio State University, health care in Columbus is state-of-the-art. The Battelle Memorial Institute also pursues new frontiers of medical and other technologies, and Children's Hospital enjoys a national reputation for its excellent pediatric care.

Columbus is the home of the newest member of the National Hockey League, the Columbus Blue Jackets. In addition, it is the home of the Columbus Crew, a major league professional soccer team. The city is also the home of one of the most popular stops on the PGA tour, the Memorial Tournament.

Airtime from Columbus to:

Atlanta	75 minutes
Boston	105
Chicago	60
Dallas	135
Los Angeles	240
Miami	135
New York	90

SHORT NORTH: ONE OF OHIO'S BEST TURN-AROUND NEIGHBORHOODS

The Short North has more urban vitality—as measured by shops, bars, restaurants, galleries, and people on the sidewalks at night—than anywhere else in Columbus. Just 20 years ago, this was a depressed neighborhood whose most conspicuous inhabitants were derelicts. Its only real asset was a relatively intact wall of shabby late 19th- and early 20th-century buildings. So what happened? A few important early steps included the rehabbed Short North Tavern's opening in 1981 and offering chamber music and poetry readings. Art galleries launched a Gallery Hop that still draws big crowds on the first Saturday of the month. Expansion northward, led by art galleries moving for lower rents, is ongoing. The Victorian Gate, at 663 North High Street, an apartment and retail complex, is a new, 1990s development, very much in the scale of the older surrounding neighborhood; it was built on a long-vacant lot. The Victorian Gate has been so successful that it's hard to believe it took seven years to realize—mostly because prospective lenders saw it as too risky because it wasn't in the suburbs. In 1997 author James Kunstler told a Columbus audience that Victorian Gate was probably the country's best urban in-fill development; he wrote about it in his book, *Home from Nowhere*. Great as the Short North is now, becoming great was a slow process involving hundreds of people. Turnaround neighborhoods that stay turned around are not one-man shows or overnight wonders. —*Jane Ware, from Building Ohio, Vol. I*

Why O, why O, Christopher Columbus, Ohio?

discovering Columbus

The most remarkable thing about the naming of Columbus, Ohio, was that no one at the time thought it was remarkable. Christian Zacher, an English professor who has probed the matter thoroughly, says both the choice of the site and the name of the city can be directly traced to Joseph Foos, tavern owner and state senator. Why Foos picked the name is another matter.

Foos was one of those self-educated and restless "doers" who materialized out of the southern mountains just in time to forever shape the crude institutions of the Ohio frontier. In 1812, Foos was the state senator from Franklinton, the first seat of Franklin County and an ever-so-humble settlement on the low west bank of the Scioto River. In Franklinton, Foos had a tavern and a ferry service across the river. On the east side, there wasn't anything but a "high bank," unbroken forest, and a big dream. Like so many Ohio dreams, it was a real estate scheme promoted by four sharp-eyed men to give land on the "high bank" side to the infant state of Ohio for a new permanent state capital. They offered to put up a statehouse, offices, and a penitentiary, guaranteed to be worth $50,000 or Ohio could have its money back.

As the local representative, Foos took himself off to Zanesville where the peripatetic legislature was sitting in the winter of 1812. Within two months, Foos had outmaneuvered everyone. He secured the necessary votes for the "high bank" site by offering the Chillicothe faction the "temporary" state capital for the seven years it would take to build the permanent one, "the first notable case of log-rolling legislation in the young state," according to a 1912 account. That done, "High Bank, Ohio" did not have a great ring as the name for a new capital city. On February 20th, a proposal to make matters worse by naming it "Ohio City" failed by three votes. Then the legislature adjourned for the evening.

What happened overnight is unknowable. Professor Zacher could find no records nor correspondence to throw light on the evening's discussions or libations. Zacher can only conclude that the name of the Admiral of the Oceans and all its Columbian derivatives were on the American national mind. Columbus and Columbia were popular material for songs and poems. In 1812, Christopher Columbus was also symbol of a non-British origin for a young republic that had just fought one war and was about to fight another with Britain. Thus the Italian navigator was on the mind of Joseph Foos. By morning, it was on the majority mind of the legislature. Foos's motion to name the capital "Columbus" went home 24–10.

By hitting upon the person of Christopher Columbus as the namesake of the new capital, Joseph Foos forever put the city in the same historical boat with the "discoverer" of the New World. That connection with the Italian-born but Spanish-sent navigator has led to a fair amount of public statuary in Columbus, the naming of Aragon and Barcelona Streets, the use of actors dressed as Columbus in local advertising selling everything from beer to window guards, and the address of St. Anthony's Hospital at 1492 East Broad Street.

—John Fleischman

drawing by Frank Elmer

Located at the confluence of the Mad, Stillwater, and Great Miami rivers, Dayton was originally supposed to be called Venice, a name indicative of its watery site as well as the ambitions of the land speculators who hoped to bring settlers to the area in 1789. Their plans went awry, however, and in 1795, the land was sold to Colonel Israel Ludlow and Generals Jonathan Dayton, James Wilkinson, and Arthur St. Clair, who was governor of the Northwest Territory. "Venice" was thus abandoned for "Dayton," which supposedly was chosen from the owners' surnames because it made the best-sounding town name. As for Ludlow, Wilkinson, and St. Clair, they settled for lending their names to the streets, and on April 1, 1796, when the first settlers finally did arrive, they landed on the Great Miami at the foot of St. Clair Street. With the coming of the Miami and Erie Canal in the 1820s, Dayton mushroomed into a manufacturing center whose products ranged from plows to pianos. After the Civil War, however, the railroads were responsible for Dayton's first "big business"—the Barney and Smith Car Co., which produced luxury passenger cars in a 59-acre plant with 3,000 employees.

By the turn of the century, Dayton was a thriving town of industry, entrepreneurs, and inventors. Daytonians, in fact, produced three of the seminal inventions of modern times—the airplane, the cash register, and the automobile self-starter. In 1903, bicycle mechanics Orville and Wilbur Wright made Dayton the "Birthplace of Aviation" when they built and flew the first controlled, powered aircraft. Saloon keeper James Ritty devised the first cash register, but master salesman John H. Patterson's innovative marketing ideas made it so popular that it became the basis of a business—National Cash Register Co. (NCR). Electrical engineer Charles Kettering parlayed his self-starter into a major General Motors division, DELCO (Dayton Engineering Laboratories Company). Eventually General Motors located several manufacturing facilities in Dayton, one of which—Frigidaire—literally became a household word.

Even when a deluge caused Dayton's worst disaster—the murderous 1913 Flood—the residents were innovative. They raised $2 million to build a series of "dry" dams designed by Arthur Morgan. The resulting Miami Conservancy District was not only the nation's first comprehensive flood control project, but also the prototype for similar projects, including the Tennessee Valley Authority. Largely in response to the demands that the flood emergency placed on the city's leadership, 1913 was also the year that Dayton became the first major city to adopt the commission-manager form of municipal government.

During World War I, when the U.S. Army decided to build installations for aircraft

PATTERSON: THE MAN WHO INVENTED SALESMANSHIP

Dayton's secret—well-kept only because no one from the outside paid enough attention—was that it did not *become* the most American city; it had *always* been so. What made it so was the confluence of certain factors, not the least of which was the American quality of inventing itself. Dayton did not have to be a city, as Cleveland did, or Cincinnati, both of which had clear geographical mandates. Dayton was not a port city. It was not an old city. It was late-growing and experimental. It merely existed, then persuaded others it was there.

Dayton was also near to being the single-handed product of the idiosyncratic American entrepreneur, John Henry Patterson, who set out to invent the 20th century in his own image. Americans were people who wanted a new frontier. They gloried in the spirit of exploration. When they ran out of country, they turned to invention. Such a description fit Patterson, one of the premier American malcontents.

Patterson, a toll collector and coal-seller, invented modern advertising and salesmanship, originated the modern American factory, and set up most of the practices which distinguished modern American businesses from all other businesses in the world. He did this by way of the cash register, which he manufactured and sold when there was absolutely no demand for such a piece of machinery. His real product, however, was not the cash register, but *himself*.

All this occurred in the last quarter of the 19th century, a time when one man of great energy, born into certain accidents of geography and circumstance, could still seem larger than his time. In the great, open spaces of the county, in the arrogance of capital and the absence of stricture, a man like Patterson could *own* his time. It was a time when men saw their own likenesses on Rushmore and, if not there, then on the sides of newly minted coins.

Patterson was a man filled with curious proclivities. He liked the feel of the green felt of pool tables and had his underwear made of it. He spent years looking for a red pencil of precisely the right color and softness to suit him, and when he finally found such a pencil he bought enough of them to last him the rest of his life. He had his executives rise at dawn and go horseback riding because he thought a man who couldn't control horses couldn't control other men.

His factory buildings were revolutionary. They were safe. They had light and space, and Ampelopsis climbed the brickwork. He thought labor had a right to be suspicious of management, and his wages were higher than union scale.

His factory complex had a library and hospital, indergarten, community center and gardens for the children. These things were unheard of at the time.

He was both paternal and autocratic. Once, he asked one of his foremen if he was pleased with the work in his epartment. The man said he was. "All right," Patterson snapped. "You're fired."

He sometimes told his men where to buy their neckties. He was called by one of them, "a combination of Julius Caesar and Alice in Wonderland."

Most of Dayton considered him a dangerous and somewhat unstable citizen. The old man was undeterred. "It has been my privilege to be called crazy many times during my life," he said. "It is an epithet which I prize highly, for I take it as a compliment to a vision that is denied to many unfortunates . . ."

—*John Baskin*

"What, you are going to keep me locked up in Dayton, Ohio? I am not a priest, you know!"

—*Serbian President Slobodan Milosevic, upon learning that the U.S. sponsored peace talks on Bosnia would be held at Dayton's Wright-Patterson Air Force Base.*

engineering and aviator training in Dayton, the city's role a a center of innovation an technology wa assured. Toda Wright-Patterson Air Force Base is the headquar-

the high points of Dayton's history with blue-and-white "Wright Flyer" signs. The Wright Flyer III, the first practical airplane and

ters for a worldwide logistics operation and the primary research and development facility of the U.S. Air Force. Covering more than 8,000 acres on the eastern edge of Dayton (including Huffman Prairie where the Wright Brothers perfected their flying), the base has some 100 military organizations involved in a variety of defense activities. It is not only the area's largest employer, but also the source of an estimated ten percent of the state's economy.

Largely because of the Wright-Patterson presence, the Dayton metropolitan area is home to numerous advanced technology and aerospace companies. The area is the headquarters for eight major corporations, including Mead and Huffy. General Motors manufactures small trucks and a variety of automotive parts. Much of the Japanese investment—Honda, Fujitech, and others—in Ohio has taken place within a 50-mile radius of Dayton. Also in the Dayton area are 20 colleges and universities. Wright State, with an enrollment of nearly 16,000, is the largest, followed by the University of Dayton. While Wright State is one of Ohio's newest universities, UD has been in existence for 140 years and is among the ten largest Catholic-affiliated universities in the U.S. Much of the area's high tech work is done by graduates of these schools.

Given Dayton's incomparable aviation heritage, it is no surprise that some of the region's premier attractions involve flight. Hundreds of thousands of people attend the international Dayton Air Show or United States Air and Trade Show every July, while the U.S. Air Force Museum at Wright-Patterson Air Force Base chronicles the history of flight and military aviation. As Ohio's most popular free tourist attraction, the museum has an IMAX theatre and more than a million visitors every year. The Aviation Trail, a self-guided driving tour, marks

a National Historic Landmark, is on display at Carillon Park, which traces the history of transportation in the Miami Valley. With an outstanding collection of exhibits displayed on more than 60 acres of beautiful grounds, Dayton's premiere park features a 50-bell carillon and free concerts.

The Dayton Art Institute houses works from ancient Greece and Rome, Egypt, Africa, and South America and a fine East Asian collection. The Museum of Contemporary Art at Wright State University is a stop on most major art tours of contemporary art exhibits. The Dayton Museum of Natural History features a planetarium with daily shows, while SunWatch, located a few minutes from downtown Dayton, is a 12th century Indian village reconstructed on an archeological site.

Downtown, the Victoria Theatre, a splendidly refurbished opera house, has been home for many the city's cultural events since 1865. Much of that is being taken over by the Benjamin and Marian Schuster Performing Arts Center. This $120 million, 2,300 seat center is the new home for the Dayton Philharmonic Orchestra and the Dayton Opera. The Neon District is the hub of the city's night life, while the homes and shops in the Oregon District have been meticulously restored to their 19th century splendor.

Dayton boasts more green space than any other city its size, and thousands of acres of open fields, rolling hills, and running streams make the city an easy place to play. Runners and bicyclists especially like the River Corridor Bikeway downtown along the Great Miami. Outlying reserves of the Miami Conservancy District offer wonderful scenery and four seasons worth of outdoor sports.

*Source: Dayton Area Chamber of Commerce
City of Dayton Public Affairs Office*

THE URBAN OHIO DILEMMA: EVERYONE'S PROBLEM

For a while it was easy. Cities—in Ohio and elsewhere—grew and absorbed their surroundings. Most of the time it was welcomed or at least accepted, and the core city provided services and protections the smaller communities could not. Somewhere around the mid-20th century, this began to change. People moving to the suburbs were exiting the city and its problems, and the suburbs blocked the core city's ability to grow.

The highway/beltway boom enabled the development of suburbs farther out, and now the suburban governments sought to better insulate themselves from the city core.

Often segregated by race and income, these new communities wanted the amenities that come with the proximity of a big city (i.e. cultural and sporting activities) but wanted neither its problems nor additional taxes.

Cities—viewed from the edges—are seen as unable to produce good schools, good transportation, safe streets, in other words, good government. In Cincinnati only 18% of the metro population lives within city borders, but the entire area covers 13 counties, 222 municipalities and townships spread over three states. This makes it the third most politically fragmented metropolitan area in the United States. Cleveland isn't much better. Its metro area covers eight counties with 259 municipalities and townships ranking it fifth nationally while the percentage of people living within Cleveland's city limits is 17.1%. For these two cities the old method of annexation won't work. Both are hemmed in by suburbs that don't want to give up local autonomy. Changes in state law, zoning, housing, and—in some extremes—gated communities are used to block undesirable elements.

Consolidating various overlapping governmental jurisdictions is also difficult. Cincinnati did it in the mid-1800s when it used the county school system to build a county library system. It remains today, one of the nation's best. But it is difficult to imagine the suburbs of Ohio's major cities giving up control of schools, police and fire to a central bureaucracy.

As business and industry has moved out, the urban core has most often turned to entertainment and culture for revival. As a way of revitalization, some are pushing residential development in the city center. But at the same time, the surrounding suburbs are engaged in a tug of war over the same residents—and the same businesses. The result merely rearranges the chairs within the metro living room.

Regional or metropolitan planning organizations—despite some notable past failures—hold the most promise. While every major Ohio city has some form of regional planning, most of their activities have dealt with transportation issues and in most other ways they are toothless.

But the long-term quality of life will only improve through some type of regional planning, along with the awareness that everyone's fortunes are tied together.

—*Michael O'Bryant*

Toledo is located at the western tip of Lake Erie at the mouth of the Maumee River and is surrounded by some of the nation's richest agricultural land. As the fourth largest city in Ohio and the seat of Lucas County, Toledo dominates the northwestern portion of the state. The city is also at the center of a major geographic and commercial triangle formed by Chicago, Detroit and Cleveland.

"I like Cedar Lake, Indiana, or Toledo, Ohio—where I'm from—rural Missouri, Cincinnati. Any place is great where people giggle when you say you're going to vacation there."

—P.J. O'Rourke

The Maumee first served as an artery of commerce and visitation among native American Indians. However, when French scouts and missionaries employed the waterway in the same manner, a dispute over their incursions erupted with the Indians, and a string of forts was built. One was at a site just south of the present day city limits of Toledo. A second stood at what is now the intersection of Summit and Monroe Streets.

In 1763, following the French and Indian War, the French ceded most of the territory to the British, who, at the end of the Revolutionary War, turned the lands over to the newly formed United States of America. The British continued to employ agents to incite Indian violence against the settlers, however, and during the War of 1812 with the British, General William Henry Harrison arrived in the Maumee Valley and built Fort Meigs. In 1813, he ordered Commodore Perry to engage British naval forces on Lake Erie. Though outgunned and outnumbered, Perry bested the enemy near Put-in-Bay and uttered the now famous phrase, "We have met the enemy and they are ours."

With the conclusion of the war, settlement in the Maumee Valley proceeded rapidly. Two towns, Port Lawrence and Vistula, were built on the shores of Lake Erie, and when they merged, they were renamed Toledo, supposedly after an anonymous suggestion. Because both Ohio and Michigan claimed the Toledo area, it took an act of Congress to settle the bloodless "Toledo War" in 1836, giving Toledo to Ohio and the Upper Peninsula to Michigan.

Toledo owes much of its growth since that time to its location at the mouth of the largest river flowing into the Great Lakes. In the late 1830s and 1840s the opening of canals from Indiana and Cincinnati, as well as the arrival of the railroads, made Toledo a major port. Today Toledo is one of the nation's leading railroad centers and the second-largest port on the Great Lakes. The Port of Toledo, a designated Foreign Trade Zone, annually handles 15 to 20 million tons of domestic and international shipments, including iron ore and coal, grain, and general cargo. The Foreign Trade Zone status allows goods to be stored, assembled, repackaged, processed, or used in manufacturing without customs duty payments until the goods enter the domestic commerce of the Unites States. Thus, businesses can take advantage of duties on finished goods that are generally lower than those on raw materials.

The discovery of gas and oil in the area encouraged the development of the glass industry in the late 1800s. When Edward Libbey moved his New England Glass Company to Toledo, the city was on its way to becoming the "Glass Capital of the World," eventually producing everything from vases, bottles, and light bulbs to plate glass, automotive glass, and fiberglass. Similarly, Toledo's turn-of-the-century dominance in buggy and bicycle building evolved into automotive industries, and during World War II, Toledo's Willys-Overland Company designed and manufactured the Jeep. Jeeps are still made in Toledo, which is also a leading manufacturer of auto parts.

Toledo's diverse economy also includes agriculture, warehousing and distribution, refining, stampings and castings, and the manufacturing of plastics, jet engines, foods,

elevators, fabrics, batteries, paints, and chemicals. In recent years, Toledo's noted Medical College of Ohio has also attracted medical research and support companies to the area. Toledo is home to the University of Toledo, and its performing arts include the Toledo Symphony, Toledo Ballet, and Toledo Opera. In addition, international artists are assembled by the Toledo Museum of Art for its Peristyle Series of classic concerts. The internationally known Museum of Art has one of the world's finest collections of glass, as well as great works by Van Gogh, Rembrandt, El Greco, Picasso, and Hopper. Wolcott House Museum is a complex of historic buildings depicting life along the Maumee in the 1800s, and the Toledo Firefighters Museum features old-fashioned equipment. The Blair Museum of Lithophanes and Carved Waxes, one of Toledo's smallest museums, houses the world's largest collection of lithophanes, delicate and decorative translucent porcelains. The *Willis B. Boyer*,

once known as "The King of the Great Lakes Freighters," is now a floating museum docked downtown. Just west of Perrysburg, visitors can take self-guided tours of Fort Meigs, the largest walled fortification built in America.

The Old West End is Toledo's historic district; the East City has ethnic neighborhoods, shopping, and dining; and the Farmer's Market in the Warehouse District offers the fresh bounty of nearby fields. The 6,600-acre network of Toledo Area Metroparks includes prairies, forests, magnificent views of the Maumee from Towpath Trail, and Ohio's only moving sand dunes in the Oak Openings Preserve. The Toledo Zoological Gardens have the world's only underwater Hippoquarium, while the Lucas County Recreation Center is a 90-acre sports complex that is the home of the Toledo Mud Hens, the farm club team immortalized in the M*A*S*H TV series by Toledo native Jamie Farr.

—*Source: Toledo Area Chamber of Commerce*

Distances from Toledo to major markets:
Atlanta .... 720 miles
Cincinnati 210
Cleveland 112
Columbus 135
New York 583
Pittsburgh 231
Washington, D.C. 566

drawing by Frank Elmer

The Toledo Blade in downtown Toledo is a notable addition: a Renaissance Revival structure made of limestone, with Spanish details. (drawing by Frank Elmer)

Lake Erie

Williams · Fulton · Lucas · Ottawa · Lake · Ashtabula · Geauga · Cuyahoga · Trumbull · Defiance · Henry · Wood · Sandusky · Erie · Lorain · Summit · Portage · Mahoning · Paulding · Putnam · Hancock · Seneca · Huron · Medina · Van Wert · Wyandot · Crawford · Richland · Ashland · Wayne · Stark · Columbiana · Allen · Hardin · Marion · Holmes · Carroll · Jefferson · Mercer · Auglaize · Morrow · Knox · Coshocton · Tuscarawas · Harrison · Logan · Union · Delaware · Licking · Muskingum · Guernsey · Belmont · Shelby · Champaign · Franklin · Darke · Miami · Clark · Madison · Fairfield · Perry · Noble · Monroe · Morgan · Preble · Montgomery · Green · Fayette · Pickaway · Hocking · Washington · Butler · Warren · Clinton · Ross · Athens · Vinton · Meigs · Hamilton · Highland · Pike · Jackson · Gallia · Clermont · Brown · Adams · Scioto · Lawrence

Counties: Ohio's Unifying Thread*

Whether we live in a city, village or township; whether our closest political entity is incorporated or unincorporated; whether we are native Buckeyes or imports from other places, there is one thing that all Ohioans have in common: we all live within a county. Counties are the unifying thread within the fabric of our diversity as Ohioans. The role that they play in Ohio is comparable to that of the states in the federal union—counties are our internal geography, the basic unit by which we define and thus attempt to make manageable our government, social, civic, business, and often personal affairs.

*The largest places in a county are the top ten places in population, and they include townships, therefore some smaller villages and cities may not appear.

Adams

Namesake John Adams, President of the United States during the county's formation

Established July 10, 1797

County Seat West Union Village

Largest Places	2000	1990
West Union village	2,903	3,096
Tiffin township	2,212	2,089
Manchester village	2,043	2,223
Meigs township	2,014	1,919
Liberty township	1,776	1,359
Peebles village	1,739	1,782
Sprigg township	1,638	1,499
Bratton township	1,412	862
Oliver township	1,246	865
Brush Creek township	1,231	1,195

Adams County is located in the southwestern part of the state on the Ohio River. Largely rural in nature, 52.1 percent of the land is in farms. Attractions in Adams County include Serpent Mound, a 1,254-foot snake-like earthwork constructed by the Hopewell Indians between 300 B.C. and 600 A.D.; Lake Adams State Park; Adams County Heritage Center; Cairn of Peace Monument commemorating the World's Plowing Match held near Peebles in 1957; Scioto Brush Creek State Forest; Tranquility Wildlife Preserve; Governor Thomas Kirker Home, Harshaville and Kirker Covered Bridges; Wheat Ridge Amish Community; Manchester Islands National Wildlife Refuge; and the Ohio River, offering boating, skiing and fishing.

Vital Statistics

Population, 1995	27,670
Population, 2000	27,330
Net Change, 1990-2000	7.7%
Median Age	36.3
White	26,721
Black	48
Native American	187
Asian	34
Pacific Islander	9
Other	31
2 or More Races	300
Hispanic	175
Area (square miles)	584
Urban Land Cover (latest figures1994)	9%
Population Per Square Mile	46.8
Elevation (feet)	957
Average Temperature	55.3
Average Precipitation	50.27 in.

Civilian Labor Force	11,600
Trade	1,775
Construction	162
Manufacturing	1,078
Transportation & Utilities	593
Government	1,506
Services	1,116
Finance, Insurance & Real Estate	202
Per Capita Income, 1999	$16,278

Persons Below Poverty, 1997	18.3%
Retail Sales Per Capita, 1997	$4,749
Housing Units, 2000	11,82
Average Family Size	3.03
Number of Farms	1,530
Average Size of Farms (acres)	134
Average Commodity Cash Receipts per Farm	$18,173
Highway Miles	
Interstate	0
U.S. Routes	29.31
State Routes	186.83
Registered Motor Vehicles	30,834
Automobile Crashes per 1,000 people	36.81

Number of Registered Voters	17,650
Number Voted 2000 Election	10,727
Percent Voted 2000 Election	60.8%
Percent Democrat	9.3%
Percent Republican	16.4%
Non Partisan	74.1%
Number Voted 2000 Election	
Percent Voted 2000 Election	65.1%
Voting, 2000 Election	
for Bush	6,380
for Gore	3,581
for Nader	162
for Buchanan	63
Contributions to Federal Candidates, Parties, & PACs, '01-'02	
to Democrats	$2,200
to Republicans	$13,235

Allen

Namesake Colonel John Allen, who spent time there during the War of 1812

Established March 1, 1820

County Seat Lima

Largest Places	2000	1990
Lima city	40,081	45,549
American township	13,599	10,921
Bath township	9,819	10,105
Shawnee township	8,365	8,005
Delphos city	3,901	3,901
Fort Shawnee village	3,855	4,128
Bluffton village	3,719	3,206
Perry township	3,620	3,577
Marion township	2,872	2,775
Jackson township	2,632	2,288

Allen County is located in the northwest portion of the state. The Auglaize and Ottawa rivers flow through the county. Once a part of the Great Black Swamp, Allen County began as a major lumber and milling center. In the late 1800s, oil was struck near Lima and an industrial boom began which continues to the present day. Attractions in Allen county include Mennonite-founded Bluffton College, the Delphos Canal Commission Museum Center, the Delphos Historical Museum, the Museum of Postal History, Allen County Museum, Shay Locomotive, the MacDonnell House, the Lima Symphony Orchestra, and the Johnny Appleseed Metro Park District.

Adams

In 1791, Nathaniel Massie started Manchester, the Virginia Military District's first settlement. In 1838, John Locke's survey of Adams produced Ohio's first county geological map. Both were preceded by the Adenas, Indians who arrived in Adams about 800 B.C. and built the world's largest earthen effigy—the 1,254-foot Serpent Mound that snakes along the county's northeast corner.

Vital Statistics

Population, 1995 109,299
Population, 2000 108,473
Net Change, 1990-2000 .... -1.2%
Median Age 36.3
White 92,147
Black 13,225
Native American 224
Asian 601
Pacific Islander 13
Other 686
2 or More Races 1,577
Hispanic 1,545
Area (square miles) 404
Urban Land Cover (latest figures 1994) 4%
Population Per Square Mile 268.5
Elevation (feet) 827
Average Temperature 54.5
Average Precipitation .... 37.84 in.

Civilian Labor Force 52,200
    Trade 14,295
    Construction 2,698
    Mining 70
    Manufacturing 12,828
    Transportation & Utilities 2,311
    Government 6,960
    Services 18,192
    Finance, Insurance & Real Estate 1,568
    Agriculture, Forestry, Fishing 347
Per Capita Income, 1999 .... $23,631
Persons Below Poverty, 1997 .... 11.4%
Retail Sales Per Capita, 1997 .... $11,964
Housing Units, 2000 44,245
Average Family Size 3.05
Number of Farms 1,080
Average Size of Farms (acres) 185
Average Commodity Cash Receipts per Farm $45,194
Highway Miles
    Interstate 23.18
    U.S. Routes 24.17
    State Routes 136.86
Registered Motor Vehicles 114,343
Automobile Crashes per 1,000 .... 30.26

Number of Registered Voters 67,950
    Percent Democrat 8.1%
    Percent Republican 17.9%
    Non Partisan 74.0%
    Number Voted 2000 Election 44,207
    Percent Voted 2000 Election 65.1%
Voting, 2000 Election
    for Bush 28,647
    for Gore 13,996
    for Nader 760
    for Buchanan 193
Contributions to Federal Candidates, Parties, & PACs, '01-'02
    to Democrats $13,375
    to Republicans $42,208

Ashland

Namesake Named for the estate of Henry Clay, prominent Whig Presidential candidate

Established February 14, 1848

County Seat Ashland

Largest Places	2000	1990
Ashland city	21,249	20,079
Jackson township	3,197	2,084
Loudonville village	2,848	2,844
Milton township	2,431	2,059
Montgomery township	2,412	2,231
Orange township	2,276	2,113
Vermillion township	2,191	1,797
Sullivan township	2,076	1,491
Perry township	1,927	1,791
Green township	1,662	1,709

Ashland county is located in the north-central part of the state, and the Mohican River flows through the county. With 60.4 percent of the land in farms, Ashland county ranks fourth in the state in raising sheep and fifth in oats production. John Chapman, better known as Johnny Appleseed, once lived on the grounds of what is now Ashland University. Attractions in Ashland County include Mohican State Park and Lodge; Mohican  State Forest with Clear Fork Gorge, a registered National Landmark; Ashland University; Ashland County Historical Museum; Charles Mill Lake; Pleasant Hill Lake; World War II Memorial Shrine; and Johnny Appleseed Monument.

Vital Statistics

Population, 1995 51,240
Population, 2000 52,523
Net Change, 1990-2000 .... 10.6%
Median Age 36.3
White 51,231
Black 424
Native American 57
Asian 287
Pacific Islander 15
Other 112
2 or More Races 397
Hispanic 339
Area (square miles) 424.4
Urban Land Cover (latest figures 1994) 1.2%
Population Per Square Mile 123.9
Elevation 1,244
Average Temperature 52.4
Average Precipitation .... 39.08 in.

Civilian Labor Force 25,900
    Trade 3,979
    Construction 690
    Mining 34
    Manufacturing 6,643
    Transportation & Utilities 357
    Government 2,835
    Services 4,598
    Finance, Insurance & Real Estate 379
    Agriculture, Forestry, Fishing 150
Per Capita Income, 1999 .... $20,739
Persons Below Poverty, 1997 .... 8.1%

Retail Sales per Capita, 1997 .... $6,076
Housing Units, 2000 20,832
Average Family Size 3.06
Number of Farms 1,020
Average Size of Farms (acres) 175
Average Commodty Cash Receipts per Farm $52,817
Highway Miles
    Interstate 16
    U.S. Routes 71
    State Routes 172
Registered Motor Vehicles 56,832
Automobile Crashes per 1,000 .... 35.13

Number of Registered Voters 30,988
    Percent Democrat 10.3%
    Percent Republican 21.5%
    Non Partisan 68.2%
    Number Voted 2000 Election 21,535
    Percent Voted 2000 Election 69.5%
Voting, 2000 Election
    for Bush 13,533
    for Gore 6,685
    for Nader 563
    for Buchanan 374
Contributions to Federal Candidates, Parties, & PACs, '01-'02
    to Democrats $2,250
    to Republicans $30,400

Ashtabula

Namesake Ashtabula River, from Indian word meaning "fish"

Established June 7, 1807

County Seat Jefferson

Largest Places	2000	1990
Ashtabula city	20,962	21,633
Conneaut city	12,485	13,241
Geneva	6,595	6,597
Ashtabula township	6,371	6,654
Saybrooke township	5,957	5,886
Geneva township	3,689	3,814
Jefferson village	3,331	3,572
North Kingsville village	2,672	2,658
Harpersfield township	2,496	2,603
Monroe township	1,883	2,268

Ashtabula county is located in the northeast corner of the state, bordering on Pennsylvania and Lake Erie, and is the largest in area among Ohio's 88 counties. The Ashtabula and Grande rivers flow through the county and the Lake Erie ports of Ashtabula and Conneaut provide access to Great Lakes shipping. Attractions in Ashtabula County include its 12 wineries and 16 covered bridges; Pymatuning and Geneva State Parks; the Jenny Munger Gregory Memorial Museum in the Geneva-On-The-Lake resort area; Conneaut Historical Railway Museum; Shandy Hall Museum in Geneva; the Great 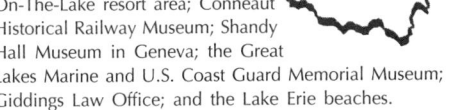 Lakes Marine and U.S. Coast Guard Memorial Museum; Giddings Law Office; and the Lake Erie beaches.

Vital Statistics
Population, 1995 102,360
Population, 2000 102,728
Net Change, 1990-2000 .... 2.9%
Median Age 37.6
White 96,635
Black 3,247
Native American 195
Asian 346
Pacific Islander 25
Other 878
2 or More Races 1,402
Hispanic 2,292
Area (square miles) 702.7
Urban Land Cover (latest figures 1994) 1.6%
Population Per Square Mile 146.3
Elevation 1,091
Average Temperature 51
Average Precipitation .... 34.53 in.

Civilian Labor Force 47,400
    Trade 7,762
    Construction 1,345
    Mining 61
    Manufacturing 10,630
    Transportation & Utilities 1,281
    Government 5,112
    Services 8,047
    Finance, Insurance & Real Estate 865
    Agriculture, Forestry, Fishing 224
Per Capita Income, 1999 .... $21,685
Persons Below Poverty, 1997 .... 13.4%
Retail Sales per Capita, 1997 .... $6,903
Housing Units, 2000 43,792
Average Family Size 3.05
Number of Farms 1,310
Average size of Farms (acres) 132
Average Commodity Cash Receipts per Farm $28,336
Highway Miles
    Interstate 29
    U.S. Routes 86
    State Routes 250
Registered Motor Vehicles 110,340
Automobile Crashes per 1,000 .... 29.66

Number of Registered Voters 66,390
    Percent Democrat 17.8%
    Percent Republican 9.9%
    Non Partisan 72.2%
    Number Voted 2000 Election 40,378
    Percent Voted 2000 Election 60.8%
Voting, 2000 Election
    for Bush 17,940
    for Gore 19,831
    for Nader 1,109
    for Buchanan 338
Contributions to Federal Candidates, Parties, & PACs, '01-'02
    to Democrats $6,180
    to Republicans $47,072

Athens

Namesake Athens, Greece, a center of learning; land in the county was dedicated to educational use

Established March 1, 1805

County Seat Athens

Largest Places	2000	1990
Athens city	21,342	21,265
Athens township	6,680	6,471
Nelsonville city	5,230	4,563
Dover township	2,730	2,615
Waterloo township	2,605	2,321
Alexander	2,590	2,345
Troy township	2,184	1,925
Glouster village	1,972	2,001
York township	1,947	1,833
Lee township	1,747	1,459

Athens County is located in the southeast portion of the state and is part of Ohio's "Appalachian Region." The Hocking River flows into the Ohio River at Athens county. The first settlement in Athens County was set up around the idea of having a university west of the Alleghenies. The Ohio University in Athens City was founded in 1808, and William Holmes  McGuffey, author of the McGuffey Readers, was one of its early presidents. Attractions in Athens County include the Wayne National Forest; Zaleski State Forest (its 28,000 acres make it Ohio's 2nd-largest state-owned forest); Burr Oak State Park and Lodge; Strouds Run State Park; Athens County Historical Society and Museum; Hocking Valley Scenic Railway; Hocking College; and the Ohio University.

Vital Statistics

Population, 1995	60,887
Population, 2000	62,223
Net Change, 1990-2000	4.5%
Median Age	25.7
White	50,812
Black	1,485
Native American	177
Asian	1,184
Pacific Islander	14
Other	224
2 or More Races	973
Hispanic	636
Area (square miles)	506.8
Urban Land Cover (latest figures 1994)	1.4%
Population Per Square Mile	122.7
Elevation	680
Average Temperature	54.1
Average Precipitation	38.46 in.

Civilian Labor Force	27,300
Trade	4,734
Construction	607
Mining	24
Manufacturing	1,160
Transportation & Utilities	358
Government	6,835
Services	3,908
Finance, Insurance & Real Estate	669
Agriculture, Fishing, Forestry	128
Per Capita Income, 1999	$18,202
Persons Below Poverty, 1997	19.1%
Retail Sales per Capita, 1997	$5,634
Housing Units, 2000	24,901
Average Family Size	2.92
Number of Farms	560
Average Size of Farms (acres)	155
Average Commodity Cash Receipts per Farm	$13,105
Highway Miles	
Interstate	0
U.S. Routes	65
State Routes	147
Registered Motor Vehicles	49,184
Automobile Crashes per 1,000	32.59

Number of Registered Voters	48,356
Percent Democrat	17.3%
Percent Republican	8.8%
Non Partisan	73.9%
Number Voted 2000 Election	25,888
Percent Voted 2000 Election	53.5%
Voting, 2000 Election	
for Bush	9,703
for Gore	13,158
for Nader	1,663
for Buchanan	743
Contributions to Federal Candidates, Parties, & PACs, '01-'02	
to Democrats	$7,150
to Republicans	$25,420

---

www. athenslegends.org

Southeastern Ohio's amateur guide to the spooks of Athens County includes stories and photographs from both the Ohio University campus, which was built over an Indian burial ground, and the surrounding area. Locations such as the former Athens Mental Health Center, Mt. Nebo, and many area graveyards provide accounts of apparitions, spectral voices, mysterious slamming doors, and flying objects, for believer and skeptic alike.

Auglaize

Namesake Named for nearby Auglaize River, from Indian word for "Fallen Timbers"

Established February 14, 1848

County Seat Wapakoneta

Largest Places	2000	1990
Wapakoneta city	9,474	9,214
St. Marys city	8,342	8,441
St. Marys township	3,457	3,145
Duchouquent township	3,111	3,127
New Bremen village	2,909	2,558
Minster village	2,794	2,650
Cridersville village	1,817	1,885
Moulton township	1,682	1,592
Union township	1,614	1,434
Washington township	1,429	1,014

Wapakoneta, the Auglaize county seat, is the birthplace of Neil Armstrong, the first man to set foot on the moon. The Armstrong Air and Space Museum in Wapakoneta the museum chronicles Ohioans' contributions to the history of flight. Recent renovations include interactive exhibits with a space shuttle landing simulator and a lunar landing simulator. Other  attractions in Auglaize County include Grand Lake Saint Marys and the canal boat, the Belle of St. Marys; the State Fish Hatchery; the Scenic Byway that follows the old canal along State Route 66; New Bremen's Bicycle Museum (with 250 vintage bikes); Loramie State Parks; and Fort Amanda Park and State Memorial.

Vital Statistics

Population, 1995 46,877
Population, 2000 46,611
Net Change, 1990-2000 .... 4.5%
Median Age 36.5
White 33,738
Black 110
Native American 86
Asian 189
Pacific Islander 13
Other 93
2 or More Races 385
Hispanic 310
Area (square miles) 401.7
Urban Land Cover (latest figures 1994) 1.7%
Population Per Square Mile 116.2
Elevation 871
Average Temperature 54.6
Average Precipitation .... 37.71 in.
Civilian Labor Force 25,000
    Trade 3,923
    Construction 1,095
    Mining 34
    Manufacturing 7,767
    Transportation & Utilities 447
    Government 2,798
    Services 2,768
    Finance, Insurance & Real Estate 465
    Agriculture, Forestry, Fishing 84
Per Capita Income, 1999 .... $25,071
Persons Below Poverty, 1997 .... 6.1%
Retail Sales per Capita $7,281
Housing Units, 2000 18,470
Average Family Size 3.11
Number of Farms 1,150
Average Size of Farms (acres) 185
Average Commodity Cash Receipts per Farm $72,898
Highway Miles
    Interstate 13
    U.S. Routes 29
    State Routes 170
Registered Motor Vehicles 49,928
Automobile Crashes per 1,000 .... 27.12
Number of Registered Voters 28,693
    Percent Democrat 9.4%
    Percent Republican 16.1%
    Non Partisan 74.4%
    Number Voted 2000 Election 20,212
    Percent Voted 2000 Election 70.4%
Voting, 2000 Election
    for Bush 13,770
    for Gore 5,564
    for Nader 372
    for Buchanan 104
Contributions to Federal Candidates, Parties, & PACs, '01-'02
    to Democrats $2,000
    to Republicans $141,777

Belmont

Namesake from French for "Beautiful Mountain"

Established September 7, 1801

County Seat St. Clairsville

Largest Places	2000	1990
Richland township	8,514	6,156
Martins Ferry city	7,226	7,990
St. Clairsville city	5,057	5,162
Bellaire city	4,892	6,028
Pultney township	4,751	4,961
Colerain township	4,438	4,602
Pease township	4,367	4,869
Barnesville village	4,225	4,326
Shadyside village	3,675	3,934
Mead township	2,405	2,250

Belmont County is located in the southeast portion of the state and is part of Ohio's "Appalachian Region." Bordering on the Ohio River, Belmont County was considered the gateway entrance for settlers moving west using Zane's Trail. The Quakers were among the first to settle in the county and today continue to run the Olney Friends School and to hold meetings in the Stillwater  Meeting House. Other attractions in Belmont County include Gay 90's Mansion and Museum; Quaker Heritage Museum; Betty Zane Statue and Grave; Benjamin Lundy House; Barbara Barbe Doll Museum; Barkcamp State Park; Piedmont and Belmont Lakes; and the Ohio River.

Vital Statistics

Population, 1995 70,379
Population, 2000 70,226
Net Change, 1990-2000 .... -1.2%
Median Age 40.9
White 66,698
Black 2,553
Native American 97
Asian 213
Pacific Islander 13
Other 109
2 or More Races 543
Hispanic 274
Area (square miles) 537.3
Urban Land Cover (latest figures 1994) 0.9%
Population Per Square Mile 130.8
Elevation 662
Average Temperature 53.6
Average Precipitation .... 42.96 in.

Civilian Labor Force 32,200
    Trade 8,198
    Construction 1,066
    Manufacturing 1,957
    Transportation & Utilities 745
    Government 3,970
    Services 5,670
    Finance, Insurance & Real Estate 1,018
    Agriculture, Forestry, Fishing 126
Per Capita Income,1999 .... $20,560
Persons Below Poverty, 1997 .... 16.3%
Retail Sales per Capita, 1997 .... $10,272

"Athens is slightly irregular. It's a small town wearing an academic tassel. A metropolis surrounded by villages with names like Mineral. A cultural watering hole that still tastes of the intoxicating Sixties..."

—Ellen Gerl

Housing Units, 2000 31,236
Average Family Size 2.90
Number of Farms 620
Average Size of Farms (acres) 240
Average Commodity Cash Receipts per Farm $22,904
Highway Miles
    Interstate 34
    U.S. Routes 32
    State Routes 217
Registered Motor Vehicles 74,867
Automobile Crashes per 1,000 .... 29.5

Number Registered Voters 51,504
    Percent Democrat 28.2%
    Percent Republican 5.3%
    Non Partisan 66.5%
    Number Voted 2000 Election 31,039
    Percent Voted 2000 Election 60.3%
Voting, 2000 Election
    for Bush 12,625
    for Gore 15,980
    for Nader 723
    for Buchanan 657
Contributions to Federal Candidates, Parties, & PACs, '01-'02
    to Democrats $7,300
    to Republicans $161,665

Carroll

The *"Fighting McCooks"* were called history's greatest fighting family—in the Civil War, four were killed and seven became generals. The "Tribe of Dan" (Major Daniel and eight sons) came from Carrollton; the "Tribe of John" (Dr. John and five sons) from Steubenville. Daniel enlisted at age 63; Dan, Jr. recited poetry as he led the Kennesaw Mountain charge.

Brown

Namesake Named for War of 1812 hero General Jacob Brown

Established March 1, 1819

County Seat Georgetown

Largest Places	2000	1990
Perry township	4,367	3,271
Georgetown village	3,691	3,627
Sterling township	3,604	2,377
Pike township	2,995	2,322
Clark township	2,650	2,245
Mount Orab	2,307	1,929
Lewis township	2,071	1,378
Green township	1,978	1,510
Ripley village	1,745	1,816
Aberdeen village	1,603	1,329

Brown County is located in the southwestern part of the state on the Ohio River. The John Rankin House in Ripley was the first stop on the "Underground Railroad," after crossing the Ohio River. Now a state memorial and open to the public, the Rankin House is said to have provided Harriet Beecher Stowe with ideas for her book, *Uncle Tom's Cabin*. Other attractions in Brown County include the Ulysses S. Grant home; Ripley Museum; Ohio Tobacco Museum; St. Martin's Ursuline Center and Chatfield College; Grant Lake State Wildlife Area; six covered bridges; Washburn Log House; and the Ohio River.

Vital Statistics
Population, 1995 30,850
Population, 2000 42,285
Net Change, 1990-2000 .... 20.9%
Median Age 35.4
White 41,474

Black 389
Native American 76
Asian 54
Pacific Islander 2
Other 35
2 or More Races 255
Hispanic 185
Area (square miles) 491.8
Urban Land Cover (latest figures 1994) 0.1%
Population Per Square Mile 85.9
Elevation 975
Average Temperature 55.3
Average Precipitation .... 50.27 in.

Civilian Labor Force 20,300
    Trade 1,694
    Construction 233
    Manufacturing 1,271
    Transportation & Utilities 372
    Government 2,063
    Services 1,484
    Finance, Insurance & Real Estate 223
    Agriculture, Forestry, Fishing 59
Per Capita Income, 1999 .... $20,699
Persons Below Poverty, 1997 .... 12%
Retail Sales per Capita $3,531
Housing Units, 2000 17,193
Average Family Size 3.09
Number of Farms 1,660
Average Size of Farms (acres) 126
Average Commodity Cash Receipts per Farm $21,057
Highway Miles
    Interstate 0
    U.S. Routes 89
    State Routes 119
Registered Motor Vehicles 50,840
Automobile Crashes per 1,000 .... 29.23

Number Registered Voters 26,955
    Percent Democrat 15.0%
    Percent Republican 8.6%
    Non Partisan 76.5%
    Number Voted 2000 Election 16,862
    Percent Voted 2000 Election 62.6%
Voting, 2000 Election
    for Bush 10,027
    for Gore 5,972
    for Nader 269
    for Buchanan 83
Contributions to Federal Candidates, Parties, & PACs, '01-'02
    to Democrats $700
    to Republicans $4,150

Butler

Namesake General Richard Butler, killed in St. Clair's 1791 defeat

Established May 1, 1803

County Seat Hamilton

Largest Places	2000	1990
Hamilton city	60,690	61,368
Union township	52,669	37,862
Middletown city	49,574	45,991
Fairfield city	42,097	39,739
Liberty township	22,005	8,701
Oxford city	21,943	18,937
Fairfield township	15,571	9,644

Trenton city	8,746	6,189
Madison township	8,611	8,547
Hanover township	7,623	7,410

Butler County is located in the southwestern part of the state on the Indiana boarder. The Great Miami River flows through the county. Attractions in Butler County include Hueston Woods State Park and State Nature Preserve; Miami University and McGuffey Museum honoring Professor William Holmes McGuffey of McGuffey Reader fame; Butler County Historical Museum; Middletown Historical Society Canal Museum; Monroe Historical Society Museum and Old Log Cabin; Governor, Congressman and Presidential candidate James M. Cox Homestead at Jacksonburg; Soldier's, Sailor's and Pioneer's Monument; Pyramid Hill Sculpture Park and Museum; Sorg Opera House; Governor Bebb Preserve; and the Great Miami River.

Vital Statistics
Population, 1995	315,601
Population, 2000	332,807
Net Change, 1990-2000	14.2%
Median Age	34.2
White	303,510
Black	17,531
Native American	693
Asian	5,147
Pacific Islander	115
Other	2,066
2 or More Races	3,745
Hispanic	4,771
Area (square miles)	467.3
Urban Land Cover (latest figures 1994)	12%
Population Per Square Mile	712.6
Elevation	653
Average Temperature	56.6
Average Precipitation	47.29 in.
Civilian Labor Force	189,300
Trade	34,863
Construction	7,873
Mining	156
Manufacturing	22,533
Transportation & Utilities	4,999
Government	18,343
Services	27,733
Finance, Insurance & Real Estate	7,604
Agriculture, Forestry, Fishing	818
Per Capita Income, 1999	$26,456
Persons Below Poverty, 1997	8.1%
Retail Sales per Capita, 1997	$6,679
Housing Units, 2000	129,733
Average Family Size	3.07
Number of Farms	1,040
Average Size of Farms (acres)	140
Average Commodity Cash Receipts per Farm	$30,502
Highway Miles	
Interstate	0
U.S. Routes	46
State Routes	173
Registered Motor Vehicles	320,588
Automobile Crashes per 1,000	28.54
Number of Registered Voters	216,275
Percent Democrat	5.0%
Percent Republican	9.7%

Non Partisan	85.3%
Number Voted 2000 Election	138,992
Percent Voted 2000 Election	64.3%
Voting, 2000 Election	
for Bush	86,587
for Gore	46,390
for Nader	2,708
for Buchanan	431
Contributions to Federal Candidates, Parties, & PACs, '01-'02	
to Democrats	$19,735
to Republicans	$488,027

Carroll

Namesake Charles Carroll, last survivor of the signers of the Declaration of Independence, who died the year the county was organized

Established January 1, 1833

County Seat Carrollton

Largest Places	2000	1990
Brown township	5,184	4,760
Carrolton village	3,190	3,042
Harrison township	2,498	2,127
Minerva village	1,898	2,086
Augusta township	1,599	1,369
Monroe township	1,588	1,384
Rose township	1,289	1,038
Center township	1,222	1,392
Malven village	1,218	1,112
Lee township	1,128	1,046

Carroll County is located in the east-central part of the state. The Atwood Lake and Leesville Lake are part of the Muskingum River Watershed Conservancy District. At Carrollton is the McCook House, the historic home of Major Daniel McCook, who, with his nine sons and the five sons of his brother, Dr. John McCook, became known as the Fighting McCooks because of their participation in the armed services prior to and especially during the Civil War. Other attractions in Carroll County include Atwood Lake Park and Lodge; Leesville Lake; the Algonquin Mill complex; Bluebird Farm and Susie's Toy Museum; the Atwood Queen Cruise Boat; and the "Elderberry Line," an 11-mile train ride between Carrollton and Minerva.

Vital Statisics
Population, 1995	28,142
Population, 2000	28,836
Net Change, 1990-2000	8.7%
Median Age	38.8
White	28,316
Black	155
Native American	93
Asian	33
Pacific Islander	7
Other	26
2 or More Races	206
Hispanic	158
Area (square miles)	394.7
Urban Land Cover (latest figures 1994)	0.3%
Population Per Square Mile	73

Elevation 1,130
Average Temperature 53.2
Average Precipitation .... 40.06 in.

Civilian Labor Force 13,700
   Trade.. 1,616
   Construction 276
   Mining 18
   Manufacturing 2,140
   Transportation & Utilities 222
   Government 944
   Services 1,158
   Finance, Insurance & Real Estate 136
   Agriculture, Forestry, Fishing 89
Per Capita Income, 1999 .... $21,652
Persons Below Poverty, 1997 .... 10.8%
Retail Sales per Capita, 1997 .... $4,491
Housing Units, 2000 13,016
Average Family Size 3.00
Number of Farms 800
Average Size of Farms (acres) 155
Average Commodity Cash Receipts per Farm $71,709
Highway Miles
   Interstate 0
   U.S. Routes 0
   State Routes 153
Registered Motor Vehicles 35,139
Automobile Crashes per 1,000 .... 28.56

Number Registered Voters 19,075
   Percent Democrat 12.1%
   Percent Republican 14.8%
   Non Partisan 73.1%
   Number Voted 2000 Election 12,576
   Percent Voted 2000 Election 65.9%
Voting, 2000 Election
   for Bush 6,732
   for Gore 4,960
   for Nader 271
   for Buchanan 207
Contributions to Federal Candidates, Parties, & PACs, '01-'02
   to Democrats $500
   to Republicans $9,475

Champaign

Namesake French word for level land

Established March 1, 1805

County Seat Urbana

Largest Places	2000	1990
Urbana city	11,613	11,353
Urbana township	3,366	3,417
Mad River township	2,650	2,353
Salem township	2,296	2,045
St. Paris village	1,998	1,842
Union township	1,788	1,525
Jackson township	1,763	1,435
Mechanicsburg village	1,744	1,803
Wayne township	1,660	1,416
Goshen township	1,639	1,369

Champaign County is located in the west-central part of the state. The Mad River flows through the county. Between 1600 and 1750, the Champaign County area was the hunting grounds for American Indian parties from the Northern and Southern Tribes. In 1789, Frontiersman Major Simon Kenton and longtime friend, Colonel Daniel Boone,

along with troops from the Logan campaign, came into the area to drive out the Indians and open the way for settlement. Simon Kenton is now buried in Urbana's Oakdale Cemetery. Attractions in Champaign County include Kiser Lake State Park; Piatt Castles; Cedar Bog; Davey Woods State Nature Preserve; Ohio Caverns; Urbana College; and Urbana High School, "The Castle."

Vital Statistics

Population, 1995 37,686
Population, 2000 38,890
Net Change 8.0%
Median Age 37
White 37,230
Black 894
Native American 120
Asian 99
Pacific Islander 8
Other 120
2 or More Races 419
Hispanic 269
Area (square miles) 428.6
Urban Land Cover (latest figures 1994) 0.5%
Population Per Square Mile 90.7
Elevation 1,087
Average Temperature 54.3
Average Precipitation .... 43.79 in.

Civilian Labor Force 20,000
   Trade 2,304
   Construction 344
   Manufacturing 3,749
   Transportation & Utilities 195
   Government 1,895
   Services 2,399
   Finance, Insurance & Real Estate 352
Per Capita Income, 1999 .... $23,769
Persons Below Poverty, 1997 .... 7.5%
Retail Sales per Capita, 1997 .... $5,358
Housing Units, 2000 15,890
Average Family Size 3.01
Number of Farms 920
Average Size of Farms (acres) 240
Average Commodity Cash Receipts per Farm $60,742
Highway Miles
   Interstate 0
   U.S. Routes 45
   State Routes 165
Registered Motor Vehicles 44,593
Automobile Crashes per 1,000 .... 28.31

Number Registered Voters 26,792
   Percent Democrat 6.7%
   Percent Republican 14.5%
   Non Partisan 78.8%
   Number Voted 2000 Election 16,035
   Percent Voted 2000 Election 59.8%
Voting, 2000 Election
   for Bush 9,220
   for Gore 5,955
   for Nader 346
   for Buchanan 80
Contributions to Federal Candidates, Parties, & PACs, '01-'02
   to Democrats $775
   to Republicans $26,750

Clark

Namesake General George Rogers Clark, who fought important Indian battles in the area

Established March 1, 1818

County Seat Springfield

Largest Places	2000	1990
Springfield city	65,358	70,487
Springfield township	13,424	13,352
Bethel township	12,934	13,255
Moorefield township	11,402	9,621
Mad River township	9,190	9,214
German township	7,012	6,670
New Carlisle	5,735	6,049
Pike township	3,521	3,367
Harmony township	3,079	2,845
Pleasant township	2,822	2,432

Clark County is located in the west-central part of the state. The Little Miami and Mad rivers flow through Clark County. In 1902, a Springfield school teacher named A.B. Graham started clubs for boys and girls to teach better farming methods and homemaking. These clubs later became nationally organized, and today are known as 4-H Clubs. Attractions in Clark County include Clifton Gristmill; George Rogers Clark Monument; Buck Creek State Park; Prairie Road Fen State Nature Preserve; Clark Lake Wildlife Area; Fairview Farms/ Crabill Homestead; Springfield Museum of Art; Springfield Symphony Orchestra; and Wittenburg University.

Vital Statistics

Population, 1995	147,731
Population, 2000	144,742
Net Change, 1990-2000	-1.9%
Median Age	37.6
White	127,541
Black	12,954
Native American	402
Asian	761
Pacific Islander	31
Other	767
2 or More Races	2,286
Hispanic	1,699
Area (square miles)	400
Urban Land Cover (latest figures 1994)	0.4%
Population Per Square Mile	361.9
Elevation	979
Average Temperature	53.7
Average Precipitation	39.32 in.

Civilian Labor Force	68,500
Trade	14,736
Construction	2,038
Mining	36
Manufacturing	13,883
Transportation & Utilities	2,584
Government	7,468
Services	14,308
Finance, Insurance & Real Estate	1,684
Agriculture, Forestry, Fishing	669

Per Capita Income, 1999	$24,791
Persons Below Poverty, 1997	12.5%
Retail Sales per Capita, 1997	$7,561
Housing Units, 2000	61,056
Average Family Size	2.97
Number of Farms	810
Average Size of Farms (acres)	231
Average Commodity Cash Receipts per Farm	$70,733
Highway Miles	
Interstate	31
U.S. Routes	58
State Routes	100
Registered Motor Vehicles	134,468
Automobile Crashes per 1,000	30.57

Number Registed Voters	89,550
Percent Democrat	10.2%
Percent Republican	11.4%
Non Partisan	78.4%
Number Voted 2000 Election	58,876
Percent Voted 2000 Election	65.7%
Voting, 2000 Election	
for Bush	27,660
for Gore	27,984
for Nader	1,347
for Buchanan	221
Contributions to Federal Candidates, Parties, & PACs, '01-'02	
to Democrats	$6,425
to Republicans	$160,216

Clermont

Namesake Named for Clermont, or Clear Mountain, France

Established December 6, 1800

County Seat Batavia

Largest Places	2000	1990
Union township	42,332	33,369
Miami township	36,632	28,199
Batavia township	15,039	11,254
Goshen township	13,663	12,697
Pierce township	10,321	8,471
Monroe township	8,236	7,762
Tate township	6,298	5,992
Milford city	6,249	5,655
Stonelick township	5,000	4,578
Wayne township	4,533	4,322

Clermont County is located in the southwestern portion of the state and is part of the Cincinnati Metropolitan Area. The east fork of the Little Miami River flows through the county, and the Ohio River provides its southern border. Attractions in Clermont County include President Ulysses S. Grant Birthplace State Memorial; Stonelick Lake; Little Miami Scenic Park; East Fork State Park; Stonelick Covered Bridge; Kelley Nature Preserve; Governor John M. Pattison House, Promont House-Milford Area Historical Society & Museum; Old Milford Village; and the Ohio River.

Vital Statistics

Population, 1995	166,941
Population, 2000	177,977
Net Change, 1990-2000	18.6%
Median Age	34.8

White 172,866
Black 1,621
Native American 333
Asian 1,129
Pacific Islander 33
Other 467
2 or More Races 1,528
Hispanic 1,547
Area (square miles) 452
Urban Land Cover (latest figures 1994) 4%
Population Per Square Mile........................ 393.8
Elevation 596
Average Temperature 56.5
Average Precipitation .... 50.07 in.

Civilian Labor Force 96,100
    Trade 14,777
    Construction 3,568
    Manufacturing 8,284
    Transportation & Utilities 1,495
    Government 6,423
    Services 11,260
    Finance, Insurance & Real Estate 2,827
Per Capita Income, 1999 .... $26,340
Persons Below Poverty, 1997 .... 6.7%
Retail Sales per Capita, 1997 .... $9,583
Housing Units, 2000 69,226
Average Family Size 3.11
Number of Farms 950
Average size of Farms (acres) 108
Average Commodity Cash Receipts per Farm $20,563
Highway Miles
    Interstate 14
    U.S. Routes 45
    State Routes 208
Registered Motor Vehicles 193,966
Automobile Crashes per 1,000 .... 31.46

Number Registered Voters 114,186
    Percent Democrat 3.5%
    Percent Republican 7.8%
    Non Partisan 88.7%
    Number Voted 2000 Election 71,242
    Percent Voted 2000 Election 62.4%
Voting, 2000 Election
    for Bush 47,129
    for Gore 20,927
    for Nader 1,303
    for Buchanan 178
Contributions to Federal Candidates, Parties, & PACs, '01-'02
    to Democrats $12,538
    to Republicans $152,875

Clinton

Namesake George Clinton, Vice President of United States when the county was formed

Established March 1, 1810

County Seat Wilmington

Largest Places	2000	1990
Wilmington city	11,921	11,199
Blanchester village	4,220	4,206
Union township	3,008	2,180
Sabina village	2,780	2,662
Vernon township	2,188	1,530
Adams township	1,901	1,592
Washington township	1,895	1,475
Chester township	1,771	1,200
Clark township	1,419	1,105
Green township	1,308	1,075

Clinton County is located in the southwest portion of the state. The Anderson, East, and Todd forks of the Little Miami River flow through the county. Many of the early settlers in Clinton County were Pennsylvania Quakers. In 1870, they established Wilmington College, which remains today as a co-educational four-year liberal arts college. Attractions in Clinton County include Caesar Creek and Cowan Lake State Parks; Murphy Theatre; Eli Harvey House; Simon Goodman Memorial Carillon; Clinton County Historical Society's Museum; the Martinsville Road Covered Bridge; and the Wilmington Peace Center.

Vital Statistics
Population, 1995 38,019
Population, 2000 40,543
Net Change, 1990-2000 .... 14.4%
Median Age 35.3
White 38,917
Black 886
Native American 107
Asian 154
Pacific Islander 1
Other 83
2 or More Races 395
Hispanic 266
Area (square miles) 410.9
Urban Land Cover (latest figures 1994) 1.3%
Population Per Square Mile......................... 98.6
Elevation 1,026
Average Temperature 53.8
Average Precipitation .... 44.37 in.

Civilian Labor Force 25,800
    Trade 3,960
    Construction 375
    Manufacturing 4,836
    Transportation & Utilities 8,687
    Government 3,024
    Services 3,257
    Finance, Insurance & Real Estate 935
Per Capita Income $25,949
Persons Below Poverty, 1997 .... 9.0%
Retail Sales per Capita, 1997 .... $11,013
Housing Units, 2000 16,577
Average Family Size 3.03
Number of Farms 860
Average Size of Farms (acres) 260
Average Commodity Cash Receipts per Farm $57,315
Highway Miles
    Interstate 15
    U.S. Routes 49
    State Routes 142
Registered Motor Vehicles 47,267
Automobile Crashes per 1,000 .... 38.75

Number Registered Voters 24,023
    Percent Democrat 5.7%
    Percent Republican 18.7%
    Non Partisan 75.6%
    Number Voted 2000 Election 15,366
    Percent Voted 2000 Election 64%
Voting, 2000 Election
    for Bush 9,824

for Gore 4,791
for Nader 325
for Buchanan 50
Contributions to Federal Candidates, Parties, & PACs, '01-'02
   to Democrats $5,222
   to Republicans $14,690

Columbiana

Namesake Combination of Columbus and Anna

Established May 1, 1803

County Seat Lisbon

Largest Places	2000	1990
East Liverpool city	13,089	13,654
Salem city	12,197	12,233
St. Clair township	7,961	7,705
Columbiana village	5,273	4,948
East Palestine city	4,917	5,168
Perry township	4,852	4,982
Knox township	4,828	4,449
Elkrun township	4,781	2,186
Liverpool township	4,374	4,746
Fairfield township	4,215	3,929

Columbiana County is located in the northeast portion of the state bordering on Pennsylvania. At the southeast corner of the county the Ohio River provides the border separating Ohio from West Virginia. Attractions in Columbiana County include Beaver Creek and Guilford Lake State Parks; Log House Museum in Columbiana; Salem Museum of Historic Interest & Memorabilia; Plymouth Street Historic Area in Hanoverton; Museum of Ceramics in East Liverpool; Old Stone House Museum in Lisbon; Scenic Vista Park; Harvey S. Firestone Park; Sandy and Beaver Canal; Cherry Valley Arboretum; Morgan's Monument; six covered bridges; and the Ohio River.

Vital Statistics

Population, 1995 111,853
Population, 2000 112,075
Net Change, 1990-2000 .... 3.5%
Median Age 38.5
White 108,071
Black 2,468
Native American 203
Asian 262
Pacific Islander 19
Other 167
2 or More Races 885
Hispanic 1,309
Area (square miles) 532.5
Urban Land Cover (latest figures 1994) 1%
Population Per Square Mile 210.7
Elevation 1,193
Average Temperature 52.5
Average Precipitation .... 37.46 in.

Civilian Labor Force 51,700
   Trade 8,045
   Construction 1,487
   Manufacturing 9,213
   Transportation & Utilities 1,745
   Mining 203
   Government 4,622
   Services 7,680
   Finance, Insurance & Real Estate 1,108
   Agriculture, Forestry, Fishing 275
Per Capita Income, 1999 .... $21,159
Persons Below Poverty, 1997 .... 13.3%
Retail Sales per Capita, 1997 .... $7,395
Housing Units, 2000 46,083
Average Family Size 3.00
Number of Farms 1,200
Average Size of Farms (acres) 130
Average Commodity Cash Receipts per Farm $41,188
Highway Miles
   Interstate 0
   U.S. Routes 50
   State Routes 252
Registered Motor Vehicles 118,411
Automobile Crashes per 1,000 .... 24.7

Number Registered Voters 74,297
   Percent Democrat 17.2%
   Percent Republican 13.1%
   Non Partisan 69.7%
   Number Voted 2000 Election 45,294
   Percent Voted 2000 Election 61%
Voting, 2000 Election
   for Bush 21,804
   for Gore 20,657
   for Nader 1,217
   for Buchanan 557
Contributions to Federal Candidates, Parties, & PACs, '01-'02
   to Democrats $2,940
   to Republicans $122,020

Coshocton

Namesake The Delaware Indian word for "Black Bear Town"

Established January 31, 1810

County Seat Coshocton

Largest Places	2000	1990
Coshocton city	11,682	12,193
West Lafayette village	2,313	2,129
Jackson township	2,045	1,947
Lafayette township	1,972	2,011
Tuscarawas township	1,798	2,151
Keene township	1,689	1,583
Crawford township	1,594	1,221
Oxford township	1,560	1,512
Bethlehem township	1,191	1,163
White Eyes township	1,078	981

Coshocton County is located in the east-central portion of the state. The Mohican and Kokosing rivers flow through the northwest part of the county and the Killbuck Creek, the Walhonding River, and the Tuscarawas River all flow into the Muskingum River at Coshocton County. Roscoe Village, now a part of Coshocton City, was once a busy port on the Ohio and Erie Canal system. The 25 brick and frame buildings, as well as a portion of the canal, have been restored, and boat rides are offered on the Monticello III canal boat. Other attractions in Coshocton County include Old Stone Fort near West Lafayette; Woodbury Wildlife Area; Johnson-Humrick

Coshocton

The name comes from three different words: one, *Goshachgunk*, which means *where the river is crossing*; two, *Koshocktoon*, which means *river crossing device* or *ferry*; and, three, *Cush-og-wenk*, which means *place of the black bear*. Put them all together, they spell *mother* or *Coshocton* or *Goshachgunkkoshock-tooncushogwenk*.

—*Dick Perry*

House Museum; Pomerene Fine Arts Center; Helmick Covered Bridge; and the 900-acre Wills Creek Lakenear Roscoe Village.

___

Vital Statistics
Population, 1995 36,244
Population, 2000 36,655
Net Change, 1990-2000 .... 3.5%
Median Age 37.8
White 35,685
Black 399
Native American 62
Asian 118
Pacific Islander 10
Other 72
2 or More Races 309
Hispanic 216
Area (square miles) 564.1
Urban Land Cover (latest figures 1994) 0.6%
Population Per Square Mile 65
Elevation 976
Average Temperature 54.3
Average Precipitation .... 38.94 in

Civilian Labor Force 17,500
    Trade 2,453
    Construction 332
    Manufacturing 4,390
    Transportation & Utilities 988
    Mining 108
    Government 1,656
    Services 3,571
    Finance, Insurance & Real Estate 272
    Agriculture, Forestry, Fishing 164
Per Capita Income, 1999 .... $21,130
Persons Below Poverty, 1997 .... 11.5%
Retail Sales per Capita, 1997 .... $5,803
Housing Units, 2000 16,107
Average Family Size 3.01
Number of Farms 950
Average Size of Farms (acres) 178
Average Commodity Cash Receipts per Farm $38,480
Highway Miles
    Interstate 0
    U.S. Routes 34
    State Routes 180
Registered Motor Vehicles 39,773
Automobile Crashes per 1,000 .... 41.69

Number Registered Voters 21,066
    Percent Democrat 14.1%
    Percent Republican 16.6%
    Non Partisan 69.1%
    Number Voted 2000 Election 14,493
    Percent Voted 2000 Election 68.8%
Voting, 2000 Election
    for Bush 8,243
    for Gore 5,594
    for Nader 295
    for Buchanan 73
Contributions to Federal Candidates, Parties, & PACs, '01-'02
    to Democrats $1,400
    to Republicans $10,460

Crawford

Namesake Colonel William Crawford, Revolutionary War Hero burned at the stake by local Indians

Established April 1, 1820

County Seat Bucyrus

Largest Places	2000	1990
Bucyrus city	13,224	13,496
Galion city	11,341	11,859
Crestline village	5,085	4,925
Polk township	2,334	2,321
Whetstone township	2,218	2,166
Jefferson township	1,613	1,598
Liberty township	1,489	1,470
Holmes township	1,330	1,397
New Washington village	987	1,057
Bucyrus township	828	1,105

Crawford County is located in the north-central portion of the state. Situated on "The Great Divide," it contains headwaters of four rivers. The Sandusky River and the Huron River flow north toward Lake Erie, and the Scioto River and the Olentangy River flow south toward the Ohio River. Attractions in Crawford County include Unger Park; Lowe-Volk Park; Sears Woods State Nature Preserve; Crestline Shunk Museum; Brownella Cottage in Galion; Scroggs House-Bucyrus Historical Society; Colonel Crawford Monument; and an annual Bratwurst Festival in August.

___

Vital Statistics
Population, 1995 47,733
Population, 2000 46,966
Net Change, 1990-2000 .... -1.9%
Median Age 38.2
White 46,022
Black 279
Native American 93
Asian 145
Pacific Islander 9
Other 113
2 or More Races 305
Hispanic 361
Area (square miles) 402.3
Urban Land Cover (latest figures 1994) 1.2%
Population Per Square Mile 116.8
Elevation 1,000
Average Temperature 52.5
Average Precipitation .... 41.5 in.

Civilian Labor Force 21,500
    Trade 3,512
    Construction 552
    Manufacturing 6,821
    Transportation & Utilities 273
    Government 2,115
    Services 3,156
    Finance, Insurance & Real Estate 690
Per Capita Income, 1999 .... $21,924
Persons Below Poverty, 1997 .... 10.1%
Retail Sales per Capita, 1997 .... $5,333

Housing Units, 2000 20,178
Average Family Size 2.94
Number of Farms 780
Average Size of Farms (acres) 291
Average Commodity Cash Receipts per Farm $79,544
Highway Miles
    Interstate 0
    U.S. Routes 21
    State Routes 178
Registered Motor Vehicles 52,683
Automobile Crashes per 1,000 .... 27.19

Number Registered Voters 31,344
    Percent Democrat 11.6%
    Percent Republican 14.5%
    Non Partisan 73.9%
    Number Voted 2000 Election 19,622
    Percent Voted 2000 Election 62.6%
Voting, 2000 Election
    for Bush 11,666
    for Gore 6,721
    for Nader 536
    for Buchanan 161
Contributions to Federal Candidates, Parties, & PACs, '01-'02
    to Democrats $1,250
    to Republicans $9,650

Cuyahoga

Namesake Cuyahoga River, from the Indian word meaning "crooked"

Established June 7, 1807

County Seat Cleveland

Largest Places	2000	1990
Cleveland city	477,459	505,616
Parma city	85,655	87,876
Lakewood city	56,646	59,718
Euclid city	52,717	54,875
Cleveland Heights city	50,769	54,052
Strongville city	43,858	35,308
North Olmsted ctiy	34,113	34,204
Westlake city	31,719	27,018
Garefield Heights city	30,734	31,739
Shaker Heights city	29,405	30,831

Cuyahoga County is located in the northeast portion of the state, and is the largest in population of Ohio's 88 counties. The Cuyahoga and Rocky rivers flow through the county. Cuyahoga County borders on Lake Erie and has many lakefront recreation and resort areas. The Port of Cleveland provides access to Great Lakes shipping and to world ports through the St. Lawrence Seaway. Attractions in Cuyahoga County include Cleveland Natural History Museum; Cleveland Museum of Art; Rock and Roll Hall of Fame; Cuyahoga Valley National Recreation Area; and professional teams—Cleveland Indians Baseball; Browns Football; Cavaliers Basketball; and Lumberjacks Hockey.

Vital Statistics
Population, 1995 1,398,169
Population, 2000 1,393,978
Net Change, 1990-2000 .... -1.3%
Median Age 37.3
White 938,863
Black 382,634
Native American 2,529
Asian 25,245
Pacific Islander 338
Other 20,962
2 or More Races 23,407
Hispanic 47,078
Area (square miles) 458
Urban Land Cover (latest figures 1994) 35%
Population Per Square Mile 3,043.6
Elevation 777
Average Temperature 53.5
Average Precipitation .... 56.2 in.

Civilian Labor Force 680,600
Employment by Industry, 2000
    Trade... 191,470
    Construction 28,871
    Manufacturing 129,765
    Transportation & Utilities 34,932
    Mining 343
    Government 84,397
    Services 261,703
    Finance, Insurance & Real Estate 68,549
    Agriculture, Forestry, Fishing 3,710
Per Capita Income, 1999 .... $32,241
Persons Below Poverty, 1997 .... 13.6%
Retail Sales per Capita, 1997 .... $9,116
Housing Units, 2000 616,903
Average Family Size 3.06
Number of Farms 180
Average Size of Farms (acres) 33
Average Commodity Cash Receipts per Farm $84,052
Highway Miles
    Interstate 113
    U.S. Routes 107
    State Routes 232
Registered Motor Vehicles 1,105,532
Automobile Crashes per 1,000 .... 27.38

Number Registered Voters 1,010,726
    Percent Democrat 18.1%
    Percent Republican 5.8%
    Non Partisan 76.2%
    Number Voted 2000 Election 590,473
    Percent Voted 2000 Election 58.1%
Voting, 2000 Election
    for Bush 192,099
    for Gore 359,913
    for Nader 16,956
    for Buchanan 3,040
Contributions to Federal Candidates, Parties, & PACs, '01-'02
    to Democrats $1,102,349
    to Republicans $1,922,718

Darke

In 1795, "Mad" Anthony Wayne negotiated the Treaty of Greenville, opening Ohio to white settlers. In the woods nearby, young Phoebe Ann Moses fired muzzleloaders and grew up to become shooting star Annie Oakley. She is buried in Brock cemetery, but Greenville's Garst Museum keeps her legend alive with the world's largest collection of Oakley memorabilia.

Darke

Namesake Revolutionary War hero General William Darke

Established January 3, 1809

County Seat Greenville

Largest Places	2000	1990
Greenville city	13,294	12,863
Greenvile township	4,831	4,439
Versailles village	2,589	2,351
Adams township	2,125	2,044
Arcanum village	2,076	1,953
Union City village	1,767	1,984
Wayne township	1,760	1,576
Twin township	1,578	1,621
Van Buren township	1,573	1,652
Washington township	1,382	1,311

Darke County is located on the Indiana border in the west-central portion of the state. The Wabash, Stillwater, and Mississinewa rivers flow through Darke County. With more than 85.5 percent of the land in farms, Darke County ranks first in the state in corn and soybean production, and second in raising hogs. Greenville is the site where the Treaty of Greenville was signed by General Anthony Wayne and the chiefs of 13 allied Indian tribes,  bringing peace to the area. Darke County is the birthplace of markswoman Annie Oakley and writer-commentator Lowell Thomas. Memorabilia from both may be found at the Garst Museum in Greenville.

Vital Statistics

Population, 1995	54,318
Population, 2000	53,309
Net Change, 1990-2000	-0.6%
Median Age	37.4
White	52,290
Black	208
Native American	89
Asian	132
Pacific Islander	12
Other	182
2 or More Races	396
Hispanic	457
Area (square miles)	600
Urban Land Cover (latest figures 1994)	1.3%
Population Per Square Mile	88.8
Elevation	1,050
Average Temperature	53.3
Average Precipitation	38.51 in.
Civilian Labor Force	29,400
Trade	4,134
Construction	1,290
Manufacturing	5,285
Transportation & Utilities	818
Government	2,140
Services	3,957
Finance, Insurance & Real Estate	709
Per Capita Income, 1999	$23,678
Persons Below Poverty, 1997	7.4%
Retail Sales per Capita, 1997	$7,103
Housing Units, 2000	21,583

Average Family Size	3.03
Number of Farms	2,010
Average Size of Farms (acres)	173
Average Commodity Cash Receipts per Farm	$110,695
Highway Miles	
Interstate	0
U.S. Routes	50
State Routes	213
Registered Motor Vehicles	66,031
Automobile Crashes per 1,000	26.69
Number Registered Voters	36,088
Percent Democrat	10.1%
Percent Republican	14.4%
Non Partisan	75.5%
Number Voted 2000 Election	23,784
Percent Voted 2000 Election	65.9%
Voting, 2000 Election	
for Bush	14,817
for Gore	7,741
for Nader	452
for Buchanan	119
Contributions to Federal Candidates, Parties, & PACs, '01-'02	
to Democrats	$23,000
to Republicans	$35,781

Defiance

Namesake Named for nearby Fort Defiance

Established April 7, 1845

County Seat Defiance

Largest Places	2000	1990
Defiance city	16,465	16,768
Hicksville village	3,649	3,664
Highland township	2,658	2,612
Noble township	2,274	2,006
Richland township	1,974	2,179
Defiance township	1,860	1,830
Tiffin township	1,705	1,772
Hicksville township	1,354	1,259
Delaware township	1,327	1,197
Washington township	1,157	1,206

Defiance County is located on the Indiana border in the northwest portion of the state. The Auglaize, Maumee, Tiffin and St. Joseph rivers flow through Defiance County. Fort Defiance, constructed in the Maumee River Valley in 1794 by General Anthony Wayne, is said to  have been so strong as to "defy the English, the Indians, and all the devils in Hell to take it." Wayne defeated the Indians at the Battle of Fallen Timbers, and in 1796 the Fort was abandoned. Attractions in Defiance County include Independence Dam State Park; Hicks Land Office; AuGlaize Village and Farm Museum; Fort Defiance Park; Defiance College; and Oxbow Lake State Wildlife Area.

Vital Statistics

Population, 1995	40.115
Population, 2000	39,500
Net Change, 1990-2000	0.4%
Median Age	36.5

White 36,575
Black 692
Native American 102
Asian 142
Pacific Islander 9
Other 1,417
2 or More Races 563
Hispanic 2,857
Area (square miles) 411
Urban Land Cover (latest figures 1994) 1%
Population Per Square Mile.................................... 96.1
Elevation 716
Average Temperature 53.5
Average Precipitation .... 36.51 in.

Civilian Labor Force 21,200
    Trade 4,794
    Construction.. 711
    Manufacturing... 6,678
    Transportation & Utilities 484
    Government 1,973
    Services 3,236
    Finance, Insurance & Real Estate 552
    Agriculture, Forestry, Fishing 65
Per Capita Income, 1999 .... $24,793
Persons Below Poverty, 1997 .... 7.1%
Retail Sales Per Capita, 1997 .... $10,617
Housing Units, 2000 16,040
Average Family Size 3.02
Number of Farms 940
Average Size of Farms (acres) 218
Average Commodity Cash Receipts per Farm $45,704
Highway Miles
    Interstate 0
    U.S. Routes 32
    State Routes 132
Registered Motor Vehicles 44,187
Automobile Crashes per 1,000 .... 43.37

Number Registered Voters 25,783
    Percent Democrat 13.5%
    Percent Republican 20.8%
    Non Partisan 75.5%
    Number Voted 2000 Election 16,610
    Percent Voted 2000 Election 64.4%
Voting, 2000 Election
    for Bush 9,540
    for Gore 6,175
    for Nader 365
    for Buchanan 99
Contributions to Federal Candidates, Parties, & PACs, '01-'02
    to Democrats $1,250
    to Republicans $13,666

Delaware

Namesake Named for Delaware Indians

Established April 1, 1807

County Seat Delaware

Largest Places	2000	1990
Delaware city	25,243	20,030
Orange township	12,464	3,789
Genoa township	11,293	4,053
Liberty township	9,182	3,790
Powell village	6,247	2,154
Westerville city (part)	5,900	1,177
Dublin city (part)	4,283	3,811
Concord township	4,088	3,363
Harlem township	3,762	3,391
Berlin township	3,313	1,978

Delaware County is located in the center of the state, and the Scioto and Olentangy rivers flow through the county. Delaware is the fastest growing county in the state. It has increased in population by 64.3 percent since the 1990 census. Before settlers arrived, Delaware and Wyandotte Indians occupied the land. Olentangy Indian Caverns served as a meeting site for both tribes. Other attractions in Delaware County include Delaware and Alum Creek State Parks; Ohio Wesleyan University; President Rutherford B. Hayes Birthplace; the Perkins Observatory; Columbus Zoo and Wyandot Lake; Jack Nicklaus Memorial Golf Tournament; and the annual Little Brown Jug Harness Races.

Vital Statistics
Population, 1994 78,958
Population, 2000 109,989
Net Change, 1990-2000 .... 64.3%
Median Age 35.3
White 103,663
Black 2,774
Native American 157
Asian 1,690
Pacific Islander 38
Other 416
2 or More Races 1,251
Hispanic 1,109
Area (square miles) 442
Urban Land Cover (latest figures 1994) 2%
Population Per Square Mile....................................... 248.8
Elevation 871
Average Temperature 54
Average Precipitation .... 32.86 in.

Civilian Labor Force 59,400
    Trade 10,259
    Construction... 2,446
    Manufacturing... 4,901
    Transportation & Utilities 553
    Mining 120
    Government 4,618
    Services 8,831
    Finance, Insurance & Real Estate 3,027
    Agriculture, Forestry, Fishing 543
Per Capita Income, 1999 .... $35,042
Persons Below Poverty, 1997 .... 4.5%
Retail Sales per Capita, 1997 .... $8,578
Housing Units, 2000 42,374
Average Family Size 3.09
Number of Farms 770
Average Size of Farms (acres) 227
Average Commodity Cash Receipts per Farm $62,311
Highway Miles
    Interstate 17
    U.S. Routes 68
    State Routes 125
Registered Motor Vehicles 93,557
Automobile Crashes per 1,000 .... 30.82

Number Registered Voters 80,132
    Percent Democrat 6.1%
    Percent Republican 18.9%

Non Partisan		75.0%
Number Voted 2000 Election		55,959
Percent Voted 2000 Election		69.8%

Voting, 2000 Election
for Bush		36,639
for Gore		17,134
for Nader		1,212
for Buchanan		162

Contributions to Federal Candidates, Parties, & PACs, '01-'02
to Democrats		$94,889
to Republicans		$217,728

Erie

Namesake the Erie Indians, whose name means "cat"

Established March 16, 1838

County Seat Sandusky

Largest Places	2000	1990
Sandusky city	27,844	29,764
Perkins township	12,578	10,793
Huron city	7,958	7,030
Vermillion city	4,937	5,483
Margaretta township	4,662	4,601
Vermillion township	4,638	4,051
Berlin township	3,017	2,628
Milan township	2,661	2,093
Huron township	2,572	2,267
Florence township	2,500	2,101

Erie County is located in the north-central portion of the state. The Huron and Vermillion rivers flow through Erie County. The Lake Erie ports of Huron and Sandusky gain access to Great Lakes shipping and world ports through the St. Lawrence Seaway. Its location on Lake Erie makes it a prime tourist area. One of the nation's largest amusement parks, Cedar  Point, provides a unique recreational area with beaches, boating, fishing, and cruises to Lake Erie Islands. Other attractions include Thomas A. Edison Birthplace; Great Lakes Historical Museum; Glacial Grooves and Inscription Rock at Kelleys Island State Park; the Merry-Go-Round Museum; and the Follett House Museum.

Population, 1995	78,805
Population, 2000	79,551
Net Change, 1990-2000	3.6%
Median Age	39.5
White	70,514
Black	6,876
Native American	164
Asian	298
Pacific Islander	4
Other	420
2 or More Races	1,275
Hispanic	1,664
Area (square miles)	255
Urban Land Cover (latest figures 1994)	6%
Population Per Square Mile	312
Elevation	264
Average Temperature	53.9
Average Precipitation	34.88 in.

Civilian Labor Force	42,500
Trade	9,530
Construction	1,533
Manufacturing	10,166
Transportation & Utilities	1,318
Mining	195
Government	5,204
Services	10,764
Finance, Insurance & Real Estate	902
Agriculture, Forestry, Fishing	515
Per Capita Income, 1999	$28,210
Persons Below Poverty, 1997	9.3%
Retail Sales per Capita, 1997	$9,313
Housing Units, 2000	35,909
Average Family Size	2.97
Number of Farms	400
Average Size of Farms (acres)	225
Average Commodity Cash Receipts per Farm	$78,299

Highway Miles
Interstate	26
U.S. Routes	42
State Routes	114
Registered Motor Vehicles	90,347
Automobile Crashes per 1,000	39.97

Number Registered Voters	55,777
Percent Democrat	13.0%
Percent Republican	10.2%
Non Partisan	76.8%
Number Voted 2000 Election	35,836
Percent Voted 2000 Election	64.2%

Voting, 2000 Election
for Bush	16,105
for Gore	17,732
for Nader	872
for Buchanan	205

Contributions to Federal Candidates, Parties, & PACs, '01-'02
to Democrats	$28,525
to Republicans	$43,546

Fairfield

Namesake Named for the beauty of its fair fields

Established December 9, 1800

County Seat Lancaster

Largest Places	2000	1990
Lancaster city	35,335	34,507
Violet township	16,893	12,968
Pickerington city	9,737	5,645
Columbus city	7,447	640
Bloom township	5,765	5,225
Pleasant township	5,039	5,060
Hocking township	4,812	4,331
Walnut township	4,545	4,270
Berne township	4,521	4,225
Greenfield township	4,456	4,023

Fairfield County is located in the central portion of the state. The Hocking River flows through the county. Colonel Ebenezer Zane, pioneer, trailblazer, and soldier, opened the area to development when he built the first national road, known as Zane's Trace, through Fairfield County. What first appeared on pioneer maps as "The Great Buffalo Swamp" is now the bed of the reservoir known as Buckeye Lake, a

popular boating and recreational area. Other attractions in Fairfield County include a number of covered bridges, some of which are still active; the Georgian Museum; the William Tecumseh Sherman House; the Wagnalls Memorial Library; and Shallenberger State Nature Preserve.

Vital Statistics

Population, 1995	117,556
Population, 2000	122,759
Net Change, 1990-2000	18.6%
Median Age	36.2
White	116,803
Black	3,274
Native American	244
Asian	890
Pacific Islander	27
Other	282
2 or More Races	1,239
Hispanic	993
Area (square miles)	505
Urban Land Cover (latest figures 1994)	1.6%
Population Per Square Mile	243.1
Elevation	844
Average Temperature	55.3
Average Precipitation	35.13 in.

Civilian Labor Force	67,900
Trade	9,516
Construction	1,834
Manufacturing	6,029
Transportation & Utilities	848
Mining	22
Government	6,942
Services	7,600
Finance, Insurance & Real Estate	1,356
Agriculture, Forestry, Fishing	416
Per Capita Income, 1999	$26,704
Persons Below Poverty, 1997	6.9%
Retail Sales per Capita, 1997	$6,927
Housing Units, 2000	47,922
Average Family Size	3.06
Number of Farms	1,190
Average Size of Farms (acres)	173
Average Commodity Cash Receipts per Farm	$37,598
Highway Miles	
Interstate	2
U.S. Routes	50
State Routes	143
Registered Motor Vehicles	124,870
Automobile Crashes per 1,000	30.65

Number Registered Voters	81,544
Percent Democrat	9.6%
Percent Republican	18.4%
Non Partisan	71.9%
Number Voted 2000 Election	54,913
Percent Voted 2000 Election	67.3%
Voting, 2000 Election	
for Bush	33,523
for Gore	19,065
for Nader	1,115
for Buchanan	168
Contributions to Federal Candidates, Parties, & PACs, '01-'02	
to Democrats	$8,366
to Republicans	$75,195

Fayette

Namesake French Marquis De LaFayette, close adviser to George Washington during the Revolutionary War

Established March 1, 1810

County Seat Washington Court House

Largest Places	2000	1990
Washington Court House city	13,524	12,983
Union township	3,808	3,718
Jefferson township	1,465	1,531
Wayne township	1,367	1,304
Jeffersonville township	1,288	1,281
Concord township	1,068	1,051
Paint township	1,031	942
Madison township	946	1,022
Perry township	945	896
Bloomingburg village	874	769

Fayette County is located in the south-central portion of the state. The Deer Creek, the Paint Creek, and the Rattlesnake Creek run through Fayette County. Fayette County is known internationally as a major horse breeding area and has one of the top standardbred horse breeding farms in the nation. Attractions in Fayette County include the Court House Murals by Archibald Willard and several outdoor murals by Harry Ahysen; Fayette County Historical Museum; Carnegie Public Library; Engine 2776 ("The Iron Horse at Rest") Locomotive in Eyman Park; and Deer Creek State Park and Lodge.

Vital Statistics

Population, 1995	28,431
Population, 2000	28,433
Net Change, 1990-2000	3.5%
Median Age	37.5
White	27,182
Black	589
Native American	44
Asian	130
Pacific Islander	2
Other	157
2 or More Races	329
Hispanic	352
Area (square miles)	407
Urban Land Cover (latest figures 1994)	0.9%
Population Per Square Mile	69.9
Elevation	980
Average Temperature	54.8
Average Precipitation	38.31 in.

Civilian Labor Force	15,100
Trade	3,951
Construction	272
Manufacturing	2,941
Transportation & Utilities	178
Government	1,523
Services	1,519
Finance, Insurance & Real Estate	293
Per Capita Income, 1999	$20,597
Persons Below Poverty, 1997	12.0%
Retail Sales per Capita, 1997	$11,559

Fairfield

The house where William Tecumseh Sherman was born in 1820 still stands in Lancaster. Named for a famed warrior, he is considered the inventor of modern warfare—in 1864, Sherman marched 60,000 Union soldiers on a path of destruction across Georgia, demoralizing the South and ruining its economy. "War," he said afterward, "is hell." No one who had been there ever disagreed.

Housing Units, 2000	11,904
Average Family Size	2.96
Number of Farms	560
Average Size of Farms (acres)	432
Average Commodity Cash Receipts per Farm	$85,630

Highway Miles
Interstate	15
U.S. Routes	69
State Routes	86
Registered Motor Vehicles	30,799
Automobile Crashes per 1,000	37.81

Number Registered Voters ... 14,713
Percent Democrat	7.3%
Percent Republican	25.4%
Non Partisan	67.2%
Number Voted 2000 Election	9,484
Percent Voted 2000 Election	64.5%

Voting, 2000 Election
for Bush	5,685
for Gore	3,363
for Nader	165
for Buchanan	37

Contributions to Federal Candidates, Parties, & PACs, '01-'02
| to Democrats | $400 |
| to Republicans | $6,350 |

Franklin

Namesake Benjamin Franklin

Established April 30, 1803

County Seat Columbus

Largest Places	2000	1990
Columbus city	702,132	632,270
Upper Arlington city	33,686	34,128
Gahanna city	32,636	27,791
Westerville city	29,418	29,092
Dublin city	27,087	12,551
Grove City city	27,075	19,661
Reynoldsburg city	26,388	24,483
Hilliard city	24,230	11,796
Whitehall city	19,201	20,572
Prairie township	17,058	16,834

Franklin County is located in the central portion of the state and is the home of the State Capital. The Olentangy river flows into the Scioto River in downtown Columbus. Attractions in Franklin County include the Ohio Statehouse; the Ohio, Palace, and Southern Theaters; the Center of Science and Industry; Wexner Center for the Arts; Martin Luther King, Jr. Performing and Cultural Arts Complex; German Village; Frank Park Conservatory & Botanical Garden; Ohio Historical Museum and Ohio Village; the James Thurber House; Capital University; The Ohio State University; Otterbein College; Blue Jackets Professional Hockey Team; and the Columbus Crew Professional Soccer Team.

Vital Statistics
| Population, 1995 | 1,011,019 |
| Population, 2000 | 1,068,978 |

Net Change, 1990-2000	11.2%
Median Age	32.5
White	806,851
Black	191,196
Native American	2,899
Asian	32,784
Pacific Islander	466
Other	10,992
2 or More Races	23,790
Hispanic	24,279
Area (square miles)	540
Urban Land Cover (latest figures 1994)	25%
Population Per Square Mile	1,979.6
Elevation	542
Average Temperature	56.4
Average Precipitation	37.57 in.

Civilian Labor Force ... 604,300
Trade	187,487
Construction	30,824
Manufacturing	65,586
Transportation & Utilities	36,161
Government	93,776
Services	207,881
Finance, Insurance & Real Estate	65,071
Agriculture, Forestry, Fishing	5,163
Per Capita Income, 1999	$30,820
Persons Below Poverty, 1997	11.1%
Retail Sales per Capita, 1997	$13,387
Housing Units, 2000	471,016
Average Family Size	3.03
Number of Farms	600
Average Size of Farms (acres)	170
Average Commodity Cash Receipts per Farm	$62,529

Highway Miles
Interstate	117
U.S. Routes	117
State Routes	122
Registered Motor Vehicles	1,072,923
Automobile Crashes per 1,000	36.97

Number Registered Voters ... 681,949
Percent Democrat	9.4%
Percent Republican	12.0%
Non Partisan	78.5%
Number Voted 2000 Election	417,800
Percent Voted 2000 Election	61.3%

Voting, 2000 Election
for Bush	197,862
for Gore	202,018
for Nader	10,702
for Buchanan	1,114

Contributions to Federal Candidates, Parties, & PACs, '01-'02
| to Democrats | $515,444 |
| to Republicans | $3,397,144 |

Fulton

Namesake Robert Fulton, inventor of the steamboat

Established April 1, 1850

County Seat Wauseon

Largest Places	2000	1990
Wauseon city	7,091	6,322
Swan Creek township	6,306	5,802
Archbold village	4,290	3,440
Swanton village	3,283	3,378
Delta village	2,930	2,849

Clinton township	2,189	2,005
German township	2,168	2,037
York township	1,788	1,611
Pike township	1,738	1,542
Fulton township	1,618	1,432

Fulton County is located on the Michigan border in the northwest portion of the state. The Tiffin River flows through Fulton County. Fulton was one of the last counties to be organized in Ohio. It was made up of part of Lucas, Henry, Defiance and Williams Counties, and Michigan. The Michigan State Line was moved north about 7 miles following the "Toledo War," a dispute between the two states over the ownership of Toledo. It was given to Ohio in 1840. The old state line runs through the center of the county. Attractions in Fulton County include Fulton Historical Museum; NYC Depot and Caboose; Harrison Lake State Park; Maumee State Forest; Goll Woods Nature Preserve; Sauder Museum; and a memorial honoring racecar driver, Barney E. Oldfield.

Vital Statistics
Population, 1995	40,846
Population, 2000	42,084
Net Change, 1990-2000	9.3%
Median Age	36.1
White	40,254
Black	103
Native American	110
Asian	175
Pacific Islander	15
Other	973
2 or More Races	454
Hispanic	2,422
Area (square miles)	407
Urban Land Cover (latest figures 1994)	0.9%
Population Per Square Mile	103.4
Elevation	723
Average Temperature	51.7
Average Precipitation	35.89 in.

Civilian Labor Force	23,500
Trade	3,835
Construction	969
Manufacturing	10,143
Transportation & Utilities	274
Government	2,169
Services	3,215
Finance, Insurance & Real Estate	472
Per Capita Income, 1999	$25,191
Persons Below Poverty, 1997	5.6%
Retails Sales per Capita, 1997	$7,104
Housing Units, 2000	16,232
Average Family Size	3.13
Number of Farms	970
Average Size of Farms (acres)	219
Average Commodity Cash Receipts per Farm	$78,252
Highway Miles	
Interstate	0
U.S. Routes	57
State Routes	85
Registered Motor Vehicles	52,502
Automobile Crashes per 1,000	31.82

Number Registered Voters	27,840
Democrat	7.7%
Republican	20.2%
Non Partisan	72.1%
Number Voted 2000 Election	19,161
Percent Voted 2000 Election	68.8%
Voting, 2000 Election	
for Bush	11,546
for Gore	6,805
for Nader	376
for Buchanan	92
Contributions to Federal Candidates, Parties, & PACs, '01-'02	
to Democrats	$1,100
to Republicans	$15,200

Gallia

Namesake Gaul, ancient name for France, given by French settlers

Established April 30, 1803

County Seat Gallipolis

Largest Places	2000	1990
Green township	5,514	5,189
Gallipolis city	4,180	4,831
Springfield township	3,181	3,201
Addison township	2,366	2,422
Clay township	1,877	1,912
Gallipolis township	1,527	1,669
Morgan township	1,341	1,332
Perry township	1,276	1,029
Raccoon township	1,253	1,124
Huntington township	1,187	1,152

Gallia County is located in the southeastern part of the state on the Ohio River and is part of Ohio's Appalachian Region. Gallia County was settled by French immigrants who had invested in Ohio land only to learn upon their arrival that their agent had absconded with all the money. General Rufus Putnam of the Ohio Company sent in a group of woodsmen from Marietta to clear land and build a settlement for the French on the Ohio River. Attractions in Gallia County include Robert C. Byrd Locks and Dam; Wayne National Forest; Elizabeth Evans Bird Sanctuary; Fortification Hill; Our House State Memorial Museum; French Art Colony; Bob Evans Farm; University of Rio Grande; and the Ohio River.

Vital Statistics
Population, 1995	32,582
Population, 2000	31,069
Net Change, 1990-2000	0.4%
Median Age	37.4
White	29,596
Black	839
Native American	134
Asian	110
Pacific Islander	6
Other	46
2 or More Races	344
Hispanic	191
Area (square miles)	469
Urban Land Cover (latest figures 1994)	1.4%

Population Per Square Mile 66.2
Elevation 576
Average Temperature 56.8
Average Precipitation .... 44.11 in.

Civilian Labor Force 15,200
    Trade 3,107
    Construction 335
    Manufacturing 1,140
    Transportation & Utilities 1,273
    Government 1,966
    Services 3,675
    Finance, Insurance & Real Estate 390
Per Capita Income, 1999 .... $19,438
Persons Below Poverty, 1997 .... 18.4%
Retail Sales per Capita, 1997 .... $8,497
Housing Units, 2000 13,498
Average Family Size 2.98
Number of Farms 830
Average Size of Farms (acres) 142
Average Commodity Cash Receipts per Farm $16,092
Highway Miles
    Interstate 0
    U.S. Routes 18
    State Routes 181
Registered Motor Vehicles 37,325
Automobile Crashes per 1,000 .... 39.07

Number of Registered Voters 21,681
    Democrat 10.6%
    Republican 26.4%
    Non Partisan 63.0%
    Number Voted 2000 Election 13,203
    Percent Voted 2000 Election 60.9%
Voting, 2000 Election
    for Bush 7,511
    for Gore 4,872
    for Nader 215
    for Buchanan 97
Contributions to Federal Candidates, Parties, & PACs, '01-'02
    to Democrats $2,950
    to Republicans $4,750

Geauga

Namesake the Indian word meaning "raccoon"

Established March 1, 1806

County Seat Chardon

Largest Places	*2000*	*1990*
Chester township	10,968	11,049
Bainbridge township	10,916	9,694
Munson township	6,450	5,775
Newbury township	5,805	5,611
Russell township	5,529	5,614
Auburn township	5,158	3,298
Chardon village	5,156	4,446
Chardon township	4,763	4,037
Middlefield township	4,418	4,111
Hambden township	4,024	3,311

Geauga County is located in the northeastern portion of the state. The Grand, the Chagrin, and the Cuyahoga rivers flow through the county. Often referred to as the "Sweetest County," Geauga has become famous around the world for its maple products. Ninety percent of all the maple syrup produced in Ohio comes from Geauga County. Attractions in Geauga County include Punderson State Park and Lodge; Six Flags Amusement Park; Geauga Park District; Geauga County Historical Museum, Century Village and Crosswoods Store; Middlefield Historical Society Inn and Depot; Reeves Victorian Home; and the Geauga County Courthouse with its electronic carillon bells.

Vital Statistics

Population, 1995 84,260
Population, 2000 90,895
Net Change, 1990-2000 .... 12.1%
Median Age 38.7
White 88,553
Black 1,110
Native American 69
Asian 385
Pacific Islander 10
Other 123
2 or More Races 645
Hispanic 538
Area (square miles) 404
Urban Land Cover (latest figures 1994) 0.1%
Population Per Square Mile 225
Elevation 408
Average Temperature 50.4
Average Precipitation .... 41.59 in.

Civilian Labor Force 48,200
    Trade 6,772
    Construction 2,168
    Manufacturing 10,628
    Transportation & Utilities 787
    Government 3,637
    Services 7,426
    Finance, Insurance & Real Estate 640
    Agriculture, Forestry, Fishing 1,113
    Mining 170
Per Capita Income, 1999 .... $34,027
Persons Below Poverty, 1997 .... 5.0%
Retail Sales per Capita, 1997 .... $6,456
Housing Units, 2000 32,805
Average Family Size 3.24
Number of Farms 710
Average Size of Farms (acres) 90
Average Commodity Cash Receipts per Farm $25,447
Highway Miles
    Interstate 0
    U.S. Routes 57
    State Routes 138
Registered Motor Vehicles 102,689
Automobile Crashes per 1,000 .... 28.03

Number of Registered Voters 62,518
    Democrat 7.5%
    Republican 12.3%
    Non Partisan 80.1%
    Number Voted 2000 Election 42,963
    Percent Voted 2000 Election 68.7%
Voting, 2000 Election
    for Bush 25,417

for Gore 15,327
for Nader 1,405
for Buchanan 236
Contributions to Federal Candidates, Parties, & PACs, '01-'02
to Democrats $27,475
to Republicans $113,645

Greene

Namesake General Nathaniel Greene, Second in Command to George Washington in the Revolutionary War

Established May 1, 1803

County Seat Xenia

Largest Places	2000	1990
Beavercreek city	37,984	33,626
Fairborn city	32,052	31,600
Xenia city	24,164	24,664
Bath township	8,877	6,979
Bellbrook city	7,009	6,511
Sugarcreek city	6,629	3,400
Xenia city	6,117	7,633
Cedarville city	3,828	3,210
Yellow Springs village	3,761	1,973
Beavercreek township	3,063	1,908

Greene County is located in the southwestern part of the state. The Little Miami River flows through it. At the turn of the 20th century, experiments in flight, including early efforts of the Wright brothers, began in a Greene County prairie that later became the home of the Wright-Patterson Air Force Museum. Attractions in Greene County include John Bryan State Park; Clifton Gorge State Nature Preserve; National African-American Museum and Cultural Center; The Paul Laurence Dunbar House; Bellbrook Historical Museum; *Bluejacket* Outdoor Drama; Antioch University; Wilberforce University; Central State College; Wright State University; Cedarville College; and the Little Miami National Scenic River.

Vital Statistics

Population, 1995 141,161
Population, 2000 147,886
Net Change, 1990-2000 .... 8.2%
Median Age 35.6
White 131,975
Black 9,414
Native American 434
Asian 2,995
Pacific Islander 51
Other 565
2 or More Races 2,452
Hispanic 1,813
Area (square miles) 415
Urban Land Cover (latest figures 1994) 4%
Population Per Square Mile 356.4
Elevation 938
Average Temperature 54.8
Average Precipitation .... 41.76 in.

Civilian Labor Force 72,600
Trade 16,485

Construction 1,799
Manufacturing 4,948
Transportation & Utilities 1,040
Government 8,538
Services 14,760
Finance, Insurance & Real Estate 1,953
Agriculture, Forestry, Fishing 431
Mining 46
Per Capita Income, 1999 .... $27,114
Persons Below Poverty, 1997 .... 7.3%
Retail Sales per Capita, 1997 .... $9,055
Housing Units, 2000 58,224
Average Family Size 3.0
Number of Farms 930
Average Size of Farms (acres) 208
Average Commodity Cash Receipts per Farm $53,987
Highway Miles
Interstate 22
U.S. Routes 82
State Routes 68
Registered Motor Vehicles 143,504
Automobile Crashes per 1,000 .... 29.73

Number of Registered Voters 98,261
Democrat 8.0%
Republican 16.3%
Non Partisan 75.7%
Number Voted 2000 Election 66,524
Percent Voted 2000 Election 67.7%
Voting, 2000 Election
for Bush 37,946
for Gore 25,059
for Nader 1,592
for Buchanan 179
Contributions to Federal Candidates, Parties, & PACs, '01-'02
to Democrats $23,952
to Republicans $220,465

Guernsey

Namesake Isle of Guernsey, homeland of many early settlers

Established March 1, 1810

County Seat Cambridge

Largest Places	2000	1990
Cambridge city	11,520	11,748
Cambridge township	3,985	4,378
Jackson township	2,825	2,863
Byesville village	2,574	2,435
Adams township	2,019	1,877
Valley township	1,939	1,935
Westland township	1,931	1,750
Center township	1,688	1,486
Richland township	1,489	974
Willes township	1,179	959

Guernsey County is located in the east-central part of the state in Ohio's Appalachian Region. Wills Creek flows through the county. Cambridge is the birthplace of Colonel John Glenn, U.S. Senator and American Astronaut. It is also the birthplace of William "Hopalong Cassidy" Boyd. Guernsey County became synonymous with quality glass in the early 1900's. Today, collectors may tour the Cambridge Glass and the Degenhart Glass Museums. Other attractions include Guernsey County Historical Museum; Salt

Fork State Park and Lodge with the largest inland beach in Ohio (2,500 feet); Seneca Lake; and the *Living Word* outdoor drama.

Vital Statistics

Population, 1995	40,246
Population, 2000	40,792
Net Change, 1990-2000	4.5%
Median Age	37.7
White	39,275
Black	623
Native American	125
Asian	122
Pacific Islander	2
Other	91
2 or More Races	554
Hispanic	254
Area (square miles)	522
Urban Land Cover (latest figures 1994)	0.6%
Population Per Square Mile	78.1
Elevation	885
Average Temperature	55.9
Average Precipitation	48.74 in

Civilian Labor Force	19,000
Trade	3,454
Construction	550
Manufacturing	2,745
Transportation & Utilities	420
Government	2,636
Services	3,878
Finance, Insurance & Real Estate	381
Agriculture, Forestry, Fishing	51
Mining	119
Per Capita Income, 1999	$18,641
Persons Below Poverty, 1997	15.4%
Retail Sales per Capita, 1997	$18,771
Housing Units, 2000	18,771
Average Family Size	3.0
Number of Farms	890
Average Size of Farms (acres)	157
Average Commodity Cash Receipts per Farm	$13,818
Highway Miles	
Interstate	52
U.S. Routes	40
State Routes	154
Registered Motor Vehicles	47,455
Automobile Crashes per 1,000	40.06

Number of Registered Voters	24,452
Democrat	16.6%
Republican	19.0%
Non Partisan	64.3%
Number Voted 2000 Election	15,855
Percent Voted 2000 Election	64.8%
Voting, 2000 Election	
for Bush	8,181
for Gore	6,643
for Nader	405
for Buchanan	120
Contributions to Federal Candidates, Parties, & PACs, '01-'02	
to Democrats	$0
to Republicans	$14,425

Hamilton

Namesake Alexander Hamilton, Secretary of the Treasury in 1790

Established January 2, 1790

County Seat Cincinnati

Largest Places	2000	1990
Cincinnati city	331,285	364,040
Colerain township	60,144	56,781
Green township	55,660	52,687
Anderson township	43,857	39,939
Springfield township	37,587	38,509
Delhi township	30,104	30,250
Norwood city	21,675	23,674
Sycamore township	19,675	20,074
Forest Park city	19,463	19,609
Symmes township	14,771	11,769

Hamilton County is in the southwestern corner of the state. The Great Miami, Little Miami, and White Water rivers flow into the Ohio River at its southern border. The Ohio River is a focal point for many activities: boating, dining, sightseeing cruises, and numerous parks. Port of Cincinnati provides access to inland shipping. Other attractions in Hamilton County include the Cincinnati Art Museum, the Taft Museum of Art, and the new Contemporary Art Museum; the Playhouse in the Park; the Cincinnati Symphony; Coney Island Park; Mt. Adams; the Riverbend Music Center; the Fire Museum; the William Howard Taft National Historic Site; the Museum Center at Union Terminal; the Cincinnati Zoo and Botanical Gardens; Cincinnati Bengals football and Cincinnati Reds baseball.

Vital Statistics

Population, 1995	863,908
Population, 2000	845,303
Net Change, 1990-2000	-2.4%
Median Age	35.5
White	616,487
Black	198,061
Native American	1,481
Asian	13,602
Pacific Islander	242
Other	4,301
2 or More Races	11,129
Hispanic	9,514
Area (square miles)	407
Urban Land Cover (latest figures 1994)	34%
Population Per Square Mile	2076.9
Elevation	543
Average Temperature	56.5
Average Precipitation	50.07 in.

Civilian Labor Force	463,300
Trade	136,964
Construction	26,373
Manufacturing	91,104
Transportation & Utilities	27,202
Government	47,021
Services	188,783
Finance, Insurance & Real Estate	39,463

        Agriculture, Forestry, Fishing 3,130
        Mining 264
Per Capita Income, 1999 .... $33,953
Persons Below Poverty, 1997 .... 11.4%
Retail Sales per Capita, 1997 .... $10,932
Housing Units, 2000 373,393
Average Family Size 3.07
Number of Farms 420
Average Size of Farms (acres) 88
Average Commodity Cash Receipts per Farm $35,048
Highway Miles
        Interstate 96
        U.S. Routes 118
        State Routes 84
Registered Motor Vehicles 767,213
Automobile Crashes per 1,000 .... 36.01

Number of Registered Voters 585,985
        Democrat 5.9%
        Republican 10.0%
        Non Partisan 84.1%
        Number Voted 2000 Election 384,336
        Percent Voted 2000 Election 65.6%
Voting, 2000 Election
        for Bush 204,175
        for Gore 161,578
        for Nader 9,222
        for Buchanan 1,084
Contributions to Federal Candidates, Parties, & PACs, '01-'02
        to Democrats $1,076,452
        to Republicans $7,500,026

Hancock

Namesake John Hancock, first man to sign the Declaration of Independence

Established April 1, 1820

County Seat Findlay

Largest Places	2000	1990
Findlay city	38,967	35,703
Liberty township	6,469	4,871
Fostoria city	3,054	3,091
Marion township	2,203	2,204
Allen township	1,797	1,643
McComb village	1,676	1,544
Arlington village	1,351	1,267
Eagle township	1,195	1,106
Orange township	1,113	1,030
Cass township	1,098	1,023

Hancock County is located in the northwest portion of the state. Several branches of the Portage River and the Blanchard River flow through the county. Once a part of the Great Black Swamp, rich farmland now occupies 81.5 percent of the county. Hancock ranks sixth among Ohio's 88 counties in the production of soybeans and wheat. Attractions in Hancock County include Van Buren State Park; the Karg Well monument; Findlay College; Tell Taylor Memorial; Hancock County Historical Museum; the Black Heritage Library; Indian Trial Caverns; Findlay Reservoir; and Ghost Town Museum Park.

Vital Statistics
Population, 1995 68,239
Population, 2000 71,295
Net Change, 1990-2000 .... 8.8%
Median Age 36.0
White 67,832
Black 789
Native American 128
Asian 867
Pacific Islander 11
Other 868
2 or More Races 800
Hispanic 2,187
Area (square miles) 531
Urban Land Cover (latest figures 1994) 1.4%
Population Per Square Mile 134.8
Elevation 847
Average Temperature 53.5
Average Precipitation .... 39.27 in.

Civilian Labor Force 43,100
        Trade 10,632
        Construction 1,456
        Manufacturing 13,711
        Transportation & Utilities 1,631
        Government 3,153
        Services 8,121
        Finance, Insurance & Real Estate 1,152
        Agriculture, Forestry, Fishing 244
        Mining 1,672
Per Capita Income, 1999 .... $28,091
Persons Below Poverty, 1997 .... 7.3%
Retail Sales per Capita, 1997 .... $11,196
Housing Units, 2000 29,785
Average Family Size 3.01
Number of Farms 1,150
Average Size of Farms (acres) 253
Average Commodity Cash Receipts per Farm $58,533
Highway Miles
        Interstate 25
        U.S. Routes 61
        State Routes 157
Registered Motor Vehicles 84,062
Automobile Crashes per 1,000 .... 37.73

Number of Registered Voters 46,334
        Democrat 5.9%
        Republican 29.7%
        Non Partisan 64.4%
        Number Voted 2000 Election 30,958
        Percent Voted 2000 Election 66.8%
Voting, 2000 Election
        for Bush 20,985
        for Gore 8,798
        for Nader 592
        for Buchanan 119
Contributions to Federal Candidates, Parties, & PACs, '01-'02
        to Democrats $3,675
        to Republicans $121,851

Hardin

Namesake General John Hardin, Revolutionary War officer killed on a peace mission

Established April 1, 1820

County Seat Kenton

Largest Places	2000	1990
Kenton city	8,336	8,356
Ada village	5,582	5,413
Pleasant township	1,662	1,835
Liberty township	1,567	1,375
Forest village	1,488	1,594
Dudley township	1,257	1,092
Buck township	1,051	1,054
Marion township	1,039	943
Dunkirk village	952	869
McDonald township	914	921

Hardin County is located in the northwest portion of the state. The Great Miami, the Scioto, the Blanchard, and the Ottawa rivers flow through it. Primarily a rural county, 82 percent of the land is in farms. Hardin ranks seventh among Ohio's 88 counties in raising hogs. Attractions in Hardin County include Ohio Northern University; the Hardin County museums; the old order Amish; the Pfeiffer Station General Store; the Mt. Victory antique shops; the Kenton Nationals (the largest coon dog field trial of its kind); the Wilson Sporting Goods Company (the makers of the NFL footballs); and Scioto River canoeing and fishing.

Vital Statistics

Population, 1995	31,558
Population, 2000	31,945
Net Change, 1990-2000	2.7%
Median Age	33.3
White	31,159
Black	224
Native American	81
Asian	138
Pacific Islander	1
Other	72
2 or More Races	270
Hispanic	248
Area (square miles)	470
Urban Land Cover (latest figures 1994)	0.5%
Population Per Square Mile	68.0
Elevation	580
Average Temperature	54.4
Average Precipitation	32.15 in

Civilian Labor Force	15,400
Trade	2,112
Construction	246
Manufacturing	2,664
Transportation & Utilities	140
Government	1,619
Services	1,730
Finance, Insurance & Real Estate	197
Per Capita Income, 1999	$19,950
Persons Below Poverty, 1997	11.5%
Retail Sales per Capita, 1997	$5,072

Housing Units, 2000	12,907
Average Family Size	3.03
Number of Farms	980
Average Size of Farms (acres)	267
Average Commodity Cash Receipts per Farm	$96,309
Highway Miles	
Interstate	0
U.S. Routes	22
State Routes	154
Registered Motor Vehicles	34,652
Automobile Crashes per 1,000	25.36

Number of Registered Voters	19,716
Democrat	10.1%
Republican	19.3%
Non Partisan	70.5%
Number Voted 2000 Election	12,159
Percent Voted 2000 Election	61.7%
Voting, 2000 Election	
for Bush	7,124
for Gore	4,557
for Nader	243
for Buchanan	57
Contributions to Federal Candidates, Parties, & PACs, '01-'02	
to Democrats	$2,500
to Republicans	$10,347

Harrison

Namesake William Henry Harrison

Established February 1, 1813

County Seat Cadiz

Largest Places	2000	1990
Cadiz village	3,308	3,439
Hopedale village	984	685
Green township	914	1,038
North township	853	966
Monroe township	827	828
Scio village	799	856
Rumley village	791	752
Jewett village	784	778
German township	767	695
Short Creek township	614	699

Harrison County is located in the east-central portion of the state. Situated on the Allegheny Plateau, Harrison County has abundant mineral wealth lying beneath its surface—coal, limestone, and sandstone, as well as petroleum and gas. Harrison County is also a noted agricultural area and ranks second among Ohio's 88 counties in sheep raising. Attractions in Harrison County include the Tappan-Moravian Scenic Trail; hiking in Harrison State Forest and Tappan Lake Park; Tappan, Clendening, and Piedmont Lakes (4,200 acres of water in the county); Puskarich Public Library and Coal Museum; the Franklin Museum; the Ourant Schoolhouse; the Coffee Cake Winery; 20,000 acres of public hunting land; and monuments to General George Armstrong Custer and screen actor Clark Gable.

Vital Statistics

Population, 1995 16,100
Population, 2000 15,856
Net Change, 1990-2000 .... -1.4%
Median Age 41.1
White 15,300
Black 348
Native American 13
Asian 17
Pacific Islander 1
Other 14
2 or More Races 163
Hispanic 59
Area (square miles) 404
Urban Land Cover (latest figures 1994) 0.2%
Population Per Square Mile 39.2
Elevation 1,280
Average Temperature 53.8
Average Precipitation .... 44.02 in.

Civilian Labor Force 6,800
   Trade 739
   Construction 74
   Manufacturing 711
   Transportation & Utilities 124
   Government 869
   Services 697
   Finance, Insurance & Real Estate 243
   Agriculture, Forestry, Fishing 58
   Mining 216
Per Capita Income, 1999 .... $23,833
Persons Below Poverty, 1997 .... 14.6%
Retail Sales per Capita, 1997 .... $3,421
Housing Units, 2000 7,680
Average Family Size 2.92
Number of Farms 480
Average Size of Farms (acres) 246
Average Commodity Cash Receipts per Farm $19,793
Highway Miles
   Interstate 0
   U.S. Routes 55
   State Routes 110
Registered Motor Vehicles 19,997
Automobile Crashes per 1,000 .... 32.29

Number of Registered Voters 11,052
   Democrat 26.6%
   Republican 14.0%
   Non Partisan 59.4%
   Number Voted 2000 Election 7,380
   Percent Voted 2000 Election 66.8%
Voting, 2000 Election
   for Bush 3,417
   for Gore 3,351
   for Nader 192
   for Buchanan 151
Contributions to Federal Candidates, Parties, & PACs, '01-'02
   to Democrats $1,600
   to Republicans $7,600

Henry

Namesake Patrick Henry, Revolutionary War hero

Established April 1, 1820

County Seat Napoleon

Largest Places	*2000*	*1990*
Napoleon city	9,318	8,884
Washington township	1,913	1,704
Deshler village	1,831	1,876
Napoleon township	1,513	1,721
Liberty township	1,296	1,149
Holgate village	1,194	1,290
Ridgeville township	1,132	1,129
Liberty township	1,109	1,084
Harrison township	1,026	1,001
Damascus township	1,020	1,095

Henry County is located in the northwest portion of the state. The Maumee River flows through it. Once a part of the Great Black Swamp, Henry County is now primarily an agricultural area with 91.6 percent of the land in farms. The county ranks third among Ohio's 88 counties in wheat production. Attractions in Henry County include Miami-Erie Canal; Robert Showman Homestead; Henry County Courthouse; Meyerholtz Wildlife Park; Mary Jane Thurston State Park; Girty Island; Indian Carvings on Turkey Foot Rock; Maumee State Forest; and the Scenic Maumee River.

Vital Statistics

Population, 1995 29,814
Population, 2000 29,210
Net Change, 1990-2000 .... 0.4%
Median Age 36.4
White 27,845
Black 169
Native American 77
Asian 124
Pacific Islander 0
Other 747
2 or More Races 248
Hispanic 1,576
Area (square miles) 417
Urban Land Cover (latest figures 1994) 0.5%
Population Per Square Mile 70
Elevation 687
Average Temperature 51.7
Average Precipitation .... 35.89 in.

Civilian Labor Force 15,800
   Trade 2,006
   Construction 615
   Manufacturing 3,666
   Transportation & Utilities 721
   Government 2,141
   Services 1,937
   Finance, Insurance & Real Estate 291
Per Capita Income, 1999 .... $18,847
Persons Below Poverty, 1997 .... 6.4%
Retail Sales per Capita, 1997 .... $6,408
Housing Units, 2000 11,622
Average Family Size 3.1

Number of Farms		950
Average Size of Farms (acres)		261
Average Commodity Cash Receipts per Farm		$69,665
Highway Miles		
Interstate		0
U.S. Routes		43
State Routes		134
Registered Motor Vehicles		36,156
Automobile Crashes per 1,000		25.54
Number of Registered Voters		19,503
Democrat		8.9%
Republican		26.6%
Non Partisan		64.5%
Number Voted 2000 Election		13,484
Percent Voted 2000 Election		69.1%
Voting, 2000 Election		
for Bush		8,530
for Gore		4,367
for Nader		258
for Buchanan		43
Contributions to Federal Candidates, Parties, & PACs, '01-'02		
to Democrats		$900
to Republicans		$8,950

Highland

Namesake the highlands between the Scioto and Little Miami Rivers

Established May 1, 1805

County Seat Hillsboro

Largest Places	2000	1990
Hillsboro city	6,368	6,235
Greenfield city	4,906	5,172
Paint township	4,112	2,908
Liberty township	3,430	2,949
Madison township	2,016	1,815
New Market township	1,941	1,480
Union township	1,710	1,037
Fairfield township	1,683	1,278
Lynchburg village	1,348	1,212
Leesburg village	1,253	1,063

Highland County is located in the southwestern part of the state. The Little Miami River flows through it. Eliza Jane Thompson successfully attacked the sale of liquor in Hillsboro in 1873, leading to the founding of the Women's Christian Temperance Union (WCTU). A section of the Highland House Museum contains memorabilia of her crusade. Another famous citizen was Milton Caniff, whose *Steve Canyon* cartoon strip was known all over the world. Other attractions in Highland County include Highland House Museum; B&O Depot in Greenfield; Lynchburg Covered Bridge; Rocky Fork and Paint Creek State Parks; Fort Hill State Memorial; Pike State Forest; Fallsville State Wildlife Area; and the Seven Caves.

Vital Statistics

Population, 1995		39,245
Population, 2000		40,875
Net Change, 1990-2000		14.4%

Median Age		36.1
White		39,599
Black		612
Native American		99
Asian		129
Pacific Islander		15
Other		62
2 or More Races		359
Hispanic		216
Area (square miles)		553
Urban Land Cover (latest figures 1994)		0.7%
Population Per Square Mile		73.9
Elevation		1,129
Average Temperature		54.4
Average Precipitation		46.84 in.
Civilian Labor Force		18,600
Trade		2,824
Construction		424
Manufacturing		3,568
Transportation & Utilities		325
Government		2,075
Services		1,615
Finance, Insurance & Real Estate		389
Agriculture, Forestry, Fishing		50
Mining		144
Per Capita Income, 1999		$19,174
Persons Below Poverty, 1997		12.5%
Retail Sales per Capita, 1997		$6,512
Housing Units, 2000		17,583
Average Family Size		3.04
Number of Farms		1,410
Average Size of Farms (acres)		174
Average Commodity Cash Receipts per Farm		$28,531
Highway Miles		
Interstate		0
U.S. Routes		56
State Routes		204
Registered Motor Vehicles		49,789
Automobile Crashes per 1,000		28.65
Number of Registered Voters		24,818
Democrat		7.5%
Republican		20.0%
Non Partisan		72.6%
Number Voted 2000 Election		15,854
Percent Voted 2000 Election		63.9%
Voting, 2000 Election		
for Bush		9,728
for Gore		5,328
for Nader		245
for Buchanan		77
Contributions to Federal Candidates, Parties, & PACs, '01-'02		
to Democrats		$3,245
to Republicans		$12,750

Hocking

Namesake Indian word for "bottle", the shape of the Hocking River

Established March 1, 1818

County Seat Logan

Largest Places	2000	1990
Logan city	6,704	6,725
Falls township	5,010	4,329
Marion township	2,411	1,950
Green township	2,280	2,041

OHIO'S AVERAGE HOURLY WAGE RATE, BY COUNTY

County	2002 Adjusted Hourly Wage Rate	County	2002 Adjusted Hourly Wage Rate
Adams	$12.00	Licking	$13.96
Allen	$14.15	Logan	$15.37
Ashland	$13.25	Lorain	$15.68
Ashtabula	$12.42	Lucas	$15.93
Athens	$13.43	Madison	$14.38
Auglaize	$15.10	Mahoning	$12.86
Belmont	$10.92	Marion	$13.97
Brown	$11.94	Medina	$14.57
Butler	$15.60	Meigs	$13.39
Carroll	$12.16	Mercer	$12.20
Champaign	$18.35	Miami	$14.27
Clark	$14.59	Monroe	$14.03
Clermont	$15.86	Montgomery	$17.08
Clinton	$15.33	Morgan	$14.47
Columbiana	$12.23	Morrow	$11.75
Coshocton	$13.32	Muskingum	$12.40
Crawford	$13.06	Noble	$12.27
Cuyahoga	$18.05	Ottawa	$13.51
Darke	$13.06	Paulding	$12.53
Defiance	$16.55	Perry	$12.17
Delaware	$16.52	Pickaway	$15.13
Erie	$15.04	Pike	$13.92
Fairfield	$12.70	Portage	$14.66
Fayette	$11.87	Preble	$13.25
Franklin	$17.32	Putnam	$12.45
Fulton	$13.68	Richland	$14.22
Gallia	$13.53	Ross	$14.52
Geauga	$14.57	Sandusky	$13.56
Greene	$13.66	Scioto	$11.71
Guernsey	$11.96	Seneca	$12.89
Hamilton	$18.57	Shelby	$16.74
Hancock	$15.67	Stark	$14.12
Hardin	$12.99	Summit	$16.26
Harrison	$11.42	Trumbull	$16.26
Henry	$13.57	Tuscarawas	$12.09
Highland	$11.73	Union	$21.44
Hocking	$11.99	Van Wert	$13.10
Holmes	$11.93	Vinton	$11.07
Huron	$13.77	Warren	$14.21
Jackson	$11.74	Washington	$13.37
Jefferson	$13.21	Wayne	$13.92
Knox	$13.61	Williams	$13.67
Lake	$15.28	Wood	$15.21
Lawrence	$10.94	Wyandot	$12.51

Perry township	2,021	1,620
Starr township	1,477	1,278
Ward township	1,474	1,358
Good Hope township	1,444	1,247
Salt Creek township	1,260	1,172
Laurel township	1,190	968

Hocking County is located in the southeast portion of the state. The Hocking River flows through the county which is best known for its Hocking Hills, which contain thick forests, cascading water falls, deep rocky gorges, and amazing rock formations. Within the Hocking Hills State Park system are Old Man's Cave, Ash Cave, Cedar Falls, Conkle's Hollow, Rock House, and Cantwell Cliffs. Other attractions in Hocking County include Schempp House Museum; Hocking Valley Scenic Railway; Lake Logan State Park; Hocking Canal Locks; Natural Rock Bridge; Saltpeter Caves; and Wayne National Forest.

Vital Statistics

Population, 1995	27,997
Population, 2000	28,241
Net Change, 1990-2000	10.6%
Median Age	37.7
White	27,547
Black	259
Native American	82
Asian	22
Pacific Islander	0
Other	22
2 or More Races	309
Hispanic	124
Area (square miles)	423
Urban Land Cover (latest figures 1994)	1.2%
Population Per Square Mile	66.8
Elevation	740
Average Temperature	54.1
Average Precipitation	38.46 in.

Civilian Labor Force	11,800
Trade	1,457
Construction	370
Manufacturing	1,700
Transportation & Utilities	191
Government	1,600
Services	1,070
Finance, Insurance & Real Estate	174
Agriculture, Forestry, Fishing	22
Mining	91
Per Capita Income	$19,174
Persons Below Poverty, 1997	12.9%
Retail Sales per Capita, 1997	$5,059
Housing Units, 2000	12,141
Average Family Size	2.98
Number of Farms	560
Average Size of Farms (acres)	114
Average Commodity Cash Receipts per Farm	$7,374
Highway Miles	
Interstate	0
U.S. Routes	19
State Routes	149
Registered Motor Vehicles	35,466
Automobile Crashes per 1,000	31.87

Number of Registered Voters	16,881
Democrat	13.6%
Republican	12.4%
Non Partisan	74.0%
Number Voted 2000 Election	11,034
Percent Voted 2000 Election	65.4%
Voting, 2000 Election	
for Bush	5,702
for Gore	4,474
for Nader	291
for Buchanan	217
Contributions to Federal Candidates, Parties, & PACs, '01-'02	
to Democrats	$1,500
to Republicans	$7,482

Holmes

Namesake Major Holmes, killed during the War of 1812

Established January 20, 1824

County Seat Millersburg

Largest Places	2000	1990
Berlin township	3,857	3,457
Salt Creek township	3,778	3,061
Clark township	3,614	2,842
Paint township	3,547	2,825
Walnut Creek township	3,530	3,044
Millersburg village	3,326	3,051
Mechanic township	2,652	2,052
Prairie township	2,399	1,846
Hardy township	2,317	2,210
Ripley township	2,194	1,730

Holmes County is located in the east-central part of the state. The Mohican River flows through the county. Primarily a farming area, 63.4 percent of the land is in farms. Holmes County ranks second in the state in oats and hay production; and in cattle and dairy farming. A group of Amish Mennonites were among the first settlers in the county. Today, their community has grown to one of the largest in the country. Their simple lifestyle, plain clothing, and horse-drawn carriages add a picturesque quality to Holmes County rural life. Attractions in Holmes County include Killbuck Marsh Wildlife Area; Ohio Amish Library; Holmes County Historical Society; and the German Culture Museum.

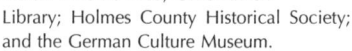

Vital Statistics

Population, 1995	36,160
Population, 2000	38,943
Net Change, 1990-2000	18.6%
Median Age	28.0
White	38,564
Black	127
Native American	22
Asian	24
Pacific Islander	3
Other	49
2 or More Races	154
Hispanic	292
Area (square miles)	423
Urban Land Cover (latest figures 1994)	0.7%

Population Per Square Mile 92.1
Elevation 1,214
Average Temperature 52.2
Average Precipitation .... 36.20 in.

Civilian Labor Force 19,100
   Trade 3,298
   Construction 951
   Manufacturing 6,527
   Transportation & Utilities 427
   Government 1,448
   Services 2,502
   Finance, Insurance & Real Estate 363
   Agriculture, Forestry, Fishing 147
   Mining 286
Per Capita Income, 1999 .... $17,591
Persons Below Poverty, 1997 .... 10%
Retail Sales per Capita, 1997 .... $6,488
Housing Units, 2000 12,280
Average Family Size 3.82
Number of Farms 1,670
Average Size of Farms (acres) 109
Average Commodity Cash Receipts per Farm $58,148
Highway Miles
   Interstate 0
   U.S. Routes 37
   State Routes 137
Registered Motor Vehicles 32,259
Automobile Crashes per 1,000 .... 29.79

Number of Registered Voters 16,766
   Democrat 8.5%
   Republican 19.4%
   Non Partisan 72.1%
   Number Voted 2000 Election 9,937
   Percent Voted 2000 Election 59.3%
Voting, 2000 Election
   for Bush 6,754
   for Gore 2,066
   for Nader 172
   for Buchanan 96
Contributions to Federal Candidates, Parties, & PACs, '01-'02
   to Democrats $1,000
   to Republicans $18,090

Huron

Namesake Huron Indians

Established March 7, 1809

County Seat Norwalk

Largest Places	2001	1990
Norwalk city	16,238	14,731
Willard city	6,806	6,210
Bellevue city	3,841	3,910
Norwalk township	3,265	2,868
New London village	2,696	2,642
New Haven township	2,011	2,120
Bronson township	1,780	1,683
Wakeman township	1,577	1,570
Townsend township	1,567	1,571
Greenwich village	1,525	1,442

Huron County is located in the north-central part of the state. The Huron and Vermillion rivers flow through the county. Huron County is within the Western Reserve Firelands area. After the American Revolution, Connecticut granted the land to settlers whose property was damaged by the British during the war. These people were known as the "fire sufferers," hence the designation, "Firelands." The county is largely agricultural—78 percent—with over 1,000 farms. Attractions in Huron County include antiques and artifacts at the Firelands Museum in Norwalk; historic Lyme Village; the Mad River and NKP Railroad Society Museum; and the Seneca Caverns.

Vital Statistics
Population, 1995 58,613
Population, 2000 59,487
Net Change, 1990-2000 .... 5.8%
Median Age 34.9
White 57,094
Black 575
Native American 106
Asian 150
Pacific Islander 5
Other 971
2 or More Races 586
Hispanic 2,117
Area (square miles) 493
Urban Land Cover (latest figures 1994) 1.6%
Population Per Square Mile 120.7
Elevation 955
Average Temperature 53.2
Average Precipitation .... 39.07 in.

Civilian Labor Force 29,800
   Trade 5,239
   Construction 1,568
   Manufacturing 10,977
   Transportation & Utilities 1,149
   Government 2,791
   Services 4,206
   Finance, Insurance & Real Estate 529
   Agriculture, Forestry, Fishing 789
Per Capita Income, 1999 .... $22,720
Persons Below Poverty, 1997 .... 8.8%
Retail Sales per Capita, 1997 .... $7,422
Housing Units, 2000 23,594
Average Family Size 3.11
Number of Farms 810
Average Size of Farms (acres) 284
Average Commodity Cash Receipts per Farm $85,865
Highway Miles
   Interstate 0
   U.S. Routes 70
   State Routes 158
Registered Motor Vehicles 70,697
Automobile Crashes per 1,000 .... 28.09

Number of Registered Voters 37,533
   Democrat 9.6%
   Republican 10.3%
   Non Partisan 80.1%
   Number Voted 2000 Election 21,788
   Percent Voted 2000 Election 58.1%
Voting, 2000 Election
   for Bush 12,286
   for Gore 8,183
   for Nader 560
   for Buchanan 213
Contributions to Federal Candidates, Parties, & PACs, '01-'02
   to Democrats $3,400
   to Republicans $25,193

Jackson

Namesake Andrew Jackson

Established March 1, 1816

County Seat Jackson

Largest Places	2000	1990
Jackson city	6,184	6,144
Wellston city	6,078	6,049
Lick township	2,682	2,433
Jefferson township	2,573	2,072
Franklin township	1,913	1,407
Scioto township	1,788	1,432
Oak Hill village	1,685	1,831
Liberty township	1,672	1,431
Coal township	1,533	1,272
Madison township	1,421	1,408

Jackson County is located in the southeastern part of the state. The Little Scioto River flows through the county. Some of the earliest settlers in the region came because of the salt licks. In 1796, Congress designated the Scioto Salt Springs in Jackson County as a U.S. salt reservation. Jackson County is known for its large apple growing farms. Every autumn the county holds its Apple Festival to celebrate the year's harvest. Other attractions include Wayne National Forest; Richland Furnace State Forest; Lake Katharine State Nature Reserve; Buckeye Furnace State Memorial; Lake Alma and Jackson Lake State Parks; Leo Petroglyph; and the Governor James A. Rhodes Birthplace.

Vital Statistics

Population, 1995	31,927
Population, 2000	32,641
Net Change, 1990-2000	8.0%
Median Age	36.3
White	31,953
Black	193
Native American	111
Asian	56
Pacific Islander	8
Other	53
2 or More Races	267
Hispanic	197
Area (square miles)	420
Urban Land Cover (latest figures 1994)	1.6%
Population Per Square Mile	77.7
Elevation	715
Average Temperature	54.7
Average Precipitation	49.32 in.

Civilian Labor Force	14,500
Trade	2,575
Construction	374
Manufacturing	3,819
Transportation & Utilities	375
Government	1,415
Services	1,658
Finance, Insurance & Real Estate	369
Per Capita Income, 1999	$18,628
Persons Below Poverty, 1997	16.4%
Retail Sales per Capita, 1997	$7,241

Housing Units, 2000	13,909
Average Family Size	3.0
Number of Farms	520
Average Size of Farms (acres)	169
Average Commodity Cash Receipts per Farm	$35,790
Highway Miles	
Interstate	0
U.S. Routes	27
State Routes	141
Registered Motor Vehicles	38,086
Automobile Crashes per 1,000	47.39

Number of Registered Voters	23,118
Democrat	6.5%
Republican	20.5%
Non Partisan	73.1%
Number Voted 2000 Election	12,918
Percent Voted 2000 Election	55.9%
Voting, 2000 Election	
for Bush	6,958
for Gore	5,131
for Nader	222
for Buchanan	90
Contributions to Federal Candidates, Parties, & PACs, '01-'02	
to Democrats	$741
to Republicans	$13,460

Jefferson

Namesake Thomas Jefferson, President at the time the county was formed

Established July 29, 1797

County Seat Steubenville

Largest Places	2000	1990
Steubenville city	19,015	22,125
Island Creek township	7,513	6,870
Toronto city	5,676	6,127
Cross Creek township	5,643	6,109
Wintersville village	4,067	4,102
Mingo Junction village	3,631	4,297
Wells township	3,128	1,552
Salem township	2,691	3,293
Knox township	2,179	2,402
Warren township	2,044	2,199

Jefferson County is located in the east-central part of the state. The Ohio River provides the eastern border of Jefferson County. The First Federal Land Office was established at Fort Steuben, now Steubenville, for the purpose of opening up the Northwest Territory to settlers. The Fort and Land Office have been reconstructed and are open to visitors. Other attractions in Jefferson County include Mt. Pleasant's historic district and the Mt. Pleasant Historical Society's day-long Pleasant Pastimes historical tour, featuring such sites as the underground railroad stops in the village. There is also the Jefferson Lake State Park; Fernwood State Forest (a 3,000-acre forest restored after strip-mining); Brush Creek Wildlife area (which now encompasses over 4,000 acres); and the Ohio River.

Vital Statistics

Population, 1995 78,262
Population, 2000 73,894
Net Change, 1990-2000 .... -8%
Median Age 41.6
White 68,341
Black 4,200
Native American 147
Asian 247
Pacific Islander 14
Other 187
2 or More Races 758
Hispanic 459
Area (square miles) 410
Urban Land Cover (latest figures 1994) 1.5%
Population Per Square Mile 180.2
Elevation 715
Average Temperature 54.8
Average Precipitation .... 41.71 in.

Civilian Labor Force 29,100
    Trade 6,141
    Construction 1,296
    Manufacturing 4,053
    Transportation & Utilities 1,776
    Government 3,790
    Services 7,346
    Finance, Insurance & Real Estate 741
    Agriculture, Forestry, Fishing 56
    Mining 67
Per Capita Income, 1999 .... $20,720
Persons Below Poverty, 1997 .... 15.5%
Retail Sales per Capita, 1997 .... $6,991
Housing Units, 2000 33,291
Average Family Size 2.88
Number of Farms 520
Average Size of Farms (acres) 156
Average Commodity Cash Receipts per Farm $14,162
Highway Miles
    Interstate 0
    U.S. Routes 19
    State Routes 154
Registered Motor Vehicles 81,495
Automobile Crashes per 1,000 .... 26.17

Number of Registered Voters 55,278
    Democrat 27.8%
    Republican 6.6%
    Non Partisan 65.6%
    Number Voted 2000 Election 35,449
    Percent Voted 2000 Election 64.1%
Voting, 2000 Election
    for Bush 15,038
    for Gore 17,488
    for Nader 897
    for Buchanan 1,048
Contributions to Federal Candidates, Parties, & PACs, '01-'02
    to Democrats $71,418
    to Republicans $38,489

Knox

Namesake Henry Knox, first Secretary of War

Established March 1, 1808

County Seat Mt. Vernon

Largest Places	2000	1990
Mount Vernon city	14,375	14,550
Howard township	4,319	2,149
Clinton township	3,326	3,502
Frederickstown village	2,428	2,443
Monroe township	2,427	2,062
Pleasant township	2,362	1,454
Morris township	1,998	1,801
Gambier village	1,871	2,073
Berlin township	1,789	1,388
Hilliar township	1,648	1,322

Knox County is located in the central portion of the state. The Kokosing and Mohican rivers flow through Knox County. Primarily an agricultural area, more than 60 percent of the land is in farms. Knox County ranks first in the state in sheep farming. Annual cash receipts from marketing of farm commodities averages $60 million. Attractions in Knox County include Kenyon College; Knox Lake; Kokosing Reservoir; Kokosing Gap Trail; Fredericktown Historical Museum; Knox County Historical Society Museum; Old Tool Crib Museum; Pearl Spring Center for American Folksong; Semple-Upham Culture and Arts Center; and the House of Daniel Emmett, composer of *Dixie*.

Vital Statistics

Population, 1995 51,009
Population, 2000 54,500
Net Change, 1990-2000 .... 14.8%
Median Age 36.5
White 53,226
Black 367
Native American 112
Asian 188
Pacific Islander 9
Other 112
2 or More Races 486
Hispanic 371
Area (square miles) 527
Urban Land Cover (latest figures 1994) 0.6%
Population Per Square Mile 103.4
Elevation 965
Average Temperature 53.3
Average Precipitation .... 40.00 in.

Civilian Labor Force 26,000
    Trade 3,799
    Construction 755
    Manufacturing 4,542
    Transportation & Utilities 429
    Government 2,705
    Services 4,372
    Finance, Insurance & Real Estate 533
    Agriculture, Forestry, Fishing 245
    Mining 98
Per Capita Income, 1999 .... $20,850
Persons Below Poverty, 1997 .... 10.1%

Knox

After Lords Kenyon and Gambier bankrolled **Bishop Philander Chase**, *he started Kenyon College in 1824 and the town of Gambier.* **Daniel Decatur Emmett**, *"Father of the Minstrel Show" and the composer of Dixie, was born and died in Mt. Vernon.* **Mary Ann Bickerdyke**, *another native, was the courageous Civil War nurse called "Mother" by thousands of soldiers.*

Retail Sales per Capita, 1997 .... $5,951
Housing Units, 2000 21,793
Average Family Size 3.03
Number of Farms 1,310
Average Size of Farms (acres) 169
Average Commodity Cash Receipts per Farm $42,896
Highway Miles
    Interstate 0
    U.S. Routes 59
    State Routes 140
Registered Motor Vehicles 60,845
Automobile Crashes per 1,000 .... 39.32

Number of Registered Voters 35,140
    Democrat 8.2%
    Republican 19.7%
    Non Partisan 72.1%
    Number Voted 2000 Election 21,488
    Percent Voted 2000 Election 61.1%
Voting, 2000 Election
    for Bush 13,393
    for Gore 7,133
    for Nader 452
    for Buchanan 123
Contributions to Federal Candidates, Parties, & PACs, '01-'02
    to Democrats $5,600
    to Republicans $74,775

Lake

Namesake Lake Erie

Established March 6, 1840

County Seat Painesville

Largest Places	2000	1990
Mentor city	50,278	47,358
Willoughby city	22,621	20,510
Eastlake city	20,255	21,161
Painesville city	17,503	16,699
Madison township	15,494	15,477
Concord township	15,282	12,432
Paineville township	15,037	13,218
Willowwick city	14,361	15,269
Wickliffe city	13,484	14,588
Wiilloughby Hills	8,595	8,427

Lake County is located in the northeast portion of the state. The Chagrin and Grand rivers flow into Lake Erie at Lake County. Its greatest asset is its location on the shores of Lake Erie. Its cultural and recreational attractions include Headlands Beach State Park; Fairport Harbor Beach; Chagrin River Harbor; Hach-Otis State Nature Preserve; Mentor Marsh; and its destination for fishermen, as the county is considered a top-ten national choice for walleye, steelhead trout, and jumbo perch. Other attractions are Lake Erie College Equestrian Center and Morley Farm; the Kirtland Temple; the Newel K. Whitney Store, Museum, and Visitor Center; North Chagrin Reservation and Squire's Castle; Holden Arboretum (one of the largest in the country); the Indian Museum of Lake County; the Fairport Harbor Lighthouse and Marine Museum; and President James A. Garfield's 29-room home, Lawnfield.

Vital Statistics
Population, 1995 223,003
Population, 2000 227,511
Net Change, 1990-2000 .... 5.6%
Median Age 38.6
White 217,041
Black 4,527
Native American 251
Asian 2,048
Pacific Islander 41
Other 1,505
2 or More Races 2,098
Hispanic 3,879
Area (square miles) 228
Urban Land Cover (latest figures 1994) 11%
Population Per Square Mile 997.9
Elevation 676
Average Temperature 54.5
Average Precipitation .... 31.00 in.

Civilian Labor Force 126,900
    Trade 26,370
    Construction 4,843
    Manufacturing 28,519
    Transportation & Utilities 2,905
    Government 11,632
    Services 22,934
    Finance, Insurance & Real Estate 3,012
    Agriculture, Forestry, Fishing 2,160
    Mining 202
Per Capita Income, 1999 .... $29,276
Persons Below Poverty, 1997 .... 5.7%
Retail Sales per Capita, 1997 .... $12,517
Housing Units, 2000 93,487
Average Family Size 3.03
Number of Farms 300
Average Size of Farms (acres) 60
Average Commodity Cash Receipts per Farm $348,433
Highway Miles
    Interstate 31
    U.S. Routes 42
    State Routes 165
Registered Motor Vehicles 237,661
Automobile Crashes per 1,000 .... 29.7

Number of Registered Voters 152,858
    Democrat 12.4%
    Republican 10.4%
    Non Partisan 77.1%
    Number Voted 2000 Election 103,347
    Percent Voted 2000 Election 67.6%
Voting, 2000 Election
    for Bush 51,747
    for Gore 46,497
    for Nader 3,166
    for Buchanan 695
Contributions to Federal Candidates, Parties, & PACs, '01-'02
    to Democrats $11,875
    to Republicans $179,933

*Wellington's **Archibald Willard** painted a national icon, The Spirit of '76. Oberlin's **Charles Martin Hall** discovered how to efficiently extract aluminum and richly endowed Oberlin College, one of the first coed campuses. Lorain's **Ernest King**, deterred from running away to sea at age seven by a batch of cookies, became the U.S. Fleet Admiral during World War II.*

Lawrence

Namesake Captain James Lawrence, Commander of U.S. frigate *Chesapeake* during War of 1812 and famous for his dying words,"Don't give up the ship."

Established December 21, 1815

County Seat Ironton

Largest Places	2000	1990
Ironton city	11,211	12,751
Rome township	8,366	7,233
Union township	7,540	7,301
Fayette township	6,750	6,661
Perry townhip	5,476	5,272
South Point township	3,742	3,823
Upper township	3,170	3,035
Elizabeth township	2,914	2,515
Lawrence township	2,574	2,484
Windsor township	2,127	1,886

Lawrence County, the southernmost county in Ohio, is strategically located on the Ohio River in the heart of the tri-state area of Ohio, Kentucky, and West Virginia. Wayne National Forest covers much of Lawrence County with Lake Vesuvius providing a recreation area. Other attractions include Dean State Park; Hanging Rock; the John Campbell House (a waystation on the Underground Railroad); Lawrence County Museum; Tour of Historic Ironton; Scottown Covered Bridge; Floodwall Murals; Riverfront Amphitheater and Shelter at South Point; Historic Old 75 Tunnel; canoeing on Symmes Creek and boating, fishing, and sightseeing on the Ohio River.

Vital Statistics

Population, 1995	64,206
Population, 2000	62,319
Net Change, 1990-2000	0.8%
Median Age	37.6
White	60,169
Black	1,302
Native American	112
Asian	117
Pacific Islander	4
Other	66
2 or More Races	549
Hispanic	355
Area (square miles)	455
Urban Land Cover (latest figures 1994)	3%
Population Per Square Mile	137.0
Elevation	604
Average Temperature	56.8
Average Precipitation	38.91 in.

Civilian Labor Force	27,000
Trade	3,511
Construction	824
Manufacturing	1,059
Transportation & Utilities	421
Government	3,581
Services	2,613
Finance, Insurance & Real Estate	366
Per Capita Income, 1999	$17,691
Persons Below Poverty, 1997	20.1%

Retail Sales per Capita, 1997	$5,604
Housing Units, 2000	27,189
Average Family Size	2.96
Number of Farms	600
Average Size of Farms (acres)	107
Average Commodity Cash Receipts per Farm	$7,441
Highway Miles	
Interstate	0
U.S. Routes	23
State Routes	167
Registered Motor Vehicles	71,478
Automobile Crashes per 1,000	27.1

Number of Registered Voters	44,032
Democrat	11.2%
Republican	14.8%
Non Partisan	74.0%
Number Voted 2000 Election	25,180
Percent Voted 2000 Election	57.2%
Voting, 2000 Election	
for Bush	12,531
for Gore	11,307
for Nader	402
for Buchanan	124
Contributions to Federal Candidates, Parties, & PACs, '01-'02	
to Democrats	$2,750
to Republicans	$21,115

Licking

Namesake Licking River, from nearby salt licks

Established March 1, 1808

County Seat Newark

Largest Places	2000	1990
Newark city	46,279	44,389
Pataskala city	10,249	3,046
Heath city	8,527	7,231
Harrison township	5,974	4,478
Granville township	5,827	3,466
Reynoldsville city	5,681	1,265
Etna township	5,410	5,484
Licking township	3,870	3,945
Johnston village	3,440	3,237
Union township	3,259	2,668

Licking County is located in the Central part of the state. The Licking River flows through the county. The Ohio Indian Art Museum at Moundbuilders State Park displays some of the artistic achievements of the Moundbuilder Indians who inhabited the region from 10,000 B.C. to 1,600 A.D. Other Moundbuilders' earthworks are located at the Flint Ridge State Memorial and Museum and the Octagon State Memorial. Other attractions in Licking County include Blackhand Gorge; Buckeye Lake; Dawes Arboretum; Granville Historical Museum; National Heisey Glass Museum; Buckeye Central Scenic Railroad; and Denison University.

Vital Statistics

Population, 1995	136,593
Population, 2000	145,491
Net Change, 1990-2000	13.4%

Licking

*Newark, site of the Hopewells' Great Circle and Octagon Earthworks, was the home of **Johnny Clem**, the "Drummer Boy of Shiloh." Homer's bright and beautiful **Victoria Claflin Woodhull** was an unabashed Women's Rights pioneer, Free Love advocate, and the first woman to run for president (against Grant in 1872).*

Marion

Marion

newspaperman

Warren Harding

once employed

Norman Thomas

as a newsboy.

Harding became

President, but

Thomas became

the nation's

conscience. A

pacifist and

socialist, Thomas

helped start the

American civil

Liberties Union

and ran for

President himself

six times on the

Socialist ticket,

dodging tomatoes

but campaigning

tirelessly for racial

equality,

disarmament, and

constitutional

freedoms.

Median Age	36.6
White	139,147
Black	2,990
Native American	435
Asian	849
Pacific Islander	29
Other	434
2 or More Races	1,607
Hispanic	1,107
Area (square miles)	687
Urban Land Cover (latest figures 1994)	1.8%
Population Per Square Mile	211.8
Elevation	836
Average Temperature	53.4
Average Precipitation	45.97 in.

Civilian Labor Force	73,100
Trade	14,552
Construction	3,133
Manufacturing	9,934
Transportation & Utilities	2,169
Government	6,709
Services	13,053
Finance, Insurance & Real Estate	3,215
Agriculture, Forestry, Fishing	1,294
Mining	108
Per Capita Income, 1999	$26,891
Persons Below Poverty, 1997	9.1%
Retail Sales per Capita, 1997	$8,484
Housing Units, 2000	58,760
Average Family Size	3.01
Number of Farms	1,530
Average Size of Farms (acres)	161
Average Commodity Cash Receipts per Farm	$86,531
Highway Miles	
Interstate	29
U.S. Routes	51
State Routes	187
Registered Motor Vehicles	175,242
Automobile Crashes per 1,000	33.45

Number of Registered Voters	98,787
Democrat	12.6%
Republican	18.3%
Non Partisan	69.0%
Number Voted 2000 Election	63,490
Percent Voted 2000 Election	64.3%

Voting, 2000 Election	
for Bush	37,180
for Gore	23,196
for Nader	1,498
for Buchanan	264
Contributions to Federal Candidates, Parties, & PACs, '01-'02	
to Democrats	$12,000
to Republicans	$155,047

Logan

Namesake General Benjamin Logan, who destroyed Mac-O-Chee Indian towns in the county in 1786

Established March 1, 1818

County Seat Bellefontaine

Largest Places	2000	1990
Bellefontaine city	13,069	12,142
Stokes township	4,293	3,935
Washington township	2,326	1,982
Jefferson township	2,012	1,809
West Liberty village	1,813	1,613
Richland township	1,648	1,336
Rushcreek township	1,648	1,371
Russells Point village	1,619	1,504
Harrison township	1,599	1,600
McArthur township	1,495	1,403

Logan County is located in the west-central portion of the state. The Mad and Great Miami rivers flow through the county. Campbell Hill, in Logan County, is the highest point in Ohio, rising 1,550 feet above sea level and is the highest point between the Rocky Mountains and the Allegheny Mountains. Indian Lake is Ohio's second largest man-made lake with over 5,800 acres of water, 69 islands, and a 29 mile natural wooded shoreline. Indian Lake State Park is a popular tourist area. Other attractions in Logan County include Piatt Castles, Mac-A-Cheek and Mac-O-Chee; Pioneer House; Ohio and Zane Caverns; and the Logan County Historical Museum.

HOMER'S LEGEND

Due north on State Route 661, through pleasant rolling countryside a dozen miles, is the humble crossroads of Homer, Ohio, a tiny footnote to national history because of the accidents of birth. A marker at the library and across the street from the Homer Cemetery gives the barest facts: *Victoria Claflin Woodhull, first woman candidate for President of the United States, 1872.* Victoria was a spiritualist, stockbroker, and an advocate of women's rights, Free Love, and legalized prostitution. She was also a newspaper publisher who printed the first English translation of the *Communist Manifesto.* Wrote a Homer woman in 1979, "Her greatest success was as a hornswoggler, which is why some people think she would have made a good president." She didn't become president, of course, Grant did, another Ohioan. Victoria moved to England, married a wealthy banker, and became, finally, something many presidents do not—a legend.

Vital Statistics

Population, 1995	45,204
Population, 2000	46,005
Net Change, 1990-2000	8.7%
Median Age	36.9
White	44,233
Black	786
Native American	94
Asian	185
Pacific Islander	13
Other	123
2 or More Races	571
Hispanic	332
Area (square miles)	458
Urban Land Cover (latest figures 1994)	0.9%
Population Per Square Mile	100.4
Elevation	1,251
Average Temperature	53.2
Average Precipitation	37.65 in.

Civilian Labor Force	28,100
Trade	4,335
Construction	758
Manufacturing	6,645
Transportation & Utilities	1,014
Government	2,220
Services	5,092
Finance, Insurance & Real Estate	568
Agriculture, Forestry, Fishing	154
Mining	45
Per Capita Income, 1999	$24,988
Persons Below Poverty, 1997	9.5%
Retail Sales per Capita, 1997	$6,739
Housing Units, 2000	21,571
Average Family Size	3.01
Number of Farms	960
Average Size of Farms (acres)	234
Average Commodity Cash Receipts per Farm	$93,651
Highway Miles	
Interstate	0
U.S. Routes	50
State Routes	183
Registered Motor Vehicles	57,476
Automobile Crashes per 1,000	37.84

Number of Registered Voters	30,494
Democrat	6.8%
Republican	22.3%
Non Partisan	70.9%
Number Voted 2000 Election	18,823
Percent Voted 2000 Election	61.7%
Voting, 2000 Election	
for Bush	11,849
for Gore	5,945
for Nader	449
for Buchanan	107
Contributions to Federal Candidates, Parties, & PACs, '01-'02	
to Democrats	$1,300
to Republicans	$16,960

Lorain

Namesake French Province of Lorraine

Established December 26, 1822

County Seat Elyria

Largest Places	2000	1990
Lorain city	68,652	71,245
Elyria city	55,953	56,746
North Ridgeville city	22,338	21,564
Avon Lake city	18,145	15,066
Amherst city	11,797	10,332
Avon city	11,446	7,337
Eaton township	9,675	6,516
Sheffield Lake city	9,371	9,825
Oberlin city	8,195	8,191
Carlisle city	7,339	7,554

Lorain County is located in the northeast portion of the state, bordering on Lake Erie. The Black River flows into Lake Erie at Lorain County. The Lake Erie Port of Lorain, an international port, offers access to Great Lakes shipping and to world markets through the St. Lawrence Seaway. Attractions in Lorain County include 21 miles of Lake Erie shoreline with beaches, cruises, boating, and fishing available to tourists; Jewel of the Port Lighthouse; Inland Seas Maritime Museum; Lorain County Historical Society & Hickories Museum; Bridgeway Trail; Findlay State Park; Lorain & West Virginia Railway; and Oberlin College.

Vital Statistics

Population, 1995	281,447
Population, 2000	284,664
Net Change, 1990-2000	5.0%
Median Age	36.5
White	243,514
Black	24,203
Native American	845
Asian	1,703
Pacific Islander	74
Other	8,160
2 or More Races	6,165
Hispanic	19,676
Area (square miles)	493
Urban Land Cover (latest figures 1994)	7%
Population Per Square Mile	577.4
Elevation	495
Average Temperature	53.1
Average Precipitation	35.20 in.

Civilian Labor Force	142,500
Trade	23,277
Construction	6,189
Manufacturing	29,616
Transportation & Utilities	3,821
Government	13,986
Services	24,201
Finance, Insurance & Real Estate	2,849
Per Capita Income, 1999	$25,712
Persons Below Poverty, 1997	10.4%
Retail Sales per Capita, 1997	$8,441
Housing Units, 2000	111,368

Average Family Size 3.08
Number of Farms 950
Average Size of Farms (acres) 147
Average Commodity Cash Receipts per Farm $82,611
Highway Miles
    Interstate 37
    U.S. Routes 47
    State Routes 223
Registered Motor Vehicles 284,163
Automobile Crashes per 1,000 .... 26.65

Number of Registered Voters 185,982
    Democrat 18.6%
    Republican 8.7%
    Non Partisan 72.7%
    Number Voted 2000 Election 114,480
    Percent Voted 2000 Election 61.6%
Voting, 2000 Election
    for Bush 47,957
    for Gore 59,809
    for Nader 3,183
    for Buchanan 745
Contributions to Federal Candidates, Parties, & PACs, '01-'02
    to Democrats $89,438
    to Republicans $159,864

Lucas

Namesake Governor Robert Lucas

Established June 20, 1835

County Seat Toledo

Largest Places	2000	1990
Toledo city	313,619	332,943
Sylvania township	25,583	22,682
Springfield township	22,817	18,835
Oregon city	19,355	18,334
Sylvania city	18,670	17,301
Maumee city	15,237	15,561
Monclova township	6,767	4,547
Waterville village	4,828	4,517
Ottawa Hills village	4,564	4,543
Washington township	3,574	3,803

Lucas County is located in the northwest portion of the state. The Port of Toledo provides access to both overseas and Great Lakes shipping. When Ohio was admitted to the Union, no reference was made as to its northern boundary. Both Ohio and Michigan claimed the western corner of Lake Erie. In 1836, the so called Toledo War was settled by Congress giving the disputed area to Ohio. Attractions in Lucas County include Maumee Bay State Park and Lodge; Mary Jane Thurston State Park; Toledo Zoological Park; Toledo Museum of Art; Center of Science and Industry; and Lake Erie.

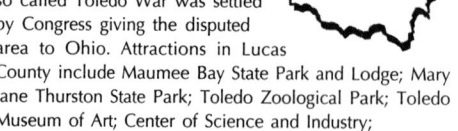

Vital Statistics
Population, 1995 455,018
Population, 2000 455,054
Net Change, 1990-2000 .... -1.6%
Median Age 35.0
White 352,678

Black 77,268
Native American 1,179
Asian 5,527
Pacific Islander 92
Other 8,468
2 or More Races 9,842
Hispanic 20,670
Area (square miles) 340
Urban Land Cover (latest figures 1994) 18%
Population Per Square Mile 1,338.4
Elevation 704
Average Temperature 53.3
Average Precipitation .... 41.86 in.

Civilian Labor Force 230,300
    Trade 63,821
    Construction 12,040
    Manufacturing 35,322
    Transportation & Utilities 11,470
    Government 26,130
    Services 77,892
    Finance, Insurance & Real Estate 9,233
    Agriculture, Forestry, Fishing 1,682
    Mining 146
Per Capita Income, 1999 .... $27,361
Persons Below Poverty, 1997 .... 13.6%
Retail Sales per Capita, 1997 .... $10,746
Housing Units, 2000 196,259
Average Family Size 3.06
Number of Farms 390
Average Size of Farms (acres) 203
Average Commodity Cash Receipts per Farm $150,525
Highway Miles
    Interstate 49
    U.S. Routes 65
    State Routes 115
Registered Motor Vehicles 435,973
Automobile Crashes per 1,000 .... 39.27

Number of Registered Voters 302,136
    Democrat 13.2%
    Republican 9.5%
    Non Partisan 77.4%
    Number Voted 2000 Election 188,419
    Percent Voted 2000 Election 62.4%
Voting, 2000 Election
    for Bush 73,342
    for Gore 108,344
    for Nader 4,227
    for Buchanan 562
Contributions to Federal Candidates, Parties, & PACs, '01-'02
    to Democrats $81,306
    to Republicans $285,618

Madison

Namesake James Madison, Fourth President of United States

Established March 1, 1810

County Seat London

Largest Places	2000	1990
London city	8,771	7,807
Somerford township	6,975	2,544
West Jefferson village	4,331	4,505
Jefferson township	2,604	2,482
Canaan township	2,496	2,309
Plain City village	1,937	1,302
Mount Sterling village	1,865	1,647

Archibald Willard began his artistic career by painting decorative motifs and scenes on wagons, carriages, and furniture manufactured by factories in Wellington. Largely an untrained artist, Willard found fame in 1876 when his life-sized oil painting of three Revolutionary War soldiers heroically playing a fife and drums through the smoke of battle debuted at the nation's 100th birthday celebration, the Centennial Exhibition in Philadelphia. Though the critics largely turned up their professional noses— one called the painting "ludicrous"—at *The Spirit of '76*, the public loved it.

Many in the crowds who flocked to see the work were moved to tears, and President Grant reportedly was so affected that he requested a private viewing to "commune" alone with the painting.

Willard, of course, found immediate fame, and he capitalized upon the painting's success by turning its patriotic appeal into a one-man industry. Varying the colors and subject's clothing, he painted at least fourteen more versions of *The Spirit of '76*, and ten of these "original copies" are known to still exist.

Willard's concept tugged so hard at the nation's heartstrings that *The Spirit of '76* had probably become the most frequently copied image in the United States—from thousands of lithographic and photographic reproductions sold at the Philadelphia Exposition to its subsequent use and reuse on cups, saucers, music boxes, and thousands of other products.

It has been patriotically recreated in Fourth of July parades and fireworks displays; it has been altered for political purposes on the cover of *Time* and the pages of *Playboy*; and it was copied on the first U.S. postage stamps commemorating the nation's bicentennial.

The Spirit of '76 is timeless, and it is everywhere. Which is exactly what Mr. Willard intended. His work, he said, "was not painted in commemoration of 1776 or 1876, or any special period in the life of our nation, but as an expression of the vital and ever-living spirit of American patriotism."

THE SPIRIT OF '76 MUSEUM— Located in one of Wellington's old cheese warehouses, this museum features a gallery of 16 paintings and murals done by Willard, a bedroom set that he decorated when he worked for a village furniture company, and an incredible collection of objects—including bathroom tissue—that have displayed the *The Spirit of '76* motif. But two of its most treasured items are the fife and drum used as models by Willard when he painted his 1876 version of *The Spirit of '76*. As he painted, Willard told Hugh Mosher to actually play that fife in order to properly capture his expression. Although the original drum exhibited in the museum is red, Willard sometimes made it blue in his later versions of the painting.

201 North Main Street; 440-647-4367. Open Apr-Oct. Sat-Sun 2:30-5.

Monroe township	1,769	1,467
Pleasant township	1,417	1,165
Union township	1,411	5,203

Madison County is located in the central portion of the state. The Big Darby and the Little Darby creeks flow through the county. Primarily an agricultural area, 88.1 percent of the land is in farms. Madison County ranks second in soybean production and third in corn production in Ohio. A Farm Science Review, held annually at the Molly Caren Agricultural Center near London, attracts exhibitors from all over Ohio and surrounding areas. Attractions in Madison County include Madison Lake State Park; Skunk Hill Mounds; Red Brick Tavern; London Fish Hatchery; Madison County Historical Society; Jonathan Alder Cabin; and the Scenic Big Darby Creek.

Vital Statistics

Population, 1995	40,878
Population, 2000	40,213
Net Change, 1990-2000	8.5%
Median Age	35.8
White	36,896
Black	2,511
Native American	80
Asian	175
Pacific Islander	6
Other	139
2 or More Races	406
Hispanic	294
Area (square miles)	465
Urban Land Cover (latest figures 1994)	0.5%
Population Per Square Mile	86.5
Elevation	985
Average Temperature	52.9
Average Precipitation	40.48 in.

Civilian Labor Force	20,900
Trade	2,566
Construction	654
Manufacturing	3,483
Transportation & Utilities	416
Government	3,004
Services	2,524
Finance, Insurance & Real Estate	204
Per Capita Income, 1999	$21,782
Persons Below Poverty, 1997	8.7%
Retail Sales per Capita, 1997	$6,791
Housing Units, 2000	14,399
Average Family Size	3.06
Number of Farms	740
Average Size of Farms (acres)	350
Average Commodity Cash Receipts per Farm	$76,248
Highway Miles	
Interstate	27
U.S. Routes	46
State Routes	124
Registered Motor Vehicles	42,600
Automobile Crashes per 1,000	28.55

Number of Registered Voters	23,221
Democrat	6.6%
Republican	16.7%
Non Partisan	76.7%
Number Voted 2000 Election	14,960

Percent Voted 2000 Election	64.4%
Voting, 2000 Election	
for Bush	8,892
for Gore	5,287
for Nader	299
for Buchanan	75
Contributions to Federal Candidates, Parties, & PACs, '01-'02	
to Democrats	$5,050
to Republicans	$43,040

Mahoning

Namesake Mahoning River, from the Indian word for "Salt Licks"

Established March 1, 1846

County Seat Youngstown

Largest Places	2000	1990
Youngstown city	82,026	95,706
Boardman township	45,518	41,796
Austintown township	38,001	36,740
Poland township	11,845	11,001
Struthers city	11,756	12,284
Campbell city	9,460	10,038
Canfield city	7,374	5,409
Canfield township	7,250	5,422
Beaver township	6,101	5,420
Springfield township	6,054	6,031

Mahoning County is located in the northeast portion of the state on the Pennsylvania border. The Mahoning River flows through the county. Discovery of pockets of iron ore and vast quantities of limestone led to Youngstown's development into a major iron and steel producing center for more than a century. The Youngstown Historical Center of Industry and Labor displays a dramatic overview of the Industry's rise and decline in the area. Other attractions in Mahoning County include Kyle Woods State Nature Preserve; War Vet Museum; Little Red Schoolhouse; Austin Log Cabin; Butler Institute of American Art; Western Reserve Village; Lake Milton; and Youngstown State University.

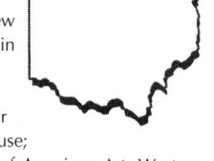

Vital Statistics

Population, 1995	262,338
Population, 2000	257,555
Net Change, 1990-2000	-2.7%
Median Age	39.7
White	208,727
Black	40,884
Native American	445
Asian	1,220
Pacific Islander	62
Other	2,656
2 or More Races	3,561
Hispanic	7,640
Area (square miles)	415
Urban Land Cover (latest figures 1994)	7%
Population Per Square Mile	620.6
Elevation	1,257
Average Temperature	52.5
Average Precipitation	37.46 in.

Civilian Labor Force 115,700
    Trade 32,127
    Construction 5,862
    Manufacturing 12,883
    Transportation & Utilities 4,867
    Government 13,755
    Services 35,133
    Finance, Insurance & Real Estate 5,037
    Agriculture, Forestry, Fishing 863
    Mining 204
Per Capita Income, 1999 .... $24,095
Persons Below Poverty, 1997 .... 14.4%
Retail Sales per Capita, 1997 .... $9,901
Housing Units, 2000 111,762
Average Family Size 3.02
Number of Farms 680
Average Size of Farms (acres) 125
Average Commodity Cash Receipts per Farm $49,143
Highway Miles
    Interstate 55
    U.S. Routes 59
    State Routes 175
Registered Motor Vehicles 263,500
Automobile Crashes per 1,000 .... 31.18

Number of Registered Voters 179,546
    Democrat 36.3%
    Republican 7.0%
    Non Partisan 56.6%
    Number Voted 2000 Election 116,889
    Percent Voted 2000 Election 65.1%
Voting, 2000 Election
    for Bush 40,460
    for Gore 69,212
    for Nader 3,322
    for Buchanan 815
Contributions to Federal Candidates, Parties, & PACs, '01-'02
    to Democrats $52,175
    to Republicans $278,432

Marion

Namesake "The Swamp Fox" of the Revolutionary War, General Francis Marion

Established April 1, 1820

County Seat Marion

Largest Places	2000	1990
Marion city	37,523	34,075
Marion township	9,590	9,489
Pleasant township	4,368	4,107
Claridon township	2,009	1,854
Richland township	1,663	1,531
Grand Prairie township	1,609	1,697
Big Island township	1,223	1,271
Prospect village	1,191	1,148
Montgomery township	1,175	1,232
Prospect township	1,016	902

Marion County is located in the central portion of the state. The Scioto and Olentangy rivers flow through the county. In 1863, a Marion County man invented a revolving hay rake that led to the manufacture of the first steam shovel in 1874. The Edward Huber Machinery Museum displays many examples of early farming and roadbuilding equipment. Other

attractions in Marion County include Delaware State Park; Warren G. Harding Home and Museum; Harding Memorial; Claridon Prairie Preserve; Killdeer and Big Island Wildlife Areas; Palace Theater; Stengel True Historical Museum; and Wyandot Popcorn Museum.

Vital Statistics
Population, 1995 65,871
Population, 2000 66,217
Net Change, 1990-2000 .... 3.0%
Median Age 37.2
White 60,987
Black 3,805
Native American 126
Asian 344
Pacific Islander 6
Other 323
2 or More Races 626
Hispanic 723
Area (square miles) 404
Urban Land Cover (latest figures 1994) 1.2%
Population Per Square Mile 163.9
Elevation 943
Average Temperature 53.6
Average Precipitation .... 37.88 in.

Civilian Labor Force 31,500
    Trade 6,288
    Construction 1,004
    Manufacturing 7,165
    Transportation & Utilities 2,259
    Government 5,743
    Services 5,071
    Finance, Insurance & Real Estate 765
    Agriculture, Forestry, Fishing 135
    Mining 52
Per Capita Income, 1999 .... $22,136
Persons Below Poverty, 1997 .... 11.9%
Retail Sales per Capita, 1997 .... $8,150
Housing Units, 2000 26,298
Average Family Size 2.98
Number of Farms 590
Average Size of Farms (acres) 375
Average Commodity Cash Receipts per Farm $94,381
Highway Miles
    Interstate 0
    U.S. Routes 20
    State Routes 181
Registered Motor Vehicles 69,958
Automobile Crashes per 1,000 .... 31.39

Number of Registered Voters 41,788
    Democrat 14.4%
    Republican 15.9%
    Non Partisan 69.6%
    Number Voted 2000 Election 25,371
    Percent Voted 2000 Election 60.7%
Voting, 2000 Election
    for Bush 13,617
    for Gore 10,370
    for Nader 588
    for Buchanan 142
Contributions to Federal Candidates, Parties, & PACs, '01-'02
    to Democrats $1,150
    to Republicans $47,013

Medina

Namesake Arabian city where Mohammed is buried

Established February 18, 1812

County Seat Medina

Largest Places	2000	1990
Brunswick city	33,388	28,230
Medina city	25,139	19,231
Wadsworth city	18,437	15,718
Medina township	7,783	4,864
Hinckley township	6,753	5,845
Brunswick Hills	5,469	4,328
Montville township	5,410	3,371
Lafayette township	4,653	3,851
Liverpool township	4,329	3,713
Sharon township	4,244	3,234

Medina County is located in the northeast portion of the state. The Rocky River and the Black River flow through the county. Medina County is the location of a unique annual occurrence. Each year on March 15, the turkey buzzards return to their summer home at Whipp's Ledges near Hinckley. This phenomenon is celebrated with an annual "Buzzard Day." Attractions in Medina County include Hinckley Reservation; Medina Public Square Historic District; Spencer Lake State Wildlife Area; Medina County Historical Society Museum; and Chippewa Lake Park.

Vital Statistics

Population, 1995	135,735
Population, 2000	151,095
Net Change, 1990-2000	23.5%
Median Age	36.6
White	146,956
Black	1,323
Native American	232
Asian	969
Pacific Islander	25
Other	375
2 or More Races	1,215
Hispanic	1,399
Area (square miles)	422
Urban Land Cover (latest figures 1994)	5%
Population Per Square Mile	358.0
Elevation	1,175
Average Temperature	51.6
Average Precipitation	40.15 in.

Civilian Labor Force	80,100
Trade	14,006
Construction	3,262
Manufacturing	12,024
Transportation & Utilities	1,470
Government	6,209
Services	12,559
Finance, Insurance & Real Estate	2,802
Agriculture, Forestry, Fishing	761
Mining	55
Per Capita Income, 1999	$28,954
Persons Below Poverty, 1997	4.9%
Retail Sales per Capita, 1997	$9,508

Housing Units, 2000	56,793
Average Family Size	3.15
Number of Farms	1,060
Average Size of Farms (acres)	107
Average Commodity Cash Receipts per Farm	$42,058
Highway Miles	
Interstate	45
U.S. Routes	39
State Routes	164
Registered Motor Vehicles	168,840
Automobile Crashes per 1,000	25.39

Number of Registered Voters	102,535
Number Voted 2000 Election	67,850
Percent Voted 2000 Election	66.2%
Voting, 2000 Election	
Democrat	8.9%
Republican	13.7%
Non Partisan	77.4%
for Bush	37,349
for Gore	26,635
for Nader	1,960
for Buchanan	532
Contributions to Federal Candidates, Parties, & PACs, '01-'02	
to Democrats	$31,659
to Republicans	$97,488

Meigs

Namesake Return Jonathan Meigs, Jr., Ohio Governor 1810-1814

Established April 1, 1819

County Seat Pomeroy

Largest Places	2000	1990
Middleport village	2,525	2,725
Chester township	2,332	2,131
Pomeroy village	1,966	2,259
Salisbury township	1,950	2,243
Rutland township	1,946	1,774
Olive township	1,874	1,727
Sutton township	1,625	1,529
Bedford township	1,212	1,097
Scipio township	1,050	1,094
Lebanon township	1,029	905

Meigs County is located in the southeast portion of the state bordering on West Virginia. The Shade River flows into the Ohio River at the Meigs County eastern border. The only Civil War battle fought in the state of Ohio or north of the Ohio River took place on Buffington Island in Meigs County. Attractions in Meigs County include Forked Run State Park; Shade River State Forest; Buffington Island State Park; McCook Monument; the Old Courthouse at Chester, which is Ohio's oldest standing courthouse; Meigs County Museum; Pomeroy Historic District; Racine Locks and Dam; The Ohio River; and the Federal-style Meigs County Courthouse.

Vital Statistics

Population, 1995	24,086
Population, 2000	23,072

Net Change, 1990-2000 .... 0.4%
Median Age 38.6
White 22,548
Black 159
Native American 62
Asian 24
Pacific Islander 0
Other 57
2 or More Races 222
Hispanic 138
Area (square miles) 429
Urban Land Cover (latest figures 1994) 0.8%
Population Per Square Mile 53.8
Elevation 607
Average Temperature 54.0
Average Precipitation .... 43.36 in.

Civilian Labor Force 8,400
    Trade 1,146
    Construction 311
    Manufacturing 149
    Transportation & Utilities 83
    Government 1,150
    Services 783
    Finance, Insurance & Real Estate 169
Per Capita Income, 1999 .... $16,426
Persons Below Poverty, 1997 .... 20.4%
Retail Sales per Capita, 1997 .... $4,747
Housing Units, 2000 10,782
Average Family Size 2.94
Number of Farms 580
Average Size of Farms (acres) 150
Average Commodity Cash Receipts per Farm $34,185
Highway Miles
    Interstate 0
    U.S. Routes 15
    State Routes 175
Registered Motor Vehicles 29,213
Automobile Crashes per 1,000 .... 27.09

Number of Registered Voters 16,242
    Democrat 12.5%
    Republican 25.1%
    Non Partisan 62.4%
    Number Voted 2000 Election 10,228
    Percent Voted 2000 Election 63%
Voting, 2000 Election
    for Bush 5,750
    for Gore 3,674
    for Nader 226
    for Buchanan 76
Contributions to Federal Candidates, Parties, & PACs, '01-'02
    to Democrats $0
    to Republicans $1,450

Mercer

Namesake Revolutionary War hero General Hugh Mercer

Established April 1, 1812

County Seat Celina

Largest Places	2000	1990
Celina city	10,303	9,650
Coldwater village	4,482	4,335
Jefferson township	2,928	3,333
Marion township	2,605	2,406
St. Henry village	2,271	1,907
Franklin township	2,112	1,927
Butler township	1,977	1,846
Granville township	1,434	1,527
Fort Recovery village	1,273	1,313
Washington township	1,218	1,259

Mercer County is located in the west-central portion of the state. The Wabash and St. Marys rivers flow through the county. Primarily an agricultural area, 88 percent of the land is in farms. Mercer County ranks first in the state in raising hogs and pigs, second in corn production, and third in raising cattle and milk cows. Grand Lake St. Marys, one of the largest man-made lakes in the U.S., was constructed in 1840 as part of the Miami-Erie Canal system. Today it is a major recreation area, attracting tourists who come to fish, boat, swim, water-ski, or just relax. Other attractions include Mercer County Historical Museum; the Fort Recovery Museum; and the Grand Lake Lighthouse.

Vital Statistics

Population, 1995 40,906
Population, 2000 40,924
Net Change, 1990-2000 .... 3.8%
Median Age 35.7
White 40,286
Black 39
Native American 105
Asian 117
Pacific Islander 9
Other 138
2 or More Races 230
Hispanic 470
Area (square miles) 463
Urban Land Cover (latest figures 1994) 1.4%
Population Per Square Mile 88.4
Elevation 858
Average Temperature 54.6
Average Precipitation .... 37.71 in.

Civilian Labor Force 19,100
Trade 4,289
    Construction 908
    Manufacturing 3,622
    Transportation & Utilities 636
    Government 2,543
    Services 2,398
    Finance, Insurance & Real Estate 648
Per Capita Income, 1999 .... $23,376
Persons Below Poverty, 1997 .... 6.5%
Retail Sales per Capita, 1997 .... $8,057
Housing Units, 2000 15,875
Average Family Size 3.24
Number of Farms 1,480
Average Size of Farms (acres) 184
Average Commodity Cash Receipts per Farm $191,306
Highway Miles
    Interstate 0
    U.S. Routes 45
    State Routes 166
Registered Motor Vehicles 49,895
Automobile Crashes per 1,000 .... 24.97

Number of Registered Voters 25,079
    Democrat 13.7%
    Republican 12.9%

Non Partisan 73.4%
Number Voted 2000 Election 18,848
Percent Voted 2000 Election 75.2%
Voting, 2000 Election
    for Bush 12,485
    for Gore 5,212
    for Nader 392
    for Buchanan 125
Contributions to Federal Candidates, Parties, & PACs, '01-'02
    to Democrats $5,000
    to Republicans $20,625

Miami

Namesake Miami Indians, Miami meaning "mother"

Established March 1, 1807

County Seat Troy

Largest Places	2000	1990
Troy city	21,999	19,478
Piqua city	20,738	20,612
Tipp city	9,221	6,027
Monroe township	6,118	6,663
Concord township	5,336	4,914
Bethel township	4,927	4,812
Union township	4,673	4,950
West Milton village	4,645	4,348
Newberry township	2,897	2,746
Covington village	2,559	2,603

Miami County is located in the west-central portion of the state. The Great Miami River and the Stillwater River flow through the county. Attractions in Miami County include Piqua Historical Area State Memorial; Fort Rowdy Museum at Covington; Union Township Historical Museum and Quaker Research Center at West Milton; Pleasant Hill Civil War Monument; Benjamin Overfield Tavern; Brukner Nature Center; Tippecanoe Historical Museum; Hoover Grist Mill; Pickawillany Monument; Charleston Falls Preserve; Stillwater Prairie Reserve; Eldean Covered Bridge; the Miami-Erie Canal Locks; and the Scenic Stillwater River.

Vital Statistics

Population, 1995 97,010
Population, 2000 98,868
Net Change, 1990-2000 .... 6.1%
Median Age 37.7
White 94,694
Black 1,932
Native American 190
Asian 780
Pacific Islander 9
Other 273
2 or More Races 990
Hispanic 721
Area (square miles) 407
Urban Land Cover (latest figures 1994) 3.9%
Population Per Square Mile 242.9
Elevation 877
Average Temperature 53.5

Average Precipitation .... 38.51 in.

Civilian Labor Force 50,500
    Trade 11,412
    Construction 1,818
    Manufacturing 15,239
    Transportation & Utilities 876
    Government 4,642
    Services 8,561
    Finance, Insurance & Real Estate 1,082
    Agriculture, Forestry, Fishing 1,079
    Mining 70
Per Capita Income, 1999 .... $27,271
Persons Below Poverty, 1997 .... 7.0%
Retail Sales per Capita, 1997 .... $8,651
Housing Units, 2000 40,545
Average Family Size 2.99
Number of Farms 1,130
Average Size of Farms (acres) 187
Average Commodity Cash Receipts per Farm $49,107
Highway Miles
    Interstate 20
    U.S. Routes 28
    State Routes 154
Registered Motor Vehicles 123,190
Automobile Crashes per 1,000 .... 31.52

Number of Registered Voters 66,765
    Democrat 6.0%
    Republican 12.9%
    Non Partisan 81.2%
Number Voted 2000 Election 43,555
Percent Voted 2000 Election 65.2%
Voting, 2000 Election
    for Bush 26,037
    for Gore 15,584
    for Nader 879
    for Buchanan 116
Contributions to Federal Candidates, Parties, & PACs, '01-'02
    to Democrats $2,400
    to Republicans $74,625

Monroe

Namesake James Monroe, presidential candidate at the time of its formation

Established January 29, 1813

County Seat Woodsfield

Largest Places	2000	1990
Woodsfield village	2,598	2,832
Center township	1,199	1,123
Lee township	1,122	1,237
Ohio township	1,032	1,134
Sunsbury township	873	861
Malaga township	845	830
Adams township	672	595
Salem township	602	590
Switzerland township	509	501
Seneca township	508	386

Monroe County is located in the southwestern part of the state on the West Virginia border. The Little Muskingum River flows through the county and the Ohio River provides its eastern border.

Troy got its name because some of its first settlers brought copies of Homer's *Iliad* and *Odyssey* with them to Ohio. Since many of them had staved off the British in George Washington's Continental Army, they had, no doubt, a ready appreciation for how well ancient Troy withstood the attacks of the Greeks.

Part of Ohio's Appalachian Region, Monroe County has been called the "Switzerland of Ohio" because of its rugged hills and early Swiss settlers. Attractions in Monroe County include Piatt Park; Keidaish Point Scenic Overlook of the Ohio River near Hannibal; Parry Museum at Woodsfield; the Knowlton Covered Bridge (at 195 feet, the 2nd-longest in Ohio); Monroe Lake and Wildlife Area; Wayne National Forest; and the Ohio River.

Vital Statistics

Population, 1995	15,388
Population, 2000	15,180
Net Change, 1990-2000	-2%
Median Age	40.8
White	14,986
Black	40
Native American	23
Asian	11
Pacific Islander	2
Other	17
2 or More Races	101
Hispanic	62
Area (square miles)	456
Urban Land Cover (latest figures 1994)	0.3%
Population Per Square Mile	33.3
Elevation	458
Average Temperature	54.5
Average Precipitation	37.15 in.

Civilian Labor Force	5,800
Trade	643
Construction	187
Manufacturing	2,310
Transportation & Utilities	134
Government	875
Services	437
Finance, Insurance & Real Estate	121
Agriculture, Forestry, Fishing	14
Mining	71
Per Capita Income, 1999	$17,702
Persons Below Poverty, 1997	16.9%
Retail Sales per Capita, 1997	$3,301
Housing Units, 2000	7,212
Average Family Size	2.96
Number of Farms	710
Average Size of Farms (acres)	162
Average Commodity Cash Receipts per Farm	$13,733
Highway Miles	
Interstate	0
U.S. Routes	0
State Routes	213
Registered Motor Vehicles	18,908
Automobile Crashes per 1,000	19.89

Number of Registered Voters	11,156
Democrat	42.4%
Republican	7.7%
Non Partisan	49.8%
Number Voted 2000 Election	7,377
Percent Voted 2000 Election	66.1%
Voting, 2000 Election	
for Bush	3,145
for Gore	3,605
for Nader	149
for Buchanan	160
Contributions to Federal Candidates, Parties, & PACs, '01-'02	
to Democrats	$1,325
to Republicans	$24,800

Montgomery

Namesake Revolutionary War hero General Richard Montgomery

Established May 1, 1803

County Seat Dayton

Largest Places	2000	1990
Dayton city	166,179	182,044
Kettering city	57,502	60,569
Huber Heights	38,177	38,686
Washington township	29,967	25,527
Trotwood city	27,420	8,816
Miami township	25,706	22,604
Harrison township	24,303	26,026
Riverside city	23,545	1,471
Centerville city	23,024	21,082
Miamisburg city	19,489	17,834

Montgomery County is located in the southwestern part of the state, and the Stillwater, the Mad, and Great Miami rivers converge there. From the bicycle shop of the Wright Brothers came the beginnings of powered flight. Today, known as the Birthplace of Aviation, Montgomery County is home to the Wright-Patterson Air Force Base. Attractions in Montgomery County include Sycamore State Park; Eastwood Lake; Aullwood Audubon Center; Germantown's Covered Bridges; the Dayton Art Institute; the Boonshoft Museum of Discovery; the new Schuster Performing Arts Center; the Carillon Historical Park; Cox Arboretum; the Paul Laurence Dunbar House; and Hawthorn Hill, home of Orville Wright.

Vital Statistics

Population, 1995	570,490
Population, 2000	559,062
Net Change, 1990-2000	-2.6%
Median Age	36.4
White	428,084
Black	111,030
Native American	1,258
Asian	7,341
Pacific Islander	196
Other	2,718
2 or More Races	8,435
Hispanic	7,096
Area (square miles)	462
Urban Land Cover (latest figures 1994)	17%
Population Per Square Mile	1210.1
Elevation	755
Average Temperature	57.8
Average Precipitation	44.33 in.

Civilian Labor Force	278,800
Trade	68,071
Construction	12,155
Manufacturing	62,412
Transportation & Utilities	17,201
Government	28,582
Services	94,675
Finance, Insurance & Real Estate	12,864
Agriculture, Forestry, Fishing	2,444

Mining 80
Per Capita Income, 1999 .... $28,113
Persons Below Poverty, 1997 .... 11.1%
Retail Sales per Capita, 1997 .... $9,797
Housing Units, 2000 248,433
Average Family Size 2.96
Number of Farms 930
Average Size of Farms (acres) 125
Average Commodity Cash Receipts per Farm $53,919
Highway Miles
    Interstate 55
    U.S. Routes 41
    State Routes 123
Registered Motor Vehicles 528,164
Automobile Crashes per 1,000 .... 24.79

Number of Registered Voters 371,790
    Democrat 10.4%
    Republican 10.5%
    Non Partisan 79.0%
    Number Voted 2000 Election 237,580
    Percent Voted 2000 Election 63.9%
Voting, 2000 Election
    for Bush 109,792
    for Gore 114,597
    for Nader 4,690
    for Buchanan 594
Contributions to Federal Candidates, Parties, & PACs, '01-'02
    to Democrats $191,279
    to Republicans $996,651

Morgan

Namesake General Daniel Morgan, friend of George Washington and Revolutionary War hero

Established December 29, 1817

County Seat McConnelsville

Largest Places	2000	1990
McConnelsville village	1,676	1,804
Windsor township	1,411	1,477
Malta township	1,268	1,190
Marion township	1,031	906
Bloom township	1,015	1,003
Homer township	976	763
York township	958	949
Morgan township	941	842
Meigsville township	894	774
Deerfield township	802	683

Morgan County is located in the southeastern part of the state. The Muskingum River flows through the county. The first settlement of Morgan County was made in 1790 at a place called Big Bottom. An Indian war party attacked the settlers killing nine men, one woman, and two children. The site of this event is now Big Bottom State Memorial Park. Attractions in Morgan County include R.V. Crews Memorial Park with the Big Muskie's bucket on display; Wolf Creek Wildlife Area; Ohio Power Recreation Land; Burr Oak State Park and Lodge; Wayne National Forest; Muskingum River State Park; Button House Museum; Opera House Theater; and Old Stockport Mill.

Vital Statistics
Population, 1995 14,602
Population, 2000 14,897
Net Change, 1990-2000 .... 5%
Median Age 38.9
White 13,952
Black 508
Native American 52
Asian 12
Pacific Islander 0
Other 39
2 or More Races 334
Hispanic 61
Area (square miles) 418
Urban Land Cover (latest figures 1994) 0.7%
Population Per Square Mile 35.6
Elevation 755
Average Temperature 54.3
Average Precipitation .... 49.74 in.

Civilian Labor Force 4,500
    Trade 657
    Construction 239
    Manufacturing 734
    Transportation & Utilities 350
    Government 700
    Services 383
    Finance, Insurance & Real Estate 104
    Agriculture, Forestry, Fishing 22
    Mining 221
Per Capita Income, 1999 .... $17,794
Persons Below Poverty, 1997 .... 15.3%
Retail Sales per Capita, 1997 .... $3,123
Housing Units, 2000 7,771
Average Family Size 2.98
Number of Farms 650
Average Size of Farms (acres) 169
Average Commodity Cash Receipts per Farm $15,626
Highway Miles
    Interstate 0
    U.S. Routes 0
    State Routes 189
Registered Motor Vehicles 18,526
Automobile Crashes per 1,000 .... 33.83

Number of Registered Voters 9,405
    Democrat 10.6%
    Republican 30.2%
    Non Partisan 59.1%
    Number Voted 2000 Election 6,158
    Percent Voted 2000 Election 65.5%
Voting, 2000 Election
    for Bush 3,451
    for Gore 2,261
    for Nader 177
    for Buchanan 72
Contributions to Federal Candidates, Parties, & PACs, '01-'02
    to Democrats $0
    to Republicans $750

Morrow

Namesake Jeremiah Morrow, Ohio Governor 1811-1826

Established March 1, 1848

County Seat Mt. Gilead

Largest Places	2000	1990
Mount Gilead village	3,290	2,846
Bennington township	2,366	1,984
Gilead township	2,141	2,178
Congress township	2,128	1,442
Harmony township	2,040	1,594
Perry township	1,970	1,646
North Bloomfield township	1,866	1,808
Cardington village	1,849	1,770
Lincoln township	1,672	1,357
Chester township	1,462	1,327

Morrow County is located in the central portion of the state. The Kokosing River flows through the county. With 62 percent of the land in farms, Morrow County ranks eighth in the state in sheep-raising. During World War I, the citizens of Morrow County sold more War Savings (Victory) bonds per capita than any other county in the state. They were duly honored and awarded the Victory Shaft Monument which stands today in Mount Gilead's town square. Other attractions in Morrow County include Mount Gilead State Park; Morrow County Courthouse and Jail; the James S. Trimble House; and the Selover Library in Chesterville.

Vital Statistics

Population, 1995	30,136
Population, 2000	31,628
Net Change, 1990-2000	14.0%
Median Age	36.5
White	31,111
Black	85
Native American	94
Asian	46
Pacific Islander	1
Other	58
2 or More Races	233
Hispanic	183
Area (square miles)	406
Urban Land Cover (latest figures 1994)	0.5%
Population Per Square Mile	77.9
Elevation	683
Average Temperature	53.6
Average Precipitation	37.88 in.

Civilian Labor Force	14,200
Trade	1,262
Construction	205
Manufacturing	1,643
Transportation & Utilities	262
Government	1,433
Services	993
Finance, Insurance & Real Estate	140
Agriculture, Forestry, Fishing	64
Mining	24
Per Capita Income, 1999	$17,776

Persons Below Poverty, 1997	10.1%
Retail Sales per Capita, 1997	$3,659
Housing Units, 2000	12,132
Average Family Size	3.09
Number of Farms	880
Average Size of Farms (acres)	198
Average Commodity Cash Receipts per Farm	$43,706
Highway Miles	
Interstate	20
U.S. Routes	26
State Routes	131
Registered Motor Vehicles	41,406
Automobile Crashes per 1,000	38.48

Number of Registered Voters	21,184
Democrat	9.6%
Republican	16.1%
Non Partisan	74.2%
Number Voted 2000 Election	13,154
Percent Voted 2000 Election	62.1%
Voting, 2000 Election	
for Bush	7,842
for Gore	4,529
for Nader	305
for Buchanan	97
Contributions to Federal Candidates, Parties, & PACs, '01-'02	
to Democrats	$1,178
to Republicans	$5,256

Muskingum

Namesake Delaware Indian word for "a town on the river side"

Established March 1, 1804

County Seat Zanesville

Largest Places	2000	1990
Zanesville city	25,586	26,788
Falls township	8,585	8,524
Newton township	5,186	4,944
Wayne township	4,455	4,514
Washington township	4,284	4,202
Muskingum township	3,813	3,343
Springfield township	3,562	3,404
Hopewell township	2,947	2,564
New Concord village	2,651	2,086
Perry township	2,420	2,086

Muskingum County is located in the east-central portion of the state. The Licking and Muskingum rivers flow through the county. New Concord is the hometown of Colonel John H. Glenn, U.S. Senator, 1974-1997. In 1962, he was the first American astronaut to orbit the earth; and in 1998, the oldest person to travel in space. Attractions in Muskingum County include National Road-Zane Grey Museum; the Y Bridge; Johnson's Mill/Salt Creek Covered Bridge; Zane's Landing Park; the Lorena Sternwheeler; the International Center for the Preservation of Wild Animals Inc. (The Wilds); Blue Rock State Park; Dillon Lake State Park; Ohio Ceramic Center; and the Muskingum River Parkway State Park.

Muskingum

Zanesville was founded in 1799 by Ebenezer Zane, who cut the first road—Zane's Trace—through the Ohio wilderness. Zane's town fostered another builder—Woolworth Building architect Cass Gilbert—and a relative, Zane Grey, whose adventurous pen romanticized the West. New Concord was home to astronaut John Glenn, the first American to orbit the earth.

Vital Statistics

Population, 1995 84,169
Population, 2000 84,585
Net Change, 1990-2000 .... 3.1%
Median Age 36.5
White 79,438
Black 3,392
Native American 180
Asian 231
Pacific Islander 17
Other 167
2 or More Races 1,160
Hispanic 436
Area (square miles) 665
Urban Land Cover (latest figures 1994) 0.1%
Population Per Square Mile 127.2
Elevation 777
Average Temperature 55.0
Average Precipitation .... 47.46 in.

Civilian Labor Force 44,600
    Trade 11,988
    Construction 1,833
    Manufacturing 10,134
    Transportation & Utilities 1,264
    Government 4,726
    Services 9,544
    Finance, Insurance & Real Estate 968
    Agriculture, Forestry, Fishing 185
    Mining 291
Per Capita Income, 1999 .... $22,055
Persons Below Poverty, 1997 .... 14.4%
Retail Sales per Capita, 1997 .... $9,334
Housing Units, 2000 35,163
Average Family Size 3.01
Number of Farms 1,220
Average Size of Farms (acres) 157
Average Commodity Cash Receipts per Farm $17,163
Highway Miles
    Interstate 27
    U.S. Routes 40
    State Routes 200
Registered Motor Vehicles 95,423
Automobile Crashes per 1,000 .... 41.63

Number of Registered Voters 54,355
    Democrat 9.3%
    Republican 14.3%
    Non Partisan 76.3%
    Number Voted 2000 Election 33,520
    Percent Voted 2000 Election 61.7%
Voting, 2000 Election
    for Bush 17,995
    for Gore 13,415
    for Nader 882
    for Buchanan 176
Contributions to Federal Candidates, Parties, & PACs, '01-'02
    to Democrats $5,950
    to Republicans $56,665

Noble

Namesake Warren P. Noble, chairman of committee on new counties in 1851

Established April 1, 1851

County Seat Caldwell

Largest Places	2000	1990
Olive township	3,429	1,527
Caldwell township	1,956	1,786
Noble township	1,750	1,714
Center township	818	831
Buffalo township	782	645
Beaver township	658	477
Wayne township	507	356
Jackson township	496	431
Seneca township	453	347
Marion township	434	434

Noble County is located in the southwestern portion of the state. On September 3, 1925, the US Navy dirigible, the U.S.S. *Shenandoah*, encountered a severe storm while crossing over the county. The ship broke apart, killing the commander and 13 crew members. One section of the craft fell near the Village of Ava where a monument has been erected in commemoration of the disaster. Attractions in Noble County include Wayne National Forest; Wolf Run Lake and State Park; Seneca Lake Park; Manchester and Parrish Covered Bridges; Site of the First Oil Well drilled in the U.S.; Caldwell House; and Heritage Park at Noble County Fairgrounds.

Vital Statistics

Population, 1995 12,096
Population, 2000 14,058
Net Change, 1990-2000 .... 24%
Median Age 35.5
White 13,010
Black 940
Native American 37
Asian 13
Pacific Islander 0
Other 4
2 or More Races 54
Hispanic 60
Area (square miles) 399
Urban Land Cover (latest figures 1994) 0.5%
Population Per Square Mile 35.2
Elevation 745
Average Temperature 54.3
Average Precipitation .... 49.74 in.

Civilian Labor Force 5,600
    Trade 707
    Construction 66
    Manufacturing 624
    Transportation & Utilities 116
    Government 1,115
    Services 603
    Finance, Insurance & Real Estate 87
Per Capita Income, 1999 .... $14,028
Persons Below Poverty, 1997 .... 15.8%

Retail Sales per Capita, 1997 .... $3,740
Housing Units, 2000 5,480
Average Family Size 3.1
Number of Farms 670
Average Size of Farms (acres) 161
Average Commodity Cash Receipts per Farm $6,562
Highway Miles
    Interstate 19
    U.S. Routes 0
    State Routes 197
Registered Motor Vehicles 15,125
Automobile Crashes per 1,000 .... 32.08

Number of Registered Voters 8,408
    Democrat 17.6%
    Republican 21.0%
    Non Partisan 61.4%
    Number Voted 2000 Election 6,210
    Percent Voted 2000 Election 73.9%
Voting, 2000 Election
    for Bush 3,435
    for Gore 2,296
    for Nader 154
    for Buchanan 75
Contributions to Federal Candidates, Parties, & PACs, '01-'02
    to Democrats $0
    to Republicans $10,700

Ottawa

Namesake Indian word for "trader"

Established March 6, 1840

County Seat Port Clinton

Largest Places	*2000*	*1990*
Port Clinton city	6,391	7,106
Danbury township	3,869	3,665
Allen township	3,297	2,888
Catawba Island township	3,157	3,148
Clay township	2,888	3,005
Oak Harbor village	2,841	2,637
Salem township	2,676	2,427
Benton township	2,232	2,046
Genoa township	2,230	2,262
Carroll township	1,931	1,735

Ottawa County is located in the northwest portion of the state on Lake Erie. The Toussaint and Portage rivers flow into Lake Erie at Ottawa County. Included in Ottawa County's land area are the Lake Erie Islands, Middle Bass with its vineyards, summer cottages and the interior wetlands being one of the most notable. Ottawa County is primarily a resort and recreation area with beaches, boating, fishing, and waterskiing. Other attractions include Johnsons Island Confederate Cemetery; the summer resort village of Put-in-Bay, as well as  Perry's Monument and Perry's Cave; the African Safari Wildlife Park; Lakeside Daisy State Nature Preserve; Catawba Island, East Harbor, South Bass Island State Park; the Lakeside Chautauqua-style summer resort; and the Marblehead Lighthouse State Park.

Vital Statistics
Population, 1995 40,591
Population, 2000 40,985
Net Change, 1990-2000 .... 2.4%
Median Age 41
White 39,576
Black 265
Native American 85
Asian 94
Pacific Islander 20
Other 589
2 or More Races 356
Hispanic 1,535
Area (square miles) 255
Urban Land Cover (latest figures 1994) 5%
Population Per Square Mile 160.7
Elevation 580
Average Temperature 53.9
Average Precipitation .... 34.88 in.

Civilian Labor Force 19,800
    Trade 4,052
    Construction 580
    Manufacturing 3,041
    Transportation & Utilities 1,691
    Government 2,072
    Services 2,921
    Finance, Insurance & Real Estate 497
    Agriculture, Forestry, Fishing 352
    Mining 126
Per Capita Income, 1999 .... $27,370
Persons Below Poverty, 1997 .... 6.9%
Retail Sales per Capita, 1997 .... $8,670
Housing Units, 2000 25,532
Average Family Size 2.92
Number of Farms 510
Average Size of Farms (acres) 208
Average Commodity Cash Receipts per Farm $47,298
Highway Miles
    Interstate 5
    U.S. Routes 0
    State Routes 140
Registered Motor Vehicles 57,249
Automobile Crashes per 1,000 .... 27.86

Number of Registered Voters 28,726
    Democrat 12.3%
    Republican 10.6%
    Non Partisan 77.1%
    Number Voted 2000 Election 20,185
    Percent Voted 2000 Election 70.3%
Voting, 2000 Election
    for Bush 9,917
    for Gore 9,485
    for Nader 432
    for Buchanan 71
Contributions to Federal Candidates, Parties, & PACs, '01-'02
    to Democrats $1,500
    to Republicans $14,000

Ottawa

Put-in-Bay was so named because Commodore Oliver Hazzard "Don't Give Up The Ship" Perry put in nearby after defeating the British in the Battle of Lake Erie. His 1813 victory yielded peaceful British-U.S. relations, and South Bass Island's Perry Peace Memorial is a tomb for the battle's casualties and the world's highest Doric column.

*Somerset's Phil
Sheridan was the
plucky Union general
whose famous ride
turned the Battle
of Clear Creek rout
into a rally that helped
assure Lincoln's
re-election.*

Paulding

Namesake John Paulding, militiaman who discovered plans for West Point in Benedict Arnold's left boot, proving that Arnold was a spy for the British

Established April 1, 1820

County Seat Paulding

Largest Places	2000	1990
Paulding village	3,595	2,605
Antwerp village	1,740	1,677
Auglaize village	1,535	1,521
Brown township	1,315	1,392
Crane township	1,314	1,278
Carryall township	1,306	1,362
Payne township	1,166	1,244
Paulding township	1,086	1,297
Jackson township	847	1,541
Emerald township	824	766

Paulding County is located in the northwest portion of the state bordering on Indiana. The Auglaize and Maumee rivers flow through the county. Paulding County was once part of the Great Black Swamp that covered much of northwest Ohio. Now, mostly fertile farmland, the county ranks fifth in the state in wheat production. Attractions in Paulding County include Paulding Ponds Wildlife Area; Black Swamp Nature Center; Black Swamp Historical Museum; John Paulding Historical Society and Museum; Otto Ehrhart Museum of Natural History; Carnegie Library; and the Scenic Maumee River.

Vital Statistics

Population, 1995	20,443
Population, 2000	20,293
Net Change, 1990-2000	-1%
Median Age	36.5
White	19,451
Black	194
Native American	58
Asian	31
Pacific Islander	3
Other	286
2 or More Races	270
Hispanic	612
Area (square miles)	416
Urban Land Cover (latest figures 1994)	0.6%
Population Per Square Mile	48.8
Elevation	732
Average Temperature	52.8
Average Precipitation	38.23 in.

Civilian Labor Force	9,900
Trade	986
Construction	101
Manufacturing	1,662
Transportation & Utilities	180
Government	1,191
Services	588
Finance, Insurance & Real Estate	124
Per Capita Income, 1999	$19,961
Persons Below Poverty, 1997	7.7%

Retail Sales per Capita, 1997	$5,063
Housing Units, 2000	8,478
Average Family Size	3.06
Number of Farms	650
Average Size of Farms (acres)	351
Average Commodity Cash Receipts per Farm	$62,251
Highway Miles	
Interstate	0
U.S. Routes	34
State Routes	134
Registered Motor Vehicles	25,748
Automobile Crashes per 1,000	26.91

Number of Registered Voters	14,104
Democrat	12.0%
Republican	16.4%
Non Partisan	71.6%
Number Voted 2000 Election	9,214
Percent Voted 2000 Election	65.3%
Voting, 2000 Election	
for Bush	5,210
for Gore	3,384
for Nader	242
for Buchanan	62
Contributions to Federal Candidates, Parties, & PACs, '01-'02	
to Democrats	$0
to Republicans	$6,400

Perry

Namesake Oliver Hazzard Perry, hero of battle of Lake Erie

Established March 1, 1818

County Seat New Lexington

Largest Places	2000	1990
New Lexington city	4,689	5,117
Thorn township	3,034	2,696
Crooksville village	2,483	2,601
Reading township	2,407	2,156
Jackson township	1,973	1,496
Hopewell township	1,965	1,516
Pike township	1,906	1,704
Harrison township	1,745	1,652
Somerset village	1,549	1,390
Clayton township	1,432	1,121

Perry County is located in the southeastern portion of the state. In 1884, a bitter contest between striking miners and strikebreakers provoked an incident at New Straitsville in Perry County. Five mine cars loaded with burning coal were shoved down mine tunnels, and the fire that resulted has burned ever since, consuming uncounted millions of tons of coal. Attractions in Perry County include Wayne National Forest; Perry State Forest; Buckeye Lake State Park; Tecumseh Lake Park; covered bridges; the McGahan Monument; the Perry County Historical Society Museum; Ohio Historical Society Pottery Museum; and General Philip Sheridan's Monument and Home.

Vital Statistics

Population, 1995	33,550
Population, 2000	34,078

Net Change, 1990-2000 .... 8%
Median Age 35
White 33,581
Black 74
Native American 95
Asian 33
Pacific Islander 4
Other 31
2 or More Races 260
Hispanic 152
Area (square miles) 410
Urban Land Cover (latest figures 1994) 1.5%
Population Per Square Mile 83.1
Elevation 955
Average Temperature 53.4
Average Precipitation .... 47.21 in.

Civilian Labor Force 14,200
    Trade 1,351
    Construction 428
    Manufacturing 1,631
    Transportation & Utilities 162
    Government 1,725
    Services 1,004
    Finance, Insurance & Real Estate 210
    Agriculture, Forestry, Fishing 71
    Mining 253
Per Capita Income, 1999 .... $16,313
Persons Below Poverty, 1997 .... 15.4%
Retail Sales per Capita, 1997 .... $3,075
Housing Units, 2000 13,655
Average Family Size 3.13
Number of Farms 740
Average Size of Farms (acres) 143
Average Commodity Cash Receipts per Farm $19,592
Highway Miles
    Interstate 0
    U.S. Routes 14
    State Routes 171
Registered Motor Vehicles 39,908
Automobile Crashes per 1,000 .... 32.78

Number of Registered Voters 18,102
    Democrat 14.8%
    Republican 14.5%
    Non Partisan 70.7%
    Number Voted 2000 Election 13,146
    Percent Voted 2000 Election 72.6%
Voting, 2000 Election
    for Bush 6,440
    for Gore 5,895
    for Nader 334
    for Buchanan 97
Contributions to Federal Candidates, Parties, & PACs, '01-'02
    to Democrats $450
    to Republicans $9,000

Pickaway

Namesake Misspelling of Piqua, prominent Indian capital city and Native American word meaning "man risen from ashes"

Established March 1, 1810

County Seat Circleville

Largest Places	2000	1990
Circleville city	13,485	11,666
Scioto township	8,120	7,553
Darby township	3,486	3,484
Ashville village	3,174	2,254
Washington township	2,951	2,662
Walnut township	2,248	2,179
Salt Creek township	2,357	1,754
Circleville township	2,300	3,488
Harrison township	2,071	2,138
Pickaway township	1,851	1,642

Pickaway County is located in the central portion of the state. The Scioto River flows though the county. Although within the Columbus Metropolitan Statistical Area, Pickaway County remains primarily a rural farming area. With 83 percent of the land in farms, it ranks fourth in the state in the production of soybeans and fifth in corn production. Attractions in Pickaway County include Deer Creek State Park and Lodge; A.W. Marion State Park; Logan Elm State Park; the Historical Museum of Pickaway County; the Ted Lewis Museum; and the Annual Circleville Pumpkin Show held in October.

Vital Statistics
Population, 1995 52,510
Population, 2000 52,727
Net Change, 1990-2000 .... 9.3%
Median Age 36.0
White 48,482
Black 3,391
Native American 148
Asian 117
Pacific Islander 17
Other 80
2 or More Races 492
Hispanic 333
Area (square miles) 502
Urban Land Cover (latest figures 1994) 1.4%
Population Per Square Mile 105.0
Elevation 695
Average Temperature 55.8
Average Precipitation .... 39.04 in.

Civilian Labor Force 25,100
    Trade 3,258
    Construction 779
    Manufacturing 4,653
    Transportation & Utilities 768
    Government 4,307
    Services 2,243
    Finance, Insurance & Real Estate 440
Per Capita Income, 1999 .... $20,364
Persons Below Poverty, 1997 .... 11.3%
Retail Sales per Capita, 1997 .... $5,392
Housing Units, 2000 18,596
Average Family Size 3.02
Number of Farms 780
Average Size of Farms (acres) 344
Average Commodity Cash Receipts per Farm $67,241
Highway Miles
    Interstate 3
    U.S. Routes 55
    State Routes 139
Registered Motor Vehicles 56,506
Automobile Crashes per 1,000 .... 34.69

Pickaway

In 1810, Circleville's settlers, finding concentric rings of Hopewell earthworks, named and planned the town accordingly. Caleb Atwater, who penned Ohio's first history in 1838, lived there, and nearby once stood the famous, but long-gone Logan Elm, where the Mingo Chief Logan gave his celebrated soliloquy lamenting his family's massacre by white men.

Number of Registered Voters		29,155
Democrat		14.2%
Republican		18.3%
Non Partisan		67.5%
Number Voted 2000 Election		17,912
Percent Voted 2000 Election		61.4%
Voting, 2000 Election		
for Bush		10,717
for Gore		6,598
for Nader		276
for Buchanan		68
Contributions to Federal Candidates, Parties, & PACs, '01-'02		
to Democrats		$700
to Republicans		$38,250

Pike

Namesake Zebulon Pike, who discovered Pike's Peak and died in the War of 1812 in Toronto

Established February 1, 1815

County Seat Waverly

Largest Places	2000	1990
Waverly city	4,433	4,477
Pee-Pee township	3,343	3,004
Pebble township	2,416	1,625
Newton township	2,006	1,587
Piketon village	1,907	1,717
Benton township	1,520	1,312
Jackson township	1,346	1,298
Sunfish township	1,317	1,091
Beaver township	1,269	1,182
Union township	1,240	1,147

Pike County is located in the south-central portion of the state. The Scioto River flows through Pike County. The construction of the Ohio-Erie Canal in the late 1820's spurred growth in Pike County. It followed a route on the west side of the Scioto River. The city of Waverly was platted alongside the canal and parts of the old locks are still present. Attractions in Pike County include Lake White State Park; Erie Canal Historic District; Pike Lake State Park and Forest; Eager Inn; Ohio Governor Robert Lucas's home; the Emmitt House Tavern; the Pike Heritage Museum; and an Annual Dogwood Festival held in April.

Vital Statistics

Population, 1995	26,775
Population, 2000	27,695
Net Change, 1990-2000	14.2%
Median Age	35.3
White	26,786
Black	246
Native American	204
Asian	51
Pacific Islander	10
Other	20
2 or More Races	378
Hispanic	155
Area (square miles)	441
Urban Land Cover (latest figures 1994)	1%
Population Per Square Mile	62.8

Elevation	556
Average Temperature	55.6
Average Precipitation	46.76 in.
Civilian Labor Force	11,800
Trade	1,807
Construction	423
Manufacturing	5,598
Transportation & Utilities	283
Government	1,694
Services	1,420
Finance, Insurance & Real Estate	217
Per Capita Income, 1999	$18,353
Persons Below Poverty, 1997	18.2%
Retail Sales per Capita, 1997	$5,578
Housing Units, 2000	11,602
Average Family Size	3.04
Number of Farms	460
Average Size of Farms (acres)	200
Average Commodity Cash Receipts per Farm	$15,328
Highway Miles	
Interstate	0
U.S. Routes	16
State Routes	134
Registered Motor Vehicles	34,443
Automobile Crashes per 1,000	30.55

Number of Registered Voters		20,396
Democrat		17.3%
Republican		12.8%
Non Partisan		70.0%
Number Voted 2000 Election		11,084
Percent Voted 2000 Election		54.3%
Voting, 2000 Election		
for Bush		5,333
for Gore		4,923
for Nader		176
for Buchanan		66
Contributions to Federal Candidates, Parties, & PACs, '01-'02		
to Democrats		$1,300
to Republicans		$3,950

Portage

Namesake From the Indian portage, a carrying path

Established June 7, 1807

County Seat Ravenna

Largest Places	2000	1990
Kent city	27,906	28,835
Aurora city	13,556	9,192
Streetsboro city	12,311	9,932
Ravenna city	11,771	12,069
Ravenna township	9,270	8,961
Brimfield township	7,963	7,554
Rootstown township	7,212	6,612
Suffield township	6,383	6,312
Shalerville township	5,976	5,270
Randolph township	5,504	4,970

Portage County is located in the northeast portion of the state. The Chagrin, Cuyahoga, and Mahoning rivers flow through the county. Attractions in Portage County include Tinkers Creek State Park; West Branch State Park; Nelson Kennedy Ledges State Park; Eagle Creek State Nature Preserve;

Brady Lake; Portage County Historical Society Museum; John Johnson Home and Farm; Kent Historical Society Museum; Historic Garretts Mill; Hiram College; and the markers and memorials commemorating the May 4, 1970, deaths of four students at Kent State University.

Vital Statistics

Population, 1995	148,899
Population, 2000	152,061
Net Change, 1990-2000	6.6%
Median Age	34.4
White	143,545
Black	4,840
Native American	277
Asian	1,246
Pacific Islander	20
Other	328
2 or More Races	1,805
Hispanic	1,093
Area (square miles)	492
Urban Land Cover (latest figures 1994)	3%
Population Per Square Mile	309.1
Elevation	1,052
Average Temperature	51.1
Average Precipitation	36.47 in.
Civilian Labor Force	83,600
Trade	11,999
Construction	2,403
Manufacturing	14,112
Transportation & Utilities	1,101
Government	11,150
Services	9,909
Finance, Insurance & Real Estate	1,021
Agriculture, Forestry, Fishing	790
Mining	300
Per Capita Income, 1999	$24,146
Persons Below Poverty, 1997	8.7%
Retail Sales per Capita, 1997	$7,435
Housing Units, 2000	60,096
Average Family Size	3.03
Number of Farms	810
Average Size of Farms (acres)	119
Average Commodity Cash Receipts per Farm	$38,381
Highway Miles	
Interstate	44
U.S. Routes	23
State Routes	204
Registered Motor Vehicles	158,956
Automobile Crashes per 1,000	31.11
Number of Registered Voters	100,554
Democrat	14.2%
Republican	8.2%
Non Partisan	77.5%
Number Voted 2000 Election	64,028
Percent Voted 2000 Election	63.7%
Voting, 2000 Election	
for Bush	28,271
for Gore	31,446
for Nader	2,340
for Buchanan	446
Contributions to Federal Candidates, Parties, & PACs, '01-'02	
to Democrats	$20,232
to Republicans	$127,169

Preble

Namesake Captain Edward Preble, naval hero of the American Revolution

Established March 1, 1808

County Seat Eaton

Largest Places	2000	1990
Eaton city	8,133	7,396
Gratis township	3,343	3,268
Gasper township	3,229	1,638
Lanier township	3,052	2,797
Harrison township	2,428	2,394
Twin township	2,315	2,303
Camden village	2,302	2,210
Washington township	2,104	1,974
Somers township	1,943	2,016
Jefferson township	1,826	1,982

Preble County is located in the southwestern portion of the state. The east fork of the Whitewater River flows into the county. Primarily a rural area, 73 percent of the land is in farms. Preble County ranks fifth in the state in raising hogs and seventh in corn production. Preble County has the only remaining double-barreled covered bridge in the state. Roberts Covered Bridge was built in 1829 and spans Seven Mile Creek. Other attractions include Hueston Woods State Park and Lodge; Rush Run Wildlife Area; Fort St. Clair State Memorial; and the Preble County Historical Society and Fine Arts Center.

Vital Statistics

Population, 1995	42,174
Population, 2000	42,337
Net Change, 1990-2000	5.5%
Median Age	37.5
White	41,691
Black	136
Native American	91
Asian	111
Pacific Islander	7
Other	47
2 or More Races	254
Hispanic	181
Area (square miles)	425
Urban Land Cover (latest figures 1994)	1.4%
Population Per Square Mile	99.6
Elevation	641
Average Temperature	54.0
Average Precipitation	42.12 in.
Civilian Labor Force	21,800
Trade	2,811
Construction	414
Manufacturing	3,485
Transportation & Utilities	339
Government	1,980
Services	1,657
Finance, Insurance & Real Estate	290
Agriculture, Forestry, Fishing	104
Mining	48
Per Capita Income, 1999	$22,272

Persons Below Poverty, 1997		8%
Retail Sales per Capita, 1997		$5,082
Housing Units, 2000		17,186
Average Family Size		3.02
Number of Farms		1,190
Average Size of Farms (acres)		179
Average Commodity Cash Receipts per Farm		$45,587
Highway Miles		
Interstate		18
U.S. Routes		61
State Routes		112
Registered Motor Vehicles		59,735
Automobile Crashes per 1,000		28.32
Number of Registered Voters		27,718
Democrat		8.0%
Republican		16.8%
Non Partisan		75.2%
Number Voted 2000 Election		18,508
Percent Voted 2000 Election		66.8%
Voting, 2000 Election		
for Bush		11,176
for Gore		6,375
for Nader		404
for Buchanan		82
Contributions to Federal Candidates, Parties, & PACs, '01-'02		
to Democrats		$2,200
to Republicans		$12,825

Putnam

Namesake Rufus Putnam, hero of Revolutionary and French and Indian War

Established April 1, 1820

County Seat Ottawa

Largest Places	*2000*	*1990*
Ottawa village	4,367	3,999
Ottawa township	2,675	2,761
Leipsic village	2,236	2,203
Columbus Grove village	2,200	2,231
Pleasant township	1,755	1,625
Jennings township	1,536	1,370
Union township	1,526	1,530
Greenburg township	1,425	1,244
Liberty township	1,304	1,253
Continental village	1,188	1,214

Putnam County is located in the northwest portion of the state. The Auglaize, Blanchard, and Ottawa rivers flow through the county. Primarily a rural area, 94 percent of the land is in farms. Putnam County ranks first in the state in processing tomatoes production, second in wheat production, and fourth in raising hogs. Attractions in Putnam County include Cascade State Park; the Round Barn at Columbus Grove; Putnam County Courthouse; Gilboa Main Street Historic District; and Ottoville Quarry Wildlife Area.

Vital Statistics

Population, 1995		35,089
Population, 2000		34,726
Net Change, 1990-2000		2.7%

Median Age		35.0
White		33,426
Black		58
Native American		53
Asian		61
Pacific Islander		2
Other		872
2 or More Races		254
Hispanic		1,521
Area (square miles)		484
Urban Land Cover (latest figures 1994)		0.8%
Population Per Square Mile		71.8
Elevation		731
Average Temperature		53.6
Average Precipitation		41.40 in.
Civilian Labor Force		20,700
Trade		2,400
Construction		931
Manufacturing		4,454
Transportation & Utilities		291
Government		1,875
Services		1,890
Finance, Insurance & Real Estate		369
Per Capita Income, 1999		$24,643
Persons Below Poverty, 1997		5.5%
Retail Sales per Capita, 1997		$5,172
Housing Units, 2000		12,753
Average Family Size		3.29
Number of Farms		1,460
Average Size of Farms (acres)		203
Average Commodity Cash Receipts per Farm		$62,733
Highway Miles		
Interstate		0
U.S. Routes		31
State Routes		178
Registered Motor Vehicles		43,237
Automobile Crashes per 1,000		21.77
Number of Registered Voters		24,105
Democrat		15.4%
Republican		17.0%
Non Partisan		67.5%
Number Voted 2000 Election		17,743
Percent Voted 2000 Election		73.6%
Voting, 2000 Election		
for Bush		12,837
for Gore		4,063
for Nader		254
for Buchanan		124
Contributions to Federal Candidates, Parties, & PACs, '01-'02		
to Democrats		$200
to Republicans		$9,425

Richland

Namesake named for richness of soil

Established March 1, 1808

County Seat Mansfield

Largest Places	*2000*	*1990*
Mansfield city	49,346	50,627
Madison township	14,680	13,286
Shelby city	9,821	9,564
Washington township	6,643	6,473
Mifflin township	6,218	6,859
Ontario village	5,303	4,026
Springfield township	4,371	4,434

Lexington village	4,165	4,124
Jackson township	2,774	2,680
Jefferson township	2,773	2,690

Richland County is located in the north-central portion of the state. The North Branch Lokosing, West Branch Huron, and the Black Fork, Clear Fork, and Rocky Fork of the Mohican River flow through the county. Author and conservationist Louis Bromfield established Malabar Farm near Lucas, Ohio, which he dedicated to developing conservation techniques. Today, the 1,000-acre estate is a state park and continues to be a working farm following Bromfield's conservationist principles. Attractions in Richland  County include Pleasant Hill Lake Park; Snow Trails and Clear Fork ski resorts; Oak Hill Cottage (Shane's Castle); Mansfield Art Center; Richland Carrousel Park; Kingwood Center; and the Richland County Museum.

Vital Statistics
Population, 1995 128,421
Population, 2000 128,852
Net Change, 1990-2000 .... 2.2%
Median Age 37.7
White 113,600
Black 12,151
Native American 263
Asian 656
Pacific Islander 38
Other 493
2 or More Races 1,651
Hispanic 1,200
Area (square miles) 497
Urban Land Cover (latest figures 1994) 3%
Population Per Square Mile 259.3
Elevation 1,109
Average Temperature 52.4
Average Precipitation .... 37.49 in.

Civilian Labor Force 61,200
    Trade 14,835
    Construction 2,084
    Manufacturing 16,111
    Transportation & Utilities 2,885
    Government 8,292
    Services 14,897
    Finance, Insurance & Real Estate 1,554
Per Capita Income, 1999 .... $22,721
Persons Below Poverty, 1997 .... 11.5%
Retail Sales per Capita, 1997 .... $9,994
Housing Units, 2000 53,062
Average Family Size 2.98
Number of Farms 1,010
Average Size of Farms (acres) 165
Average Commodity Cash Receipts per Farm $55,440
Highway Miles
    Interstate 21
    U.S. Routes 37
    State Routes 204
Registered Motor Vehicles 145,573
Automobile Crashes per 1,000 .... 37.59

Number of Registered Voters 82,059
    Democrat 13.1%
    Republican 17.8%
    Non Partisan 73.1%

Number Voted 2000 Election 54,088
Percent Voted 2000 Election 65.9%
Voting, 2000 Election
    for Bush 30,138
    for Gore 20,572
    for Nader 1,306
    for Buchanan 533
Contributions to Federal Candidates, Parties, & PACs, '01-'02
    to Democrats $13,431
    to Republicans $115,226

Ross

Namesake James Ross, unsuccessful gubernatorial candidate in Pennsylvania supported by early settlers of area

Established August 20, 1796

County Seat Chillicothe

Largest Places	2000	1990
Chillicothe city	21,796	21,923
Union township	11,750	8,160
Huntington township	6,018	5,102
Scioto township	5,940	8,731
Green township	3,460	2,543
Twin township	3,146	2,755
Concord township	3,096	2,534
Liberty township	2,476	2,126
Springfield township	2,176	2,284
Franklin township	1,671	1,655

Ross County is located in the south-central portion of the state. The Scioto River flows through the county. Chillicothe City in Ross County served at the first Capital of the State of Ohio. The State Constitutional Convention was held here in 1802. Attractions in Ross County include Great Seal, Scioto Trail, and Paint Creek State Parks; Hopewell Culture National Historical Park; Tar Hollow State Forest; Pleasant Valley Wildlife Area; the Adena State Memorial; Dr. John Harris Dental Museum;  James M. Thomas Telephone Museum; Ross County Historical Society Museums; Seven Caves; Lucy Hayes Heritage Center; and *Tecumseh!*, the Outdoor Drama.

Vital Statistics
Population, 1995 73,941
Population, 2000 73,345
Net Change, 1990-2000 .... 5.8%
Median Age 36.9
White 67,288
Black 4,544
Native American 226
Asian 259
Pacific Islander 14
Other 136
2 or More Races 878
Hispanic 429
Area (square miles) 688
Urban Land Cover (latest figures 1994) 1.3%
Population Per Square Mile 106.6
Elevation 630
Average Temperature 55.3
Average Precipitation .... 39.58 in.

Kinnickinnick, a village north of Chillicothe, at the juncture of State Route 159 and 180, finds fame with its name, one of the longest palindromes in the English language. Kinnickinnick was the Indian word for a mixture of tobacco, tree leaves, and bark enjoyed widely by both the natives and Ohio's early settlers.

Civilian Labor Force		35,300
Trade		6,652
Construction		1,014
Manufacturing		4,986
Transportation & Utilities		1,558
Government		4,987
Services		6,048
Finance, Insurance & Real Estate		527
Per Capita Income, 1999		$20,291
Persons Below Poverty, 1997		14.6%
Retail Sales per Capita, 1997		$7,771
Housing Units, 2000		29,461
Average Family Size		2.97
Number of Farms		920
Average Size of Farms (acres)		286
Average Commodity Cash Receipts per Farm		$37,825
Highway Miles		
Interstate		0
U.S. Routes		94
State Routes		122
Registered Motor Vehicles		89,809
Automobile Crashes per 1,000		40.18
Number of Registered Voters		39,400
Democrat		15.4%
Republican		15.7%
Non Partisan		68.9%
Number Voted 2000 Election		26,348
Percent Voted 2000 Election		66.9%
Voting, 2000 Election		
for Bush		13,706
for Gore		11,662
for Nader		421
for Buchanan		122
Contributions to Federal Candidates, Parties, & PACs, '01-'02		
to Democrats		$6,600
to Republicans		$23,525

Sandusky

Namesake Indian word meaning "at the cold water"

Established April 1, 1820

County Seat Fremont

Largest Places	2000	1990
Fremont city	17,375	17,648
Ballville township	6,395	6,049
Clyde city	6,064	5,776
Bellevue city	4,352	4,236
Sandusky township	4,087	4,441
Green Creek township	3,467	4,016
York township	2,512	2,401
Gibsonburg village	2,506	2,579
Woodville village	1,977	1,953
Washington township	1,769	1,654

Sandusky County is located in the north-central portion of the state. The Sandusky and Portage rivers flow through the county. Originally a part of the Great Black Swamp, Sandusky County is now a rich agricultural area with 76 percent of the land in farms. The county ranks fifth in the state in the production of tomatoes for processing. Attractions in Sandusky County include President Rutherford B. Hayes' home, Spiegel Grove; Mull Covered Bridge; Mad River and NKP Railroad Museum; Woodville Historical Museum; Sandusky County Historical Society Museum; Blue Heron Reserve; and Lake Erie's Sandusky Bay.

KNOCKEMSTIFF: WHAT'S IN A NAME?

If you take SR 772 south from Chillicothe five or six miles, then bear left at Horseback Knob, you'll drive through the tiny hamlet of Knockemstiff, Ohio, although the basic reason to do so is merely to say you've been there. "By most definitions," said one writer, "Knockemstiff is nowhere." Said another commentator, "The people who live there didn't move to Knockemstiff, Ohio; they moved to the *country*." The name itself is, according to local legend, commemorative of a rousing brawl between two women. Before the local tavern disappeared a few years ago, there was some debate as to how rough Knockemstiff actually was. The bartender said then that the young fellows couldn't fight as well as their fathers, and the bar was only rough when there was a *band*. The locals still describe Knockemstiff with pride, saying it is the kind of place where "If you want to raise a dog, you can raise a dog." The place is notable largely for its name, of course, and from a refrain from the tavern, circa 1975, which goes:

I went to Knockemstiff Fair,
All of the drunks were there.
Joe Muldoon, by the light of the moon,
Was cutting Bob Rafferty's hair...

Vital Statistics

Population, 1995 62,997
Population, 2000 61,792
Net Change, 1990-2000 .... -0.3%
Median Age 37.3
White 56,974
Black 1,650
Native American 80
Asian 177
Pacific Islander 5
Other 1,913
2 or More Races 993
Hispanic 4,298
Area (square miles) 409
Urban Land Cover (latest figures 1994) 3%
Population Per Square Mile 151.1
Elevation 636
Average Temperature 53.9
Average Precipitation .... 35.25 in.

Civilian Labor Force 30,900
   Trade 5,261
   Construction 1,000
   Manufacturing 10,424
   Transportation & Utilities 537
   Government 3,385
   Services 5,443
   Finance, Insurance & Real Estate 674
   Agriculture, Forestry, Fishing 449
Per Capita Income, 1999 .... $23,315
Persons Below Poverty, 1997 .... 9.5%
Retail Sales per Capita, 1997 .... $7,541
Housing Units, 2000 25,253
Average Family Size 3.04
Number of Farms 920
Average Size of Farms (acres) 225
Average Commodity Cash Receipts per Farm $63,106
Highway Miles
   Interstate 27
   U.S. Routes 63
   State Routes 112
Registered Motor Vehicles 72,512
Automobile Crashes per 1,000 .... 40.81

Number of Registered Voters 40,769
   Democrat 12.5%
   Republican 17.5%
   Non Partisan 70.0%
   Number Voted 2000 Election 26,441
   Percent Voted 2000 Election 64.9%
Voting, 2000 Election
   for Bush 13,699
   for Gore 11,146
   for Nader 587
   for Buchanan 157
Contributions to Federal Candidates, Parties, & PACs, '01-'02
   to Democrats $1,730
   to Republicans $17,600

Scioto

Namesake Indian word for "deer"

Established May 1, 1803

County Seat Portsmouth

Largest Places	2000	1990
Portsmouth city	20,909	22,676
Porter township	9,892	9,687
Washington township	5,971	6,171
Harrison township	4,497	4,316
Valley township	4,256	4,785
Green township	4,079	3,758
Madison township	3,794	3,351
Clay township	3,792	4,000
Rush township	3,144	2,887
Jefferson township	2,751	2,536

Scioto County is located in the south-central portion of the state on the Ohio River. The Scioto River flows into the Ohio River at Portsmouth. Scioto County's rolling hills and valleys and its richly forested land have led some to refer to the area as "The Little Smokies." Attractions in Scioto County include Wayne National Forest; Shawnee State Forest, Park, and Lodge; Brush Creek Forest; Bear, Wolfden, Turkey Creek, Roosevelt, and Pond Lick Lakes; Philip Moore Stone House; 1820 House and Scioto County Historical Society; Historic Boneyfiddle District; Southern Ohio Museum and Cultural Center; Vern Riffe Center for the Arts; Shawnee State University; Floodwall Murals depicting the history of Portsmouth and surrounding area; and the Ohio River.

Vital Statistics

Population, 1995 81,414
Population, 2000 79,195
Net Change, 1990-2000 .... -1.4%
Median Age 36.7
White 75,139
Black 2,163
Native American 502
Asian 189
Pacific Islander 19
Other 144
2 or More Races 1,039
Hispanic 477
Area (square miles) 612
Urban Land Cover (latest figures 1994) 1.6%
Population Per Square Mile 129.4
Elevation 559
Average Temperature 56.8
Average Precipitation .... 38.91 in.

Civilian Labor Force 32,800
   Trade 6,627
   Construction 1,254
   Manufacturing 2,687
   Transportation & Utilities 800
   Government 5,232
   Services 7,499
   Finance, Insurance & Real Estate 711
   Agriculture, Forestry, Fishing 166

Mining 20	
Per Capita Income, 1999 .... $18,978	
Persons Below Poverty, 1997 .... 21%	
Retail Sales per Capita, 1997 .... $6,687	
Housing Units, 2000 34,054	
Average Family Size 2.96	
Number of Farms 740	
Average Size of Farms (acres) 143	
Average Commodity Cash Receipts per Farm $21,392	
Highway Miles	

Highway Miles
Interstate 0
U.S. Routes 61
State Routes 140
Registered Motor Vehicles 88,441
Automobile Crashes per 1,000 .... 37.01

Number of Registered Voters 49,719
Democrat 11.8%
Republican 10.4%
Non Partisan 77.8%
Number Voted 2000 Election 30,786
Percent Voted 2000 Election 61.9%
Voting, 2000 Election
for Bush 15,022
for Gore 13,997
for Nader 590
for Buchanan 159
Contributions to Federal Candidates, Parties, & PACs, '01-'02
to Democrats $3,677
to Republicans $16,275

Seneca

Namesake The Seneca Indians, who had a reservation there

Established April 1, 1820

County Seat Tiffin

Largest Places	2000	1990
Tiffin city	18,135	18,604
Fostoria city	10,035	10,848
Clinton township	4,188	4,055
Hopewell township	2,874	2,976
Loudon township	2,395	2,475
Eden township	2,020	1,996
Pleasant township	1,685	1,594
Jackson township	1,640	1,747
Seneca township	1,585	1,515
Big Spring township	1,565	1,448

Seneca County is located in the north-central portion of the state. The Sandusky River flows through the county. Discovery of natural gas in 1887 brought a rush of glass companies to the area. Today, many of the original glass artifacts from Fostoria and Tiffin glassmakers are displayed in Fostoria's Glass Heritage Gallery and at the Seneca County Museum. Other attractions in Seneca County include Seneca Caverns; Sorrowful Mother Shrine; Springville Marsh State Nature Preserve; Seneca County Museum; the Indian Maiden Bronze Statue in Tiffin; Valentine's Village; and Heidelberg College.

Vital Statistics
Population, 1995 60,369
Population, 2000 58,683
Net Change, 1990-2000 .... -1.8%
Median Age 36.3
White 55,770
Black 1,033
Native American 103
Asian 222
Pacific Islander 5
Other 817
2 or More Races 733
Hispanic 1,972
Area (square miles) 551
Urban Land Cover (latest figures 1994) 1.4%
Population Per Square Mile 106.5
Elevation 766
Average Temperature 53.9
Average Precipitation .... 39.95 in.

Civilian Labor Force 28,300
Trade 4,581
Construction 899
Manufacturing 6,570
Transportation & Utilities 893
Government 3,088
Services 5,467
Finance, Insurance & Real Estate 727
Agriculture, Forestry, Fishing 295
Mining 120
Per Capita Income, 1999 .... $21,695
Persons Below Poverty, 1997 .... 9.6%
Retail Sales per Capita, 1997 .... $6,778
Housing Units, 2000 23,692
Average Family Size 3.04
Number of Farms 1,360
Average Size of Farms (acres) 220
Average Commodity Cash Receipts per Farm $50,549
Highway Miles
Interstate 0
U.S. Routes 45
State Routes 177
Registered Motor Vehicles 67,557
Automobile Crashes per 1,000 .... 33.01

Number of Registered Voters 35,917
Democrat 14.4%
Republican 21.9%
Non Partisan 63.6%
Number Voted 2000 Election 24,931
Percent Voted 2000 Election 69.4%
Voting, 2000 Election
for Bush 13,863
for Gore 9,512
for Nader 666
for Buchanan 183
Contributions to Federal Candidates, Parties, & PACs, '01-'02
to Democrats $1,575
to Republicans $37,860

Shelby

Namesake General Isaac Shelby, first Governor of Kentucky

Established April 1, 1819

County Seat Sidney

Largest Places	2000	1990
Sidney city	20,211	18,710
Cynthian township	1,972	1,762
Salem township	1,910	1,699
Loramie township	1,887	1,748
Washington township	1,875	1,641
Franklin township	1,773	1,602
McLean township	1,738	1,650
Turtle Creek township	1,583	1,301
Van Buren township	1,424	1,622
Orange township	1,419	1,183

Shelby County is located in the west-central portion of the state. The Great Miami River flows through the county. Agriculture plays an important role in Shelby County's economy with cash receipts from farm marketings totaling more than $70 million each year. Shelby ranks high among the 88 counties in dairy farming and the raising of cattle and calves. Attractions in Shelby County include Lake Loramie State Park; Gross Woods Nature Reserve; Jackson Center Community Museum; Lockington Reserve; Tawawa Park; Whitby Mansion; the Shelby County Historical Society; and the Wilderness Trail Museum in Fort Loramie.

Vital Statistics

Population, 1995	47,079
Population, 2000	47,910
Net Change, 1990-2000	6.7%
Median Age	34.8
White	46,011
Black	714
Native American	80
Asian	464
Pacific Islander	25
Other	113
2 or More Races	503
Hispanic	383
Area (square miles)	409
Urban Land Cover (latest figures 1994)	1.6%
Population Per Square Mile	117.1
Elevation	1,030
Average Temperature	53.3
Average Precipitation	37.76 in.

Civilian Labor Force	28,600
Trade	4,858
Construction	1,417
Manufacturing	14,770
Transportation & Utilities	641
Government	2,604
Services	3,838
Finance, Insurance & Real Estate	361
Per Capita Income, 1999	$25,520
Persons Below Poverty, 1997	7.6%
Retail Sales per Capita, 1997	$6,545

Housing Units, 2000	16,682
Average Family Size	3.13
Number of Farms	1,090
Average Size of Farms (acres)	196
Average Commodity Cash Receipts per Farm	$65,392
Highway Miles	
Interstate	21
U.S. Routes	0
State Routes	144
Registered Motor Vehicles	58,586
Automobile Crashes per 1,000	37.1

Number of Registered Voters	29,578
Democrat	13.6%
Republican	11.2%
Non Partisan	75.1%
Number Voted 2000 Election	19,670
Percent Voted 2000 Election	66.5%
Voting, 2000 Election	
for Bush	12,476
for Gore	6,593
for Nader	392
for Buchanan	115
Contributions to Federal Candidates, Parties, & PACs, '01-'02	
to Democrats	$19,520
to Republicans	$20,450

Stark

Namesake General John Stark, Revolutionary War hero

Established February 13, 1808

County Seat Canton

Largest Places	2000	1990
Canton city	80,806	84,161
Jackson township	37,484	31,774
Plain township	25,543	34,318
Massillon city	31,325	31,007
Perry township	29,167	30,307
Lake township	23,718	20,312
Alliance city	23,195	23,304
North Canton	16,369	14,748
Canton township	13,402	13,672
Nimishillen township	9,098	9,492

Stark County is located in the northeast portion of the state. The Tuscarawas River flows through it. The National Football League was founded in 1920 in Canton, Ohio. In the early 1960's, the city was chosen as the site for the Professional Football Hall of Fame. Twin enshrinement halls honor the greats of professional football fame. Other attractions in Stark County include Quail Hollow State Park; the President William McKinley National Memorial; the McKinley Museum of History, Science, and Industry; Canton Museum of Art; Classic Car Museum; the Hoover Historical Center's vacuum cleaner museum (including the first commercially successful portable electric vacuum cleaner); the Ohio Military Museum at Massillon; Spring Hill Historic Home; and the St. Helena III Canal Boat at Canal Fulton.

Stark

In 1894, Massillon's **Jacob Coxey**, *a wealthy businessman and currency reformer, led the first protest march on Washington, D.C. Unemployment was the issue that moved the 500 members of "Coxey's Army", and his proposals for federal assistance and public works jobs anticipated the New Deal by 40 years.*

Vital Statistics

Population, 1995	375,553
Population, 2000	378,098
Net Change, 1990-2000	2.9%
Median Age	38.2
White	341,342
Black	27,219
Native American	920
Asian	2,059
Pacific Islander	57
Other	1,098
2 or More Races	5,403
Hispanic	3,492
Area (square miles)	576
Urban Land Cover (latest figures 1994)	5%
Population Per Square Mile	656.4
Elevation	959
Average Temperature	52.5
Average Precipitation	37.46 in.

Civilian Labor Force	190,100
Trade	44,472
Construction	8,547
Manufacturing	43,236
Transportation & Utilities	4,197
Government	18,059
Services	48,327
Finance, Insurance & Real Estate	6,714
Agriculture, Forestry, Fishing	1,182
Mining	467
Per Capita Income, 1999	$25,214
Persons Below Poverty, 1997	10.5%
Retail Sales per Capita, 1997	$9,821
Housing Units, 2000	157,024
Average Family Size	3.00
Number of Farms	1,300
Average Size of Farms (acres)	115
Average Commodity Cash Receipts per Farm	$65,726
Highway Miles	
Interstate	19
U.S. Routes	72
State Routes	232
Registered Motor Vehicles	418,942
Automobile Crashes per 1,000	31.67

Number of Registered Voters	240,794
Democrat	16.2%
Republican	14.2%
Non Partisan	69.6%
Number Voted 2000 Election	163,061
Percent Voted 2000 Election	67.7%
Voting, 2000 Election	
for Bush	78,153
for Gore	75,308
for Nader	4,032
for Buchanan	1,499
Contributions to Federal Candidates, Parties, & PACs, '01-'02	
to Democrats	$42,087
to Republicans	$1,064,798

Summit

Namesake Portage Summit, the highest land along the Ohio Canal

Established March 3, 1840

County Seat Akron

Largest Places	2000	1990
Akron city	217,074	223,019
Cuyahoga Falls city	49,374	48,950
Stow city	32,139	27,702
Barberton city	27,899	27,623
Green city	22,817	3,553
Hudson city	22,439	5,159
Tallmadge city	16,180	14,870
Springfield township	15,168	14,773
Copley township	13,641	11,130
Franklin township	12,339	14,910

Summit County is located in the northeast portion of the state. The Cuyahoga, Tuscarawas, and Rocky rivers flow through the county. Once known as the "Rubber Capital of the World," Akron today is recognized as a world leader in polymer research. The University of Akron's Institute of Polymer Science is internationally acclaimed. Attractions in Summit County include Cuyahoga Valley National Recreation Area; Portage Lakes State Park; the Akron Art Museum; Akron Zoological Park; Blossom Music Center; Stan Hywet Hall and Gardens; F.A. Seiberling Naturealm (a 104-acre nature center and arboretum); the Goodyear World of Rubber Exhibit; and the National Inventors Hall of Fame at Inventure Place.

Vital Statistics

Population, 1995	530,135
Population, 2000	542,899
Net Change, 1990-2000	5.4%
Median Age	37.2
White	453,336
Black	71,608
Native American	1,086
Asian	7,641
Pacific Islander	100
Other	1,590
2 or More Races	7,538
Hispanic	4,781
Area (square miles)	413
Urban Land Cover (latest figures 1994)	14%
Population Per Square Mile	1,314.5
Elevation	985
Average Temperature	52.4
Average Precipitation	40.28 in.

Civilian Labor Force	282,100
Trade	70,649
Construction	11,498
Manufacturing	49,740
Transportation & Utilities	13,740
Government	27,850
Services	76,258
Finance, Insurance & Real Estate	13,085

Agriculture, Forestry, Fishing 1,972
Mining 280
Per Capita Income, 1999 .... $29,187
Persons Below Poverty, 1997 .... 10.9%
Retail Sales per Capita, 1997 .... $10,280
Housing Units, 2000 203,880
Average Family Size 3.02
Number of Farms 310
Average Size of Farms (acres) 61
Average Commodity Cash Receipts per Farm $39,183
Highway Miles
    Interstate 90
    U.S. Routes 6
    State Routes 185
Registered Motor Vehicles 527,006
Automobile Crashes per 1,000 .... 25.7

Number of Registered Voters 354,189
    Democrat 16.4%
    Republican 9.5%
    Non Partisan 74.1%
    Number Voted 2000 Election 232,252
    Percent Voted 2000 Election 65.6%
Voting, 2000 Election
    for Bush 96,721
    for Gore 119,759
    for Nader 5,955
    for Buchanan 1,363
Contributions to Federal Candidates, Parties, & PACs, '01-'02
    to Democrats $385,522
    to Republicans $2,131,485

Trumbull

Namesake Connecticut Governor Jonathan Trumbull

Established July 10, 1800

County Seat Warren

Largest Places	2000	1990
Warren city	46,832	50,793
Niles city	20,932	21,128
Howland township	17,546	18,005
Liberty township	12,661	13,189
Girard city	10,902	11,304
Brookfield township	9,921	10,474
Champion township	9,762	9,189
Weatherfield township	8,677	9,430
Hubbard city	8,284	8,248
Warren township	7,817	6,867

Trumbull County is located in northeast portion of the state on the Pennsylvania border. The Grand and Mahoning rivers flow through the country. Clarence Darrow, born in Kinsman, Ohio, was a skillful advocate in many dramatic trials including the 1925 Scopes "Monkey" Trial. The historic site, the Clarence Darrow Octagon House, is located in Kinsman. Other attractions in Trumbull County include the W.D. Packard Car Museum; Mosquito Lake State Park; National McKinley Birthplace Memorial Library and Museum; the Workshops of Gerald E. Henn, basketmaker; Newton Falls Covered Bridge; and the Trumbull County Historical Society Museum.

Vital Statistics
Population, 1995 228,417
Population, 2000 225,116
Net Change, 1990-2000 .... -1.2%
Median Age 39.0
White 203,084
Black 17,778
Native American 333
Asian 1,014
Pacific Islander 34
Other 472
2 or More Races 2,401
Hispanic 1,794
Area (square miles) 616
Urban Land Cover (latest figures 1994) 4%
Population Per Square Mile 365.4
Elevation 880
Average Temperature 52.1
Average Precipitation .... 37.56 in.

Civilian Labor Force 110,900
    Trade 22,551
    Construction 2,924
    Manufacturing 30,894
    Transportation & Utilities 2,909
    Government 10,779
    Services 20,966
    Finance, Insurance & Real Estate 2,882
    Agriculture, Forestry, Fishing 577
    Mining 88
Per Capita Income, 1999 .... $25,022
Persons Below Poverty, 1997 .... 11.2%
Retail Sales per Capita, 1997 .... $8,551
Housing Units, 2000 95,117
Average Family Size 3.02
Number of Farms 1,000
Average Size of Farms (acres) 124
Average Commodity Cash Receipts per Farm $28,816
Highway Miles
    Interstate 23
    U.S. Routes 32
    State Routes 302
Registered Motor Vehicles 255,276
Automobile Crashes per 1,000 .... 26.93

Number of Registered Voters 145,019
    Democrat 31.4%
    Republican 7.0%
    Non Partisan 61.5%
    Number Voted 2000 Election 98,440
    Percent Voted 2000 Election 67.9%
Voting, 2000 Election
    for Bush 34,654
    for Gore 57,643
    for Nader 2,749
    for Buchanan 844
Contributions to Federal Candidates, Parties, & PACs, '01-'02
    to Democrats $82,835
    to Republicans $145,963

Trumbull

Born near Kinsman, **Clarence Darrow** *was America's most famous criminal lawyer. In 1925, he debated silver-tongued William Jennings Bryan during Tennessee's sensational "monkey trial." Defending the right to teach evolution, Darrow "lost" when his client was found guilty, but he triumphed in focusing national attention on a social issue.*

Tuscarawas

Namesake Indian word meaning, "open mouth"

Established March 15, 1808

County Seat New Philadelphia

Largest Places	2000	1990
New Philadelphia city	17,056	15,698
Dover city	12,210	11,329
Uhrichville city	5,662	5,604
Dover township	4,485	4,251
Goshen township	4,225	4,677
Lawrence township	4,154	3,205
Newcomerstown village	4,008	4,012
Dennison village	2,992	3,282
Sandy township	2,513	2,437
Strasburg village	2,310	1,995

Tuscarawas County is located in the east-central portion of the state. The Tuscarawas River flows through the county. Schoenbrunn Village was settled by a Moravian minister in 1772, and he converted many Delaware Indians to Christianity. The Christian Delawares set up another community called Gnadenhutten. During the American Revolution, the Indians at Schoenbrunn were driven out, and the Gnadenhutten Delawares were massacred. Both villages have been restored, and the story of the settlement and the massacre is told in the outdoor production, *Trumpet in the Land.*

Other attractions in Tuscarawas County include Atwood Lake; Fort Laurens State Park and Museum; and a restored 19th century commune at Zoar.

Vital Statistics

Population, 1995	87,323
Population, 2000	90,914
Net Change, 1990-2000	8.1%
Median Age	37.9
White	88,976
Black	663
Native American	154
Asian	220
Pacific Islander	43
Other	195
2 or More Races	663
Hispanic	650
Area (square miles)	568
Urban Land Cover (latest figures 1994)	1.6%
Population Per Square Mile	160.1
Elevation	1,031
Average Temperature	53.2
Average Precipitation	40.06 in.

Civilian Labor Force	44,400
Trade	9,980
Construction	1,699
Manufacturing	9,215
Transportation & Utilities	1,325
Government	4,642
Services	7,977
Finance, Insurance & Real Estate	1,038
Agriculture, Forestry, Fishing	411
Mining	437

Per Capita Income, 1999	$21,708
Persons Below Poverty, 1997	10.2%
Retail Sales per Capita, 1997	$8,615
Housing Units, 2000	38,113
Average Family Size	3.01
Number of Farms	1,080
Average Size of Farms (acres)	143
Average Commodity Cash Receipts per Farm	$60,016
Highway Miles	
Interstate	35
U.S. Routes	39
State Routes	141
Registered Motor Vehicles	109,855
Automobile Crashes per 1,000	34.66

Number of Registered Voters	57,546
Democrat	21.1%
Republican	8.8%
Non Partisan	70.0%
Number Voted 2000 Election	38,246
Percent Voted 2000 Election	66.5%
Voting, 2000 Election	
for Bush	19,549
for Gore	15,879
for Nader	1,061
for Buchanan	420
Contributions to Federal Candidates, Parties, & PACs, '01-'02	
to Democrats	$10,700
to Republicans	$29,775

Union

Namesake From the union of parts of four counties

Established April 1, 1820

County Seat Marysville

Largest Places	2000	1990
Marysville city	15,942	9,656
Jerome township	3,033	2,519
Dover township	2,331	2,067
Richwood township	2,156	2,186
Liberty township	1,705	1,221
Darby township	1,634	1,292
Paris township	1,617	2,368
Allen township	1,518	901
Taylor township	1,444	1,266
Claibourne township	1,265	1,113

Union County is in the central portion of the state. The Big Darby and Little Darby creeks flow through the county. Although Marysville is a thriving, urban city due to several large and small industries located there, the county is primarily rural with 73 percent of the land in farms. Attractions in Union County include Union County Courthouse; Richwood Park and Lake; Union County Historical Society and Museum; Houston House at Marysville; Bigelow Cemetery Prairie State Nature Preserve; covered bridges; the Scenic Big Darby Creek; and an annual Balloon Festival in August.

Vital Statistics

Population, 1994	36,520
Population, 2000	40,909
Net Change, 1990-2000	28.0%
Median Age	34.5
White	38,965
Black	1,149
Native American	75
Asian	221
Pacific Islander	7
Other	92
2 or More Races	400
Hispanic	309
Area (square miles)	437.0
Urban Land Cover (latest figures 1994)	.7%
Population Per Square Mile	93.6
Elevation	935
Average Temperature	54.9
Average Precipitation	32.32 in.

Civilian Labor Force	18,400
Trade	3,254
Construction	737
Manufacturing	11,700
Transportation & Utilities	1,011
Government	2,911
Services	3,053
Finance, Insurance & Real Estate	430
Per Capita Income, 1999	$23,776
Persons Below Poverty, 1997	6.7%
Retail Sales per Capita, 1997	$7,186
Housing Units, 2000	15,217
Average Family Size	3.11
Number of Farms	930
Average Size of Farms (acres)	245
Average Commodity Cash Receipts per Farm	$58,108
Highway Miles	
Interstate	0
U.S. Routes	51
State Routes	146
Registered Motor Vehicles	54,780
Automobile Crashes per 1,000	30.04

Number of Registered Voters	25,981
Democrat	6.3%
Republican	27.4%
Non Partisan	66.3%
Number Voted 2000 Election	17,288
Percent Voted 2000 Election	66.5%
Voting, 2000 Election	
for Bush	11,502
for Gore	5,040
for Nader	336
for Buchanan	64
Contributions to Federal Candidates, Parties, & PACs, '01-'02	
to Democrats	$1,250
to Republicans	$36,600

Van Wert

Namesake Isaac Van Wert, helped capture Major John Andre, the British officer who was Benedict Arnold's intermediary

Established April 1, 1820

County Seat Van Wert

Largest Places	***2000***	***1990***
Van Wert city	10,690	10,891
Delphos city	3,043	3,192
Pleasant township	2,233	2,112
Washington township	1,592	1,561
Ridge township	1,311	1,198
Convoy village	1,110	1,200
Harrison township	1,085	1,019
Willshire township	1,057	1,076
Tully township	1,009	934
Liberty township	912	1,152

Van Wert County is located in the northwestern portion of the state. The Little Auglaize and St. Marys rivers flow through the county. Primarily a rural area, 90 percent of the land is in farms. Van Wert County ranks ninth in the state in soybean production. Attractions in Van Wert County include Wassenberg Art Center; Brumback Library (the first county library in the U.S.); the Central Fire Museum; Civic Theater; George Marsh Homestead and Marsh Foundation School; the Van Wert Historical Museum; and the Pennsylvania Railroad Caboose.

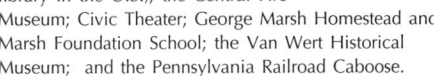

Vital Statistics

Population, 1995	30,463
Population, 2000	29,659
Net Change, 1990-2000	-2.6%
Median Age	37.6
White	28,896
Black	222
Native American	33
Asian	57
Pacific Islander	0
Other	223
2 or More Races	228
Hispanic	462
Area (square miles)	410
Urban Land Cover (latest figures 1994)	1.1%
Population Per Square Mile	72.3
Elevation	795
Average Temperature	54.4
Average Precipitation	37.12 in.

Civilian Labor Force	16,900
Trade	2,832
Construction	328
Manufacturing	4,701
Transportation & Utilities	222
Government	1,374
Services	2,221
Finance, Insurance & Real Estate	587
Per Capita Income, 1999	$22,916
Persons Below Poverty, 1997	6.4%
Retail Sales per Capita, 1997	$6,838

Housing Units, 2000 12,363
Average Family Size 3.0
Number of Farms 810
Average Size of Farms (acres) 312
Average Commodity Cash Receipts per Farm $75,257
Highway Miles
    Interstate 0
    U.S. Routes 71
    State Routes 97
Registered Motor Vehicles 36,457
Automobile Crashes per 1,000 .... 30.08

Number of Registered Voters 21,841
    Democrat 8.8%
    Republican 29.3%
    Non Partisan 61.7%
    Number Voted 2000 Election 13,471
    Percent Voted 2000 Election 61.7%
Voting, 2000 Election
    for Bush 8,679
    for Gore 4,209
    for Nader 216
    for Buchanan 62
Contributions to Federal Candidates, Parties, & PACs, '01-'02
    to Democrats $1,850
    to Republicans $7,903

Vinton

Namesake Early Ohio Statesman, Samuel Finley Vinton

Established March 23, 1850

County Seat McArthur

Largest Places	2000	1990
McArthur village	1,888	1,541
Richland township	1,667	1,241
Elk township	1,246	1,142
Clinton township	1,174	884
Harrison township	1,030	938
Hamden village	871	877
Swan township	796	696
Wilkesville township	737	750
Jackson township	714	541
Knox township	599	443

Vinton County is located in the southeastern portion of the
state. Salt Creek and Raccoon Creek flow though the
county. Attractions in Vinton
County include Wayne National
Forest; Tar Hollow State Forest;
Zaleski State Forest and Park;
Lake Hope State Park and Lodge;
Lake Alma State Park; Lake
Rupert Wildlife Area; Mead
Corporation Wildlife Area; Hope
Furnace; Richland Furnace; Cox,
Mt. Olive, Tinker, Arbaugh, and Ponn covered bridges; and
100 mile-long Raccoon Creek, the longest creek in the U.S.

Vital Statistics
Population, 1995 12,072
Population, 2000 12,806
Net Change, 1990-2000 .... 15.4%
Median Age 35.5
White 12,560
Black 45

Native American 58
Asian 11
Pacific Islander 0
Other 10
2 or More Races 122
Hispanic 60
Area (square miles) 414
Urban Land Cover (latest figures 1994) 6%
Population Per Square Mile 30.9
Elevation 681
Average Temperature 54.1
Average Precipitation .... 38.46 in.

Civilian Labor Force 3,800
    Trade 310
    Construction 79
    Manufacturing 586
    Transportation & Utilities 108
    Government 798
    Services 311
    Finance, Insurance & Real Estate 134
Per Capita Income, 1999 .... $16,423
Persons Below Poverty, 1997 .... 18.7%
Retail Sales per Capita, 1997 .... $2,260
Housing Units, 2000 5,653
Average Family Size 3.04
Number of Farms 300
Average Size of Farms (acres) 170
Average Commodity Cash Receipts per Farm $89,083
Highway Miles
    Interstate 0
    U.S. Routes 30
    State Routes 127
Registered Motor Vehicles 16,666
Automobile Crashes per 1,000 .... 39.36

Number of Registered Voters 8,595
    Democrat 14.5%
    Republican 19.9%
    Non Partisan 65.6%
    Number Voted 2000 Election 5,184
    Percent Voted 2000 Election 60.3%
Voting, 2000 Election
    for Bush 2,720
    for Gore 2,037
    for Nader 110
    for Buchanan 42
Contributions to Federal Candidates, Parties, & PACs, '01-'02
    to Democrats $200
    to Republicans $1,650

Warren

Namesake General Joseph Warren, killed at Bunker Hill

Established May 1, 1803

County Seat Lebanon

Largest Places	2000	1990
Deerfield township	25,515	15,039
Mason city	22,016	11,452
Lebanon city	16,962	10,453
Springboro city	12,227	6,590
Turtlecreek township	12,114	10,319
Franklin city	11,396	11,026
Franklin township	9,947	11,840
Clear Creek township	8,747	6,757
Hamilton township	8,645	5,430

Carlisle village
4,876
4,610

Warren County is located in the southeastern portion of the state. The Little Miami and Great Miami rivers flow through the county. Attractions in Warren County include Caesar Creek Lake State Park; Spring Valley Wildlife Area; Scenic Little Miami State Park; Fort Ancient State Memorial; Warren County Historical Society Museum; Glendower State Memorial; Ohio's oldest inn—The Golden Lamb; Indiana & Ohio Scenic Railway excursions between Mason and Lebanon; Paramount's Kings Island Theme Park; and the Annual Ohio Renaissance Festival, held late August to mid-October weekends.

Vital Statistics

Population, 1995 131,295
Population, 2000 158,383
Net Change, 1990-2000 .... 39%
Median Age 35.2
White 149,919
Black 4,327
Native American 282
Asian 1,991
Pacific Islander 47
Other 485
2 or More Races 1,332
Hispanic 1,633
Area (square miles) 400
Urban Land Cover (latest figures 1994) 4%
Population Per Square Mile 396
Elevation 805
Average Temperature 54.7
Average Precipitation .... 40.99 in.

Civilian Labor Force 81,300
  Trade 16,865
  Construction 2,243
  Manufacturing 13,383
  Transportation & Utilities 766
  Government 6,926
  Services 15,748
  Finance, Insurance & Real Estate 2,989
  Agriculture, Forestry, Fishing 755
  Mining 108
Per Capita Income, 1999 .... $28,402
Persons Below Poverty, 1997 .... 5.6%
Retail Sales per Capita, 1997 .... $7,941
Housing Units, 2000 58,692
Average Family Size 3.12
Number of Farms 900
Average Size of Farms (acres) 148
Average Commodity Cash Receipts per Farm $36,482
Highway Miles
  Interstate 34
  U.S. Routes 45
  State Routes 138
Registered Motor Vehicles 166,418
Automobile Crashes per 1,000 .... 27.6

Number of Registered Voters 96,538
  Democrat 4.8%
  Republican 15.4%
  Non Partisan 79.7%
  Number Voted 2000 Election 70,109
  Percent Voted 2000 Election 72.6%
Voting, 2000 Election
  for Bush 48,318
  for Gore 19,142
  for Nader 1,067
  for Buchanan 207
Contributions to Federal Candidates, Parties, & PACs, '01-'02
  to Democrats $24,025
  to Republicans $206,347

Warren

*Lebanon's **Golden Lamb** is Ohio's oldest inn. Since 1803, it has accommodated ten presidents and the likes of **Daniel Webster**, **Henry Clay**, **Mark Twain**, and **Clement Vallandigham**, the Copperhead who accidentally shot himself in his room. In 1842, **Charles Dickens** left disgusted when offered only ice water as a libation.*

WARREN COUNTY: FAMOUS BREEDING GROUND

Warren County is no longer referred to as "Hog Heaven" as it was in the middle of the 19th century, for which the tourist bureau is thankful, but it's the home of one of America's most notable breeds—the Poland China. The breed began early in the 1800s when the Lebanon Shakers began selective breeding's tedious process. They were after a fat hog, rather than the stringy razorbacks that were rugged enough for the long market treks. By mid–century, the Shakers had their hog—a docile creature that was a miracle of protein conversion. Its name seems to have been an amalgam of the eastern breed known as the Big China, and the nationality of the Polish farmer and Warren County pig-breeder, Asher Asher, who is said to have been the one to break the Shaker monopoly. At any rate, in 1876, America's first pedigree for a Poland China was written—for a sow named Lady Pugh, an appropriate name for such porker royalty, in both deference and onomatopoeia. There's still a monument to it all, perhaps the only such monument in the world, a bronze plaque on a marble shaft just north of SR 122, on the Cincinnati-Dayton Road, on what was once the farm of the fair Lady Pugh. "When you consider the work that gets done in America each morning on the human energy generated from ham and eggs," wrote Frank Seidel, "it hardly seems strange that there should be a monument to a pig."

Washington

Namesake George Washington

Established July 27, 1788

County Seat Marietta

Largest Places	2000	1990
Marietta city	14,515	15,026
Belpre city	6,660	6,796
Marietta township	4,673	4,453
Muskingum township	4,627	4,764
Belpre township	4,192	4,208
Warren townhip	4,044	3,872
Dunham township	2,505	2,224
Waterford township	2,426	2,257
Barlow township	2,417	1,982
Newport township	2,176	2,077

Washington County is located in the southeastern portion of the state, and unites the Muskingum, Little Hocking, and Little Muskingum rivers with the Ohio River. During the early 1800's, shipbuilding became a thriving business in Marietta. Full-rigged ocean-going vessels were built and launched at the mouth of the Muskingum River and floated down the Ohio River to the Mississippi River, then on to the ocean and world ports. Attractions in Washington County include Wayne National Forest; Blennerhassett Island Historical State Park; the Ohio River Museum; Showboat Becky Thatcher; W.P. Snyder Riverboat; the Valley Gem Sternwheeler; and the Campus Martius Museum of the Northwest Territory.

Vital Statistics
Population, 1995	63,836
Population, 2000	63,251
Net Change, 1990-2000	1.6%
Median Age	39.1
White	61,563
Black	585
Native American	151
Asian	274
Pacific Islander	29
Other	85
2 or More Races	564
Hispanic	324
Area (square miles)	635
Urban Land Cover (latest figures 1994)	2%
Population Per Square Mile	99.6
Elevation	891
Average Temperature	55.3
Average Precipitation	44.69 in.
Civilian Labor Force	32,700
Trade	6,088
Construction	1,603
Manufacturing	5,553
Transportation & Utilities	855
Government	3,142
Services	5,714
Finance, Insurance & Real Estate	843
Agriculture, Forestry, Fishing	272
Mining	262
Per Capita Income, 1999	$22,298
Persons Below Poverty, 1997	12.3%
Retail Sales per Capita, 1997	$7,879
Housing Units, 2000	27,760
Average Family Size	2.93
Number of Farms	1,000
Average Size of Farms (acres)	147
Average Commodity Cash Receipts per Farm	$20,643
Highway Miles	
Interstate	18
U.S. Routes	11
State Routes	244
Registered Motor Vehicles	78,435
Automobile Crashes per 1,000	30.17
Number of Registered Voters	40,969
Democrat	11.2%
Republican	23.3%
Non Partisan	65.5%
Number Voted 2000 Election	27,080
Percent Voted 2000 Election	66.1%
Voting, 2000 Election	
for Bush	15,342
for Gore	10,383
for Nader	571
for Buchanan	108
Contributions to Federal Candidates, Parties, & PACs, '01-'02	
to Democrats	$5,850
to Republicans	$51,651

Wayne

Namesake General Anthony Wayne

Established August 15, 1796

County Seat Wooster

Largest Places	2000	1990
Wooster city	24,811	22,191
Orrville city	8,551	7,712
Chippewa township	7,078	6,504
Rittman city	6,208	6,037
East Union township	5,528	4,973
Wooster township	5,250	4,918
Sugar Creek township	4,897	4,413
Wayne township	4,034	3,958
Green township	3,511	3,602
Franklin township	3,485	2,747

Wayne County is located in the northeast portion of the state. The Muddy Fork of the Mohican River flows through the county. Primarily a farming area, Wayne County ranks first in the state in the production of oats, hay, cattle, and dairy products. The county is home to the Ohio Agricultural Research and Development Center. Research at the Center follows the development of the Agricultural products from farm to the consumer's dinner table. Attractions in Wayne County include Killbuck Marsh Wildlife Area; Johnson Woods State Nature Preserve; Shreve Lake; and Wayne County Historical Society Complex.

MARIETTA: A COLONY OF FAVORABLE AUSPICES

Local vanity here holds that the Marquis de Lafayette's triumphant tour of the U.S. in 1825 made him America's first tourist and that his itinerary included Marietta. The aging French hero of the American Revolution did stay in Marietta, actually, stopping overnight, no doubt, to see his old comrades from the battles of Brandywine and Yorktown.

The founders of this town were no rude trappers or rough pioneers, but the cream of New England's social crop—educated, eminently civilized fellows. They were Revolutionary War veterans and friends of Washington, men rich with the ideals of liberty who went home to find their prospects poor.

When the Northwest Ordinance of 1787 opened up the land beyond the Alleghenies for settlement, they traded their Continental Army I.O.U.s for 1.5 million acres of Ohio wilderness and headed down the Ohio River on a flatboat to start a settlement at the mouth of the Muskingum River. Like good soldiers, they left their women and children safe at home, while they faced the uncertainties of Indians and dark forests.

As a nod to the part France played in the Revolution's success, they named their settlement for its Queen, Marie Antoinette. And Washington gave them his blessing, saying that "no colony in America was settled under such favorable auspices."

Though squatters and soldiers had gone into Ohio before them, Marietta was the first permanent American settlement in the Northwest Territory. The civilization that they started in April, 1788, was the test case for law and order and government in the Northwest Territory, the first crack in the wilderness, whence came the states of Ohio, Indiana, Michigan, Illinois, and Wisconsin.

Their leader was Rufus Putman, the general who had engineered the fortifications at Bunker Hill and West Point. At Marietta, he built the Campus Martius, a blockhouse strong enough to make Marietta last and to give the founding New Englanders a lasting influence in the town. "If you don't have flatboat splinters in your bottom," says one resident, "you're considered a newcomer."

Old General Putnam ambitiously brought in shipbuilders, but since the railroads and highways bypassed Marietta for most of its history, the town stayed small and still retains much of its original Yankee flavor. Though the streets of Marietta tell three centuries of living history, the rivers will always punctuate this place founded on a flatboat. Years ago when Marietta got a telephone exchange, it was built to be carried by elevator from floor to floor—just in case of a flood.

"As a town, Marietta had a distinctly martial character, rather like an ancient Roman fort in the land of the barbarians—a comparison enhanced by the Latin names chosen by the ex-soldiers (many of whom were Dartmouth and Harvard graduates), such as Campus Martius for the fort, Cecelia, Quadranaou and Capitolium for the open spaces, and Sacra Via for the wide road leading up from the river to the town. The remaining streets were named for Washington and other revolutionary generals."

—Richard Lingaman, Small Town America

Vital Statistics

Population, 1995	107,526
Population, 2000	111,564
Net Change, 1990-2000	10%
Median Age	35.4
White	107,677
Black	1,749
Native American	183
Asian	740
Pacific Islander	15
Other	264
2 or More Races	936
Hispanic	837
Area (square miles)	555
Urban Land Cover (latest figures 1994)	1.8%
Population Per Square Mile	201
Elevation	1,083
Average Temperature	52.1
Average Precipitation	40.6 in.

Civilian Labor Force	57,200
Trade	10,342
Construction	2,460
Manufacturing	16,181
Transportation & Utilities	1,544
Government	6,737
Services	8,464
Finance, Insurance & Real Estate	1,556
Agriculture, Forestry, Fishing	590
Mining	359
Per Capita Income, 1999	$23,776
Persons Below Poverty, 1997	8.8%
Retail Sales per Capita, 1997	$7,321
Housing Units, 2000	42,324
Average Family Size	3.17
Number of Farms	1,840
Average Size of Farms (acres)	137
Average Commodity Cash Receipts per Farm	$95,543
Highway Miles	
Interstate	7
U.S. Routes	58
State Routes	187
Registered Motor Vehicles	123,940
Automobile Crashes per 1,000	29.01

Number of Registered Voters	62,395
Democrat	9.9%
Republican	17.6%
Non Partisan	72.6%
Number Voted 2000 Election	43,141
Percent Voted 2000 Election	69.2%
Voting, 2000 Election	
for Bush	25,901
for Gore	14,779
for Nader	1,171
for Buchanan	398
Contributions to Federal Candidates, Parties, & PACs, '01-'02	
to Democrats	$55,679
to Republicans	$140,392

Williams

Namesake David Williams, one of three militiamen who captured Major John Andre with Benedict Arnold's traitorous plans for West Point in his possession

Established April 1, 1820

County Seat Bryan

Largest Places	2000	1990
Bryan city	8,333	8,348
Montpelier village	4,320	4,299
Center township	3,056	3,055
Pulaski township	2,628	2,647
Edgerton village	2,117	1,896
Jefferson township	1,969	1,787
Springfield township	1,821	1,139
West Unity village	1,790	1,677
Pioneer village	1,460	1,287
Superior township	1,452	1,280

Williams County is located in the northwest corner of the state. The St. Joseph and Tiffin rivers flow through the county. Primarily a rural area, 75 percent of the land is in farms. From the marketing of farm commodities, Williams County has annual cash receipts of over $45 million. Attractions in Williams County include Nettle Lake Mound Group; Lake La Su An Wildlife Area; Fountain City Historic District; the Quaker church;  Beaver Creek Wildlife Area; Bryan Downtown Historic District; Kunkle Log House; and the Williams County Courthouse.

Vital Statistics

Population, 1995	37,846
Population, 2000	39,188
Net Change, 1990-2000	6%
Median Age	36.9
White	37,821
Black	283
Native American	89
Asian	202
Pacific Islander	3
Other	466
2 or More Races	324
Hispanic	1,049
Area (square miles)	422
Urban Land Cover (latest figures 1994)	1.2%
Population Per Square Mile	92.9
Elevation	861
Average Temperature	52.6
Average Precipitation	39.35 in.

Civilian Labor Force	21,100
Trade	3,257
Construction	534
Manufacturing	9,631
Transportation & Utilities	602
Government	2,121
Services	2,882
Finance, Insurance & Real Estate	421
Per Capita Income, 1999	$25,226
Persons Below Poverty, 1997	6.8%

Retail Sales per Capita, 1997 .... $6,001
Housing Units, 2000 16,140
Average Family Size 3.00
Number of Farms 950
Average Size of Farms (acres) 225
Average Commodity Cash Receipts per Farm $47,407
Highway Miles
    Interstate 22
    U.S. Routes 81
    State Routes 105
Registered Motor Vehicles 46,458
Automobile Crashes per 1,000 .... 36.18

Number of Registered Voters 26,683
    Democrat 6.0%
    Republican 18.9%
    Non Partisan 75.1%
    Number Voted 2000 Election 16,170
    Percent Voted 2000 Election 60.6%
Voting, 2000 Election
    for Bush 9,941
    for Gore 5,454
    for Nader 347
    for Buchanan 101
Contributions to Federal Candidates, Parties, & PACs, '01-'02
    to Democrats $1,650
    to Republicans $75,025

Wood

Namesake Colonel Wood, engineer of Fort Meigs

Established April 1, 1820

County Seat Bowling Green

Largest Places	2000	1990
Bowling Green city	29,636	28,176
Perrysburg city	16,945	12,551
Perrysburg township	13,613	13,176
Lake township	6,643	6,632
Rossford city	6,406	5,861
Northwood city	5,471	5,506
North Baltimore village	3,361	3,139
Troy township	3,357	3,000
Walbridge village	2,546	2,736
Middletown township	1,960	1,911

Wood County is located in the northwest portion of the state. The Maumee and Portage rivers flow through the county. With 77 percent of the land in farms, Wood County ranks first in the state in the production of wheat, second in processing tomatoes, third in soybeans, and fourth in corn production.  Attractions in Wood County include the reconstructed Fort Meigs State Memorial; Mary Jane Thurston State Park; Missionary Island Wildlife Area; Wood County Historical Museum; the Oliver Hazzard Perry Monument; and the Bowling Green State University.

Vital Statistics
Population, 1995 115,934
Population, 2000 121,065
Net Change, 1990-2000 .... 6.9%
Median Age 32.6

White 114,802
Black 1,540
Native American 274
Asian 1,247
Pacific Islander 18
Other 1,756
2 or More Races 1,428
Hispanic 4,033
Area (square miles) 617
Urban Land Cover (latest figures 1994) 2%
Population Per Square Mile 196.2
Elevation 860
Average Temperature 53.3
Average Precipitation .... 37.45 in.

Civilian Labor Force 67,700
    Trade 13,161
    Construction 3,226
    Manufacturing 15,257
    Transportation & Utilities 2,255
    Government 9,897
    Services 11,978
    Finance, Insurance & Real Estate 1,281
    Agriculture, Forestry, Fishing 531
    Mining 60
Per Capita Income, 1999 .... $26,737
Persons Below Poverty, 1997 .... 7.1%
Retail Sales per Capita, 1997 .... $8,000
Housing Units, 2000 47,468
Average Family Size 3.04
Number of Farms 1,190
Average Size of Farms (acres) 271
Average Commodity Cash Receipts per Farm $73,835
Highway Miles
    Interstate 55
    U.S. Routes 61
    State Routes 206
Registered Motor Vehicles 127,849
Automobile Crashes per 1,000 .... 32.68

Number of Registered Voters 84,715
    Democrat 9.2%
    Republican 12.6%
    Non Partisan 78.0%
    Number Voted 2000 Election 52,832
    Percent Voted 2000 Election 62.4%
Voting, 2000 Election
    for Bush 27,504
    for Gore 22,687
    for Nader 1,536
    for Buchanan 210
Contributions to Federal Candidates, Parties, & PACs, '01-'02
    to Democrats $16,900
    to Republicans $68,310

Wyandot

Namesake Wyandot Indians

Established February 3, 1845

County Seat Upper Sandusky

Largest Places	2000	1990
Upper Sandusky city	6,533	5,906
Carey village	3,901	3,684
Tymochtee township	1,186	1,127
Crawford township	1,719	1,265
Salem township	1,055	963
Sycamore village	914	919
Crane township	861	1,029
Pitt township	833	776
Nevada village	814	849
Eden township	751	677

Wyandot County is located in the northwest portion of the state. The Sandusky River flows through the county. Primarily a rural area, 80 percent of the land is in farms. Wyandot County has annual cash receipts of over $55 million from the marketing of farm commodities. Major attractions in Wyandot County include Chief Tarhe Monument; Killdeer Plains Wildlife Area; Springville Marsh State Nature Preserve; McCutchen Overland Inn; the Parker and Swartz covered bridges; and the Wyandot Historical Society and Museum.

Vital Statistics

Population, 1995	22,732
Population, 2000	22,908
Net Change, 1990-2000	2.9%
Median Age	37.4
White	22,429
Black	32
Native American	19
Asian	115
Pacific Islander	1
Other	169
2 or More Races	143
Hispanic	334
Area (square miles)	406
Urban Land Cover (latest figures 1994)	4%

Population Per Square Mile	56.4
Elevation	1,083
Average Temperature	53.7
Average Precipitation	32.5 in.
Civilian Labor Force	12,300
Trade	1,809
Construction	547
Manufacturing	4,477
Transportation & Utilities	224
Government	1,257
Services	1,257
Finance, Insurance & Real Estate	281
Agriculture, Forestry, Fishing	113
Mining	252
Per Capita Income, 1999	$22,183
Persons Below Poverty, 1997	7%
Retail Sales per Capita, 1997	$4,833
Housing Units, 2000	9,324
Average Family Size	3.03
Number of Farms	700
Average Size of Farms (acres)	309
Average Commodity Cash Receipts per Farm	$79,177
Highway Miles	
Interstate	0
U.S. Routes	46
State Routes	152
Registered Motor Vehicles	29,958
Automobile Crashes per 1,000	34.79
Number of Registered Voters	15,130
Democrat	10.2%
Republican	24.6%
Non Partisan	65.3%
Number Voted 2000 Election	10,059
Percent Voted 2000 Election	66.5%
Voting, 2000 Election	
for Bush	6,113
for Gore	3,397
for Nader	191
for Buchanan	70
Contributions to Federal Candidates, Parties, & PACs, '01-'02	
to Democrats	$700
to Republicans	$7,550

Sources: Ohio County Profiles, February, 2002, Ohio Department of Development, Office of Strategic Research; 2000 Estimates of Ohio's population, Ohio Department of Development; U.S. Department of Commerce, General Population Characteristics, 2000; County and City Data Book, 2000, U.S. Department of Commerce, Economics and Statistics Administration, Bureau of the Census

AWAY IN A MANGER

In 1750, as Britain and France sparred over North America, Christopher Gist entered Ohio to survey the wilderness and cajole Indians for the Ohio Company. In December, at a Wyandot village near today's Coshocton, Gist narrated the Nativity story, thus conducting Ohio's first Protestant Christmas service and convincing the Wyandots—who thought Christ was French—to befriend the British.

A PRONOUNCING GAZETEER FOR THE UNINITIATED

Beallsville (BELZ-vil),
Monroe County

Bellefontaine
(Behl-FOWN-tin),
Logan County

Berlin (BURR-lin),
Holmes County

Cadiz (KAY-diz),
Harrison County

Cairo (KAY-row)
Allen County

Cairo (KAYR-oh)
Stark County

Cincinnati
(Since-in-NADDY),
Hamilton County

Coshocton
The name, says Dick
Perry, comes from three
different words: (1)
Goshachgunk, which
means where the river is
crossing; (2) Koshocktoon,
which means river crossing
device or ferry; and, (3)

Cush-og-wenk, which
means place of the black
bear. Put them all
together, they spell mother
or Coshocton or:
Goshachgunkko-
shocktooncusho-
gwenk.

Dayton (DATE-un),
Montgomery County

Elida (Eh-LEYE-duh),
Allen County

Gallipolis
(Gal-a-puh-LEECE)
Gallia County

Genoa (Gin-OH-a),
Ottawa County

Gratiot (GRAY-shot),
Licking/Muskingum
Counties

Greenwich (GREEN-wich),
Huron County

Houston (HOUSE-tin),
Shelby County

Lima (LIE-mah),
Allen County

Louisville (LOO-ihs-vil),
Stark County

Mantua (MANT-uh-way),
Portage County

Marseilles (Mar-SALES)
Wyandot County

Medina (Meh-DIE-nuh),
Medina County

Milan (MEYE-lan),
Erie County

Ohio (Uh-HIA)

Palestine (Pal-uh-steen),
Darke County

Rio Grande
(RYE-oh GRAND),
Gallia County

Russia (ROO-shi),
Shelby County

Versailles (Vur-sales),
Darke County

Vienna (Vy-EN-uh),
Trumbull County

—Sources: *The Serene
Cincinnatians; The Buckeye
Country;* "A Pronouncing
Gazateer," *Ohio Magazine,* Gene
Logsdon; Associated Press, Jeri
Waters

*Children from
northern Ohio who
hear adults say
Chillicothe think
they are hearing
'Chillacoffee' and
sometimes they are.
Trying to pronounce
the last syllable
correctly is arduous,
even for a native.
The 'th' is not
spoken as hard as in
the word 'theory'
nor yet as soft as in
the word 'thee.'
Best just to say
'Chillacoffee' and
everyone will know
exactly where you
are talking about.*

—Gene Logsdon

763

"HELLO, TV WEATHER DEPARTMENT? I'D LIKE A WORD WITH MR. DOPPLER!"

As these 19th century studies in high coloring passed from generation to generation, everyday weather wisdom became an accepted science. As weather—particularly bad weather—seriously affected most areas of agrarian life, the study of its patterns became a preoccupation. A weather-wise man who could predict the seasons was not only smarter than most but apt to grow richer. Under such circumstances, serious conclusions were drawn from the thickness of husks on ears of corn, the length of hair on the furry caterpillar, the degree of activity of squirrels gathering nuts in the fall and the thickness of the skin of an apple.

Simple adages were invented. "The full moon eats clouds" refers to the fact that, in the evening, cumulus clouds tend to disappear. "When pigs lie in the mud, no fear of flood" alludes to the fact that once the hog is out, the worst has passed. But not all are accurate. To date, no Ohioan has been able to prove that caterpillar fuzz correlates with the thermometer, although one man north of Salem claims his grandmother once insulated her husband's pants with caterpillar fur and that it snowed all winter.

Unfortunately, early the next spring, his pants grew wings and disappeared.

Of all weather forecasting tools, the least reliable comes from a thickset, grizzled marmot better known as a groundhog. There are Ohioans who make a strong case that the groundhog legend did not originate on Gobbler's Knob in Quarryville, Pennsylvania, or Punxsutawney, or at Sun Prairie, Wisconsin. The origination, they claim, comes from a hill in Wood County about 20 yards from the anthropology department at

by Jay Paris

Bowling Green State University. The reason is that in the dead of winter, Wood County is usually the warmest place in the state—an average five degrees warmer than Cincinnati and seven degrees warmer than Columbus.

The result of this is that groundhogs of intelligence and superior breeding begin to migrate toward Toledo, leaving their more stupid cousins behind. By the turn of the century it was well known that one could rarely catch a woodchuck in Wood County. Of the few trophies collected, all were found to have lighter coats and bigger brains. As the rest of America foolishly watches groundhog shadows in Pennsylvania and Wisconsin, the people of Wood County never need to wander past Bowling Green.

During the middle of the 19th century, when groundhogs were migrating north and caterpillar fur was stuffed into pants, the rudiments of meteorology emerged. Much was theorized but little was known about the relationship between climate and land masses. As the discipline developed, the path on which weather lore traveled began to narrow. In 1868, this became especially true when Ohio took a giant step in leading the way.

It began when an impertinent young meteorologist named Cleveland Abbe found himself with little to do in Puklova, Russia. He had been sent to measure the cold and snow and had not been disappointed. But neither was he challenged and so he began to conjure ways to foretell the weather. In 1868, weather forecasting was nonexistent. There were no weather maps and the few efforts that had been made to document climatological conditions were local endeavors that had no effect on the United States at large.

Abbe theorized that winds prevailed across America and that air masses, like the oceans, were connected. By tracking their movements, probabilities could be deduced to revolutionize the way people understood weather. From his cabin in Puklova, he dreamed of creating a United States weather bureau that would analyze and foretell weather from around the country, maybe even the world. Being young and brash, Abbe resolved to create such a network as soon as he could return to the United States.

A year later, he was transferred to Cincinnati. With unstoppable self-confidence he assaulted community groups, the newspapers, his associates, and anybody on the streets of Cincinnati who would listen to any detail of his plan. One of those infected by his ardor was Frank A. Armstrong, the manager of the Cincinnati Western Union office. Armstrong thought Abbe was madly obsessed but recognized his brilliance and even helped him devise a weather code usable over the wire. It was soon shown to executives at Western Union who agreed that it had merit if someone else would pay for it. Abbe sought the support of the Cincinnati Chamber of Commerce, who anted up the necessary funds. In return, Abbe promised the chamber that the nation's weather would soon be told to the world from Cincinnati's doorstep.

On September 1, 1869, it was agreed that 20 participating weather stations would forward their reports to Abbe. By September 2, he had only two reports, one from his assistant. Abbe wired each participant for an explanation. All responded that the weather was fine; there was nothing to report. Abbe hotly replied that it didn't matter what the conditions were, as long as they could breathe the air, he wanted to know its temperature. All agreed, except the Chicago Board of Trade, which felt that what mattered in Chicago would not in Cincinnati. He then published his first new edition of the Cincinnati Weather Bulletin, predicting rather hopefully that easterly and southerly wind would prevail in America.

Within twenty months of his arrival in Ohio, Abbe had cajoled, convinced or overwhelmed 33 weather observatories into forwarding their weather reports to Cincinnati where it was then broadcast to the nation. There were still holdouts, including Chicago, that Abbe continued to stalk and convert.

In December of 1869, 15 months after his experiment began, a congressman from Wisconsin introduced a bill authorizing the secretary of war to provide a national weather bureau. On February 9, 1870, Ulysses Grant signed the bill, officially creating a national

weather service under the jurisdiction of the U.S. Army Signal corps. The budget for the fiscal year was $15,000. A year later, Cleveland Abbe left Cincinnati to become the special weather assistant to the chief signal officer.

In the century that has followed Cleveland Abbe's innovations, there have been innumerable technical advancements to dissect Ohio's weather. Barographs have turned into radarscopes and telepsychrometers relayed by laser satellites. But the method in which the raw data is collected remains exactly the same as Cleveland Abbe planned it. Every day throughout Ohio, 250 volunteers bring the official weather readings in from official weather sheds and file them into a gigantic official computer in Asheville, North Carolina. There are no excuses for missing a day. The equipment is simple, devoid of electronics. The system is as reliable as it is straightforward, much like the volunteers who maintain it.

In 1948, Ray Diederich of Elyria, Ohio, became a weather observer because he and his father couldn't agree upon how cold it had become. Ray decided that the way to settle it was to volunteer for the weather service, which would make his readings official. If all of Elyria, the National Weather Service, and the secretary of commerce believed him, so would his father. He wrote the National Weather Service and found that he was welcome to participate but there was no money for equipment. Ray explained that accuracy mattered more than money and offered to buy the equipment himself. The National Weather Service recognized that Diederich was the kind of person they were looking for. Ray soon acquired a minimum-maximum thermometer, a rain gauge, and the shed that the bureau required to store them.

The Diederichs understood observation. Ray had made a great uncle who never planted in the spring until a certain walnut tree on his farm became silver-tipped. Another uncle taught him how to cut open a hailstone to count its rings and his mother convinced him that animals could smell earthquakes days before they happened, even though the theory had never been tested in Elyria.

As Ray became an experienced weather observer, he also became fascinated with storms. He professed a desire to be in a tornado and once in Korea even stayed up all night, hoping to watch a typhoon strike his ship. He eventually learned to read clouds as a kind of weather Braille. What he observed began to astound him. He noticed that sometimes when it sprinkled in Elyria, it poured in Parma. Or when Hudson and Solon got an inch of rain, Parma received four, even though few miles separated the communities. He began to believe that Parma could be the cloudiest place in Ohio, maybe even the cloudiest place in America, outside of the Pacific Northwest.

He began to study the intricate topography of Cleveland. With each new storm, he became more certain there was a relationship between topography and weather, which he called the Cleveland Shear Effect. The essence of his theory was that the four major river valleys dissecting Cuyahoga County tended to suck storms blowing across Lake Erie into the lap of downtown Parma. For his weather discoveries the Elyria paper, *The Chronicle-Telegram*, heralded Ray Diederich as a weather soothsayer. When the temperatures were published, it was Ray Diederich's temperature and no one else's would do. The officials at the Ohio Weather Bureau knew little of the Cleveland Shear Effect except to note that there may be no weather in the world quite like Cleveland's.

Greater Cleveland is the only place in America where it can be sunny in Elyria, rain in Parma, kill jack rabbits with hailstones in Mayfield Heights, and snow in Chardon—all on the same afternoon. Because Cleveland's eastern shoreline makes a cut to the north, prevailing westerly winds crossing the lake push large wet clouds onto the shoreline that discharge at the first opportunity. If not sheared into Parma, they continue past Euclid into the higher elevations of Geauga County where between October and May it always seems to be snowing. The average snowfall in Chardon is over 100 inches per year, compared to 20 inches in Cincinnati, 28 inches in Columbus or even 65 inches in Richmond Heights, which is only 11 miles away.

There used to be a saying that they didn't move snow in Chardon until it was two years old.

Now the village has three snowplows to clear 13 miles of road, a ratio of equipment to road surface only matched by International Falls, Minnesota, and sections of Fairbanks, Alaska. By common agreement there seems to be only two ways to view winter there: either invigorating or interminable. The interminables generally move down the road to Burton. The invigorated more or less like living in the state's weather anomaly, bizarre as it is.

Bert Barnum was a life-long resident of Chardon and operated a shoe store in the center of town where boots sold briskly in the winter and many of the town's historians stopped to sit. Bert battled the snow for the first 30 or 40 years of his life, resigned himself to it for another ten, then finally began to enjoy it. From 1927 to 1930, he hauled *The Plain Dealer* from Painesville to Burton, through the path of the snow that was always within ten miles of downtown Chardon. He recalled that it was always there—the strange wall of snow—waiting for him one quarter of a mile south of Route 322. He finished unloading his truck in Burton, on green grass, and started home. At the hill by the Lake County line, he watched the curtain appear, akin to an approaching thunderstorm, until he was in it, snapping on his high beams and defrosting the windshield. The storm hung over him as he rode home, continuing in spurts until the cooling effect of evening drove off the clouds.

One time, Shorty Wilman, a very long-legged neighbor of Bert's decided to walk to Chardon from Fowler Mills after having breakfast with the mayor's daughter. It was sunny and dry when he started but within a half-mile he saw a great wall of snow waiting for him. It looked huge and white and cold. He loped up to it, even glared into its space but could see nothing. Taking a long breath, he waded into the storm until he couldn't stand it, which was not long, maybe several hundred yards, and then decided to retreat directly east toward his uncle's farm.

When he got there, the barn, which sat on the north side of the property, was covered with 19 inches of snow while the vegetable garden, on the south side of the house, was bare. Shorty asked his uncle if he could borrow a horse as he

was already two hours late, but when he went behind the barn to retrieve it, the nag was so cold that he had to return for a whip just to wake her up.

Among Bert Barnum's associates there was always an unresolved debate about which snowstorm was the most ruthless ever to hit Chardon and, to a lesser degree, the rest of the state. They defined ruthless as hellish, ill-disposed, heartless and demanding, qualities that were better left to judgment than to statistics. If the contest was ever to be resolved, all agreed that no place in Ohio deserved to host the final arguments more than Chardon's shoe store. In the midst of many wet gales, Bert had withdrawn to the back section, near the wingtip boxes, to hear stories of blizzards.

According to Chardon's historians, there were really only two contenders: the early November storm of 1913 and the Thanksgiving storm of 1950. B.J. Shanower, an occasional visitor in Chardon and reliable weather consultant, was 24 years old when the storm of 1913 struck. In 1900, he thought he had seen the worst ever when 25 inches of snow fell in the same number of hours after the oat harvest. He was certain there would never be an unannounced blizzard of that intensity again. But when he awoke on November 9, 1913, he suspected that he had been wrong.

They say it snowed for three days in Cleveland, four in Burton and six in Chardon. "I started my milk route on Sunday morning in the hardest snow I've ever seen and finished the next Thursday as it was tapering off," said Mr. Shanower, who was 94 years old. "The C & E took 11 hours to go six miles before it gave in. The passengers, about a dozen strong, formed a chain and walked to the nearest farmhouse, which belonged to the former school superintendent's widow.

"Being on a main thoroughfare, group after group got diverted into her living room and I think 22 spent the first night. Quite a number for a widow. A few tried coming and going for food, but most stayed for five days. It was a wet snow and the air was heavier than I've ever seen it, before or since. I remember how the wind pushed on the house. I can still hear the thud

of our clock hitting out the seconds. By the end there were four feet on the level and drifts as high as houses. Why this would happen in Ohio in early November, I've never figured out."

Stanlae Merritt, another frequenter of Bert's, served the county engineers for 47 years. He concurred that the storm of 1913 was the most unusual of his lifetime, with the possible exception of the storm in 1926 that blew apart a bank in Elyria, scattering its checking accounts over three counties. One set was even found near Chardon as they scraped off the last of the winter ice. But that storm was made of twisters, not snowflakes, and did awful things all over Geauga County. Ed Clinton on Nash Road was milking his cows when it brought down his barn without putting a mark on him or the cow he was cleaning. When he went to tell his wife, he found his house on another location across the road. Only one window broke as it went on its way.

But as damaging as the storm was, it was still early November and Ohio weather quickly turned warm, even in Chardon. Four feet of snow became three feet of slush. B.J. Shanower left a rowboat by Route 168. But the floodwaters eventually rescinded and by Thanksgiving, it was gone. Much like the storm of 1913, the blizzard of 1950 arrived from the south without much warning. As it reached Lake Erie, it stalled, unloading more snow on Ohio than any storm in history. The infant boom was in motion and, over the long weekend many expectant mothers produced a contingent of blizzard babies who began life in snow banks and on the rear seats of stalled vehicles. Papers around the state featured headlines proclaiming the hardships. "Baby Girl Literally Born in Snow Drift," read the Elyria *Chronicle-Telegram*. "Father Delivers Little Shaver in Blizzard" from Leetonia and "Birth Saga in Philo" from a paper in Perry County.

As many of these snow babies took their first breath, the most outlandish occurrence of the storm began on the Ohio State playing field. Michigan had arrived to play Ohio State for the Big Ten rivalry, the championship, and a berth in the Rose Bowl. Both teams were highly ranked although OSU was favored.

Three hours before the kickoff, the temperature on the field was 11 degrees and winds gusted to 55 miles per hour. The ground was already frozen and so was the tarp that covered it. When Richard Larkins, the OSU athletic director, called the Ohio Weather Service for a prediction, they forecast minor flurries, tapering off by early afternoon. With 82,500 tickets sold and the biggest press contingent ever to see the season finale, Larkins wanted to be optimistic. As a last democratic gesture, he polled each team to see whether they wanted to play or postpone. The Ohio State players were eager but the Michigan players were adamant. The decision was made to play.

When the snow bowl got underway, the reporters in the press box couldn't see the field. Larkins assigned six maintenance men to shovel the goal lines whenever they began to disappear. The shovelers never stopped. Ohio State's ticket-takers claimed that 50,000 fans attended the game but, if that were so, most never found their seats. Thousands more departed from their homes around the state, hoping to make the

> **The more I traveled eastward the higher the snowdrifts were piled at curbside, because for some strange reason the East Side always got a lot more snow than the West. This phenomenon was referred to mysteriously as "the lake effect" by TV weathermen, but no one ever bothered explaining it to my satisfaction or anyone else's. It's one of those things you accept when you live here, like each year's disappointments over the Cavs and the Indians, or jokes about the river catching on fire.**
> **Milo, Pepper Pike**

kickoff, but listened to the game from the interior of snowbanks.

Ohio State's golden player in 1950 was an All-American from Elyria named Vic Janowicz. Working from Ohio State's single-wing formation, Janowicz called the plays, was the league's leading passer and rusher, the team punter, field goal kicker, punt and kickoff return specialist and was considered to be the best defensive back in college football. As Janowicz stood in his end zone facing the blast, waiting for a Michigan punt he wouldn't be able to see until the ball had almost completed its trajectory, he knew he was playing a sport unlike any he had ever practiced, particularly football. There was no visibility, no footing, no passing game, and no penalties. Just defense.

In complete contrast to the predictions, the storm's intensity grew each quarter. By half time, the stadium was nearly empty and the wind chill was 40 below zero. Snow was ankle deep when the OSU band took the field, and two inches above that when the Michigan band looked for a place to hide.

Midway through the third quarter, Janowicz ran over the left tackle, tripped, and fumbled the ball. In the dim blizzard light, scoured by sheets of snow, the Michigan defense piled on, thinking he still had it. Even the officials thought he had it. Only Janowicz knew it was buried somewhere on the field. Squirming out from a ton of Michigan defense, Janowicz hunted for the ball and nonchalantly made the recovery before anyone started a controversy.

In the fourth quarter, Janowicz could no longer see his center when punting, so he was forced to take the ball from seven yards behind the line of scrimmage. At the gun, Michigan had blocked two punts, one for a touchdown and one for a safety. Janowicz had kicked a 27-yard goal, but it wasn't enough. The teams had punted 45 times. Michigan had scored nine points without making a first down or completing a pass, while rushing for 27 yards. Ohio State had completed three passes for 25 yards and rushed for another 16. The following Monday, Ohio State students hung Athletic Director Larkins in effigy. One student was arrested for putting his head through the side window of a police cruiser, and only the appearance of university president, Howard Bevis, stopped others from doing the same.

In Chardon that hellish Thanksgiving weekend, the radios played the Ohio State fight song through the static of it all. Bert Barnum had to stand on his counter to see over the drifts piled next to the sidewalks. He did it every few minutes for the first day of the storm, even though there wasn't anything to see. On Sunday, the drifts on the square grew so high that the afternoon light could not enter his store, leaving him quietly among his shoes.

Thirty-four years later, the promise of winter was again upon Chardon. For two years it had hardly snowed in Ohio and the verdure of summer hadn't worn off. In Bert Barnum's store, the town's weather-wise gathered to anticipate the long overdue punishment. As always, the final debate, the one that stayed unresolved, was about how hard it had ever snowed.

"Nineteen hundred and fifty was the worst of any century," one man said.

"Yes," said another, a bit older, "except for the disaster that took us by surprise in '33. For my money, we have never seen the likes of, before or since."

"No," argued an older man, who was a boy when the November storm of 1913 hit. "Thirteen was absolutely the most wicked blizzard God has ever put on humanity. It puts the rest in mothballs."

"Oh, I doubt it," said the eldest member, surveying the youth of the group. "The storm of February 8, 1878, was worse. My father said that it snowed so hard that a section of Zanesville disappeared for a week. The ice underneath it barely even thawed for Memorial Day, flooding the Ohio River so badly that Marietta moved downstream two and a quarter feet. Only the blizzard of February 2, 1818, could even possibly compete. According to my father's father, raging clouds stalled right at the Mansfield interchange and didn't move for 11 days. Fifteen feet of snow fell from the sky, Fortunately, most of it blew up to Canada and onto the polar cap where they say you can still find traces of the blasted thing today."

—Jay Paris

June 24—What is generally conceded to be the most intense rainfall in Ohio history deluges southwestern Canton Township in Stark County—12 inches in 80 minutes. Hyberbolic *Canton Repository* says four feet of water fell in three minutes, but most reliable estimates hold that, indeed, one foot in an hour and a half was likely. Wayne County reports unofficially—but reliably—that 14.8 inches fell in Chester Township during the night of July 4-5, 1969, resulting in floods that kill 14 people.

1884

February 10—Coldest temperature in Ohio history set by official recording in Milligan near New Lexington—minus-39 degrees; reports of frozen thermometers (the alcohol used in them freezes at -39). At Jackson, unofficial reports of -42. Boats frozen in Ohio River, although Coal Run minister cuts hole in Muskingum River to baptize three of his flock.

1899

March 23-27—Called Ohio's worst weather disaster, the Flood of 1913 deluges the whole length of Ohio's largest rivers and kills an estimated 467 people. Miami River is 18 feet deep in Dayton's train station, some 1,500 horses drown, and 45,000 books are lost at the public library where water reaches 16 feet deep. Over 40,000 homes are flooded in Ohio, over 2,000 destroyed, and losses are estimated at $113 million ($2,043,119,764.71 in 2003 dollars).

1913

June 28—Deadliest tornado in Ohio history strikes Lorain and Sandusky, kills estimated 85 people. All downtown businesses and more than a thousand homes damaged in Lorain, and State Theater collapses, killing 15, largest ever tornado death toll in one Ohio building. Nine city blocks badly damaged in Sandusky as Sandusky Yacht Club blown into bay and B&O worker crushed between two freight cars blown together.

1924

June 5—Most destructive hailstorm in Ohio since September 27, 1850, strikes Martins Ferry. For 20 miles across northern Belmont County, hail reported as big as three or four inches scores gutters, car roofs, and housetops, with even slate roofs broken. Paint is chipped off houses, thousands of windows broken, branches ripped from trees, and drifts of hail a foot deep do not melt for two days. "A Republican asked a Democratic friend whether this was part of the New Deal," reported the *Martins Ferry Daily Times*. "The Roosevelt adherent stopped the argument by stating that the iceball shower was due to Republicans still controlling the Weather Bureau."

1933

July 21—Gallipolis weather station reports 113 degrees, the highest temperature ever officially recorded in Ohio. Gallipolis *Daily Tribune* reports that, as news topic, hellish weather obliterated Feds' fatal shooting of desperado John Dillinger in Chicago.

1934

January 26—Greatest Ohio River flood inundates river towns from Gallipolis to Cincinnati, where waters crested at 28 feet above flood stage, creating 50,000 homeless.

1937

by Thomas & Jeanne Schmidlin

1950   *September 24*—Smoke from large forest fires in northwestern Canada drift across Ohio causing "almost midnight blackness through the entire state," says Cleveland *Plain Dealer*. From noon until midafternoon, people drive with headlights on, and the Indians-Tigers game at Cleveland Stadium is played under lights. Even birds, tricked by the conditions, go to roost in the afternoon.

1950   *November 23-27*—Deepest snowstorm in Ohio history, covering almost all of the state with more than 10 inches, with some of eastern Ohio getting as much as 35 inches; drifts of 25 feet in the upper Ohio Valley. Although movement across the state is virtually stopped, OSU plays Michigan in Columbus in temperatures of five degrees and winds of 40 miles an hour. Michigan wins 9-3, after the two teams punt a total of 45 times.

1974   *April 3*—Xenia, Ohio, becomes national benchmark for tornado destruction when "superbreakout" of 148 tornadoes across 13 states kills 315 people and injures 6,000. The 12 tornadoes in Ohio cause most damage, killing 36 people, injuring 2,100, with more than 4,000 homes and 639 businesses destroyed or seriously damaged. Xenia's, the first and most destructive tornado, cuts 32-mile swath through the city and northeast, killing what amounts to one person for each mile of its passing. Half the city's buildings are damaged, 300 homes destroyed, as are nine churches. Seven of 12 Xenia schools are destroyed or damaged and school buses blow onto the high school stage where students moments before are rehearsing a play.

1977   *January 28*—Coldest winter of the century; wind chills below -50 with blowing snow closing both state and secondary roads, isolating entire counties.

1978   *January 26*—Worst winter storm in Ohio history shuts down transportation, schools, businesses, and industry for two days. Temperatures fall 30 degrees in two hours and wind gusts of 82 miles an hour at Cleveland Hopkins Airport sets a Cleveland record. Thousands of trees and hundres of miles of electric wires blow down; 51 dead. All air flights are stopped for at least two days, and I-75 is closed for three days. The entire Ohio Turnpike is closed for first time in its history. Food supplies are stopped and shortages of milk, eggs, and bread ensue. National Guard helicopters deliver 80,000 loaves of bread to six cities; 45 Guard helicopters fly 2,700 rescue missions. Federal troops are airlifted into Ohio with arctic gear and heavy equipment to clear highways.

1990   *June 14*—Deadliest flood since 1969 sweeps down Appalachian valleys in Belmont County and kill 26 people in village of Shadyside. Flash flooding over in 30 minutes after wall of water six feet high pours down steep valley creekbeds. Debris, including two bodies, creates 15-acre island of debris behind Hannibal Dam on the Ohio, 30 miles downstream.

1992   *July 12*—Most tornadoes ever in a single day in Ohio—28—part of record month in which 44 tornadoes strike the state, and record year of 61.

from Thunder in the Heartland by Thomas W. Schmidlin & Jeanne Appelhans Schmidlin, The Kent State University Press, Kent, Ohio, 1996, with permission of the Kent State University Press.

WEATHER REPORTS GET START IN UNPREDICTABLE CINCINNATI

If you don't like the weather in Cincinnati, the saying goes, just wait a minute. Although meteorologists insist there's nothing unique about it, most Cincinnatians are certain it's especially unpredictable. Cleveland Abbe thought the opposite. For him, Cincinnati was "the city closest to the United States" in terms of weather. As the man who created the first weather reports, he ought to have known.

Mr. Abbe came to Cincinnati in 1868 as the director of the Cincinnati Observatory in Mount Adams. For the 30-year-old astronomer, there was no more prestigious job than to head the largest observatory in America. But when he arrived in Cincinnati, the observatory was impoverished. The building and equipment were run down and the atmosphere over the city was so heavily choked with smoke and coal dust that the telescope was all but useless.

When Mr. Abbe gave his first annual report to the Cincinnati Chamber of Commerce, he made two suggestions: move the observatory out of the city and concentrate on meteorology.

The key to weather forecasting was the telegraph. It was customary for telegraph operators to include their community's weather in transmissions, and Western Union made that information available to customers. The Smithsonian Institution had been taking weather information via telegraph for 13 years. Civil War armies relied on telegraphed weather reports. No one had thought of gathering weather information from a number of sites and processing the information to calculate the probability of weather patterns. What better location than Cincinnati, the nation's population center, to produce daily weather reports, charted on a weather map?

Most Chamber members treated the idea as a joke but its president, John Gano, saw its potential. A sudden warm spell in winter slaughtering season could mean thousands of pounds of spoiled pork at the city's meat-packing houses. Millions of dollars worth of produce were lost to storm-related steamboat accidents each year. In 1869 alone, 1,914 vessels were wrecked by storms, floods and ice.

The Chamber authorized Mr. Abbe to set up a weather bureau for three months at a cost of $300. The *Cincinnati Commercial* signed a contract to publish them. Knowing that weather moves from west to east, Mr. Abbe supplied 25 Western Union telegraphic stations as far away as Leavenworth, Kansas, with barometers, self-registering maximum and minimum temperature thermometers, and rain gauges.

The weather reports caused great excitement. Five months after the Cincinnati weather reports began, the National Weather Service Bill became law. By the end of 1870, less than two years after arriving in Cincinnati, Mr. Abbe was summoned to Washington to establish a U.S. Army weather service, which became the National Weather Bureau. ～

—*by Owen Findsen*

Cleveland Abbe's predecessor at the Cincinnati Observatory, Ormsby Mitchell, had been nicknamed "Old Star," and Chamber of Commerce members decided Mr. Abbe needed a nickname, too. Because he placed great emphasis on the word "probability" in his reports, they dubbed him "Old Prob."

The climate of Ohio is classified as humid-continental warm summer type. The general characteristics of Ohio climate are: (1) pronounced seasonal shifts of temperature; (2) alternation of high and low pressure air masses that produce irregularly spaced changes of weather; (3) a winter season which is dominated by polar continental air masses that produce dry cold weather, but which is broken intermittently by brief interjections of tropical maritime air bringing wet warmer weather; (4) a summer season dominated alternately by tropical maritime and continental tropical air masses producing high temperatures and frequently high humidity; (5) somewhat higher rainfall in the summer half of the year than in the winter; (6) considerable annual range of temperature; (7) small diurnal range of temperature, especially in summer; (8) prevailing winds from the west, northwest, or southwest; (9) moderate cloud cover in summer and a much higher percentage of cloudiness in winter; (10) occasional tornados, especially in the early spring. Ohio's latitudinal and continental location has made it experience the frigidity of the Arctic and the torridness of the humid tropics.

Temperature

Temperatures in Ohio are generally moderate. Daily maximum temperatures average about 37°F in January and almost 85°F in July. Daily minimum temperatures for the same months are around 22°F and 62°F, respectively. In general, spring temperatures are somewhat lower than autumn temperatures, although both seasons are characterized by moderate temperatures. Hot weather in southern Ohio, especially along the Ohio River, is much more common than in northern Ohio. Extremely cold temperatures are not common in Ohio. Only a narrow zone in the northeastern portion of the state regularly has temperatures of zero or below on more than six days each year. However, the lowest officially recorded temperature in Ohio was in Perry County on February 10, 1899, when the mercury plunged to -39°F. Unusually cold temperatures have also occurred in the summer season. On June 23, 1902, snow fell at several recording stations in northern Ohio and in August, 1942, considerable agricultural damage was experienced in northeastern Ohio from freezing temperatures. The most unusual weather in Ohio history, however, was undoubtedly that of 1816, sometimes characterized throughout northeastern United States as "the year without a summer." Snow fell during every month and despite the fact that winters were unusually mild, freezing temperatures occurred throughout the summer, virtually destroying all crops.

Precipitation

As with temperature, precipitation totals are moderate. The average annual precipitation in Ohio is between 30 and 40 inches. On average, thunderstorms occur on 41 days annually, predominantly in the summer half of the year. The autumn season is normally the driest period of the year. Much of the winter precipitation is received in the form of snow, and snowfall is relatively light, with only the extreme northeast receiving over 40 inches annually. Annual precipitation can vary about 14 or 15 inches from the average. The annual total, however, is normally sufficient to support plant growth. Occasional periods of exceptionally high rainfall are experienced. The least amounts of precipitation are received along the western end of Lake Erie from Toledo to Sandusky Bay.

Sunshine

Located as Ohio is, roughly halfway between equator and pole in the northern hemisphere, the amount of daylight varies greatly from season to season. In Columbus, which because of its central location may be taken as representative of the entire state, the longest day of the year is 15 hours and 1 minute, while the shortest is only 9 hours and 19 minutes. However, because of varying combinations of cloud cover, rain or snow, fog, haze, and air pollution, the sun is always partially obscured so that on the average, no part of the state receives total sunshine from sunrise to sunset.

Weather Hazards

Two aspects of Ohio climate—flooding and tornadoes—deserve mention because of the hazards which they present. Although floods occur every year in some part of Ohio, only two years in the 20th century have seen widespread major flooding—1913 and 1959. In both years two major floods occurred. In January 1913 the Ohio River crested at Wheeling almost nine feet above flood stage and six days later at Cincinnati over 12 feet above. The January floods were only a prelude, however, to the devastation experienced from March 23 to March 27, 1913, a period which brought the worst floods in Ohio history. Not until January, 1959 did floods approach the levels of 1913. Every stream in the state reached flood level or exceeded it from January 21 to 24, 1959. Tornadoes may occur anytime, but are most frequent in spring. These very destructive wind storms are normally of rather small extent, and fortunately affect only small areas. However, within the area in which the storm cell touches the ground, destruction may be almost complete. Probably the most destructive single tornado in Ohio history is that widely known as "the Lorain tornado," which struck on June 28, 1924. The storm swept across Sandusky, out over the bay, and then, veering, smashed directly across the city of Lorain, leaving 85 persons dead in its wake.

Source: Edited with the Permission of The Ohio Department of Natural Resources from Ohio—An American Heartland, *by Allen G. Noble and Albert J. Korsok*

State Average Temperature and Annual Precipitation

Year	Temp. °F	Precip. Inches	Year	Temp. °F	Precip. Inches	Year	Temp. °F	Precip. Inches
1883	NA	45.57	1912	48.78	37.84	1939	52.27	37.31
1884	NA	36.59	1913	51.51	45.03	1940	49.17	37.92
1885	NA	37.73	1914	50.10	35.20	1941	52.03	31.60
1886	NA	37.84	1915	50.03	40.77	1942	51.01	38.73
1887	NA	34.78	1916	50.21	37.14	1943	50.07	35.53
1888	NA	38.52	1917	47.10	36.43	1944	51.35	33.03
1889	NA	33.45	1918	50.70	36.32	1945	50.25	44.58
1890	NA	50.37	1919	51.48	40.34	1946	52.36	35.38
1891	NA	38.87	1920	49.54	37.29	1947	50.23	40.62
1892	NA	37.15	1921	53.83	42.78	1948	50.94	42.07
1893	NA	39.60	1922	52.01	36.83	1949	53.01	37.35
1894	NA	29.72	1923	50.58	39.00	1950	49.88	47.68
1895	49.22	28.28	1924	48.48	37.19	1951	50.53	40.61
1896	50.98	39.40	1925	50.62	34.14	1952	52.13	35.37
1897	50.69	38.33	1926	49.18	43.67	1953	52.91	28.57
1898	51.39	43.56	1927	51.27	43.19	1954	52.11	36.40
1899	50.67	34.05	1928	50.31	35.03	1955	51.91	36.06
1900	51.38	32.74	1929	49.58	45.91	1956	51.21	40.49
1901	49.33	31.27	1930	51.66	26.59	1957	51.29	39.83
1902	49.88	37.19	1931	53.45	37.79	1958	48.93	39.14
1903	49.66	36.18	1932	51.88	36.94	1959	51.89	40.61
1904	47.79	35.67	1933	52.54	38.28	1960	49.73	30.12
1905	49.17	40.28	1934	51.60	26.66	1961	50.49	40.34
1906	50.79	37.08	1935	50.55	40.41	1962	49.87	33.38
1907	48.79	43.34	1936	50.84	33.46	1963	48.87	26.84
1908	51.28	34.39	1937	50.36	44.50	1964	51.23	37.44
1909	50.10	42.59	1938	52.79	39.29	1965	50.79	37.06
1910	49.57	35.99						
1911	51.75	42.80						

1966	49.53	36.60		1985	50.40	40.25
1967	49.85	35.44		1986	51.79	39.05
1968	50.02	38.85		1987	52.28	31.38
1969	49.60	36.39		1988	50.43	31.51
1970	50.81	37.68		1989	49.50	42.57
1971	50.81	33.63		1990	52.75	51.53
1972	49.61	42.50		1991	53.13	31.91
1973	52.41	41.55		1992	50.28	39.98
1974	50.55	40.39		1993	50.51	38.96
1975	51.27	42.85		1994	50.47	35.68
1976	49.03	33.74		1995	50.33	39.10
1977	50.11	39.01		1996	49.5	46.97
1978	48.38	38.43		1997	49.1	38.62
1979	48.95	45.17		1998	54.1	40.28
1980	49.33	39.78		1999	52.3	33.53
1981	49.63	39.56		2000	50.8	40.76
1982	50.44	37.70		2001	53.4	37.83
1983	51.08	40.43		2002	52.7	39.51
1984	50.33	36.87				

* NA indicates not available

Source: Midwest Weather Center &
David H. Cashell, Hydrologist

The wettest

Year	Annual Precipitation (inches)
1990	51.53
1890	50.37
1950	47.68
1929	45.91
1883	45.57
1979	45.17
1913	45.03
1945	44.58
1937	44.50
1926	43.67

The warmest

Year	Average Annual Temperature
1921	53.83°F
1931	53.45°F
1991	53.13"F
1949	53.01°F
1953	52.91°F
1938	52.79°F
1933	52.54°F
1973	52.41°F
1946	52.36°F
1987	52.28°F

Normal Precipitation

Month	Precipitation
Jan.	2.18
Feb.	2.19
Mar.	3.29
Apr.	3.45
May	3.98
Jun.	3.72
Jul.	4.08
Aug.	3.58
Sep.	3.12
Oct.	2.52
Nov.	3.13
Dec.	2.91
Annual	*38.15*

Normal Temperatures

Month	Temperature
Jan.	25.4
Feb.	28.4
Mar.	39.2
Apr.	49.6
May	59.9
Jun	68.6
Jul.	72.5
Aug.	70.7
Sep.	64.2
Oct.	52.7
Nov.	42.0
Dec.	31.0

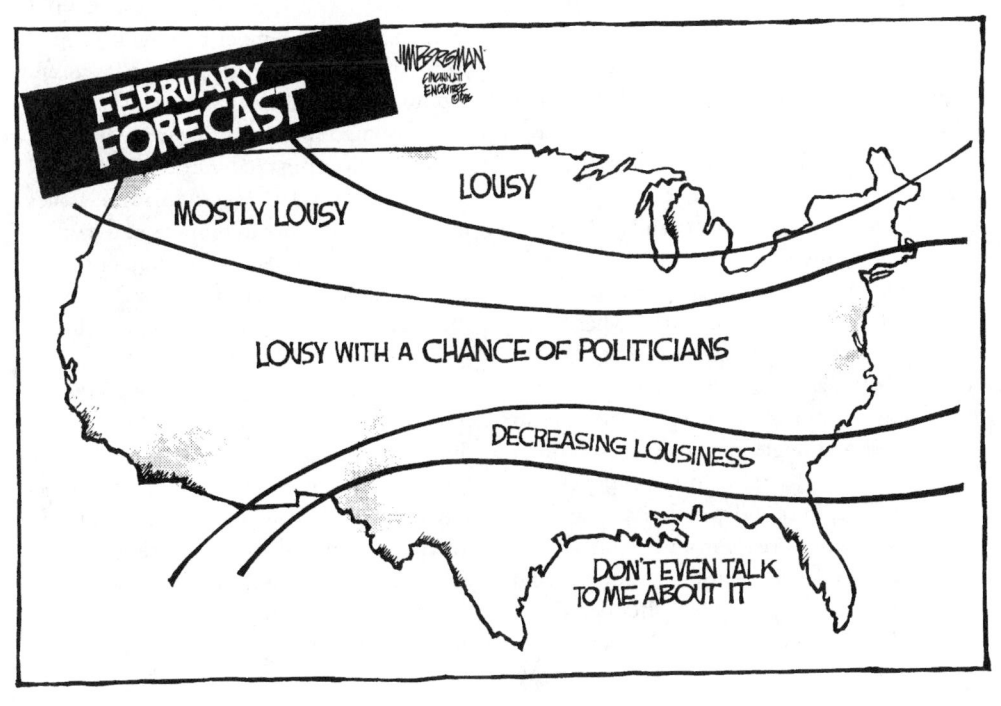

Ohio at age 200 has the landscape it deserves. When it joined the Union in 1803, it was still a sprawling, pristine wilderness bounded in the north by majestic Lake Erie and in the south and east by its namesake river, the fabled thoroughfare for western travelers and commerce. Ohio represented the fledgling western vanguard of an expanding United States, which doubled its size that year with the purchase of the Louisiana Territory from France for a pittance. Ohio's inhabitants numbered slightly more than 70,000 whites, plus a few thousand Native Americans, a human inventory roughly equal in number to modern-day Lorain.

Ohio now teems with 11 million folk, but we must count the many millions of yore who gave the state its present facade. In 1803, life expectancy in Ohio was less than 40 years. People then often succumbed to ailments arising from their confrontation with the natural environment, such as malaria, ague (fever), starvation, exhaustion, cholera, and typhus, conditions preventable and curable today.

Today, we also confront illness or death born of our environment, only these maladies stem from our conquest of nature and seem incurable. Unlike early 19th century Ohioans, we can be stricken by eating mercury-laden fish, drinking well-water contaminated by diesel fuel, breathing coal dust, asbestos and smog, and from exposure to toxic chemicals and radioactive matter carelessly buried in the ground.

The formidable pioneers and Indians living here at the dawn of statehood would not recognize this busy, noisy, crowded and spoiled place. We can only guess what they would say about our treatment of the land. Would they toast us for our mighty cities and technological achievements or reproach us for wantonness and neglect? Did we betray their legacy, or endorse it? As always, it depends on whom you trust and whether you are upstream or downstream from trouble.

In the late 1990s, Marion was downwind of everything. Everyone there shuddered in March 1998 when a U.S. Army Corps of Engineers backhoe unearthed a cesspool of lethal poisons behind River Valley High School. The petroleum odor and black ooze that drifted to the surface confirmed rumors, nightmares, and allegations that for nearly four decades youngsters had been exposed to more than 75 hazardous chemical contaminants buried a few feet beneath the school's athletic fields. Talk about fear factor.

Adding to Marion's angst, the U.S. Environmental Protection Agency had begun employing $400,000 of Superfund money for an emergency cleanup of creosote, a wood preservative that had poisoned the grounds at an abandoned lumber treatment plant formerly owned by Baker Wood Preserving Company, just a half-mile northwest of downtown. This oily, pungent agent, known as polycyclic aromatic hydrocarbon (PAH), causes cancer in lab rats, and nausea, rashes, dizziness, headaches in humans and harm to internal organs. Soil there contained more than 100,000 parts per million of PAHs, among the highest concentrations of that pollutant in the nation.

Cleanup contractors removed 3,000 tons of contaminated soil to a hazardous waste dump in Michigan. Worse still, the filth had fouled a three-mile stretch of the Little Scioto River, making it one of the state's dirtiest streams. Luckily, the lethal leaking occurred a half-mile downstream from pumps that supply the city with drinking water. The final cost of the cleanup could be $7 million.

www. epa.gov/Region5/

This is Ohio's region, and this deep site includes hot topics, publications, summaries of laws, and ways to submit questions and complaints. (Top queries are about mold, treated wood, and the West Nile Virus.) Ohio EPA may be found at www. epa.state.oh.us/

by Stephen Ostrander

Each Ohioan generates one scrap tire annually; these tires are the equivalent of 77 million gallons of oil, or 15,000 BTUs per pound of scrap rubber. In Ohio, there are 100 known illegal tire dumps with an estimated 30 to 40 million tires. The good news: 61 percent of Ohio's tires are recycled, more than twice the national average.

—*Scrap Tire Management Council, ODNR*

The four-day fire that burned five to seven million tires in 1999 spread smelly sooty smoke for dozens of miles across rural Wyandot County, heretofore famous for its prolific corn harvest. National television coverage of the fire on "Bald Tire Mountain" transformed Ohio from tire manufacturing center to used tire capital of the country.

The heaps at the 100-acre Kirby tire dump may have totaled 20 million tires. Health concerns became forefront when several deaths and illnesses due to West Nile virus, St. Louis encephalitis, and other diseases were linked to mosquitoes breeding in rainwater pooling in old tires.

With green lights and extra funding (state legislators hiked the tire disposal fee to $1), Ohio EPA moved quickly. Since the Kirby fire, more than 16 million tires from eight dumps have been buried, shredded, retreaded, recycled or otherwise put out of commission.

More than six million passenger tire equivalents (one PTE equals 20 pounds of rubber) have been removed from the Kirby site alone (though several million PTEs remain).

EPA also has cracked down on used tire reporting compliance. In 2000, scrap tire dealers accounted for 15.8 million PTEs, up from nine million PTEs in 1997. That's progress, because in 1987, nearly half of all tires were uncounted and probably waywardly dumped.

EPA hopes to clean up 1.5 billion tires by the end of the decade, an ambitious goal considering Ohio generates 12-14 million scrap tires a year.

Top Ten Landfills (Tons Dumped in 2000)

American Electric Power, Gavin Plant (Gallia, Jackson, Vinton, Meigs SWCD), 2,864,924 tons

Rumpke Waste Inc. (Hamilton SWCD), 1,957,133 tons

AMS American Landfill (Stark, Tuscarawas, Wayne Joint SWCD), 1,450,986 tons

BFI Carbon Limestone Landfill (Mahoning SWCD), 1,376,173 tons

American Electric Power, Conesville Plant (Coshocton, Fairfield, Perry, Licking SWCD), 1,015,061 tons

Zimmer Industrial SW Landfill (Adams, Clermont SWCD), 981,762 tons

WMC Stoney Hollow Landfill (Montgomery SWCD), 906,016 tons

WMI Countywide R&D Landfill
(Stark, Tuscarawas, Wayne Joint SWCD),
        863,137 tons
Solid Waste Authority of Central Ohio
(Franklin SWCD),
        854,196 tons
WMI Suburban R & D Landfill
(Coshocton, Fairfield, Perry Licking SWCD),
        787,193

Ohio Superfund Sites, 2003

Arcanum Iron & Metal/Darke
Allied Chemical & Ironton Coke/Lawrence
Alsco Anaconda/Tuscarawas
Big D Campground/Ashtabula
Bowers Landfill/Pickaway
Buckeye Reclamation/Belmont
Chem-Dyne Corporation/Butler
Chemical & Minerals Reclamation Inc./
        Cuyahoga
E.H. Schilling Landfill/Coshocton
Feed Materials Production (Fernald Uranium
        Plant)/Hamilton-Butler
Fields Brook/Ashtabula
Fultz Landfill/Guernsey
Industrial Excess Landfill/Stark
Laskin/Poplar Oil/Ashtabula
Miami County Incinerator/Miami
Mound Plant (U.S. Dept. of Energy)/
        Montgomery

Nease Chemical/Columbiana
New Lyme Landfill/Ashtabula
North Sanitary Landfill/Montgomery
Old Mill Rock Creek/Ashtabula
Ormet Corporation/Monroe
Powell Road Landfill/Montgomery
Pristine Inc./Hamilton
Reilly Tar & Chemical Corporation/
        Tuscarawas
Republic Steel Corp. Quarry/Lorain
Sanitary Landfill Company/Montgomery
Skinner Landfill/Butler
South Point Ethanol Plant/Lawrence
Summit National/Portage
TRW Inc. (Minerva Plant)/Stark
United Scrap Lead Company/Miami
Van Dale Junkyard/Washington
Wright-Patterson Air Force Base/
        Greene-Montgomery
Zanesville Well Field/Muskingum

National Priority List Cleanup Sites
Baker Wood Products/Marion
Eagle-Picher Site/Fulton
Envirosafe/Lucas
Greiner's Lagoon/Sandusky
John Mercer Drum/Licking*
Lammers Barrel Factory/Greene
Master Metals, Inc./Cuyahoga
Valleycrest Landfill/Montgomery
Vernay Industries/Greene
*Completed project
—Source: U.S. Environmental Protection Agency

Almost 500,000 children in Ohio live within a few blocks of a known or suspected hazardous waste site.

—*The Plain Dealer*

GARBAGE: OHIO'S UNDERWORLD

The Ins and Outs of Garbage
Out-of-state solid waste dumped in Ohio in 2000: 1,774,139 tons
Ohio solid waste dumped in other states in 2000: 800,767 tons
Leading exporters of solid waste to Ohio: New York (466,423 tons),
        Pennsylvania (427,722 tons)
Leading importer of solid waste from Ohio: Kentucky (400,000 tons)

Picking Through Ohio's Trash Heap
Total garbage dumped in landfills in 2000: 19.7 million tons
Total garbage dumped in landfills in 1984: 10 million tons

In 2000, the average Ohioan threw away 4.59 pounds of garbage a day. Per capita garbage disposal was highest in Lucas County, Hamilton, and Wood counties (more than seven pounds per person); lowest in Holmes and Athens counties (2.32 and 2.67 pounds per person, respectively). In 2000, Franklin County residents tossed away an average of 6.37 pounds of trash, some 4.17 pounds more than in 1992.

—*Source: Ohio Environmental Protection Agency*

"GENTLEMEN, THESE ENVIRONMENTAL KOOKS ARE GETTING REALLY OBNOXIOUS...."

In 2003, Ohio had 33 counties with failing grades in air pollution—the highest of any state. A 2002 study ranked Ohio 2nd only to California for the number of times monitors measured ozone levels above the national health standard.

—American Lung Association, U.S. Public Interest Research Group

Unquestionably, the Ohio EPA, which marked its 30th anniversary in 2002, has substantially purged the air we breathe. The agency has reported that between 1992 and 2000 toxic air emissions—notably carbon monoxide, nitrogen oxide, sulfur dioxide, lead, ozone (a.k.a. smog), and particulates (the main pollutants the U.S. EPA measures to judge air quality)—dropped 50 percent.

Specifically, carbon monoxide emissions fell 61 percent; sulfur dioxide, down 52 percent; nitrogen oxide, down 15 percent; and soot, down 22 percent. More encouraging, toxic releases declined another 13.4 percent in 2001, in spite of a U.S. Environmental Protection Agency-mandated increase in the number of facilities and hazardous chemicals monitored. The trend likely will continue because in 2002 Ohio EPA enacted tougher regulations forcing power plants and industrial boilers to yearly remove an additional 114,000 tons of nitrogen oxide from the air, beginning in 2004.

The statistics sound great until Ohio is compared to the national picture. The Environmental Defense Fund (EDF) still ranks Ohio near the top for defiling the air and elevating the risk of cancer. EDF's 2000 environmental scorecard listed Ohio as the 11th worst state in "added cancer risk," a category estimating an individual's chance of contracting cancer from a lifetime exposure to foul air.

Under this projection, 730 Ohioans per million (or 7,300 statewide) will get cancer from air pollution. EDF reported that 1,671,291 Ohioans are being exposed to levels of hazardous air pollution that exceed the Clean Air Act's so-called "cancer risk" goal.

The U.S. Public Interest Research Group painted a gloomier picture in 2002 when it ranked Ohio's electric power plants first (worst) nationally for spewing sulfur dioxide and nitrogen oxide, and third in carbon dioxide and mercury emissions. The environmental watchdog ranked Columbus-based American Electric Power second nationally in sulfur dioxide, mercury, and carbon dioxide emissions; and third in nitrogen oxide emissions.

Ohioans assuredly will become more focused on smog (ground level ozone) and its consequences after more stringent federal monitoring standards take over in April 2004. The new standards, welcomed by environmentalists and regulators alike, will require

Ohio EPA to measure smog over eight-hour periods instead of the one-hour standard established a quarter century ago.

Any metropolitan area that exceeds the new level four times during any three-year span will be deemed out of compliance, requiring it to adopt remedial programs to improve air quality. Ohio EPA began eight-hour monitoring in 2002, partly to brace public officials for the bad news.

Under the eight-hour standard the Cincinnati area topped the "acceptable" smog level 109 days, compared to five days under the old program. Elsewhere, monitors indicated that Central Ohio surpassed the new level a third of the time between June and September 2002. Based on these maiden tests, 32 of Ohio's 88 counties may flunk federal standards in 2004 and be forced to develop mitigation plans.

The worst place for lungs in Ohio may be Jefferson County, where a state-leading 16.6 million pounds of toxic chemicals was jettisoned into the air, according to the U.S Environmental Protection Agency, 2002 Toxic Release Inventory. Based on that sad statistic, the EDF ranked Jefferson County the second most likely place in Ohio (after Coshocton County) for a human to be stricken with cancer caused by lethal chemicals.

An estimated 1,920 Ohioans die annually from soot emissions from power plants, according to the Clear the Air Task Force and the U.S. Public Interest Research Group.

Ohio power plants rank:
—First nationally in sulfur dioxide emissions, a cause of acid rain and sooty air.
—First nationally in nitrogen oxide emissions, a cause of smog and acid rain.
—Third nationally in carbon dioxide emissions, a contributor to global warming.
—Third nationally in mercury emissions, a toxic element.

Ohio's Dirtiest Power Plants (tons of emissions)

W.H. Sammis, owned by FirstEnergy, Jefferson County
—5th worst nationally in nitrogen oxide
—6th worst nationally in sulfur dioxide
Conesville, owned by American Electric Power, Coshocton County
—7th worst nationally in sulfur dioxide
—12th worst nationally in mercury
General G.M. Gavin, owned by American Electric Power, Gallia County
—9th worst nationally in nitrogen oxide
—9th worst nationally in mercury
—19th worst nationally in carbon dioxide
Kyger Creek, owned by Ohio Valley Electric Cooperative, Gallia County
—10th worst nationally in sulfur dioxide
Eastlake, owned by FirstEnergy, Lake County
—13th worst nationally in sulfur dioxide
—29th worst nationally in mercury
J.M. Stuart, owned by Dayton Power & Light, Adams County
—11th worst nationally in carbon dioxide
—22nd worst nationally in sulfur dioxide
—30th worst nationally in mercury
Cardinal, Ohio Rural Electric Cooperatives, Jefferson County
—14th worst nationally in sulfur dioxide
Muskingum River, American Electric Power, Morgan County
—25th worst nationally in sulfur dioxide

—Sources: U.S. Public Interest Research Group report "Lethal Legacy" (2000); Ohio Environmental Council

Three-eighths of an inch of steel is all that kept the aged Davis-Besse power plant's reactor near Toledo from exploding in early 2002 and becoming the nation's worst nuclear disaster in nearly a quarter century. Just as scary, the Nuclear Regulatory Agency, the federal bureaucracy in charge of safety at the nation's nuclear facilities, had gambled dangerously with our health and safety. The NRC knew for months that the leaky and encrusted reactor could blow at any time, but instead of closing the troubled plant as it had mandated in December 2001, it allowed the utility to postpone an inspection until a scheduled shutdown for refueling in February 2002.

During the stoppage, inspectors fortunately stumbled on a football-sized cavity in the reactor's lid and cracks in shafts that enclosed radioactive fuel rods. For the umpteenth time in its 26-year history the wayward nuke plant, located two dozen miles east of Toledo, would be shut down indefinitely for expensive repairs. The six-inch thick steel lid had been corroded by acidic coolant that chills the super-hot reactor. If the lid had burst, the coolant would have geysered into the containment building, a gymnasium-sized concrete enclosure designed to prevent radiation releases, and set off bells and whistles in the control room.

The plant's owner, Cleveland-based FirstEnergy, said a rapid loss of coolant would have automatically triggered a safe shutdown of the reactor. Spare coolant would have been sprayed on the reactor as sump pumps recirculated jettisoned coolant that had pooled beneath the reactor.

No meltdown.

No radiation.

No injuries.

No worry.

However, even the mildest critics argue that given FirstEnergy's poor safety, operating and maintenance records and the old clunker's many repairs and design flaws, nobody should trust the plant's failsafe procedures, nor the vigilance of the owner and the regulator.

Deposits of crystalline boric acid, an ingredient in the coolant, appeared on the reactor lid as early as 1996. Rust-colored liquid, a sure sign of corrosion, started spewing three years later. Workers used crowbars to chop off the crust in 2000. In spite of these obvious warnings, Davis-Besse's ailments went untreated. The NRC

figured FirstEnergy was handling any problems; and the utility, not hearing complaints from the NRC, figured there weren't any.

In the summer of 2001, the NRC learned about corrosion problems at Davis-Besse's sister plants in other states and ordered their shut down on December 31, 2001. Pressured by FirstEnergy, the regulatory agency postponed Davis-Besse's stoppage until mid-February, praying that the plant would not blow its top.

Critics thought the faulty lid finally would bring down the curtain on Davis-Besse, a.k.a. "Lemon (or mistake) on the Lake" for the numerous costly fiascos that has sidelined it for much of its life. FirstEnergy, however, surprised many when it decided—for $400 million—to fix the pariah. (The utility whined that it had to spend an extra $10-$15 million each month Davis-Besse was benched).

The plant was scheduled to restart in the summer of 2003. Not surprisingly, the out-of-state energy giants that have purchased other seasoned nuclear facilities have not been keen on buying the boondoggle, so FirstEnergy, needing to recoup yet another investment on the "lemon," is likely to run it until its operating license expires in 2017.

Meanwhile, the rest of us ask why nobody can pull the plug on Davis-Besse. The same-old story, from the same-old people continues, leaving us trusting those who failed us before and hoping the nuke-plant-turned-Rube- Goldberg-contraption is not a time bomb with a short fuse.

ELSEWHERE, Ohio's "powers that be" reached the breaking point with an incorrigible super-sized egg producing enterprise whose numerous scandals gave many pause to wonder if megafarms can ever be desirable, responsible, and governable.

After years of legal parrying with Buckeye Egg Farm, a billion-dollar company spread among five counties, the Ohio Environmental Protection Agency delivered the apparent *coup de gras* in 2002 by revoking the megafarm's operating permits. The bureaucratic sleight-of-hand followed the ninth contempt charge the Ohio Attorney General has issued against the recalcitrant egg producer since 1983.

The unlucky neighbors who have lived downwind from a BEF factory endured odors that gagged maggots. In 2000, a dozen of them won a lawsuit requiring the owner, German egg baron Anton Pohlman, to personally pay two-thirds of the $19.7 million settlement.

Over the years, the Licking County-based enterprise repeatedly has been blamed for air and water pollution, fly and beetle infestations of biblical proportions, manure spills, fish kills and reselling out-of-date eggs. Animal rights groups charged it with cruelty for the way it confined and treated some 14 million hens. It got busted for improperly piling dead hens and chicks in fields.

After a September 2000 tornado flattened some barns, it had to dispose of 600,000 fowl. For awhile, BEF ducked knockout punches by acting contrite, paying fines, prolonging legal battles, and settling nuisance lawsuits, but as the broken promises, contempt citations, and public pressure mounted, oversight agencies and courts seemingly rallied to put Buckeye Egg Farm on ice in 2002.

Buckeye Egg Farm appealed the revocations, giving Pohlman time to wing back to Germany and hand the keys over to a management firm whose task was to sell BEF. Meanwhile, the Ohio legislature devolved regulation of megafarms from the EPA to the Ohio Department of Agriculture, which announced it would keep Buckeye Egg Farm's permits in limbo in case a new, more responsible owner should emerge.

Violations and behavior aside, the egg firm was an economic boon, for it employed 500 people at its peak and purchased $30 million worth of grain a year.

In January 2003, Maryland-based Ise America, a subsidiary of egg producing giant Ise Japan, announced its willingness to buy the former nuisance, provided the agriculture department, the new fox watching the henhouse, freed the permits.

Whatever the outcome—a reconstituted egg farm, an extinct business, or some murky middle ground—it will be the fruit of the age-old battle, pitting corporate interests against environmental welfare.

In the spring of 2002, scientists aboard the Lake Guardian, the U.S. Environmental Protection Agency's boat monitoring Lake Erie's water quality, reported that they had found a large "dead zone," an area devoid of life, deep in the lake's Central Basin between Cleveland and Erie, Pennsylvania. The resulting headlines caused folks along Ohio's north shore to wonder if Lake Erie, one of the environmental movement's most remarkable rehab projects, was backsliding to the early 1980s when 90 percent of the basin was declared dead.

Such a relapse would set back the tourism and sport fishing industries which have experienced boon times for a decade. There was talk that complacency had beset the coalition of the state, federal and Canadian officials entrusted to monitor the lake. Critics, on the other hand, characterized "dead zone" headlines as hyperbole, reckless and premature.

Nevertheless, "dead zone" touched the right buttons. Backed by a $2 million U.S.-Canada research grant, a flotilla of boats equipped with probes, monitors, labs, chemists and biologists embarked in June to determine the cause of Erie's burgeoning case of anoxia, or depletion of oxygen.

The scientists discovered wide "clouds" of algae and other tiny plants suspended near the bottom, a tipoff that levels of phosphorus and nitrogen, the nutrients for algae, had ballooned again. Anoxia naturally occurs every year when the lake bottom gets buried by rotting plant matter, which is decomposed by oxygen-consuming bacteria and fungi. July and August are the peak months for anoxia, but it normally disappears by mid-September after cooler temperatures churn the lake water. Prolonged and spreading anoxia can produce the fish kills, thicker algae blooms, and make beaches putrid, as many were in the 1970s.

Although researchers gathered a treasury of data, the source of the latest "dead zone" remains a conundrum. It may take scientists years to know if its recent enlargement is a fluke, a temporary phenomenon, or a long-term problem; or whether it is caused by pollution or natural causes.

For example, researchers have been baffled by the rapid algae bloom because $8 billion spent

on sewage treatment plants since the late 1970s reportedly has reduced the annual phosphate load from 24,000 tons to 11,000 tons.

If so, why then have the Canadians been recording levels of phosphate leaving the lake at Niagara Falls, which exceed the amount entering upstream from known sources, such as farm runoff and sewage plants?

Could Erie be generating its own algae nutrients?

Some experts blame tiny quagga mussels, the latest of 146 foreign plants and animals that have invaded the lake's ecosystem since 1830. This prolific critter may be expelling waste containing phosphorus, which in turn feeds algae and swells the "dead zone." Other invasive creatures, such as round gobies (small fish) and zebra mussels, also may be altering the lake's biota in unknown ways.

Some theories allege that ozone depletion in the atmosphere, ultraviolet radiation, global warming, lower water levels, and higher water temperatures are contributing factors. Though unique, Erie is a big organism influenced by three larger lakes, thousands of streams, millions of people, international shipping (source of most of the lake's invasive species), and natural forces not clearly understood.

Is Erie coming out of remission and showing us that the therapy of the previous 20 years was unable to cure deeper wounds? Could the "dead zone" be a biological marker, a sign of an impending ecological crash? Or is the ancient lake, of which we know so little, simply battling indigestion? The answers will spring from statistics, the lens through we view all things, except for beauty.

Lake Erie, of course, is healthy only if its major tributaries are clean. The U.S. EPA has categorized portions of four Ohio rivers flowing in Erie—Cuyahoga, Ashtabula, Black and Maumee—as "areas of concern" for pollution. Remedial work is underway to restore the Cuyahoga River downstream from Cuyahoga Falls (including the section through Cuyahoga Valley National Park); the lower two miles of the Ashtabula River and its harbor; the entire watershed of the Black River; and the Maumee River and its branches in Lucas County.

In spite of these nagging problems, Ohio EPA can report a significant overall improvement in the water quality of Ohio streams. Currently, nearly 55 percent of Ohio river miles monitored fully meet aquatic life uses, meaning they contain thriving and diverse animal and plant populations and are safe for recreation.

Before 1988, only 34 percent of the monitored miles met that criteria. The Scioto River, once a stinky and oxygen-depleted current, now supports several rare species. More than half of the remaining monitored river miles continue to improve.

Even the Little Scioto River, the state's filthiest stream, is expected to rebound after a $7 million rehab project, proving again that the sins of the past can be purified.

Ohio's dirtiest streams

Don't wade or swim in these streams nor eat fish from them due to high levels of contamination.

Black River, Lorain County, from Downtown Lorain to Lake Erie.
Little Scioto River, Marion County, from State Route 739 to Holland Road.
Mahoning River, Trumbull and Mahoning counties, from Warren to Pennsylvania border.
Middle Fork of *Little Beaver Creek*, Columbiana County, from State Route 14 to State Route 11.
Ottawa River, Lucas County, from I-475 to Maumee Bay.

part i

Toxic Chemical Pollution

Worst Counties for Releasing Chemicals into Air, Land, Water
Washington, 24,693,815 pounds
Lucas, 20,858,689 pounds
Jefferson, 18,561,588 pounds
Allen, 18,491,290 pounds
Sandusky, 17,825,063 pounds

Least Polluting Counties
Greene, 493 pounds
Mercer, 300 pounds
Carroll, 208 pounds

Worst Counties for Releasing Chemicals into Air
Jefferson, 16,635,128 pounds
Brown, 14,212,284 pounds
Washington, 13,584,040 pounds
Gallia, 9,086,691 pounds
Hamilton, 8,421,045

Worst Counties for Releasing Chemicals into Water
Coshocton, 4,733,120 pounds
Washington, 1,024,846 pounds
Stark, 720,159 pounds
Allen, 154,938 pounds
Butler, 147,663 pounds

Worst Counties for Releasing Chemicals into Land
Lucas, 17,431,892 pounds
Washington, 10,084,929 pounds
Gallia, 3,568,481 pounds
Brown, 3,127,475 pounds
Cuyahoga, 2,421,982 pounds

Source: U.S. Environmental Protection Agency, 2002 Toxic Release Inventory

Counties where cancer risk from toxic emissions is highest: *Coshocton, Jefferson, Washington, Lake, Gallia.*

Counties where cancer risk from toxic emission is lowest: *Jackson, Clinton*

—*Source: Environmental Defense Fund, 2002*

part ii

Ohio's dirtiest streams

Eating bottom-feeding fish (catfish, suckers, carp) caught from sections of these streams is a health risk due to high concentrations of hazardous chemicals.

Dicks Creek, Middletown
          to Great Miami River
Great Miami River, Dayton
          to Ohio River
Lake Erie
Lake Nesmith, Summit County
Maumee River, Lucas County,
                    Waterville
                    to Lake Erie
Ohio River
Portage Canal, Summit County
Summit Lake, Summit County
—*Source: Ohio Department of Health, Ohio EPA*

Ohio's container: Is it half-empty or half-full?

The oil slick that burst into raging flames atop the Cuyahoga River in June 1969 is one of those "turning point" events in American history. The hellish images dancing in Cleveland's industrial heartland, which symbolized the nation's disgraceful disregard for the natural environment, seem forever branded in the American psyche. Pundits thereafter maligned the Cuyahoga as "ooze" river whose soup would decay a man before drowning him. The fire became a burning cross on America's conscience; and turned a nascent environmental movement into a *cause célèbre*.

Ohioans shamed by it suffered more humiliations in the early 1970s when scientists declared Lake Erie "dead" and the Ohio River a slow-moving cesspool, both victims of prolonged pollution and neglect.

Fortunately, the gruesome events inspired nationwide reforms, ranging from the simple volunteer acts of recycling the Sunday newspaper and car pooling to legislation controlling emissions from cars and power plants. The environment became a national crusade to save the planet and our soul.

Three years after the Cuyahoga River calamity, state legislators put the newly-created Ohio Environmental Protection Agency (OEPA) in charge of rehabilitating the state's fouled environment and image, and keeping both clean. Since its onset, however, the noble mission of the multifaceted agency has been fraught with conflict and complexity. Whenever ardent environmentalists have claimed that it lacked the funds, zeal and backbone to be an effective protector, industries and municipalities, the major polluters, have complained that it overregulated, mandated costly corrections too swiftly, and threatened local economies.

Over the years, intervening federal and state agencies, politicians, and courts, whose actions have opposed OEPA as often as they have been allied with it, have paradoxically energized, stifled, streamlined, complicated, reconstituted, polarized and politicized environmental progress in Ohio. While some players proudly attribute a modicum of progress to consensus, others wonder if a distressed environment can survive the politics of give and take.

So, what is the state of Ohio's environment one baby step into the third millennium, two centuries into statehood, and three decades into institutionalized repair? It depends on whether you judge a container half empty or half full.

—Stephen Ostrander

Almost 500,000 children in Ohio live within a few blocks of a known or suspected hazardous waste site.

—*The Plain Dealer*

"WELL, AT LEAST WE'RE DOWN TO ONE BAG OF TRASH...."

Ohio's Worst Occurrences

The Cholera Epidemics
1800's, Entire state
Thousands died
International Plague

Ohio Penitentiary Fire
April 21, 1930, Columbus
322 killed
Deadliest U.S. prison fire

Collinwood School Fire
March 4, 1908, Collinwood
172 children, 2 teachers killed
Deadliest U.S. school fire

East Ohio Gas Company Explosion and Fire
October 20, 1944, Cleveland
130 dead, 20 city blocks devastated
Worst fire in Cleveland history

Cleveland Clinic Fire
May 15, 1929, Cleveland
123 killed
Deadliest U.S. hospital fire

Ashtabula Bridge Collapse
December 29, 1876, Ashtabula
92 killed
Deadliest Ohio rail accident

Millfield Mine Explosion
November 5, 1930, Millfield, Athens County
82 killed
Deadliest Ohio mine accident

Lorain Tornado
June 28, 1924, Lorain
85 killed
Worst Ohio twister

1913 Flood
March 23-28, Great Miami
and Scioto River Valleys
467+ died
Worst Ohio flood

The 1937 Flood
January, 1937, Ohio River Valley
250+ dead
Major U.S. natural disaster

The Nursing Home Fires
November 22, 1963, Fitchville;
63 killed
January 9, 1970, Marietta
32 killed
First and second most deadly
U.S. nursing home fires

The Xenia Tornado
April 3, 1974, Xenia
34 killed
Focal point of a national disaster

1978 Blizzard
January 26, 1978, Entire state
51 dead
Most severe snow storm in Ohio history

The Shadyside Flood
June 14, 1990, Shadyside
26 killed
A once-in-500-years storm

National class disasters have struck Ohio several times. Disasters almost by definition always strike, a most revealing verb, for it tells how helpless folks feel when calamity suddenly confronts them. But whenever disasters have loosened their grip on the wheel of their own fortune, Ohioans have seized the moment during those tragic times and reacted variously to regain control.

When the first cholera epidemics reached Ohio in 1832, the Governor appealed to the Almighty. He declared a day of fasting and prayer, and Columbus folks hoped that gathering in churches would spare them from the plague. Given the contagiousness of the disease, of course, such congregations were quite counterproductive, and the time would have been better spent in simply washing their hands. A few years later, a Cincinnati woman tried running away from cholera. After sewing her money in her skirt, she took off for the country, but cholera caught her anyway. Folks were so anxious to get her diseased body buried that they didn't even bother to take the gold coins out of her hem.

Disasters have also brought out the best in Ohioans, as people rise to even the nastiest occasions. After the 1913 flood washed away most of Dayton, a relief committee asked Lib Hedges, the city's eminently successful madam, for a modest donation. Lib groused about her own losses for a while, then blurted out, "I'll give $2,000 and not a damned cent more."

And during that flood, National Cash Register President John Henry Patterson became his city's savior. In a single morning, he shifted his production line from business machines to boats and turned his factory into a hospital and relief center. Mothers who gave birth in the "maternity ward" gratefully named their babies "Cash."

But fright and flight and floods aside, consider the sterling reaction of Columbus reporter William Cunningham when a prisoner

asked him to notify his family that he had survived the Ohio Penitentiary fire:

"What shall I wire?" asked Cunningham.

"You make it up," said the prisoner.

"How about escaped?" he asked.

Ah yes, *escaped*. Given the circumstances, can there be a better response whenever disaster strikes?

THE CHOLERA EPIDEMICS
thousands died—international plague
1800s, entire state

Cholera was the scourge of the 19th century, a disease that began in India and spread over the world in successive waves of epidemic. The United States might have gotten off lightly, except for the Industrial Revolution. The advent of rapid transportation and mushrooming urban populations only fueled the contagion.

Cholera traveled to Ohio via the Ohio River and Lake Erie, then was carried inland by canal and stagecoach traffic. People did not know that the cholera bacteria thrives in human waste, a near-suicidal ignorance considering that public sanitation was minimal for most of the century. What they did know—and feared—was that the disease spread like wildfire and that death, given the violence of the gastrointestinal symptoms, came with merciful swiftness.

The worst year for Ohio was 1849, when cholera raged in all states east of the Rocky Mountains. Cholera never discriminated. It took 120 in the village of Eaton and 8,000 in the city of Cincinnati. It claimed the innocent—Harriet Beecher Stowe's baby son—as well as the damned—116 inmates of the Ohio Penitentiary in Columbus. It delayed the fun of the Ohio State Fair and the business of Cincinnati, where city fathers vainly tried to purify the air with sulphur fires on the streetcorners. Stephens Collins Foster wrote to his worried mother that he was quite well in the city, but for Mrs. Stowe, cholera was the last straw. After her young Samuel died, she left Cincinnati for good.

OHIO PENITENTIARY FIRE
322 killed—deadliest U.S. prison fire
April 21, 1930, Columbus

A warden once compared the hoary Ohio Penitentiary to the Bastille, and its massive stone walls 24 feet high did render the place a grim rock of cages that witnessed torture, epidemic, and execution. But the blackest moment came when a fire apparently started by inmates to divert attention from an escape plan got out of control. Most of the dead were prisoners locked in the 'living hell' of cell blocks G and H, where 'black smoke was choking the breath out of men,' and "steel bars turned so red hot that human beings were being boiled alive."

Prison officials later drew fire of their own for not holding fire drills or unlocking imperiled inmates with all due speed, and the National Guard had to maintain order among the bitter survivors. Ironically, the burnt section of the prison had been considered "fireproof," and it might well have been except for the wooden roof, which was inexplicably made doubly deadly by a heavy, and highly flammable, tarpaulin covering.

COLLINWOOD SCHOOL FIRE
172 children, 2 teachers killed
deadliest U.S. school fire
March 4, 1908, Collinwood

Fire inspectors blamed the blaze on an overheated steam pipe and the death toll on panic. The rush to escape Lakeview Elementary turned into a stampede, and scores of young bodies were found piled against the doors. Of the 300 or so children in attendance, only 80 escaped harm. Most pitiful of all, perhaps, were the 19 who could not be identified and had to be buried in a common grave.

Lakeview Elementary was built mostly of wood; too many pupils were crowded inside; there was only one fire escape; and the narrow hallways not only impeded safe exit but also acted as giant flues. The school's tragedy taught a cruel lesson, and the entire nation paid attention with beefed up school fire laws and safety standards.

EAST OHIO GAS COMPANY EXPLOSION AND FIRE
130 dead, 20 city blocks devastated
October 20, 1944, Cleveland

Since the war effort fairly devoured natural gas, patriotism could justify building a liquification and storage plant in the middle of the blue collar neighborhood. Because such a commercial gas facility had never been built before, the plant was something of an experiment, and the people living between East 55th and 67th streets became unwitting guinea pigs in a catastrophe. The storage tanks developed cracks, and leaking gas spread a surreptitious carpet of death throughout the neighborhood. As the gas invaded basements and sewers, houses suddenly began exploding. The subsequent fire storm did not even spare the birds. The intense heat reached high into the sky and scorched them out of the air.

CLEVELAND CLINIC FIRE
123 killed—deadliest U.S. hospital fire
May 15, 1929
Cleveland

Overheated x-ray film touched off explosions that sent staff and patients jumping for their lives from the windows and roof. The burning film released nitrogen dioxide, a gas which causes severe lung edema, and deadly yellow clouds rolled through the clinic. The noxious fumes repelled fireman at the doors and forced them to enter the building through a skylight. A physician exposed to the gas died a few hours later; others lingered for days. Every automobile in the city was commandeered to transport victims, and an SOS went out to 30 cities for oxygen tents. In the aftermath, Cleveland firemen got gas masks, and the nation got new ways of handling and storing hazardous materials, in particular nitrocellulose x-ray film.

ASHTABULA BRIDGE COLLAPSE
92 killed—deadliest Ohio rail accident
December 29, 1876, Ashtabula

The bridge spanned a deep gorge just east of town, and it fell on a bitter night when the snow was coming down fast and the ill-fated Pacific Express No. 5 was running late. The double track wooden bridge had been built by the Lake Shore and Southern Railroad. Amasa Stone, the railroad president, held the patent on the bridge's iron Howe trusses and was largely responsible for its design. Though experts later concluded that the heavy snow caused a derailment that in turn placed ruinous stress on the bridge, Mr. Stone never escaped personal blame for one of the worst accidents in the history of U.S. railroads.

The breaking point of the bridge, however, proved to be a turning point in bridge engineering. The horror of Ashtabula and the spectacular collapse three years later of Scotland's Tay Bridge offered vivid proof that iron could not support the railroad's ever-increasing loads. Iron was the real culprit at Ashtabula, and the disaster there accelerated the transition to steel bridge construction.

MILLFIELD MINE EXPLOSION
82 killed—deadliest Ohio mine accident
November 5, 1930
Millfield, Athens County

The Sunday Creek Coal Company first learned that there was a problem at Mine No. 6 when a farmer telephoned that he had just seen a man being blown out of the new air shaft. A short circuit touched off a pocket of methane gas shortly before noon. It took four hours of digging through debris before rescuers could bring in the canaries and another three hours before they found the first body. In addition to the burned and suffocated miners, the Sunday Creek president and several other company officers perished. They had been inspecting the air shaft, recently installed in what they thought was the safest mine for miles.

LORAIN TORNADO
85 killed—worst Ohio twister
June 28, 1924, Lorain

A musical was in progress when a tornado took the roof off Sandusky's State Theatre about 5 p.m. The house went dark, and the stunned audience dodged bricks and broken glass, but the pianist gamely kept on playing. After delivering its initial blow to Sandusky, the twister traveled 25 miles across Lake Erie and saved the knockout punch for Lorain: 200 stores and 500 houses destroyed, more than 1,000 people injured, and about one-fourth of the town—some 10,000—homeless. Because Governor Donahey would not seek federal relief funds, the citizens of Lorain rebuilt the town with their own money and donations from fellow Ohioans.

1913 FLOOD
467 + died—worst Ohio flood
March 23-28
Great Miami and Scioto River Valleys

Spring rains and a thaw had already saturated the ground, then an Easter Week cloudburst turned the rivers and tributaries wild. Though a hundred Ohio cities were inundated, low-lying Dayton (whose founders had ignored the Indians' flood warnings) was hardest hit. Four waterways converge within a mile there, and on March 25, the city was deluged with 1.5 million gallons of water per second, an incredible torrent that equalled an entire month's flow over Niagara Falls. River gauges registered a record-setting 29 feet, and fires and explosions added to the toll of dead and injured. But Daytonians pulled themselves up by their own soggy bootstraps, pledging personal funds as seed money for dams that have not only kept them dry ever since but have also been a national flood protection model.

THE 1937 FLOOD
250 + dead—major U.S. natural disaster
January, 1937
Ohio River Valley

Someone once wrote that folks along the Ohio River monitor the water level the way that New Yorkers spot gold and Southerners cotton. On January 26, the river watchers got an eyeful as the Ohio crested at a record 79.99 feet, after weeks of unrelenting rain poured an estimated 60 billion tons of water into the valley. The river simply could not hold it all, and the tremendous overflow flooded more than 12,000 square miles of land. From Marietta to the Mississippi River, water closed every bridge, except for Cincinnati's Suspension Bridge, which residents heroically protected with sandbags, even as floating gasoline sparked the city's greatest fire on "Black Sunday." The widespread destruction proved that flood prevention in the Ohio Valley was no longer a local option, and the federal government began to enact the nation's fledgling Flood Control Act.

THE NURSING HOME FIRES
63 and 32 killed—first and second most deadly U.S. nursing home fires
November 22, 1963; January 9, 1970
Fitchville; Marietta

The blazes at Golden Age Nursing Home and Harmar House seemed especially dastardly because they trapped the ill and the infirm, a situation that resulted in nursing homes being required to have automatic sprinkler systems to give residents a fighting chance. So far, so good: Harmar House was Ohio's last multiple fatality nursing home fire.

THE XENIA TORNADO
34 killed—focal point of a national disaster
April 3, 1974, Xenia

When two unusually strong fronts—one warm and moist, one cold and dry—collided over the Midwest, they spawned an epidemic of tornadoes from Alabama to Ontario, the likes of which the United States had not seen in nearly a century. At least 148 twisters touched down in 24 hours, killing 309 persons and injuring another 5,000. In Xenia, a huge twister roared for an agonizing 35 minutes. During each of those minutes, it wreaked $3 million worth of havoc, but Xenians counted one big blessing: the tornado devastated the schools after their children had been dismissed.

1978 BLIZZARD
51 dead—most severe snowstorm in Ohio history
January 26, 1978, entire state

When two low pressure systems met over southern Ohio, they precipitated a once-in-a-lifetime blizzard for the Great Lakes States. In Ohio, ten inches of new snow piled on top of the foot or so already on the ground, temperatures dropped 40 degrees in a few hours, and sustained winds of 50 to 70 miles per hour whipped up white-out conditions and 25-foot snow drifts.

Governor James Rhodes called it the state's worst disaster ever, and he had plenty of evidence: hundreds of thousands of people stranded without food, fuel, or electricity; the Ohio Turnpike completely shut down for the first time; and business, commerce, and society brought to a screeching halt. In all, the blizzard cost Ohioans some $100 million.

SHADYSIDE FLOOD
26 killed—once-in-500 years storm
June 14, 1990
Shadyside

Over Belmont County on the evening of June 14, a localized "high efficiency" storm estimated to be ten miles high poured out five inches of rain in less than 30 minutes. The deluge turned the usually docile streams of Ohio's Appalachian foothills into raging walls of water as much as 20 feet tall. The sudden violence of Pipe and Wegee Creeks caught residents of the wooded hollows by surprise and many were trapped when the water burst through their homes. The two-story house that landed on a bridge on Pike Creek was just one of the hundreds of homes destroyed.

CINCINNATI SHIP IN AMERICA'S WORST MARITIME DISASTER

It was the nation's worst maritime disaster yet, surprisingly, one of the least known. The *Sultana* was launched from Cincinnati's Litherburg Shipyard in 1863, built for a Cincinnati captain. In the pre-dawn hours of April 27, 1865, overloaded with Union soldiers on their way back north, its boiler exploded, killing as many as 1,800 of its 2,400 passengers—including some 800 Ohioans. Most of the dead were men who had just been paroled from the Confederacy's worst prison camps, and were on their way to civilian life. Author Jerry Potter said there were accusations from Army officers who charged that their colleagues accepted bribes from steamboat captains to carry as many men as possible. The charges were never properly investigated. The boat, said Potter, was designed to hold only 376. The explosion happened in the Mississippi north of Memphis and bodies of the soldiers floated to the surface for weeks after the explosion. The disaster was overshadowed by the war's end and the assassination of President Lincoln and received little attention, particularly in the eastern newspapers. Sadly, it became only a small footnote in history. The sinking of the *Sultana*, however, was a tragedy that eclipsed even the *Titanic*, whose death toll was 1,522. The U.S. Customs Office in Memphis said 1,547 died on the *Sultana*; other estimates ran as high as 1,800. The last of the survivors died, forgotten, in the 1930s. ✍

Sultana tragedy

Sunday, November 7, 2003

Ohio Daily Paragon

Our Motto: Silence is the virtue of fools

Buckeye Publisher Assembles All-Star Cast After Daring Raid on Buckeye Media Moguls; Incidents of Garment-rending and Teeth-gnashing Reported from Ohio Capitals of Fourth Estate

By Thomas Suddes
Special to the Daily Paragon

The Ohio Daily Paragon is a mythical newspaper invented by one of Ohio's top journalists, is the paper everyone would read. And you read it here first.

Like MGM's one-time boast, Ohio's newspapers offer a reader "more stars than there are in heaven," but they don't all shimmer in the same constellation: For that, imagine *The Ohio Paragon*, a mythical mirror reflecting the sparkle—attitude, *gravitas* and, yes, idiosyncrasy—in the biggest Buckeye State dailies.

Photographically, for example, an Ohioan would be hard-pressed to find better news pictures anywhere than those routinely offered by the *Columbus Dispatch*, whose art (to use print-shop lingo) sets a regional standard for composition, impact and reproduction. *The Paragon* would showcase many of them.

The *Dispatch*, heir to its proud sister, the frankly Republican *Ohio State Journal* (closed in 1959), is also as close to a paper of state-political record as Ohio gets, because Ohio's General Assembly—unlike Congress—publishes no detailed record of debates. *The Paragon* could, after a fashion, by relaying the *Dispatch*'s insights.

Lean Dayton Political Machine Lauded for Gas Mileage

For concise but nonetheless thorough coverage of state politics, the *Dayton Daily News*'s lean but productive Columbus operation is often just the thing, depending on the day or issue. But *The Paragon* would have to choose its state reportage wisely. That's because, embodying Nathan Bedford Forrest's battlefield philosophy, the competing *Cleveland Plain Dealer* bureau is usually on a given Columbus story first, and with the most people.

Among big editorial pages, none is as idiosyncratic as the *Toledo Blade*'s, whose targets, if unwise, swiftly learn the peril of fighting a foe that buys ink in barrels, The Blade's opinions are the remembered voice in the Ohioana Babel. *The Paragon*, reserving its cautionary prerogatives, could garnish its smorgasbord with the *Blade*'s evergreen blasts.

Meanwhile, on its pages, the *Dayton Daily News*—the "Dayton Daily Worker," to unhappy Ohio conservatives—beats the drum for the New Deal, the Great Society and every other cathartic in Democrats' first-aid kit, regardless of "sell by" dates and the purported death of American liberalism. Those spices, too, would pepper *The Paragon*'s stewpot, as would John S. Knight's *Akron Beacon Journal*, whose editorial page that, on any given day, is Ohio's most quietly intellectual.

Cleveland Bench Strength Routs Statewide Competition

As for the sporting news, the *Plain Dealer* fields an impressive front line with good bench strength, providing wider coverage than most and with a larger hole—including a once-a-week golf section and a prep sports insert. *The Paragon* might also finish out its sports staff with a sports feature writer purloined from the *Akron Beacon Journal*, the *Dayton Daily News*, or the *Cincinnati Post*, each of which has a worthy house headliner.

For attitude—Take sass with your news?—nothing in Ohio matches sports, arts and consumer pages of the *Cleveland Plain Dealer*, which is not only Ohio's most widely circulated

Anne O'Hare McCormick of Dayton, in 1936, was the first woman on the New York Times editorial board

paper but circulates in the state's most populous, rambunctious—and cultured—region.

Wrapped into *The Paragon* would be the Cleveland giant's music and architecture criticism, its food and wine coverage, and—alternately with the *Columbus Dispatch*'s concise and usually dead-on Washington report—stories reported by the *Plain Dealer*'s big Washington staff.

Meanwhile, in the department of life's diversion, the *Cincinnati Enquirer* provides an ample guide to the many entertainments, festivals and such that proliferate in what it calls the "Tristate"—the conjunction of Ohio's border with those of Kentucky and Indiana. In its regional round-ups, *The Paragon* would include those, so much less somber than much of what other Ohio papers consider news.

And the *Youngstown Vindicator*, long "the People's Paper," a paper of record for that region's rambunctious politics, would freshen *The Paragon*, too, offering enough "believe it or not counterpoint" to rival Ripley's famous feature.

The state's numerous weeklies range from the typographical serenity of, say, the *Yellow Springs News*, to the in-their-faces clutter of urban alternative papers, heirs of the underground press that surfaced in the 1960s.

But while most Americans may or may not get their news—actually, their headlines—from television, Ohio newspaper readers mostly get their news from the state's big papers.

Ohio's big dailies, which range in circulation from the *Plain Dealer* to the *Canton Repository*, sell 59 of every 100 daily papers that Ohioans buy, and 72 of every 100 Sunday papers. All told, regardless of a paper's circulation, Ohio's 80-plus dailies sell about 2.4 million copies every weekday—about 2.7 million copies on Sundays.

Cincinnati David Dukes it out With Crosstown Goliath

Still, head-to-head newspaper competition among Ohio dailies continues, perhaps appropriately, only in the birthplace of Ohio newspapering, Cincinnati. There, the Gannett chain's *Cincinnati Enquirer* and the feisty but far smaller *Cincinnati Post* duke it out Mondays through Saturdays. (The *Post* doesn't publish on Sundays.)

According to historian Osman C. Hooper, Ohio's first newspaper, William Maxwell's *Centinel of the North-Western Territory*, debuted in Cincinnati in 1793, when George Washington was president and Philadelphia was America's capital. Ohio's first daily, was the

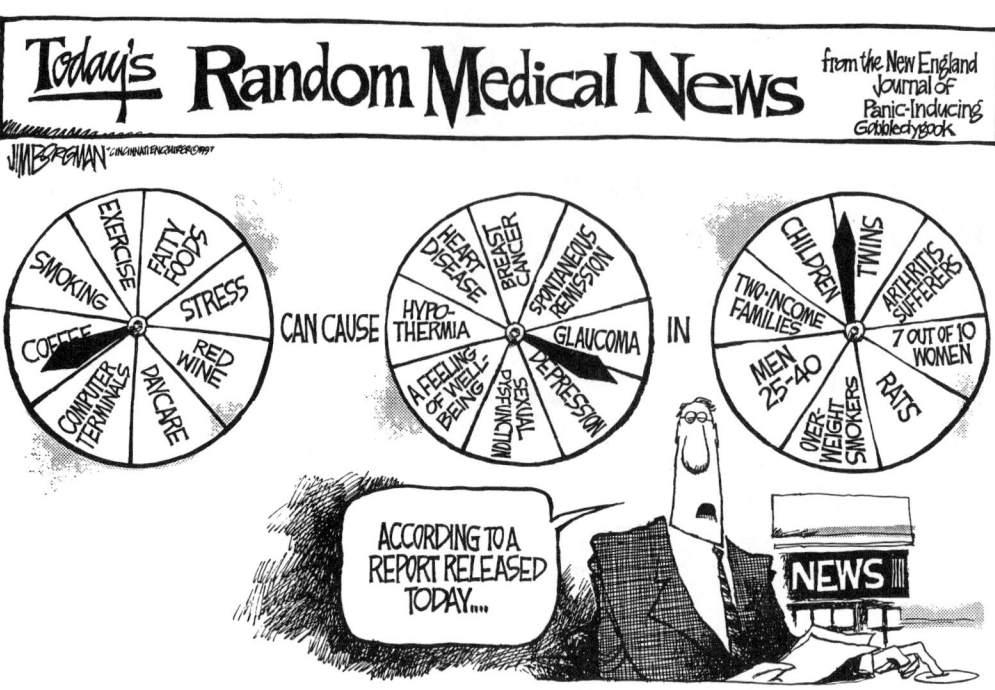

Today's **Random Medical News** from the New England Journal of Panic-Inducing Gobbledygook

JIMBORGMAN ©Cincinnati Enquirer ©1997

CAN CAUSE ... IN ...

ACCORDING TO A REPORT RELEASED TODAY....

NEWS

Cincinnati Commercial Register, which appeared in 1826, while John Quincy Adams lived in the White House and 750,000 people lived in Ohio.

The *Cincinnati Post* is the last Ohio daily published by the Scripps Howard chain. At its in-state peak in the 1930s, Scripps also published dailies in Akron, Cleveland, Columbus, Toledo and Youngstown. Scripps's Ohio editors, and the chain's Statehouse bureau (closed in 2002), were sparkplugs of Ohio's Progressive Era reforms, before the First World War.

Lip From Scripps Sinks Statehouse Ship

In 1911, for instance, the Ohio Senate, enraged by Scripps coverage of legislative corruption and the chain's refusal to betray Statehouse sources, voted 24-8 to bar Scripps reporters from the Senate floor for the final hours of the 79th Ohio General Assembly. Looking back 50 years later, Hoyt L. Warner, a leading historian of Ohio's Progressive era, concluded that Ohio's Gilded Age "conservatives recognized and feared the influence of [Scripps-group] papers."

Scripps reportage also haunted Ohio's scoundrels for much of the remainder of the 20th century.

By some measures, notably invigorated political coverage, Ohio's most improved big newspaper today may be the *Canton Repository* under new owners, California-based Copley Press, publisher of the *San Diego Union-Tribune*. Before Copley bought the *Repository* in 2000, the Canton paper had dulled as a link in the Anglo-Canadian Thomson chain.

The Thomson media empire's founder was the gleefully philistine Roy Thomson, an Ontario-born salesman, whose journalistic creed was, "I am in business to make money, and I buy more newspapers to make more money to buy more newspapers," and favorite music, he said, was "the sound of radio commercials at $10 a whack."

1985—The Columbus Citizen-Journal ceases publication. Charlotte Curtis called its staff "oddly exotic." The senior reporter was a former railroad engineer, she said. The obituary editor sobbed when anyone phoned in a death notice, the news editor was a failed Olympic hurdler, and the managing editor, having coined "flash flood", dreamed of leaving to work for Life magazine. It was, she said, "a buggy whip in a jet age, and a frayed buggy whip at that."

strip artists

Ohioans like to claim that among their populace was the fellow who drew the first color comic strip— Lancaster native Richard Outcault who, in 1895, started drawing "Hogan's Alley," whose protagonist was a big-eared little boy who wore a saffron nightgown.

The truth is, there's no way to know exactly what the first color comic actually was but Outcault drew the first well-known one and was the artist who firmly established its basic tenets. The strip began as a panel but the format soon changed into a sequence with dialogue in balloons, which soon became a staple of the comic strip form. The pioneer Outcault had created the first continuing comic strip character, as well as fathering the child or "kid" strip, which saw its fullest expression a century later when another Ohioan, Bill Watterson, created Calvin and Hobbes, a 6-year-old whose hilariously embattled early-life stance is aided and abetted by a stuffed tiger.

Outcault himself did not rest on the laurels of creating the kid strip; he also concocted the long-lived Buster Brown, which began in 1902. Foppish Buster, a counterweight to the marginally literate Yellow Kid, was a kind of parody of Little Lord Fauntleroy and each strip displayed a prank for which he is justly dealt.

Outcault went to McMicken University in Cincinnati before taking off for New York, and historians say his famous Yellow Kid was born when the foreman of the pressroom needed a patch of white space in which the presses could print yellow. Outcault's urchin, with his white nightgown, seemed the perfect candidate for the tallow-drying process.

That, of course, was said to have been the origin of "yellow journalism," a term applied ever since to newspapers given to lurid splashes of salacious reporting.

At the time, Pulitzer was waging a circulation war with William Randolph Hearst, and Outcault alternately hired his services to both of them. When the rivalry between the newspaper barons escalated to sensationalism, the phrase "yellow journalism" became *de rigueur*.

Outcault's urban stew would not regularly become a part of the comic strip menu because gritty realism was not a staple of the newspaper strip. What did remain as a staple, however, was the American sense of humor and fanciful expression that saw the Yellow Kid's nightshirt emblazoned with ever-changing dialogue. This inventive use of urban slang in itself might also have presaged the later century's explosion of expressive tee-shirts and self-promotions.

Another Ohio expatriot, Winsor McCay, had also begun his career in Cincinnati, drawing murals for the Vine Street Dime Museum. Trailing Outcault to New York, McCay drew Little Nemo in Slumberland for the *New York Herald* in 1905. It was called "the most beautifully drawn and aesthetically pleasing Sunday page ever to grace the weekly color supplements."

McCay's strip was the first extended comic narrative—its story unfolded over a five-year period—and his elegant line anticipated the dreamscapes of the Surrealist artists. He is also recognized as the father of the American animated cartoon. ✍

Spare the rod (but not the antennae)

By the time the average Ohio child becomes a teenager, his or her television habits will be such that he or she will have witnessed 18,000 murders.

—National Issues Forum, "Kids Who Commit Crimes"

The moment	The background	The context	The quote
1860s—Joseph Medill helped found the Republican Party, and send Lincoln to the White House.	Grew up on a Stark County farm, and in 1852 began the first morning newspaper in Cleveland.	Credited with persuading Lincoln into making a stand against slavery and securing his nomination at 1860 National Convention in Chicago. He built the *Chicago Tribune* into one of America's best newspapers.	His final words, before dying of heart failure: "What is the news this morning?"
1888—Carr Vattel Van Anda, a Georgetown, Ohio, boy, becomes "one of the greatest managing editors of his time and perhaps of all time."	Built his own makeshift printing press by the time he was ten.	His leadership was credited with making the *New York Times* the foremost news operation in the country, and developing it as the "newspaper of record."	"All the news that's fit to print."
1890—Isaac Kauffman Funk, and partner Adam Wagnalls, begin work on A Standard Dictionary of the English Language.	Another Ohio farmer's son, from Clifton.	Funk hired several hundred staffers, working for over three years to produce a major dictionary advance, in that it stressed "correct spellings of words, their most common meanings, and pronunciation."	"Look *that* up in your Funk and Wagnalls."
1908—Percy Hunter Hammond, Cadiz, Ohio, becomes drama critic of the *Chicago Tribune*. Salary: $8 a week.	Considered the first of American journalism's 'sophisticates', he "practiced the 'light touch' with a pretense of Oxonian learning which seemed to be laughing at itself."	As a theatrical journalist, his reviews heralded the end of "the old style pontifical school of play reviewing and the beginning of the modern era." He became America's most influential drama critic.	His critique of a musical he found tedious: "I find I have knocked everything but the chorus girls' knees, and there God anticipated me."
1920—James Thurber begins work at the *Columbus Dispatch*, where his editor said the perfect story lead was: "John Holtsapple, prominent Columbus galosh manufacturer, died of complications last night at his home, 396 N. Persimmon Blvd."	Thurber's editor addressed him as "Author," and "Phi Beta Kappa." Afterward, Thurber said he had an recurring anxiety dream about him: "He runs up to my desk with a shoe in his hand and says, 'We've got just ten minutes to get this shoe in the paper!'"	Considered the finest American humorist since Mark Twain. With his terse, eccentric writings on the foibles of humanity, he became the first major writer to build an entire career as a writer of short pieces.	"It is always apparent to Thurber that at the very moment one's heart is caught in an embrace, one's foot may be caught in a piano stool." —E.B. White

The moment	The background	The context	The quote
1939—Scotty Reston begins 50-year association with New York Times, joining the Times' London bureau on September 1, 1939, as Hitler's armies march into Poland.	During high school years in Dayton, Ohio, caddies at Dayton Country Club, becoming good enough to win—twice—Ohio's public links golf championship. First job: sports editor, Springfield Daily News, $10 a week.	Winning Pulitzers in 1945 and 1957, the recipient of 28 honorary degrees, Reston was called the most influential American journalist of his generation.	"What I try to do is write a letter to a friend who doesn't have time to find out all the goofy things that go on in Washington." 1939
1940—On his 10th anniversary on the air, Lowell Thomas was broadcasting each night to an audience of 10 million.	The folksy Thomas, born just north of Greenville, Ohio in the hamlet of Woodington, called himself an entertainer rather than a journalist.	His voice may have been heard by more people than any voice in history, his total radio audience estimated at 70 billion.	Recognizing he was on the air at dinnertime, he said, "I never felt it was my responsibility to destroy the digestive system of the American people."
1942—Earl Wilson launches his gossip column in the New York Post.	Begins writing sports for the Lima Republican-Gazette for $1.50 a week while in high school before going off to OSU's journalism school.	In 40 years, the dean of the gossip columnists, syndicated in 300 newspapers, writes 11,424 columns.	"My mother was shrewd enough when I was young to hint that it would be agriculture's gain if I left farming."
1949—Eugenia Sheppard sees her women's pages become a daily feature of the New York Herald Tribune.	She was a Columbus native whose first brush with fashion occurs at the Columbus School for Girls.	She transformed fashion news "from a dry description of clothes to a spirited discussion of the lives of the people involved in the international fashion industry," and her personalized reporting signalled the beginning of modern fashion reporting.	"She maintained her influence despite her bad eyesight and her refusal to wear eyeglasses."
1965— Charlotte Curtis begins her 25-year career with the New York Times.	She said she was "the little girl from Ohio" who always kept her Ohio driver's license.	The first woman to appear on the Times' masthead.	"I'd walk over my own grandmother for a story."
1980—Ted Turner begins the Cable News Network.	Turner's mother was the granddaughter of Cincinnati's first chain grocer.	CNN revolutionized mass communications by bringing instantaneous 24-hour news to a global audience, thereby changing the dynamics between people and their governments.	"Ted Turner is a mixture of genius and jackass." 1980

Old waves

Oldest TV station in Ohio—WLWT-TV, Cincinnati, since 1948

Oldest radio station in Ohio—WHK-AM, Cleveland, 1921

Oldest public TV station in Ohio—WCET-TV, Cincinnati, 1954

Oldest public radio station in Ohio—WOSU-AM, Columbus, 1922

**Getting public information from city
and state agencies would be a lot easier were
it not for Ohio's public-records law, say groups
that promote openness in government.
The Chicago-based Better Government
Association, formed by businessmen 79 years
ago to fight corrupt city administrations,
recently gave Ohio a grade of "D" and ranked its public-
records law 41ˢᵗ out of 50 for failing to make it easier
to obtain state and local records.**

Ohio's law got low marks for requiring only that records be released in a "reasonable" amount of time, which is ambiguous and can lead to excessive delays, the association said. Ohio also scored poorly for its appeals process, which requires going to court if a government refuses to turn over records—a costly, time-consuming process. In addition, it lost points for not having a procedure to move records disputes to the front of a court docket, important for time-sensitive documents. And it lacked specific punishments for agencies that drag their heels.

Ohio won praise for only one component of its law—the part that allows attorneys fees to be awarded under certain circumstances, such as a city's deliberate failure to comply with open-records requests.

"While it's disappointing, it's not surprising," said State Sen. Dan Brady, Democrat of Cleveland, who has pushed for more openness and blames the Republican-dominated Statehouse and governor's office. "They have come to see the state and its documents and its institutions as belonging to their party rather than to the public."

But Mark Weaver, a former Ohio deputy attorney general, said the legislature has balanced the public's right to know with the need to protect certain functions of government. He cited the Ohio Supreme Court's unanimous ruling in 2000 that Columbus did not have to release names, addresses, phone numbers, photos and health information for about 25,000 children.

Recreation officials used the database to issue ID cards to children using Columbus swimming pools. A radio talk show host asked to use it to recruit for the Boy Scouts.

While Weaver assumed the radio host's motives were pure, he said releasing the database would mean "anyone would be able to get it, including all the people on the registered sex offender list."

The court agreed, and just to be safe, the state legislature passed a bill excluding such information from Ohio's public records laws.

Watchdog groups and news organizations say the public cannot effectively keep an eye on the government without ready access to documents such as government payrolls, travel and personnel records, crime reports, and health department inspections. Examinations of public records have helped expose corruption, cost overruns, abuses in government-licensed nursing homes, even theft against the government.

"We put these people in. We give them enormous sums of money, and they run our government," said Terry Norton, executive director of the Better Government Association. "And the bigger it gets, the more important it is for us, through the media and our own means, to find out what is the government doing in our name, and with our money."

—by Stephen Koff, permission of *The Plain Dealer*

www. *ohionews.org*

Links to most of the newspapers in Ohio, from the *Akron Beacon Journal* to the *Zanesville Times-Recorder*, as well as many of the weekly newspapers.

Ask Mr. Sunshine

Everything you wanted to know about the Ohio Public Records Act.

DEAR MR. SUNSHINE,
   What is a public record?

A public record is a document created or received by a city, county, state or federal agency. It must exist in a "fixed medium," which is finely tuned legalese for paper, videotape, audiotape, computer files, film or microfilm. The document must be used to carry out the duties and responsibilities of a public office. In other words, the doodles the city airport director draws while listening to constituent complaints are not public records, but the memo his fawning assistant drafts to have the drawing framed certainly is.

DEAR MR. SUNSHINE,
   Who can make a public records request?

Anyone. It doesn't matter if you're a born-again hot dog vendor, a voo-doo economist or a death row inmate.

DEAR MR. SUNSHINE,
   Do I have to make a public records request in writing? Do I have to state a reason for wanting the records?

You're dealing with politicians, judges and lawyers here, so the magic word isn't "Please." It's "Ohio Revised Code 149.43." As in "I want the combination to the mayor's safe pursuant to Ohio Revised Code 149.43."

Your request does not have to be in writing. You can walk into any public office during business hours and ask to inspect records. You do not have to give your name or a reason for requesting those records.

You can also make a request over the telephone. But the clerk, dispatcher, administrative assistant, records keeper or bureaucrat who answers your call has rights, too. That harried public employee does not have to read you the records over the telephone, or fax them, or ship them by overnight mail, or e-mail them to you.

For a thorough discussion of public records protocol, you can visit *www.ag.state.oh.us/online%5Fpublications/2002YellowBookno.pdf* and download a copy of the 2000 *Yellow Book*, a free guide published by the attorney general's office to traverse the complex world of government records.

The first ship-to-shore radio broadcast in the world took place at Put-in-Bay in July of 1907. Inventor Lee DeForest and Frank Butler, in an extensively remodeled yacht, sent results of a regatta as the boats crossed the finish line. Results were then sent to newspapers on the mainland by telephone and telegraph cables. Carrier pigeons had been used the year before.

DEAR MR. SUNSHINE,

> Once I've made my request, am I entitled to:
> (a) An "I Got Burned by the Ohio Sunshine Law" T-shirt?
> (b) A recording of the attorney general and the assistant general singing "Ain't No Sunshine"?
> (c) Prompt inspection of the documents I requested, as well as copies of those documents which, if I ask, will be mailed to me?

My Final Answer is (C).

DEAR MR. SUNSHINE,

> How much can I be charged for copies of public documents?

In 1994, the Ohio Supreme Court ruled in *Warren Newspapers, Inc. v. Hutson* that public agencies do not have to provide copies of records free of charge, but they can charge only their actual cost for making copies, a figure the state attorney general's office has set at 5 cents a page. However, a random telephone survey of public agencies in the Cleveland area shows little conformity with that recommendation. The Cleveland Police Department toes the line by charging 5 cents a page for copies, while the Westlake Police Department quoted us 25 cents a page, and those high rollers in the Bratenahl Police Department are asking 50 cents a page. In 2001, Summit County was ordered to reimburse residents because it was charging 50 cents for a photocopy of a public document.

DEAR MR. SUNSHINE,

> Aren't some public records exempt from disclosure?

They sure are.

So-called "public records" that only the government can access include parental-notification bypass records of minors seeking an abortion; child abuse reports; academic records other than your own; taxpayer records; sealed court documents; trade secrets; medical records; ongoing criminal and civil investigations; the addresses, telephone numbers and other personal information of law enforcement officers and their wives, ex-wives and their children; probation and parole records; adoption records; DNA database records; intellectual property records at public universities; and juvenile court proceedings.

—Christopher Evans, permission of *The Plain Dealer*

OHIO'S JANUARIUS MACGAHAN: THE LIBERATOR OF BULGARIA

When **Januarius Aloysius MacGahan** was born to Irish immigrants in New Lexington in 1844, no one in Perry County would have predicted that the day of his humble birth would become a national holiday in Bulgaria. Indeed, it probably would not have, if MacGahan had done the sensible thing and found a town job or assumed the yoke of an Ohio yeoman. But after the New Lexington school board turned down his application for a teaching job, MacGahan's failure to do the expected was the catalyst that eventually took him to Europe, where he learned nine languages and was hired in 1870 by *The New York Herald* to report on the Franco-Prussian War.

Nationalism was not only kicking the underpinnings out from under Europe's old empires, but also creating new ones, and MacGahan followed the armies that were remaking the map of the continent. The ongoing fighting, plus improved communications and transportation, made the last quarter of the 19th century a golden age for war correspondents, and MacGahan, with his sense of adventure and ability to put a story in perspective, became one of the best.

His adventures were legendary—riding 2,000 miles on horseback across the Central Asian steppes, escaping the guillotine in France, searching the Arctic for a lost explorer. Russia became his surrogate motherland. He was a favorite in Czar Alexander II's court, married into the nobility, and learned to "ride and shoot like a Cossack."

When Turkey cruelly smashed freedom fighters in Bulgaria, MacGahan funneled his moral outrage at the atrocities he witnessed into searing dispatches that not only nudged the Czar into rescuing Bulgaria, but also kept the British from stopping him.

MacGahan's pen had unleashed powerful swords, and he became known as "the virtual author of the Russo-Turkish War." Historian Henry Howe wrote that the grateful Bulgarians "ran after him as he rode through the streets of the towns and villages . . . kissing his boots, saddle, bridle and even the little pet horse that he rode."

MacGahan died, somewhat anti-climactically for an adventurer, in his bed from typhus in 1878 at the age of 33. His wife had him buried in Fern near Constantinople, but in 1884, the Ohio General Assembly arranged for his remains to be returned to New Lexington. His body lay in state in both the New York City Hall and the state capitol rotunda in Columbus, before MacGahan was finally laid to rest in New Lexington's Maplewood Cemetery. ↶

—*Damaine Vonada*

If it were not for Januarius MacGahan, the restless Ohioan, Bulgaria could still be a Turkish province.

805

The original Seven Wonders of the Ancient World—the Colossus of Rhodes, the Hanging Gardens of Babylon and so on—were all man-made and all ancient even to the Ancients. Two thousand years later and 4,000 miles away, the new American continent was a land of many wonders, from the Grand Canyon to Old Faithful, but they were largely natural wonders. Mark Twain pronounced Niagara Falls "marvelously well done," but only a handful of the New World's wonders could qualify under the Ancient's standards—man-made and truly old. The Seven Wonders of Ohio have been chosen serendipitously. We have traversed ancient to modern; natural to man-made, coming up with an agreeable mix whose bottom line reads, "We would travel across the state to see it." In addition, we have added some lesser wonders—meaning, "We'd travel across the state to see it, but only if the weather was nice and a good restaurant was close by."

Step right up and see the marvels of the Great Buckeye State, all positively guaranteed to leave the most hardened tourist slack-jawed in awe.

Glacial Grooves

When Kelleys Island quarrymen uncovered the glacial grooves in the 1830's, they had no idea what they'd unearthed—only that there were deep, sinuous furrows, twisted and polished to a fine sheen, as though by some giant sculptor. For the next 40 years, as geological theorists argued their Ice-Age notions, the island was a mecca for scientists seeking proof that, indeed, some 30,000 years ago a great ice sheet had formed in Northern Canada, accumulating to such depth and weight that it spread itself outward and downward, over the eons, in a succession of melts and freezes that gouged and tortured the face of the Earth. Through the accidents of geology, the grooves on what became Kelleys were buried until the quarry men came.

Visiting scientists marveled at the intricacy of the Kelleys Island grooves, which were considered to be the most spectacular anywhere in the world. But the quarry owner was pragmatic. When he had exhausted the island's other limestone deposits, the grooves themselves seemed too valuable to ignore. So he hired a photographer to record them, then he proceeded to quarry the rocks.

Yet the quarry owner was not entirely callous: he left intact a short section, which was deeded to the state in 1932. In 1971, the Ohio Historical Society excavated another long stretch—some 400 feet long, 34 feet wide and 15 feet deep. Now, as a protected site, the Kelleys Island Glacial Grooves can be seen and enjoyed but never again despoiled.

Serpent Mound

Ohio has one of the best and one of the most ancient of the true wonders—the Great Serpent Mound in what is now Adams County.

It was the work of a prehistoric Indian people we call the Adena. The name is Greek. It was slapped on these people by archaeologists digging in the grounds of the Chillicothe home of Ohio's early governor Thomas Worthington. The archaeologists took the Greek name for Paradise that Worthington had applied to his house and gave it to the Mound Builders whose remains they were disinterring.

The Adena came into the paradise of the Ohio Valley around 800 B.C., when the blind Greek poet Homer was still composing his epics of the Trojan War. They vanished from Ohio

sometime after A.D. 500, about the time the Saxons were invading Britain.

The Adena were rudimentary farmers but first-rate earth movers. The Great Serpent was their masterpiece. An earthen sculpture of an open-mouthed snake 1,254 feet long and still four feet high after centuries in the open atop a bluff overlooking Ohio Brush Creek, the Great Serpent is the largest "effigy" mound of its type in the world, both ancient and modern. While we know that the Adena built it, we know little else. Why they put so much labor into its construction and what they did with it once it was finished are only two questions atop a lengthy list of Adena unknowns.

Still it was a minor triumph of science that we acknowledge today that the Serpent was the work of prehistoric Indians. Our pioneer forefathers would not even entertain the notion that so impressive a wonder could be the work of an Indian people at all. Finding the serpent overgrown by 1,500 years of forest, the pioneers brushed aside the idea that its builders could be remotely related to the historic "savages"—the Miami, the Shawnee and the Wyandot—who were so vigorously driven from the Ohio country. Surely, they reasoned, the mound was the creation of a lost civilized "white" race who were wiped out by later "red" barbarians. The learned men of the frontier turned to fantasy to supply mound builders from across the sea—Vikings, Phoenicians, wandering lost tribes of Israel, even the Almighty Himself. Reverend Landen West of Pleasant Hill, Ohio, decided that the Serpent was raised by the actual hand of God to mark the place where Eve yielded to the pomological temptations of the biblical serpent.

Scientists have long since examined the Serpent from nose to tail, confirming a few facts but raising many more questions. The Serpent, though, still has a hold on the public imagination. In 1984, Battelle Institute released a study of how to indelibly mark our hazardous waste dumps so that the warning to stay away would come through loud and clear a thousand years from now. Battelle singled out the Serpent Mound as such an immutable monument, likely to survive war, nature and neglect.

A decade ago, the Serpent became a rallying point in a nationwide celebration of something called a "harmonic convergence" by thousands of so-called New Age devotees. They sang and snaked around the Serpent, attracting heavy media coverage while giving the site custodians conniptions. Usually, the Serpent is a much quieter place. Indeed, it is all but forgotten by adult Ohioans who find their wonders today in theme parks and on video. But the Great Serpent is still an eerie creature, an enigma made from the earth in ancient time, a wonder of Ohio and of the world.

Our Amish

We call them "Dutch," which they are not, and the Amish call us "English," which many of us are not. We have almost bear-like curiosity about them, while the Amish see the economic sense of catering to our fascination but remain fearful of being crushed under our big feet.

The Amish are Ohio's biggest "non-commercial" tourist attraction. Outside the theme parks, museums, sports events, and zoos, nothing pulls the tourists like Amish country. Strangely enough, our Amish are not as widely known nationally as the more famous or at least better advertised "Pennsylvania Dutch." Yet Ohio has the largest Amish community in the world, roughly 60,000 Ohio Amish compared to about 15,000 Pennsylvania "Dutch," and approximately 90,000 Amish worldwide. Ohio Amish center themselves in Holmes County, although there are Amish communities scattered about every rural quarter of the state. Because there are so many Amish in east-central Ohio, their communities are big enough to attract a tourist trade without being overwhelmed by it.

Nonetheless, we English think we know Amish when we see it—the poke bonnets on the women, the bearded menfolk and, of course, the horses and enclosed black buggies. And we can't seem to get enough of it—dumplings, dolls, pies, cheese and quilts. It is a healthy two-way trade. By and large, the Ohio Amish are prospering. On their picturesque small-scale horse-and-hand-worked farms, sweat replaces bank equity. Yet, more and more Amish now work in factories or directly in the tourist trade.

The Amish way is fascinating. They live their distinctive life for their own reasons, but for us, Amish Ohio is a country of wonder where we can see again into a labor-intensive way of life that most of our ancestors gave up without regret long ago. It is peaceful, beautiful, well-cared-for country. From the Amish, we can see how far we have come and how far we still have to go to catch up with them.

Akron's Airdock

In 1929, the Goodyear Zeppelin Corporation built the world's biggest freestanding building in which to build the world's biggest airship, the *USS Akron*.

The Airdock proved to be the more durable structure, for the *USS Akron* went down at sea 18 months after it was completed, but the Airdock, on Akron's southeast side, survives. For most of its lifetime, the Airdock was off-limits and under wraps. But it's hard to hide a building so big that the entire AFC Central Division could play simultaneous football games inside it. The Airdock is a major tourist attraction on the rare occasions when the public is permitted to enter.

At an open house in 1986, 175,000 people came to see it, forming the largest crowd ever gathered in one place at one time in northern Ohio. There was plenty of room in the vast egg-shaped interior that rises 22 stories high and 1,175 feet long behind sliding doors that weigh 1,200 tons each.

For many, it was a nostalgic occasion, for the Airdock is merely a shell of its former self: Goodyear no longer owns it, and airships are no longer made, or stored, within its steel-clad walls. The new owner, Loral Systems Group, uses the Airdock primarily for storage and office space. The engineering marvel is an industrial has-been.

The Y-Bridge

Here, it's the idea that's wondrous, as much as the steel-and-concrete reality, for Zanesville's fifth and newest Y-bridge looks like an ordinary bridge, except that it begins as one and ends up as two.

Zanesville's unique geography demands a Y-shaped bridge to span the Muskingum, which flows in from the north, and is joined by the Licking, which flows in from the west. A less imaginative people might have preferred to make the crossing with multiple bridges, but the town's first bridge builder, Moses Dillon saw the Y-shaped possibilities in 1813 and thought, "Why not?"

He began his bridge at the foot of Main Street on the east bank of the Muskingum, ran it along stone piers to the middle of the confluence with the Licking, where one span turned left to become West Main Street, while the other turned right to become Linden Avenue—thereby giving rise to Zanesville's longest-running practical joke: "Oh? You want to know the way to Columbus?

Well, just drive to the middle of the bridge and turn left."

Dillon's bridge lasted only four years before a flood ripped it out. The second one went the same way. If one flooded river is dangerous, two can be deadly, as bridge-builder Ebenezer Buckingham discovered first-hand during the construction of Zanesville's third Y-bridge, when some of the supports collapsed and a span fell into the river.

But Zanesville remained true to its Y-bridge commitment—and reaped the publicity benefits. When the fourth bridge opened in 1902, a merchant offered $100 worth of furniture to the first couple who volunteered to be married midstream. Ripley's "Believe It or Not" immortalized the Zanesville bridge as "the only bridge in the world which you can cross and still be on the same side of the river."

When the next span was constructed in 1984, there was no question what form it should take. Zanesville remains America's Y-Bridge City; the official stationery touts the bridge, and the police even wear a "Y" on their shoulder patches. As Moses Dillon once asked, "Why not?"

Monarch Migration

The monarch butterfly, the only butterfly to migrate a great distance, has been doing just that, at least, since the last Ice Age 10,000 years ago. Each fall, when the days shorten and the temperature falls, several million eastern butterflies begin a 2,500-mile journey to their ancestral homes in Mexico. (Monarchs west of the Rockies—a much smaller number—head for Pacific Grove and other areas of California.) Ohio is a major breeding ground, and western Ohio is a major flyway for monarchs from Ontario; several hundred thousand monarch butterflies create a wondrous sight as they hopscotch across Kelleys and the Bass Islands on their way to the Ohio mainland.

Where are they going? Actually, their goal is twofold. They stop on the islands for a brief rest after crossing Lake Erie and snack on wildflowers. Then they're off for their journey to Mexico.

Doris Stifel, a member of the research team from the Cleveland Museum of Natural History, placed tiny wing tags on 3,400 monarchs at Maumee Bay State Park in the fall of 1987. One tagged by Stifel on Kelleys Island was found five days later in Texas, a trip that would mean that the monarch averaged 200 miles a day

on its journey south.

In early March, the monarchs rouse themselves from the Mexican Oyamel fir trees where they've huddled for warmth all winter and begin to follow the wildflowers north. By late May or early June the monarchs again reach the northern coast of Ohio.

The view of the migration in process is wondrous to behold as well as to contemplate—intrinsic natural proof that, indeed, you can go home again.

The Blue Hole of Castalia

Rainbow brook trout and brown trout the size of torpedoes coexist peacefully with the tourists who feed them at one of Ohio's natural wonders. Indians had medicine camps here long before Major Robert Rogers found the site in 1761. Named for the celebrated fountain in Greece, the dead water is visible 50-60 feet down, but divers have never been able to locate the bottom. Floods and drought have no effect on the spring's 7,519 gallons per minute—enough to supply a city of 75,000—and the temperature, a constant 48 degrees, summer and winter, is perfect for the imported fish who survive because of aerating water wheels and the kindness of strangers. In recent years, the original Hole fell prey to regulations and dwindling receipts but was supplanted by the discovery of a second, almost identical Hole next door at Castalia Fish Hatchery, run by the state. The mystery is back and better than ever.

Some lesser Wonders

The Crowns of Carey

Over 50,000 pilgrims a year travel to Our Lady of Consolation Shrine (designated by the Vatican as the only minor basilica in Ohio), where they believe that praying before the statue of Mary and Jesus with their jewel-encrusted crowns produces healing miracles. It gained momentum in 1916 when a blind man was healed of his affliction. The jewels were stolen last fall, and some were returned, damaged, five days later. It will take a miracle to find the rest of them.

Port of Toledo

It's the greatest international inland port on the Great Lakes and stretches across the largest river—the Maumee—flowing into the Great Lakes. The harbor is filled with huge ships; the shipyard is filled with the enormous machinery for loading and unloading them. It's the only port on the Great Lakes where you can see two cars loaded with coal lifted into the air and dumped at one time into a freighter.

Cincinnati Suspension Bridge

Called one of the major engineering triumphs of its time, it was the creation of German immigrant John A. Roebling, an aloof engineering genius who spent 22 years, from blueprint to completion, working on the bridge. It was the prototype of Roebling's more famous Brooklyn Bridge. Though thousands have never traveled to see the Cincinnati version, many more have traveled across it.

Perry's Victory Memorial

The memorial column of Roman Doric design rising 352 feet above Lake Erie on South Bass Island is one of the tallest towers of its kind in the world. Its construction from 1912 to 1915, which cost about $1 million and took many months and ingenious labor to complete, commemorates the War of 1812's Battle of Lake Erie, which took about 3 hours and 68 lives. The agreement it represents—to never build forts or maintain armed forces along the American-Canadian border—has held for over 170 years.

Anatomiae Universae Icones

Paul Mascagnii was noted for the study of the development of the lymphatic system. But between 1823 and 1832 he took time to produce six 91-page books weighing over 60 pounds each, the largest medical books in the U.S. One copy now sits on the counter in the History of the Health Sciences Library and Museum at the University of Cincinnati, where, if one were to stack three single plates showing the human anatomy above one another, it would depict a person at least six feet tall. It's located not far from another famous book, *The Medical Reports of the Effects of Water, Cold and Warm, as a Remedy in Fever and Febrile Diseases*, by James Currie, known as the longest (145 years) overdue library book in the world.

Places
Greater Ohio

A tomato farmer up Cleveland way was being asked about the market for his Ohio greenhouse crop. He allowed that three quarters of the local output was shipped out of state. "New York, Philadelphia, St. Louis, Lexington," he said, "…you know, greater Ohio."

Well, we know. But don't tell *them*. The outlanders of Greater Ohio may seem superior, but secretly they measure themselves against us. Believing Cleveland has no future, they count on San Francisco. Thinking Columbus provincial and without culture, they settle on Houston. Convinced that Cincinnati is smug and insular, they wall themselves on Manhattan Island.

Yet at night, they startle awake, crying, "But what of Ohio? What of her cities, her rich lands, her resourceful multitudes?" Meantime, we keep on growing children, sunrises, redbud trees, and tomatoes. The trick to living here is to see what *is* and not what is somewhere else. Live here. For we are central; Ohio, the inner kingdom. Everywhere else is without.

Views
The true test is to see Ohio as she truly is.

There is a view of Ohio the love of which is a pure and true test of Ohioness. The bounteous recognition of it should be the essential test by which a true Buckeye earns citizenship. The view is this: the long, flat limitless expanse of Ohio countryside that takes places most nakedly on the northwestern side of the state and goes on so far that off in the clear and intergalactic distance one can see the woodsmoke curling lazily upward from Rocky Mountain ski lodges. It is an unfettered view, crossing fields as broad and deep as the pioneer instinct that brought our forefathers out here to see it. It is at its apogee in early February, when the empty and expansive fields are rimed with frost, and the trees form a silver border off in that limitless distance, as beautiful as any Chinese etching. "The land will be laid out like tile," an adopted Ohio writer once wrote, "sheets of earth fitted at field corner, a flat and stormless ocean upon which farmers sail on tides of ear and stalk." Surely that fellow is now one of us.

The Lone Prairie

Ohio BC—Before Columbus, Before Cleveland, Before Cincinnati—was mostly trees. The territory was 95 percent forested when American settlers came into the land and in an epic feat of largely manual labor reduced the tree cover to 14 percent in a century and a half. But Ohio was not all forest. Statistically small but immensely important to our provincial biological diversity were the Ohio prairie "islands," pockets of grassland standing out in a sea of trees.

Today the trees are coming back; Ohio is now about 27 percent forested—the highest percentage in 100 years—but much of the prairie land is gone forever, except for a few pockets in park districts and pioneer cemeteries and along railroad rights of way. But if you choose your season and your location, there are still patches where you can lose yourself in head-high prairie grass and think about the breaking of this land.

North-South-East-West

The most intriguing view north from Ohio can be had by standing near Cleveland's Lakefront Airport, watching Ohio surfers shooting the curls on Lake Erie. The most intriguing view east begins above East Liverpool by looking down at the old, narrow and still privately owned silver toll bridge over the Ohio River. The most intriguing view south (actually southwest) is to be had in Letart Falls in Meigs County, where the perfectly placid Ohio today flows unruffled over the rapids that were, in days of low water during the last century and for a good piece of this one, the bane and dread of rivermen. The Army Corps of Engineers' navigational dams on the Ohio covered the rapids, making travel less perilous but removing from sight forever one of the river's most spectacular and dangerous reaches. The most intriguing view west occurs in Union City, Ohio, when peering across the road into Union City, Indiana. Given the right disjunction between daylight-saving time in Ohio and plain old Eastern Standard Time in Indiana, you are looking across an hour and the vagaries of running a state line through the middle of a town.

by John Baskin Juliann Evans, John Fleischman, Sue Gorisek, and Marcy Hawley.

From the Lake to the River, from sports to culture, Ohio has a wealth of activities to meet any taste. The state has two of the world's great amusement parks and the world's greatest military museum. It showcases invention and inventors; those who took us into space and onto the moon; seven presidents and others who changed our world. In Ohio we can explore our natural wonders and visit the exotic in zoos or natural areas. Look into our past at the many restored villages and homes, roll through the countryside on a vintage train, or harken back to a slower time on a canal boat or riverboat. Reach back into the past or look into the future. It's Ohio, get out and do it.

The first 20 miles of the Buckeye Trail were begun in 1959 in Hocking County, growing from that inauspicious beginning to 1,280 miles in a continuous loop passing through the most scenic country in 40 of Ohio's 88 counties. Its southern terminus is in Cincinnati's Eden Park, with a view across the Ohio River into Kentucky. The hardy volunteers of the Trail Association manage the entire loop, as well as sponsoring events both social and educational. www.buckeyetrail.org

Ohio Travel Information Centers

All but one of the state's travel information centers are located on major highways (one is located in the Statehouse on the lower level). Each is staffed by professional travel counselors to aid the public in finding housing and destinations in Ohio. At each location three to four hundred tourism brochures are available. They serve over a million people yearly from all 50 states and many foreign countries.

www.dot.state.oh.us/tic/ticmap/htm
Distribution: 614.351.5517

Statehouse (Franklin County)—614-728-9707

I-70 West (Belmont County)—740-782-1644

I-70 East (Preble County)—937-437-0978

I-71 North (Warren County)—513-932-9293

I-71 South (Warren County)—513-932-3538

I-75 North (Butler County)—513-777-2083

I-75 North (Wood County)—419-686-3191

I-75 South (Wood County)—419-686-5001

I-77 North (Washington County)—740-373-8806

I-80 West (Trumbull County)—330-534-9144

I-90 West (Ashtabula County)—440-593-6298

SR23 (Scioto County)—740-259-3670

Ohio's scenic byways

www.ohiobyways.com

Accommodation Line Byway
The byway follows a portion of the route used by the Accommodation Line Stagecoach which operated in the 1820s and 1830s. The route is 10.4 miles long beginning at SR 73 and Main Street in Waynesville and goes north to Spring Valley Road.

Amish County Byway
The byway is a series of routes which take travelers through the Amish country of Holmes County. The routes include:
SR 63 (18 miles) from the Coshocton/Holmes county line to SR 557 and on to SR 39.
US 62 (18 miles) from Millersburg to the Holmes/Stark county line.
SR 83 (26 miles) north from the Holmes/Wayne county line.
SR 241 (13 miles) from Millersburg to the Holmes/Wayne county line.
SR 515 (7 miles) from Walnut Creek to US 62.

Canal Way Ohio Byway (110 miles)
    Also a national scenic byway, it starts at Cleveland's Carter Road Lift Bridge and extends south to I-77 in Tuscarawas County. The byway follows the Ohio and Erie Canal.

Heritage Corridors of Bath
    The byway follows 12 roads within Bath township in Summit County passing by historic structures, state nature preserves and part of the Cuyahoga Valley National Recreation Area.

Historic National Road (225 miles)
    The byway follows National Road (US Route 40) across the entire width of the state. Built in the early 1800s it was the nation's first federally supported road.

Jefferson County Byway (15 miles)
    The byway is a combination greenway, recreation trail and area of historical interest. The route follows SR 150 and 674.

Land of the Cross Tipped Churches Byway (38.4 miles)
    The byway passes through Shelby, Auglaize and Mercer counties. Beginning at McCartyville take SR 119 to Fort Recovery. Then proceed north on SR 49 to SR 28 at Walbash.

Maumee Valley Byway (60 miles)
    The byway begins in Defiance and follows SR 424 east through Napoleon to US 6. There it stops until it resumes again just west of Waterville on River Road to Maumee where it ends at the site of the British Fort Miamis, now a city park.

Miami and Erie Canal Scenic Byway (50 miles)
    The byway follows SR 66 from Johnson Farm in Piqua, continues northward until it ends in Delphos.

Morgan County Byway (39 miles)
    The byway begins on SR 78 at Burr Oak State Park, continues northeast along SR 83 to SR 284 and ends at the Muskingum/Morgan County line.

Ohio River Scenic Byway (452 Miles)
    The byway—also a national scenic byway—runs the length of the Ohio across 14 counties.

Olentangy Heritage Byway (10.5 miles)
    The shortest of the state's scenic byways it begins at I-270 in Franklin County and follows Olentangy River north (primarily on SR 315) to US 23.

Tappan-Moravian Trail Scenic Byway (55 miles)
    The byway begins on US 250 at Stock TR 313. Using mostly township and county roads it goes through Deersville, Feed Springs, Scio, Jewett, and New Rumley.

Welsh Scenic Byway (34 miles)
    The byway goes through Gallia and Jackson counties along US 35, SR 325 and 223.

Attractions
Z o o s & T h e m e P a r k s

African Safari Wildlife Park
236 Lightner Road
Port Clinton, OH 43452
419-732-3606
www.AfricanSafariWildlifePark.com
Drive-through safari with giraffe, zebra, elephants and bird shows.

Akron Zoo
500 Edgewood Avenue
Akron, OH 44307
330-375-2525
www.akronzoo.com
Zoo houses over 200 animals, featuring a bear and wolf exhibit and an exotic bird collection.

The Beach Waterpark
2590 Water Park Drive
Mason, Ohio 45040
513-398-SWIM
www.thebeachwaterpark.com
One of the nation's top waterparks with 35 acres of water slides and attractions.

Cedar Point
One Cedar Point Drive
Sandusky, OH 44870
419-627-2350
www.cedarpoint.com
One of the nation's premier amusement parks, including 12 roller coasters, theatres, animals and animal attractions, mile-long sandy beach on Lake Erie.

Cincinnati Zoo & Botanical Garden
3400 Vine Street
Cincinnati, OH 45220
513-281-4700
800-944-4776
www.cincinnatizoo.org
World-renowned zoo, including famous collection of white tigers, reptiles, children's zoo.

Cleveland Metroparks Zoo
3900 Wildlife Way
Cleveland, OH 44109
216-661-6500
www.clemetzoo.com
Featuring a 2-acre rainforest exhibit, the Zoo also includes live aquatic mammals, invertebrates, reptiles, amphibians, and fishes from around the world.

Ohio has eight resort parks, notable among them being Maumee Bay Lodge, situated in an unique ecosystem of meadows and wetlands created by the convergence of Lake Erie and the land mass. The lodge, cabins, and golf course are situated in the midst of this natural system. Tips for getting rooms at the state resorts: lowest call volume is between 10 a.m. and 3 p.m. and best day to call is Sunday. Worst day is Monday. Best days to arrive: Sunday and Thursday. The two weeks after Memorial Day and before Labor Day are slow periods and good rooms are often available.

Columbus Zoo
9990 Riverside Drive
Powell, OH 43065
614-465-3550
www.colzoo.org
Hundred-acre zoo with 40 buildings and 31,500 specimens; the only zoo in the world housing four generations of gorillas; new North American exhibit.

Coney Island
6201 Kellogg Avenue
Cincinnati, OH 45228
513-232-8230
www.coneyislandpark.com
Family entertainment complex.

Great Bear Lodge
4600 Milan Road
Sandusky, Ohio 44870
888-779-2327
www.greatbearlodge.com
One of the nation's largest indoor waterparks at over 33,000 sq. ft. It boasts of five pools, seven waterslides and a 48 foot tall dipping bucket which dumps 1,000 gallons of water.

Paramount's Kings Island
6300 Kings Island Drive
Kings Island, OH 45034
800-288-0808
www.pki.com
Six hundred-acre family entertainment center with theme park and 15-acre water park.

Pioneer Waterland, Wet & Dry Adventure Park
10661 Kile Road
Chardon, OH 44024
440-951-7227
440-285-0910
www.pioneerwaterland.com
Water park with a six-acre natural lake, six-story high waterslides, and other activities.

Six Flags Worlds Adventure
Route 43
Aurora, OH 44202
330-562-8303
www.sixflags.com
Entertainment facility featuring roller coasters and other rides, live shows, water area, dining.

Toledo Zoo
2700 Broadway
Toledo, OH 43614
419-385-5721
www.toledozoo.org
Reptiles, aquarium, birds, mammals, petting zoo, picnic area, greenhouse, and botanical gardens.

The Wilds
14000 International Road
Cumberland, OH
740-638-5030

www.thewilds.org
Opened to the public in 1994, The Wilds spans nearly 10,000 acres of reclaimed, surface-mined land. Thousands of acres have been developed and divided into large sections where African, Asian, and North American species are managed. Visitors may observe the many groups of animals on guided safaris, or explore the natural settings surrounding the Johnson Visitor Center.

Wyandot Lake
10101 Riverside Drive
Powell, OH 43065
800-328-9283
www.sixflags.com/parks/wyandotlake/index.asp
A collection of classic rides along with 14 towering water slide rides.

The Rock Hall

Speciality museums

Ashtabula Marine Museum
1071 Walnut Street
Ashtabula, OH 44004
440-964-6847
The 1896 lighthouse keeper's quarters on shore is now the Great Lakes Marine & U.S. Coast Guard Memorial Museum (also known as the Ashtabula Marine Museum), and the lighthouse preservation society has applied to the federal government for ownership in 2003. It plans on having tours of the lighthouse.

African American Museum
1765 Crawford Road
Cleveland, OH 44106
216-791-1700
www.aamcleveland.org
Located in the historical Hough Community, the museum is a place of African and African American culture in the heart of Cleveland.

Black Heritage Library and Museum
817 Harmon Street
Findlay, OH 45840
419-423-4954
African-American culture and the contributions of Black Ohioans to the state's history are on display here.

Tourism spending in Ohio was $23.1 billion in 2001 and $24.7 billion in 2001. It also generated $3.5 billion annually in state and local taxes.

Campus Martius Museum
Washington & Second Streets
Marietta, OH 45750
800-860-0145 or 740-373-3750
Whatever possessed Rufus Putnam to leave the civilized delights of Massachusetts at age 50 and go to a howling wilderness in Ohio ultimately rendered him the Founding Father of Marietta, a distinction that years ago inspired a successful grassroots campaign to preserve, protect, and defend his home from the wrecking ball. Today, the Rufus Putnam House and another Marietta original, the Ohio Land Company Office, are the featured attractions at this museum built on the site of the Campus Martius, a fortified complex of "curtain wall" houses that Putnam designed to preserve, protect and defend the first Mariettans from the Indians. A millwright by trade, Putnam got a crash course in military engineering during the Revolution when Washington buttonholed him to defend Boston's Dorchester Heights. Borrowing a French book on fortifications, he learned how to build an *abatis* to hasten the British retreat. When Putnam got to Ohio, he constructed not only an *abatis* but also palisades and a stockade fence to defend the Campus Martius. The old boy knew what he was doing: the Indians never attacked those first settlers, which is a primary reason why the museum today can boast such a fine collection of their furnishings and tools.

Canton Classic Car Museum
555 Market Avenue South
Canton, OH 44702
330-455-3603
www.cantonclassiccar.org
Antique, classic and collector cars; classic car rentals.

Carillon Historical Park
1000 Carillon Blvd.
Dayton, OH 45409
937-293-2841
www.carillonpark.org
Sixty-one-acre park with displays and museums. Exhibits include Conestoga wagon, the 1905 Wright "B" Flyer (the world's first practical airplane), replica of Wright Brothers' bicycle shop. Adjacent to Deeds Carillon, one of only six true carillons in America.

Carriage Hill Metropark & Farm
7800 Shull Road
Dayton, OH 45424
937-879-0461
www.dayton.net/Audubon/carghl.htm
Rural history portrayed in historic farmhouse and outbuildings.

COASTING HOME: OHIO'S WORLD RANKING

Wooden Roller Coasters

		World rank
Son of Beast *(Kings Island)*		
Tallest	218'	1
Largest Drop	214'	1
Longest	7,032	2
Fastest	78.3 mph	1
Angle of Descent	55.7 degrees	4
Mean Streak *(Cedar Point)*		
Tallest	151'	4
Largest Drop	155'	3
Longest	5,427'	3
Fastest	65 mph	7
The Beast *(Kings Island)*		
Largest Drop	141'	7
Longest	7,400'	1

Steel Roller Coasters

		World rank
Top Thrill Dragster *(Cedar Point)*		
Tallest	420'	1
Largest Drop	400'	1
Fastest	120 mph	1
Angle of Descent	90 degrees	1
Millennium Force *(Cedar Point)*		
Largest Drop	300'	3
Batman Knight Flight *(Six Flags)*		
Vertical Loop	142'	1

Shuttle Roller Coasters*

Wicked Twister *(Cedar Point)*		
Tallest	215'	6
Fastest	72 mph	3
Angle of Descent	90 degrees	1
Superman Ultimate Escape *(Six Flags)*		
Fastest	70 mph	8
Angle of Descent	90 degrees	1

*incomplete circuit requires the train to go both backward and forward

Cedar Point was rated in 2003 the nation's best amusement park by industry publication, Amusement Today. It was the 6th year in a row the nation's largest amusement park was so designated. Cedar Point draws 3 million visitors a year and its 68 rides can move 100,000 people an hour.

Ohio's Roller Coasters

Coaster	Location	Type	Description	Year Built	Height	Track Length	Speed (mph)
Adventure Express	Kings Island	Steel	Mine Train	1991	63'	2,963'	35
Batman Knight Flight	Six Flags	Steel	Multielement	2000	161'	4,210'	65
The Beast*	Kings Island	Wood	Terrain	1979	141'	7,400'	65
The Beastie	Kings Island	Wood	Junior	1972	38'	1,350'	30
Big Dipper	Six Flags	Wood	Out & Back	1926	65'	2,680'	32
Blue Streak	Cedar Point	Wood	Out & Back	1964	78'	2,558'	40
Boa Squeeze	Wonderpark	Steel	Junior	2001	–	–	–
The Brat	Erieview Park	Steel	Junior	–	12'	280'	
Cedar Creek Mine Ride	Cedar Point	Steel	Mine Train	1969	48'	2,540'	42
Corkscrew	Cedar Point	Steel	Loop	1976	85'	2,050'	48
Disaster Transport	Cedar Point	Steel	Bobsled	1985	63'	1,932'	40
Double Loop	Six Flags	Steel	Double Loop	1977	90'	1,800'	35
Face Off	Kings Island	Steel	Shuttle	1999	138'	985'	55
Gemini	Cedar Point	Steel	2 Track Racer	1978	125'	3,935'	60
Iron Dragon	Cedar Point	Steel	Suspended	1987	76'	2,800'	40
Jr. Gemini	Cedar Point	Steel	Junior	1979	19'	443'	6
Kiddie Roller Coaster	Dover Lake	Steel	Junior	–	–	–	–
King Cobra	Kings Island	Steel	Standing	1984	95'	2,210'	50
Little Dipper	LeSourdsville	Steel	Junior	1968	12'	280'	–
Little Dipper	Memphis Kiddie Park	Steel	Junior	1952	12'	280'	8
Magnum XL-200	Cedar Point	Steel	Out & back	1989	205'	5,106'	72
Mantis	Cedar Point	Steel	Standing	1996	145'	3,900'	57
Mean Streak	Cedar Point	Wood	Twister	1991	160'	5,427'	65
Millennium Force	Cedar Point	Steel	Hypercoaster	2000	310'	6,595'	93
Mind Eraser	Six Flags	Steel	Boomerang	1996	125'	875'	48
Mini Coaster	Tuscora Park	Steel	–	–	–	–	–
Outer Limits/Flight of Fear	Kings Island	Steel	Indoor Looper	1996	-	2,600'	54
Pepsi Python	Coney Island	Steel	Zyklon	1996	33'	1,100'	–

Coaster	Location	Type	Description	Year Built	Height	Track Length	Speed (mph)
Python Pit	Jeepers! Randal Park	Steel	Junior	2000	13'	300'	8
Racer	Kings Island	Wood	Out & Back	1972	88'	3,415'	61
Raging Wolf Bobs	Six Flags	Wood	Out & Back	1988	80'	3,426'	45
Raptor	Cedar Point	Steel	Inverted	1994	137'	3,790'	57
Road Runner Express	Six Flags	Steel	Junior	2000	26'	1,164'	22
Rugrats Runaway Reptar	Kings Island	Steel	Inverted	2001	52'	1,129'	25
Scooby's Ghoster Coaster	Kings Island	Steel	Jr., Suspended	1998	35'	450'	–
Screechin' Eagle	LeSourdsville	Wood	Out & Back	1927	78'	2,640'	40
Sea Dragon	Wyandot Lake	Wood	Junior	1956	37'	1,300'	25
Serial Thriller	Six Flags	Steel	Suspended	1998	105'	2,172'	50
Serpent	LeSourdsville	Steel	Galaxi	1972	45'	1,919'	30
Son of Beast**	Kings Island	Wood	Twister	2000	218'	7,032'	92
Superman Ultimate Escape	Six Flags	Steel	Shuttle	2000	181	640'	70
Teddy Bear	Stricker's	Wood	Junior	1996	25'	850'	–
Top Cat's Taxi Jam	Kings Island	Steel	Junior	1992	8'	199'	–
Top Gun	Kings Island	Steel	Suspended	1993	100'	2,352'	51
Top Thrill Dragster***	Cedar Point	Steel	Out & Back	2003	420'	2,800'	120
Tornado	Stricker's	Wood	Out & Back	1993	55'	2,080'	–
The Villain	Six Flags	Wood	Out & Back	2000	122'	3,900'	60
Vortex	Kings Island	Steel	Multielement	1987	148'	3,800'	55
Wicked Twister	Cedar Point	Steel	Shuttle	2002	215'	2,700'	72
Woodstock Express	Cedar Point	Steel	Twister	1999	38"	1,100'	25
X-Flight	Six Flags	Steel	Out & Back	2001	115'	3,340'	51

*The world's longest coaster ride—The Beast, 4 minutes, 30 seconds

**The world's tallest, fastest and only looping wooden coaster—Son of Beast, 7,032 feet, 92 mph

***The world's tallest, fastest coaster—Top Thrill Dragster, 42-stories. 120 mph

Robert Ward, a bank clerk from Brecksville, in midsummer 2003 set the unofficial season record for riding Cedar Point's Magnum XL-200 coaster—1,194 times, breaking the old record of 901 rides in 2001 by Dan Haverlock, a Streetsboro grocery clerk. Haverlock still holds the all-time Magnum record—2,400 rides since 1997.

Central Ohio Fire Museum & Learning Center
260 North Fourth Street
Columbus, Ohio 43215-2511
614-464-4099
www.fire.ci.columbus.oh.us/museum.htm
E-mail: cofmuseum@aol.com
Housed in a restored 1908 firehouse the museum houses a collection of hand-drawn, horse-drawn and motorized fire apparatus.

COSI-Columbus (Center of Science and Industry)
333 West Broad Street
Columbus, OH 43215
888-819-2674
www.cosi.org
Technology museum, which features seven learning worlds, including a time-traveler exhibit, and archaeological dig and an underwater exhibit.

COSI-Toledo (Center of Science and Industry)
One Discovery Way
Toledo, OH
419-244-2674
www.cosi.og
A technology museum featuring seven hands-on learning worlds.

Cincinnati Fire Museum
315 West Court Street
Cincinnati, OH 45202
513-621-5553
www.cincyfiremuseum.com
Located in a 1907 National Register firehouse, the museum offers a panorama of the entire course of American fire-fighting, a natural place for it since Cincinnati, in 1853, became the first city to use fulltime paid city employees as firefighters. In addition, Cincinnati inventors Able Shawk and Alexander Latta created "Uncle Joe Ross," the first successful steam fire engine, which had the capacity of the six biggest double-engine hand pumpers. The Queen City became famous world-wide for the design, development and manufacture of firefighting apparatus, and the museum demonstrates everything, from leather fire buckets to the oldest surviving fire engine in Cincinnati, an 1836 Hunneman hand pumper.

Cincinnati Museum Center
1301 Western Avenue
Cincinnati, OH 45203
513-287-7000
800-733-2077
www.cincymuseum.org
Housed in Cincinnati's historic Union Terminal the museum center is an complex of three museums as well as an OMNIMAX theater and the Cincinnati Historical Society Library.

Cinergy Children's Museum
An interactive museum for children of all ages.

Cincinnati History Society Museum
Full sized replica of the Cincinnati riverfront of the 1800s complete with riverboat as well as other exhibits about the "Queen City."

Cincinnati Museum of Natural History & Science
A glacier you can walk around, a cavern, and live bat colony along with other exhibits.

The Citizens Motorcar Company: America's Packard Museum
420 South Ludlow
Dayton, OH
937-226-1710
www.americaspackardmuseum.org
The world's only restored Packard dealership operating as a museum, which also offers limousine service from a fleet of Packards, including the 1925 LeBaron speedster convertible and a 1948 Packard taxi.

Cleveland Museum of Natural History
1 Wade Oval, University Circle
Cleveland, OH 44106
216-231-4600
800-317-9155
www.cmnh.org
Ohio's largest natural science museum. Displays include mounted dinosaur, exhibits of prehistoric and North American Indian life.

Crawford Auto-Aviation Museum
10825 East Boulevard
Cleveland, OH 44106
216-721-5722
www.wrhs.org
Part of the Western Reserve Historical Society, it is a collection of more than 200 restored vehicles, from the 1890s to the present; restoration shop in operation.

Dawes Arboretum
7770 Jacksontown Road Southeast, (SR 13)
Newark, OH 43056
800-443-2937 or 740-323-2355
www.dawesarb.org
Ohioan Beman Dawes struck it rich when he hit oil in West Virginia and started the Pure Oil Company. In time, however, his enduring legacy might prove to be his 1,000-plus acre arboretum on this great swell of Licking County earth, sloping wonderfully down into well-tended farms. Dawes had five homes at one time, but Daweswood was his favorite. He found it one day when he had driven out from Newark and saw some lumbermen cutting trees, and bought the land to stop them. His commitment to trees never waned and today a large part of the arboretum is stately with old hardwoods. After seeing a tree dedication in England, Dawes initiated the ritual here, calling upon his notable friends, and first plantings were gifts of Admiral Byrd, Orville Wright, General Pershing, Red Grange, and over 60 others. The arboretum, second in size in Ohio only to Cleveland's Holden Arboretum, is deeded to increase the general love and knowledge of trees

and shrubs, therefore it is not as "showy" as arboretums given to flowering displays. It has a lovely driving and/or walking tour, one of the northernmost Cypress swamps, the world's largest lettered hedge (complete with a tower to climb and take a good look), and what has been called one of the best Japanese gardens in America. Among its peers, though, Dawes is known for being a pioneer in the use of computerized records; its plant list is computer accessible, for instance. It is a great area resource, offering more and cheaper horticultural education than any other arboretum in the country. It has a splendid array of programs, aids both amateurs and professionals in propagating more unusual species, and maintains a 3,000-volume library. Dawes and his wife are buried in the arboretum and while we have no first-hand knowledge of the view, he left the rest of us with a notable one.

Degenhart Paperweight & Glass Museum
65323 Highland Hill Road
Cambridge, OH 43725
740-432-2626
www.degenhartmuseum.com
Collections of paperweights, ceramics and glass. Exhibits focus on glassmaking techniques.

Fairport Marine Museum and Lighthouse
129 Second Street
Fairport Harbor, OH 44077
440-354-4825
www.ncweb.com/org/fhlh/
Marine relics housed in 1871 lighthouse and adjacent light keeper's cottage.

First Ladies' National Historic Site
331 Market Avenue South
Canton, OH 44702
330-452-0876
www.firstladies.org
The only national institution dedicated to the contributions of the nation's First Ladies.

HUBERT'S PORCH: STILL THERE. COME SIT A SPELL.

The late Hubert Robinson wanted a front porch so he tore out the bay window and built one. A sign out front now reads, "Hubert's porch, adults welcome" and so they come and sit, reflecting on the memory of Hubert and Oese Robinson, people who saved everything. The house is as they left it, an unorthodox museum to, as one visitor put it, "this woman who saved all her stuff."

It is also a gentle, genuine, and somehow touching monument to the lives of two ostensibly ordinary people. Hubert was the last-of-the-line scion of a wealthy Granville pioneering family but he became a plumber with something of a drinking problem. He was still much loved, managed to put the original plumbing in many of the village's houses, and kept the village fire engine repaired. His wife, Oese, was "a poor country girl from Jacktown," given lessons in deportment by her mother-in-law.

When the family fortune—and its goods—fell to the Robinsons, Oese did what any self-respecting woman would have done in those post–war times: she modernized the kitchen, even to providing herself with a view, which she painted on one wall and put a window frame around. The museum wisely kept the kitchen exactly as Oese left it, as well as their early 1950s television, which is still sitting anachronistically in the Victorian parlor.

Visitors enter the Robinson's house and, if they're past a certain age, say "Do you remember we had one of these when we got married?" Oese and Hubert, however, will likely have two. Oese's lace stockpile alone has over a thousand items in it. She also has a collection of over 125 hats, and the daguerreotypes of Marcus Root, Hubert's step-great uncle from Granville who is credited with writing the first book on the history of photography (It's called *The Camera and the Pencil* and was published in 1864).

Different items are featured each month and one of the favorite displays is the narrated program featuring live models wearing the family's Victorian underwear. The wives of local executives do most of the modeling as they tend to remain perpetually size 6 and thus do not—as the Victorians sometimes did—feel the necessity of having ribs removed.

121 South Main; 740-587-0373; www.granville.oh.us/newsite/discover/museums.cfm

Follett House Museum
404 Wayne Street at East Adams
Sandusky, OH 44870
419-627-9608
www.sandusky.lib.oh.us/old/follett_house.html
It took three years to build the Follett home, even though the stone came from a quarry in Memorial Park right across the street. It's an 1830s Greek Revival that once had 20 rooms and now has only 11, the last nine removed because the owners thought it would be easier to sell the house. Now owned by the public library, it's filled with the things the library collected since 1902. Look for the glass cane collection in the basement, one-of-a-kind examples of what a local glass blower from the Sandusky Glass Plant made as souvenirs from leftover glass. In the attic is a Civil War collection with artifacts from Johnson's Island. The view of the island— from the "Captain's Walk"—once the Civil War prisoner-of-war camp, is juxtaposed with the other landmark, Cedar Point Amusement Park, a fortress of a different sort.

Garst Museum
205 North Broadway
Greenville, OH 45331
937-548-5250
www.garstmuseum.org
The museum features Annie Oakley, Lowell Thomas, the Treaty of Greeneville, and Zach Landsdowne.

Goodyear World of Rubber
1201 East Market Street
Akron, OH 44305
330-796-7117
Rubber's history and the development of the vulcanization process.

Great Lakes Science Center
601 Erieside Avenue (*at North Coast Harbor*)
Cleveland, OH 44114
216-694-2000
www.greatscience.com
350 interactive exhibits on three floors and a five story OMNIMAX Theater in a 165,000 square-foot building.

Greene County Historical Society
74 West Church Street
Xenia, OH 45385
937-372-4606

Restored James Galloway log house, built in 1798; period furnishings.

The Health Museum of Cleveland
8911 Euclid Avenue
Cleveland, OH 44106-2039
216-231-5010
www.healthmuseum.org
The museum is devoted to the human body and a healthy life-style.

Hoover Historical Center
1875 Easton Street
North Canton, OH 44720
330-499-0287
Home of founder of Hoover Co., restored to Victorian era; world's largest collection of antique and early vacuum cleaners.

Hopewell Culture National Historical Park
16062 State Rte. 104
Chillicothe, OH 45601
740-774-1125
www.nps.gov/hocu/index.htm
23 Burial mounds constructed by Hopewell Indians 200 B.C.-500 A.D.; Visitor Center contains educational exhibits and an observation deck.

Hower House
60 Fir Hill/the University of Akron
Akron, OH 44325-2401
330-972-6909
www3.uakron.edu/howerhse
The 28-room home of Henry Hower, built in 1871 is one of the nation's finest examples of Second Empire Italianate architecture.

Inland Seas Museum
480 Main Street
Vermilion, OH 44089
440-967-3467
www.inlandseas.org
Museum of Great Lakes history, located on Lake Erie overlooking Vermilion Harbor.

International Women's Air & Space Museum
Burke Lakefront Airport
Room 165
1501 North Marginal Road
Cleveland, OH 44114
216-623-1111
www.iwasm.org
Amelia Earhart, Jacqueline Cochran, Katharine

This is one of the best small-town house museums in the state, and also one of the largest—100,000 items—which is not to say that quantity has been sacrificed for quality. One of the rarest items—only a handful are known to exist—is a Confederate jacket bribed off the back of a guard allowing Nelson Purdum, a Ross County farmer, to escape home to Chillicothe. Here is the Constitution Table, upon which the State's beginnings were signed; Charles Pont's Megalethoscope, the home entertainment device of the 1860s; the patent model of the 1884 coal hopper car; a wonderful toy collection; and a piston-driven fan run off alcohol and thereby perfectly encapsulating America's industrial schizophrenia, cooling ourselves by means of a heat-producing device.

It is a good, full, quirky collection in rooms wonderfully busy with quickly shifting times and artifacts. The museum is actually a complex of three buildings, the other two being a library, and a house of antique clothing. The Franklin House, a large Moorish home filled with two centuries of antique dresses, hats, shoes and fans, is also one of the best collections in Ohio, with exhibits constantly changing. Some of the dresses, recovered from Chillicothe attics, were brought here from Paris in the late 1700s.

The McKell Library is the museum's collection of illuminated manuscripts, early illustrated books, and prints. They were collected by Col. David McCandless McKell, an old military man with a passion for children's books. A Chillicothean who became a noted American bibliophile, he used his books as a working library, sharing it with friends and students.

Since many of the items in the museum complex came out of Chillicothe homes, it provides a context for seeing Chillicothe—along with Cincinnati and Lexington—as one of three cultural centers of the Ohio Valley in the first part of the 19th century, a designation it has been reluctant to give up.

45 West Fifth Street
Chillicothe, OH 45601
740-772-1936
www.rosscountyhistorical.org

Chillicothe is not a town that has made itself into a 'theme' in order to survive, therefore its charm is less fragrantly stated, which is, of course, charm of an entirely different kind. The reason for visiting Chillicothe is to slow down and use its continuity to understand how Ohioans lived in the first part of this century. The best way to do this is by walking around in the town, letting it reveal itself slowly, in its detail, its architecture, its odd little nooks and crannies, its very atmosphere.

—Particular Places, Volume I

Wright, the WASPs, women astronauts, and the women of Desert Storm are featured in exhibits dedicated to the world of women in aviation.

Invent Now
221 South Broadway
Akron, OH 44308-1505
800-968-4332
www.invent.org
Home of the National Inventors Hall of Fame, the 77,000 square foot attraction contains 23,000 sq. ft. of interactive exhibit space dedicated to innovative ideas past, present and future.

Jack Nicklaus Museum
2355 Olentangy River Road
Columbus, OH 43210
614-247-5959
www.nicklausmuseum.org/
A museum dedicated to the life and accomplishments of the greatest golfer of all time.

Karl E. Limper Geology Museum
Shideler Hall, Miami University
Corner of Patterson Avenue and Spring Street
Oxford, OH 45056
513-529-3220
Ask Joe Marak how long he has been curator of this small gem of a museum and he begins, "Since many, many years ago, when the earth was very young and still almost molten…" Obviously, he jests, but they do think in terms of Eras and Epoch here, especially the Ordovician Period of 450 million years ago when invertebrates such as clams, snails, and trilobites flourished. Well-preserved Ordovician fossils are found in such quantity in Southwest Ohio that geologists consider the area a classic site, and this fortuitously located museum owns one of the nation's finest and largest—some 180,000 specimens—collections of them. But even if you don't know a placoderm from a cyclocystoid, the museum is worth a visit. Mr. Marak will not only gladly explain everything but also show you several thousand splendid specimens of minerals, rocks, and meteorites.

Kelton House Museum and Garden
586 East Town Street
Columbus, OH 43215
614-464-2022
www.keltonhouse.com
A grand victorian home where authentically costumed guides give tours.

The McKinley Museum
800 McKinley Monument Drive NW
Canton, OH 44708
330-455-7043
www.mckinleymuseum.org
The Ramsayer Research Library of the McKinley Museum is a depository of McKinley's personal and professional life—photographs, correspondence, books, magazines and papers. The Stark County Historical Society maintains a 50,000-piece collection related to Stark County and regional Ohio culture, including the fossils, rocks and live animals which make up Discover World, the museum's hands-on science center.

Merry-Go-Round Museum
(West Washington and Jackson
Sandusky, OH 44870
419-626-6111
www.merrygoroundmuseum.org
Sandusky has the only carousel museum with a working carousel in it and a full-time in-house restorer working on it. Inconspicuously housed in the 1920s neoclassical post office, the life of a 1948 Herschell-Spillman carousel has been saved through the grass roots effort of Sanduskians whose summer memories can now be extended through adulthood and winter. Thirty other carousel animal originals and two chariots are on display, as well as Gustave Dentzel's original workshop, purchased from a Florida collector and shipped north tool by tool, his sign included. An elaborately carved M.C. Illions' sleigh, miniature carousels and miniature carousel rides and changing exhibits from Cedar Point all add up to about a half million dollars of inventory. Probably one of the finest collections ever put together by noncollectors, it's due merit for a group who lunged for the brass ring and got it, an axiom, by the way, which came from an actual brass ring on carousels; riders who were able to grab it won a free ride.

Motorcycle Hall of Fame Museum
13515 Yarmouth Drive
Pickerington, OH 43147
614-856-2222
The museum exhibits over 50 motorcycles, as well as memorabilia.

National Cambridge Collectors Museum
136 South Ninth Street
Cambridge, OH 43725
740-432-4245
www.cambridgeglass.org
World's largest collection of Cambridge Glass, large collection of Cambridge Pottery.

National Heisey Glass Museum
169 West Church Streets
Newark, OH 43055
740-345-2932
www.heiseymuseum.org
Museum of glassware produced in Newark from 1895-1957; housed in an 1830s residence.
(see also *Arts, Ohio*, page 265)

National McKinley Library & Museum
40 North Main Street
Niles, OH 44446
330-652-1704
www.mckinley.lib.oh.us
The McKinley Museum is part of the National McKinley Birthplace Memorial and consists of memorabilia from President William McKinley's early life in Niles; Civil War and Spanish-American War artifacts; campaign materials and presidential items. The other wing of the memorial houses the McKinley Memorial Library, a public library named after the President.

National Packard Museum
1899 Mahoning Avenue NW
Warren, Ohio 44482
330-394-1899
www.packardmuseum.org
A museum dedicated to the Packard automobile, family and Packard electric.

National Road /Zane Grey Museum
8850 East Pike
Norwich, OH 43767
740-872-3143
www.ohiohistory.org/places/natroad/
Display in miniature depicts construction and evolution of the National Road. Museum also commemorates life and career of Ohio writer, Zane Grey. Exhibits include Conestoga wagon, a carriage, an early bicycle and antique automobiles.

Neil Armstrong Air & Space Museum
Just west of I-75 at exit 111 (Bellefontaine Street)
Wapakoneta, OH 45895-0978
419-738-8811
800-860-0142
www.artcom.com/museums/vs/mr/45895.htm
Contemporary museum in Neil Armstrong's

hometown chronicles the history of flight.
On display is the 1946 Aeronca 7AC Champion in which Armstrong learned to fly; the Gemini VIII spacecraft flown by Armstrong and David Scott in 1966, in which they successfully completed the first rendezvous and docking in space; Apollo 11 artifacts; and a rock collected from the Sea of Tranquility in 1969. Among exhibits listed as visitor favorites is the imitation spacecraft, in which visitor is strapped into a moveable shuttle that creates the illusion of space. Multimedia presentations in the museum's Astro-theater display sights and sounds of space against a starry background.

Ohio Ceramic Center
SR 93 at CR 96 between Roseville and Crooksville in Perry County
740-697-7021
800-752-2604
www.ohiohistory.org/places/ohceram
The center is devoted to the history of pottery. Each of the five buildings houses exhibits of the different types of pottery made in the area.

Ohio Historical Center and Village
1985 Velma Avenue, I-71 and 17th Avenue
Columbus, OH 43211
614-297-2300
www.ohiohistory.org/places/ohc/
Exhibits on history, archaeology and natural history from the ice age to the space age.

Ohio-Hocking Forestry Museum
Hocking College
3301 Hocking Parkway
Nelsonville, OH
740-753-3591
If you've ever wondered how the great hardwood forests were subdued before subjugation went painlessly high-tech then this museum is for you. It's a premier collection of the equipment, historical to contemporary, of the instruments used to tame, for better or worse, the great Ohio forests. The collection includes 16 different kinds of two-man saws, primitive instruments that certainly gave the forests a fighting chance. There's everything here from a German Stihl chainsaw that was torched apart and smuggled into America in pieces during World War II, to an entire reassembled fire tower.

Ohio Railway Museum
990 Proprietors Road
Worthington, OH 43085
614-885-7345
www.ohiorailwaymuseum.org
Collection of equipment and other material tracing railroad history.

Ohio River Museum
601 Second Street
Marietta, OH 45750
740-373-3717
800-860-0145
www.ohiohistory.org/places/ohriver/
Because this three-building complex is built on piers anchored in the Muskingum, visitors literally experience a river museum. That is just fine with the Sons & Daughters of the Pioneering Rivermen, who began this museum 50 years ago by exhibiting riverboat memorabilia in a landlocked basement corner of the Campus Martius Museum. As their collection grew, so did the exhibit's concept, evolving into the award-winning architecture of today's museum, which is designed to treat visitors to a steamboat perspective. The Sons & Daughters, a group preserving the nation's colorful river and steamboat heritage, have provided much of the collection, including the 22-foot model of a circa 1900 steamboat that is authentic down to the doorknobs. On the model's maiden voyage, the builder fired up the gasoline engine and actually sat on the bow while the miniature paddlewheel moved him down river. Children especially like the "hand's-on" exhibits, but the real crowd-pleaser is the school of carp that takes up summer residence beside the towboat *W.P. Snyder, Jr.* in order to feed on bread that visitors cast upon the waters. Museum director John Briley says the carp—like the swallows at Capistrano or the buzzards of Hinckley, Ohio—are so fond of the locale that every April 19, they faithfully return to Marietta.

Ohio Veterans Hall of Fame Museum
3416 Columbus Avenue
Sandusky, Ohio 44870
419-625-2454 ext. 447
www.state.oh.us/gova/hallfame.htm
Located on the first floor of the I.F Mack Building at the Ohio Veterans Home, the museum contains military artifacts, memorabilia dating to the Civil War, and a library.

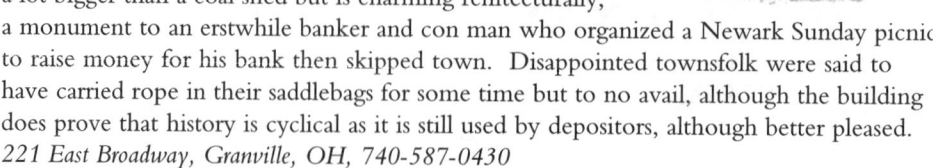

Rock and Roll Hall of Fame and Museum
1 Key Plaza
Cleveland, OH 44114
216-781-7625/800-493-7655
www.rockhall.com
Dedicated to the heritage of rock and roll, the $84 million, 150,000 square foot museum

ROBBY HUNTER'S ODD MUSEUM: GRANVILLE LEGACY

This 27-room Avery-Downer mansion has been in architectural books since the turn of the century; the Smithsonian calls it one of the two best examples of Greek Revival interiors in America. It's an exacting copy of two ancient Greek temples and while restoration is ongoing, visitors can still browse through the period-decorated rooms filled with Robby Hunter's collections of early furniture, paintings, carpets, silver and china, and items of Ohio craft. Hunter was a master forager—among his other accomplishments he collected for Henry Ford's Dearborn Village—and he filled the old mansion with his expert finds. Once, he took out part of his own stairwell in order to get into the house an organ he had just bought. He liked to point out some new piece by saying, "This came from Mama's bedroom," which prompted one villager to say, "My God, Mama's bedroom must be the size of Grand Central Station." It also has—little noted—what curator Paul Goudy says is "the outstanding example of Greek Revival outhouse architecture." It is a small building to the rear that, indeed, contains the museum facilities, and was once a Newark bank building. It is not a lot bigger than a coal shed but is charming rchitecturally, a monument to an erstwhile banker and con man who organized a Newark Sunday picnic to raise money for his bank then skipped town. Disappointed townsfolk were said to have carried rope in their saddlebags for some time but to no avail, although the building does prove that history is cyclical as it is still used by depositors, although better pleased.
221 East Broadway, Granville, OH, 740-587-0430

was designed by I. M. Pei. The collection spans a century and includes everything from early blues shouters to instruments, lyrics, stage props, and childhood memorabilia representing nearly every major rock and roll artist.

Santa Maria
West Broad Street and Marconi Blvd.
Columbus, OH 43215
614-645-8760
www.santamaria.org
A full scale replica of the flagship of Christopher Columbus located in downtown Columbus.

Shaker Historical Museum
16740 South Park Boulevard
Shaker Heights, OH 44120
216-921-1201
800-860-6078
www.cwru.edu/affil/shakhist/shaker.htm
Collection of artifacts from local and other Shaker Colonies of the 19th Century; general collection of area historical material.

Spirit of '76 Museum
201 North Main Street, P.O. Box 76
Wellington, OH 44090
440-647-4367
Museum dedicated to Archibald M. Willard, artist who painted "The Spirit of '76;" artworks and historical artifacts.

Temperance Tavern Museum
221 West Canal Street
Newcomerstown, OH 43832
740-498-7735
Fifteen miles east of Coshocton on State Route 36 (and only two miles west of I-77) is the consummate small-town museum, the Temperance Tavern Museum, a hands-on personal repository of the townspeople's past, perpetuated with their time, money and artifacts. For this, thank Dorothea Marshall for her foresight and loyalty to Newcomerstown history, some of which she made herself when she changed the wet pants of a little boy named Woody Hayes. The pants are not in the museum, but Mr. Hayes' bronzed football shoes are. Canal boats used to cruise by the front door on what was once the very beginning of the Ohio-Erie Canal. Travelers were taken down the stone steps to the kitchen. The huge fireplace and the original black walnut table are still there. Behind the fireplace it's completely open all the way up to the third floor. Once, they lowered a child with a camera down the opening. The picture showed nothing but a great hiding place for black slaves heading north. Everything in the museum ("Why, we have *twice* as much as that one in Roscoe Village") is loaned or is a gift of a Newcomerstown resident. And the rule is, any resident coming to the door, whether child or adult, asking to display whatever it is they have, is granted that request. Because of this, you can find an outfit worn to Warren G. Harding's inaugural,

the dress worn by the first woman postmaster, the original drum used in the Newscomerstown Hyperion Band, an entire skeleton of an Indian girl with a metal plate in her skull, virgins' lamps dug up in the Holy Land in 1921, a piece of rare, old barbed wire from Delaware County and the largest collection of Cy Young memorabilia, including the pair of shoes he had on when he died and the wood he chopped the last week he was alive.

Toledo Firefighters Museum
918 Sylvania Avenue
Toledo, OH 43612
419-478-3473
www.toledofiremuseum.com
The museum contains restored fire equipment, antique fire toys, uniform and other fire related displays.

United States Air Force Museum
Wright-Patterson Air Force Base
1100 Spaatz Street
Dayton, OH 45433
937-255-3286
www.wpafb.af.mil/museum
With the home of the Wright Brothers only a few miles away, you might expect the collection here to be top notch, and it is. As the largest museum in the world dedicated to military aviation, hanger-sized buildings hold exhibits as old as the legend of Icarus and as new as the proposed National Aero-Space Plane; as poignant as spoons made by prisoners of war, and as personal as Billy Mitchell's binoculars; as small as the World War I carrier pigeon "Stumpy John," and as large as the World War II-era B-36, a bomber so huge that a museum building had to be completed around it. This trove of memorabilia is a mecca for aviation buffs and every year more than a million of them make the pilgrimage here to celebrate the ascent of man that Orville and Wilbur began. In fact, the museum is the most popular free attraction in Ohio, certainly because of the unsurpassed displays but also because visitors are made most welcome here, thanks to amenities such as the excellent aviation book store and model shop, free films in the Museum Theatre, on-site café, outdoor picnic tables and even baby strollers and wheelchairs.
Enter Wright-Patterson Air Force Base via Gate 28-B off Springfield Pike east of Woodman Drive.

Director's favorites:
1. The Royal Air Force "Spitfire,"
credited with saving England during World War II.
2. The F-94C, the Lockheed "Starfire,"
an early jet fighter.
3. The P-51D "Mustang," which escorted bombers into Germany in World War II.
4. The PT-17, a biplane trainer from the 1930s.
5. The B-17G, the "Flying Fortress,"
the glamour bomber of World War II.

Air apparent

The largest community event in the Dayton area is the Dayton Air Fair, which has its origins in barnstorming pilots performing for a few thousand spectators in the early '70s at the old Montgomery County Airport. The fair officially began in 1975 when its official launching attracted 65,000 people and began a run that made it the largest air show in the world. Today, its budget is $1 million and the 2003 event brought in over 160,000 spectators. Organized by the non-profit United States Air and Trade Show, Inc., it has a fulltime staff assisted by over 500 volunteers—physicians and fire chiefs, auto mechanics and secretaries—some of whom have worked for 20-plus years.

The Wagnalls Memorial
150 East Columbus Street
Lithopolis, OH 43136
614-837-4765
www.wagnalls.lib.oh.us
Three public libraries and a community center
housed in ornate Tudor/Gothic stone buildings.

Warren County Historical Society Museum
105 S. Broadway
Lebanon, OH
513-932-1817
www.wchsmuseum.com
In the early part of the century, when schools
didn't have gyms, this was the equivalent of the
downtown Y. But when the local historical society
took it over, it became a model hometown
museum. Out came the gymnasium bleachers and
in went a village green, an idea borrowed from
the Henry Ford museum. Surrounding the green
are shops and craft houses, tiny but so realistic as
to imagine it's business as usual. Elsewhere in the
building are prehistoric Indian items, farm tools,
and a seven-room Shaker collection, said to be the
largest anywhere, and known worldwide. This is
by far one of the more interesting museums in the
state, and a great place to see what lifestyles
through several generations used to be.

Warther Carvings
331 Karl Avenue
Dover, OH 44622
330-343-7513
Collection of hand-carved historical pieces, Swiss-
style gardens, railroad park.

Western Reserve Historical Society
10825 East Boulevard
Cleveland, OH 44106
216-721-5722
www.wrhs.org/
Exhibits and period settings tracing American
cultural history, with emphasis on Western Reserve;
extensive genealogical collection.

S.S. Willis B. Boyer Museum Ship
26 Main Street
P.O Box 50406
Toledo, OH 43605-3068
419-936-3070
www.internationalpark.org
A 617-foot ship which once reigned as "King of the
Freighters" now is open for tours as a museum.

Wyandot Popcorn Museum
169 East Church Street
Marion, OH 43302
740-387-4255
www.wyandotpopcornmus.com
Devoted to the popcorn industry, the museum
houses the world's largest collection of popcorn
antiques.

Historic sites
Kingwood

Blennerhassett Island State Historical Park
The island is in the Ohio River, two miles west
of Parkersburg, West Virginia.
137 Juliana St.
Parkersburg, WV 26101-5331
304-420-4800
800-225-5998
www.blennerhassettislandstatepark.com

Archaeologists found the Blennerhassett foundations in 1973 (the 7,000 square-foot Palladian style
mansion burned in 1811), and it was painstakingly
restored. A 20-minute sternwheeler ride takes
visitors to the island where guides in period
costumes tell the bizarre story of the Irish
aristocrat who allowed Aaron Burr to use his
island to recruit soldiers for Burr's alleged scheme
of invading Mexico and separating the trans-
Appalachian states from the Union to create
a vast new empire. Blennerhassett fled when
President Jefferson proclaimed Burr's intentions—
whatever they were—treasonous; he was released
after the government failed to convict, but his
fortunes were ruined.

Chateau Laroche
12025 Shore Drive
Loveland, OH 45140
513-683-4686
www.dupontcastle.com/castles/laroche.htm
A Norman-style castle begun in 1929 along the
Little Miami River, it took 51 years for one man,
Harry Andrews, to build out of limestone rocks and
bricks shaped from milkcartons.

Clifton Mill
75 Water Street
Clifton, OH 45316
937-767-5501
www.cliftonmill.com
America's largest water-powered mill, established
in 1802, producing wheat and corn products.
Country store.

Edison Birthplace
10 North Edison Drive
Milan, OH 44846
419-499-2968
www.milanhistory.org
The home where inventor Thomas Edison spent his

early years displays family photos and examples of his inventiveness.

Grant Homestead
219 East Grant Avenue
Georgetown, OH 45121
937-378-4222
www.usgrantboyhoodhome.org
This national landmark was the boyhood home of U.S. Grant who lived here from the age of 1 to the age of 17 when he left to attend West Point. *The Grant Birthplace* (513-553-4911) is at Point Pleasant, five miles east of New Richmond. It's a three-room cottage small enough to take an extensive tour of the U.S. on a railroad flatcar, which it once did.

Rutherford B. Hayes Presidential Center
Speigel Grove
Freemont, OH 43420-2796
419-332-2081
800-998-7737
President Rutherford B. Hayes home is the first Presidential museum and library. The Hayes Research Library contains 100,000 volumes with an emphasis on the late 19th century.

Kingwood Center
900 Park Avenue, W.
Mansfield, OH 44906
419-522-0211
www.kingwoodcenter.org
Industrialist Charles Kelley King's home accented by a 47-acre garden. A popular spring attraction is the 50,000 tulips.

Kirtland Temple Historical Center
9020 Chillicothe Road
Kirtland, OH 44094
440-256-3318
www.Kirtlandtemple.org
First temple in world built by followers of Mormon leader Joseph Smith, Jr.

Lawnfield / James A. Garfield
National Historical Site
8095 Mentor Avenue
Mentor, OH 44060
440-255-8722
www.wrhs.org/lawnfield/default.asp
Among Lake County's most notable buildings is "Lawnfield", the Victorian manse that was once the home of James Garfield. Thousands of people came by train to hear him campaign for the Presidency from his front porch. Now they come to see the family possessions, including Garfield's Congressional desk, his Presidential china, and the waxed funeral wreath Queen Victoria sent after he was assassinated.

Malabar Farm State Park/Big House
4050 Bromfield Road
Lucas, OH 44843
419-892-2784
www.malabarfarm.org
Restored home of Pulitzer Prize-winning author Louis Bromfield.

Mansfield Reformatory
100 Reformatory Road
Mansfield, OH 44905
419-522-2644
www.mrps.org/index2.html
Opened in 1886 the former Ohio State reformatory was built to resemble a medieval chateaux. No longer housing prisoners it is now open for tours. The prison was also featured in four motion pictures, *Harry and Walter, Tango and Cash, Shawshank Redemption,* and *Air Force One.*

Marblehead Lighthouse
C/O Lake Erie Islands State Park
4049 E. Moores Dock Road
Port Clinton, OH 43452
419-797-4530
www.dnr.state.oh.us/parks/parks/marblehead.htm
U.S. Government-constructed lighthouse; picnic grounds. Tours given on the second Saturday of the month June through September.

Ohio Historical Center
1982 Velma Avenue (Juncture of I-71 and 17th Ave.)
Columbus, OH 43211
614-297-2300
www.ohiohistory.org
Aside from being the headquarters of one of the country's largest historic site networks, the center's prehistoric exhibits were described by the *Smithsonian Guide to Historic America* as "probably the finest museum in America devoted to pre-European history." Exhibits feature the state's natural environment and the historical period since the 1700's. The 1 1/2 acres of exhibit space showcase items from the society's collection of over two million artifacts, and about ten temporary exhibits each year. The center houses a 300-seat auditorium, a research library, state archives, and the Ohio Historic Preservation Office.

Perkins Stone Mansion/John Brown Home
550 Copley Road
Akron, OH 44320
330-535-1120
1837 Greek Revival stone house with original and period furnishings; next-door to home of abolitionist John Brown.

Perry's Victory & International Peace Memorial
Bayview Avenue, P.O. Box 549
Put-in-Bay, OH 43456
419-285-2184
www.nps.gov/pevi
352 feet Doric column commemorating Oliver Hazzard Perry's naval victory.

ROSCOE VILLAGE: TRIBUTE TO AN INCREDIBLE LABOR

The 308-mile canal from Cleveland to Portsmouth, with 152 locks, cost $4.7 million and took nine years to build. It, along with its parallel canal and branches in Western Ohio, was the largest canal system in the world at the time. Thank Alfred Kelley and his crews of Irish laborers for this. The Irish immigrants got 30 cents a day and a jigger of whiskey every five hours. With picks, shovels and wheelbarrows they completed over 1,000 miles of canals, their aqueducts and locks.

And because of them, there evolved the little town of Roscoe, one of the pivotal points on the Ohio–Erie Canal. Its success lasted 20 years, until the railroad, whose pieces the canal carried to their destinations, put an end to the need for a canal system. And, as water breathed life into the canals, water also finally washed them away.

The 1913 flood ended the declining system for good. Fifty-five years later, Edward and Frances Montgomery mourned these remnants as they made their daily drive from Roscoe Hill down through the village. So they restored the canal's tollhouse and began a foundation to restore the village. Now commercialism thrives once again in Roscoe Village, drawing some 175,000 visitors annually.

Over 20 homes and buildings have been upgraded and filled with sweets, cheeses, musical instruments, gifts and eateries. Most buildings are brick, with stepped gables typical of the canal era, and there are tidy gardens of flowers, herbs and vegetables dotting the landscape. Festivals are common, May through December, and visitors on this easy walking tour are greeted by shopkeepers in costumes of the Canal Era.

Without pests, dust and lack of amenities, here is a place where, at the end of Whitewoman Street the traveler can see the Parthenon of the canal era—Triple Locks—gateless and grassy, but with "well-built sides, straight and true."

From here, follow the worn path from the end of the parking lot to the footbridge on the site of the Walhonding River—to the restored one-mile stretch of canal that now carries the Monticello III.

Here, if you will, pause to consider Mr. Kelly, his Irish immigrants, all who toiled, and those who died, to create this abandoned dream.

—381 Hill Street; Coshocton, OH
740-622-9310 or 800-877-1830
www.roscoevillage.com

Piatt Castles
10051 Township Road 47
P.O. Box 497
West Liberty, OH 43357
937-465-2821
Norman-style castle built in 1864, with original furnishings and art collection and a Flemish castle built in 1879 furnished with European and oriental antiques. Although the decidedly different architectural vision of Abram and Donn Piatt has dazzled visitors for more than a century and a half, their castles were not opened to public tours until about 1912. The story goes that curious people doing business at the estate repeatedly asked Abram's son, William, if they could go inside. Since that man's castle really *was* his home, William repeatedly turned them down. Eventually, the requests got so bothersome that William decided he could discourage his friends and neighbors by asking them for money when they wanted to see the castle. Much to his surprise, they paid willingly, and the castle tour business was born.

Sherman House
137 East Main Street
Lancaster, Ohio 43130
740-687-5891
www.shermanhouse.org
This National Historic Landmark is filled with fascinating mementos from the life of Civil War General William Tecumseh Sherman, and Senator John Sherman, the architect of the antitrust law that bears his name.

Sherwood-Davidson House Museum
North Sixth Street
Newark, Oh 43055
740-345-6525
One of the finest examples of Federal architecture in the Ohio Valley, furnished with items from the 18th and 19th century. Upstairs gallery with changing exhibits.

Stan Hywet Hall & Gardens
714 North Portage Path
Akron, OH 44303
330-836-5533
www.stanhywet.org
The 65-room country estate is known as one of the finest examples of Tudor Revival architecture in America. It sits on 70 acres of gardens and grounds designed by renowed American landscape architect, Warren Manning, and is considered one of the finest remaining examples of his private work in America.

William Howard Taft National Historic Site
2038 Auburn Avenue
Cincinnati, OH 45219
513-684-3262
www.nps.gov/wiho
The Federal-style home is the birthplace of the only person who was both a president and a Chief Justice of the Supreme Court.

AuGlaize Village
12296 Krouse Road
P.O. Box 801
Defiance, OH 43512
419-784-0107
419-782-7255
www.defiance-online.com/auglaize
A 19th century restored village with two farms, military, natural history and archaeology museums. Special events.

Caesar's Creek Pioneer Village
Waynesville, OH 45068
513-897-1120
www.caesarscreekvillage.org
In the 1960s, U.S. Army Corps of Engineers began work on a flood control dam creating Caesar Creek State Park and an enormous lake. In the process, they emptied the hundred-year-old village of New Burlington of its inhabitants, tore down their buildings and erased it from existence. Not far away in the woods, they uncovered several *log* homes under layers of siding. *These* were saved. A rather paradoxical beginning for the Caesar's Creek Pioneer Village. Since 1973, over 18 buildings and structures have been found in surrounding counties and moved to the 17-acre village. Arranged more like a New England village, with buildings around a village green, there are nice examples of a variety of 19th century structures. The earliest cabin, dating back to the late 1700s, is the only settler's cabin known to still exist in Ohio. High points are the annual events, at least a dozen from February until October: maple syrup making, old machinery days, frontier food and pioneer music.

Century Village
14653 East Park Street
Burton, OH 44021
440-834-1492
Restored 19th century village with 16 buildings, including a church, barn, law house and black smith shop.

Fort Recovery/St. Clair's Battlefield
Fort Recovery Museum
One Fort Site Street
Fort Recovery, OH 45846
419-375-4649
www.artcom.com/museums/newones/
45846-a.htm
This 12-mile diversion onto State Route 119 West is well worth the drive. On the land behind what is now Fort Site Street, behind Wayne Street and a monument business, 2,000 Indians left 900 white men dead or wounded in just three hours. The dead were buried where they were found when General Anthony Wayne arrived two years later in 1793, to build the fort. In 1851, on "bone burying day" they were dug up and placed in Pioneer Cemetery, only to be removed 61 years later to Monument Park. That's where the tall spire is now. At the fort site is a reconstructed garrison and a marker where a black walnut stake was found, showing the western terminus of the Greenville Treaty line. The stake is in the museum, and even the most casual student of history could be moved by the magnitude of the event, should he care to press the museum caretaker for the gory details.

German Village
624 South Third Street
Columbus, OH 43206
E-Mail: tours@germanvillage.com
www.germanvillage.com
Restored 19th century community containing private homes, shops and restaurants. Guided tours available.

Hale Farm & Village
2686 Oak Hill Road
Bath, OH 44210
330-666-3711
www.wrhs.org/halefarm/default.asp
Complex of restored buildings depicting mid-19th century rural life; working farm with livestock; authentic crafts demonstrations.

Historic Lyme Village
5001 State Rte. 4
Box 342
Bellevue, OH 44811
419-483-4949
www.lymevillage.com
A collection of buildings from the pioneer, Williamsburg and Victorian eras.

Ohio Village
1985 Velma Avenue, I-71 and 17th Avenue
Columbus, OH 43211
614-297-2300
www.ohiohistory.org/places/ohvillag/
Reconstructed mid-19th century village with working crafts people restored inn with restaurant.

Piqua Historical Area
9845 North Hardin Road
Piqua, OH 45356
937-773-2522
www.ohiohistory.org/places/piqua
Restored farm with residence, barn, springhouse; Indian museum; canal boat.

Roscoe Village
381 Hill Street
Coshocton, OH 43812
800-877-1830
www.roscoevillage.com
Restored 1830s Ohio and Erie Canal town; encourages visitor participation.

Sauder Farm & Craft Village
State Rte. 2, P.O. Box 342
Archbold, OH 43502
800-590-9755
www.saudervillage.org
Farm and craft village reliving northwest Ohio's great Black Swamp of the late 1800s.

Schoenbrunn Village
East High Avenue
New Philadelphia, OH 44663
330-339-3636
800-752-2711
www.ohiohistory.org/places/schoenbr/
Missionary village abandoned in 1877, now reconstructed; 18 log structures, Ohio's first schoolhouse, and guided tours.

Sharon Woods Village
Sharon Woods Park
11450 Lebanon Pike
Cincinnati, OH 45241
513-563-1986
Reconstructed 1880s Ohio village including farm houses, train station, doctor's office.

Sunwatch
2301 West River Road
Dayton, OH 45418
937-268-8199
www.sunwatch.org
A National Historic Landmark, this reconstruction of a prehistoric Indian village shows the heritage and culture of early Americans.

Zoar Village
198 Main Street
Zoar, OH 44697
330-874-3211
800-262-6195
www.zca.org
Eight buildings built by Zoar separatists, a German religious communal group, from 1817-1898. tours led by costumed guides; State Memorial.

The 1953 Ohio State Fair celebrated Ohio's 150th anniversary as a state with an elaborate pageant titled "The Seventeenth Star," a subtle reference to Ohio's status as the 17th state admitted to the Union. The pageant, said to be the world's largest, was anything but subtle—500 performers decked out in costumes worth $100,000, on a 243-foot custom-made stage, acting out a two-hour production that told the story of Ohio from Moundbuilders to modern times in words and music.

Governor Frank Lausche even made a token appearance—in a ruffled, purple velvet waistcoat—as Thomas Worthington, Ohio's founding father. In the Arts and Crafts Building, Mrs. Walter Baldauf of Marion displayed a quilt that took her two years to complete. She had painstakingly reproduced in needlework the signatures of 143 famous people, including Mamie Eisenhower, Groucho Marx, and General Douglas MacArthur. Her ambition received two blue ribbons.

The 1953 fair was also favored with a sculpture made entirely of butter, by J.S. Wallace. He juxtaposed a contemporary cow and milking machine with an 1803-vintage cow, farmer, small boy, and a cat enjoying a squirt of fresh milk. The Butter Cow and Calf became something of a landmark—if not a trademark—at the Ohio State Fair.

The custom developed of adding a third executed-in-butter figure as a sign of the times. Thus the buttery bovines were joined in their refrigerated glass showcase by such figures as John Glenn, Darth Vader, and Dave Thomas.

The state fair got underway as far back as 1845, when friends of agriculture gathered in Columbus for an Agriculture Convention. Its Board of Agriculture assumed the goal of promoting exhibitions of farm products at the county and district levels, and the first of several district fairs was held October 20-21, 1847, in Wilmington. The second district fair was held in Xenia, September 20-21, 1848.

The first Ohio State Fair was held the first week in October of 1849 at Camp Washington, about three miles from what was then the center of Cincinnati, on the Miami Canal. Despite a small deficit, between 25,000 and 30,000 people traveled from varying distances.

The state's new annual event was held in several cities around Ohio, and in 1886, it found a permanent home in Columbus. Since, the fairgrounds have expanded from the original 115 acres to 360.

In 1895 it set a standard for other state fairs with the addition of electricity. The milestone event was advertised in the Fair Bulletin this way: "Determined that Ohio shall be the first with respect to introducing advanced ideas for state fairs, the board has erected on the grounds An Immense Electric Plant." That decision paved the way for night racing, concerts, and exhibitions.

More than two million people enjoy the facility and its more than 200 annual events, in addition to the Fair, and more than 18,000 youths participate in the annual Junior Fair, making it the largest in the country.

One of the state fair staples has been the butter cow, a sculpted constant since the tradition began in the 1920s. Dan Ross, the preeminent butter artist, made his cows near life size, weighing over 500 pounds. In time, the cows were joined by people and in 2003, the Wright Brothers made it into butter, right down to their high-cholesterol mustaches and neckties. It took six Cincinnati-based artists 250 hours and about a ton of butter to create them. The newly-minted Wrights were a larger-than-life 6-foot-3 and 250 buttery pounds each.

Natural wonders

Cantwell Cliffs
State Route 374, north of SR 180
Logan, OH 43138
www.heartofhocking.com/Cantwell_Cliffs.htm
This 150-foot high palisade offers a Hobson's choice of approaches. If visitors follow the valley trail, they face a long hike and hundreds of steps, but they are rewarded with the view and the advantage of gravity on the return trip. Those who approach from above have the view without effort, but as they descend the stairs into the gorge, they most remember that he who goes down must come back up. Although these cliffs may be beautifully tranquil now, that was not always so. Years ago, Farmer Cantwell was harassed by two tobacco-stealing Indians until he finally convinced them to break the habit by locking them in his barn. It is said that the last Indian in Hocking County died under a cherry tree at the bottom of Cantwell Cliffs.

Conkles Hollow
State Route 374, south of SR 678
Logan, OH 43138
www.heartofhocking.com/Conkles_Hollow.htm
We don't know who he was, where he came from, or what became of him. We only know that he made himself immortal in the Hocking Hills by stopping long enough to carve his name and the date in the gorge, "W.J. Conkle 1797." Perhaps, like some 16th century conquistador planting a flag on a rich discovery, Conkle was trying to claim the view, for most folks agree that it is the best in the county. And the best place to take in that view is from the observation platform located in the middle of Rim Trail, a two-mile path that winds past the Hollow's graceful ferns, over the footbridges, across the boardwalks, and—just for gasps—along the edge of the 200-foot high cliffs.

Cedar Falls
Old State Route 374 in Hocking Hills
State Park and Forest
Logan, OH 43138
www.hockinghills.com/parks.htm
Bring your camera to Cedar Falls. Everyone else does. Voted most photogenic by most everyone, this waterfall is a healthy but safe (in spite of the cliff warning sign) falls to visit. From the parking lot, the gentle trail winds through hemlocks (the pioneers didn't know their trees), along a tumbling creek and over a footbridge. Turn north and 200 yards ahead are the falls, almost completely surrounded by sheer cliffs. In January, it's a frozen mass of ice, in spring it's a torrent, in late summer, it practically disappears. A beautiful hike through a primeval area called Queer Creek connects it to Old Man's Cave and very few people know about it. Try this. Go back to the footbridge and turn south. Look carefully. There's a three to four foot ramp where the trail goes around a cliff. Now you're at the beginning of a valley whose closest likeness would be in the Smokey Mountains. Spectacular formations and dozens of waterfalls in wet weather guide you all the way to Old Man's Cave. A terrific B & B, The Inn at Cedar Falls, is just across the road. It's widely known for the proprietor's gourmet cooking; call for reservations. 740-385-7489.

Cedar Bog Nature Preserve
Four miles south of Urbana on U.S. Route 68, then west on Woodburn Road for one mile
Urbana, OH 43078-9417
937-484-3744 or 800-860-0147
www.cedarbog.org
According to on-site naturalist Terry Jaworski, visiting Cedar Bog is like seeing Ohio as the mastodons saw it at the end of the Ice Age. Cedar Bog is frozen in time, a remnant of the last glacier, which destroyed the ancient Teays River and

www. 1800hocking.com

Good, workaday site by the Hocking Hills Tourism Association that charts the handsome lay of the Land of Ahhs. Covers everything from rentals (cabins, B&Bs, chalets, with links to their own sites, with prices and pictures), to events, shopping, dining, and natural attractions.

filled with limestone gravel the valley where it once flowed. Cool ground water rising to the surface of the gravel in much the same way that water bubbles from a leak in a garden hose formed the swampy "bog," which is actually a fen through which water flows rather than accumulates. Cedar Bog was Ohio's first nature preserve, and the cool, sweet water supply—the temperature is a constant 54F all year round—makes it the only fen in the state that is still surrounded by an Ice Age community of woody plants that includes northern white cedar and dwarf birch. Cedar Bog is a National Natural Landmark, and public access is limited in order to safeguard this unique, 10,000-year-old geologic and botanical area. Guided tours, however, are conducted via a well-designed boardwalk that takes visitors over the bog and past the plants and animals (many of which are rare and endangered) that it harbors—lady's-slipper orchids that bloom in the spring, yellow cinquefoil, blue fringed gentians, Milbert's tortoise shell butterflies, spotted turtles, massasauga rattlesnakes, sedges (which have edges), and grasses (which are round).

Fort Ancient State Memorial
6123 State Route 350 east
Oregonia, OH 45054
513-932-4421 or 800-283-8904
www.ohiohistory.org/places/ftancien/
Long recognized as one of the outstanding prehistoric sites in America, the Fort Ancient Earthworks hunker in a 700-acre park overlooking the Little Miami gorge. It has been accurately called "eerily beautiful, especially in fall," and the site contains three and a half miles of earthen walls that enclose over a hundred acres; it is probably the most notable vista in this part of Ohio. The Fort Ancient culture ostensibly gets the credit for the earthworks but they were actually constructed by the much older Hopewell Indians, who inhabited the area from around 300 B.C. to 600 A.D. The Fort Ancients were the last prehistoric Native Americans who occupied the Ohio Valley before the coming of the first Europeans. They arrived in Ohio around 1,000 A.D., took over the mortgage on the earthworks and became generally considered uninteresting, if not actually "degenerate," the poor end of a larger cultural group called the Mississippian. In reality, the Fort Ancients were probably the first settled people in the valley, certainly the first farmers, and they gave us the gift of corn-growing. Archaeological digs have shown that

the Fort Ancients also had a coherent astronomy, as well as building skills, even if they did not create their own earthworks. The historian Harlan Hatcher called the earthworks here, "the most intriguing of them all." In his time, their purpose was considered to have been defensive but later revelations assert they were ceremonial. In the summer of 1820, an archaeologist named Caleb Atwater suggested that the site here was a great arena for athletic competition, thus delivering a thesis for the original Buckeye.

Hocking Hills State Park
Park office: 20160 State Route 664
Logan, OH 43138
740-385-6841 (park office)
740-385-6165 (camp office)
www.hockinghillspark.com
You've probably already heard all the standard adjectives for the scenery at Hocking Hills State Park—beautiful, breathtaking, gorgeous, glorious, colorful, spectacular. Well, they're all true. Southeast Ohio abounds with nature preserves and parks, but none are grander than the wooded cliffs and rugged gorges of Hocking country. Located only fifteen miles west of Logan, the Hocking Hills rock formations are a panorama of Ohio geology. More than 300 million years ago, an ocean covered the region, and feeder streams deposited layers of sand in a delta, which with time hardened into a sedimentary rock called sandstone. Subsequently, the earth heaved upward, creating the Appalachian Mountains and the hills of Hocking County. About two million years ago, glaciers moved over most of what is now Ohio. Those massive ice sheets stopped short of the State Park, but when they melted, the running water eroded the hills. Weak, crumbly areas of the sandstone washed away. Left behind was a water-resistant stratum known as Black Hand Sandstone, a true Rock of Ages, which forms every craggy dip and peak in today's landscape. You can read this rough-hewn corner of Ohio like a natural history. Before the glaciers, the long-gone Teays River brought in seeds of plant species from the south; then the ice carried northern flora to the area. Thanks to this botanical quirk, yews and mayflowers grow in the cool, damp valleys of Hocking Hills, while mountain laurel flourishes in the high places. One of the park naturalists even likes to brag that "the Hocking Hills are Canada in the valleys and Carolina and Tennessee on the ridges."

From upper left, counterclockwise: historic photograph of boulder seven miles north of Ironton; Conkles Hollow; and Lake Logan

The Mound builders:
This land was their land

HOPEWELL CULTURE NATIONAL HISTORIC MONUMENT—This spot is one of the earliest settled geographies in America and the center of mound building activity in the country, with over 500 mounds accounted for in the area. The Mound Builders were two distinct groups of Indians, the Hopewell and the Adena, the latter being a more modest but older people, having arrived in the Ohio Valley about 800 B.C. The Hopewell emerged about a hundred years before the birth of Christ. When the white man ran into them, he did so archaeologically and not very accurately. The white dilemma, as usual, centered around notions of real estate, thus if the historic Indians of the Northwest Territory were legitimate descendants of the once-grand civilization of the Mound Builders—and could not be written off as inherently savage—then our claim to empire would be seen as exactly what it was: a land grab.

So we invented splendid theories, notably about such things as the Ten Lost Tribes of Israel, promulgated mostly by backwoods clergymen. To one Pleasant Hill man of the cloth, the Great Serpent Mound was the site of the Garden of Eden and the effigy was made by the hand of God to mark original sin. The Ross County Historical Society Museum, as a matter of fact, had in recent years a sporadic visitor who extolled the Serpent Mound as evidence of an extra-terrestrial visit to Earth. The society has thus far resisted collecting his notes and papers. In 1848 a Chillicothe newspaper editor and his companion surveyed hundreds of the mounds and their report put Chillicothe on the map of international scientific interest.

Meanwhile, though, the mounds were being plumbed by expert and nonexpert alike, plowed over, and built upon. It was a splendid tribute to the Hopewell that not even the U.S. Army could completely destroy their works when during World War I it built a huge complex on the present-day monument site. The remains of that camp lie just outside—the VA hospital and a state prison—all monuments to incarceration, of one kind or another.

The Mound City grounds, one of only five Ohio national monuments, has preserved 23 mounds in one 13-acre tract, more of a concentration than anywhere else in America. Even with the knowledge of our civilization pushing at the edges of the ancient necropolis, on just the right early autumn afternoon, slightly before dusk, the large grassy field of mounds, ringed by woodland, can be very effecting. An incredible labor went into the elaborate burials where the rulers were covered in mica brought back from North Carolina and laid to rest with artifacts traded as far away as the Rockies. The Mound Builders, called by some "the Egyptians of the United States," were obsessed with a well-stocked afterlife, and if we have reversed this notion, we still share a powerful kinship. In our time, it is

www. *ohioarchaeology.org*

Site of the Ohio Archaeology Council contains maps and history of most historical parks and archaeological sites in Ohio. Events, publications, research papers, as well as deep list of links, particularly ones to "virtual archaeology" sites worldwide.

imminently worthwhile standing in a quiet field, on one of the biggest pieces of prehistoric America still above ground, and contemplating life and work that went diligently on 2,000 years before us.

FORT HILL AND THE SERPENT MOUND—For the true devotee, there are two other notable monuments within a short drive southwest of Chillicothe. The nearest of these, off State Route 41 outside Cynthiana, is Fort Hill.

The uninitiated, after seeing a few carefully mowed and managed mounds, tend to think they are all the same. But Fort Hill gives visitors a whiff of the early mystery. Fort Hill is a hilltop enclosure "fort" and a steep hiking trail takes the visitor up the heavily wooded slope where the Hopewell piled dirt and rocks 50 feet deep in places to raise a rampart around the summit. Fort Hill is "conjectively" Hopewell as it contains no burials, living sites, nor any evidence that it was used as a fortress. Compared to other well-groomed and level sites, this one is half lost in forest. Only when one walks along the rampart, which is over a mile-and-a-half around, can the effort of creating it be imagined. Thousands of baskets were lugged up the slope, an epic labor animated and directed by a cult or culture that is still at the very limits of our understanding. You can sit in the momentary quiet, listening to the wind through the trees and imagine this as the pioneers found it. You can think of old Squier and Davis running their survey lines through these woods and, point by point, a massive monument emerged, an earthwork of such size and permanence that it could survive a thousand years to put us in our place as only the latest, not the last, people to shape Ohio.

A little farther south is the Great Serpent Mound, best known of the prehistoric earthworks in the Ohio Valley. While most of Ohio's notable earthworks are Hopewell, the Serpent Mound, thought to be the largest effigy earthwork in the world, is attributed to the Adena, our first moundbuilders. It is 1,254 feet long and four feet high, atop a bluff in Ross County, and its age is believed to be about two-and-a-half millennia. Its name refers to its reptilian coil, with a "mouth" that seems to be grasping a large egg-like oval.

In 1886, when the site was about to be destroyed, Harvard professor F.W. Putnam bought a year's option on it and persuaded a group of wealthy Boston matrons to put up money to save it. In 1888, Ohio passed the country's first law protecting archaeological sites, and the Serpent Mound is thought to be the first park in America created to save such an earthwork. For over a hundred years—scant time by Adena and Hopewell standards—the mound has been a favorite spot for hiking, picnics, and reunions.

HOPEWELL CULTURE NATIONAL HISTORIC MONUMENT: *16062 State Route 104 North; 740-774-1125. Open year round. Labor Day-mid-June, 8-5; extended hours in summer.*

FORT HILL: *State Route 41, three miles south of Cynthiana; 937-588-3221.*

SERPENT MOUND: *six miles south of Fort Hill, at Locust Grove, turn west (right) on SR 73. Go four miles. 937-587-2796.*

The Great Serpent Mound in Ross County, the largerst serpent effigy in the world, was probably built by the Adena people who disappeared from Ohio around the second century A.D. after 900 years of residence. The serpent confounded early settlers who spun elaborate fantasies about its meaning, including the tale that the great snake marked the Garden of Eden.

Inscription Rock, on the south shore of Kelleys Island, is a flat-topped limestone slab displaying carvings of animals and human figures, discovered partly buried in the shoreline in 1833. The rock's surface is covered with one of the finest examples of aboriginal art in the Great Lakes region. Known as a petroglyph, no one is sure what the unusual drawings depicted. The most widely accepted theory is that the large rock was used as a "message stone" where various Native Americans would make drawings noting that they'd been there, how the hunting or fishing had been and/or where they were headed next.

—Kelleys Island Historical Association

Inscription Rock, Kelleys Island
Kelleys Island, Ohio 43438
(Just east of downtown)
www.kelleysislandhistorical.org/island_places/inscription_rock.htm
Right on the shoreline on Water Street at Addison Road is the famous rock, now dimly inscribed in pictographs by the carvings of long-ago Indians. This quiet waterfront park is an appropriate place to consider the peculiar nature of island time, which runs more slowly than mainland time, for here is where Jake Hay had his repair shop. Jake was known for slowness tempered with generosity. He freely loaned out his tools and shop so his customers could make their own repairs when they grew tired of waiting for him.

Johnson's Island
Johnson's Island, OH 43440
419-448-2327
www.johnsonsisland.com
By the end of the Civil War almost 15,000 Confederate prisoners were jailed in the prison on this tiny 275-acre island in Sandusky Bay, just off the peninsula that faces Cedar Point. According to historian Harlan Hatcher, the camp was a rather grim village, especially in mid-winter when the temperatures sometimes went under 20 below zero. A worse fate was the monotony of the place. The prisoners were guarded inside and out, inside by, among others, the famous "Gray Beard Brigade," a Federal unit that contained octogenarians (one had 15 sons in the Union army), and outside by a gunboat. When the prison closed in 1865, 206 Confederate soldiers were left, buried in that lonely spot. Most of them had died of pneumonia. For a long while, the island—and the soldiers—were forgotten. Then the people of Sandusky, wartime passions cooled, re-marked the graves with marble headstones, and installed a statue of a soldier pointing his Confederate flag toward his homeland. None of the prison buildings still stands; the last part of the fort, a pigsty, was burned before World War II. The only warring today is against real estate developers, a bigger headache to the historically-minded than vandals, who don't seem to want to pay the 50 cents toll it takes to use the mile-long causeway from the mainland.

John Bryan State Park and Clifton Gorge State Nature Preserve
Yellow Springs, OH 45387
937-767-1274
3790 State Route 370
www.dnr.state.oh.us/dnap/location/clifton.html
You probably won't find a better natural area in Ohio than this pristine state park and its steep gorge. Beautiful? Incredibly, from the Little Miami River's 130-foot plummet near diverse and often unexpected—this is one of the few places in the state where the red baneberry grows—plants that flourish on the dolomite walls of the gorge. Historic? Of course, naturally as well as socially.

The area's natural history began with the glaciers, whose meltwater carved the gorge and left behind a trove of plant species. Human history here peaked during the last century when the rush of the river through the narrow gorge made it an ideal site for mills and thus the industrial hub of Greene County. Before that, the gorge was the province of the Shawnee, who late in the 1780's captured frontiersman Cornelius Darnell, a crony of Daniel Boone. Darnell escaped by jumping across the gorge, a death-defying feat that made him a local legend. Such leaps, of course, are discouraged today, as is climbing on the tall cliffs. In fact, the southern part of Clifton Gorge is such a hallowed preserve that even walking through it is by permission only. Therefore, plan your picnics and fishing for the other gorgeous grounds of John Bryan State Park, which is named for the farmer who once owned the land. Campgrounds now occupy the site of the enterprising Mr. Bryan's famous barn, a five-story behemoth that he built to be the largest in the world. When he willed his farm to Ohio in 1916, the state turned down the gift because Mr. Bryan, an atheist, had attached a proviso banning religious services. But his generosity eventually overshadowed his philosophy, and the state accepted his land for a park where the only worship today is to the glories of Mother Nature.

Newark Earthworks
99 Cooper Avenue (State Route 79 south and Hopewell)
Newark, OH 43055
740-344-1919
800-600-7174
www.ohiohistory.org/places/newarkearthworks/index.cfm
This 66-acre park contains the remnants of what has been called "the most elaborate and complicated earthworks in prehistoric times in America," which, while anachronistic, serves to suggest its importance in the Ohio earthworks inventory. The white man's encroachments destroyed much of it but, fortunately, left segments, including the great ceremonial circle, 1,200 feet in diameter and walls eight to 14 feet high, enclosing over 26 acres. Ohio's first state fair was held in the circle, which, ironically, helped save it. It's a wonderful natural area now, wooded with maples, dogwood and old beeches, and the best time to visit is in early spring or late fall, and the visitor can walk the circle and ponder our connection to this ancient people. The works were built by the Hopewell, Ohio's first great architectural firm, probably about 2,000 years ago. Archaeologists think the works were "civic centers" for the Indians of the area, used in a seasonal context for ceremony, religion, and trade. There is also a museum—America's first devoted exclusively to prehistoric American Indian art— where the history of Ohio's prehistoric cultures are carved in rock, pottery, pipes and ornamentation. Nearby is the Octagon State Memorial (Parkview Road), part of the same original complex. It is a

preserved circle and an octagon, six to eight feet high, tied together. The entire memorial is 138 acres, but it is also a private golf course with part of the greens inside the enclosures, demonstrating conclusively the correlation between religion and recreation. As far as can be determined, this is the only Ohio memorial to irony.

The Old Man's Cave Gorge at Hocking Hills State Park
State Route 664, 14 miles west of Logan, OH 43138
www.hockinghills.com/parks.htm

In 1939, the old travel writer, Claude Shafer, said, "Here you climb ladders, cross bridges, and drop into weird nooks and shadowy crannies, go into ecstasies at the ferns and moss, admire the pretty creek and waterfall, and shout to hear the echo. Your mind wanders and you get an eerie feeling in the semidarkness and you sort of wish you were home in bed with the covers over your head." An accurate description. But with a child or two along there's no time for idyllic contemplation. The trails invite movement and sometimes that means alongside a rim trail that drops two or three hundred feet. But if you can strike a balance between overreaction and passivity, the falls at Old Man's Cave cover some of the best rock scenery in southwestern Ohio. Begin at the stone bridge—to the east side—and walk across the rim, there's a pathway down to the bottom of the plunge pool. You're crossing over bridges and yet there are bridges above you. There's a sluice, then more rim trails, some little falls and finally it plunges over Lower Falls 50-60 feet. Just before the plunge is Old Man's Cave.

Ohio Caverns
2210 East State Route 245
West Liberty, OH 43357
937-465-4017
http://cavern.com/ohiocaverns/
Carved by an ancient underground river, these caverns are not only the largest in Ohio, but arguably the most colorful in the nation. Yet they were unknown until 1897, when a teenage farmhand noticed a sinkhole in a field and started digging. The slow drip of surface water through the limestone caverns over tens of millions of years has produced spectacular accumulations of calcite crystals on the floor (stalagmites) and ceiling (stalactites). These milky white formations provide a striking contrast to the colorful cavern walls, where stunning shades of red, orange, and yellow plus purple, brown, and black have been produced by oxides of iron and manganese found in the earth above the caverns. At just a shade under five feet long, the caverns' carrot-shaped, 400-pound Crystal King is the largest stalactite in Ohio. Since the caverns' crystals are still "growing" at the rate of one cubic inch every 500 to 1000 years, the 250,000-year-old Crystal King should reach its full five foot length in several decades. The caverns also have the nation's only dual formations, consisting of both iron oxide and calcite producing individual stalactites. Touching the beautifully preserved stalactites and stalagmites is prohibited because they are quite fragile, but the tour guides do have a six-and-a-half pound, 4,000-year-old specimen called the pet rock for visitors who want to get a feel for the crystals. Tours usually last about an hour, during which you'll descend 103 feet under the ground along well-lighted passages that take full advantage of the caverns' natural beauty. Since the temperature inside the caverns is a constant 54 degrees all year, take along a sweater or jacket, even in the summer. For most of this century, the caverns have been owned by members of the Smith-Evans family, who have done a remarkable job of preserving the beauty of both the caverns and the park-like grounds where they are located. The grassy, 35-acre hilltop setting is open to the public during daylight hours and has pavilions where people can picnic or simply enjoy a fine, pastoral view of the countryside.

Ottawa National Wildlife Refuge
14000 West State Route 2
Oak Harbor, OH 43449
419-898-0014
http://midwest.fws.gov/ottawa/ottawa.html
For birds of passage, this is Ohio's rest stop of choice. Thousands of birds of multiple family lineages use this marsh, woodlands and beachfront during their journey along the Mississippi fly-way. In February, the place is thick with swans coming in from Texas and Florida. The thousand resident Canada geese swell to 8,000 during migration, and in March, the place is reed-to-reed with ducks. It is probably the finest place in Ohio to

watch migratory birds when, during the peak season in October, one can see as many as a hundred different kinds of birds on a single morning. The ONWR, a sort of oasis around an oasis, wraps around Crane Creek State Park, a place where birders can swim, picnic, and walk the boardwalk through the woodlands. There are over nine miles of pathways and an observation deck. But go to the office first. The telescope there is permanently focused on an American Bald Eagle's nest one-and-one-half miles away.

Rock Bridge
On Dalton Road, off State Route 33, between SRs 374 and 180
Logan, OH 43138
www.dnr.state.oh.us/dnap/arches/default.htm#rockbridge
Ohio and Virginia have long sparred over the right to claim the title "Mother of Presidents" for producing the nation's most Chief Executives. Apparently, the rivalry also extends to rock bridges: Ohio can claim at least 16 of them, but Virginia's "Natural Bridge" is more famous, mostly because Thomas Jefferson discovered it. The Hocking Hills Rock Bridge, which is the largest one in the state, came to the attention of the world in a much humbler manner. At the turn of the century, this 100-foot sandstone span was a favorite excursion stop on the Hocking Valley Railroad, whose conductors sang out, "Rock Bridge, Rock Bridge, all out for the Rock Bridge!" Their announcements were so successful that the name of the adjacent town was forgotten and permanently changed to Rockbridge.

Seneca Caverns
15248 East Thompson, TR178
Bellevue, OH 44811
419-483-6711
www.senecacavernsohio.com
Seneca Caverns was discovered in June 1872 by two boys hunting rabbits. When their dog disappeared in a brush pile, the boys discovered an opening, which was actually a natural sinkhole. The boys fell through the opening, landed in the cave, found their dog, and crawled back up to the cave entrance. In 1933, after the discovery of a series of passageways and rooms not previously known to exist, including an underground river, Seneca Caverns was opened to the public.

Zane Caverns
7092 State Rte. 540
Bellefontaine, OH 43311
937-592-9592
www.zaneshawneecaverns.org
The first Native American owned and operated museum in Ohio, featuring Hopewell, Fort Ancient and Ancient to early historic Shawnee artifacts. There are also the rare formations known as cave pearls and found nowhere else in Ohio, and a Bat Educational Module to teach children about the bats that live in the cave. Campsites available.

Sporting venues

Paul Brown Stadium

Canal Park
300 South Main Street
Akron, OH
800-972-3767
Home to the Akron Aeros AA baseball team.

Cleveland Browns Stadium
1085 West Third Street
Cleveland, OH
440-891-5000
www.clevelandbrowns.com
Home of the Cleveland Browns of the NFL.

Columbus Crew Stadium
One Black and Gold Blvd.
Columbus, OH
614-447-2739
www.thecrew.com
Home of the Columbus Crew of Major League Soccer.

Convocation Center, Cleveland State University
4400 Renaissance Pkwy
Cleveland, OH
216-896-1140
www.clevelandforce.com
The home of the Cleveland Force of the Major Indoor Soccer League.

Cooper Stadium
1155 West Mound Street
Columbus, OH
614-462-5250
www.clippersbaseball.com
Home of the Columbus Clippers AAA affiliate of the New York Yankees baseball team.

THE GOOD FIGHT TO PROTECT A WOODEN-TRUSSED HERITAGE

In 1809, Ohio's first documented wooden through truss bridge was built over Little Beaver Creek in Columbiana County. More than 3,000 wooden truss and combination truss bridges, covered and uncovered, were built to serve Ohio's highways, railroads, and canals. Many were lost to vandalism, especially arson. Others were removed or bypassed by transportation experts because they were no longer a viable option for modern traffic.

By 1953, a listing by the Ohio Covered Bridge Committee of the Ohio Historical Society showed that the state had 353 1/2 covered bridges left, the 1/2 being shared by Preble County, Ohio, and Union County, Indiana. The 1961 Ohio Covered Bridge Map showed only 226 covered bridges, but from that time on, fewer bridges were removed, largely because of the preservation efforts of the Ohio Covered Bridge Committee and the Southern and Northern Ohio Covered Bridge associations.

Of all the state's bridges, Vinton County's Humpback Covered Bridge is one of the most scenic. In southern Montgomery County, in the little town of Germantown, is a unique covered bridge that is actually a suspension bridge. There is as much metal as wood in its trusses, and while it has always had a roof, it has never been sided as are most covered bridges. It was built in 1865 and is maintained as an historic site.

The Roberts Bridge, Ohio's oldest covered bridge and last two-lane covered structure, was built in 1829 and set on fire by arsonists in 1986. Although badly damaged, the Burr trusses of the Roberts Bridge continued to hold. After several years of fundraising efforts, the bridge was moved in late 1990 to span Seven Mile Creek in the Preble County town of Eaton.

Ohio's last "village" covered bridge is in the heart of Newton Falls in Trumbull County, where it spans the east branch of the Mahoning River. This Town Lattice truss, built in 1832, is one of Ohio's oldest covered bridges.

The numbering system identifying Ohio's covered bridges was developed in the 1940s by John A. Diehl and is now in use world-wide. The first number (35) stands for the state, the next number is for the county, and the final number for the specific bridge. Thus, 35-84-24 denotes a covered bridge in Ohio in Washington County known as the Hills Bridge. This tracking system is effective because many covered bridges have the same name, but no two ever have the same number.

Ohio now has 136 covered bridges located in 43 counties. Over half still carry traffic. Some have been moved to college campuses, fairgrounds or parks, and about a dozen are on private property. The rest are still on the original sites and often have been abandoned.

The best news is that the old art has been given new life by the state's preservationists and craftspeople: they're not only preserving the old but building anew. Ashtabula has built four new covered bridges and is planning one that will have the fourth-longest span in the world, which will be the county's 17th. Others were built in the late 1990s in Jefferson, Miami, Cuyahoga, and Williams, and as recently as 2000 in Fairfield (now with 13), and 2002 in Fulton. ✎

—*Bureau of Environmental Services, Ohio Department of Transportation, from The Second Ohio Historic Bridge Inventory; website, with good links—*
http://members.aol.com/jreinhl/

Only two states have more covered bridges than Ohio, and Ashtabula County helps keep Ohio's rating intact. Not only has the county preserved its bridges, it has built new ones. The construction of its 1983 bridge brought people from all across the country and gave birth to Ashtabula's annual Covered Bridge Festival, held every October to coincide with the fall foliage.
www.coveredbridgefestival.org

Fifth Third Field
220 North Patterson Blvd.
Dayton, OH
937-228-2287
www.daytondragons.com
Home of a Class A minor league affiliate of the
Cincinnati Reds.

Fifth Third Field
406 Washington Street
Toledo, OH
419-725-4367
www.mudhens.com
Home of the AAA minor league baseball team the
Toledo Mud Hens.

Great American Ball Park
Cincinnati Riverfront
Cincinnati, OH
513-765-7400
www.cincinnatireds.com
The home field of the Cincinnati Reds of the
National League.

Gund Arena
200 Huron Road
Cleveland, OH
216-420-2200
www.gundarena.com
The home of the Cleveland Barons of the American
Hockey League, Cleveland Cavaliers of the NBA,
and the Cleveland Rockers of the WNBA.

Jacobs Field
2401 Ontario Street
Cleveland, OH
216-420-4636
www.indians.com
The home of the Cleveland Indians of the American
League, the Jake is a true urban ballpark, placed
intimately within the physical boundaries of three
main streets downtown Cleveland streets and built
to replace the famous old stadium known affection-
ately as "The Mistake on the Lake that had been
home to the Indians since it was built in 1932 as the
intended home for the Olympics, which never
arrived. Despite its contemporary luxuries, the Jake
has its classic touches—an asymmetrical field only
partially enclosed, so that fans can look out into the
city. The seats down both lines are angled toward
home plate, the bullpens are raised above the
playing field so fans can watch warmups, and
there's a picnic area behind the outfield fence. The
Jake's intimate confines seat 43,345 (the old

stadium held a record 74,000) and in its first year ,
Cleveland averaged over 39,000 fans per game.

Lake County Captains
35300 Vine Street
Eastlake, OH
440-975-8085
www.captainsbaseball.com
The home of the Indian's Class A baseball team.

The Little Brown Jug
At the Delaware County Fairgrounds
off U.S. 23 north
236 Pennsylvania Avenue
Delaware, OH 43015
740-362-3851 or 800-335-3247
www.littlebrownjug.com
Harness racing began informally on the country
roads of Ohio, Kentucky, and Tennessee in the
late 1800s, and the competition eventually moved
to county fairs and then commercial tracks. The
last major harness racing event still held at a
county fairgrounds is the Little Brown Jug, which
draws international attention—and more than
50,000 people—to the Delaware County Fair
every September as the main event in five days of
Grand Circuit races. Named for a famous horse
that once raced on the back roads after church on
Sunday, its official trophy is a plain, but highly
prized brown jug with a bronze plaque. Since the
Jug began in 1946, it has grown into *the* major
race for 3-year-old pacers, and the crown jewel
in harness racing's Triple Crown. A win—or loss—
on Jug Day can make—or break—a horse's
career. Although it is the most prestigious event
in the world of harness racing, the classic is very
much a Delaware event, albeit one that has been
masterfully promoted by the community.
Considered the fastest half-mile track in the world,
the Little Brown Jug racetrack was the work of a
local man, R.K. McNamara; the first Jug was won
by Ensign Hanover, driven by Delaware's own
Wayne "Curly" Smart; and the sights and sounds of
the country fair provide a very homegrown
backdrop for the manicured track and its crisp
white buildings. But perhaps the most telling local
element of all is the tradition that Delawareans
have of reserving a spot along the track by
chaining lawn chairs to the fence and leaving
them there from one year's Jug to the next.

Nationwide Arena
200 West Nationwide Blvd.
Columbus, OH
614-246-2000
www.bluejackets.com
Home of the Columbus Blue Jackets of the NHL.

Paul Brown Stadium
One Paul Brown Stadium
Cincinnati, OH
513-621-8383
www.bengals.com
Home of the Cincinanati Bengals of the NFL.

NICHOLAS LONGWORTH: MAKING OHIO WINE AN INDUSTRY

Nicholas Longworth's particular genius was to behold pearls where others saw only swine. Early on, he earmarked half of his earnings for land speculation, often snatching up for a pittance Cincinnati real estate others rejected as worthless. One early acquisition was 30 acres between Sixth and Seventh streets. The owner had dismissed it as "not worth shucks," and Longworth got the parcel in a swap for two used, but perfectly good, stills. Fifty years later, that downtown property was worth $2 million.

His investment acumen allowed Longworth to abandon his law practice and apply his energies to grapes. He sent for thousands of French vine cuttings and soon discovered what Jefferson had known 20 years before; the vinifera grapes were difficult to cultivate in America. After the viniferas failed, he began experimenting with the native labruscas that East Coast winegrowers had so long scorned. In 1825, Longworth received cuttings of a grape called the Catawba. Discovered along a North Carolina river, this "wonder grape" readily established a second home on the banks of the Ohio. Longworth sampled its first wine three years later and was so impressed with its light, semi-sweet taste that he dedicated himself to cultivating the Catawba.

It was not a misplaced devotion. In 1842, he made America's first champagne—"sparkling Catawba." It was immortalized in verse—"Ode to Catawba"—by the famous poet, Henry Wadsworth Longfellow. By mid-century, vineyards stretched along the Ohio from Cincinnati for 40 miles. Nineteen out of every 20 vines were Catawbas, and Longworth was either buying or growing almost every grape. Even with more than 500,000 bottles of white Catawba and sparkling Catawba champagne in his cellars, he could scarcely meet the demand from the eastern states, California, Europe, and South America. With a single native grape, Longworth had elevated American wine from a farm product to an industry. Cincinnati had become the horticultural center of what was then known as "The West." Longworth had become the father of American winemaking, as well as one of the wealthiest men in America.

The year 1859 was a very good year for Longworth, his wine, and for Ohio. With 568,000 gallons bottled, the state supplied one third of the nation's wine and out-produced California two-to-one. Aspiring California vintners even ventured to grow Catawbas in their vinifera-ideal climate, and some sent a shipment of grapes to Cincinnati for the now legendary Mr. Longworth's opinion.

Longworth spent most mornings working in his garden, pruning knife in hand. Visitors often mistook him for the groundskeeper. Longworth offered to show them around, allowing that he was sure the owner wouldn't mind. Afterward, they customarily tipped him a dime, which Longworth always pocketed with his most humble thanks. He told his family that since he was a lawyer, the coins gained in the garden were probably the only honest money he ever made.

In the ensuing decades, between diseases attacking the wines and the ravages of the Civil War, most of the magnificent vineyards were abandoned. It was nearly a hundred years before the Ohio River valley returned to its place in Ohio's viticultural history. In the 1970s, newly re-discovered French American hybrids were planted on Tarula Farms near Clarksville, and these plantings began a new chapter in Midwestern winemaking. Now, hundreds of acres from West Virginia to Missouri trace their beginnings to those original Tarula Farms' vineyards. ◡

—*Damaine Vonada*

wonder grape

The Longworth tradition lives on and can be explored by following the Longworth Heritage Wine Trail, the assembly of southwest Ohio vintners recognized for making some of the nation's best late harvest wines, known as "ice wines." Find the tour at www.ohiowines.org.